A Dictionary of
Sociology

FOURTH EDITION

Edited by JOHN SCOTT
Previous editions also edited by
GORDON MARSHALL

T0087771

OXFORD
UNIVERSITY PRESS

OXFORD
UNIVERSITY PRESS

Great Clarendon Street, Oxford, OX2 6DP,
United Kingdom

Oxford University Press is a department of the University of Oxford.
It furthers the University's objective of excellence in research, scholarship,
and education by publishing worldwide. Oxford is a registered trade mark of
Oxford University Press in the UK and in certain other countries

© Oxford University Press 1994, 1998, 2005, 2009, 2014

The moral rights of the authors have been asserted

First published 1994
Second edition 1998
Third edition 2005
Third edition revised 2009
Fourth edition 2014

Published in the United States of America by Oxford University Press
198 Madison Avenue, New York, NY 10016, United States of America

British Library Cataloguing in Publication Data
Data available

Library of Congress Control Number: 2014942679

ISBN 978-0-19-968358-1
e-book ISBN 978-0-19-104755-8

Printed and bound by CPI Group (UK) Ltd, Croydon, CR0 4YY

Preface to the first edition

This dictionary, an entirely new compilation, has been written by a distinguished team of sociologists from one of the leading departments of sociology in Europe. It is intended primarily for those who are relatively new to the discipline.

To simplify the use of the dictionary abbreviations have been avoided in the text. An asterisk (*) placed before a word in a definition indicates that additional relevant information will be found under this heading. Some entries simply refer the reader to another entry, indicating either that they are synonyms, or that they are most conveniently explained, together with related terms, in one of the dictionary's longer articles. As a rule, nouns with an associated qualifying adjective may be searched for under either word; thus, for example, 'nuclear family' is also entered as 'family, nuclear'. All the major entries and many of the shorter ones mention at least one bibliographical source which will allow the reader to pursue the relevant literature independently. Such references should be of interest to American and British students alike, despite the distinctive histories of the discipline in these countries, although some entries do point readers on either side of the Atlantic in slightly different directions.

Sociology itself has a clear theoretical core but an irretrievably opaque perimeter. Arguably, this is one of the subject's principal merits, since it facilitates study of genuinely interdisciplinary problems—which include many if not most social issues. Sociologists are therefore likely to encounter the terminology of adjoining specialisms such as economics, psychology, and anthropology. For this reason the dictionary contains a number of entries that relate mainly to cognate disciplines but which will also be useful to the student of sociology.

In recent years, dictionaries of sociology have included an increasing proportion of entries devoted to brief biographical sketches of contemporary practitioners of the discipline, although these often amount to little more than a date of birth, institutional affiliation, and short list of publications. The rationale for this practice is not at all obvious, since the dictionaries in question are intended to provide a guide to the content and terminology of the subject, rather than an annotated list of its proponents. Moreover, pilot research for this dictionary showed that it was in practice impossible to reach a consensus among one's peers as to who were the 'leading contemporary sociologists', partly because of the diversity of the subject itself. The dictionary therefore includes 'names' only in those cases where the individuals concerned have themselves become sociological subjects—mostly because of their influence upon the subsequent history of the discipline. A further criterion is that living authorities have been excluded. Entries will therefore be found under, for example, 'Weber, Max' and 'Goffman, Erving', but not 'Merton, Robert K.' or 'Goldthorpe, John H.' Arguably, this excludes from consideration a number of contemporary sociologists, the corpus of whose work has already become a subject for study within the discipline. Anthony Giddens, Jürgen Habermas, and Pierre Bourdieu are obvious examples. Some readers may think this makes only biological but not intellectual sense. In practice, however, the inclusion of any living sociologists as subjects merely reintroduces irresolvable disputes about who, among the current generation, are sufficiently influential—or controversial—to constitute proper 'topics' for inclusion. Naturally, the work of all these writers is here discussed in the context of wider substantive entries, as for example under the headings of critical theory (Habermas), anomie (Merton), and social mobility (Goldthorpe).

All the contributors to the dictionary were, at the time of its inception, on the staff of the Department of Sociology at the University of Essex, Colchester, UK. The fact that many have since moved on is entirely coincidental.

Preface to the second edition

For this edition I have revised and expanded much of the original text. More than 150 new entries—including several substantial essays—have been added. As a result the new volume is some 45 000 words longer than its predecessor.

I have also corrected a few minor errors drawn to my attention by users of the dictionary. I should therefore like to take this opportunity for thanking the many readers who wrote either to me or to Oxford University Press, often with helpful suggestions for improvements, sometimes merely to express their admiration for the finished product. One correspondent from India proposed the inclusion of a consolidated bibliography, but I am not persuaded that this is as useful to students as is my current practice of citing appropriate references in the context of individual entries, so in this matter the format of the earlier edition has been retained. Nor—having read more about the subject—can I agree with the late Professor Hans Eysenck, who took the trouble to send a thoughtful letter explaining why he felt at least one of the entries gave an unbalanced account of the evidence for and against genetic differences in human behaviour, although the discussion of 'intelligence' has been extended to include some of the more recent (and still controversial) literature on this topic.

Once again I have been the major contributor of entries, although several friends and former colleagues at the Department of Sociology of the University of Essex were kind enough to pen specialist pieces for this new edition: Tony Coxon, Ian Craib, Diana Gittins, Catherine Hakim, Maggy Lee, Sean Nixon, and Nigel South. The dictionary has been greatly improved by their entries and advice. Any remaining deficiencies are entirely my own responsibility.

Oxford
1997

Preface to the third edition

The third edition of *The Oxford Dictionary of Sociology* sees a change of editor but, I hope, not a change of style or approach. In editing the dictionary I have sought to retain the strong and distinctive style established by Gordon Marshall that has made it the leading reference book in its field. I have gone through every entry in the dictionary and have modified entries to reflect current concerns and to update their content. In doing so, I have deleted some of the less useful entries or have incorporated their content into other parts of the dictionary. Some existing entries have been completely rewritten. In introducing new entries to the dictionary I have sought to increase the coverage of topics that have increased in importance since the initial planning of the dictionary. The dictionary has, as a result, grown considerably in length. I have begun to introduce some biographical entries on living sociologists. There is not enough space for a comprehensive coverage of contemporary theorists and researchers, so I have concentrated on those who figure centrally in the areas covered in the dictionary. I hope that it will be possible to expand this coverage in future editions of the dictionary.

I owe a great debt to the massive amount of work undertaken by Gordon Marshall in securing the core entries of the dictionary for the first two editions. His efforts have made my task that much easier. I have relied considerably on colleagues at the University of Essex for many of the new entries, but am also grateful to colleagues elsewhere who have provided new or updated entries. In addition to those entries that I produced myself, draft entries for this third edition of the dictionary were supplied by Eamonn Carrabine, Bob Connell, Tony Coxon, Miriam Glucksmann, Johs Hjellebrekke, Paul Iganski, Stina Lyon, David McCrone, Alison Pilnick, Lucinda Platt, Ken Plummer, Nirmal Puwar, David Rose, Susie Scott, Sanjay Sharma, Nigel South, Liz Stanley, Rob Stones, Tiziana Terranova, and Frank Webster.

John Scott
University of Essex
2004

Preface to the third edition revised

This new edition of the dictionary now includes Internet links to online sources of information, available through the Oxford University Press dedicated website. I have concentrated on supplying the links for the most important and most authoritative sources of further information available on the Internet. A number of these sources are general links to specialized providers of information, and all Internet sources need to be treated with caution. The sites have been chosen to provide the most reliable and impartial information appropriate to the dictionary.

John Scott
University of Essex
2008

Preface to the fourth edition

The Oxford Dictionary of Sociology has grown in scope and coverage since its first edition twenty years ago. First Gordon Marshall, then the two of us together, and finally I alone have included a wider range of topics, added more living sociologists, and sought to improve its style and usability.

A major innovation for the revision to the third edition was the use of internet links that related the *Dictionary* to its online partner and allows a direct click-through to carefully selected sites that are known to be reliable. This innovation has been retained in the present edition. As more and more material becomes available online it is more than ever useful to have a reliable guide to these sources. I have sought to ensure that the links are up-to-date but the publishers would be grateful for any comments on difficulties in using these sites so that the links can be rectified as soon as possible. Please also let us know the sites that you have found especially useful and that you think might be shared with other users of the *Dictionary*.

A significant change in this issue is that a number of the less used, very technical entries have been shortened or deleted to allow a number of new entries to be included and for coverage of newer areas to be expanded, such as intersectionality, Islamophobia, climate change, and social media, as well as new biographical entries on figures such as bel hooks, Ann Oakley, Stanley Cohen, and Randall Collins. I hope that you will find this change useful.

The *Dictionary* includes many cross references indicated by an in-text asterisk marker (in the print edition) and a list of 'See also' sources. These are important ways of finding material and readers are encouraged to follow these in the same way that you might follow an online link on a web page: indeed, the online version allows you to do exactly this. If you do find 'missing' entries that you think a future edition should include, the publishers would again be glad to hear any suggestions.

The *Dictionary* is a reference source, but I hope that you will also find it readable. I hope that you will get much pleasure and value from simply browsing the entries and following the links.

John Scott
University of Copenhagen and University of Exeter
2014

Contributors

Contributors to various editions of this dictionary, some of whom are no longer with us, have provided the raw materials from which the current edition has been compiled. The publishers and editors are grateful to all of them for their help in ensuring the success of the dictionary.

Diane Barthel
Ted Benton
David Bouchier
John Brewer
Joan Busfield
Eamonn Carrabine
Raewyn Connell
Tony Coxon
Ian Craib
Fiona Devine
Judith Ennew
Pete Fussey
Diana Gittins
Miriam Glucksmann
Roger Goodman
Judith Green
Catherine Hakim
Michael Harloe
Johs Hjellebrekke
Paul Iganski
David Inglis
George Kolankiewicz
David Lee
Maggy Lee
Stina Lyon
Dennis Marsden
Gordon Marshall
David McCrone
Mary McIntosh

Graham Meikle
Maxine Molyneux
Lydia Morris
Sean Nixon
Judith Okely
Alison Pilnick
Lucinda Platt
Ken Plummer
Nirmal Puwar
Kate Reynolds
David Rose
Tania Saeed
Colin Samson
Sanjay Sharma
Alison Scott
Jacqueline Scott
John Scott
Susie Scott
Nigel South
Liz Stanley
Rob Stones
Oriel Sullivan
Tiziana Terranova
Bryan Turner
Frank Webster
Richard Wilson
Anthony Woodiwiss
Nira Yuval-Davis

Useful websites

(⊕) SEE WEB LINKS

This is a web-linked dictionary. To access the websites below, go to the dictionary's web page at http://www.oup.com/uk/reference/resources/sociology, click on **Web links** in the Resources section and click straight through to the relevant websites.

Intute

- A very useful starting point if you are reviewing the literature in a particular area of sociology. Intute is a collection of online resources for all the disciplines of the social sciences, and by following the links you can find articles and papers, datasets, books, journals and organizations related to your area of interest. It is an archive and is no longer being updated.

British Sociological Association (BSA)

- The BSA is the main professional association for sociologists in the UK, and aims to provide information and services for its members. It is worth visiting this site to acquire an understanding of the nature of sociology and how the discipline is different from others in the social sciences. The BSA organizes conferences and workshops to bring together sociologists throughout the world, and publishes two major journals which may be familiar to you. Students can join the BSA for a reduced rate and enjoy all the benefits of membership.

theory.org

- An entertaining introduction to contemporary social theory, written by David Gauntlett at the University of Leeds. A very accessible site showing the basics of some of the more innovative and unconventional theories.

SocioSite, University of Amsterdam

- This site lists a number of sociologists and their main ideas, including excerpts from the original texts.

Social Theory Pages

- A very helpful page of links to websites about the key thinkers, prepared by Jim Spickard at the University of Redlands. It includes links to resources on both classic and contemporary theory, as well as to some other major sites such as SocioSite.

UK Data Service

- The UK Data Archive, housed at the University of Essex, contains a wider selection of quantitative data from social science research. You can browse the catalogue to find abstracts and methodological details of each study, and registered users can order a copy of the original data sets. There is also a bank of data from the major national surveys, including the British Crime Survey and the Social Attitudes Survey.

- The Service also includes the Qualidata archive that collects and disseminates qualitative data from a wide range of research projects. You can use the 'Qualicat' catalogue to search for data on a particular topic, or locate datasets from some of the classic studies in sociology.

Social Research Update

- Another online store of articles about research methods, published and maintained by the Department of Sociology at the University of Surrey. The articles are relatively short, and the website is easy to navigate. It contains accounts of new and less conventional methods, such as visual ethnography and Internet-based research, alongside a number of other substantive issues in methodology.

ability The power to perform a mental or physical task—either before or after training. Social psychologists usually distinguish ability from aptitude, the natural capacity to acquire or learn a body of knowledge as measured in an aptitude test. Sociologists would probably distinguish ability and *skill, the former being relatively specialized and task-specific, the latter referring to a wider set of learned techniques that can be applied to a number of cognate tasks.

abolitionism A term originally associated with a call for the abolition of slavery on the grounds of its inhumanity (see, for example, the arguments of William Wilberforce, 1759–1833). More recently extended to arguments for the abolition of prisons and imprisonment. The latter stance developed within Scandinavian criminology (see T. Mathiesen, *The Politics of Abolition*, 1974) but has since been taken up within wider *critical criminology. Abolitionists argue that prisons are ineffective, their justification untenable, and their violations of human rights widespread. The abolitionist stance rejects mere reform on the grounds that this perpetuates and legitimates the existing system. Abolitionism proposes new responses to crime, offending, and disputes—for example community-based alternatives to incarceration—and argues that the urge to punish and inflict pain must be challenged.

absolute deprivation *See* DEPRIVATION.

absolute mobility *See* MOBILITY, SOCIAL.

absolute poverty *See* POVERTY.

absolutism (absolutist state) A strong and centralized form of state typical of societies in the process of transition from *feudalism to *capitalism and in which power is concentrated in the person of a monarch who has at his or her disposal a centralized administrative apparatus. The label has been applied to a wide variety of *states, ranging from 16th-century Tudor England to 19th-century Meiji Japan. This definition is not uncontroversial: the label has also been applied to Tsarist Russia, where the transition was from feudalism to *communism, and some would deny that Japan was ever a feudal society in anything other than the loosest sense. A useful overview can be found in Perry Anderson's *Lineages of the Absolute State* (1974).

There has also been great controversy over the role that absolutist states played in the transition to capitalism. Many historians have seen the absolutist state as preparing the way for capitalism and have sometimes preferred the term 'enlightened despotism'. (Others, however, have limited this term to the promotion of Enlightenment rationalism in states such as Prussia and Austria. Most Marxists have (at least until relatively recently) tended to see absolutism as an obstacle to the development of capitalism. The problem that both parties to this dispute have had to address is the variability in the historical outcomes. Within continental Europe, for example, the rise of absolutist states appears to have been associated with both a rapid transition to capitalism in the West, and an intensification of feudal domination in the East.

For Max *Weber (*General Economic History*, 1919–20) and for non-Marxist scholars more generally, an explanation for the progressive role played by the absolutist or 'rational state' can be found in the immense contribution that these regimes made to the increasing predictability of action within their territories as they bureaucratized their own administrations, introduced elements of the rule of law, monopolized the legitimate use of force, and used this force to extend their jurisdiction throughout society. Weber's response to the divergent outcomes of absolutism in Eastern and Western Europe was to portray what happened in the East as a delay rather than a regression, and to explain it as the result of the state's lack of allies in the wider society, which in turn reflected the more general economic and cultural backwardness of these societies.

The response of Marxists (such as Maurice Dobb, Eric Hobsbawm, and Perry Anderson) to this line of argument, has been to suggest that it owes more to the tendency amongst non-Marxists to accord analytical privilege to the political realm, than it does to sound historical research. Given that the absolute monarchs and their most powerful supporters were always representatives of the feudal nobility, so Marxists have argued, it is the short-lived absolutisms of Western Europe (and especially of England and Holland) that require explanation, rather than the long-lasting ones of the East. The explanation that they provide revolves around the bold and controversial claim that the majority of continental states experienced a prolonged economic crisis during the 16th century, a crisis from which England and Holland were spared. As a result, the feudal nobility in every society except those two was able to crush or constrain its capitalist rivals. For this reason, it was possible for the bourgeois classes of England and Holland to gain an early advantage over their potential competitors, an advantage that they enhanced still further by overturning their absolute monarchies in relatively short order. Putting to one side the many empirical objections that this thesis has encountered, it is important to note that it rests on an analytical privileging of the economic realm that is arguably no more justified than the privileging of the political realm to which its proponents have rightly objected. Perhaps the most successful exception to both strictures is A. Lublinskaya's, *French Absolutism: The Crucial Phase, 1620–1629* (1968).

abstracted empiricism A term coined by C. Wright Mills in *The Sociological Imagination* (1959) to refer to the work of those sociologists who equate a strong and rigid *empiricism with science and make a fetish of survey-generated numerical data and quantitative research techniques. Mills saw this as having become the dominant style of social research in the United States during the

1940s and 1950s. It is empirical research abstracted from theoretical reflection. While Mills recognized the importance of empirical data, including numerical data and statistical analysis, in sociological work, he insisted that they are not sufficient for sociological analysis. Sociological accounts must always be theoretically informed. Mills held that *surveys, in particular, tend to restrict data to those concerning individuals and their attributes and so make it difficult to conceive of social *structure or to undertake comparative historical analyses. A fascinating historical account of the origins of abstracted empiricism will be found R. Bannister, *Sociology and Scientism: The American Quest for Objectivity, 1880–1949* (1987).

accommodation *See* ASSIMILATION.

accounts *See* VOCABULARIES OF MOTIVE.

acculturation *See* ASSIMILATION.

accumulation *See* CAPITAL ACCUMULATION.

acephalous A term used to describe the political system of societies without centralized state authority—such as, for example, traditional African lineage political systems (see J. Middleton and D. Tait, *Tribes without Rulers*, 1958). Authority is wielded at the level of the clan, lineage, or lineage segment. For this reason these 'headless' societies are often referred to by the alternative term 'segmented'.

achieved status *See* STATUS, ACHIEVED.

achievement The successful accomplishment or performance of a socially defined task or goal. Talcott *Parsons (in *Social Theory and Modern Society*, 1967) suggests that modern societies use indices of achievement—examination credentials or success in role-based tasks—rather than ascriptive criteria to recruit, select, and evaluate individuals for particular *roles. However, research demonstrates the continued influence of *ascription in social *stratification, notably in relation to such factors as race and sex. There is an interesting cross-disciplinary discussion of the concept and interpretation of achievement, its relationship to creativity and innovation, and its role in explaining economic growth in England and Japan since the 17th century, in Penelope Gouk (ed.), *Wellsprings of Achievement* (1995). *See also* ACHIEVEMENT MOTIVATION; MERITOCRACY; STATUS, ACHIEVED.

achievement motivation Defined as the need to perform well or the striving for success, and evidenced by persistence and effort in the face of difficulties, achievement motivation is regarded as a central human motivation. Psychologist David McClelland (*The Achieving Society*, 1961) controversially hypothesized that it was related to economic growth and, for a period during the 1950s and 1960s, a lack of achievement motivation was widely proposed as explanation for the lack of economic development in the Third World. This was most notable among certain American *modernization theorists, and their thesis was much criticized by *dependency theorists such as Andre Gunder Frank (*Latin America: Underdevelopment or Revolution*, 1969). *See also* WORK ETHIC.

act (action, social act) *See* ACTION THEORY; MEANING; PARSONS; WEBER, MAX.

actionalism A term generally associated with the name of French sociologist Alain Touraine, and not to be confused with the 'action frame of reference' (*see* ACTION THEORY) proposed by Talcott Parsons. Beginning in the 1960s, Touraine developed a radical new theoretical framework, most fully described in *The Self-Production of Society* (1973). In his own words, Touraine aimed to 'replace a sociology of society with a sociology of actors'. His purpose was to overcome what he saw as a false division in sociology between objective and subjective, or system and action approaches. Actionalism places the social actor at the centre of theoretical attention, including theories of structural and historical phenomena. Actors are not simply the components of social systems, but the agents of those systems. Groups and collectivities such as social classes are treated not as mere categories but as dynamic sets of relationships among social actors. This dynamic aspect of actionalism is what Touraine calls historicity (a term adapted from Jean-Paul *Sartre) and referring to the ability of a society to act on itself, and the quality of history as a human activity. The sociologist is an agent of historicity—not a neutral observer—and has a stake in the conflicts of his or her society.

This led Touraine to the method of '*sociological interventionism', in which sociologists study social change movements by participating in them directly. An actionalist sociology, Touraine believes, is diverse and full of conflicts, but is more legitimate because of its active engagement in social change processes.

In concrete terms, the actionalist approach attempts to explain how social values are shaped, and thus how social *change is accomplished, by identifying in each historical epoch the 'historical subject' (collective actor) that carries the capacity for accomplishing revolutionary change by organizing itself into a *social movement. In his earlier studies, Touraine argued that historical subjects attain the necessary self-awareness through the experience of productive work, seeing the key social movement expressing the historical subject of capitalism as organized labour. However, in later studies he broadened his conception of 'production' and extended the theory to other social movements, including those organized by women, students, nuclear protesters, and nationalists. Touraine's analysis of social movements can be found in his *The Voice and the Eye* (1978).

action frame of reference *See* ACTION THEORY.

action research A type of research in which the researcher is also a change agent. It is often used in local communities or by consultants working in companies, as part of the change process itself. The research subjects are invited to participate at various stages of a relatively fast-moving sequence of research-action-research-action. There is an iterative process of investigating a problem, using *case-study methods, loosely defined; presenting the analysis, with one or more proposed solutions, to the subjects or group leaders; deciding which course of action to follow and implementing it; followed by further investigations to assess the outcomes and identify unanticipated problems and possible solutions to them; and finally followed by further action to refine and extend the new policies or activities. The process can be extended indefinitely, as the original focus of concern gradually moves to other related areas. The British community development programmes of the 1970s are an interesting example (see particularly the Coventry CDP Final Report, 1975).

action theory (action frame of reference) These terms are not interchangeable but are closely related and carry a number of implications about the way we regard sociology as a science. It has been common, for example, to juxtapose action to structure as alternative starting-points for sociological investigation. Action theories are those that start from or see the major object for sociology as human action. A defining quality of action is that, unlike behaviour, it carries a subjective meaning for the actor. These approaches, therefore, concern themselves with the *meaning of action and its *interpretation. Sociology gives a rational, coherent account of people's actions, thoughts, and relationships. Action theories include Weberian sociology, phenomenological sociology, symbolic interactionism, ethnomethodology, rational choice theory, and structuration theory (all of which are dealt with under separate headings in this dictionary).

The action frame of reference is associated with the name of Talcott *Parsons, whose theory starts with a systematic analysis of action that sees the social actor as choosing between different means and ends, in an environment which limits choice both physically and socially. The most important social limitations on choice are *norms and *values. From this, Parsons built up an elaborate model of the *social system, and his theory stressed the determining role of norms and values rather more than the choosing actor. Critics of Parsons such as John *Rex (*Key Problems of Sociological Theory*, 1962) have rejected this view but have retained the underlying action frame of reference as the basis of their own action theories.

Action theories in contemporary sociology have raised three different concerns. First is the nature of *rationality and rational action itself. This arises from of Weber's work and poses questions about the possibility of causal explanations of action. (Are the reasons for doing something a cause in the same way that heating a piece of metal causes it to expand?) It also addresses the issue of whether there are any absolute criteria of rationality, or whether sociological explanations are always in some sense culturally relative. *Rational choice theory takes up some of these problems in a more substantive way. The second concern is the taken-for-granted rules and stock of knowledge that underlie action—a theme pursued notably by ethnomethodology and phenomenology. The third, addressed by symbolic interactionism, is the learning and negotiation of *meaning that goes on between actors. Many important approaches are reviewed in Ira Cohen, 'Theories of Action and Praxis' in Turner (ed.), *The Blackwell Companion to Social Theory* (2000).

actor (social actor) *See* ACTION THEORY; AGENCY; SELF; SUBJECT.

adaptation A term widely used in evolutionary theory to describe the outcome of the process of natural selection. Genetic variations in biological species are seen as selected on the basis of their capacity to promote or inhibit survival in a particular environment. Those variations that allow a species to survive do so by allowing them to adapt to the pressures and opportunities of their particular environment. In much social *evolutionism a similar approach was adopted, with cultural innovations being seen as the objects of environmental selection and as the means through which social groups may be able to adapt to their physical and social environment. Talcott *Parsons took adaptation as one of the four functional prerequisites of any system of action—the others were goal attainment, *integration, and latency, forming the so-called AGIL scheme. *See also* FUNCTIONALISM.

Addams, Jane (1860–1935) Addams was an American sociologist of central importance to the work of the *Chicago School in the late 19th and early 20th centuries. A powerful influence on many other women in sociology, such as Charlotte Perkins Gilman and Emily Greene Balch, in 1889 she set up a social settlement in Chicago, Hull House to support social work and community activities. This was partly inspired by London's Toynbee Hall, but was more woman-influenced, more egalitarian, and less religious. Addams argued that one of the main problems for women was trying to manage the conflicting demands of family and society, and she believed social settlements were one way to resolve the problem. Hull House was an important sociological centre for the University of Chicago, and also attracted other leading social theorists, Marxists, anarchists, and socialists. A spokeswoman for women and working-class immigrants in particular, Addams was a cultural feminist who saw female values as inherently superior to those of men, and argued that a more productive and more peaceful society could be built by drawing on, and integrating, such values. Her commitment to pacifism made her a social pariah during the First World War, although in 1931 she was awarded the Nobel Peace Prize. See Emily Cooper Johnson (ed.), *Jane Addams: A Centennial Reader* (1960), and Mary Jo Deegan, *Jane Addams and the Men of the Chicago School* (1989).

((⊕)) SEE WEB LINKS
- A classic article by Jane Addams on the idea of the social settlement: 'A Function of the Social Settlement.' (Subscription)

addiction *See* DRINKING AND ALCOHOLISM; DRUGS.

administrative theory (classical administrative theory) An early form of *organization theory, pioneered mainly by Henri Fayol (1841–1925) in his *Administration industrielle et générale*, 1916), which was concerned principally with achieving the 'most rational' organization for coordinating the various tasks specified within a complex *division of labour. The translation of this book into English as *General and Industrial Management* (1949) implies that Fayol was concerned mainly with business management, although he himself made it clear that his ideas about management were intended to apply to all formal organizations, including political and religious undertakings. Expressing the French 'administration' as 'management' has also led to the alternative designation of this approach as the 'classical school of scientific management', more recent exponents of which include Lyndall Urwick and Peter F. Drucker.

Fayol identified the key functions of management as those of forecasting and planning. The most rational and efficient organizations were, in his view, those that implemented plans that facilitated 'unity, continuity, flexibility, precision, command and control'. Universal principles of administration could be distilled from these objectives. These include the key elements of the scalar chain (authority and responsibility flowing in an unbroken line from the chief executive to the shop floor); unity of command (each person has only one supervisor with whom he or she communicates); a pyramid of prescribed control (first-line supervisors have a limited number of functions and subordinates, with second-line supervisors controlling a prescribed number of first-line supervisors, and so on up to the chief executive); unity of direction (people engaged in similar activities must pursue a common objective in line with the overall plan); specialization of tasks (allowing individuals to build up a specific expertise and so be more productive); and, finally, subordination of individual interests to the general interest of the organization. This list is not exhaustive, but illustrates the key proposition of administrative theory, which is that a functionally specific and hierarchical structure offers the most efficient means of securing organizational objectives (see M. B. Brodie, *Fayol on Administration*, 1967).

Classical administrative theory, like its near-contemporary the *scientific management approach, rests on the premise that organizations are unproblematically rational and (effectively) closed systems. In other words, organizations are assumed to have unambiguous and unitary objectives that the individuals within them pursue routinely by obeying the rules and fulfilling their role expectations according to the prescribed blueprint and structure. Moreover, in the attempt to maximize efficiency, it is only variables within that structure that need to be considered and manipulated. The interaction of the organization with its environment, together with the various factors that are external to the organization but nevertheless have consequences for its internal functioning, are systematically ignored. Clearly, both perspectives take a rather deterministic view of social action, since each assumes that individuals will maximize organizational efficiency, independently of their own welfare, and with no thought for the relationship between the collective goal and their own particular purposes. *Human Relations Theory in organizational analysis, an otherwise diverse group of writers and approaches, is united by its opposition to precisely this assumption. Despite such criticisms, the classical theory of administration has exerted considerable influence on the fields of business studies and public administration, and it still provides the basic concepts that many managers use in clarifying their objectives.

adolescence First introduced as a concept in social psychology by G. Stanley Hall (in *Adolescence*, 1904). The term has been used to refer to the emotional and behavioural states supposedly associated with becoming adult; the phase in the *life-cycle before the physical changes associated with puberty are socially recognized; and the transition in status from childhood to adulthood.

Typically, in modern industrial societies, young people are sexually mature well before society acknowledges them as adults in other respects; and, because of education and training, they remain dependent on parents and guardians. Consequently, adolescence has been seen as a time of peak emotional turbulence (see J. S. *Coleman, *The Nature of Adolescence*, 1980). Sociologists do not see this as an exclusively biological process in which physical change itself brings about behavioural change. Rather, biological maturation is recognized as real but also as socially constructed in relation to social norms and values. This means that adolescence itself is a culturally relative condition. In the recent past in Europe children frequently had to move into adulthood as soon as they could do useful work and without passing through a stage of adolescence.

Anthropologists too describe numerous examples (especially in *age-set societies) where the transition to adulthood is abrupt, marked by clear *rites of passage, and relatively free from alleged adolescent problems. Surveys and other field studies in the industrialized West itself have cast doubt on the ideas that adolescence is typically any more stressful than any other stage in life or that the majority of teenagers are rebellious. The treatment of adolescence as a social problem may say more about the stereotypes of youth in the adult world and indicate a *moral panic about *youth culture (see Frank Coffield et al., *Growing Up at the Margins*, 1986). For an overview of the literature see Patricia Noller and Victor Callan, *The Adolescent in the Family* (1991).

Adorno, Theodor Wiesengrund (1903–69) A leading member of the Frankfurt Institute of Social Research, who worked in America during the Second World War, returning to West Germany after the allied victory. He was a man of immense learning, and complex, often obscure and difficult ideas. His work covered aesthetic theory, literary and musical theory, general cultural criticism, social psychology, and philosophy. A major work was (with numerous others) *The Authoritarian Personality* (1950), a (much criticized) empirical and theoretical investigation into the psychological roots of authoritarianism.

With other members of the Frankfurt Institute he engaged critically with Marxism and sought to incorporate a sophisticated conception of culture and individual psychology into the revisionist strands of Marxism that were developed by such writers as *Lukács. His aesthetic and cultural criticism and his philosophy were concerned with form rather than content: the form of a work of art, or of a system of ideas, offered the clearest demonstration of the limits and contradictions imposed upon us by society, as well as of the possibilities it offers. He particularly developed this idea in relation to music and wider trends in culture, where he saw a polarisation between artistic culture and the development of popular, mass culture and *mass society (see R. Witkin, *Adorno on Music*, 1998; *Adorno on Popular Culture*, 2002). His own difficult writing style was allegedly an attempt to avoid what he saw as the false integration of his ideas into modern industrial society. Perhaps the clearest statement of his view of modernity can be found in *Minima Moralia* (1951), a collection of aphorisms, which state that the notion of totality was once part of a liberating philosophy, but over the last century has been absorbed into a totalizing *social system, a

real or potentially *totalitarian regime. For examples of his cultural criticism
see *Prisms* (1955) and, with Max Horkheimer, *The Culture Industry Revisited*,
ed. J. Bernstein (1992). Adorno's introductory lectures on sociology from 1968
have been published as *Introduction to Sociology* (published 2000). *See also*
AUTHORITARIAN PERSONALITY; CRITICAL THEORY.

(⊕) SEE WEB LINKS
• A selection of extracts from works by Adorno on music and the culture industry.

advocacy research One kind of descriptive *policy research, carried out by
people who are deeply concerned about certain social problems, such as poverty
or rape. Their studies seek to measure social problems with a view to heightening
public awareness of them and providing a catalyst for policy proposals and other
action to ameliorate the problem in question. Critics sometimes suggest that
advocacy research studies bend their research methods in order to inflate the
magnitude of the social problem described, and thereby enhance the case for
public action to address the issue. See Neil Gilbert's article: 'Advocacy Research
and Social Policy', *Crime and Justice* (1997).

affect (affective, affectivity) An affect is an emotion. In sociology the use of
the term generally implies that an action is being or has been carried out for
emotional gratification. Affectivity *versus* affective neutrality is one of Talcott
Parsons's so-called pattern variables for the classification and analysis of societies. This was used to explore the relationship between cognitive and emotional
action orientations and social relations. For example, in their discussion of *Class
Awareness in the United States* (1983), Mary R. Jackman and Robert W. Jackman
discuss 'affective class bonds'; namely, 'the issue of whether subjective social
class encompasses a feeling of emotional attachment', rather than being merely a
matter of nominal identification. *See also* AFFECTIVE INDIVIDUALISM.

affective individualism A change in family life, said to have accompanied
the demographic, industrial, and capitalist revolutions that occurred in
18th-century England, and has since been experienced widely in other modernized and modernizing countries. The term affective individualism describes the
formation of *marriage ties on the basis of personal attraction, guided by norms
of romantic attachment rather than being arranged by parents.

A number of authorities (including L. Stone, *The Family, Sex and Marriage in
England, 1500–1800*, 1977) have argued that the 18th century saw a revolution in
familial norms. Hitherto, families (even nuclear *families) were deeply embedded in a wider network of community involvements (including close relationships with other kin), so that the family was not a major focus of emotional
attachment and dependence for its members. Among other things, therefore, sex
was instrumental (necessary to propagate children) rather than a source of
pleasure; as indeed was marriage itself (which was undertaken for economic or
political reasons, rather than feelings of romantic attraction). For reasons connected with *industrialization (the precise causality varies between accounts),
this form of family life gave way rapidly to the 'closed domesticated nuclear
form', characterized by intimate emotional or affective bonds, domestic privacy,

a preoccupation with love and with the rearing of children for expressive rather than instrumental reasons. By extension, this process is said to have accompanied the spread of *capitalism and industrialization throughout the globe.

The theory of affective individualism as an invention of modern societies has been strongly challenged—most notably by Alan Macfarlane (see *The Culture of Capitalism*, 1987)—mainly on the grounds that it posits as revolutionary a series of changes that were incremental and long pre-dated the processes of industrialization. *See also* FAMILY, SOCIOLOGY OF.

affine (affinity) *See* KINSHIP.

affirmative action *See* POSITIVE DISCRIMINATION.

affluence *See* EMBOURGEOISEMENT.

affluent worker *See* EMBOURGEOISEMENT.

ageing, sociology of The physiological process of growing older has vital social and cultural dimensions which affect what is often seen as a purely biological inevitability. Age is also a cultural category and its meaning and significance vary both historically and cross-culturally. The sociology of ageing did not feature in standard sociology textbooks until recently. Like sex or gender, age tended to be seen as a purely 'natural' division, or else as a 'problem' reserved for social policy. By contrast, considerable sociological attention has been paid to *youth culture.

In Western capitalism, a wage-labour system means fixed retirement from external production, thus categorizing the aged as non-productive, and a burden. In research priorities, *gerontology, with its medical model of ageing, has been influential. Sociological research in Britain has focused on the aged as isolates or in state institutions. Demographic changes—with increasing longevity, a declining birth-rate, and a greater proportion of the population over 65 in the West—have stimulated both a *moral panic and new interest in the consumer and political potential of the elderly.

Stereotyping and an assumed homogeneity among the aged are to be challenged. Class, race, and gender, as well as culture, counter biological factors. For example, old age is not perceived as an impediment for males with supreme political power in either communist or capitalist states. In numerous articles on the social relations of old people, Ethel Shanas has criticized what has been termed the acquiescent functionalism of much writing on ageing and the family life of the elderly, a tradition which legitimates *ageism by excluding the elderly from the *labour market and other significant social *roles. By contrast, Shanas's own research seems to demonstrate that ageing is a process of *deprivation, leading to what has been called 'structured dependency' (see Shanas et al., *Old People in Three Industrialised Societies*, 1968, and Shanas and M. B. Sussman (eds.), *Family, Bureaucracy and the Elderly*, 1977).

There is growing research interest in this field, not only in the experience and ethnography of the aged, but also in the specific constructions of 'old age' across cultures and through time (see, for example, M. W. Riley, 'On the Significance of Age in Sociology', *American Sociological Review*, 1987).

(⊕) SEE WEB LINKS
• A portal site with links to numerous sites on aspects of ageing.

ageism Discrimination, or the holding of irrational and prejudicial views about individuals or groups, based on their age. It involves *stereotypical assumptions about a person's or group's physical or mental capacities and is often associated with derogatory language. These are most commonly applied to the elderly. Organizations such as the Grey Panthers have emerged in the United States to combat *discrimination against the elderly and to fight for their *rights.

age sets (age grades) Broad age-bands that define the social *status, permitted *roles, and activities of those belonging to them and that include all the members of the society in the particular age category. Transitions from one age grade to the next are often major collectively organized social events with *rites of passage marking the change of social status and role. Although the term has sometimes been applied in the modern industrial context, it is more commonly used in reference to pre-industrial societies where an age-grade system of stratification (dividing members into youths, maidens, elders, and so forth) is superimposed on the organizing tribal, lineage, or clan structure, and class differences do not exist.

age stratification A system of inequalities linked to age that involves the formation of *age sets. As a form of *stratification, it is most usefully distinguished from mere inequality. In Western societies, for example, both the old and the young are perceived and treated as relatively incompetent and excluded from much social life as distinct statuses, but they do not comprise unified and cohesive social strata. *See also* AGEISM.

agency The term agency is often juxtaposed to *structure and is often no more than a synonym for action, emphasizing implicitly the undetermined nature of human action, as opposed to the alleged determinism of structural theories. If it has a wider meaning, it is to draw attention to the psychological and social psychological make-up of the actor, and to imply the capacity for willed (voluntary) action.

Sociological theories are often characterized by the relative emphasis they place on agency or structure—and in terms, therefore, of an agency versus structure debate. Some recent theorists have intervened in the debate in a conscious attempt to transcend this *dualism. The French sociologist Pierre *Bourdieu is a good example. His insistence that the objective and subjective aspects of social life are inescapably bound together leads him to challenge the dualism of macro versus micro and structure versus agency (*Outline of a Theory of Practice*, 1977).

Another writer to have addressed this issue is Anthony *Giddens in his theory of *structuration. Similarly, the American sociologist Jeffrey Alexander argues for a multidimensional sociology that brings together the two levels of analysis, most notably in his four-volume *Theoretical Logic in Sociology* (1984). *See also* ACTION THEORY; STRUCTURATION.

aggregate Large collections of people may act as groups, with some degree of common purpose, but they may also act as non-organized aggregates. For example, an audience or crowd may be said to be an aggregate, in so far as its members lack any organization or persisting pattern of social relationships. The term is also used more broadly in reference to research or analysis that deals only with aggregate data, which consist of statistics produced for broad groups or categories (for example certain types of persons, households, or companies), and in which the characteristics of individual respondents (persons, households, or companies) are no longer identifiable. *See also* COLLECTIVE BEHAVIOUR; MICRODATA.

aggregate data *See* AGGREGATE (COLLECTIVITY).

aggression Acts of hostility, injury, violence, or extreme self-assertion. There are several competing theories as to why people may become aggressive. Many of these are biological. Thus, for example, the philosopher Thomas *Hobbes argued that people were by nature violent and avoided a 'war of all against all' only by considerable ingenuity and effort. Many schools of psychology share this assumption, and argue that aggression is obviated by exhaustive processes of education or *socialization, combined with a generous measure of *social control. That is, social learning is not sufficient, and people must be continually rewarded for their civilized behaviour and punished for unacceptably aggressive conduct.

Most sociological theories of aggression root it not in the biological substructure or psychological superstructure of the individual, but in his or her relationship to the social environment. Probably the most popular of these is the so-called frustration-aggression hypothesis or theory, which states that aggressive behaviour results when purposeful activity is interrupted (see the classic statement in J. Dollard et al., *Frustration and Aggression*, 1939). Thus, for example, children may attack other children who take their toys from them. This theory has, however, been criticized for its inability to explain the circumstances under which frustration leads to outcomes other than aggression. (Some children may simply sulk quietly under these circumstances.) The frustration-aggression thesis has also been identified with the earlier work of Sigmund *Freud, who argued that frustration—the blocking of pleasure-seeking or pain-avoiding activities—always leads to aggression, either towards the perceived source of interference, or (if inhibited) displaced onto another object. Freud later suggested that aggression was the product of a death instinct (called Thanatos) that operates alongside the life instinct that he called libido or Eros.

A third group of theories—learning theories—view violence as the result of *successful* socialization and social control. That is, aggressive behaviour in general and violent behaviour in particular occur where they are expected, even in the absence of frustration. For example, members of a *subculture may learn to behave in accordance with *norms of violence which have been presented to them as socially desirable, as in cases where the use of force (such as fist-fighting) is associated with masculinity. Similarly, soldiers at the front in times of war and teenagers in a *gang may feel violence is acceptable and the done thing, because they have been brought up to believe this to be the case, expect to win approval and prestige if they fight well, and wish to avoid censure should they 'chicken out'. *See also* DIFFERENTIAL ASSOCIATION.

agnate (agnation) In Roman law, *agnati* were a group of males and females who were related through a common ancestor, and thus came under a single family authority. The modern use in social anthropology relates to patrilineal (or male) descent, but the element of male authority has been lost. An agnate is thus a blood relative in the patrilineal (or male) line. Agnation refers to a kinship system in which relationship is traced exclusively through the male line. In current anthropological usage the term *patrilineal is preferred.

agrarian capitalism *See* CAPITALISM.

agrarianism Agrarian societies are those that combine horticulture and animal husbandry in systems of farming. Agrarianism also refers to the romanticization of the rural farm as the ideal place for family life. *See also* RURAL SOCIOLOGY.

agreement, method of *See* MILL, JOHN STUART.

agribusiness A large-scale *capitalist farming and food-processing organization and enterprise (producing fertilizers, pesticides, or machinery) that shares many characteristics of other advanced industries. These include, for example, the use of advanced science and technology, techniques of mass production, and extensive vertical and horizontal integration of processes and *corporations. Thus, for example, one might find a frozen-food corporation, having long-term contracts with an array of large farms, using computers to plan production of highly specialized produce to order, and being supplied with inorganic fertilizers and other materials by a company also owned by the food corporation. These are increasingly organized on a global scale and with a global division of labour. The effects of agribusiness in the United States are discussed in Richard Merrill (ed.), *Radical Agriculture* (1976) and Susan George, *How the Other Half Dies* (1976). *See also* RURAL SOCIOLOGY.

agriculture, sociology of *See* RURAL SOCIOLOGY.

AIDS The Acquired Immune Deficiency Syndrome is a complex of symptoms and ultimately deadly infections caused by the Human Immuno-deficiency Viruses (HIV). An initial period of high infectivity is followed after some three months by the appearance of HIV antibodies that signal a reaction to the HIV infection and on which the main tests for the condition are based. Following what are often years of symptom-free living, the body finally succumbs to what are normally rare and unusual diseases—especially PCP (Pneumocystis Carinii Pneumonia) and KS (Kaposi's Sarcoma). The main vehicles of transmission are the bodily fluids, especially blood (blood-transfusion, intravenous drug uses, and vertical transmission from mother to child) and semen, chiefly by means of penetrative sexual intercourse (homosexual or heterosexual). UNAIDS distinguishes three zones and patterns of infection: Asia (now the principal growth area of infection), the African continent (initial discovery and primarily heterosexual in form), and industrialized Western nations (where the pandemic was recognized and defined in the 1980s). In the West, transmission was primarily by homosexual intercourse, and intravenous drug needle-sharing, but transmission is now primarily heterosexual. By 2010 an estimated 39 m people had been infected by HIV (over a half of whom were women and two-thirds of whom were in Sub-Saharan Africa) and over 20 m had died in 20 years. Rapid advances in treatments now make the infection chronic rather than acute in the West, but they are expensive and rarely available where most needed outside the West.

Sociology has contributed in various ways to the understanding and control of AIDS/HIV infection. Studies of sexual networks of transmission were crucial for identifying the virus in 1982. It has also informed national and large-scale studies of sexual and drug-taking behaviour, both KABP (Knowledge, Attitudes, Behaviour and Practices) and more innovative and qualitative research necessary to find out and monitor the prevalence and incidence of high-risk behaviour and risk-taking activity. Techniques to identify and sample 'hidden populations' such as non-gay-identified men who have sex with men and illegal drug-taking activity have depended chiefly on sociological and anthropological methodologies. Theories of risk-taking have also developed from early reliance on the Health Belief Model to contextual and strategic aspects and collective and community response.

(⊕) SEE WEB LINKS
• A United Nations site providing statistical and other information on HIV/AIDS.

alcoholism See DRINKING AND ALCOHOLISM.

alienation In the most general terms, this concept describes the estrangement of individuals from one another, or from a specific situation or process. It is central to the writings of Karl *Marx, and Marxists have explored the philosophical, sociological, and psychological dimensions to his argument. (These are most usefully expounded in Istvan Meszaros, *Marx's Concept of Alienation*, 1970, and John Torrance, *Estrangement, Alienation and Exploitation*, 1977.)

Alienation as a philosophical concept has its roots in *Hegel. It was Hegel's view of the movement of ideas through history and their externalization, objectification, and reappropriation in knowledge that provided Marx with his revolutionary imperative. Turning Hegel on his head and building a *materialist vision, Marx argued that labour defines the 'species being'; the needs, powers, and potential of human beings. It is human labour power that is externalised and objectified in the form of material objects and social relations. This alienation of labour dehumanizes people and is reappropriated on a fully human basis only with the advent of *communism, which represents the complete return of individuals to themselves as social beings.

This philosophical conception of alienation permeates Marx's writings, though there has been much debate over the extent to which his early concerns continued to shape his later arguments. However, sociological discussion of the term relates more to his argument that externalisation and estrangement are consequences of social structures that oppress people, denying them their essential humanity. Alienation is an objective condition inherent in the social and economic arrangements of *capitalism. All forms of production result in objectification, a process in which people manufacture goods that embody their creative talents yet come to stand apart from their creators. Alienation is the distorted form taken by that humanity's objectification of its species-being. Under capitalism, the fruits of production belong to the employers, who expropriate the surplus created by others and in so doing generate alienated labour. Marx attributes four characteristics to such labour: alienation of the worker from his or her 'species essence' as a human being rather than an animal; alienation between workers, since capitalism reduces labour to a commodity to be competitively traded on the market; alienation of the worker from the product itself, which is appropriated by the capitalist, and so escapes the worker's control; and, finally, alienation from the act of production itself, such that work comes to be a meaningless activity, offering little or no intrinsic satisfaction. The last of these generates the psychological discussion of alienation as a subjectively identifiable state of mind, involving feelings of powerlessness, isolation, and discontent at work—especially when this takes place within the context of large, impersonal, bureaucratic social organizations.

It is impossible to extricate Marx's ideas about alienation from his wider sociological discussion of the *division of labour, the evolution of private *property relations, and the emergence of conflicting *classes. In the Marxian terminology, alienation is an objectively verifiable state of affairs, inherent in the specific social relations of capitalist production. However, many researchers have tended to neglect these structural considerations, and have focused on its specifically cognitive and attitudinal characteristics. The 'psychological state' of alienation was said by Melvin Seeman ('On the Meaning of Alienation', *American Sociological Review*, 1959) to comprise the dimensions of powerlessness, meaninglessness, isolation, normlessness, and self-estrangement. In a famous study of factory workers, Robert Blauner attempted to link these dimensions of subjective alienation to particular types of work situation, arguing that the technologies associated with craft, machine, assembly-line, and continuous-process production show a curvilinear association with alienation. That is, 'in the early period, dominated by craft industry, alienation is at its lowest level and the worker's freedom at a maximum. Freedom declines and the curve of alienation...rises sharply in the period of machine industry. The alienation curve continues upward to its highest point in the assembly-line technologies of the 20th century...in this extreme situation, a depersonalised worker, estranged from himself and larger collectives, goes through the motions of work in the regimented milieu of the conveyer belt for the sole purpose of earning his

a

bread...But with automated industry there is a countertrend...automation increases the worker's control over his work process and checks the further division of labour and growth of large factories' (*Alienation and Freedom*, 1964). At this juncture, the discussion of alienation becomes part of a larger debate about the subjective experience of work generally, and *job satisfaction in particular. See also WORK, SUBJECTIVE EXPERIENCE OF.

alliance theory Generally associated with the structuralist anthropologist Claude Lévi-Strauss, the theory argues that in *kinship systems, inheritance and the continuation of the vertical line (descent) are less important than the horizontal links (alliances) and relationships of reciprocity and exchange that are brought about by marriage between different groups.

Allport, Gordon W. (1897-1967) A leading American social psychologist who became head of the Harvard Department of Psychology in 1938. His most significant contribution was a theory of *personality that highlighted the *self and the 'proprium', the latter defined as 'all the regions of our life that we regard as peculiarly ours' (see *Becoming*, 1955). He also undertook studies of the importance of *prejudice as a historical and cultural, as well as a psychological, phenomenon, reviewed the importance of *personal documents in social science (such as his collection of *Letters from Jenny*, 1965), and he championed the *ideographic method.

altercasting A concept introduced by Eugene A. Weinstein and Paul Deutsch-berger (*Sociometry*, 1963) and used within *role theory and *dramaturgical sociology to describe the process of the casting of the other (alter) into a particular role. It highlights the fact that the way in which one acts towards others has a definite pattern and may constrain what the other can do.

alternative movement *See* SOCIAL MOVEMENTS.

alternative technology *See* APPROPRIATE TECHNOLOGIES.

Althusser, Louis (1918-90) One of the most original and influential of 20th-century Marxist social philosophers, Louis Althusser provoked a spectacular, but deeply controversial renewal of Marxist scholarship across a whole range of humanities and social science disciplines. His most important work, and the height of his influence, spanned the 1960s and 1970s. Viewed in political terms, his project was to provide an analysis and critique of the Stalinist distortion of Marxism. Althusser differed sharply from many contemporary Marxist critics of *Stalinism in refusing to employ the rhetoric (as he saw it) of merely *humanist moral condemnation. Instead, a 'rigorously scientific' analysis of the causes and consequences of Stalinism was seen to be a necessity, if political opposition to it was to be effective.

The quest for a scientific approach to the understanding of history took Althusser in two directions: first, to a rereading of the classic texts of the Marxian tradition; and, second, to a philosophical consideration of the nature of science, and how to distinguish it from other forms of knowledge or discourse (*see*

IDEOLOGY). Althusser's view of science was an ambitious attempt to recognize
science as a social practice in which knowledge is produced, and so as a part of
the history of those societies within which it is conducted. At the same time,
Althusser retained from the *materialist tradition of Marxism the insistence that
the real world exists prior to, and independently of, our historically and socially
produced knowledge of it. Ideology also alludes to this independently existing
reality, but does so, according to Althusser, in a way quite different from science.
In ideology, individual 'subjects' are provided with a way of imagining or recognizing themselves and their relation to the society in which they are situated. This
mode of recognition—or misrecognition—serves primarily to orient practical
conduct. In the case of the *dominant ideology, it does so in ways that tend to
reproduce and preserve the prevailing system of social domination.

Althusser's view of science was put to work in his rereading of the classic
Marxian texts. The most famously controversial outcome of this process was the
proclaimed 'epistemological break' between the earlier (pre-1845) and mature
writings of Marx. The philosophical humanism of the early Marx, according to
which history was to be understood as a process of progressive human self-
realization through the concept of *alienation, was rejected as a prescientific
'theoretical ideology'. Only after Marx's 'settling of accounts' with his earlier
philosophical position did the beginnings of a new and scientific approach to
the understanding of human history emerge in his writings. This new approach—
*historical materialism—did not arise fully formed, and Althusser and his asso-
ciates employed a method of 'symptomatic reading' to recover the basic structure of concepts (the 'problematic') that underlay Marx's science of history.
During the 1960s Althusser and his close colleagues produced a series of texts
(*For Marx, Reading Capital*, and *Lenin and Philosophy* were probably the most
influential) in which rigorous definitions and applications of these concepts were
attempted. In part, this was a matter of reworking already well-established
Marxian concepts such as forces and relations of production, modes of production, ideology, the state, and social formation (all of which are treated separately
in this dictionary).

Amidst this reworking of established concepts, Althusser was also addressing
long-standing lacunae and failings in Marxist theory. First, there is the question
of *economic determinism (or 'economism'). Drawing on indications in texts by
Marx and Engels themselves, together with then influential *structuralist ideas,
Althusser advanced a view of social wholes as 'decentered structures in dominance'. This means that *societies are seen as ordered combinations of economic, ideological, and political practices, none of which is reducible to any of
the others, and each of which has its own specific weight in the shaping of the
whole ('structural causality').

The view of history as a linear sequence of modes of production through which
humankind passes *en route* to communist self-realization had become identified
with Marxist orthodoxy. Althusser rejected this as a *historicist ideology, and
claimed to uncover an anti-historicist view of history as a 'process without a
subject' in Marx's later writings. For Althusser, the major historical transitions are
always contingent, always exceptional outcomes of the *overdetermination or

'condensation' of a multiplicity of contradictions affecting a social order. Accordingly, the quasi-religious certainty that 'history is on our side' should have no place in a Marxist understanding of history.

Althusser's most controversial position was his stand against 'theoretical humanism': his view of the relation between subjects and society. Not only is the view of history as a process of human self-realization to be rejected, but so also is any notion of autonomous individual agency, as the source or basis of social life. Individuals are 'bearers' of social relations, their sense of *self an outcome of the social process of 'interpellation' (or 'hailing'), which is itself the *modus operandi* of the dominant ideology. Althusser's apparent denial of individual autonomy provoked much criticism.

These Althusserian ideas were influential in fields as diverse as literary and film criticism, political sociology, anthropology, feminist social theory, epistemology, cultural studies, and sociology of development. From 1967 onwards, however, Althusser produced a spate of self-critical writings, many bearing the imprint of the radical student movement of the time. Althusser appeared to retract his earlier commitment to a theory of the nature of science, viewing philosophy rather as a practice of mediating between science and politics. Along with this went a deepening of his scepticism concerning the scientific status even of much in the mature writings of Marx himself. This is discussed in Ted Benton, *The Rise and Fall of Structural Marxism* (1984).

As his autobiography reveals, Althusser had always been psychologically unstable. A period of deep depression in 1980 resulted in his killing his wife Hélène, and he spent the final decade of his life in obscurity, most of it in a Paris mental hospital.

altruism A term introduced by Auguste *Comte to refer to behaviour that takes account of the interests of others, usually treated as in opposition to egoism, selfishness, and *individualism. There are extensive theoretical and empirical research literatures in social psychology, economics, political behaviour, and sociobiology (as well as sociology) on altruism, its sources and consequences, and on whether altruistic behaviour is ultimately reducible to and explained by egoistic motives. Research on altruism is also relevant to exchange theory and *rational choice theory, public policy-making, and the voluntary sector. Studies have focused on blood donation; acts of bravery in wars and other conflicts; spontaneous acts of helping strangers in public situations compared to help offered to family and friends; the willingness of citizens to tax themselves for the benefit of others; participation in voluntary non-profit organizations; and giving money to charities.

Research seems to confirm that people do have regard to the interests and needs of others, make sacrifices for their children and even non-kin, and contribute to *public goods. Other social animals also display altruistic behaviour (for example, birds give predator alarms) and some research has suggested that there is a hereditary, genetic component in altruism. Sociobiologists have identified selection processes that lead to the establishment and perpetuation of 'altruistic' genes in populations. In addition, socialization in the family and community encourages people to adhere to public-spirited values and engage in helping behaviour. People who do voluntary work generally give altruistic reasons for becoming involved in such activities (such as a desire to help others). But self-oriented reasons are often simultaneously present, such as the desire to gain work experience, enjoyment of social contacts, and an interest in the particular activity in question. For some people, involvement in charity work confers the prestige, power in the community, and self-fulfilment that others obtain from employment. Similarly, studies of corporate philanthropy conclude that charitable donations are good for business, with enlightened self-interest rather than altruism being the driving factor in firms' public activities. In many cultures, gift-giving is used to enhance prestige, or even defines a person's social status.

Economists are concerned with the '*free rider' problem in the provision or use of public goods, such as the problem of the person who benefits from public TV but does not contribute his or her share of the costs through taxes, or the country that regularly exceeds its allocated fishing quota and so depletes fish stocks for all other countries fishing in the same seas. Sociologists are concerned rather with the development of *trust and co-operation in relationships, and the impact of social norms and group identity on decision-making in social dilemmas. These issues are often studied through decision-making in the *Prisoner's Dilemma game, with variable results from short-term studies.

Research based on Prisoner's Dilemma simulations has shown that, in the long run, altruism and selfishness are not always or necessarily mutually exclusive choices. In his *Evolution of Cooperation* (1984) R. Axelrod showed how cooperation can evolve in a society of completely self-interested individuals, in effect that altruism and individualism are not necessarily in conflict in human society where public goods are of benefit to all, including people who do not use them directly. Axelrod carried out a series of computer simulations to assess the effectiveness of various strategies in Prisoner's Dilemma, an issue which is usually studied with laboratory experiments of short duration. Contrary to expectation, one of the simplest strategies, named TIT FOR TAT, emerged repeatedly as the winner, owing to a combination of being nice, retaliatory, forgiving, and clear. By using computer simulations of the competing strategies, the game could be run for a much longer time and with a larger number of diverse players than in laboratory experiments, thus approximating to evolution in the long term. For a useful overview of relevant literature see J. A. Piliavin and H.-W. Charng, 'Altruism', *Annual Review of Sociology* (1990). *See also* GIFT RELATIONSHIP; SUICIDE.

altruistic suicide *See* SUICIDE.

ambivalence The coexistence, in one person, of opposing emotions or attitudes. Sigmund Freud often refers to the individual oscillating between love and hate for the same object or person. In sociology, the *dual consciousness thesis posits a subordinate class that holds apparently inconsistent beliefs or values, resulting in an ambivalent attitude to some of the central institutions in society.

amnesia, retrograde *See* RETROGRADE AMNESIA.

amoral familism Social action persistently oriented to the economic interests of the nuclear *family. In a controversial account of *poverty in a village in southern Italy (*The Moral Basis of a Backward Society*, 1958), Edward C. Banfield argued that the backwardness of the community was to be explained 'largely but not entirely' by 'the inability of the villagers to act together for their common good or, indeed, for any end transcending the immediate, material interest of the nuclear family'. This was attributed to the ethos of 'amoral familism' that had been produced by the combination of a high death rate, certain land-tenure conditions, and the absence of the institution of the extended *family. Banfield's thesis provoked considerable debate about the nature of 'familism' and the role of *culture generally in preventing or facilitating economic development (*see* DEVELOPMENT, SOCIOLOGY OF).

amplification of deviance *See* DEVIANCE AMPLIFICATION.

analysis of variance *See* CAUSAL MODELLING, VARIATION (STATISTICAL).

analytical Marxism A term sometimes applied to the writings of sociologists and social theorists who attempted during the 1980s and 1990s to revitalize European and North American *Marxist sociology by combining the methodological tenets of *Marxism with a variety of alternative approaches. Key figures are Erik Olin Wright, Jon Elster, and John Roemer. Individual members of this loosely defined group have, to varying degrees and at different times, adopted the positivist covering law account of causal explanation (*see* CAUSE)—Wright's work has sometimes been referred to rather disdainfully as 'multiple-regression Marxism'—methodological *individualism, and *rational choice theory. Their commitment to abandoning some of the philosophically untenable positions of earlier Marxisms is neatly captured in their self-description as 'No Bullshit Marxists'. Critics claim that, when the objectionable principles of Marxism (such as its *historicism and *economic determinism) are jettisoned, nothing that is distinctively Marxist remains (since all that seems to hold the members together is a commitment to clarity). For a sympathetic overview see Tom Mayer, *Analytical Marxism* (1994).

analytic induction A method of qualitative research introduced by Florian Znaniecki that employs a systematic and exhaustive examination of a limited number of cases in order to identify similarities and so produce generalizations. Donald Cressey, who employs the method in his book *Other People's Money* (1953), suggested the stages of analytic induction are: defining the field; hypothesizing an explanation; studying one case to see if it fits the facts; modifying the hypothesis or the definitions in the light of this; and reviewing further cases. According to Cressey, 'this procedure of examining cases, re-defining the phenomenon and reformulating the hypothesis is continued until a universal relationship is established'. *See also* GROUNDED THEORY; INDUCTION; SYMBOLIC INTERACTIONISM.

anarchism An array of philosophical and political positions arguing that human societies function best without government or authority, and that suggest that the natural state of people is one of living together harmoniously and freely, without such intervention. Anarchy is said not to lead to chaos but to 'spontaneous order'. The philosophy takes many forms and covers the whole political spectrum from extreme right to extreme left, the former seeking to diminish the influence of the *state in order that *free-market principles might prevail, the latter arguing that the state will wither away under true *communism. Proponents of *voluntary associations and mutual aid fall somewhere between. Good overviews of the theory of anarchism can be found in texts of that name by David Miller (1984) and Alan Ritter (1980).

In modern times, Jean-Jacques *Rousseau's romantic claim that we are born free but then everywhere found in chains is one of the first statements of anarchism, whilst the first person to evolve a systematic theory of anarchism was the English rationalist William Godwin. During the 19th century, Pierre-Joseph *Proudhon (influenced in part by Godwin) developed a theory of anarchism that provided much of the basis for French *syndicalism, arguing for the ideal of an ordered society of small units, functioning without central government, and organized instead on the federal principle of 'mutualism'—or equitable exchange between self-governing associations of producers. Proudhon's disciple Mikhail Bakunin, in dispute with Karl Marx, favoured the destruction of state power and advocated violence to achieve this end. He too insisted that the reconstruction of society has to be achieved from the bottom upwards by free associations or federations of workers. Like Proudhon, Bakunin maintained that all political parties are 'varieties of absolutism', and so was opposed to organized political action by a revolutionary vanguard on behalf of the *proletariat. The extent to which anarchism challenges other political philosophies on the right and left alike is evident in Peter Kropotkin's observation that 'Throughout the history of our civilisation, two traditions, two opposed tendencies have been in conflict: the Roman tradition and the popular tradition, the imperial tradition and the federalist tradition, the authoritarian and the libertarian tradition' (*Modern Science and Anarchism*, 1912). Kropotkin, a Russian aristocrat, was himself an advocate of a 'communist anarchism' which was opposed to centralized mass production, and favoured instead an ideal of small communities in which industry and agriculture would be combined and an education allowing each individual to develop to his or her full potential would be integral to the production process. Like most anarchists he tended to idealize primitive communities in his writings.

Anarchist influences are often evident in contemporary discussions of *communes and communalism, 'direct action', workers' control, decentralization, and federalism. Anarchist philosophy and practice has also played a role (usually a minor one) in the *trade-union movement, the Spanish Civil War, the Hungarian Uprising of 1956, the events of May 1968 in France, in Gandhian techniques of non-violent protest, and in much latter-day terrorism.

An interesting link with social *ecology is made in the writings of the Canadian anarchist Murray Bookchin. After thirty years of political activism, beginning with the Spanish Civil War, Bookchin emerged in the 1960s as a distinctive voice within the radical ecological movement. His theories, usually described as part of the communitarian anarchist tradition, have been developed in twenty or so books including *Post Scarcity Anarchism* (1971), *Towards an Ecological Society* (1980), *The Rise of Urbanization and the Decline of Citizenship* (1984), *The Modern Crisis* (2nd edn., 1987) and *The Philosophy of Social Ecology* (1990).

Although rarely acknowledged as such, much social scientific writing can be seen as embodying elements of anarchist thought. This includes the *symbolic interactionists and their view of society as spontaneous order, the *anti-psychiatry of Thomas Szasz, the free-market views of *laissez-faire economics, the anti-systemic stress on decentered power in *Michel Foucault, and the theories of *post-structuralism and *postmodernism.

anarchy, epistemological *See* METHODOLOGICAL PLURALISM.

ancestry *See* DESCENT GROUPS.

androgyny An androgynous individual is one who unites the characteristics of both sexes. Androgyny has been of interest to some sociologists who study *gender because it makes problematic the taken-for-granted assumptions of what it is to be a man or a woman. Examples include Harold Garfinkel's case-study of 'Agnes' or Michel Foucault's historical dossier on Herculine Barbine. More commonly it provides the subject-matter of much science fiction (see e.g. M. Piercey's *Woman at the Edge of Time*). Some feminists advocate cultural or psychological (rather than physical) androgyny as an alternative to *patriarchy. Androgynous styles have long been embraced in popular culture, especially since the 1960s, epitomized in singers such as David Bowie, Freddie Mercury, Michael Jackson, and Annie Lennox.

animism *See* TOTEMISM.

Annales School An influential school of French historians, formed around the journal *Annales: économies, sociétés, civilisations*, which was founded by Lucien Febvre and Marc *Bloch at the University of Strasburg in 1929. The Annales School attempted to develop a 'total history' as a critique of existing historical methodology, which offered merely a chronology of events. They turned attention away from political history towards a macro-historical analysis of societies over long time-periods. The Annales School, which included Maurice Halbwachs, André Siegfried, Fernand *Braudel, Emmanuel Le Roy Ladurie, and Georges Duby, had the following characteristics: it was interdisciplinary; it was concerned to study very long historical periods (*la longue durée*) and social structure; some members of the School employed quantitative methods; and they examined the interaction between geographical environment, material culture, and society.

The work of the original members is represented by Bloch, who attempted a total analysis of medieval society in his *Feudal Society* (1961). The two most influential works in the later period have been Braudel's study of the Mediterranean (*The Mediterranean and the Mediterranean World in the Age of Philip II*,

1949) and Le Roy Ladurie's analysis of fourteenth-century village life (*Montaillou*, 1975). The School has influenced historical sociology, especially the *world-system theory of Immanuel Wallerstein (see, for example, his three-volume study of *The Modern World-System*, 1974, 1980, and 1989). Critics have argued that the Annales School neglected political processes. The Annales approach has similar interdisciplinary concerns to *historical materialism, the historical sociology of Max *Weber in his *The Agrarian Sociology of Ancient Civilisations* (1924), and the figurational sociology of Norbert *Elias in *The Court Society* (1969).

anomic suicide *See* ANOMIE.

anomie (anomy) An absence, breakdown, confusion, or conflict in the *norms of a society. The term *anomia* is scattered throughout classical Greek writings, where it may be linked to the adjective *anomos*, meaning 'without law'. It has since assumed a wider and often negative connotation of breakdown and catastrophe. In sociology the term is most frequently identified with the work of Émile *Durkheim and Robert *Merton.

In Durkheim's writings the concept appears prominently in *The Division of Labour in Society* and *Suicide*. In the former, anomie emerges through society's transition from mechanical to organic solidarity. Normally, an increasing *division of labour brings about social integration through organic solidarity, but if economic change is too fast for the growth of moral regulation to keep pace with increasing differentiation and specialization then an abnormal or pathological division of labour occurs. This is the anomic division of labour. The argument is further developed in the discussion of *suicide, where anomie is one of the four causes of suicide identified. Anomic suicide occurs in organic societies when economic depression or boom leads to a lessening of normative regulation. At such times, people are less closely locked into their society and their basic desires may become limitless and confused. At this point, anomie results in a psychological state of disorder and meaninglessness. The concept is often contrasted with Marx's idea of *alienation.

Robert Merton's work shifted the meaning somewhat. Merton wanted to produce a sociological account of *deviance: of how social structures and cultural values exert definite pressures to conform, yet create disjunctions and contradictions that make deviance a necessary outcome. In his classic essay on 'Social Structure and Anomie' (in *Social Theory and Social Structure*, 1957), he discusses the American Dream of 'log cabin to White House', the truly open society where enormous upward social mobility and financial rewards are possible. According to Merton, the American value-system creates almost universal striving for success, especially economic success, and specifies a range of normatively approved means for securing this goal (most notably, educational attainment and hard work). However, the structure of economic resources in that society enables only certain privileged groups and classes to succeed through these means. This creates feelings of relative *deprivation among many poorer individuals, who then turn to various forms of individual deviance that seem to offer alternative means to the same desired ends. In other words anomie occurs as a disjunction between means and goals. The true conformist will be the person who has access to both the legitimate means and the approved goals. However, in a celebrated typology of modes of individual adaptations to anomie, Merton also discusses innovation (keeping goals, but rejecting legitimate means, as in theft); retreatism (rejecting or withdrawing from goals and means, as in drug use); ritualism (keeping to legitimate means becomes a goal in itself, as in the case of a slavish bureaucrat); and, finally, rebellion (rejecting both means and goals, and substituting new ones, as in political radicalism).

Merton's theory has been much criticized for assuming too much consensus and social integration, but it has been very influential, especially in theories of crime and delinquency. For example, in Albert Cohen's theory of *status frustration (*Delinquent Boys*, 1956) and R. Cloward and L. Ohlin's theory of differential *opportunity structures (*Delinquency and Opportunity*, 1961), delinquency is seen as the outcome of a situation of strain or anomie in the social structure. The concept of anomie has also been applied to a range of other areas, discussed critically in a volume edited by Marshall B. Clinard, *Anomie and Deviant Behaviour* (1964), and more recently in Marco Orrù, *Anomie: History and Meanings* (1987). *See also* SUBCULTURE.

anthropology *See* SOCIAL ANTHROPOLOGY.

anthropomorphism Attribution of human characteristics to things that are not human.

anticipatory socialization In contrast to more formal training, anticipatory *socialization involves the informal adoption of *norms or behaviour appropriate to a *status not yet achieved by the individuals concerned, so providing them with experience of a *role they have yet to assume. For example, children may anticipate parenthood by observing their parents as role models, and the careerist may anticipate promotion by emulating the occupational behaviour of his or her superiors.

anti-naturalism *See* NATURALISM.

antinomianism The belief that one's religious commitments or faith exempt one from the legal or moral codes of the wider society (hence 'anti-norms'). Antinomianism has been a characteristic of particular *sects throughout the history of Christianity. Most notably, certain radical Protestant sectarians of the 16th and 17th centuries extended the Calvinist doctrine of predestination in this way, arguing that those who possessed an inner certainty of their own election are no longer capable of sin and are therefore freed from the restrictions of conventional conduct. More recent examples include the Oneida Community in the 19th century, and the Children of God in the present day. Antinomianism is usually associated with unorthodox sexual or marital practices, such as plural marriage (the Oneida Community) or sexual activity outside marriage (the Children of God), the latter being justified on the grounds that it brings others to salvation.

anti-psychiatry A term coined in the 1960s for writers who are highly critical of the ideas and practice of *psychiatry. Precisely who is included within this group (which is always theoretically and politically heterogeneous) tends to vary. Frequently mentioned are the radical libertarian Thomas Szasz, the more left-wing, existentialist-inclined Ronald *Laing and his colleague David Cooper, and the Italian mental health reformer Franco Basaglia. Two sociologists who have written on mental illness—Erving *Goffman and Thomas Scheff—are also often included, as is Michel *Foucault. All of these writers, from their divergent stances, view madness and *mental illness as socially constructed, and emphasize the way in which psychiatry functions as an agency of *social control that constrains and coerces individuals, especially in institutional contexts.

The work of Szasz is typical. In *The Myth of Mental Illness* (1961) he forcefully denounced the application of the language of illness to human thought and conduct, regarding it as mystifying processes of social control. He held that mental illnesses (except for organic disorders) are 'problems in living' and are to be analysed in terms of social rules and role-playing. Numerous subsequent books reaffirm his message, calling for private, contractual psychiatry to replace state coercion.

In the United States and United Kingdom, acceptance of policies of *community care largely predated 1960s anti-psychiatry. In Italy, however, anti-psychiatry was an important influence on the reforming programme that culminated in the radical legislation of 1978, which introduced community care on a national basis.

anti-urbanism An intellectual strand of social science writing that is critical of the city as a social form. Negative attitudes to urbanization—and the 'pastoral myth' of the countryside—predate the industrial revolution. However, as Robert Nisbet has observed, 'revulsion for the city, fear of it as a force in culture, and forebodings with respect to the psychological conditions surrounding it' date from the 19th century. While some radicals (notably Karl *Marx and Friedrich *Engels) saw aspects of *urbanization as socially progressive, for liberals and conservatives it posed problems of *social control. Classical sociology reflected these concerns. According to Nisbet, 'the city...form[ed] the context of most sociological propositions relating to disorganisation, alienation, and mental isolation—all stigmata of loss of community and membership' (*The Sociological Tradition*, 1966).

The presumed breakdown of traditional *communities in urban societies was a powerful theme in the work of Auguste *Comte, Frédéric Le Play, and Émile *Durkheim. More specifically, anti-urbanism affected the development of rural and *urban sociology: Ferdinand *Tönnies's suggestion that cities were prime locations for *Gesellschaftlich* (instrumental and associational) social relations was developed by Georg *Simmel ('The Metropolis and Mental Life', 1903), whose work strongly influenced the *Chicago urban sociologists. Raymond Williams (*The Country and the City*, 1975) has shown that this has also been a theme in literary and historical writing, each generation feeling that it is uniquely poised at the point of communal breakdown.

a

Contemporary sociology largely rejects anti-urbanism. It is now generally recognized that the growth of cities, and the varied forms of social association occurring within them, are both consequences of the emergence of modern industrial societies. The city, in other words, is 'a mirror of ... history, class structure and culture' (R. Glass, *Clichés of Urban Doom*, 1989). *See also* COMMUNITARIANISM, COMMUNITY STUDIES.

apartheid *See* SEGREGATION.

applied sociology *See* POLICY RESEARCH.

appropriate technologies Because of the permanent over-supply of labour in contemporary developing societies, some sociologists (and economists) have argued that the labour-saving (often capital-intensive) techniques of *production that are associated with technological innovation and development in the West, are inapplicable in most *Third World contexts. Rather, the labour surplus suggests a bias in favour of labour-intensive and capital-saving techniques, exemplified in 'appropriate' (sometimes called 'alternative' or 'intermediate') technologies. The example of China is often cited in this context, since the particular combination of the factors of production in that country has encouraged Chinese governments to build roads using large numbers of people armed with shovels, rather than fewer people equipped with (expensive) bulldozers. All manner of goods and services can be produced by labour-intensive technologies, which offer full employment, self-sufficiency, and (possibly indirectly) greater equality. However, because capital-intensive methods of production promise higher net output and therefore higher rates of growth, they are often favoured despite yielding a lower volume of present employment. *See also* TECHNOLOGY.

aptitude *See* ABILITY.

Ardrey, Robert (1908–80) Author of a series of best-selling books on human and animal nature (*African Genesis*, 1961, *The Territorial Imperative*, 1966, and *The Social Contract*, 1970). In the 1950s he became deeply interested in R. A. Dart's discoveries of fossil hominids in Kenya, and combined a view of humans as descended from 'a race of terrestrial, flesh-eating, killer apes' with evidence on territoriality, dominance, and aggression in non-human animals to argue for the instinctual basis of *human nature. The popular reception of Ardrey's work was undoubtedly connected with its politically conservative response to the challenges and conflicts of the 1960s, and it remains an exemplar of the *biological reductionism to which many sociologists object. *See also* SOCIOBIOLOGY.

aristocracy *See* UPPER CLASS.

aristocracy of labour *See* LABOUR ARISTOCRACY.

arithmetic mean *See* CENTRAL TENDENCY (MEASURES OF).

arms control *See* DISARMAMENT.

Aron, Raymond (1905–83) Professor of sociology at the Sorbonne from 1955 to 1968 and for some years a prominent member of the *Mont Pelerin Society (although he later resigned). He was instrumental in introducing German sociology (especially Tönnies, Simmel, and Weber) to French social science in his *German Sociology* (1935). He also wrote an influential introduction to sociological theory (*Main Currents in Sociological Thought*, 1960 and 1962) in which he gave a special emphasis to the work of Alexis de *Tocqueville. Aron disagreed profoundly with *Marxism as a social science, and it was partly on these grounds that he was often a target of criticism from within the dominant Marxist paradigm in post-war French social philosophy. Aron, by contrast, was more impressed by the work of Max *Weber, an influence that is evident in publications such as *Eighteen Lectures on Industrial Society* (1956). He played an important part in the debate that followed the student protests of 1968 (see *The Elusive Revolution*, 1968), and also wrote more generally about the nature of power, political elites, and political organizations. He had a specific interest in the work of Vilfredo *Pareto on elites.

Aron's work is distinctive because of the attention that he gave to international relations and war—topics that have been rather neglected by sociologists. This interest is reflected in *Peace and War* (1962) and *Clausewitz* (1985).

artefacts, statistical and methodological A statistical artefact is an inference that results from *bias in the collection or manipulation of data. The implication is that the findings do not reflect the real world but are, rather, an unintended consequence of *measurement error. When the findings from a particular study are deemed to be—at least in part—a result of the particular research technique employed (*see* RESEARCH DESIGN), rather than an accurate representation of the world, they are sometimes said to be a methodological artefact.

asceticism (this-worldly) *See* PROTESTANT ETHIC THESIS.

ascribed status *See* ASCRIPTION; STATUS, ACHIEVED.

ascription In allocating *roles and *statuses, or imputing allegedly natural behaviours, cultures make varying use of kinship, age, sex, and ethnicity. Such ascribed characteristics cannot be changed by individual effort, although *social movements and *states attempt periodically to challenge the disadvantages and *stereotypes arising from nepotism, *ageism, *sexism, and *racism. *See also* ACHIEVEMENT; PARSONS; STATUS, ACHIEVED.

Asiatic mode of production Of all Karl *Marx's conceptions of the modes of production that he considered to have provided the *base for the various forms of society known to human history, this was perhaps the least developed, and is certainly the one that has given rise to the most controversy.

The term 'Asiatic society' has sometimes been used to refer to all non-Western social forms other than 'primitive-communism' and slavery, whilst at others it (or its more common synonym *oriental despotism) has been seen as applicable only to the cases of Japan and China. Underlying this referential variation was a conceptual variation. Especially in their earlier work, Marx and *Engels stressed the dominant role that the *state played in such societies because of its monopoly of land ownership, its control over irrigation systems, or its sheer political and military power. At other times—and this is what allowed them to broaden the range of societies to which the term was applied in most of their later work—they suggested that it was the communal nature of landholding that isolated the inhabitants of different villages from one another and so made them prey to state domination.

The subsequent status of the concept among Marxists and non-Marxists alike has varied with changes in the political climate. Between the two world wars, the idea was disavowed by Soviet-influenced Marxists, who probably saw it as an obstacle to the Soviet Union's political ambitions in and for the Far East. In the Cold War climate of the 1950s, Karl Wittfogel disinterred the concept in his *Oriental Despotism* (1957), suggesting that the real reason for its unpopularity in the Soviet Union was the uncomfortable similarity between it and the reality of Stalin's Russia.

During the 1960s the concept excited some interest on the part of Western Marxists, who hoped that it might provide them with a means of avoiding a Eurocentric conception of social development. In the 1970s, however, such hopes were exposed to a barrage of criticism from structuralist Marxism, largely explaining the concept's current eclipse. For example, Perry Anderson subjected the concept to a major critique in his *Lineages of the Absolutist State* (1974), while Barry Hindess and Paul Hirst made it the object of a (rather more controversial) theoretical critique in their *Precapitalist Modes of Production* (1975). Finally, Edward Said delivered what appears to have been the *coup de grâce*, by arguing that, in formulating the concept, Marx and Engels were the unwitting bearers of a noxious discourse that he termed 'orientalism' (see his 1979 book of the same name).

assimilation A term synonymous with acculturation, used to describe the process by which an outsider, immigrant, or subordinate group becomes indistinguishably integrated into the dominant host society. In early American studies of race relations (such as those of Robert *Park), the term was contrasted with accommodation (whereby the subordinate group simply conformed to the expectations of the dominant group), competition (in which it set up its own values in opposition to the mainstream), and extermination and exclusion (which saw no room for interaction between subordinate and dominant groups). Assimilation implied that the subordinate group actually came to accept and internalize the *values and *culture of the dominant group. This view of the process developed in part out of American concerns about the growing number of immigrants to that society, and has been criticized for exaggerating the importance of the values of the dominant group, and for neglecting the ability of new or subordinate groups both to affect these values (thereby creating a *melting-pot culture) or else to live alongside it while adhering to its own values (in a *multicultural society).

association *See* PLURALISM; VOLUNTARY ASSOCIATIONS.

associational democracy *See* PLURALISM.

association coefficients A number used to indicate the degree to which two *variables or attributes are related. Two basic types are covariation measures and dis/similarity measures. Statistical associations and measures of *correlation are not in themselves evidence of causal relationships, which must be identified by theoretical reasoning and models. In practice, statistical associations are often treated as equivalent to establishing causal links, with textbooks warning against *spurious correlations. Statistical measures become less important in the research process as our knowledge of causal mechanisms becomes more complete, although they remain useful for assigning quantitative values to a model of a causal process.

asymmetrical causal processes An irreversible or one-way causation process. Once A has been set in motion and caused B, the new situation becomes permanent, and cannot be reversed by eliminating or reducing A after the event. For example, breaking and frying an egg produces an omelette, but the process cannot be reversed to produce an unbroken raw egg from an omelette. Asymmetrical causal processes are more common in the social world than in the physical world, invalidate many of the assumptions underlying statistical inference and social statistics, and pose special problems in *policy research. See Stanley Lieberson, *Making it Count* (1985).

atomism A philosophical position that views the world as composed of discrete atomistic elements, and reduces knowledge to observation of the smallest of these. For example, individual human beings may be seen as the elements of social structures and social institutions. In strict atomism, the basic elements do not have causal powers: the relations between them are external and contingent. However an atomistic view of society may be combined with a *voluntaristic explanation of social phenomena.

attitudes Variously defined as an orientation (towards a person, situation, institution, or social process) that is held to be indicative of an underlying *value or belief, or, among those who insist that attitudes can only be inferred from observed behaviour, as a tendency to act in a certain (more or less consistent) way towards persons and situations. Milton Rokeach's much-quoted definition (*Beliefs, Attitudes and Values*, 1976) embraces both tendencies and describes an attitude as 'a relatively enduring organization of beliefs around an object or situation predisposing one to respond in some preferential manner'.

Social psychologists and sociologists have invested a great deal of effort in the measurement of attitudes, opinions, and views and on the identification and measurement of the more deeply held and less volatile values that underlie them. Attitudes are studied both as a substitute for measuring behaviour directly and because they are (sometimes) assumed to predict behaviour. Some social scientists treat them as important variables in their own right, key features of the individual, as reflected for example in the so-called *authoritarian personality.

The sheer volume of attitudinal research is not difficult to explain. Consider, for example, the phenomenon of race discrimination. It is not easy to observe instances of discrimination, and isolated incidents, while illustrative, may not be representative. The alternative in surveys is to ask people to report their behaviour, but this runs into difficulties with situations that have never arisen, or are purely hypothetical. The other approach is then to collect attitudinal data on people's predispositions and stated values, the advantage being that the questions seem to be appropriate for everyone.

In reality, however, many people do not have well-developed or even superficial opinions on topics that may interest the sociologist. Some would argue that the idea of attitudes is closely tied to the culture of Western industrial society, in which citizens are regularly invited to express their views on public issues, both directly and through the ballot box. What is certain is that attitude scales developed in Western societies do not function in the same way in other cultures. Even a standard and simple *job-satisfaction question attracts a different pattern of response as soon as it is used beyond the confines of Western industrial societies—in Japan for example. There is some debate about the *ethnocentrism and broader cross-cultural validity of many attitude scales that have been developed over the past eight decades.

At the simplest level, attitude questions invite people to agree or disagree, approve or disapprove, say Yes or No to something. More sophisticated techniques for measuring attitudes include the well-established and easy to use Likert scale, Thurstone scale, semantic differential scale, and Guttman scale. A huge variety of personality tests, attitude and aptitude scales have been developed in the United States and Europe for commercial use by employers and recruitment agencies, as part of the staff selection process. Attitude scales of various types are sometimes used in *opinion polls, occasionally in simplified form. Attitude research shades into studies of reported behaviour, sociometric scales, the sociology of knowledge, research on motivations, preferences, aims and objectives, which are also causally linked to behaviour, and the whole range of social psychological research.

One of the longest-running disputes in social-scientific research concerns the relationship between attitudes and action. What are the behavioural implications of holding particular attitudes? This debate, which has taken place mostly among social psychologists, has culminated in the view that attitudes are merely one of the factors that influence behaviour (see Icek Ajzen and Martin Fishbein, *Understanding Attitudes and Predicting Social Behavior*, 1980). However, there is widespread disagreement both about where attitudes stand in this list of factors, and how they relate to the many other variables in the equation. After exhaustively reviewing the literature, Richard Eiser (*Social Psychology: Attitudes, Cognition and Social Behaviour*, 1986) was able to conclude only that 'attitudes, in short, have behavioural implications', and that 'the question of which specific behaviours are implied by a particular attitude, however, will depend on circumstances, and is therefore an empirical one'.

For a useful summary of the major contributions to this debate, together with a discussion of other salient issues in attitude research, see Richard Eiser and J. van der Pligt, *Attitudes and Decisions* (1988). *See also* EQUAL APPEARING INTERVALS; PROTESTANT ETHIC THESIS.

attitudinal consistency *See* COGNITIVE CONSISTENCY.

attribution theory Attribution theory deals with the rules that most people use when they attempt to infer the causes of behaviour they observe. In general, people tend to attribute their own behaviour to the situation or circumstances (social *environment) in which they find themselves, while they attribute other people's behaviour to *personality factors. An excellent sociological discussion of this phenomenon, as it emerges in the context of beliefs about the causes of poverty and wealth, will be found in James R. Kluegel and Eliot R. Smith's *Beliefs about Inequality: Americans' Views of What is and What Ought to Be* (1986).

authenticity A concept common in *existentialist philosophy, involving the idea of a life led in and through the recognition of our human condition (most importantly that we will die), and our total responsibility for our choices and actions (as opposed, for example, to the claim that society makes us what we are). *See also* EXISTENTIAL SOCIOLOGY.

authoritarian (authoritarianism) *See* AUTHORITARIAN PERSONALITY.

authoritarian personality A term coined by Theodor *Adorno and his associates through a book of the same name first published in 1950, to describe a personality type characterized by (among other things) extreme conformity, submissiveness to authority, rigidity, and arrogance towards those considered inferior.

Adorno and colleagues conducted extensive empirical research on anti-semitic, ethnocentric, and fascist personalities. In attempting to explain why some people are more susceptible to *fascism and authoritarian belief-systems than others, Adorno devised several *attitude scales that revealed a clustering of traits that he termed authoritarianism. Several scales were constructed (ethnocentric, anti-semitic, fascist) and part of the interest in the study came from examining these scales. During interviews with more than 2000 respondents, a close association was found between such factors as ethnocentrism, rigid adherence to conventional values, a submissive attitude towards the moral authority of the in-group, a readiness to punish, opposition to the imaginative and tender-minded, belief in fatalistic theories, and an unwillingness to tolerate ambiguity. Intensive interviewing and the use of *Thematic Apperception Tests identified the authoritarian personality with a family pattern of rigidity, discipline, external rules, and fearful subservience to the demands of parents, which were analysed in Freudian terms.

The Authoritarian Personality is a classic study of *prejudice, *defence mechanisms, and *scapegoating. The term itself has entered everyday language, even though the original research has attracted considerable criticism. Among other weaknesses, critics have suggested that the Adorno study measures only an authoritarianism of the right, and fails to consider the wider 'closed mind' of both left and right alike; that it tends, like all theories of scapegoating, to reduce complex historical processes to psychological needs; and that it is based on flawed scales and samples. For a detailed exposition and critique see John Madge, *The Origins of Scientific Sociology* (1962). *See also* CRITICAL THEORY.

authoritarian populism *See* POPULISM.

authoritative power *See* ORGANIZATIONAL REACH.

authority *See* CHARISMA; DOMINATION; LEGITIMACY; POWER.

autobiography *See* LIFE-HISTORY.

autocracy A regime in which power is concentrated in the person of a single individual—as, for example, in the case of 'the Stalinist autocracy'. The term is thus loosely applied, and will be found in discussions of a variety of state structures and political regimes, including in particular *totalitarian, *fascist, *real socialist, and monarchical examples. *See also* STALINISM.

automation In theory, a workerless system of manufacture; in practice, a series of individual computer-controlled or robotic machine tools, with electro-mechanical link operations replacing transfer by hand. Research on the modern *labour process suggests that automation displaces, rather than replaces, human labour and skill—to maintenance, planning, distribution, and ancillary work.

average (averaging) *See* CENTRAL TENDENCY (MEASURES OF).

aversion therapy A therapy based on classical *conditioning, in which a maladaptive behaviour (such as drinking alcohol or smoking) is associated with an unpleasant event (for example an electric shock). It is now generally regarded as outmoded by other forms of therapy more acceptable to contemporary social values. *See also* BEHAVIOURISM.

avoidance relationships A generic term applied to certain potentially difficult or stressful affinal ('by marriage') secondary relationships in extended families. These relationships are, to a differing degree in different societies, subject to strain—either because of the potential for (threatening) sexual relations or because of lack of a specified role content for incumbents. Typically, strain is avoided by physical avoidance; by codifying the relationship so that it is subject to minute regulation of correct behaviour and precise requirements; or by 'personalization', whereby the parties involved are expected to create a working relationship, merely on the basis of their own goodwill and personalities. The custom takes many forms. Among the African Galla, for example, a man must not mention the name of his mother-in-law, drink from a cup she has used, or eat food prepared by her, although he can address her directly.

Where this custom of maintaining a respectful distance between certain relatives occurs, there is also frequently associated with it a directly contrary relation of familiarity, usually called a 'joking relationship'. Thus, a man might have an avoidance relationship with his wife's parents, but a *joking relationship with her brothers and sisters.

awareness context A concept developed by Barney Glaser and Anselm Strauss in *Awareness of Dying* (1965), to facilitate analysis of 'the total combination of what each interactant in a situation knows about the identity of the other and his own identity in the eyes of the other', and in this way to aid understanding of the social organization of knowledge and awareness.

axiom (axiomatic) An axiom is an assumption, postulate, universally received principle, or self-evident truth. Most sociological theories rest on one or more undemonstrated axioms, for example, that all human action is rational, or—as in the case of *Marxism—that the class struggle is the motor of history. Some sociologists refer to such axiomatic beliefs as 'domain assumptions' or 'metatheoretical beliefs'. Thus, for example, in *Metatheorizing in Sociology* (1991) the American sociologist George Ritzer takes social theories themselves as the object of study, classifying and comparing them to produce a history of sociology that traces the rise and demise of sociological *paradigms and their central postulates.

Bachelard, Gaston (1894-1962) A founding figure in the historically oriented French tradition in philosophy of science, Bachelard was also concerned with the characteristics of creative thought in the arts. Like Thomas Kuhn, Bachelard argued against a pervasive view of science as continuously cumulative knowledge. He saw science passing through sharp ruptures or breaks in its history, each new phase of scientific practice requiring the abandonment of previous *epistemologies. In general, the advance of a science is a struggle against the 'epistemological obstacles' constituted by extra-scientific *ideologies, which include philosophical (mis)representations of science itself. Bachelard's work was important in shaping the ideas of many French intellectuals of a younger generation, most notably Louis *Althusser and Michel *Foucault. *See also* PARADIGM.

backward-sloping supply curve for labour An economic concept that measures the preference for increased leisure over increased remuneration. It is found when wage incentives are offered to improve *productivity and labourers respond by working shorter hours to earn the same money rather than working harder or longer to earn more money.

Max Weber discussed this phenomenon in *General Economic History* (1919-20), seeing it as an example of economic *traditionalism that runs counter to modern capitalist rationality. Sociological research has produced a variety of alternative explanations for the persistence of this traditionalism in modern societies. It may be a consequence of perceived opportunities for saving, investment, and social mobility, reflect familial obligations regarding the distribution of rewards, or resentment against new patterns of authority. If non-monetary rewards are considered, the backward-sloping supply curve is as consistent with the maximization of individual welfare as a positively sloped curve in other contexts (see M. P. Miracle, 'Interpretation of Backward-Sloping Labour Supply Curves in Africa', *Economic Development and Cultural Change*, 1976). *See also* ECONOMIC MAN.

Balch, Emily Greene (1867-1961) An American sociologist who pioneered the concept of *role and the use of statistical techniques in sociology. She carried out important comparative analyses of immigrant life in both Europe and America, and forged links between feminism, pacifism, and peaceful arbitration. In 1892 she co-founded a social settlement in Boston—Dennison House—with Vida Scudder and Helena Dudley. Balch was active in numerous women's trade-union activities, and from the start Dennison House became a centre for women workers. Her commitment to world peace during the First World War created much furore and subsequent ostracism, including the termination of her professorship at Wellesley College, although her work in this field was finally given recognition in 1946, when she was awarded the Nobel Peace Prize. Balch combined both statistical data and sociological theory in her important study *Public Assistance of the Poor in France* (1893), at a time when few other sociologists were doing so. However, her best-known volume is *Our Slavic Fellow Citizens* (1910), which pre-dated and in some ways complemented the much-praised and more widely recognized work of the Chicago sociologists W. I. Thomas and Florian Znaniecki on *The Polish Peasant in Europe and America* (1918–20).

banks, data *See* DATA ARCHIVE.

banks, development *See* DEVELOPMENT BANKS.

bar chart A graphic means of displaying a *frequency distribution of quantitative data. Blocks proportional in width to the size of the categories are raised along the horizontal axis. The height of each block is then adjusted so that its area is proportional to the relative frequency of its category. The chart appears as a series of bars of varying height, as in the hypothetical example in the first figure, which shows the number of births in a hospital for each day of the week.

A similar type of chart is the histogram, which uses numerical categories on a continuous scale. The second figure is a histogram showing the monthly spending of a group of teenagers attending a summer camp.

These and other visual means of presenting data (such as the *pie-chart) are normally found where researchers wish to convey the basic information contained in a frequency distribution at a glance or in a simplified form. For this reason they are widely used in magazines and newspapers. *See also* MEASUREMENT.

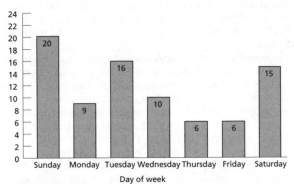

A bar chart showing frequency of births by day of week

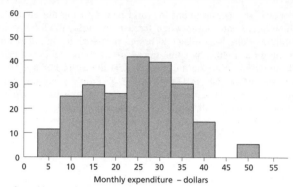

A histogram of monthly expenditure

Barnard, Chester I. (1886–1961) An American industrialist and administrator who was interested in the comparative study of *organizations and wrote classic and influential studies of their workings (see *The Function of the Executive*, 1938, and *Organization and Management*, 1948). Barnard argued that organizations are inherently co-operative systems—in sharp contrast to previous approaches, such as *administrative theory, that stressed their hierarchical, rule-bound, and authoritarian nature.

base A term referring to Karl *Marx's idea of a 'real foundation, on which rises a legal and political superstructure and to which correspond definite forms of social consciousness' in his Preface to the *Contribution to the Critique of Political Economy* (1859). Discussion of the term has revolved around the two issues of the composition of the base and its relation to the *superstructure. Marx himself wrote that the base comprised 'relations of production which correspond to a definite stage of development of their material productive forces. The sum total of these relations of production constitutes the economic structure of society'. What has been at issue is the meaning of 'correspond' and the composition of the 'relations of production'.

Earlier generations of Marxists tended to understand 'correspond' as meaning 'determine', and to see the *relations of production of production as purely economic in the sense of material production itself. Their more recent successors have not only softened the sense of determination implied by 'correspond', but have also reversed the direction of any determining current so that it flows from the relations to the material forces of production (see, for example, the writings of Louis *Althusser). Furthermore, they have pushed the question of the nature of the relations one step back, by asking whether it is correct to suppose that economic relations can ever be understood as purely matters of material production when they necessarily also involve (at a minimum) both managerial power relations and ideological relations (see, for example, Michael Burawoy, *The Politics of Production*, 1985).

As regards the relation of the base to the superstructure, here too, earlier generations tended to assume that the former more or less unproblematically determined the latter. Taking their cue from some clarificatory comments made by Marx and Engels themselves, their successors have emphasized what has been termed the *relative autonomy of the various aspects of the superstructure, and their capacity to react back on the base—while nevertheless still maintaining that, in Althusser's words, 'the economic is determinant in the last instance'. Examples here would include Ernesto Laclau, *Politics and Ideology in Marxist Theory* (1977) and Bob Jessop, *The Capitalist State* (1982). Needless to say, this terminology has prompted endless and acrimonious debate (mostly between Marxists and their critics but also, to a lesser extent, within Marxism itself), about how—precisely—these propositions ought to be interpreted. In other words, how much autonomy is implied by the term 'relative', and what (or when) is 'the last instance'?

In a controversial defence of *Karl Marx's Theory of History* (1978), the philosopher G. A. Cohen has argued that Marx saw base and superstructure as elements in, a *functional explanation. Although opinions vary, it is at least arguable that this puts an end to the debate about the explanatory priority of forces and relations of production, and accommodates arguments for the relative autonomy of superstructures—at least in so far as deciding what Marx meant is concerned. *See also* IDEOLOGY; MODE OF PRODUCTION; SOCIAL FORMATION.

Bauman, Zygmunt (1925–2017) Born in 1925 in Poland, of Jewish descent, Bauman was forced by the rise of Nazism to leave his homeland in 1939. He was educated in Soviet Russia, fought with the Red Army against the Germans during the Second World War and emigrated to the West in 1968 after being sacked from the University of Warsaw for his criticisms of the regime. He became Professor of Sociology at Leeds University in 1971 and was an Emeritus Professor both at Leeds and, since the collapse of communism, at the University of Warsaw. A prolific writer, Bauman was one of the most influential and interesting contributors to an understanding of the nature of contemporary society and the transition from *modernity to postmodernity.

In a complex, globalized world of radical cultural pluralization Bauman has championed an interpretative approach to the social sciences against the judging, legislative imperative of modernism (see *Legislators and Interpreters*, 1987). His dissection of the lethal brew of the modernist ideology of social engineering with the bureaucratic and political capability to pursue it won him the Amalfi prize for *Modernity and the Holocaust* (1989). In the age of seductive consumerism, rapid technological change, complexity, contingency and ambiguity that he labelled *Liquid Modernity* (2000) he believed that the ethical codes inherited from a less frenetic modernity cannot provide effective social norms, and in books such as *Postmodern Ethics* (1993) he argued for a re-discovery of a deeper moral impulse shorn of rigid ethical codes. He explored the liquidity, or fluidity, of contemporary modernity in a series of books on identity, community, consumption, fear, inequality, and culture.

Becker, Howard (1928–   ) A major contributor to *labelling theory and *symbolic interactionism. His early work drew upon his own experiences of performing as a jazz pianist, where he observed the patterns of negotiated order followed by musicians. His observations of music making and of drug use among musicians led to his presentation of a labelling theory of deviance in *Outsiders* (1963). Here it was argued that there are no inherently deviant individuals or acts but rather that 'social groups create deviance by making the rules whose infraction constitutes deviance'. This focus on the way identities are formed in interaction is also reflected in studies of medical students and undergraduate culture (*Boys in White*, with others, 1961; *Making the Grade*, with Blanche Geer and Everett C. Hughes, 1968, reprinted with a new introduction 1995), and his studies of *Art Worlds* (1982). He returned to his ethnographic study of jazz musicians in *Do You Know?* (with Robert Faulkner, 2009). Becker has also debunked some of the myths about academic writing, theory, and research in *Writing for Social Scientists* (1986), *Tricks of the Trade* (1989), and *Telling About Society* (2007).

( ) SEE WEB LINKS
• Howard Becker's home page, containing some recent papers and providing the opportunity to communicate with him.

behaviour *See* BEHAVIOURISM; SOCIAL BEHAVIOURISM.

behaviourism An approach in psychology that denies (with greater or lesser insistence) that consciousness has any relevance to the understanding of human behaviour. Behaviour is seen in terms of an identifiable and measurable response to external or internal, recognizable, and measurable stimuli. The response can be modified by reward or various forms of discouragement—a process known as *conditioning. Behaviourism is thus both a theoretical orientation, of enormous influence in academic psychology, and a practical technique used to alter what is perceived as undesirable conduct.

Behaviourism blossomed at the beginning of the 20th century as a reaction against the then dominant introspectionism. While introspectionism concentrated on the study of consciousness through self-examination, behaviourism rejected the idea that states of consciousness could be apprehended. In the first behaviourist manifesto (*Behaviourism*, 1913), John B. Watson argued that introspection was unreliable because self-reports may be vague and subjective, and the data thus obtained cannot be independently verified. Behaviourists, basing their arguments on the philosophical foundations of logical *positivism, then proposed that all that can truly be known is what is observed through the senses. They staunchly maintained that observable behaviour is the only legitimate subject-matter for psychology and that observation is best achieved through conducting controlled experiments. In practice, such experiments often use animals, under the assumption that the characteristics of animal behaviour can fruitfully be generalized to humans (see, for example, Watson's *The Psychological Care of Infant and Child*, 1938).

The behaviourist project can be illustrated by the influential work of the Russian psychologist Ivan Pavlov, who was awarded the Nobel Prize in 1904, for his work on the process of digestion in dogs. Pavlov conducted a number of experiments on dogs that purported to show that reflexes could be learned, or (in behaviourist terminology) 'conditioned'. In Pavlov's experiments, the animals were exposed to the sight or smell of food, thus eliciting salivation. They were then exposed to the ringing of a bell at the same time as the food was produced. This stimulated further salivation. Finally, the dogs were exposed only to the ringing of the bell, which produced salivation even though no food was present. Pavlov and other behaviourists have taken this and similar experiments as proof of the idea that reflexes can be conditioned through environmental stimuli. Their conclusion is, then that both animal and human behaviour works according to a stimulus-response model. Subsequent behaviourists, such as B. F. Skinner in the United States and Hans Eysenck in Britain, have elaborated on these premises in their own work (see Skinner's *About Behaviourism*, 1973, or any one of Eysenck's numerous books and articles about mental illness—or 'abnormal behaviour' as he prefers to call such conditions). Skinner also outlined his own behaviourist social utopia in *Walden Two* (1948), a novel that paints a picture of a society controlled by operant techniques.

As a direct application of behaviourist theories, aversion therapy, desensitization, and operant conditioning are among the behaviourist techniques used within the health, mental health, and prison services. Aversion therapy involves the use of a noxious physical stimulation or punishment to reduce the frequency of unwanted behaviour. Electric shocks and injections of apomorphine have been used in attempts to make patients averse to certain anti-social behaviours. Desensitization, used particularly in the treatment of phobias, is a psychological therapy in which the practitioner steers the patient through an 'anxiety hierarchy', with the intention of allowing the patient to become less sensitive to the feared object or event. Operant conditioning involves the systematic manipulation of the consequences of a behaviour through rewards and punishments so as to modify the subsequent behaviour. At present there is extensive and intensive controversy about both the effectiveness and the ethics of all these techniques.

Behaviourism represents an extreme environmentalist position as regards the question of what guides human actions. According to behaviourists, all behaviour is learned through association and conditioning of one kind or another, and this same behaviour can therefore be unlearned or altered by external (environmental) manipulations. As might be expected, the theory has been regarded with suspicion or rejected outright by sociologists, who see it as a rigidly individualistic approach and hold that it is very difficult to carry out a sociological study without taking some account of how people think about the social world. For example, a criticism of behaviourism voiced by George Herbert *Mead was that it can account only for what people are doing, not what they are thinking or feeling. It therefore ignores the many aspects of human conduct that may not be readily amenable to observation. For a long time, however, behaviourism dominated theoretical and clinical psychology, especially under the influence of Skinner, although cognitive psychology now seems to be replacing it as the central orthodoxy.

Elements of behaviourism do nevertheless appear in sociology: George Homans's exchange theory borrowed from some of Skinner's work, and more often there are generalized behavioural assumptions implicit in some theories of *socialization. George Herbert Mead's *Mind, Self and Society* (1934) is about consciousness, yet Mead often called himself a *social behaviourist, and *symbolic interactionism can indeed be seen as propounding the view that society, as a structure of social roles, conditions people into acceptable social behaviour. It must be emphasized, however, that this is a very loose usage of the term, and a very general form of behaviourism. *See also* NEO-POSITIVISM.

behaviour therapy A form of *psychotherapy, originally resting upon *behaviourist principles, and using the techniques of classical and instrumental *conditioning. The therapist tries to change the conditions that maintain the maladaptive behaviour. Recently, however, behaviour therapists have paid increasing attention to thoughts and thought processes and the treatment is referred to as cognitive behavioural therapy.

Benedict, Ruth Fulton (1887-1948) A student of Franz *Boas at Columbia University, Benedict conducted her first fieldwork in the early 1920s and developed a strong interest in comparative studies. She was subsequently influenced by psychological theory and is closely associated with the so-called *culture-and-personality approach in American anthropology. Her best-known works are probably *Patterns of Culture* (1934), on native American *Zuñi*, and *The Chrysanthemum and the Sword* (1946), on Japan.

benefits, welfare *See* SELECTIVE VERSUS UNIVERSAL BENEFITS; WELFARE.

Benjamin, Walter (1892-1940) A literary critic associated with the Frankfurt School of *critical theory in the 1930s, taken up by sociologists of literature in the 1970s, mainly because of his analysis of the material aspects of literary production (see J. Roberts, *Walter Benjamin*, 1982). Best known for his arguments about the nature of artistic creation and production and his analysis of cultured bourgeois street life in the large city.

Bentham, Jeremy (1748-1832) Often regarded as the founder of modern *utilitarianism, Bentham is best known for his texts on legal philosophy, and his programmes of social (especially penal) reform. He was a leading figure in classical *criminology, which attempted to make the legal system more rational, and devised the idea of the panopticon—a design for the organization and architecture of prisons that facilitates maximum surveillance and control of the inmates.

Bernstein, Eduard (1850-1932) The leading 'revisionist' thinker of the German Social Democratic Party, who sought to eliminate the anachronistic assumptions of Marxist orthodoxy from the party's ideology. Philosophically a follower of *neo-Kantianism, he rejected the *positivism and *evolutionism, as well as the residual *Hegelianism, that he detected in orthodox *Marxism. He challenged the immiseration and *proletarianization theses as descriptions of tendencies within capitalist societies, as well as the amorality, fatalism, and political pessimism that underpinned them. For Bernstein, then, *socialism represented not just a distant goal, but also an ethical ideal that possessed far more than mere inspirational significance in the present. Despite his often misread statement that 'the movement is everything, the goal nothing', Bernstein came to stand for a socialist gradualism that should be distinguished from mere reformism (see P. Gay's book *The Dilemma of Democratic Socialism*, 1952). *See also* KAUTSKY.

Beveridge Report December 1942 saw the publication of a *Report on Social Insurance and Allied Services*, the fruits of a committee chaired by Sir William Beveridge and subsequently known as The Beveridge Report. The report was enthusiastically received, selling 635 000 at two shillings each in the days following its release. This report came to be regarded as the blueprint of the British welfare state and continues to be invoked as a way of summarizing the post-war settlement and the establishment of the British welfare state, among both sociologists and politicians. In fact, though, the report dealt only with one aspect of the welfare state: how national insurance should function to cover periods of non-employment through sickness, unemployment, or old age, and the related question of providing a safety-net level of income through national assistance for those without resources and not covered by the insurance provision. Although the subject of the report was relatively narrowly defined, Beveridge did make assumptions about other areas of the welfare state that were essential to both the report's vision and its calculations. Memorably, the report spoke of the need to defeat the five 'giants' of 'disease', 'ignorance', 'squalor', 'idleness', and 'want' through comprehensive health and education provision, a coherent housing (and house-building) policy and measures to prevent long-term unemployment, as well as putting into practice the provisions of the report that were aimed at tackling 'want'. In fact, the report's assumptions of expenditure both on national insurance and assistance and on other areas outside the direct scope of the report, such as the establishment of family allowances, led the government (and the treasury in particular) to disown responsibility for the committee's conclusions and to make clear that the report was Beveridge's individual contribution. However, the popularity with which the report was greeted made this position hard to maintain. The years following the report were, indeed, to see legislation on education (1944), family allowances (1945), a new National Health Service (1946), as well as on national insurance (1946) and national assistance (1948), alongside an initial commitment to *Keynesian management of employment.

Beveridge had long been wedded to the principles of covering employment risks through an insurance system, as he had been involved in putting together the 1911 National Insurance Act. However, in the 1942 proposals he moved away from an actuarial system of insurance (where people could receive only amounts in proportion to what they had contributed) to a system of risk pooling, whereby all would pay flat-rate contributions and flat-rate payments would be made as long as the need existed. The flat-rate contribution for flat-rate benefit has been slightly modified, but still essentially underlies the current system of pensions and benefits for unemployment and sickness.

Beveridge's plans for insurance assumed a family form of male breadwinner and dependent wife and children. Allowances therefore were anticipated to need to cover the earner's wife as well as dependent children. Moreover, wives who did work could opt to pay a lower rate of contributions (with consequent lower, individual returns at pension age). The gendered assumptions underlying these arrangements have been criticized as have the deleterious effects on some women's subsequent incomes in old age. Beveridge has also been criticized for setting the rates of benefit lower than would be needed for subsistence-level support, with consequences for generations of claimants. Nevertheless, though the report may have been less revolutionary than Beveridge claimed, it established the principles of the British social security and influenced the systems of other countries.

An understanding of the development of Beveridge's thought and a detailed account of the genesis of the report can be found in José Harris's biography, *William Beveridge* (1977). An evaluation of Beveridge's contribution both in Britain and beyond can be found in J. Hills, J. Ditch and H. Glennerster (eds.) *Beveridge and Social Security: An International Retrospective* (1994).

((⊕)) SEE WEB LINKS
• Includes a substantial extract from the Report.

bias *See* INTERVIEW BIAS; INTERVIEWER BIAS; NON-RESPONSE; OBJECTIVE; OBSERVER BIAS; PREJUDICE; SAMPLE SELECTION BIAS; SAMPLING ERROR.

bilateral descent *See* DESCENT GROUPS.

bimodal distribution *See* CENTRAL TENDENCY (MEASURES OF).

binomial distribution A probability distribution for the occurrence of a specific event which either occurs or not—such as winning a race. The binomial distribution may be symmetrical (like the *normal distribution), but is otherwise skewed. *See also* DISTRIBUTION (STATISTICAL OR FREQUENCY).

biography *See* LIFE-HISTORY; PERSONAL DOCUMENTS.

biological analogy *See* ORGANIC (OR BIOLOGICAL) ANALOGY.

biological reductionism (biologism) A theoretical approach that aims to explain all social or cultural phenomena in biological terms, denying them any causal autonomy. Twentieth-century incarnations of biological reductionism have relied to varying degrees on Darwin's theory of evolution and principles of natural selection. Within the human sciences, there have been attempts to explain observed differences in group behaviour—such as performance on *intelligence tests, rates of *mental illness, intergenerational *poverty, male dominance or *patriarchy, and propensity for *crime—as being biologically determined, by claiming that groups have different biological capacities or evolutionary trajectories. The theories of Social *Darwinism, *eugenics, and *sociobiology often involve biological reductionism. A recognition of the importance of biological conditions and *human nature need not involve biological reductionism. *See also* ARDREY.

bio-medical model *See* MEDICAL MODEL.

Bion, Wilfred (1897–1979) One of the better-known British Kleinian psycho-analysts (*see* KLEIN, MELANIE) for whom psychoanalysis dealt less with defences against feeling than with defences against thought. From a sociological point of view, his most important work was on group processes and, in particular, the unconscious alliances that groups form in order to resist accomplishing their tasks. Bion called these alliances 'basic assumption groups' and listed depen-dency (waiting for the leader to do everything); flight-fight (finding an external enemy or scapegoat to distract attention), and pairing (where two members form a relationship that seems to offer a solution to the group's problems). See especially his *Experiences in Groups* (1961).

bio-psycho-social model *See* MEDICAL MODEL.

biotic competition *See* URBAN ECOLOGY.

bipartite (bipartisan) Affecting two parties ('bipartite agreement') or divided into two parts. The term is mostly employed in reference to formal economic and political negotiations and arrangements. For example, a number of social scien-tists have pointed to bipartisanship as a factor explaining the lack of success of third parties (such as Socialist and People's Parties) in the United States, citing the difficulties faced by any new political party within an established two-party system. In such systems, the more conservative parties find it relatively easy to incorporate, as their own, parts of the platforms of the more reform oriented third parties, thus undermining their appeal to the electorate. (See, for example, W. Sombart's *Why is there No Socialism in the United States?*, 1906.)

birth cohort *See* COHORT.

birth rate A measure designed to provide information on the comparative fertility of different populations, most commonly used in demographic analysis. A number of different calculations of varying sophistication may be used. The most well-known—the 'crude birth rate'—is simply the number of live births in a year per 1000 population. This measure takes no account of the age structure of a population, which affects the numbers of women capable of giving birth in any year, and does not therefore yield particularly accurate comparisons. Adjusting the measure for age and sex differences allows meaningful comparisons to be made between geographical areas or social groups. The 'general fertility rate' is the birth rate per thousand women of child-bearing age, calculated as the number of live births divided by the female population aged 15–44 years, times 1000. This more sophisticated measure of the birth rate takes account of factors such as age structure, but more data about the population are required for its calculation.

black economy That portion of *employment within the market economy that is not fully covered by *official statistics because of some degree of under-reporting. This is often connected with tax evasion or illegal employment practices. Unfortunately, economic statistics are imperfect, so that gaps and inconsistencies are due more often to data-quality problems than to unreported black economy activity. Guesstimates of the size of the black economy are inflated by the substantial amounts of non-market work and marginal work in the *informal economy.

Black Report An influential Report of the Working Group on Inequalities in Health (under the chairmanship of Sir Douglas Black) submitted to the British Government in 1980. The Report synthesized much evidence, hitherto available mainly in academic journals and in a fragmented form, and suggested that Britain's health service was failing to reduce social (particularly *class) inequalities in health.

For example, the Report argued that working-class men and women are significantly more likely than are those in the managerial or professional classes to die early, and that children born into working-class homes are exposed to higher risks of early mortality, illness, and injury than are those coming from middle-class backgrounds. More controversially, it suggested that although many absolute improvements in the various rates had been achieved over time, some class differentials in health outcomes had actually increased over the period of thirty years or so since the National Health Service was first established. It argued that this was due, not so much to the flawed workings of the *health-care system itself, or to restricted access to health-care facilities, as to social inequalities such as those to be found in housing and working conditions, in the distribution of incomes, and in opportunities for educational advancement. The authors of the Report concluded that health standards could be improved and equalized only by major initiatives in community health, preventive medicine, and primary care, and (more importantly) by radical shifts in *social policy in order to improve the standard of living of the working classes.

The Conservative government that received the Report made strenuous efforts to suppress it, although these simply created intense media interest. When the findings were finally published (as P. Townsend and N. Davidson, *Inequalities in Health*, 1982) they became the focus for a protracted debate among epidemiologists, sociologists, and public health experts. On one hand, the Report stimulated further research into class and other persisting social inequalities in health, including comparative studies that examined Britain in relation to industrialized societies elsewhere. On the other, critics suggested that the Report's tendency to focus upon mortality (death) rates overlooked the complexities of the relationship between these and morbidity (sickness) rates, in particular the possibility that inequalities in death rates may have only a weak relationship to inequalities in health. (For example, *mental illness rarely results in death, but has a significant although complex relationship to social class.)

Whatever the weaknesses of the Report, it was important in promoting interest in the sociology of *health and illness, and provides a good illustration of the way in which sociologists can inform social policy by means of *policy research. In the longer term, its greatest sociological significance may lie in the fact that it acted as a catalyst for a vigorous discussion of the methodological problems involved in epidemiological work, including: the use of the Registrar-General's (that is the British Government's official) occupational classification as a measure of social class (some commentators argued that the Report actually underestimated class differentials in health because of the class heterogeneity of some of the Registrar-General's categories); the implications of social mobility for health (is poor health more common among the working classes and the poor because sick people are likely to be steadily downwardly mobile?); and the difficulties of interpreting complex causal interactions between differences in life-style (smoking, diet, leisure activities, and the like) and effects attributable to social class as such.

A useful discussion of some of the issues that have emerged as a result of the debate prompted by Black will be found in D. Vågerö and R. Illsley, 'Explaining Health Inequalities: Beyond Black and Barker', *European Sociological Review* (1995). As a measure of how much more sophisticated that debate has now become, the original Report can usefully be compared with recent studies such as that by M. Bartley et al., 'Measuring Inequalities in Health' (*Sociology of Health and Illness*, 1996), which examines trends in mortality in Britain in terms both of the conventional Registrar-General's class categories and the newer and more robust *Goldthorpe class scheme.

blank-slate or blank-paper hypothesis *See* TABULA RASA.

Bloch, Marc (1886–1944) A distinguished French medieval historian and geographer, co-founder of the *Annales School, and therefore an important influence on historical sociology such as the *world-systems theory of Immanuel Wallerstein. Bloch was an enthusiast of 'totalizing' approaches that emphasized the underlying movements in whole societies rather than either the activities of particular individuals or the chronology of specific events. His major works were *French Rural History: An Essay on its Basic Characteristics* (1931) and *Feudal Society* (1939–40). His comparative and, as he saw it, scientific approach to history, and his enthusiasm for the use of as wide a variety of data-sources as possible, is evident in his text on *The Historian's Craft* (1949). *See also* FEUDALISM.

blockbusting Defined by Gregory Squires (*Blockbusting in Baltimore*, 1994) as 'the intentional action of a real estate speculator to place an African American resident in a house on a previously all-white block for the express purpose of panicking whites into selling for the profit to be gained by buying low and selling high'. Blockbusting occurs when there is racial prejudice on the part of White residents, underpinned by an institutionalized dual housing market, whereby lenders and realtors are involved in 'a silent conspiracy on race and residency' in order to maintain racially exclusive neighbourhoods. For reasons of self-interested short-term economic gain, realtors sometimes violate this unwritten agreement, and offer African Americans housing opportunities in hitherto exclusively White areas. The argument is reminiscent of Rex and Moore's much earlier account of *housing classes, and by implicitly reviving the perspective of *urban managerialism, it provides a corrective to those in sociology and policy-making who view urban processes in entirely cultural or structural terms.

blue-collar work *See* MANUAL VERSUS NON-MANUAL DISTINCTION.

Blumer, Herbert (1900–86) Blumer studied at the University of Chicago and taught George Herbert *Mead's classes after the latter's death in the early 1930s. In an overview article on the nature of social psychology in *Man and Society* (edited by W. Schmidt, 1937), he coined the term *symbolic interactionism— hence literally becoming the founder of this tradition. Later, when he held the first Chair of Sociology at the University of California at Berkeley, he influenced several generations of interactionist sociologists as well as encouraging diversity in one of North America's leading sociology departments. He held many important offices, including the presidency of both the American Sociological Association and the Society for the Study of Social Problems.

His abiding concern was that sociology should become the down-to-earth study of group life. He outlined this position in various essays collected together in *Symbolic Interactionism* (1969) and his views on Mead were published posthumously as *George Herbert Mead and Human Conduct* (2004). Blumer disliked the tendency for sociologists to analyse phenomena that they had not witnessed first-hand, and had a particular abhorrence of abstract, grand theory. Instead, he advocated a methodology that would explore and inspect the rich variety of social experience, as it was lived; would build up 'sensitizing concepts' from experience; that would produce theories directly grounded in empirical data; and would determine the relevance of such theories by a continual return to the evidence. He is often seen as inspiring the idea of *grounded theory. Substantively, he was interested in the mass media, fashion, collective behaviour, industrial relations, race relations, and life-history research. His work is appraised in an edition of the journal *Symbolic Interaction* (1988) published shortly after his death.

Boas, Franz (1858–1942) A German-born anthropologist, initially a student of geography, who founded modern cultural anthropology (*see* SOCIAL ANTHROPOLOGY) in the United States. He and his students came to dominate American anthropology for the first three decades of the 20th century. Boas revolutionized fieldwork methodology, relying on analysis of local texts, linguistics, and training local representative researchers to document their own *culture. His *Primitive Art* (1927) greatly influenced later approaches to examining the material culture of peoples.

Using these methods Boas produced an enormous amount of ethnographic data on native American cultures of the Pacific Northwest. He gave priority to empirical ethnographic investigation over any search for scientific laws of cause and effect in culture. Boas was a cultural relativist, arguing that culture should be understood in terms of its own framework of meaning, rather than being judged by outside investigators according to the values of their own culture. He exposed and undermined the more extravagant claims of evolutionary theory as espoused by Edward *Tylor and James *Frazer. Instead, Boas insisted on the study of cultures as wholes, as systems of many interrelated parts. His later interest in psychology served as a precursor to the *culture and personality approach. His other principal works include *Race, Language and Culture* (1940), and *The Mind* *of Primitive Man* (1911). George Stocking discussed much useful background on Boas and his approach in *Volksgeist as Method and Ethic* (1996).

body language A term used in social psychology to refer to the gestures, facial expressions, and bodily postures adopted by people in social interaction. Just as oral and written *language expresses our ideas, thoughts, and emotions, so our bodies are said to express a series of unspoken (some say unconsciously articulated) messages, by means of posture and suchlike. The alternative term 'kinesics' (R. L. Birdwhistell, *Kinesics and Context*, 1970) is sometimes used in psychology, to refer both to the body movements which convey information in the absence of speech, and the study of such movements. *See also* NON-VERBAL COMMUNICATION.

body, sociology of the Influenced by the writings of Michel *Foucault, which assert sociology's neglect of the body, sociologists who practise this relatively new specialism analyse humans as embodied persons—not just as actors with values and attitudes. They explore the varied cultural meanings attached to bodies, and the way they are controlled, regulated, and reproduced, paying especial attention to illness, disease, and sexuality. A good introduction to the field is Bryan S. Turner's *The Body and Society* (1996). The study of the body has developed into a very broad strand in modern sociological research. It includes such diverse themes as sex therapy, contemporary dance, the body-building industry, the management of children, use of food, and images of lesbians and gays. These apparently esoteric themes are usually connected to central issues of social theory, such as those of control, order, and ideology. Sociologists of the body have also made an increasing contribution to the study of *illness and to *medical sociology. The scope of this increasingly popular specialism is illustrated in the range of topics addressed in Sue Scott and David Morgan (eds.), *Body Matters* (1993). *See also* EMOTION, SOCIOLOGY OF; FOOD, SOCIOLOGICAL STUDIES OF; GENDER; NATURE VERSUS NURTURE DEBATE.

(⊕) SEE WEB LINKS
• The journal *Body & Society*, the leading source for research in this area (subscription).

bonded labour *See* PATRON–CLIENT RELATIONSHIP.

bonding A term referring to the mutual identification of mother and child and the circumstances in which this develops. Sometimes it is used to describe the formation of other close relationships.

Booth, Charles (1840–1916) A Victorian businessman and social reformer who produced the first major empirical survey of the *Life and Labour of the People of London*, in seventeen volumes between 1891 and 1903. Using a subsistence definition of *poverty he found (contrary to his expectations) that nearly 31 per cent of those surveyed were living in poverty. His work was the first major survey in British sociology and has influenced all subsequent debates on poverty. Much useful material on Booth's studies can be found in David Englander and Rosemary O'Day (eds.), *Retrieved Riches: Social Investigation in Britain, 1840–1914* (1995).

(⊕) SEE WEB LINKS

- An online archive of Booth's original data and notebooks covering the London survey.

Bosanquet, Helen (Helen Dendy 1860–1926) An important figure in poor relief at a time of increasing activism and conceptual development in this area. A core member of the Charity Organisation Society (COS), she worked closely with its Secretary and dominant force, C. S. Loch. It was through the COS that she met her husband, philosopher and fellow activist, Bernard Bosanquet. The COS aimed to rationalize philanthropic endeavour and instil principles of self-help into its recipients. Through its development of case work, it laid the foundations of the social work profession. Bosanquet described the formation and principles of the COS in *Social Work in London 1869–1912* (1914).

Appointed to the Royal Commission on the Poor Law in 1905, investigating the system of provision for the destitute that had come under increasing criticism, she contributed to the subsequent majority report and published a summary of it as *The Poor Law Report of 1909* (1909). The report argued for a synthesis of the systems of public and voluntary support which would combine coherent and consistent criteria for relief with sensitivity to the particular circumstances of the claimants (including moral evaluation and consideration of possible negative effects of relief). Bosanquet's other writings include *Rich and Poor* (1896) and *The Family* (1915).

Bouglé, Celestin Charles Alfred (1870–1940) A close associate of Émile *Durkheim who undertook studies of egalitarianism, democracy, socialism, a general study of social values (*The Evolution of Values*, 1922), and a review of sociology in Germany. His most important work was a study of the Indian caste system (*Essays on the Caste System*, 1908). In this study he showed that the mechanical solidarity (*see* DIVISION OF LABOUR) of the hierarchical caste system confines people within specific social groups and gives them only a very restricted freedom of action. This was a major influence on the later work of Louis Dumont (*Homo Hierarchicus*, 1966). He was a supporter of *anarchism and edited the complete works of Pierre Proudhon, who he saw as proposing important sociological ideas.

boundary debate *See* CONTRADICTORY CLASS LOCATION.

boundary maintenance The ways in which societies (or *social systems) maintain distinctions between themselves and others. Many have suggested that, by studying the ways in which a society attempts to define its inherently ambiguous—and hence potentially dangerous—peripheral areas, it is possible to obtain a better understanding of what constitutes its key cultural *values.

bounded rationality According to the rational exchange postulates associated with the *organizational theory of Herbert A. Simon (see *Models of Bounded Rationality*, 1982), there are cognitive limits to the ability of people to pursue wholly rational purposeful behaviour. Rather than seek the optimal solution, actors *satisfice; that is, they accept a solution which is 'good enough' within a so-called 'zone of indifference'.

Bourdieu, Pierre (1930–2002) The most influential French sociologist of the second half of the 20th century, who by his early thirties had been nominated Director of Studies at the prestigious École des Hautes Études en Sciences Sociales in Paris. Born in a small market town in the agricultural region of the Bearn in the Pyrenees, where his father was a postman, this marginal early setting left its mark on all of Bourdieu's work. The region had much in common with Kabylia, the mountainous southern area of Algeria, where he carried out fieldwork training as an anthropologist, and that provided the empirical basis for major theoretical works such as *Outline of a Theory of Practice* (1972) and *The Logic of Practice* (1980).

Bourdieu developed a theory combining the objectivism of *Durkheim with the subjectivism of *phenomenology. He developed an idea of socialization through the concept of *habitus, which emphasized the skills and the ways of looking at the world that people acquire within the unequal social structures around them. He saw human capacities and opportunities as embodied in forms of social, economic, and cultural 'capital' generated within the particular structural 'fields' in which they are located.

In his empirical studies, Bourdieu explored the cultural and power dynamics of various interlinked social fields. In *The State Nobility* (1989), for example, Bourdieu analysed the elite world of the *grandes écoles*, the educational conduits for those at the highest levels in government, business, the professions, and administration in France. Adding sophisticated cultural, lifestyle, and status dimensions to insights from *Marxism, he argued that the cultural capital of the dominant *class give it an arbitrary advantage over other groups in gaining educational access and credentials. *Distinction* (1979) drew on the same theoretical ingredients to probe the underlying links between the aesthetic tastes of consumers and class position, whilst *The Rules of Art* (1992) likewise places the subjective views of producers within the objective, historical circumstances of the relevant literary or artistic field in which they strive to make their mark. *See also* CULTURAL CAPITAL; SOCIAL CAPITAL.

bourgeoisie A French term, originating in the 16th century, to refer to the body of urban freemen and corresponding to the English term burghers. It gradually became interchangeable with the term capitalist class as it was taken up in international discourse, especially amongst Marxists. Current usage refers to the owners of the means of production in *capitalist societies—although the supposed separation of *ownership and control has led some writers to completely reject the term.

Daniel Bell's highly influential article on the decline of family capitalism (reprinted in his *The End of Ideology*, 1960) saw the *entrepreneur disappearing as an identifiable directing force in the *corporation or enterprise and being replaced by internal managers. This *managerial revolution, he argued, made the concept of the bourgeoisie redundant.

The counter-response to this has been twofold. On one hand, it has been argued that empirical studies demonstrate that the powers of individual owners have not declined much, and certainly not as radically as has been claimed. On the contrary, according to these researchers, the more widespread share owner-ship only means that it is now often possible to have a very significant impact on the manner in which the still very considerable powers of boards of directors are exercised (for example with regard to investment decisions), whilst owning only a single-figure percentage of the shares. Moreover, as has been argued more recently by those interested in ownership networks, because of the power that comes with the ownership of relatively small parcels of shares, especially if these shares are in large, market-dominating companies, it is possible that their owners may come to exercise power far beyond the confines of their base company, either through that company's holdings, or as owners on their own account. For these writers, the concept of a bourgeoisie or capitalist class is still important. (See, for example, Beth Mintz and Michael Schwartz in *The Power Structure of American Business* (1985) or J. Scott's *Who Rules Britain?*, 1990.) *See also* MAN-AGERIAL REVOLUTION; MIDDLE CLASS.

bourgeoisie, petite *See* PETITE BOURGEOISIE.

Bowlby, John E. (1907–90) A British *psychoanalyst famous for his work on the early separation of an infant from his or her mother, positing a biological attachment need to explain both the infant's immediate responses, and later adult behaviour. His work, whilst controversial amongst feminists, was influen-tial in changing practices in nurseries and children's wards in hospitals. The most succinct summary is in *A Secure Base* (1988).

bracketing *See* PHENOMENOLOGY.

Branford, Victor Verasis (1863–1930) A British sociologist and founder of the Sociological Society in 1903. Born in Northampton but brought up in Edin-burgh, he studied at Edinburgh University and came under the influence of Patrick Geddes. Inspired by Geddes's project for establishing sociology in Britain, Branford participated enthusiastically in the Edinburgh summer schools. Sup-porting himself as an accountant and banker's agent, he took on the organiza-tional role for promoting Geddes's vision of an integrative and comprehensive social science. In addition to forming the Sociological Society he established an annual publication that became the *Sociological Review*, and edited a series of books.

From 1908 to 1913 he was heavily involved in his business activities, develop-ing the railway industry in South America and working from offices in London and New York. He married, as his second wife, Sybella Gurney, a pioneer of the cooperative and garden-city movements. He returned to a more active role in the Sociological Society, which had been subject to many splits and dissensions and had an uneasy relationship with the sociology that was being established at the

London School of Economics. Geddes's and Branford's view of sociology became increasingly marginal to the view of the subject being established by Hobhouse and the Society was largely moribund by the 1930s.

Branford published a psycho-biography of St Columba, a collection of essays based on an American lecture tour, and cooperated with Geddes in completing studies of the development of modernity, most notably *The Coming Polity* (1917). He was a pioneer in developmental sociology, an early advocate of psychoanalysis, and set out a system theory that aimed to provide a wider framework for Geddes's regional ideas. This theory drew on ideas shared with his associates John Hobson and Thorstein Veblen. Branford is the only British sociologist to have been made an honorary member of the American Sociological Society. His life and works are discussed in John Scott and Ray Bromley *Envisioning Sociology: Victor Branford, Patrick Geddes, and the Quest for Social Reconstruction* (2013).

Braudel, Fernand (1902–85) A leading member of the *Annales School of French history, best known for his *magnum opus The Mediterranean and the Mediterranean World in the Age of Philip II* (1949), although his *Capitalism and Material Life, 1400–1800* (1967) is more accessible.

Braudel's monumental studies of nascent *capitalism are replete with typologies of economies and cultures. However, the organizing principle of his work was a distinction between different levels of historical time within which change takes place at different speeds, most notably the threefold distinction between *histoire événementielle, histoire conjoncturelle,* and *histoire structural*: the histories of events, conjunctures, and structures. 'History,' he claimed, 'exists at different levels...On the surface the history of events works itself out in the short term; it is a sort of micro-history. Halfway down, a history of conjunctures follows a broader, slower rhythm. So far that has above all been studied in its developments on the material plane, in economic cycles and intercycles...And over and above the "recitatif" of the conjuncture, structural history, or the history of the *longue durée*, enquires into whole centuries at a time...It functions along the border between the moving and the immobile, and because of the long-standing stability of its values, in appears unchanging when compared with all the histories which flow and work themselves out more swiftly, and which in the final analysis gravitate around it' (*On History*, 1980). The last of these generates a 'geohistory' of the environment, a history of material life as consisting of 'repeated actions, empirical processes, old methods and solutions handed down from time immemorial, like money or the separation of town from country'.

Although Braudel was a major influence on *world-systems theory, his work has been criticized by some for its imprecision as regards causality, and by others for its implicit *historical materialism.

bride-price (bride-wealth) The money or goods given by the kin of the groom to the kin of the bride on marriage. Although it is sometimes seen as compensatory payment to the natal family for the upbringing of the daughter, it varies in form and meaning across cultures. In some, the 'bride-price' may become the property of the bride, and is treated as an insurance against divorce.

Buddhism A salvation religion, founded in north India in the fifth century BCE—the exact dates are the subject of scholarly controversy—by Siddhartha Gautama, known as the Buddha (meaning Enlightened One). Buddhism as taught by the Buddha was a universalist humanism not unconnected with the emergence of urban culture in north India. Buddhist teaching involves reverence for the so-called Three Jewels: the Buddha himself; the Dharma or doctrine taught by him; and the Monastic Community (monks and nuns who renounce the married household to live out the doctrine in full). According to this teaching, anyone (male or female, high-born or low) can escape from the endless cycle of rebirths by following the practice of morality, meditation, and insight.

Today, two main types of Buddhism survive. Theravada Buddhism is found in Burma, Thailand, Laos, Cambodia, and Sri Lanka. It is the more conservative form: it has few and simple rituals and focuses on the worship of the Buddha itself. Mahayana Buddhism is a slightly later development found in Nepal, Tibet, China, Mongolia, Korea, Japan, and Vietnam. It has a more elaborate ritual, a baroque pantheon of saints (bodhisattvas), more numerous scriptures, and (sometimes) a married clergy. Mahayana Buddhists believe that their form of Buddhism offers an easier route to salvation than that provided by Theravada Buddhism. Although Buddhism is a form of religious individualism, it has always accepted spiritual hierarchies, the most dramatic of which was the Mahayana theocratic state, whose Dalai Lamas ruled Tibet for many centuries. Missionaries and migrants have carried both forms of Buddhism throughout the world. In the modern world, new forms of Buddhism have arisen which combine it with nationalism, socialism, rationalism, and even social welfare activities.

Bukharin, Nikolai (1888–1938) A leading Bolshevik theorist who saw his work as a contribution to sociology. His earliest works included *Economic Theory of the Leisure Class*, 1914) and *Imperialism and World Economy* (1915), the latter having a major influence on *Lenin's theory of imperialism. After the Russian revolution he co-authored the officially sponsored *ABC of Communism* (1920) and during the 1920s he tried to reconcile historical materialism with mainstream sociology, producing a general theoretical statement in *Historical Materialism: A Study in Sociology* (1924). This book drew on emerging ideas of systems and *equilibrium to reconstruct some key Marxist arguments. His political views were supported by Josef Stalin (*See* STALINISM) during the 1920s but the two came into conflict during the 1930s and Bukharin was executed following a show trial.

bureaucracy A body of administrative officials, and the procedures and tasks involved in a particular system of administration, for example, a *state or formal organization. Max *Weber did not invent the concept of bureaucracy (the term was coined in France at the beginning of the 19th century) but he is generally recognized as having made the most original contribution to the study of the phenomenon. Almost alone, among early contributors, his treatment is not pejorative.

Although the concept is usually understood as one of Weber's *ideal types concerned with rational and efficient organization, comprising specific attributes for both positions and personnel, it is much more than this. Its full value can be gleaned only by seeing bureaucracy both as an outcome of the broader process of *rationalization and as related to Weber's work on *democracy and *domination. Domination, or the legitimate and institutionalized exercise of power, requires some kind of administration, and therefore a role for the functionary interposed between leader and electorate within a democratic system. The type of organization which emerges depends on the nature of the legitimation elaborated when those in power justify their power to their subordinates. Bureaucracy develops when that legitimation is of the rational-legal type, emphasizing the impersonal exercise of power according to rational rules.

The characteristics of bureaucracy are: a hierarchy of offices and the channelling of communication through hierarchical levels; files and secrecy; clearly defined spheres of authority determined by general rules and governed by regulations; and the administrative separation of official activities from private affairs. Bureaucratic officials, according to Weber, are appointed from above (rather than elected); enjoy life-long tenure and high status; have a fixed salary and retirement pension; and a vocation and sense of loyalty to their career and office.

Bureaucracy has a purely technical superiority over all other forms of domination. This does not necessarily imply that it has the greatest efficiency in goal attainment, as rationality and efficiency must always be measured in relation to a clearly stated objective. Above all else, bureaucracy is tied to the capitalist market economy, which demands the unambiguous and continuous discharge of public and private administration. Bureaucracy implies rationality, and this in turn implies calculability, which minimizes uncertainty in risk-taking activities. Such calculability also involves mass democracy, a levelling process by which all become formally equal before the law, so that arbitrary treatment diminishes.

Weber's pessimistic view of the rationalization process is evident in his concern about the indestructibility of fully established bureaucratic structures. Once in place, the rulers cannot dispense with the trained personnel, as the example of post-communist Eastern Europe illustrates clearly. The professional bureaucrats are also chained to their activity and thus seek its perpetuation. Finally, politicians (elected or otherwise) must increasingly take the position of a dilettante with respect to the expert bureaucrat, who wields administrative secrecy as a weapon against public scrutiny and oversight. Bureaucratic knowledge is thus *power, not only in the sense of expert knowledge, but also as concealed knowledge which enables officials to hide behind routines and procedures. Not surprisingly, the term has since come to be used in reference to every situation in which officials wield excessive power, or the organizational structure itself malfunctions. Bureaucracies can cease to be efficient, in terms of the purposes for which they are intended, when personnel proliferate beyond what is needed for the task in hand; when responsibilities are shunned and passed around the system; when rules, formalities, and files proliferate, again beyond what is necessary; and when officials stick rigidly to the letter of the regulations without regard for the purpose they are supposed to serve (in other words slavish adherence to the bureaucratic means becomes an end in itself).

Bureaucracy tends to breed experts with educational credentials who, Weber was concerned, could emerge as a self-recruiting caste. In a Marxian aside, Weber argued that capitalism and socialism can be subsumed under the broader process of bureaucratization; namely, the separation from the means of production, destruction, research, and administration of the worker, soldier, academic, and administrator respectively.

Stanislav Andreski (*Max Weber's Insights and Errors*, 1984) has argued that there are in fact now four distinct meanings which can be attached to the term. 'Bureaucracy' can refer to the set of people who perform the administrative functions in the manner described by Weber; the network of relationships in which they are enmeshed; the amount of power they wield as a body; and the various kinds of malfunctioning of the administrative machine. Andreski himself argued that the term ought to be reserved for the third of the aforementioned meanings: that is, 'the condition when the power of the administrators is greater than that of any other group of leaders or holders of authority'. Weber himself did not live to see a complete bureaucracy in this sense—the first example being the depersonalized government of the Soviet Union after the death of Stalin. However, the Chinese Empire offers a pre-industrial approximation: no other class could challenge the mandarins, although their power was subject to and limited by the prerogative of the emperor and his relatives (an unstable form of political domination which Weber refers to as *patrimonialism).

Without a doubt Weber's writings on the nature of bureaucracy not only became a fruitful source of what emerged as *organization theory but also contributed to the study of the conditions for the democratic exercise of power in an increasingly complex world. Though conceptually untidy, and in places empirically questionable, his studies of bureaucracy are unrivalled as a survey of the development and functioning of administrative machines. While most of the other early sociologists foresaw progressive movements towards democracy and liberty, Weber could see only increasing bureaucratization, and in that sense his analysis has stood the test of time. However, his treatment is scattered, and by no means an easy introduction to the subject. The best starting-point for the student of sociology is still Martin Albrow's *Bureaucracy* (1970).

bureaucratic orientation to work *See* WORK, SUBJECTIVE EXPERIENCE OF.

bureaucratic socialism *See* COMMUNISM.

Burgess, Ernest W. (1886–1966) Born in Canada, Burgess taught at Chicago University from 1916 until his retirement in 1952. He was a major influence on the development of the *Chicago School, stressing the value of empirical research, and pioneering the study of the city (with Robert Park), delinquency (with Clifford Shaw), and family life. Many of his most influential writings will be found in *The Basic Writings of Ernest W. Burgess* (1974) edited by Donald J. Bogue. *See also* CONCENTRIC ZONE THEORY.

business cycle Recurring economic cycles, involving a period of above-average growth (expansionist phase), followed by one of lower than average growth (recession), then one of negative growth (depression). Modern economists generally assume that the 'normal', 'classic', or 'Juglar' cycle lasts approximately five years, but there is no consensus as to its causes, indeed there are some who have argued that the fluctuations themselves are random rather than uniform in character. The Russian-born American development economist Simon Kuznets also identified a longer economic cycle ('Kuznets cycle') lasting some fifteen to twenty years. So-called Kondratieff cycles (named after the Russian economist who developed the idea in the 1920s) consist of 'long wave' cycles of boom and recession averaging half a century or so, fuelled by major technological and industrial advances, such as the advent of steam power. These cycles are often linked to developments in the *world-system (see, for example, Christopher Chase-Dunn and Peter Grimes, 'World-Systems Analysis', *Annual Review of Sociology*, 1995).

Business Improvement Districts (BIDs) A strategy for mobilizing private funding in order to improve the environment of city centres. First established in Canada and then the USA in the 1970s, BIDs are now found in many other countries. Businesses in an area can hold a ballot to secure agreement to the levy of a mandatory tax or business rate for the improvement of the urban environment (refurbishment of public amenities, installation of security cameras, and so forth). The tax is collected by the local authority, but handed over to a board run by the private sector, which spends the money on urban renewal projects. By 2013 there were 180 BIDs in the UK, where they cover major shopping areas (such as Oxford Street in London) and many city centres.

Enthusiasts argue that BIDs should be judged by their results, and claim that these typically will include a cleaner, friendlier, and safer urban space, a reduction in crime, and re-invigoration of the economic life of hitherto depressed areas. Sceptics point to higher property values and argue that BIDs are undemocratic and may result in a form of *gentrification that merely dispossesses and displaces the inner-city poor. *See also* CONCENTRIC ZONE THEORY; URBAN SOCIOLOGY.

Cambridge scale *See* CAMSIS SCALE.

CAMSIS scale The Cambridge scale of stratification was devised in the early 1970s and was redesigned in a more general form as the CAMSIS scale. It is based on the assumption that a continuous measure of social inequality is a better approach to social *stratification than the categorical approaches used in the *Goldthorpe class scheme, and the *NS-SEC classification.

The scale is constructed from measures of similarity and difference between occupations, as reflected in the typical interaction patterns of their incumbents, through such relations as friendship choices and inter-marriage. These are measured by their frequency for occupations, and occupations receive a score on a single dimension on a scale from 0 to 100. Originally constructed through the use of *multi-dimensional scaling techniques, the scale is now derived from *correspondence analysis. The scale has been used in studies of social mobility and as a general measure of distance within a system of social stratification. The scale was first presented in A. Stewart, B. Blackburn, and K. Prandy, *Social Stratification and Occupations* (1980) and the more recent version has been discussed in W. Bottero and K. Prandy, 'Social Interaction, Distance, and Stratification' (*British Journal of Sociology*, 2003).

(⊕) SEE WEB LINKS
• The official site for the Cambridge Social Interaction and Stratification Scale.

CAPI (Computer Assisted Personal Interviewing) *See* SURVEY (SOCIAL SURVEY).

capital One of four factors of production, according to modern economics, the others being land, labour, and enterprise. That capital is not simply a sum of money was the great discovery of early *political economy, which stressed that any expansion in the wealth of a society involved an expansion of its productive powers. Capital therefore consists of tools, machinery, plant, and any other humanly made material or equipment that, not being used for immediate consumption, contributes to or enhances productive work. Since Adam *Smith it has also been customary to distinguish between circulating capital and fixed capital. The former is used to purchase commodities, chiefly raw materials and labour effort, and sell them again as a product at a profit. The latter, for example machines and tools, yields a profit without circulating further.

According to Karl *Marx, *capital accumulation supplies the dynamic specific to the capitalist mode of production. This depends on the *exploitation of workers through the extraction of surplus value (*see* LABOUR THEORY OF VALUE).

In *Capital* (1867), Marx argued that the accumulation process tends to result in the concentration of capital in a few hands and that this occurs simultaneously with the *proletarianization and immiseration of the bulk of the labour-force.

Mainstream economists and sociologists continue to regard capital formation and accumulation as necessary for any form of *industrialization. Moreover, because the development of *capitalism has proceeded somewhat differently from Marx's expectation, it has become necessary, even for Marxists, to distinguish between various capital functions—in particular between capital ownership and managerial control. In recent sociological work, the concept of capital has been extended from this economic meaning to human, cultural, social, and other forms of capital. *See also* CORPORATION; CULTURAL CAPITAL; HUMAN CAPITAL THEORY; LABOUR THEORY OF VALUE; MANAGERIAL REVOLUTION; OWNERSHIP AND CONTROL; SOCIAL CAPITAL.

capital accumulation Within *Marxism, this is the central dynamic of capitalist development and refers to the process whereby *capital is expanded through the production, appropriation, and realization of *surplus value. It cannot be understood apart from capitalist *relations of production. In conventional economics, it is also an important component of *economic growth, referring to a country's net investment in fixed assets: equipment, machinery, inventories, buildings, social overhead capital, and overseas assets.

capital-intensive production Techniques of *production in which the capital-labour ratio—the proportion of *capital (machinery, equipment, inventories) relative to *labour—is high. The term is frequently used in the development literature to characterize the nature of the *industrialization process and to examine its consequences for growth in employment *vis-à-vis* output.

capitalism A system of wage-labour and commodity production for sale, exchange, and profit, rather than for the immediate need of the producers. Plentiful examples of capitalism in the pre-modern era exist but, typically, capitalist exchanges were restrained by political and religious control. What has impressed students of modernity is the huge and largely unregulated dominance of capitalist enterprise (with its related monetary and market networks) across political and cultural frontiers. Capitalism provided the principal, but not the only means of *industrialization, and should not be confused with it.

The list of defining attributes of capitalism still derives largely from the pioneering writings of Karl *Marx and Max *Weber. Weber considered market exchange as the defining characteristic of capitalism. Thus, in the modern West, capitalism typically means calculating rationality, accumulation of wealth through deferred gratification, and the separation of economic and social relations. The other institutions necessary to capitalism include: private property, formally free labour, a network of *markets for raw materials, labour produce, and an extensive monetary system. Marx, on the other hand, had taken the production relations as the crucial explanatory mechanism underlying exchange relations. Following Adam *Smith he distinguished the intrinsic use of commodities from their exchange value in the *market. Capital is created by purchasing commodities (raw material, machinery, labour) and combining them into a new commodity with an exchange value higher than the sum of the original purchase. This is made possible by the use of labour-power that, under capitalism, has itself become a commodity. According to Marx, labour-power is used exploitatively: its exchange value, as reflected in the wage, is less than the value it produces for the capitalist. The difference, so-called surplus value, is retained by the capitalist and added to the stock of capital. The cycle recurs *ad infinitum* and is the basis of class conflict. Marx's identification of capitalism with *exploitation relies on the thesis that labour is the source of all value, and therefore profit. This is contested in mainstream economics and even by many Marxists.

The concept of capitalism now has little analytic value by itself because of the extremely wide expanse of historical time over which it might be applied. The insight to be gained from describing both mid-Victorian and late 20th-century Britain as capitalist is limited. The same applies to its wide geographical and cultural scope, since it is not self-evidently helpful to explain the momentum of contemporary societies as different as Japan, Sweden, and Australia, simply in terms of their possession of a capitalist system of production. More precision can be gained by specifying types of capitalism according to either qualitative or quantitative factors.

Qualitative classifications show that capital can be accumulated by several different methods. Thus mercantile capitalism is a system of trading for profit, typically in commodities produced by non-capitalist production methods. Agrarian capitalism is exemplified by the activities of the British landowning gentry during the 17th and 19th centuries, who oversaw a transformation from a system of production for subsistence into one of the production of cash crops for the market. Industrial capitalism is capitalism's classic or stereotypical form. It entails manufacture by means of a factory system with an intricate division of labour within and between work processes; the creation of designated workplaces and factories; de-skilling of traditional handicraft skills; and the routinization of work tasks. Financial or pecuniary capitalism subordinates the capitalist productive process to the circulation of money and monetary assets and hence to the accumulation of money profits. It presupposes a highly developed banking system, an equity market, and corporate holdings of wealth through share ownership. As Thorstein Veblen pointed out, whole industrial complexes as well as buildings and land, become the subject of speculative profit and loss. State capitalism occurs where some element of government-created or government-led enterprise has been necessary to initiate both industrialism and capitalism. Even in nominally *communist economies, or in the developing world, state enterprise finds itself beholden to the pressures of international trade and finance, or the managerial constraints of capitalist production methods.

Quantitative classification aims to reflect the extensive variation in the scale of capital accumulation and in the concentration of the economic power of capital. Petty capitalism is a system in which the owner of capital is also a worker, and the system is nominally classless. Entrepreneurial capitalism exists when capital accumulation makes possible a division between owners and employees. The entrepreneurial business class typical of this phase consists of individuals who wholly or substantially own and also control (manage) their undertakings Corporate or monopoly capitalism is the outgrowth of shareholding, limited individual liability, and the concentration of capital into large impersonally owned monopolistic or oligopolistic holdings through banks and finance houses. It is identified with the growth of *corporations and a division of labour, supposedly through shareholding, between owners and managers.

James Fulcher's *Capitalism* (2004) is the best short introduction, while Tom Bottomore's *Theories of Modern Capitalism* (1985) remains a good introductory overview of this vast topic. Contemporary empirical material and debates are covered in John Scott's *Corporate Business and Capitalist Classes* (1997). For a provocative and detailed analysis of the contemporary international financial scene see Susan Strange, *Casino Capitalism* (1986). Strange's observations suggest that many sociological models of capitalist exchanges may in fact be rather selective, referring mainly to entrepreneurial or corporate industrial capitalism, and ignoring the vast speculative activity associated with modern money and commodity markets. *See also* ENTREPRENEUR; LABOUR THEORY OF VALUE.

((⊕)) SEE WEB LINKS

• An article on cultural influences in producing variant forms of capitalism, by Gordon Redding: 'The thick description and comparison of societal systems of capitalism.' (Subscription)

capitalism, disorganized *See* DISORGANIZED CAPITALISM.

capitalism, spirit of *See* PROTESTANT ETHIC THESIS.

capitalism, state *See* STATE CAPITALISM.

capitalist (capitalist class) *See* BOURGEOISIE; OWNERSHIP AND CONTROL.

carceral organization *See* INCARCERATION.

career A patterned sequence of occupational *roles through which individuals move over the course of a working life, implying increased prestige and other rewards, although not excluding downward occupational and social mobility.

The sociological concept of career began its life in the study of *occupations conducted by sociologists such as Oswald Hall and Everett Hughes in the 1940s and was further refined within the *symbolic interactionist tradition, where it was applied outside the occupational context. Thus, Howard Becker in *Outsiders* (1963) applied the concept to the stages of 'becoming a marijuana smoker', whereby smokers learned the technique, learned to perceive the effects, and finally learned to enjoy the experience.

In studies of careers, the aim is to uncover the recurrent or typical contingencies and problems awaiting someone who continues in a course of action. A distinction can be made between the objective career line, in which the recurrent problems of adjustment facing someone on a particular path of change can be predicted (for example, the stages involved in becoming a student, a doctor, or a member of a religious sect); and the subjective career or interpretive acts taken by people as they move through these changes. Erving Goffman highlighted this distinction in *Asylums* (1961), insisting that the value of the career concept is its very two-sidedness where 'one side is linked to internal matters held dearly and closely, such as image of self and felt identity; [and] the other side concerns official position, jural relations and style of life, and is part of a publicly accessible institutional complex'. Goffman focused his attention on the 'moral career' of the mental patient through the three phases of prepatient, patient, and post-patient. Goffman's work, however, was particularly concerned with the shifts in subjective images of the sense of *self experienced by patients: how, for example, they are stripped of an earlier sense of *identity when others define them as 'mad'; how this sense of self is undermined and degraded on arrival in a mental hospital; and how patients begin to build a new imagery of the self and a new identity.

career mobility *See* MOBILITY, SOCIAL.

cargo cult *See* MILLENARIANISM.

cartel *See* MONOPOLY.

case Any single unit selected for observation or analysis by a researcher. For example, in a study of the division of household tasks among eighty couples, each couple is a separate case. Similarly, in a sample survey, individual respondents or interviewees are cases. Cross-national comparative analysis might feature nations as cases.

case history A sociological method analogous to medical case histories, tracing a phenomenon through one example or many, and enabling comparative and longitudinal analysis. The extended history of a selected case may be one of a number in a *case-study research project, providing an enormously detailed and substantiated account, with reference to some specific characteristic or experience. The most common type is the *life history of an individual a *post hoc* account of the antecedents, causes, consequences, contextual factors, perceptions, and attitudes associated with some key feature of the person or their experience—such as the fact of their being an immigrant, criminal, or charismatic leader. By their nature, such case histories give greater emphasis to personal characteristics than to structural factors, and to specific processes rather than general patterns. Case histories sometimes take as their unit of study a group, organization, or community, and are thus closely allied to the case study. A single case history is often used to generate hypotheses for further study. Case histories are also used extensively in *psychiatry, *social work, *criminology, and clinical psychology.

case study (**case-study method**) A research design that takes as its subject a single case or a few selected examples of a social entity—such as communities, social groups, employers, events, life-histories, families, work teams, roles, or relationships—and employs a variety of methods to study them. The criteria that inform the selection of the case or cases for a study are a crucial part of the research design and its theoretical rigour. Case studies include descriptive reports on typical, illustrative, or deviant examples; descriptions of good practice in policy research; evaluations of policies after implementation in an organization; studies that focus on extreme or strategic cases; the rigorous test of a well-defined *hypothesis through the use of carefully selected contrasting cases; and studies of *natural experiments. The methods used to assemble information are determined in part by ease of access and whether the study is accepted by the subjects, and case studies can use any of the principal sociological methods. There are no standard formats for reporting the methods used, the data collected, and the results from case studies, but quantitative methods are less common than qualitative. *See also* CASE HISTORY; COMMUNITY STUDIES.

casework The earliest and possibly most widely discussed method of social work, pioneered originally by Octavia Hill in the London Charity Organization Society (1869), but given its first systematic statement by Mary Richmond in her book *Social Diagnosis* (1917). Whilst an emphasis is placed upon meeting the needs and solving the problems of the individual person, and there is a broad affinity to *psychoanalysis, casework harbours a range of different theoretical traditions. It is one of the major methods of *social work—the others being group work and community work. The former involves the social worker in the activities and situation of a small group of clients facing common or similar difficulties; the latter places the social worker in a neighbourhood area, to act as a resource for, and mobilizer of, local activists.

cash crop (cash-crop production) A cash crop is a horticultural product that is grown exclusively for sale on a money market, rather than for subsistence or barter. Cash-crop production may entail monoculture (the production of a single crop for the market), with the result that farmers are dependent on the success of this crop to generate sufficient income to cover their subsistence needs.

cash nexus The reduction (under *capitalism) of all human relationships, but especially relations of production, to monetary exchange. The term occurs most frequently in the writings of Karl *Marx and is still used primarily by Marxists. *See also* CAPITAL.

caste Its basis is the traditional Hindu idea of the five *varna*: Brahmin, Kshatriya, Vaishya, Shudra, and Untouchable. Within each *varna* there are myriad *jati*, which are small endogamous groups, tied to a defining occupation, based in a village or group of villages, and which provide for the element of mobility within a system where otherwise birth determines social rank. The term 'caste' has been used to refer to both the *varna* and the *jati*. The *varna* system provides the system of values, the *jati* its functional organization and practice. *Jatis* may seek promotion within the hierarchy by adopting the practices of higher *varna*, which can result in promotion within their *varna* but not between *varna*, a process known as sanskritization. It is believed that mobility between *varna* can be achieved only through rebirth, where the successful practice of the caste code or *dharma* earns for the individual an increased *karma* and therefore higher status at rebirth.

The major dividing-line between and within the various castes centres around the rules of pollution. These affect commensality (sharing and preparing of food), intermarriage, and any form of social intercourse. Since pollution of food is most likely, the higher *varna* tend towards vegetarianism, and are also teetotal. For this reason too, meat consumption is gradated, with distinctions being made between mutton, pork, and beef. Spatial segregation is a natural consequence of the *jati* system, and the segmentation inherent in the system and its attendant rules are overseen by a caste court. The caste system has been able to assimilate non-caste, non-Hindu outsiders very successfully. Since independence in 1947, the Indian state has attempted to break down caste divisions and to improve the position of the untouchables (now called *Dalit*). In practice caste retains an important role in the social structure of India and Indian overseas communities.

Max Weber attempted to convert the term into an ideal type of rigid hierarchical social *stratification, based on extreme *closure criteria. He saw it as synonymous with ethnic *status stratification and as one end of a continuum that contrasted status honour stratification with commercial *classes and the *market. Possibly the clearest definition is that proffered by André Béteille, who describes a caste as 'a small and named group of persons characterized by endogamy, hereditary membership and a specific style of life which sometimes includes the pursuit by tradition of a particular occupation and is usually associated with a more or less distinct ritual status in a hierarchical system, based on concepts of purity and pollution' (*Caste, Class and Power*, 1965). Some sociologists have attempted (controversially) to extend the term to apply it to the analysis of the South African system of apartheid, and even to the system of racial segregation in some parts of the United States during the 20th century. A good general account can be found in Chris Smaje, *Natural Hierarchies: The Historical Sociology of Race and Caste* (2000). *See also* CASTE SCHOOL OF RACE RELATIONS; HINDUISM.

caste school of race relations The label sometimes attached to those authors who applied the term *caste to the separation between Whites and Blacks in the United States. The most notable publications in this mould are W. Lloyd Warner's 'American Caste and Class' (*American Journal of Sociology*, 1936), John Dollard's *Caste and Class in a Southern Town* (1937), and Gunnar Myrdal's *An American Dilemma* (1944).

This interpretation of American race relations provoked a furious (though fairly short-lived) controversy. Myrdal defended his analysis by claiming that 'the scientifically important difference between the terms "caste" and "class" . . . is . . . a relatively large difference in freedom of movement between groups'. He also disputed whether (as critics of the School tended to claim) the Hindu caste system was characterized by less fluidity and less conflict than relations between Whites and Blacks in the United States.

The most sustained criticism of the school is Oliver C. *Cox's *Caste, Class and Race* (1948), in which the author points to a fundamental difference between the Indian and American situations, in that caste divisions in the former are a coherent system based on the principle of *inequality, whereas the 'colour bar' in America actually contradicted the *egalitarian principles of the system within which it occurred.

category A key aspect of the *measurement process involves placing observations of measurements into groups or categories on the basis of unequivocally shared features. Hence a category is a homogeneous grouping of data. For example, the *variable 'sex' might have two categories, male and female; the variable 'social class' might have three categories, upper, middle, and working. The number of categories and the rule for assigning cases or observations to the appropriate category depend on the theory being used. *See also* CODING; RULES OF CORRESPONDENCE.

catharsis Literally 'cleansing' or 'purging', in psychoanalysis the term refers to a release of emotions that reduces underlying tensions and anxieties. Sigmund *Freud initially suggested that catharsis could be accomplished through the simple re-enactment of the distressing early experiences that occasioned subsequent pathology. Later he argued that active processes of repression inhibited cathartic re-enactments.

cathexis A charge of psychic energy. The term is particularly associated with Sigmund *Freud, who used it to refer to the investment of libidinal (sexual) energy in ideas, persons, or things. These 'object-cathexes' were counterposed by anti-cathexes: forces employed by the ego in the process of repression. *See also* PSYCHOANALYSIS.

CATI (Computer Assisted Telephone Interviewing) *See* SURVEY (SOCIAL SURVEY).

causal modelling A causal model is an abstract representation of real-world dynamics that attempts to describe the causal and other relationships, among a set of variables. The best-known form of causal modelling is *path analysis, which was adopted in the 1960s by American sociologists such as Otis Dudley Duncan. Most causal modelling is associated with quantitative *survey research (see the classic text by H. M. Blalock, *Causal Inferences in Nonexperimental Research*, 1964).

Causal models are generally based on *structural equations and are analysed using *regression techniques. However, a simpler way to understand the principle of causal models is to think of them as hypotheses about the presence, sign, and direction of influence for the relations of all pairs of variables in a set. Usually these relations are mapped in diagrams or flow graphs as in the simple example shown.

Even when there are only three variables under examination many different models of their relationship are possible. Thus, investigating all the different possible models is an important step in the analysis of data, and in linking sociological theory to empirical research.

Causal models incorporate the idea of multiple causality, that is, there can be more than one cause for any particular effect. For example, how a person votes may be related to social class, age, sex, ethnicity, and so on. Moreover, some of the independent or explanatory variables could be related to one another. For example, ethnicity and class may be related, so that the effect of ethnicity on vote is both direct and indirect (through class)—as shown in the figure. This example also serves to show the importance of thinking about such models before data are collected. Theorizing in this way tells us what data we need to collect to test our model.

Causal models include a residual or error term to account for the variance in a *dependent variable left unexplained. There are, after all, many other social characteristics that affect how people vote, apart from those of age, sex, and class. It is also important to note that the causal model assumes a hierarchy—age, sex, and class cause vote, but vote does not cause age, sex, and class. Finally, it should be noted that causal models do not prove that one variable is caused by the effect of others. All the model can do is to indicate whether it is compatible with the data; and, if so, what the strengths of the causal effects are, given the model being used.

Herbert Asher's *Causal Modelling* (2nd edn., 1990) gives a short—but highly technical—introduction to the logic and tools of causal models. *See also* MULTI-LEVEL MODELS; MULTIVARIATE ANALYSIS.

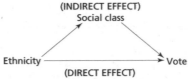

Casual modelling. Diagram showing hypothetical direct and indirect (through class) effects of ethnicity on voting behaviour

cause (causal explanation) In non-specialist contexts, to ask for the cause of some particular happening is to ask what made it happen, or brought it about. To give a causal explanation is to answer such questions, usually by specifying some prior event, condition, or state of affairs without which the problematic event would not have occurred. In more specialist, scientific or philosophical contexts, the concepts of cause and causal explanation have been the focus of sustained attempts to achieve analytical rigour. The scientific revolution of the 16th and 17th centuries recognized two forms of causation. The commonsense meaning was called 'efficient causation' and was seen as the exclusive form of causation in the natural world. Many such as Thomas *Hobbes extended this idea to the whole of the human world. Others, however, recognized that explanations of human actions may involve explanations in terms of the *goals or purposes to which they lead. This formed the basis of the distinction between the natural sciences and the human sciences.

Those who followed Hobbes's view of the human sciences tended to take David *Hume's *empiricist view of efficient causality as the regular association, or 'constant conjunction', of phenomena in our experience. If events of type *B* are regularly preceded by events of type *A*, then we may identify *A* as the cause of *B*.

But this drastic narrowing-down of causal explanation to what could be established by the evidence of the senses only served to underline the gap between scientific claims and their basis in evidence. Hume famously posed the intractable problem of *induction; namely, how do we know that regularities in our experience so far will be continued into the future? Or, more generally, how can we make justifiable inferences from our finite evidence to the universal claims embodied in causal laws? Hume appeared content to acknowledge that no such rational justification could be found, but empiricist philosophy since Hume has been littered with failed attempts to solve this problem. It should be noted that, in the absence of a solution to the problem of induction, empiricist philosophy can give no rational justification for *counterfactuals, scientific prediction, or for the application of scientific knowledge in new technologies.

But there are other difficulties faced by the empiricist view of causality, now commonly referred to as the 'covering law' account (that is, the event to be explained is shown to be 'covered' by a law linking events of that type with events of some other type). The most obvious of these is that events may be regularly associated with one another without one being the cause of the other (in the sense of bringing it about, or making it happen). The association may be coincidental; or, more likely, there may be some more complicated causal connection between them (such as that both are effects of some so-far undetected common cause). A related problem is that even where the evidence suggests a direct causal relation between two phenomena, it may not be possible to establish which is the cause, and which is the effect.

Another problem for the empiricist view of causality is that constant conjunctions in the flow of our experience of nature are actually quite unusual. For example, seeds commonly germinate as temperature rises in the spring. However, they do not always do so. Empiricist philosophers respond to this kind of problem by making the account more complicated; several conditions (such as sufficient moisture, changes in day-length, past exposure of the seed to sub-zero temperature, and so forth) may have to be specified in order that the constant conjunction may be stated as a universal law. Which of these conditions we call the cause will depend on the context of the inquiry, as will those that may be regarded as given, or background conditions. It should be noted, however, that the process of drawing up this list of individually necessary and jointly sufficient conditions will involve experimental methods that are not applicable in many fields of inquiry, including (many would argue) large parts of social science. Here, scientists working under the influence of empiricist philosophy have devised substitutes for experimentation, usually involving analysis of statistical relationships.

Yet another difficulty with the empiricist view of causality is that it does not adequately represent a large and important part of what scientists take themselves to be doing when they search for explanations. For example, observed regularities governing the germination of seeds may be only the starting-point for a scientific investigation of what makes seeds germinate. This investigation, for example, would take us into the internal structure of the seed, its tissues and cellular structure, the genetic mechanisms that regulate the secretion of growth hormones, and the biochemistry of their action on cell nuclei. Most of the great conceptual innovations of modern science—gravitation, atomic theory, natural selection, quantum mechanics, and so on—have consisted in postulating underlying mechanisms that explain observable regularities. These alternative forms of causal explanation have been explored in *realism.

In the human sciences, the philosophical influence of this empiricism has been very strong, especially in Britain and the United States. In the absence of any general utility of experimental method, the search for causal explanation has tended to take the form of statistical analysis of large-scale data-sets. Though methods of data collection and analysis have become extremely sophisticated, it is arguable that the concepts of causality commonly involved still suffer from the general limitations of the empiricist covering law model. However, such methods are also criticized in some quarters as inappropriate to the distinctive subject-matter of the social sciences. Human social action is purposive and goal oriented. Various traditions of interpretive sociology and anthropology, often rooted in German *neo-Kantianism, take this 'teleological' view. In its more extreme forms, interpretivism denies the applicability of causal explanation, favouring instead methods aimed at the interpretive understanding of social communication. *See also* CAUSAL MODELLING; CONVENTIONALISM; DEPENDENT VARIABLE; INDEPENDENT VARIABLE; INTERPRETATION; REALISM; SEQUENCE ANALYSIS.

cell (cell entry) *See* CONTINGENCY TABLE.

census A complete and individual enumeration of all cases of the type specified within defined boundaries at a single point in time; a 100 per cent count of some social entity or type of event. This stands in contrast to a sample *survey in which only part of a *population is included. A census can range from a simple head count to the collection of more sophisticated information, on every member (in theory at least) of a population.

In order to achieve such complete coverage, national censuses usually require compulsion, an obligation to participate and cooperate in providing the information required, and are therefore the preserve of national governments. National censuses have been undertaken only relatively recently (the first British Census took place in 1801). Other bodies that attempt censuses—for example of all members of an association—may achieve high levels of co-operation, but are unlikely to achieve complete coverage due to the absence of any compulsion to participate, resulting in some degree of non-response.

Most countries carry out a population and housing census every ten years with compulsory participation to ensure total coverage and a complete head count. Population data in inter-censal years must then be inferred from projections or from sample surveys. Some countries also have other national censuses, for example of employment or business activities, or industrial output. Censuses may be carried out annually, or at other intervals, instead of every ten years, although there are obvious constraints of logistics and finance. In recent years, therefore, there have been experiments in applying *sampling techniques to national censuses. This means that the 100 per cent count is limited to identifying all relevant cases and a questionnaire survey is undertaken for only a specified proportion of all cases.

( ) SEE WEB LINKS
• The official government site for the UK census.
• The US Census Bureau.

central business district (CBD) *See* CONCENTRIC ZONE THEORY.

central tendency (measures of) A statistical term applied to the central value in a frequency *distribution. Commonly referred to as the average, it is usual to identify three different measures: the mean, the median, and the mode. The mean is the most well-known, and is obtained by adding together all the individual values in a set of measurements, then dividing the sum by the total number of cases in the set. The mean is the measurement of central tendency most people have in mind when they talk about 'the average'. However, if a particular distribution is highly skewed (that is, if there are several numbers of extreme value at one or other end of the series), then it may make more sense to calculate the median. This is literally the middle value in a series of numbers, the point that neither exceeds nor is exceeded by more than 50% of the total observations. The third measure of central tendency, the mode, is used to describe the most frequently occurring category of a non-numeric variable (for example voting intention). It is less frequently employed than the mean or median. *See also* SKEWNESS.

centre-periphery model The centre-periphery (or core-periphery) model is a spatial metaphor that describes and attempts to explain the structural relationship between the advanced or metropolitan 'centre' and a less developed 'periphery', either within a particular country, or (more commonly) as applied to the relationship between capitalist and developing societies. The former usage is common in political geography, political sociology, and studies of *labour markets. An influential early example was the work of Alfred *Weber on industrial location (*Theory of the Location of Industries*, 1909).

In sociology, however, centre-periphery models are most likely to be encountered in studies of economic *underdevelopment and *dependency and tend to draw on the *Marxist tradition of analysis. The use of the centre-periphery model in this context assumes that the world system of production and distribution is the unit of analysis. It also assumes that underdevelopment is not a simple descriptive term that refers to a backward, traditional economy, but rather a concept rooted in a general theory of *imperialism.

According to the centre-periphery model, underdevelopment is not a result of the persistence of traditionalism, but is produced as a necessary feature of the development of *capitalism in the central capitalist countries and its continued reproduction on a world scale. The theory assumes a central core of capitalist countries, in which the economy is determined by *market forces, there is a high organic composition of capital, and wage levels are relatively high. In the peripheral countries, on the other hand, there is a low organic composition of capital and wage levels do not meet the cost of reproduction of labour. Indeed, the cost of reproduction of the labour force may be subsidized by non-capitalist economies, particularly rural subsistence production. Likewise, in peripheral economies, production and distribution may be determined largely by non-market forces such as *kinship or *patron-client relations.

The centre-periphery model thus suggests that the global economy is characterized by a structured relationship between economic centres that, by using military, political, and trade power, extract an economic surplus from the subordinate peripheral countries. One major factor in this is the inequality between wage-levels between core and periphery, which makes it profitable for capitalist enterprises to locate part or all of their production in underdeveloped regions. The extraction of profit depends on part of the cost of the reproduction of the labour force being met in the non-capitalist sector rather than through wages from employment in the capitalist sector. According to proponents of the core-periphery model, the appearance that capitalism is developing traditional and backward societies by locating enterprises in underdeveloped regions masks the structural relationship by which capital develops and prospers at the expense (or progressive underdevelopment) of non-capitalist economies.

The centre-periphery model has led to two main debates. The first concerns the elaboration of a theory of modes of production that attempts to conceptualize different economic forms in terms of their characteristic relationship between production and distribution. The other tries to tease out the exact links between particular areas of the centre and periphery through examining the articulation of different modes of production. The centre-periphery model is also implicated in various types of *world-system theories (see, for example, A. G. Frank, *Dependent Accumulation*, 1978, and S. Amin, *Unequal Development*, 1976). *See also* ECONOMIC DUALISM; NEO-COLONIALISM.

chain migration *See* MIGRATION, SOCIOLOGICAL STUDIES OF.

change (social change) One of the central problems of *sociology, where history is not seen simply as a succession of separate events (as depicted in some narrative accounts) but as a structured process in which it may be possible to identify a specific direction or tendency.

The first attempts at sociological analysis in the middle of the 19th century were prompted by the need to explain two great waves of change that were sweeping across Europe: namely, *industrialization, and the expansion of *democracy and human *rights in the wake of the American and French Revolutions. Auguste *Comte, in his theory of social dynamics, proposed that societies changed through a series of predictable stages based on developments in human knowledge. Herbert *Spencer offered a theory of change that was *evolutionary, based on population growth and *structural differentiation. Karl *Marx contended that the most significant social changes were revolutionary in nature, and were brought about by the struggle for supremacy between economic classes. The general tendency of 19th-century theories of social change was towards *historicism and *utopianism.

Theories of social change proliferated and became more complex, without ever wholly transcending these early formulations. In the modern world we recognize that societies are never static, and that social, political, and cultural changes constantly occur. Change can be initiated by governments through legislative or executive action (for example, legislating for equal pay or declaring a war), by citizens organized in *social movements (for example trade unionism, feminism), by cultural diffusion from one area to another (as in military conquest, migration, colonialism), or by the intended or unintended consequences of technology (such as the invention of the motor car, antibiotics, television, and computers), or environmental factors (such as drought, famine, and international shifts in economic or political advantage).

Social change theories now encompass a very broad range of phenomena, including short-term and long-term, large-scale and small-scale changes, and variations from the level of global society to that of the family. Dramatic structural and economic changes such as occurred in Eastern Europe and the former Soviet Union at the beginning of the 1990s are only one part of the field. Sociologists are also interested in changes that affect norms, values, behaviour, cultural meanings, and social relationships.

One predominant theory of social change is *functionalism, associated with the names of Talcott Parsons and Wilbert E. Moore. If society is viewed as a complex and interconnected pattern of functions, change can be explained as an epiphenomenon of its constant search for *equilibrium. For example, mass unemployment may generate a welfare system, or racial conflict may generate legislative action. The ramifications of any particular social change are endless and unpredictable, but all can be understood as social adjustments to some imbalance or maladjustment within the social organism.

A systematic functionalist attempt to specify the structural determinants of change can be found in the work of the American sociologist Neil J. Smelser (1930–2017). In his study of *Social Change in the Industrial Revolution* (1959), he analysed the interrelationship between the growth and organization of the cotton industry and the structure of the family, during the industrialization process in 19th-century England, proposing an explanation of the differentiation of social systems in terms of the way in which industries and families respond to forces for change. In his subsequent writings, for example *Theory of Collective Behaviour* (1963), Smelser both refined this model and applied it to a variety of types of collective action. A good summary can be found in the essay 'Toward a General Theory of Social Change' (in his *Essays in Sociological Explanation*, 1968). More recently, in *Social Paralysis and Social Change* (1991), he applied his theory of social change in a study of working-class education in England.

Marxist and *conflict theory traditions have developed along different lines, although they share important underlying assumptions with functionalism. They place more emphasis on the ability of human beings to actively influence their own fates through political action and relate group conflict to structural contradictions. Conflict theories in general explain social change as the outcome of a struggle for advantage between classes, races, or other groups, rather than a search for consensus. Daniel Bell's *Cultural Contradictions of Capitalism* (1976) gives an interesting example of the conflict perspective by suggesting that change in the modern world arises out of the tension between three 'realms' of social reality which operate on different principles and move towards different goals: the techno-economic structure (science, industry, and the economy); the political system; and culture. Bell showed that change is often uneven and partial. An example is so-called cultural lag, where the development of culture falls out of step with developments in technology, politics, or economics.

The problems presented by the empirical study of social change are formidable. Historical data are invariably incomplete or biased, and long-term studies of ongoing change are expensive and difficult. *Official statistics, documentary sources, repeated *surveys, and *panel studies are among the tools the student of social change must use. The whole area of social change is well-covered in Anthony Smith's *The Concept of Social Change* (1973) and the more recent *The Sociology of Social Change* (1994) by Piotr Sztompka.

The 19th-century equation of change with moral *progress is no longer widely accepted. Change may be regressive, or destructive, or confused by cultural lag. It remains an open question to what extent sociologists can explain or predict social change, and therefore to what extent societies can ever reliably initiate or control change in directions deemed socially desirable, or in any direction at all.

charisma In his famous typology of forms of authority (or 'non-coercive compliance'), Max *Weber distinguished traditional, charismatic, and rational-legal types. The first of these depends on the leader delivering a traditional message or holding a traditionally sanctioned office. By contrast, charismatic authority disrupts tradition, and rests only on support for the person of the leader. Weber defines charisma as 'a certain quality of an individual personality by virtue of which he is set apart from ordinary men and treated as endowed with supernatural, super-human, or at least specifically exceptional powers or qualities. These are such as are not accessible to the ordinary person, but are regarded as of divine origin or as exemplary, and on the basis of them the individual concerned is treated as leader' (*Economy and Society*, 1920). In Weber's view, most previous societies were characterized by traditional authority structures, periodically punctured by outbursts of charisma. In modern societies with rational-legal forms of authority, Weber saw the charismatic demagogue as the main counterweight to bureaucratic rigidity. Charisma is therefore unusual (outside of the routine and everyday), spontaneous (by contrast with established social forms), and creative of new movements and new structures. Being a source of instability and innovation, charisma is a force for social change. Although vested in actual persons, charismatic leadership conveys to beholders qualities of the sacred, and followers respond by recognizing that it is their duty to serve the leader. Charisma is alien to the established institutions of society. As Weber puts it, 'from a substantive point of view, every charismatic authority would have to subscribe to the proposition, "It is written . . . but I say unto you . . . "'. The concept has been widely used in both religious and political sociology (case studies are reported in the essay on 'Charismatic Leadership' reproduced in R. Bendix and G. Roth (eds.), *Scholarship and Partisanship*, 1971). Archetypical charismatic figures include Jesus Christ and Adolf Hitler. Although the concept is intended to highlight certain aspects of the relationship between leader and followers, it does tend to point also to an irrational element in the behaviour of the latter, and on that basis has been subject to some criticism (see R. Bendix, *Max Weber*, 1960).

Charismatic phenomena are temporary and unstable. In the short term, the leader may change his or her mind, possibly in response to being 'moved by the Spirit'. In the longer term he or she will die. For that reason, charismatic authority is often 'routinized' during the lifetime of the new leader, so that he or she will be succeeded either by a *bureaucracy vested with rational-legal authority or by a return to the institutionalized structures of tradition to which the charismatic impetus has now been incorporated. (See A. Bryman, *Charisma and Leadership in Organizations*, 1992.)

chattel slavery *See* SLAVERY.

Chicago sociology (Chicago School) A tradition of sociology associated with the University of Chicago for the first four decades of the 20th century and that dominated North American sociology throughout this period. It was the first department of sociology to be established (in 1892 by Albion *Small), and with it came the first main sociological journal, the *American Journal of Sociology* in 1895, the establishing of the American Sociological Association in 1905, the first major student text by Robert Park and Ernest Burgess in *Introduction to the Science of Sociology* (1921), a large graduate school, and an important series of research monographs. Much of this is catalogued in the many histories written about the 'Chicago School'. (The best of these include R. E. L. Faris, *Chicago Sociology*, 1967; M. Bulmer, *The Chicago School of Sociology*, 1984; A. Abbott, *Department and Discipline*, 1999.)

The tradition was heavily informed by philosophical *pragmatism, the direct observation of experience, and the analysis of urban social processes. It is most frequently identified with these three themes.

First, and most commonly, Chicago sociology was firmly committed to direct *fieldwork and empirical study. In contrast to some of the more abstract and theoretical tendencies of many of the earlier North American sociologists, especially the Social *Darwinians, Robert Park told his students to 'go and sit in the lounges of the luxury hotels and on the doorsteps of the flophouses; sit on the Gold Coast settees and on the slum shakedowns; sit in the Orchestra Hall and in the Star and Garter Burlesque. In short, go get the seat of your pants dirty in real research'. Such a directive led not only to a large number of now classic empirical studies of sociology—Frederic Thrasher's *The Gang* (1927), Clifford Shaw's *The Jack Roller* (1930), Nels Anderson's *The Hobo* (1923), or Harvey Zorbaugh's *The Gold Coast and the Slum* (1929) are typical examples—but also to considerable experimentation in research methods. Of particular note was the development of *participant observation and the *case study method.

However, it is a mistake to see Chicago simply as the home of qualitative methods, as its sociologists also pioneered the use of social *surveys and community-based statistical research, the quantitative mapping of social areas, and the creation of local community fact books. In short, a strong tradition of quantitative method was also developed at Chicago, linked especially to William

*Ogburn. Nor was Chicago sociology atheoretical. Everett C. Hughes, a leading member of the Chicago School and pioneer of the sociology of occupations and professions in the 1940s, was instrumental in introducing explicit theory into the later Chicago sociology. Hughes himself wrote several classic articles investigating the subjective consequences of work for the individual and the strategies for pursuing status and earnings in workplaces (see *Men and their Work*, 1958, jointly authored with Helen McGill Hughes).

A second core theme of sociology at Chicago was its concern with the study of the city. It was in Chicago—one of the fastest-growing cities in North America at the turn of the century, with all its attendant problems of immigration, *delinquency, *crime, and social problems—that the sociological study of the city came into its own. Much of *urban sociology has its roots in this tradition, both descriptively through a mapping of the areas of the city (into a series of zones arranged in a concentric circle from an inner city zone to an outer commuter belt), and theoretically in terms of attempting to explain the dynamics of city growth and change. Its *urban ecology has close links with environmental determinism (*see* ENVIRONMENT).

A third theme to emerge from Chicago was a distinctive form of social psychology, derived in part from the allied department of philosophy, and especially the work of George Herbert *Mead. This was a tradition that focused on the creation and organization of the *self, and that later came to be identified through the writing of Herbert *Blumer as *symbolic interactionism. *See also* FORMALISM; FRAZIER, EDWARD FRANKLIN; SEQUENCE ANALYSIS; URBAN ECOLOGY.

child abuse In its most general sense, child abuse refers to the maltreatment or injury of a child by an adult or adults. Such abuse can be physical, emotional, sexual, or a combination of all three. It might be perpetrated by one person or by several, within a family or outside it, and in public or in private. Child abuse is widely acknowledged as causing (often) severe emotional and psychological damage to victims, damage that, because of widespread imposition of secrecy by abusers, sometimes does not become manifest for many years. In this broad sense it points to an abuse of *power between different age-groups. Historical evidence shows clearly that child abuse of all kinds has existed for centuries, although how it has been defined varies enormously. What was regarded as firm discipline fifty years ago is today considered abusive.

It is useful to differentiate physical abuse of children—child abuse or 'baby battering'—from child sexual abuse. Baby battering became an issue of widespread concern and the basis of a *moral panic in the 1960s, as discussed in particular by R. and C. Kempe in the USA (see their *Child Abuse*, 1983), who saw it as indicative of 'dysfunctional' families. Later investigations found that baby battering, as well as physical violence within families generally, was strongly associated with families living in poverty, although some contend that middle-class family violence is simply kept more hidden and secretive. The deaths in Britain of infants Maria Colwell in 1973, Jasmine Beckford in 1984, Victoria Climbié in 2000, and Peter Connelly ('Baby P') in 2007 created public outcry and raised controversial issues about what constituted appropriate interventions in families by social workers (*see* SOCIAL WORK).

In contrast with baby battering, which seems to be class-related, the evidence pertaining to child *sexual* abuse suggests that it occurs within all social classes. Most victims are girls, though boys are also abused. The majority of abusers are men, although there is evidence that a very small proportion of women also abuse children sexually. Collecting reliable data for child sexual abuse is notoriously difficult, particularly as most experts agree that the majority of cases are never reported. Estimates range from 10 per cent to 90 per cent of all children having experienced some form of sexual abuse. One problem for researchers is that there is no single legal category of 'sexual abuse'; it includes rape, buggery, unlawful intercourse with a minor, and incest (defined narrowly as the father having full sexual intercourse with a child). Much debate has focused on what exactly does constitute sexual abuse, and whether or not children can be trusted to tell the truth, particularly in court situations.

These issues came to the fore in a crisis in Cleveland (UK) in 1987, when over 200 children were reported by a paediatrician to have been sexually abused, but the local police, unwilling to accept such a possibility, refused to act on the doctors' evidence. Although it was later decided that some children had been wrongly diagnosed, evidence upheld the view that the majority of children had indeed been abused. At the time, however, it was the paediatrician and social workers, rather than the abusers, who were criticized. The episode resulted in widespread public debate about the role of the family in child-rearing, the nature of privacy and power relations in families, and balance between children's rights as against those of parents. Less discussed, but no less relevant, were issues relating to children as parents' property, male violence, and the erotic nature of some power relations (see B. Campbell, *Unofficial Secrets—Child Sexual Abuse: The Cleveland Case*, 1988).

There are three main models of child sexual abuse. The psychological model, which is concerned primarily with male offenders, sees the perpetrators as suffering from personality disorder. This model disregards the victims and the social context in which abuse occurs. The *family systems model, by contrast, treats the family as a single entity, rather than focusing on the individuals within it, or the histories of particular family members. Families where abuse occurs are seen as 'dysfunctional'. This view presupposes such a thing as a 'normal' family and implicitly labels families that do not appear to be normal as pathological or deviant. The feminist model regards sexual abuse as an aspect of a wider power system of male dominance over women and children, and integral part of which is male violence. Such a model recognizes inequality in general, particularly the abuse of power between age groups, and presupposes different forms of intervention, but it does not offer any obvious solution for the minority of women who abuse children.

Good accounts of child abuse, which situate the phenomenon in its wider sociopolitical context, will be found in N. Parton, *The Politics of Child Abuse* (1985) and D. Gittins, *The Family in Question* (2nd edn., 1993), *The Child in Question* (1997), and S. Scott, *The Politics and Experience of Ritual Abuse* (2001).

Childe, Vere Gordon (1892–1957) Born in Australia, Childe became professor successively in the Universities of Edinburgh and London, and was a leading figure in mid-20th-century archaeology. Known for his Marxist emphasis on the importance of the economy, Childe nevertheless also stressed the importance of society and culture, rather than artefacts. He was a great popularizer of archaeology, particularly through his well-written comparative accounts of human prehistory, such as *Man Makes Himself* (1956).

childhood The term 'child' can be used to mean either an offspring or someone who has not reached full economic and jural status as an adult in a society. Individuals in the latter state are passing through an age-related period known as childhood.

Childhood is not simply a stage of biological immaturity but is also socially constructed in various ways in different societies and at different historical periods. The French historian Phillipe Ariés (*Centuries of Childhood*, 1962), was the first to point out that modern Western childhood is unique in the way it 'quarantines' children from the world of adults, so that childhood is associated with play and education, rather than work and economic responsibility. Other writers have pointed out that childhood is constructed on the inabilities of children as political, intellectual, sexual, or economic beings, despite empirical evidence to the contrary. This construction implies that children must be protected (primarily by women) in the family, which serves the needs of capitalist states for the reproduction and socialization of the labour-force, at minimum cost to the state. The child also provides state agencies with the excuse to intervene in irregular families, and to change or dismember them, if they do not comply with certain norms.

Studies in the sociology of childhood indicate that the term is a powerful symbol in the construction of modern, Western society. The term is highly ambiguous, which helps its symbolic functioning. On one hand, children are the cherished and valued possessions of the parents; on the other, they are a cost and burden on society (and particularly on women). In the 1980s, through the 'discovery' of *child abuse and also the development of the United Nations Convention on the Rights of the Child, a new approach—stressing the rights, strengths and capabilities of children—has arisen in sociology, to challenge the prevailing image of childhood.

For different reasons, childhood has been a major topic of analysis in *psychoanalysis, *linguistics, the sociology of *education, and in the study of primary *socialization and *gender differentiation. For an overview of the field see Allison James and Alan Prout (eds.), *Constructing and Reconstructing Childhood* (1990).

chiliasm The doctrine or belief that Christ will reign on earth for 1000 years. There are numerous examples of chiliast cults and sectarian movements in the history of the Christian Church. In the medieval period, for example, the Taborites (led by the Bohemian priest Martin Huska) preached an imminent period of catastrophe to be followed by the advent of Christ and a New Age of His rule on earth (see H. Kaminsky, 'Chiliasm and the Hussite Revolution', *Church History*, 1957). Chiliasm is therefore a specific form of *millenarianism and shares many of the same characteristics. Thus, in anticipation of the Second Coming, chiliast communities tend to secede from the larger social order, not only spiritually but also physically, often living (as did the Taborites for a time) in a state of collective emancipation—recognizing no traditional authorities, norms, or legal restraints, shunning family and home, and turning over material possessions to common funds.

Christianity A world religion that regards Jesus Christ as its founder, Christianity was originally a social movement in *Judaism, emerging in Jerusalem during the Roman occupation. With the destruction of Jerusalem in 70 CE, Christianity became increasingly a religion of Gentiles, partly as a consequence of the preaching of the apostle Paul and his establishment of Gentile churches. In Rome, these Christian groups became the targets of political repression, especially under Nero. This persecution resulted in new institutions of martyrdom and sainthood. Although Christianity spread among the lower classes, it eventually won favour among the powerful, and in 313 CE, Constantine established it as the religion of the Roman Empire. Thus, Karl *Kautsky's argument (*Foundations of Christianity: A Study of Christian Origins*, 1908) that early Christianity was a proletarian religion requires qualification.

Christianity is based on the belief in an omnipotent and just God who is responsible for all creation. Although humanity has sinned, and therefore fallen from grace, salvation from punishment has been made possible by God's mercy in sending a saviour—Jesus Christ—to atone for these sins. Christians therefore believe that faith in Christ as the Son of God ensures everlasting salvation. However, Christianity has no single organizational structure. By the 11th century, there was a clear divide between Western and Eastern Orthodoxy. The bishop of Rome was transformed into a Pope with authority over Western Christendom. The Roman Catholic Church had a major impact on Western culture, especially through the educational function of monasteries. There was a profound split in the Church as a consequence of the Protestant Reformation in the 16th and 17th centuries. Contemporary Christianity is, then, an extraordinarily diverse system of beliefs, embodying various doctrines emphasizing not only faith but also all manner of good works. A fascinating account of the historical emergence of the doctrines and organization of the Christian Church is given in Elaine Pagels's book, *The Gnostic Gospels* (1979).

Much of the sociology of religion has been concerned with the social consequences of specifically Christian beliefs. Max Weber's *protestant ethic thesis is one of the best-known examples. There has also been much debate about the impact of Christianity on Western civilization generally, for example in promoting *democracy or scientific innovation, and about the contemporary *secularization of the Christian religion. *See also* CHILIASM; CHURCH; RELIGION, SOCIOLOGY OF; SECT.

chromosomes A biological term referring to the units of information in human cells. The nuclei of the body cells of humans and other complex animals and plants contain a number of pairs of thread-like structures called chromosomes. These carry the *genes, the basic units of material inheritance, arranged in a linear sequence. It is the inheritance of specific chromosomes from each of the two parents that ensures the continual redistribution of genetic material among offspring. This is the basis of genetic variation as a factor in the biological evolution of species.

church A church is any form of association organized around religious beliefs, and the word can also be used to refer to the buildings in which such religious activity takes place. To give a more specific meaning, the term 'ecclesia' is sometimes preferred. This refers to a large, bureaucratic, and hierarchical religious organization with a priesthood, sacraments, and formal liturgy. Lay participation, especially in worship, is not necessarily encouraged. An ecclesia is organized around an orthodox doctrine and claims spiritual authority over all those who live within its jurisdiction. Individuals are born into the church and become permanent members through such rituals as infant baptism. The ecclesia is accommodated to existing social arrangements and regards the state as a necessary aspect of political control over society. The ecclesia or church as an ideal type is typically contrasted with the *sect, the *cult, and the *denomination.

circulation mobility *See* MOBILITY, SOCIAL.

circulation of elites *See* ELITE.

citizenship In political and legal theory, citizenship refers to the *rights and duties of the members of a nation-state or city. In some historical contexts, a citizen was any member of a city; that is, an urban collectivity with relative immunity from the demands of a monarch or state. In classical Greece, citizenship was limited to free men, who had a right to participate in political debate because they contributed, often through military service, to the direct support of the city-state. Many have argued that citizenship has expanded with democratization to include a wider definition of the citizen regardless of sex, age, or ethnicity. The concept was revived in the context of the modern *state, notably during the French and American Revolutions, and was gradually identified more with rights than obligations.

In sociology, recent theories of citizenship have drawn their inspiration from T. H. *Marshall, who defined citizenship as a status which is enjoyed by a person who is a full member of a community. Citizenship has three components: civil, political, and social. *Civil rights are necessary for individual freedoms and are institutionalized in the law courts. Political citizenship guarantees the right to participate in the exercise of political power in the community, either by voting, or by holding political office. Social citizenship is the right to participate in an appropriate standard of living; this right is embodied in the *welfare and educational systems of modern societies. The important feature of Marshall's theory was his view that there was a permanent tension or contradiction between the principles of citizenship and the operation of the capitalist *market. *Capitalism inevitably involves inequalities between social *classes, while citizenship involves some redistribution of resources, because of rights that are shared equally by all.

Marshall's theory has given rise to much dispute. Critics argue that it is a description of the English experience only, and it is not a comparative analysis of citizenship; that it has an *evolutionary and *teleological view of the inevitable expansion of citizenship, and does not examine social processes that undermine citizenship; it does not address gender differences in the experience of citizenship; it fails to address other types of citizenship, such as economic citizenship; and it is not clear about the causes of the expansion of citizenship. Some sociologists believe that Marshall's argument can be rescued from these criticisms if the original theory is modified. The continuing debate is reflected in the papers collected in M. Bulmer and A. M. Rees (eds.), *Citizenship Today: The Contemporary Relevance of T. H. Marshall* (1996).

There are very different traditions of citizenship in different societies. Active citizenship, that is based on the achievement of rights through social struggle, is very different from the passive citizenship which is handed down from above by the state (see R. Bendix, *Nation-Building and Citizenship*, 1964). There are also very different theoretical approaches to understanding the structure of the public and private realm in conceptions of citizenship. For Talcott Parsons the growth of citizenship is a measure of the *modernization of society because it is based on values of universalism and *achievement. These different theoretical traditions are primarily the product of two opposed views of citizenship: it is either viewed as an aspect of bourgeois *liberalism, in which case it involves a conservative view of social participation, or it is treated as a feature of radical democratic politics; it is either dismissed as a mere reform of capitalism, or it is regarded as a fundamental plank of *democracy. Recently, sociologists have gone beyond these traditional theories of democracy, liberalism, and *civil society, to ask questions about the changing relationships between individuals, communities, and states such as whether *globalization will replace state citizenship with a truly universal conception of human rights in a world in which the nation-state is increasingly subject to influences from supranational institutions. (Speculative answers to this and related questions will be found in Bryan S. Turner (ed.), *Citizenship and Social Theory*, 1993.) Jack Barbalet's *Citizenship* (1988) is an excellent discussion of the (now extensive) literature surrounding the concept. *See also* INDUSTRIAL DEMOCRACY.

city, sociology of the *See* URBAN SOCIOLOGY.

civic nationalism *See* NATIONALISM.

civil disobedience The refusal by all or part of a community to pay taxes or obey the laws and regulations of the *state, in an attempt to change government policy by non-violent means. The Gandhian protests against British Rule in India are one obvious example. More recently, substantial numbers of British voters refused to pay a community charge (or so-called poll tax) to fund the spending of local government, and successfully forced a change in the system of taxation. More generally, however, civil disobedience shades into other (sometimes violent) forms of collective protest (such as *riots), so that the precise boundaries of the phenomenon can be difficult to identify. What are intended to be peaceful protests against particular taxes may (for whatever reason) turn into violent episodes; indeed, it is often in the state's interest to label such activity in precisely this way, in order to discredit the participants. *See also* PASSIVE RESISTANCE.

civilizing process *See* ELIAS, NORBERT.

civil liberties *See* CIVIL RIGHTS.

civil religion (civil religion thesis) In the 1960s a number of sociologists (including Talcott Parsons, Edward Shils, and Robert Bellah) distinguished civil religion from institutional, church-based religion, arguing that societies such as contemporary America were attaching *sacred qualities to certain of their institutional arrangements and historical events. Thus, in the case of the United States, the extensive immigration from Europe was analogous to the Jewish Exodus, and the Civil War a rebirth through bloodshed and an expiation of old sins. The theme of American civil religion was therefore one of Americans as the new Chosen People (see, for example, Bellah's 'Civil Religion in America', in W. G. McLoughlin and R. N. Bellah (eds.), *Religion in America*, 1968). Similarly, in a famous (and much criticized) article on the monarchy in Britain, Edward Shils and Michael Young identified what they argued were religious aspects of the apparently secular *rituals surrounding the coronation ('The Meaning of the Coronation', *Sociological Review*, 1953). The basic idea behind these and other variants of the 'civil religion thesis' is that in advanced industrial societies, which are increasingly secular in terms of institutional religions, civic religions (such as the celebration of the *state or *civil society) now serve the same *functions of prescribing the overall values of society, providing social cohesion, and facilitating emotional expression. In other words, civil religions offer a 'functional equivalent' or 'functional alternative' to institutional religions, since they meet the same needs within the *social system. Both arguments (about civil religion in particular and functional alternatives in general) were subject to the charges of *evolutionism, *teleology, *tautology, and empirical untestability laid against normative functionalism as a whole. *See also* SECULARIZATION.

civil rights *Rights that are recognized as belonging to all individuals in a society, that can be upheld by appeal to the law, and that are not subject to arbitrary denial either by individuals or the state. They are usually defended in terms of the protection of the individual from the *state, and subject to clear limits, themselves identified in relation to the rights of others or the common good.

Although the idea of rights being embodied for citizens in legal doctrines was hardly new, it took on a new meaning in the 20th century, as a result of the Civil Rights Movement. The distinctively modern form of civil rights is often dated from the American Civil War, after which slaves gained the right of freedom. It is embodied in the Civil Rights Legislation of the late 20th century—such as the 1964 Civil Rights Act in the United States. The history of this legislation is discussed in M. Berger, *Equality by Statute* (1978). *See also* CITIZENSHIP; CIVIL SOCIETY.

civil society There are several competing definitions of what this concept involves. However, its key attributes are that it refers to public life rather than private or household-based activities; it is juxtaposed to the family and the state; and it exists within the framework of the rule of law. Most authorities seem to have in mind the realm of public participation in voluntary associations, the mass media, professional associations, and trade unions.

Interposed between the individual (or *family) and the *state for some thinkers (such as *Hegel), it is a temporary phenomenon, to be transcended when particular and common *interests combined. For others it is the realm of the particular counterpoised to the state, whereas for Antonio *Gramsci it was the bastion of class *hegemony, and ultimately (though not unequivocally) support-ive of the state. More recent usage has drawn on the experience of the collapse of *communism in Eastern Europe, and the apparent atrophy or non-existence of the 'meso' level of social relations in the articulation of interests between the private realm of the domestic and the totalizing realm of the state.

Civil society is always seen as dynamic and as involving *social movements. It can also be seen as the dynamic side of *citizenship that, combining as it does achieved rights and obligations, finds them practised, scrutinized, revamped, and redefined at the level of civil society. Thus, freedom of speech as an essential *civil right depends on the culture and organization of publishers, journalists, and the reading public at large, both for the manner in which it is legitimized and for its scope and intensity. An excellent edited collection on this topic is Z. A. Pelczynski, *The State and Civil Society* (1984), and the debate is explored at a transnational level in J. Keane, *Global Civil Society* (2003).

clan A clan is a unilineal kin group that is usually exogamous, claiming descent from a common ancestor, and is often represented by a totem. Clans are of either matrilineal or patrilineal descent, depending on whether descent is traced through the female or the male line. A clan is usually segmented into lineages, which are the branches of descent from a common ancestor. Classic works on clans include A. L. Kroeber, *Zuni Kin and Clan* (1917), Raymond Firth, *We, the Tikopia* (1936), and E. E. Evans-Pritchard, *The Nuer* (1940). *See also* PHRATRY.

class *See* BOURGEOISIE; CLASS AWARENESS; CLASS CONSCIOUSNESS; CLASS IMAGERY; CLASS INTEREST; CLASS POSITION; CLASS SITUATION; CONTRADICTORY CLASS LOCA-TION; FALSE CONSCIOUSNESS; HOUSING CLASS; MARX, KARL; MIDDLE CLASS; PETITE BOURGEOISIE; PROLETARIAT; STATUS; STRATIFICATION; UNDERCLASS; WORKING CLASS.

class awareness A term—broadly synonymous with 'class identification'—referring to the subjective definition and interpretation of social *class in the public consciousness. Sociological investigations of class awareness therefore examine the class labels (if any) that are commonly used in popular discourse; the extent to which people personally identify with these labels; which factors determine identification with particular classes; and the implications of class identities for broader political orientations and social behaviour generally. The term has a much wider currency in the United States than in Britain or Europe, mainly because it carries less of the ideological baggage associated with the Marxist notion of *class consciousness, although there are obvious overlaps between the two concepts and indeed in the relevant sociological literatures. For example, and rather confusedly, Reeve Vanneman and Lynn Weber Cannon (*The American Perception of Class*, 1987) argue that lack of an organized working-class movement in the United States does not mean that American workers lack class consciousness, by which the authors actually mean awareness. It is doubtful whether this minimal conception of class consciousness would be accepted by Marxists or other class analysts. A more typical (and probably the best) treatment of the American material are Mary R. Jackman and Robert W. Jackman's *Class Awareness in the United States* (1983) and Paul Kingston's *The Classless Society* (2000). *See also* CLASS IMAGERY.

class consciousness A term originating in Marxist theory and referring to a sense of shared identity and common purpose among the members of a *class. Marx saw this in terms of the development of a 'class in itself' (a category of people having a common relation to the means of production) into a 'class for itself' (a group organized in conscious and active pursuit of its own *interests). The emphasis in Marxist analysis has been on the development of revolutionary class consciousness among workers through their concentration in factories, their ease of communication, a distinctive way of life and cultural activities, and engagement in political struggle, all of which bring the *working class into conflict with the capitalist class or *bourgeoisie. It is only when these objective features generate a consciousness of common *interests rooted in the process of production and lead to practical action through political representation, that it is possible to speak of class consciousness in the Marxian sense. The idea of a unified and class-conscious *proletariat found in *The Manifesto of the Communist Party* (1848) is replaced in some other Marxist writings by a more complex view of 'class fractions' tied to particular market situations and having varied forms of consciousness and political orientation.

However many the hints about the historical contingency of class consciousness that one can find in Marx, his emphasis is still upon the inevitability of real interests being pursued, even if sometimes the means come accidentally to hand—as with the Paris Commune. Here too, Marx saw only 'delusive prejudice' rather than real interest separating peasant from proletarian, and predicted that rural producers had as a class fraction entered their period of decay. Most conceptions of proletarian class consciousness depict its development as an explosion of mass consciousness—culminating in some sort of latter-day equivalent of the storming of the Winter Palace.

A number of empirically orientated Marxists have attempted to ground class consciousness in everyday cultural practices, shop-floor collective action, and local forms of social organization. Michael Burawoy's celebrated study of *Manufacturing Consent: Changes in the Labor Process under Monopoly Capitalism* (1979) is an early example and had much in common with the understanding of class to be found in the work of the English historian E. P. Thompson, who viewed class consciousness and class formation as cultural expressions embodied in the development of neighbourhood solidarism, mutual aid societies, social clubs, class-specific forms of leisure, and so forth (see *The Making of the English Working Class*, 1968).

In an interesting attempt to introduce *rational choice theory into Marxist analysis, John Elster ('Marxism, Functionalism and Game theory', *Theory and*

Society, 1982) has argued that a class-conscious class is one that has solved the free-rider problem. That is, class consciousness is the ability of class organizations to pursue class objectives by controlling sectional struggles, and is therefore an attribute of organizations rather than consensus among individuals: it is the capacity of a class to behave as a collective actor. From this point of view, what is at issue is the capacity of class organizations (such as *trade unions) to mobilize members behind centrally organized initiatives on behalf of class rather than particular interests; and, once mobilized, to hold in check groups who would '*free ride' or pursue sectional gains at the collective expense. Almost paradoxically, therefore, class consciousness implies the absence of industrial *militancy and spontaneous mass action, since class objectives are pursued by a highly centralized labour organization. *See also* CLASS INTEREST; COLLECTIVE ACTION; SOCIAL CLASS.

class dealignment *See* CONSUMPTION SECTORS; VOTING BEHAVIOUR.

classical conditioning *See* CONDITIONING.

classical criminology *See* CRIMINOLOGY, CLASSICAL.

classical economic theory *See* LAISSEZ-FAIRE ECONOMICS; MALTHUS; MILL; SMITH.

classification *See* TAXONOMY.

class imagery The commonsense or everyday beliefs about social *class held by ordinary members of society—particularly in respect of the number, size, and characteristics of the various classes in their society. Studies of social *stratification often distinguish objective and subjective structure, the former pertaining to relationships of *power or privilege, the latter being the domain of class imagery. The term itself dates from 1957 and gained British currency through David *Lockwood's influential research on working-class *images of society (see M. Bulmer (ed.), *Working-class Images of Society*, 1975).

Where Marxist views see class consciousness or awareness of the class structure as arising from class conflict and the experience of social *inequality, with any departure from a conception based on class interest deemed to be *false consciousness, more recent sociological views highlight different perceptions of the class structure and recognize variations in the extent to which these images are dichotomous (a simple 'us' *versus* 'them') or are multiple and finely graded. Different bases for these images or models (such as power and money) have been described, but in most cases systematic class images are difficult to identify empirically. The most recent studies of class imagery suggest that there exists a more fluid, complex, and open stock of such class and occupational images and meanings than is usually assumed, and that individuals use different imagery and conceptions for different purposes and strategies (see, for example, N. Britten, 'Class Imagery in a National Sample of Women and Men', *British Journal of Sociology*, 1984).

class interest The basic concept of class interest derives from Karl *Marx's theory of social class. Marx argued that the social relations that define *class generate inherently opposing interests. Hence, for example, the *interests of the *bourgeoisie are different from and antagonistic towards those of the *proletariat. It is in the interests of the bourgeois class to exploit the proletariat and in the interests of the proletariat to overthrow the bourgeoisie. Note that this definition of interest is inbuilt to the definition of class: classes have objective interests. As the American Marxist Erik Olin Wright puts it, 'class structure is . . . a terrain of social relations that determine objective material interests of actors, and class struggle is understood as the forms of social practices which attempt to realize those interests [and] class consciousness can be understood as the subjective processes that shape intentional choices with respect to those interests and struggles' (see his *Classes*, 1985). Here it is possible to see the role assigned to the concept of class interests within a Marxist theory of class action.

However, there are many problems with this concept. In particular, it is more satisfactory to examine how far objective conditions actually exist, which are sufficiently similar for there to be the possibility of common interests emerging. What form those interests might take also becomes an empirical question. Hence, for example, David *Lockwood has noted how workers form attachments to (rather than antagonisms against) the existing form of capitalist society through the activities of *trade unions. John H. Goldthorpe, on the other hand, argues that whether or not individuals become conscious of possessing a class identity, and seek to pursue common class interests with others similarly placed, will depend in part upon the nature and degree of 'demographic class formation', the extent to which classes exist on the basis of patterns of mobility and association (see *Social Mobility and Class Structure in Modern Britain*, 1980). But neither Goldthorpe nor Lockwood assumes that there are objective class interests. Rather, each argues that the interests pursued by a class or its representatives are contingent upon a complex pattern of historical and political circumstances, and emerge out of social action rather than being an inherent condition of such action. In particular, people have to assume social *identities as members of a class, before it becomes possible for sociologists to identify its interests.

class situation Class situation was defined by Max *Weber as the particular causal component in *life chances that results from a person's location in property and market relations. Marxists call this class position or class location. In a study of *class consciousness among clerical workers (*The Blackcoated Worker*, 1958; 2nd edn., 1989), the British sociologist David *Lockwood introduced an influential view of class situation that distinguished the market situation ('the economic position narrowly conceived, consisting of source and size of income, degree of job-security, and opportunity for upward occupational mobility') and the work situation ('the set of social relationships in which the individual is involved at work by virtue of his position in the division of labour'). Like Weber, he also distinguished the status situation ('the position of the individual in the hierarchy of prestige in the society at large'). It was the particular combination of experiences originating in class and status situations that, according to Lockwood, constituted the principal determinants of class consciousness among clerks. *See also* GOLDTHORPE CLASS SCHEME; SOCIAL CLASS; SOCIAL STATUS.

classroom interaction (**classroom behaviour**) Describes the form and content of behaviour or social interaction in the classroom. In particular, research on gender, class, and 'race' in education has examined the relationship between teachers and students in classrooms. A variety of methods have been used to investigate the amount and type of 'teacher-time' received by different groups of students. Much of the research has then sought to relate this to different educational experiences and outcomes among particular groups. For example, some studies showed that boys received a disproportionate amount of the teachers' time, sat in different places in the classroom, and were more highly regarded by teachers, which may go some way towards explaining the educational differential between men and women. More recently, focus has shifted to examining the role of the school as a whole on student experiences as well as behaviour outside the classroom, such as bullying and racial and sexual harassment. *See also* EDUCATION, SOCIOLOGY OF.

clergy A generic term used for ordained religious leaders, deriving from 'clericus', a clerk in Holy Orders (bishop, priest, or deacon). In the Christian tradition, ordination creates a *status, but not necessarily a specific *role or *occupation.

clientelism (**client-patron relationship**) *See* PATRON-CLIENT RELATIONSHIP.

climate change The link made within sociology between climate and culture goes back to the writings of the 18th-century European Enlightenment, most notably in Scotland with Adam Ferguson and in France with Baron de Montesquieu, and it has long been recognized that climate has effects in society. These range from its influence on social behaviours, like food availability and cuisine, work habits, forms of available employment, and leisure pursuits, to types of social relationships, such as its impact on family life and on different lifestyle choices, amongst many others. Social anthropology has particularly captured through detailed ethnographic research the ways in which extremes of climate mediate culture and social relations, including notions of time, the ownership of wealth, and everyday cultural practices. However, the emergence of climate change in the late 20th century as a critical problem for the future of humankind has seen this relationship explored from the reverse position, the impact of society on climate. This remains a two-way, reciprocal relationship in that climate changes in turn rebound in society to have potentially enormous damaging effects on ecosystems and social systems alike. It was only in 2008 that Lever-Tracy complained that outside of environmental sociology, the discipline ignored global warming. By 2010 the American Sociological Association had set up a task force on sociology and global climate change, and in the same year the British Sociological Association established its Climate Change Study Group. Heavily carbon-reliant economies and carbon-reliant transport systems are obvious examples of the way society impacts on climate, but so are certain forms of agriculture in arid regions that result in the intensification of deserts (so-called desertification) or the clearance of natural forests to make way for agriculture, both of which deprive the land of natural forms of carbon capture.

So reliant on carbon are most economies in the Global North, through the motor car, air transport and carbon-rich forms of electricity generation, that the debate about climate change overlaps with the debate about global patterns of inequality and poverty in the Global South. The Global South is likely to experience the worst effects of climate change, such as rising sea levels, food insecurity, pollution, desertification and water shortage, yet its own rush to industrial development as a solution to global poverty only encourages its reliance on carbon economies and carbon-rich lifestyles. The connection between climate change and global inequality is thus not simple or amenable to easy solutions, and climate change is now recognized as a global problem, requiring global responses. Sociology's recent intervention in the climate change debate, therefore, is an important one. Disagreement within climate change science over whether climate changes are human-made or naturally occurring cyclical phenomena is not the most important issue. Greenhouse gases generated by carbon-intensive societies are partly responsible for distorting the climate, and sociology can help understand how climate changes will impact on local societies and cultures and what social, political, and economic re-arrangements can be made to help alleviate these effects. Sociologists have thus made significant contributions to understanding the consequences of carbon-reliant economies and of motor car-reliant cultures and behaviours, to rethinking transport policies, and to town and city planning in order to try to reduce carbon use, and to the development of alternative policies of sustainable development and environmental protection. Issues like the political sociology of climate change, and the emergence of climate protection social movements, are also amenable to sociological investigation. However, climate change poses an interesting challenge to sociology's practices as a discipline. A sociological perspective on climate change in isolation from other approaches can reveal only so much. The study of climate change calls for new forms of interdisciplinary collaboration that extend across the traditional nature-culture divide and require social scientists to work with those whom they considered strangers in the past, such as environmental scientists, oceanographers, biologists, physical geographers, and others. Meaningful contributions to climate change science by sociologists also require changes to other forms of practice, especially greater engagement with governments, policymakers, civil servants, and international agencies, which threaten the distance most sociologists like to keep from power elites. Climate change is as much a challenge to sociology as to global society.

These issues are explored in Anthony Giddens, *The Politics of Climate Change* (2009) and John Urry, *Climate Change and Society* (2011).

(⊕) SEE WEB LINKS
• The British Sociological Association Study Group on Climate Change.

clinical sociology A term, analogous to clinical psychology, introduced in 1931 by Chicago sociologist Louis *Wirth, for the work of sociologists employed in clinical settings alongside social workers, psychologists, and psychiatrists. Clinical sociology involves the use of sociological knowledge to aid diagnosis, treatment, teaching, and research. However, the practice of employing clinical sociologists is not widespread.

closed shop A system of *trade-union job control in which getting and holding employment is contingent on being a member of the union either before entry or on engagement. Pre-entry shops require union membership before a worker can be hired; post-entry and agency shops require workers to become members after taking up employment. Now illegal as such in the United States, Britain, and some European societies (on the grounds that compulsory membership is an infringement of *civil rights), closed shops are nevertheless not without advantages to employers as a device for informal management of labour relations. Consequently, there are several forms of union-management agreement (UMA) that constitute a closed shop in all but name.

closed society *See* OPEN SOCIETIES AND CLOSED SOCIETIES.

closure (social closure) Identified in the writings of Max *Weber, and more recently resurrected by the British sociologist Frank Parkin, the concept emerged as an alternative to *Marxist theories of *inequality and of how the latter is generated, maintained, and transformed (see Parkin's *Marxism and Class Theory*, 1979). Weber saw closure as one of the means by which commercial and property classes move along a continuum of legitimation and reproduction of life-chances in the direction of social class formation. Later exponents of this view saw closure as the basis of all inequality, be it that of material reward, *status honour including *ethnicity, *caste, and even the *nomenklatura* system of communist regimes.

Closure functions through the twin mechanisms of *exclusion and inclusion and can be founded upon individualistic or collective criteria. It is based on the *power of one group to deny access to reward, or positive life-chances, to another group on the basis of criteria that the former seek to justify. The selection of these criteria of exclusion and inclusion—be they educational credentials, party membership, skin colour, religious identity, property, social origins, manners and style of life, or region—and their imposition, contribute to explaining the boundaries of inequality and the strategies of usurpation on the part of the excluded, as much as the patterns of *domination and the legitimizing *ideologies for inequality. Processes of social closure involve marginalization (or exclusion), on one hand, and incorporation (inclusion) on the other.

Since closure is about mobilizing power to exclude others from privileges or rewards, students of the process tend to assume that power is itself an attribute of closure, and rarely investigate the sources of that power. Thus, an educational elite may be assumed to have the power to exclude those without the relevant credentials. Often, however, there are competing modes of closure that conflict with each other. Furthermore, *elites defined by one criterion (say, education) may not always seek the obvious (in this case educational) means to achieve closure—attempting to exclude people, instead, on other grounds (such as those of gender or ethnicity). One other problem with closure theories stems from the uneven distribution of reward within a group practising closure, as for example in the case of the communist *nomenklatura*, where rewards to those in the lower reaches were questionable to say the least. The best overall assessment of closure theory is Raymond Murphy's *Social Closure: The Theory of Monopolization and Exclusion* (1988).

cluster analysis A form of *multivariate analysis, of which the purpose is to divide a set of objects (such as variables or individuals), characterized by a number of attributes, into a set of clusters or categories in such a way that the objects in a cluster are maximally similar to each other and maximally different from the other objects on the measured attributes.

codes, cultural The various means whereby societies or social groups organize and produce meanings and meaningfulness. Each society or group makes sense of an otherwise meaningless world by projecting meaning onto it. Codes are the systems devised and then used for meaning-making. Two principal sociological approaches to understanding what cultural codes are and how they work have developed, one deriving from *Saussure's structural linguistics and the other from *Durkheim's structural sociology. Both have been influential in subsequent sociological thinking, especially in the sub-field of the sociology of culture.

According to Saussure, each particular language is a code. It is made up of signifiers (words either verbal or written), each of which makes sense only in relation to all the other signifiers in the system of which it is a part (that is, a particular language). The signifiers are organized in patterned ways, through the rules of grammar. Signifiers refer not to objects in the world, but to 'signifieds', which are the ideas that a particular language has of those objects. Although speakers of the language generally assume that the words they use transparently refer to 'reality', the reality they perceive and that they think is 'natural' is actually a product of the language these speakers use. Thus the world the speakers of a language experience is constructed by linguistic codes, generally below the conscious awareness of those speakers. For an outsider to understand a group that uses a particular language, the code or codes embodied in it will have to be 'cracked', i.e. the logic of the codes will have to be identified and the codes will have to be translated into the codes of the language of the outsider. Only by penetrating the codes in and through which a language works can an outsider truly understand how a language—and by extension, a culture—'encodes' the world and renders it meaningful for group members.

Saussure indicated that there were codes that were not purely linguistic in nature, but that operated in ways like linguistic codes. For example, in a particular society or group, hand and other bodily gestures operate according to a code. The discipline of semiotics, which Saussure envisaged would be a major science of the 20th century, would study these various social/cultural codes, showing how they patterned and organized the actions of individuals. This was a project taken up by Michel *Foucault, whose studies of 'discourses' are essentially studies of the codes that underpin particular cultural forms, and Roland Barthes in his semiotics of the 1950s and early 1960s. This united a Saussurean focus on the codes that structure the various spheres of modern society with a neo-Marxist emphasis on 'revealing' both the operation of these codes at sub-conscious levels and their ideological character in coding reality for the majority in ways that serve the power interests of dominant groups. This approach to reading 'texts', such as forms of popular culture, with the intent of revealing the encoding of forms of social power within them, subsequently became highly influential in cultural studies from the 1980s onwards. But this method raises a problem of interpretation—how can the semiotician prove her or his reading of the presence and operation of particular codes when normally codes operate in a highly subterranean manner?

Saussurian semiotics assumes that, just as a language fundamentally constrains what its speakers can and cannot perceive and think, so too do all codes fundamentally constrain what individual agents can or cannot do. In this vision, codes powerfully structure social relations and individuals' actions. Saussure's approach struggles to deal with the opposite possibility of how social relations and individual actions may either change or challenge codes. This also raises the problem of how individuals or groups can become reflexively aware of the codes they live by, possibly subjecting codes to conscious strategies of reflection or contestation. From the later 1970s, *cultural studies, especially in the UK, endeavoured to move towards more dynamic understandings of how cultural codes can be changed and challenged as much as simply unintentionally reproduced. Dick Hebdige's study of 'rebellious' youth groups such as punks understood them as engaged in a partly self-aware form of warfare against mainstream culture's codes, seeking to challenge these by developing alternative codes, such as novel and provocative dress codes. Stuart Hall's influential essay of 1980, 'Encoding/Decoding', argued that while media in a capitalist society encode texts such as TV news in ways that are highly ideologically loaded, their acceptance or rejection by particular social groups depends on the forms of decoding those groups work with, and these are rooted in the total life conditions of the group. This approach became highly influential in later studies of media audiences. It was taken up by writers such as Michel de Certeau and John Fiske, who claimed that the codes of the powerful are rarely or never accepted by subordinate groups. These views resonated with the post-structuralist turn in cultural studies in the mid-1980s and after, which was inspired by claims by Jacques Derrida and others that linguistic systems are far more self-contradictory, ever-changing, and unstable than Saussure envisaged.

An alternative, though in some ways overlapping, conception of cultural codes was offered by Durkheim. In his later work on religion, which has affinities with Saussure's writings of the same period, culture is seen to encode reality through the deployment of collective classifications structured by binary oppositions. Each society or group has its own distinctive worldview, which is centred around certain definitions of universal binaries such as good/bad, moral/immoral, acceptable/unacceptable, and so on. Through these dyads, symbolic boundaries are drawn, both between the group and the others defined to be outside of it, and within the group itself, for example dividing 'normal' people from 'criminals'. Such encoding of reality is regularly reinforced through social rituals, which periodically refresh actors' commitments to these boundaries.

Much subsequent Durkheim-inspired sociology has investigated how binary codes have been deployed to draw symbolic boundaries, and thus to enact processes of social inclusion and exclusion. The alleged autonomous power of cultural codes to structure societies has been promoted by Jeffrey C. Alexander and the Yale School of Cultural Sociology. This approach rejects what it takes to be the mainstream view in sociology, namely that social structures shape and direct cultural codes; instead, the creative power of cultural binaries is emphasized, especially those instances where politically progressive cultural codes, as in the US civil rights movement, have reformed societies in what are taken as beneficial ways. This approach stands in apparently stark contrast to the position of Pierre *Bourdieu. The latter is notable for combining a Durkheimian sense of cultural binaries with a post-Saussurean focus on how dominant class ideologies are encoded into many cultural forms, especially the institutions of 'high culture'. It is the Saussurean element in Bourdieu's thinking—where viewers of artworks are assumed to decode those works in class-based ways—that has come in for most criticism in recent years. The current orthodoxy in the sociology of culture assumes that while the Durkheimian understanding of cultural codes still has some vitality, the Saussurean version is now too narrow and constraining to be of much use to sociologists on its own.

Useful discussions of cultural codes can be found in Daniel Chandler's *Semiotics: The Basics* (2007) and Paul Cobley's edited collection *The Routledge Companion to Semiotics* (2009). *See also* ELABORATED AND RESTRICTED SPEECH CODES; SEMIOLOGY.

co-determination A translation of the German term *mitbestimmung*, which refers to the form of workers' participation in *management practised in Germany since 1951. Under the terms of the law passed in that year, employees have a right to participate not just in the management of the workplace but also in that of the company as a whole, through elected board representatives. With the notable exception of Britain, this model has inspired similar schemes throughout much of the rest of Europe. *See also* INDUSTRIAL DEMOCRACY.

coding The transformation of observations into categories and classifications, assigning a number or symbol to each item of information or section of a statement, to enable quantitative analysis to be carried out subsequently. While coding is an important part of many types of research, it is most commonly thought of as an essential element within survey research.

Much coding work in sample surveys can be undertaken by the interviewer, who marks up or circles responses on an interview schedule, but some has to be done after the interview by trained coders.

Coding is essential for the analysis of responses to surveys and most questionnaires provide space for the codes connected with each reply. However, coding can be applied to other types of information, such as depth interviews or observed interactions, and it is an important aspect of *conversation analysis. When qualitative coding is applied to the substantive content of communications, such as newspapers or political speeches, it is called *content analysis.

coefficient *See* ASSOCIATION COEFFICIENTS.

coercion *See* POWER.

coercive power *See* COMPLIANCE.

cognate (cognatic) Having a common ancestor who can be traced back bilaterally through either the male or female line; that is, descent is not unilineal. *See also* DESCENT GROUPS.

cognition (cognitive) The process of knowing (thinking), sometimes distinguished from affect (emotion) and conation or volition (striving), in a triad of mental processes. Cognitive psychology, which focuses on the use and handling of information (often employing computer models), is now the dominant approach within academic *psychology, and has replaced and transformed older *behaviourist approaches.

cognitive consistency The experience of holding thoughts, attitudes, or of acting in ways that are not mutually contradictory. The cognitive consistency versus inconsistency polarity, along with consonance versus dissonance and balance versus imbalance, has been employed widely by social psychologists in the analysis of *attitude change. Theorists assume a desire for cognitive consistency, arguing that cognitive inconsistencies—a mis-match between *cognitions—are uncomfortable, and can motivate attitude change. However, the consequence may also be denial and rationalization. *See also* COGNITIVE DISSONANCE.

cognitive dissonance A major cognitive theory propounded by Leon Festinger in *A Theory of Cognitive Dissonance* (1957). The theory addresses competing, contradictory, or opposing elements of *cognition and *behaviour: for example, why do people continue smoking, when they know that smoking damages health? Festinger suggests that individuals do not believe so much out of logic as out of psychological need—a kind of psycho-logic. He argues that, striving for harmony and balance, there is a drive towards consonance amongst cognitions. Dissonance reduction may happen either through a change in a person's behaviour or a shift in attitude; thus, in the example cited above, either they stop smoking, or else modify their knowledge, for example to the belief that 'most people who smoke don't die young and so aren't really at risk'. The theory is almost *tautological in postulating some inner need for consistency, and has been criticized for ambiguity, but it has been enormously influential. L. Festinger, H. W. Riecken, and S. Schachter illustrated this theory in their study of a religious sect (*When Prophecy Fails*, 1956). *See also* COGNITIVE THEORY.

cognitive psychology *See* COGNITION; COGNITIVE THEORY; PIAGET, JEAN.

cognitive sociology A version of *ethnomethodology that examines the problematic nature of 'meaning' in everyday life, and seeks to integrate ethnomethodology with linguistics (deep structures), on one hand, and traditional sociology (normative or surface rules) on the other. The major proponent is the

American sociologist Aaron V. Cicourel, who has studied many apparently diverse phenomena—including crime, deafness, education, and research methods—in an attempt to identify the underlying social organization and 'negotiated order' of everyday life.

cognitive theory A major cluster of theories in social *psychology that focus upon the links between mental processes (such as perception, memory, attitudes, or decision-making), and social behaviour. At a general level such theories are opposed to *behaviourism, and suggest that human beings are active in selecting stimuli, constructing meanings, and making sense of their worlds. There are many branches of cognitive theory, including Fritz *Heider's cognitive balance theory, Leon Festinger's *cognitive dissonance theory, George Kelly's *personal construct theory, and *attribution theory (see J. R. Eiser, *Cognitive Social Psychology*, 1980).

cohabitation An arrangement whereby couples who are not legally married live together as husband and wife. Frequent in previous eras, cohabitation has increased markedly in the United States and Britain since the 1960s. It is now common before *marriage and is often an alternative to marriage. Cohabitation has become so widespread that the term itself is now rarely used.

Cohen, Stanley Hymie (1942–2013) Born in South Africa but spent the first part of his career in Britain, where he worked at Durham and Essex Universities. Following a period in Israel from 1980 to 1996 as Director of the Institute of Criminology at the Hebrew University of Jerusalem, he became Professor of Sociology at the London School of Economics. He was a leading member of the National Deviancy Conference in the 1960s and early 1970s, using ideas from American *symbolic interactionism to reorientate British criminology. His first major work was *Folk Devils and Moral Panics* (1972), based on his PhD, in which he reported on the ways in which the police and the mass media reported the Bank-Holiday fights between 'mods' and 'rockers' at British seaside resorts. Popularizing the term *moral panic, Cohen provided a radical focus to *labelling theory. In particular, he helped to make the idea of *social control central to concerns with crime and deviance. This was taken further in his *Visions of Social Control* (1985), in which he allied his earlier concerns with arguments taken from Michel *Foucault. This served to emphasize the importance of issues of power in social control and, in particular, the key role of states and state power. His later work was especially concerned with human rights and the 'denial' of emotional concerns. In his *States of Denial* (2001) he explored reactions to atrocities, suffering, injustice, and the violation of human rights, reflecting on his own experiences and observations in South Africa and Israel.

cohort rates *See* FERTILITY.

Coleman, James S. (1926–95) A much honoured American sociologist, prolific author and co-author of numerous monographs and scholarly papers (some 28 books and more than 300 articles), who was for much of his professional life associated with the University of Chicago. He served as President of the

American Sociological Association in 1991–2. Major themes in his work include the social organization of education, *adolescence, and *youth (*The Adolescent Society*, 1961, *Youth: Transition to Adulthood*, 1973, *Becoming Adult in a Changing Society*, 1985), the role of families, communities, and religious institutions in education, and the idea of *social capital (*Equality of Educational Opportunity*— the so-called *Coleman Report—1966, *High School Achievement*, 1982, *Public and Private High Schools*, 1987), the social theory of simulation games, collective decision-making, and *collective action, models of purposive action and markets in *mathematical sociology (*Introduction to Mathematical Sociology*, 1964; *The Mathematics of Collective Action*, 1973), and theories of rational action (*Foundations of Social Theory*, 1990). In addition, he was a co-author of *Union Democracy* (1956), a classic of political sociology; a leading exponent of applied sociology committed to *policy research in the social sciences; and wrote monographs on (among other things) *Community Conflict* (1957) and *Medical Innovation* (1966), which he described as being more or less 'single-shot activities' rather than recurring themes in his work.

It is probably too soon to judge the lasting influence of his *magnum opus* on *The Foundations of Social Theory*. Many admirers have already hailed the work as a 'foundation effort' within sociology, to be placed on a par with earlier attempts by Durkheim and Parsons, who also sought to provide a unifying theoretical and methodological basis for the discipline. Others question whether *rational-choice theory—the broad umbrella under which Coleman constructed his models and explanations—can provide a satisfactory solution to the long-standing sociological concern of solving the problem of *social order by explaining how individually rational actions systematically generate regularities in macro-level outcomes.

Coleman Report An influential and controversial study, mandated in the Civil Rights Act of 1964, published by the US Government in 1966 as *Equality of Educational Opportunity*, and directed by the sociologist James Coleman. The report was based on a survey of educational opportunity using a national sample of almost 650 000 students and teachers in more than 3 000 schools). A landmark in *policy research, it was one of the first social scientific studies specifically commissioned by Congress in order to inform government policy, following those done on the military during the Second World War. The research design adopted for the investigation changed the whole direction of policy research in education and was widely imitated by later researchers. The results shaped school desegregation policy for many years following publication.

The study began with the controversial and innovative premise that *equality of opportunity should be assessed by equality of outcome rather than equality of input. The researchers therefore collected data on both the educational resources available to different groups of children and students' achievements as measured by test scores. For the first time it was possible to provide an informed answer to the question of how much, and in what ways, schools were able to overcome the inequalities (notably those associated with race) with which children came to school. The report showed that variations in school quality (as indexed by the usual measures such as per pupil expenditure, size of school library, and so on) showed little association with levels of educational attainment when students of similar social backgrounds were compared across schools. It concluded that a student's educational attainment was related to his or her own family background and also (less strongly) to the class and ethnic backgrounds of the other students in the school. These findings had clear implications for *social engineering, suggesting that opportunities could best be equalized through strategies of desegregation in schools (for example by busing). They challenged a major plank of Lyndon Johnson's vision for the 'Great Society': namely that increased spending on education could rectify social deficits.

The report was a focus of controversy for many years.

However, considering both the constraints of time under which he and his colleagues worked and the limited agenda set by the government bureaucrats who monitored the study, all but one of the major findings generated by Coleman have withstood subsequent examination. Subsequent reanalysis showed that a *coding error had led to greater evidence of peer effects in schools than was actually the case, a particularly unfortunate error as this finding was often cited as evidence to support policies of forced integration and busing as the most effective way of ending racial *segregation and raising Black educational achievement.

There is an excellent summary and appraisal of the Coleman Report, together with an account of research that followed in its wake, in the article on 'Coleman's Contributions to Education', in J. Clark (ed.), *James S. Coleman* (1996).

collective action Action taken by a group or organization in pursuit of members' perceived shared interests. It seems logical to expect that people who have an *interest in common will act on it—for example that pensioners will act for higher pensions, or miners for greater underground safety. This is not always the case, and many people who stand to benefit from a given collective action will refuse to join in. This seems to run against the assumption of *rationality in human behaviour, and presents a particular problem for students of politics and *social movements.

In 1965 Mancur Olson offered an explanation in *The Logic of Collective Action*. Olson argued that rational self-interest often leads to inaction, in so far as individuals will benefit from concessions made to the whole group, whether they themselves have been active or not. If pensions are raised after a campaign by senior citizens, all pensioners will gain, including those who do nothing. Olson called this the *free-rider problem, and it is important because it undermines the ability of interest groups and social movements to mobilize large numbers of citizens. If those citizens are poor, the costs of participation are relatively high for them, and they are even more likely to remain passive. The only answer to the free-rider problem is for the movement to offer extra incentives to participate, beyond the goals themselves. These incentives may take the form of recognition, prestige, or the psychological rewards of participation itself.

The nature of rational choice has been a conundrum for sociology since Max Weber's writings on the problem. One attempt to model the process is shown in rational calculus or *game theory, which tries to show how, in concrete social situations, actors will try to maximize their rewards and minimize their costs. However, few people are so careful, controlled, and well-informed that their actions will fit the rational-choice model (*see* RATIONAL CHOICE THEORY). Acts of bravery and commitment lie outside its explanatory power, as do acts based on ignorance or impulse. Large areas of collective action clearly require explanations of a more complex type. A good overview of the field is given in Russell Hardin's *Collective Action* (1982). *See also* CLASS CONSCIOUSNESS; CLASS INTEREST; COLLECTIVE BEHAVIOUR; REBELLION; STRIKE.

collective and distributive power In his essay on 'The Distribution of Power in American Society' (in *Structure and Process in Modern Societies*, 1960), Talcott *Parsons distinguishes the distributive aspects of *power ('power by A over B'), from its collective aspects ('the power of A and B together'). In distributive power situations, the relationship between A and B is a zero-sum game: there is a fixed amount of power to be distributed among participants, and for one member to gain power another must lose. In collective power situations, co-operating individuals can enhance their joint power over a third party.

collective bargaining A system for the fixing of earnings and conditions of employment, in which the processes of price (or wage) competition in the *labour market between individual workers and individual employers is replaced, either in whole or in part, by rule-fixing. These rules are of two kinds: procedural, regulating the forms and institutions under which collective negotiations are to be conducted; and substantive, regulating the actual content of particular agreements. Typically, collective bargaining occurs between *trade unions and an employer, or organization of employers. However, during the 20th century, governments and the law in industrial societies have increasingly become parties to both the procedural and the substantive aspects. Bargaining may therefore take place at the workplace, company, regional, or industry levels. Britain is unusual in having no legal compulsion on employers to bargain in this way and collective agreements are rarely directly enforceable in the courts.

collective behaviour Potentially a very wide-ranging field of study that deals with the ways in which the behaviour of groups emerges as responses to problematic circumstances and situations. At one extreme this can mean the study of coordinated and organized *social movements; at the other, it refers to the seemingly spontaneous eruption of common behavioural patterns, as for example in episodes of mass hysteria. Between these are responses to natural disasters, riots, lynchings, crazes, fads, fashions, rumours, booms, panics, and even *rebellions or revolutions. Many of these phenomena are dealt with under separate headings in this dictionary.

The earliest theories of collective behaviour are to be found in crowd psychology. Gustave Le Bon, in *The Crowd: A Study of the Popular Mind* (1895), argued that a crowd is a real collective entity since 'it forms a single being, and is subjected to the law of the mental unity of crowds'. He suggested that all individual responses are lost in crowds, and that a 'collective mind' emerges and makes people 'feel, think and act in a manner quite different from that in which each individual of them would'. Crowds act in this way because of anonymity (which reduces the sense of personal responsibility), contagion (as ideas move rapidly through a group), and through suggestibility (whereby the unconscious aspects of the personality come to the fore).

Many subsequent studies of *crowds, *riots, mobs, and similar collective disturbances—including, for example, contributions by Gabriel *Tarde and Sigmund *Freud—do little more than elaborate Le Bon's contagion hypothesis. Freud followed Le Bon's description of the crowd mentality as impulsive, changeable, and irritable, as incapable of sustained attention, criticism, or perseverance, and as governed by a sense of omnipotence, exaggerated feelings, magical formulas, and illusions. He explained group participation in terms of the psychoanalytic theories of the instinct-object relationships in the individual and the primal horde. As he puts it, 'The uncanny and coercive characteristics of group formation, which are shown in the phenomena of suggestion that accompany them, may...be traced back to the fact of their origin from the primal horde. The leader of the group is still the dreaded primal father; the group still wishes to be governed by unrestricted force; it has an extreme passion for authority... it has a thirst for obedience. The primal father is the group ideal, which governs the ego in the place of the ego ideal' ('Group Psychology and the Analysis of the Ego'). According to Freud, these features together with the loss of consciousness, dominance of the mind by emotions, and the impulsiveness of crowds, 'correspond to a state of regression to a primitive mental activity'.

A more sociological approach to collective behaviour is evident in Neil Smelser's 'value-added schema' (see *Theory of Collective Behaviour*, 1963), which suggests that the determinants of collective behaviour involve: structural conduciveness (conditions of permissiveness under which collective behaviour is seen as legitimate); structural strain (such as economic *deprivation); growth and spread of a generalized belief (for example a mass hysteria, delusion, or creation of a *folk devil); precipitating factors (specific events—such as a fight set against the background of an explosive race situation—which confirms the earlier generalized belief); the mobilization of the participants for action (through effective leadership, in a social movement, or a single dramatic event such as a rumour of a panic sell by a leading holder of shares in a company); and the counter forces of *social control set up by the wider society to prevent and inhibit other factors. According to Smelser, the last of these is of particular importance as 'once an episode of collective behaviour has appeared, its duration and severity are determined by the response of the agencies of social control'.

Smelser's sixth determinant attaches the same importance to social control as do transactional (notably *labelling) theories of deviance. Within the interactionist tradition more generally, special attention has been paid to social typing, and to the way in which *role models are created and diffused in the wider society (see, for example, R. H. Turner and L. M. Killian, *Collective Behaviour*, 1957). This volume also includes some of the earliest sociological work on fads and fashions. Collective behaviour is sometimes contrasted with narrower theories of *collective action that stress the importance of rational motivations to act. *See also* COLLECTIVE ACTION; RATIONAL CHOICE THEORY; SUBCULTURE.

collective conscience Defined by Émile *Durkheim as 'the body of beliefs and sentiments common to the average of members of a society', its form and content varies according to whether society is characterized by mechanical or organic solidarity. In the former, the collective conscience is extensive and strong, ranging far and wide into people's lives, controlling them in detail through various religious or other traditional sanctions. It emphasizes the primacy of society over the individual and his or her dignity. However, the growth of a division of labour and *individualism leads to the collective conscience becoming less extensive, weaker in its grip on the individual, secular, and sanctioned through the imposition of general rule rather than specific codes. This could be observed in the replacement of repressive by restitutive systems of law. Whereas the former punishes for the violation of solidarity itself, the latter is geared to maintaining normal contact and social intercourse. Durkheim's argument is that a society-wide collective conscience can hold a segmental society together, but a more differentiated society must be held together by a more differentiated moral consciousness. He saw this as based on occupational groups and the specialized norms issuing from them. The collective conscience becomes a diffuse, abstract 'cult of the individual' that, as a *civil religion, supplies ultimate principles and justifications but cannot bear the whole weight of social cohesion. *See also* ANOMIE; DIVISION OF LABOUR; DYNAMIC DENSITY.

collective consumption A central concept in neo-Marxist urban social theories developed in the late 1960s and 1970s. Manuel Castells and others argued that advanced capitalism required increasing state involvement in the so-called means of collective consumption. To reproduce an adequate labour force, provision of individual means of consumption (commodities such as food and clothing) was no longer enough; services such as education and mass transportation were also needed. Unlike individual commodities, the latter were consumed collectively, as services used by many people rather than goods consumed individually. Particular features of collective consumption, notably the state's role in its provision and the opportunities it appeared to offer for the political mobilization of consumers, underlay the significance of the concept for these urban social theories.

Subsequently, however, the distinction between collective and individual consumption was much disputed. It is difficult, for example, to see just how services such as education are **consumed** 'collectively'—although they may be **provided** collectively. As used in practice, therefore, the term collective consumption now has no very precise meaning and is a misnomer, although it normally refers to services (rather than goods) that are directly provided by state agencies instead of by the market; or, at least, to services provided with considerable state involvement, for example through subsidies or regulation. Later writers have developed more complex classifications of the social organization of consumption, and have used these to analyse the nature of urban politics and the role of so-called *consumption sector cleavages in social stratification and in determining political attitudes. For an overview see Peter Saunders, *Social Theory and the Urban Question* (1986). *See also* URBAN SOCIOLOGY.

collective good *See* PUBLIC GOOD.

collective representations The ideas, beliefs, and values elaborated by a collectivity and that are not reducible to individual constituents. They are central to Émile *Durkheim's search for the sources of social solidarity. The concept develops Durkheim's earlier notion of '*collective conscience'. In *The Elementary Forms of the Religious Life* (1912), these representations are seen as being created through the intense interaction of religious *rituals, and being richer than individual activities they come to be autonomous of the group from which they emerged. Collective representations help to order and make sense of the world, but they also express, symbolize, and interpret social relationships. Collective representations inhibit and stimulate social action. Their force or authority comes from their being within all of us and yet external to the individual. Durkheim explained great value transformations (such as the propagation of Enlightenment values in the French revolution) by reference to the power of this 'coming together' (or *dynamic density), whereby the religious world is rooted in collective life, leaving the profane to the individual. Assembly of an intense kind generates collective representations, which then survive the disintegration of this higher collective life as *sacred and therefore morally coercive beliefs, values, and symbols.

collectivism A term with a general and a variety of specific applications. In the most common usage it refers to any political or socio-economic theory or practice that encourages communal or state ownership and control of the means of production and distribution. Particular applications vary greatly since there are numerous examples of collectivist organizations.

Farmers organized into collectives were, until recently, a significant social group in the former USSR. These farms controlled the labour inputs of members, fixed rates of remuneration, and determined the content of agricultural production. Many were the result of a violent forced collectivization of peasant and family-owned farms during the Stalinist period. Agricultural collectives in China have had a more varied history. One of the most popular schemes was a 'responsibility system' introduced in the 1980s, whereby individual peasant households signed a contract by which the land still belonged technically to the collective, but was assigned to individual households for their own use. These contracts specified obligations on either side, for example with respect to the provision of tools and equipment, payment of taxes, and meeting of production quotas. A particularly interesting form of collective—the workers' self-management of the economy—emerged in Tito's Yugoslavia. However, sociological research confirmed that the theoretically democratic distribution of influence within the enterprise was not matched by the real power of Workers' Councils, which tended in practice to be largely symbolic.

The collectivist critique of liberal and other theories of *individualism argues that *market relationships are competitive, tend also therefore to be divisive, and undermine those communal bonds that are necessary between individuals if they are to cope with misfortunes to which all are in principle vulnerable. For example, social welfare theorists argue that unrestrained free exchange causes *welfare problems, as evidenced by the housing market which fails to provide shelter to those in demonstrable need. One of the most celebrated collectivist defences of the *welfare state was made by Richard Titmuss (see *The Gift Relationship*, 1970), who argued that welfare systems should be defended by reference to arguments about altruism. His argument was that people should receive welfare as a gift from strangers, an expression of social solidarity, rather than as an entitlement or right derived from a complex network of reciprocal relationships. Thus, in the case of blood donations, Titmuss maintained that if this 'most sacred' of commodities were to be commercialized then the moral bonds between individuals would become wholly contaminated by calculations of self-interest and market price. As he puts it, 'In not asking for or expecting any payment of money those donors signified their belief in the willingness of men to act altruistically in the future, and to combine together to make a gift freely should they have need for it. By expressing confidence in the behaviour of future unknown strangers they were thus denying the Hobbesian thesis that men are devoid of any instinctive moral sense'. This communitarian view of welfare as an expression of the common values that bind otherwise disparate individuals together may be contrasted with the more individualistic conception of welfare derived from the theory of *citizenship. The latter implies that claims to welfare resources are simply an extension of the legal and political *rights characteristic of liberal democracies and, therefore, that collective welfare is quite consistent with the theory of liberal pluralism. Welfare states are simply adjuncts to markets; that is, rational deprivation-alleviating institutions and policies, resting on the individualistic principles of reciprocal obligations and exchange. Communitarianism, by contrast, embodies a vision of a social order that fosters intimate communal bonds.

   See also GIFT RELATIONSHIP; WELFARE STATE.

Collins, Randall (1941–) An American sociologist who has developed a distinctive form of *conflict theory. Grounded in the *symbolic interactionism of Blumer and *Goffman, he has sought to develop their ideas into a sociology that combines micro and macro perspectives. He has himself worked at both levels. His earliest work in *Conflict Sociology* (1975) was particularly directed at issues of education and stratification, where Collins explored ideas of credentialism and power. He has extended this work into investigations in historical sociology that have looked at issues of democracy, militarism, and globalization. In 1998 he produced *The Sociology of Philosophies* in which he set out an intellectual history of Eastern and Western thought from classical China and Greece to the contemporary world, using ideas from the sociology of science and *network analysis. He has developed these ideas in a series of essays on science, philosophy, and culture. In 2004 he produced *Interaction Ritual Chains*, a book that took up Goffman's analysis of ritual and developed it into a systematic account of the concatenation of action sequences into large-scale structures. In his most recent book *Violence* (2008) he applies Goffman's ideas to the production of violence in everyday situations and makes a major contribution to the understanding of emotions.

colonialism The establishment by more developed countries of formal political authority over areas of Asia, Africa, Australasia, and Latin America. It is distinct from spheres of influence, indirect forms of control, *semi-colonialism, and *neo-colonialism.

Colonialism was practised by Spain, Portugal, Britain, France, and the Netherlands in the Americas from the fifteenth century onwards, and extended to virtually all of Asia and Africa during the 19th century. It was usually (but not necessarily) accompanied by the settling of White populations in these territories, the exploitation of local economic resources for metropolitan use, and sometimes both together. The term is often used as a synonym for *imperialism although the latter covers other informal mechanisms of control.

In addition to debates about the causes, benefits, and impact of imperialism, discussion of colonialism has covered a wide range of issues including: the different mechanisms of colonial control and the contrast between the assimilationist policies of France and Portugal and the more segregated policies of Britain; the social and economic impact on colonized countries, resulting from the destruction of old social, economic, and political systems and the development of new ones; the 19th-century discourse of domination around the idea of the 'civilizing mission' and the related rise of racism; the issue of why colonialism ended in the post-1945 period, involving a consideration of the relative weights of international pressure from both the United States and USSR, the rise of nationalist movements demanding independence in colonies, and the exhaustion of the European colonial powers after the Second World War.

colonialism, internal *See* INTERNAL COLONIALISM.

command economy Not to be confused with its associated feature the planned economy, the paradigm case is the neo-Stalinist, centrally directed, state-owned economy of the Soviet Union. A continuum can be elaborated, within which *communist economic systems can be located in terms of whether they seek to centralize all or some of the decisions relating to macroeconomic policy, enterprise-level activity, and household behaviour concerning employment and consumption. The type of economy that existed in post-revolutionary Russia faced with civil war between 1918 and 1921—namely war communism—centralizes all of the above spheres of decision-making. The command economy centralizes the first two dimensions but leaves some scope for local-level decisions as regards the third. So-called market socialism decentralizes all three—although state ownership remains. Many of the pathologies attributed to planned (or 'administered', 'managed', or 'non-market') economies are in fact evident only in the specifically command version. *See also* STALINISM.

commodification Within Marxist theory this refers to the production of commodities for exchange (via the *market) as opposed to direct use by the producer. It signals the conversion of use-values into exchange-values and heralds a change in production relations. In conventional terms it can be described as the process whereby goods and services that were formerly used for subsistence purposes are bought and sold in the market. These terms are widely used in *Third World studies, for example, when subsistence peasants begin to sell their produce for cash. The term has also been used by Jürgen *Habermas to refer to the transfer of services such as health and welfare from systems of state provision to systems of private-sector, market-based provision. *See also* COMMODITY FETISHISM.

commodity chains A network of economic links that integrates transnational labour processes and corporations involved in the global sourcing and global marketing of products. Commodity chain analysis—sometimes also known as the 'global commodity chains' (GCC) approach—is a development of the *world-system perspective. It challenges the assumption that capitalism is contained within nation-states by tracking the organizational, geographical, and cultural dimensions of world-wide chains for the manufacture and distribution of goods such as clothing, automobiles, food, and drugs. A distinction is sometimes made between producer-driven (transnational corporation) and buyer-driven (retailer/ trading company) commodity chains. For a summary statement and series of case studies see Gary Gereffi and Miguel Korzeniewicz (eds.), *Commodity Chains and Global Capitalism* (1994). *See also* GLOBALIZATION.

commodity fetishism An idea elaborated by Karl *Marx early in the first volume of *Capital*. He makes a distinction between use-value and exchange-value: the former is a judgement about the usefulness of an object; the latter is what that same object will fetch in exchange on the market. Money provides the medium of exchange, and brings different objects into relations of equality with each other—one meal in a restaurant, for example, might equal four paperback books. Exchange-values depend upon the ratio of the labour times currently needed to produce the objects. This in turn refers us to the social *division of labour and the complex relationships of interdependence that exist in *capitalist society. These complex relationships, however, are not obvious to those partic-ipating in *market exchanges who see only the resulting relationships (of price) between commodities. They therefore mistakenly view these relationships as autonomous, and as governing rather than dependent on the social division of labour, and the relations it establishes between different and unequal producers. When generalized, this delusion is the commodity fetishism that Marx criticized in bourgeois economics, which took economic value to be an intrinsic property of commodities, like their use-value.

The commodity is a fetish, in the sense that it is endowed with the powers of human beings, so it seems that what happens to us depends upon the state and movement of the market. György *Lukács extended the theory into the idea of reification: all human relationships and experience come to be perceived as commodities and we treat them as things. Commodity fetishism is one aspect of the analysis of *ideology in capitalist societies: the real underlying relation-ships are hidden from our perception and we build our understanding of the world only on appearances.

commonsense knowledge The routine knowledge people have of their everyday world and activities. Different sociological approaches adopt different attitudes to commonsense knowledge. The concept is central to Alfred Schutz's *phenomenological sociology, where it refers to organized and 'typified' stocks of taken-for-granted knowledge upon which activities are based and that, in the 'natural attitude', are not questioned. This idea forms the basis of Peter Berger and Thomas Luckmann's theory (*The Social Construction of Reality*, 1967). For *ethnomethodologists, commonsense or 'tacit' knowledge is a constant achievement, in which people draw on implicit rules of 'how to carry on' and which produce a sense of organization and coherence. Anthony *Giddens builds this idea into his theory of *structuration (*The Constitution of Society*, 1984). For *symbolic interactionists and other interpretive sociologists, there is a less rigorous analysis of commonsense knowledge, but the central aim of sociology is seen as explicating and elaborating people's conceptions of the social world.

However, some sociologists see commonsense knowledge as different from, if not opposed to, sociological understanding. For Émile *Durkheim, sociology must break free of the prejudices of commonsense perceptions before it can produce scientific knowledge of the social world. For Marxists, much commonsense knowledge is ideological, or at least very limited in its understanding of the world. These approaches tend to emphasize the scientific nature of sociology and, in the case of Marxists, the importance of the revolutionary party in organizing and guiding the working class.

commune Refers to either a group of people sharing life and work, typically a *utopian community in which members attempt to found a new social order based on a vision of an ideal society (as in the Israeli *kibbutzim), or, in some countries, to a territorial administrative unit referring to a subdivision of a canton. The latter usage was adopted by the Jacobin regime in the French Revolution, extended to other insurrectionist bodies such as the Paris Commune of 1871, and to several other countries including Italy. In the post-war period it has also referred to Chinese units of territorial administration.

However, sociological interest in communes focuses mainly on the commune in the first sense; namely, the attempt to create new, shared, *egalitarian living and working relationships. Among the questions posed by these experiments is whether behavioural patterns and power relations (such as those based on gender) are significantly transformed in a more socially egalitarian context. Andrew Rigby (*Alternative Realities*, 1973) has offered a useful six-fold typology of communes: self-actualizing communes offer members the opportunity to create a new social order by realizing their full potential as individuals within the context of the communal group; communes for mutual support attempt to promote a sense of solidarity that members feel they have been unable to discover in the world at large; activist communes provide an urban base from which members can venture forth to involve themselves in social and political activity in the outside world; practical communes define their purpose at least partly in terms of the economic and other material advantages they offer to members; therapeutic communes, as the name implies, offer some form of care and attention to those who are considered to have particular needs; and religious communes are defined by their members primarily in religious terms. These categories are, of course, not mutually exclusive.

communication The process of establishing meaning, found in all social situations, and hence a very wide-ranging concern of social scientists generally. Conventionally studied by social psychologists, semiologists, students of *mass media, and linguists, communication studies has increasingly become established as a field of inquiry in its own right, and is often allied to cultural studies.

Communication occurs through at least five modes. Intrapersonal communication concerns internal conversations with one's *self. Interpersonal communication concerns *face-to-face interaction, such as that analysed by Erving Goffman, and often involves paralanguages such as body movements (*see* BODY LANGUAGE) and spatial arrangements. Group communication involves the study of *group dynamics. Mass communication involves messages sent from mass sources in mass ways to mass audiences, often to make mass money. A fifth and growing form of communication has been called extrapersonal communication and concerns communicating with non-humans: this could mean 'talking to the animals', but most frequently it refers to the way we communicate with machines, computers, and high technology (for example through video games, bank-teller machines, or mobile phones).

Communications research often works from a simple model that asks 'who says what in which channel to whom and with what effects?' The resulting description of the 'communication structure' that exists in every (simple or complex) social system is sometimes criticized for depicting too linear a flow since feedback loops can occur at all stages of communication. Nevertheless, the central components usually involve senders (producers), messages (codes), and receivers (audiences). A distinction must also be made between the formal and actual structures of communication. The former is defined by publicly recognized social *roles (such as the hierarchy of offices in a bureaucratic organization) whereas the latter refers to the structure of *interaction as it actually occurs (which may include various forms of informal communication through unofficial channels). *See also* CODES; CONTENT ANALYSIS; CRITICAL THEORY; CYBERSOCIETY; INTERNET; LANGUAGE.

communication, non-verbal *See* NON-VERBAL COMMUNICATION.

communism A political doctrine, originating in the French Revolution, according to which human society can be organized on the basis of the common ownership of economic resources by the direct producers or workers. The theory of communism was developed systematically by Karl *Marx and Friedrich *Engels in the 1840s, who asserted that human society underwent development through a series of historical stages or *modes of production, and that out of the development of *capitalism and the organized activity of the working class would emerge a communist society or workers' state as the culmination of history. Marx gave only the most general indication as to what constituted a communist society, and later writers modified his vision by allotting a central place to the state in the organizing of such societies, and by arguing for a prolonged transition period of *socialism prior to the attainment of full communism. For that reason, the People's Republic of China, Cuba, and the former USSR are often described as 'state socialist'. This usage indicates that they are judged to have realized part of the socialist programme by abolishing private property and establishing state control over the economy; however, they are not considered truly socialist (or communist), because they have not established political democracy. However, they are sometimes also referred to as forms of *state capitalism. What both terms point to is the recognition that these societies fall far short of Marx's utopian communist ideal—and usually involve a heavily centralized and undemocratic political apparatus in which the state bureaucratic elite acts as a surrogate capitalist class. Thus, and to add further to the terminological confusion, they are sometimes also known as 'bureaucratic socialist' or 'state monopoly capitalist' societies. Non-Marxists have applied the term communism to any society ruled by a communist party and to any parties aspiring to create such a society. One of the best histories of the communist movement and communist societies is Fernando Claudin's *The Communist Movement: From Comintern to Cominform* (1975).

Theories within Marxism as to why communism was not achieved after socialist revolutions have pointed to such factors as the pressure of external capitalist states, the relative backwardness of the societies in which the revolutions occurred, and the emergence of a bureaucratic stratum or class that arrested and diverted the transition process in its own interests. Communist societies were seen by most sociologists as being distinct from capitalist states in important political and ideological respects, involving as they did the concentration of decision-making in a small and secretive leadership; state domination of the economy; the limitation of all independent political and social activity; and a higher reliance on coercion than was present in liberal democracies. However, the extent to which the economic bases of the two types of system are in practice distinct has always been a hotly debated issue, with some writers arguing that the technological imperatives of advanced *industrialism yielded great similarities at the level of the productive unit and its organization.

While critics applied the concept *totalitarian to these societies, more sympathetic analysts identified possibilities for independent political activity within them, and stressed their continued evolution up to the point of the dissolution of the USSR and its satellites in Eastern Europe during the late 1980s. *See also* REAL SOCIALISM.

communitarian (communitarianism) A political theory stressing the moral values of *community. Popularized during the early 1990s by a small group of mainly American social scientists linked by a common hostility to the philosophies of *liberalism and *libertarianism. The sociologist Amitai Etzioni was one of the prominent founders of this movement (see his *The New Golden Rule: Community and Morality in a Democratic Society*, 1996). Etzioni argues that the advanced industrial societies of the capitalist West suffer from 'rampant moral confusion and social anarchy' because individuals have been given too much freedom and not enough responsibilities. Etzioni and other communitarians are in favour of more obligations and fewer rights. They tend to shun economic explanations of social problems, preferring instead to blame everything from crime to excessive consumerism on the moral decline of the family, much of which they trace to the increasing employment of women outside the home. Etzioni claims this has created a 'parenting deficit' that prevents 'effective personality formation' in infants, increasing reliance on child-care facilities that often amount to little more than 'kennels for kids', and in due course producing a generation of young people who lack the moral fibre to resist crime, drugs, and early sex.

Communitarians deny that they are advocating a return to the 1950s-style division of labour (formal employment for men, back into the home for women), and proffer instead a range of 'pro-family practices and policies', such as Etzioni's ideas for 'peer marriage' (a two-parent family, in which each partner has the same rights to extended 'family leave' after the birth of children, underwritten by a hardening of the laws against divorce). More broadly, communitarians favour a social order in which 'the community' identifies the common good, and persuades its members to act towards it. In this way arguments in favour of (say) safer driving will succeed because they have moral force.

Communitarians claim to have influenced the development of social policy in America (Etzioni was a policy adviser to the Clinton administrations) and Britain (where communitarian ideas found favour with New Labour). Community policing, for example, is a policy consistent with communitarian ideals. Critics have suggested that communitarian arguments are both vague and naïve. Who will pay for extended parental leave of absence from employment? What if 'the community' endorses values such as *homophobia or *racialism? What happens to dissenters, who refuse to conform to the ideals of the two-parent family and marriage for life, and are not persuaded by exhortation alone? Communitarian social policies are also said to be authoritarian in effect if not intention. *See also* COMMUNE.

(⊕) SEE WEB LINKS

• A website associated with the communitarian ideas of Etzioni.

community The concept of community concerns a particularly constituted set of social relationships based on something that the participants have in common—usually a common sense of identity. It is frequently used to denote a wide-ranging solidarity over a rather undefined area of life and interests. According to Robert Nisbet (*The Sociological Tradition*, 1966), it was the most fundamental and far-reaching of the core ideas incorporated in the discipline's foundations, principally because concern with the loss of community was central to 19th-century sociology. The sociological content of community has, however, remained a matter for endless dispute.

These disputes flow from what Nisbet describes as the rediscovered symbolism of community in 19th-century thought, which identified this form of social association with the Good Society, and with all forms of relationship that are characterized by a high degree of personal intimacy, emotional depth, moral commitment, social cohesion, and continuity in time. It was feared that these were precisely the features that were disappearing in the transition from a rural-based society to an urban-industrial one. This alleged loss of community was central to the work of Ferdinand *Tönnies, often regarded as the founder of the theory of community. In the book *Community and Civil Society* (originally *Gemeinschaft und Gesellschaft*) Tönnies presented ideal-typical pictures of these forms of social association, contrasting the solidaristic nature of social relations in the former, with the large-scale and impersonal relations thought to characterize industrializing societies.

One difficulty for the sociology of community ensuing from these intellectual origins is that it has frequently been used to identify and at the same time endorse a particular form of social interaction. A second is that there is no clear and widely accepted definition of just what characteristic features of social interaction constitute the solidaristic relations typical of so-called communities. These value-laden but imprecise circumstances go a long way to explaining a third difficulty: the empirical identification of communities. The term has been used in the sociological literature to refer directly to types of population settlements (such as villages or physically bounded urban neighbourhoods); to supposedly ideal-typical ways of life in such places; and to social networks whose members share some common characteristic apart from or in addition to a common location (such as ethnicity or occupation). Frequently the term is used in ways that contain all these elements—as, for example, in 'traditional inner-city working-class communities'. At one time the problems of defining the concept of community provided the basis for a thriving sociological industry. In a classic contribution to this debate, George A. Hillery analysed no fewer than 94 definitions of the concept, although his conclusions were hardly enlightening since he was able only to extract from these a classification that distinguished sixteen different and characteristic elements. These included geographical area, self-sufficiency, kinship, consciousness of kind, common life-styles, and various intensive types of social interaction. Somewhat despairingly, perhaps, Hillery concluded from his review that 'There is one element, however, which can be found in all of the concepts . . . all of the definitions deal with people. Beyond this common basis, there is no agreement' ('Definitions of Community: Areas of Agreement', *Rural Sociology*, 1955). And see G. Crow and G. Allen, *Community Life*, 1994). *See also* ANTI-URBANISM; COMMUNITY POWER; COMMUNITY STUDIES.

community care An imprecise and much abused concept embracing a diverse set of policies for dependent persons—particularly those chronically dependent by virtue of age, mental illness, or mental or physical handicap—that involve, in some way or another, looking after them in the community. In its most general sense, the community is here merely negatively defined as 'not the institution'; that is, not the large-scale, long-stay institution, such as the asylum or workhouse. Inherent in the concept is, therefore, a contrast between old institutional policies that encourage the separation of people from the community (ordinary everyday life), and new policies according to which individuals should be cared for and integrated into community life as far as possible. This basic opposition is associated with contrasting stereotypes: the vast, impersonal, isolated, impoverishing, harsh, and bureaucratic institution, on one hand, and on the other the friendly, supportive, enriching, and caring (with its connotations of love) *community. It is this contrasting imagery that gives the notion of community care such strong symbolic power, accounts for the ready acceptance of policies put forward in its name, and that can distract attention from any precise examination of the care, if any, that is provided.

The actual character of community-care provisions varies enormously and changes over time. Only detailed knowledge of service arrangements and policies allows us to determine their exact nature. In its early usage in the 1930s, community care referred to the boarding out (fostering) of those identified as mentally subnormal. Here and elsewhere the model was that of publicly funded and administered alternatives to institutional care. After the Second World War, when community care became a very widely accepted policy objective, it still referred to publicly provided services, including 'half-way' houses and small residential units for the chronically dependent, or units in general hospitals for those with acute problems. Not surprisingly, the main obstacle to policy implementation was the capital investment required, in a context of low capital expenditure on state welfare services.

Studies showed that in Britain the implementation of community-care policies was slow compared with the more rapid spread in the United States. Although some new state-funded services, such as Community Mental Health Centres (which in practice primarily dealt with acute problems), were established in the United States, many people with chronic problems were still discharged into private facilities such as nursing homes and boarding houses. The introduction of community care consequently went hand in hand with the *privatization of care—a trend exacerbated in the 1970s by the cutbacks in federal support for facilities like CMHCs.

A similar pattern emerged in Britain from the mid-1970s, prompted by the state's *fiscal crisis, and compounded by public expenditure cuts. Community care increasingly meant private care, whether provided by commercial or charitable groups, or family and friends—a transformation that ensured that public expenditure pressures accelerated rather than curtailed policy implementation. It also ensured that, with the run-down in public services, many individuals faced neglect and marginalization (rather than enjoying care and support) in the community, or else experienced a process of 'trans-institutionalization', discharged from one (large-scale) institution only to end up in another—albeit smaller. The marked failures of community care in Europe and the United States, as well as its somewhat limited successes, are now well documented.

community, moral *See* MORAL COMMUNITY.

community power *Power arising in and distributed among the members of a locality. A major contribution to competing theories of power comes from the community power debate—arguments about how and by whom power is exerted in local democratic polities.

One view is that local power is exercised by an *elite—such as local officials, politicians, and leading business interests—and is manifest in its public and private decision-making on public policies (see F. Hunter's classic *Community*

Power Structure, 1953). However, some political scientists reject this 'stratification theory' of power, and deny that an upper-class elite rules, in its own interests, through subordinate officially recognized political and civic leaders. Robert Dahl's study of New Haven (*Who Governs*, 1961) concluded that the advent of representative democracy shifted power from an élite to various organized interest groups—from oligarchy to *pluralism. Differently constituted groups rule depending on the issue in question.

Lukes reanalyses a 'two-dimensional' study of community responses to air pollution that, he argues, indicates that real interests can sometimes be identified empirically where *counterfactual instances arise, that is, where the processes and structures that deny the expression of real interests are (for whatever reason) temporarily rendered ineffective (a phenomenon illustrated in J. Gaventa's *Power and Powerlessness*, 1980). His analysis, which has been extensively criticized, transcends the initial confines of the community power debate and addresses the nature of social power generally.

For a critical summary of research on community power and a re-examination of Dahl's findings see G. W. Domhoff's *Who Really Rules?*, 1978. *See also* COMMUNITY STUDIES; NATURAL EXPERIMENT.

community safety A concept that is sometimes used interchangeably with that of 'crime prevention' in criminological debates. The argument that the *community can be both the cause (as, for instance, in some of the writings of the *Chicago School) and the solution of the *crime problem is not new. Ironically, at a time when critiques of *post-industrial or *mass society are mourning the loss of 'traditional communities', the idea that tackling criminal victimization is the responsibility of a broad base within the community has regained prominence in criminal justice policies and practices. Communities have been given a role in local crime prevention through the emphasis on physical measures to reduce the rate of crime. Members of the community are encouraged to take a share in *deviance control by cooperating with the police and fulfilling their moral obligations as active *citizens. However, critics of this philosophy have argued that the idea of citizen involvement in community safety programmes presumes both that we can identify and agree upon who the citizens are that make up a community, and what the crime concerns are for such citizens. In reality, some ethnic, gender, and age-groups are less visible, and (it is argued) their needs are therefore taken less seriously than are those of others in the 'community'.

community studies The ambiguities of the term *community make any wholly coherent sociological definition of communities, and hence the scope and limits for their empirical study, impossible to achieve. In practice, most self-proclaimed community studies have been concerned with examining patterns of social interaction in geographically confined locations, such as villages and urban neighbourhoods. The impact of externally generated change has often been a key concern of these studies. Some sociologists use community studies as a means of exploring, at a manageable local level, wider social processes and structures—such as class or power structures. Others focus on the impact of the spatial proximity of people in a given locality on patterns of social interaction. A wide range of methods has been used, but participant observation, the use of key informants, and social anthropological techniques have been prominent.

The links between community studies, on one hand, and rural and urban sociology, on the other, have (unsurprisingly) been particularly close. For example, concepts of community were incorporated in Robert Redfield's *folk-urban continuum, and in the *urban ecology of the Chicago School; while, conversely, many of the classic community studies were inspired by such theoretical perspectives. However, much scepticism has been expressed concerning the alleged typicality of those community studies that claimed to provide case-studies of wider social processes.

Various attempts have been made to rethink the content and purpose of community studies by abandoning the normative overtones that the concept of community has so frequently carried. The philosopher Raymond Plant has also argued that the concept is 'essentially contested' and therefore necessarily comprises both a descriptive and an evaluative dimension. In an article entitled 'The Myth of Community Studies' (*British Journal of Sociology*, 20, 1969). Margaret Stacey proposed abandoning the concept altogether, and reformulating the terrain conventionally occupied by community studies as the examination of locally based and interrelated sets of social institutions, or local social systems. These social systems are not however conceived in isolation from more widely operative social structures and processes.

Stacey's paper appeared at a time when *urban sociology in particular was turning sharply away from what appeared to be the abstracted micro-sociology of community studies to consider how macro-social processes shaped the sorts of locations that had been the targets of many such studies. Its impact was therefore limited. However there was a later revival of interest in 'locality studies' (as they were now termed) among urban sociologists. The reasons for this are complex but they stem in large part from geographical work that emphasizes the significance of locally varying social, economic, and political structures in the explanation of changing patterns of industrial location. There is also now some more general sociological concern with the spatial aspects of social organization, notably in Anthony Giddens's theory of *structuration, which incorporates the concept of 'locale'—defined as the 'physical settings associated with the "typical interactions" composing . . . collectivities as social systems'. Among such locales are those which contain—in more or less complex forms—the types of local social system referred to by Stacey. The best introductions to the debate on community are C. Bell and H. Newby's *Community Studies* (1972) and G. Crow and G. Allen's *Community Life* (1994), but see the useful overview in Crow's 'Community Studies: Fifty Years of Theorization' (*Sociological Research Online*, 2002). *See also* COMMUNITY POWER.

compadrazgo *Compadrazgo* is best described as a system of fictive kinship, with its origins in the medieval Catholic Church in Europe. It can be loosely translated as 'godparenthood'. Through baptism of a child into the Christian Church, *compadrazgo* sets up a relationship between the child's biological mother and father and (possibly unrelated) persons who become spiritual parents. The latter sponsor the child's acceptance into the Church and, theoretically at least, are responsible for his or her religious education.

It is in the Catholic cultures of the Mediterranean and in Latin America that *compadrazgo* can be said to be an institution with economic and political significance.

Co-parents with political and economic resources are sought by the biological parents of a child in order to ensure political protection and economic support for the whole family, or perhaps financial support for the child, for example in the form of help with school fees. Persons of political and economic standing in the community often have a large number of godchildren, which not only demonstrates their high status, but also entails that they can count on the labour services and political support of numerous others. The unequal reciprocal system thus established is the basis of many of the widespread *patron-client relationship systems in these areas. The strength of *compadrazgo* (as an alternative to kinship or the state) as an organizing principle can be seen in the role it plays in the Mafia.

comparative sociology (comparative method) All sociology is implicitly comparative, since social phenomena are invariably held in some way to be typical, representative, or unique, all of which imply appropriate comparison. Émile *Durkheim was therefore correct to insist that 'comparative sociology is not a particular branch of sociology; it is sociology itself, in so far as it ceases to be purely descriptive and aspires to account for facts' (*The Rules of Sociological Method*, 1895). Consequently, there is no one comparative method, since all research techniques can be used to facilitate comparison.

Where a sociological analysis is explicitly held to be comparative, this usually involves the study of particular social processes across nation-states, or across different types of society (such as capitalist and state socialist). Much of what is normally referred to as comparative sociology is perhaps more accurately described as cross-national research. In his Presidential Address of 1987 to the American Sociological Association, Melvin L. Kohn delivered a manifesto for this form of research ('Cross-National Research as an Analytical Strategy', *American Sociological Review*, 1987).

Two general orientations to this type of comparative analysis are evident in the literature. First, there are those studies that seek similarity, usually starting from some well-defined a priori general theory that is then tested in different social (and possibly historical) contexts. Much *functionalist inspired research, for example almost the whole corpus of *modernization theory, takes this form. Similarly, *structuralists in both sociology and anthropology have attempted to identify the models and general processes that underlie the apparently different orderings of experience in different societies, as for example in the work of structural Marxists. The danger of this approach is that context is ignored in the search for illustrations of allegedly universal propositions.

At the other extreme are studies that search for variance. These emphasize the specific historicity of societies, reject the search for general theories or laws, and use comparative research to shed light on the differences between cultures in order to understand better the specific arrangements that are found within each. Max *Weber's comparative sociology offers a good example. Correspondingly, the problem here is that sociological explanation may be sacrificed on the altar of context, so that one arrives at the conclusion that cross-cultural or cross-national differences in particular social phenomena are entirely the result of historical contingency. The division of labour, crime rates, organization of religion (or whatever) are different in Britain and Germany because Britain is Britain and not Germany. The units of analysis (in this case nation-states) are simply so many case studies to be interpreted.

In a stimulating analysis of this dilemma, A. Przeworski and H. Teune (*The Logic of Comparative Social Inquiry*, 1970) have argued that the objective of comparative sociological research should be one of replacing the names of nations with the names of variables. That is, the *explanans of particular dependent variables which differ cross-nationally should be rooted not simply in the different histories of the societies involved, but in specific national characteristics (such as degree of income inequality or type of political regime) that can be subsumed under variable names about which the sociologist can meaningfully generalize.

Much comparative research relies on *multivariate statistical techniques in order to answer questions about (for example) cross-national variation in levels of class awareness. In *The Comparative Method* (1987), Charles Ragin advocates an alternative (or, as he sees it, complementary) logic of qualitative comparative method, based on a technique of data reduction that uses algebra to simplify complex data structures in a systematic and holistic manner. This approach is case-oriented, rather than variable-oriented, and historical rather than abstractly causal. It cross-classifies types of social situations against historical outcomes, in the attempt to identify patterns of multiple conjunctural causation (preferably by exhaustive consideration of all possible combinations of present and absent social conditions).

The logical and methodological problems of comparative research are best discussed in the context of substantive comparative analyses. Exemplary texts include Else Oyen (ed.), *Comparative Methodology* (1990) and Charles C. Ragin (ed.), *Issues and Alternatives in Comparative Social Research* (1991). *See also* CAUSE; COUNTERFACTUAL; HISTORICAL SOCIOLOGY; MILL; QUALITATIVE COMPARATIVE ANALYSIS.

compensatory education Programmes for targeting special resources and schooling at so-called problem groups, in the belief that carefully designed *curricula (for example in language skills) will overcome the supposed cognitive and motivational deficit experienced by children from deprived backgrounds. Frequently linked with *human capital theory, the assumption of such education is that underachievement is an individual problem, and that schools can in some way compensate for structured social *inequality.

complementarity hypothesis The literature on small-group formation contains two major hypotheses about the determinants of attraction between individuals. The first of these—the similarity thesis—suggests that people are drawn together because of similarities in their personal characteristics (attitudes, ages, interests and so forth). Theodore M. Newcomb's study of friendship formation at college (*The Acquaintance Process*, 1961) supports this view. The second hypothesis maintains that interpersonal attraction takes place on the grounds of complementarity of characteristics between individuals. For example, Robert Francis Winch's investigation of married couples (*Mate-Selection: A Study of Complementary Needs*, 1958) suggested that 'social needs' (such as deference, aggressiveness, and exhibitionism) should be complementary rather than similar, if marriages are to work. If one partner is low in a particular attribute then the other should be high. Furthermore, certain combinations of attributes are favoured, such as high deference and high dominance. Later modifications of this thesis took into account additional variables (such as mutual gratification of social needs and the social context of relationships).

compliance (types of compliance) The organizational sociologist Amitai Etzioni distinguished three means by which organizations (*see* ORGANIZATION THEORY) could secure compliance from their members—essentially three types of *power by which organizations could be classified. Coercive power, based on physical means, rests on the real or potential use of physical force to enforce compliance with orders. Remunerative or utilitarian power rests on the material means provided by money or some other reward that the members desire and the organization controls. Finally, normative or identitive power uses symbolic means to secure loyalty, by manipulating symbols such as prestige or affections. Typically, prison regimes employ the first of these means, business organizations the second, and collegiate organizations the third.

Etzioni also argued that three kinds of involvement by members could be identified in organizations—alienative, calculative, and moral—covering the range from negative to positive feelings among participants. These do not correspond to the types of compliance on a one-to-one basis; rather, when cross-classified against the latter, they yield a nine-fold typology of compliance relationships, embracing six cells in which the dominant power system does not correspond to the involvement of the members, thus inducing strain towards congruence in one or other dimension. Thus, for example, universities, which are organized around symbolic power, do not function effectively when calculative involvement becomes the norm among teaching staff (see Etzioni's *A Comparative Analysis of Complex Organisations*, 1961).

comprador A Portuguese term, literally 'buyer', used to denote the main indigenous agent in trading houses on the China coast. By extension, 'comprador bourgeoisie' is a term used for a social *class deemed to be compliant with foreign interests, and uninterested in developing the national economy. It is usually contrasted with the class of the 'national bourgeoisie' that is considered to have this potential.

Comte, Auguste (1798–1857) A French social theorist who coined the term 'sociology'. After studying the natural sciences at the École Polytechnique in

Paris, Comte became Henri *Saint-Simon's secretary in 1817. In the course of what proved to be a somewhat fraught relationship (it ended acrimoniously in 1824 after a dispute over authorship credits), Comte was able to begin the development of what he described as his 'positivist philosophy'. Many of those who have invoked Comte's name but not read his work have been misled by his use of this term. Although Comte took the natural sciences as his model, he intended the term to suggest that his approach was a positive rather than a negative one, and not (as is more commonly supposed) that he embraced any sort of *empiricism.

For Comte, his Enlightenment predecessors had been too critical of the social conditions they confronted, and as a result they had failed to appreciate not simply the beneficent nature of certain institutions but also and more importantly the interrelated nature of all of them. On this basis, he came to define the object of his interest as the social whole, and to label the science of this new object initially 'social physics' and latterly *sociology.

Between 1820 and 1826 Comte produced his first essays in this new discipline. He grounded his writings in a set of metaphysical and methodological protocols. (See, for example, the collection entitled *The Crisis of Industrial Civilisation*, edited and translated by Ronald Fletcher.) In these essays, he sought to explain the instability of the Europe in which he lived as the product of an interrupted and therefore incomplete transition between social structures of a 'theological' or 'military' type, and those of a 'scientific-industrial' type. He referred to this transitional phase of social development as the 'metaphysical stage', and specified its overcoming as the purpose of sociology, which as the synthetic and therefore the most difficult of the sciences he dubbed 'the queen of the sciences'. This 'Law of the Three Stages' inspired numerous attempts at *evolutionary sociology in the 19th century. In his subsequent six-volume *Cours de philosophie positive* (1830–42) he identified the specific objects of sociological inquiry as economic life, ruling ideas, forms of individuality, family structure, the division of labour, language, and religion. He organized his discussion of these topics in terms of a highly influential distinction between 'social statics' (the requirements for *social order) and 'social dynamics' (the determinants of social *change).

In his later six-volume *System of Positive Polity* (1850–54) he set out a system of sociological analysis that was to be developed and promoted through a Church of Humanity under Comte's spiritual leadership. These ideas had considerable international influence and a number of affiliated Comtist 'churches' were formed across the world. His specifically methodological and sociological ideas had a growing influence in various positivist and secularist debating societies of the late 19th century, though it was his methodology rather than his sociology that had a more lasting influence. The most important intellectual biography of Comte is the three-volume study by Mary Pickering, *Auguste Comte: An Intellectual Biography* (1993 and 2009). *See also* POSITIVISM.

SEE WEB LINKS

- A French site covering all aspects of Comte's work, including key texts (in French and English).

concentric zone theory A view of the ecological structure of the city that, in the words of its authors, 'represents an ideal construction of the tendencies of any... city to expand radially from its central business district' (R. Park and E. Burgess, *The City*, 1925). The theory posits concentric zones round the central area, defined by their residential composition, moving from the very poor and socially deviant of the inner *zone of transition, to a peripheral suburban commuter ring.

*Burgess himself argued that this structure is the result of competition between users for land—a process analogous to the *ecological competition between biological species for territory. In human societies, these 'biotic' processes are overlaid by cultural processes that limit the conflict and social disorganization resulting from unfettered territorial competition. Control is exercised through the division of the population into distinctive groups, defined by common ethnic identity, occupational status, or economic position. Within each zone, groups occupy particular *natural areas, so forming an 'urban mosaic' of local communities. Social and economic mobility cause changes in the pattern of territorial occupation, via the ecological processes of invasion, domination, and succession.

More complex views of urban structure and typologies of natural areas have subsequently been proposed, aided by the advent of large data-sets and computer technology. Much of this *social area analysis, which stresses purely spatial processes, has ignored the wider issues of social process and structure that concerned Burgess and his colleagues in their distinctive contribution to the development of urban sociology. *See also* CHICAGO SOCIOLOGY; HOUSING CLASS; INVASION-SUCCESSION MODEL; URBAN ECOLOGY.

concepts The terminological means by which social scientists seek to analyse social phenomena, to classify the objects of the observed world, impart meaning through explanation to these phenomena, and formulate higher-level propositions on the basis of these observations. Concepts have themselves been categorized in many ways, for example one distinction is between those which describe directly observable phenomena, and those which signify inferred phenomena. The malleability of concepts is attested to by the fact that there is controversy over their definition and indeed there may exist a class of such concepts termed 'essentially contested concepts'. These are concepts that are both descriptive and evaluative and so carry emotional or theoretically loaded overtones. Such terms as *exploitation, *alienation, *discrimination, *power, and *class bring with them a heavy baggage of values (see S. Nowak, *Methodology of Sociological Research*, 1977).

concomitant variation, method of *See* MILL.

concrete operations stage *See* PIAGET.

conditioning A term employed by behaviourist psychologists within the frame-work of stimulus–response (S–R) models of learning. It refers to the process whereby new stimulus–response connections are established.

*Behaviourists conventionally distinguish two types of conditioning. In classical or Type-S conditioning, first identified by Ivan Pavlov in his famous experiments with dogs, a new stimulus is linked to an already existing response. The new S–R connection is established by contiguously pairing the new, formerly neutral, stimulus with an old one that already provokes the response. In Pavlov's experiments, the old, unconditioned (or unconditional) response (UCS) of food in the mouth provokes a reflex unconditioned (unconditional) response (UCR) of salivation. When this stimulus is repeatedly paired with a new one (the sound of a bell) this new stimulus alone will, in time, produce salivation. A new connection is, therefore, established between a conditioned (conditional) stimulus (CS), the sound of the bell, and a conditioned response (CR), salivation. In this process, the pairing of food with the sound of the bell serves to strengthen or reinforce the new S–R connection—that is, to make the occurrence of the response of salivation to the sound of the bell more likely. Frequent repetition of the new stimulus without reinforcement (food) leads to extinction of the conditioned response.

In operant, instrumental, or Type–R conditioning, a new response is established to a formerly neutral stimulus. This response is encouraged by the introduction of some reinforcement of that response whenever it occurs. The approach is commonly associated with the American psychologists E. L. Thorndike (*Animal Intelligence*, 1911) and B. F. Skinner (*The Behaviour of Organisms*, 1938). In Skinner's well-known experiments with rats in cages, the pressing of a bar is reinforced by giving a pellet of food (the reinforcing stimulus) whenever the bar is pressed. Reinforcement utilizing pleasure is termed positive reinforcement. Where the reinforcement takes the form of avoiding something that is unpleasant (an electric shock, a disagreeable taste) it is termed negative reinforcement. Where a reinforcer derives its value through learning it is termed a secondary reinforcer. For example, if a rat learns to obtain tokens to secure food, the tokens may be used as secondary reinforcers in conditioning some new response. Operant conditioning has also been used as a basis of therapy for humans. Subjects learn that certain patterns of behaviour have desirable consequences, that is they are rewarded, and this increases the likelihood of the behaviour occurring in the future.

Much of the debate amongst learning theorists has concerned the interpretation of the empirical observations made in studies of conditioning. Early behaviourists developed analyses of conditioning that suggested it was a simple, unconscious, and automatic process. However, a number of experiments provided convincing evidence that cognitive processes were involved in establishing the stimulus-response connections observed in conditioning studies. In academic psychology from the 1960s onwards, the increasing emphasis on cognition and information processing has shifted attention away from studies of conditioning in animals and humans, and from conceptualizing learning in terms of stimulus-response models.

Condorcet, Marie-Jean-Antoine-Nicolas de Caritat, Marquis de

(1743–94) A leading contributor to the *Encyclopedie* (1751–65), and first supporter then victim of the French Revolution, Condorcet is chiefly remembered for his theory of human *progress. This was presented in his *Sketch for a Historical Picture of the Progress of the Human Mind*, written while in hiding. He distinguished a series of ten progressive epochs or phases in human history, and like many of his contemporaries, emphasized the indefinitely progressive potentiality of the growth of science and mathematics. His radical social and political ideas were one of the main targets of criticism in Thomas *Malthus's *Essay on the Principle of Population*, in which the latter argued that all such well-meant projects must founder on the disproportion between population growth and natural limits to the supply of food.

confidence intervals (confidence limits) The *values measured for a sample of individual cases are always spread across a range of values. When the spread of values corresponds to the *binomial distribution, its known properties can be used to estimate the confidence that can be placed on a judgement about how close a measured value is to the actual value in the population. The degree of confidence can be expressed as a percentage level. *See also* CENTRAL TENDENCY (MEASURES OF); VARIATION (STATISTICAL).

conflict (social conflict) *See* COMPETITION, ECONOMIC AND SOCIAL; CONFLICT THEORY; CONSENSUS; INDUSTRIAL CONFLICT; MILITARY AND MILITARISM; POWER.

conflict, industrial *See* INDUSTRIAL CONFLICT.

conflict theory Conflict has always been central to sociological theory and analysis. Some of the earliest approaches included Ludwig *Gumplowicz's theory of ethnic conflict and Gaetano Mosca's theory of conflict between elites and masses. Many have seen *Marx's theory of class as providing a conflict theory of social change. Today, however, the term conflict theory is more often used to refer to the sociological writings of opponents to the dominance of structural functionalism in the two decades after the Second World War. Its proponents drew on Max *Weber and (to a lesser extent) Karl *Marx to construct their arguments emphasizing the importance of *power and *interests over *norms and *values. They look at the ways in which the pursuit of interests generates various types of conflict as normal aspects of social life, rather than as abnormal or dysfunctional occurrences. In *Class and Class Conflict in Industrial Society* (1959)—a standard work of conflict theory—Ralf Dahrendorf argued that classes in the advanced 'post-capitalist' societies of Britain, Germany, and the United States had to be derived 'from positions in associations co-ordinated by authority', and that these societies were therefore characterized by disputes about 'participation in or exclusion from the exercise of authority'.

The claims of conflict theory against *functionalism were comparatively modest compared with later criticisms. For example, Dahrendorf argued that structural functionalism was not so much wrong as partial: that power or authority within a social system was not simply integrative, something that emerges from the system in order to keep it together, but also divisive, something that has to be imposed over conflicting interests. At the same time he argued, again against Marx, that social conflict was multi-faceted and does not congeal around one central issue.

Conflict theorists did not claim to present any general theory of society but emphasized coercion rather than *consensus as the basis of social order. John

Rex, in *Key Problems of Sociological Theory* (1961), offered a version of conflict theory owing rather more to Marx. The works of C. Wright *Mills and Alvin *Gouldner took a similar orientation to the centrality of conflict. The most effective contribution from this period is David Lockwood's paper on *system integration and *social integration and (in G. K. Zollschan and W. Hirsch (eds.), *Explorations in Social Change*, 1964). Lockwood argues that we can distinguish between system integration, which refers to relationships between different parts of the social system, the economy, and political system; and social integration, which refers to norms and values. Structural functionalism tends to run both together and gives priority to social integration: if that persists then the assumption is that system integration is also present. Lockwood points out that social integration can exist without system integration. An economic crisis, for example, can indicate the existence of system conflict, but does not automatically lead to a breakdown in social integration. Lewis Coser's *The Functions of Social Conflict* (1956) attempts to incorporate the analysis of social conflict into structural-functionalism, seeing it as a process of tension management, or as part of a process of reintegration in response to social *change. Randall Collins's more recent version of conflict theory (in his *Conflict Sociology*, 1975) is distinguished by the fact that it is rooted in the microlevel concerns of individual actors; indeed he claims his theoretical roots lie in *phenomenology.

With the emergence of *Marxism as a major force in social theory during the 1960s, this debate largely faded away, and conflict theory merged into the more general Marxist and Weberian tendencies in social theory. In modern sociology, the conflict tradition is represented (in very different ways) by such developments as Anthony Giddens's *structuration theory, and by *rational choice theory. *See also* SYSTEM INTEGRATION AND SOCIAL INTEGRATION.

conformity Conformity is the tendency of people to make their actions comply with prevailing *norms or expectations, despite their personal beliefs or preferences. It may also refer to a tendency to alter beliefs in line with those of others. Some social psychologists have argued that there are distinct conformist personalities that are the result of particular patterns of *socialization, while others have focused on the social pressures existing in a group, organization, or leader, or because of the perceived expectations of others in general. Experiments conducted by Solomon E. Asch, an American *gestalt psychologist, involved a series of small-group studies in which subjects were asked to answer a basic puzzle (for example on the length of a line) when others provided a manifestly incorrect answer. Many subjects felt under pressure to give the same incorrect answer; however, the majority resisted pressures to conform, and even those who acquiesced offered reasonable explanations for doing so, despite subsequently expressed doubts about their behaviour (see his *Social Psychology*, 1952). Asch argues that the results confirm his view of *human nature, which is of human beings as creative and rational organisms, in contrast to the tradition that views them as passive and responding only to environmental pressures. The concept of conformity was also used by Robert Merton in *Social Theory and Social Structure* (1968) to refer to acceptance of cultural goals and the legitimate or approved means of achieving them. *See also* AUTHORITARIAN PERSONALITY.

Confucianism A philosophy that contains elements of religious practice, founded by Confucius in the sixth to fifth centuries BCE. Its influence in China was paramount, but it has also been significant in Korea, Japan, Vietnam, Hong Kong, Singapore, and Taiwan as a source of learning and an ethical code.

Confucius (551–479 BCE) taught the necessary actions for harmony and order during a time of political violence and social disorder. During the Han dynasty (206 BCE–220 CE) his teachings (compiled by his disciples in the *Analects*) became state orthodoxy in China and remained so until 1911. Confucianism taught that nobility was not to be attained through inheritance but by following the correct rituals and acts of filial piety, reciprocity, and righteousness. In particular, juniors (such as subjects or sons) should show loyalty to seniors (rulers, fathers), while seniors should show benevolence to juniors. This idea was extended by Mencius (*c.* 371–289 BCE), the 'second sage of Confucianism', to suggest that humans were essentially good (the idea of original virtue), and that it was appropriate for subjects to rebel against unjust rulers. Significantly, the latter idea was never introduced into Japan, where loyalty to the Emperor was made paramount.

Although today practised actively as a religion only in South Korea, the influence of Confucianism on the ethical, legal, political, and educational systems of the above-named countries remains considerable. Robert Bellah (*Tokugawa Religion*, 1957) has argued that Confucianism may have had a similar role in the development of modern Japan as did the *protestant ethic in Europe (an interpretation which is at odds with that of Max Weber in *The Religion of China*, 1916). Others have argued that Confucianism's emphasis on harmony, respect for authority, loyalty, benevolence, meritocracy, literacy, and scholarship, lies behind the recent economic growth of Japan and the newly industrializing countries (NICs) of East Asia.

conjugal role *See* ROLE, CONJUGAL.

conjuncture A term used by so-called structural Marxists (see Louis *Althusser) to refer to the concrete state of political-economic and especially class relations, in a specific society, at a particular point in time (as in 'specific historical conjuncture'). The term also appears in the historical studies of the *Annales School.

connotative versus denotative meaning Connotative meaning refers to the associations, overtones, and feel that a concept has, rather than what it refers to explicitly (or denotes, hence denotative meaning). Two words with the same reference or definition may have different connotations. Connotative meaning is often researched using the *semantic differential, based in part on the phenomenon of synaesthesia, where experience in one sense is perceived with (or replaces) another modality: for example, where a sound is perceived as a colour or emotion, as in blue or sad music. *See also* DISCOURSE.

connubium A system of marital exchanges, for example between two bands or tribes, by which the men of one group must marry the women of the other (and vice versa). There are several interpretations of these arrangements, for example relating them to the *incest taboo, the formation of political alliances, and attempts to define the symbolic boundaries of groups.

consanguinity A consanguine relationship is a kin relationship based on descent from a common (male or female) ancestor, who may not necessarily be a blood relation. Social anthropologists point out that fictive relationships can be just as important as actual biological ties when tracing consanguinity (as is often the case with *clans). A. R. *Radcliffe-Brown argued that *kinship is a better term than consanguinity, because it does not imply a blood relationship.

consciousness, class *See* CLASS CONSCIOUSNESS.

consensual union A form of cohabitation by a man and a woman who live together as married but whose relationship is not formally ratified by the dominant laws and religion of the country. The offspring of a consensual union are illegitimate in law. In some parts of the *Third World, customary marriages are not recognized by the state, and are defined as consensual unions in *official statistics. *See also* MARRIAGE.

consensus The term consensus refers to a commonly agreed position, conclusion, or set of values, and is normally used with reference either to *group dynamics or to broad agreement in *public opinion. More generally, it refers to the sharing of a set of ideas, norms, and values among the members of a whole society. It is in this sense that it has come to be associated with the normative *functionalism of Talcott *Parsons (see, for example, *The Social System*, 1951).

In so far as sociological theory is concerned with the problem of *social order, it is possible to identify two broadly differing approaches in the history of the discipline, one of which emphasizes conflict and coercion while the other assumes a degree of social consensus in the form of agreement over *values and *norms. Whilst value consensus is seen as the basis of social order, the true explanatory focus is the process of *socialization through the vehicle of the family, an activity upon which normative functionalists placed great emphasis.

It was commonplace, during the 1960s, to speak of the debate between the consensus and conflict schools. Enthusiasts of the former approach tended to be critical of any kind of social determinism and to argue instead that social theory must accommodate intention and choice at the level of individual action. Society should therefore be seen as the expression of a system of *values and *norms that have been developed and institutionalized over time by its members. Thus, in Parsons's own writings, 'integration' is cited as one of four key requirements for the functioning of society. *Conflict theory was the counterpart to the consensus view of social order and was developed in opposition to Parsonian functionalism in the late 1950s and early 1960s. This approach rejects the assumption of shared norms and values as the basis for social order, and points instead to the balance of *power between conflicting interests, both political and economic. With hindsight it is clear that, on many issues, the two groups of protagonists were simply talking past each other.

consensus theory *See* CONSENSUS; FUNCTION.

conservatism An everyday notion meaning to 'preserve' or 'keep intact' and that has, at least in Europe and the United States since the 19th century, come to be associated with a set of political principles. The major problem in defining the concept is that many conservatives themselves deny conservatism is an abstract theory or *ideology; rather, they defend their judgements on the grounds of tradition, historical experience, and gradualism. Typically, conservatives eschew comprehensive visions of the good society, and favour instead the pragmatism of piecemeal social reform.

That said, modern conservatism tends to draw on two somewhat contradictory intellectual strands, namely the organic conservatism of the Middle Ages and the *libertarian conservatism of writers such as Edmund Burke. The former harks back to the medieval ideal of the close-knit local *community, a stable social hierarchy with rank ascribed at birth rather than achieved (*see* ASCRIPTION), dominated by aristocratic *paternalism towards the poor, and a network of reciprocal rights and obligations linking benevolent master and deferential servant (*see* DEFERENCE). By comparison, Burke (an 18th-century English political theorist) favoured *laissez-faire economics, unregulated *capitalism, and minimal state intervention in economic affairs. Whereas organic conservatism emphasizes 'one nation', libertarians endorse the *individualism of autonomous individuals following their own self-interest, usually on the grounds of individual freedom, social justice, and (long-term) collective welfare.

These strands have proved difficult to reconcile in the long term, though Burke himself wrote a passionate defence of the organic political and social traditions of 18th-century Britain, denouncing the French Revolution, and showing how liberal principles can be justified in an already liberal society. Modern conservatives have grappled to balance the two and offered a full range of hybrids. A useful study of conservative thought is Robert Nisbet's *Conservatism* (1986).

conspicuous consumption *See* LEISURE CLASS.

constant conjunction *See* CAUSE.

constructionism (constructivism) *See* SOCIAL CONSTRUCTIONISM.

consumer society A term sometimes applied to modern Western societies and suggesting that they are increasingly organized around their consumption (of goods and leisure) rather than the *production of materials and services. Factors implicated in this development include increasing affluence, *embourgeoisement, the emergence of a mass *popular culture, growing *privatism, the demise of social class, *consumption sectors sectors and cleavages, and growing *individualism. As will be clear from a reading of those entries in this dictionary to which the reader has just been referred, most of these trends are highly questionable, and it is in any case not clear whether, were they to be realized, the new consumer society would display those features of *egalitarianism that some of its proponents have envisaged. Consumerism may simply underline the distinction between rich and poor—as, for example, in the phenomenon of conspicuous consumption. *See also* CONSUMPTION, SOCIOLOGY OF.

consumption sectors (consumption cleavages) Social divisions created by the way in which material goods and services—especially major items such as housing, health, and education—are consumed in advanced *capitalist societies.

The possible significance of patterns of consumption in determining social *stratification was recognized by Max Weber, who observed that *status groups are 'stratified according to the principles of their consumption of goods'. Similarly, Thorstein *Veblen analysed the conspicuous consumption of the so-called *leisure class. Debates about *housing classes and *collective consumption during the 1960s and 1970s led some sociologists to claim that consumption-based cleavages had become more significant than production-based divisions. In Britain this claim has been reinforced by studies that claim to show that, during the 1980s, the public/private housing-tenure divide became more important than social class in determining *voting behaviour (the so-called dealignment thesis).

According to a leading theorist of consumption cleavages, 'a sociological analysis of the different patterns of consumption—state provision in kind, state provision in cash, self-provisioning, and marketed or privatized provisioning—is... central to an understanding of certain key features of contemporary social organization' (P. Saunders, *Social Theory and the Urban Question*, 1986). In practice, discussion has concentrated on private (market) and socialized (state) provision, since (according to Saunders) the main consumption-based division in contemporary capitalist societies is between those who satisfy their needs through personal ownership and those who remain reliant on socialized state provision. Moreover, given the choice, those who can afford to do so choose privatized and market-based, in preference to socialized, consumption—for example of housing, health care, and education. This undermines political support for *welfare regimes (and parties that promote them) and has negative effects on the quality of what welfare institutions provide for those who remain dependent on them. This creates a major social division between a 'marginalised and stigmatised minority... cast adrift on the water-logged raft of what remains of the welfare state', and a privatized majority, with increasing freedom to choose among better-quality market-based consumption possibilities.

There are many criticisms of this theory of sectional cleavages. Increasingly, sociologists accept the need for a closer analysis of the relationship between differing modes of consumption and possible social divisions these create, but many reject Saunders's conclusions about the merits and demerits of privatized and socialized provision. A majority would probably question whether consumption cleavages rather than (say) social class determine life chances and political alignments, though there is a growing amount of evidence concerning their importance in social identity. There is, however, evidence that consumption cleavages are class dependent rather than independent determinants of social processes. Some critics have argued that the theory is ethnocentric (being mainly concerned with the situation in

Britain); others argue that the distinction between socialized and market-based consumption is unrealistic, since the public sector frequently supports apparently privatized consumption. Empirical studies have also shown that attitudes to welfarism vary according to the particular social service under discussion and that the major determinant of voting behaviour (at least in Britain) is still social class. The debate about these findings has led to some further refinements of the original theory that, together with developments elsewhere in sociology, has contributed to a growing volume of literature on the sociology of *consumption.

consumption, sociology of A diverse field of sociology that developed rapidly during the 1980s. Its substantive focus is the material culture (especially the mass culture) of advanced *capitalist societies. The essays collected together in Stephen Edgell et al. (eds.), *Consumption Matters* (1996) are a good illustration of the diversity of the field, and a good introduction to central issues is Daniel Miller's *Consumption and Its Consequences* (2012).

Proponents of the sociology of consumption tend to argue that it provides an alternative focus for much of the work carried out in the tradition of *urban sociology, a new approach to the analysis of social *inequality and political alignments, and (sometimes) the basis for a wholesale revolution in sociological thinking. Their general complaint is that sociology has been dominated by the 19th-century concerns of the classical theorists—*alienation, *bureaucracy, social *class, the *division of labour, and other characteristics of early industrial capitalism—all of which emphasize *production as the source of social meaning and the basis of *social order or *conflict. By contrast, if one takes seriously the late capitalist phenomenon of mass consumption, then (to quote the critique by H. F. Moorhouse) 'it should no longer be possible for analysts to operate with a notion of an alienation based on paid labour pervading all contemporary life, nor should it be possible to privilege the factory, office, shop or mine as *the* crucial site of human experience and self understanding, though this is continually done in a lot of sociological and most Marxist theorizing' (see 'American Automobiles and Workers' Dreams', *Sociological Review*, 1983). In short, sociologists have produced too many studies of what it is like to work for Ford, and too few of what it means to own, drive, or customize a Ford.

This self-conscious attempt to challenge some of the basic assumptions of sociology has encouraged studies of topics as diverse as those of leisure, fashion, niche marketing, tourism, and the heritage industry. Many of these are less original than is claimed, since they tend to echo themes such as *commodity fetishism, *materialism, *structural differentiation, inequality, *privatism, and *individualism, all of which were familiar to the classical theorists themselves. The interpretation of the symbolic significance of cultural artefacts (such as automobiles) does tend, however, to draw heavily on more recent *structuralist and *post-structuralist writings by authors such as Roland Barthes, Claude Lévi-Strauss, and Jean Baudrillard. Recent work on consumption has explored our relationship to food (see Warde et al., *Trust in Food: an institutional and comparative analysis*, 2007) and to technologies aimed at cleanliness (E. Shove, *Comfort, Cleanliness and Convenience,* 2003), while the work of *Bourdieu has been explored in T. Bennett et al., *Culture, Class, and Distinction* (2009).

In so far as the very diverse literature has a central unifying theme then this is provided by the common contention that consumption shapes social relations and social meanings in no less authentic a manner than does production; or, as Daniel Miller puts it, the sociology of consumption 'translates the object from . . . being a symbol of estrangement and price value to being an artefact invested with particular inseparable connotations' (*Material Culture and Mass Consumption,* 1987).

Discussion in Britain—and to a lesser extent some other European countries— has tended to focus on the particular claim that there is a major and novel *consumption cleavage in advanced capitalist societies, between a majority of people who provide for their consumption requirements through the market, and a minority who remain reliant on (increasingly inadequate) state provision. This cleavage is argued to be as important (possibly more so) as earlier divisions such as social class, and is said to influence political attitudes, material life-chances, and cultural identities in parallel fashion. Critics have replied by insisting that the individual's position in the realm of consumption is still importantly influenced by his or her position in the *labour market—and is therefore reducible to the more traditional cleavages associated with production. This, in turn, has provoked the counterclaim that state intervention in provisions such as housing, education, health, and transport introduces a dimension of inequality not directly affected by relations of production. However, it can be argued that even if this were the case, dependence on state provision is itself a factor of weakness in the labour market. Critics have also argued that the realm of consumption, once divorced from relations of production, does not of itself generate social inequality. *See also* EMBOURGEOISEMENT; INFORMAL ECONOMY; LEISURE CLASS; POPULAR CULTURE.

contagion *See* COLLECTIVE BEHAVIOUR.

content analysis A method for identifying the meaning of a text by reducing it to a much smaller summary or representation of its principal themes or ideas. Bernard Berelson (*Content Analysis in Communication Research,* 1952) saw it as an 'objective, systematic and quantitative' method, though others have recognized more qualitative elements. The technique was largely developed in the 1940s for propaganda and communication studies ('Who says what to whom and with what effect?', as Harold Lasswell puts it in his essay on 'Describing the Contents of Communication', in Lasswell et al. (eds.), *Propaganda, Communication and Public Opinion,* 1946), and has increasingly made use of ideas from linguistics and information science.

In its simplest form, content analysis consists of word counts, using the frequency with which words appear as a measure of their significance in the meaning of the message. The basic form consists of word frequency tabulations, but more grammatical and semantic methods have increasingly been sought. These advanced approaches attempt to count variants and inflections under a root word (such that 'am', 'are', 'is', 'will', 'was', 'were', and 'been' are seen as variants of 'be'), and to 'disambiguate', or distinguish between different meanings of a word spelt the same (such as 'a *bit* of a hole', 'a 16-*bit* machine', 'he *bit* it off'). More ambitiously, content analysis seeks to identify general semantic concepts (such as 'achievement' or 'religion'), stylistic characteristics (including understatement or overstatement), and themes (for example 'religion as a conservative force'). *See also* CODING.

contest and sponsored mobility Alternative patterns of intergenerational social ascent through schooling. Under a system of contest mobility individuals have, within a basic framework of rules, a wide range of strategies or routes they can pursue in order to attain credentials associated with high status. Under a system of sponsored mobility the alternatives are minimal and typically controlled by an elite. The former is seen as more *egalitarian, since it implies open contest or competition, with selection delayed as long as possible. Under the latter, recruits are chosen early by those who are already established and who sponsor their rapid rise, and exclusion is practised against the rest. Ralph H. Turner, who proposed the distinction in the early 1960s, made the controversial claim that, in the United States, contest mobility is the more predominant, compared with the stronger emphasis on sponsorship in Britain and other European societies. *See also* CLOSURE.

contextual models *See* MULTI-LEVEL MODELS.

contingency table Contingency tables, often referred to as cross-classifications or cross-tabulations, describe and analyse the relationship between two or more *variables in a data-set. Cell entries give the number of cases (persons, households, or other unit of analysis) that combine particular values of the two variables. Marginal totals (or 'marginals') give the total number of cases found in each category of the variables. Normally, cell entries are expressed as either row or column percentages, with the total numbers of cases shown in the marginals. These elements are shown here in tabular form.

COLUMN VARIABLE

		variable A	variable B	
ROW VARIABLE	variable X	cell entry	cell entry	row marginal
	variable Y	cell entry	cell entry	row marginal
		column marginal	column marginal	Total number

The example is a typical 2 × 2 cross-tabulation, but contingency tables can take more complex forms with three or more variables and several categories of each. The analysis of complex contingency tables is nowadays normally undertaken using the mathematical techniques of *loglinear analysis. *See also* MULTIVARIATE ANALYSIS; TABULAR PRESENTATION.

contingency theory A strand of *organization theory (sometimes also known as the 'rational systems perspective'), the leading practitioners of which were Tom Burns, Joan *Woodward, Paul Lawrence, and Jay Lorsch, an otherwise theoretically eclectic group who were nevertheless united in their belief that no single organizational structure was inherently more efficient than all others. Rather, since organizations differed in the tasks they performed and environments they faced, the appropriate organizational structure was in each case a function of such factors as technology, market, and the predictability of tasks.

In *The Management of Innovation* (1961), Burns and his co-author G. Stalker examined the impact of technical innovation on electronics companies, and attributed the differential adaptability of firms to the prevailing system of management. They devised an influential typology of 'mechanical' and 'organic' (or 'organismic') systems of management. In mechanical management systems, decision-making takes place within a tightly controlled and familiar normative framework, in which: individual employees are responsible for well-defined tasks; functions are precisely defined; control, authority, and communication are hierarchical; interaction between members is typically vertical (between subordinate and superior); there is an insistence on loyalty to and obedience of superiors; and a greater importance is attached to internal (local) than to general (cosmopolitan) experience and skills. Organic management systems display characteristics that are the obverse of these: continual adjustment and redefinition of tasks through interaction with others; network structures of control, authority, and communication; a lateral rather than vertical direction of communication through the organization, involving frequent communications between people of different rank, with communications taking the form of consultations rather than command; and so forth. Burns and Stalker argued that the former structure was only suited to 'a concern for which technical and market conditions approximated very closely to stability'. Changing market and technological conditions, which create unforeseen problems and tasks that cannot therefore be described functionally or distributed automatically throughout a clearly demarcated structure, required an organic system of management.

Lawrence and Lorsch (*Organization and Environment*, 1967) summarize the key idea in the statement that there is no 'one best way' to organize a given technical process, an explicit challenge to the assumption made by the *scientific management approach that science can always identify the quickest and best way to perform work-tasks.

contract labour Normally refers to workers who are hired for a specific task and a finite period. In *Third World countries the term sometimes refers to a system whereby workers are hired by an intermediary—the labour contractor—who supplies them to the employer for a fee. Such workers are often bound to the contractor by a variety of mechanisms and their freedom of movement may thus be restricted.

contractarianism A mode of reasoning, derived from social contract theories, that purports to deduce moral principles from the rational choices of abstract individuals ('rational contractors') deliberating under conditions of ignorance and uncertainly. The most prominent contemporary example will be found in John Rawls's *A Theory of Justice* (1972). *See also* JUSTICE, SOCIAL.

contraculture *See* COUNTER CULTURE; SUBCULTURE.

contradiction Originally a logical term taken up by G. W. F. *Hegel to explain the nature of the *dialectical movement in the history of thought, whereby a thesis necessarily produces its antithesis (opposite), and results in a synthesis that contains and advances upon the initially antagonistic (contradictory) ideas. As his own work developed, Karl *Marx provided himself with the means to move on from this to a method of understanding conceptualizing social development in terms of the antagonisms or contradictions between material forces. Friedrich *Engels later made this *materialism into a rather deterministic theory referred to in orthodox Marxism as 'dialectical materialism'. Its usage therein represents the principal justification for the term's subsequent canonical status within Marxist discourses of an orthodox kind.

The concept is now widely (and more loosely) used in sociological theory to refer to structural oppositions and antagonisms. For example, in *The Cultural Contradictions of Capitalism* (1979), the American sociologist Daniel Bell identified a growing contradiction in advanced Western societies between its social *structure (its economy, technology, occupational system) and its *culture (the symbolic expression of meanings), each of which is governed by a different 'axial principle'. The former calls for functional rationality, efficiency, self-control, deferred gratification, and dedication to a career, whereas the latter fosters attitudes of conspicuous display, prodigality, and hedonism.

contradictory class location During the 1970s class analysis, particularly that influenced by Marxism, was preoccupied with the problem of assigning *class situations to those 'intermediate' roles (such as manager, supervisor, or salaried professional) that seemed to be neither unambiguously of the *bourgeoisie nor of the *proletariat, and so generated a series of 'boundary problems' in class schemes. The resulting literature (the so-called boundary debate), with extensive contributions from Nicos *Poulantzas, Guglielmo Carchedi, and John and Barbara Ehrenreich, is cogently summarized in Nicholas Abercrombie and John Urry's *Capital, Labour, and the Middle Classes* (1983). By far the most sustained attempt to solve these boundary issues was Erik Olin Wright's theory of 'contradictory class locations'.

Wright, an American Marxist, argued that in each *mode of production certain basic social classes are defined by being completely polarized within the relevant social *relations of production. Under *capitalism, for example, the *working class is wholly dispossessed of the means of production, must sell its labour-power to the *bourgeoisie, and so is both exploited and dominated by it. However, in the absence of wholesale polarization, contradictory situations or locations within a mode of production also arise. Managers have contradictory interests as a class: like workers, they are exploited by capitalists (who make a profit from managerial work), yet like capitalists themselves they dominate and control workers. Moreover, concrete social formations rarely comprise a single mode of production, so that capitalist societies, for example, typically contain certain non-capitalist forms of production relations. Most obviously, they inherit the legacy of simple commodity production, in which direct producers own and control their own productive means—the *petite bourgeoisie or own-account workers more common to feudal societies. Certain class relations interpenetrate both modes of production and so constitute contradictory relations between them. Small employers, for example, are simultaneously petit bourgeois and capitalist, in that they are self-employed direct producers, but also employers and therefore exploiters of labour power. Similarly, an extensive group of so-called 'semi-autonomous employees' (such as salaried professionals) do not own productive means, but still exercise considerable control over their activities within production: they are, therefore, in a contradictory class location defined by elements of both proletarian and petit bourgeois existence.

Wright's theory has been refined during the course both of several lengthy theoretical works, and a major empirical programme of class analysis, involving research teams in countries throughout the world (see in particular his *Classes*, 1985, and *Class Counts*, 1997).

Wright's reformulation of the concept of class has been controversial, both within Marxism and without, and has been criticized as static, mechanical, deterministic, and (in common with the arguments of most other *structuralists) devoid of human agency. However, it has also generated enthusiastic support, notably among those who see in it a corrective to the excessive individualism of the alternative *status attainment tradition of class analysis in the United States. Wright's *The Debate on Classes* (1989) gives a good overview of the arguments and the enormous secondary literature generated by his project. *See also* MIDDLE CLASS.

control group A group used for comparison with another, either because it represents the most common or typical case, or because it illustrates the absence of some phenomenon being studied. Human beings are not inert, lifeless matter, and hence cannot be studied simply by carrying out before-and-after studies around some experimental stimulus applied to them. Many other developments and changes will be occurring spontaneously at the same time, as people go about their lives, and it is difficult to disentangle the effects of one particular stimulus from all the others affecting people, as individuals or as groups, at the same time. The solution is to identify a group, or social aggregate, that serves as a control group in providing information on characteristics or changes in a base-line situation that is as close to 'ordinary' as possible, or illustrates social behaviour in the absence of the key factor of interest. For example, in an investigation of medical treatment the group being studied receives the treatment being tested and a control group receives no treatment or an ineffective (placebo) treatment, and hence provides baseline information on spontaneous developments against which the effects of the experimental treatment can be measured. Control groups can be created at the *sampling stage, through statistical manipulation of the data-set, or during analysis. The most rigorous type is experimental control, when there is a random allocation to groups.

control, social *See* SOCIAL CONTROL.

conurbation A term coined by Patrick *Geddes in 1915 to describe large-scale city regions such as Greater London, New York/Boston, or the Ruhr. It is not a statistically based concept, but normally refers to one city or a conglomerate of very large cities surrounded by extensive suburbs, and which forms a continuous urban and industrial built-up environment. In most cases, transportation systems develop to link all districts within the conurbation, so as to create a single urban labour market or travel-to-work area. Alternative terms are urban agglomeration and, in the United States, metropolitan area.

conventionalism The view that the adoption by the relevant scientific community of one theory rather than its rival(s) is a matter of mere convention.

It is now widely accepted in the philosophy of science that even the best-established scientific laws and theories are not fully confirmed by the factual evidence upon which they are based. In part, this is because such laws and theories are usually universal in scope, and so make claims that of necessity go beyond any finite set of evidence for them. Also, the evidence is itself conceptualized and described in terms that are informed by theory. If this is so, choice between rival theories is never determined by the facts and logic alone.

Against conventionalism, it is possible to argue that, in the absence of conclusive proof of a logical or factual kind, there may still be good reasons for accepting one theory as more plausible, better supported by the evidence, and so on, than any available alternative.

convergence thesis *See* INDUSTRIAL SOCIETY.

conversation analysis A research method that takes conversations in real-life settings as the object of study, and as a window onto the roles, social relationships, and power relations of participants.

Derived largely from *ethnomethodology and *sociolinguistics, it starts from the premise that conversations are one of the central activities of social life and that much social life is organized through them. Conversation analysis therefore sets out to record patterns of conversation in order to detect underlying rules that enable communication to proceed in a largely orderly fashion. It focuses on the structure, cadences, and other characteristics of verbal interactions, usually in dyads or very small groups. The subject matter of the discussion is noted, but can be unimportant, and is not itself the main focus of analysis (as in *content analysis). The method normally involves making tape recordings or video recordings of conversations, which are then subjected to detailed analysis. Research findings have proved useful in elucidating many hidden aspects of human interaction, such as how turns to talk are allocated, the duration of pauses, silences, and speech, and when interruptions are permitted.

An excellent introduction to the leading practitioners (such as Emmanuel A. Shegloff and Harvey Sacks) and principal themes is I. Hutchby and R. Wooffitt, *Conversation Analysis* (1988), while a practical guide can be found in P. Ten Have *Doing Conversation Analysis* (1999). Sacks's own work can be found in the posthumously published *Lectures on Conversation* (1965–72, pub. 1992).

conversion In religious terms, this refers to sudden and dramatic experience of God that brings about a profound change in a person's religious status. For example, in Protestant, *evangelical Christianity, there is an emphasis on personal and emotional experience of God, and thus on the importance of a conversion. In sociological terms, conversion refers to the process by which a person achieves membership of a religious group; it is common to contrast the achievement of Christian membership of a *sect by a conversion experience, and of a *church by training and ritual. In some branches of *Judaism conversion is achieved by circumcision. Sociologists argue that in fact individual conversion is normally preceded by a period of preparation or socialization.

The term can also be used in a more general sense to mean the acquisition of a new *role or *ideology. This general sense would embrace, for example, the idea of conversion to socialism. *See also* RELIGIOUS REVIVAL.

Cooley, Charles Horton (1864–1929) Cooley was one of the first generation of American sociologists, but an eccentric who differed from most of his peers. Whereas the majority of the pioneers were Social *Darwinists, Cooley was a less mechanical evolutionist: most were aiming to make sociology a rigorously objective science, while Cooley was more concerned with introspection and imagination—one of the earliest of *humanistic sociologists.

Cooley sought to abolish the dualisms of society/individual and body/mind, emphasizing instead their interconnections, and conceptualizing them as functional and organic wholes. The root problem of social science was the mutual interrelationship between the individual and social order. In his view, the concepts of the 'individual' and of 'society' could be defined only in relationship to each other, since human life was essentially a matter of social intercourse—of society shaping the individual and individuals shaping society. However, his critics did not see him as being successful in this enterprise, ultimately siding too much with the individual and *idealism.

Cooley launched his career 'in defiance of categories', refusing to label himself a sociologist, and seeking instead to merge history, philosophy, and social psychology. Two of his concepts have, nevertheless, captured the sociological imagination. The first is the *looking-glass self: the way in which the individual's sense of self is 'mirrored' and reflected through others. This was an idea later to be greatly expanded by William *James and George Herbert *Mead in their attempts to build a general theory of the *self. The second of Cooley's lasting concepts is that of the 'primary group', characterized by close, intimate, face-to-face interaction, which Cooley contrasted with the larger and more disparate 'nucleated group' (subsequently referred to more commonly as the 'secondary group'), whose members were rarely if ever all in direct contact. (Families or friendship circles are typical primary groups; trade unions and political parties are characteristically secondary groups.)

Cooley was both a student and professor at the University of Michigan. His major works are *Human Nature and the Social Order* (1902), *Social Organisation* (1909), and *Social Process* (1918). *See also* SYMBOLIC INTERACTIONISM.

Coolidge, Mary Elizabeth Burroughs Roberts Smith (1860–1945) Coolidge was the first American full-time professor of sociology. A statistician of women's poverty, she was also an authority on feminism, social welfare, Victorian sexuality, Chinese immigration to the United States, and Native Americans. Her major study *Chinese Immigration* (1909) was highly regarded in both America and China. This combined an analysis of both law and history to document race relations between this exploited minority group and the wider White community. A further study of a minority people, *The Rain Makers: Indians of Arizona and New Mexico* (1929), provided important photographic and other documentation of a group much neglected and oppressed at the time. In 1912 she published a systematic and comprehensive, but also controversial, study of gender—*Why Women are So*. In this she argued that women are socially constructed as a distinct group, and that their life-chances are seriously curtailed and constrained by dress, language, and the market place: all factors that were subsequently addressed by second-wave *feminism. Coolidge was an active leader of the San Francisco women's struggle for the vote, and believed that sociology could and should play an active part in documenting social problems and inequalities, which could then inform and encourage reform and improvement. Passionately concerned with women's poverty, she carried out many analyses of old age, poverty, catastrophic disasters, and the workings of the criminal courts.

cooperative An alternative form of organization to the *capitalist system, found in some decentralized forms of *socialism, but also sustainable on a successful basis within capitalism itself. There are two kinds: producer (or worker) cooperatives, which constitute a form of worker self-management, and consumer cooperatives, in which customers share in the profits in relation to purchases. The cooperative movement grew out of ideas formulated in the early 19th century by Robert Owen in Britain and Charles Fourier in France, and has spread throughout the world, with particular success in the United States. Cooperatives include farming cooperatives (for marketing, processing, and purchasing), retailer-owned wholesale cooperatives, mutual insurance companies, credit and banking cooperatives, housing cooperatives, consumer goods shops, and group health and medical schemes. Historically, cooperatives tend to have experienced difficulty in raising funds for long-term investment, ensuring that an adequate proportion of the profit is reinvested rather than distributed among the membership, and reconciling their democratic ideals with management expertise.

co-optation A term devised by Philip Selznick (see *TVA and the Grass Roots*, 1949), to refer to a political process found especially in formally democratic or committee-governed organizations and systems, as a way of managing opposition and so preserving stability and the organization. Non-elected outsiders are 'co-opted' by being given formal or informal power on the grounds of their status, specialist knowledge, or potential ability to threaten essential commitments or goals.

core–periphery model *See* CENTRE-PERIPHERY MODEL.

corporate capitalism *See* CAPITALISM.

corporate crime Frequently (and unhelpfully) used interchangeably with the term *white-collar crime, corporate crime should be seen as distinct. It is crime committed on behalf of or by a *corporation, not against it (though competing businesses may be the victims). The term does not necessarily mean that criminal law is violated. The insight offered is into the ways in which corporate businesses can cause major social, financial, and physical harm, yet face few or no legal sanctions. Such crime can be intentional or the result of indifference or inefficiency. Examples include price-fixing cartels, long-term fraud, industrial accidents, and pollution. There have recently been extensions of this idea to that of corporate manslaughter, where a corporation is held responsible for the death of customers or service users.

corporate groups *See* CORPORATE SOCIETY.

corporate society (corporatism) These terms refer to a type of society in which various large-scale corporate organizations with powerful vested interests are involved in the economic, social, and political decision-making process. Examples of groups of people acting jointly in their interest include business groups, the *professions, *trade unions, and *pressure groups. Sociologists have usually concentrated their attention on economic *corporations, especially large multinational corporations that have grown over the course of the 20th century, and on the extent to which they enjoy control over the economy or are themselves controlled by democratic processes.

The evidence suggests that business corporations have considerable power in the *market, but they may also be constrained by competition in the market, and by the *state. Corporate groups are interdependent. In the 1970s, it was argued that a corporatist relationship existed between employers' associations and trade unions, which, along with the state, were jointly involved in economic decision-making. Corporatism was especially evident in West Germany, the Scandinavian countries, and to a lesser extent Britain. Corporate groups were said to enjoy a say in making national policy decisions in return for controlling their members. In relation to the trade unions, there has been much debate as to whether corporatism was a form of working-class *incorporation, or an expression of worker power. In the harsher economic climate of the 1980s, however, corporatism all but disappeared, especially in Britain, when trade unions were almost entirely excluded from the policy process. The various interpretations of corporatism are spelled out fully in *Order and Conflict in Contemporary Capitalism* (1984), edited by John H. Goldthorpe.

It should be noted that theories of corporatism are sometimes called 'neocorporatist theory', to distinguish them from the *normative theory of the corporate state espoused in the early 20th century by the Roman Catholic Church, Italian Fascist Party, and others.

corporation The legal form of business organization for both capitalist and public enterprise, often referred to as the joint stock company or simply the company. Large corporations in the private sector involve joint-stock (share) ownership and have both individual, personal shareholders and impersonal financial shareholders. In the public sector they typically result from state nationalization and ownership of assets. The term is sometimes, and rather misleadingly, used to refer to any formal organization. *See also* CAPITALISM; MANAGERIAL REVOLUTION; OWNERSHIP AND CONTROL.

corporatism *See* CORPORATE SOCIETY.

correlation An association between *variables. If a change in the amount of one *variable is accompanied by a comparable change in the amount of another variable, and the latter change does not occur in the absence of the former change, then the variables are said to be correlated. This method of analysis was first discussed by philosopher John Stuart *Mill, and anthropologist Edward *Tylor Correlations may be positive (increase in one variable is associated with increase in the other) or negative (increase in one variable is associated with decrease in the other). When two (or more) variables are correlated, but there is no causal link between them, then the correlation is said to be *spurious: both may be affected by a third variable. *See also* ASSOCIATION COEFFICIENTS; CAUSAL MODELLING; CURVI-LINEAR RELATIONSHIP; MULTIVARIATE ANALYSIS; SPURIOUS CORRELATION.

correspondence analysis A statistical method for analysing cross-tabulated data by finding a geometrical representation of the structures of the table. Such tables might combine, for example, social class and music preference. The rows and columns of the table are depicted as clouds of points in a multidimensional space, one point for each row or column, as shown in the Figure. Well-known applications of correspondence analysis are the diagrams presented by Pierre Bourdieu in *Distinction*, 1979).

For recent authoritative presentations of the principles and applications see Benzécri, *Correspondence Analysis Handbook* (1992) and Brigitte Le Roux and Henry Rouanet, *Geometric Data Analysis* (2004).

cost-benefit analysis A method of setting out the factors that need to be taken into account in making choices about major investments in public-sector projects. The objective is to assign monetary values and so weight all costs and all benefits, social and economic, so that one can see clearly whether the benefits exceed the costs of a venture. The method is normally applied to major public projects such as a new dam, airport, urban motorway, university, or a scheme for the unemployed, but the approach could in principle be applied to other private-sector investments or personal choices, as an aid to decision-making. The appraisal differs from commercial project appraisal because costs and benefits to all members of society are included—not only the monetary expenditures and receipts of the investor—so that, for example, environmental costs and the costs of social severance are included with other diffuse social costs and benefits.

The main difficulty with cost-benefit analysis is how to assign monetary values to social costs and benefits, especially when these affect different social groups, users and non-users, of the proposed facility. The objection most often raised is that it gives a spurious air of economic rationality and objectivity to decisions that are necessarily social and political in nature.

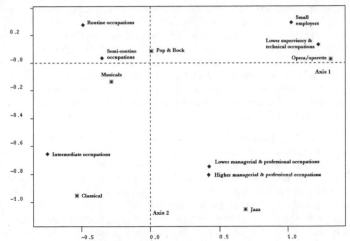

Correspondence analysis. The association between social class position and music preferences

counter culture When *subcultures specifically stand in direct opposition to the dominant *culture of the society in which they are located, rejecting its most important values and norms and endorsing their opposites, they are sometimes termed 'contra-cultures' or 'counter-cultures'. The term was popularly applied to the student and hippy cultures identified with the youth conflicts around 1968, but it can have a wider usage.

counterfactual A proposition that states what would have followed had the actual sequence of events or circumstances been different. Thus, to claim that the Battle of Alamein altered the outcome of the Second World War is to imply the counterfactual that, had victory in the desert actually gone to the defeated German forces, then the Allies would have lost the War.

Counterfactual reasoning is inherent in causal explanation: the identification of a *cause implies that, other things being equal, things would have happened differently in its absence. It is frequently claimed that any meaningful and falsifiable sociological proposition will necessarily have a corresponding counterfactual. In practice, however, it may be difficult to assess the plausibility of the counterfactual claim, which can often be supported only indirectly by comparative analysis of similar circumstances elsewhere that (for some identifiable reason) yielded different outcomes.

Many sociological claims (for example those relating to the allegedly functional consequences of certain social institutions) are notoriously without counterfactuals. If the argument is put that the state in capitalist society serves the long-term interests of capital, then it is difficult to see how this statement can be subject to *falsification, unless one can specify both what the precise interests of capital are and what would count as evidence of the state acting against these interests.

counter-movement An organized response to a *social movement, with the purpose of blocking the movement's activities, resisting change, and presenting alternative points of view. Counter-movements may be spontaneous expressions of public feeling, or fronts for interest groups. *Feminism, for example, has given rise to several counter-movements in the United States, including Pro-Life (anti-abortion), and the successful anti-ERA (Equal Rights Amendment) movement. Other examples of counter-movements include those against fascism and racism in many European countries, and conservative movements against the dismantling of communism in the former USSR.

countervailing power A term first used by American economist John Kenneth Galbraith in *American Capitalism: The Concept of Countervailing Power* (1952) to describe one aspect of the *power system in a mature capitalist *democracy. In the theory of *pluralism, powerful groups and interests maintain a rough balance, none being strong enough to dominate all the others. In *mixed economies, Galbraith proposed that a similar balance of powers had superseded *laissez-faire capitalism and pure *market competition. Trade unions, consumer organizations, trade associations and government regulation formed a system of countervailing power against the monopolistic powers of big business (*see* MONOPOLY). This idea was important in theories of *corporatism.

coup d'état A violent and immediate seizure of *state power, usually by armed forces, and with the implication of being undemocratic and unconstitutional. Successful examples occurred in Greece in 1967, Chile in 1973, and in Turkey in 1980, and Pakistan in 2006. An unsuccessful attempt was made at a *coup d'état* in Russia in 1991. The best overview will be found in Edward Luttwak's *Coup d'État* (1968).

covert observation *Participant observation carried out without the explicit awareness and agreement of the social unit being studied. This entails finding some self-explanatory role within the research setting in order to mask the researcher's true purpose. It may be used because research access to the social unit would normally be denied, or to ensure that the researcher's presence does not affect the behaviour of those being observed. Examples include Laud Humphries's covert observations of homosexual encounters (*Tearoom Trade*, 1970), and work by Leon Festinger and his colleagues, who observed a religious cult by pretending to become adherents to its beliefs (*When Prophecy Fails*, 1956). The method raises potentially serious ethical problems. Martin Bulmer's *Social Research Ethics* (1982) examines the merits and dilemmas of covert participant observation, as illustrated by a variety of well-known American and British studies. *See also* RESEARCH ETHICS.

Cox, Oliver Cromwell (1901–74) An African American sociologist from Trinidad who produced a controversial critique of the caste interpretation of race relations that had gained popularity in post-war American sociology. In his book *Caste, Class, and Race* (1948) he stressed the need to consider the link between racism and the social and economic system. By tracing racism to the origins and dynamics of capitalism as a world system he provided a materialist interpretation of race. He also wrote *Foundations of Capitalism* (1959), *Capitalism and American Leadership* (1962), and *Capitalism as a System* (1964).

credential inflation *See* DIPLOMA DISEASE.

credentialism A process of social selection in which *class advantage and social *status are linked to the possession of academic qualifications. Credentialism expresses the ideology that qualifications reflect either the expertise or attributes necessary for social ascent or the occupancy of certain roles. It is said that an unintended consequence of credentialism, especially in developing societies, is credential inflation or so-called *diploma disease. For a case study of the United States see Randall Collins, *The Credential Society* (1979). *See also* MERITOCRACY.

crime A crime is held to be an offence that goes beyond the personal and into the public sphere, breaking prohibitory rules or laws, to which legitimate punishments or sanctions are attached, and that requires the intervention of a public authority (the state or a local body). Ideally, the latter administers a formal system for dealing with crime, and employs representative officers (for example a police force) to act on its behalf. In terms of law and jurisprudence, being guilty of the committing of a criminal act usually involves evil intent or conscious recklessness, although there are some exceptions in law. Where such conscious intent can be shown to be missing (as, for example, in the cases of children or the insane) then the offence is not a crime and will not attract the usual punishment (although some form of detention or therapeutic treatment may follow).

For crime to be known as such it must come to the notice of, and be processed through, an administrative system or enforcement agency. It must be reported and recorded by the police (or other investigator); it may then become part of the *criminal statistics. Reported crimes may or may not be investigated and so may or may not result in a court case. Thus, *crime rates are socially constructed, and also leave out hidden or unreported crime. The latter can include, for example, unreported instances of domestic violence, attacks on ethnic minorities, indecent assault, and rape. Self-report studies of those involved in delinquency and criminality have confirmed that a large proportion of such behaviour is not officially recorded. A more recent wave of studies of victims of crime has also supported the view that the hidden crime figure is very large. One could also include here various forms of economic crime, from workplace theft to large-scale fraud, industrial pollution, and contravention of health and safety legislation, all of which may not be officially recorded as crime but, according to some criminologists, contribute significantly to the hidden crime that affects society. What some have termed *victimless crimes or crimes without victims (for example those involving drugs, prostitution, and illegal gambling) may break laws but go unreported because those involved enter into implicit agreements that support the transaction (see E. Schur, *Crimes Without Victims*, 1965).

A legal definition of crime may therefore not be sufficient. What a society defines as crime is socially constructed and highly relative. Its definition and accepted aetiology (or cause) can be influenced by ideas of morality (in relation to responsibility), and by religious faith (the sinful nature of crime), as well as competing scientific claims as to its origins.

The perpetration of crime can be an individual act or be talked of in organizational terms (see M. McIntosh, *The Organization of Crime*, 1975). The concept can also be loosely applied to actions that offend against a set of principles but that do not necessarily involve the breaking of a law—such as, for example, crimes of the powerful and crimes of the state. States can, of course, use the category crime and the criminal law for their own political purposes: exceptions to and expansions of the law can quickly be introduced in times of national emergency or in the interests of the state. The example of Nazi Germany provides a clear illustration of this process. Some anthropological and sociological studies would suggest that adopting a definition of crime derived from law, legitimated by the *state, and administered by a *bureaucracy, is *ethnocentric and narrow, and that a wider consideration of the breaking of *norms and the exercise of *social control in simpler societies without formal law is illuminating. *See also* CORPORATE CRIME; WHITE-COLLAR CRIME.

crime rate A measure of change in recorded *crime, over a given period of time, based upon *official statistics for offences or offender rates. It enables comparison of variations across offences or areas, and can be produced for selected offences (such as car theft), or as a general measure. Recorded rates are open to criticism as unreliable, reflecting personal and institutional biases, changes in law and police practice, and distortion caused by *moral panics about (for example) mugging (see S. Hall et al., *Policing the Crisis*, 1978). *See also* CRIMINAL STATISTICS; INDEX CRIME.

crimes of the state *See* POLITICAL CRIME.

criminal statistics First produced in France in 1827 and regularly for England and Wales since 1837, such statistics once held to reflect accurately the incidence of crime in society. Like all *official statistics, they are now interpreted with caution. Criminal statistics are based on notifiable (triable by jury) recorded offences, and can be drawn from aggregate data recorded by official agencies such as the police and courts, but also from criminological research studies. Limitations have been confirmed by the national British Crime Surveys (begun in 1982 and annual since 2000), which have produced data on typically unreported and hidden crime such as vandalism. Even victim surveys can have difficulty eliciting data about some crimes such as rape and sexual attack. Localized *surveys suggest that both routinely compiled criminal statistics and national survey data seriously under-record crime generally and crimes such as rape in particular.

Most sociologists recognize that the criminal statistics are the product of a complex process. Society must first define a behaviour as criminal, but the definition of a criminal act can change over time, and between jurisdictions. To enter the statistics a *crime must be reported and recorded, but the public do not report all offences, while changes in police procedure, or simple human error, can mean no record is made. The outcome of a court case, and hence the statistical recording of a conviction or otherwise, also depends upon a complex mix of ingredients. Some would argue, therefore, that criminal statistics are less a picture of the incidence of crime than an indicator of what the authorities regard as the most important offences, what the police actually find it manageable to police, and what kind of offence the court system tends to process with convictions resulting. Nevertheless, after a period of criticism and distrust, use of criminal statistics has been regaining broad acceptance. *See also* CRIME RATE; OFFICIAL STATISTICS.

(⊕) SEE WEB LINKS
- Reports on official statistics on crime in the UK.
- The US Department of Justice.

criminology Most literally, the study of *crime, its perpetrators, and its causes. Relatedly, an interest in crime prevention, and in the deterrence, treatment, and punishment of offenders (see M. Maguire et al., *The Oxford Handbook of Criminology*, 5th edn., 2012).

Approaches and theoretical traditions are diverse. Thus, criminology as the study of crime will be interested in the distribution of crime, and in the techniques and organization of crime. Criminology as the study of criminals might seek explanations for criminal behaviour in biology, psychology, or in the political economy of society. The related sociology of *law may be interested in the processes of making and breaking laws and in issues such as proportionality— making the punishment fit the crime. During the 1960s and early 1970s, a sociology of *deviance developed as a source of sociological opposition to the law-enforcement and establishment-orientation or traditional criminology, and as an epistemological critique of unquestioned assumptions about what constitutes crime. The approach placed crime within a wider framework of forms of deviance such as mental illness, political conflict, and other forms of non-conformity. In the 1970s and 1980s external and internal influences on criminology encouraged the development of critical criminology and feminist criminology (*See* CRIMINOLOGY, CRITICAL; CRIMINOLOGY, FEMINIST). The latter drew attention to the near invisibility of women in criminological work and gave significant impetus to rectifying the past neglect of victims of crime. Generally speaking, the politics of these new positions has been identified with supporting and asserting the rights of minority groups.

Sometimes seen as a sub-field of sociology, sometimes as a discipline in itself, criminology is clearly a mixed but dynamic enterprise, drawing on sociology, economics, history, psychology, and anthropology. Some commentators have suggested that its principal concern ought to be the study of the production and disruption of order: in other words, of control rather than crime. Some critics have announced the death of criminology. Yet others argue that such announcements are premature, and are promoting new directions in crime prevention, and critical and realist criminology (*see* CRIMINOLOGY, REALIST). John Hagan et al., *Criminological Controversies* (1996), provides an excellent introduction to the theoretical and empirical issues that dominate the field. *See also* LABELLING; CRIMINOLOGY, POSITIVIST.

criminology, classical Originating in 18th-century philosophy, classicism views both criminality and the administration of criminal justice as premised upon principles of rationality, choice, responsibility, and the deterrent power of punishment. It is usually associated with the work of Cesare Beccaria (1738–94; for example, see his *Dei delitti e delle pene*, 1764) and conventionally interpreted as the advocacy of a humane alternative to the arbitrary and unjustly severe sentencing and punishment of offenders. Underpinning this rationalist approach was an attempt to achieve administrative uniformity, a scale of punishments proportionate to the objective harm caused by the offence, and a belief in the aim of punishment as deterrence not retribution. A social contract is held to be agreed between the individual and society—and deemed to be a rational agreement in everyone's interest. To break the contract, and in so doing the laws of society, demonstrates free will and choice; but it is also a failure to meet one's social responsibilities, which must be met by appropriate punishment on behalf of society, in order to deter others.

Orthodox classicism was criticized for not taking account of circumstances, either of the offender, or in which the offence itself was committed. Critics maintained that, for this reason, punishment that is unvarying, or laid down according to a fixed scale, will be unjust. In this way other considerations are raised, for example the issue of causation (whether environmental or biological), and classicist free-will rationality comes eventually to be replaced by 19th-century positivist criminology (*see* CRIMINOLOGY, POSITIVIST) as a dominant perspective. However, the classical perspective has been adapted over time, and a contemporary neo-classical form remains influential in some areas—for example in debates about responsibility for crime. The best recent appraisal of the tradition is Bob Roshier's *Controlling Crime: The Classical Perspective in Criminology* (1989).

criminology, critical Also termed radical criminology, this perspective emerged in the early 1970s, as an explicitly politicized body of work. Drawing on varieties of *Marxism (and in some cases *anarchism), it adopted a *conflict perspective and placed emphasis on the oppressive power of the *state, its control over the definition and prosecution of *crime, and the exploitation of the powerless by *capital. Crime was viewed and explained as a product of the social and historical processes related to capitalism itself. The standard treatment is given in Ian Taylor, Paul Walton, and Jock Young, *The New Criminology* (1973). Critical of both the *behaviourism of positivist criminology (*see* CRIMINOLOGY, POSITIVIST) and the apolitical and narrow vision of *labelling theory, it was in its turn criticized for being too polemical, neglecting gender and race issues, romanticizing the criminal as someone engaged in political resistance to capital and the state, and concentrating on control and neglecting crime and its victims.

As it developed in the 1970s and 1980s, critical criminology rediscovered its own (lengthy) radical history (see, for example, G. Rusche and O. Kirchhimer, *Punishment and Social Structure*, 1939). It has allied itself with cultural studies in work around *race, racism, and the state, and studies of youth *subcultures. It has also strengthened its commitment to the abolition of prisons and greater accountability of the police, with a series of studies of institutions of the criminal justice system, including, for example, prison regimes, deaths in police custody, sexism and racism in the criminal justice process. Despite this, the approach is dismissed by some as mere Left Idealism, particularly by those involved in the development of realist criminology. *See also* CRIMINOLOGY, REALIST; NEW PENOLOGY.

criminology, environmental The study of 'crime and place'; that is, of the spatial patterning of crime and victimization (*see* VICTIMOLOGY). Early advocates included the Dutch sociologist Willem Bonger, and environmental criminology later became associated with the work of the *Chicago School on urban ecology, and with such developments in crime prevention as the notions of 'defensible space', 'target hardening', and, most recently, zero tolerance. However, with the emergence of theories of late-modernity and the *risk society, 'green' (environmental) issues have become more prominent—a context in which the notions of environmental crime and criminology tend more often to refer to crimes against the natural environment, animal life, and human communities (for example the dumping of toxic waste). This emerging area of sociological research also raises questions of human *rights and issues related to *ecopopulism.

criminology, feminist A self-conscious corrective to mainstream *criminology and *deviance theories (of various kinds), and one with the triple goals of critique, research, and reformulation of the field of inquiry. It emerged during the 1970s, partly as an outgrowth of both the *women's movement and *feminism, but also as a response to the so-called new deviance theory and critical criminology (*see* CRIMINOLOGY, CRITICAL), which, whilst aiming to be radical and innovative, had continued to ignore women. In Britain the first major publication of feminist criminology was Carol Smart's *Women, Crime and Criminology* (1976), which critically reviewed the field to that time. In the United States there was a more controversial start, with several studies suggesting that the *crime rate amongst women was increasing, alongside the development of the new feminist consciousness (see, for example, F. Adler's *Sisters in Crime*, 1975, or the somewhat less controversial R. Simon, *Women and Crime*, 1975).

Research and theory now cover a wide range of areas. The initial critiques examined the neglect of the study of women in the fields of *crime and control, and also reviewed the few studies which did exist, in order to reveal their patriarchal and sexist foundations (studies, for example, such as O. Pollak's *The Criminality of Women*). From this start, attempts were made to see if women could be incorporated into the mainstream of deviance theory, for example by asking whether *anomie theory or *subcultural theory could make sense of *gangs comprised entirely of girls.

Feminist criminology brought with it not just a revitalized interest in established areas of research, such as female offenders, differential court responses to women offenders, and women's prisons (all traditionally areas of male inquiry); it also helped to develop a number of newer areas of study. For example, it looked at the way in which women's deviance was more often prone to both sexualization and medicalization, and investigated new areas of control (such as the regulation of women's bodies, their reproductive cycles, their private and personal lives, and their sexuality). Thus, in one key feminist analysis, the thesis was propounded by Susan Brownmiller and others that fear of rape was a central mechanism in the control of women's lives (*Against her Will*, 1975).

The most general contribution of feminist criminology has been to open up the topic of gender relations for criminological study. Since crime is overwhelmingly committed by men, the fundamental question that it poses concerns the links between gender relations and crime: namely, what is it about gender that creates the tendency for crime to be a predominantly male phenomenon?

criminology, positivist A term applied—often by critics—to criminology committed to the practical application of theory and research, that claims scientific status for its quantitative methodology, and that looks for the determining causes of *crime and misbehaviour, which are held to be discoverable in the physical, genetic, psychological, or moral make-up of those pre-disposed to such acts. Hypothesis-testing, empirical investigation, classification, and categorization are its hallmarks. This perspective developed as a reaction to the view of classical criminology (*see* CRIMINOLOGY, CLASSICAL) that the criminal is a rational actor, exercising free will.

Early key figures were the Italian criminologists Enrico Ferri (*The Positive School of Criminology*, 1901), Raffaele Garofalo (1852–1934), and Cesare Lombroso (*L'uomo delinquente*, 1876). The last of these proposed that criminals exhibit certain physical stigmata, which also identify them as 'throwbacks' to some early primitive humanity or animal state. This may be termed biological positivism, and as a strand of *criminology it has remained strong, represented (for example) in work by Eleanor and Sheldon Gluecks in the 1950s linking propensity to commit crime to body size and shape, the XYY chromosome theory where the presence of an additional chromosome is held to determine criminality, or the work of Hans Eysenck, who has argued that 'criminality is obviously a continuous trait of the same kind as intelligence, or height, or weight'. Some *evolutionary psychologists have made similar claims.

Critics argue that the approach is *value-loaded rather than *objective, dealing with social constructs rather than scientific facts, and tied to a *behaviourist view of humanity that overlooks the importance of beliefs, values, and purpose.

criminology, realist Sometimes termed 'Left Realism', realist criminology emerged in the mid-1980s, in the work of Jock Young and others in Britain (see, for example, the special issue of *Contemporary Crises*, 1988). Its proponents emphasize social causes of *crime, and interaction between agencies of *social control (such as the police and courts), the offender, the victim, and the public.

They consider the restricted choices facing individuals in tightly structured circumstances, and draw strongly upon theories of relative *deprivation and *subcultures.

critical theory In sociology, critical theory is most closely associated with the Frankfurt Institute of Social Research, although its origins can be traced back through Hegelianism and Western Marxism generally. The term now describes a very diverse strand of *Marxism that, over the past fifty years or so, has drawn on a wide range of other influences including *psychoanalysis and *system theory.

The central principles of critical theory can perhaps be defined most clearly in contrast to some of the principles of 20th-century *positivism—indeed its proponents have sometimes referred to it as a negative philosophy. Critical theory employs a *dialectical method of thought, in which contradictions continually appear and disappear into new syntheses. For Hegel, history was moving relentlessly towards a rational conclusion; the Marxist appropriation of Hegel gradually eliminated the idea of inevitability and linked the process to human *praxis. The most complete statement of this view can be found in the early work of György *Lukács, whose ideas were developed into critical theory by Marxists at Frankfurt.

As opposed to the idea that knowledge comes from our sense-experience, critical theory is a form of *rationalism: that is, critical theorists maintain that the source of our knowledge and the source of our common humanity is the fact that we are all rational beings. From the idea of rationality it is possible to deduce the basic form of a rational society. By virtue of being human we all possess the quality or potentiality of rational thought. A rational society, therefore, is one in which we all participate in order to create and transform our environment. This provides us with a standard by which we can criticize societies that exist in the present: a society that excludes groups from economic and political participation, or that systematically renders groups powerless, is an irrational society. In the work of Jürgen Habermas, the major modern representative of the school, a rather different model can be found. Habermas works not from our possession of rational faculties but from the fact that we all use language. He invokes an 'ideal speech situation' in which all have equal access to information and public debate. In terms of theoretical argument, critical theory works dialectically, not juxtaposing one set of truth claims to another, but by searching out the internal contradictions and the gaps in a system of thought, and pushing these contradictions to the point where something different emerges. This is sometimes referred to as an internal critique. The fact that we are all symbol-using animals living and working together indicates an ideal in which communication is free and not distorted by social inequalities, external oppression, or internal repression.

The Frankfurt Institute of Social Research was founded in 1923 as a centre for socialist research. Its leading figures emigrated to America with the rise of Hitler and several remained there after the War. The central figures were Theodor *Adorno, Max *Horkheimer, and Herbert *Marcuse. (The classic statement is *Dialectic of Enlightenment* by Adorno and Horkheimer, 1947). A number of other famous names were associated with it, including Leo Lowenthal, Karl Wittfogel, and Erich Fromm. From the beginning, the school was critical of orthodox Marxism, offering an analysis of ideology and politics and abandoning traditional forms of economic explanation. For the classic critical theory of the founders of the Frankfurt School, the main targets were so-called instrumental reason, and the particular *totalitarian form of domination that they saw developing in modern industrial society. Instrumental reason sees the world, including other people, in terms of how it can be exploited. It involves the separation of fact from value and the relegation of values to an unimportant role in knowledge and life. This way of thinking is typical of industrial society and (according to critical theorists) is intimately linked to structures of domination. (See the collectively produced *Aspects of Sociology*, 1956.)

Frankfurt critical theory has the reputation of being pessimistic. The argument is that capitalism has managed to overcome many of its contradictions and the working class has been incorporated into the system. Marcuse saw other minority groups on the fringe of the system—ethnic groups or perhaps even students— as providing possible foci for opposition, but Adorno seemed to see few signs of hope beyond avant-garde culture, which at least forced people to think. Some of the group's most famous work—such as *The Authoritarian Personality* (Adorno et al., 1950) and Marcuse's *Eros and Civilisation* (1955)—drew on psychoanalysis to provide a theory of *ideology that explains not only how people come to be dominated but why they need to be dominated.

Habermas trained under Adorno, but achieved much of his influence after the first generation of critical theorists had died or ceased to be active. His work still maintains a critical dimension, but he differs from the first generation of critical theorists in his desire to construct a systematic social theory and his willingness to grant instrumental thought a legitimate place in his scheme. He draws on the systematic theory of Talcott *Parsons and on psychoanalysis to construct an 'emancipatory science'. This is a science that not only produces knowledge, but also enables us to become aware of and to change ourselves, and thus to remove inequalities and distortions in communication. In *Knowledge and Human Interests* (1968), he distinguishes three so-called cognitive interests that human beings share: a technical interest, in knowing and controlling our environment, which gives rise to the empirical (primarily the natural) sciences; a practical interest in being able to understand each other and work together, which gives rise to the hermeneutic sciences; and an emancipatory interest, which involves our desire to rid ourselves of distortions in understanding and communication and gives rise to the critical sciences such as psychoanalysis.

Behind this is a fairly radical revision of the orthodox Marxist view of the nature of human existence. Habermas regards work as important but sees it as generating only the first of these cognitive interests. We are also, importantly, symbol-using animals: this generates the other two. For Habermas, this means that we cannot maintain any form of economic-determinist argument, except perhaps for the historically limited period of early capitalism.

Drawing on a wide variety of disciplines he develops a broad evolutionary theory of history. Evolutionary stages are seen in terms of increasing levels of universality, each level setting new problems and offering new possibilities, and each type of society governed by a particular institutional complex. For example, tribal society is dominated by kinship institutions, and late capitalism by state institutions. His analysis of capitalism identifies a number of crises through which the system moves. In early capitalism, which he analyses in terms similar to that of Marx, economic crises present the main problem. Political intervention to deal with economic problems produces what he calls a rationality crisis, based on the impossibility of constructing a stable social order on the basis of an unstable market economy, and this in turn can lead to a legitimation crisis in which the state loses legitimacy because it cannot reconcile the conflicting demands made upon it by the requirement to plan the economic system. If, however, the state is successful in reconciling the different interests, the *work ethic and competitive drive are weakened, leading to a motivation crisis that also threatens social integration. These ideas are spelled out in *Legitimation Crisis* (1973) and in the two volumes of his *The Theory of Communicative Action* (1981).

The best introduction to critical theory is David Held's (1980) book of that name. The history of the Frankfurt School is meticulously documented in Martin Jay's *The Dialectical Imagination* (1973) and, more recently, Rolf Wiggeraus's *The Frankfurt School* (1995). Some fairly telling criticisms—especially of the work of those writers at the centre of this tradition (Horkheimer, Marcuse, Adorno, and Habermas)—are spelled out in Alex Honneth's article on 'Critical Theory' (in A. Giddens and J. Turner (eds.), *Social Theory Today*, 1987).

cross-class family *See* MOBILITY, SOCIAL.

cross cousin In kinship theory, cross cousin is a term used to describe first cousins whose related parents are of the opposite sex. In other words the mother of one is the sister of the father of the other. Societies vary as to whether they forbid or prefer marriages between cross cousins. The term was introduced by Edward *Tylor, but used extensively by Claude *Lévi-Strauss to examine the 'elementary structures of kinship', by which he meant the rules that govern preferences and proscriptions about marriage between *parallel cousins and cross cousin.

cross-sectional analysis (**cross-sectional data**) Statistical analysis that provides information on the characteristics of, and statistical relationships between, individual units of study at a specified moment in time (the moment of data collection). Sometimes referred to as a 'snapshot' approach, cross-sectional analysis cannot therefore provide information on change or processes over time, for which purpose a longitudinal study design is required. *See also* PANEL STUDY.

cross tabulation (**cross classification**) *See* CONTINGENCY TABLE.

crowding A collective or *public good is said to suffer from crowding if the ratio of individual benefit to total cost declines as the number of people who use or enjoy the good increases; in short, the more who enjoy it, the less each enjoys it. A good example is highways, public goods that become less attractive as more people use them, until the point at which people reckon it is not worth their while attempting to travel by car.

crowds First studied by early social psychologists such as Gustav Le Bon (*The Crowd*, 1895) and Gabriel *Tarde, who suggested the origins of crowd behaviour in instincts of imitation and processes of contagion. Sociological research on crowds is now part of the study of *collective behaviour. It is argued that people do things in mobs and crowds that they would not do on their own or in more formal settings. They are particularly swayed by group pressure and emotional commitment. Crowds usually involve large numbers of people, in close proximity, with a common concern. They may be focused and instrumental, having a clear goal, such as attending a rally; or they may be expressive, where the group aims to produce its own emotional or expressive satisfaction, as for example in the case of a dancing crowd at a carnival. This line is not always easy to draw, as can be seen in the case of *riots: some have argued that riots are expressive and purely emotional, an outburst of senseless rage and destruction; others have suggested riots are instrumental, being either a political statement, or a criminal act of theft and destruction. These distinctions are not always clear. Others, no less ambiguous, concern the differences between focused crowds (having a specific object or goal), and diffuse crowds (uncertain, suggestible, and in which milling and rumour is common). An important series of such clarifications may be found in Ralph H. Turner and Lewis M. Killian's *Collective Behaviour* (1957). *See also* EMERGENT NORMS.

cult In the anthropological meaning, a cult is a set of practices and beliefs of a group, in relation to a local god. In sociology, it is a small group of religious activists, whose beliefs are typically syncretic, esoteric, and individualistic. Although it is related to the concept of a *sect, the cult is not in Western society associated with mainstream *Christianity. As a scientific term, it is often difficult to dissociate the idea of a cult from its common sense pejorative significance, and it does not have a precise scientific meaning. Cultic practices appear to satisfy the needs of alienated sections of urban, middle-class youth. Cultic membership among young people is typically transitory, spasmodic, and irregular. Research suggests that young people often have multiple cult memberships. In Western societies, cults have proliferated in the post-war period, and are often associated with the *counter culture. *See also* NEW RELIGIONS; SECULARIZATION.

cultural anthropology *See* SOCIAL ANTHROPOLOGY.

cultural assimilation *See* ASSIMILATION.

cultural capital A term introduced by Pierre *Bourdieu to refer to the symbols, ideas, tastes, and preferences that can be strategically used as resources in social action. By analogy with economic *capital, such resources can be invested and accumulated and can be converted into other forms. Bourdieu sees this cultural capital as formed into a 'habitus', an embodied socialized tendency or disposition to act, think, or feel in a particular way. Thus, middle-class parents are able to endow their children with the linguistic and cultural competences that will give them a greater likelihood of success at school and at university. Working-class children, without access to such cultural resources, are less likely to be successful in the educational system. Thus, education reproduces class inequalities. Bourdieu sees the distribution of economic and cultural capital as reinforcing each other. Educational success—reflecting initial cultural capital—is the means through which superior, higher-paying occupations can be attained, and the income earned through these jobs may allow the successful to purchase a private education for their children and so enhance their chances of educational success. This 'conversion' of one form of capital into another is central to the intragenerational or intergenerational reproduction of class differences. Bourdieu recognizes a number of other forms of capital, most notably the *social capital of contacts and connections.

cultural diffusion *See* DIFFUSION.

cultural integration *See* ASSIMILATION.

cultural lag A concept and theory developed by William F. *Ogburn as part of a wider theory of technological *evolutionism. It suggests that there is a gap between the technical development of a society and its moral and legal institutions. The failure of the latter to keep pace with the former is said, in certain societies, to explain (at least some) social conflict and problems.

cultural materialism A macro-theory in anthropology that sees most aspects of human culture as explainable in material terms. Its most systematic formulation is in the two closing chapters of Marvin Harris's exhaustive survey of the development of anthropological theories of *culture (*The Rise of Anthropological Theory*, 1968). Harris, an American anthropologist, claimed that his purpose in writing the book was 'to reassert the methodological priority of the search for the laws of history in the science of man', specifically to prove that 'the analogue of the Darwinian strategy in the realm of socio-cultural phenomena is the principle of techno-environmental and techno-economic determinism'. This holds that similar technologies applied to similar environments tend to produce similar arrangements for the production and distribution of goods, which in turn tend to support similar sorts of social groupings, who organize and explain their activities in terms of similar systems of beliefs and values. In this fashion, the principle assigns research priority to the study of the material conditions of socio-cultural life, in much the same way (according to Harris) as the principle of *natural selection accords priority to the study of differential reproductive success. He claims that this makes the former a 'statement of a basic research strategy' rather than a specific 'law of society'. Critics have observed that, despite Harris's attempts to avoid *historicism and to exclude any reference to the Hegelian *dialectic, his materialist approach to the study of culture shares the same characteristics as the *materialism of Marx and Engels: namely, that as a concrete research strategy it soon falls foul of empirical findings that falsify its basic premise, and as a pseudo-law of history it must be framed at such an abstract level that it claims everything but says nothing.

cultural pluralism *See* MULTI-CULTURAL SOCIETY.

cultural relativism Cultural relativists assert that concepts are socially constructed and vary cross-culturally. These concepts may include such fundamental notions as what is considered true or morally correct, and what constitutes knowledge or even reality itself. In 'Understanding a Primitive Society' (*American Philosophical Quarterly*, 1964), Peter Winch argues that our sense of reality is a social construction, based upon the prevailing discourse of a society. Thus, cultural relativists reject the *rationalist and universal premises of grand theories such as *functionalism, *Marxism, or Freudian *psychoanalysis.

Cultural relativism draws on the tradition of linguistic philosophers such as Ludwig *Wittgenstein and Willard Quine, and on the work of linguists and anthropologists such as Benjamin Whorf and Edward Sapir. These writers have contended that if *language constructs the world, then reality is not independently existing, but is shaped by cultural and linguistic categories. Two cultures can thus be incommensurable since their worldviews are based on quite different languages. Paul Feyerabend (in *Against Method*, 1975) says that there are cultures so different from the West that they are incomprehensible to outsiders, who therefore cannot translate them into their own terms. More recently, the arguments of postmodernists have also advanced claims of cultural relativism.

This has major implications for the study of non-Western societies. If importing a Western rationalist approach is *ethnocentric, then we must understand cultural patterns in their own terms, adopting an insider's view of the culture. *Ethnography thus becomes a process of uncovering the meanings by which people construct reality and translating this knowledge into the discourse of the field-worker's own society. *See also* INTERPRETATION; SAPIR-WHORF HYPOTHESIS.

cultural studies A developing area of academic interest, sometimes taught as a distinctive university or college qualification, that lies at the interface between social sciences such as sociology and humanities such as literature. It is principally concerned with the nature of mass culture and the workings of culture industries. Among other things, therefore, it embraces the study of *popular culture, *communication, *consumer society, the *mass media, *leisure, *postmodernism, and aspects of literary and sociological theory that address the construction of *identity and *ideology. Typical of those whose writings are considered central to the field (although they themselves might deny the applicability of this label to their work) would be Jürgen Habermas, Stuart Hall, Pierre Bourdieu, Jean Baudrillard, and Jean-François Lyotard.

As a field of interest, cultural studies seems to lack a distinctive or coherent disciplinary core, and over the years it has borrowed both its substantive topics and theoretical orientations increasingly freely from other areas of scholarship. Recently, some critics have claimed that it now exerts a pernicious influence on teaching and research in sociology, political science, and social history, by encouraging them to abandon structural concerns. However, proponents argue that cultural studies has revitalized sociology: first, by exposing its obsession with concepts related to the world of production and, second, by alerting researchers to the real concerns of ordinary people in the contemporary world.

It is clear that British (and to a lesser extent American) sociology took a pronounced renewal of interest in cultural matters in the early 1990s. A good overview of some of the key issues and debates in this arena will be found in *The Polity Reader in Cultural Theory* (1993). *See also* CONSUMPTION, SOCIOLOGY OF; KNOWLEDGE, SOCIOLOGY OF.

cultural theory This term has been applied to diverse attempts to conceptualize and understand the dynamics of *culture. Historically these have involved arguments about the relationship between culture and nature, culture and society (including material social processes), the split between high and low culture, and the interplay between cultural tradition and cultural difference and diversity. Cultural theory has also been marked by an engagement with concepts that have often been taken to cover some of the same ground signified by the notion of culture itself. Prominent here have been the concepts of *ideology and consciousness (particularly its collective forms).

The works of Raymond Williams (*The Long Revolution*, 1961) and E. P. Thompson (*The Making of the English Working Class*, 1963) have been particularly influential in the development of post-war British cultural theory. Williams's emphasis on culture as a 'whole way of life' and Thompson's emphasis on culture as the way in which groups 'handle' the raw material of social and material existence opened up new ways of thinking about culture—in particular uncoupling the concept from a narrow literary and aesthetic reference. Both Williams and Thompson studied the lived dimension of culture and the active and collective process of fashioning meaningful ways of life.

The so-called culturalist reading of the term developed by both Thompson and Williams was subsequently challenged by other more obviously structuralist interpretations. These emphasized the external symbolic structures of culture, as embodied in cultural languages and *cultural codes, rather than its lived forms. In this formulation culture could be read as a signifying system through which the social world was mapped. The structuralist version of cultural theory was also strongly informed by Louis *Althusser's version of Marxism. Althusser offered a reworking of Marxist theories of ideology which gave greater scope to the efficacy of the ideological realm. In particular he emphasized the *relative autonomy of the ideological or cultural domain whilst holding on to the principle of the ultimately determining character of economic relations and processes.

The concern to recognize the efficacy of cultural practices in Althusser's writings was further developed within cultural theory by the appropriation of the ideas of Antonio Gramsci. Gramsci's work opened up new ways of conceptualizing the role of culture and cultural practices in class formations and class alliances and, in particular, gave great weight to the role of culture in securing forms of political and moral leadership and authority (*hegemony). The influence of Gramsci's ideas was particularly important in helping cultural theory move beyond the impasse created by the tensions between competing culturalist and structuralist perspectives in the 1970s (see, for example, Stuart Hall et al., *Policing the Crisis*, 1978).

As Gramsci's importance has waned within cultural theory, so that of Michel *Foucault has increased. A central thrust of Foucault's influence has been to shape a more discursive understanding of cultural languages and of the interconnection between power and representation (see Sean Nixon, *Hard Looks*, 1996). Foucault's influence has also been obvious in arguments about the historically specific character of culture and its development as both an object and instrument of government (see L. Grossberg et al. (eds.), *Cultural Studies*, 1992).

The interplay between race, ethnicity, and culture has also emerged as a central concern of contemporary cultural theory. This has often been via a critique of the forms of ethnicity assumed within the tradition of British cultural theory associated with Williams and Thompson—or what Paul Gilroy has termed the morbid fascination with Englishness (see his *Ain't No Black in the Union Jack*, 1987). It has also challenged the incipient *nationalism of conceptions of culture which link it to particular bounded national territories. In place of this, writers such as Gilroy have emphasized instead the transnational movement and mixing of cultures. Gilroy's notion of the 'Black Atlantic' represents an attempt to envisage cultural processes outside the restrictions imposed by nationally delimited conceptions of culture. In this sense, it has much in common with Edward Said's work on orientalism, which examines not only the internal dynamics but also the external determinants of cultures. In Said's *Orientalism* (1978), Western conceptions of culture and civilization are depicted as having been formed against a process of naming and symbolically subordinating the Oriental.

Feminist arguments have also exerted an important influence on recent cultural theory. Looming large here has been the interplay between feminism and psychoanalysis. This has led to much discussion about the ways in which gender identities are formed within cultural languages and through cultural practices. Recent work on memory, fantasy, and gender performance has been especially suggestive (see P. Adams and E. Cowie, *The Women in Question*, 1993; and J. Butler, *Bodies that Matter*, 1993). *See also* CLASS CONSCIOUSNESS; FALSE CONSCIOUSNESS.

cultural transmission theory *See* SUBCULTURE.

culture When social scientists use the term culture they tend to be talking about a less restrictive concept than that implied in everyday speech. In social science, culture is all that in human society which is socially rather than biologically transmitted, whereas the commonsense usage tends to point only to the arts. Culture is thus a general term for the symbolic and learned aspects of human society, although some animal *behaviourists now assert that certain primates have at least the capacity for culture.

Social anthropological ideas of culture are based to a great extent on the definition given by Edward *Tylor in 1871, in which he referred to a learned complex of knowledge, belief, art, morals, law, and custom. Some writers make distinctions within this category. German usage distinguishes between *Kultur* and *Zivilisation*, the former referring to symbols and values, while the latter refers to technical, economic, and political ideas and organization.

Archaeological usage, though acknowledging the wholeness of human societies, makes a distinction between material culture (or artefacts) and the non-material or adaptive culture transmitted by teaching and tradition. Only material culture is accessible to archaeology, whereas adaptive culture is the subject of history, sociology, and anthropology.

19th-century anthropologists, such as Tylor and Lewis Henry *Morgan, saw culture as a conscious creation of human rationality. Civilization and culture, in this conception, show a progressive tendency towards what are regarded as higher moral values, and this enabled the Victorian mind to construct a hierarchy of cultures or civilizations that provided a rationale for colonial activities by apparently higher-order Western civilizations.

Contemporary ideas of culture arose through the work of field anthropologists such as Franz *Boas, around the turn of the century, and tend towards *relativism. The intention is to describe, compare, and contrast cultures, rather than rank them, although Boas and some later North American anthropologists have also been interested in the processes by which cultural traits may be borrowed or otherwise transmitted between societies. This has led to the development of the idea of culture areas, and a comparative ethnography of North America, both of which are largely absent in British social anthropology. For the latter, culture is generally taken to mean a collection of ideas and symbols that is generally distinguished in the discipline from social *structure, and this distinction is also central to European and North American sociological usages of the term.

In cultural anthropology, analysis of culture may proceed at three levels: learned patterns of behaviour; aspects of culture that act below conscious levels (such as the deep level of grammar and syntax in language, of which a native language speaker is seldom aware); and patterns of thought and perception, that are also culturally determined. An interesting review of approaches to culture is Adam Kuper's *Culture: The Anthropologists' Account* (1999). *See also* CONSUMPTION, SOCIOLOGY OF; CULTURE AND PERSONALITY SCHOOL; CULTURAL RELATIVISM; CULTURAL STUDIES; CULTURAL THEORY; EVOLUTIONARY UNIVERSALS; PARSONS; POPULAR CULTURE.

culture and personality school A development in the study of *socialization that arose principally in the United States in the 1930s. The theory combined elements of psychology, anthropology, and sociology, but principally involved the application of *psychoanalytic principles to *ethnographic material. Drawing on Freudian theory (see Freud's *Civilization and its Discontents*, 1930), it emphasized the cultural moulding of the *personality and focused on the development of the individual. Culture-and-personality theorists argued that personality types were created in socialization, and they placed particular emphasis on child-rearing practices such as feeding, weaning, and toilet training. The perspective is best demonstrated in the work of anthropologists such as Gregory Bateson, Ruth *Benedict, Geoffrey Gorer, and Margaret *Mead. Mead, in particular, has become associated with the main tenet of the school: that different cultures (or societies) produce different personality types as a result of different socialization practices. Her controversial findings—notably that *sex roles are culturally rather than biologically determined—influenced a generation of American sociologists to re-examine their cultural assumptions about the roles of men and women in society.

Numerous other studies offer variations on this theme. In *The Psychological Frontiers of Society* (1945), Abram Kardiner looked at the way in which personality types are present in cultural patterns. Kardiner and his colleagues argued that religion and politics are screens on to which the basic personality-orientation of a society is projected. In 'Anthropology and the Abnormal' (*Journal of General Psychology*, 1934), Ruth *Benedict examined social deviance, and drew attention to the fact that a highly valued personality type in one society may be considered deviant in another. She argued that different societies have different means for dealing with whatever behaviour is considered abnormal—and that this changes over time.

The culture and personality school was particularly important in the wartime National Character Studies, undertaken in an attempt to understand the character (and hence the strategies) of the Axis Powers, one result of which was Benedict's classic account of the Japanese, *The Chrysanthemum and the Sword* (1946). Mead's parallel account of the United States was published as *And Keep Your Powder Dry* (1942). After 1950 greater emphasis was placed on the use of statistics in demonstrating connections between child-rearing practices, personality, and *culture. Thus, in *Child Training and Personality* (1953), John Whiting and Irving Child used a large cross-cultural sample to show the alleged connection between experiences of early childhood and systems of curing illness.

In the post-war period, the School came increasingly to be criticized for exaggerating the congruence of personality types within any given society; for ignoring the significance of relationships that exist between cultures; and, most seriously, for reifying culture rather than viewing it as a social construction. It also proved difficult to demonstrate the connections between early child-rearing practices and later adult personality traits. Culture-and-personality studies have little currency in contemporary anthropology and sociology, even in the United States, to which their influence has mostly been confined. The influence of the School has not, however, entirely disappeared.

culture area *See* CULTURE.

culture of poverty *See* FATALISM; LEWIS, OSCAR; POVERTY.

culture, popular *See* POPULAR CULTURE.

culture shock A term coined in the 1960s to refer to the experience of those suddenly immersed in a *culture very different from their own. The term generally implies a negative reaction (physical, cognitive, and psychological) to moving within or between societies, but some authors have suggested it may have benefits for the individual concerned. Those who become partially, or fully, immersed in a new culture may suffer return culture shock when re-entering their own society.

curriculum The curriculum comprises the subjects and courses taught in any educational institution. It is a formal statement, by the institution, of what is to be learned. In English and Welsh schools, following the 1988 Education Reform Act, the curriculum is determined nationally and consists of a number of core subjects that must be studied by all school students (See P. Wexler, *Sociology of the Curriculum*, 1991). *See also* HIDDEN CURRICULUM.

curvilinear relationship A relationship between two or more variables that is depicted graphically by anything other than a straight line. For example an accelerating rate of increase in deaths with age is represented by a steepening curve. Curvilinear relationships are very variable, and more complex and less easily identified than simple linear relationships. *See also* CORRELATION.

customs Customs are established ways of thinking and acting in societies. They are the cultural traditions that *Sumner referred to as the folkways. They have been studied at various levels. *Ethnographic accounts detail the routine minutiae of daily life. At a greater level of complexity the rules implicit in these routines can be analysed and cultural patterns discerned in repetitive acts. Finally, custom can be taken to mean the distinctive nature of a whole *culture, or of a culture area (a geographical area in which the inhabitants share a common culture—which may embrace a number of *subcultures).

cyber ethnography A relatively new method of data collection that involves applying the techniques of classic anthropology and ethnography to the online world. It has developed as the Internet has become a more widely used tool of social research, both as a means for gathering data and as an object of study in its own right. Cyber ethnographers conduct largely qualitative studies of online communities and of the kind of interaction that goes on in cyberspace. This might involve participant observation in chat rooms, multi-user domains, email distribution lists, forums, and bulletin boards, as well as techniques of online interviewing, conferencing and other types of computer-mediated communication.

The overall aim of cyber-ethnographic studies is to immerse oneself in the virtual world that the participants have created, in order to understand how they experience social interaction and devise ways of regulating social order. Some examples of this are the work of Katie ward (*sic*) on two feminist online communities (in *Sociological Research Online*, 1999), Paul Hodkinson's study of *Goth: Identity, Style and Subculture* (2002), and a study by Nicholas Pleace et al. of an alcoholics' support group (*Sociological Research Online*, 2000).

The unique position of the cyber-ethnographer in relation to their informants makes this method quite distinct from ethnographies of social settings in the offline world. ward identifies some of the methodological differences between the two and their implications for social epistemology. First, the environment in which the researcher is immersed is not pre-determined and stable; online communities are constantly redefined as members enter and leave, and so tend to have a fluctuating membership. This means that the researcher may have only a transitory relationship with their participants and must be reflexive about the way that their own presence throughout the study might change the dynamics of the group. Secondly, the more anonymous character of interaction in cyberspace and its ephemeral nature over time may mean that participants become 'disinhibited', disclosing more personal information than they would in face-to-face interviews. It also opens up the possibility of identity deception, both by participants (see Judith Donath in P. Kollock and M. Smith (eds.), *Communities in Cyberspace*, 1996) and by the researcher, who can 'lurk' invisibly in virtual communities while 'harvesting' their data. Both of these issues have serious ethical implications, and there is an ongoing debate about the perceived privacy of some online encounters versus their public accessibility (see S. King in *The Information Society*, 1996). Nevertheless, cyber ethnography has created an original and effective way of finding out about interaction online, and so has increased our understanding of a relatively new phenomenon of social life.

cybernetic hierarchy *See* Parsons; social system.

cybernetics The study of communication among machines, animals, and men, particularly the role of feedback information in the process of control. In the social sciences, the theory links *social control closely to the nature and function of *communication, and has been deployed most widely in the study of formal organizations. *See also* Parsons; social system.

cybersociety The mesh ('space' or 'virtual reality') of electronically based communications created by the world-wide network of computer users. Although it is conventional to distinguish between 'information technology' (the term applied to any computer-based application or process, such as is found in the case of office automation), on one hand, and 'telecommunications technology' (for example fax machines or video conferencing), on the other, the multi-media integration of almost all technologies of communication via computers has effectively made this distinction redundant. The newer terminology of cyberspace refers to both developments.

Computer-mediated social interaction became increasingly prominent in the organization of everyday life in the late 20th century. Electronic mail and the creation of the *Internet have made possible such things as online shopping, Web-based 'chat-rooms', and personalized video pornography in the home. The implications of this explosion in communications for work, leisure, and politics are a matter of controversy among sociologists (see, for example, Steven G. Jones (ed.), *CyberSociety*, 1994).

Curiously, one of the most thought-provoking statements about the possible sociological characteristics of a thoroughgoing cybersociety is the novel *The Naked Sun*, written by the prolific science-fiction author Isaac Asimov and first published (in 1956) while computer development was still in its infancy. The story features a distant world in which people 'view' each other remotely via 'trimensional images' and are only exceptionally involved in direct face-to-face physical contact. It also contains a good deal of speculation about the role of sociologists in this and other no less abnormal societies (in Asimov's novel, people on Earth, by contrast, live underground in vast over-populated caves of steel, and are terrified of open spaces and contact with fresh air), and includes the immortal line, spoken in response to the need to send an Earthly representative to other planets in order to save the human species, that the ruling authorities 'had better send a sociologist'.

cyborg A term introduced by electronic engineers Manfred Clynes and Nathan Kline in the 1960s to refer to cybernetically enhanced organisms (*see* CYBERNET-ICS) capable of surviving in extraterrestrial environments. It was argued that advances in engineering would make it possible to alter or replace human functions with mechanical parts and computer-controlled systems. This idea inspired much science fiction writing, including *Robocop*, the bionic man Steve Austin in *The Six Million Dollar Man*, Luke Skywalker in *Star Wars*, *Inspector Gadget*, and the Borgs in *Star Trek*. More prosaically, the term came to be applied to those fitted with the various mechanical modifications that were actually becoming possible, such as artificial legs, visual sensors, and cochlear implants.

The word was taken up by Donna Haraway in 1985 (reprinted in *Simians, Cyborgs and Women: The Reinvention of Nature*, 1991) to refer to the growing integration of human beings into mechanical systems that makes us all cyborgs. Through reliance on mechanical divisions of labour, systems of transport, networks of telecommunications, and systems of bio-engineering, the boundaries between humans and machines have become difficult to draw. Advances in technology become ways in which human bodies are socially constructed and reconstructed, taking us further away from any idea of essential biological attributes of sex and race.

cycle of deprivation A theory popularized in the 1970s to explain the persistence of poverty and other forms of socio-economic disadvantage through generations. The theory postulates that 'family pathology' is the principal mechanism for transmitting social *deprivation intergenerationally, and that this explains the persistence of bad housing, low education attainment, and unemployment in poorer households and communities. In essence the argument is that deprivation and welfare dependency are, if not quite the fault of the poor, then certainly without serious structural origins—an interpretation that has much in common with the earlier culture of poverty (*see* FATALISM) thesis, though placing less emphasis on individual and community pathologies. Extensive empirical research has largely undermined the credibility of the thesis (see M. Rutter and N. Madge, *Cycles of Disadvantage*, 1976).

cyclical change *See* BUSINESS CYCLE.

cyclical unemployment *See* UNEMPLOYMENT.

dangerous classes A term taken from the title of the book (*The Dangerous Classes of New York*) published in 1872 by the American social reformer Charles Loring Brace. His 'dangerous classes' included the vagabonds, waifs, predatory criminals, vagrants, and prostitutes that emerged out of the poor *underclass in late 19th-century New York City. Sociologists and criminologists have sometimes argued that contemporary policing policies (for example in relation to drugs control) are still informed by this concept, and contain a hidden agenda which aims either to identify 'public enemies' who can be blamed for various economic and social problems, or to suppress members of today's 'dangerous classes' (immigrants, youths, various minority groups) in the interests of public order and security (see, for example, Diana Gordon, *The Return of the Dangerous Classes*, 1994).

dark figure of crime The term 'dark figure' came to prominence in the 1960s and 1970s, to describe the unknown mass of unreported and unrecorded offences, which in turn exposed the limitations of using official statistics to measure crime. The traditional method of gathering data is based on those crimes recorded by the police and the courts, a practice that dates back to the 19th century, as European governments sought to compile detailed information over many different aspects of their populations' lives. In England and Wales, the statistical series compiled annually by the Home Office from data returned by criminal justice agencies has constituted the 'official statistics' since the 1850s. Despite occasional changes their format has remained remarkably consistent over most of this time.

Up until the late 1950s the official crime rates remained generally low, after which point the rates began to soar, generating much political debate and media attention. Crime quickly became a major focus of public concern and policy making, at which point the problems posed by the extent and character of the 'dark figure' took shape. The use of the term 'dark' was significant, not simply because it is 'obscure' but also as 'it is construed as malign, the combination of these attributes occasioning considerable anxiety' (C. Valier, 'Criminal Detection and the Weight of the Past: Critical Notes on Foucault, Subjectivity and Preventative Control', *Theoretical Criminology*, 2001: 432). Furthermore, sociologists were highlighting how official agencies were, by processing some events as criminal and not others, themselves acting as key filters and primary definers of the crime problem.

From the late 1960s in the USA initially, but later elsewhere around the world, interviewing citizens about their personal experiences of crime became commonplace. In addition to trying to obtain a more accurate view of victimization levels these national household crime surveys provide information on the public's belief and attitudes towards crime, policing, punishment and prevention. The British Crime Survey (BCS) was first carried out in 1982 and has been repeated at regular intervals since. Now it is an annual survey and conducted on a rolling basis, with a significantly enlarged sample size. The key aim was to find out the extent of unreported crime, while challenging popular perceptions of the stereotypical crime victim and to highlight the relatively low risks of serious crime.

Accompanying national surveys were an increasing number of local crime surveys, which in the UK were conducted in various places, like Bristol, Sheffield, Merseyside, Islington, and Edinburgh, from the 1980s onwards. These surveys sought to rectify what were seen as the two main deficiencies of the BCS—its underestimation of the impact of criminal victimization and its inability to uncover 'hidden' crimes like domestic violence. By using national averages, the BCS highlighted that a large proportion of the dark figure was composed of offences that were perceived by the victim as trivial, and that was their reason for not reporting them to the police. However, findings in high-crime areas of inner cities reveal that the major reason why victims did not report crimes was because they felt the police would be unable to do anything. In these settings a 'large number of victimisations, therefore, genuinely belong to the dark figure as defined by the victims and *are* seen as a matter for the police' (Jock Young, 'Risk of Crime and Fear of Crime', in M. Maguire and J. Pointing (eds.), *Victims of Crime: A New Deal?* 1988: 167). Here the drive is to explain victimization through a form of class analysis, which in some early versions is thoroughly 'genderless', and underplayed the extent of racism and homophobia experienced in these social worlds. These issues are explored in J. Goodey, *Victims and Victimology: Research, Policy and Practice*, 2005).

Feminists challenged the conceptual thinking underpinning these surveys for not adequately grasping women's experiences and fears of sexual danger. By using alternative research methodologies significant empirical evidence was unearthed that debunked 'the myth of the safe home' and the extent of 'ordinary violence' women regularly face and manage across public and private domains (see Betsy Stanko, *Everyday Violence*, 1990). Such work was aimed at discovering the size of the dark figure of sexual crimes and domestic violence, while revealing how women actively and routinely negotiate risk and danger in their daily lives. Others are critical as these surveys are incapable of uncovering reliable data on the extent to which people are harmed by crimes of the powerful, which are often hidden or difficult to detect, such as deaths caused by poisoning from corporate pollution. Despite these difficulties, victim surveys have played an important role in providing better estimates of the extent of crime than those found in the official statistics, while giving important insights into how victims experience crime and the criminal justice system.

Darwinism (Social Darwinism) Darwinism is the belief in the theory of evolution by means of natural selection, developed separately by Charles Darwin and Alfred Wallace, and subsequently popularized in Darwin's two great works on evolution: *On the Origin of Species by Means of Natural Selection* (1859) and *The Descent of Man* (1871). The original version of the theory proposed that, since population numbers remained stable whilst reproduction occurred at a higher than replacement rate, there must be some systematic selective mechanism involved in the process, by which certain individuals perished and others survived. The mechanism advanced was that of 'natural selection': those individuals better suited to their environment survive, whilst others who are less well adapted die. Over time this process results in species formation. Not until thirty or so years later was the actual mechanism of heredity—the individual *gene— widely recognized and incorporated into existing theory to inaugurate modern neo-Darwinism.

At the time of its writing, Darwin and Wallace's theory formed just one thread in an existing discourse about evolution more generally, which included the social *evolutionism of Herbert *Spencer. Many writers on society, influenced by Spencer, eagerly absorbed Darwin's 'scientific' theory into their own writings, and it was Spencer himself who coined the phrase (commonly attributed to Darwin) 'the survival of the fittest', to explain the historical development of societies. Towards the end of the 19th century there arose, in the United States and Britain, a movement based upon the incorporation of notions of survival of the fittest into social theory. The most well-known manifestation of this Social Darwinist movement was *eugenics. In its most extreme manifestation, members of the Eugenic Society wrote pamphlets variously advocating the compulsory sterilization or incarceration of large subgroups of the population and selective breeding among the rest, in order to improve the genetic quality of the population as a whole.

More recently, Darwinian theory has been a focus of controversy, for certain scientists are now convinced that the slow process of natural selection as Darwin proposed it is insufficient to account for species formation, which (they claim) must arise from some process that operates more rapidly. It is still the case, however, that the vast majority of practising biologists and genetic scientists remain committed neo-Darwinists. Many important contributions are discussed in D. P. Crook, *Darwinism, War, and History: The Debate over the Biology of War from the Origin of Species to the First World War* (1994). *See also* GUMPLOWICZ; MILITARY AND MILITARISM.

data Plural of datum, a fact or statistic. Hence data are records of observations. These might take a number of forms: for example, scores in IQ tests, interview records, fieldwork diaries, or taped interviews. All of these provide data, that is, observations from which inferences may be drawn, via analysis.

data archive (data bank) A storage and retrieval facility or service for social scientific *data. Data archiving has grown in parallel with the development of secondary analysis as a recognized field of social research. The International Federation of Data Organizations for the Social Sciences (IFDO) was founded as recently as 1977 by four North American and seven European data archives. These archives act as lending libraries for machine-readable information collected by academics and government agencies. In the vast majority of cases, the information in question is derived from social *surveys (most data archives are in fact survey archives), although there are now archives that store the taped interviews obtained by *oral historians and others. Survey archives are often depositories for *official statistics, including *censuses, as well as non-official data-sets such as *opinion polls and academic surveys. In Britain, for example, the Economic and Social Research Council established such an archive (the UK Data Archive) at the University of Essex in the late 1960s. Similar archives exist at many universities in America and Europe.

All data archives have three primary functions: the collection, storage, and preservation of data in electronic form, the dissemination of data within the national social science community and across international boundaries, and the development of facilities and techniques of analysis to encourage the widest and most intensive possible use of data. Different archives attach different degrees of importance to these objectives: some operate a broad acquisition policy whereas others are more selective; some make access to the data-sets easy by publishing detailed catalogues of holdings; others specialize in *secondary analysis conducted by in-house researchers.

Data archives are a rich source of inexpensive and publicly available information. However, unless the data-sets held by the archive are fully documented (with complete and detailed codebooks, for example), then the researcher engaged in secondary analysis may be unaware of important limitations on how the original information was collected and how it may legitimately be used.

Davis-Moore thesis *See* FUNCTIONAL THEORY OF STRATIFICATION.

dealignment (dealignment thesis) *See* CONSUMPTION SECTORS.

death rate *See* MORTALITY rate.

de Beauvoir, Simone (1908–86) A Parisian-born philosopher and novelist who graduated from the École Normale Supérieure. She is most celebrated for her two-volume *The Second Sex* (1949), published in a new and complete translation in 2010. This was a wide-ranging analysis of the subordination of women, examining biological, historical, and ethnographic aspects. 'Woman is made not born,' she argued. Literature and belief systems revealed that women are always seen as the 'other' to man as subject. Women, she concluded, are seen as nature while man is seen as culture. Such claims rest sometimes on Eurocentric ideological assumptions disguised as universals. Many descriptions of women's existence were in effect vivid details from de Beauvoir's first-hand experience and observations of mid-century Paris and gave authenticity to her text. The book inspired thousands of women readers at a time when the question of women's subordination seemed to have disappeared. There has since been a growth of *feminist perspectives in many specialisms; there have been few such multidisciplined studies.

De Beauvoir also wrote novels, her earliest being *She Came to Stay* (1943). *The Mandarins* (1954) received the Prix Goncourt. An *existentialist philosopher, she explored moral and political dilemmas in essays and plays. There were also autobiographical volumes; for example *Memoirs of a Dutiful Daughter* (1958), *The Prime of Life* (1960), and accounts of both her mother's death (*A Very Easy Death*, 1964) and that of her long-term companion Jean-Paul *Sartre (*Adieux*, 1981).

debt bondage *See* PATRON-CLIENT RELATIONSHIP.

decarceration The process of removing people from institutions such as prisons or mental hospitals—the opposite of *incarceration. In the middle of the 20th century, this became a central feature in the reorganization of *social control, and is closely allied to programmes of *community care and *community control. The reasons for this change are discussed in Andrew Scull's controversial book *Decarceration* (1984). A linked concept is transcarceration, in which people are moved sideways from one kind of institution to another.

decentred self *See* ALTHUSSER; DESCARTES; STRUCTURALISM.

decision-making *See* COMMUNITY POWER; CONTINGENCY THEORY; COST-BENEFIT ANALYSIS; GAME THEORY; ORGANIZATION THEORY; POLITICAL PARTIES; POWER; SATISFICING.

decomposition of capital *See* OWNERSHIP AND CONTROL.

decomposition of labour The process of differentiation within the working class, such that it is no longer a homogeneous group, but is instead stratified internally by skill level. An early statement of the thesis will be found in Ralf Dahrendorf (*Class and Class Conflict in Industrial Society*, 1959), although this has now been superseded by debates about *labour-market segmentation and the extent to which the industrial proletariat of capitalist societies has always been internally divided (notably the so-called *labour aristocracy debate).

deconstruction *See* POST-STRUCTURALISM.

deduction (deductive) The use of logical rules to arrive at a set of premises from which certain conclusions must follow. Deduction begins with *theory, moves to *hypotheses derived from the theory, and then tests hypotheses via prediction and observations. This approach to testing and theory is often referred to as the hypothetico-deductive method, and since it emphasizes hypotheses, prediction, and testing, is sometimes held to be the method *par excellence* of science. *See also* INDUCTION.

defence mechanisms Unconscious psychological mechanisms, delineated by Sigmund *Freud, that the ego uses to defend the individual from unacceptable instinctual impulses which must be hidden from consciousness. Best-known are repression and *projection; others include regression, *reaction formation, intro-jection, and *displacement. Although widely criticized, these concepts have been incorporated into everyday psychological understandings. *See also* PSYCHOANALYSIS.

deference Part of the Weberian armoury of concepts dealing with *legitimacy, deference has been defined by Howard Newby (*The Deferential Worker*, 1977) as 'the form of social interaction that occurs in situations involving the exercise of traditional authority'. Submissive behaviour—but not necessarily, according to Newby, a normative endorsement of the status quo—is required on the part of the subordinate actor or group. A deferential performance need not imply deferential attitudes—merely a conforming to expectations within an unequal power relationship.

As with all concepts of legitimacy, deference requires reference both to those claiming as much as to those ascribing legitimacy to an order, and this in turn led Newby to coin the phrase 'the deferential dialectic' to describe the manner in which the superior 'defined, evaluated and managed the relationship from above', as much as it was being 'interpreted, appraised and manipulated from below'. The face-to-face nature of the deferential relationship, and the overt inequality apparent at every turn, suggest that the traditional order within which this relationship is played out is grounded in the most morally powerful of values. Property ownership, with its hereditary overtones as in the case of family farms and the tied cottage, rural religiosity, and respect for natural forces, may all combine in a constellation of such values. The erosion of deferential behaviour amongst industrial workers has been caused by the disappearance of those same conditions for the exercise of such relationships and the collapse of the economic and moral basis to the order that maintained them. *See also* IMAGES OF SOCIETY.

deferred gratification The ideological principle which encourages individuals and groups to postpone immediate consumption or pleasure in order to work, train, invest, or gain in some other way an enhanced return at a future date. Deferred gratification is an essential principle behind *capital accumulation and implicit in any system of *industrialization.

definition of the situation A concept first developed by William Isaac Thomas and Florian Znaniecki in *The Polish Peasant in Europe and America* (1918–20), and now central to *symbolic interactionism. It is the idea that people's actions are shaped more by the subjective meaning given to their situation than by the purely objective aspects of the situation. Individuals construct the meaning of a situation on the basis of their experiences, needs, and wishes, and also on the basis of the customs and beliefs of their social group. Most significantly the concept was used to formulate an early version of the *self-fulfilling prophecy: Thomas and Znaniecki argued that when people define situations as real, they are real in their consequences for all concerned.

definition, operational *See* OPERATIONAL DEFINITION.

degradation ceremony Introduced by Harold Garfinkel in his article on 'Conditions of Successful Degradation Ceremonies' (*American Journal of Sociology*, 1956), the term degradation ceremony (or 'status degradation ceremony') refers to communicative work directed towards transforming an individual's total *identity into an identity lower in the relevant group's scheme of social types. Garfinkel argued that the structural conditions of moral indignation and shame—and hence the conditions of status degradation—are universal to all societies. Law courts are one example where degradation ceremonies are carried out publicly by professional degraders (lawyers and judges) as an occupational routine. Public denunciations undertaken in other social settings may be just as effective. The term highlights the importance of *societal reaction in the defining of *deviance in everyday life. *See also* LABELLING; STATUS; STIGMA; SYMBOLIC INTERACTIONISM.

degradation-of-work thesis The proposition that skilled work has declined in importance with the rise of capitalist *industrialization—most notably during the 20th century and following the rise of the *scientific management movement. The most notable proponents of this thesis have been neo-Marxists such as Georges *Friedmann and Harry Braverman. The latter argues that private capitalists pursue increased control over their workforces, both as a means of increasing labour productivity by extracting greater profits, and for the political purpose of subduing the *working class. The principal means for securing this control is said to be the separation of conception and execution. That is, appropriation of all planning and design knowledge by managers, with the workers being delegated only the responsibility for operating pre-programmed machinery and performing routinized and *de-skilled tasks. This process was characterized as the 'degradation of work' because it stripped formerly skilled employees (for example craft-workers and clerical workers) both of their *skills and their self-respect. The thesis formed the core of the so-called *labour process debate that preoccupied neo-Marxist sociologists of work during the 1980s. *See also* PROLETARIANIZATION.

deindustrialization The diminishing proportion of either national production or the labour-force of the richest Western nations engaged in the primary and secondary *industrial sectors. The extent of, and reasons for, deindustrialization are a matter of controversy. Though some such trend is evident in all the major Western economies, in only a few (notably Britain) has it coincided with falling investment, and an absolute decline in manufacturing capacity.

deism *See* THEISM.

Deleuze, Gilles (1925–95) French philosopher who studied philosophy at the Sorbonne, where he also taught history of philosophy between 1957 and 1964, and taught at the University of Lyon, the University of Vincennes (at the behest of his good friend Michel Foucault), and finally at the University of Paris VII where he stayed until his retirement in 1987. Author of many studies of classical philosophers from Kant and Hume to Spinoza, Leibniz, Nietzsche, and Bergson, he is probably most famous for his collaborative work with psychiatrist and political activist Felix *Guattari with whom he co-authored the two influential and widely read volumes on 'Capitalism and Schizophrenia': *Anti-Oedipus* (1972) and *A Thousand Plateaus* (1980). These can be considered as the first texts of philosophy to conceptually engage with the political events of 1968. In the final stages of a serious pulmonary illness which he suffered for almost 30 years, he took his own life in 1995.

Deleuze can be described as a philosopher of becoming. Following Henri Bergson, he argued that material composites undergo qualitative changes when divided and/or extended. Since for Deleuze, variations, intensities, speed, and affects constitute the plane of immanence, an exclusive emphasis on extensive multiplicities ends up reproducing an image of thought and matter devoid of becoming (*see* RHIZOME). He criticized Hegelian dialectics (including its Marxist reformulation) for having produced a false image of movement, devoid of any real intensive and expressive capacity of deterritorialization, or what he called 'lines of flight'. As an alternative to transcendental representation, hermeneutics, and Marxist concepts of infrastructure and superstructure, he advocated a flat ontology of lines, surfaces, planes, folds, sets, intensive variations, and divergent/convergent series. In his later work with Guattari, becoming was more explicitly associated with an active ethics of desire—understood as an impersonal and transversal tendency to deterritorialization and destratification through a logic of connections and assemblages.

Although he is usually described as a *post-structuralist, he had significant differences from other post-structuralist thinkers such as Jacques Derrida and Jacques Lacan. As such, and in spite of his association with *postmodernism, Deleuze's work constitutes an alternative to postmodern theories and he can be characterized as a 'constructivist' rather than a 'constructionist'. *See also* SOCIAL CONSTRUCTIONISM.

delinquency Literally misdeed, guilt, or neglect of duty, and hence in this sense not strictly defined by law. However, particularly when referred to as juvenile delinquency, the term is often used to embrace a broad range of behaviour, from that found offensive to respectable values (noisy teenage gatherings, truancy) to petty and occasionally more serious crime (such as shop-lifting, breaking and entering, and car theft).

Typically, the delinquent has been seen as an urban male, usually working class, aged between 12 and 20, associated with a variety of anti-social behaviours, membership of a *gang, and having a history of trouble with the authorities and of *recidivism. A high proportion of serious (indictable) offences are committed by people in this age-group, and so, on one hand, the 'problem' of delinquency is one that always seems clearly demonstrable and inviting obvious explanations. Yet, on the other, the sociological literature and range of explanatory approaches is wide—drawing, for example, on the diverse theories of anomie, the Chicago School, the gang, delinquent drift, deviance amplification, differential association, differential opportunity, moral panics, and subcultures (all of which are treated under separate entries elsewhere in this dictionary). Psychology and psychiatry also offer various approaches: influences here include parental or maternal deprivation, and measures of intelligence and personality (for all of which again see separate entries). It is often held that the problem is new or getting worse, but late 19th-and early 20th-century British and American society saw similar waves of delinquency. (A good account of these is given in G. Pearson, *Hooligan: A History of Respectable Fears*, 1983.) In the past, studies of delinquent youth largely neglected questions of race and gender, an omission which is only slowly being addressed. *See also* DRIFT.

Delphy, Christine (1941–   ) A French feminist and sociologist. Active in the 'events' of May 1968, she played a major part in the development of the women's movement and was the key figure in formulating a 'materialist feminism': an approach to gender that takes seriously Marx's materialist analysis of class and production. Delphy argued that women occupy a position within material relations of production based on the performance of domestic labour. This constitutes them as a 'sex class' structured by institutionalized patriarchal relations of marriage and motherhood. Her ideas were set out in an influential paper on 'The Main Enemy' in 1970 and were incorporated into the book *Close to Home* published in 1984. Her numerous articles have been published in the two-volume collection entitled *L'Ennemi principal* (1998 and 2001). An important study of her work is Stevi Jackson's *Christine Delphy* (1996).

demobilization *See* MOBILIZATION.

democracy So many political systems and ideologies claim the virtue of democracy that the word has become virtually meaningless in its everyday use; the label is used to legitimize almost every kind of political power arrangement.

The origins of democracy as an idea and a practice go back to the city-states of Greece in the 5th century BCE. At that time, it meant simply 'rule of the citizens' (the *demos*), and was designed to allow all citizens to have a voice in decisions that would affect all. This right was exercised at mass meetings, and approximated to what we would today call direct democracy. It is important to remember three things about this ancient Greek democracy: first, that it excluded women and a large class of slaves; second, that the demos acted as a collective or social body, rather than as isolated individuals; and, third, that this kind of collective decision-making could work only as long as the citizen body remained relatively small and homogeneous. Kirkpatrick Sale in *Human Scale* (1980), building on the empirical work of Robert Dahl, has suggested that true democracy is difficult in groups larger than 10 000, and impossible in populations above 50 000: most West Europeans and Americans live in towns and cities larger than this. In fact the classic age of Greek democracy lasted only for about 200 years, in city-states of a few thousand privileged citizens, and was destroyed by invasion and war. Its long-term durability in the face of population growth was never tested.

Contemporary democracies are all very different from the ancient Greek model. The pattern that emerged in England in the 17th century and slowly became the model for the world was one of representative democracy. Here, citizens elect politicians who promise to represent the interests of those citizens in debates and decisions, which typically take place in some central national forum such as a parliament or congress. Thus, ideally, the parliament becomes a miniature *demos*.

In practice, politicians in a democracy usually belong to parties that propose general policies or programmes, rather than responding to citizens on an issue-by-issue basis. Parties thus become independent centres of *power. The experience of the 20th century seems to show that citizens' views are best represented by the proliferation of many small parties—as in Italy or Israel; but government can be carried on more efficiently where there are only two, or at most three parties—as in Britain or the United States. This is one of the many paradoxes of democracy which have engaged the attention of sociologists and political scientists.

Although there are many one-party systems in the world that claim to be democratic on the basis that they represent the collective will of the people, it is widely agreed that real inter-party competition and real representation of different interests is a necessary condition of democracy. Other necessary conditions include: free and fair elections, a genuine choice between candidates and polities, real parliamentary power, the separation of powers, *civil rights for all citizens, and the rule of law. There is room for unlimited disagreement about the exact meaning of any and all of these conditions, which is why democracy continues to be the focus of intense public and academic debate. Researchers have explored the nature of the *state as a sociological entity, *political socialization, *voting behaviour and political participation, the relationships between democracy and economic systems, and the manipulation of *public opinion.

However, the main thrust of research has been to investigate the reality of democracy itself—how widely power is distributed, and what role ordinary citizens play. In 1956 Robert A. Dahl published *A Preface to Democratic Theory* in which he argued that the modern industrial states are not classical democracies so much as polyarchies—shifting coalitions of powerful interest groups. In modern conditions, democracy had to be seen as an outcome of the pluralistic competition of interest groups and associations. This sparked off two decades of intense research and analysis on *pluralism. C. Wright *Mills produced *The Power Elite* (1956) which took the critique of democracy much further by claiming that, in the United States, democratic political practices had been obliterated by a *power elite consisting of the institutional leaders of big business, the military, and what Mills called 'the political directorate' (the executive branch of government). Citizens had become docile and powerless in this *mass society.

The counterpart of elite and class-rule theories of democracy has been the conservative tradition which, from Plato to Burke, has been suspicious of democracy as a dangerous and inefficient system which could easily lead to mob rule. The origins of popular democracy in the French Revolution of 1789 gave force to this view.

In the modern democracies there is little consensus about just how strong the voice of the people can or should be in a constitutional democracy. Politicians routinely ignore massive public opinion majorities—for example the majority for capital punishment or a balanced budget in the United States, or the majority against full integration into Europe, or against health privatization in Britain. Democracy mixes uneasily with traditional *paternalism, international *corporate capitalism, and *welfare statism. Indeed, the complexity of political and economic decision-making today presents a formidable barrier to real public participation. In the future, new electronic techniques for supplying information and testing public opinion may bring democracy a little closer to its participatory origins.

Useful introductions to the voluminous literature surrounding these issues are Jack Lively's *Democracy* (1975) and the collection edited by Graeme Duncan, *Democratic Theory and Practice* (1983). See also BUREAUCRACY; INDUSTRIAL DEMOCRACY.

democracy, industrial *See* INDUSTRIAL DEMOCRACY.

democracy, participatory *See* PARTICIPATORY DEMOCRACY.

democratic socialism *See* STATE CAPITALISM.

demographic transition The pattern of transition, observed in many areas of the developed world, between two demographic regimes: the first, termed traditional, in which levels of *fertility and *mortality are high; and the second or modern regime in which levels of fertility and mortality are low. According to demographic transition theory, developed from the observation of this pattern in Europe and associated with the name of Frank W. Notestein, mortality should decline first, leading to a period of fairly rapid population growth (as occurred in Great Britain in the first half of the 19th century for example), followed by a subsequent decline in fertility to similarly low levels (see, for example, 'Population—the Long View', in T. W. Schultz (ed.), *Food for the World*, 1945). Much effort has been devoted to debating whether the demographic transition will follow a similar pattern in developing countries, and the implications of the question of whether the growth of population at intermediate stages of the transition acted as a stimulus to the Industrial Revolution, or was merely a consequence of *economic development and *modernization.

demography The study of human populations, their growth and decline, due to changing patterns of *migration, *fertility and *mortality, and characteristics such as the *sex ratio, dependency ratio, and age structure. The subject is sometimes divided for further elucidation into 'formal demography', meaning the formal statistical analysis of population parameters and dynamics, and 'population studies', the wider investigation of the causes and consequences of population structures and change. It is in the latter area that many demographers have interests which overlap with those of sociologists, and in much sociological investigation demographic analysis forms an important component in the description and understanding of human societies.

The methodology consists of analysis of databases of *official statistics from births, deaths, and marriage registration, and from population *censuses. Demographers seek ultimately to produce population projections, that is, forecasts not only of the size of the population over coming decades, but also its changing age-structure, which can be important for social policy and labour-market policy. For example, if the dependent population (children under school-leaving age and people over retirement age) is growing relative to the population of working age which has to support it financially, there may be major implications for taxation, social insurance, and fiscal policy. If the population of working age is declining in absolute numbers, there may be a case for government policy to encourage a larger percentage (of women especially) to enter employment. Thus demographic statistics and analyses provide the essential underpinning for many other types of study. For this reason population censuses were the very first type of systematic social enquiry to be developed.

Analyses of *vital statistics do, however, have their limitations. In particular, they cannot supply information on the motivations, value-systems, or aims and preferences underlying changes in the *birth rate, which is a key factor in population growth. In recent years, there have been concerted efforts to develop and carry out interview surveys on fertility orientations and behaviour. These cover issues such as the preferred number of children in a family, the effects of household income and women's employment on their fertility, attitudes to contraception and its use—all factors affecting the timing and spacing of births. The World Fertility Survey in the 1970s established standards of data collection and analysis for an important addition to the demographer's repertoire of data sources and research analyses. *See also* HISTORICAL DEMOGRAPHY; SOCIAL DEMOGRAPHY.

SEE WEB LINKS
• The United Nations site for its Population Division, containing data and policy proposals.

denomination (denominationalization) A denomination is a religious organization that, in the church-sect typology, stands midway between the *church type and the *sect type. It is a voluntary association with a formal *bureaucracy. There is a trained ministry and lay participation is restricted to particular limited activities. It is tolerant about belief and practice, and expulsion of members who deviate from orthodoxy is rare. Individual commitment is not intense, and recruitment is through *socialization. Denominationalization refers to the historical process by which certain sects (such as the Methodists) acquired the characteristics of a denomination without necessarily becoming a church. The classic source is R. Niebuhr, *The Social Sources of Denominationalism* (1929).

denotative meaning *See* CONNOTATIVE VERSUS DENOTATIVE MEANING.

density The degree of aggregation, concentration, or crowding within a defined geographical or social space, measured in different ways. The population density of an area is measured by the number of persons usually resident in the area or, sometimes, by the number of persons working in an area (the day-time population density). Trade-union membership density is the percentage of all workers at a particular workplace, or in a company, who are union members. In *network analysis, density refers to the proportion of all possible connections among members of the network that actually exist: more dense networks have a higher level of connection. *See also* DYNAMIC DENSITY.

dependence (dependency) The state of being connected to and subordinate to someone or something. The opposite of self-reliance, this term may be encountered in a variety of sociological contexts.

In the study of *economic growth and the sociology of *development, it describes a situation in which the less developed countries (LDCs) literally depend on inputs from the advanced industrial states in order to achieve growth. This can take the form of financial and technical aid, expertise, or military support. Dependency is judged by so-called *dependency theorists and others to be a limiting condition which is detrimental to the long-term economic and political interests of *Third World states.

In a medical context, the term is synonymous with addiction, the most common forms of dependency being associated with *drug addiction and alcoholism (*see* DRINKING AND ALCOHOLISM). Individuals are sometimes described as being emotionally dependent, financially dependent, or politically dependent on others. Much research has also been done on the social consequences for relationships between the sexes of the financial dependence of many married women on their husbands (especially if the former are not involved in paid employment). *See also* COMPADRAZGO; PATRON-CLIENT RELATIONSHIP; DEPENDENT VARIABLE.

dependency theory A set of theories which maintained that the failure of *Third World states to achieve adequate and sustainable levels of development resulted from their *dependence on the advanced capitalist world.

Dependency theories developed in opposition to the optimistic claims of *modernization theory which saw the less developed countries being able to catch up with the West. They stressed that Western societies had an interest in maintaining their advantaged position in relation to the LDCs and had the financial and technical wherewithal to do so. A variety of different accounts of the relationship between the advanced and less developed states evolved within the broad framework of dependency theory, ranging from the stagnationism and 'surplus drain' theory of Andre Gunder Frank (which predicted erroneously that the Third World would be unable to achieve significant levels of *industrialization), to the more cautious pessimism of those who envisaged a measure of growth based on 'associated dependent' relations with the West.

The major contribution to dependency theory was undoubtedly that of Frank, a German economist of development who devised and popularized the phrase 'the development of underdevelopment', describing what he saw as the deformed and dependent economies of the peripheral states—in his terminology the 'satellites' of the more advanced 'metropolises'. In *Capitalism and Underdevelopment in Latin America* (1969), he argued that the Third World was doomed to stagnation because the surplus it produced was appropriated by the advanced capitalist countries, through agencies such as transnational corporations. Frank himself insisted that growth could only be achieved by severing ties with capitalism and pursuing auto-centric socialist development strategies.

Dependency theory was flawed by an overemphasis on economic factors and in some versions a necessitarian logic based on the idea of a 'surplus drain' (extraction and appropriation of profits) from the LDCs to the rich and powerful nations. None the less, it had the merit of drawing attention to the international dimension of development, and brought the power relations between states under scrutiny. The emergence of the newly industrializing countries (NICs) as a group of successful late developers challenged the validity of the core assumptions of dependency theory, demonstrating that successful late industrialization was possible under certain circumstances, and suggesting the need for a more sophisticated and disaggregated approach to Third World development. *See also* DEVELOPMENT, SOCIOLOGY OF.

dependent variable Within a particular study, analysis, or model, a dependent variable is the social element whose characteristics or variations are to be explained by reference to the influence of other, prior, so-called *independent variables. For example, a person's income (dependent variable) may vary according to age and social class (independent variables). The value of dependent variables can often be predicted using some form of *causal modelling. Whether a *variable is treated as dependent or independent is determined by the theoretical framework and focus of a study.

depression (clinical depression) Mental states characterized by feelings of sadness, hopelessness, and loss of interest, experienced by most individuals. They are deemed clinical (that is a *mental illness) if they are persistent, severe, and out of proportion to any identifiable precipitant. The term depression entered *psychiatric classification primarily as a symptom of melancholia (the predecessor to depression) and has only featured as a diagnostic label since the end of the 19th century (initially in the term manic depression).

The precise differentiation of types of depression varies. In the post-war period it has been common to distinguish reactive and endogenous depression. With reactive depression—a *neurosis—there is an identifiable precipitant, but the response is exaggerated. With endogenous depression—a *psychosis—there is not; instead the illness appears to arise from within. Under the heading of 'Affective Disorders', the APA *Manual of Mental Disorders* distinguishes bi-polar (manic depression) and unipolar disorders (depression).

The various types of depression are now the most frequently diagnosed mental illnesses, and are more common in women than men (with a usual ratio of two to one). There are undoubtedly biochemical changes associated with depressive states (though work on the biochemistry of depression has not been very successful) and the most widely used treatments are physical—drugs or ECT (electro-convulsive therapy). However, the case for the importance of social factors in the aetiology of depression is strong. George Brown and Tirril Harris's study of the *Social Origins of Depression* (1978) demonstrated very clearly that adverse *life-events and other *stress-inducing occurrences, when combined with situationally generated vulnerability, increased the chances of clinical depression (both reactive and endogenous).

depression, neurotic *See* NEUROTIC DEPRESSION.

deprivation Literally the taking away of something or the state of being dispossessed, the term is loosely used for the condition of not having something, whether or not it was previously possessed, with the implication that the person in question could reasonably expect to have it. It involves loss or being excluded from things that are typically available to others. Of what precisely the individual is deprived varies, but basic welfare needs for food, housing, education, and emotional care (*see* MATERNAL DEPRIVATION) receive much of the attention. This is most usefully seen in relation to standards of *citizenship (J. Scott, *Poverty and Wealth*, 1994).

Like the narrower notion of *poverty, deprivation can be viewed in absolute or relative terms. Absolute deprivation refers to the loss or absence of the means to satisfy the basic needs for survival—food, clothing, and shelter. The term relative deprivation refers to deprivations experienced when individuals compare themselves with others: that is, individuals who lack something compare themselves with those who have it, and in so doing feel a sense of deprivation. Consequently, relative deprivation not only involves comparison, it is also usually defined in subjective terms. The concept is intimately linked with that of a comparative *reference group—the group with whom the individual or set of individuals compare themselves—the selection of reference group being crucial to the degree of relative deprivation.

The concept of relative deprivation was introduced by Samuel Stouffer and his co-workers in their classic social psychological study *The American Soldier* (1949); it was also used by Robert K. Merton in his standard text *Social Theory and Social Structure* (1949), and was widely used by sociologists in the 1950s and 1960s. Not surprisingly it was invoked in discussions of poverty and in the arguments about the need for relative definitions of poverty. It was also employed by W. G. Runciman in his important study *Relative Deprivation and Social Justice* (1966). This focused on institutionalized inequalities and people's awareness of them, and on the question of which inequalities ought to be perceived and resented, by standards of social *justice. More recently, the link between social inequalities and the experience of relative deprivation has been put forward as the explanatory mechanism that accounts for international differences in *life expectancy, the argument being that high levels of inequality lead via relative deprivation to lowered life expectancy.

Sociological debates have tended to focus on subjectively experienced relative deprivation. In the field of social policy, however, externally assessed material and cultural deprivations have been the focus in studies of *poverty. One important issue has been the extent to which deprivation is transmitted from one generation to the next. In this context the idea of a *cycle of deprivation has been employed to refer to the intergenerational transmission of deprivation, primarily through family behaviours, values, and practices. This idea suggests the importance of personal and familial pathology—as opposed to structural inequalities—in accounting for deprivation, and has led to considerable debate and criticism (see M. Rutter and N. Madge, *Cycles of Disadvantage*, 1976, and Z. Ferge and S. M. Miller, *Dynamics of Deprivation*, 1987). The term multiple deprivation is used where deprivations extend across a wide range of social needs. For a useful review of the extensive literature see Joan N. Gurney and Kathleen J. Tierney, 'Relative Deprivation and Social Movements: A Critical Look at Twenty Years of Theory and Research', *Sociological Quarterly* (1982).

deprivation, maternal *See* MATERNAL DEPRIVATION.

Deprivation-Satiation Proposition *See* SUCCESS PROPOSITION.

derivations *See* ELITE theory.

Descartes, René (1596–1650) Together with Immanuel *Kant and David *Hume, the French philosopher René Descartes is one of the founding figures of modern Western philosophy. Descartes also made significant contributions to mathematics and the science of mechanics. He is best known for his *Discourse on Method* and *Meditations*, two texts in which he employed his method of systematic doubt so as to arrive at some indubitable foundation from which certain knowledge could be deduced. Famously, Descartes discovered he could doubt virtually everything, save that in doubting, and so thinking, he must at least exist. However, the existence thus asserted was not his bodily existence, but rather the existence of the *self as a 'thinking thing'. Descartes required proof of the existence of God, to restore his confidence in the existence of material bodies, defined by their spatial existence. This metaphysical view of the world as composed of extended material bodies, on one hand, and souls or minds defined by thought, on the other, is known as *dualism. The adjective used to refer to Descartes is 'Cartesian'.

Descartes himself, and successive dualist philosophers of mind, have experienced great difficulty in accounting coherently for the special connection between mind and body that constitutes the human person. The influence of body-mind dualism is pervasive throughout the contemporary social sciences (for example, in Max *Weber's distinction between behaviour and meaningful action). It has led to great difficulties in dealing adequately with either human embodiment or ecological issues. *Pschoanalysis and recent *structuralist approaches in social science, which affect to 'de-centre' the human subject, often start out by explicitly rejecting Descartes's assumption of the 'transparency' of the self to reflection. Finally, Descartes is now frequently criticized as advocating a view of animals as non-conscious complex machines, thus allegedly excluding animals from direct moral concern, and sustaining an untenable gulf between human and animal nature. *See also* METAPHYSICS.

descent (descent theory) *See* KINSHIP.

descent groups These are kin groups who are lineal descendants of a common ancestor. Unilineal descent is either *matrilineal (if traced through the mother) or *patrilineal (traced through the father's line). Bilateral descent can be traced through either line. Although the local discourse of descent often stresses its biological foundations, this should be seen as culturally constructed, since fictitious biological relationships are sometimes created. *See also* CLAN; KINSHIP; PARALLEL DESCENT.

descent, parallel *See* PARALLEL DESCENT.

deschooling A movement associated with the writings of Ivan Illich (*Deschooling Society*, 1971) and Paulo Freire (*Pedagogy of the Oppressed*, 1970), although critiques of the role of the educational system in the development process had been presented earlier, by René Dumont (*False Start in Africa*, 1962) among others. The movement was influential during the 1970s, especially in the United States, although Illich and Freire both wrote from a Latin American perspective. The central ideas are that education and learning permeate all life-experiences and social relationships, and are not the monopoly of the formal educational system; that in the *Third World it is essential for the *curriculum to build on pupils' own experiences and provide relevant knowledge and skills; and that conventional educational systems serve in practice to demean and exclude many social groups (for example the poor) and to create institutional dependence. Wider political arguments are developed from this position. *See also* EDUCATION, SOCIOLOGY OF.

descriptive statistics *See* INFERENTIAL STATISTICS.

desire Desire refers to the psychological aspects of sexuality, particularly fantasies, operating both consciously and unconsciously. It is distinct from both the biological aspects of sexuality—the body and its sensations, its ability to reproduce, and sexual acts—and the social and political aspects, including sexual identity and sexual relationships.

Although we experience pleasure and pain through our bodies, arguably much of this is in fact a result of the psychological aspects of fantasy and desire. Psychoanalytic theory has explored these issues in particular, and in recent years the French psychoanalyst Jacques *Lacan challenged Sigmund *Freud's theory of biological 'drives', arguing instead that sexuality and desire are primarily sites for the production—and transgression—of meaning, and that desire is a result of cultural meanings and *representations as much as any physiological expression. In particular, he sees desire as a metonym; that is, a word used in a transferred sense—'metonymy' being a figure of speech, and an important concept in *semiology, in which the name of one thing is substituted for another to which it is related, for example an effect for a cause, or as in the substitution of 'the bottle' for 'drink'. *See also* NEED.

de-skilling A term that summarizes the central ideas of Harry Braverman's *Labour and Monopoly Capital: The Degradation of Work in the 20th Century* (1974). His thesis was that *capitalist forms of *production reduce the cost of labour by breaking down complex work processes into smaller, simpler, and unskilled tasks. This continuous fragmentation process replaces the skilled craft worker by unskilled labour requiring little training, so that jobs in the secondary sector of the *labour market are substituted for jobs in the primary sector. In consequence, wages and employment conditions are pushed down to the lower levels typical of the secondary sector; *unemployment and insecure employment become widespread; and people in the de-skilled jobs become *alienated from their work.

The thesis has attracted a lot of interest among academic social scientists, especially in Britain, and it has provided the framework for case-study research on work organization and change within workplaces, particularly in the declining manufacturing sector (see P. Thompson, *The Nature of Work: An Introduction to Debates on the Labour Process*, 1983, for an overview). Studies based on nationally representative statistics on the workforce tend not to substantiate Braverman's conclusion about the direction of change in the *occupational structure and the consequences of a shift away from manufacturing to service-sector industries: while certain skilled occupations are disappearing, others experience skills upgrading, and newer occupations, such as computer programming and systems analysis, expand rapidly. *See also* DEGRADATION OF WORK THESIS; INDUSTRIAL SECTOR; LABOUR PROCESS; PROLETARIANIZATION; SCIENTIFIC MANAGEMENT; SKILL.

despotism *See* ABSOLUTISM.

determinism *See* BIOLOGICAL REDUCTIONISM; CULTURE AND PERSONALITY SCHOOL; ECONOMIC DETERMINISM; HISTORICISM; LABELLING; SOCIAL AREA ANALYSIS; SOCIOBIOLOGY; TECHNOLOGICAL DETERMINISM.

deterrence In *criminology deterrent and preventive measures can overlap, since both aim to discourage certain acts or place restrictions on the rational choices of others. The threat of imprisonment, for example, may be held to be a deterrent and hence preventive of crime. The threat of arrest, trial, conviction, and punishment may be viewed as a general deterrent. Deterrence, as a general objective, is also invoked to justify punishment. Imprisonment is assumed to be a powerful deterrent but its effectiveness in persuading potential offenders to avoid crime is disputed. However, prison also seeks to reform, and may be said to deter crime if an individual commits no further crime after release. Nevertheless, in most modern penal systems, *recidivism is high. Also used in the sociology of the *military to refer to the use of threatened force (such as nuclear weapons) to prevent attack.

development, sociology of The application of social theory and analysis to societies (usually in the *Third World) that are undergoing a late transition to capitalist *industrialization. It has been particularly concerned with analysing the social effects of development on class relations and on social groups such as the *peasantry and the urban poor.

Development studies emerged as a distinct area of research in the post-war period, and was associated with the growing concern for the political and *economic development of the post-colonial world. The first sociological account of development was *modernization theory, which held that the less developed countries would eventually catch up with the industrialized world, providing they emulated the economic and social systems of Western *capitalism. Based largely on the theoretical premises of structural *functionalism, modernization theory conceptualized development as a staged transition from tradition to modernity, to be brought about at the economic level by the operations of the *market and foreign investment; at the social level by the adoption of appropriate western institutions, values, and behaviours; and at the political level by the implementation of parliamentary *democracy. A product of the Cold War, and motivated by the concern to challenge socialist ideas in the post-colonial world, modernization theory was criticized for its optimism, over-simplification, and *ethnocentrism. It was displaced in the late 1960s as the most popular sociological analysis of development by the *dependency approach. This was in turn charged with over-simplification and with merely inverting the assumptions of the previous orthodoxy.

Criticism of these approaches has left the sociology of development as a fragmented field in which various competing and more modest theories jostle for supremacy. In recent years there has been a growing awareness that the nation-state cannot be analysed in isolation from the international context. The field also has significant and growing overlaps with the sociological debates about *globalization and the *environment (see, for example, John Brohman's *Popular Development*, 1996). There has also been a renewed analytic emphasis on the interdependency and integration among nations, not just in terms of economic processes, but also at the level of culture and ideology. For example, in *The Westernization of the World* (1996), Serge Latouche argues that the concept of 'Third World development' is rooted in specifically Western ideas of technical progress and the accumulation of capital. This leads to development policies which destroy the cultures of non-Western populations. In particular, Latouche maintains that the drive towards global uniformity in cultures, life-styles, and 'mentalities' has been responsible for endemic civil wars, ecological disasters, and the widespread national debt throughout the Third World. David E. Apter's *Rethinking Development* (1987) gives a good overview of the more established literature. *See also* CENTRE-PERIPHERY MODEL.

development banks Financial institutions established by states and private interests, for the particular purpose of promoting *economic growth, often having preferential interest rates and terms of repayment. Examples include the Inter-American Development Bank, International Development Agency, and European Bank for Reconstruction and Development.

development, uneven *See* UNEVEN DEVELOPMENT.

deviance, sociology of Commonsensically, deviance has been seen as an attribute, as something inherent in a certain kind of behaviour or person: the delinquent, the homosexual, the mentally ill, and so forth. Indeed, this was a position which had a certain credence in the earlier writings of the *social pathology theorists, and which is still important in some clinical and *criminological research. For sociologists, however, deviance is best viewed, not as a type of person, but rather as a formal property of social situations and social systems. There is no fixed agreement on the substance of deviance—even murder or incest are accepted at times—but there are two interrelated properties that help characterize the phenomenon.

The first refers to deviance as a pattern of norm violation, and a range of *norms are then specified such that religious norms give rise to heretics, legal norms to criminals, health norms to the sick, cultural norms to the eccentric, and so forth. Since norms emerge in most social situations, such a definition is very wide-ranging, and enters every sphere of social life.

A second property highlights deviance as a *stigma construct, a label bestowed upon certain classes of behaviour at certain times, which then become devalued, discredited, and often excluded. This characteristic can also be seen as very wide-ranging: people may make friends deviant simply because they belch or talk too much; whilst terrorists may become political martyrs in the eyes of those who share their particular values. The study of deviance here is concerned primarily with the construction, application, and impact of stigma labels.

Within both approaches—norm violation and stigma construct—deviance is a shifting, ambiguous, and volatile concept. Precisely who or what is deviant depends upon a firm understanding of the norms and *labelling process in particular social contexts. Despite these inherent difficulties with the term, an enormous sociological literature has been generated by research on deviance.

The work of Émile *Durkheim is generally considered the most fruitful starting-point for the contemporary analysis of deviance. In his work, two major and somewhat antagonistic issues emerge, both of which signpost subsequent trends. One is his focus on *anomie: a state of normlessness and breakdown that emerges most conspicuously at times of rapid social change. Anomie indicates a strain, a breakdown, within a social order or social structure. This concept shifts the focus away from the deviant as a type of person to the suggestion that deviance is a feature of certain kinds of social structure. It is an idea followed through in a host of subsequent writings: in theories of *delinquency as a consequence of strains within the social order (as in the work of Robert Merton and anomie theory); as a consequence of the breakdown of parts of the city (see ZONE OF TRANSITION); and in the idea of *subcultures.

Durkheim's second concern is his focus upon the functions of deviance. In *The Rules of Sociological Method* (1895) he suggests that 'crime is normal because a society exempt from it is utterly impossible'. Deviance is bound up with the very conditions for a society; far from deviance being abnormal or pathological in itself, every society needs deviance. This seemingly paradoxical claim about the normality of deviance is propounded by Durkheim on several grounds. First there is a broad statistical argument: empirically, all known societies do have their deviance, and the rate of deviance often remains relatively stable over periods of time (though Durkheim certainly agrees that there can be abnormally high rates which need to be checked). But why is deviance universal? In line with Durkheim's more general functional analysis he suggests that deviance fulfils a number of important functions. Citing Socrates, he argues that one of these functions is to bring about change: today's deviants are signs of tomorrow's world. This is not true of all deviance—some is apologetic and fits readily into the existing social order. But deviance that is radical, challenging, and threatening is often so precisely because it suggests a different vision of the social world, one that may increasingly come to be: the reforming Christian sects of the 16th century, for example, quickly became the established Churches of subsequent eras. But in contrast to the function of facilitating change there is also a major function of solidarity and cohesion secured by deviance: people unite against a common enemy.

Durkheim's work has been very influential but there have been many other sociological traditions within which the issue of deviance has also been addressed in some depth. Members of the so-called *Chicago School examined deviance as part of a normal learning process of cultural transmission, most fruitfully in the later work of Edwin Sutherland, and in terms of the general theory of *differential association. Those within the *symbolic interactionist tradition were particularly concerned with the processes through which deviance was socially constructed. Ultimately this interest gave rise to labelling theory and *social constructionism. Other strands of thought have seen deviance as a form of social *conflict, and there have been attempts recently to link it to *Marxism and the sociology of *law, feminist *criminology, and Michel *Foucault and *discourse theory.

Throughout the late 1960s and much of the 1970s, deviance theory was one of the most fertile and controversial fields of sociology, but by the 1980s debate had become largely institutionalized and interest somewhat diminished. In the opinion of some observers the rather boisterous specialism gradually matured. Alternatively, in the view of many of the self-proclaimed radicals within the field, the sociology of deviance simply became yet another sociological orthodoxy. However one judges this process, the story itself is well documented in Stephen J. Pfohl, *Images of Deviance and Social Control: A Sociological History* (1985). *See also* CAREER; CRIME; DEVIANCE AMPLIFICATION; DEVIANCE DISAVOWAL.

deviance amplification Introduced by Leslie Wilkins in his book *Social Deviance* (1967), the concept suggests that a small initial deviation may spiral into ever-increasing significance through processes of *labelling and over-reacting. It was initially linked to *cybernetics and feedback loops, but was used most extensively within the labelling theory of deviance. However, by far the most systematic defence and application of the theory will be found in Jason Ditton's *Controlology* (1979), a critique of 'half-hearted' labelling theories which attempts 'to extend Wilkins's model to the point at which control may be seen to be operating *independently* of crime (rather than within a mutually causal framework) on the basis that such liberation will constitute an adequate prepositional basis for a fully-fledged labelling theory'.

deviance disavowal A refusal, on the part of those who have been labelled deviant, to accept this characterization. The concept was originally developed with reference to so-called social deviants, such as the physically handicapped, who had a strong interest in attempting to minimize the *stigma of *deviance in order either to appear normal or to normalize their interactions and relationships with the able-bodied. It is now used more widely, notably within the *labelling perspective, to apply to all forms of deviant behaviour.

deviant career *See* CAREER.

deviant subculture *See* SUBCULTURE.

Dewey, John (1859–1952) Over a long life spanning nearly a century, Dewey was one of America's leading philosophers, responsible for developing and refining philosophical *pragmatism. Rejecting much of classical European and *essentialist philosophy, Dewey stressed the importance of linking theories to active participation in the world, and to practical problem-solving (instrumentalism). His work exemplifies the North American approach to problem-solving and it has been especially influential in progressive theories of education. For example, in *Democracy and Education* (1916) Dewey stressed the importance of child-centred learning, where the experiences of the child are seen as valuable in establishing problems, and where thoughtful continuity of such experiences allows the child to exert increasing control over his or her life.

diachrony *See* Saussure; structuralism.

dialectic (dialectical materialism) *See* Engels; Gurvitch; Hegel; historical materialism; Marx; materialism.

diaspora (diaspora studies) A diaspora is a dispersion of people throughout the world. The term was first applied collectively to the Jews scattered after the Babylonian captivity, and in the modern period to Jews living outside of Palestine and latterly Israel, but has now been extended to include the situation of any widely spread migrant group.

During the late 1980s and 1990s, diaspora studies of *trans*national experiences and communities developed as a self-conscious critique of earlier sociological approaches to *inter*national migration, this shift in terminology reflecting the more general turn towards *globalization as a theme in macrosociology (although *postmodernism and *post-structuralism are also evident influences). Proponents argue that improvements in transport (such as cheap air fares) and communications (electronic mail, satellite television, the *Internet) have made it possible for diaspora communities, scattered across the globe, to sustain their own distinctive identities, life-styles, and economic ties. The rigid territorial nationalism that defines modern nation-states has in this way been replaced by a series of shifting and contested boundaries. Diaspora studies has spawned many new terms ('imagined communities', 'global ethnospaces', 'preimmigration crucibles') which describe these transnational influences, and the networks and communities under study, to substitute for the conventional terminology of immigration and assimilation. Typical studies would include Paul Gilroy's *The Black Atlantic* (1993) and Nancy Abelmann and John Lie's *Blue Dreams: Korean Americans and the Los Angeles Riots* (1995).

Enthusiasts argue that the new diaspora studies detail the complexity, diversity, and fluidity of migrant identities and experiences in a more realistic way than did the older mechanistic theories and models of international migration (which, it is claimed, emphasized unidirectional flows and influences, uprooting of migrants from their societies and cultures of origin, and *assimilation via the *melting pot into the new host culture). Critics point to the creation of pointless neologisms, abstruse theoretical terminology, apparent disregard for numbers and generalizations, and a tendency to ignore earlier sociological studies of *migration (especially where these document complex structures of opportunity and migrant networks in ways that prefigure the new diaspora studies themselves). It is also said that the new diaspora studies unwarrantably overlook structural economic and political influences upon migration. Certainly, many are focused principally upon personal narratives of migrants, and document mainly the popular culture of the diaspora community.

diaspora identities *See* IDENTITY.

dichotomy Any variable which has only two categories. In theory these categories are meant to be mutually exclusive. The variable 'sex', with its two categories of 'male' and 'female', is a good example. There are numerous well-known examples of dichotomies in sociology: Tönnies's *Gemeinschaft* and *Gesellschaft*, Durkheim's *mechanical and organic solidarity, and so on. A variable with more than two categories is called a polytomy. Sometimes, in order to simplify analysis, polytomous variables are collapsed—the number of categories is reduced by merging adjacent codes—to a dichotomy.

dictatorship of the proletariat *See* LENIN.

difference Although increasingly employed with reference to ethnic, class, and age divisions within social groups, the term 'difference' was initially used by 'second wave' *feminist writers, who defined the term politically, seeing it as a polarity both between women and men and among women themselves. Kate Millett and Shulamith Firestone viewed women's differences from men as a principal manifestation of women's oppression by men. Others see the term as referring more to the fact that women have a different experience of work, love, and family, indeed a different psychology, from that of men. It is also used in the negative sense of social *exclusion and subordination, although radical feminists such as Mary Daly see it as a positive phenomenon, difference as a cause to embrace and celebrate. Black feminists such as Audre Lorde have attacked the misleading universalism of feminism and stressed the deep differences existing between women at all levels, especially with regard to access to scarce resources and power, as a result of ethnic differences and divisions based on class and sexual orientation. In recent years there has been a growing multiplicity of women celebrating differences, but some argue this results in a loss of homogeneity in the women's movement, while others point out that the politically neutral notion of difference to a great extent disguises social *inequality—both between women and men, and among women themselves.

difference principle *See* JUSTICE, SOCIAL.

differential association A theory of *crime and *delinquency pioneered by Edwin Sutherland in the 1930s, as a response to the dominant multi-factorial approaches to crime causation, associated particularly with the work of Eleanor and Sheldon Glueck. In contrast to their account, which identified long lists of factors that might contribute to crime causation, Sutherland aimed to build an integrated and sociological theory that stressed that crime is basically a learned phenomenon. The theory was elaborated and refined in various editions of Sutherland's highly influential textbook *Principles of Criminology* (later co-authored with Donald Cressey), and came to be presented in nine propositions, the most central of which argued that 'a person becomes delinquent because of an excess of definitions favourable to violation of law over definitions unfavour-able to violation of law'. People learn criminal behaviour through contact with others who define criminality in favourable ways. Arguably, therefore, the theory is as much one of differential definitions as differential association.

The theory was highly influential in *deviance and delinquency research, making the explanation of crime largely a matter of ordinary learning processes, rather than biological predisposition. Although it was frequently attacked for being too general and failing to deal adequately with individualistic crimes like embezzlement, the proponents of the theory responded by making it ever more refined and testable, as well as applying it to a wider range of individual deviant phenomena, often using the *vocabulary of motives argument to clarify the social nature of even solitary crimes.

differentiation, social or structural *See* STRUCTURAL DIFFERENTIATION.

diffused power *See* ORGANIZATIONAL REACH.

diffusion (diffusionism) Diffusion refers to the spread of traits and attributes from one *culture to another through contact between different societies. Diffu-sion theory developed in the 18th and 19th centuries, in opposition to *evolu-tionary theory, both being concerned with the origins of human culture. Diffusionists such as Robert *Lowie (*The History of Ethnological Theory*, 1937) saw cultures as patchworks of borrowed traits, the superior traits moving out from the centre, like the ripples from a stone thrown into a pond. The movement of these cultural traits could be reconstructed by assuming that the traits most widely distributed are the oldest.

Some diffusionists sought to prove that all human culture originated in one place and spread out from there by diffusion. The similarities between Mayan temples and Egyptian pyramids led anthropologists like W. Perry (1887–1949) and Elliot Smith (1871–1937) to argue that Egypt was the fount of human culture (see, for example, W. J. Perry, *The Growth of Civilization*, 1926).

Anthropology has largely moved away from this debate, seeing most cultural traits in disparate areas as having developed independently, and criticizing the diffusionists for extracting cultural artefacts from their context. For example, although the Mayan temples and Egyptian pyramids share a similarity of form, they have completely different religious functions. Some of the original interests of the diffusionists have continued to be pursued by the American historical school of anthropology. *See also* GALTON'S PROBLEM.

Dilthey, Wilhelm (1833–1911) A German philosopher, one of the great precursors of the interpretative tradition in sociology, Dilthey's central preoccu-pation was with the creation of an adequate philosophical foundation for knowl-edge in the human or historical sciences. For him, the world of human history and culture consisted of 'expressions' of human life-experience (*Erlebnis*) which are to be apprehended and understood in ways quite different from and irreducible to the methods of the natural sciences. His early conviction that psychology could play the part of a foundational science for the human sciences was eventually displaced in favour of a hermeneutic approach (*see* INTERPRETATION) to institutions, religions, buildings, and so on, as so many 'objectifications' of life experience. *See also GEISTESWISSENSCHAFTEN* and *NATURWISSENSCHAFTEN*; IDEOGRAPHIC VERSUS NOMOTHETIC APPROACHES.

diploma disease A term developed by Ronald Dore as part of a critique of the excessive reliance on the selection process in formal educational institutions (and hence on educational qualifications) as evidence of ability, training, and merit for entry to particular occupations, careers, or internal labour markets. This phenomenon is sometimes referred to as credential inflation. As an unintended consequence of the belief that educational certificates are the key to obtaining the best-paid and most secure jobs, individuals may come to strive for constantly higher credentials in order to procure jobs which previously did not demand these, and for which their education does not in any case prepare them. Education thereby becomes merely a ritualistic process of accumulating qualifications. *See also* MERITOCRACY.

direct (causal) effect *See* CAUSAL MODELLING.

direct democracy *See* PARTICIPATORY DEMOCRACY.

disability A disadvantage that is caused for the physically impaired by particular forms of social organization. An impairment is a loss or lack of functioning, such as blindness, paralysis, or mental subnormality—that, unlike illness, is usually permanent. According to the social model of disability (see Michael Oliver, *The Politics of Disablement*, 1990), disability consists of a failure on the part of a society to provide appropriate services and facilities that meet the needs of those with particular impairments. This often involves *stigmatizing the impairment. Disabled persons often need extra financial and personal support (which is too often inadequate to sustain their *rights), and are a key group in *social security and *welfare programmes.

 SEE WEB LINKS
• The disability archive at Leeds University.

disarmament The process or policy of reducing levels of armaments, especially in the nuclear age, with the implication that possession of arms itself stimulates conflict. It is distinct from arms control—the negotiation of limits on armaments by participant states. Variants of the policy include unilateral and multilateral, partial and complete, nuclear and conventional disarmament.

disasters, sociological aspects of Natural disasters—volcanoes, earthquakes, tidal waves—disrupt all or part of societies, provoking refugees, collapse of production and distribution systems, and intensified competition for resources. Man-made disasters (notably war) involve social causes as well as these consequences—with the implication that they are avoidable. So-called disaster research examines the social and psychological impact of these occurrences among those involved.

Some sociologists (most notably Robert Merton) have argued that disaster sites offer important opportunities for sociological research and the construction of social theory, since the resulting conditions of collective stress compress social processes into an uncommonly brief time span; make usually private behaviour public and therefore more amenable to study; and generally highlight aspects of social systems and processes that are normally obscured by the routine of everyday life. Research has established that disasters have typical phases (such as the warning, threat, impact, inventory, rescue, remedy, and recovery phases); that certain types of collective behaviour tend to be associated with each phase; and that the precise form taken by each phase is affected by the characteristics of previous stages. (Thus, for example, the scale of the remedy operation is in part a function of the degree of identification with the victims.) A good comprehensive account of this literature is G. W. Baker and D. W. Chapman's *Man and Society in Disaster* (1962), and a typical case study is Kai Erikson's *Everything in its Path* (1976), which investigates the individual trauma (state of shock) and collective trauma (loss of communality) that followed a flood in previously tightly knit mountain communities in West Virginia.

discourse (discourse analysis) The study of *language, its structure, functions, and patterns in use. For Ferdinand de *Saussure, language in use as 'speech' (or *parole*) could not serve as the object of study for linguistics. As compared to the underlying system of rules of a 'tongue' (or *langue*), speech is individualized, contingent, and therefore intangible. Eventually, however, some of Saussure's successors in linguistics as well as in the wider *structuralist tradition did turn their attention to *parole*, in the hope of discovering, behind it, additional structures to those of *langue*; structures that, in other words, would facilitate the completion of the analysis of meaning, and so allow *semantics to take account of the connotative (secondary or implied) as well as the denotative (intended or explicitly signified) dimension of language.

In the event, the reversal of the privilege accorded by Saussure to the denotative over the connotative became one of the distinguishing characteristics of *post-structuralism, and it is the sense given to the term discourse within this body of thought (rather than within linguistics) that has come to exercise a powerful influence in sociology. For this reason, then, discourse analysis in sociology has been more concerned to uncover the large patterning of thought that structures whole texts, rather than the finer patterning that structures sentences, and which concerns linguists.

As Roland Barthes pointed out in the conclusion to his *Mythologies* (1957), what one is confronted with in *parole* is a chain of 'signifiers' rather than one of 'signs'. What is more, these signifiers often appear to mean more than is suggested by dictionary definitions. Barthes's suggestion was that, in order to discover what this might be, one has to be able to reconstruct the additional sets of underlying relations that determine the actual use of signifiers in particular contexts. Barthes himself termed these additional sets of relations 'myths'—a term he and others later rejected because of its negative and economic-reductionist connotations.

It was Michel *Foucault who eventually provided a conception of the additional structures that determine language use (and, indeed, although this is far less often acknowledged, of the sociological constraints upon them). This sits happily alongside the positive and non-reductionist conception of the *ideological realm that commands wide support today. According to Foucault in his methodological text *The Archaeology of Knowledge* (1969), these additional structures are made possible by historically produced, loosely structured combinations of concerns, concepts, themes, and types of statement, which he terms 'discursive formations'. Although such formations are far more loosely structured than the discourses they make possible, they are sufficiently determining to allow the differentiation of connotative structures from one another, for example, of sociology from racism and from the law.

What gives these formations their structuring quality are the particular conditions which made and still make them possible. These 'rules of formation of a discursive formation' include, so far as the objects they allow to be addressed are concerned, each of the following: the social or institutional contexts wherein they emerge, most often as the loci or sources of concern of some kind; the social identities of those who have or gain authority to pronounce on such problems and their causes; and the 'grids of specification', the intellectual templates so to speak, which are used to separate off the particular objects of concern from the many others with which each is intertwined in reality.

In order to indicate that the discourses produced in such ways add meaning to *langue*, Foucault describes their joint product not as a sentence, but as a 'statement'. He then defines this as a series of signs which, first, assumes the particular subject position given by the relevant discursive formation; second, projects a certain dynamic on to the set of signifiers that constitute it; and, finally, possesses a definite materialism by virtue of being recognizably different from other statements. A discourse is thus 'a group of statements insofar as they are made possible by the same discursive formation'.

Despite the formidable nature of the intellectual underpinning made necessary by the counter-intuitive nature of nonrepresentationalist conceptions of social phenomena, and (ironically) its own somewhat opaque language (some idea of which can be gained from the terminology introduced in this entry), discourse analysis is not a horrendously difficult exercise, as Jonathan Potter and Margaret Wetherell make clear in the excellent discussion of its methodology contained in their *Discourse and Social Psychology* (1987). For an example of an empirical study see David Silverman's *Discourses of Counselling* (1997), a study of the conversations between HIV counsellors and their clients that draws on the sociological traditions of *interactionism, *conversation analysis, and *ethnomethodology. An introduction to the whole area is David Howarth's *Discourse* (2000). *See also* CONNOTATIVE VERSUS DENOTATIVE MEANING; SEMIOLOGY.

discretionary income *See* INCOME DISTRIBUTION.

discrimination This concept—which in common usage means simply 'treating unfairly'—occurs most commonly in sociology in the context of theories of ethnic and race relations. Early sociologists (such as William G. *Sumner and Franklin H.*Giddings) viewed discrimination as an expression of *ethnocentrism—in other words a cultural phenomenon of 'dislike of the unlike'. This interpretation is consistent with studies of *stereotyping that show how relations between ethnic and racial groups are affected by the socially derived beliefs each holds about the other. However, most sociological analyses of discrimination concentrate on patterns of dominance and oppression, viewed as expressions of a struggle for *power and privilege.

There is considerable disagreement about the structural sources of these inter-ethnic and inter-racial struggles. Marxists argue that capitalist societies create *racialism to assist *exploitation (see, for example, M. Nikolinakos, 'Notes Towards an Economic Theory of Racism', *Race*, 1973). A derivative of this approach is the argument that discrimination is often the result of *internal colonialism (as illustrated in R. Blauner's article on 'Internal Colonialism and the Ghetto Revolt', *Social Problems*, 1969). Theories of segmented or split labour markets (such as that proposed by E. Bonachich, 'A Theory of Ethnic Antagonism: The Split Labour Market', *American Sociological Review*, 1972; *see also* LABOUR-MARKET SEGMENTATION) offer another interpretation of discrimination, suggesting that capitalists benefit by forcing a distinction between cheap insecure labour and higher-paid secure labour, and that it is often convenient to draw from different ethnic or racial groups in constructing these categories. Finally, there are those who have argued that discrimination results from tendencies towards *authoritarianism (however caused) among the poorer sections of any population (as, for example, in A. W. Smith's 'Racial Tolerance as a Function of Group Position', *American Sociological Review*, 1981).

In recent years, the concept of discrimination has also been applied widely in the study of relationships between the sexes, where parallel sorts of arguments have often been deployed. Thus, research suggests that women are more likely to be located in the secondary sector of split labour markets, and (according to some) may even form an *industrial reserve army. Rather more specialist studies have also looked at discrimination against the elderly (*ageism) and those with disabilities. *See also* INSTITUTIONAL RACISM; PREJUDICE; SEXISM.

discrimination, institutionalized *See* INSTITUTIONALIZED DISCRIMINATION.

discrimination, positive *See* POSITIVE DISCRIMINATION.

discursive formation *See* DISCOURSE.

disease *See* HEALTH AND ILLNESS, SOCIOLOGY OF; MEDICINE, SOCIOLOGY OF.

disequilibrium *See* EQUILIBRIUM.

disorganized capitalism A term used to describe the fragmentation of socio-economic groups in the economy, *state, and *civil society of advanced capitalism (see, for example, S. Lash and J. Urry, *The End of Organised*

Capitalism, 1987; C. Offe, *Disorganized Capitalism*, 1985). The organized inter-action of *capital (into *corporations) and labour (into *trade unions) character-istic of *corporate society and finance *capitalism has allegedly broken down—principally as a result of economic restructuring and recession. It is argued that changes in the *occupational structure, the demise of full *employment, growing divisions between the employed and *unemployed, the growth of the *service industries and the increasing size of the *informal sector have had profound implications for the political process in liberal democracies. Interrelated prob-lems in the state include the failure of *corporatist organizations to fulfil their objectives, difficulties of managing both political demands and distributional conflicts, and *class dealignment. As a consequence, liberal-democratic assump-tions about political participation and representation are undermined. Finally, economic and political disorganization has implications for the nature of civil society, notably by encouraging the growth of a *postmodern culture, which is linked to fragmented specific interest groups other than social classes.

dispersion, measures of *See* VARIATION (STATISTICAL).

displacement A process whereby strong negative or positive emotions directed towards an object or person are, because they are for some reason blocked, redirected on to another object or person. *See also* DEFENCE MECHA-NISMS; PSYCHOANALYSIS.

disposable income *See* INCOME DISTRIBUTION.

dissimilarity, measures of *See* ASSOCIATION COEFFICIENTS.

dissonance *See* COGNITIVE DISSONANCE.

distribution (statistical or frequency) A series of figures presenting all observed *values (as raw numbers or proportion of cases) for a *variable in a quantitative data-set—enabling a quick visual appreciation of the distribution of the data. The frequency distribution may be further illustrated by use of graphics such as a *pie-chart or *histogram.

A frequency or statistical distribution using observed data should not be confused with mathematical probability distributions, which are hypothetical distributions, the form of which is determined by algebraic formulae. The corre-spondence between an observed frequency distribution and various hypothetical mathematical distributions will often determine the type of statistical analysis performed on particular data.

Frequency distributions from a *survey data-set are usually the first output from the clean and edited data-set, showing the response totals for each possible reply to each question in the *questionnaire. Empirically observed distributions can be analysed using measures of dispersion and other statistical tools devel-oped from the three main forms of probability distribution: *binomial, *Poisson, and *normal (Gaussian).

distributive justice *See* JUSTICE, SOCIAL.

distributive power *See* COLLECTIVE AND DISTRIBUTIVE POWER.

divination Divination is an act that tries to foretell the future or discover the origin of a situation—usually of a calamity or illness. It does this through the consultation of an oracle or deity by a religious specialist, the diviner.

division of labour One of the oldest concepts in the social sciences. It denotes any stable organization, co-ordinating individuals, or groups carrying out different, but integrated activities. Its first and most celebrated use was in classical *political economy, the precursor to modern economics. According to Adam *Smith, division of productive labour greatly increases the wealth-creating capacity of a society. Unrestrained by government or administrative rules, the free *market encourages producers to specialize in activities where they have a natural advantage. By specializing, they benefit from greater dexterity, more efficient use of materials and time, and from mechanization. Simultaneously, the hidden hand of competition penalizes insufficiently specialized (by implication inefficient) producers, and encourages the prudent (rational) *exchange of goods and services.

However, there can be different principles of specialization. Economics emphasizes specialization according to productivity, or quantity produced in relation to the costs of production. *Organization theory, however, has long recognized that in practice conflicting criteria govern the division even of productive tasks. Considerations of the mental health of the worker (psychological efficiency) or the management of industrial unrest (social efficiency) actually limit the over-detailed specialization of tasks. Outside of productive organization, specialization may well be according to some qualitative criterion, whereby scale and quantitative productivity are relatively discounted (for example in medicine or education). Socio-geographers have also explored the spatial division of activity and power between different regions and localities.

Co-ordination is itself a troublesome concept. The early political economists assumed that a single factor (market competition between prudent individuals) was enough to bring differentiated activities together so as to maximize public well-being. Yet they also recognized that a division of labour could take place on a number of levels, between different sectors of the economy, between occupations, or between individual tasks. To this, classical sociology added the notion that modern societies as a whole are characterized by an extensive social division of labour, involving the specialization and interdependence of whole institutions and social processes. The extension of market competition, which is by definition divisive, is inadequate to explain the co-ordination of modern societies.

Despite their many differences in outlook, the common theme of sociology's founders was that the division of labour is held together by *power relations, *ideology, and moral regulation. Karl *Marx, for example, argued that market processes express an underlying division of class power that is a property of the whole socio-economic complex and encompasses individual motives and actions. Class seriously distorts the division of labour as it might occur naturally between isolated and roughly equal individual producers. Antagonistic relations of production originated in the first place from the division of labour, because of arbitrary inequalities of advantage in exchange, and the ensuing dependence of the weaker on the stronger. In turn, the subsequent form of the division of labour in any particular era reflects the struggle over the distribution of the surplus product, between the owners and non-owners of the means of production.

Émile *Durkheim's principal interest in the division of labour concerned its moral consequences, that is, its effect on the underlying solidarity of the society that should restrain individual egoism, ruthlessness, and licence. Although historians and anthropologists have subsequently questioned the idea that premodern societies lacked a division of labour, Durkheim argued that traditional societies are integrated by so-called mechanical solidarity, in which emphasis is placed on the values and cognitive symbols common to the clan or tribe. Individuals and institutions are thus relatively undifferentiated. Modern societies, he claimed, require the development of organic solidarity, in which beliefs and values emphasize individuality, encourage specialist talents in individuals, and the differentiation of activities in institutions. But although the economic division of labour may have initiated such a way of life, by itself the unregulated market loosens restraint on individual desires, undermines the establishment of social *trust, and produces abnormal forms of the division of labour. This is the source of his celebrated concept of *anomie, and of the forced division of labour associated with class and political conflict. Full organic solidarity will require appropriate education; legal restraint on inheritance and other unjust contracts; and intermediary institutions to integrate individuals into occupational and industrial life.

With the possible exceptions of Friedrich *Engels and Thorstein *Veblen, the division of labour by sex or *gender received only scant attention from the so-called founding fathers of sociology. Yet *patriarchy is arguably the oldest example of a forced or exploitative division of social activities. Most societies operate a broad division of labour between men and women, in terms of their social, religious, and political functions, and specifically in relation to the work they perform. In the context of paid employment this is called occupational segregation; it is typically far more pronounced than segregation on the basis of race or religion in the *labour market. A distinction is usually drawn between vertical and horizontal occupational segregation. Horizontal segregation arises when men and women do different types of work: in industrial societies jobs involving heavy manual labour are usually done by men, and women are concentrated in social welfare services. Vertical segregation arises when men have a near monopoly of the higher *status occupations that offer greater authority and better rewards, while women are concentrated in the lower-status jobs. (It is never the other way round.) Even in societies where horizontal occupational segregation is eroded by policies emphasizing social equality, a high degree of vertical occupational segregation persists. In an extremely important paper ('Why Work? Gender and the "Total Social Organisation of Labour"', *Gender, Work and Organisation*, 1995), Miriam Glucksmann has developed these insights into the idea of the total social organization of labour to refer to the interconnections between formal and informal work, including domestic work and voluntary work, in complex interweaving circuits.

Recent feminist analysis has drawn on both power and moral types of explanation in order to explore invidious distinctions almost universally made between men's and women's social labour and social position, and the form the division of labour by gender has taken in industrial societies. Power inequality is evident in the way the system of industrial production for many years existed alongside, and arguably relied upon, the domestication of women and their unpaid household labour. Persistent inequalities of reward, and the segmentation of labour markets into areas of men's and women's work, are only slowly diminishing. Moral control is at work in the ideologies of the family, myths of romantic love, the duties of motherhood, and supposedly natural differences between the sexes which the *socialization of boys and girls still encourages. Thus, despite modern doctrines of natural *rights, women have often (until recently at least) been excluded from the legal and political guarantees which Durkheim considered to be essential if the division of labour was to be accompanied by organic solidarity. *See also* DEPRIVATION; DISCRIMINATION; DOMESTIC DIVISION OF LABOUR; LABOUR-MARKET SEGMENTATION; SOCIAL ORDER.

division of labour, domestic *See* DOMESTIC DIVISION OF LABOUR.

division of labour, international *See* INTERNATIONAL DIVISION OF LABOUR.

division of labour, sexual *See* SEXUAL DIVISION OF LABOUR.

divorce The formal legal dissolution of a legally constituted *marriage. The conditions necessary to terminate a marriage in divorce vary widely from culture to culture and over time. In certain societies the rights of men and women in this respect are still highly unequal, but there appears to be a move in Western societies towards an acceptance of the idea of irretrievable breakdown of a marriage as suitable grounds for divorce. One of the most significant trends in the wake of this liberalization of divorce laws has been the increasing propensity for divorce proceedings to be initiated by women. In addition, it should be noted that definitions of what constitute marriage and divorce also vary widely, and that in Western societies divorce is increasingly preceded by extended periods of separation between partners, which renders the legal procedure increasingly less relevant.

In the United States and Britain over the past two decades, concern over rising *divorce rates has frequently reached the status of a *moral panic, and it is often stated that, given the continuation of current rates, over one in three marriages contracted will end in divorce. However, these calculations must be considered in the light of high rates of remarriage among divorcees, and an increasing propensity to establish common-law rather than formalized legal unions among those groups most at risk of divorce (for example the young). Of course, the statistics say nothing of the social difficulties and personal suffering faced by many people experiencing the effects of divorce, including the children of broken marriages. Another well-publicized statistic indicates that one in five children in Britain, by the age of 16, will have experienced the divorce or separation of their parents, given current rates. In *Social Origins of Depression* (1978), George Brown and Tirril Harris identified divorce of parents as one of the more stressful life-events likely to have been experienced by women suffering from neurotic depressive conditions. The deleterious effects on divorcing individuals of legal wrangling over children and housing is also well documented.

The basic statistics, and some of their social policy implications, are discussed in Janet Finch, *Family Obligations and Social Change* (1989). *See also* FAMILY, SOCIOLOGY OF.

divorce rate A measure designed to provide information on the comparative propensity to *divorce in different populations. The crude divorce rate for a particular year is calculated by dividing the number of divorces occurring within a population over the year, by the average or mid-year population for that year, expressed times 1000. However, as in the case of the crude birth rate, this measure takes no account of the age-structure of populations, and therefore of the population at risk. A more refined measure divides the number of divorces by the number of marriages in a given year (times 1000).

The divorce rate is sometimes used as an indicator of social stress in a society. However, in countries where separation characteristically precedes formal legal divorce, divorce rates are increasingly less relevant as a measure of the actual experience of individuals in a population. *See also* MARRIAGE.

documentary research Research that uses personal and official documents as a source material. Documents used by social scientists may include such things as newspapers, diaries, stamps, directories, handbills, maps, government statistical publications, photographs, paintings, CDs, tapes, and computer files.

The most important consideration in using documents is their quality as evidence on social meanings and social relations. Unlike survey questionnaires or interview transcripts, documents have generally been compiled for purposes other than research, and their value must be thoroughly assessed before they can be used. It has been suggested that documents must be assessed against four criteria: authenticity, credibility, representativeness, and meaning (see John Scott, *A Matter of Record*, 1990). The criterion of *authenticity* involves assessing documents for their soundness and authorship. Soundness refers to whether the document is complete and whether it is an original or a sound copy. Authorship concerns issues of forgery or fraud and matters of collective or institutional authorship. Authorship is assessed through both internal evidence on vocabulary and literary style and external evidence from chemical tests on paper and ink. The criterion of *credibility* concerns the sincerity and accuracy of a document. All documents are selective, as it is impossible to construct accounts independent of particular standpoints, but they can be more or less credible as accounts, depending on the motives from which a point of view is adopted and whether the account gives an accurate report from that standpoint. To assess the accuracy of a report it is necessary to look at the conditions under which it was compiled and, in particular, how close the author was to the events reported. The criterion of *representativeness* involves an assessment of the survival and availability of relevant documents. It is important to know whether the documents consulted are representative of all the relevant documents that once existed, and this depends upon what proportion of the relevant documents have been stored or retained and whether they are available for researchers to use. The availability of official documents may often be limited by considerations of confidentiality and official secrecy. The *meaning* of documents is the most important matter and arises at two levels. The first level is the literal understanding of a document, by which is meant its physical readability, whether it is in a language that can be read, and such issues as dating. Once this practical matter has been resolved the more fundamental interpretative meaning must be addressed. Interpretation is a hermeneutic task through which an appreciation of the social and cultural context and forms of discourse that structure a text is reached. This involves methods of textual analysis and *content analysis.

A useful recent overview of documentary research can be found in Lindsay Prior's *Using Documents in Social Research* (2003). Scott's *A Matter of Record* covers the issues involved in handling a range of documents, while Ken Plummer's *Documents of Life, 2* (2001) gives good coverage of *personal documents. *See also* LIFE HISTORY; PERSONAL DOCUMENTS.

domain assumptions *See* AXIOM.

domestic colonialism *See* INTERNAL (OR DOMESTIC) COLONIALISM.

domestic division of labour The division of tasks, roles, and duties within the household. With the increased entry of married women into formal *employment, sociologists began to look more closely at the processes that linked home and workplace, including the question of whether or not women's increased involvement in paid labour led to a renegotiation of the 'traditional' domestic roles and organization of *domestic labour. A huge empirical and theoretical literature was then generated in a relatively short time.

Early studies cast doubts on the optimistic view (advanced, for example, by Michael Young and Peter Wilmott in *The Symmetrical Family*, 1973) that, especially among the middle classes, husband and wife were increasingly sharing in the complementary (hitherto largely segregated) tasks of earning a wage and running a household. Thus, Robert O. Blood and Donald M. Wolfe (*Husbands and Wives*, 1960) found that, among a large sample of families in Detroit, the sex segregation of domestic tasks was largely unchanged: men performed outdoor tasks requiring 'mechanical aptitude' while women did *housework. Similar findings are reported in Ann Oakley's *The Sociology of Housework* (1974) and Stephen Edgell's *Middle Class Couples* (1980). Research by Rhona and Robert N. Rapoport on *dual-career marriages drew attention to the *role conflict confronting the women, a conflict which frequently resulted in them shouldering a 'double burden' of accepting primary responsibility for traditional domestic labour, but also holding down a paid job.

More recent studies have documented in great detail the extent to which the traditional allocation of domestic tasks to women remains largely unaltered. An excellent summary of the findings from this explosion of research is Lydia Morris's *The Workings of the Household* (1990). She concludes that the American and British studies produce parallel findings, the most important of which are as follows: women, including employed women, continue to bear the main burden of domestic work; men's (slightly) increased participation in domestic labour does not offset women's increased employment; women in part-time employment fare worst, possibly because of a life-cycle effect, which creates extra work associated with caring for young children; men tend nevertheless to be more involved with domestic tasks at this stage of the *life cycle than at other stages; there is relative stability in the level of housework time expended by men whether the wife works or not. Differences in emphasis and on points of detail across these studies are interesting, but insignificant when set against the central and often confirmed finding echoed by Sarah F. Berk, to the effect that 'husband's employment activities and the individual characteristics that establish husbands in the occupational sphere are the most critical determinants of total household market time . . . [whilst] . . . few married men engage in significant amounts of household labour and child care' (*The Gender Factory*, 1985). *See also* CONJUGAL ROLE; HOUSEHOLD ALLOCATIVE SYSTEM; SEX ROLES; SEXUAL DIVISION OF LABOUR.

domestic labour A concept developed within feminist theory to analyse the significance of the unpaid work performed by women in the home. Within Marxist feminism, domestic labour is sometimes referred to as 'reproductive labour', after Friedrich Engels's distinction between productive (value-creating) work and work aimed at re-creating the worker or the capacity to work. Most definitions of domestic labour equate it with *housework but some include 'emotional work' such as tension management and caring. Considerable debate took place in the 1970s as to whether this labour should be considered productive or unproductive in the classic Marxian sense, and whether it should be seen to benefit men or *capitalism, or indeed both. Despite disagreement as to how precisely to conceptualize such labour, and about its substantive significance, it is widely recognized as providing an important basis for inequality between the sexes, entailing some degree of *exploitation of women by men, and constituting a significant if hidden subsidy to the economy. *See also* HOMEWORK; PATRIARCHY.

domestic violence Specifically male violence (physical or psychological) against women, the term was popularized by feminists in the 1970s, some of whom established refuges for battered women, and who argued that domestic violence is a reflection of *gender inequalities in *power and of women's oppression. More broadly, the term encompasses any violence within the family, although violence against children is usually described specifically as child abuse. Typically, the police have been reluctant to intervene in incidents involving domestic violence, preferring to regard the family as a private realm.

dominant culture Whereas *traditional societies can be characterized by a high consistency of cultural traits and *customs, modern societies are often a conglomeration of different, often competing, *cultures and *subcultures. In such a situation of diversity, a dominant culture is one whose values, language, and ways of behaving are imposed on a subordinate culture or cultures through economic or political power. This may be achieved through legal or political suppression of other sets of values and patterns of behaviour, or by monopolizing the media of communication.

dominant ideology thesis Proponents of the thesis identify *ideology, a term used (in this context) synonymously with concepts such as shared belief systems, ultimate *values, and common *culture, as the mainstay of *social order in advanced capitalist societies. The argument assumes that, in class-stratified societies, the ruling class controls the production of ideas as well as material production. It propagates a set of coherent beliefs which dominate subordinate meaning systems and, as a consequence, shapes working-class consciousness in the interests of the status quo. The dominant class effectively diffuses a *false consciousness among the masses who are thus rendered incapable of defending their own *class interests. In other words, a dominant ideology functions to incorporate the *working class into *capitalist society, thereby maintaining social cohesion.

While Talcott *Parsons and other *normative functionalists have long been associated with cultural accounts of social integration, it has been noted that neo-Marxists such as Louis *Althusser, Antonio *Gramsci, and Jürgen Habermas also relied on theories of a dominant ideology in their writings on capitalist societies. Moreover, with the possible exception of Gramsci, they give a functionalist account of the role of such an ideology in their explanations of social stability. Neo-Marxists, it has been argued, have come increasingly to depend on the concept of ideology to explain the lack of revolutionary working-class consciousness in advanced capitalist societies: the absence of revolutionary struggle is explained primarily by the ideological *incorporation of the working class. Functionalist and Marxist explanations of how societies cohere have thus become rather similar over the course of the 20th century—a somewhat ironic development since neither *Durkheim nor *Marx neglected the role of economic and political coercion in their own accounts of social stability and instability.

Numerous theoretical and empirical problems have been identified with the dominant ideology thesis. Rarely has a dominant ideology been clearly identified and its principal characteristics properly defined. The thesis suggests that an overarching ideology dictates the way in which the subordinate classes view society, yet its proponents have consistently failed to explain the processes by which the ruling class imposes such an ideology on the masses. Instead, they proffer a somewhat derisory picture of a falsely conscious working class, easily lulled into accepting an unequal distribution of material resources and political power. It is not surprising, therefore, to find that such a vague and imprecise thesis has been almost impossible to *operationalize and substantiate empirically.

Many sociologists question the importance which has been attached to the role of a dominant ideology in recent accounts of social order. For example, Nicholas Abercrombie and his colleagues (*The Dominant Ideology Thesis*, 1980) maintain that dominant ideologies are rarely transmitted effectively throughout social structures, and that their principal effects are on superordinate rather than subordinate classes. In feudal and early capitalist societies such ideologies functioned to maintain the control of the dominant class over wealth—but at the level of the *elites themselves. Both the *feudal manor and capitalist family firm depended on the conservation and accumulation of property. Private possession of land and capital required a stable marriage system, with unambiguous rules about inheritance, legitimacy, and remarriage. The dominant ideology was a complex of legal, moral, and religious values which had the required effect of preserving wealth. Among feudal ruling classes, for example, Catholicism and the system of honour provided ideological guarantees that children would remain loyal to family holdings. By comparison the *peasantry (and in early capitalism the factory workforce) were co-opted by the sheer exigencies of labouring to live—the 'dull compulsion of economic relations'. Even in late capitalism the 'iron cage' of everyday life offers a better explanation of working-class quiescence than does ideological incorporation. Moral pluralism and a great diversity of political, social, and cultural deviance can readily be tolerated because the compliance of subordinate strata is secured by economic constraint, political coercion, and the *bureaucratic mechanisms of school, family, workplace, and prison. The persistence of conflict in capitalist societies also suggests that a dominant ideology is not functionally all-embracing.

In short, the consequences of a dominant ideology for social order have almost certainly been overstated, and the sources of social cohesion are to be found also in economic compulsion and interdependence, legal and political coercion, the constraints of everyday routine, and (perhaps) *fatalism. *See also* DOMINANT CULTURE; DUAL CONSCIOUSNESS.

dominant value system *See* DUAL CONSCIOUSNESS.

domination Rule by coercion or noncoercive compliance. Individuals or groups may exercise *power over others—domination—either by brute force or because that power is accepted as legitimate by those who are subject to it. Max *Weber identified three pure types of 'legitimate domination', otherwise termed types of authority, and classified these according to the grounds on which their claims to legitimacy were based. These types are: rational-legal (legitimacy claimed from a generally agreed set of rules and procedures); traditional (legitimacy based on continuity over time); and charismatic (legitimacy based on the extraordinary personal qualities of the leader). *See also* BUREAUCRACY; CHARISMA; LEGITIMACY.

doubling-time The time it takes for a population of a given size to double its size—which is nowadays measured in decades rather than centuries.

dramaturgy (dramaturgical perspective) A theoretical position, often allied to *symbolic interactionism, *role theory, and the work of Erving *Goffman, that uses the stage and the theatre as its key organizing metaphor. The idea that 'all the world is a stage and all the people players' is hardly new, having a long lineage which includes Greek theatre, Shakespeare, and Machiavelli. In modern sociology, the idea was most fully explored by Goffman, whose study of the micro order of interaction highlighted the ways in which people are engaged in *impression management. But although he is the most central contributor to this field there have been others: either developing particular aspects of the theory, as for example the application of the concept of 'script' to sexuality (in the work of John Gagnon (1931–2016) and William Simon, *Sexual Conduct,* 1973), applying it to particular research problems such as the study of soccer hooligans (reported in Peter Marsh et al., *The Rules of Disorder,* 1978), or in political symbolism (as exemplified in Peter M. Hall's 'The Presidency and Impression Management', *Studies in Symbolic Interaction* 1979).

dream work *See* PSYCHOANALYSIS.

drift Movement in and out of particular forms of behaviour without any necessary commitment to it. Originally used in relation to delinquency by David Matza (*Delinquency and Drift,* 1964), who argued that *delinquency does not emerge as a result of strongly deterministic forces, but rather through a gentle weakening of the moral ties of society, which allowed some young people to drift into delinquency. Only a minority become committed to full-time delinquent careers. *See also* DELINQUENCY; VOCABULARIES OF MOTIVE.

drinking and alcoholism A depressant intoxicant, alcohol is a popular drink in the leisure time of most cultures; it is also held in high regard as a key part of many religious and secular ceremonies and *rituals. Alcohol is a disinhibitor and can impair judgement. In moderation the former effect is often socially valued, but this carries implications for health by increasing the possibility of accidents, unsafe sex, and such like. Some cultures forbid alcohol use for reasons of religion (for example Muslims), whilst some countries (such as Finland) have sought to impose tight regulations on its availability for social reasons. The best known failure of total prohibition is the United States in the 1920s. Since the Second World War, spending on alcohol has risen in most advanced industrial societies, as part of the rising proportion of household finances available for leisure pursuits. Drinking in the home has increased, though drink remains associated with either sophistication and escape or masculine values and camaraderie. Public houses and bars often retain a sense of being masculine territory. Drinking carries various symbolic meanings, for example 'round-buying' and other rituals involve reciprocity, inclusion, and exclusion.

Alcoholism was coined as a term to denote a special medically diagnosable condition of serious *dependence upon or addiction to alcohol. Dating from the mid-19th century, acceptance of the term is the cornerstone of the self-help philosophy of groups like Alcoholics Anonymous, founded in the United States in the 1930s. Alcoholism has been described as a disease, a genetic disorder, a psychological problem, and as the product of the dysfunctional family. Undoubtedly, drink and its heavy consumption are related to the incidence of petty and serious crime (especially violence and motor accidents), health problems, and workplace injuries. However, the term alcoholism has been justifiably criticized in recent years: the World Health Organization and others would no longer accept its description as a disease, and a broader set of perspectives, including social and cultural theory, now generally inform work on alcohol dependence.

drives, innate and acquired Energizing forces directed towards a particular *goal or objective. Drives may be viewed as innate (physiological) or acquired (learned). In the former case the term is sometimes used as an alternative to instinct—though drive suggests less pre-patterning of behaviour. It is arguably a better translation of Sigmund Freud's *trieb* than is instinct. *See also* NEED.

drugs (drug addiction) These terms generally refer to illegal drugs, although the social significance of alcohol, tobacco, and tranquillizers should be noted (for example regarding health). The diverse origins of illegal drugs include natural plants and manufactured synthetics. Research shows that patterns of use, behaviour, and subjective experience will be influenced by particular properties of drugs but also by social factors, such as *culture and expectations (see, for example, Institute for the Study of Drug Dependence, London, *Drug Abuse Briefing*, 1991). Most commonly used is cannabis, but greatest social concern is aroused by heroin, and more recently crack/cocaine, LSD, amphetamine, and ecstasy. Prohibitions on drug use are relatively recent; use of opiates as remedies and intoxicants was common during the 19th century (see V. Berridge and G. Edwards, *Opium and the People*, 1987).

The concept of addiction is unhelpful: it suggests a *dependency with grave consequences for the individual and society. Not all drug-users develop dependency nor do such consequences inevitably follow; the term 'problem drug-user' is therefore increasingly favoured. Regarding *crime, the dominant thesis is that regular drug use, coupled with the illegality of supply, forces users to commit crime to pay for drugs; however, whether drug use leads to involvement in crime, or involvement in delinquent life-styles introduces a person to drug use, is debated. HIV transmission via shared syringes has encouraged the aim of minimizing harm associated with use, challenging the traditional pursuit of abstinence. Calls for decriminalization are regularly made, but legislative change seems unlikely, at least in the short term.

(⊕)) SEE WEB LINKS
• Release: a campaigning pressure group in the field of drug use.

dual-career marriage Marriages in which both partners pursue occupational *careers. Such marriages are still relatively rare, and findings about dual-career *marriages may not generalize to dual-earner families (where both partners are formally *employed but only one—usually the male—pursues a career), which are now the norm. However, empirical studies suggest that both career women and those with less rewarding jobs appear to work a double shift, combining home and work responsibilities. *See also* DOMESTIC DIVISION OF LABOUR.

dual consciousness A term used to describe the world view of people who simultaneously hold two apparently inconsistent sets of beliefs. It is particularly associated with the ideas of *Gramsci. This is usually ascribed to the fact that people receive a set of beliefs through general *socialization into a *dominant culture but have another set of beliefs based on their own practical experiences of life. It is often said that the *working class is most prone to dual consciousness because the everyday experience of working-class life runs counter to many received beliefs about society. Thus, for example, it is possible for workers to agree that strikes are usually caused by malcontents, extremists, and agitators (received beliefs), but to relate their own experiences of strikes to genuine grievances (practical experience). In Frank Parkin's *Class Inequality and Political Order* (1972) the terms 'dominant value system' and 'subordinate value system' serve to make this same distinction. The former refers to the fact that 'the social and political definitions of those in dominant positions tend to become objectified and enshrined in the macro institutional orders, so providing the moral framework of the entire social system'. The generating milieu of the latter is the local working-class community. Parkin describes the subordinate value system as 'essentially accommodative; that is to say its representation of the class structure and inequality emphasizes various modes of adaptation, rather than full endorsement of, or opposition to, the *status quo'*. See also DOMINANT IDE-OLOGY THESIS.

dual-earner families (dual-earner marriages) *See* DUAL-CAREER MARRIAGE.

dual economy *See* ECONOMIC DUALISM; INTERNAL COLONIALISM; LABOUR MARKET; LABOUR-MARKET SEGMENTATION.

dual labour market *See* LABOUR MARKET; LABOUR-MARKET SEGMENTATION.

dualism Any theory that identifies an irreducible distinction between two classes of thing. Those of most interest to sociologists are ethical dualism, which states an irreducible difference between statements of fact and *value-judgements; explanatory dualism, which holds that while natural events have causes, human actions can only be explained by reference to motives or reasons; the doctrine that mind and matter exist as independent entities; and the idea of the religious and the secular being parallel and independent spheres of life, governed by different laws. *See also* DESCARTES, RENÉ.

dualism, economic *See* ECONOMIC DUALISM.

Du Bois, William Edward Burghardt (1868–1963) A Black American intellectual and activist whose work, though largely ignored by modern sociologists, prefigures some of the classic themes of early American sociology.

Du Bois studied at the Universities of Harvard and Berlin (Max Weber was an admirer), contributed to the *American Journal of Sociology*, chaired the Department of Sociology at Atlanta University, and published the first systematic sociological studies of African American communities. His *The Philadelphia Negro* is a comprehensive report on what nowadays would be called the Black urban underclass. It pre-dates W. I.*Thomas and Florian Znaniecki's *The Polish Peasant* by more than twenty years and could serve equally well as the *locus classicus* of American urban ethnography. In a famous article published in *Atlantic Monthly* in 1897 (and reprinted in his *Souls of Black Folk*, 1899/1903), Du Bois formulated a theory of *dual consciousness that shows the influence of William *James's ideas about the self (James taught Du Bois at Harvard), noting that 'it is a peculiar sensation, this double-consciousness, this sense of always looking at one's self through the eyes of others, of measuring one's soul by the tape of a world that looks on in amused contempt and pity. One feels this twoness—an American, a negro; two souls, two thoughts, two unreconciled strivings; two warring ideals in one dark body, whose dogged strength keeps it from being torn asunder.'

Du Bois was a co-founder of the NAACP (National Association for the Advancement of Colored People) and a major figure in the renaissance of Harlem as a cultural centre in the 1920s. He was, however, much criticized for his support for African American participation in the First World War. He moved to Ghana in 1961 and renounced his US citizenship. His contribution to the development of sociology is described in the two-volume biography by D. L. Lewis, *W. E. B. Du Bois* (1993 and 2000).

Durkheim, Émile (1858–1917) The most famous French sociologist, long acknowledged as the founding figure of *functionalism, but more recently hailed by leading authorities on *structuralism, *sociolinguistics (*see* CONVERSATION ANALYSIS), and *postmodernism, all of whom have found in Durkheim's writings ideas and sentiments which are easy to incorporate.

Born of Jewish parents (his father was a rabbi), Durkheim was educated at the École Normale Supérieure, where he studied philosophy. After teaching this subject in provincial *lycées* for five years he obtained a post as a lecturer in social science and education at the University of Bordeaux in 1887. Ten years later he helped found *L'Année sociologique*, soon to become the most prestigious sociological journal in France, and a focus for an influential Durkheimian school of thought. Durkheim published regularly in the journal until his relatively early death, from a stroke, at the age of 59.

Despite a brilliant career as a teacher and researcher, and the publication of a series of controversial monographs which sketched out the methods and subject-matter of the new science of sociology, it was a full fifteen years before Durkheim was eventually called to a Chair in Paris. Some have suggested that, in this, he was a victim of the anti-semitism of French intellectual life. However, it is also true that his single-minded championing of sociology as the most important social science gained him many enemies in the educational establishment, and his career is littered with bitter controversies involving those who rejected his vision of sociology.

Most of his major monographs were translated into English after his death and are, remarkably, still in print even in translation. The impelling logic of *The Division of Labour in Society* (1893), his controversial doctoral thesis defended after his stint in *lycée* teaching, was swiftly followed by *The Rules of Sociological Method* (1895). Durkheim here stressed that sociology as a science would be characterized by observation (rather than abstract theory), the study of social (rather than psychological) facts, and provide both functional and causal explanations. His principles were applied in the complex and multidimensional argument of *Suicide* (1897), in which he seeks to demonstrate that this apparently most personal of acts is ultimately determined by society, and that the suicide-rate is therefore a 'social fact'. He deploys an aetiological explanation in which the effects (suicides) are evidence of the underlying social currents. His lifelong interest in morality and moral authority (evident, for example, in the depiction of mechanical and organic solidarity in his doctoral thesis) culminated almost inevitably in writings on religion. The conclusion that 'collective' individuals worship society, stated most forcefully in *The Elementary Forms of the Religious Life* (1912), is an apt epitaph for his work. Other major texts on socialism, morality, and education were published posthumously.

Throughout these publications one is struck by the breadth of vision displayed by Durkheim in his remorseless search for the social and moral bases of the emerging industrial society. He continues to be reappraised by commentators from both the left and right of the political spectrum. His label as a conservative thinker has long ago been discarded—rightly so, in the light of his contributions to the theory of equality of opportunity, evident for example in his writings on education.

Steven Lukes conveniently identifies the key concepts, dichotomies, and arguments that identify the Durkheimian heritage. *Collective conscience, *collective representations, and *social facts were concepts which argued for the distinctiveness of sociology against other social sciences (notably psychology). These concepts were suited to the object of sociological explanation—namely, collective phenomena not reducible to the individual actor or psyche. Furthermore, the central problem for sociology was to explicate the relationship between the individual and society, recognizing that these analytical levels were distinct. The association created by individuals has its own characteristics, its own 'facticity', which can only be explained by social facts located at that level. His strong opposition to methodological *individualism pushed him in the direction of a holism which occasionally appeared to reify society itself (a charge also levelled against subsequent functionalists who looked at society in a similarly holistic way). Other dichotomies flowed from this key coupling of individual and society. For example, in the distinction between the *sacred and the profane, the former was created by the collectivity while the latter expressed the private and individual life. The former was moral whereas the latter was sensual.

Durkheim saw his task as the creation of a science of sociology, with its own subject-matter, methodology, and explanatory models. In this he continued the work of *Comte and *Saint-Simon. Likewise, his concern for what might be termed social engineering derived from his belief that sociology could and should intervene scientifically, when social development did not produce order *sui generis*. He read and absorbed the work of his near contemporaries, including Karl Marx, and this perhaps explains why his thought has variously been depicted as *idealist, *realist, *positivist and *evolutionist. In truth his intellectual and personal concerns refracted these views into a *mélange* of concepts peculiarly his own. Lukes's biography gives an appreciative assessment. By comparison, Raymond Aron systematically treats all of Durkheim's major works to a thoughtful but fairly savage criticism, in his *Main Currents in Sociological Thought*, ii (1967). The key intellectual biographies are those of Steven Lukes (*Émile Durkheim: His Life and Work*, 1973) and Marcel Fournier (*Émile Durkheim: A Biography*, 2007). *See also* ANOMIE; DIVISION OF LABOUR; DYNAMIC DENSITY; FATALISM; INFLATION; LAW, SOCIOLOGY OF; MORAL COMMUNITY; ORGANIC (OR BIOLOGICAL) ANALOGY; RELIGION, SOCIOLOGY OF; RITUAL; SOCIAL ORDER; SOCIAL SOLIDARITY; SUICIDE; TAXONOMY.

SEE WEB LINKS
• The British Centre for Durkheimian Studies, University of Oxford.

dyad The dyad, a group of two members, is the smallest possible social group: if one person opts out the group ceases to exist. Two people can form an intimacy not found in larger groups, but the dyad also involves other basic elements of social exchange, such as rivalry, reciprocity, and power. *See also* TRIAD.

dynamic density In Émile *Durkheim's writings on the emergence of organic solidarity from mechanical solidarity, he identified certain conditions for the transition to the former: volume (or population growth), the concentration of people, and finally the increase in the intensity of communication which would emerge out of these two factors. Increased intensity of communication served to break down the segmented structures of society, overcome the opaque nature of social milieux, and in due course develop *social differentiation. Durkheim places enormous store on dynamic density—observability, contiguity, and constant social contact—as the pre-condition for and guarantor of social and moral consensus. Moral or dynamic density, by fostering interaction, not only creates the *division of labour, but is the condition for its continued existence. Employer, employee, state, and society must all be in proximate contact, so as to be aware of each other's interdependence, and also to create the moral regulation that acts as the social glue for *social integration.

dysfunction (dysfunctional) Terms used to deal with tensions in the *social system. Something is dysfunctional if it inhibits or disrupts the working of the system as a whole or another part of the system; for example, if teenage *anomie disrupts the labour market or education system, then it may be said to be dysfunctional for the society. *See also* FUNCTION.

ecological competition A term derived from the biological sciences to denote the process of interaction between social groups, each seeking to gain access to a limited supply of the necessities of life, such as living space. *See also* CONCENTRIC ZONE THEORY; ECOLOGY; HUMAN ECOLOGY; URBAN ECOLOGY.

ecological fallacy The spurious inference of individual characteristics from group-level characteristics. The classic presentation is by W. S. Robinson in 'Ecological Correlations and the Behaviour of Individuals' (*American Sociological Review*, 1950), which demonstrates the inconsistencies between correlations at differing levels of aggregation. For example, a strong association between unemployment rates and crime-rates may be observed in data for police districts, but the statistical association will be much weaker and may not occur at all in data for particular component smaller neighbourhoods, or in survey microdata. More generally, a strong association between two factors in aggregate data cannot be taken as evidence of a causal link at the individual level. One of the most famous examples of ecological reasoning is Émile Durkheim's *Suicide* (see H. C. Selvin, 'Durkheim's *Suicide*: Further Thoughts on a Methodological Classic', in R. A. Nisbet (ed.), *Émile Durkheim*, 1965).

ecological invasion A term referring to the process by which social groups or activities which are better adapted to a given environment than are its existing inhabitants or activities enter and eventually dominate it. *See also* CONCENTRIC ZONE THEORY; ECOLOGY; HUMAN ECOLOGY; URBAN ECOLOGY.

ecological succession A term used in *urban ecology, denoting the replacement of one dominant group or activity by another, following an invasion of the territory of the latter by the former. *See also* CONCENTRIC ZONE THEORY; ECOLOGY; HUMAN ECOLOGY.

ecology Ecology is the scientific study of the interactions that determine the territorial distribution and abundance of organisms. The term was first used scientifically in 1869 by the German biologist Haekel in a study of plant ecology. Darwin's theory of the evolution of species inspired the development of ecology. According to Darwin, evolution is driven by reproduction and inheritance on one hand, and by natural selection on the other. Natural selection eliminates species least able to survive the struggle for existence because they fail to adapt to changing environments. An important aspect of the latter—alongside factors such as climate and topography—is the presence of other species competing for limited territory or other resources. However, unfettered competition is normally limited, as species are also interdependent, related to each other symbiotically in a 'web of life', the result of successful adaptation to each other and to the natural environment (although certain species are dominant). This equilibrium is temporarily upset when newly dominant species emerge. The concepts of invasion, domination, and succession have been used to analyse the stages of this process.

Ecological perspectives have had considerable influence well beyond the biological sciences, for example in medical *epidemiology, the psychology of architecture and design, and *human geography. Late 20th-century concern about the impact of human activities on the environment has resulted in new social and political ecology movements and the growing salience of so-called green issues generally—all of these being topics for sociological research. However, the main influence of ecological concepts on sociological theory occurred between the 1920s and the 1940s in the United States, initially through the development of *urban ecology by Chicago sociologists. The ecological perspective was subsequently applied more widely and the terms human or social ecology have often been used in this context. Some *human ecologists were critical of the emphasis placed by the early Chicago sociologists on competition between human groups for territorial advantage (based on a rather unidimensional view of Darwinian natural selection) and suggested a broader remit for study, namely, the form and development of different types of human *community (not necessarily spatially bounded), with particular reference to the ways in which they adapt to their environments through cooperative and competitive social relationships.

The relationship between ecological theories and sociology has been limited, and is stronger in North America than in Europe, still influencing, for example, some American urban and rural sociology. Indeed, it has been claimed that the ecological perspective transcends any individual social science, as it deals with processes which underlie all these disciplines. Recent sociological theory is scarcely influenced by its particular use of the biological analogy, although the concern with adaption, interdependence, and equilibrium also characterizes *structural-functional sociology. *See also* DARWINISM; ECOLOGICAL COMPETITION; ECOLOGICAL INVASION; ECOLOGICAL SUCCESSION; ENVIRONMENT; INVASION-SUCCESSION MODEL; NATURAL AREA.

ecology, human *See* HUMAN ECOLOGY.

ecology, urban *See* URBAN ECOLOGY.

econometrics Economic analysis using a combination of empirical data, techniques of statistical estimation, and (usually) some form of *multivariate analysis, such as *regression analysis, applied to economic theory. Econometric models of the economy are used in forecasting and policy analysis.

economic activity *See* EMPLOYMENT.

economic determinism A philosophical and theoretical position most commonly associated with the Marxist assertion that social phenomena have their roots in the relations of production.

According to Karl *Marx the *relations of production constitute the *base upon which a legal and political *superstructure rests. They also structure social relations between classes, producing corresponding forms of social consciousness. Thus, as Marx puts it, 'the mode of production of material life conditions the social, political and intellectual life process in general' ('Preface' to *A Contribution to the Critique of Political Economy*, 1859). This and similar propositions have been the source of much debate about the nature and degree of economic determinism. At one extreme, it might be argued that all social, political and cultural life can be 'read off' from the relations of production, and that the social consciousness of the individual is determined by his or her position in the economic structure. Such a view challenges the notion of free will and individual autonomy, and has been criticized accordingly. Alternatively, the relations of production could be seen merely as a constraining factor in the development of the superstructure, defining no more than the broad parameters to which the superstructure and individual consciousness will loosely correspond.

These points were elaborated by Friedrich *Engels after Marx's death, such that economic relations were denied any automatic determining effect, but seen rather as exerting a 'decisive influence'. Engels's phraseology has been the focus of much debate within Marxism and the source of much criticism by non-Marxists. At the heart of the criticism is the desire to assert the power of ideas and the potential of autonomous individuals to effect social *change. *See also* Althusser.

economic development *See* economic growth.

economic dualism A way of conceptualizing the existence of two (sometimes more) separate but symbiotic sets of economic processes or *markets within the same political or national social framework. In *Third World societies, for example, a dual economy is formed by the coexistence of peasant subsistence agriculture and cash production of basic commodities or industrial goods for the international market. An analogous division exists in highly industrialized economies between the corporate core and peripheral firms and *labour markets. *See also* labour-market segmentation.

economic growth The growth of national income, or the output of goods and services per head of population, with output conventionally measured by the Gross National Product (GNP). The alternative term economic development is often used in relation to *Third World societies. Economic growth does not necessarily lead to growth in consumption and improved distribution of wealth and public welfare; it depends on how the increased output is used, and by whom.

Economists have devoted much effort to producing theories of economic growth which might guide policy-making in developing countries and in industrial societies. Theories place varying degrees of emphasis on capital investment, the economic infrastructure, manpower planning and education, and the relative roles of government and the private sector. *See also* entrepreneur; sustainable development.

economic man A term used in classical economic theory (*see* LAISSEZ-FAIRE ECONOMICS), denoting the individual's rational deployment of labour or resources in the marketplace, in systematic pursuit of his or her own self-interest. The term is intended to apply to both men and women but could be argued to reflect an implicit assumption of the primacy of male activity in the *market. *See also* POLITICAL ECONOMY; RATIONAL CHOICE THEORY.

economic sociology The fundamental problem in economics is to explain how the limited productive resources and effort of a society are allocated among the wide range of alternative uses to which they might be put. Conventional economic theory seeks to address this issue by adopting a position of methodological *individualism. It also makes a number of abstract assumptions for purposes of analysis. First, relationships of competition exist between the producers of a commodity, between its consumers, and between producers and consumers collectively, the whole constituting a set of *market relationships. Second, both competition and economic co-operation are outcomes of the rational pursuit of economic advantage by individuals and groups. This is the paradigmatic example of a *rational choice theory. Third, the propositions of the theory do not simply describe the institutions and motivations of so-called market societies alone; they formalize what is an inevitable and natural set of determining influences in any society, as soon as the issue of scarce resources (means) and competing possible uses (ends) arises.

Economic sociology can also be said to be concerned with resource allocation; and, like economics, it can trace its origins to classical *political economy. However, early sociology was very often a critique of the tendencies towards individualism and abstraction within political economy, on which economics subsequently built. For example, Karl *Marx was among the first to claim that resource allocation through unregulated market competition is fundamentally anarchic rather than orderly, and reproduces already existing inequalities of *class power and privilege. In modern times, a similar view has been taken of market discrimination in relation to *race and *gender. Such arguments mean that the investigator is obliged to approach society with a degree of methodological holism which is unacceptable to many economists.

Another influential controversy is the link between economics and various versions of *liberal political theory in which state regulation of economic and social policy is rejected as an infringement of individual liberty. It is claimed that welfare is more likely to be maximized by encouraging free enterprise and unrestricted market competition. This view is associated with *neo-classical economics which argues that the fundamental momentum of a competitive economy is towards optimum distribution of resources and equalization of the incomes of factors of production. It is a serious mistake, however, to assume that intellectual criticism of this orthodoxy in economic theory amounts in itself either to an attack on liberal political values or (a criticism often levelled at sociological thought) inevitably implies an underlying socialistic bias. On the contrary, many of the sociological critics of competitive market theories have themselves subscribed to the broader values of liberalism and individualism, yet at the same time have argued either that neoclassical theory is intellectually inadequate or that political reliance on supposed laws of the marketplace will have unintended consequences which place liberal values in jeopardy. Examples include Max *Weber on *bureaucracy and Émile Durkheim on *anomie. Moreover, a similar controversy has existed within modern economics itself, especially since the revolution in economic theory initiated by John Maynard Keynes and his followers. *Keynesian economics claimed that the equilibrium of a whole economy may occur at a point where aggregate resources are less than optimally utilized–even though individual markets are in *equilibrium.

Sociology has shared with economic history (and with the so-called institutional heresy within economics itself) an interest in the origin and variability of actual markets and other economic institutions. Markets and banking, for example, both presuppose a relatively stable currency, codified and effective law, and normative standards of conduct. A degree of moral order, together with interpersonal *trust, is a necessary pre-condition for sound money, dependable contracts, and economic transactions in general. The need to account for the non-contractual pre-conditions of contractual exchanges was acknowledged by early political economists, but with the increasing formalization and abstraction of market theory was overlooked, and only taken up later by sociologists from Durkheim onwards. Market institutions also presuppose the presence in individuals and groups of the appropriate economic motivations. But, far from being a universal human motive, the calculative and sustained pursuit of economic advantage and profit, so essential to the idea of the competitive economy, may have flourished only under the rather unusual, possibly unique, religious and moral conditions found at the onset of the modern age. Sociologists tend therefore to be highly critical of the suggestion that the supposed laws of the market are universally valid, rather than (at best) merely descriptive of a particular historical situation and type of society, namely modern *capitalism and *industrialization.

Because the causal factors advanced by conventional economics may themselves stand in need of causal explanation, some sociologists have gone so far as to claim that economic theory cannot stand alone, or even that a separate discipline of economics is unnecessary. Such sociological imperialism risks self-contradiction. On one hand, sociologists commonly compare societies in terms of their economic institutions; on the other, the meaning and nature of economic activities is held to be wholly relative to individual cases. The (mainly Marxist) attempt to solve this problem by equating economic activity with productive activity overlooks the fact that, in all societies, many undoubtedly productive activities, notably domestic and reproductive tasks performed by women, are considered to be of little economic value. Economists can thus argue that their treatment of scarcity and resource allocation as a universal and self-contained societal problem is indeed valid.

Sociologists are arguably better placed to address the interconnections between the economy, the political system, social structures, ideological systems, and culture. Examples might include the linkages between the international *division of labour, inter-state relations, and multinational firms; the relationship between *patriarchy, as a set of social institutions, and the economy; or the classic example of the thesis about a direct link between the *protestant ethic and the rise of capitalism in Western Europe. Sociologists have contributed a substantial body of theoretical and empirical work on particular features of the economy and *labour market, particularly at the micro-level, including the study of power relations in the labour market as a whole and in the workplace; *industrial conflict and its resolution; explaining the development and impact of *pressure groups, *trade unions, and other associations, and analysis of their role in *industrial relations; studies of *social movements such as demands for desegregation and equality of opportunity in education, *training, and the workforce; studies of *management, *entrepreneurs, firms, and corporate behaviour; analysis of social and technical innovation processes and the diffusion of knowledge and technical innovations; studies of work organization and social processes in the workplace, and their effects on productivity or *job satisfaction, including theses about *de-skilling and *socio-technical systems; research on social and economic relationships within households, and the implications of *household work strategies and family financial management systems on workforce participation and attitudes to pay; issues of preferences and tastes, work orientations, and value systems which affect labour-market behaviour and consumer behaviour; the wider objectives of management that make *satisficing strategies more common than profit-maximizing ones; and the nature of *work outside the market economy, including domestic work and work in the *informal economy. Finally, sociologists' strengths in empirical research mean they are usually better placed than economists to collect data and conduct studies to test theories and arguments about economic activity developed by economists, particularly in relation to decision-making processes, both implicit and explicit.

An early, but still useful, attempt to map the contours of this major area of sociology is Neil Smelser's *The Sociology of Economic Life* (2nd edn., 1976). A rather partial account of a 'new economic sociology' is summarized in Richard Swedberg's *Principles of Economic Sociology* (2003) and in an edited collection by Smelser and Swedberg (*Handbook of Economic Sociology*, 2nd. ed., 2004). Important studies of classic views of the area are Swedberg's *Max Weber and the Idea of Economic Sociology* (2000) and Philippe Steiner's *Durkheim and the Birth of Economic Sociology* (2005).

( ) SEE WEB LINKS

• European Electronic Newsletter on Economic Sociology (a free online journal).

economics *See* ECONOMIC GROWTH; ECONOMIC SOCIOLOGY; EMPLOYMENT; GIFT RELATIONSHIP; HUMAN CAPITAL THEORY; INFLATION; INFORMAL ECONOMY; KEYNESIAN ECONOMICS; LABOUR MARKET; LABOUR-MARKET SEGMENTATION; LAISSEZ-FAIRE ECONOMICS; MALTHUS; MILL; MONETARISM; NEO-CLASSICAL ECONOMICS; PARETO PRINCIPLE; POLITICAL ECONOMY; RATIONAL CHOICE THEORY; SMITH; SUSTAINABLE DEVELOPMENT; UTILITARIANISM; UTILITY.

economic traditionalism *See* BACKWARD-SLOPING SUPPLY CURVE FOR LABOUR.

economism A Marxist term, originally used to denote a trade-union-based political strategy, but nowadays more commonly used to characterize an economically reductionist argument. *See also* ECONOMIC DETERMINISM; MODE OF PRODUCTION; REDUCTIONISM.

economy, black *See* BLACK ECONOMY.

economy, command *See* COMMAND ECONOMY.

economy, informal *See* INFORMAL ECONOMY.

economy, mixed *See* MIXED ECONOMY.

economy, positional *See* POSITIONAL ECONOMY.

economy, subsistence *See* SUBSISTENCE ECONOMY.

ecopopulism The term sometimes applied to the contemporary environmental justice movement, or development during the 1980s (notably in the United States) of thousands of community groups who developed a national co-ordinating infrastructure, in order to protest against inappropriate dumping of hazardous wastes, use of pesticides, and other environmentally damaging toxic substances. Opponents sometimes use the alternative epithet BANANA (build absolutely nothing anywhere near anything).

educability A term sometimes used in the sociology of education in an attempt to avoid begging the vexed *nature versus nurture controversy surrounding *intelligence. It is intended simply to refer to observed variations among school pupils in their capacity to accomplish teacher-imposed intellectual tasks.

education, sociology of Education is a philosophical as well as a sociological concept, denoting ideologies, curricula, and pedagogical techniques of the inculcation and management of knowledge and the social reproduction of personalities and cultures. In practice, the sociology of education is mostly concerned with schooling, and especially the mass schooling systems of modern industrial societies, including the expansion of higher, further, adult, and continuing education. School organization and pedagogy has drawn upon at least four competing educational philosophies: elitist or Platonic; open or encyclopedic; vocational; and civic (as exemplified by American pragmatist education for democracy and the polytechnic school systems of Marxist state socialism). Sociologists argue that the power structure and needs of individual societies determine which of these is emphasized.

Systematic sociology of education can be traced to Émile *Durkheim's pioneering studies of moral education as a basis for organic solidarity and Max *Weber's analysis of the Chinese literati as an apparatus of political control. But the first major expansion of the subject after the Second World War was associated with technological *functionalism in America, *egalitarian reform of opportunity in Europe, and *human-capital theory in economics. These all asserted a causal linkage between amounts of schooling and the economic advancement of both individuals and societies. They also implied that, with *industrialization, the need for technologically educated labour progressively undermines class and other *ascriptive systems of *stratification, and that educational *credentialism promotes social *mobility. However, statistical and field research in numerous societies uncovered a persistent link between social class origins and achievement, and suggested that only limited social mobility occurred through schooling. As a result, intense controversy developed over the determinants of the *educability of groups disadvantaged by class and ethnic background. Sociological studies pointed to a wide range of material, cultural, and cognitive factors likely to depress intellectual development. Other work showed how patterns of schooling reflected, rather than challenged, class stratification and racial and sexual *discrimination.

That school learning is an unmitigated good was even more profoundly challenged with the general collapse of functionalism from the late 1960s onwards. Neo-Marxists argued that school education simply produced a docile labour-force essential to late-capitalist class relations. Advocates of *deschooling argued that, for the world's poor, schools merely created institutional dependence on professional educators. In particular, the deschoolers drew on a growing research literature revealing numerous counter-productive effects of human-capital-inspired development programmes for the *Third World. An analogous challenge, combining research and ideology, was mounted against human-capital compensatory programmes for the urban poor of the industrialized West. *Phenomenological and interactionist (*see* SYMBOLIC INTERACTIONISM) perspectives in the 1970s were associated with a so-called new sociology of education (*see* M. F. D. Young (ed.), *Knowledge and Control*, 1971). This emphasized several important dimensions of knowledge management through schooling: in school classroom interaction; by the professionalizing of the teaching process; through the bureaucratization of school organization; and, at the cultural level, where the links between the sociology of education and the sociology of *knowledge are more immediately visible.

The extent to which education can in principle operate as a means of *social engineering—for example in pursuit of greater *equality in society—is contested in the work of the American sociologist Christopher Jencks. This investigates the determinants of economic success; that is, the relative effects of family background, cognitive skills, length and type of schooling, race, and personality on subsequent occupational status and earnings. In two acclaimed though controversial (co-authored) texts, Jencks and his colleagues argued that people from similar family backgrounds and with similar test scores were scattered across almost as wide a range of occupational destinations and incomes as those with disparate origins and social characteristics, thus suggesting that attempts to equalize outcomes through education were likely to prove ineffective. Direct intervention in the market processes distributing incomes was necessary for successful social engineering (see *Inequality: A Reassessment of the Effects of Family and Schooling in America*, 1972, and *Who Gets Ahead? Determinants of Economic Success in America*, 1979).

This is a consistently popular area of the discipline, from the point of view of both research and teaching, so the literature is correspondingly large. Good general texts include Roland Meighan et al., *A Sociology of Educating* (2nd edn., 1986) and Philip Wexler, *Social Analysis of Education: After the New Sociology* (1987). For a highly original case study see Diego Gambetta, *Were they Pushed or did they Jump? Individual Decision Mechanisms in Education* (1987). *See also* CLASSROOM INTERACTION; COLEMAN REPORT; COMPENSATORY EDUCATION; CONTEST AND SPONSORED MOBILITY; CULTURAL CAPITAL; CURRICULUM; DEWEY; DIPLOMA DISEASE; HIDDEN CURRICULUM; PEDAGOGY; SCHOOL CLASS; SOCIALISM; TRACKING.

effort bargaining A term first used by Hilde Behrend ('The Effort Bargain', *Industrial and Labour Relations Review*, 1957), popularized by W. Baldamus (*Efficiency and Effort*, 1961), in relation to the competing *rationalities behind *employment that emerged from studies of *incentive payment systems. The latter assume that workers seek to maximize money income and thus share in the managerial definition of rational action. Field studies in industrial sociology and psychology revealed that workers typically restrict output (that is, produce less than the technically possible level for maximum short-run earnings), because they do not expect any dramatic change in their average earnings level. Synthesizing the results of such work, Baldamus argued that because workers do not expect long-run fluctuations in their overall income, it is rational for them to minimize the wage disparity between the amount of effort required by a particular task and the average rate of pay. Different social classes in fact will entertain conflicting values regarding the notion of a fair day's work for a fair day's pay. Incentive schemes may even encourage workers to conceal the level of actual effort from work-study engineers and management. Today it is recognized that effort bargaining has important implications for the conduct of *labour relations, since wage-effort comparisons between groups was endemic to *collective bargaining itself, as well as attempts by modern governments to run incomes policies.

egalitarianism A doctrine which sees equality of condition, outcome, reward, and privilege as a desirable goal of social organization. The bases for such beliefs have been religious and secular, and have ranged from crude slogans such as 'we all have the same stomachs, and only one of those', to more sophisticated Marxian statements about societies moving from the organizing principle of 'from each according to their abilities to each according to their work' (*socialism) to 'from each according to their abilities to each according to their needs' (*communism). But even this form of equality demands unequal treatment. *Positive discrimination may have as its goal either the preparation of a 'level playing-field' or the facilitation of an endless series of draws with no winners or losers. Given the multi-dimensional nature of inequality and its seemingly ineluctable nature some socialist writers have sought to find equality in the unequal but inconsistent distribution of several facets of *inequality. Prestige, income, education, and any other goods could be so arranged that their various levels of distribution balanced out, thus minimizing any sense of *relative deprivation. In practice, however, this has involved the allocation of unacceptable levels of power to the state, the agency that is invariably charged with manipulating these social scales. *See also* JUSTICE, SOCIAL.

ego *See* PSYCHOANALYSIS.

egocentrism Referring to the idea of being self-centred, the term is used in the writings of social psychologists such as Jean *Piaget and Lawrence Kohlberg to refer to a stage in the development of thought or morality that is entirely self-focused.

egoism *See* INDIVIDUALISM; SUICIDE.

egoistic suicide *See* SUICIDE.

elaborated and restricted speech codes A distinction formulated by Basil Bernstein, a leading figure in the sociology of education, that contrasts the so-called formal language of middle-class children with the public language of the working class (see his *Class, Codes and Control*, 1971-7). These linguistic codes were said to be correlated with class differences in family organization, *power, and control. The elaborated code of the middle class is institutionalized in schools. This results in 'culturally induced backwardness' among working-class children. Bernstein's research projects at the London University Institute of Education appeared to confirm these ideas, but the results of replication by others in Britain and the United States have been more ambivalent. His work has also been criticized, rather unfairly, for an implicit disdain for working-class life.

Bernstein was one of the first sociologists to place the problem of knowledge at the centre of the study of educational process. This was taken up by the 'new' sociology of education of the early 1970s. His work is usually discussed in two phases, though it is underlain throughout by concerns that reflect the influence of Émile *Durkheim's analysis of social symbols, classification, and cognitive processes. The earlier studies of social class and linguistic codes did much to initiate a sociology of *language. His later works deal with the classification and framing of educational knowledge. Classification refers to the variability of boundaries in curriculum content (for example between school subjects); framing addresses the relative openness of teacher-pupil relationships. These concerns led Bernstein to a critique of progressive classroom pedagogies because of their invisible link to middle-class rather than working-class child-rearing styles.

elective affinity A term used by Max *Weber to describe the relationship between Protestantism and capitalism (in *The Protestant Ethic and the Spirit of Capitalism*, 1905). It refers to the resonance or coherence between aspects of the teachings of Protestantism and the ethos of the capitalist enterprise: the contents of one system of meaning engender a tendency for adherents to build and pursue the other system of meaning. The actors concerned may not be consciously aware of this affinity. The concept has remained firmly tied to Weber's work although it has been used loosely by other sociologists, often in situations where it seems likely that there is an association or connection between systems of belief operating in different spheres of life. (see R. H. Howe, 'Max Weber's

Elective Affinities', *American Journal of Sociology*, 1978). *See also* PROTESTANT
ETHIC THESIS.

Elias, Norbert (1897–1990) Studied under Alfred *Weber and worked as
teaching assistant to Karl *Mannheim at Frankfurt University. Of Jewish origin,
his career was disrupted by the rise of National Socialism in Germany. Elias
managed to complete his Habilitation thesis on *The Court Society* (published only
in 1969) but fled from Germany in 1933. He eventually became a lecturer in
sociology at the University of Leicester, in England, in 1954. He retired in 1962,
and was Professor of Sociology at the University of Ghana from 1962 to 1964. His
major work, *The Civilising Process*, was published in 1939 in German and was
long neglected until its republication in German in 1969 and its translation into
English in 1978 and 1982. From 1979 to 1984, he was a Fellow at the Centre for
Interdisciplinary Research at the University of Bielefeld. He divided his final years
between homes in Leicester, Bielefeld, and Amsterdam. He was awarded the
Theodor W. Adorno Prize in 1977, and the Amalfi Prize for sociology in 1988, for
his study *The Society of Individuals*. His work was relatively neglected in his
lifetime, but particular schools of 'figurational sociology' have arisen since then.

   Two key principles dominated his sociology. First, he was concerned to understand the process of civilization, which he defined as a process whereby external
restraints on behaviour are replaced by internal, moral regulation. Second, he
criticized *functionalism and *structuralism for their tendency to reify social
processes, and argued instead for figurational or processual sociology; that is, a
conceptualization of the constant and endless processual flux of all social relationships. Hence he wrote about 'civilizing processes' rather than 'civilization'.
His work has been criticized on two principal counts. First, it is not clear what is
the cause or mechanism that produces these civilizing processes. Second, it is
objected that his theory is not supported by empirical evidence, since modern
societies are very uncivilized in terms of everyday violence and brutality.

   Among his numerous other publications are *What is Sociology?* (1970), *The
Loneliness of the Dying* (1982), *Involvement and Detachment* (1987), *An Essay on
Time* (1984), and *The Germans* (1989).

elite (elite theory) Sometimes spelled with an accent, the word has now been
anglicized in its sociological usage. The term is often loosely used to refer to any
superior or privileged group, but it more properly refers to groups defined by
their superior *power. An elite is a ruling minority. It was the work of two 19th-
century Italians—Gaetano *Mosca and Vilfredo *Pareto—that turned the observation that for much of recorded human history the few have ruled the many into
an important contribution to modern political sociology. For Mosca, whose *Ele-
menti di scienza politica* of 1896 (translated as *The Ruling Class* in 1939) was the
first statement of the theory, the distinguishing mark of the rulers and therefore
the explanation for their political dominance over the ruled lay in the rulers'
superior organization. The dominance so achieved is justified through a set of
values ('the political formula') that gives it *legitimation. The composition of the
ruling elite reflects the balance of power among the underlying social forces.

Although he is usually considered to have derived the idea from Mosca, it was Pareto who, by naming the ruling few 'the elite', gained much of the credit for the theory's creation. However, Pareto went on to develop the idea as part of his own sociology. Where Mosca related elite composition and circulation to a changing balance of social forces, Pareto saw this as reflecting an underlying distribution of psychological qualities. He held that social action is determined by one or other of six basic 'sentiments' or 'residues'. These are typically rationalized by more intellectual sets of ideas (for example, democracy, nationalism, and liberty) that he terms 'derivations' and which correspond to Mosca's idea of the 'political formula'. Amongst the residues two were far more important than the others: the 'residue of the persistence of aggregates', which stimulated courage and strength; and the 'residue of combinations', which stimulated cunning and compromise. Borrowing from Machiavelli, Pareto termed those rulers moved by the first of these residues 'lions' and those moved by the second 'foxes', and then used this distinction to formulate his theory of the 'circulation of elites'. According to this theory, every society is founded in violence and therefore by lions, but as it settles down the need for their courage and strength declines. Eventually, this need is replaced by an even more compelling one for the subtler skills of the foxes, who then become the rulers. The rule of the foxes remains in place until the society's identity and sense of direction become so unclear that a need for more leonine qualities once again arises.

The idea of a ruling elite, generally without the psychological assumptions made by Pareto, has been used by those who seek to complement or to avoid the Marxian emphasis on purely economic power. Thus, C. Wright Mills's *The Power Elite* (1956) looked at the balance among political, economic, and military leaders in the ruling elite, while 'democratic elitists' (see P. Bachrach, *The Theory of Democratic Elitism*, 1967) point to the competition among elite groups as central to *pluralist theories.

For a review of both the extensive literature on elite theory, and the substantive material deriving from studies of *bureaucracy, business, the military, and *community power, see Geraint Parry, *Political Elites* (1969). A contemporary approach can be found in John Scott's 'Modes of power and the re-conceptualization of elites' (in Savage and Williams (eds.), *Remembering Elites*, 2008). *See also* MICHELS; POWER ELITE.

elite, power *See* POWER ELITE.

embeddedness A concept that challenges disciplinary boundaries between economics and sociology, by suggesting that no 'pure' realm of the economic exists. Economic activities, institutions, and processes are historically specific, shaped by and inseparable from their contextual social relations. This is sometimes contrasted with a view of modern societies as increasingly structurally differentiated. The argument builds on the economic anthropology of Karl Polanyi (in K. Polanyi, C. M. Arensberg, and H. Pearson (eds.), *Trade and Market in the Early Empires*, 1957) who distinguished between reciprocity, redistribution, and exchange as socially embedded modes of economic activity, that might be expressed or conducted through kinship, religious, political, or other relations. Since the 1980s economic sociology has developed this approach in a number of directions, especially in relation to advanced industrial societies. The determining impact of personal social networks on firm, market, and trading activity has been a major focus of study. Attention has also been drawn to the continuing significance of forms of informal exchange, the household and other non-market economies, where economic are embedded in non-economic relations.

embourgeoisement (embourgeoisement thesis) Embourgeoisement is the process by which *bourgeois aspirations, and a bourgeois standard and style of life, become institutionalized among the *working class. The phenomenon is said to undermine working-class consciousness and so frustrate the historical mission of the *proletariat as an agency of revolutionary *social change.

The concept itself has Marxian origins. In the late 1880s, Friedrich *Engels attempted to explain the failure of the British working class to exploit the franchise of 1867 in terms of the workers' 'craving for respectability', and enjoyment of a standard of living sufficient to encourage bourgeois values, lifestyles, and political ideals. Orthodox Marxists since have often deployed this argument as an explanation for working-class quiescence under capitalism.

However, the proposition attained a much wider credibility when it was taken up by (mainly North American) liberals such as S. M. Lipset and Clark Kerr, during the two decades following the Second World War. Proponents formulated the thesis of embourgeoisement in a variety of ways and identified a range of disparate causal mechanisms behind the process itself. In its most general formulation, however, the thesis claimed that the sectoral transformation in the structure of *employment—the move from manufacturing to services, and from unskilled labouring to the new knowledge-based occupations—created high levels of class mobility, and led to a shrinkage of the working class, considered as a proportion of the economically active population. Advanced Western societies were therefore literally becoming more middle class, in the demographic sense at least, if none other.

Additionally, however, tendencies intrinsic to production (notably *automation) were granting manual workers greater control over their work and undermining their sense of workplace *alienation. Urban renewal after the war led to the dissolution of long-established, tightly knit, often occupationally homogeneous working-class communities in the inner cities, as workers spilled out into the less dense, more heterogeneous suburbs of the new commuting areas. *Official statistics of this period purported also to show a 'homogenization' of incomes and living standards, both because of the high-wage and full-employment-based expansion in Western economies, and the redistributive social policies pursued by welfare-minded social democratic states. This was the era of 'high mass consumption' and the 'affluent society': ownership of consumer durables became widespread and even manual workers could realistically aspire to car-ownership and purchasing their own home. A mass-market of 'middle-income' consumers was created.

These objective changes allegedly prompted, in turn, the homogenization of lifestyles and social values. Increased income facilitated working-class participation in *middle-class styles of dress, leisure practices, and styles of décor. Finally, the increase in incomes and integration of rank-and-file workers into their employing organizations as skilled operatives together changed the workers' attitudes and values, fostering a new identification with the objectives of the capitalist enterprise, a weakening of the traditional loyalties to workmates, *trade union, and class, and the growth of a typically middle-class concern with *status. Workers became family-minded and home-centred rather than neighbourhood-centred and collectivist. Conservative values came to dominate their world-views: manual workers now sought security and respectability, and by individualistic rather than solidaristic means. Ultimately, this translated into *voting behaviour, as the old class-based parties of the Left were abandoned in favour of the bourgeois or petit-bourgeois parties of the political Right. British politicians such as Anthony Crosland (*The Conservative Enemy*, 1962) saw this as explaining Labour's electoral failures during the 1950s.

The clearest statement of this thesis is Ferdynand Zweig's *The Worker in an Affluent Society* (1961), which has the additional virtue of being empirically grounded, since Zweig conducted interviews with workers in five British firms. Most other proponents of embourgeoisement argued principally on the basis of speculation and anecdote.

The thesis prompted a number of important sociological studies in the 1960s. These were generally more rigorous than the original statements and greatly undermined the credibility of the argument. The most notable of the critical treatments were probably the so-called Affluent Worker Studies in Britain, carried out by John H. Goldthorpe, David Lockwood, Frank Bechhofer, and Jennifer Platt (see especially *The Affluent Worker in the Class Structure*, 1969); Bennett M. Berger's study of a *Working-Class Suburb* (1960) in the United States; and, for France, Richard F. Hamilton's *Affluence and the French Worker in the Fourth Republic* (1967). The most comprehensive re-examination of this debate for Britain is Fiona Devine's *Affluent Workers Revisited* (1992). These and a host of similar studies showed convincingly that the working classes of the advanced West were not as wealthy as their middle-class peers, retained important aspects of their proletarian identities, and still had distinctive social values, political ideals, and styles of life.

Although theories of embourgeoisement were widely held to be discredited during the 1970s, they made a curious return in the midst of the recessionary 1980s, when commentators of both the extreme Right and Left argued that working-class support for the policies of right-wing governments across Europe and North America provided testimony to a new consensus around middle-class *norms, *values, and *lifestyles. This view was central to the building of 'new Labour' in Britain. *See also* CONSUMPTION, SOCIOLOGY OF; INCORPORATION; LABOUR ARISTOCRACY; PRIVATISM; SUBURBANISM.

emergence (emergent properties) Emergence is the process by means of which a number of divergent elements are synthesized and organized into a new form. As a concept it has been particularly prominent in *evolutionary theory. However, it is also widely deployed in *symbolic interactionism, which also aims to capture the processual and adaptive nature of social life. In the writings of both

George Herbert *Mead and Herbert *Blumer the interaction of body, mind, self, and society constantly leads to emergence. From this point of view, society itself is an emergent, as are all social objects. An excellent discussion can be found in Dave Elder-Vass's *The Causal Power of Social Structures: Emergence, Structure and Agency* (2010).

emergent norms Standards of behaviour that are gradually established by people who have come together into a group. Thus, for example, Ralph Turner and Lewis Killian (*Collective Behaviour*, 1993) suggest that crowds consist of individuals with different *attitudes, motives (*see* VOCABULARIES OF MOTIVE), and *values, but the ambiguity of the crowd situation encourages the development of a group *norm (for that particular circumstance) which creates an illusion of unanimity of purpose and uniformity of behaviour.

emic and etic analysis A distinction borrowed by anthropologists from linguistics. An emic analysis concentrates on describing the indigenous values of a particular society while an etic one applies broader theoretical models across a number of societies. The emic approach became popular in the late 1960s as part of the movement towards *cultural relativism. In practice, anthropological research has always entailed a mixture of emic and etic approaches.

emigration *See* MIGRATION, SOCIOLOGICAL STUDIES OF.

emotional labour For Arlie Hochschild (*The Managed Heart*, 1983), this is the work done with feelings, as part of paid *employment. In addition to exercising their physical and cognitive capacities, they must exercise specific emotional abilities. People in many of the personal service occupations—such as airline stewardesses, waitresses, bartenders, and such like—are paid to 'sell their emotions', showing 'appropriate' behaviour towards their customers. Emotions here can become a commodity. As with all labour, this is subject to *management control. Arguably, more and more work in the Western world is of this type, particularly in those occupations dominated by women. *See also* EMOTION, SOCIOLOGY OF.

emotion, sociology of Although a concern with emotion is present in much early sociology, the sociological study of emotions emerged as a distinctive subfield within the discipline only during the 1970s, in part at least as a self-conscious response to a sociology that (in the eyes of some) had become overly concerned with the *cognitive and *rational. It examines such emotions as shame and pride, love and hate, awe and wonder, boredom and melancholy, and asks questions about how these are culturally patterned, experienced, acquired, transformed, managed in daily life, and legitimated through accounts. At its most general, then, the specialism examines the links between feelings, on one hand, and *cultures, *structures, and interactions (*see* ACTION THEORY) on the other.

Three models of analysis are common. The first (or organismic) suggests that feelings happen within the person, are experienced bodily, and then interpreted. The second or constructionist position maintains that feelings are socially constructed, and that they do not apply to internal states but are in fact cultural meanings given to sensations, since the same sensation may be given very different meanings. (Pain, love, and anger, for example, are not universals, but are given different meanings in different cultures, and are often experienced differently.) The final position is that of the interactionist who interprets feelings as an emergent property of the interaction between environment and body.

Two pioneering works in this field illustrate the sorts of research that will be found here. Arlie Hochschild's *The Managed Heart* (1983) is a study of airline cabin crew in the United States, which highlights the ways in which those who practise this particular occupation are required to express particular emotions (it is *emotional labour), and are guided by *feeling rules. Thomas Scheff suggests that 'shame is the primary social emotion', and in his work examines both the ubiquity of this emotion, and the 'spiral of shame and rage' often generated by it in social interaction (see especially *Microsociology*, 1990). The terrain and topics of interest are clearly mapped in T. Kemper (ed.), *Research Agendas in the Sociology of Emotions* (1990).

emotion work The effort that a person has to exercise in order to appropriately engage in *emotional labour and other forms of action in which feeling is demonstrated.

empathy The ability to identify with and understand others, particularly on an emotional level. It involves imagining yourself in the place of another and, therefore, appreciating how they feel. Empathy is a useful basis for arriving at explanatory hypotheses. In sociology, Max Weber's concept of *verstehen* (understanding) was based around the argument that empathy with another did not require any emotional or political sympathy with them: we do not have to approve of those emotions that we can understand in others. William Outhwaite's *Understanding Social Life: The Method Called Verstehen* (1975) is still the best commentary. *See also* MEANING.

empirical As applied to statements, particular research projects, or even to general approaches to research, the term 'empirical' implies a close relationship to sensory experience, observation, or experiment. Sometimes the term is contrasted with abstract or theoretical, sometimes with dogmatic, or sometimes with scholarly. In its derogatory uses, lack of attention to matters of principle or *theory is implied. As a term of approval, for example from the standpoint of *empiricism, the term implies practical relevance, or testability, as against bookish scholasticism or groundless speculation.

empiricism In sociology, the term empiricism is often used, loosely, to describe an orientation to research which emphasizes the collection of facts and observations, at the expense of conceptual reflection and theoretical enquiry. More rigorously, empiricism is the name given to a philosophical tradition which, in its modern form, developed in the context of the scientific revolution of the 17th century. Though by no means all of the early empiricists were advocates of the new science, empiricism subsequently developed in close symbiotic association with modern science. In sociology, empiricism has been widely adopted as a philosophical approach by those who advocate methodological *naturalism: the development of sociology as a scientific discipline.

In its early forms (in the work of John *Locke, David *Hume, and others) empiricism was primarily an *epistemology: a theory of the nature, scope, and limits of human knowledge. As such, it included a theory of the mind and its workings which has subsequently been displaced by the development of *cognitive psychology. What remains of empiricism as a philosophical theory is primarily the thesis that substantive human knowledge is limited to what may be tested (confirmed or validated) by empirical observation. What may be known a priori, or independently of all experience, is restricted to analytical statements— for example, statements that offer definitions of technical concepts, or, as Hume put it, which state 'relations of ideas'. Empiricism defended the privileged status of science as the only form of human enquiry in which knowledge-claims were based upon, or were permanently open to, testing in terms of empirical observation and experiment. Theology and speculative *metaphysics, by contrast, made bogus claims to knowledge on the basis of faith, intuition, or 'pure' reason.

Though empiricists are keen to demonstrate their opposition to metaphysics, it may be argued that empiricism itself carries an implicit metaphysics: namely, that the ultimate (knowable) realities are the fleeting sensory impressions (or 'sense-data') against which all genuine knowledge-claims are to be tested. The most radical forms of empiricism, then, are liable to be sceptical about the knowability not only of the objects of scientific knowledge, but also the things and beings of commonsense experience. Thus, the distinctive 20th-century form of empiricism, the logical empiricism or positivism of the *Vienna Circle, followed upon the deep uncertainties of the turn-of-the-century revolution in physical science. In general, empiricists have raised the standard of empirical testability as a means of defending science, and combating the claims of, first metaphysics and theology, and more recently pseudo-sciences such as *Marxism and *psychoanalysis. Their difficulty has been to do so in a way which does not rule out all, or most, genuine science by the same criterion.

empiricism, abstracted *See* ABSTRACTED EMPIRICISM.

empiricism, logical *See* VERIFICATION; VIENNA CIRCLE.

employer strategies This term refers to patterns of employers' decision-making regarding work organization within firms (for example forms of control over labour, job structures, and payment systems). Originally developed within *Marxism to refer to employers' responses to capital-labour conflicts, it is currently used in the *labour process and *labour-market segmentation literatures to stress the intervention of employers in a supposedly impersonal labour market, and the variety in their forms of decision-making.

employment The supply of labour by persons of either sex for the production and processing of all primary products (such as the characteristic products of agriculture, forestry, and fishing); the processing of primary commodities to produce such goods as flour, cheese, wine, cloth, or furniture, whether for the market, for barter, or for own consumption; and for the production of all other goods and services for the market. This broad definition ensures that the concept is applicable to statistics on *market economies, *command economies, *mixed economies, and *subsistence economies. It covers the production of goods and services normally intended for sale on the market, goods and services supplied by government agencies and the nonprofit sector, and certain types of production for own consumption (non-market production). In Western industrial societies, a much narrower definition is conventionally applied in *official statistics—namely work for pay, profit, or family gain, within a specified reference-week—thus limiting the concept to work in the market economy, which is reflected in national economic accounts and gross national product. Employment can also be defined with reference to a person's usual activities rather than their current activities.

Sociologists frequently ignore these precise, and essentially economic definitions of employment (often termed economic activity by economists), in favour of the much more general notion of *work, which has a different, wider meaning. Many disagreements and debates have their origin in a failure to distinguish clearly between work and employment. To make matters worse, work is regularly used as a synonym for paid employment or market work in everyday discourse, and in social science reports. Hence, for example, work-rates are synonymous with labour-force participation rates and economic activity rates in scientific (especially economic) papers. *See also* BLACK ECONOMY; HOUSEHOLD WORK STRATEGY; LABOUR MARKET; LABOUR RELATIONS; OCCUPATIONAL SEGREGATION; WAGE-LABOUR.

(⊕) SEE WEB LINKS
• A gateway to official statistics on employment.

employment, flexible *See* FLEXIBLE EMPLOYMENT.

employment status The legal status and classification of someone in *employment as either an employee or working on their own account (self-employed). In practice, most classifications of employment status in *official statistics expand this simple two-fold distinction into a fuller typology that identifies large employers, small employers, the self-employed without any employees, unpaid family workers contributing labour to a family farm or business, partners in a legally defined partnership, apprentices and supervisors, as well as ordinary employees.

The sociological distinction between capitalists and employees is clouded in most classifications of employment status, as those who employ workers are classified by their specific legal status, as employees of their own incorporated companies; however, some countries ignore the legal status in favour of the social reality. Practice varies because this concept is not wholly defined by the economic framework that dominates *labour-market statistics.

enclave A term used in under-development and *dependency theories to refer to parts of a *Third World economy that are based on production for export and are controlled and managed by foreign capital. The enclave is thought to have few linkages with the national economy and thus to have little impact on internal growth.

enculturation A term from American cultural anthropology that is virtually synonymous with *socialization. It refers to the idea that, to be a full member of any *culture or *subculture, individuals have constantly to learn and use, both formally and informally, the patterns of cultural behaviour prescribed by that culture.

end-of-ideology thesis Although not originated by the American sociologist Daniel Bell, this very controversial thesis is commonly identified with him, thanks to the publication in 1960 of a book of his essays entitled *The End of Ideology*. The central thrust of the thesis is suggested by the subtitle of this book: 'On the Exhaustion of Political Ideas in the Fifties'. Bell's argument is that the great political *ideologies of the 19th century, *liberalism and *socialism especially, each of which he conceives of as 'a set of beliefs, infused with passion, and seek[ing] to transform the whole of a way of life', finally lost their ability to mobilize the people of the advanced *industrial societies in the 1950s. This, he suggests, happened for two main reasons. First, because of the failure of these ideologies to prevent war, economic depression, and political oppression. And second, because of the modifications to capitalism brought about by the changes summarized by the term *welfare state. Although Bell acknowledged the continuing and indeed increased importance of ideology in 'the rising states of Asia and Africa', his conclusion was that in the industrialized West, social improvement would and could only come through what he was later to term '"piecemeal" change in a social-democratic direction'.

endogamy The preferred or prescribed practice of marrying within the defined kin-group, be it clan, lineage, village, or social class. The opposite principle is exogamy: the preferred or prescribed practice of marriage outside the kin group, the boundaries of which are often defined by the incest taboo. The latter principle is most clearly expressed in the Arapesh saying, recorded by Margaret *Mead, which states: 'Your own mother, your own sister, your own pigs, your own yams you have piled up, you may not eat. | Other people's mothers, other people's sisters, other people's pigs, other people's yams that they have piled up, you may eat.'

Engels, Friedrich (1820–95) A 19th-century philosopher, socialist, manufacturer, and co-founder of *Marxism. The best introduction to his life and work is Tristram Hunt's *The Frock-Coated Communist: The Revolutionary Life of Friedrich Engels* (2010).

Born into a family of well-to-do mill-owners in Rhineland, Engels very soon took up a critical stance against the conservatism of his background, and went on to establish the intellectual partnership with Karl *Marx for which he is most well-known. So close was the cooperation between them that it is often difficult to be sure what should be attributed to either partner. Their early influences in the radical Young Hegelian circle, and conversion to *socialism and *communism in the early 1840s, ran in close parallel. It seems to have been Engels's *Outlines of a Critique of Political Economy* (1844) which set Marx off on his life-long researches into that subject. The culmination of this research was Marx's *Capital*. Only one volume of this was published in Marx's lifetime, and it was Engels's contribution, after Marx's death, to prepare for publication the drafts of the remaining two volumes.

Following their (relatively minor) involvement in the unsuccessful uprisings of 1848, both Marx and Engels went into exile in England. Until 1869 Engels was preoccupied with the family business in Manchester, but he was at least able to offer Marx's family desperately needed financial support, while Marx continued with his studies. From the 1870s onwards Engels was able to give more time to intellectual and political work. His advice was much sought by the leaders of the international working-class movement, and he was particularly closely involved with the development of the German socialist movement from 1875 onwards. The books and pamphlets in which he expounded his and Marx's approach to history, politics, and philosophy were extremely widely read, and were more influential even than Marx's own work in forming the image of Marxism as a systematic world-view held by successive generations of socialist and communist militants.

However, Engels's contribution went well beyond merely popularizing the work of his mentor. His *Condition of the Working Class in England* (1845) remains a classic work of social and economic investigation. It is particularly noteworthy for its pioneering exposition of the links between poverty, environmental degradation, and ill-health, consequent upon modern industrialism. Engels's late work also contained much originality. His *Origin of the Family, Private Property and the State* (1884) extended the range of *historical material-ism to engage with current work in anthropology. This work was especially significant in its attempt to explain the history of women's subordination 'materialistically' in terms of the institutions of private property and monogamy. Despite its flaws, this work is still considered worthy of serious attention by many contemporary feminists. Engels's later years were also much taken up with following developments in the natural sciences and engaging with the political and philosophical implications of those developments. *Dialectical materialism was the term invented by Engels to encapsulate his attempt to sustain a form of *materialism which was sufficiently open and flexible to address these new developments. His use of ideas from physics tended to give his work a rather mechanistic character. Engels's ideas were subsequently converted into a dogmatic ideology by the leadership of the Soviet state. *See also* EMBOURGEOISE-MENT; MATRIARCHY.

Enlightenment, The The period when European thought became concerned with reason, experience, scepticism of religious and traditional authority, and a gradual emergence of the ideals of secular, liberal, and democratic societies. Often dated from the publication of Isaac Newton's *Principia Mathematica* in 1686 and John *Locke's *Essay Concerning Human Understanding* and *Two Treatises on Government* three years later, some argue it began earlier, in the 17th century, with the works of Bacon and *Hobbes in England, and in France, with *Descartes's emphasis on unaided reason. It is the 18th century, however, which is generally seen as the heyday of the Enlightenment, especially in France, with the *Encyclopédie* and anti-clerical *encyclopédistes* such as *Rousseau, Diderot,

*Montesquieu, and Voltaire. David *Hume, a Scottish philosopher, aimed to bring the experimental method into the study of the human mind, and believed natural science, culminating in Newtonian mechanics, could find a few basic principles which would make it possible to discern order in the apparent chaos of natural systems. Adam *Smith, in *The Wealth of Nations*, outlined his optimistic ideas about free markets in the economy and the benefits of a division of labour. The German philosopher Immanuel *Kant argued that knowledge of space and time is subjective, and distinguished between things as they are in themselves and things as they appear to us, thus separating out experience and thought.

There were many strands to the Enlightenment, running through literature and the arts, science, religion, and philosophy. Overall, however, it is equated with a *materialist view of humanity, an optimism about the possibility of rational and scientific knowledge, progress through education, and a *utilitarian approach to ethics and society. Theodor *Adorno and Max *Horkheimer have argued in *The Dialectic of Enlightenment* (1972) that there is a hidden logic of domination and oppression behind Enlightenment rationality. The desire to control nature, which was at the core of the Enlightenment, also entailed the domination of human beings. The legacy of the Enlightenment, if thoroughly analysed and understood, can be seen as the triumph of an instrumental rationality that led to the development of a bureaucratic rationality from which some argue there is no escape. *See also* EMPIRICISM; EPISTEMOLOGY; PROGRESS; SCOTTISH ENLIGHTENMENT.

enterprise society (enterprise culture) A term used in the 1980s to refer to those countries in which the state made a conscious attempt to promote the qualities of self-reliance, innovation, and individual *achievement. Governments in Britain and the United States implemented a series of economic and social reforms, including the deregulation of industry and *privatization of public utilities, in order to revitalize the (as they saw it) moribund organizational culture of late 20th-century *corporate society. These policies were intended to promote economic *competition, reduce the influence of the *state in economic life, constrain public expenditure, and encourage individuals to take responsibility for their own welfare, mainly by promoting the adoption of *market principles wherever possible. It is doubtful if this programme had any long-term effect on *entrepreneurship or the *work ethic, although it contributed in some countries to a retrenchment of the *welfare state. See the collection of papers in Russell Keat and Nicholas Abercrombie (eds.), *The Enterprise Culture* (1991).

entitlement *See* JUSTICE, SOCIAL.

entrepreneur (entrepreneurship) There are at least four distinct meanings given to this term, which overlap only in part. At a basic level, an entrepreneur is a person who owns and runs a business—not necessarily a new, small, growing, or successful business. Economists define the entrepreneur as a person who risks *capital and other resources in the hope of substantial financial gain, or as someone who specializes in taking judgemental decisions about the use and coordination of scarce resources. The emphasis is on calculated risk-taking.

Sociologists define the entrepreneur as a creative innovator in the business sphere, in contrast to the conventional business-owner, capitalist, or professional manager, who conforms more often to established procedures and objectives. This conception originated with Joseph *Schumpeter, who defined entrepreneurs as individuals who develop and implement new combinations of the means of production, a function which he described as fundamental to economic development in his book *The Theory of Economic Development* (1934). Finally, the term is sometimes used more loosely to refer to the owner or creator of a new, small, growing, and successful business, or even to any person who sets up a small business, or changes from an employee job to being self-employed, even though neither need involve any significant degree of innovation or capital investment.

The 1980s saw the development of the concept of *intra*preneurs; that is, people working alone or in teams who remained employees within the organization or firm for which they worked, but took responsibility for some innovation, costly exercise or risky development, or even for a routine subset of activities, in the expectation of additional personal financial reward for successful ventures and profitable operations. At the extreme, intrapreneurs shade into employees whose earnings depend heavily on bonus and commission payments, or other *incentive payments—such as sales personnel.

Theories about entrepreneurial behaviour concern the relative importance of personality traits, social marginality, the 'artisan' or 'craftsman' orientation to work, sources of risk capital, the economic environment, and institutions. Theories of *economic growth do not always attach importance to entrepreneurs. Sociological interest in entrepreneurship has declined steadily with the emergence of *monopoly capitalism and the rise of the modern business *corporation. However, the American economic sociologist Ronald S. Burt has conducted a number of analyses of envy and entrepreneurial opportunities in competitive environments, notably via the application of concepts derived from *network analysis (see *Corporate Profits and Cooptation*, 1983, and *Social Contagion and Innovation*, 1988).

entrepreneurial capitalism *See* CAPITALISM.

environment, sociology of The environment is literally 'that which environs or surrounds', and the term is used in various ways in academic discourse. In biology and psychology, environment is frequently juxtaposed to *heredity, in an exhaustive division of the causes that shape the character of living things. Heredity refers to what is genetically transmitted, environment to what is given externally. Much of the debate has focused on their relative importance, and environment itself is usually given little substantive content. In other usages the environment is simply the (delimited) social context in which the individual (or any living organism) is located, and the emphasis is on issues of adaptation and adjustment to this environment, as in Jean *Piaget's work on cognitive development.

Writing on the environment in early sociology saw the physical environment as a major determinant of patterns of social life and has often been characterized as environmental determinism. The most sophisticated writers emphasized that the environment merely sets fundamental limiting conditions on possible courses of action. Examples of such work include Frederic le Play and Patrick *Geddes. In France, the work of Paul Vidal de la Blache and Lucien Febvre established a regional focus for social studies and found its best expression in the work of the *Annales School. American work on environmental influences, such as that of Ellen Semple, exercised a great influence on the *urban ecology of the *Chicago School.

The natural environment, for all its potential significance to sociology as the territory in which human action occurs and as itself modified by human agency has featured in sociological thinking mainly in references to the heredity versus environment debate. Significantly, the current social and political attention given to the environment concentrates on the physical world—on towns, houses, the countryside, and natural resources such as air and water—albeit an environment recognized to be not just a matter of nature but also of human intervention. In this interpretation, the term contrasts with concepts like *community, *society, and social *group that highlight social relations rather than physical and material conditions. However, it is precisely the focus on the specificities and impact of the material world and on the way it is socially constructed that produces the potential for an environmental sociology.

Since the 1980s, the sociology of the environment has emerged as an identifiable specialism within the discipline, although it is still rather loosely defined. Among the topics likely to be encountered in any of the standard texts now available will be the following: the role of *industrialism in generating environmental degradation; the structural and social origins of environmental movements (*see* SOCIAL MOVEMENTS); the content and influence of Green politics and parties; the environmental implications of *urbanization and *globalization; the problems of securing *sustainable development; and wider theoretical issues such as the possible conflict between a non-exploitative approach to nature and the continued commitment to Enlightenment values such as those of *democracy, human *rights, and the pursuit of *progress. (See, for example, Tim Hayward, *Ecological Thought*, 1995, and David Goldblatt, *Social Theory and the Environment*, 1996.) Several strands of this literature deal with the built environment and lead into discussions of *culture (especially *popular culture). For example, in his study of the links between environmental and social change, as these are evident in the use of commercial space, Mark Gottdiener (*The Theming of America*, 1996) depicts 'themed spaces' (everything from Graceland and Disneyworld to local shopping malls) as a barrage of familiar and comforting symbols that are intended to make consumers feel good, and to part them systematically from their money in the interests of sustaining economic growth. Recent discussions have concerned such issues as global climate change and the *risk society. *See also* HUMAN GEOGRAPHY.

environmental criminology *See* CRIMINOLOGY, ENVIRONMENTAL.

environmental sociology *See* ENVIRONMENT.

epidemiology The analysis of the incidence and spread of disease within populations, with the aim of establishing causality. The modern science of epidemiology is often said to have originated with John Snow's identification of a particular source of drinking water as the cause of the 1849 cholera epidemic in London. More recently, linkages between smoking and lung cancer, between heart disease and certain fats, and between the contraceptive pill and breast cancer, have all been established through epidemiological research.

epistemological anarchy *See* METHODOLOGICAL PLURALISM.

epistemology The philosophical theory of knowledge—of how we know what we know. Epistemology is generally characterized by a division between two competing schools of thought: *rationalism and *empiricism. Both traditions of thought received their most systematic philosophical expressions in the context of the scientific revolution of the 17th century. Both approaches were concerned with finding secure foundations for knowledge, and clearly distinguishing such well-grounded knowledge from mere prejudice, belief, or opinion. The model of certainty which impressed the rationalists (*Descartes, Leibniz, and Spinoza) was that found in the formal demonstrations of logic and mathematics. They sought to reconstruct critically the total of human knowledge by the employment of such 'pure' reasoning from indubitable axioms or foundations (hence Descartes's 'I think therefore I am'). The empiricists (*Locke, Berkeley, and *Hume) took direct acquaintance with the 'impressions' of sense-experience as their bedrock of infallible knowledge. Disputes between rationalists and empiricists centred especially on the possibility of innate knowledge, of knowledge acquired a priori, or independently of experience. Empiricists vigorously denied this, advocating their view of the human mind as a blank sheet or *tabula rasa*, until marked by the impressions of sensory experience.

The 18th-century German philosopher Immanuel *Kant is widely held to have achieved a transcendence of this conflict of ideas, insisting that a framework of basic organizing concepts (space, time, causality, and others) could not be acquired by experience alone, yet was necessary for us to be able to interpret the world of experience at all. These concepts were therefore prior to experience, but nevertheless (a nod in the direction of the empiricists) they could only be used to make objective judgements within the bounds of possible experience.

It is arguable that all theoretical and empirical approaches in sociology presuppose (explicitly or implicitly) some epistemological position or other. Large-scale quantitative research is often (though wrongly) characterized in terms of *empiricist or *positivist epistemology, whilst the main opposition to positivism has derived (directly or indirectly) from the Kantian tradition. Whereas Kant thought the basic conceptual structure (the 'categories' and 'forms of intuition') underlying objective judgements about the world were necessary and therefore universal, many of Kant's successors in the human sciences have historically or socio-culturally relativized his position. Accordingly, it is common for sociological anti-positivists to argue that some conceptual or theoretical framework must be presupposed in any empirical research or factual judgement, but that there are several competing conceptual frameworks, and no neutral standpoint can be found from which to adjudicate between them. Arguments such as this lead to epistemological *relativism, *conventionalism, or agnosticism. Another argument, deriving from 19th-century neo-Kantianism, emphasizes the qualitatively different form of understanding involved in intersubjective communication and the interpretation of meaning (compared with the objective understanding we have of the material world). This form of understanding has its own conceptual and methodological conditions of possibility which may be philosophically analysed, as in *phenomenological and hermeneutic *philosophies of social science. Critical (or transcendental) *realists (such as Roy Bhaskar (1944–2014)) also draw upon Kant's method of argument, and recognize the necessity of prior conceptual organization for all empirical knowledge. They nevertheless insist upon the knowability of realities which exist and act independently of our knowledge of them. This philosophical tradition is claimed by its adherents to offer a defence of *naturalism, whilst at the same time accepting the main arguments of the Kantians against positivism and empiricism.

Some *post-structuralists, impatient with the apparently interminable disputes among rival epistemologies, have sought to avoid epistemology entirely. The main argument for doing so begins with a premise which is common ground to most non-positivist philosophers of social science. This is that we have no direct or unmediated access to the realities about which our theories claim to provide knowledge. Some form of conceptual or linguistic ordering is necessary for even the most basic reports of our experiences or observations. We cannot step outside of language or discourse so as to check whether our *discourse does, after all, correspond to reality. The conclusion which is then drawn from this axiom is that the classical epistemological question as to the adequacy of our discourse to the reality it purports to represent is in principle unanswerable and therefore misconceived. These post-structuralists are then led to deny the knowability of any reality beyond, or independent of, discourse, thence into an oscillation between epistemological agnosticism and *metaphysical *idealism. Of course, it does not at all follow from the widely accepted claim that language (or 'discourse') is necessary to our knowledge of the world, that we cannot then know the world. This would be as if someone were to say that, because we have no way of telling what colour things are other than by looking at them, we cannot know what colour they (*really*) are! So far, attempts to avoid epistemology appear to have yielded only yet more terminologically impenetrable epistemologies.

equality (social equality) *See* DEMOCRACY; EGALITARIANISM; JUSTICE, SOCIAL; SOCIALISM.

equality of opportunity *See* JUSTICE, SOCIAL.

equilibrium (social equilibrium) In normative *functionalist theory generally, and the work of Talcott *Parsons in particular, the commonplace concept of equilibrium (a state of balance in which opposing forces or tendencies neutralize each other) is given a more specific meaning. It applies, in particular, to what Parsons calls a 'boundary-maintaining system': that is, a social system that 'maintains certain constancies of pattern', relative to its environment. Two types of constancy are identified—static (unchanging), and moving, the latter of which Parsons describes as 'an orderly process of social change' (see *The Social System*, 1951). The tendency of *social systems towards equilibrium is built into the premises of (and later the very definitions of a society proffered by) Parsonian theory, which uses the terms 'moving equilibrium' and 'disequilibrium' to describe departures from a static equilibrium. *See also* CHANGE, SOCIAL; CONSENSUS; SYSTEM INTEGRATION AND SOCIAL INTEGRATION.

equity theory *See* JUSTICE, SOCIAL.

eschatological Beliefs about the 'last things' and a religious end (and judgement) to the world. They form a significant part of the Judaeo-Christian tradition and tend to be stressed most strongly by *fundamentalist and *sectarian—especially Adventist—movements. *See also* MILLENARIANISM.

essentialism A philosophical term which has been used in a variety of ways. According to Karl Popper (*Conjectures and Refutations*, 1969), essentialists make the twin claims that it is possible to establish definitively the truth of a scientific theory, and that scientists can arrive at complete explanations by discovering the essence or reality that lies behind the appearance of a phenomenon. However, the term is also applied to the theory of descriptions which states that definitions are descriptions of the essential properties of things, and that one can evaluate attempts at definitions in terms of the falsity or truth of the descriptions given by them. From this point of view, science requires the discovery of such essences, and thus of correct definitions. The contemporary usage of the term is largely pejorative, since most philosophers of science accept that descriptions and knowledge are provisional, and that facts (like truth and reality) are always conceptualized in terms which are informed by *theory. *See also* CONVENTIONALISM; RELATIVISM.

estate A social stratum to which are attached specific rights and duties sustained by the force of legal sanction. The most obvious examples are the peasants, serfs, burghers, clergy, and nobility of the post-feudal states of continental Europe. For example, early-modern France distinguished the nobles, clergy, and the 'Third Estate' until the late 18th century. The term is often (though controversially) applied to the system of *stratification in feudal Europe, though feudal strata were characterized more by personal bonds of vassalage, rather than shared political rights and obligations. It should be noted, for example, that the distinguished historian of *feudalism Marc Bloch refers to the strata of the feudal order simply as 'classes'.

Estate systems of stratification are rigid in their prescription of economic duties, political rights, and social convention, although typically they are not closed to social mobility. Unlike in *caste systems, the estate does not necessarily renew itself from within: the clergy in pre-revolutionary France, for example, was an 'open estate'.

Sociological usage of the term dates back to Ferdinand *Tönnies's distinction between estates and classes (or 'communal' and 'societal' collectivities). In *Economy and Society* (1922) Max *Weber cites the estates of medieval Europe as paradigmatic examples of *status groups. In the same vein, T. H. *Marshall defined an estate as 'a group of people having the same status, in the sense in which that word is used by lawyers. A status in this sense is a position to which is attached a bundle of rights and duties, privileges and obligations, legal capacities or incapacities, which are publicly recognized and which can be defined and enforced by public authority and in many cases by courts of law' ('The Nature and Determinants of Social Status', in *Class, Citizenship, and Social Development*, 1964). However, like most of the other main sociological concepts for studying systems of stratification, that of estate is a matter of some dispute.

ethical dualism *See* DUALISM.

ethics A branch of philosophy concerned with moral principles and values, with what ought to be the case and how people ought to live their lives. Ethical philosophers are concerned with the ideas of 'good' and 'bad' as they apply to human affairs. Ethics is contrasted with science, which is concerned with describing reality as it actually exists. This distinction has given rise to the notion that social science should be *value free or value neutral. In practice, however, both the means and goals of social science investigation are intrinsically bound up with ethical considerations. Much ethical philosophy has sought to discover absolute foundations for moral judgements, but most recent work holds that this is impossible. Contemporary ethical thought, therefore, tends to adopt a stand-point of *relativism. A key text in ethical thought is Alisdair MacIntyre's *After Virtue* (1981).

The abandonment of the idea that there are absolute and fundamental ethical standards means that there is no clear consensus on a complete set of ethical rules to be followed when conducting research involving human subjects. There are, however, some generally agreed professional guidelines based on ideas of protecting individual autonomy and freedom. One of the basic tenets is that subjects should normally have their privacy protected through the practice of informed consent. This would rule out any observation of private behaviour without the explicit and fully informed permission of the person to be observed. Furthermore, subjects should not be exposed to unnecessary stress, or manipu-lation, or personal risk. The researcher is also responsible for preserving the confidentiality of any information that could identify subjects. The protection of data, so that anonymity is assured, is an increasing concern and is now subject to certain legal requirements. Ethical principles guide not only the conduct, but also the presentation of research, and there are ethical implications concerning how the results might be used. Sociologists may never face the dilemma of Oppen-heimer developing the atomic bomb, but knowledge is never neutral and is always linked to power. *See also* RELATIVISM; RESEARCH.

ethnicity (ethnic group) Individuals who consider themselves, or are consid-ered by others, to share common cultural characteristics that differentiate them from the other collectivities in a *society, and from which they develop their distinctive behaviour, form an ethnic group.

The term ethnicity was coined in contradistinction to *race, which is often seen in biological terms. Members of an ethnic group may be identifiable in terms of racial attributes, but they may also share other cultural characteristics such as religion, occupation, language, or politics. Ethnic groups should also be distinguished from social *classes, since membership generally cross-cuts the socio-economic *stratification within society, encompassing individuals who share (or are perceived to share) common characteristics that supersede class. The Jews in the United States thus constitute a typical ethnic group, since they include individuals of different racial origins (from East Europe to North Africa), social classes, mother-tongues, political beliefs, and religious commitment (from orthodox to atheist), yet still consider themselves to share a common Jewish identity that distinguishes them from, while not necessarily placing them in opposition to, wider American society.

Ethnic groups are therefore fluid in composition and subject to changes in definition. New ethnic groups are constantly being formed as populations move between countries. Indians in Britain, for example, constitute an ethnic group—although as individuals in India they would be seen to be members of quite different groups in terms of *caste and *language. The concept of ethnicity is particularly important when it forms the basis for social *discrimination (as, for example, in the case of Jews in Nazi Germany) or for independence movements (as in the Soviet Union).

The relevant literature is voluminous. John Rex and David Mason's *Theories of Race and Ethnic Relations* (1986) demonstrates the range and diversity of current approaches in the field. Michael Banton's *Racial and Ethnic Competition* (1983) is an excellent summary of the American and British substantive literature. For Britain, David Mason's *Race and Ethnicity in Modern Britain* (2000) is a useful source. For America see Nathan Glazer, *Ethnic Dilemmas, 1964–1982* (1983). Anthony Smith's *The Ethnic Revival* (1981) demonstrates the importance of the concept to a sociological understanding of conflict and change in the modern world. Frank Bean and Marta Tienda's *The Hispanic Population in the United States* (1990) uses quantitative data in a case study of ethnicity in modern America. Ira Katznelson's history of the urban politics of Northern Manhattan (*City Trenches*, 1981) is a case study of the interaction of ethnicity and class. *See also* CULTURE; NATIONALISM.

(⊕) SEE WEB LINKS

• The Centre for Research in Ethnic Relations: the leading UK research centre.

ethnic nationalism *See* NATIONALISM.

ethnocentricism Sometimes described as the cardinal sin of the *comparative method, this is the practice of studying and making judgements about other societies in terms of one's own cultural assumptions or bias. Ethnocentricism often suggests that the way something is done in other societies is inferior to the way it is done in one's own society. It is only by escaping the preconception that there is one correct way of organizing things that sociologists can begin to analyse the practices of other *cultures in the context in which they are performed. Avoidance of ethnocentricism quickly became one of the main tenets of *social anthropology and comparative sociology after the turn of the century. However, pushed to extremes, this principle can make comparative analyses so *relativistic that it becomes impossible to apply any universal cognitive or evaluative criteria—such as, for example, criteria of *rationality or universal moral standards. *See also* OBSERVER BIAS.

ethnography A term usually applied to the acts both of observing directly the behaviour of a social group and producing a written description thereof. Sometimes also referred to as fieldwork, the term is most commonly linked with the research techniques of *social anthropology, although sociologists involved in a *community study would certainly do fieldwork, as might those doing almost any form of *case study. The principal technique of ethnographic research is *participant observation. A classic example is William Foote Whyte's study of the social structure of an Italian slum district in an American city (*Street Corner Society*, 1943). Subsequently, Whyte also wrote a fine piece of descriptive methodology, reflecting on his ethnographic work (*Learning from the Field: A Guide from Experience*, 1984). Useful texts are Martyn Hammersley and Paul Atkinson, *Ethnography: Principles in Practice* (2nd ed., 1995) and John Brewer, *Ethnography* (2000).

ethnomedicine 'Folk' ideas and practices concerning the care and treatment of illness available within particular (usually non-Western) cultures—that is, outside the framework of professionalized, regulated scientific medicine. They commonly involve empirically based natural remedies, frequently from plants, and healing *rituals with a supernatural element. Often deemed unscientific, such methods of healing are increasingly shown to have some value.

ethnomethodology A sociological approach that emerged from the breakdown of the so-called orthodox consensus in the mid-1960s. The label was coined by the American sociologist Harold Garfinkel, who laid the foundations of ethnomethodology as a theory and as a self-conscious critique of all conventional sociology. Ethnomethodology draws on a varied philosophical background: *phenomenology on one hand and *Wittgenstein and linguistic philosophy on the other. Explaining the origins of the term, he suggests that '"ethno" seemed to refer, somehow or other, to the availability to a member of common-sense knowledge of his society . . . If it were "ethno-botany", then it had to do somehow or other with his knowledge of and his grasp of what were for members adequate methods for dealing with botanical matters . . . and the notion of "ethnomethodology" was taken in this sense' ('The Origins of the Term "Ethnomethodology"', in R. J. Hill and K. S. Crittenden (eds.), *Proceedings of the Purdue Symposium on Ethnomethodology*, 1968). This is indeed the rationale behind the name: 'ology' (the study of) 'ethno' (people's) 'method' (methods) of creating *social order. This interest led Garfinkel to analyse, in great detail, the methods used by people in *everyday life to account for (or make sense of) their activities—both to themselves and others. These unconventional (some might say esoteric) researches are reported in *Studies in Ethnomethodology* (1967), where Garfinkel gives the most concise definition of his studies, as being 'directed to the tasks of learning how members' actual, ordinary activities consist of methods to make practical actions, practical circumstances, commonsense knowledge of social structures, and practical sociological reasoning analysable'.

For a decade or more after the publication of Garfinkel's text, ethnomethodology was the subject of fierce and often bitter debate. It has now settled into an accepted but minority preoccupation, although some of its insights have been taken into the centre of sociological theory, particularly through the work of Anthony Giddens.

Social life, and the apparently stable phenomena and relationships in which it exists, are seen by ethnomethodologists as a constant achievement through the use of language. It is something that together we create and recreate continuously. The emphasis is on doing things: we 'do' friendship, being a sociologist, walking along the street, and everything else. At one time it was common to distinguish linguistic from situational ethnomethodology, but this is no more than a difference in emphasis, the basis for both tendencies resting firmly in the use of language.

There are two central ideas in ethnomethodology: indexicality and reflexivity. The first is the insight that there is no such thing as a clear, extensive definition of any word or concept in a language, since meaning comes from reference to other words and to the context in which the words are spoken. It is always possible to ask 'What do you mean?' about a statement, and then go on indefinitely, asking the same question to whatever answer is given. There is no final answer. Much of Garfinkel's early work consisted of sending his students out on exercises that establish the fact that we create and maintain a sense of meaning and existence in social life which is not actually there. One such exercise was to ask 'What do you mean?' relentlessly during conversations. The result is that people become distressed and angry when the taken-for-granted rules we use for establishing meaning are undermined. They lose their sense of social reality.

Reflexivity refers to the fact that our sense of order is a result of conversational processes: it is created in talk. Yet we usually think of ourselves as describing the order already existing around us. For ethnomethodologists, to describe a situation is at the same time to create it.

Both ideas formed part of a radical critique of all conventional sociology—which explains the bitterness of some of the arguments that ensued. According to ethnomethodologists, conventional sociologists are constructing a sense of social order in the same way as a layperson: namely, meanings are regarded as substantive and unproblematic. Consequently they are taken for granted. By contrast, ethnomethodologists argue that the proper task of sociology is to sort out the interpretive rules by means of which we establish our sense of order, rather than engage in reflexively establishing that sense. In this way, conventional sociology becomes an object of study for ethnomethodology, in the same way as any other human social activity is an object of study. Thus, Garfinkel's book contains both an essay on *coding answers to sociological interviews and an essay on trans-sexuality, the activities sharing an equal status as ways of producing social reality.

The example of so-called glossing illustrates the sort of interpretive procedure in which ethnomethodology is interested. In everyday life glossing means avoiding the issue. For ethnomethodologists, all talk is glossing, since the issue cannot be directly stated. In glossing, we employ a range of taken-for-granted rules, such as the 'etcetera rule', which adds to every other rule a clause which says 'except in reasonable circumstances'. Harvey Sachs, who specialized in *conversation analysis, stated numerous similar rules, including the one which states that, generally, only one person speaks at a time, and that if this rule is broken it is only for a very short period.

A common criticism of ethnomethodology is that it does not tell us anything very important. By definition, the big political and social issues of the day are beyond its scope, since the concern is with how we constitute this world, rather than what we constitute it as being. It is argued that the rules it draws out are also comparatively low level and merely tell us what we already know. The most influential criticism by conventional sociologists are John H. *Goldthorpe's 'A Revolution in Sociology?' (*Sociology*, 1973), James S. Coleman's review of Garfinkel's book in the *American Sociological Review* (1968), and Lewis A. Coser's celebrated presidential address to the American Sociological Association in 1975 ('Two Methods in Search of a Substance', *American Sociological Review*).

Although ethnomethodological work continues, especially as *conversation analysis, it is neither as prominent, nor as controversial as hitherto. On the other hand, a modified version of some of its insights is now almost taken-for-granted: there is, for example, a much wider recognition among sociologists of the problematic nature of *meaning and of the way in which our talk does contribute to the creation of our social reality. Meanwhile, ethnomethodology has become a relatively prosperous alternative discipline, with its own conferences, journals, and centres of excellence. (An excellent overview of contemporary work is John Heritage's essay on 'Ethnomethodology' in Anthony Giddens and Jonathan H. Turner (eds.), *Social Theory Today*, 1987.)

Among ethnomethodologists Aaron Cicourel has been most concerned with establishing a relationship with conventional sociology (see *Cognitive Sociology*, 1973). The most systematic attempt to integrate ethnomethodological insights into sociology can be found in the work of Anthony Giddens, particularly in *New Rules of Sociological Method* (1976), and *The Constitution of Society* (1984). He stops short of seeing social reality and societies as constructions of talk, but recognizes that taken-for-granted rules of talk and action are fundamental to social order, and employs a notion of rule similar to that of ethnomethodology as a way of understanding both social *action and social *structure and bringing the two together. *See also* COGNITIVE SOCIOLOGY; COMMONSENSE KNOWLEDGE.

ethology Pioneered by Konrad Lorenz and Nikolaas Tinbergen, ethology applies *evolutionary theory to early animal and childhood human behaviour, in order to examine its instinctive and adaptive nature. Its roots go back to Charles Darwin's *Origin of Species by Means of Natural Selection* (1859). Lorenz is usually credited with its discovery in the early 1930s. He is best-known for his studies of 'imprinting' and the instinctive basis of animal and human behaviour.

His work had more impact on psychologists (as in John *Bowlby's research on attachment and loss) than on sociologists: the latter usually argue that studies of animal behaviour are of little relevance in understanding human society.

Ethology became immensely popular during the 1960s in popular books such as Desmond Morris's *The Naked Ape* (1967). In this and his subsequent work, Morris sought to demonstrate the similarity, and hence the evolutionary significance, of certain aspects of human and animal behaviour. Critics have pointed to the reductionist assumptions behind much of the popular ethology of the 1950s and 1960s, which is regarded as one of the precursors of *sociobiology and *evolutionary psychology.

eufunction (eufunctional) A eufunctional activity (from the Greek *eu* meaning 'well') is one which contributes to the maintenance or survival of another social activity or of the *social system as a whole. The term is now largely obsolete, having been replaced by the simple reference to an activity being functional or having a particular *function, the implication being that the objective consequence of the activity in question for the wider social system is indeed positive, in the sense of contributing to the maintenance of *social order and stability. The contrast, in the cases of both the older and modern terminology, is with the concept of *dysfunction—a term applied in functionalist sociology to activities that are deemed to contribute to the disturbance of existing social patterns and structures.

eugenics From the Greek *eu* (well) and *gens* (to produce), eugenics refers to the manipulation of the processes of evolutionary selection, in order to improve a particular genetic stock or population. This may be achieved either through 'negative' eugenics (for example the provision of screening facilities to pregnant mothers, in order to detect and prevent the inheritance of deleterious recessive genetic conditions), or through 'positive' eugenics (in which certain groups may be selected for, or prevented from, reproducing). The latter is generally considered ethically unacceptable; the former is an area of ethical controversy. The Eugenic Society achieved notoriety in the early years of the 20th century for advocating various forms of positive eugenics in order to improve the genetic quality of the national populations in Britain and the United States. Many members of the Eugenics Society, however, were interested in the consequences of genetic differences in populations and pursued policies of, for example, educational reform rather than biological intervention. *See also* DARWINISM; GENE.

evaluation research A type of policy research devoted to assessing the consequences, intended and unintended, of a new policy programme or of an existing set of policies and practices, including measurement of the extent to which stated goals and objectives are being met, and measurement of displacement and substitution effects. Evaluation research became a self-identified field during the 1960s, and has common roots with the War on Poverty. (It was obviously useful to know the impact of the various social programmes to combat discrimination, deprivation, and other perceived social ills.) Because evaluation research tends to be applied, interdisciplinary, and methodologically opportunistic, practitioners tend to publish via specialized outlets such as the journals *Evaluation Review* (formerly *Evaluation Quarterly*) and *New Directions in Program Evaluation*. Many of these issues are discussed in Ray Pawson and Nick Tilley, *Realistic Evaluation* (1998).

evaluative theory *See* NORMATIVE THEORY.

evangelical This term is derived from the Greek word *euaggelion* meaning 'Gospel' or good news (of the salvation of human beings from sin). In sociological terms, it refers to those movements in Protestantism that are concerned with religious revival through an emphasis on the Bible, preaching, personal conversion, and salvation through faith in Jesus Christ. *See also* RELIGIOUS REVIVAL.

Evans-Pritchard, Sir Edward Evan (1902–73) A leading British social anthropologist who undertook *ethnographic studies of a number of African societies. He viewed *social anthropology as a humanistic rather than a scientific study of society—perhaps, it is thought, because his first degree was in history. Because of this belief he distanced himself from A. R. *Radcliffe-Brown (whom he succeeded as Professor of Social Anthropology at the University of Oxford between 1945 and 1970) and other *functionalists who sought to generate laws or theories about societies in general. By introducing a historical element to his work, Evans-Pritchard showed how societies change and manage change over time, which represented a major advance on the static analyses of functionalism. At the same time, however, he was concerned to describe societies holistically, and in this sense can be seen as a follower of Émile Durkheim.

Perhaps most importantly, however, Evans-Pritchard played a major role in shifting the focus of anthropology from the study of the function of *rituals in society to an examination of the *meaning ascribed to rituals by members of that society. He saw one of the main tasks of anthropology to be the translation of one *culture into terms understandable to members of another culture. This he achieved most memorably in the two early monographs which made his reputation and are still popular today—*Witchcraft, Oracles and Magic among the Azande* (1937) and *The Nuer* (1940).

If Evans-Pritchard was less concerned to be scientific than was Radcliffe-Brown, his work was nevertheless more theoretical than that of Bronislaw *Malinowski, from whom he learned his enthusiasm for intensive fieldwork methods. The volume he edited with Meyer *Fortes (*African Political Systems*, 1940) revolutionized political anthropology, and many of Evans-Pritchard's later writings (such as *Essays in Social Anthropology*, 1964) were about the relationship between anthropology and other social sciences, including sociology. They constitute important contributions to the *sociology of knowledge, and offer provocative statements of the problems of subjectivity in social research, and of the need for comparative analysis. The sociological significance of his writings, especially for theories of *language, *rational action, and *religion, is clearly explained in Mary Douglas's commentary on his life and work (*Evans-Pritchard*, 1980). *See also* MAGIC, WITCHCRAFT, AND SORCERY.

evolutionary psychology A development from *sociobiology, sharing many of its concerns. At its most extreme it holds that all human attributes and behaviour are determined by genetic factors, though more sophisticated approaches recognize that genetic influences operate only in relation to specific environmental factors and conditions. What unites most evolutionary psychologists is a hostility to sociological explanations, which they see as denying any part for biological conditions. *Social constructionism is a major target. The leading advocate of this view is Steven Pinker in his books *The Language Instinct* (1994) and *The Blank Slate* (2002).

Evolutionary psychologists have recently tried to incorporate social factors into their account by emphasizing the similarity between biological genes and cultural 'memes' or symbols, seeing these as the objects of natural selection through a process of imitation (see Susan Blackmore's *The Meme Machine*, 1999). Such arguments completely ignore the fact that it was a sociologist, Gabriel *Tarde, who first proposed this mechanism and that the idea of the natural selection of cultural symbols has been central to sociological analysis ever since the classical writers. *See also* EUGENICS; HUMAN GENOME.

evolutionary universals In his later writings, Talcott *Parsons tied his *functionalist theory (notably the four so-called 'systems problems') to an *evolutionary perspective, exemplified in his twin volumes on *Societies* (1966) and *The System of Modern Societies* (1971). He argued that, like biological organisms, societies progress through their 'capacity for generalized adaptation' to their *environment. This is achieved mainly through processes of *structural differentiation; that is, the development of specialized institutions to perform the social functions necessary to meet increasingly specialized needs. However, this increasing complexity then requires new modes of integration, in order to coordinate the new and more specialized elements. This is achieved through the 'cybernetic hierarchy', which involves increased information exchange or the growth of knowledge. (In this way *culture comes to be the dominant influence on the *social system in Parsons's work.)

Evolution is a move from traditional to modern societies, and progress can be charted by the development (structural differentiation) of evolutionary universals such as bureaucratic organization, money and market complexes, stratification, and the emergence of generalized universalistic norms. Each of these enables a society to adapt more efficiently to its environment (see 'Evolutionary Universals in Society', *American Sociological Review*, 1964).

evolutionism (evolutionary theory) In the 19th century, evolutionism was a current of thought based on a *biological analogy, but distinguished from Darwinian theory by its deterministic nature. Darwin's general theory of evolution claims that natural species evolve through variation and natural selection, a process that is not necessarily progressive. However, in the evolutionary theory espoused by Victorian social scientists, human societies were bound to improve, change was progressive, and led to further civilization and moral improvement of human society. Such theories were central to the 19th-century approach to society and political life. They underpinned *colonialism and are still deeply entrenched in Western thought. Kenneth Bock's essay on 'Theories of Progress, Development, Evolution' (in T. Bottomore and R. Nisbet (eds.), *A History of Sociological Analysis*, 1979) gives a good history and overview.

Although evolutionary theory in sociology is attributed to Herbert *Spencer, it is clear that it was taken for granted by writers as diverse as Karl *Marx, Friedrich *Engels, Émile *Durkheim, and V. Gordon *Childe. The fact that it can be traced in the work of both radical and conservative theorists is indicative of the profound cultural importance of evolutionism for Western thought. *See also* CHANGE, SOCIAL; DARWINISM; EVOLUTIONARY UNIVERSALS; FRAZER, SIR JAMES GEORGE; MATRIARCHY; MORGAN; PARSONS; PROGRESS; SOCIAL ANTHROPOLOGY.

exchange *See* GIFT RELATIONSHIP; RATIONAL CHOICE THEORY.

exchange mobility *See* MOBILITY, SOCIAL.

exchange value *See* CAPITALISM; COMMODIFICATION.

exclusion (social exclusion) A process by which individuals or households experience *deprivation, either of resources (such as income), or of social links to the wider *community or society. During the 1980s, the language of social exclusion came increasingly to be used alongside (and sometimes to replace) that of *poverty, especially in discussions of *social policy in Europe. It is not immediately obvious what is gained by this shift in terminology, since the former concept is no less controversial than the latter, and is commonly used to refer to the same cluster of *social problems associated with (for example) *unemployment, low income, poor housing, deficient health, or social isolation.

At least three broad and overlapping usages have emerged in this context. The first of these defines social exclusion in relation to social *rights and to the barriers or processes by which people are prevented from exercising these. This understanding of the term leads researchers readily into discussions of *civil society and to modern notions of *citizenship. A second strand in the literature reveals a broadly Durkheimian frame of reference. Here, authors conceptualize social exclusion as a state of social or normative isolation from the wider society, and refer this to related notions such as those of *anomie and so to problems of *social integration. Finally, the term has been applied to situations of extreme *marginalization, especially in the setting of *multi-cultural societies. *See also* CLOSURE.

(⊕) SEE WEB LINKS
- The Social Exclusion Task Force, formerly the Social Exclusion Unit: the UK government agency responding to deprivation.

existentialism A loose philosophical label applied to the work of, amongst others, Søren Kierkegaard, Friedrich *Nietzsche, Martin *Heidegger, and Jean-Paul *Sartre. It refers to the systematic investigation of the nature of human existence, giving priority to immediate experiences of aloneness, death, and moral responsibility. *See also* EXISTENTIAL SOCIOLOGY.

existential sociology A mainly American (especially West Coast) school of sociology, which has emerged as a rejection of most orthodox scientific versions of sociology, claiming as its roots the European existential philosophies of Søren Kierkegaard, Friedrich *Nietzsche, Martin *Heidegger, and Jean-Paul *Sartre, as well as the *phenomenology of Husserl and Schutz. The claim is usually made that the grand laws of the Enlightenment may become new tyrannies, and need to be challenged by looking at life as it is lived, with all its angst and even terror. In some of the writings of its proponents, the world is without meaning, and the sociologist is charged with the study of the processes by which people make sense of their lives and milieu. In this, it has some similarities with the philosophies of Max *Weber and (more obviously perhaps) *symbolic interactionism, a claim made by Edward Tiryakian in his book *Sociologism and Existentialism* (1962).

The most recent proponents of this sociology stress intimate familiarity with the experiences of everyday life. Two books published in 1970 identified the new sociology. Jack Douglas's collection of readings on *Understanding Everyday Life* distinguished the traditional sociologies from a range of newer ones, while Stanford M. Lyman and Marvin B. Scott's *A Sociology of the Absurd* provided essays on such topics as *time, space, and accounts, which highlighted the new approach and its areas of inquiry. More recent works such as Jack Douglas and J. Johnson's *Existential Sociology* (1977) and J. Kortaba and A. Fontana's *The Existential Self in Society* (1984) take this position further.

Existential sociology claims to study human beings in their natural settings and in all their complexities, most importantly incorporating their brute bodies and feelings into the picture, two areas that are often neglected elsewhere in sociology.

To date very few sociologists have followed in this tradition, and it has many critics who accuse it of creating yet another schism, of avoiding the central concerns of classical sociology, and of vulgarizing the tradition of existential philosophy developed in Europe. *See also* EXISTENTIALISM.

exogamy *See* ENDOGAMY.

experiment (experimental design, experimental method) *See* CONTROL (EXPERIMENTAL); CONTROL GROUP; EXPERIMENTER EFFECTS; FIELD EXPERIMENT; NATURAL EXPERIMENT.

experimenter effects A term used in psychology to highlight the ways in which an experimenter or researcher may influence the outcome of an experiment through his or her presence. The most celebrated instance in sociology is probably that of the so-called *Hawthorne experiments conducted by Elton Mayo and his colleagues.

explanandum and explanans (explicandum and explicans) That which needs to be explained (explanandum) and that which contains the explanation (explanans)—either as a cause, antecedent event, or necessary condition.

explanation *See* CAUSAL MODELLING; CAUSE; INTERPRETATION; MEANING; REALISM.

explanatory dualism *See* DUALISM.

explanatory reduction *See* REDUCTIONISM.

exploitation The use for unacceptable purposes of an economic resource, be it land, labour, or market position. Thus, a *monopolist could use control of the market to charge consumers excessive prices, or an owner could utilize land in such a way as to damage the natural resources. In orthodox economics the term has virtually no place. In *Marxism exploitation is central, and is defined in terms of the *labour theory of value, to denote the extraction of surplus value, or the difference between the value of what a worker receives in wages and that which is produced and appropriated by the capitalist. *See also* FEUDALISM; PATRON–CLIENT RELATIONSHIP.

exponential growth Growth at an increasing (geometrical) rate, as in the case of compound interest rates. Thomas *Malthus (*Essay on the Principle of Population*, 1789) pointed out that if food resources increase in linear (arithmetical) ratio, and population increases exponentially, extinction is inevitable.

expressive ties and instrumental ties A distinction sometimes employed to characterize social relationships considered to be an end in themselves as against those which are goal-oriented. Thus, for example, expressive ties involve a commitment to the other person, arising perhaps out of kinship or feelings of love, whereas instrumental ties involve cooperation merely in order to achieve some limited and immediate goal (such as the relationship between salesperson and customer).

extended family *See* FAMILY, EXTENDED.

extensive power *See* ORGANIZATIONAL REACH.

external labour market *See* LABOUR MARKET; LABOUR-MARKET SEGMENTATION.

externality (externalities) In economic theory it is generally recognized that some of the costs and benefits of economic activities (production, exchange, and the like) are not reflected in market prices. So, for example, air pollution caused by the activity of a company may be experienced as a cost by local residents or by society as a whole, but since clean air does not figure in the costs of production as calculated by the company, the latter has no incentive to reduce its polluting activity. Such costs and benefits which are not expressed in market prices are termed 'externalities'. Policy problems implicit in social and environmental externalities in *market economies are conventionally addressed by economists in the form of strategies for assigning market values to non-market variables and so 'internalizing' them, for example through taxation of pollution or scarce-resource use. Recent developments in environmental economics tend to exhibit the limitations of the concept of externality in the face of the systemic character of environmental-economic interactions (see, for example, E. B. Barbier *Economics, Natural-Resource Scarcity and Development*, 1989).

externalization A concept used by *phenomenological and some *Marxist sociologists to describe how human beings imprint their ideas and projects on the outside world. For example Peter Berger and Thomas Luckmann, in *The Social Construction of Reality* (1966), view social processes as a *dialectic of externalization and internalization.

extrinsic satisfaction *See* WORK, SUBJECTIVE EXPERIENCE OF.

extroversion and introversion A polarity in descriptions of *personality, which has a long history, although the terms themselves only became popular in the 19th century. Extroversion (literally turning outwards) is typified by outgoing, sociable, impulsive behaviour; introversion (turning inwards) by reflective, withdrawn, responsible behaviour. The psychoanalyst Carl Gustav *Jung linked extroversion with hysterical tendencies, introversion with depression and anxiety, the contrast underpinning his differentiation of personality types. Hans J. Eysenck, employing *psychometric techniques and *factor analysis, identified two major dimensions of personality and labelled the poles of one dimension extroversion and introversion. Individuals are located at points along the dimensions, the two axes enabling the full mapping of personality differences, and identification of personality types.

Fabianism Fabianism describes a broad central tendency in English collectivist thinking about social policy which is essentially non-revolutionary, pragmatic, rational, with a belief in government intervention and the perfectibility of the *welfare state; it is strongly associated with the English tradition of empirical research. The Fabian Society, founded in 1884 by (among others) Beatrice and Sidney *Webb and George Bernard Shaw, took its name from Fabius, a Roman general whose motto was 'slow but sure'. Avoiding both revolutionary *Marxism and Owenite *utopianism, the early Fabians embraced a programme of 'municipal socialism' and state control of the conditions of labour, to be achieved by the Labour Party with *trade-union backing. Political influence was mainly exerted indirectly through marshalling facts in policy-related publications and journalism. Nevertheless, in 1945 over half the members of parliament for the Labour Party were Fabians. Although always concerned with socialist ideals of equality, freedom, and fellowship, Fabian writings have ranged from Richard H. Tawney's *egalitarianism, in the 1920s, to the revisionism of Anthony Crosland in the 1950s. Fabianism, when wrongly bracketed with *social administration, is sometimes criticized as untheoretical, nationalistic, incremental, bureaucratic, and elitist, being addressed mainly to British politicians and civil servants rather than wider issues, grass-roots politics, and the common people. However this criticism seriously underrates the historical influence and continuing strength of the left-wing empirical tradition in the Fabian Society. *See also* COLLECTIVISM; SOCIALISM.

face-to-face interaction The process in which co-present individuals influence each other's actions; or, as it is defined by Erving *Goffman (in *The Presentation of Self in Everyday Life*, 1959), 'the reciprocal influence of individuals upon one another's actions when in one another's immediate physical presence'.

fact There is no generalized opposition between the everyday and sociological uses of the term fact. Both suggest that any statement which is true can be described as a fact. For example, it is a fact that British law prohibits murder, that Russia possesses nuclear weapons, and that wealth in America is distributed unequally. However, there is a considerable social science literature on the relationship between facts and *theories, or interpretations based on facts. It is for this reason that social science generalizations are often contested. Most sociologists would also accept that many of the most interesting *social facts are theory impregnated; that is, they imply certain assumptions about what is significant in society, and how best to conceptualize this. Facts are also considered to be provisional—considered true until shown otherwise. The boundary between fact and assertion is also hard to draw—although many would argue that *falsifiability provides a useful criterion for the social sciences.

factor analysis A family of statistical techniques for exploring data, generally used to simplify the procedures of analysis, mainly by examining the internal structure of a set of *variables in order to identify any underlying constructs. The most common version is so-called principal component factor analysis.

The most common use is to identify underlying factors in individual attitudinal, cognitive, or evaluative characteristics. For example, respondents who are in favour of capital punishment may also be opposed to equality of opportunity for racial minorities, opposed to abortion, and may favour the outlawing of trade unions and the right to strike, so that these items are all intercorrelated. Similarly, we might expect that those who endorse these (in the British context) right-wing political values may also support right-wing economic values, such as the privatization of all state-owned utilities, reduction of welfare state benefits, and suspending of minimum-wage legislation. Where these characteristics do go together, they are said either to be a factor, or to load on to an underlying factor—in this case with what one might call the factor 'authoritarian conservatism'.

Among the many texts, the most accessible is Paul Kline's *An Easy Guide to Factor Analysis* (1994). *See also* CORRESPONDENCE ANALYSIS.

factory system A system of *manufacturing involving the concentration of materials, fixed capital, and a labour-force, in one or more workplaces or plants. The reasons why factory production developed and largely displaced scattered domestic manufacture are a matter of debate in economic and social history. As a productive system it possesses three main types of *efficiency gains for the owner or controller: economic, by allowing advantages of scale, while reducing the costs of distribution of raw materials and finished product; technical, by making possible the *deskilling of craft labour, and the use of machines; and managerial, by increasing the scope for disciplined control of the *effort bargain. *See also* CAPITALISM.

fact, social *See* SOCIAL FACT.

falangism Literally 'phalanxism', a right-wing Spanish movement that developed in the early 1930s under the leadership of José Primo de Rivera, and sought to reproduce German and Italian *fascism in Spain. Opposed to the Republican regime, it supported Franco's Nationalist coup of 1936, but became only a minor element in his regime.

fallacy of composition The (mistaken) assumption that, if an action is in the collective *interest of a *group, and if members of that group are *rational, then the group must be (in the same sense) collectively rational—and will therefore act in its interest, just as each of its individual rational members would do. The fallacy has been demonstrated by *game theorists and theorists of *public goods.

fallacy of misplaced concreteness *See* REIFICATION.

false consciousness A *Marxist concept, referring to thinking that confirms human servitude, rather than emancipating the species essence. It refers to the purpose served by thought in the collective life of humanity. False consciousness hinders the universal class of the *proletariat in its liberating and developmental role and it leads the bourgeoisie to misleadingly cast its sectional outlook as a universally valid view.

In *The 18th Brumaire of Louis Bonaparte* (1852), Karl *Marx writes of 'the phrases and fantasies of the parties and their real organization and real interests, between their conception of themselves and what they really are', which appears to suggest the commonsense (and mistaken) interpretation of false consciousness, as a wrong self-perception of *interests and *identity. However, these superstructures of illusion inhibit class (emancipating) action, by obscuring both the role of reason and its object in the historical process.

Within the class process, Marx's description of the manner in which the ruling ideas of an ascendant class come to exert *hegemony on a broader class basis than that exercised by the previous ruling class, has led to further misunderstanding of what is meant by false consciousness. These ruling ideas are progressively more emancipating although still expressing a class interest. They are subversive of the ruling class itself in that their liberating thrust cannot ultimately be turned into a force for consolidating class power. False consciousness is also often mistakenly associated with consumerism and economic instrumentalism (*see* WORK, SUBJECTIVE EXPERIENCE OF).

In the writings of György *Lukács there exists the distinction between class opportunism, where the struggle is with effects and not with causes of class situation (with the parts and not the whole, the symptoms and not the thing itself), actual consciousness, and real class consciousness. The last of these allegedly becomes obvious in periods of crisis, when the reified forms that fetter the proletariat and its reified consciousness are overcome, through objective necessity and the emergence of the 'class for itself'. Lukács in particular identified the workers' councils as the signifier of the class consciousness that was overcoming bourgeois consciousness.

David *Lockwood (*Solidarity and Schism*, 1992) examines the Marxist problem of 'end-shift', or the relation between class position, actual consciousness, class action, and potential consciousness. Eschewing discussions of revolutionary practice, and elaborating the relationship between immediate and fundamental interests, Lockwood criticizes the attribution by Marxists of standards of *rationality that are a necessary prerequisite for the proletariat to overcome false consciousness. This not only overlooks such factors as the *status order but also relegates nonrational action to the *utilitarian depository of ignorance or error. An interesting elaboration of the idea can be found in Joseph Gabel's *False Consciousness* (1962, trans. 1975). *See also* DOMINANT IDEOLOGY THESIS; COMMODITY FETISHISM; IDEOLOGY; REIFICATION.

falsification (falsificationism) To falsify a knowledge-claim is to provide evidence that it is false. Since the time of David *Hume, *empiricist philosophy of science has struggled with the problem of *induction: namely, how is it possible to justify inference, from a finite set of instances, to the truth of a universal law whose scope is potentially infinite? In the absence of a convincing answer to this question, our everyday and scientific belief in a regular, ordered, and predictable universe must seem to be a physiologically indispensable, but still irrational, habit of mind.

The original approach to this problem pioneered by Karl *Popper involved a reasoned rejection of the question itself. Popper accepted that the problem of induction was insoluble, but it did not follow that science was irrational, or that it could not progress. Instead of seeing discovery of the truth as the aim of science, we should, rather, see scientific activity as a systematic attempt to 'falsify'—or refute—bold and imaginative conjectures about the nature of the world.

Popper's formulation of this principle is widely acknowledged as one of the most original contributions to the modern philosophy of science. His work is often assimilated to the logical positivism of the *Vienna Circle, but Popper was in fact (correctly) viewed by the latter as 'the official opposition'. Certainly, Popper shared with the Vienna Circle a concern with what differentiated science from other approaches to knowledge and belief, and with passionate advocacy of scientific method. However, he differed from them in several important respects. First, he did not equate testability or scientificity with 'meaningfulness'. For him, *metaphysics, *religion, *myth, and other forms of discourse which fell on the 'wrong' side of the science/non-science division were still meaningful, and might even be true. Such systems of thought in any case formed the indispensable prehistory of properly scientific modes of enquiry. Furthermore, Popper did not follow the logical positivists in their search for indubitable 'basic statements' which reported sense-experience, and were crucial to *verification.

Popper rejected the most characteristic doctrine of empiricism, in arguing (following Kant) that all descriptions of experiences involve selection and interpretation in terms of some prior conceptual framework, or theory. The model of scientific advance as an inductive process of generalization from particular experiences must therefore be rejected. Popper's alternative model is eloquently captured in the title of one of his books—*Conjectures and Refutations* (1963). Scientific theories are invented, by a process which cannot be captured by any logical scheme. Once invented, their scientific status is established by their fruitfulness in allowing the deduction of hypotheses which are 'empirically contentful'. By this, Popper means that they should be highly improbable (in the sense that they rule out as impossible many happenings which might otherwise seem possible), and at the same time be clear and unambiguous in specifying what they rule out. In Popper's version, the empirical testing of a theory is not a matter of finding evidence to support or confirm it, but rather a matter of systematically attempting to show it to be false—a logic of refutation or falsification. In this way Popper avoids the problem of induction which had bedevilled the attempt to justify science in terms of the idea of empirical verification. Popper's position is based on recognition of a very simple asymmetry between the logic of verification and that of falsification in relation to the law-like generalizations of science: universal claims always go beyond what is strictly justified by the (finite) body of evidence for them, but may be decisively refuted by a single counter-instance.

But the situation is more complex than this. Most especially, although the logic of falsification may be simple, its methodology is not. An observation which appears to challenge an established theory may itself be challenged as fraudulent, methodologically suspect, and so on, and will always leave advocates of the theory a range of choices to modify their theory, short of wholesale abandonment. Popper is fully aware of this, and is inclined to present falsificationism as a normative injunction, rather than as a description of the actual practice of scientists. Nevertheless, choice between rival theories is never an arbitrary matter. Although all scientific knowledge must be considered provisional (there is no conclusive proof or disproof), scientists properly prefer, among rival theories which are so far unfalsified and account for the known facts, that theory which has most empirical content.

Popper's colleague, Imre Lakatos, developed a still more complex form of falsificationism in response to the historically based *conventionalist arguments of Thomas S. Kuhn, Paul Feyerabend, and others (see 'Falsification and the Methodology of Scientific Research Programmes', in I. Lakatos and A. Musgrave (eds.), *Criticism and the Growth of Knowledge*, 1970). Popper set out a comprehensive statement of his views in *Objective Knowledge* (1972).

family, conjugal The conjugal family refers to a family system of spouses and their dependent children. In such systems, because the social emphasis is placed primarily on the marital relationship, families are relatively independent of the wider *kinship network. Consequently, divorce rates tend to be high. In this context, the term has come increasingly to be applied also to partners who are in a long-term relationship, but who are not actually married. *See also* FAMILY, EXTENDED.

family, extended This term refers to a family system in which several generations live in one *household. Nostalgia for the extended family is based largely on myth, as in Western, non-agrarian societies such households are rare. Conversely, even in *conjugal families, wider *kinship obligations can be strong. *See also* FAMILY, SOCIOLOGY OF.

family, nuclear The term nuclear family is used to refer to a unit consisting of spouses and their dependent children. Early accounts of the family emphasized the biological imperative underpinning the nuclear family. Anthropological studies reinforce the 'naturalness' of the nuclear family and George P. Murdock asserts that it is a 'universal human grouping' (*Social Structure*, 1949). Murdock attributes this to the nuclear family's utility in performing tasks necessary to the survival of the species and to social continuity: namely, the regulation of sexual relationships, reproduction, the socialization of children, and economic cooperation between the sexes. Sociologists emphasize that biology is not sufficient for understanding family forms and insist that it is also necessary to examine how the nuclear family is shaped by ideological, political, and economic processes.

The *structural-functionalist interpretation of the family (see Talcott Parsons and Robert Bales, *Family, Socialization and Interaction Process*, 1955) is still important because so much subsequent family sociology is a reaction against functionalism. However, the argument that the isolated nuclear family developed in response to the needs of a mature industrial economy is now widely rejected, because of evidence of historical and cross-cultural variation. *Parsons argues that the nuclear family fits industrial needs because, on one hand, it allows families to be mobile and economically independent of the wider kin group; and, on the other hand, it ensures that in an individualistic and impersonal world, adults and children have a stable, if limited, set of affective relationships. William Goode (*The Family*, 1964) also emphasizes that a nuclear family serves industrial society well in providing what Christopher Lasch calls a *Haven in a Heartless World* (1977). However, Goode also warns that family forms and functions change, as a result of individual desires and initiatives.

The 'family as a haven' thesis raises the question of haven for whom? By treating the family as a unified entity, the realities of *power are ignored. Husband, wife, parents, and children all have different interests and differential power. Michael Young and Peter Willmott claimed, in *The Symmetrical Family* (1973), that the nuclear family is becoming more egalitarian, with more flexible *sex-role division. However, this optimistic view has been rejected by many feminist authors, who argue that the family is a repressive institution, especially for women. What is clear is that, with rising divorce rates and the ageing of the population, the nuclear family is no longer the norm in either Britain or America. An adult will usually experience nuclear families twice: once as a child in his or her family of origin; and, after a period of independence, as a parent in his or her family of marriage (see C. C. Harris, *The Family and Industrial Society*, 1983). Nuclear families are therefore increasingly associated only with certain stages in the *life-course and are less durable than in the past. They may also have a different role structure now that the majority of married women and mothers are in paid employment. Nevertheless, the nuclear family seems a remarkably resilient institution, surviving various social upheavals and adapting to social change. *See also* AFFECTIVE INDIVIDUALISM; FAMILY, SOCIOLOGY OF; MARRIAGE; ROLE, CONJUGAL.

family, sociology of The family is an intimate domestic group made up of people related to one another by bonds of blood, sexual mating, or legal ties. It has been a very resilient social unit that has survived and adapted through time. Yet, on both sides of the Atlantic, there have been loud claims that families are in decline, and there have even been those who welcome the so-called demise of the family, because it is viewed as an oppressive and bankrupt institution. Nevertheless, family sociology continues to thrive, and is producing a wide range of research that is demythologizing our beliefs about family systems of the past; and expanding our understanding of the diversity of family life, not only between individual nations, but also between various classes, ethnic groups, and regions. More studies are crossing discipline boundaries, looking at the interrelationship of family life and *work, and how micro-family relationships are affected by macro-social and economic changes. Family sociology is also incorporating the *life-cycle perspective, exploring how families differ at various stages, from early *marriage through to old age. Finally, there is an increasing amount of research concerning different family forms, such as lone-parent and reconstituted families; and, inevitably, family sociology has become closely entwined with practical policy concerns.

In recent years there has been a radical reappraisal of the state of the contemporary family and of the desirability of its survival. One strand of this criticism has been to view the family as a bolster for capitalist society (see E. Zaretsky, *Capitalism, the Family, and Personal Life*, 1976). A second is the view that the conjugal *family oppresses and represses individuality (as argued by, for example, R. D. Laing, *The Politics of the Family*, 1971). A third line of criticism can be found in the work of feminist authors, ranging from writers like Jessie Bernard and Ann Oakley, who tend to focus on the nature and consequences of current *sex-role divisions in the contemporary family, through to the more radical critique of Michelle Barrett and Mary McIntosh (*The Anti-Social Family*, 1982), who regard the family as not only oppressive to women but also an antisocial institution.

Historical studies of families have laid to rest some of the myths about family life of the past. For example, it is a mistake to presume that the nuclear *family emerged in response to *industrialization, replacing a pre-existing extended *family system. Research has indicated that, throughout most of Western Europe, the nuclear family type preceded the early formation of *capitalism. Moreover, the romantic image of a close and stable family unit in bygone ages proves unfounded, and studies such as Philippe Aries's *Centuries of Childhood* (1962) make it quite apparent that the emphasis on intimacy in modern family life is relatively new.

Although there is clearly some continuity of family form over time it is wrong to downplay the diversity of family life. Different ethnic and religious groups hold quite different values and beliefs, and these differences affect not only gender-role conceptions, the internal family division of labour and child-rearing, but also attitudes to work and other social institutions. Similar differences emerge for families of different class backgrounds. Working-class families have been associated with more segregated *conjugal roles, although even working-class marriages are now claimed to be symmetrical (see Michael Young and Peter Willmott, *The Symmetrical Family*, 1973). Child-raising orientations also vary by social class, with studies by John (Newson) and Elizabeth Newson in England and by Melvin Kohn in America showing that the middle classes tend to emphasize autonomy and the working class value obedience in their respective offspring. Kohn attributes this difference in orientation to the father's occupation, making it clear that family relationships and work roles interconnect.

Families and work have often been conceptualized as separate spheres, with women being linked to the home and men to the workplace. This separation was unfortunately perpetuated by the sociology of the family being conducted as a separate enterprise from the sociology of work and occupations. Clearly, however, the divide makes no sense, and the increased participation of married women in the workplace has highlighted the importance of work and family transactions. Early work by Rhona (Rapoport) and Robert N. Rapoport on *dual-career families has expanded into studies exploring the benefits and strains of families with dual-earners. There are, however, many questions still to be answered concerning the interaction of family and work. For example, how do families affect transitions in and out of the *labour market? How do workplace policies and events affect family life? And how do work-family arrangements differ through the life-cycle?

Research concerned with the life-cycle of families parallels the growing interest in individual life-course analysis. A key concept is family time, which addresses the timing and sequence of transitions such as marriage and parenthood, and how such timings are precipitated both by individual family members and by society at large. The timings of earlier events (such as age of first marriage) are shown to have a great impact on later outcomes (such as divorce). Family transitions also have economic consequences. For example, research in the United States has revealed how women and children face a high risk of poverty following divorce.

The proportion of single-parent families rose dramatically during the second half of the 20th century. Social research can play an important role in revealing how society can aid single-parent families to adjust and survive—and not just in financial terms. Many children will at some stage live in a single-parent *household and it is damaging to view such families as pathological or deviant. Reconstituted families are also coming under scrutiny and, as yet, many important questions remain unanswered. For example, to what degree does a remarriage terminate the existing child-grandparent relationship, and how does this affect the transfer of equity, inheritance, and family culture across the generations?

Inevitably, in family sociology, the line between social research and policy tends to be blurred. There is a long tradition of excellent family studies that combine both theory and practical concerns (see, for example, P. Townsend, *The Family Life of Old People*, 1957, or J. Finch, *Family Obligations and Social Change*, 1989). The questions facing family sociologists of the future will undoubtedly be different, as changing circumstances bring new problems to light. However, one thing is clear: regardless of changes in its size, shape, membership, or form, if past experience is any guide then families are here to stay. Good overviews of the area are David Morgan's *Family Connections* (1996) and Fiona Williams's *Rethinking Families* (2004). *See also* AFFECTIVE INDIVIDUALISM; HOUSEHOLD ALLOCATIVE SYSTEM; HOUSEHOLD WORK STRATEGY.

(⊕) SEE WEB LINKS

• The Morgan Centre for the Study of Relationships and Personal Life, University of Manchester.

family, stem Through field studies of family organization, Frédéric Le Play (1806–82) claimed to have distinguished four fundamental family types: namely, patriarchal, unstable, particularist and stem. The stem family was described as a more flexible modification of the patriarchal type. It was said to be typical of Central Europe, Spain, and Scandinavia; was the ideal for stability and prosperity; and consisted of six or seven members, typically free labourers or farm tenants, with clear intergenerational inheritance of either tenancy or smallholding.

family, symmetrical A family form identified by Peter Willmott and Michael Young in the early 1970s and said to be increasingly common, in which the *domestic division of labour is less marked, and the home more central to social life and social identities. However, feminist scholarship of the same period highlighted continued inequalities of the domestic division of labour, and the thesis has found little empirical support. *See also* ROLE, CONJUGAL.

family therapy A form of treatment favoured by some *social workers and *psychotherapists. It shifts attention away from the individual's problems to the family viewed as an interdependent system. Treatment involves analysing and interpreting the observed intra-familial dynamics. Feminists argue it ignores inequalities in power between the sexes, so contributing to tendencies to blame, devalue, and subordinate women.

family wage This was an objective adopted by male *trade unionists at the turn of the 19th century in their fight for improved wages. It is based on the argument that a wage should be sufficient to maintain a wife and children. There was considerable female support for this view—although nowadays it is often cited as a factor in explanations of women's disadvantaged position in the *labour market.

fascism Originally, the term denoted only the Italian political party founded by Benito Mussolini in the aftermath of World War I, and the state that was created during the 1920s following the party's seizure of power, although in ordinary usage it has since become a generic term used to refer to almost any *authoritarian right-wing *ideology, *political party, or *state. It nevertheless retains a certain precision within *political sociology. In the latter context, it has come to refer to parties, ideologies, or states that either advocate or embody a typically terroristic domination of a fused state apparatus, within which there is no separation of powers or rule of law, by a single party infused with a frequently racist and always nationalist petit-bourgeois ideology. On this basis, the German Nazi (National Socialist) Party founded by Adolf Hitler, the ideology he elaborated, and state that he created after his seizure of power, have become the archetypes of fascism in place of their Italian equivalents. Naturally, there were many variations on the fascist themes current in inter-war Europe, and these are concisely discussed in Eugen Weber, *Varieties of Fascism*, 1964.

Striking as this broadening of reference and change of archetype has been, it has not aroused much controversy, at least in sociological circles. Certainly, it has not provoked nearly as much controversy as that which has raged around the causes and significance of fascism in general, and of its temporary German and Italian successes in particular. It is true that almost all those who have sought to explain the rise of fascism in the inter-war years have regarded it as the product of a crisis associated with some type of transitional process. But what they have signally failed to agree about is the nature of the crises and transitions involved.

For the majority of liberal sociologists (such as Ralf Dahrendorf and Reinhard Bendix, addressing the case of Germany or A. W. Salamone and Frederico Chabod that of Italy) the pertinent transitional process was that which was occurring—or, better, failing to occur—at the level of values. The general process that is involved here is often referred to as one of *modernization. More concretely, since the chief bearers of the liberal-democratic values that are considered to be appropriate to modern societies are the *bourgeoisie and their *middle-class allies, such scholars have focused their attention on the failure of these groups to establish their social dominance or keep faith with their values.

Within such an analytical framework it is not surprising that what are typically identified as the 'fatal crises' turn out to be essentially political in nature. Thus, in the case of both societies, emphasis is given to the ways in which the *legitimacy of what were newly established liberal-democratic regimes was undermined. Among the most important factors cited in this regard are: tensions arising from what were termed in Italy 'lost territories'; the heavy financial burdens imposed by war reparations (Germany) and the repayment of war loans (Italy); the shared experience of a hyper-inflation which wiped out the savings of the middle classes; the uncertainty and instability that in both cases resulted from the political fragmentation caused by the existence of electoral systems based on proportional representation; and, finally, miscalculations on the part of the bourgeois parties as to the seriousness of the fascist threat.

By contrast, Marxist-inclined writers have traditionally identified the pertinent transition process as an economic one, and have focused instead on the difficulties encountered by both Italy and Germany in making the transition between the competitive and monopoly stages of *capitalist development. More recently, they have also stressed the contribution made to these difficulties by the belated passing of *absolutism, as for example in the work of Barrington Moore (see his *The Social Origins of Dictatorship and Democracy*, 1966).

By far the most sophisticated Marxist analysis is that to be found scattered through the pages of Antonio *Gramsci's *Prison Notebooks* (1929–35)—although, because of the conditions under which Gramsci wrote, his account is not worked out in great empirical detail and is sometimes rather too elusive for contemporary readers. Guided by the particular interpretation of the *relative autonomy of politics and ideology that he brought to Marxism with his concept of *hegemony, Gramsci formulated a whole series of middle-range concepts ('passive revolution', 'catastrophic equilibrium', 'fordism', and 'Caesarism') which he uses to chart and explain the interaction of economic, political and ideological factors in the aetiology of Italian fascism. In the 1970s several structuralist Marxists sought with mixed success both to develop Gramsci's ideas, and to apply them to the German and other cases. Nicos *Poulantzas was by far the most ambitious and prominent of these (see his *Fascism and Dictatorship*, 1970).

Many historians as well as sociologists continue to be attracted to the study of fascism, because of its horrific dramatic interest, its implications for the development of civilization, its suitability for comparative study, and feared recurrence. It provides an almost unrivalled opportunity for sociologists and others to investigate some of the most profound and disturbing aspects of the modern world, as illustrated in Michael Mann's *Fascists* (2004). *See also* FALANGISM.

fatalism A system of beliefs which holds that everything has its appointed outcome, that this cannot be avoided by effort or foreknowledge, and must merely be accepted as an unavoidable fact of life. The phenomenon has been somewhat neglected by sociologists, although fatalism is often identified as a characteristic of *poverty, chronic illness, and *unemployment. Thus, for example, Oscar Lewis maintains that it is a central characteristic of the 'culture of poverty' (see *The Children of Sanchez*, 1961). Similarly, in her discussion of 'the passive worker thesis' (the idea that women are generally more stable, passive, and fundamentally exploitable workers than men), Kate Purcell argues that women's behaviour at work is informed by 'a fatalistic approach to life', fostered by gender *socialization and women's biology, and reinforced particularly by women manual workers' work and class circumstances ('Female Manual Workers, Fatalism and the Reinforcement of Inequalities', in David Robbins (ed.), *Rethinking Social Inequality*, 1982).

In his study of *Suicide* (1897), Émile *Durkheim defines fatalistic suicide (as in the case of suicides committed by slaves) in terms of excessive regulation of the wants of individuals, a situation in which the future is 'pitilessly blocked and passions violently choked by oppressive discipline'. Hope is diminished to the extent that even life itself becomes a matter of indifference. In an extension of the Durkheimian discussion, David *Lockwood (*Solidarity and Schism*, 1992) suggests that fatalism is a matter of degree, and can result from either 'physical or moral despotism'; that is, from force of circumstances such as the condition of *slavery, or the constraints imposed by a system of explicitly fatalistic beliefs such as those embraced by the *Hindu doctrine of *karma-samsara-moksha*. Fatalism grounded in a specifically fatalistic ideology (such as Hindu soteriology) engenders an ethical commitment. By comparison the existential fatalism induced by slavery is grounded primarily in ritual rather than beliefs, and the subordinate strata do not approve of their condition but judge it merely to be unalterable. In both cases, however, 'what is especially conducive to a fatalistic attitude is not so much the degree of oppressive discipline involved, but rather the fact that social constraint is experienced as an external, inevitable and impersonal condition'.

fatherhood An apparently commonsense concept, but one which is too often used loosely by sociologists, since it could mean: a man through whom ties of filiation ('being the child of') are traced; a man through whom property rights are traced; a man whose acknowledged (not necessarily genetic) relationship to the child establishes its full social membership within the society; a man whose acknowledged relationship to the child establishes its social group membership within a society; or any combination of these. Different societies, with different systems of descent and transmission of rights, employ the term differently.

Featherman-Jones-Hauser hypothesis This states that there exists a cross-national similarity of social *mobility rates at the level of underlying 'relative mobility chances', such that in all societies having a nuclear family system and market economy, the mobility pattern will be 'basically the same' (see D. L. Featherman, F. L. Jones, and R. M. Hauser, 'Assumptions of Social Mobility Research in the US: The Case of Occupational Status', *Social Science Research*, 1975). The argument has since been much disputed.

The terminological inexactitude of the hypothesis has meant that debate about its empirical standing has been lively. On one hand, there are those such as Erikson and Goldthorpe (*The Constant Flux*, 1992) who argue that the weaker (verbal) formulation is essentially sound, and that the key features of cross-nationally common fluidity patterns can be represented in a so-called 'core model'. Although their data for fifteen countries show some cross-national variations in relative rates that are not captured by this model, these are relatively minor. On the other hand, Harry Ganzeboom, Ruud Luijkx, and Donald Treiman have argued that analysis of 149 intergenerational class mobility tables from 35 countries 'suggests that the hypothesis of common social fluidity is simply incorrect'. Their results seem to show that 'the between-country variance accounts for about one third of the total variance in the mobility parameters, indicating that there are significant between-country differences' ('Intergenerational Class Mobility in Comparative Perspective', *Research in Social Stratification and Mobility*, 1989).

It is difficult to arbitrate between these and other similarly competing accounts, not only because they tend to adopt different criteria as to what constitutes mobility regimes that are 'basically the same', but also because they have invariably been arrived at from an analysis of alternative data-sets, coded to class schemes (including *Goldthorpe class schemes) of varying complexity and reliability, and conducted on the basis of competing statistical tools. It does seem to be generally agreed, however, that the cross-nationally common element in relative mobility chances heavily predominates over the cross-nationally variable one.

fecundity The biological capacity for reproduction of individuals or populations. In demography, fecundity (as the potential for childbearing) is contrasted with *fertility, or actual childbearing. The infecund are those who cannot have children though they may have been fertile and/or fecund in the past.

federalism A political system and philosophy that, within a particular nation-state, recognizes a central government for the whole country and autonomous regional governments for constituent states or provinces. The powers and functions of government are divided between the two levels. Federal systems must embody a means of resolving conflict between the centre and regions or between any two regions. Regional authorities are given specific duties and protected by *rights from encroachment by the centre. Both levels of government have the right to legislate for tax. Switzerland and the United States are contemporary examples of federal political systems. The term is sometimes also applied to commercial and other organizations, as for example in the case of federal (as against centralized) labour movements, but its main application is with regard to systems of government.

feedback *See* CYBERNETICS; EQUILIBRIUM.

feeling rules A concept developed by Arlie Hochschild (*The Managed Heart*, 1983) to draw attention to the existence of 'rules about what feeling is or is not appropriate to a given social setting'. *See also* EMOTION, SOCIOLOGY OF.

femininity A summary term, contrasted with *masculinity, for the distinctive ways of acting and feeling on the part of women. Precisely what characteristics are listed varies, though passivity, dependence, and weakness are usually mentioned. Sociologists point to the social origins of femininity and female subjectivity, and stress their ideological role, but discussions of femininity have often lapsed into *essentialism.

feminism (feminist theory) A social movement, combining theory with political practice, which seeks to achieve equality between men and women. Its origins in 18th-century England are associated with Mary Wollstonecraft's plea for the rights of women. At the turn of the 20th century the term referred to suffragettes and other campaigners for votes for women and women's access to education and the professions. After the achievement of the vote (1920 in the United States and 1928 in Britain), active feminism was less in evidence until it burst onto the scene again in the late 1960s across North America and Europe in the wake of the civil rights, student, and anti-imperialist movements. Many key concerns of what became known as 'second wave feminism' had been prefigured in Simone *de Beauvoir's *The Second Sex* (1949), a foundational text which remains a crucial influence on contemporary feminist thought. Her recognition that 'one is not born, but rather becomes, a woman' became the basis for the distinction between sex and gender. Her argument that women were defined in relation to men, but unequally, so that 'woman' was the negation or 'Other' of 'man', resonated in later feminist theories, as did her understanding that femininity and masculinity are both discursive and material.

The writings of Kate Millett, Betty Friedan, Valerie Solanas, Shulamith Firestone, and Juliet Mitchell echoed the concerns of the emergent Women's Liberation Movement. They drew attention to varied forms and sites of female subordination and male power (from reproductive technologies and socialization practices to laws and cultural representations), and to the ways that marriage and motherhood confined women to the 'private sphere'. All this prevented women from realizing their potential and contributed to their acceptance and even interiorization of inferiority. The WLM was a grass-roots movement, composed of many locally based groups that came together in campaigns and national conferences. At the first British national conference in 1970, four demands were formulated: for equal pay, for equal education and opportunity, for 24-hour nurseries, and for free contraception and abortion on demand. The last was later altered to women's right to control their bodies (in recognition that fertility control was routinely imposed on minority ethnic women even if white women had difficulty accessing it) and a fifth added, demanding financial independence. Campaigns ranged from rape crisis and women's aid to support for night cleaners and machinists at Fords, and solidarity campaigns with women's struggles in Chile, Argentina, South Africa, and Mozambique. Publications took the form of pamphlets, newsletters, and magazines, the best-known in Britain being *Shrew, Spare Rib*, and *Red Rag*. Members were predominantly young and well educated: the post-war generation whose experience of higher education led them to expect an equality that they did not find in reality. In recognition of the slogan 'the personal is political', many groups undertook 'consciousness-raising', attempting to understand through collective discussion how their own lives and consciousness had been shaped. This gave the possibility of acknowledging as social and so challenging politically what had previously been experienced as personal and individual.

Cross-cutting differences of theory and politics are a feature of the feminist movement. The greatest division has been between those aiming for emancipation and equal rights within the present system and those whose goal was liberation and transformation of the prevailing sex/gender system. Overlying this were debates about equality and difference (whether women and men were the same or different, and should have similar or different treatment) and the primacy of patriarchy or capitalism as causes of gender subordination. For radical feminists who prioritized patriarchy, men were 'the main enemy' (Delphy) and there was no question of combining with (male) trade unions or political groups to achieve change, as there was for socialist feminists. In addition, separatists critiqued 'compulsory heterosexuality' (Adrienne Rich) and argued for feminists to become lesbian. But socialist feminists also criticized the 'anti-social family' (Barrett and McIntosh) and romantic love as oppressive institutions. Within each broad grouping there were also significant divisions. Shulamith Firestone and Christine Delphy were both radical feminists. The former argued that the basis of patriarchy lay in the 'dialectic of sex' or 'sex-class' that 'sprang from a biological reality'. To overcome it required seizing the means of reproduction, and freeing women from their biology through reproductive technology. The latter avoided such essentialism, locating the material basis for women's oppression in the 'family mode of production' where husbands appropriated their wives' labour. Socialist feminists differed in how they conceptualized the relation between capitalism and patriarchy, as two analytically separate systems, each of which has an independent effect (Juliet Mitchell and Heidi Hartmann), or as so completely fused that they formed a single system of capitalist patriarchy (Zillah Eisenstein), and also in their understanding of institutional location of the two principles. Divergent views of political engagement accompanied all these differences of analysis.

Second-wave feminism had a significant impact on sociology in the 1980s, although the first attempts to introduce feminist perspectives were resisted and often ridiculed. Gradually junior academics set up women's studies groups, and challenged 'malestream' sociological thinking for its gender blindness, under the guise of gender neutrality. Meg Stacey criticized the 'founding fathers' for their exclusive concern with 'the public domain . . . affairs of state and the market place which in the mid-19th century were not affairs with which women were allowed to be concerned . . . the authors were all men working in that domain and addressing other members of it'. Ann Oakley (*Sex, Gender and Society*, 1972,

The Sociology of Housework, 1974) emphasized that gender was socially constructed, introduced domestic labour and childbirth as topics for sociological study, and championed qualitative and egalitarian research methods. As well as opening up new terrain for sociological analysis, feminists criticized then-dominant writings on class, work, and crime for the distorted analysis that resulted from their lack of gender awareness. As sociology acknowledged its omission, the tendency to 'add on' women to substantive areas of study gradually gave way to adoption of a gendered framework of analysis. The key debates in early feminist sociology closely reflected those of the feminist movement, notably equality versus difference and capitalism versus patriarchy (e.g. Sylvia Walby, *Patriarchy at Work*, 1986).

By the time feminism gained a place in the academy, it was in decline as a social movement: acceptability increased as militancy dissipated. By the 1980s, second-wave feminism had passed its peak as a (relatively) unified and confident movement. Formal achievements included anti-discrimination and equal pay legislation and abortion reform. In the ensuing decade questions of identity and difference became a preoccupation, shifting the political terrain to the 'politics of location' and 'identity politics' where aims were based on the position or identity of activists rather than an ultimate goal. Considerable theoretical attention was devoted to the formation of gendered subjectivity, male and female, informed by recent developments in psychoanalytic thinking.

Anglo-Saxon feminism was seriously challenged by Black women's critique that it had universalized the position of White Western women by implying that what explains their particular situation explains that of all women. White feminism was charged (by bell hooks, Angela Davis, Chandra Mohanty) with being simplistic and Eurocentric, if not racist, for ignoring the enormous differences between women that arose from imperialism, racism, and the historical legacy of slavery. Such differences rendered the basic concepts of feminist theory inappropriate to Black and Third World women. Hazel Carby's influential chapter (in *The Empire Strikes Back*, 1982) used historical evidence to question basic feminist ideas such as the distinction between re/production, the priority accorded to the family as the origin of women's oppression, and the assumption that all men were patriarchal. If women were not a homogeneous grouping, there could be no aspiration to unitary theory or practice. Each group would need to be analysed in terms of its own particularity. This recognition was the stimulus for a flowering of Black, minority ethnic, and post-colonial feminisms in the developed and developing world, while at the same time forcing White feminism into self-critique (Chilla Bulbeck, *Re-orienting Western Feminisms*, 1997). Differences between women, rather than between men and women, became a central focus, and the theoretical challenge was to conceptualize the intersection of multiple cross-cutting social divisions, for example as a 'matrix of domination' (Patricia Hill Collins, *Black Feminist Thought*, 1990).

The 'Black' critique was reinforced by postmodernism and post-structuralism. These approaches questioned the very underpinnings of Western feminism as a modernist Enlightenment project reliant on the suspect category 'woman'. If the meaning of 'woman' in relation to 'man' is tied to particular contexts, there could be no universal category that applied through time and space, nor general theory (Michele Barrett and Anne Phillips, *Destabilizing Theory*, 1992). The sex/gender dichotomy was equally challenged, notably by Judith Butler and her influential conceptualization of gender as 'provisional' and 'performative' (*Gender Trouble*, 1990). The focus on culture, language, identity, and transgression is also characteristic of the attempt by 'post-feminism' at the dissolution of gender.

Since the 1990s feminist and gender theory shared a concern with femininities and masculinities in the plural and became further integrated, for example in the important work of Bob Connell. Degrees in women's or gender studies proliferated. While the voice of Anglo-Saxon feminism is loudest in the academy, feminist political movements are gaining strength in East Asia, the Indian subcontinent, and parts of Africa. Many issues familiar to second-wave feminists are again on the agenda, but posed in a manner appropriate to their specific circumstances. In the West, the world encountered by young women is very different today from 1970, a legacy in part of the feminist movement. Sexuality and women's place in private and public life have been transformed in ways now almost taken for granted. *See also* CRIMINOLOGY, FEMINIST; CULTURAL THEORY; METHODOLOGY, FEMINIST; MOTHERHOOD.

(⊕) SEE WEB LINKS
• The Women's Library (formerly the Fawcett Library): a major archive and source of information on feminism and women's history.

feminist criminology *See* CRIMINOLOGY, FEMINIST.

feminist methodology *See* METHODOLOGY, FEMINIST.

Ferguson, Adam (1724–1816) Though less revered as a philosopher than his fellow luminary of the *Scottish Enlightenment, David *Hume, Ferguson has a better claim to be considered among the founders of modern sociology. His critique of the 'self-interest' view of *human nature followed Hume's lead, but Ferguson took his view of humans as inescapably social in nature forward into a critical analysis of the new commercial civilization then displacing the older clan-based society of the Scottish Highlands. His views on the effects of the *division of labour were significant precursors of later work on this topic by Karl *Marx and Émile *Durkheim, and the concepts of self-estrangement and *alienation are also prefigured in Ferguson's writings. *See also* INTERESTS.

fertility (fertility rate) The actual level of childbearing of an individual or population. There are different ways of measuring the fertility of a population. The simplest measure, the crude *birth rate, relates the number of live births in a given year to the total population size in that year. More complex measures relate the year's births to more restricted populations, usually childbearing women, to yield a better index of underlying fertility. The denominator may be all women of childbearing years (commonly set at 15 to 44) or women in more specific age-bands (age-specific fertility rates). Fertility rates may be combined with *mortality rates to generate an overall reproduction rate.

Historically there has been a long-term decline in levels of fertility in industrial societies, a decline that is associated with economic development and restructuring, reductions in child mortality, changes in welfare provision and the economic and social value of children, and the changing social position of women.

fetishism of commodities *See* COMMODITY FETISHISM.

feudalism Some historians have argued that feudalism is a technical term that can be applied only to Western European institutions of the Middle Ages. Others (including most sociologists) have conceptualized the phenomenon in a more abstract way, as a general method of political organization, and one which can therefore be identified in other times and places (such as Tokugawa Japan).

The term originated in 17th-century England as a way of talking about a mode of landholding that was then rapidly disappearing. In the 18th and 19th centuries it was widely taken up by legal scholars and in this way entered the vocabularies of the founders of sociology. Although the founders typically used the term to refer to the type of society from whence *capitalism had emerged in Western Europe, none of them explicitly formulated a fully developed concept of feudalism. However, as will become apparent below, highly influential embryos of such a concept may be derived without much difficulty from the historical writings of both Karl *Marx and Max *Weber.

There have been and there remain disputes about how the concept of feudalism should be formulated. All of the specifically sociological conceptualizations are nomothetic (generalizing) in character. The best-known ideographic (individualizing) formulation is that arrived at by the French historian Marc *Bloch in his *Feudal Society* (1961). Bloch's account deserves some attention, not only because it has been highly influential in itself, but also because the contrast between it and the various sociological alternatives illustrates some of the central disputes about concept formation in the social sciences.

Bloch's methodological premise is that each society is unique and has to be understood in its own terms. (He only grudgingly admits, mentioning Japan specifically, that something like feudalism may have existed outside of the West European context.) His work is also profoundly *empiricist and *humanist in Louis *Althusser's senses of these terms. The consequences of these premises are apparent in his formulation of the core relation of feudalism—vassalage. In the course of a highly detailed study of France during the Middle Ages, he defines vassalage as 'the warrior ideal', or a contract of mutual benefit freely entered into 'by two living men confronting each other'. From this relationship all the other characteristics of feudal societies follow: hereditary succession; enfeoffment (the granting of land by lords to their vassals); the fragmentation of authority; and the existence of a confinable and taxable but otherwise self-disciplining peasantry. What inevitably (but regrettably in Bloch's view) followed from the institutionalization of vassalage, was the tarnishing of 'the purity of the (original) obligation', and the gradual dissolution of the way of life constructed around it.

Almost by definition, no properly sociological approach to social phenomena is likely to start from the assumption that each society must be considered separately and as wholly unique, and this certainly has proved to be the case in the literature relating to feudalism in Western Europe (if not in Japan). On the contrary, the *sine qua non* of most macro-sociological explanation is the assumption of comparability, and what differentiates explanations from one another is whether they depend upon comparisons that were made before or after the formulation of the concepts upon which they rest; that is, whether they depend upon empiricist or realist modes of formulation, respectively.

Where the formulation is empiricist, as in the case of the contributors to the collection edited by Joseph Strayer and Rushton Coulborn (*Feudalism in History*, 1956), a large number of cases of possible feudalisms are compared and any shared characteristics are then formed into a generalization. Interestingly, in this case the generalization is to all intents and purposes the same as that produced by Bloch, minus the romanticism and, by the same token, any means of grasping the internal dynamics of the system.

Because it is not a straightforward empirical generalization Weber's *ideal type of feudalism does not share this weakness. Although it is nowhere explicitly formulated, this ideal-type may be extracted relatively easily from the discussions of feudal social relations to be found in Weber's *Economy and Society* (1920) and *General Economic History* (1919–20). In Weberian terms, feudalism represented an instance of the routinization of *charisma, in the context of a traditional mode of *domination. Thus, power was organized in a *patrimonial manner, underpinned by a system of enfeoffment, and rested upon a system of exploitation whereby serfs (unfree peasants) were forced, in exchange for the right to work land, to pay varying and often multiple forms of rent (in labour, cash, or kind) to their lords. According to Weber it was the last of these, the struggles over rent, that gave the system its internal dynamic.

There is some textual evidence to suggest that Weber derived his concept of feudal rent from that constructed by Marx on the basis of the latter's *realist mode of concept formation. Certainly, there are striking similarities between the two concepts, as well as in the reasoning used in their support. Most importantly, both theorists explain why *exploitation took the form of rents extracted on the basis of the lords' superior might by arguing that the lords had no alternative, given their exclusion from the process of production. However, in their book *Precapitalist Modes of Production* (1975), Barry Hindess and Paul Hirst argue that Marx would have, or at least should have, revised this argument, in the light of the advances he made in refining his general concept of *mode of production in *Capital*. They support this stance by arguing that feudal lords did in fact play an important role in the production process. On this basis, then, Hindess and Hirst argue that the importance ascribed by Marx and others to political coercion as the critical component of feudalism should be rejected, as a sign of conceptual underdevelopment, and replaced by a specification of the economic relations which allowed the lords to extract surplus product from the serfs.

field experiment An *experiment carried out in a 'natural' setting. That is, unlike in the case of laboratory experiments, the setting is not created by the researcher. It is less artificial than laboratory experiments, fewer variables are controlled, and so inferences are often difficult. Field experiments are relatively rare, as identifying settings where experimental intervention is both feasible and ethical is difficult. For a review and discussion of examples see Catherine Hakim, *Research Design* (1987).

field theory An approach developed by German-American psychologist Kurt Lewin in the 1950s, influenced by *Gestalt theory. Individual behaviour is seen as determined by the totality of the individual's situation—their psychological field or life-space. This contains the individual with *goals, *needs, and their perceived *environment, and can be represented in diagrams. The classic secondary discussion is Harold Mey's *Field Theory* (1972), while a recent discussion is John Martin, 'What is Field Theory?', *American Journal of Sociology* (2003).

fieldwork Data collection for any study that involves talking to people or asking them questions about their activities and views, sometimes including attempts at systematic observation of their behaviour. Fieldwork ranges from large-scale *survey interviewing by hundreds of professional interviewers, to the lone researcher recording information collected through *participant observation in a small-scale *case study (see R. G. Burgess, *In the Field: An Introduction to Field Research*, 1984). The term is sometimes extended to any research activity that takes one out of the office and into the 'field' that is the subject of study.

figurational sociology *See* ELIAS, NORBERT.

figure-ground contrast *See* PERCEPTION.

finance capitalism *See* CAPITALISM; OWNERSHIP AND CONTROL.

first-order constructs *See* PHENOMENOLOGY.

First World The term was originally applied to the first group of countries to *industrialize and to achieve high levels of growth and a rising standard of living for their populations, thus covering North America, Western Europe, Japan, and Australasia. *See also* THIRD WORLD.

fiscal crisis (of the state) A term coined by James O'Connor (*The Fiscal Crisis of the State*, 1973), to denote the 'structural gap' in advanced capitalist societies between state revenues and expenses, which leads to economic, social, and political crises. Now used more widely to describe such fiscal difficulties. For example, in *Contradictions of the Welfare State* (1984) and *Disorganized Capitalism* (1985), the German sociologist Claus Offe examines the legitimation problems of advanced welfare-capitalist societies, and what he calls the 'crises of crisis management'; namely, the problems faced by states in attempting to manage the socio-political problems (notably the fiscal crises, demand overload, and decline of the 'achievement principle') that he sees as being inherent in such social systems.

fixed capital *See* CAPITAL.

fixed-choice question *See* CLOSED RESPONSE.

flexibility, labour-market *See* LABOUR-MARKET FLEXIBILITY.

flexible employment Said increasingly to characterize the industrial firms and economies of the *post-industrial world, it assumes two forms. Functional flexibility (or post-fordism) means the adaptation of work organization, skills, and machinery, so as to cope with the constantly changing market and technological environment of the global economy of the late 20th century. So-called *flexible firms are also said to adopt numerical flexibility, using non-standard forms of *employment to allow rapid changes in labour recruitment and discharge, in the face of product-market fluctuations. Only equivocal empirical evidence exists of flexible employment growth; likewise, that it is due to long-term change, rather than relatively short-term cyclical influences. *See also* FORDISM.

flexible work (flexible production, flexible specialization) These terms are part of a widespread debate about changing industrial structure and work organization. It is argued that increasing national and international competition is forcing greater flexibility on firms in order to respond more quickly to changes in the product-market. This includes greater flexibility in employment levels (numerical flexibility), job tasks and skills (functional flexibility), and payment systems (financial flexibility). Flexible specialization implies small, decentralized firms oriented towards niche markets, rather than (as in *fordism) large, centralized, mass-production firms. Much of the debate has been prompted by studies of Japanese manufacturing and corporations (see R. Dore, *Flexible Rigidities*, 1986). For a case study of the international automobile industry see Rebecca Morales, *Flexible Production* (1994). *See also* FLEXIBLE EMPLOYMENT; JUST-IN-TIME SYSTEM; SOCIO-TECHNICAL SYSTEM.

focused interaction A concept applied to the coordinating of face-to-face interaction by two or more actors. The contrast is with unfocused interaction, which is communication by gestures and signals that arises simply through actors being co-present, as in the case for example of *body language. The distinction is used by Erving *Goffman, in his description of the *framing of interaction, and Anthony Giddens builds the idea into his structuration theory.

focus groups Focus groups have a long history in social and commercial market research, beginning with studies on audience response to radio and other mass media by Paul *Lazarsfeld and Robert *Merton in the 1940s and '50s. There was a resurgence of interest in the later decades of the 20th century, and they remain a popular method, particularly in the fields of media research and medical sociology. Typically, a focus group consists of between five and eight people, with a facilitator (sometimes called a moderator) who leads a discussion on a particular topic by providing tasks for the group to undertake, asking questions, prompting answers and managing the flow of talk. Formats vary, but typically, after introductions, the session starts with an 'ice-breaking' exercise, such as inviting each member of the group to name their favourite television programme, and some 'focusing' tasks, in which the group is asked to respond to stimuli such as newspaper headlines or photographs. Participants may also be asked to rank or sort these stimuli. These focusing tasks are a useful technique for accessing participants' tacit knowledge about the topic, as the process of persuading other members of what items belong together, or how they are ordered in hierarchies, entails making explicit their normative views about categorization or priority. This allows the researcher to see what resources the group draws on to make distinctions, and what sources of evidence are credible in discussions. A series of questions and follow-up prompts for discussion then move from the more general to the more specific on the topic of interest. At the end, participants might also complete a questionnaire, to record demographic details of who took part and sometimes to also record individual responses to similar prompts used in the group discussion.

The composition of each focus group can be heterogeneous, with participants deliberately recruited to include a range of different backgrounds within each group, if the researcher is interested in eliciting diverse views. Alternatively, it may be advantageous to have more homogeneous participants, who share particular social or demographic characteristics, such as gender, ethnicity, or political views. The sensitivity of the topic, and what kind of data the researcher needs, will influence how much heterogeneity is desirable. Homogeneous groups are often more appropriate for discussions of experiences which might be stigmatized by wider society. Although focus groups traditionally consisted of strangers, the use of pre-existing groups, such as workmates, or friends, is a format that is particularly useful in social research for generating data on not just what people say, but on how decisions are made, and how opinions are formed within the kinds of interaction that would happen in everyday life.

Like individual interviews, focus groups can also be more or less structured. Tightly structured protocols will generate similar data from every group in the study, and may use prompts to ensure all participants are enabled to make a contribution on each question. In less-structured ones, the facilitator manages the interaction less intrusively, allowing the participants to set the agenda to some extent, and the discussion to flow more naturally, with participants interacting with each other, rather than through the facilitator. This has the advantage of generating more naturalistic talk, but will reduce the input of less confident members and risks the discussion moving into less pertinent topics.

Focus groups present greater logistic challenges than individual interviews, in terms of finding enough participants with the required experiences or characteristics who can attend at a specified time and place, and booking a suitable venue. One solution is virtual groups, where the interaction is conducted online, either through web-based discussion boards, or in real time, through linking up via Skype or commercially available virtual meeting software. Such techniques are useful for particularly sensitive issues, where participants welcome the anonymity provided by online discussion, or for geographically dispersed or less mobile participants.

The composition of the group, the degree of structure in the protocol, and the setting will all influence the kind of data generated. Social actors prioritize different aspects of their experiences and views depending on where they are, who they are talking to (whether those people are 'the same' or 'different' on particular characteristics), and what aspects of their identity have been foregrounded in the recruitment.

The key difference between data from a focus group and that from an individual interview is access to interaction between the participants. This is a real advantage for research where it is important to investigate how knowledge is generated, shared, and perhaps changed in social life, as participants challenge or agree with each other's views. Close analysis of a discussion enables the researcher to see how views are formed, which kinds of evidence are persuasive, or how strongly dissenting views are silenced. This interaction is less advantageous if the topic or population of interest is one where private accounts are needed, or where marginal voices need to be heard. For very sensitive topics, focus groups raise some ethical issues, especially if using pre-existing groups. Although the research team can protect the confidentiality of disclosures, it is not possible to ensure that all members of the group will, and care should be taken to guard against 'over-disclosure' of private information.

Data from a focus group study is usually analysed qualitatively, using some version of thematic analysis or discourse analysis, depending on the needs of the researcher, to explore transcripts of the audio-recorded discussion. Analysis requires careful attention to the interaction, taking into account the context in which opinions are offered, challenged, and changed. The unit of analysis for a focus group study is properly the group, not the individuals within the group. Given the challenges of organizing the groups, and of analysis, the sample size of a focus group study is generally small, depending on how segmented the groups are in terms of gender, experiences, or other characteristics.

There are many texts on focus groups. One of the best overviews of the practical and methodological issues raised by the use of focus groups is M. Bloor et al. *Focus Groups in Social Research* (2001).

folk devils A term employed most famously by Stanley Cohen in his study of the *moral panic over the 'Mods' and 'Rockers' *subcultures in England during the 1960s (see *Folk Devils and Moral Panics*, 1972). Drawing upon *interactionist approaches to the sociology of *collective behaviour, Cohen suggests that societies build a gallery of social types that provides examples of types of behaviour to be avoided and to be emulated. Those groups seen as deviant, and that are objects of disapproval, occupy 'a constant position as folk devils: visible reminders of what we should not be'. The term has since been used widely in other studies of representations of *deviance. Some of the general issues are covered in Orrin E. Klapp's *Heroes, Villains, and Fools* (1962). *See also* LABELLING.

folk society An ideal type referring to 'primitive' agrarian societies in all historical periods which, it is assumed, have none of the economic or socio-cultural characteristics of 'modern' urban-industrial societies. The concept is often criticized on theoretical and empirical grounds and for its ideological bias. *See also* FOLK-URBAN CONTINUUM.

folk-urban continuum A concept relating to the transition from rural to urban societies. Investigation of the social, cultural, and economic characteristics of individual societies allows them to be positioned at different points along an evolutionary path. *See also* FOLK SOCIETY.

folkways A term associated with the work of William Graham *Sumner, whose major contribution to sociology was his analysis of the nature, origins, and significance of folkways and *mores. The former are group habits (or customs). In Sumner's view, societies develop (by trial and error) the particular ways of acting that are suited to their milieu; these ways of behaving are repeated and produce habits (in individuals) and customs (in groups); and these habits—or folkways—then become the commonly accepted ways of doing things in that society. Sumner is vague about the precise origins of folkways, and inconsistent in stating their relationship to mores, which are essentially folkways embodying moral imperatives about what is right and true. Sometimes the two terms are opposed, but occasionally folkways are deemed to include all commonly accepted ways of thinking, including mores (see *Folkways*, 1906).

food, sociological studies of An area of sociology that, with some significant exceptions (as in the work of Norbert Elias on table-manners), is of very recent interest, despite the quite widespread and long-standing attention to the *rituals surrounding food in the work of *social anthropologists. (Claude Lévi-Strauss's studies, such as *The Raw and the Cooked*, 1970, are a notable illustration of the latter.) The anthropological interest in food no doubt arises from the attention to the details of everyday life that are a feature of *ethnographic studies. The prohibitions and prescriptions relating to food provide a useful vehicle for the examination of cultural differences. Without the same concern to describe the full detail of everyday behaviour, so much of which is taken for granted, ideas and practices concerning food have until recently generally seemed of little significance to sociologists, except in the context either of studies of poverty and deprivation, or of the study of agriculture and industry.

The expanding sociological interest in food stems most obviously from, and is a reflection of, the growing social and cultural significance of food in affluent industrial societies. Whereas the preparation and consumption of food may often have been seen simply as the meeting of a biological *need, they are now seen as of diverse cultural and social significance. On one hand, they are regarded as of major significance to the individual's bodily health, with diet identified as a key health-related behaviour, and a range of studies now examining many aspects of food and diet. There has also been an enormous increase in eating disorders, such as anorexia nervosa and bulimia, which are more frequently detected in women than men and are seen as in part a reflection of the cultural significance attached to diet and the *body. On the other hand, the preparation and consumption of food within the home are seen as important aspects of the gender-based *division of labour and distribution of resources. In addition, the consumption of food in the public sphere is not only an increasingly common leisure activity, but is also seen to be important to the maintenance of the social networks surrounding paid employment (*see* Alan Warde and Lydia Martens, *Eating Out*, 2000).

The sociology of food is therefore likely to be an expanding area of research for some years to come. Jack Goody's *Cooking, Cuisine and Class* (1982) and Stephen Mennell's *All Manners of Food* (1985) give good—though quite different—impressions of the field. *See also* CONSUMPTION, SOCIOLOGY OF.

forces of production Marxist political economy makes an analytical distinction between two aspects of economic activity. On one hand are the 'social relations' of production, which relate to the maintenance of social domination, the extraction of an economic surplus, and the exploitation of labour. On the other hand, there are the 'forces of production', those elements and relations that are necessary, whatever the social structure, if materials, objects, and forces, drawn from nature, are to be modified into a form suitable to meet some human purpose. There is no agreement about the exact scope of the term 'forces of production', but at various times Marx and Engels included the following: 'raw materials', the bodies or substances to be worked upon in the labour-process, and always considered by Marx and Engels to be the products of prior expenditures of human labour; 'instruments of production', the tools or machinery employed in modifying raw materials (including in some versions, human organs themselves); the human capacity for work ('labour power'), a function of bodily organization, fitness, skill, knowledge, and suchlike; and, finally, the forms of social division and coordination of labour required by the particular characteristics of a given labour-process (sometimes called 'technical relations' of production). A further category of requirements for production—land, air, water, and other broadly environmental or contextual conditions—was recognized by Marx and Engels, but often mistakenly included among the instruments of production. Marx and Engels postulated a long-run historical trend in human societies, dramatically accelerated by *capitalism, for the forces of production (combined human productive powers) to develop. This developmental process would enhance humanity's capacity to control and regulate nature, and so meet universal human needs with a minimum of expenditure of unrewarding effort. This state of developed productive forces was to be a precondition for the future *communist realm of freedom beyond scarcity and the necessity for labour.

fordism As defined by Antonio *Gramsci, this refers to a form of productive organization thought to be typical of advanced capitalism and exemplified by Henry Ford's system of mass automobile production. This allied labour management according to the principles of *scientific management ('Taylorism') with a wider reorganization of production and marketing, involving a moving assembly line, standardized outputs, and demand stimulation by a combination of low prices, high wages, advertising, and consumer credit. Gramsci suggested that high levels of production could only be sustained by 'tempering compulsion . . . with persuasion'. Fordism provided workers with high wages and rising levels of consumption in exchange for an intensified work regime.

Many subsequent theorists have used the concept in analysing the industrial and social order of full employment, mass production, the welfare state, and rising standards of consumption, which characterized advanced capitalist societies after the Second World War. However, the term is used variously to refer to assembly-line mass production, certain leading sectors of industry, a *hegemonic form of industrial organization, or a 'mode of regulation'—the meaning of which probably comes closest to that intended by Gramsci.

Following the economic crises of the 1970s and 1980s, with associated changes in the social and technical organization of production and the alleged coming of *post-industrial society, some suggest that fordism is in terminal crisis, being succeeded by 'post-fordism', based on so-called *flexible production systems. This new terminology also carries varying meanings according to the context of use and author. *See also* REGULATION THEORY.

foreign aid The transfer of state resources through loans, grants, or provision of goods, from more to less developed countries, for development or emergency relief purposes. This can be done on a bilateral basis, or through multilateral bodies such as United Nations agencies, the European Economic Community, or World Bank. From the 1970s it has increasingly been queried as a means of promoting *economic growth.

formalism (formal sociology) In sociology, a theoretical approach that traces its origins to Georg *Simmel. It aims to capture the underlying forms of social relations, and thus to provide a 'geometry of social life'. Followers of Simmel in Germany included Leopold von Wiese and Alfred Vierkandt.

Simmel distinguished the 'content' of social life (wars, families, education, politics) from its 'forms' (such as, for example, conflict), which cut across all such areas, and through which social life is patterned. Conflict, as a social form, may be found in situations as diverse as those of family life and politics, and to it certain common features will accrue. Contents vary—but forms emerge as the central organizing features of social life. Among the forms central to Simmel's ideas are the significance of numbers for group alignments (isolated individuals, *dyads, *triads), patterns of superordination and subordination, group relationships (conflicts, competitions, coalitions), *identities and *roles (the stranger, the poor), disclosures (secrets, the secret society), and evaluations (prices, exchanges).

Most sociology concentrates upon content: there are sociologies of education, the family, the media, and so forth. Formalism shuns this approach to sociology, by cutting across such topics, and seeking to identify generic processes and patterns through which they are socially constituted: *stigma, *stratification, and secrecy, for instance, may be forms cutting through the substantive areas of education, family, and media. The best general commentary on Simmel's formal sociology remains Nicholas Spykman's *The Social Theory of Georg Simmel* (1925).

After Simmel and his immediate followers, the earliest development of such an approach was to be found in the work of the Chicago interactionists. Robert Park was a student of Simmel's, and brought to Chicago a concern both to study the richness of the empirical world as revealed in the city, and a concern to detect the patterns of city life. The most popular textbook of the day (Park and Burgess's *An Introduction to Sociology*) is largely organized according to 'forms'.

Barney Glaser and Anselm Strauss have attempted to develop formal sociology in their work on dying, moving from a rich substantive area of research (cancer wards and the dying process), to a more sustained theoretical analysis of common forms (such as status passages and awareness contexts). For example, moving from a detailed case study of a dying patient, they were able to seek comparisons with other major status changes in order to develop a formal theory of status passage, which postulated many features in common with other status passages (see *Status Passage*, 1967). From a grounded substantive study came more comparative, abstract, and formal theory. More recently, Robert Prus ('Generic Social Processes', *Journal of Contemporary Ethnography*, 1987) has outlined five key dimensions of group life that are needed for a processual generic sociology: acquiring perspectives, achieving identity, being involved, doing activity, and experiencing relationships.

There have been a number of other attempts to construct a formal theory of social life, including John Lofland's *Doing Social Life* (1976) and Carl Couch's *Constructing Social Life* (1975), as well as more specific case studies, such as Lewis Coser's *The Functions of Social Conflict* (1956). Erving Goffman's *Stigma* (1961) is sometimes seen as owing a great deal to formal sociology.

There is some dispute about the role and nature of formal sociology. Some see it as seeking fixed structures of an obdurate social order; others view it as depicting the very interactions out of which social life is constituted; while for many it is simply an analytic device produced by sociologists seeking to impose order on an otherwise chaotic universe. *See also* SYMBOLIC INTERACTIONISM.

formal justice *See* JUSTICE, SOCIAL.

formal operations stage *See* PIAGET.

formal organization *See* FORMAL STRUCTURE.

formal rationality As defined by Max Weber in his account of the *market and *bureaucracy, this refers to the extent of impersonal quantitative calculation (that is, risk assessment) that is possible and applied. Money is the best means for ensuring such calculability within a particular institutional order. The concept is best understood in contradistinction to (as well as in the context of) 'substantive rationality', which involves acting in relation to some ultimate values, be they status, egalitarian, social justice, or indeed any infinite variety of value-scales by which to judge the outcome of actions. Given certain substantive conditions—such as legal formalism, separation of employees from the means of production and administration, free labour, and a system of property rights—formal rationality refers to the calculability of means and procedures, substantive rationality to the value of ends or outcomes. The two are in constant tension, in so far as social action is oriented to ends, beliefs, and value commitment.

formal structure (formal organization) A term first used by the *human relations movement for the managerial blueprint, organizational chart, or chain of authority and *communication in an organization. It may be contrasted with the informal organization or system of human relations through which the organization actually operates, and which typically departs (sometimes widely) from the formal structure. *See also* ORGANIZATION THEORY.

Fortes, Meyer (1906–83) A South African social anthropologist, passionate defender of *structural-functionalism, who spent much of his working life in

Britain. His ethnographic work was concerned especially with the kinship system of the Tallensi of Northern Ghana (*The Web of Kinship among the Tallensi*, 1949) and *segmentary political systems (*African Political Systems*, 1940).

Foucault, Michel (1926–84) A French *post-structuralist philosopher, professor of 'the history of systems of thought', who had a major impact on sociology from the mid 1970s onwards. His work defies easy description and characterization. The one major intellectual influence on his work was probably *Nietzsche.

The most straightforward way to approach Foucault's work is to read his case-studies of madness, medicine, prisons, and sexuality. In *Madness and Civilization* (1961), he charts the emergence of a world of reason and unreason, symbolized in the segregating asylum and the birth of *psychiatry. The book spans the period that was Foucault's principal concern: the Middle Ages through the Renaissance to the Modern Period starting with the early 19th century. In *The Birth of the Clinic* (1963) he charts the shifts from the anatomo-classical method to modern scientific medicine. As 'the gaze' shifts from outside the body to inside it, medicine becomes the founding science of humanity, and the human being becomes an 'object of positive knowledge'. In *Discipline and Punish* (1975) Foucault examines changes in penal regimes, the 'micro-physics of power' from the public execution of the classical era to the timetable of the modern prison, from the regulation of the body to the regulation of the soul. The strategies of confinement in the prison eventually become the model for the whole of modern society: a regime of observation, surveillance, classification, hierarchy, rules, discipline, and social control. *The History of Sexuality* (vol. i, 1976) was to appear in six volumes but was incomplete at the time of Foucault's death. It is in this work that Foucault's much debated account of power is most clearly stated in the proposition that 'discursive formations' (structures of knowledge or *epistemes*) both constitute and exert power over social objects (including human bodies).

These four studies are probably the most accessible to students. However none can be seen as a straightforward history of *progress. Rather, Foucault's aim is to demonstrate major shifts in the *discourses through which such topics become constituted: to show how new 'regimes of truth' order our knowledge, our categorization systems, our beliefs, and our practices. Foucault's work therefore moves well beyond the case study to broader theoretical speculations, about the organization of knowledge and power in the modern world, and the implications of particular discursive formations for *social control (see especially *The Archaeology of Knowledge*, 1969, and *The Order of Things*, 1966).

Foucault's writing has been described both as profoundly original and hopelessly opaque. It achieved enormous popular status and some of his studies became best-sellers. There has also developed a substantial industry of critical commentary and analysis. Alan Sheridan's *Foucault: The Will to Truth* (1980) provides probably the most systematic, sympathetic, and accessible overview of the literature. Didier Eribon's *Michel Foucault* (1997) situates his life and ideas in their intellectual milieu. *See also* SURVEILLANCE.

(((⊕))) SEE WEB LINKS

• The Michel Foucault Archives (in several languages).

frame (framing, frame analysis) In *Frame Analysis* (1974), Erving Goffman defines a 'frame' as 'definitions of the situation [that] are built up in accordance with the principles of organization which govern events—at least social ones—and our subjective involvement in them'. Frame analysis is therefore concerned with the organization of experience. In a wider context, there is a considerable body of research literature (mainly in social psychology but also in sociology) to suggest that people's responses to questionnaire or interview items are partly dependent on how they 'frame' the questions, most notably whether a particular query is defined as being a distant issue of 'macro' or systemic concern, or a 'micro' issue that affects individuals directly. Similar 'framing' effects have been observed as a result of issues being defined as aspects of the economic rather than the non-economic spheres of life, the perceived time-horizon involved, and the definition of the imputed goals that are imagined to be the objectives of particular interactions (see, for example, W. Arts et al., 'Income and the Idea of Justice: Principles, Judgements and their Framing', *Journal of Economic Psychology*, 1991).

Frankfurt School (of social theory) *See* CRITICAL THEORY.

Frazer, Sir James George (1854–1941) Born and educated in Scotland, Frazer came to Cambridge to carry out research in 1879, remaining there for the rest of his long career. Originally trained as a classicist, he came to comparative anthropology under the influence of the work of W. Robertson-Smith and Edward Tylor, although this was based on correspondence with travellers, rather than on fieldwork, and focused almost exclusively on religion and systems of belief.

Frazer was best known in his lifetime for the much read and many-volumed *Golden Bough* (1890), in which he examined the meaning of divine sacrifice, compulsively adding more and more examples from ethnography, folklore, mythology, and the Bible. Espousing an *evolutionary approach, he claimed to have discovered the intellectual history of human societies, progressing from *magic, through *religion, to science. He viewed the last of these as a return to magical techniques and logic—but using correct (empirically tested) hypotheses and methodologies. It has been suggested that the huge popularity of his work rested on the implication that *Christianity is simply a form of magic, an idea that appealed to emerging rationalistic philosophy. His books are little read now, although it is generally acknowledged that his work stimulated ethnographic activity world-wide.

Frazier, Edward Franklin (1894–1962) A member of the *Chicago School of Sociology, former President of the American Sociological Society, and author of numerous studies of black family life in urban America, including *The Negro Family in the United States* (1939), *The Negro in the United States* (1949), and *Black Bourgeoisie* (1957). In the last of these, Frazier described the black business class in the USA as a 'lumpen-bourgeoisie', which exaggerated its economic well-being to help create a world of make-believe into which its members could escape from their inferiority and inconsequence in American society. (The term 'lumpen-bourgeoisie' had been used slightly earlier by C. Wright Mills in his *White Collar* (1951), to designate the multitude of white firms 'with a high death rate, which do a fraction of the total business done in their lines and engage a considerably larger proportion of people than their quota of business'.) Although sometimes accused of being empirically suspect, Frazier's work ranges far beyond its overt subject-matter of race relations, and makes a number of stimulating and still controversial points about the values and culture of modern Americans.

free association *See* PSYCHOANALYSIS.

free market *See* MARKET.

free rider A person who takes advantage of a *public good, or other collectively funded benefit, while avoiding any personal cost, or evading personal contributions to collective funding. Fare-dodging on the railway is (literally) free riding; as is, for example, benefiting from a wage increase that results from strike action in which one took no part. *See also* COLLECTIVE ACTION.

free will *See* VOLUNTARISM.

frequency distribution *See* DISTRIBUTION (STATISTICAL OR FREQUENCY).

frequency polygon *See* BAR CHART.

Freud, Sigmund (1856–1939) Famous as the founder of the psychoanalytic movement, Freud developed the basic ideas that still underlie *psychoanalysis, in all its variants. His influence on modern *psychology has also been immense but often indirect. He has been regarded with at least suspicion, often hostility, by mainstream psychology, which has been dominated by *behaviourist and, more recently, *cognitive approaches.

Born in Vienna, Freud took up a medical career and worked as a neurologist, becoming increasingly interested in psychology, hypnosis, and the 'talking cure'. It was not until *The Interpretation of Dreams* (1899–1900) that he made the leap into what is now the centre of psychoanalytic theory. For the rest of his life he wrote prolifically and devoted much time and energy to organizing the psycho-analytic movement, which experienced several famous schisms, in particular those associated with the ideas of Alfred Adler and Carl Gustav *Jung. He died in exile in London, having left Austria in 1938, five years after his books had been burned in Berlin.

Freud developed a model of the personality as consisting of three aspects or elements. The conscious element that orients a person to the requirements of action in the external world is referred to as the ego. The ego must also cope with the unconscious drives originating in the id, and it is the wishes and desires generated by the id that may be denied or repressed back into the unconscious. This repression originates in the internalized expectations of parents and others that form the superego or conscience. The interplay between the ego, the id, and the superego shapes human behaviour, and Freud traced this in his analyses of phenomena such as everyday behaviour, slips of the tongue, dreams, and religion. A more detailed account of psychoanalytic theory can be found elsewhere in this dictionary. The present entry will concentrate on Freud's contribution to sociological thinking. Four different approaches to society can be found in his work.

The first, and least acceptable to modern sociology, suggests that human society and the human individual develop through the same evolutionary stages. This type of analysis usually focuses on the evolution of religion as the manifestation of the social superego (see *Totem and Taboo*, 1913; *Moses and Monotheism*, 1939; and *The Future of an Illusion*, 1927).

The second theory which is sometimes incorporated into sociology sees society in terms of the repression and *sublimation of the instincts; that is, the potentially destructive sexual and aggressive instincts are sublimated into socially useful activities, such as friendship in the former case, and the struggle against external enemies in the latter. Freud saw this as an ambivalent relation. Sublimation involves sacrificing the immediate gratification of our desires, and therefore creates a degree of misery: the greater the level of civilization, the greater the misery (see especially *Civilization and its Discontents*, 1930). This thesis was taken up by Talcott Parsons as part of his theory of *socialization (see his *Essays in Sociological Theory*, 1949) and from a radical point of view by Herbert Marcuse (in *Eros and Civilization*, 1955).

Thirdly, Freud's theory of the development of sexuality from polymorphous perversity through the oedipal stage to relative heterosexuality has been developed into a theory of the origins of civilization (which is also how Freud thought of it), and employed by some modern feminists in explaining the existence of *patriarchy. Juliet Mitchell's *Psychoanalysis and Feminism* (1975) is typical.

Finally, in *Group Psychology and the Analysis of the Ego* (1921), Freud offers a way of conceptualizing social relations in terms of identifications, introjections, and projections. This too has been used by modern feminists writing about *gender. An example is Nancy Chodorow's *The Reproduction of Mothering* (1978). *See also* AGGRESSION; KLEIN, MELANIE; NARCISSISM.

(⊕) SEE WEB LINKS

• The Freud Museum, London, with links to many useful resources.

frictional unemployment *See* UNEMPLOYMENT.

Friedmann, Georges (1902–77) A French sociologist, originator, and the driving-force behind the *Sociologie du Travail in early post-war France; also a trenchant critic of the *scientific management movement. Sociologie du Travail developed out of Friedmann's seminars on the nature and evolution of the *labour process; several leading investigators (including Michael Crozier and Alain Touraine) were strongly influenced by him; and much of the subsequent research programme was shaped by his way of selecting and posing problems.

The major part of Friedmann's huge published output was his critique of fragmented labour and *technicism. His studies of work fragmentation and the destruction of craft skills prefigure the much later (and more widely known) critique of *de-skilling in the work of Harry Braverman. Fragmented work, according to Friedmann (and Braverman), is a characteristic of *capitalism, produced by the drive to separate execution from control, and thus de-skill workers. By comparison, skilled craft work is not only more interesting, but results in a moral and ethical transformation of the individuals so employed: its technical features exercise an educational and humanizing force on practitioners. Friedmann, who was rather obsessed with skilled work and the craft, believed strongly enough in this thesis to take an apprenticeship himself as a metal-worker. He is best known to sociologists as the author of *The Anatomy of Work* (1961) and *Industrial Society: The Emergence of the Human Problems of Automation* (1964). *See also* DEGRADATION-OF-WORK THESIS.

friendship Although friendship is a common term in modern cultures it has not been studied much by social scientists. The word is loosely applied in Anglophone society, although there seems to be general agreement that it has a deeper meaning in Europe than in North America. Arguably, in non-Western cultures, it has a more explicit meaning and is used as the basis of structured social relationships. In all contexts, friendship is not a kin term, but it does imply some type of reciprocity and obligation between otherwise unrelated individuals, although this varies according to situation and context. Friendships can range from the relatively casual, depending on shared activity or setting (such as a sports club), to deep and enduring relationships of mutual support.

The systematic study of friendship has two main strands. The first is the social-psychological study of the ways in which children develop friendships, and the correlation of types of friendship with chronological age in childhood. Studies of friendship among adults concentrate on patterns of sociability and tend to focus on class differences. Graham Allan (*Friendship: Developing a Sociological Perspective*, 1989) claims that working-class friendship choices are dominated by kin links, although neighbours and workmates also feature. The middle classes, on the other hand, have a greater fascination with personal relations and a wider, more conscious choice of friends. Recent innovative studies are those of Liz Spencer and Ray Pahl (*Rethinking Friendship: Hidden Solidarities Today, 2006*) and David Morgan (*Acquaintances: The Space Between Intimates and Strangers*, 2009).

Fromm, Erich (1900–80) A Marxist and psychoanalyst who studied sociology under Alfred Weber and worked at the Institute of Social Research while it was in exile in the United States during the 1930s (*see* CRITICAL THEORY). He worked on a social, humanistic version of *psychoanalysis and contributed to *Horkheimer's early study of authoritarianism. He broke with the Frankfurt theorists and published his *Escape from Freedom* (1941), in which he set out a distinctive social psychology that owed a great deal to the ideas on *alienation in *Marx's early manuscripts, which had recently been published. He saw people 'escaping' from their human capacity for freedom through such pathological states as authoritarianism, conformity, and aggression. His other key work *The Sane Society* (1955) extended his critique of the psychological consequences of *capitalism and proposed a socialist society as the means to mental health. His later work included *The Anatomy of Human Destructiveness* (1973), which enlarged his analysis of human aggression. *See also* PSYCHOANALYSIS.

function (functionalism) Although the use of the concepts of function and functionalism is usually associated with the work of Talcott Parsons in modern sociology, there is a long tradition of functional explanation in studying societies, and a form of modified functionalism is now undergoing a revival. Among the founders of sociology, Émile Durkheim is most closely associated with functionalism, since he often employs analogies with biology. The most prominent of these is an *organic analogy, in which society is seen as an organic whole, each of its constituent parts working to maintain the others, just as the parts of the body also work to maintain each other and the body as a whole. This idea is basic to his conception of organic solidarity. Durkheim did distinguish between functional and historical explanations and recognized the need for both. A functional explanation accounts for the existence of a phenomenon or the carrying out of an action in terms of its consequences—its contribution to maintaining a stable social whole. For example, a functional explanation of the existence of crime is that it serves to mark out and reinforce (through punishment) the boundaries of socially acceptable behaviour, so that crime is therefore a normal feature of social life. Similarly, religious institutions serve to generate and maintain social solidarity. Historical explanations are an account of the chronological development of the same phenomena or actions. Modern functionalism, through the work of Robert Merton, distinguishes between manifest functions (intended consequences or consequences of which the participants are aware) and latent functions (unintended consequences of which the participants are unaware). The latter may or may not be generally beneficial.

There has been a strong and often explicit functionalism present in *sociology and *social anthropology throughout most of this century. There has also been an implicit functionalism in the more determinist forms of Marxist theory, where so-called surface features of the social formation (such as political systems, ideologies, and trade unions), are seen as produced and by, and in order to maintain, the underlying relations of production. However, probably the most famous functionalist analysis in sociology is the so-called *functional theory of social stratification offered by Kingsley Davis and Wilbert Moore, although Davis also wrote a functionalist textbook, *Human Society* (1949), and made a spirited defence of functionalism in his Presidential Address to the American Sociological Association in 1959 (see 'The Myth of Functional Analysis as a Special Method in Sociology and Anthropology', *American Sociological Review*, 1959). Herbert J. Gans's celebrated essay on 'The Positive Functions of Poverty' (*American Journal of Sociology*, 1972), said by some to have been written as a parody of structural-functionalism, is actually a superb example of ideologically neutral functional analysis.

In the late 1960s functionalism came under sustained attack from various sources. It was argued that this approach could not account for social *change, or for structural contradictions and *conflict in societies, and that its reliance on stability and on the organic analogy rendered it ideologically conservative: it became fashionable to refer to functionalism as *consensus theory. This particular group of criticisms is not entirely accurate. Parsons's evolutionary theory, seeing historical development in terms of the *differentiation and reintegration of systems and sub-systems, can account for change and at least for temporary conflict until the reintegration takes place. The existence of functional explanations in *Marxism indicates that they can exist alongside a recognition of contradictions in *social systems. Durkheim himself was able to combine functionalist explanations with a sometimes radical form of guild socialism.

The principal criticisms of functionalism have been *epistemological and *ontological. The epistemological argument is that a functionalist explanation is not an explanation at all in that it does not identify causal mechanisms and processes; it is, instead, assumed that social institutions are adequately explained in terms of their putative effects. The ontological arguments have to do with what we think is the nature of *society itself. Some theorists, who are happy to accept that society has an existence over and above individuals, nevertheless also argue that we cannot attribute needs (for example Parsons's four, famous, so-called functional prerequisites of *adaptation, goal attainment, *integration, and latency) to a society as such, since that is to grant societies the same qualities as human beings. Furthermore, even if we can attribute needs to a society, it does not follow that because these needs exist they will be met. It requires a proper historical and causal explanation to show why and how they are met. Anthony Giddens argues that all functionalist explanations can be rewritten as historical accounts of human action and its consequences; that is, human individuals and their actions are the only reality, and we cannot regard societies or systems as having an existence over and above individuals.

For most of the 1970s and a good part of the 1980s, it seemed as if functionalism as a school of thought and as a way of understanding and explaining social phenomena had disappeared, but during recent years there have been some interesting attempts at a revival: in America under the impetus of Jeffrey Alexander; in Germany in the work of Niklas Luhman; and, in Britain, in an interesting revision of Marxism by the philosopher G. A. Cohen.

Alexander argues (in *Neofunctionalism*, 1985) that functionalism is perhaps best understood as a broad school (rather like Marxism), in which there are many variations of approach, rather than a systematic theory in the manner of Parsons. He maintains that we should not take it as providing explanations, but as a description which focuses on the symbiotic relationships between social institutions and their environment, taking *equilibrium (stability) as a reference-point for analysis, rather than as something which necessarily exists in reality, and treating structural differentiation as a major form of social change. This effectively strips functionalism of any the determinism. For Alexander, functionalism is simply one approach among many, and has the virtue of focusing attention on aspects of the social ignored elsewhere. Luhmann has elaborated a comprehensive *system theory that has been applied to a range of sociological topics such as law, religion, and the mass media.

Cohen's argument (in *Inquiry*, 1982) takes up a position which can be found in a different form in Durkheim's work. He suggests that societies can be seen, not as having needs in the way that individuals can be said to have needs, but as having what he calls dispositional facts; that is, features of a social environment which encourage the continued existence of a particular institution, but did not actually cause that institution to come into existence. Cohen's example is racism, which historically might be the result of a range of factors, but which survives because once in existence it helps the capitalist system to survive, by dividing the working class and making *social control easier. In a rather similar way Jon Elster, a leading exponent of modern rational-choice theory, argues that we have to employ a functionalist explanation to show why capitalist firms on average adopt a policy of profit maximization. Independently of how they come into existence, the market selects for survival those that come closest to this optimal strategy, and thus imposes it upon them (see *Ulysses and the Sirens*, 1979). Functionalism, then, still has a place in sociology—albeit a more restricted place than when the Parsonsian version was dominant. *See also* DEVIANCE, SOCIOLOGY OF; DEVELOPMENT, SOCIOLOGY OF; DIVISION OF LABOUR; MALINOWSKI; RADCLIFFE-BROWN; SYSTEM INTEGRATION AND SOCIAL INTEGRATION; SYSTEM THEORY.

functional equivalents *See* CIVIL RELIGION.

functional imperatives (functional prerequisites) *See* PARSONS; SYSTEMS THEORY.

functional inequality *See* FUNCTIONAL THEORY OF STRATIFICATION; JUSTICE, SOCIAL.

functional rationality A concept originating in the work of Max Weber and used by Jürgen Habermas in his development of Parsonsian social theory. It refers to the rationality of the social system, developing by differentiation and reintegration through the media of money and power, and now 'colonizing' the rationality of the 'life-world' of interpersonal relationships. *See also* CRITICAL THEORY; PARSONS.

functional theory of stratification In a classic article outlining 'Some Principles of Stratification' (*American Sociological Review*, 1945), Kingsley Davis and Wilbert Moore argued that unequal social and economic rewards were an 'unconsciously evolved device' by which societies ensured that talented individuals were supplied with the motivation to undertake training that would guarantee that important social *roles were properly fulfilled. In this way, the most important *functions would be performed by the most talented persons, and the greatest rewards go to those positions which required most training and were most important for maintenance of the *social system.

The theory was (and remains) highly influential but has generated enormous controversy. (M. Tumin's *Readings on Social Stratification*, 1970, offers a good selection of the classic contributions to the debate.) Davis and Moore's argument is based on the functionalist premise that *social order rests on consensual values which define collective goals that are in the general interest. In order to encourage those who are best able to realize these goals it is necessary to offer unequal rewards. Both of these propositions have allegedly been found empirically wanting. Critics have also suggested that the theory is simply an apologia for inequality. Some also maintain that it is tautological (circular), since it proposes that the occupations and other social roles which are most highly rewarded are most important to social stability, and then cites the high levels of reward as evidence of their social importance. What was lacking throughout the lengthy debate, and has yet to be found, is a criterion of 'social importance' that is conceptually independent of the rewards being allocated. Nevertheless, the theory continues to inform important topics of sociological discussion, including for example the literatures on *social mobility and social *justice. *See also* STATUS ATTAINMENT.

function, latent *See* FUNCTION.

function, manifest *See* FUNCTION.

fundamentalism (religious) A movement or belief calling for a return to the basic texts or 'fundamentals' of revealed religion—usually contrasted, therefore, with modernism and liberalism in religion. The term has been applied to Protestant trends within *Christianity, since the 1920s, and recently to trends within *Islam. Despite its theological character it is usually linked to projects of social reform and the acquisition of political power.

futurology The attempt to forecast the future by constructing theories of history is as old as philosophy itself. But the systematic practice of futurology—projecting statistical trends in order to construct realistic future scenarios—dates from the 1950s and is a distinctively social scientific enterprise. Early predictions such as those of Herman Kahn and Anthony Wiener in *The Year 2000* (1967) tended to be optimistic, and even *utopian.

This pattern changed with the Club of Rome's report on *The Limits to Growth* (1972). Futurology in the 1980s and 1990s has been more pessimistic, and sometimes apocalyptic, focusing on negative trends in population, environment, and social order. However, positive predictions can still be found in books like *American Renaissance* by Marvin Cetron and Owen Davies (1989).

Most forecasting depends on identifying historical trends and patterns, and projecting them into the future. The simplest forecasts focus on a specific vector of change, like population or technology. These may offer more or less definite answers about the future: world population will definitely grow by one billion in the next decade; technology will definitely become more sophisticated, and so on. Other vectors like economic performance, drug use, crime, religious belief, or social attitudes are far more difficult to predict. Sophisticated modelling systems can take many variables into account, but they offer so many branching pathways of change that their usefulness is limited. Futurology in general is interesting as a speculative exercise, but has little or no scientific basis, and has an almost complete record of predictive failure.

Galton's problem The Galton problem is named after Francis Galton, the 19th-century British polymath, who became embroiled in a celebrated exchange about the logic of *comparative analysis with the anthropologist Edward *Tylor. In 1889, Tylor published an article that purported to show clear correlations between the economic and familial institutions of a wide range of past and present societies, and attempted to explain these in terms of their *functions. Galton's rejoinder argued that correlations between social institutions might not only arise under pressure of functional exigencies (that is, through processes operating within societies), but also as an effect of cultural *diffusion between societies. In this way he questioned Tylor's assumption that each of his national *cases represented an independent observation (see the debate in the *Journal of the Royal Anthropological Institute*, 1889).

This problem of distinguishing between autonomous institutional development on one hand, and institutional development influenced by cultural diffusion on the other, remains a central issue in comparative macrosociology. For example, it is plausible to argue that the national institutions associated with the emergence of modern welfare states have in different ways been influenced by the examples of the Beveridge Plan for post-1945 Britain, 19th-century Bismarckian social policy in Germany, or the contemporary so-called Scandinavian model. Indeed, some observers argue that the process of *globalization, the emergence of the *world-system, and policies of certain *multinational corporations and political organizations are accelerating and intensifying the effects of cultural diffusion, to the point at which these undermine the very possibility of a comparative macrosociology based on 'independent' national observations: we may be moving towards a world in which N=1.

Empirically, the problems posed for cross-national comparative analysis by processes of cultural diffusion seem to vary across different spheres of social life, being particularly pronounced in the study of economic and social policy (where governments purposively do often emulate each other). Similarly, it is clear that theorists wishing to develop general accounts of *rebellion that emphasize indigenous causes must recognize that revolutionaries have everywhere learned from each other, so that (for example) the course of the Chinese revolution was in part shaped by the earlier Russian experience. Elsewhere, however, such as in the study of class differentials in educational attainment, there is evidence to suggest that national variations are in fact largely attributable to processes of social selection which are distinctive to indigenous institutions—despite the apparent cross-national similarities in programmes of educational expansion and reform. It is also possible to model cross-national interdependence into comparative macrosociology, for example by using event-history analysis to study how institutional and policy development is affected both by domestic factors, and by the timing of cross-national influences of particular kinds.

For an excellent discussion of the implications of Galton's problem for the methodology of comparative macrosociology, of both a case-oriented (qualitative) and variable-oriented (quantitative) kind, and of wider problems of theory development and testing in this field, see the symposium in volume 16 of the journal *Comparative Social Research* (1997). *See also* COMPARATIVE SOCIOLOGY; FUNCTION.

game theory A development in *rational choice theory that is concerned with the rational behaviour of two or more people in circumstances where their *interests are, at least in part, conflicting. In *The Theory of Games and Economic Behaviour* (1947), John Von Neumann and Oskar Morgenstern attempted to develop a theory covering both zero-sum games and non-zero-sum games. In this context a 'game' is any social situation where interaction occurs between at least two 'players' who are competing with each other at least some of the time. Such situations might include marriage, war, rivalry between political parties, the labour market, and more specifically employer-worker negotiations. The key contribution of game theory is to provide an abstract mathematical theory to model what choices are possible, or likely, in situations with certain common features (such as the number of participants, or players, and whether the 'prize' is of fixed size or is variable).

Zero-sum games represent circumstances in which the gain of one participant is the loss of another; that is, situations where the size of the 'cake' is fixed, and everyone seeks to get as large a slice of it as possible. Two-person zero-sum games were the first to be studied by Von Neumann, who showed that in certain cases there would be a relatively stable equilibrium point (or minimax-maximin combination), at which one player's optimum choice met the other's.

In non-zero-sum or non-constant-sum games, it may pay all or some of the participants to cooperate actively to increase the total benefits achieved, so analysis focuses on the formation of coalitions and their outcomes. In effect, collaboration increases the size of the cake, but participants cannot always predict their rival's choice. The most famous examples are the well-known *Prisoner's Dilemma and (more recent) *Problem (or Tragedy) of the Commons, both of which capture clearly situations in which choices that maximize each individual's self-interest produce the worst possible outcome overall. Only if each participant chooses what is in the collective interest, rather than narrow self-interest, will the collective optimum result be achieved. In most laboratory experiments based on these games, nearly two-thirds of all subjects make the selfish, or distrustful choice; the cooperative outcome is achieved in a small minority of cases. However, they have been run on a vast scale using computer simulations to assess the effectiveness of various strategies pitted against each other; and, on this longer time-horizon, cooperation was found to evolve in a society of completely self-interested individuals.

The mathematical models of game theory have mainly been used in economics, but the general theory and concepts have had an influence in all the social sciences that study situations of conflict, competition, and potential cooperation (notably, for example, in studies of the military and of voting and electoral alliances). See Robert Gibbons, *A Primer in Game Theory* (1992) and Kenneth G. Binmore, *Fun and Games* (1992).

gangs Frederic M. Thrasher (*The Gang*, 1927) challenged earlier images of gangs as simply loose groups of street-roaming law-breakers, and presented an analysis influenced by the approach of the *Chicago School: gangs as structured groups of working-class youth, bound by loyalty, territoriality, and a hierarchy. Furthermore, the formation of gangs reflects social dynamics, such as identity search in the face of urban change; thus, to quote Thrasher, 'the gang develops as one manifestation of the economic, moral and cultural frontier, which marks the interstice [between areas of the city]'. Other key works include William Foote Whyte, *Street-Corner Society* (1955) and Albert K. Cohen, *Delinquent Boys* (1955). Questions of race and gender were neglected until recently. *See also* DELINQUENCY; SUBCULTURE; YOUTH CULTURE.

gatekeeping The hierarchical structure of *formal organizations places certain individuals or groups in crucial positions from which they can control access to goods, services, or information. They therefore wield *power far in excess of their formal authority. Sociologists have examined this phenomenon in numerous contexts. One example is provided by the *urban managerialist perspective on the city, a label applied to a number of studies in the 1960s and 1970s, all of which made the broad claim that 'urban managers' (such as planners and local government officials) played a crucial role as gatekeepers in controlling access to urban resources (housing, land, permissions to build, and so forth).

gay studies *See* LESBIAN AND GAY STUDIES.

gaze A term associated with Foucault's account of surveillance, referring to structured ways of seeing and interpreting the social world. The concept of gaze is increasingly seen as being important to the discussion of more traditional sociological topics, such as that of the family. Thus, for example, drawing on Michel *Foucault's theory of the *panopticon, as well as Bryan Turner's writings about the body, David H. J. Morgan has argued that the parental gaze over children is an important aspect of surveillance within families (see *Family Connections: An Introduction to Family Studies*, 1996). Laura Mulvey introduced an influential theory of the gaze in 'Visual Pleasure and Narrative Cinema' in *Screen magazine* (1975). She argued that women are objectified and *stereotyped on the screen because of the way cinema is structured around three male ways of looking—or 'gazes'. First, the way the camera looks in any filmed situation is voyeuristic, as most films are made by men; second, there is the gaze of men within a particular film itself, which is structured to make women appear as objects of their gaze; third, there is the gaze of the actual male spectator. Mulvey's theory was much influenced by Jacques Lacan's ideas about psychoanalysis.

It has become important in feminist art theory and it has since been argued there is a female gaze as well as a male gaze.

Sociologists are increasingly beginning to consider the importance of visual representation in everyday life; arguably the distinction between social analysis and visual representation has become less clear-cut. Elizabeth Chaplin's *Sociology and Visual Representation* (1994) contains a good discussion of some key areas, as does Gillian Rose's *Visual Methodologies* (2001).

Geddes, Sir Patrick (1854–1932) A Scottish polymath. His background was in biology and *ecology, and he went on to develop an account of the effects of the environment on human settlements. Drawing on ideas from Frédéric Le Play, he saw strong links between 'place', 'work', and community. His work pioneered an ecological orientation to environmental and social policy. His approach to sociology placed social phenomena in the 'regional' context of their natural environment and saw cultural processes of 'synergy' shaping regional social structures. He explored urban social processes and coined the term 'conurbation' as a way of understanding modern metropolitan-industrial regions. An important figure in British sociology in the early years of the 20th century, some of his ideas have had a great influence on urban-planning theory and practice. He was active in many political groups and advocated a centrist 'third way'. His sociological ideas are explored in John Scott and Ray Bromley *Envisioning Sociology: Victor Branford, Patrick Geddes, and the Quest for Social Reconstruction* (2013). *See also* Branford, Victor Verasis.

(⊕) SEE WEB LINKS
• The Sir Patrick Geddes Memorial Trust, Scotland, encompassing his life and work.

Geiger, Theodore (1891–1952) A German sociologist who taught mainly in Denmark. He produced important studies of changes in class structure, seeing class relations dissolving in a 'melting pot' to produce a mass society. His study of social *mobility in Denmark (*Soziale Umschichtungen in einer dänischen Mittelstadt*, 1951) was a classic critique of the *status-attainment tradition of taking *occupational prestige as the sole basis of mobility analysis. Much of his work has not been translated into English, but some has been translated and extracted in *Theodor Geiger on Social Order and Mass Society* (1969).

Geisteswissenschaften* and *Naturwissenschaften German words used to denote respectively the human (or social) sciences and the natural sciences. For some three decades prior to the outbreak of the First World War, German academic life was dominated by a number of related disputes about methodology (the so-called *Methodenstreit*), the most general (and probably the most important) of which dealt with the relationship between the natural and the cultural (or historical) sciences. The philosopher Wilhelm Windelband, arguing from the premise that reality is indivisible, proposed an a priori logical distinction between natural and social sciences on the basis of their methods. Natural sciences, according to Windelband, use a 'nomothetic' or generalizing method, since they seek to discover law-like and general relationships and properties, whereas social or cultural sciences employ an *ideographic or individualizing procedure, since they are interested in the nonrecurring events in reality and the particular or unique aspects of any phenomenon. Wilhelm *Dilthey, on the other hand, contrasted *Naturwissenschaften* and *Geisteswissenschaften* in terms of their subject-matter, this criterion following logically from the alternative premiss that reality can be divided into autonomous sectors—a fundamental distinction being that between the realms of 'nature' and of 'human spirit'—with each sector being the prerogative of a separate category of sciences.

The most interesting contribution to this debate, from the point of view of sociology, is probably that of Heinrich Rickert (1863–1936), the *neo-Kantian professor of philosophy at Freiberg and then Heidelberg, a contemporary and friend of Max Weber. Rickert's theory of concept formation in the sciences (as described in *Die Grenzen der naturwissenschaftlichen Begriffsbildung: Eine logische Einleitung in die historischen Wissenschaften*, 1902, and *Science and History: A Critique of Positivist Epistemology*, 1898–1902) was a strong influence on Weber's methodological writings and substantive analyses (notably, for example, the *ideal-typical methodology employed in the essays on *The Protestant Ethic and the Spirit of Capitalism*). The sociological significance of the *Methodenstreit* is explained in Werner J. Cahnman, 'Max Weber and the Methodological Controversy in the Social Sciences', in Cahnman and Alvin Boskoff (eds.), *Sociology and History* (1964).

Gellner, Ernest (1925–95) Although Gellner was born in Czechoslovakia, his family (who had Jewish origins) left immediately after the German occupation in 1939, and he spent most of his working life in England. Between 1949 and 1984 he taught sociology then philosophy at the London School of Economics, before moving to a professorship of Social Anthropology at the University of Cambridge. In 1993 he returned to Prague to become full-time Director of the Centre for the Study of Nationalism at the Central European University.

His writings are enormously wide-ranging. His first book was a critique of linguistic philosophy (*Words and Things*, 1959), which he condemned as complacent, unimaginative, and parochial. In *Thought and Change* (1964) he proposed the controversial thesis that social orders are seen to be legitimate only when they meet the requirements of affluence and nationalism. (Gellner's later writings attempted to insert the idea of liberty into this otherwise harsh conception of modernity.) An ethnography of the North African Berber (*Saints of the Atlas*, 1969), critical studies of psychoanalysis (*The Psychoanalytic Movement*, 1985) and of Soviet ideology (*State and Society in Soviet Thought*, 1988), and many essays and books on *nationalism, Muslim society, relativism, pluralism, and the methodology of the social sciences followed. Just before his death he completed volumes on nationalism (*Nationalism Observed*) and on Wittgenstein and Malinowski (*Language and Solitude*), although a study of the conditions for successful transitions from socialism to democracy remained unfinished.

This prolific output is difficult to characterize. One unifying thread is a defence of rationalism against relativism in the social sciences. Another is a long-standing interest in nationalism, of whose horrors Gellner was keenly aware, but whose influence on the development of citizenship he saw as decisive. His own influence on Anglo-Saxon sociology is evident in the publications of successive generations of British and American historical sociologists and social theorists whom he taught. Gellner's life and work are discussed in John Hall's *Ernest Gellner: An Intellectual Biography* (2010).

Gemeinschaft* and *Gesellschaft Usually taken in tandem, these German terms generally refer to Ferdinand *Tönnies's 'community' and 'society' couplet, although the latter is sometimes also translated as 'association' (see Tönnies, *Gemeinschaft und Gesellschaft*, 1887). According to Tönnies's thesis on European modernization, the passage from the former to the latter proceeds through a rationalizing process, involving a move from relationships based upon family and guild to those based on rationality and calculation. *Gemeinschaft* was the world of close, emotional, face-to-face ties, attachment to place, ascribed social status, and a homogeneous and regulated community. *Gesellschaft* has come to be linked with urbanism, industrial life, mobility, heterogeneity, and impersonality. Much of the debate about the concept of *community has been structured in these terms (see C. Bell and H. Newby, *Community Studies*, 1971).

In essence, the concepts constitute *ideal types, as do similar notions of tradition and modernity. In practice, elements of both are to be found in differing proportions in most social relations and societies. The intellectual heritage of the concepts of traditional and modern societies is usually traced to Émile Durkheim's distinction between mechanical and organic solidarity (and the attendant forms of *collective conscience), but is also (and perhaps most clearly) to be found in the writings of Max Weber, where status, connubium, commensality, and style of life contrast with interests, economic groups, and classes. Parsonian value-orientations—for example the distinctions between particularism and universalism, ascription and achievement—also grew out of this basic pair of polar concepts, all geared to understanding the essence of institutional and agency change attendant on *modernization. *See also* PARSONS.

gender discrimination *See* GENDER, SOCIOLOGY OF.

gender roles *See* GENDER, SOCIOLOGY OF.

gender segregation (in employment) This term refers to the unequal distribution of men and women in the occupational structure—sometimes also (and more accurately) called 'occupational segregation by sex'. There are two forms: 'vertical segregation' describes the clustering of men at the top of occupational hierarchies and of women at the bottom; 'horizontal segregation' describes the fact that at the same occupational level (that is within occupational classes, or even occupations themselves) men and women have different job tasks. Degrees of sex segregation vary inversely with the level of aggregation of data. *See also* LABOUR MARKET; LABOUR-MARKET SEGMENTATION; OCCUPATIONAL SEGREGATION.

gender, sociology of According to Ann Oakley, who introduced the term to sociology, '"Sex" refers to the biological division into male and female; "gender" to the parallel and socially unequal division into femininity and masculinity' (see *Sex, Gender and Society*, 1972). Gender draws attention, therefore, to the socially constructed aspects of differences between women and men. But the term gender has since become extended to refer not only to individual identity and personality but also, at the symbolic level, to cultural ideals and *stereotypes of *masculinity and *femininity and, at the structural level, to the sexual *division of labour in institutions and organizations.

In the 1970s, sociological and psychological interest was focused upon demonstrating that gender exists; that is to say, upon showing that the differences and divisions between men and women cannot be accounted for by biological difference, and that the culturally dominant ideas about masculinity and femininity are stereotypes which correspond only crudely to reality. It was shown that there are huge cross-cultural variations in ideas about gender and in the *roles of men and women. There were studies of the ways in which baby boys and girls are turned into adult men and women by the processes of *socialization in child-rearing, education, youth culture, employment practices, and family ideology. At the structural level, there were studies of the unequal division of labour in the household, even between women and men who both have full-time jobs outside, and of discrimination in employment, where sex (rather than individual skills and qualifications) plays a large part in determining types of job and chances of promotion. More recently, interest has turned to the changing formations of gender at the cultural level. Much of this work has been interdisciplinary, drawing upon anthropology, history, art, literature, film, and cultural studies to explore issues such as the interconnections between ideas of racial purity, White women's sexual purity, and Black masculinity in the United States; or the myth of *motherhood as natural and universal. Much of this literature is reviewed in Sara Delamont's *The Sociology of Women* (1980).

There have been two major kinds of criticism of the concept of gender. The first is that it is based upon a false dichotomy between the biological and the social. This relates to a general criticism that sociology has tended to see the social as disembodied, with the infant as a *tabula rasa upon which socialization may write at will, to produce social consciousness and action (as in the work of Émile Durkheim). Following the more recent writings of Michel Foucault, sociologists are now less inclined to take the *body for granted, and to see it rather as an object of social analysis, recognizing that the social meaning of the body has changed through history. But in a sense this too can be another means by which biology is discounted and biological science dismissed as merely a social discourse. One criticism of the sex versus gender distinction has been Foucauldian, denying that there is a biological difference—sex—that is in any sense outside of the social. On the other hand, there is the criticism that would reassert biological difference as being extra-social, and argue against a view of gender that discounts the true significance of the body. The sex/gender distinction, it is said, is linked to a particular form of feminist politics that seeks the eradication of gender and a move towards *androgyny; it leaves little space, for instance, for other feminist concerns with the biological politics of menstruation, contraception, reproductive technology, abortion, or the management of childbirth.

The second kind of criticism relates to the way in which the concept of gender focuses on differences between women and men at the expense of power and domination. Some writers would prefer to use the term *patriarchy as the main organizing concept, in order to keep the question of power to the fore, both analytically and politically. There are many problems with this term, but the important one to note here is that it conflates sex and gender by treating a biological category as a social one: women and men are treated as pre-consti-tuted groups in the description of patriarchy, and the biology of procreation is often used in the explanation of it.

On a lighter note, 'gender' has been criticized as a prudish way of avoiding the word 'sex'. This is clearly not the case when it is used correctly in sociology, but it is true that it has entered everyday speech in this sense, when people talk (for example) about 'the opposite gender'. Some sociologists, too, are guilty of this when they refer to 'gender roles' or 'gender discrimination'.

The term gender can be used fruitfully with some awareness of these problems. If it is recognized that there is a need to consider biological difference and structures of power in relation to the elaborate social construc-tion of difference, then the concept of gender has the great advantages that it encourages a study of masculinity as well as femininity, the relations between the sexes as well as the social position of women, and a recognition of historical and cultural variety and change rather than a universalizing analy-sis. *See also* DOMESTIC DIVISION OF LABOUR; FAMILY, SOCIOLOGY OF; GENDER SEGREGATION (IN EMPLOYMENT).

gender stereotypes These are one-sided and exaggerated images of men and women which are deployed repeatedly in everyday life. They are found commonly in the mass media because they operate as a widely understood shorthand. Sociologists often see *stereotyping as part of the process by which children are socialized into *sex roles and by which adults and children are denied opportunities for more individually varied development.

gene (genotype) The fundamental unit of biological inheritance. In sexually reproducing species every individual's genotype is composed of half of each biological parent's genes. This underlying genetic structure combines in complex ways with a wide variety of environmental influences to produce the individual phenotype—or outward appearance. Modern evolutionary theory rests on the premiss of genetic inheritance, but this did not constitute part of Darwin's original formulation. It was not until some thirty years after the publication of the *Origin of Species*, when the significance of the work of Mendel was recog-nized, that genes (the actual carriers of genetic information) were first identified.

Biochemical technology has subsequently advanced to the stage where it is now possible, via genetic engineering techniques, to alter the composition of human genetic material—although the ethical problems involved mean that only limited applications have been permitted.

The implications of these findings for the social sciences are discussed in Richard Dawkins's *The Selfish Gene* (1976), a book which did much to popularize the *socio-biological vision of Edward O. Wilson. In Dawkins's volume, the unit of natural selection is identified as the gene itself, with the individual organism representing merely a survival machine or carrier for its genetic cargo. If the argument is taken to its logical conclusion then the imperatives of gene survival and reproduction determine all behaviour. The inherent *reductionism of this position has been the focus of much criticism. *See also* CHROMOSOMES; DARWINISM; EUGENICS; HEREDITY; MEME.

genealogy An important tool in kinship theory and a vital part of the political organization of kinship-based societies. A genealogy is the means of tracing real or fictive *kinship links across and between generations.

generalized other *See* SELF.

generation A generation is a form of age group consisting of those members of a society who were born at approximately the same time. A closely related idea is that of the cohort, which refers to any group or category sharing a particular time-specific attribute or characteristic. Thus, a generation is a birth cohort, and such categories are frequently used in analyses of trends in social mobility. Cohort analysis is a method of study in which measures for one or more cohorts are compared at different time intervals. In recent years there has been an increasing interest in generational analyses which examine the contribution of emerging age groups to social change. Karl *Mannheim, in his essay on *The Problem of Generations* (1952), describes how people located in the same generation may see the world in very different ways from their counterparts in earlier generations. Thus the unique experiences common to each generation group allows for social change. In a more recent work, *Children of the Great Depression* (1974), Glenn H. Elder shows how the generation brought up in a time of great frugality had a very different view of the world from those raised in a time of economic prosperity. Generation is also used to refer to the period that elapses between one generation and the next. Studies of differences in the *socialization of successive generations have disagreed about the extent of continuity or discontinuity of both values and behaviour, although inter-generational conflict is a pervasive theme. Within any one generation, however, there can also be conflicting views of reality, in part due to other social characteristics such as sex, ethnicity, and social class. A further question of interest concerns the persistence of generational identities; for example, what happens to participants of youthful protest movements when they reach middle age? Thus research on life course and *ageing is closely linked to the interest in generations. Useful overviews of work on generations are Jane Pilcher's *Age and Generation in Modern Britain*

(1995) and Judith Burnett's *Generations: The Time Machine in Theory and Practice* (2010). *See also* AGE GRADES.

generic social processes *See* FORMALISM.

genetic modification A genetically modified (GM) organism is one that has been genetically engineered. Genetic engineering involves the introduction of changes into the genetic material, or the transfer of parts of the genetic material from one cell to another. This transfer can take place between different types of cell, for example, from animal to plant or micro-organism to plant. Gene therapy involves genetic modification of the *human genome in an attempt to treat or cure human genetic disorders, but the most visible and socially contentious use of this technology in the UK has been to produce GM crop plants for food. The aim has been to introduce desirable characteristics into plants, for example, high crop yield, increased nutritional value, or resistance to drought or pests. However, opponents of GM foods have highlighted uncertainties over the long-term consequences for the environment and for human health. Potential benefits for *Third World agriculture have commonly been cited, but these tend to assume that Third World hunger is solely a problem of food production. Attempts to patent modified crop plants and their products by biotechnology companies have led to debates over the 'ownership' of naturally occurring entities and accusations of 'biopiracy', where local knowledge and biological resources are exploited for commercial gain.

genetics *See* GENE; GENETIC MODIFICATION; HEREDITY; HUMAN GENOME.

genocide A term devised during the Second World War by Raphael Lemkin and adopted by the United Nations Convention in 1948. to refer to the large-scale systematic destruction of whole populations. Sociologists have been most concerned with five matters: how to *define* the term; its typological manifestations; the conditions which give rise to genocide; a historical analysis of it; and the consequences of genocide, not just for the victims, but also for the perpetrators. (The best general discussion is F. Chalk and K. Jonassohn's *The History and Sociology of Genocide*, 1989.)

Irving Horowitz (in *Taking Lives: Genocide and State Power*, 1980) defines genocide as the 'structural and systematic destruction of innocent people by a state bureaucratic apparatus'. Genocide usually entails an outgroup or pariah group being defined as less than fully human, and the existence of a centralized bureaucratic authority capable of administering the deaths in a large-scale and impersonal way. In the past this has often meant the slaughtering of whole populations in war or the sacrifice of large groups for religious purposes (for example in Carthage, where the younger sons were sacrificed to the gods). Often, in earlier periods, the consequences for the perpetrators of such large-scale murders were minimal. There are many controversies around what constitutes a genocide. Should the witchcraft purges throughout Europe in the 16th and 17th centuries be seen as genocide? The bombing of Hiroshima could also be included, if one is concerned with all forms of 'death on a large scale', but this was an (almost) unique and distinct form.

Some have suggested that the conditions for genocide coincide with the conditions of modernity, and indeed that the 20th century—far from being a century of progress—was decisively the age of genocide. This may be overstated, as there have certainly been many other cases of genocide throughout history. The Nazi Holocaust, Stalin's purges, and the 'Year Zero' or 'killing fields' activities of the Khmer Rouge in Cambodia are frequently cited as instances of modern 'ideological' genocide. In a celebrated study of the Holocaust (*Modernity and the Holocaust*, 1990), Zygmunt *Bauman has argued that the Nazi mass exterminations were symptomatic of the dark side of modernity, of conditions ripe for large-scale bureaucracies, mass technology, and ideological control. Where particular ethnic groups within a territory are the objects of genocide with the aim of eliminating them from that territory (either by death or forced migration), this has sometimes been referred to as 'ethnic cleansing'. A major and important study is Mick Mann's *The Dark Side of Democracy: Explaining Ethnic Cleansing* (2005).

( ) SEE WEB LINKS

• Institute for the Study of Genocide: a source of materials and policy proposals organized by an interdisciplinary group of academics.

gens *See* PHRATRY.

gentrification The upgrading of decaying, normally inner-city housing, involving physical renovation, the displacement of low-status occupants by higher-income groups, and (frequently) tenure change from private rental to home ownership. The term was first used by the British urban sociologist Ruth Glass (*London: Aspects of Change*, 1964).

gentry A term applied to the stratum immediately below the peerage (*see* UPPER CLASS) in the social hierarchy of late medieval and early modern Britain. Untitled, the gentry were a grouping whose wealth lay in landholding, mineral rights, or rents from urban property. They were tied loosely to the nobility by marriage ties and similar lifestyles, and to the *middle class by family ties and their interest in farming. At various times this rather diffuse stratum has been held to have played a decisive part in English history; for example, by sponsoring the agricultural revolution and the commercialization of farming during the 17th century, and (conversely) offering a 'gentlemanly ideal' to the sons of 19th-century industrialists (a factor which is sometimes said to have contributed to Britain's relative lack of success in manufacturing). The term continued to be used into the 20th century to describe old landowning families without peerages.

geography *See* HUMAN GEOGRAPHY.

gerontocracy Rule by old men. A term introduced by social anthropologists in the 1930s to describe certain societies in Africa south of the Sahara, in which social stratification was based on *age sets or age grades, public roles were allocated by age grade (as well as gender), with governance functions allocated to the oldest age group. The term is now used more generally to describe societies in which the most senior decision-making and political roles are dominated by the oldest males, with negative consequences in periods of rapid change and instability, when innovation and flexibility are at a premium.

gerontology The study of the processes of *ageing, old age, and the elderly. Frequently viewed as a branch of biology, with a focus on the role of genetic factors (the extent to which ageing is pre-programmed), the study of the social aspects of ageing, sometimes termed social gerontology, is now well established. Interest in ageing has grown enormously with 20th-century demographic changes. Increases in life expectancy and reductions in childbearing have transformed the age-structures of the population of advanced industrial societies, increasing significantly the proportions of the elderly (usually defined as persons aged 65 or over). Since the use of many forms of welfare provision (especially health care, personal social services, and state benefits) rises markedly amongst those over 65, increases in the numbers of the elderly (especially in the growing numbers of those aged 75 or over) are of major concern to policy-makers and policy analysts.

However, although policy issues are of great importance, the sociological contribution to gerontology comes from the study and analysis of age as a social category, and of the way in which the structures of society shape the ageing process, including the way it is experienced by individuals. The status of the elderly varies significantly across time, place, and social arrangements, including the extent to which retirement policies, pension provisions, and housing can foster independence or generate dependence, with important implications for physical and psychological health. There is growing awareness of the salience both of stratification by age and of *ageism in society.

Gesellschaft See GEMEINSCHAFT and GESELLSCHAFT.

Gestalt theory An early 20th-century development in psychology and an alternative to *empiricist theories of perception and knowledge. A gestalt is a coherent whole with its own laws, seen as a construct of the perceiving mind and eye, not as given in reality. (*Gestalt* is a German word meaning pattern, form, or configuration.) Gestalt theory argues that the functioning of the various parts of a social entity is determined by the behaviour and nature of the whole, seeks to organize human and social phenomena in terms of larger units of analysis, and is therefore opposed to atomism (or analysis of 'wholes' in terms of their constituent and simpler parts). It is a background influence in much *phenomenological sociology. *See also* FIELD THEORY.

gesture Part of George Herbert *Mead's theory of the *self. A gesture is the act of an organism that stimulates a response on the part of other organisms: a dog growling may provoke another dog to growl, and a 'conversation of gestures' ensues. Such responses are merely impulsive or instinctive for most animals; among humans, the process depends upon significant symbols and vocal gestures, which call up more complex reflective responses.

ghetto An inner-urban area characterized by the spatial concentration of disadvantage. The term is often associated with particular *ethnic groups—for example black North Americans—and was originally applied to the urbanized Jewish populations of Europe. The classic study is by Louis Wirth, who argued that the ghetto could only be understood as a social psychological as well as an ecological phenomenon, since 'it [the ghetto] is not so much a physical fact as it is a state of mind' (*The Ghetto*, 1928). In this respect, much of Wirth's analysis prefigures his later classical essay on 'Urbanism as a Way of Life' (*American Journal of Sociology*, 1938), and should be read against this broader theoretical background. *See also* URBAN SOCIOLOGY; URBANISM.

Giddens, Anthony (1938–) Internationally famous British sociologist, innovative publisher, public intellectual, former Director of the London School of Economics, Giddens has produced a remarkable succession of seminal contributions to social theory. In the 1970s he introduced what he called *structuration theory, providing an original, counter-intuitive, means of combining *structure and *agency by placing *hermeneutics and *phenomenology at the core of the conception of structure (see *The Constitution of Society*, 1984). In the same year, 1985, as Giddens became Cambridge University's first head of the new faculty of Social and Political Sciences, he founded Polity Press. Closely involved with commissioning and editing, Giddens was instrumental in making many of the continental European and American sources for his own philosophical and theoretical syntheses accessible to a much wider audience. His extensive *historical sociology, also developed during the late 1970s and 1980s, famously challenged core ingredients of historical materialism and argued for a distinctively pluralistic and non-teleological approach to causation (see *The Nation State and Violence* (1985).

Four major works on *late modernity and its politics written in the 1990s, beginning with *The Consequences of Modernity*, dissected and analysed the major institutional forces and life experiences of the 'runaway world', highlighting the central roles played in contemporary life by institutional *reflexivity, *risk, *trust, and powerful abstract systems that have little respect for local contexts. More recently, his role as a public intellectual has come to the fore with a series of popularly targeted publications, such as *The Third Way: The Renewal of Social Democracy*, that began life as an attempt to give logical rigour to a series of seminars he was involved in with Tony Blair, the Clintons, and members of the British and American cabinets during the late 1990s. Politics in late modernity, argues Giddens, needs still to be utopian in its aspirations but to temper this with a greater sense of the limits to the possible. This is because of the limits to the tractability of abstract systems, the inevitability of unintended consequences, and—the paradox of institutional reflexivity—the constant undermining of a stable environment by the very ideas, lessons and theories that are meant to give it some stability. Following his retirement from the LSE he joined the House of Lords as a Labour peer.

(⊕) SEE WEB LINKS

- Giddens' Reith Lectures of 1999, including an interview and lectures on contemporary modernity.

Giddings, Franklin H. (1855–1931) An early American sociologist who applied the evolutionary ideas of Herbert Spencer in comparative and historical analyses. Although his texts now seem dated (see for example *Principles of Sociology*, 1896; *Elements of Sociology*, 1898; *Studies in the Theory of Human Society*, 1922; and *The Scientific Study of Human Society*, 1924), his work displays several characteristic traits of mainstream American sociology, including an emphasis on quantification and an interest in the theories of psychologists. His earlier work is characterized by psychological evolutionism; his later studies by an enthusiasm for quantification and behaviourism that provided an important stimulus to American *neo-positivism.

gift relationship Social scientists usually regard a gift as an expression of the relationship between donor and recipient. In *The Gift* (1954) Marcel *Mauss argued that gifts are widely obligatory and reciprocal. This behaviour could not be explained in terms of the 'rational economic man' model espoused in much Western formal economic thought. Mauss asserted that the economic is insep-arable from other social fields. In every society, economic relations are infused with values and moral relations, and it is misguided to separate the rational and the non-rational—or affection and self-interest. Mauss came to the conclusion that economic value has a religious origin, a perspective shared by his mentor, Émile Durkheim. The *utilitarian values of things are renounced in order to gain social *status; so ceremonial values transcend economic values. To give an example from the fieldwork of Bronislaw Malinowski, people in the Trobriand Isles deny their desire to eat yams, and stockpile them in order to give them away and gain prestige. Among the Kwiakutl of the American Pacific Northwest, such conspicuous *ritual gift-giving reached epic proportions in the so-called potlatch, when vast quantities of possessions would be destroyed (see H. Codere, *Fighting with Property*, 1950). In both of these societies the gift relationship has been seen by anthropologists to be a major political institution.

Marshall Sahlins (*Stone Age Economics*, 1972) created a typology of gift-giving relations in different societies, ranging from the gratuitous gift at one pole, to the exploitative relationship at the other. Generalized reciprocity refers to the Euro-pean ideal of gift-giving, where one does not give in order to receive, and the return of the gift is not constrained by time, quality, or quantity. Generalized reciprocity usually operates within a kin network. Balanced reciprocity, on the other hand, expresses a continuation of social relations in a way it does not within the family, signifying more non-contractual, long-term relationships. In this form, equivalents must be exchanged within a relatively short time-scale, as with the buying of drinks in a bar: there may be some temporary imbalances but these cannot be tolerated indefinitely. Sahlins's third category is negative reci-procity, where each party is looking to maximize his or her own advantage, at the expense of the other.

The above analyses of gift-giving have been developed primarily in relation to so-called *traditional societies, yet 5 per cent of consumer expenditure in the United Kingdom is on gifts, and the proportion of gift-goods in the modern West is as high as in more traditional societies.

Gifts of money in Western societies can be problematic, since they may focus attention upon the economic value of the gift, rather than its symbolic meaning. It is for this reason that, at least in most Western societies, the use of money as a Christmas gift is highly circumscribed, and generally acceptable only if it passes down a status hierarchy, such as from older to younger generations within a family. If a gift of money conforms to this pattern it can reflect a recognized difference in *status without loss of face for the recipient and is an accepted means of expressing affection by providing for his or her material needs. By comparison, it would generally be judged unacceptable for a grandchild to give a grandparent money, since this runs the risk of commodifying affection (see T. Caplow, 'Christmas Gifts and Kin Networks', *American Sociological Review*, 1982).

Monetary gifts also help illustrate the way in which taboos may act to maintain the barrier between the economic and other spheres of life. For example, V. Zelizer ('Human Values and the Market', *American Journal of Sociology*, 1978) describes the 'repackaging' that had to be done before the idea of life insurance became acceptable to modern Americans. Initially this form of commercialization—putting a price on someone's life—was strongly resisted. Life insurance was therefore very difficult to sell. However, the problem was overcome by changing the apparent meaning of the insurance money, so that instead of an economic transaction between the buyer and the company, life insurance was redefined as a means by which a man could express love for his family, through continuing to provide for them after his death. In this new *definition of the situation, rather than death becoming commodified by its association with market exchange, the money paid out for life insurance itself became a (nearly sacred) gift—a one-way transfer from father to family.

The modern phenomenon of gift-giving (including the making of charitable donations) continues to be a somewhat under-researched phenomenon among sociologists, by comparison with (say) psychologists, who have conducted systematic studies of the meaning of gifts and of the social acceptability of various goods involved in different sorts of gift relationships. An interesting account, however, is that of Richard Titmuss (*The Gift Relationship*, 1970), who looked at the nonmonetary motivations involved in blood donation. *See also* EXCHANGE THEORY; KULA RING.

Gilman, Charlotte Perkins (1860–1935) Gilman was an American writer who published a huge range of work across a broad spectrum of disciplines, including sociology, literature, political science, economics, and women's studies. Her best-known volume is *The Yellow Wallpaper* (1892), written after her nervous breakdown in 1885. It can be taken as a semi-autobiographical record of psychiatric treatment and the descent into 'madness', but can also be interpreted as a metaphorical account of women's situation generally, and particularly that of married women in a patriarchal society. Her more specifically sociological work addressed the culturally repressed status of women and how this impeded full intellectual development.

Like Harriet Martineau in her earlier works, and also some contemporary radical feminists, Gilman suggests an analogy between women's social situation and slavery. She rejected Herbert Spencer's theory of social determinism, and maintained that humans are dynamic agents that are not determined by inherited traits or ruthless competition, but can plan and direct their own destiny. She subscribed to Lester Frank Ward's gynecocentric theory, which saw women as the original and dominant form of the species, with men serving only as assistants in the fertilization process. She thus dismissed the basic tenets of *Marxism because she saw sex as a more fundamental social division than class, arguing that women's social repression is a direct result of their singular role of *motherhood, a role that impedes and minimizes creativity and expression.

Children, she believed, should be entrusted to childcare experts, and she saw strong state agencies as essential to maintaining a more just society for women. Similarly, she argued that private housekeeping was both inefficient and wasteful, and suggested that households and the economy generally would be more productive if women worked in the labour force and cooperative kitchens were set up for the mass-preparation of food. Gilman published some 2173 written works, including *Herland* (1915), and *The Home: Its Work and Influences* (1903). Perhaps her most important studies on women and work were *Women and Economics* (1898) and *The Man-Made World* (1914).

Ginsberg, Morris (1889–1970) An early professor of sociology in Britain, notable mainly for his influence on generations of inter-war and post-war sociologists at the London School of Economics and Political Science. He collaborated in an important study in comparative sociology (Hobhouse, Wheeler, and Ginsburg, *The Material Culture and Social Institutions of the Simpler People*, 1914) and produced an early textbook on *Sociology* (1934). A close follower of *Hobhouse, he wrote on such topics as 'The Idea of Progress', 'The Nature of Responsibility', and 'The Unity of Mankind' (see his three volumes of *Essays in Sociology and Social Philosophy*, 1947–61).

Glass, David V. (1911–78) A British sociologist who is justly famous for his pioneering work on *demography and *social mobility. His landmark study of *Social Mobility in Britain* (1954) was based on a sample of men and women interviewed in 1949. He and his colleagues found a fairly stable social structure showing a high degree of association between the status of fathers and sons; mobility concentrated at intermediate levels, where it tended to be both short-range, and rather transitory; and no evidence of an increase in social mobility in the first half of the century. Glass called for an *egalitarian opportunity structure to create a more just society than he observed, although he recognized that equal opportunities policies in education and employment did not necessarily undermine differential access to privilege, where distributional inequalities in resources persisted. His many other publications include *Population Policies and Movements in Europe* (1940), *The Trend and Pattern of Fertility in Britain* (1954), and *Numbering the People* (1973).

Glass (Durant), Ruth (1912–90) A British urban sociologist, former Director of Research at the influential Centre for Urban Research, University of London. Her publications include *Watling: A Social Survey* (1939), *Middlesbrough: The*

Social Background of a Plan (1947), *Newcomers: The West Indians in London* (1960), and a much reprinted (and telling) attack on the *anti-urbanism of the British generally, and of British social anthropology and sociology in particular ('Urban Sociology in Great Britain', *Current Sociology*, 1955).

global commodity chains *See* COMMODITY CHAINS.

globalization (globalization theory) Globalization theory examines the emergence of a global cultural system. It suggests that global culture is brought about by a variety of social and cultural developments: the existence of a world-satellite information system; the emergence of global patterns of consumption and consumerism; the cultivation of cosmopolitan lifestyles; the emergence of global sport such as the Olympic Games, world football competitions, and international tennis matches; the spread of world tourism; the decline of the sovereignty of the nation-state; the growth of a global military system; recognition of a world-wide ecological crisis; the development of world-wide health problems such as AIDS; the emergence of world political systems such as the League of Nations and the United Nations; the creation of global political movements such as Marxism; extension of the concept of human rights; and the complex interchange between world religions. More importantly, globalism involves a new consciousness of the world as a single place. Globalization has been described, therefore, as 'the concrete structuration of the world as a whole': that is, a growing awareness at a global level that 'the world' is a continuously constructed environment. Perhaps the most concise definition suggests that globalization is 'a social process in which the constraints of geography on social and cultural arrangements recede and in which people are becoming increasingly aware that they are receding' (Malcolm Waters, *Globalization*, 1995).

Globalization is thus more than merely the sociology of international relations. It is also distinct from the *world-systems theory which has analysed the growth of global economic interdependence—and which claims that cultural globalism is simply the consequence of economic globalism. It is also important to avoid confusing the globalization thesis with an earlier argument about the *convergence of nation-states towards a unified and coherent form of industrial society. Contemporary views of globalization see it as comprising two entirely contradictory processes of homogenization and differentiation in which there is a complex interaction between localism and globalism and that there are powerful movements of resistance against globalization processes.

The proponents of the argument are critical of traditional sociology which continues to focus on the nation-state rather than the world as a system of societies. However, there are problems with globalization theory. What, for example, is the distinction between globalization and modern patterns of *imperialism? There are also difficulties in specifying the relationships between economic and cultural globalization, and between globalization and *modernization. An important recent statement of a globalization perspective is that of David Held and colleagues in *Global Transformations: Politics, Economics and Culture* (1999), amplified in the contributions to Held's *Global Transformations Reader* (2nd edn. 2003).

Globalism increasingly became part of the conventional wisdom of sociologists during the 1990s. Almost every subject of sociological interest that could be given a global gloss was so endowed. Thus, for example, in a single issue of the journal *Contemporary Sociology* (September 1996), there were reviews of books on such diverse subjects as the Women's Movement, the international economy, biological reproduction, immigration, apartheid, racism, the forest products industry, transnational corporations, the production and distribution of food, central banks and international monetary arrangements, American foreign policy, the growth of Third World cities, and value-change in advanced societies—all of which contained the words 'global', 'globalization', or 'globalism' in their titles.

It is undoubtedly true that, on a planet in which the same fashion accessories (such as designer training-shoes) are manufactured and sold across every continent, one can send and receive electronic mail from the middle of a forest in Brazil, eat McDonald's hamburgers in Moscow as well as Manchester, and pay for all this using a Mastercard linked to a bank account in Madras, then the world does indeed appear to be increasingly 'globalized'. However, the excessive use of this term as a sociological buzzword had largely emptied it of analytical and explanatory value, as a perusal of many of the studies mentioned above will reveal. *See also* COMMODITY CHAINS; CYBERSOCIETY; DEVELOPMENT, SOCIOLOGY OF; ENVIRONMENT; FLEXIBLE EMPLOYMENT; FLEXIBLE WORK; INTERNATIONAL DIVISION OF LABOUR; INTERNET; MULTINATIONAL CORPORATION; NEOCOLONIALISM.

glocalization Introduced by Roland Robertson (*Globalization*, 1992) to refer to 'global localization'. This is the process through which global processes, such as the activities of a transnational enterprise, result in the provision of locally specific goods and services and communicates locally specific information back to the global system.

glossing *See* ETHNOMETHODOLOGY.

goal (goals) The end-results towards which an individual or *collective action is directed. The term is commonplace in sociology, although its logical and explanatory status varies greatly, according to context and authorship. Numerous typologies exist, so that it is possible to distinguish between (for example) the informal goals of individuals, and the explicitly stated objectives of *formal organizations; between personal and superordinate goals (the former pertaining to individuals and the latter to a common aim which cannot be attained without a cooperative effort between individuals or groups); or between permissive and prescriptive goals (a distinction employed by Talcott Parsons). Most schools of thought in sociology assume that social action is (to a greater or lesser degree) goal-directed, although the terminology of goals is most frequently encountered in *normative functionalist writings, where it is generally argued that the ends (goals) of social action are largely set by the institutionalized *value-systems of societies (which define the *roles and *statuses that comprise the *social system). This same literature developed the related concepts of goal differentiation (distinctions between the specific goals that are morally approved for different individuals); goal generalization (the tendency for social systems to define expectations attached to roles in such a way that, whatever the wide variety of particular goals held by individuals within a role, these are channelled into a single kind of role-specific activity); and goal displacement (the process by which the particular means selected to achieve a goal become ends in themselves, as for example in the case of *bureaucracies, where adherence to set procedures becomes a primary objective of officials rather than a means by which they can accomplish whatever tasks the organization has been set). *See also* ACTION THEORY; RATIONAL CHOICE THEORY; TELEOLOGY.

goal attainment One of the four functional prerequisites in Talcott Parsons's theory of action systems. Along with *adaptation, *integration, latency it forms the so-called AGIL scheme. Goal attainment is the process through which human and other resources are mobilized for the attainment of collective goals and purposes. In a social system, the goal attainment functions are met through political activities and mobilization occurs through the generation and exercise of *power. *See also* FUNCTIONALISM.

goal differentiation *See* GOAL.

goal displacement The substitution by an organization, of the *goal or goals which it was established to serve, for other goals. The latter frequently serve the interests of employees. First noted by Robert Michels in a classic study of the German Social Democratic Party (*Political Parties*, 1911). *See also* ORGANIZATION THEORY.

goal generalization *See* GOAL.

Goffman, Erving (1922–82) The most influential micro-sociologist of the 1960s and 1970s, Goffman pioneered the *dramaturgical perspective for sociology. The influences on his work were many. After completing his first degree at the University of Toronto he pursued graduate work at Chicago during the late 1940s. Here he came under the influence of the *symbolic interactionists, especially Everett Hughes and Herbert Blumer, as well as neo-Durkheimians such as Lloyd Warner, Edward Shils, and Edward Banfield, and of *social anthropology. In this way, his attention was drawn to the importance of *symbol and *ritual in everyday life, and to the research techniques of *participant observation.

He conducted his first major fieldwork study on one of the Shetland Islands off Scotland (whilst based in Edinburgh). His observations of everyday life in this crofting community subsequently informed his highly influential *The Presentation of Self in Everyday Life* (1959) in which he outlines his dramaturgical framework. In this early work Goffman analyses social life via the metaphor of the theatre, and is concerned with the ways in which people play *roles, and manage the impressions they present to each other in different settings. He also reveals his abiding concern with the interaction order—with what people do when they are in the presence of others.

His next two books continued his dramaturgical interest but applied this framework to the field of deviance. *Stigma* (1964) provides a formal analysis of the features of those who experience *stigma, whilst *Asylums* (1961) reports on fieldwork inside a mental hospital, and traces the moral *career of a mental patient. From this case study, he developed a more general account of the workings of *total institutions. Both these studies were also very influential in the development of *labelling theory, the latter being particularly relevant to the critique of *institutionalization, and perhaps having some impact in encouraging the process of *decarceration.

Many of Goffman's other studies, including *Encounters* (1961), *Behaviour in Public Places* (1963), and *Relations in Public* (1971), pursued the themes of dramaturgical analysis, and provided a dictionary of new sociological concepts that facilitate understanding of the minute details of face-to-face interaction. These have influenced a whole generation of scholars interested in studying everyday life. But by the late 1960s Goffman's works also showed signs of an increasing interest in *phenomenology and *sociolinguistics. Thus, in *Frame Analysis* (1974), there is an attempt to depict the organization of consciousness, and in *Forms of Talk* (1981) language becomes a major focus.

Although Goffman has had many followers he remains unique in the annals of sociology. He broke almost all the rules of conventional methodology: his sources were unclear; his fieldwork seems minimal, and he was happier with novels and biography, than with scientific observation; his style was not that of the scientific report but of the essayist; and he was frustratingly unsystematic. Likewise, he is very hard to place in terms of social theory. Sometimes he is seen as developing a distinct school of symbolic interactionism, sometimes as a *formalist following in the tradition of Georg *Simmel, and sometimes even as a *functionalist of the microorder, because of his concern with the functions of rituals (especially talk) in everyday life. He appears to have had a notoriously difficult temperament, which adds to the popular view of him as an intellectual maverick.

He has had more than his share of critics. Apart from the confusions raised above, he has consistently been accused of neglecting the wider *macrosociological concerns of social structure, class, and the economy in his writings—a charge he accepted, saying that these were not his concerns, but they were more important than his concerns! Others accused him of conservatism, because of his emphasis on the importance of ritual, order, and (in his later works) gender, for preserving aspects of the status quo. In Alvin Gouldner's *Coming Crisis of Western Sociology* he is depicted as an apologist for capitalism, overly cynical, and far too concerned with the trivial. However, others found his work too radical, since its constant demonstration of the fragile nature of routine life seemed akin to *anarchism or *ethnomethodology.

Goffman's prime contribution lies in showing the deeply textured way in which societies are ordered through a multiplicity of human interactions. He developed an array of concepts to help us see this, and through his writings challenged the aridity of a methodologically sophisticated sociology lacking in much substance. He attempted ceaselessly to show that the interaction order was the bridge between the micro and the macro concerns of social life and sociology. His last paper, 'The Interaction Order' (*American Sociological Review*, 1983), lays out a summary of his major arguments. It is too soon to judge whether the corpus of his work, which was so widely influential in his lifetime, will become a significant influence on sociology in the future. See Thomas Scheff's, *Goffman Unbound: A New Paradigm for Social science* (2006). *See also* FRAME; IMPRESSION MANAGEMENT.

(⊕) SEE WEB LINKS
• A comprehensive bibliography of Goffman's articles and books.

Goldmann, Lucien (1913–1970) A Romanian *Marxist philosopher and literary critic, pupil and follower of György *Lukács, he also worked closely with Jean Piaget. He worked mainly in France and is best known for his sociology of literature, in particular *The Hidden God* (1955), a study of Pascal and Racine. In later life he became an important critic of *structuralism. His general approach to culture is set out in *Cultural Creation* (1970).

Goldthorpe class scheme A categorization which allocates individuals and families into social classes, devised mainly by the English sociologist John Goldthorpe. The scheme is used increasingly widely throughout Europe, Australasia, and North America, notably in the study of social *mobility and in the analysis of *class more generally. Because of its complex genealogy it is variously referred to in the literature as the Goldthorpe, Erikson-Goldthorpe, EGP (Erikson-Goldthorpe-Portocarero), and CASMIN (Comparative Study of Social Mobility in Industrial Nations) typology.

For the Oxford Social Mobility Study of England and Wales in the early 1970s, Goldthorpe developed a sevenfold scheme, the categories of which were said 'to combine occupational categories whose members would appear, in the light of the available evidence, to be typically comparable, on one hand, in terms of their sources and levels of income, their degree of economic security and chances of economic advancement [*market situation]; and, on the other hand in their location within the systems of authority and control governing the processes of production in which they are engaged, and hence in their degree of autonomy in performing their work-tasks and roles [*work situation]' (see *Social Mobility and Class Structure in Modern Britain*, 1980). The subsequent requirements of conducting comparative research involving nations having occupational structures quite different from that found in Britain led Goldthorpe and his colleagues in the later CASMIN Project to subdivide some of the original class categories. In a series of revisions to the initial framework, routine non-manual employees were subdivided into clerical (higher) and personal service (lower) categories; the *petite bourgeoisie of own-account workers was separated into its constituent elements of small proprietors with employees, small proprietors without employees, and farmers and smallholders; and agricultural workers were distinguished from other rank-and-file semi-skilled and unskilled manual labourers. These amendments yielded the now standard elevenfold Goldthorpe class scheme shown in the table.

The Goldthorpe Class Categories

I	Higher-grade professionals, administrators, and officials; managers in large industrial establishments; large proprietors
II	Lower-grade professionals, administrators, and officials; higher-grade technicians; managers in small industrial establishments; supervisors of non-manual employees
IIIa	Routine non-manual employees, higher grade (administration and commerce)
IIIb	Routine non-manual employees, lower grade (sales and services)
IVa	Small proprietors, artisans, etc., with employees
IVb	Small proprietors, artisans, etc., without employees
IVc	Farmers and smallholders; other self-employed workers in primary production
V	Lower-grade technicians; supervisors of manual workers
VI	Skilled manual workers
VIIa	Semi-skilled and unskilled manual workers (not in agriculture, etc.)
VIIb	Agricultural and other workers in primary production

As the categories of the schema have been refined over the years, so too have its conceptual and theoretical foundations. For example, in their report of the findings from the CASMIN Project, Erikson and Goldthorpe (*The Constant Flux*, 1992) state that the rationale of the schema is 'to differentiate positions within *labour markets* and *production units* or, more specifically . . . to differentiate such positions in terms of the *employment relations* they entail'. For this reason it is important to distinguish between the self-employed and employees. However, within the fairly heterogeneous category of employee, it is also possible to make 'meaningful distinctions' according to differences in (what has now become) 'the labour contract and the conditions of employment'. In their words, 'employment relationships regulated by a labour contract entail a relatively short-term and specific exchange of money for effort. Employees supply more or less discrete amounts of labour, under the supervision of the employer or of the employer's agents, in return for wages which are calculated on a "piece" or time basis. In contrast, employment relationships within a bureaucratic context involve a longer-term and generally more diffuse exchange. Employees render service to their employing organisation in return for "compensation" which takes the form not only of reward for work done, through a salary and various perquisites, but also comprises important *prospective* elements—for example, salary increments on an established scale, assurances of security both in employment and, through pension rights, after retirement, and, above all, well-defined career opportunities'.

It is clear that, despite these changes in terminology, the nature of the employment relationship has always been central to the scheme. As Erikson and Goldthorpe insist, it is 'the distinction between employees involved in a service relationship with their employer and those whose employment relationships are essentially regulated by a labour contract that underlies the way in which, within our class schema, different classes have been delineated'. So-called *service-class (or salariat) occupations offer incremental advancement, employment security, and the possibility of exchanging commitment to the job against a high level of trust on the part of employers. *Working-class occupations, on the other hand, tend to have closely regulated payment arrangements and to be subject to routine and greater supervision. If the circumstances of those who buy labour, and of those who neither buy the labour of others nor sell their own (that is, employers and the self-employed respectively), are also taken into account, then the origins and basic structure of the classification can readily be grasped.

Despite its increasing popularity and use, the scheme has been the subject of intensive criticism and much controversy, although a good deal of this has been misconceived. It is often suggested that the service-class category is of limited value in empirical analyses because it is too broad, failing to distinguish between the employment situations of the capitalists on one hand, and the mass of professional and managerial employees on the other. Indeed, a major limitation of the scheme is its neglect of propertied class situations other than those of the small proprietors. Critics have also argued that the scheme lacks *validity: because (in research practice) people are allocated to social classes on the basis of their *employment status and the title of their *occupation, the classification may not in fact measure those characteristics (relations or conditions of employment) that are central to Goldthorpe's concept of class. Feminist critics have claimed that, because the original categories were designed for an investigation into social mobility among men, it is male conditions of employment that inform the algorithm which is used to construct the classes. This is said to make the categories (and any analysis on which they are based) sex-specific.

These and other criticisms have prompted a huge secondary literature, involving extensive validation studies of the scheme, a debate about the relationship between class inequality and *gender segregation, investigations of the cross-national and temporal *reliability of the categories, and of the strengths and weaknesses of alternative *operationalizations of Goldthorpe's concept of class. All of these issues and most of the related literature are discussed at length in Gordon Marshall et al., *Against the Odds? Social Class and Social Justice in Industrial Societies* (1997). *See also* BOURGEOISIE; MANUAL VERSUS NON-MANUAL DISTINCTION; NATIONAL STATISTICS SOCIO-ECONOMIC CLASSIFICATION.

Goldthorpe, John H. (1935–) British sociologist, a class analyst with a particular interest in social *mobility. Drawing on earlier work by David *Lockwood with whom he collaborated on *The Affluent Worker* studies (1968–9), developed a class schema for use in mobility research. In adapted form this schema now forms the basis of the UK government's official social class schema, the *National Statistics Socio-economic Classification. At the centre of Goldthorpe's intellectual concerns has been a rejection of *historicism whether in its liberal form (the 'logic of industrialism') or its Marxist alternative. Attached to both the Weberian separation of politics from sociology and the Popperian philosophy of science, he is a strong advocate of sociology as social *science* and a *falsificationist approach. Goldthorpe argues for the search for empirical regularities as revealed through multivariate analysis of large-scale survey data and the explanation of regularities via a form of *rational action theory. For

Goldthorpe, sociological problems arise when we observe and establish significant social regularities that are nevertheless opaque. The role of scientific sociology is to explain these regularities and remove their puzzling character. In using rational action theory, Goldthorpe specifically rejects the explanation of social phenomena in terms of general, covering laws in favour of accounting for causal processes and the mechanisms that produce them.

goodness of fit A statistical term used to indicate the correspondence between an observed *distribution and a *model or hypothetical mathematical distribution. *See also* SIGNIFICANCE TESTS.

Gouldner, Alvin W. (1920–81) An American sociologist who eventually became as much a critical intellectual as a sociologist. His early work was recognized as important within the then orthodox sociological framework, especially *Patterns of Industrial Bureaucracy* (1954), but even at that stage he adopted a critical attitude towards the dominant functionalist perspective. His essay 'Anti-Minotaur: The Myth of a Value-Free Sociology', published in 1964, was a controversial interpretation of Max Weber's work, arguing that Weber did not believe sociology was capable of simple *objectivity, although his name was often erroneously used to support such a proposition.

From the beginning Gouldner was influenced by European traditions of thought (see *Enter Plato*, 1967) and he himself eventually settled in Europe. His most influential work was *The Coming Crisis of Western Sociology* (1970). This offers a substantial and exhaustive argument for a so-called reflexive sociology. Against the view that science in general and sociology in particular is concerned with producing objective truths, Gouldner argued that knowledge is not independent of the knower, and that sociology is intimately bound up with the political and socio-economic context in which it exists. It is therefore important to be aware of this connection and of sociology's role as part of the way we look at ourselves and our future. The book was critical of all the mainstream approaches of modern sociology, but the major part was devoted to a systematic critique of Parsonian *structural-functionalism.

His later work did not have the same impact but pursues similar themes. He insisted on a need for at least an attempt at a totalizing theoretical critique of modern culture and was concerned with the nature of *intellectuals as a new class. His criticism of *Marxism and of intellectuals made a distinction between those who see themselves as producing objective knowledge about society and history, on one hand, and on the other critical thinkers who are less concerned with objective truth than with understanding history in order to change it. His sympathies clearly lie with the latter. In this context, he argued that *ideology should not be taken simply as falsehood used in the interests of a dominant group, although this is often the case: it is developed by intellectuals but has a wider reach and depth and can also become a means of social transformation. These ideas are expounded in *The Dialectic of Ideology and Technology* (1976), *The Two Marxisms* (1980), and *Against Fragmentation* (1985).

governmentality Introduced in the later work of Michel Foucault as a more refined way of understanding his earlier idea of power/knowledge. Government refers to a complex set of processes through which human behaviour is systematically controlled in ever wider areas of social and personal life. For Foucault, such government is not limited to the body of state ministers, or even to the state, but permeates the whole of a society and operates through dispersed mechanisms of power. It comprises both sovereign powers of command, of the kind that figure in traditional *political science and *political sociology, and disciplinary powers of training and self-control. Sovereign power is coercive and repressive, involving exclusion through external controls and inducements. Disciplinary power, on the other hand, concerns the formation of motives, desires, and character in individuals through techniques of the self. Disciplined individuals have acquired the habits, capacities, and skills that allow them to act in socially appropriate ways without the need for any exercise of external, coercive power. Disciplinary power developed in the modern period through such means as schools, hospitals, military barracks, and prisons, and a particularly important focus is the family itself. It is through the disciplinary agency of the family that selves and bodies are regulated at the most intimate level. Foucault traces the emergence of a whole array of 'experts', based in scientific 'disciplines' and involved in the disciplining of individuals. It is through all these means that governmentality takes place. A particularly interesting account of governmentality can be found in *Political Power beyond the State* by Nikolas Rose and Peter Miller (1991) and in Nikolas Rose 's *Powers of Freedom* (1999).

Gramsci, Antonio (1891–1937) A prominent Italian Marxist theorist and noted critic of *economic determinism. After a childhood marked by poverty and ill-health, Gramsci entered the University of Turin, where he seems to have been a particularly talented student of language-related matters. However, because of continuing poverty and deepening political involvements, he left the university in 1915 after four years of study and without graduating. Thereafter he became, in turn, an influential journalist, a prominent political activist and parliamentarian, the leader of the Italian Communist Party (1924–6), and, finally, a political prisoner in Mussolini's gaols (1926–37).

Without denying in any way his immense political importance before and after his death, it nevertheless seems reasonable to say that his current exalted reputation amongst Marxist social scientists rests on the writings now known as *The Prison Notebooks* (1929–35, edited and translated into English in 1971). Among the topics discussed in the notebooks are: *intellectuals, education, Italian history, *political parties, *fascism, *hegemony, and *fordism.

These, then, are the ideas and concepts that made Gramsci a pivotal figure in the debates and developments within Marxist social science during the 1970s— as, first, Nicos *Poulantzas used them to develop his political sociology; and, later, numerous others used them as a conceptual bridge connecting the Marxist tradition with that of *discourse analysis. A good introduction to his life and work, which discusses most of the sociological concepts and topics mentioned above, is James Joll's *Gramsci* (1977). *See also* IDEOLOGY.

grand theory A term coined by C. Wright *Mills in *The Sociological Imagination* (1959) to refer to the form of highly abstract theorizing in which the formal organization and arrangement of *concepts takes priority over understanding the social world. His main target was Parsonsian systems theory.

green revolution A popular term referring to a particular type of technical change in *Third World agriculture arising from improved genetic material, intensive fertilizer use, and controlled irrigation. Mainly associated with wheat and rice production and widely diffused in South and East Asia and Latin America, but not Sub-Saharan Africa.

Gross National Product (GNP) A measure of the total flow of output in any economy during a specified time-period. The aim is to measure final products—the consumer goods and services which constitute the ultimate aim of all productive work and the measure excludes intermediate goods and services that are used as inputs in the production of further goods and services—such as the use of flour to make bread for sale. GNP excludes the value of large amounts of consumption work and other types of work. *See also* INFORMAL ECONOMY.

grounded theory An idea pioneered by Barney Glaser and Anselm Strauss (in their book *The Discovery of Grounded Theory*, 1967) in which *theory is developed from close observation of the world. In contrast to formal or abstract theory, which is developed by deducing (according to logical rules) hypotheses that are then tested against observations, the grounded approach argues for *inductive theory-building: that is, developing theoretical ideas from observations of the data themselves. Glaser and Strauss argue that such theory should construct 'sensitizing concepts' from observation, drawing out comparisons with other linked areas (in a process they call the constant comparative method), and should sample theoretically (for example by sampling critical cases). The approach is closely linked to *symbolic interactionism. It has often been incorrectly invoked by researchers who enter the field without theoretically informed research questions. Grounded theory does not mean 'no theory'.

group (social group) A number of individuals, defined by formal or informal criteria of membership, who share a feeling of unity or are bound together in relatively stable patterns of interaction. The latter criterion is necessary in order to distinguish social groups from other *aggregates dealt with by sociologists which are grouped only in the statistical sense that they share some socially relevant characteristic (including, for example, social categories such as suburban residents or junior managers). However, the term is one of the most widely used in sociology, and will often be found applied to combinations of people who may or may not share a feeling of unity (as in social class groups) and may or may not be involved in regular social interaction (as in the case of members of certain ethnic groups). *See also* COOLEY; DESCENT GROUPS; DYAD; GROUP DYNAMICS; OUT-GROUP; PARIAH GROUP; PEER GROUP; PRESSURE GROUPS; REFERENCE GROUP; STATUS GROUP; SUMNER; TRIAD.

group dynamics In one sense, all sociology is about group dynamics, but the term is usually applied to the structure of, and processes within, small face-to-face groups. The terrain is largely occupied by psychologists, but is integrated into sociology, mainly through the work of Talcott Parsons and the American social psychologist Robert F. Bales (see *Family, Socialisation and Interaction Process*, 1955, and *Working Papers in the Theory of Action*, 1953). Bales's related publications include *Interaction Process Analysis: A Method for the Study of Small Groups* (1950), and *SYMLOG: A System for Multiple Level Observation of Groups* (1979).

group marriage The idea of group marriage probably originated in the incorrect observations of 18th-century explorers (such as Cook) of the sexual habits of Polynesian societies. Lewis Henry Morgan suggested that group marriage, in which sexual and reproductive rights in a group of women were acquired by a group of men, was the original family form. Friedrich Engels also used this notion in his evolutionary theory of the family and the development of the state.

group therapy A psychotherapeutic technique usually involving six to eight subjects in the presence of one or two psychotherapists. There are many different types, although as Mark Aveline points out ('The Group Therapies in Perspective', *Free Association*, 1990), most assume that the origin of psychological difficulties lies in patterns of poor social relationships.

group work *See* CASEWORK.

Guattari, Félix (1930–1992) French psychoanalyst and political activist. He abandoned his studies of commercial pharmacy in 1948 to study philosophy at the Sorbonne but broke off his studies to pursue a career in psychiatry and psychoanalysis and never received his undergraduate degree. Actively involved with the *antipsychiatry movement, he was a co-founder (with Jean Oury (1924–2014)) of the experimental clinic La Borde. He studied and underwent therapy with Jacques Lacan but dissociated himself from Lacan's group later on. He started or was involved with numerous political associations and movements. He is best known for his collaboration with Gilles Deleuze, and in particular for the two volumes of 'Capitalism and Schizophrenia' (*Anti-Oedipus*, 1972; and *A Thousand Plateaus*, 1980). He is the author of *The Molecular Revolution* (1977); *The Three Ecologies* (1989); *Chaosmos* (1992); and, with Antonio Negri, *Communists Like Us* (1990). Guattari started as a radical psychiatrist working on the relation between society, mental illness, institutions, and groups. In this context, he absorbed the insights of Lacanian psychoanalysis only to later reject the centrality attributed by the former to 'lack' or 'fading' in the formation of the unconscious. To the Lacanian understanding of the unconscious, he opposed a mechanistic and molecular understanding of desire as constitutive of social and material assemblages. He also polemicized against the Marxist underestimation of subjectivity; and opposed the signifying semiotics of Ferdinand de Saussure, preferring the *semiotics of Charles Peirce and Louis Hjemslev.

guerrilla A Spanish term meaning 'little war', universally applied to low-level or irregular warfare, using social, political, and geographical advantages against conventionally superior forces. It is often associated with resistance by *peasants, and was developed as a form of revolutionary and anti-colonial movement in the post-1945 period, based on the theories of guerrilla warfare propounded by Mao Zedong and Che Guevara. The idea is much romanticized but has had some practical successes.

guilds (gilds) Medieval trade associations that sought to regulate trade and to protect the interests of employers and which in some countries survive vestigially as curious gentlemen's clubs. The 19th-century view that they could be seen as precursors of *trade unions is now seldom advanced. The Guild Socialism of the early 20th century drew on medieval ideas to propose that industrial unions and other economic groups should manage major industries and form the basis of a larger political democracy. A contemporary form of this view is Paul Hirst's *Associative Democracy* (1994).

Gumplowicz, Ludwig (1838–1909) A Polish sociologist, Social *Darwinist, and *materialist, who argued that social evolution represented a struggle for economic resources resulting in the survival of the fittest. This struggle is characterized by conflict between (in an evolutionary sequence) racial groups, nation-states, and classes. He influenced the elitist theory of Gaetano Mosca, but little of his work has been translated into English (the notable exception being his *Grundriss der Soziologie*, 1885). His writings have been discredited by their authoritarian and racist overtones, although theorists of global processes have recognized his contribution in drawing attention to large-scale social conflicts such as conquests and wars. *See also* MILITARY and MILITARISM.

Gurvitch, Georges (1896–1965) A Russian-born sociologist, who spent most of his professional life in France, and exerted a strong influence on the development of French sociology. Although some of his work has been translated into English (see, for example, his *Sociology of Law*, 1942, and *The Spectrum of Social Time*, 1958), it is largely alien territory to American and British sociologists, mainly because of its strongly philosophical character. Gurvitch described his approach as 'hyper-empiric dialectics' (the *dialectical method grounded in reality), and was critical of Hegel and Marx for recognizing only one form of dialectics (polarization and then synthesis of opposites), whereas he claimed to have identified five: complementarity (in which two apparently distinct elements are part of a larger whole); mutual involvement, in which elements interpenetrate each other; ambiguity and ambivalence, where there is both attraction and repulsion; polarization of opposites (as in the Hegelian dialectic); and reciprocity of perspectives, or differentiation between parallel manifestations of the same elements.

Habermas, Jürgen (1929–) Trained by Theodor *Adorno at Frankfurt, Habermas has been seen as a member of the second generation of *critical theorists. Apart from a short period in Sternberg, he taught at the University of Frankfurt from the 1960s until his retirement in 1994. He wrote on philosophical anthropology and the philosophy of the social sciences during the 1960s, but produced the essays of *Towards a Rational Society* in 1968–9. In these essays he allied Max Weber's account of rationalization through instrumental technique with Marx's analysis of labour and developed a powerful critique of technological domination. The argument was elaborated in association with Claus Offe and others and was set out in summary form in *Legitimation Crisis* (1973), which made clear the extent of his theoretical differences from Marx. Habermas argued that economic crisis tendencies had been resolved through the growth of state expenditure and the willingness of states to plan this expenditure to offset the upturns and downturns of the economic cycle. The price of this, however, was that the crisis tendencies were translated into the state itself, where they appeared as increasingly intractable fiscal crises that were exacerbated by growing motivational and legitimation problems.

Habermas continued to develop the basis of his argument and presented this in the two volumes of *The Theory of Communicative Action* (1981). Here he drew on theories of language and communication, together with ideas from *phenomenology and *symbolic interactionism, to construct a comprehensive *system theory able to grasp the operations of political and economic systems and also the socio-cultural lifeworld. His later work concentrated on philosophical issues surrounding the concepts of Enlightenment and modernity, especially as these are apparent in the work of *Derrida (see *The Philosophical Discourse of Modernity*, 1985). This led to much debate with Derrida over issues of militarism, terrorism, and the future of Europe. Habermas set out his own views on Europe in *Europe: The Faltering Project* (2009) and *The Crisis of the European Union* (2012).

(⊕) SEE WEB LINKS
• The Habermas Forum, including up-to-date information, and links to resources.

habitus A set of acquired dispositions of thought, behaviour, and taste, which is said by Pierre Bourdieu (*Outline of Theory and Practice*, 1977) to constitute the link between social *structures and social practice (or social action). The concept offers a possible basis for a cultural approach to structural inequality and permits a focus on the 'embodiment' of cultural representations in human habits and routines. Although seen as originating in the work of Bourdieu, the concept was first used by Norbert Elias in 1939. Anthony Giddens attempts a similar task with his concept of 'structure'. The best exposition will be found in Richard Jenkins's *Pierre Bourdieu* (1992).

Halbwachs, Maurice (1877–1945) An early French sociologist, much influenced by Émile Durkheim (see his *Les Causes du Suicide*, 1930), and one of the first in that country to write systematically about the nature of social class and the collective structures of class consciousness (see *The Psychology of Social Class*, 1938). Halbwachs pioneered studies of the spatial organization of social processes in his *Population and Society: Introduction to Social Morphology* (1938). His most innovative work concerned the nature of collective memories

Halévy thesis The argument advanced by the historian Élie Halévy (see *A History of the English People in the 19th Century*, 1962), that the stability of English society during the late 18th and 19th centuries (when the rest of Europe experienced revolutionary upheaval) was in significant part due to the influence of Methodism, which taught the working classes the bourgeois virtues of thrift, sobriety, and individual *achievement. By preaching individual rather than collective salvation, and personal rather than political change, Methodism also defused incipient tendencies to popular revolt. According to Halévy, it offered a ladder of opportunity to respectable members of the lower orders, and helped prevent the social and ideological polarization of English society in the wake of the process of *industrialization. In short, this is a variation on the theme of *embourgeoisement, and one which has proved no less controversial among historians than has its later and more familiar sociological counterparts.

halo effect This refers to a common bias in the impressions people form of others, by which attributes are often generalized. Implicitly nice people, for example, are assumed to have all nice attributes. This can lead to misleading judgements: for example, clever people may falsely be assumed to be knowledgeable about everything.

Haraway, Donna Jeanne (1944–) An American specialist in the history and philosophy of science who applies a feminist perspective to the understanding of science and technology. She has taught at the University of Hawaii, Johns Hopkins University, and the University of California at Santa Cruz. She first came to international prominence through the publication of 'A Cyborg Manifesto' (1985), in which she argues against essentialist views of gender, emphasising the way in which gender categories are constructed through scientific and technical discourses and practices. She took up the idea of the cyborg as an entity in which human and machine elements are combined through specific technical practices. The thesis that she develops provides a radical critique of the modern technological consciousness and the uses of technology. Her background is in zoology and in *Primate Visions: Gender, Race, and Nature in the World of Modern Science* (1989), which includes a revised version of her earlier essay, she criticises orthodox views in primatology and their popular uses to justify particular views of gender and race. Her most recent reflections on human-animal relations are in *When Species Meet* (2008).

(⊕) SEE WEB LINKS

• Her own website is at http://people.ucsc.edu/~haraway/

hate crimes Crimes committed out of racial, religious, or sexual *prejudice, which target minority groups, and which often violate anti-discrimination laws. Such crimes are usually crimes of violence motivated against (for example) women, Jews, Blacks, or gays. During the 1980s legislation was developed around the idea of hate crimes, raising the question of whether the motivation behind an act should make it more or less punishable. A useful review of issues is Paul Iganski (ed.), *The Hate Debate* (2002).

Hawthorne studies The experiments that inspired Elton Mayo and others to develop the *Human Relations Movement. From 1924 the Western Electric Company of Chicago, influenced by *scientific management theories, measured the impact of different working conditions (such as levels of lighting, payment systems, and hours of work) on output. The researchers, Fritz Roethlisberger and William J. Dickson, concluded that variations in output were not caused by changing physical conditions or material rewards but partly by the experiments themselves. The special treatment required by experimental participation convinced workers that *management had a particular interest in them. This raised morale and led to increased *productivity. The term 'Hawthorne effect' is now widely used to refer to the behaviour-modifying effects of being the subject of social investigation, regardless of the context of the investigation. More generally, the researchers concluded that supervisory style greatly affected worker productivity.

Later work, involving covert observation of working practices, showed how the pace and organization of work is regulated by informal social *norms and organization among workers. These studies led Mayo to claim that workers are not primarily motivated by economic factors but by management styles and informal work organization. Enhanced productivity therefore depends on management sensitivity to, and manipulation of, the 'human relations' of production. Critics point to methodological defects in the Hawthorne experiments and question the key conclusion drawn from them—that economic factors are less important in determining productivity than the degree of psychological satisfaction which work provides. The best discussion of the studies is still to be found in John Madge's *The Origins of Scientific Sociology* (1963). *See also* EXPERIMENTER EFFECTS.

Hayek, Friedrich A. (1900–92) Born in Vienna, where he later gained doctorates in law and political science, Hayek taught for many years at the London School of Economics and Political Science and the University of Chicago, before returning to Austria in 1962. In an ironic coupling, he was awarded the Nobel Prize in economics jointly with Gunnar Myrdal. The irony arises because Hayek was even better known for his immoderate free-market *liberalism than Myrdal was for his measured social democratic views. Given his later fame as the leading theorist of the anti-Keynesian *monetarism that became influential in the 1980s, it is appropriate that his first book was entitled *Monetary Theory and the Trade Cycle* (1933), and that he used the ideas set out therein to criticize Keynes's *Treatise on Money* (1930). His substantive work is based on a theory of action (modified from that of Carl Menger and Ludwig von Mises) according to which individuals are knowledgeable, rational agents whose rule-following acts have unintended consequences at the collective level. This can be seen as an elaboration of the argument of Adam *Smith and as providing a basis for some of the arguments of functionalist writers such as Robert *Merton who, nevertheless, do not fully accept his strong emphasis on *rational choice.

In 1944 Hayek published the book that for the first time gained him a wider public, *The Road to Serfdom*. In it he drew out the political consequences of his *laissez-faire economics, stressing in particular that centralized economic planning threatened the very liberties that were then being fought for. Hayek continued to elaborate his views in a more positive manner, publishing *The Constitution of Liberty* (1960) and his three-volume *Law, Legislation and Liberty* (1982). *See also* JUSTICE, SOCIAL; LIBERTARIANISM; MONT PELERIN SOCIETY.

head of household This term is used in official surveys to refer to the principal earner in any *household but has often been applied simply to the senior male in the role of husband and (perhaps) father. The practice of taking the senior adult male of a household as the 'head' has been much criticized—at least in most industrialized countries—for its implicit assumption of male primacy. For example, the literature on social class is characterized by a long-standing controversy about the appropriate unit of analysis, a debate which turns on the acceptability or otherwise of classifying a whole household, in class terms, according to the class position of its (usually male) head of household. The term is now rarely used in sociological analysis.

health and illness, sociology of A field of sociology concerned with the social dimensions of health and illness, it covers three main areas: namely, the conceptualization of health and illness; the study of their measurement and social distribution; and the explanation of patterns of health and illness. Clarification of the concepts of health and illness is the starting-point of sociological discussion in the field, with emphasis given to the cultural variability of the boundaries of health and illness, to the multifaceted nature of the concepts, and to their evaluative nature. Ill-health refers to a bodily or mental state that is deemed undesirable, consequently intervention to ameliorate or remedy that condition can be justified—a position analysed most fully by Talcott Parsons in his influential discussion of sickness as a social *role in which processes of social regulation and social control play an important part.

The measurement of patterns of health and illness is far from easy, even when definitions have been agreed. Researchers employ two main sources when measuring ill-health—*official statistics and *community surveys. Official statistics provide data on persons who have had some contact with the health services—so-called 'treated' cases. This means that, whilst the data are more readily accessible, they are contaminated by illness behaviour; that is, by people's willingness to use health services, their access to services, their perception of their illness, and so forth. Community surveys avoid this problem by screening general populations independently of health service contact. However, they usually rely on various self-report scales for measuring ill-health, and the relation between these measures and clinically defined sickness is problematic. Not surprisingly perhaps, *mortality statistics are often used as a substitute measure of *morbidity statistics on the grounds that in developed societies where many people die from degenerative conditions, the age at which an individual dies offers some measure of their lifetime health. Given the limitations of these different measures it is necessary, where possible, to examine a range of data in analysing the social distribution of sickness.

There can be no doubt, whatever the difficulties of measurement, that there are major differences in patterns of health and illness between societies, over time, and within a particular society. Historically, there have been long-term reductions in mortality in industrial societies, and on average life-expectancies are considerably higher in developed than developing societies. Ill-health and mortality are also related to age and sex. The young and the old are more vulnerable to sickness and death, and in most societies women live longer than men, though by some indices women experience more ill-health. There are also major differences by social class and ethnicity within societies. For example, the landmark study *Inequalities in Health: The Black Report* (P. Townsend and N. Davidson, 1982) found that in Britain death rates of those aged 15 to 60 were some two and a half times as high for a person in social class V than in class I, and there is no sign of these differences declining.

Explaining these patterns of health and illness, or the distribution of specific illnesses, is far from easy. It is fashionable among the public and the medical profession to focus on so-called 'health-related behaviours', especially alcohol consumption, smoking, diet, and exercise, and the importance of these behaviours is, on the whole, quite well supported. However, sociologists generally seek to move beyond these individual behaviours, and to understand health and illness in terms of the broader features of society. Whilst the focus on health-related behaviours directs our attention to cultural factors determining patterns of consumption, as well as to the material resources that enable or inhibit particular patterns of consumption, there has also been considerable attention given to the impact of the productive process on health and illness, not only via occurrences such as industrial and environmental pollution or accidents at work, but also via stress-related diseases.

Though the evidence is often open to different interpretations, what is very clear is that social factors play a major part in generating health and illness. For example, epidemiological studies support the idea that autonomy and control at work are important factors in the aetiology of heart disease, and some suggest that what has been called the 'effort-reward imbalance'—a work situation involving high demands but with low career prospects, job security, and financial reward—may also be a significant contributory factor. Reductions in opportunities for career advancement and differences in control over work have been linked to a number of other adverse consequences for health. Some studies show that pension rights may be important in explaining mortality differentials among adult and retired men and women from different class backgrounds.

A good overview of the field is given in Ellen Annandale, *The Sociology of Health and Medicine* (1988). *See also* BLACK REPORT; SICK ROLE.

(⊕) SEE WEB LINKS
- The Wellcome Trust Centre for the History of Medicine at UCL: a useful starting point for information.
- The Department of Health (UK), with links to publications and statistics.

health-care system A term used rather loosely to refer to the arrangements in a given society for the provision of health-care (both preventive and curative) whether organized into a coherent system or not. The term may embrace informal as well as formal (paid) care and care by non-specialists as well as specialists.

health-maintenance organization (HMO) A type of health-care organization developed in the USA, initially on cooperative principles, now increasingly run by profit-making corporations. Unlike fee-for-service medicine, HMOs (a 1970s term) are group practices, providing relatively comprehensive (primary and hospital) services for a standard prepayment, so helping to reduce costs and increasing medical incentives to health maintenance.

health-related behaviour *See* HEALTH AND ILLNESS, SOCIOLOGY OF.

Hegel, Georg Wilhelm Friedrich (1770–1831) A German *idealist philosopher whose major influence on the development of sociological thought has been through Karl *Marx and *Marxism. He developed a philosophy of history, particularly of the history of thought, which he saw as a determinant of social and political history. History is seen as a *dialectical movement towards rational truth. This involves an initial standpoint (the thesis) that is partial and generates a counter-position (its antithesis). The two partial truths are reconciled in a synthesis of the two that is an improvement that, nevertheless, remains a partial view in the longer term. Truth is seen in relation to a totality in which the meaning of each proposition depends upon its relationship to others. The movement of history is then seen as the estrangement or objectification of the mind from itself and the subsequent transcendence of that estrangement. Hegel held that the bourgeois state of his period represented the final transcendence of divisions in history and went hand in hand with the development of truth as a whole. A good starting-point for those interested in Hegel's philosophy is his volume on *The Phenomenology of Spirit* (1807). Peter Singer's *Hegel* (1983) is an excellent commentary on the man and his work.

Karl Marx, in a famous phrase, 'stood Hegel on his head', giving priority to economic, social, and political history over the history of ideas, but maintaining something of the same dialectical method. His concept of *alienation owes much to Hegel's concept of objectification and estrangement, and his analysis of the succession of modes of production was a formulation of Hegel's idea of development. Hegel's influence and mode of reasoning can also be found in the Marxism of György Lukács and the Frankfurt School (*see* CRITICAL THEORY).

hegemonic masculinity Refers to the existence of multiple definitions of masculinity and, at the same time, to hierarchies of power, authority, and recognition among men, and between men and women. At any given time, one form of masculinity rather than others is likely to be culturally exalted. Hegemonic masculinity is the configuration of gender practice that embodies the currently accepted answer to the problem of the legitimacy of patriarchy—which guarantees (or is taken to guarantee) the dominant position of men and the subordination of women.

The most visible bearers of hegemonic masculinity are not always the most powerful people. They may be exemplars, like film actors or sporting heroes, or even fantasy figures, like film characters. Nevertheless, hegemony is only likely to be established if there is some correspondence between cultural ideal and institutional power. So the top levels of business, the military, and government provide a fairly convincing corporate display of masculinity, very little shaken by feminist women or dissenting men.

Violence often underpins or supports authority. A capacity for violence, or a willingness to endorse violence, is still an important feature of hegemonic masculinity in contemporary Western culture. When conditions for the defence of patriarchy change, the bases for the dominance of a particular masculinity are eroded. New groups may challenge old solutions and construct a new hegemony. The dominance of any group of men may be challenged by women. Hegemony, then, is a historically mobile relation.

Where there is a pattern of hegemonic masculinity, there are also subordinated or marginalized masculinities. The most important case in contemporary European/American society is the dominance of heterosexual men and the subordination of homosexual men. Gay men are collectively subordinated to straight men by an array of practices, including political and cultural exclusion, cultural abuse, street violence (ranging from intimidation to murder), economic discrimination, and personal boycotts. Some heterosexual men and boys too are expelled from the circle of legitimacy, in a process marked by a rich vocabulary of abuse: wimp, nerd, pantywaist, dweeb, geek, Milquetoast, and so on.

The number of men rigorously practising the hegemonic pattern in its entirety may be quite small. Yet the majority of men gain from its hegemony, since they benefit from the advantages men in general gain from the overall subordination of women. Masculinities constructed in ways that realize this patriarchal dividend, without the tensions or risks of being the frontline troops of patriarchy, may be regarded as 'complicit' rather than hegemonic. A useful discussion is R. W. Connell, *Masculinities* (1995).

hegemony This concept is to be understood in the context of Karl Marx's historical materialism. It refers to the ideal representation of the *interests of the ruling-class as universal interests. The cumulative nature of the universalization of ideas not only broadens the scope of each ruling-class hegemony but at the same time sharpens the conflict between it and each subsequent ascendant class until such a time as a class (the *proletariat) emerges which really does represent the universal interest. According to Marx, each ruling class does actually represent a broader range of interests than its predecessors, by providing (for example) avenues of social mobility into a higher class; hence, it comes to power not only on the illusion of the common interest, but also because it does in fact serve a broader range of interests. Likewise, the ideas which express the dominant material relationships within and between classes also take a firmer grip, and for that reason are all the more embedded, providing no obvious alternatives. However, in due course the specific class interests of the ruling class become apparent, demanding a more radical negation for its transcendence.

The major vehicle for bourgeois hegemony is *civil society. Antonio *Gramsci locates hegemony within the role of the 'private' or non-state levels of the superstructure, distinguishing this social hegemony from the use of force, as the principal means of maintaining *social order in capitalist societies. Seen in Weberian terms, it would correspond to the 'myth of natural superiority', or the legitimating of a status order. It is, in short, the manufacturing of consent. Cultural hegemony, which is generally identified as the major dimension of this manipulation, involves the production of ways of thinking and seeing, and of excluding alternative visions and *discourses. For that same reason it is difficult to identify what are non-hegemonic modes of reasoning and penetrative analysis, especially since hegemony permeates all of the levels distinguished in Marx's schema, from the basic items of *labour-power and *capital, through the connections of *commodity fetishism, into the fractions of classes and politics. According to Marxists, therefore, hegemony has to be confronted at every level. The same conceptual as well as methodological strictures as apply to *false consciousness and its transcendence must be applied in the case of hegemony.

The sociological significance of the concept, and some idea of its use in empirical research on *ideology, is demonstrated in Joseph Femia, 'Hegemony and Consciousness in the Thought of Antonio Gramsci', *Political Studies* (1975). An excellent overview can be found in John Hoffman's *The Gramscian Challenge* (1984). *See also* DOMINANT IDEOLOGY THESIS.

Heidegger, Martin (1889–1976) A German *existentialist philosopher, who adopted Edmund Husserl's *phenomenological method, in order to investigate the nature of human existence. His most significant work is *Being and Time* (1926), which was an important influence on *postmodernism, and a source for Anthony Giddens's ideas about time and space.

Heider, Fritz (1896–1988) A psychologist who was born in Vienna and, after a period in Germany, emigrated to the United States. Heider's most influential work is *The Psychology of Interpersonal Relations* (1958) in which he uses concepts from *Gestalt psychology to develop his theory of balance and causal attribution. *Cognitive dissonance and *attribution theory both stem directly from Heider's work.

heredity The passing down by genetic transmission of the characteristics of plants or animals from one generation to the next. The idea of biologically transmitted similarities is an old one. However, ideas as to the means of this transmission and its malleability by environmental influences have changed. Present-day ideas are grounded in research on genetics (a term first coined in 1905 for the science of heredity) that has its origins in Mendel's classic studies cross-breeding peas. This and other research provided the missing link in Charles Darwin's theory of natural selection by specifying the mechanism through which species variation and similarity could occur.

The impact of such ideas on the study of human behaviour was considerable. Francis Galton, a cousin of Darwin, explored the role of heredity in accounting for individual differences in *personality and *intelligence. He also introduced the term *eugenics for the body of knowledge that could be used to direct human evolution—an interventionist strategy that has remained highly controversial. Subsequent academic debate, juxtaposing heredity and *environment in an exhaustive specification of causal factors, has continued the attempt to assess the relative contributions of genetics and environment in the causation of human characteristics and behaviour, with individual differences receiving much of the research attention. Twin studies, comparing monozygotic or MZ (identical) twins with dizygotic or DZ (non-identical) twins have been widely employed, although the methodological difficulties are considerable. However, whilst the attempt to quantify the genetic or environmental contribution to differences between individuals continues, there is increasing recognition that both genetics and environment are essential to all human behaviour. *See also* DARWINISM; GENE; HUMAN GENOME; NATURE VERSUS NURTURE DEBATE; SOCIOBIOLOGY.

hermeneutics *See* INTERPRETATION.

Herskovitz, Melville Jean (1895–1963) An American economic anthropologist who was influenced by Franz *Boas and A. A. Goldenweiser during his studies at Columbia University, and himself taught at Northwestern University. He is probably best known for his research into the retention of Africanisms in Afro-American *culture (see *The Myth of the Negro Past*, 1941) and his writing on economic anthropology (*Economic Anthropology: A Study in Comparative Economics*, 1952). He criticized the early theory that the individual must be the starting-point of economic analysis, without himself retreating to economic determinism, and pointed to the importance of looking at how individuals make an economic choice in the face of social constraints and resources and cultural values.

heterosexism A diverse set of social practices—from the linguistic to the physical, in the public sphere and the private sphere, covert and overt—in an array of social arenas (including work, school, church), in which the binary distinction of homosexual (attracted to members of the same sex) versus heterosexual (attracted to members of the opposite sex) is at work in such a way that heterosexuality is privileged. Allied concepts include those of 'compulsory heterosexuality'—and the more psychological notion of *homophobia. *See also* HEGEMONIC MASCULINITY.

heuristic device Any procedure which involves the use of an artificial construct to assist in the exploration of social phenomena. It usually involves assumptions derived from extant empirical research. For example, *ideal types have been used as a way of setting out the defining characteristics of a social phenomenon, so that its salient features might be stated as clearly and explicitly as possible. A heuristic device is, then, a form of preliminary analysis. Such devices have proved especially useful in studies of social *change, by defining benchmarks, around which variation and differences can then be situated. In this context, a heuristic device is usually employed for analytical clarity, although it can also have explanatory value as a *model.

hidden crime *See* CRIME; DARK FIGURE OF CRIME

hidden curriculum In education, the hidden curriculum refers to the way in which cultural values and attitudes (such as obedience to authority, punctuality, and delayed gratification) are transmitted, through the structure of teaching and the organization of schools. This is different from the manifest or formal *curriculum that is subject-based or topic-based. Philip Jackson's classic work on *Life in the Classroom* (1968) points to three aspects of the hidden curriculum: crowds, praise, and power. In classrooms, pupils are exposed to the delay and self-denial that goes with being one of a crowd; the constant evaluation and competition with others; and the fundamental distinction between the powerful and the powerless, with the teacher being effectively the infant's first boss. Much sociological research has been concerned with undesirable aspects of the hidden curriculum, whereby schools are said to sustain inequality, through *sexism, *racism, and class bias. If, as Émile Durkheim postulated, schools reflect the larger society of which they are a part, it is not surprising that, for good or for ill, the hidden curriculum reflects the *values that permeate the other societal systems that interact with education.

hierarchy of credibility A concept introduced by Howard S. Becker (in 'Whose Side are we on?', *Social Problems*, 1967), to capture social inequalities and the moral hierarchy of society. For Becker, those at the top (of an organization or a society) are seen to be more credible, those at the bottom less so. Indeed, the 'underdogs' may be completely discredited and pathologized, and often do not have a voice at all. He argued, as part of a wider debate in deviancy theory about the role of *values in sociological research, that it may be the sociologist's task to help the marginalized 'underdogs' to find a voice.

Hilferding, Rudolf (1877–1941) A leading member of the so-called Austro-Marxists (others were Karl Renner and Otto Bauer), who is best known for his analysis of *Finance Capital* (1910). He served as German Minister of Finance during the 1920s but, as a Jew and a Marxist, went into exile when the Nazis came to power. He was arrested in occupied France and was imprisoned by the Nazis in 1941, dying in prison after Gestapo interrogation.

Hilferding produced an influential critique of Eugen von Böhm-Bawerk's critical discussion of Marxist economics and went on to show how the Marxian framework could be updated to explain the emerging economic trends at the end of the 19th century. His ideas had a great influence on the theories of imperialism constructed by *Bukharin and *Lenin. His central argument was that concentration and monopolization characterized both industry and banking, and that banking capital was increasingly dominant over industrial capital. Enterprises of all kinds were tied into circuits of 'finance capital', within which a small knot of finance capitalists could exercise control. Finance capital was the basis of the overseas imperial expansion of capitalist monopolies. *See also* BOURGEOISIE; OWNERSHIP AND CONTROL.

h

Hinduism A belief-system with a history stretching back some 5000 years, and practised today by approximately five hundred million people, mainly in India. This religious tradition is very diversified: there is no generally acknowledged single teacher or creed, and some commentators speak of the Hindu tradition embracing several religions, while not a few question whether the Western concept of *religion is at all applicable in this context.

The distinctive features of Hindu religion (its vast complexity aside) are the *caste system and the view of life referred to by the term *samsara*. Hindus think of their present life as merely one in a succession of lives, taking various forms, not all human and not all lived on this earth. This is linked to the concept of *karma*, which denotes a moral causation whereby what and where a person is today is largely a consequence of how he or she has conducted him- or herself in all of his or her past lives, especially in regard to *dharma* (or sacred law). Finally, the associated concept of *moksha* signifies emancipation from the bonds of present existence, to be attained through transcending *avidya* (ignorance) and *maya* (illusion). However, these basic ideas have not existed from the beginning of the tradition, and some scholars apply the term Hinduism only to the beliefs and practices which were established around the beginning of the Christian era.

The disparate nature of Hinduism is well illustrated in Hindu scripture, which includes the Vedas (knowledgeable texts written some two thousand years before the Christian era), a mixture of hymns to various Gods, philosophical texts, and prose dealing with rituals; and the enormously diverse *smirti*, which include the great Hindu epics, manuals and law-books, as well as popular stories and legends. Not surprisingly, no fewer than twelve schools are described as orthodox, including Sankhya dualism (which names no god), Sankara non-dualism (which embodies a qualified belief in god), and the theism of Ramanuja (which posits no belief in god). There are numerous well-established sectarian movements, such as the Jains and *bhakti*, who appeal for different reasons to different castes.

Sociological interest in Hinduism has mainly taken the form of studies of the *caste system, as an extreme form of ascriptive stratification, and speculations about the likely consequences of Hindu beliefs for the development of rational capitalism of the Western type. The latter tradition was initiated by Max Weber's essays on the 'Economic Ethics of the World Religions' (1916–19, the relevant sections being translated as *The Religion of India*, 1958), which argue that Hinduism effectively blocked this form of economic development. The debate about Weber's interpretation continues today (see, for example, G. R. Madan, *Western Sociologists on Indian Society*, 1979). The classic study of caste is Louis Dumont's *Homo Hierarchicus* (1970), although this makes the controversial claim that the Indian caste system cannot be analysed in terms of concepts applicable to other forms of social *stratification, a claim that would seem to be undermined by anthropological and historical research demonstrating that social mobility processes of a kind familiar elsewhere (involving *status usurpation resulting from status incongruities associated with shifts in the distribution of power) were also endemic in the traditional caste order.

The literatures on stratification and religion come together in the dispute about whether or not Weber's claim that a form of *fatalism, arising out of the belief in the *karma* doctrine of compensation, was a major factor in stabilizing the caste system—despite its extreme inequalities of condition and social rigidity. This issue is pursued in David Lockwood's essay on 'Fatalism: Durkheim's Hidden Theory of Order', in Anthony Giddens and Gavin Mackenzie (eds.), *Class and the Division of Labour* (1983).

histogram *See* BAR CHART.

historical demography The study of the size and structure of past populations and of the historical relationship between demographic, economic, and social changes. Measuring the demographic characteristics of populations prior to the advent of the *census and national vital registration presents a major challenge since available data are often fragmentary. It is necessary to draw on a range of sources, such as ecclesiastical registers, bills of mortality, wills, tombstones, military records, property lists, and so forth, and painstakingly reconstruct a demographic picture of the period.

Attempts to measure the demographic characteristics of past populations predate the second half of the 20th century. However, historical demography emerged as a distinctive branch of *demography in the post-war period, and was associated with the development of new techniques for studying historical populations, particularly the method of family reconstitution pioneered by Louis Henry of the French Institut d'Études Démographiques in the 1950s. Henry used parish registers, first of the Genevan bourgeoisie and then of the peasantry in Crulai in Normandy, to reconstruct the demographic experiences of families in these communities. His approach to family reconstitution involves taking a particular marriage pair and tracing information about their birth, their parents, the marriage, their own childbearing, and their deaths, a procedure repeated for each family in turn.

In the United Kingdom, E. A. Wrigley employed the same techniques to study families in Colyton in Devon, using parish registers covering the period 1538–1837. His influential article on 'Family Limitation in Pre-Industrial England' (*English History Review*, 1966) argued that birth control was widespread and that families were able to respond to social and economic pressures by delaying childbearing and restricting family size. Together with Peter Laslett, he established the Cambridge Group for the History of Population and Social Structure, which since 1964 has served as the focal point for historical demography in Britain. Work from groups such as this has done much to challenge established views about *family and *household life in the 17th and 18th centuries. Laslett's work in particular set new and formidably high standards for the use of quantitative historical materials in analyses of the Western family (see *The World we have Lost*, 1965; *Household and Family in Past Time*, 1972; and *Family Life and Illicit Love in Earlier Generations*, 1977). However, it should be noted that his rediscovery of the nuclear family as the norm in pre-industrial England has since been challenged by several critics (both sociologists and historians), who have argued that the existence of small households as a unit of residential organization, and small (that is nuclear) families as a framework of meaning for everyday life are not necessarily one and the same thing. *See also* SOCIAL DEMOGRAPHY.

historical materialism A term applied by Karl Marx himself to his theory of society and history. 'Historical' entailed the analysis of how particular forms of society had come into existence, and the specific historical contexts within which apparently universal or eternal social forms—state, religion, market, and so forth—were located. *Materialism denoted the rejection of Hegelian *idealism and the primacy of socio-economic processes and relations. A sustained attempt to defend Marx's account of the determining role in history played by the productive forces is made by William H. Shaw (*Marx's Theory of History*, 1978). *See also* BASE; ECONOMIC DETERMINISM; FORCES OF PRODUCTION; HISTORICISM; LABOUR THEORY OF VALUE; MARXISM; MODE OF PRODUCTION; RELATIONS OF PRODUCTION; SUPERSTRUCTURE.

historical sociology The term commonly applied to sociological analysis based on historical data sources—either primary (such as original documents in archives) or secondary (the written history produced by historians themselves). Historical sociologists see social *change as a structured process of development but do not accept *evolutionism and its view of long-term change.

There has been widespread and sometimes acrimonious methodological debate among historians and sociologists as to the boundaries and relationship between the two disciplines. In the early 1960s E. H. Carr (*What is History?*) argued that 'The more sociological history becomes and the more historical sociology becomes, the better for both. Let the frontier between them be kept open for two-way traffic.' However, Carr's views can be contrasted with those of Charles Wilson (Professor of Modern History at the University of Cambridge), who used the occasion of his inaugural lecture (in 1964) to observe that 'the economic historian and historical sociologist have, it seems, never had things so much their own way ... There is, I think, no great harm done if they go on talking their latest professional jargon to each other in private; if economic historians prattle of liquidity, variables, or backward sloping curves, or sociologists of motivation, elites and social roles. Provided always that we return to some common plain language which recovers this specialized shorthand for purposes of civilized intercourse and ultimate history'. The less controversial view of most sociologists and historians is probably that aired by Philip Abrams (*Historical Sociology*, 1980), who argued that 'history and sociology are and always have been the same thing', so that any dispute about their relationship to each other was merely a matter of prevailing institutional arrangements rather than one of intellectual substance. History tends to be individualizing (*ideographic) and to describe singular or unique phenomena, whereas sociology is generalizing (nomothetic) in formulating theories that apply to categories of phenomena, but this is a matter of emphasis rather than a hard-and-fast principle of method, since (to quote Anthony Giddens, *Central Problems in Social Theory*, 1979) 'there simply are no logical or even methodological distinctions between the social sciences and history—appropriately conceived'. The common objective of practitioners in both disciplines is a *causal analysis of the *meaningful behaviour of individuals and groups, with a proper appreciation of process, context, and *change.

Notwithstanding these *epistemological matters, the major issue confronting historical sociologists relates to the practical difficulties of using primary historical materials as evidence, since (as E. P. Thompson so eloquently put it) we cannot interview tombstones. Such materials include public and private written documents such as official reports, surveys, parish registers, records of organizations, letters, and diaries. Among other things, the researcher needs to establish the authenticity of documents, identifying their authorship and degree of completeness; the credibility of documents, given likely sources of error and distortion, the possible motives of their authors, and the different conditions under which each testament was produced; and the representativeness of the various surviving documentary materials. In other words issues of *reliability are especially acute. The question of *validity is also to the fore, since few surviving sources were constructed for precisely the purposes which the modern researcher has in mind, so that he or she is usually attempting to establish the meaning of data by reading 'against the grain' of the purposes for which they were originally compiled.

It is often the case, therefore, that extant historical data cannot directly answer the questions which are asked of them by the sociologist. In particular, it has proved very difficult for the historical sociologist to explore the subjective aspects of behaviour, especially given the traditional reliance on written documents as sources of evidence. People's motives for action, the meaning and feeling they might attach to (for example) their relationships with kin, their *attitudes, *values, and beliefs, and the *salience of all of these things in their daily lives, have proved among the most elusive of quarries. Such subtleties cannot easily be recovered from the *official statistics and semi-official records which are by far the most common source of information regarding individual and collective behaviour. While *oral histories, diaries, letters, novels, and so forth can give us an impression of the 'temper' of a particular time, they are themselves often partial and have methodological problems of their own which restrict the extent to which the historical sociologist is able to draw inferences from these materials.

Such scepticism should apply, of course, to secondary as well as primary historical materials. There is an unfortunate tendency among some historical sociologists to treat the written accounts produced by historians as if these were somehow unproblematic collations of the historical facts about particular episodes. Such accounts are then raided to provide illustrations with which to fill the empty boxes provided by preconceived sociological models and theories. Historical sociology on this grand scale—in which one ignores the specific historicity (or context) of events, ignores disputes surrounding the interpretation of the original data offered by the historian.

Despite this methodological controversy—or perhaps one should say fuelling it—some of the most prominent works in recent years have been within the domain of historical sociology. These include Barrington Moore's *The Social Origins of Dictatorship and Democracy* (1966), Immanuel Wallerstein's *The Modern World System* (1974, 1980), Michael Mann's *The Sources of Social Power* (1986), and Theda Skocpol's *States and Social Revolutions* (1979), all of which have provoked an enormous secondary literature and no little controversy.

Moore's text exemplifies this sort of work and was significant as the first of a new wave of historical sociology in the late 1960s. The central argument of the book is that it was variations in three sets of social relations which determined whether particular nation-states took a democratic or dictatorial route to modernity. On the basis of sustained reflection on the transition from *feudalism to *capitalism in a range of societies which includes England, France, Germany, Japan, Russia, China, and India, Moore suggests that the critical sets of relations are the following: the relations between the landed aristocracy and the monarchy, which remained evenly balanced where there was a democratic outcome; the relations between the aristocracy and the peasantry, which involved the granting of considerable autonomy to the latter, where there was a democratic outcome; the relations between the aristocracy and the urban bourgeoisie, which were mutually supportive *vis-à-vis* the monarchy, where there was a democratic outcome.

The best overview of the area is the *Handbook of Historical Sociology* edited by Gerard Delanty and Engin Isin (2003) *See also* CHANGE; DOCUMENTARY RESEARCH.

historicism According to Karl Popper, historicism is 'an approach to the social sciences which assumes that *historical prediction* is their principal aim, and which assumes that this aim is attainable by discovering the "rhythms" or the "patterns", the "laws" or the "trends" that underlie the evolution of history'

(*The Poverty of Historicism*, 1957). Historicism is therefore the belief in laws of history, of social development, or of *progress. Political ideologies such as *fascism and *communism are often said to be erected upon historicist foundations.

Popper's critique of historicism has several aspects. He rejects the view that predictions can be made about the future course of history in the form of unconditional prophecies, holding that scientific predictions must be conditional in character. In an independent argument, Popper claims that human history is also radically unpredictable, because of its dependence upon knowledge. New knowledge cannot be predicted because to do so would be to be already in possession of it. He held that *Marxism is to be rejected because of its determinism and historicism, and because its predictions have turned out to be false. It is at best a former scientific conjecture that has been subsequently falsified. To continue to adhere to Marxism in the face of its empirical refutation is, in Popper's view, to abandon science in favour of metaphysical or quasi-religious faith.

history, social *See* SOCIAL HISTORY.

Hobbes, Thomas (1588–1679) An English philosopher and social theorist of the Enlightenment. Hobbes's most influential writings in political philosophy span the period of the English Civil War, and are widely interpreted as an intellectual response to the experience of political instability and personal insecurity. His major work *Leviathan* (1651) offered a justification for absolute political authority that purported to be a deduction from *human nature. Hobbes's account of human nature was an extraordinarily thoroughgoing and ingenious extension of the science of mechanics (as learned from Galileo). According to Hobbes, the whole range of human psychological attributes—sense-perception, memory, imagination, thought, speech, and the passions—were effects of the motions of the minute particles of matter of which we, like other material bodies, are composed. On this view of our nature, action is governed by the passions, which are in turn classified as 'aversions' and 'appetites'. These passions are the basis of moral judgement, and issue in actions whose tendency is self-preservation.

In Hobbes's view, then, human action is governed by the twin passions of fear of death and desire for power. If we imagine humans living in a 'state of nature' prior to the establishment of any law or political power to keep them 'in awe', each individual, lacking any reason for expecting goodwill from the others, will be caught up in a restless pursuit of ever more power. In such a situation, the desire for security on the part of each individual must issue in perpetual antagonism and instability, a state in which (to use Hobbes's famous phrase) life would be 'solitary, poor, nasty, brutish and short'. But humans are possessed of rationality and foresight (capacities which Hobbes characteristically accounts for in mechanical terms). They are thus able to recognize that their security would be better guaranteed by a voluntary act of giving over their individual powers to an individual or group who would thereby be established as a sovereign power over all of them. On Hobbes's bleak view of human nature, the sole function of government is to guarantee the security of the national citizen.

In his own day, Hobbes was able to make himself acceptable to Royalists and Parliamentarians alike. Subsequently, his *materialistic view of human nature and political power has been praised by Marxists, whilst his view of humans as essentially self-interested and his *authoritarian view of the minimal state have been popular with the political right. He was one of the earliest and most brilliant exponents of a *naturalistic approach to social science. Hobbes's political philosophy remains influential in the study of international relations. *See also* SOCIAL CONTRACT.

Hobhouse, Leonard Trelawny (1864–1929) An early British sociologist and social philosopher, author of a four-volumed *evolutionary treatise on the *Principles of Sociology* (1918–24), and a number of other comparative studies of societies. His *The Elements of Social Justice* (1922) contains a stimulating discussion of the relationship between individual freedoms and an economically regulating state. He was a strong supporter of 'New *Liberalism' and developed an account of liberal *citizenship that influenced his colleague T. H. Marshall.

Hobson, John Atkinson (1858–1940) A much underrated economic sociologist, closely allied with the Fabian writers and with Leonard Hobhouse, but developing a very independent line. He produced *The Evolution of Modern Capitalism* (1894) and *Imperialism* (1902), in which he pioneered arguments later taken up by Rudolf Hilferding and others. His general economic theory of 'underconsumption' anticipated many of the ideas later set out by Maynard Keynes. In *The Social Problem* (1901), *Work and Wealth* (1914), and *Wealth and Life* (1929) he explored the welfare issues around the question of poverty and its economic causes. His iconoclastic style brought him close in approach to Thorstein Veblen, on whom he produced a book (1936).

holism *See* INDIVIDUALISM.

Homans, George C. (1910–89) An American social theorist, probably best known for his argument that theory should be based on a series of propositions about individual behaviour, which were to be derived from 'covering laws'. For Homans, the most general covering laws are found in behavioural psychology. In *Social Behaviour: Its Elementary Forms* (1964), Homans puts forward a set of propositions which form the basis of his *rational choice theory of exchange, which states that individual assessments of costs and benefits are the basis of such social phenomena as competition and cooperation, authority, and conformity. Exchange theory, with individuals rather than groups, institutions, or societies as its starting-point, and with its ultimate grounding in behavioural psychology, attracted considerable criticism from the start but several later theorists have been strongly influenced by it. Besides his contributions to social theory, Homans maintained a lifelong interest in the study of small groups, industrial sociology, and historical sociology. He was President of the American Sociological Association in 1964. His other major publications include *English Villagers of the Thirteenth Century* (1941), *The Human Group* (1950), *Sentiments and Activities*

(1962), *Certainties and Doubts* (1987), and his autobiography, *Coming to my Senses* (1984). *See also* BEHAVIOURISM; CAUSE; SUCCESS PROPOSITION.

homework (homeworking) A form of wage work undertaken by family members in their own homes, for large or small firms, usually on a piece-rate basis. Not to be confused with schoolchildren's tasks set by the school to be undertaken at home, nor with unpaid *domestic labour, the latter referring to the goods and services (including *housework) produced within the home for consumption by household members. *See also* OUTWORK.

homophobia A term coined by George Weinberg (1935–2017), in *Society and the Healthy Homosexual* (1972), to refer to the psychological fear of homosexuality. Scaling devices have been used to measure it, and a number of studies have pointed to the characteristic 'homophobia personality', after the fashion of Adorno's *authoritarian personality. However, the concept is very limited as it focuses upon a psychological attribute, and tends to neglect the wider structural sources of the homosexual taboo. The word 'homophobic' has been taken up in popular discussion to refer to overt prejudice or discrimination against gay men.

homosexuality The term homosexual describes those who have sex with, or are sexually attracted to, persons of the same (Greek: *homo*) sex. It was devised in 1869 by a Hungarian doctor (Benkert), as part of the emerging medical and scientific discourse around sexuality, discussed by Michel Foucault in his *History of Sexuality* (1976). During the following century, a great deal of scientific writing was concerned with depicting homosexuality as a morbid pathology, although several more sympathetic strands of thought did emerge during the early part of the 20th century. For Sigmund Freud homosexuality was not an illness; for Alfred Kinsey it was a statistically widespread phenomenon; William H. Masters and Virginia E. Johnson saw it as physiologically normal; and, by 1973, it was no longer classified as a disease by the American Psychiatric Association.

In modern Western usage, male homosexuals are referred to as 'gay' and female homosexuals as 'lesbian'. In all societies men have had sex with men (and probably women with women, though this is less well documented), but having this behaviour as a basis for a social—and especially an organizing or life-long—*identity is a recent and Western phenomenon. Other societies have had other arrangements: generation-specific (and often mandatory) ritualist homosexuality in Melanesia; age- and role-specific relationships (Ancient Greece); and specified inter-role or third-role identity (American Indian Berdache). Even in well-documented Western societies, the varieties of homosexual identity, arrangements, and lifestyles show considerable diversity, including episodic and time-limited activity (for example same-sex institutions), admixture with heterosexual activity (bisexuals and married gays), and wholly casual and anonymous encounters ('cottaging' and 'cruising').

Although the shift in both popular attitudes towards homosexuality and the social organization of homosexual identity and *subculture must be seen largely as a consequence of the rise of a lesbian and gay movement, the sociological analysis of this field has proved important. The pathbreaking article was by Mary

McIntosh ('The Homosexual Role', *Social Problems*, 1968), in which she argued that homosexuality was not a condition at all, but a social *role which has emerged since the 17th century in the Western world—a proposition which sponsored the so-called social constructionist theory of homosexuality.

It is useful to distinguish homosexual behaviour, feelings, and identity, which may or may not be congruent. Estimates of prevalence are notoriously difficult to establish due to the stigmatized and often socially invisible nature of the gay and lesbian identities. The pioneering studies by Kinsey in the United States in the 1930s and 1940s introduced a seven-point scale, ranging from exclusively heterosexual to exclusively homosexual, and showed that changes in the definition of what counts as homosexual behaviour lead to estimates of male homosexuality between 4 per cent (life-long, exclusively homosexual activity) and more than 40 per cent (some significant homosexual activity to orgasm during sexually active life). Recent studies converge on a figure between 6 and 12 per cent for those exclusively or predominantly homosexual for most or all of their sexually active life.

Studies of the aetiology of homosexuality, though extensive, are inconclusive and make little sense outside the context of the aetiology of sexual orientation in general. Much sociological attention has been focused instead on the nature of homosexual identity and whether it is primarily inherent (essentialism) or socially elicited and moulded (constructionism). For an overview see Jeffrey Weeks, *Against Nature* (1991). *See also* HETEROSEXISM; HOMOPHOBIA; SEX, SOCIOLOGICAL STUDIES OF.

hooks, bell (1952–) The pen name, always in lower case, of Gloria Jean Watkins, an American feminist writer who has explored the relationship between gender, race, and class and pioneered views on intersectionality. Her background is in English literature, but her interdisciplinary approach to literary texts has given her an influence across the humanities and social sciences. Her first book was *Ain't I a Woman?: Black Women and Feminism* (1981), which brought together themes that she had been exploring since the rise of the women's movement in the 1970s. Writing from a postmodernist perspective, she examined sexism and racism in the context of images of women and the disadvantaging and marginalizing of black women. *Feminist Theory: From Margin to Center* (1984) explored further the issues of marginalization. Working in a Department of African and African-American Studies, she has continued to investigate issues facing black women in education and in cultural production. She sees an intrinsic link between theory and practice and has been an outspoken critic of government policies.

hooligan (hooliganism) The word 'hooligan' emerged in the late 1890s and literally meant *gangs of rowdy youths. But as Geoff Pearson demonstrates in *Hooligan: A History of Respectable Fears* (1983), the term also encapsulated wider anxieties about the state of the nation's youth and the breakdown of traditions of order and stability in late Victorian England. Fears about hooligans, their territorial gang fights, and their distinctive dress style went hand in hand with anxieties ranging from the failure to instil stable work habits among working-class youths, and perceived decline in the national character, to the lowered morality of the new 'city type' or urban degenerate. The destruction of what were held to have been previously stable traditions of *family and *community, resulting in hooliganism and widespread *juvenile delinquency, was to become a common background theme informing a number of schemes (including the Boy Scout movement) to reclaim the hooligans. Hooliganism, then and now, is almost invariably seen as an entirely unprecedented and alien phenomenon—as well as a threat to the 'British way of life'. For a classic account of *moral panics and the processes which generate other *folk devils such as Teddy Boys and Hell's Angels see S. Cohen, *Folk Devils and Moral Panics* (1972).

horizontal integration *See* INDUSTRIAL INTEGRATION.

Horkheimer, Max (1895–1973) A leading member of the Frankfurt Institute for Social Research, he is best known in sociology for his critique of the dominant rationality of late *capitalism. His most important books are (with *Adorno) *Dialectic of Enlightenment* (1941), *The Eclipse of Reason* (1947), and *Critique of Instrumental Reason* (1967).

horticulture (horticultural societies) Horticulture is the system of production that depends on the cultivation of plants. Horticultural societies are those in which this system predominates. *See also* AGRARIANISM; AGRARIAN SOCIETIES.

hospice An institution specializing in care of the dying. The focus is on the management of pain and suffering (often by controlled medication) and in dealing with the prospect of death. In the United Kingdom the hospice movement developed in the 1980s. Most hospices are charitably funded, small-scale institutions, providing short-term care.

household A group of persons sharing a home or living space, who aggregate and share their incomes, as evidenced by the fact that they regularly take meals together—the 'common cooking-pot' definition. Most households consist of one person living alone, a nuclear *family, an *extended family, or a group of un-related people. The definition is sometimes varied so as to exclude, or include, households of non-related people who may set very variable limits, in practice, to the extent of their income-sharing or common expenditure.

household allocative system A term first coined by Jan Pahl, in a series of articles written in the 1980s, to describe the distribution of financial resources within households. The Pahl model provided a more sophisticated understanding of intrahousehold dynamics than had previously been attempted.

Five systems were identified for married couples, ranging from a 'whole-wage system' (where a single earner controls finances and dispenses a housekeeping allocation), to 'independent management' of separate incomes (with each partner taking responsibility for certain items of expenditure). 'Pooling' systems were either male-controlled or female-controlled—according to who managed and who had ultimate control over decisions on expenditure (see J. Pahl, *Money and Marriage*, 1989).

Recently the concept has been criticized on several grounds. It is evident, for example, that there are substantial difficulties involved in assigning couples to a predefined categorization of systems. In addition it is highly probable that systems are more flexible over time than has been recognized from *cross-sectional data. Moreover, the categorization refers only to couple households, and not to more extended households or to inter-household allocations. And, finally, the only resources considered are financial. More recent contributions have therefore been concerned with extending and refining the Pahl model, to encompass more flexible allocative arrangements, different types of household, a wider range of goods, services, and responsibilities than the purely financial, and the implications of online systems. See Jan Pahl, *Invisible Money: Family Finances in the Electronic Economy* (1999).

household dynamics A reference both to changes in *households (for example, changing household composition) and to the reasons for and patterns of such changes in terms of relations between household members. Research seeking to explain the timing and reasons for young people leaving their parental home would, at least in part, be a study of household dynamics.

household, head of *See* HEAD OF HOUSEHOLD.

household work strategy In essence, the *division of labour between members of a household, whether implicit or the result of explicit decision-making, with the alternatives weighed up in a simplified type of *cost-benefit analysis. It is a plan for the relative deployment of household members' time between the three domains of *employment: in the market economy, including home-based self-employment second jobs, in order to obtain money to buy goods and services in the market; domestic production work, such as cultivating a vegetable patch or raising chickens, purely to supply food to the household; and domestic consumption work to provide goods and services directly within the household, such as cooking meals, child-care, household repairs, or the manufacture of clothes and gifts. Household work strategies may vary over the *life cycle, as household members age, or with the economic environment; they may be imposed by one person or be decided collectively.

The term was devised by Ray Pahl in his book *Divisions of Labour* (1984). His original use of the term refers to the division of labour between household members; the individual's own plan for allocating time to work within and outside the household; and all sources of labour used by a household, including work by relatives on a gift or barter basis, and bought-in services such as child-care and cleaning purchased from non-household members. His usage also involves other concepts, such as 'household self-provisioning' or 'informal work' that bear no direct relationship to the conventional economic terms for different types of market and non-market work.

housework Until relatively recently, sociologists studied women as paid employees outside the home, or as wives and mothers—but did not consider unpaid *domestic labour (the various tasks of cleaning, cooking, and so forth, associated with child-care and maintaining the *household) as a job analogous to any other kind of work. It was not until the 1960s and 1970s that systematic research was undertaken which applied to domestic labour the analytical tools of the sociology of *industry and *work. An early example is Helene Z. Lopata's *Occupation: Housework* (1971).

Studies such as Ann Oakley's *The Sociology of Housework* (1974) have since raised questions about housewives' satisfaction and dissatisfaction with the various domestic tasks; routines for maintaining standards of cleanliness and order; the self-image of women who did this sort of work; the monotony, fragmentation, and pace of activity during the day (work conditions); social interaction among housewives; self-reward (*job satisfaction) in housework; and social-class differences and similarities in all of these. Typically, a majority of respondents in these studies are found to be dissatisfied with housework, which is the aspect of being a housewife which is most disliked. Housewives tend to have a long working week, to perceive their role as having low social prestige, and to feel particularly dissatisfied with it when they have experienced work satisfaction in a previous (paid) job. On the other hand, according to Oakley at least, these predominantly negative feelings about housework (low job satisfaction) contrast with a typically positive orientation to (or high identification with) the housewife *role itself. This apparent paradox arises because 'women locate their orientation to the housewife role within the context of a general view of masculine and feminine roles, according to which the place of each sex is clearly and differently defined', and within which the equation of *femininity with housewifery is axiomatic. *See also* DOMESTIC DIVISION OF LABOUR.

housing class A concept that emerged from a study of Sparkbrook, an inner-city area of Birmingham (UK), conducted by John Rex and Robert Moore during the 1960s (see *Race, Community and Conflict*, 1967). In this study, urban social groups are conceptualized in terms of a struggle over the allocation of scarce resources, the main focus being access to desirable *suburban housing. In Birmingham *ethnicity was a key issue in determining access, linked both with disadvantage in the market and the bureaucratic regulation of public-sector housing allocation. (Immigrants to the city from abroad lacked the sizeable and secure income necessary to raise a loan for house purchase, and were excluded from local authority housing by a prior-residence qualification, which forced them into substandard multi-occupied dwellings supplied by private landlords in the inner city.) The outcome of this struggle is expressed in terms of the formation of different housing classes. Class is used here in the Weberian sense of being based on common *life chances.

The concept of housing class has been subject to much criticism. One objection is that position in the housing *market is in fact determined by position in the *labour market; that is, by social-*class position with reference to the sphere of production. Similarly, other critics have argued that there are status-linked advantages and disadvantages which determine this struggle for housing, and that these are the real source of the problems faced by particular ethnic groups. A further criticism has been directed at Rex and Moore's proposition that 'the basic process underlying urban social interaction is competition for scarce and desired types of housing'. This assumes a unitary value system (the suburban ideal) which, subsequent empirical research suggests, may not in fact exist. Different residential outcomes may reflect (at least in part) different housing preferences and styles of life. However, most criticisms address the problems common to any attempt to produce a ranked classification of social groupings, notably those of how the categories themselves are defined and how to incorporate the possibility of different prospects for those currently occupying identical positions. For all its problems, the concept has highlighted the importance of considering property, of all types, in schemes of class analysis.

The theory of housing classes is thoroughly explored from the point of view of urban social theory in Peter Saunders, *Social Theory and the Urban Question* (1983) and assessed against the background of the literature on race in Michael Banton, *Racial and Ethnic Competition* (1983).

housing, sociological studies of There is not, nor can there be, any uniquely defined sociology of housing. The nature of housing as a physical artefact, its spatial distribution and the terms of its occupancy (physical, legal, financial), are affected by social *structures and processes. Conversely, these features of housing have social effects. Thus housing may be seen both as a social construct and as socially causative. A wide range of sociological research considers housing in one or other of these contexts. At least five areas of study may be identified. First, the influence of *culture and social divisions (class, gender, and so forth) on housing design. Second, how the distribution of social groups across residential locations is affected by social structures and processes, as for example in studies of *urban ecology. Third, how the physical nature of housing and spatial relations between housing units affect patterns of social interaction at the micro-level, that is within and between individual households. Fourth, determinants of housing provision in differently constituted societies (socialist, capitalist, underdeveloped), how these patterns vary cross-nationally and temporally, and the significance of forms of provision for wider social processes (for example, the role of squatter housing in the development of *informal economies, political processes, and *social movements in *Third World cities). Finally, the role of housing in creating or maintaining social divisions or social solidarity, involving (for example) studies of the relationship between housing and class, community, status, gender, race, or forms of consumption. *See also* CONSUMPTION SECTORS; HOUSING CLASS.

human-capital theory This is a modern extension of Adam Smith's explanation of wage differentials by the so-called net (dis)advantages between different employments. The costs of learning the job are a very important component of net advantage and have led economists such as Gary S. Becker and Jacob Mincer to claim that, other things being equal, personal incomes vary according to the amount of investment in human capital; that is, the education and training undertaken by individuals or groups of workers. A further expectation is that widespread investment in human capital creates in the labour-force the skill-base indispensable for *economic growth. The survival of the human-capital reservoir was said, for example, to explain the rapid reconstruction achieved by the defeated powers of the Second World War.

Human capital arises out of any activity able to raise individual worker *productivity. In practice full-time education is, too readily, taken as the principal example. For workers, investment in human capital involves both direct costs, and costs in foregone earnings. Workers making the investment decisions compare the attractiveness of alternative future income and consumption streams, some of which offer enhanced future income, in exchange for higher present training costs and deferred consumption. Returns on societal investment in human capital may in principle be calculated in an analogous way.

Even in economics, critics of human-capital theory point to the difficulty of measuring key concepts, including future income and the central idea of human capital itself. Not all investments in education guarantee an advance in productivity as judged by employers or the market. In particular, there is the problem of measuring both worker productivity and the future income attached to *career openings, except in near-tautological fashion by reference to actual earnings differences which the theory purports to explain. Empirical studies have suggested that, though some of the observed variation in earnings is likely to be due to skills learned, the proportion of unexplained variance is still high, and must be an attribute of the imperfect structure and functioning of the *labour market, rather than of the productivities of the individuals constituting the labour supply.

Human-capital theory has attracted much criticism from sociologists of education and training. In the Marxist renaissance of the 1960s, it was attacked for legitimating so-called bourgeois *individualism, especially in the United States where the theory originated and flourished. It was also accused of blaming individuals for the defects of the system, making pseudo-capitalists out of workers, and fudging the real conflict of *interest between the two. However, even discounting these essentially political criticisms, human-capital theory can be regarded as a species of *rational choice theory and open to a standard critique, by sociologists, of individualist explanations of economic phenomena. *See also* CULTURAL CAPITAL; SOCIAL CAPITAL.

human ecology The study of the relationships between individuals, social groups, and their social *environments. Systematic study of human (or, as it is sometimes termed, 'social') ecology was initiated by Robert Park and the other *Chicago sociologists who applied concepts taken from plant and animal ecology in their development of *urban ecology.

In its later forms (see A. Hawley, *Human Ecology*, 1950) human ecology rejects any simple application to human societies of the competitive and evolutionary mechanisms by which biologists explain the distribution of species in varying physical environments. Instead it is 'a logical extension of the system of thought and the techniques of investigation developed in the study of the collective life of lower organisms to the study of man'. This involves examining how human groups produce particular patterns of social relationships when adapting to their environment. Adaptation exhibits basic characteristics thought to be inherent properties of any *social system: namely, human interdependence, and functionally differentiated social institutions, including dominant institutions performing certain key functions. Under normal circumstances social change is limited to that required to restore *equilibrium conditions. Ecologists such as Hawley sought ecological explanations of human behaviour and culture as well as of spatial patterns (see his *The Changing Shape of Metropolitan America*, 1955, and *Urban Society*, 1971).

Human ecology is often claimed as a general approach, useful for the study of social life in a variety of disciplines, including social anthropology, human geography, and urban economics. Its direct influence on contemporary sociological thought is limited, although it has obvious affinities with structural-functional theory, notably in its emphasis on the adaptive mechanisms by which social equilibrium is maintained, seeing these as an inevitable basis for social existence, and largely discounting the more radical possibilities for social *change occurring through human agency. *See also* URBAN ECOLOGY.

human genome The term used to collectively describe all of the (approximately 30 000) genes found in humans. The human genome was sequenced and mapped by the Human Genome Project (HGP), an international collaborative effort that began formally in 1990 and published the completed sequence in April 2003. Current and potential applications of this information include improved diagnosis of disease, earlier detection of genetic predispositions to disease, improved drug design and treatment, and gene therapy. However, there are also important social concerns to address as use of the HGP data becomes more widespread (see Alison Pilnick, *Genetics and Society*, 2002). These include the possibility of 'geneticization', where individuals may become objectified and the genome, rather than the person, becomes the focus of attention. This objectification can lead to genetic discrimination, where distinctions are made between those genomes that are considered to be more or less desirable, for example, for employment, insurance, or reproductive purposes. The boundaries of health and illness are also potentially changed. From a *reductionist genetic perspective, health is no longer defined by lack of symptoms, feelings or the bodily effects of disease, but by the presence or absence of particular genetic variations that can occur in the human genome. The focus on genetic information arising from the HGP has raised fears of a resurgence of strong forms of *eugenics.

human geography Geography is generally defined as the science that describes the earth's surface, its form and physical features, its natural and political divisions, climates, and productions. This broad-ranging discipline has numerous points of contact with the natural and the social sciences. In the case of the latter the sub-discipline of social or human geography is particularly pertinent.

Human geography was pioneered by the French geographer Paul Vidal de la Blache (*Human Geography*, 1918)., though a broadly similar development of social geography occurred in Germany, influenced by Friedrich Ratzel. Unlike physical geography, which is concerned principally with the description and analysis of the land, human geography focuses on the interaction between human populations and the territories in which they live. This relationship has been marginalized in mainstream sociological theory and research (except by rural and urban sociologists), though it was central to Durkheim's concept of social morphology. The recent rapprochement between sociology and geography resulted from the impact of *Marxism on human geography (see especially D. Harvey, *Social Justice and the City*, 1973) and on *urban sociology. Subsequently there has been a more wide-ranging discussion concerning the significance of spatially defined relationships for social structure and process (and vice versa). A notable contribution has been made by Anthony Giddens's incorporation of space (and time) in his theory of social *structuration. This work, in turn, has influenced (together with *realist epistemology) the development of so-called critical or postmodern geography, which attempts a reconstruction of the theoretical basis for geography, parallel to that attempted by Giddens for sociology. Important recent works include Edward Soja's *Postmodern Geographies: Reassertion of Space in Critical Social Theory* (1989) and Andrew Leyshon and Nigel Thrift's *Money and Space: Geographies of Monetary Transformation* (1997). Relations between geographical and sociological ideas are addressed in John Scott's *Conceptualising the Social World* (2011, Chapters 3 and 5).

humanism A very wide-ranging set of philosophies that have at their core the belief that human interests and dignity should be of primary importance. Its roots are usually traced to ancient Greece, but seeds are also observed elsewhere: in the Renaissance concern with directing attention away from God and spirituality towards the study of 'men' and their work in art, literature, and history; in the progressive Enlightenment concerns with *rationality; and in the Modernist movement with its belief in the death of God.

With variations, the humanist philosophies stress with Protagoras that 'man is the measure of all things', or with Alexander Pope that 'the proper study of mankind is man'. Most commonly, humanism involves a rejection of *religions which place a God at the centre of their thought. Humanist Associations throughout the world (as embodied, for example, in the journal the *Humanist*) affirm that 'the nature of the world is such that human intention and activity may play the determining role in human enterprise, subject only to the conditioning factors of the environing situation' (C. W. Reese, *The Meaning of Humanism*, 1945).

Humanism appears in many forms in contemporary social science. For example, there is a *Marxist humanism usually associated with the early writings of Karl Marx and their influence on Lukács, Adorno, and other *critical theorists. Humanistic psychology, sometimes called the Third Force, stands in contrast to both *behaviourism and *psychoanalysis, and focuses upon the *self and its potential, as for example in the work of Gordon Allport, William James, and A. H. Maslow. There is also a *humanistic sociology, identified with the works of C. Wright Mills, Alfred McClung Lee, and others.

From the 1970s onwards a strong critique of humanism emerged in the writings of *structuralists and *deconstructionists. The work of Michel Foucault, for example, provided an 'archaeology' of the growth of the knowledges which centred themselves upon a human subject; the semiological work of Jacques Derrida and Roland Barthes proclaimed the death of the author, and the 'decentred' nature of things, thus removing the human subject from the centrepoint of creativity; and Louis *Althusser claimed that a belief in the human being was an epistemological disaster, an 'idealism of the essence', and a 'myth of bourgeois ideology'. However, despite such attacks, humanism has remained a pervasive influence on Western thought.

humanistic sociology Those sociologists who are opposed to (as they see it) mechanistic, overly technical, abstracted, and career-seeking approaches, and who attempt instead to provide a social analysis 'in the service of humanity', acting as 'critics, demystifiers, reporters and clarifiers' (see Alfred McClung Lee, *Sociology for Whom?*, 1978). C. Wright Mills is often cited as a major example, and since the 1970s there has been an Association for Humanist Sociology based in the United States, with its own journal *Humanity and Society*. Ken Plummer, in his introduction to the problems and literature of a humanistic method (*Documents of Life*, 1983), outlines four criteria for humanistic sociology: it pays 'tribute to human subjectivity and creativity showing how individuals respond to social constraints and actively assemble social worlds'; deals with 'concrete human experiences—talk, feelings, actions—through their social, and especially economic, organization'; shows a 'naturalistic "intimate familiarity" with such experiences'; and a 'self awareness by the sociologist of the ultimate moral and political role in moving towards a social structure in which there is less exploitation, oppression and injustice'.

human nature A variety of sociological writers refer to the concept of human nature in different contexts. Most frequently, however, the term implies a recognition of some core and loosely determining characteristics which are assumed to underlie human action and consciousness. The exact composition of these elements is a matter of debate. Some social and political theorists (such as Thomas Hobbes, Charles Darwin (*see* DARWINISM), Sigmund Freud, and *utilitarians generally) have invested human nature with selfish and egoistic motives, perhaps emanating from deeper biological imperatives. Others—such as Jean-Jacques Rousseau, Karl Marx, and Peter Kropotkin—have linked human nature in varying degrees to cooperation and altruism. The most influential perspective in sociology, typified for example by the work of Max Weber, has been to view human nature as a consequence of human histories and experience, rather than any predetermined essence. Indeed, many recent social theorists (including Michel Foucault, *social constructionists, and *postmodernists generally) have rejected the very notion of human nature itself.

human relations theory An approach in the sociology of *industry originating in the United States before the Second World War, whose influence spread to Britain for a short period after it. Human relations comprised both an academic literature of varying quality and a set of prescriptions for managerial practice supposedly based upon it. Authority for the ideas in both components was initially developed out of the so-called *Hawthorne experiments (or studies) that were carried out in Chicago from the mid-1920s to the early 1940s, under the aegis of the Western Electric Company, and in conjunction with the Harvard Business School.

Academically, human relations theory sought both causes and solutions within the workplace, for worker dissatisfaction, trade-union *militancy, *industrial conflict, and even *anomie within the wider community. Because, for a time, human relations and industrial sociology were virtually synonymous, the latter also tended until recently to study in-plant factors in isolation. However, human relations theorists have also been noted for a willingness to downplay the role of economic motivations even within the workplace itself, and to stress instead the supposed logic of sentiments affecting worker behaviour. Sentiments, and work-group norms deriving from them, create an informal structure within any organization that cuts across the goals and prescriptions of the organization's *formal structure, which is dictated by the contrasting managerial logic of efficiency.

Within this broad analysis there is considerable variation. The naïve ideas of Elton Mayo, based on vulgarization of the social theories of Vilfredo *Pareto and Émile Durkheim, are commonly taken as the major theoretical statements of the movement. They assert that market industrial societies suffer from a loss of empathy and community feeling that is (mistakenly) characterized by Mayo as anomie. Workers attempt to compensate for this by seeking social satisfactions in the workplace. But the formal structures and payment systems established under the vogue for *scientific management fail to meet this need, with the result that supervision and productivity goals are resisted.

Mayo's analysis depends on an interpretation of the results of the Hawthorne studies that does not wholly coincide with that of F. J. Roethlisberger and W. J. Dickson, the authors of the main report on the experiments themselves (*Management and the Worker*, 1949). In turn, the compatibility of their own interpretation with the actual findings as presented in the report itself, has been challenged by various authors. In particular, it has been argued that the findings do not confirm the authors' thesis that workers attach more importance to the social than to the economic rewards of work. The main interest of *Management and the Worker* today is, first, as a historical document showing the reaction against *behaviourist and economic approaches to the industrial worker in social science; and, secondly, as a warning of the methodological traps awaiting unwary field-workers, especially in the industrial context. The most famous of these is the so-called Hawthorne Effect, in which the very act of setting up and conducting research produces reactions in the subjects, which are then reported as findings about social reality.

Greater methodological sophistication is to be found in the various *ethno-graphic studies of W. Lloyd Warner, Melville Dalton, Donald Roy, and William Foote Whyte. All of these researchers developed or modified Human Relations doctrine in some way. Warner conducted a classic study of a major strike, caused by job losses and de-skilling characteristic of industrial decline and recession, among a hitherto quiescent labour force. Dalton and Roy both carried out influential research by means of participant observation that showed how this method could illuminate the behaviour of industrial work-groups. Roy's work, especially, demonstrated that workers' treatment of pay incentive schemes is economically rational once allowance has been made for their long-term income-expectations. Whyte's studies were among the first to acknowledge the effects of technology and work organization on industrial behaviour and job satisfaction.

Very little of the above work was carried out as entirely disinterested science: the search for successful management techniques to boost worker productivity is often explicitly acknowledged by Human Relations writers. This aspect was so prominent at one point that the perspective was dubbed 'cow sociology'—from the saying that contented cows give the most milk. *Managements were urged to enrich the experience of work by enlarging its content and understanding workers' problems. For Mayo, therapeutic counselling was the principal means of mollifying workers' antagonism to managerial plans; for other writers, effective employee-centred supervision provided the key. Increasingly, theorists working within the tradition prescribed participatory styles of management or even self-supervision by workers, in order to give a veneer of *industrial democracy and to humanize employment (especially in factories). Nevertheless, no writer within the movement abandoned the idea that management constitutes a legitimate scientific elite, or ever proposed a permanent shift of effective control to the workforce. Ultimately, therefore, human relations managerial techniques were criticized as manipulative and as a classic example of a method of managerial control which one author has called management by responsible autonomy. The much later Quality of Worklife Movement is thought by some observers of management theory to be a recrudescence of Human Relations. The same might be said for the 1980s fad for so-called Japanization and for post-*fordist management styles. Indeed, Japanese quality circles are a development of human relations prescriptions imported into Japanese companies from the United States after the Second World War, and developed there more successfully than in their country of origin.

There is an excellent account of the human relations approach—or, rather, two excellent accounts—in separate editions of Michael Rose's *Industrial Behaviour* (1975, 1988).

human rights See RIGHTS.

Hume, David (1711-76) The most significant philosopher of the *Scottish Enlightenment and founding figure of empiricism, Hume is best remembered for his 'constant conjunction' account of causality, and the associated problem of induction. Hume is also remembered for his insistence that moral values could never be deduced from factual premises (no inference from 'is' to 'ought') and for his rejection of the 'self-interest' view of *human nature and morality. He also attempted to lay the foundations for an empirical science of human nature. *See also* CAUSE.

hunter-gatherer (hunting and gathering societies) A mode of subsistence dependent on the exploitation of wild or non-domesticated food resources. This has been the means of subsistence for 99 per cent of humankind's history, and involves the hunting of animals, fishing, and the gathering of wild fruit, plants, honey, and insects. Many hunting and gathering societies comprised small *nomadic bands, although others have shown greater social organization. The few surviving contemporary groups cannot be seen as offering a window on the past since they have their own history. For example, some have been pushed into marginal environments by invading groups and policies of ethnocide, while others were formerly agriculturalists.

Hunting and gathering groups are often organized about a division of labour by sex, with hunting done mainly by men, and gathering done by women. While meat is usually a source of prestige, gathering produces the indispensable food, thus suggesting that members might be more accurately labelled gatherer-hunters.

The popular image of early hunting and gathering groups struggling for survival, to the detriment of all other concerns, is a myth. There is no relation between a society's technology and the complexity of its intellectual and creative pursuits: many of these groups had a rich religious and artistic life. Indeed, Marshall Sahlins has suggested they were the 'original affluent society' (in *Stone Age Economics*, 1972), since they only needed to devote a few hours each day to subsistence activities in order to satisfy their limited material wants, thus leaving considerable periods of leisure.

SEE WEB LINKS
• A BBC site with video links on New Guinea hunter-gatherers and the threat from the logging industry to their way of life.

Husserl, Edmund Gustav Albert (1859–1938) *See* PHENOMENOLOGY.

hybridity A central feature of colonial racism has been the need to categorize and separate 'races'. The spurious belief of distinct 'races' in 19th-century discourses of scientific racism was based upon an immutable boundary between White Europeans and its racial 'others'. The term hybridity has been used to describe a condition in which these boundaries of identity are crossed, resulting in illegitimate racial mixing. Derogatory names such as 'half-breed' and 'mongrel' signify these negative racial encounters. The purity and fixity of a 'white' identity has been maintained by labelling those mixed 'others' as both racially and culturally impure. The anxiety over racial mixing or miscegenation led hybrids to be associated with disease and moral decay. The existence of inter-sexual relations—the illicit union of 'Whites' with 'Blacks'—also revealed a hidden colonial desire for the racial 'other' (Robert Young, *Colonial Desire*, 1995).

More recently, hybridity has been re-appropriated by social and cultural critics. Its transformation into a positive condition of cultural change and creativity has attempted to challenge fixed or essentialist accounts of identity and culture. The racialized claims of purity of origins have been undermined by a view that implies that the crossing of racial and cultural boundaries is a normative feature of societal development. Hybridity acknowledges that identity is formed through an encounter with difference. In particular, the condition of cultural hybridity has been highlighted by examining the post-colonial cultures of migrants which are based on fusions and translations of existing elements. The most developed theorization of hybridity by Homi Bhabha (*The Location of Culture*, 1994) does not consider it as merely fusing existing cultural elements.

Rather, hybridity refers to the process of the emergence of a culture, in which its elements are being continually transformed or translated through irrepressible encounters. Hybridity offers the potential to undermine existing forms of cultural authority and representation.

However, positive accounts of hybridity have been criticized for failing to consider other social differences of class, gender, or location (Giyatri Spivak, *In Other Worlds*, 1988). There is a danger that some accounts of hybridity banally celebrate everyday cultural mixing, instead of analysing the relations of power which produce social differences and political antagonisms. *See also* IDENTITY.

hydraulic hypothesis (hydraulic society) *See* ORIENTAL DESPOTISM.

hypothesis (hypothesis testing) A hypothesis is an untested statement about the relationship (usually of association or causation) between *concepts within a given *theory. Hypothesis testing involves the testing of a hypothesis in a scientific manner, and hence requires a precise statement of the supposed relationship between the concepts under investigation, and the data which would need to be collected for the testing to take place. Hypothesis testing is perhaps best seen as involving *falsificationism. *See also* DEDUCTION.

hypothetico-deductive method *See* DEDUCTION.

iatrogenesis Literally 'doctor-generated', the term refers to sickness produced by medical activity. Widely recognized as a phenomenon, the debate is over its extent. The term was introduced into social science by Ivan Illich (*Medical Nemesis*, 1976), as part of his more general attack on industrial society and in particular its technological and bureaucratic institutions, for limiting freedom and justice and for corrupting and incapacitating individuals. Illich claims that iatrogenesis outweighs any positive benefits of medicine. He distinguishes three major types of iatrogenesis. Clinical iatrogenesis concerns ill-health contracted in hospital—largely the unwanted side-effects of medications and doctor ignorance, neglect, or malpractice, which poison, maim, or even kill the patient. Social iatrogenesis refers to the process by which 'medical practice sponsors sickness by reinforcing a morbid society that encourages people to become consumers of curative, preventive, industrial and environmental medicine'. It makes people hypochondriac and too willing to place themselves at the mercy of medical experts—a dependence on the medical profession that allegedly undermines individual capacities. Finally, cultural iatrogenesis implies that societies weaken the will of their members, by paralysing 'healthy responses to suffering, impairment and death'. Here, the whole culture becomes 'overmedicalized', with doctors assuming the role of priest, and political and social problems entering the medical domain.

Illich's arguments may be placed in the context of wider debates about the excessive *professionalizing and *bureaucratization of modern life. Other sociologists (such as Jack Douglas) have suggested that medicine is not the only sphere in which the activities of the professionals may have unintended consequences: attempts at intervention in other social problems sometimes seem merely to exacerbate the original difficulties. This is also part of the *labelling theory of deviance. *See also* MEDICALIZATION.

id *See* PSYCHOANALYSIS.

idealism A term used to refer to a position in the philosophy of the social sciences that assumes the social world, like all other objects of external perception, consists of ideas originating from some source or other. Examples of such sources would be *Hegel's 'Geist', Berkeley's God, or (most commonly in sociology) the minds of individual human beings. In other words, what idealism asserts *ontologically is that society exists only in so far as human beings think that it exists. And what it asserts *epistemologically is that the proper way to gain knowledge of society is through the investigation of this thinking.

The position set out by Peter Winch in his *The Idea of a Social Science* (1958) comes closest to that of pure idealism in contemporary social science, although some versions of *discourse analysis are also good approximations. More commonly, however, sociologists drawn to idealism have followed one of two courses: either they have based themselves on a synthetic ontology which assumes the coexistence of mental and material phenomena in the social world, and have combined this with a largely *empiricist epistemology (as, some have argued, in the case of Max Weber); or, they have combined an idealist ontology with an empiricist stress on the epistemological primacy to be accorded to observation (as, perhaps, in *symbolic interactionism and *ethnomethodology).

ideal speech situation *See* CRITICAL THEORY.

ideal type Ideal types in sociology are most closely associated with the name of Max *Weber, although as a method of investigation and explanation they are more commonly found in economics, for example in the concept of the perfect market. For Weber, the construction of an ideal type was clearly a *heuristic device, or method of investigation. An ideal type is neither an average type nor a simple description of the most commonly found features of real-world phenomena. Thus one does not construct an ideal type of *bureaucracy by finding the features that are shared by real bureaucracies. Nor is ideal used normatively in the sense of a desirable objective.

Ideal types are worked out with reference to the real world, but involve a selection of those elements that are most *rational or which fit together in the most rational way. Thus the ideal type of bureaucracy embraces those aspects of real bureaucratic organizations that fit together in a coherent means-end chain.

Implicit in Weber's work is the view that constructing an ideal type is a way of learning about the real world. This is situated within a rationalist view of the human sciences: namely, that we all share a rational faculty, and the fact that we can think and act rationally gives order to the world. Thus, by constructing a rational ideal type, we learn something of how the world works. We can then learn more, by comparing the ideal type with reality, looking at how and why the real bureaucracy might differ from the ideal type. We do not end with a model of what a bureaucracy is, or of what it should be, but of what it might be if it were entirely rational. In this way we can learn much from the sources of apparent irrationalities in real bureaucracies.

The method is a difficult one and owes much to the *neo-Kantian philosophical tradition from which Weber came. Anglo-Saxon sociologists have had trouble with it, and often treat ideal types as a sort of hypothetical model that can be tested against reality, thus giving Weber's account (at least) a distinctly *positivist gloss. The best account will be found in Susan J. Hekman, *Weber, The Ideal Type, and Contemporary Social Theory* (1983). *See also* IMAGES OF SOCIETY.

identity Although the term identity has a long history—deriving from the Latin root *idem* implying sameness and continuity—it was not until the 20th century that the term came into popular usage. Discussions of identity take two major forms—psychodynamic and sociological. A central thrust of both traditions has been to challenge essentialist understandings of the concept. These assume a unique core or essence to identity—the 'real me'—which is coherent and remains more or less the same throughout life. Against this the emphasis within both sociological and psychoanalytic theories has been, to varying degrees, the invented and constructed character of identity.

The psychodynamic tradition emerges with *Freud's theory of identification, through which the child comes to assimilate (or introject) external persons or objects, usually the superego of the parent. Psychodynamic theory stresses the inner core of a psychic structure as having a continuous (though often conflicting) identity. Erik Erikson saw identity as a process 'located' in the core of the individual, and yet also in the core of his or her communal culture, hence making a connection between community and individual. He developed the term *identity crisis during the Second World War, in reference to patients who had 'lost a sense of personal sameness and historical continuity', and subsequently generalized it to a whole stage of life (as part of his epigenetic life-stage model of the eight life-stages of man). Here, youth is identified as a universal crisis period of potential identity confusion. Subsequently, the term 'identity crisis' has moved into common parlance.

The sociological tradition of identity theory is linked to *symbolic interactionism and emerges from the pragmatic theory of the *self discussed by William *James and George Herbert *Mead. The self is a distinctively human capacity that enables people to reflect on their nature and the social world through communication and language. Both James and Mead see the self as a process with two phases: the 'I', which is knower, inner, subjective, creative, determining, and unknowable; and the 'Me', which is the more known, outer, determined, and social phase. Identification, here, is a process of naming, of placing ourselves in socially constructed categories, with language holding a central position in this process. In the later works of Erving *Goffman and Peter Berger, identity is stated clearly to be 'socially bestowed, socially sustained and socially transformed' (Berger, *Invitation to Sociology*, 1966).

Developments in social theory associated with *structuralism and *poststructuralism share the concern with language and representation more broadly which was integral to the symbolic interactionist approach to identity. Structuralism and post-structuralism, however, more assertively emphasize the constitutive or deeply formative role of language and representation in the making of identity. Underpinning both structuralism and post-structuralism are the insights of the Swiss structural linguist Ferdinand de *Saussure (see *The Course in General Linguistics*, 1949). Saussure's work emphasized the way meaning in language was produced, not through the intention of the speaking or writing subject, but by the interplay of signs. Language itself was a structured system which produced meaning. In a radical formulation, Saussure suggested that it was language which effectively spoke the individual by subjecting him or her to its rules, rather than the other way around. Saussure's account of language has been used to argue that all social and cultural meanings are produced within language or systems of representation more generally. In other words the world around us, and our place in it, is given meaning—made meaningful—within representation.

In an important sense, therefore, who we are—our sense of identity—is shaped by the meanings attached to particular attributes, capacities, and forms of conduct.

The French philosopher Michel *Foucault, building on the broad thrust of Saussure's arguments, took this account of identity further through his work on *discourse or discursive formations. Discourse, for Foucault, shaped ways of talking about or representing or knowing a particular object. In his work on the growth of the modern prison, for example, he argued that penal discourses (such as criminology) produced a distinct set of ways of talking about and knowing the criminal and the criminal mind (see his *Discipline and Punish*, 1977). Importantly, for Foucault, these discourses furnished positions for *agency and identity. They did so both for the knowing subject (the expert criminologist) and for the known (the criminal). The raw material for identity, then, was formed within discourses, taken up and inhabited by an individual, shaping and forming a sense of identity in the process.

Foucault's work also introduces an element that has become central to recent accounts of identity. This is the insistence that individuals inhabit multiple identities. There are two key dimensions to this assertion. The first—and most important to Foucault himself—is that different discourses generate particular and often divergent positions for agency and identity. Discourses associated with religion, the state, sport, or consumption produce discrete and often contradictory versions of the self. We are, within this perspective, each addressed by a range of possible versions of ourselves: as devout believer, as taxpayer, football supporter, or hedonist. The second dimension is that the multiple identities we inhabit in relation to a range of social practices are themselves linked to larger structures of identity. What is usually cited here are structures like class, ethnicity, 'race', gender, and sexuality. It is important to note, however, that these different identities are not discrete—they interact with each other. As Catherine Hall has shown in relation to 19th-century middle-class men in Britain, their masculinity was dependent upon and secured not only through class-based dispositions, but also through particular kinds of ethnicity ('Englishness') and race ('whiteness') (see *White, Male and Middle Class*, 1993). Gender, ethnicity, and race, as in this example, are not partitioned but interwoven.

A further development of this concern with the interfusing of identities has emphasized the hybridity of cultural identities. The notion of hybridity suggests—most importantly in relation to 'racial' and ethnic identities—that identities are not pure but the product of mixing, fusion, and creolization. Underlying this account of identity is an attention to the mixing and movement of cultures. Figuring prominently in this are the diverse forms of cultural traffic—from the slave trade to the contemporary circulation of media forms—which have helped to shape the modern world (see, for example, Paul Gilroy, *Black Atlantic*, 1993). The resulting fusion or hybridity of identities is not the product of the *assimilation of one culture or cultural tradition by another, but the production of something new. Studies of the hybridity of cultural identity are closely allied to accounts of diaspora identities. Diaspora is a term that was initially used to refer to the dispersal of Jewish people across the globe, but is now regularly used to describe a Black diaspora, the movement and trafficking of people of African origins across continents. Diaspora identities are shaped by this sense of having been, in Salman Rushdie's phrase, 'borne across the world' (see his *Imaginary Homelands*, 1991); of being 'in' but not entirely (or only) 'of' the West.

A different conception of identity is stressed by the French psychoanalyst Jacques *Lacan. Lacan developed Freud's work via the influence of Saussure and emphasized the split and alienated aspects of identity. In what is, in large degree, a rigorous reworking of Freud's writings on *narcissism, Lacan defines the infant's first sense of itself (its first self-identification) as coming through its imaginary positioning by its own mirror-image (see his essay on 'The Mirror Phase as Formative of the Function of the "I"', 1968). Looking at its own reflection, or literally reflected in its mother's eyes, Lacan argues that the infant misrecognizes itself as its mirror-image; and is taken in by its own image in a moment of *gestalt. Lacan describes this as an instance of primary narcissistic identification, and it is for him the basis and prototype of all future identifications. The splitting or misrecognition at the heart of this process is exemplary for Lacan; it establishes the subject's enduring relation to the visual field as an alienated or decentred experience, a split between the external 'ideal ego' (the mirror-image) and the internalized 'ego ideal'.

Discussions of identity have been prominent in sociology and have spawned a huge literature, including many plays and novels, in which the quest for identity or the breakdown of the self are primary themes. These accounts tend to divide into two main camps: an optimistic and a pessimistic version. For the optimists, the modern world has brought with it increasing individuality and choice over a wider range of identities. Thus, people are more likely to *self-actualize: to discover an inner self which is not artificially imposed by tradition, culture or religion; and to embark upon quests for greater individuality, self-understanding, flexibility, and difference. By contrast, pessimists portray a *mass society of estrangement: for example, the psychodynamic tradition highlights the loss of boundaries between self and culture, and the rise of the *narcissistic personality; while the sociologists see a trend towards fragmentation, homelessness, and meaninglessness, and bemoan the loss of authority in the public world through the growth of self-absorption and selfishness.

There is, therefore, no clear concept of identity in modern sociology. It is used widely and loosely in reference to one's sense of self, and one's feelings and ideas about oneself, as for example in the terms 'gender identity' or 'class identity'. It is sometimes assumed that our identity comes from the expectations attached to the social *roles that we occupy, and which we then internalize, so that it is formed through the process of *socialization. Alternatively, it is elsewhere assumed that we construct our identities more actively out of the materials presented to us during socialization, or in our various roles. However, Goffman's work (in particular *The Presentation of Self in Everyday Life* (1959), which looks at the complex ways in which we present ourselves to other people, a process which might be termed identity management) raises a crucial issue that is unresolved in all camps: namely, the question of whether or not there is an authentic self or identity behind the various masks which we present to others. *See also* PERSON-ALITY; PSYCHOANALYSIS; REFLEXIVE MODERNIZATION.

identity crisis This concept is most fully developed by the American psycho-analyst Erik Erikson. He uses it to refer to a crisis, having interlocking psycho-logical and sociological aspects, in an individual's sense of self. Erikson sees such crises as common in the *adolescent stage of development, when no clear social *role has yet been developed, and the youth is more than a child but not yet an adult. Psychologically, this is complemented by a reworking of earlier stages of development, particularly in relation to sexuality and the ability to form intimate relationships outside the family. (See, for example, his *Life History and the Historical Moment*, 1975.)

ideographic versus nomothetic approaches The former term refers to those methods which highlight the unique elements of the individual phenom-enon—the historically particular—as in much of history and biography. The contrast is with the nomothetic, which seeks to provide more general law-like statements about social life, usually by emulating the logic and methodology of the natural sciences. The distinction hails from the German philosopher Wilhelm *Windelband, and provoked an acrimonious debate (the so-called *Methoden-streit*) in late 19th-century Germany and Austria, between proponents of gener-alizing and individualizing approaches to the social, historical, and cultural sciences. Many of Max *Weber's methodological writings are directed towards this debate, notably his theory of concept formation and ideal types, although the issues have also been popularized via the psychological writings of Gordon *Allport. *See also* GEISTESWISSENSCHAFTEN and NATURWISSENSCHAFTEN; LIFE-HISTORY.

ideological state apparatus A term developed by the Marxist theorist Louis *Althusser to denote institutions such as education, the churches, family, media, trade unions, and law that were formally outside state control but which served to transmit the values of the *state, to *interpellate those individuals affected by them, and to maintain order in a society, above all to reproduce capitalist *relations of production. In contemporary capitalist societies education has replaced the Church as the principal ideological state apparatus. Among Marxists, the term is contrasted with the so-called 'repressive state apparatus' of the armed forces and police, and is allotted a major role in securing compliance within developed capitalist societies. Beyond reproducing the assumption that the state itself reflects a particular class interest, the theory of ideological state apparatus has also been criticized for simplifying relations between these insti-tutions and the state, and underestimating their autonomy or potential for such autonomy. It also allowed too facile an equation of challenging authority within education with weakening the capitalist system as a whole.

ideology This term has a long, complex, and extraordinarily rich history. As a specifically sociological concept, it originated in the work of Karl *Marx, and to this day its deployment in a particular sociological analysis remains a sign that such analysis is either Marxist or strongly influenced by *Marxism. This said, it is important to bear in mind that the social phenomenon to which the concept refers—the realm of ideas or culture, in general, and that of political ideas or political culture more specifically—together with the relationship between the realm of ideas and those of politics and economics, have also been discussed at length within other sociological traditions. What is more, these other discussions (especially those amongst Weberians, Durkheimians, and structuralists), have not infrequently had a considerable impact on Marxist conceptualizations of ideology (as well as vice versa).

Much of the complexity of the concept's history, and therefore the difficulties encountered by those who are asked to define it, is a consequence of the underdeveloped and partial nature of Marx's various fragmentary and sometimes conflicting discussions of the phenomenon to which it refers. In *The German Ideology* (1846), Marx was concerned to explain not simply why he was no longer a *Hegelian idealist of any kind, but also why he and so many others had for so long been in the thrall of such ideas. In essence, and putting to one side all the ambiguities that subsequent commentators have reasonably and unreasonably claimed to descry, his argument was that the principal substantive tenet of Hegel's idealism (namely the belief that ideas were the motive force of history) was not in any sense Reason's final coming to consciousness of itself; rather, this tenet was the product of a history that had hitherto been hidden from view, especially from that of intellectuals like himself, and as such it was an ideological doctrine. This hidden history was that history of 'real, active men' that he was soon to refer to as the 'history of class struggles', and the reason it had proved to be particularly difficult for the intellectuals to discern was because, to paraphrase Marx, they tended to be concerned with the ruling ideas of the epoch, which as in any epoch were the ideas of the ruling class.

In sum, then, this argument contains the following: first, the embryo of Marx's *base versus *superstructure model of society, with its suggestion that the realm of ideas is distinguishable from and determined by that of the economy; and, second, the notion that what makes some (the ruling) ideas ideological is the fact that they hide things to the benefit of the ruling class.

Marx's most sustained effort to explain the nature of the link between the economic and ideational realms, as well as how the ideas of the ruling class become ruling ideas, may be found at the end of the first chapter of *Capital* (1867). First, he explains the basic mechanism whereby there can occur a difference between how things really are in the economy and the wider society, and how people think they are. This he does by making an analogy with 'the mist-enveloped regions of the religious world'. He then argues that 'in that world the productions of the human brain appear as independent beings endowed with life, and entering into relation both with one another and the human race'. Finally, he concludes, as it is with ideas then 'so it is in the world of commodities with the products of men's hands. This I call the Fetishism which attaches itself to the products of labour (in capitalist societies).'

The net result of the occurrence of this fetishism is that what people (including, he points out particularly, bourgeois economists, Christian clerics, and lawyers) think is going on is simply the buying and selling of things whose values are intrinsic to the things themselves. In fact, Marx suggests, these values are the product of certain relations between people that are obscured from them, by all the buying, selling, litigating, and justifying which, as he states at the beginning of the following chapter, they have to engage in by virtue of the fact that 'commodities cannot go to market and make exchanges on their own account'. Thus, people in capitalist societies necessarily come to regard apparently equal (or neutral) *market exchanges as the basic relationships within their societies, whereas in fact, according to Marx, the more basic relationships are the profoundly unequal ones that occur within 'the hidden abode of production'. In this way, then, 'the class which is the ruling material force of society . . . [becomes] . . . its ruling intellectual force'.

The metaphor of the fetish and Marx's specification of how fetishism occurs in capitalist societies have continued to have a great if sometimes very divergent influence amongst Marxist scholars. For example, György *Lukács utilizes it both in his theory of *false consciousness and his proposals as to how this might best be overcome. Lukács's treatment was also influenced by Weber. By contrast, and in his case influenced somewhat by Durkheim and the *structuralist tradition, Louis *Althusser developed Marx's ideas to produce both a conception of the ideological relation as in a rather special sense an 'imaginary relation', and a specification of the mechanism whereby people or subjects are positioned within such a relation as one of *interpellation.

More recently, numerous scholars, often under the influence of Antonio *Gramsci's notion of *hegemony, have sought to incorporate various linguistic and other concepts of *discourse analysis into the theory of ideology. Their hope is that this will enable them to investigate what might be termed the internal life of the ideological realm, and so give some content to what many have termed its *relative autonomy. In so doing, their hope is also that they might be able to provide more detailed and sophisticated accounts of how it is that a society's 'ruling ideas' are produced—more sophisticated, that is, than those explanations that are possible on the basis of the theory of *commodity fetishism, and its associated notion that such ideas must necessarily be those of the ruling class. Nevertheless, the theory of fetishism still has its defenders, for whom any such dalliance with *post-structuralism and *postmodernism is heretical.

The sociological literature on ideology is extraordinarily dense. Jorge Larrain's *The Concept of Ideology* (1979) and Terry Eagleton's *Ideology* (1991) are both reasonably accessible. *See also* DOMINANT IDEOLOGY THESIS; DUAL CONSCIOUSNESS; GOULDNER; HEGEMONY; IDEOLOGICAL STATE APPARATUS.

(⊕) SEE WEB LINKS
- A key paper by George Lichtheim: 'The Concept of Ideology.' (Subscription)

illness *See* HEALTH AND ILLNESS, SOCIOLOGY OF.

images of society In the *Sociological Review* for 1966, the British sociologist David *Lockwood published an article on 'Sources of Variation in Working-Class Images of Society', in which he drew together the findings from a range of existing studies of social imagery, voting behaviour, industrial sociology, and community life. From these, Lockwood derived an influential typology of the 'world-views' or 'social consciousness' of manual workers, distinguishing between the 'traditional proletarian', 'deferential traditionalist', and 'privatized instrumentalist' types.

The first of these is associated with mining, shipbuilding, or some similar such industry which typically gathers its labour-force into solidary communities, relatively isolated from the wider society. These workers tend therefore to be members of 'occupational communities': that is, social networks that are characterized by a high degree of *job satisfaction among those involved, who also share strong attachments to primary work groups, and are committed to workplace relationships which carry over into the sphere of leisure. These sorts of manual workers reside in 'traditional working-class communities', comprising closely knit cliques of workmates who are also friends, neighbours, and relatives. Their circumstances are said to promote mutual aid, sociability, cohesion, and *collectivism. Finally, they display a proletarian consciousness rooted in a power-based image of society, which makes a simple distinction between 'us' and 'them'.

Deferential traditionalists, by comparison, proffer a prestige or hierarchical model of society in which people are ranked according to *status. Characteristically, these sorts of manual workers defer to their 'betters' (status superiors) both socially and politically, for example by voting for traditional right-wing parties on the grounds that the established elites in society can be trusted to pursue national as opposed to sectional or class interests. According to Lockwood, this world-view is common among employees in small-scale family enterprises, or in work situations where *paternalistic forms of industrial authority are prevalent, as for example among farm labourers. Typically, such workers live in small communities comprising a 'local status system', in which people tend to accord to individuals a position as individuals, within a localized hierarchy of prestige within which 'everyone knows his or her place'.

Finally, there are privatized instrumentalists who have a predominantly monetary orientation to work and a home-centred and family-centred (privatized) suburban lifestyle, which together foster a pecuniary image of society in which class divisions are seen principally in terms of income and material possessions. These workers are attracted to jobs mainly for extrinsic (economic) reasons, are rarely members of solidary work-groups, and only infrequently socialize with their workmates. Their attachments to trade unions and left-wing political parties are less solidaristic and more instrumental (calculating) than those of the traditional proletarians, since they are 'devoid of all sense of participation in a class movement seeking structural changes in society', and conditional instead upon the ability of the workers' organizations and parties to improve their material circumstances (a type of sectional militancy which Lockwood termed 'instrumental collectivism').

Lockwood was ambivalent about the status of his argument, since he claimed both that it presented a series of *ideal types which were sociological rather than historical concepts, but also that the image of society propounded by privatized instrumentalists of the age of post-war affluence was 'prototypical' of manual workers in general, in that the pecuniary world-view was rapidly replacing those of the traditional proletarians and deferential traditionalists of an earlier era. Nevertheless, both his typology and the highly original synthesis of many of the themes of post-war British sociology on which it rested acted as benchmarks for innumerable studies of British working-class life for more than a decade, and Lockwood's analysis continues to influence researchers on both sides of the Atlantic even today. *See also* DEFERENCE; EMBOURGEOISEMENT; WORK, SUBJECTIVE EXPERIENCE OF.

imagined community Benedict Anderson (1936–2015), in his book *Imagined Communities: Reflections on the Origin and Spread of Nationalism* (2nd edn., 1991, originally 1983) referred to the nation as an imagined political community. It is imagined because: (*a*) the members never know or meet most of their fellow-members, yet in the minds of each lives the image of their communion; (*b*) it is *limited* because even the largest of them has finite, if elastic, boundaries, beyond which lie other nations; (*c*) it is *sovereign* because its members have the right to govern themselves; (*d*) it is a *community* because the nation is always conceived as a deep, horizontal comradeship, despite abiding social inequality between members. Anderson emphasized that the nation is 'imagined' not 'imaginary', that it does not imply fabrication and falsity but a process of cultural or ideological construction and creativity.

Criticisms of the concept include the fact that it does not develop the ways in which this process of 'imagining' is carried out and sustained—for example, by institutional mechanisms that sustain and shape the belief in a people's distinctiveness—that it underplays the contested nature of 'nation' in social-political terms; and that it reifies nation in time and space.

immanence *See* TRANSCENDENTALISM.

immigration *See* MIGRATION, SOCIOLOGICAL STUDIES OF; RACE, SOCIOLOGY OF.

imperialism Literally 'empire-ism', a term originally used in the 1860s to denote the political and military aspirations of Napoleon III in France, and later applied to Great Power rivalry in general, involving military competition and the acquisition of colonial territories in Africa and Asia. More recently, it has been used increasingly (now almost exclusively) to refer to the domination of colonial by more developed countries, and hence as a synonym for *colonialism.

Theories of imperialism seek to provide explanations for the expansion of European control after 1870. They fall into three broad categories. The sociological theory of Joseph *Schumpeter, drawing on a tradition of liberal thought, sees imperial policies as unnecessary and counter-productive. It analyses imperialism as a reflection of the existence of a pre-industrial and precapitalist social stratum within the imperial countries, a landed and military aristocracy, whose atavistic ideals and social position impel them towards something that is not in the interests of modern capitalist society. *Marxist and more broadly economic theories see imperialism as a necessary product of capitalist industrialization and the limits which this has reached in the more developed countries. Here, imperialism represents either the search for markets, for pre-capitalist societies to subjugate, or for low wages or higher investment returns. For *Lenin, drawing on John *Hobson and Nikolai Bukharin, imperialism (in the sense of colonialism) was the 'highest stage' of *capitalism, and its abolition would spell the end of capitalism as a whole. Finally, strategic or political theories of imperialism see the expansion of the 1870s as but one of many such historical phenomena, in which more powerful states, for a variety of reasons (many of them non-economic) and through different mechanisms, seek to subject weaker states to their control; that is, there is nothing specifically economic or capitalist about the phenomenon. In this sense the term would cover such ancient empires as the Persian and Roman, as well as the Soviet bloc up to 1990, and informal empires such as those constituted by the economic influence of the United States in Latin America. *See also* NEO-COLONIALISM.

impression formation A social psychological term referring to the way in which strangers develop perceptions of each other. A long tradition of (largely experimental) studies have investigated the impact of initial impressions. These have identified phenomena such as *primacy effects and *halo effects.

impression management A *dramaturgical concept, introduced by Erving *Goffman in *The Presentation of Self in Everyday Life* (1959). It highlights the ways in which persons in the company of others strive to present an image of themselves in particular ways. *See also* ALTERCASTING; IDENTITY.

incarceration The process of being institutionalized, by a carceral organization such as the prison service, in a prison, mental hospital, juvenile detention centre, or other carceral institution that isolates inmates from the wider society. *See also* DECARCERATION; INSTITUTIONALIZATION.

incentive payments Payment by results: any method—such as individual piecework—of paying workers above a basic minimum and in relation to their output or *productivity. Schemes may apply to individuals, small groups, or (as with some so-called profit-related pay arrangements) to entire workforces. Incentive payments require precise and acceptable measures of output and assume that workers are always motivated to maximize short-run money earnings. The aim, often unrealized, is to increase workers' effort and commitments to their tasks. *See also* EFFORT BARGAINING; HUMAN RELATIONS THEORY; SCIENTIFIC MANAGEMENT.

incest taboo The prohibition of sexual relations between immediate relatives, usually between parents and children, and between siblings. The prohibition usually extends to persons adopted into or marrying into any of these primary relationships, and is thus attributed to a need to limit sexual activity to a single generation within the nuclear family group (to avoid conflict), as well as to the fear of inbreeding.

inclusion *See* CLOSURE.

income distribution There are two types—functional and size. The functional distribution of national income shows how the total is made up of income from land, labour, and capital, or the contribution of each factor of production to the national income. In this context, income redistribution concerns arguments about whether profits should be reduced to augment employment income, for example. The size distribution of personal income shows the distribution of direct financial resources received by individuals, families, and households. This is now the most common meaning of the term. The focus is on the receipt of money income, excluding the social wage income implied by access to public goods such as state-funded education and health services.

There is no precise agreed definition of personal income, and no unambiguous operational definition setting out which items are to be included or excluded, and in what manner. Definitions tend to rely in practice on whatever information is available within administrative records, regular *surveys of income and expenditure, and other sources within *official statistics. One of the most common definitions is thus the earnings distribution, because data on the wages and salaries of employees and the earnings and profits of the self-employed are available from many surveys. But the definition of personal income goes wider than this and can include profits of firms in the private sector when distributed as dividends (but not the profits of state enterprises); earnings in kind and fringe benefits (such as free housing, free meals, subsidized loans or the use of a company car); unearned income from investments; income from sub-letting and other imputed income from home ownership; income maintenance payments from the state and any other benefits or insurance receipts. A distinction is drawn between income and wealth, which is the net value of all assets which can be assigned to individuals, but in reality income and capital are not separate entities and can be converted one to the other. This is an important source of practical difficulty in defining income as visible money income.

Earnings and income can be measured as current income (such as income in the last week or previous twelve months), or as usual or normal income, which will differ in cases where the current income is untypical for any reason, such as sickness or unemployment. An important distinction is made between the pre-tax and after-tax income distributions, between original incomes and disposable incomes. The distribution of original income shows the position before any income redistribution policies take effect, and always displays the widest dispersion of income. The distribution of disposable (or net) income shows the position after deducting taxes, social insurance contributions, and any other obligatory deductions from original income, then adding income maintenance and related benefits. Disposable income provides a broad measure of spending power, as distinct from discretionary income, which is disposable income less necessary expenditure on housing, travel-to-work, and similar unavoidable costs.

The distribution of income is studied to assess the redistribution effects of government fiscal and social *welfare policies; as a key factor in patterns of consumption; as a measure of economic and hence social inequality, and one that is more accessible to researchers than the distribution of wealth; and to measure *poverty. It is sometimes used to study the unanticipated effects of policies overtly concerned with quite different matters, such as divorce or ill-health. Economists are interested in the pattern of income distribution as an independent variable in its own right, for example whether greater income inequalities lead to higher savings, or whether industrialization leads to reduced income inequalities.

Most of the (many) methodological problems of investigating income distribution, especially changes therein, are discussed in A. B. Atkinson (ed.), *Wealth, Income and Inequality* (1980). The evidence for Britain is usefully summarized in W. D. Rubinstein, *Wealth and Inequality in Britain* (1986), and in Daniel Dorling et al., *Poverty, Wealth and Place in Britain, 1968 to 2005* (2007). *See also* LORENZ CURVE.

(⊕) SEE WEB LINKS
• Official National Statistics on income and wealth for the UK.
• The US Census, with information on income distribution.

incommensurability *Measurement requires common units of measurement along a single continuum or scale for comparing 'objects'. If these requirements are not met then the apparent measurements are said to be incommensurable.

incorporation The process whereby social groups, classes, and individuals are integrated into a larger social entity. This can be seen as being achieved either through the extension of rights and the subsequent exacting of obligations, as in *citizenship communities, or through mechanisms such as *social mobility, intermarriage, and urban desegregation. As with social *closure, incorporation implies marginalized groups, elite-mass relations, and co-optation. The term has been widely employed in discussions about the allegedly revolutionary role of the *proletariat, a historical mission which (it is claimed by some) has been frustrated by the incorporation of this class, via the mechanisms of the welfare state, political representation, home ownership, and more recently share ownership. *See also* CORPORATE SOCIETY.

independence *See* STATISTICAL INDEPENDENCE.

independent variable Within a particular study, analysis, or model, the independent (or explanatory) *variable is the social element whose characteristics or variations shape and determine the dependent variable: for example, the age of marriage can help explain the likelihood of divorce. In an experimental situation, independent variables can be systematically manipulated, so that the effect on the *dependent variable can be observed. Whether a variable is treated as dependent or independent is determined by the theoretical framework and focus of a study, but independent variables must precede the dependent variable, and should have causal powers. *See also* CAUSAL MODELLING.

index A quantitative social, economic, or political measure, often a weighted combination of a number of selected individual *indicators for the domain of interest. One example is the Federal Bureau of Investigation's uniform crime index for the USA. Many countries have some kind of retail prices index which measures the rate of inflation in consumer goods. Indexes usually employ standardization to facilitate comparisons, for example showing the initial year of the time-series as base 100, or using the national figure as base 100 for presenting sub-national figures—as illustrated by standard *mortality rates.

While these and many other simple indices are useful to sociologists interested in studying trends via *longitudinal analysis, other more complex indices are of dubious utility, including (for example) the many available indices of *deprivation and *poverty. In the first place, the technical problems of combining multiple indicators of (say) deprivation into a meaningful single index are considerable. To mention only the most obvious, indicators may be closely correlated, although reflecting quite different processes; weighting, ranking, and collapsing of indicators is inevitably contentious, since these can all be done in many different ways (involving expert opinion, *factor analysis, *cluster analysis, and so on); and, finally, the causal analysis is undermined by the ecological problems (*see* ECOLOGICAL FALLACY) inherent in the resulting index (most clearly in the attempt to explain individual behaviour by reference to aggregated, usually district-level, data). In addition, many different indices have been created to cover the degree, extent, and intensity of deprivation, so that problems of interpreting the scores are further aggravated. The problems then involved in standardizing indicators across (say) countries simply underline the technical difficulties of creating meaningful composite indices.

Moreover, the availability of a growing range of sophisticated techniques for *multivariate analysis renders these sort of composite indices increasingly obsolete. If relevant data are collected about (for example) unemployment, values, ethnicity, income, size and type of family, welfare dependency, and suchlike, from a sufficiently large sample, then the causal relationships between these characteristics can properly be treated as an empirical issue via the family of *regression and other statistical techniques for *causal modelling. The connections between structural location, behaviour, and beliefs can then be a matter for empirical investigation, and the researcher no longer needs to decide—a priori—how many of these attributes should be compounded before some putative condition of 'deprivation' is established.

Of course, politicians like to see league tables that rank local areas, hospitals, or universities in terms of a single index score purporting to reflect their relative strength or weakness because such tables seem to provide a firm basis for public spending (and one that is easily understood). Sociologically dubious indices continue, therefore, to be a prominent feature of much *policy research (see the report by UK Department of the Environment, 1991 *Deprivation Index: A Review of Approaches and a Matrix of Results*, 1995). However, whether they are good social science is quite another matter, and it is hard to see how such exercises help illuminate those causal relationships which constitute the primary interest of sociological research.

index crime The Federal Bureau of Investigation's uniform crime *index in the USA is composed of seven index crimes: murder and non-negligent manslaughter, forcible rape, robbery, aggravated assault, burglary, larceny (theft), and motor vehicle theft.

indexicality *See* ETHNOMETHODOLOGY; PEIRCE.

indicator A quantitative measure which reflects change in some aspect of the economy or of society—such as *mortality rates, measures of job segregation, or the retail price index. In the 1960s and 1970s, effort was invested in developing systems of *social indicators, to monitor and evaluate *social policy.

individualism Broadly any set of ideas emphasizing the importance of the individual and the individual's interests, the term is used to characterize a range of ideas, philosophies, and doctrines. It is, for example, employed to describe a political philosophy usually described as 'liberal individualism' that stresses the importance of the individual and the value attached to individual freedom and individual choice. This philosophy is frequently contrasted with *collectivism, where the collective rather than the individual good is paramount. Thus, the American sociologist Robert N. Bellah and his colleagues proposed the controversial thesis, owing much to Durkheim's account of *anomie and egoism, that American individualism is becoming excessive, since it is destroying the moral integrity of that society (see *Habits of the Heart*, 1985). The term is also used to characterize certain religious ideas, as in the phrase 'Protestant individualism', since Protestant churches historically have emphasized the relationship of God and individual as being one that is not mediated by the organization of the Church itself. This view has also been put forward from a different theoretical basis by Ulrich Beck and Zygmunt *Bauman. Their argument is that the growth of *reflexive modernization has undermined social bonds and exposed individuals to the anxieties involved in making their own choices.

While sociologists frequently use the term as a description of the philosophy of a particular social or political group within society, they also use it to characterize an approach to social phenomena within their discipline. So-called methodological individualism refers to the position adopted by those who argue that, in studying society, sociologists must not only (inevitably) study individuals, but also that the explanations of the social phenomena they study—phenomena such as social classes, power, the educational system, or whatever—must be formulated as, or reducible to, the characteristics of individuals. This position stands in marked contrast to 'methodological holism', the theoretical principle that each social entity (group, institution, society) has a totality that is distinct, and cannot be understood by studying merely its individual component elements. (An example would be Émile Durkheim's claim that *social facts can be studied and explained independently of the individual.)

The debate over methodological individualism reflects an underlying tension about the relation between the society and the individual. This tension is, however, now more commonly analysed in terms of *structure and *agency: discussions of methodological individualism as such are less common. *See also* LIBERALISM; SOCIAL CAPITAL.

induction (inductive) The inverse of *deduction. Induction begins from particular observations from which empirical generalizations are made. These generalizations then form the basis for *theory-building. So-called *analytic induction is common in qualitative studies within sociology. This method requires that every case examined in a piece of research substantiates a *hypothesis. The researcher formulates a general hypothesis from observation of initial cases; investigates subsequent cases in the search for a negative instance; and reformulates the hypothesis to cope with those confounding cases that are encountered. The process is deemed to be exhausted when no new discrepant cases can be found—a necessarily rather subjective judgement—and the (now revised) generalization is allowed to stand. *See also* CAUSE.

industrial action Certain sanctions available to groups of workers and employers in dispute with each other over employment conditions. A *strike is a refusal by workers to continue working, usually involving a walk-out or concerted non-attendance at the workplace. Wildcat strikes are short and begin without notice. Unofficial strikes are called without formal approval from the workers' trade union. Sit-down strikes or sit-ins differ in that strikers remain on the employer's premises. Other sanctions available to workers and their trade unions include the work-to-rule, in which an officious and punctilious observation of factory or office rules is made to inconvenience management; go-slows in which work is carried out more slowly than normal; overtime bans in which workers refuse to work more than their standard hours; and blacking in which workers refuse to work with particular products or services. Aside from disciplinary action against individuals, the main equivalent sanction available to employers is the lock-out, in which the employer either dismisses workers or prevents them from entering the workplace. Measures of industrial action are often taken to be indicators of *industrial conflict, though this is a broader and more difficult notion. Information on strikes and lock-outs, including numbers of disputes, numbers of working days lost, and numbers of workers involved, is available for many countries, though care is needed in analysis because of differing statistical definitions. Measures of other forms of industrial action are much less widely available.

industrial capitalism *See* CAPITALISM.

industrial conflict A term that refers to all expressions of dissatisfaction within the employment relationship, especially those pertaining to the employment contract, and the *effort bargain. The many different kinds of industrial conflict may be divided into two broad classes—informal and formal.

Informal industrial conflict is so labelled because it is not based on any systematic organization, results directly from a sense of grievance, and supposedly is wholly expressive in nature. Many forms of industrial sabotage that appear irrational would constitute industrial conflict in this sense, as would purely individualized and even unconscious forms of protest, including absenteeism, frequent job-changing, negligence, and even accidents at work. Industrial sociologists have also regarded spontaneous walk-outs and strikes as examples of informal industrial conflict, as well as the constant opposition to management expressed in workgroup norms regulating output, restrictive practices, secrecy, or other guarded treatment of superiors. The idea of informal industrial conflict thus draws attention to the roots of behaviour which may appear incomprehensible from the point of view of management. Used too widely, however, it loses its vigour.

Formal industrial conflict is reserved for organized expressions of conflict articulated through a *trade-union or other worker representative. Its supposed purpose is strategic or instrumental rather than (or as well as) expressive and may often involve workers who, by themselves, have no feelings or personal involvement regarding the issues at stake in the dispute. Its characteristic form is the organized *strike: that is, a withdrawal of labour such as to constitute a temporary breach of contract, using the collective strength of the workforce to avoid sanctions and achieve adjustments to pay or conditions of work. Strikes may be reinforced by other types of formal sanction such as the go-slow and work to rule. They may be confined to those directly affected or may take the form of sympathy strikes by workers in related jobs and industries. Strikes are deemed to be official if they have been called at the behest of the union leadership and in accordance with the law and with procedural *collective-bargaining agreements. The term unofficial or 'wildcat' is applied to strikes waged through unrecognized leaders such as shop stewards, or by a nonrecognized union, or in some other way which breaches established collective-bargaining laws and procedures. Obviously, there is not a clear distinction in practice between wildcat strikes and some of the more collective forms of unofficial conflict.

At one time there was much debate in industrial sociology about the term strike-proneness—epitomizing the search for structural causes of industrial conflict. Attempts were made to link patterns of strike activity with industry type, with the degree of isolation and class homogeneity of the work community, with the use of mass-production technologies, the bureaucratization of management, and the structuring of work groups. Though weak correlations have been found with some of these factors, the frequency and incidence of strikes and similar forms of unrest is so erratic that plenty of discrepant occurrences could be found. Economists have had some success linking long-term strike patterns to economic indicators but they, like other investigators in this mould, are hampered by the varying quality and scope of national and international strike statistics. The conclusions tend therefore to be pitched at a highly general level. A fundamental objection to such structural explanations is that the more overt forms of industrial conflict have to be socially organized as well as provoked. Hence, explanations of them have to bear in mind the strategic considerations perceived by workers and their leaders, as well as the meaning of *industrial action, which can (and clearly does) vary greatly between industrial relations cultures. It is said, for example, that the wearing of red hats during work is as serious an expression of dissent in the Japanese context as a protracted strike is in the British.

The theoretical and case-study literature is vast. A useful collection of studies can be found in David Metcalf and Simon Milner's *New Perspectives on Industrial Disputes* (1993). *See also* KERR-SIEGEL HYPOTHESIS; WORK, SUBJECTIVE EXPERIENCE OF.

industrial democracy An ideal in which *citizenship rights in employment are held to include partial or complete participation by the workforce in the running of an industrial or commercial organization. The term, and others associated with it, is often laden with ideological overtones. At one extreme, industrial democracy implies workers' control over industry, perhaps linked with worker ownership of the *means of production, as exemplified by producer *co-operatives. Another approach is the appointment of worker or *trade-union representatives to company boards or governing bodies. For others, industrial democracy takes the form of 'worker participation', such as *collective bargaining in which trade unions operate as a kind of permanent opposition to *managements. In this model managements are seen to propose, employees and their unions offer reactions and if necessary opposition, and negotiation subsequently leads to collective agreements more or less satisfactory to both sides. A fourth approach places less stress on power-sharing and more on consultation and communication: managers are seen as retaining all responsibility for decisions but make arrangements to consult worker representatives before changes are introduced. These and other approaches to industrial democracy which involve representative structures on the workers' side are often described as examples of indirect democracy. Where individual workers represent themselves without such intermediaries direct democracy is said to exist. An example would be an autonomous work group in a factory or office, charged with making its decisions about work organization and planning independently of higher management, but which is sufficiently small for all its members to take a personal direct part in influencing the group's decisions.

Industrial democracy challenges not only the characteristically authoritarian and bureaucratic structures of the *capitalist enterprise but also centralizing tendencies in the planned economies of *socialist regimes. Without participation, it is argued, worker *alienation will persist. Critics claim, however, that participation may be used as a manipulative device to control workers' efforts or to weaken trade-union organization and unity. Actual examples testify that the degree of power achieved by or delegated to the workforce is a crucial consideration. Sceptics argue that, even in the extensive worker self-management of the decentralized state socialism of Yugoslavia, underlying party control was retained. The alternative of worker co-operatives, notably the Mondragon experiment in Spain, has attracted much interest. In Germany, a system of *codetermination has been introduced as a result of labour-movement pressure to find a middle way between capitalism and socialism, and has influenced the labour policies of most countries in the European Community. Profit-sharing and share-ownership schemes may be regarded as examples of management-initiated systems of participation, which also include self-managed work-groups and teams, participatory leadership styles reflecting the ideas of the *Human Relations Movement, and the quality circles based on Japanese practice.

(⊕) SEE WEB LINKS
- The Mondragon co-operative in Spain.

industrial integration The tendency to link formerly separate firms, enterprises, or production processes, in order to reap economies of scale or finance. Integration may be vertical, combining separate stages in the manufacture of a finished good or provision of a service; or horizontal, combining ownership and control of activities within separate markets.

industrialism (industrialization) Both words denote the transition in methods of *production which has been responsible for the vastly increased wealth-creating capacity of modern societies compared with traditional systems. It should be noted that, although industrialization is generally thought of as something affecting the *manufacturing of goods, it is reasonable and indeed necessary to apply the term industrial to modern methods of raising *productivity in agriculture and other industrial sectors, and in administrative contexts. It is important to add that industrialism is not the same thing as *capitalism, for although capitalism was the first and principal agent of industrialization, it is not the only one. Capitalism pre-dated industrialization and arguably varies more in fundamental form over time and from society to society.

There has been a reasonable degree of agreement about typical features of industrialism but less about which ones are essential. Typical characteristics, all of which are discussed elsewhere in this dictionary, include a division of labour; cultural rationalization; a factory system and mechanization; the universal application of scientific methods to problem-solving; time discipline and deferred gratification; bureaucracy and administration by rules; and a socially and geographically mobile labour-force.

However, any such list of features is bound to raise the question whether a particular item is the result of industrialism as such, or should be attributed either to the coexistence of capitalism or the fact that capitalist societies were the first to industrialize. Much the same might be said of several other features of modernity which are variously attributed to capitalism or industrialization, including the indefinite expansion of markets, the growth of the money economy and the calculating out-look behind scientific rationalism, and the industrial spirit itself. *See also* INDUSTRIAL SECTOR; INDUSTRIAL SOCIETY.

industrial relations *See* LABOUR RELATIONS.

industrial reserve army This term derives from Karl *Marx's writing and refers to a disadvantaged section of the *proletariat. These workers perform two functions: to regulate wages by the implicit threat posed by available labour; and to supply labour for sudden expansions in production. As the reserve army decreases then wages increase—and vice versa. There has been considerable recent debate about the role of women as reserve labour. *See also* LABOUR-MARKET SEGMENTATION.

Industrial Revolution, The This term, introduced by the economic historian Arnold Toynbee, is used to refer to the period of rapid social, economic, demographic, and technological change that took place in Britain from the latter half of the 18th century to the first half of the 19th century. There is much debate and disagreement over the precise characteristics of the Industrial Revolution, but broadly speaking it defines the transformation of Britain from a predominantly rural and agrarian society to an increasingly urban one based on manufacturing and industry. Although the term always refers to Britain (usually

England), which was the first industrial nation, the phrase 'Second Industrial Revolution' is sometimes used to refer to the *industrialization of other countries, especially Germany and the USA, during the latter part of the 19th and early 20th centuries.

The most important features of the revolution in Britain were as follows: first, there was a so-called 'demographic transition' from the late 18th century, which was characterized by a decrease in mortality rates, a declining age at marriage, a marked growth in population, and an increasing rate of migration from rural to urban areas. The escalating numbers of people who came to the rapidly expanding urban areas provided much of the labour force for the new manufacturing industries, and formed the basis of a new industrial working *class.

Second, there was a revolution in transportation. In the 18th century this was effected through the construction of canals and an improved road system, while from the first half of the 19th century the invention and development of the railway system radically improved the ease and speed with which goods could be transported. This meant food could be brought more readily from rural to urban areas, thereby satisfying growing demands from the new and expanding urban centres. As industry developed, the improved transportation network also became crucial for the extraction and transportation of raw materials, and the distribution of finished industrial products.

Third, an agricultural revolution improved farming techniques, which generated both increased agricultural production and growing prosperity for the farming classes. This resulted in rising demand in the countryside for better clothing and household goods, which stimulated urban industry and distribution, and was in turn aided by improved transportation facilities. As farmers became wealthier, they increasingly adopted the ways of, and identified with, the urban middle classes, and boundaries between the two groups became even less clear through intermarriage. Farmers often provided capital for industrial enterprises, their sons frequently trained in urban-based professions, and the urban middle classes tended more and more to idealize the rural way of life, often moving into the countryside when they could.

Fourth, increasingly large investments of capital, particularly in textiles, coal mining, and metal industries, partly facilitated by the expansion and development of colonial markets and outposts, enabled the growth of powerful manufacturing industries that in turn relied on, and were strengthened by, both expanding internal markets and exports overseas. The textile industry, for instance, relied on raw material from America; finished goods were sold internally but also abroad, especially in India, where British colonial rule was able virtually to destroy the once flourishing Indian textile industry by forbidding the export of Indian textiles.

Fifth, technological inventions and developments, in particular that of steam power, were crucial to the operation of trains, ships, and the larger factories, although recent research suggests that much industrial production was on a small scale and often not mechanized until late in the 19th century.

These radical changes, deemed revolutionary because of the speed at which many of them occurred, were all interrelated, although they developed at varying rates and in very different ways according to region and area. The desire to understand and analyse such sweeping and unprecedented change provided a catalyst for early sociologists to develop a raft of theories relating to the *division of labour, *capitalism, and *bureaucracy. *Comte, *Spencer, *Marx, *Engels, and later *Durkheim and *Weber were all arguably responding to, and seeking to explain, the changes which accompanied industrialism, and altered not only the infrastructure but also the whole way of life of Britain, over an unusually short period of time.

There are long-standing controversies (mainly involving historians) about the causes and consequences of the Industrial Revolution (see, for example, R. M. Hartwell (ed.), *The Causes of the Industrial Revolution in England*, 1967). Among numerous available statements one lasting classic is E. J. Hobsbawm's *Industry and Empire* (1968). Leonore Davidoff and Catherine Hall, in *Family Fortunes* (1987), give a detailed historical account of the interrelationships between the development of capitalism, urban industrial society, class, and family structures.

industrial sector Classification of the (changing) composition of economic activities with the passage from early to late *industrialization. Rationalization and expansion of the primary sector (that part of the economy concerned with the extraction of natural resources) characteristically precedes the rapid growth of the secondary sector (that part of the economy concerned with the manufacture of goods from the raw materials supplied by primary-sector industries), which then becomes the major source of occupation and employment. Late (advanced or mature) industrialization is associated with the expansion of the tertiary sector (that part of a country's economy concerned with the provision of services). There are, however, important exceptions and qualifications to this broad pattern.

The primary economic sector therefore includes agriculture, horticulture, forestry, and fishing; the extraction of oils, minerals, and natural gas, mining and quarrying; and the water industry. These may also be referred to as primary industries. Note that the term 'primary sector' is used in a different way in *labour-market segmentation theory. Which concept is intended should be clear from the context.

The secondary economic sector is often termed the *manufacturing sector or manufacturing industries. The construction industry is sometimes included, but sometimes treated as a separate category, on the grounds that it covers repairs and other services as well as basic construction of new buildings and dwellings. Again, the concept is used with a different meaning in labour-market segmentation theory, and here too the intended meaning should be clear from the context.

The tertiary sector includes, for example, the leisure industry, financial services, education and health services, transport, and communication. Often this is called the service sector or service industries. *See also* DEINDUSTRIALIZATION; INDUSTRIALISM.

industrial society A key element in *modernity, it is important to distinguish the descriptive from the analytical uses of this term. At a descriptive level, an industrial society is simply one displaying the characteristic features of *industrialism, as listed under that heading. However, the term is also used in the abstract to denote the thesis that a definite type of society exists whose culture, institutions, and development are determined by its industrial production process. As such, theories of industrial society constitute a species of *technological determinism, or scientific evolutionism. It is claimed that the logic of applied science, or of the technical processes based on scientific expertise and values, makes necessary certain fundamental and irreversible modifications to the traditional culture and institutions of a society. This view is expressed in the writings of Claude-Henri de *Saint-Simon and by many 19th-century social theorists, including Auguste *Comte, Herbert *Spencer, and Émile *Durkheim. But the most influential example in classical sociology is to be found in Max *Weber's interpretation of the *modernization of the Western world as progressive *rationalization, and the disenchantment of the traditional magical and supernatural systems of beliefs and values which once gave meaning to human life. For Weber's critics, however, a profound metaphysical pathos—a deeply pessimistic but unsubstantiated moral philosophy—underlies his claim that *bureaucracy is inescapable in modern industrial society and politics.

The industrial society thesis assumed a much more tangible shape in the writings of post-war, mostly American, *functionalist sociologists and industrial-relations specialists. These writers claimed to be following Durkheim in arguing that the cohesion and similarity of industrial societies depended on a social consensus, in each case around the same set of organizing *values and *norms. But in talking about the contents of these norms they were influenced by Weber, and stressed the rationalistic, impersonal (or universalistic) aspects of these societies, the primacy they gave to rationalized production of material goods and services, and the emphasis they placed on *deferred gratification. Such societies, it was claimed, would tend over time to base the allocation of people to positions on their *achievements, especially their education and technical competence, rather than on traditional *ascriptive characteristics such as family connections, race, or gender. Simultaneously, mechanization and technical development would raise living standards and render many unpleasant manual jobs unnecessary, resulting in the *embourgeoisement of the manual working class. The combined effect of all these factors would be that the dichotomous class structure typical of early *capitalist industrialism would be replaced by a more divergent and less polarized system of occupational stratification. Marked class conflict in the workplace and industry would, under mature industrialism, be replaced by institutionalized industrial conflict and *collective bargaining. Political consequences would follow, for the complexity and diversity of industrial stratification implies a dispersal of power, referred to by these theorists as *pluralism. Basically, this means the demise of authoritarian political systems, and their replacement by representative non-ideological mass parties. These predictions were synthesized in the work of a group of so-called convergence theorists who claimed that, because of the alleged logic of industrialism and its technology, capitalist and communist societies alike would develop into something resembling the ideal pattern of mature pluralist industrialism described above.

Critics of this theory have noted that the general features it ascribes to mature industrialism correspond very closely to the ideal picture which Cold War propaganda had painted in the United States. However, alternative and less blatantly ideological models of mature industrialism can be developed, by revising the assumptions made about the logic of the industrialization process. Students of Japanese society, for example, noted the persistence of ascriptive elements in the industrial culture of that country, elements which appeared to be compatible with a high rate of technological advance, aided organizational functioning, and prevented industrial unrest. They argued that emergent tendencies in the labour markets, in the labour relations, and in the industrial enterprises of societies like the United States and Britain suggested that these nations might well be converging on a quasi-Japanese model of mature industrialism. The pattern of Japanese industrialism and industrial management has kept alive the search for universal and convergent trends affecting a number of highly industrialized societies in the form of theories of *post-industrialism.

The notion of an abstract type of industrial society, with causal implications for the study of contemporary social change, is open to the same objections as its celebrated rival, the theory of capitalist society. Arguably, both are over-generalized, and cover too large an expanse of time and space to be of value for rigorous analysis. Even when reduced in scope they tend to ignore the specifics of history and culture. In particular, similar technologies injected into different social and cultural meaning systems may mean that individual nations coexist as similarly industrialized states, but remain vastly different entities in most other respects. The analytical usage of industrial society considered above is also open to objection on the grounds that its pedigree as a species of *evolutionary theory implies the following: that the principal processes of social change are endogenous rather than exogenous; that the most decisive processes of social *change are economic or material, rather than cultural, political, or military in nature; and that a *society is the same thing as the nation-state. None of these statements would go unquestioned today.

The classic statement of the industrial society thesis is to be found in Clark Kerr et al., *Industrialism and Industrial Man* (1960, 1973). A useful discussion of theories of post-industrialism is Krishan Kumar's *From Post-Industrial to Post-modern Society* (1995). *See also* REFLEXIVE MODERNIZATION.

industrial sociology *See* INDUSTRY, SOCIOLOGY OF.

industry, sociology of A loosely defined, but well-established sub-special-ism within sociology, which can trace its origins back to the discipline's founders. Its expansion in the 20th century was encouraged by the hope of certain company *managements, notably in the United States, that sociological and psychological research might yield a set of management and supervisory techniques which could be used to prevent workplace conflict and raise *productivity. Though its potential applications still impinge on the subject, later practitioners fought hard to establish the area as an independent field of academic study, which (from a variety of theoretical perspectives) accepts the inevitability of a so-called pluralism of interests in industrial work situations, and concerns itself with the consequences.

A major problem for industrial sociologists is to define their central term—industry. In practice, despite some important exceptions, a great deal of research in the subject has been about factory workers and factory work situations. It is far from clear how far these findings can be generalized; or indeed, under what circumstances the label 'industrial' is appropriately applied to non-factory work. The preoccupation with factories and manufacturing also resulted for a time in a tendency to over-emphasize the causal effects of workplace factors, especially technology and production methods, on worker and management behaviour both inside and outside the plant. Even today, there is considerable research on the internal and external effects of *automation, information technology, and *flexible methods of work organization. The result has been a tendency to *technological determinism, and to the making of inferences about macroscopic change in industrial society, from findings gleaned in a few (usually large and possibly unrepresentative) industrial plants. A curious additional feature is that, because industrial sociology impinges on management education and theory, some of these over-generalizations have a self-fulfilling effect.

The explanatory emphasis on technology and methods of work organization has provided an important rationale for describing studies of non-factory work as industrial sociology. But, with the shift of research from (typically male) manual factory workers, the idea that factors within the workplace have an identifiable and independent causal influence on people's actions has been questioned. An important example is provided by research on white-collar workers. Clerks, technicians, and other white-collar workers have formed a growing proportion of employees in modern societies, as a result of the growth in company size, the expansion of public and financial administration, and the general increase in professional and service employment. However, it is clear that the attitude and behaviour of such workers towards (say) management or *trade unionism, as well as the values with which they view their *employment, are very different from those of their blue-collar counterparts, and are consonant with a higher class and status situation. A considerable body of literature attempted to explain these differences, and hence to say something about the dynamics of social *stratification, by reference to workplace factors. These factors included the more personal dealings white-collar workers have with management, their greater personal autonomy, and the better remuneration and promotion prospects they were said to enjoy. It was also claimed that, as the many offices and white-collar workplaces became larger, more impersonal, and more automated, so the workers were becoming more like factory workers both in their objective work situation and in their subjective response to it. Recent research has revealed a more complicated picture from which the following findings have clearly emerged: social background and self-selection may be as important as workplace variables in shaping the characteristic attitudes and industrial relations of white-collar workers; technological change in offices was accompanied by major readjustments in the external labour market for white-collar workers, which made it difficult or even unnecessary to separate out 'in-house' causal influences from external ones; not the least important of the labour-market changes was a shift to the employment of women, especially part-timers returning after a period spent at home. Thus, under the pressure of engaging with non-factory research agendas, the traditional approach of the industrial sociologist to this important topic tended to collapse into other well-established sub-specialisms: the sociology of *class and *status cultures, of *labour-market structures, and of *gender.

In recent years, the need for industrial sociologists to begin their inquiries outside the factory gates has been emphasized by a disparate range of studies which suggest that the effect of technology, work organization, and other workplace variables, is itself culturally and socially specific. For example, comparative surveys have examined factories with identical technologies, in different national and cultural milieux. The findings show that it is these factors (especially politics and the industrial relations system) rather than technology or organization, which exert the primary influence on behaviour, even within the plants themselves. Other comparative research has suggested that labour-management practices, job structures, training, skills, and supervision are all profoundly affected by the complex of political, legal, and educational regulation in a society, even to the extent of shaping overall national economic performance. Again, industrial sociology as such tends to be absorbed, this time into historical and comparative research on patterns of industrial culture.

Arguably, then, industrial sociology is a rather old-fashioned term. Nevertheless, courses and texts on the subject, especially in conjunction with management or trade-union education, continue to offer a welcome and interesting introduction to the sociological perspective for many who might otherwise not encounter it. Conventionally, such courses treat areas which these days, for reasons given above, and because of the expansion of the literature, have tended to become subspecialisms in their own right, and for which separate entries will be found in this dictionary. Keith Grint, *The Sociology of Work* (1991) and John Eldridge et al., *Industrial Sociology and Economic Crisis* (1991) are among the textbooks which still attempt to cover the field as a whole. *See also* ECONOMIC SOCIOLOGY; HUMAN RELATIONS THEORY; INDUSTRIAL CONFLICT; INDUSTRIAL DEMOCRACY; REGULATION THEORY; SCIENTIFIC MANAGEMENT; SOCIOLOGIE DU TRAVAIL; WORK, SUBJECTIVE EXPERIENCE OF.

inequality (social inequality) Unequal rewards or opportunities for different individuals within a group or groups within a society. If equality is judged in terms of legal equality, equality of opportunity, or equality of outcome, then inequality is a constant feature of the human condition. Addressing the question whether it is also a necessary feature of modern societies brings to the fore a number of longstanding debates between *liberals, *Marxists, *functionalists, and others.

According to liberals such as Friedrich *Hayek, inequality is the price to be paid for the dynamic *economic growth that is characteristic of *capitalism. The societies of *real socialism (the then actually existing communist states of the Soviet Bloc), committed as they were to the *historicism of the class struggle, sought to ameliorate if not abolish these inequalities, but in fact merely generated novel forms of their own, which were in turn less productive of economic growth and social *welfare, and subsequently collapsed under the weight of social discontent. However, the arguments propounded by functionalists provide a rationale for inequality, but not (as is sometimes claimed) a proof of its universality and inevitability. In fact, many of the functionalist tenets may now have to face up to a form of *egalitarianism which is no longer hampered by the odium of its communistic connotations. It will not be unstated competition between socio-economic systems that defines the agenda as regards inequality, but rather an investigation of which inequalities are justifiable on their own terms, rather than in comparison to some utopian-based alternative. The realities of social-class-determined inequalities of educational achievement, *morbidity and *mortality rates, and more generally of *social mobility, will have to confront the growing problems of the *underclass, of generational inequalities, and inequalities produced by the *globalization of capitalism, all of which will be seen as part of the social consequences of the 'peace dividend'. As societies in the post-Cold-War era come to be graded along the criteria of the political democratic audit, so also will the 'quality of life' scale be applied both internally and externally, and the extent and nature of inequality will be scrutinized.

Currently, the existence of inequality, its causes and consequences, particularly as they relate to social *class, *gender, *ethnicity, and locality, continues to occupy the sociological foreground. The implications of inequality for well-being are interestingly discussed in Richard Wilkinson and Kate Pickett's *The Spirit Level: Why Equality is Better for Everyone* (2010). *See also* FUNCTIONAL THEORY OF STRATIFICATION; INCOME DISTRIBUTION; JUSTICE, SOCIAL; POWER; STRATIFICATION.

infancy (infant development) Derived from the Latin word *infans*, meaning 'unable to speak', infancy is the earliest period in the human life-span, usually taken to extend from birth through to the end of the first year. In demography, for example, infant *mortality rates measure the deaths during the first year following birth. Similarly in psychology, infancy commonly refers to the first year of life, although the term is sometimes used more loosely to cover the first two or three years of life. In law, infancy as a legal status is typically more extensive, as the young child is usually deemed legally incapable of speaking long after language skills have developed.

Apart from their interest in infant mortality rates, sociologists rarely give much attention to infancy and usually do not treat it as a distinctive period in the *life-cycle, subsuming it within the period of *childhood. However, there is some sociological interest in psychological research on infant and child development, particularly because of its relevance to controversies about the relative importance of nature and nurture in explaining human behaviour.

Psychologists commonly regard the period of infancy as crucial to individual development and hence to adult behaviour. Sigmund *Freud, emphasizing both innate tendencies and social and psychological experience, viewed the first five years of life as determining the individual's subsequent personality and emotional development, and regarded the experiences of the first year as essential to satisfactory ego development—ideas developed more fully by psychoanalytic theorists such as Melanie *Klein. Other writers have focused on cognitive development. Jean *Piaget's specification of stages of cognitive development, based on his detailed observations, has been especially influential. Recent research on infancy increasingly suggests that infants have considerable cognitive capacities—capacities which selectively regulate their experiences of the *environment. *See also* MATERNAL DEPRIVATION; NATURE VERSUS NURTURE DEBATE.

infant mortality rate *See* MORTALITY RATE.

inflation A rise in the general level of prices in an economy which, if it continues, must bring about an increase in the money supply. Economists have offered a number of different explanations for inflation, and though it is generally accepted that excess aggregate demand is typically responsible ('too much money chasing too few goods'), there is no accepted version of how this situation is created in the first place. A major axis of debate is about whether inflation is demand-led or induced by rising costs. Among the factors said to contribute to the latter are excess money-wage increases, administered price increases, import cost rises, rigidity in the distribution of investment and resources between industrial sectors, and inflationary expectations. What does seem clear is that, although inflation does not affect the real value of average living standards, it tends to redistribute real living standards among groups in an arbitrary way according to their ability to adjust the money value of their incomes to the general rise in the price-level. This engenders social tensions and conflict and these consequences have also attracted the interest of sociologists.

Though early sociological studies of inflation claimed to be addressing unexamined residual categories in economic theory, most later accounts sought not to displace, but rather to supplement the work of economists. The inflation-causing factors emphasized as the basis of difference between inflation-prone and price-stable industrial cultures may be classed as normative and structural. The normative argument, clearly influenced by Emile *Durkheim's concept of egoism, is that in a *market society, inequalities in income are not governed by some moral standard of a fair day's work for a fair day's pay. They reflect, instead, arbitrary variations in the market power of both individuals and organized groups. The extent to which resentment is engendered will depend on the degree to which there is a general acceptance of *individualism and competitiveness as values in themselves. Resentment, in turn, sets off leap-frogging attempts by groups to advance their relative standing.

However, the effect of normative causes will be mediated by various structural factors, notably the extent to which the differential ability of groups to enhance their incomes is stabilized or regulated by law and institutional controls that promote *trust between groups; the productive capacity of the economy, especially the degree to which claims are pursued against a surplus that is growing rapidly, or is fixed or increasing only slowly; and whether gains in profitability are reinvested in income-earning industrial capacity or siphoned off into financial speculation whose returns are not enjoyed by the workforce at large.

The best summary of the sociological literature on inflation is Michael Gilbert's *Inflation and Social Conflict* (1986).

informal care Care given to dependent persons, such as the sick and elderly, outside the framework of organized, paid, professional work. Attention to the importance of informal care has increased with the adoption of *community care policies which place increasing reliance on care provided by family, relatives, and friends, often women.

informal economy As used by sociologists, the term refers to non-market work, in some cases with the addition of *black economy work (which is market work strictly defined). Economists are more likely to use the term as an alternative label for the hidden, underground, or black economy which is imperfectly measured within the *Gross National Product. These incompatible uses are the source of many misunderstandings and confusion in debates, particularly in non-disciplinary, interdisciplinary, or policy contexts.

There is a great variety of non-market work encompassed by the sociological term informal economy: unpaid *domestic work, consumption work, non-market productive labour, community service work, producing goods and services that are bartered or offered as *gifts within extended families or communities, non-legal commerce (in drugs for example), and work on which income tax may not be paid in full (a matter for speculation more often than factual knowledge). Some writers even include market work that is home-based, and thus seems to them to be linked more to household activities, than to the abstract concept of paid employment. The only thing these activities have in common is that they are not covered at all, or only partially, by *official statistics on *employment. Sociologists often assume that this reveals a failure or inadequacy of the statistics in question; in fact the exclusions are in most cases intentional, and derive from the fact that *labour-market statistics are constructed within an economic theoretical framework, rather than a sociological framework.

Economists have always been aware that the total volume of productive work and consumption work are greater than that measured by official statistics of employment and Gross National Product. They reserve the term 'black economy' for that portion which should be included but may not be fully reported due to tax evasion. The term 'marginal' work or workers is reserved for those people (usually women, and numbering millions in Britain and some other countries) who have very small earnings from employment and are thus, perfectly legitimately, excluded from income tax and social insurance systems, and from related statistics. But in industrial societies, by far the largest volume of work excluded from definitions of employment and GNP consists of consumption work. In *Economics and the Public Purpose* (1973), the economist John Kenneth Galbraith pointed out that the conversion of women into a crypto-servant class was essential for the development and continued growth of the modern economy: the limits on consumption are severe unless the work can be delegated; the conversion of women from productive work in pre-industrial societies to the role of housewives who administer household consumption, opens up the possibility of indefinitely increasing consumption in market economies, and also contributes to the continuous expansion of service industries. The servant role of women is thus seen as critical for the continuing expansion of consumption in the modern economy.

In the 1980s social scientists became interested in the many types of work excluded from official statistics of employment, and attempted (with partial success) to classify and measure them. Few sociologists fully understand the concepts and operational definitions underlying employment statistics, and operational definitions differ between countries, leading to confusion over boundaries and overlapping definitions between types of informal non-market work and paid employment. For example, if one distinguishes between domestic production work, leisure activities, and domestic consumption work in the *household work strategy, the close relationship between participation in the market economy and non-market work becomes clear.

informal-sector theories This is the dominant paradigm in use for explaining *poverty and *inequality in *Third World cities. There have been many versions since its first formulation in 1971, but most focus on differences in *productivity and earnings associated with large- and small-scale enterprises. Employment in large-scale (formal) enterprises is associated with high wages, high skill levels, modern technology, unionization, and social security protection, while small-scale (informal) enterprises lack these characteristics. The term 'formal' is often taken to mean waged and salaried labour, while 'informal' refers to self-employment, one-person enterprises, artisanal production, and domestic service. Note, however, that in this literature both terms refer to paid, officially registered employment, although in advanced industrial societies 'informal' work has been taken to mean work that is not declared to official censors or the tax system, and may even include unpaid labour in the household. *See also* INFORMAL ECONOMY; LABOUR-MARKET SEGMENTATION.

informal social controls *See* SANCTION.

informant *See* RESPONDENT.

information society A concept that responds to the expansion and ubiquity of information. The term has been in use since the 1970s, but has gained in popularity and is now widely used in social and political policy. Sustained and accelerated growth of media, of education provision and participation, as well as computer communications technologies has led many to posit that the attendant information explosion distinguishes a new epoch. The information society is one in which information is the defining feature, unlike the industrial society where steam power and fossil fuels were distinguishing elements.

While the term is used frequently, it is imprecise on inspection. There are six analytically separate definitional criteria used by commentators on the information society.

1. *Technological.* The most common definition is to highlight an increase in information and communications technologies (ICTs) as signalling the emergence of an information society. It is suggested, often implicitly, that ICTs both define and create the information society. Technological measures appear robust, but on examination they are vague (e.g. they range from photocopiers to PCs, the Internet to video games, to digitalization in general).

2. *Economic.* This suggests that the information society is one in which the contribution of information businesses and trades (e.g. publishing, entertainment, consultancies) has expanded over time to now outweigh manufacture and agriculture in terms of contribution to Gross National Product. Generally such analysts adopt the term information economy to describe a situation in which information industries command the major proportion of GNP.

3. *Occupational.* This approach is most closely associated with Daniel Bell's theory of post-industrialism. Bell's book *The Coming of Post-Industrial Society* (1973) delineates an information society as one in which most jobs are informational. Thus occupations such as researchers, lawyers, counsellors, and teachers are information intensive, involving information production, analysis, and communication, and the outcome is a changed condition rather than an object. This is in contrast with industrial society jobs such as machine operation and mining where the product is a physical good and the labour is largely manual.

4. *Spatial.* Here the stress is on networks along which information flows. Information networks have profound effects on the organization of time and space, as well as on other relations, allowing real-time communication on a planetary scale. Manuel Castells's (1942–) trilogy *The Information Age* (1996-8) is the major statement of this position. It is synonymous with what he terms a network society. The metaphor of *mobilities* along *scapes* (e.g. roads, rail, telecommunications systems which enable movements) may be thought central to information societies (see John Urry, *Sociology Beyond Societies*, 2000).

5. *Cultural.* This approach is one which stresses the growth of symbols and signs over recent decades, an information society being one in which there is pervasive television, advertising, a plethora of lifestyles, multiple ethnicities, many hybridized musical expressions, the world wide web, and so on. It is associated closely with Cultural Studies and interest in *postmodernism.

6. *Theory.* This suggests that an information society is one in which theoretical information/knowledge (that which is abstract, generalizable, and codified in texts) takes precedence over the practical and is constitutive of virtually everything that is done. This is contrasted with previous societies in which practical exigencies, know-how, and custom predominated. A useful overview of debates is Frank Webster's *Theories of the Information Society* (3rd edition, 2006). *See also* CYBERSOCIETY; INTERNET.

information technology (IT) *See* CYBERSOCIETY.

in-group *See* OUT-GROUP.

initiation (initiation rites) *Rituals associated with the passage from *child-hood to adulthood, from one *age-set to another, or the entry into membership of secret societies. Aspects of initiation influenced van Gennep's study of *rites of passage. Rituals for the change of status from childhood to adulthood often involve physical change such as circumcision. In other ways the initiate has to undergo pain and humiliation. Rites associated with girls and women often affirm male control of reproductive powers.

inner city *See* ZONE OF (OR IN) TRANSITION.

inner-directedness *See* OTHER-DIRECTEDNESS.

instincts Species-characteristic patterns of behaviour considered innate and predetermined rather than learned—a product of nature not nurture. What human behaviour, if any, is deemed instinctive varies between authors. Sigmund *Freud's formulation of two primary instincts (drives)—life and death (Eros and Thanatos)—is well known. Sociologists tend to emphasize social learning, and either eschew the concept or see it as a more plastic and flexible biological tendency. A classic source is Ronald Fletcher *Instinct in Man* (1957). *See also* NATURE VERSUS NURTURE DEBATE; SOCIOBIOLOGY.

institution (social institution) The use of the term institution in sociology, meaning established aspects of society, is close to that in common English usage. However, there have been some changes over time in the exact conceptualization of the term, and there are differences in the analytical precision with which it is used.

In some ways an institution can be seen as a sort of 'super-custom', a set of *mores, *folkways, and patterns of behaviour that deals with major social inter-ests: law, church, and family for example. Thus, a social institution is a cluster of specialized normative expectations and consists of all the *structural components of a *society through which the main concerns and activities are organized, and social needs (such as those for order, belief, and reproduction) are met. This was certainly the sense in which the term was used by Herbert *Spencer and Talcott *Parsons, for both of whom it was central to the notion of society as an organism or functioning system. However, as the functionalist perspective gave way to ideas based on society as being in a state of flux, with less consensus over values, so the strong Parsonian association between institution and *function also with-ered away.

The current concept of institution is more fluid, seeing kinship or religion, for instance, as comprising changing patterns of behaviour based on relatively more stable *value systems. This allows sociologists to consider the moral ambivalence of human behaviour as well as its creative effects on social *change.

The term is often used to refer to a group or organization, as in Erving *Goff-man's studies of the mental hospital as a *total institution (see *Asylums*, 1961).

However, an institution is strictly the underlying normative pattern in terms of which a group is organized, rather than the group itself. This may be confusing, but the dual usage is probably too deeply entrenched to alter. The meaning will usually be clear from the context. *See also* SOCIAL STRUCTURE.

institutionalism *See* INSTITUTIONALIZATION.

institutionalization A term used in two distinct senses. In its first sense it refers to the building and embedding of an *institution. In its second sense it describes the adverse psychological effects on individuals of residence in long-stay organizations such as mental hospitals and prisons. The most frequently mentioned effects of the latter are dependency, passivity, and lethargy, though their precise causes are debated. These effects are sometimes termed institutionalism.

institutionalization of (class) conflict The thesis that, in the advanced *capitalist societies, *class conflict has been institutionalized; that is, has become regulated or controlled, and has therefore declined. This is said to result from the separation of political and industrial conflict (so that disputes in one sphere no longer reinforce lines of schism in the other) and by the extension of *citizenship rights and greater equality of opportunity. Liberal political theorists often advanced this argument during the 1950s and 1960s. A good sociological example is Ralf Dahrendorf's *Conflict after Class* (1967). *See also* INCORPORATION.

institutionalized discrimination A long tradition of studies in sociology has shown that *discrimination against some groups in society can result from the majority simply adhering unthinkingly to the existing organizational and institutional rules or social *norms. *Prejudice, *stereotyping, and covert or overt hostility need not be factors in the exploitation of one group by another, or in the unfair distribution of rewards. Institutionalized *sexism and *institutional racism are the most common manifestations of this phenomenon. *See also* UNINTENDED OR UNANTICIPATED CONSEQUENCES.

institutional racism In a remarkable episode in the history of ideas the concept of 'institutional racism' emerged in the context of radical political struggle and the Black Power movement in the United States in the 1960s and then traversed three decades, two continents, and the social class structure to be adopted by a member of the British nobility. In 1999, Lord Macpherson of Cluny concluded, in his inquiry report on the racist murder of Stephen Lawrence in South London in 1993, that London's Metropolitan Police Service was guilty of 'institutional racism'. However, the concept of 'institutional racism' used in the Macpherson report was far removed from its origins, and across the decades it has been afflicted with analytic ambiguity.

Early conceptualization focused upon the structural relationship between Black and White Americans in the United States, and specifically the material inequality between the two groups. At its core, the early formulation described the exclusion of Black people from 'equal participation in the society's institutions' (Robert Blauner, *Racial Oppression in America*, 1972). The concept extended further than this, however, to refer to a pattern of subordination of Blacks by

Whites at the societal level that was the outcome of the interaction of a number of social institutions, such as systems of education, policing, and the labour market.

This focus on structural inequality and outcomes was shared by the many early analyses of institutional racism. David Wellman's analysis presented in his book *Portraits of White Racism* (1977), for instance, can be distinguished by the emphasis given to group conflicts between Whites and Blacks that maintain structural inequality. Wellman's view was that racism is: 'a structural relationship based on the subordination of one racial group by another. Given this perspective, the determining feature of race relations is not prejudice toward blacks, but rather the superior position of whites and the institutions—ideological as well as structural which maintain it.' The emphasis given to exclusionary processes that do not have any racial motive was strongly echoed over twenty years later in the Macpherson Inquiry's notion of institutional racism as consisting of: 'the collective failure of an organisation to provide an appropriate and professional service to people because of their colour, culture or ethnic origin. It can be seen or detected in processes, attitudes and behaviour which amount to discrimination through unwitting prejudice, ignorance, thoughtlessness, and racist stereotyping which disadvantage minority ethnic people.' The juxtaposition of 'unwitting prejudice, ignorance, thoughtlessness' alongside 'racist stereotyping', however, is emblematic of what some critics regard as one of the significant analytical weaknesses of conceptualizations of institutional racism: a lack of clarity about the connection between intention and outcome in relation to the production of 'racial' inequality. This is a serious limitation as the presence or absence of a connection clearly has implications for strategies of policy intervention. There appears to have been no consensus, however, about the relationship between intention and outcome in the early literature. For instance, Carmichael and Hamilton—two of the earliest exponents of the concept of 'institutional racism'—appeared to draw a very close connection between motive and action when they argued that: 'Institutional racism relies on the active and pervasive operation of anti-black attitudes and practices. A sense of superior group position prevails: whites are "better" than blacks; therefore blacks should be subordinated to whites. This is a racist attitude and it permeates the society, on both the individual and institutional level, covertly and overtly.' (*Black Power: the Politics of Liberation in America*, 1967).

In contrast, Robert Blauner appears to have placed far less significance on the link between intent and action, as he argued that institutional racism 'arises out of indirect processes and from actions that are usually non-intentional, in contrast to "individual" racism, which tends to be more direct and volitional'. David Wellman went further still by proposing that any activity or process—irrespective of intentionality—which preserves or inhibits challenges to the racial status quo could be conceptualized as racism.

Another enduring ambiguity affecting conceptualization of 'institutional racism' concerns the use and meaning of the term 'institution'. In the early literature examples of 'institutional racism' have on one hand involved processes operating at the societal level, and on the other hand they have also been reduced to the attitudes and activities of individuals. The confusion generated by such ambiguity was notable in Lord Scarman's observation in his report on the 1981 Brixton disorders that: 'It was alleged by some of those who made representations to me that Britain is an institutionally racist society. If, by that is meant that it is a society which knowingly, as a matter of policy, discriminates against black people, I reject the allegation. If, however, the suggestion being made is that practices may be adopted by public bodies as well as private individuals which are unwittingly discriminatory against black people, then this is an allegation which deserves serious consideration, and, where proved, swift remedy' (*The Brixton Disorders*, Cmnd. 8427, 1981).

Clearly if the concept of 'institutional racism' is interpreted as signifying an apartheid-like social system of explicit racial discrimination pursued by a state and its agents, it is so extreme that it will be readily rejected by critics. However, when 'institutional racism' is used to conceptualize the production of racial inequality through the norms, values, culture, and normal practices of an organization, then collective culpability is far easier to swallow, as evidenced by the confessions of guilt made by police forces following the Macpherson inquiry.

(⊕) SEE WEB LINKS
- The Macpherson report on the murder of Stephen Lawrence: a report that popularized the term 'institutional racism'.

institution, total *See* TOTAL INSTITUTION.

instrumental collectivism *See* IMAGES OF SOCIETY.

instrumentalism *See* WORK, SUBJECTIVE EXPERIENCE OF.

integration, industrial *See* INDUSTRIAL INTEGRATION.

integration (social) In *functionalist theory, the term integration is fundamental, and describes 'a mode of relation of the units of a system by virtue of which, on one hand, they act so as collectively to avoid disrupting the system and making it impossible to maintain its stability, and, on the other hand, to "cooperate" to promote its functioning as a unity' (Talcott *Parsons, *Essays in Sociological Theory*, 1954). For other writers, the focus tends to be on the integration and cooperation of groups and individuals rather than the integration of *institutions. David *Lockwood has distinguished social integration, in the narrow sense of the integration of individuals, from system integration. *See also* EQUILIBRIUM; SYSTEM INTEGRATION AND SOCIAL INTEGRATION.

intellectuals In modern societies intellectuals do not form a clearly defined group. Traditionally, the intellectual's role has been that of the thinker and truth-seeker. In simple societies they might be priests or *shamans. In Europe, from the Renaissance to the 19th century, they were the creators of high culture, the philosophers, and the scientific innovators of their times. Brilliant groups of intellectuals like those who joined Diderot in the production of the great French Encyclopaedia (1751–75)—d'Alembert, Montesquieu, Voltaire, Rousseau, and others—literally changed history by introducing new ideas and new knowledge into their tradition-bound societies.

Intellectual life flourished under two conditions: the relative independence of intellectuals themselves, and the unique position they held in societies that were largely illiterate. *Democracy, mass literacy, and *bureaucratization have all tended to undermine the role of the independent intellectual. In fact, intellectuals have become increasingly unpopular. Richard Hofstadter, in *Anti-Intellectualism in American Life* (1962), explored the mistrust of intellectual talents in a practical, materialistic society. More recent critics like Paul Johnson (*Intellectuals*, 1988) and Steve Kimball (*Tenured Radicals*, 1988) dismiss intellectuals as unrealistic and even dangerous dreamers.

The heirs to the intellectual tradition work mainly in large organizations—usually universities—which are not hospitable to new or challenging ideas. Academics are by necessity careerists first and intellectuals second. Russell Jacoby's book *The Last Intellectuals* (1987) portrays the decline of independent intellectuals in the 20th century, and their absorption into the bureaucratic, salaried world of government institutions.

Others have suggested a whole new role for intellectuals in *post-industrial society. Daniel Bell in *The Coming of Post-Industrial Society* (1964) and Alvin Gouldner in *The New Class and the Future of Intellectuals* (1981) have argued that the 'knowledge society' of the future will give intellectuals a central and honoured status.

Intellectual life continues to flourish on the margins of society, in the play of ideas in serious journals and books, films, videos, and computer networks. The true intellectual is not so much performing a role as expressing a particular personality, and those qualities will find an outlet under any social conditions. As Albert Camus put it, 'An intellectual is a person whose mind watches itself.'

intelligence (intelligence testing) A well-trampled arena of combat between the advocates of the supremacy of nature and nurture, intelligence is commonly thought of as synonymous with the Intelligence Quotient (IQ), devised originally by Alfred Binet in early 20th-century France, for the purpose of identifying schoolchildren in need of remedial attention. IQ tests were subsequently developed in the United States into a measure designed to provide a unitary indicator of an individual's innate intelligence. They are standardized around an average of 100 and are calculated separately for men and women.

Many advocates of IQ testing assume that the usual battery of IQ tests combine to produce a measure of intelligence which is genetically transmitted and consequently immutable. Critics argue that the tests were not originally intended to provide a fixed measure of intelligence, unamenable to improvement, and that the assumption that a unitary measure can be provided at all is an unjustifiable reification of a culture-bound concept. Much effort and energy has been invested in this debate, but no convincing conclusions have been evinced in either direction, and estimates of the heritability of IQ still range between zero and 80 per cent.

There have also been well-publicized accusations that one of the most influential contributors to the debate in the middle years of the century, Sir Cyril Burt, fabricated his results to make it appear that the heritable component accounted for the vast majority (around 80 per cent) of variability in IQ scores. Protagonists include Hans Eysenck, a psychologist who maintains a belief in a high heritable component for IQ, and Leon Kamin, a human geneticist who argues that the debate is unlikely ever to be conclusive, and in any case is misconceived for the reasons given above (see Eysenck and Kamin, *Intelligence: The Battle for the Mind*, 1981). In one analysis which provoked fierce controversy, Arthur R. Jensen ('How Much Can We Boost IQ and Educational Achievement?', *Harvard Educational Review*, 1969) argued that intelligence is largely explained by genetic factors, and that the poverty of American Blacks was not sufficient to explain away the differences in their test performances in relation to Whites. Critics argued that Jensen's data were unsound and the implications of his study unwarranted.

More recently, the relationship between IQ and social class has also become a focus for renewed academic discussion, after being many years in abeyance.

Similarly, Richard Herrnstein and Charles Murray's controversial account of the relationship between intelligence and both class and race in America (*The Bell Curve*, 1994) argues that IQ is a good indicator of natural ability, and appears to be a largely inherited trait. Here too, sceptics have replied by assembling no little evidence which casts doubt on both of these propositions, and have concluded that educational attainment and IQ scores are both products, not only of putatively natural or genetic origins, but also of socially determined influences. Most obviously, the results of intelligence tests are (at least in part) a reflection of attributes such as miscellaneous information picked up at home and on television, and of the inclination (mainly instilled by school teaching) to try harder at this particular task than at any other. In other words, test results are partly a function of socialization, substantial aspects of which are already influenced by existing inequalities in the distribution of resources between different classes and ethnic groups. The argument here is that, as John Miner (*Intelligence in the United States*, 1957) long ago observed, 'no test item that has ever been devised taps native potential directly, independent of the past life and learning of the respondent'. The most sustained of the many critiques of Herrnstein and Murray's study will be found in Claude S. Fischer et al., *Inequality by Design* (1996), which argues that social inequalities depend more on social circumstances and the structure of society than they do on IQ, which is itself a social product. In particular, social policies set the 'rules of the game' within which individual abilities and effort matter, and it is these that perpetuate the differences between rich and poor. *See also* DARWINISM; EUGENICS; HEREDITY.

intelligentsia Nowadays this term is loosely applied to any educated stratum of society—normally including *intellectuals and *managers—which has an interest in ideas. Historically, the use of the term has been more restricted, and although its origins are contested they are usually sought in early 19th-century Russian and Polish usage. However, as a social category it differed in the two countries, for obvious historical reasons.

Formed from the déclassé elements of major estates in 19th-century Russia, the intelligentsia were at first marginally located, between Tsarist *autocracy and the *peasant masses. Their procedures of inclusion (*see* CLOSURE) nevertheless borrowed from *gentry manners, and later added the imprimatur of educational qualifications, which were superseding military and other credentials. Both attributes tended to cut the stratum off from the bulk of society, towards which they none the less felt they had a mission of responsibility. In the Polish case, it was the maintenance of the national spirit, its *intelligens* or self-consciousness, during the century of partition where Polish nationhood survived with only a rump state to bolster it, that explains the emergence of this group.

In the absence of an indigenous *bourgeoisie in Eastern Europe, and given the role of the state and foreign capital, there emerged complex intelligentsia ethos: of *nationalism coupled with a Western orientation, anti-industrialism and emphasis upon cultural and *humanistic values, criticism of the state, adherence to the gentry style of life, and criteria of good breeding demanded of the intelligentsia proper. These represented, in the words of one commentator, the 'universal concomitant of the confrontation of a traditional society with a modern West'. After the advent of *communism it was easy to see how, as some commentators have observed, the intelligentsia in its anti-bourgeois, anti-capitalist ethos was compatible with Marxism. However, in the dominated countries of the Soviet bloc, that other feature of the intelligentsia—its sense of mission as a vehicle of national values—served to undermine the communist order.

It is a moot question whether, with the advent of market economies, capitalism will finally transform parts of the intelligentsia into its Western equivalent; namely, a loose category of intellectuals, rather than a solid social stratum. In the West, some critics have argued that the modern salariat or *service class, if it tends to closure through self-recruitment and various forms of *credentialism, could create a Western intelligentsia, distinguished—by its style of life, sense of status honour, and patterns of intermarriage—from the mass of *post-industrial, late-capitalist society.

interaction (social) *See* ACTION THEORY; CYBERSOCIETY; DRAMATURGY; FORMALISM; NEGOTIATED ORDER; SYSTEM INTEGRATION AND SOCIAL INTEGRATION; SYMBOLIC INTERACTIONISM.

interactionism (interactionist perspective) *See* SEQUENCE ANALYSIS; SYMBOLIC INTERACTIONISM.

interest groups A valuable element of *democracy is the ability and willingness of citizens to organize on their own behalf, and to seek to influence legislatures, government agencies, and *public opinion. Citizens so organized are often termed interest groups (a label which can also be synonymous with the terms *pressure group, lobby, party, political action committee, and *social movement).

Interest groups are voluntary associations with specific and narrowly defined goals, which may be moderate or radical, local or international in scope. Professional and trade associations work as interest groups, as do activist groups like the ecology movement. Interest groups may represent one segment of the public (such as pensioners or students), or they may represent a value (for example anti-abortion), at which point they shade into ideological or *moral crusades.

From the democratic point of view, the limitation of interest groups is that they tend to represent mainly the wealthier and better-educated sections of the public, leaving the poor and minorities largely unrepresented. In Washington DC, for example, some 11000 interest-group organizations compete for the attention of 535 legislators. Almost all these organizations represent business, financial, and professional interests.

interests In everyday speech the word interests has three main interrelated meanings. Someone may be said to be interested in a topic, in the sense that it excites his or her attention, or curiosity. The usage has had little specialist significance in the social sciences. In its second usage, interests may be used as a synonym for property, or investments. This usage is closely related to a more pervasive usage, according to which interests include whatever contributes to the general well-being, or fulfilment of the purposes of some individual. These latter usages have been very influential in philosophy and the social sciences.

Thomas *Hobbes's political philosophy is founded upon a *materialist view of human nature according to which self-preservation is the underlying motivation of all action. This self-interest view of human motivation was also widely assumed in the discipline of *political economy. It was challenged by David *Hume, Adam *Ferguson, and others on several grounds. Humans were by nature social, so that no clear distinction could be made between self-interest and the interests of others. Ferguson particularly criticizes the association of interests with economic wealth and material possessions, arguing that virtues such as courage, honesty, and loyalty are much more highly valued attributes of the self, and so should take pride of place in any adequate account of interests.

Ferguson notwithstanding, the materialist tradition of conceptualizing interests primarily in relation to material wealth or political power and dissociating them from the sphere of values and principles has persisted, both in common-sense usage and in social and political science. However, a significant shift which took place in the 19th century, especially in the context of the *historical materialism of Marx and Engels, was the attribution of interests to hypothetical collective actors—social classes and fractions. This practice has subsequently been generalized in such fields as industrial sociology, political sociology, and the sociology of the professions, so as to apply to any group with identifiable common economic or social advantages to protect, or disadvantages to overcome.

The great utility of the concept of interests is its apparent ability to link analysis of the objective conditions of life of individuals or groups with their patterns of belief and action. It remains, however, a matter of dispute whether interests can justifiably be attributed to an individual or group without prior knowledge of their beliefs and intentions. If this cannot be done, then much of the apparent power of explanations in terms of interests dissolves into vacuity. Most sociologists would also argue that an individual's sense of social *identity must precede his or her conception of self-interest—and for this reason interests can only be defined subjectively rather than (as some, especially certain Marxists, have claimed) objectively. *See also* CLASS INTEREST.

intergenerational mobility *See* MOBILITY, SOCIAL.

interlocking directorship An interlocking directorship (or interlock) is created when an individual who sits on the board of directors of one business organization takes a board seat with another. Interlocks are seen as possible bases of corporate control and coordination and as indicators of economic *power. US writers often use the term 'interlocking directorate' to refer to an interlock, though the term should strictly be used to refer to the whole system of interlocks rather than to individual interlocking directorships.

An extensive literature on the causes and consequences of corporate interlocks has developed since early studies in the 1960s. Some investigators suggest that within-industry interlocks are established in order to restrict competition in the *market. Others propose that interlocks between financial institutions and business corporations perform a monitoring function by which the former control the profitability of their investments. Critics argue that the quantitative indicators used by most researchers fail to capture the complexity and dynamics of boardroom and inter-firm relations. For this reason it has proved difficult to establish convincing causal links between the structure of interlocking directorates and corporate behaviour in the market (see Mark Mizruchi, 'What do Interlocks Do? An Analysis, Critique, and Assessment of Research on Interlocking Directorates', *Annual Review of Sociology*, 1996). *See also* OWNERSHIP AND CONTROL.

( ) SEE WEB LINKS
- A review of research by Mark Mizruchi, in *Annual Review of Sociology*. (Subscription)

intermediate technology *See* APPROPRIATE TECHNOLOGIES.

internal labour market *See* LABOUR MARKET; LABOUR-MARKET SEGMENTATION.

internal migration Population shifts which occur within nation-states as labour migrates towards growth poles in the economy. Since the 1950s these shifts of population have often been of significant proportions—especially in developing countries. They have accompanied the processes of *urbanization and *industrialization and have involved large-scale movements of people from rural to urban areas. Debate has centred on whether 'push' or 'pull' factors are more important in explaining internal migration, and on the processes of *proletarianization and depeasantization, which are seen to be a consequence. *See also* MIGRATION, SOCIOLOGICAL STUDIES OF.

internal (or domestic) colonialism A term used widely to characterize exploitative relationships between a 'centre' and 'periphery' within a single nation-state or society. It has been applied to White-Black relations in the United States, Indian-White and Indian-Mestizo relations in Latin America, and has also been used to describe the exploitative relationship between the Soviet state and Soviet society (particularly the conditions of the *peasantry under forced collectivization and the working class under imposed industrialization). The situation of the Celtic fringe in British national development during the past four centuries has also been depicted in these terms (see M. Hechter, *Internal Colonialism*, 1975). The term is now largely discredited, mainly because of the obvious difficulties in drawing parallels with *colonialism strictly defined. For example, the latter involves the control and exploitation of the majority of a nation by a minority of outsiders, whereas in America the Black population is a numerical minority and was, originally, the 'outside' group. However, advocates of the theory argue that these sorts of differences are less significant than the core stock of common experiences that have been shared by oppressed (often racialized) minorities throughout the world, and have defended the use of the term vigorously (see, for example, R. Blauner's *Racial Oppression in America*, 1972).

international division of labour The specialization of particular countries in distinct branches of production, whether this be in certain products, or in selected parts of the production process. The concept suggests that the spread of *markets and production processes world-wide creates (as indeed this same process has done within particular economies) a growing differentiation of economic activity. However, whereas in orthodox economics the *division of labour as such is seen as providing mutual benefit for these specialized branches of activity, alternative analyses of the international division of labour stress the inequalities and structured hierarchies which it creates. Thus, Folker Fröbel and his colleagues (*The New International Division of Labour*, 1980), analysing the industrialization of selected *Third World countries in the late 1970s, showed how this involved the creation of a new (often mainly feminine) working class that worked for lower wages and in inferior conditions on new electrical and other assembly lines. Some theories and studies of *post-industrial society suggest that a significant proportion of industrial activity, and particularly its ecologically damaging and low-skill elements, are being shifted to intermediate and developing countries ('the new international division of labour'). *See also* LABOUR-MARKET SEGMENTATION.

Internet A global network of computers (also known as the World Wide Web) which allows instantaneous access to an expanding number of individual Web sites offering information about practically anything and everything—including the contents of daily newspapers, the price of goods, library holdings, commodity prices, sports news and gossip, eroticism, and various *social media. It is increasingly used for selling goods through dedicated online stores and for viewing television and listening to radio.

The Internet is a product of the Cold War. It was originally developed by the Government of the United States during the 1970s as a means of sharing information and protecting communications in the event of a nuclear attack. During the 1980s it developed quickly, first into an academic exchange network, then as a means of mass electronic communication available in principle to anyone having access to a personal computer and a telephone line. In 1995 approximately 1 million people were using the Web. Two years later this total had reached an estimated 40 million. Between 1993 and 1997 the number of accessible pages on the Web grew from around 130000 to more than 30 million, and by 2000 the total exceeded 2 billion. Most sites currently offer free access though there may be a charge for access to copies of print-based material such as newspapers and journals.

Most users find information by using one of many 'search engines' that are available. These are fast computers that produce organized lists of relevant Web sites in response to a query about particular topics or key-words. For example, typing in the name of a multinational corporation (such as 'Sony' or 'Nissan') will generate dozens of sites giving information about the company's current products, economic performance, manufacturing capacity, retailing outlets, and so forth. Many of these will be 'official', being maintained by the company or its agents, but some will be unofficial sites supported by enthusiasts or critics.

Use of the Internet continues to grow rapidly all over the world. The social implications of this are contested. It has been argued that the Internet is the greatest technological development of the 20th century, comparable in importance to (say) the invention of printing, or even of electricity. It could change the way economies function, for example by depressing prices (as customers increasingly have the facility to search the globe for the cheapest products), holding down wages (some tasks can be farmed out electronically to cheap *labour markets), or making it possible for people to work from home. There are companies which subcontract routine administrative work (such as maintaining their personnel records) via the Internet to *Third World agencies which can pay computer staff lower wages than would be required in the West. Increasingly, it is possible to shop online (for example to buy airline tickets direct from airlines), and this may affect the structure of retailing. Some forecasts suggest that the resulting so-called technological deflation may depress prices by as much as 25 or 30 per cent over the next decade.

There are also many sites where one can search for a job. This is said to be affecting the US labour market, since people on the East Coast can explore vacancies in the West that they otherwise would not be aware of, and vice versa. The increasing availability of digital products (including online magazines and films) may lead to an under-recording of economic activity by conventional measures (such as *Gross National Product) and may make it difficult for governments to collect certain taxes. Some observers maintain that the existence of the Web makes *totalitarian regimes less likely to succeed, because the effects of propaganda can readily be countered by accessing alternative sources of information on the Web, and it has even been suggested that this will make new forms of *participatory democracy possible in the near future.

Sceptics argue that much of the information available on the Internet is trivial. They also point out that global 'Netizenship' is restricted to those who can afford a personal computer, a Wi-Fi router to link it to the world's telephone lines, and who can then pay the associated running costs. It is estimated that in Britain, for example, 80 per cent of households have Internet access and almost two thirds of adults have Internet access through a mobile device such as a smartphone. Knowledge of English is virtually a prerequisite of Net use. This information revolution could therefore be creating a new international division of the world into a small group of 'information-rich' countries and individuals and a dispossessed majority who will be excluded from this particular form of *power. The computers which serve the system also seem to be permanently on the edge of collapsing under the weight of demand. New capacity constantly has to be installed. Users often complain of information overload.

At the time of writing, there are signs that some of these shortcomings may be overcome by the mass production of cheap network computers and tablet computers (which do not contain expensive components such as hard drives), and by making television a medium through which the Web can be accessed. The biggest change, however, has been the integration of the Web with mobile phones, opening up a variety of possible uses. This may make the Internet a truly universal and affordable source of information. If the problem of finding a secure method for payment of goods bought over the Web is also solved then the prospects for transforming retailing and other markets will also be dramatically enhanced. On the history of the Internet, and its possible implications for the organization of work, leisure, and politics, see Rob Shields (ed.), *Cultures of Internet* (1996) and Sherry Turkle, *Life on the Screen: Identity in the Age of the Internet* (1995). *See also* CYBER-SOCIETY; TELECOMMUTING.

interpellation Within Louis *Althusser's conception of the constitution of *identity, this is the process by which agents (individuals) acquire their self-awareness as subjects, and the skills and attributes necessary for their social placement. It literally means the 'calling out' or identification of someone. Within the theory of *discourse analysis the term refers to the *ascription of such characteristics.

interpersonal comparisons *See* REFERENCE GROUP.

interpretation (interpretive sociology) In one sense, any statement is an interpretation: if I call this thing in front of me a desk (rather than a dressing table) then I am interpreting a battery of sense impressions; if I say I feel happy (rather than, say, drunk) then I am interpreting certain physical sensations and a mental state. Not all sociologists recognize such a wide use of the word. Some, for example, use it more narrowly as in the sense of interpreting statistical data.

Interpretive sociology is a term usually confined to those sociological approaches that regard *meaning and *action as the prime objects of sociology. These differ in the extent to which they view interpretation as problematic. *Symbolic interactionism and much Weberian sociology, for example, generally interprets meaning on a commonsense level. *Phenomenological sociology possesses a quite elaborate theory of interpretation, as do *ethnomethodology, hermeneutics, and *structuralism. Interpretive theories differ as well in the degree to which they go beyond the actor's own understanding of what he or she is doing.

For Max *Weber (*The Methodology of the Social Sciences*, 1904–17), *verstehen* ('understanding' of people's actions) is the method *par excellence* of sociology. Understanding and interpretation are closely related, and most sociologists would now recognize that some interpretation is involved in all acts of understanding, although some maintain a more naïve view that there are unproblematic meanings in social reality which can be directly understood. Weber distinguishes descriptive understanding (for example 'John is walking across the room and opening a window') and explanatory understanding ('He is opening the window in order to ventilate this stuffy room'). In fact, both statements require an interpretation of what is happening, the second merely going rather further than the first. It is argued that the more complete our understanding or interpretation, the closer we are to a full explanation of an action. Alfred Schutz (in *The Phenomenology of the Social World*, 1932) develops a more elaborate conception by extending Weber's work and exploring the formation of goals from the stream of experience. This leads him to distinguish 'because' motives (which lie in past experience) from 'in order to' motives (which point to a future state of affairs that the actor wishes to bring about).

Most modern sociological conceptions of understanding recognize that it is also a process of interpretation. Some try to avoid this, by arguing that what we should be searching out are the rules by means of which we understand and interpret, since these remain the same whatever the content of interpretations. This lies behind Peter Winch's idea that all social action is rule-following; as well as the ethnomethodological focus on conversational rules; the concerns of structuralism with the rules which enable the production of meaning from an underlying structure; and, less obviously, the interest of *post-structuralism in the constant and shifting play of meanings. Anthony Giddens (in *The Constitution of Society*, 1984) argues that all explicitly formulated rules become sites for interpretation, and the rules that are most basic to human action and interaction are not formulated, but rather, as far as the actor is concerned, are pre-conscious. They are, therefore, like the rules that govern mathematical progressions, and tell us how to proceed in the same way. Thus, given the beginning of a sequence (say 2, 4, 6, 8), we know how it continues (10, 12, 14) without necessarily knowing the rule which governs this progression.

Hermeneutics is the science of interpretation and maintains an interest in the content as well as the form of what is being interpreted. The term itself originated with the practice of interpreting sacred texts. It works on the principle that we can only understand the meaning of a statement in relation to a whole discourse or world-view of which it forms a part: for example, we can only understand (say) the statements of monetarist economics, in the context of all the other contemporary cultural phenomena to which they are related. We have to refer to the whole to understand the parts and the parts to understand the whole—the so-called hermeneutic circle. This in turn involves putting ourselves in the position of the author of the text and looking at the meaning of what is produced in relation to its context. Whereas biblical interpretation aimed at the correct meaning, it is now generally acknowledged that there is no such entity, although many philosophers hold that an approximation to the truth is possible. The German hermeneutic philosopher Hans-Georg Gadamer, for example, argues this is possible through a shared tradition (*Truth and Method*, 1960).

It should be evident by now that the systematic investigation of interpretation is largely the province of the *philosophy of social science, and its influence on sociological investigation is variable. Perhaps its most important contribution has been to the problem of understanding other cultures, given the possibilities for *cultural relativism. If we take Winch's position, for example, we must understand a culture in its own terms, through its own rules, and without imposing the framework of our own culture. In a classic paper on 'Understanding a Primitive Society' (in B. Wilson, *Rationality*, 1970) he argues that we cannot make any judgement about the truth or otherwise of Azande beliefs about witchcraft. In Azande society, there are witches and witchcraft, whereas in our society we have science and scientists. The two are just different and one is not superior to the other by any transcendent standard: for us, science is better, but for the Azande witchcraft is better. All we can do is understand, this being made possible by the fact that we share a common human condition, since each society has to find a way of regulating and dealing with the birth of new members, sexual relations, and death.

For those approaches that posit the existence of a social structure independent of people's conception of their social world, the problem of the nature of understanding is much less important.

intersectionality Intersectionality theory explores how the differential situatedness of social agents influences the ways they affect and are affected by various social, economic, and political projects. The term emerged from the field of critical legal studies, in the writings of the critical race feminist Kimberlé Williams Crenshaw (1989). At nearly the same time, the sociologist Patricia Hill *Collins was preparing her landmark work, *Black Feminist Thought* (1990), which characterized intersections of race, class, and gender as mutually reinforcing sites of power relations. As a development of feminist standpoint theory, it claims it is vital to account for the social positioning of the social agent and challenge any false objectivity that implies a non-positioned standpoint: situated gaze, situated knowledge, and situated imagination construct differently the ways we see the world. What could also be called intersectional analysis was in fact developing at roughly the same time among European and post-colonial writers. Although many of the early writings on intersectionality related to marginalized and racialized women, intersectionality analysis applies to everyone, in the same way that not only 'Blacks' have 'race' or only women have 'gender'. Those interested in a more comprehensive and transformative approach to social justice—whether legal scholars, feminist theorists, political theorists, social psychologists, policymakers, or human rights advocates—have used the language and tenets of intersectionality to more effectively articulate injustice and advocate positive social change. The idea is one of the outcomes of the mobilization and proliferation of identity group struggles for recognition (see Charles Taylor, *Multiculturalism and 'the Politics of Recognition'*, 1992, and Nancy Fraser, *Justice Interruptus*, 1997).

Intersectionality analysis can involve focusing on identities (e.g. black, woman), on categories of difference (e.g. race, gender), on processes of differentiation (how subjectivities and social differences are produced via discourses and practices such as racialization and gendering), or on systems of domination (racism, colonialism, sexism, patriarchy). Intersectionality analysis is important in all spheres of life, all scales of social context, and all facets of social locations.

It is not just about social inequalities but also about the dynamics of power which affect and are affected by these inequalities.

Intersectionality analysis relates standpoints to the distribution of power and other resources in society. As such, it constitutes what in sociology is known as a *stratification theory relating to the differential hierarchical locations of individuals and groupings of people on grids of power. Recent work by Anthias ('Intersectional what? Social divisions, Intersectionality and levels of analysis', *Ethnicities*, 2013) and Yuval-Davis, 'Beyond the Recognition and Re-distribution Dichotomy: Intersectionality and Stratification', in Lutz et al. (eds.), *Framing Intersectionality*, 2011) claims that intersectionality is the most valid approach to the sociological study of social stratification because it does not reduce the complexity of power constructions into a single social division as has often been the case in stratification theories.

As with any theoretical approach, the theorization of intersectionality varies widely, even within sociology itself. The main debates focus around several central questions that are crucial for any analysis. One debate concerns the relationship between the different axes of power. The term 'intersectionality' invokes an intersection of pathways yet most of the sociological writings on intesectionality see these axes, although separate ontologically and irreducible to each other, as mutually constituting each other in each concrete historical case and subject. Another debate relates to the number of axes of power that should be taken into account in each intersectional analysis. Writers have varied from focusing exclusively on race and gender to considering fourteen social divisions. The answer, of course, varies in different situations and forms of analysis. Some social divisions (e.g. gender, class, race/ethnicity) are more universal while others (e.g. (dis)ability, (un)documented migrants) might be important in specific situations. An important recent development in intersectionality studies is its relationship to complexity theories in order to explore the operation of intersectionality at different levels of social structure. While intersectional relations exist in all social spheres and need to be analysed in specific spatial and temporal contexts, it is important to differentiate between levels of abstraction when carrying out an intersectional analysis so as to avoid reducing the ontological levels of analysis into each other.

A methodological debate within intersectionality relates to a differentiation made between 'inter-categorical' and 'intra-categorical' approaches. By an inter-categorical approach is means focusing on the way the intersection of different social divisions affects a particular social behaviour or the distribution of resources. Intra-categorical studies, on the other hand, are less occupied with the relationships among various social divisions and problematize the meaning and boundaries of the categories themselves in a particular place and time. These two approaches are not mutually exclusive and instead call for an intersectionality approach that combines the sensitivity and dynamism of the intra-categorical case study approach with the more macro socio-economic perspective of the inter-categorical approach.

It is vital to remember, then, that constructions, deconstructions, and reconstructions of complex and contested power relations are situated. The meanings of social power structures are different for people who are intersectionally differentially socially located. As meanings and values are related to social locations they cannot be reduced to these or to the associated identities or emotional attachments. The everyday is a social context in which these issues can be observed but we should never forget the intra-categorical explorations of meanings not only in particular situations but comparatively and globally.

Important recent discussions of intersectionality include Nira Yuval-Davis, 'Intersectionality and feminist politics', *European Journal of Women's Studies*, 2006; and Sylvia Walby, *Globality and Inequalities: Complexity and Contested Modernities*, 2009. *See also* FEMINISM; STRATIFICATION

intersubjectivity A term used primarily in *phenomenological sociology to refer to the mutual constitution of social relationships. It suggests that people can reach consensus about knowledge or about what they have experienced in their *life-world—at least as a working agreement if not a claim to *objectivity. An excellent overview is Nick Crossley's *Intersubjectivity: The Fabric of Social Becoming* (1996).

intertextuality First introduced by the *semiotic writer Julia Kristeva to redirect the attention of literary theorists from the author and his or her influences. Texts, she argued, have to be seen as systems of *signs that exist in relation to other systems of signs. Any single text is the outcome of transformations of earlier texts and is involved in the production of further texts. Hence, attention must focus on the relations between texts—literary analysis must be intertextual. Using the ideas of text and sign system more broadly, *post-structuralist writers see all cultural analysis as intertextual.

intervening variable A *variable, used in the process of explaining an observed relationship between an *independent and *dependent variable(s), such that $X \rightarrow T \rightarrow Y$—where T is the intervening variable which is used to explain the $X \rightarrow Y$ relationship. For example, if X is age and Y is reading ability, the causal relationship between X and Y might be explained by the intervening variable T, say education, which explains the $X \rightarrow Y$ link. Hence X is an indirect cause of Y through the intervening variable T: T predicts Y but is simultaneously predicted by X.

interview A social interaction that results in a transfer of information from the interviewee to an interviewer or researcher. Interviews may be personal, conducted face to face, or by telephone (which has certain advantages for more sensitive topics), or may be conducted at one remove through a postal, email, or online *questionnaire (which gives people more time to consider their replies). The questions put to interviewees may treat them as a respondent who supplies information about their own circumstances, activities, and attitudes, or as an informant who supplies factual information about social phenomena within their experience and knowledge, such as the number of rooms in their home, an estimate of their total household income, characteristics of their local community, trade union, or employer. Less commonly, people are invited to be proxy informants for a respondent who is not available, such as a wife answering questions on her husband's job.

Interviews vary in style and format, from the structured interview based on a questionnaire (which is typical in sample *surveys), to the unstructured interview based on a list of topics to be covered, to the depth interview or qualitative interview which may last hours and range widely around the topics in an interview guide. A somewhat different approach to interviewing consists of the group discussion, in which four to twelve people discuss the topic of interest to the researcher, under the guidance of the researcher (*see* FOCUS GROUPS).

The research interview has some similarities to other interview situations, such as job selection interviews, in that it is an interaction between unequals rather than an ordinary conversation: the topics are chosen by the researcher and interviewers must reveal nothing of themselves in case this biases responses. Researcher control over the interview is greatly increased by the use of computer-based questionnaires for personal and telephone interviews, such as Computer-Assisted Telephone Interviewing (CATI) systems. *See also* INTERVIEW BIAS; INTERVIEWER BIAS.

interview bias Biases that appear in research findings because of the social nature of the interview. There are three major sources of such bias: the interviewer (who may, for example, have prejudices or ask leading questions); the respondent (who may wish to lie or evade questions); and the actual interview situation itself (especially the physical and social setting). *See also* INTERVIEWER BIAS.

interviewer bias The distortion of response to a personal or telephone *interview which results from differential reactions to the social style and personality of interviewers or to their presentation of particular questions. The use of fixed-wording questions is one method of reducing interviewer bias. Anthropological research and case-studies are also affected by the problem, which is exacerbated by the *self-fulfilling prophecy, when the researcher is also the interviewer. *See also* INTERVIEW BIAS.

intimacy (intimacies) A complex sphere of 'inmost' relationships with self and others that are not usually minor or incidental (though they may be transitory) and which usually touch the personal world very deeply. They are our closest relationships with friends, family, children, lovers, but they are also the deep and important experiences we have with self (which are never exactly solitary): our feelings, our bodies, our emotions, our identities.

Theodore Zeldin in *The Intimate History of Humanity* (1994) suggests three kinds of intimacy emerging over time. Initially it was linked to space and objects such as 'an intimate room into which one withdrew from the hubbub of relatives and neighbors', or intimate souvenirs and relics 'like a lock of hair which one cherished as though there was magic in them'. Later came a more romantic meaning in which a union of two souls—centrally through sexual intercourse—became the core. More recently still he suggests the term flags a partnership in the search for truth, a union of minds.

This latter meaning is not unlike the way in which sociologist Lynn Jamieson sees the term at work today. In her book *Intimacy* (1998), she suggests intimacy involves a very special 'sort of knowing, loving and being close to another person' which in the late 20th century depended upon a kind of 'disclosure and disclosing'. Generally, it involves close association, privileged knowledge of each other, and a general 'loving, sharing and caring'. In the modern world, for Jamieson, there are four paradigmatic forms of intimacy involving: couple relationships, friends and kin relationship, parent-child relationships, and sexual relationships. In contrast, some discussions of intimacy may take us away from 'positive' relations and head us into other areas. Elizabeth Stanko's work, for example, on women's experiences of male violence is called *Intimate Intrusions* (1985), and actually takes us into a very different sphere: of rape and abuse, an issue so central to the women's movement across the world. And in a sense this does connect back to the original meaning of the word 'inmost'—rape, after all, is an inmost violation of the being and the body.

It is common to suggest that sociology does not have much to say on such seemingly individualistic phenomena but in fact, at least since Durkheim's classic study of *Suicide*, the role of the social in shaping personal bonds and the intimate life has become increasingly recognized. In sociology, the analysis of families, sexualities, the body, friendships, and gender have all become key areas of debate in recent times.

Part of this prominence is linked to an interest in how such intimacies have been changing. Thus, Anthony Giddens talks of *The Transformation of Intimacy* (1992) and argues that there has been a democratization of the personal life in late modern societies. Bill Simon talks of *Postmodern Sexualities*—as we move increasingly away from a reproductive goal of sex to more pluralistic and varied ones. And Jeffrey Weeks, in *Invented Moralities*, sees a diverse array of 'experiments in living' as part of the making a new world order, one in which gay and lesbian relations become increasingly common and accepted.

intragenerational mobility *See* MOBILITY, SOCIAL.

intrapreneur *See* ENTREPRENEUR.

introspection The process of looking into one's mind, to examine one's own thoughts, feelings, and experiences. Data from introspection can be of some value in examining mental processes, but our introspection may not be accurate, and many mental processes are not accessible to conscious introspection. *See also* BEHAVIOURISM.

introspectionism *See* BEHAVIOURISM.

introversion *See* EXTROVERSION AND INTROVERSION.

invasion-succession model A theoretical construct, setting out the sequence of competitive social actions by which a human group or social activity comes to occupy and dominate a territory, formerly dominated by another group or activity. *See also* CONCENTRIC ZONE THEORY; ECOLOGY; HUMAN ECOLOGY; URBAN ECOLOGY.

inverse correlation *See* CORRELATION.

invisible hand An expression deriving from Adam *Smith's economic treatise on *The Wealth of Nations* (1776). It refers to the idea that when individuals pursue their own self-interest for gain in business their actions are led by an unseen force ('invisible hand') to promote the general good of society. Smith argued that, with some exceptions such as *monopolies, individual economic action supplies benefits to society when it is allowed to progress without hindrance from the state. This contention has often supplied ammunition to those who would promote *laissez-faire capitalism and are opposed to state intervention in the economy and in *civil society generally. Alfred Chandler (*Strategy and Structure*, 1962) has argued that the growth of large-scale *corporations and monopolized markets has allowed greater social planning by the 'visible hand' of the corporate leadership. *See also* ECONOMIC SOCIOLOGY; JUSTICE, SOCIAL; RATIONAL CHOICE THEORY.

invisible religion This concept, which is associated with Thomas Luckmann (*The Invisible Religion*, 1963), involves the notion that *religion is still an important feature of modern society, but it should not be defined narrowly as churchgoing behaviour. Religion involves the creation of meaning, which becomes objective in *culture, and thereby transcends immediate experience. *See also* SECULARIZATION.

involvement (types of involvement) *See* COMPLIANCE.

iron law of oligarchy *See* MICHELS; POLITICAL SOCIOLOGY.

Islam One of three great *monotheistic religions of the world (the others being *Judaism and *Christianity). It originated in 7th-century Arabia with the prophet Muhammad, who first converted the trading cities of Mecca and Medina, and then rallied the hitherto polytheistic tribal population. Within a century Islam had spread through conquest to Persia, much of the Middle East, North Africa, and Spain. It is represented by a succession of great empires: Ummayad to 750, Abbasid to 1258, and Ottoman to 1918. Today it encompasses around 45 countries and one billion or so people.

Islam is based on the principle of submission to Allah or God, its holy texts are the Koran (the word of God as revealed to Muhammad by an angel), and the Hadith or sayings of the Prophet. There are five main principles or 'pillars' of Islam: the affirmation that there is no God but God, and that Muhammad is his prophet; prayer five times a day; *zakat*, the giving of alms; fasting in the month of Ramadan; and *hajj* or pilgrimage to Mecca at least once in a lifetime. *Jihad*, or holy war, is sometimes regarded as another obligation of Muslims, but it does not have the same status, and is often interpreted as referring to a process of spiritual improvement rather than combat with non-Muslims.

Islam differs from Christianity in having no clerical hierarchy, in enforcing a number of prohibitions to do with diet, and in paying special attention to the status and clothing of women. Since the seventh century, it has been divided into a Sunni faction and a minority Shi'ite school, the latter dominant in Iran. The interpretation of Islam in the contemporary world has ranged from those who want to harmonize it with Western economic and political values to those who seek a return to the model of the seventh century. The Islamic revolution of Iran (1979) represented an attempt to pursue the latter path.

Sociological analysis of Islam was advanced by Max *Weber who identified two principal differences with Christianity: the lack of an ethic of this-worldly asceticism, and the domination of *patrimonial or prebendary relations, through which the state inhibited the growth of private property. Both served to prevent the development of capitalism. This interpretation was later challenged in several works by Maxime Rodinson, who saw Islam as continent and its failure to evolve to capitalism as due to other factors, including international pressures. Later work on Islam focused on the debate between those who identified a distinct sociology of Islam derived from the Koran and other texts, and those who stressed the variety and contingency of Islamic social and political practices. A third area of interpretation was that of the rise of Islamic political movements in the 1970s and 1980s. Some saw this as a popular mobilization, using an Islamic idiom, against foreign domination; others viewed it as a retrospective usage of Islamic symbols by certain social groups (particularly clergy, merchants, and intellectuals) threatened by the processes of *secularization and *modernization.

Islamophobia A form of discrimination against Muslims and their religion, Islam. It is an expression of fear, hatred, or intolerance towards Muslims and their religious beliefs and practices. Etymologically, Chris Allen and Jocelyne Cesari have traced the term to a French article by Etienne Dinet and Slima Ben Ibrahim in the early 20th century, but the modern-day understanding of Islamophobia and its usage in academic, media, and policy discourse was influenced by the Runnymede Trust report *Islamophobia: A Challenge for Us All* (1994), which defined it as 'unfounded hostility towards Islam' often the result of 'closed views' about Islam. The Trust became the first organization to provide an institutionalized definition of Islamophobia. However, the definition was limited, providing general guidance about Islamophobia without capturing the multidimensional aspects of discrimination against Muslims and Islam that could be indirect or psychological.

For academics such as Tariq Modood, Nasar Meer, and Salman Sayyid, Islamophobia is a *racialization of Muslims, where individuals are reduced to their religious and cultural identifiers, defined and confined within socially constructed categories that move beyond the biological yet restrict Muslim identities within the limits of their religious identifiers such as the veil and the beard. Muslims, by virtue of social characteristics rather than simply biology, are racialized in media and political discourse, with the Muslim veil equated with oppression, and the bearded man a fundamentalist. The nature of such racialization is both physical and psychological. Islamophobia takes the form of physical attacks and verbal altercations, as well as psychological control through what David Tyrer calls 'racialized governance' (in *The Politics of Islamophobia: Race, Power and Fantasy*, 2013). Such racialization results in categories of the acceptable or unacceptable Muslim, often externally defined by state actors, yet internalized by Muslims who need to prove their normality within society. Islamophobia in the Western context is further influenced by the historical interaction between the West and Islam, in particular Arabs from the time of the Crusades to colonialism, as captured in Edward Said's groundbreaking work *Orientalism* (1978). The barbaric and backward Muslim of the Orientalist imagination continues into the 21st century. This imagination is further fuelled by a history of racism between immigrants from the Commonwealth and the host community at the colonialist centre; a history that continues to define the interaction between the West and its Muslim communities.

After the tragedies of 11 September 2001, the Commission on British Muslims and Islamophobia further expanded the definition of Islamophobia to highlight how the sociopolitical climate of the 'War on Terror' contributed to a negative perception of Muslims and Islam. This 'War on Terror' has resulted in what Stuart Croft called a 'securitization' of Islam and Muslims that further contributes to discrimination against Muslims. With images of the bearded Muslim terrorist and the oppressed veiled female inundating media and political discourse about Islam and terrorism, Muslims and their religion continue to be stereotyped as violent and destructive within the social imagination. Therefore, in the post 9/11 socio-political milieu Islamophobia takes the form of a both racializing and securitizing discourse about Muslims and Islam.

The term however has proven problematic, viewed as a hindrance towards constructive criticism of Islam. Detractors fear that a critique of Islamic practices or beliefs can be deemed Islamophobic, limiting any discussion about the religion. Hence, a term such as anti-Muslim is suggested as opposed to Islamophobia as it captures discrimination and abuse against Muslims without limiting any criticism of Islam as a religious ideology. Further problematic considerations are comparisons between Islamophobia and anti-Semitism, where critics and defenders challenge the nature of this comparison in light of the distinct historical experiences of Islam and Judaism. For this reason, the exact meaning of Islamophobia continues to be debated amongst academics and policymakers alike.

Jacobson, Roman Osipovic (1896-1982) A member of the Prague linguistic circle, developing the structuralist linguistics of Ferdinand de *Saussure, and who argued in particular for the fundamental status of binary oppositions (see his *Selected Writings*, 1962 ff.). He was an important influence on Claude Lévi-Strauss and modern *structuralism generally.

James, William (1842-1910) An American philosopher of the pragmatist school, and brother of the novelist Henry James. Notable mainly for his unusual accomplishment in significantly influencing the development both of *neo-positivism and *symbolic interactionism, via his view that the empirical consequences of an idea constitute its meaning. *See also* PEIRCE; PRAGMATISM (PHILOSOPHY OF).

Janowitz, Morris (1919-88) An American sociologist, student at Chicago University in the mid-1940s, then Professor in a number of North American departments. He was the author of numerous books, including *The Professional Soldier* (1946), *Sociology and the Military Establishment* (1959), *Social Control of the Welfare State* (1976), *The Last Half-Century* (1978), and *The Reconstruction of Patriotism* (1983). Janowitz will be remembered as probably the leading sociologist of the military, and for his argument that the transition from early to advanced industrial society created forms of institutional organizations that made *democracy harder to sustain, although he also researched and published significant studies on the topics of urban and political sociology, race and ethnic relations, and sociological theory generally. A useful selection of his papers—prefaced by an excellent biographical introduction—is James Burk's *Morris Janowitz—On Social Organization and Social Control* (1991). *See also* MILITARY AND MILITARISM.

job evaluation This is a system of job classification which determines grading structures and pay scales according to characteristics of the job (skill, discretion, responsibility) rather than the employee. Job evaluation is favoured by the equal opportunities lobby because of its potential for reducing employee-based biases. In practice, however, many job-evaluation schemes simply reinforce *prejudices and existing *inequalities by the particular interpretation that is placed upon what counts as *skill. Thus, for example, in segmented labour markets (*see* LABOUR-MARKET SEGMENTATION), jobs in which men are in a majority tend to be evaluated more highly than those in which women predominate (see A. Pollert, *Girls, Wives, Factory Lives*, 1981).

job satisfaction This is conventionally measured in interview *surveys by asking a question along the lines of 'How happy are you, overall, with your job?', with 80–90 per cent of adults in industrial societies routinely responding that they are 'satisfied'. Dissatisfaction is more often voiced in relation to specific aspects of a job, such as pay, promotion prospects, or conveniently flexible hours of work. Although job dissatisfaction, as defined by the standard question, is rare, research shows that it is closely associated with worker behaviour such as absence from work, job change, and labour turnover. *See also* WORK, SUBJECTIVE EXPERIENCE OF.

joint conjugal roles Joint conjugal roles are those where the husband and wife carry out many activities together and with a minimum of task differentiation and separation of interests. Marriages in which couples share activities and have an overlapping social network are thought to be more stable. This key idea was set out by Elizabeth Bott in her *Family and Social Network* (1957). *See also* ROLE, CONJUGAL; SEGREGATED CONJUGAL ROLES.

joking relationships Clearly defined relationships of reciprocal, ritual, mildly abusive behaviour, between persons who are not only permitted but expected to behave in ways that would be offensive or insulting to persons not so related. These relationships express a form of friendliness by a show of mild hostility. Joking relatives are expected not to take offence but to respond in kind.

Joking relationships are therefore the obverse of *avoidance relationships and are often found in the same social context. It has frequently been argued, indeed, that they serve the same social function. For example, A. R. Radcliffe-Brown (*African Systems of Kinship and Marriage*, 1950) maintains that 'in the building of social structures means must be provided for avoiding, limiting, controlling, or settling conflict. In the new structural situation resulting from marriage . . . while there is a union of the husband and wife the two families . . . remain separated, only linked together by their separate connection with the new family . . . It is the separateness of the two groups, together with the need of maintaining friendly relations between them, that has to provide the basis for their personal relations'. In this situation, the social separation of the man and his wife's relatives is symbolically represented in sham hostility and the readiness not to take offence, both governed by strict conventions. Thus, for example, in agnatic (descended by male links from the same male ancestor) kinship systems, it is often considered appropriate for a sister's son to express symbolically his relationship to his uncle in joking customs of privileged familiarity (a situation found among the Winnebago and certain other North American tribes). Similarly, among the patrilineal Hutu of northern Rwanda, a joking relationship exists between a man and his matrilateral cross-cousins, male or female, whereas his behaviour towards his female patrilateral cross-cousins has to be kept discreet and formal.

Judaism A *monotheistic world religion with origins in the prophetic activities of the Jews in relation to the God Yahweh. It is important to distinguish early biblical Judaism, before the fall of the Temple in 70CE, and later Judaism which was focused on the synagogue. Judaism was organized around religious teachers (the rabbis) and religious knowledge was contained in the Torah or teaching (especially the first five books of the Hebrew Bible). Judaism, which was based on the idea of a sacred covenant between Yahweh and his people, produced profound *messianic movements throughout history.

In the Middle Ages, there were a number of important mystical movements, such as the Kabbalah, which gave an esoteric reading to traditional Jewish theology. In the 19th century, there were attempts to change and reform many traditional practices, giving rise to the creation of two separate religious movements, Reform and Conservative Judaism. The destruction of European Jewish communities in the Holocaust and the creation of the modern state of Israel in 1948 transformed Judaism in the 20th century.

Sociologists have been particularly interested in the nature of Jewish prophecy (see, for example, M. Weber, *Ancient Judaism*, 1917-19), the relationship between Judaism and capitalism (see W. Sombart, *The Jews and Modern Capitalism*, 1911), and more recently the implications of the Holocaust for established social theories (see Z. Bauman, *Modernity and the Holocaust*, 1990). *See also* CHRISTIANITY.

Jung, Carl Gustav (1875-1961) Swiss *psychologist and *psychoanalyst. For some time Sigmund *Freud's heir apparent, he eventually split from Freud in 1913, after disagreeing in particular about the importance of sexuality. His work is considered more spiritual than Freud's, offering analyses of the *life-cycle and *symbolism, and by comparison remains curiously ignored by sociologists. Good introductions to his work are Anthony Storr, *Jung* (1986) and Anthony Stevens, *On Jung* (1990).

justice *See* CRIMINOLOGY; JUSTICE, SOCIAL.

justice, social Arguments about justice feature not only in sociology, but also in *philosophy, *political science, *social policy, *psychology, and of course *law itself. Justice is a central moral standard in social life, is generally held to have a prominent role in social theory and social action, and so it is perhaps not surprising that all the social sciences have examined the concept at some length. (The best multi-disciplinary overview is R. L. Cohen's edited collection entitled *Justice: Views from the Social Sciences*, 1986.)

It is conventional to distinguish 'formal justice' (the law) and material justice (morality and politics), although some theorists of justice treat the two concepts as parallel or overlapping, and argue that since legal or criminal justice concerns the distribution of penalties to the guilty, it has much in common with social justice, which deals with the allocation of scarce goods (and 'bads') to a population: both are premised on the ideas of due process, impartiality, and distribution according to appropriate criteria. In older literature, a distinction is usually drawn between social (or as it is frequently termed 'distributive') justice, and retributive justice. The latter holds that the guilty should be punished simply because wrong-doing as such ought to be punished, regardless of the consequences of doing so in terms of deterring further misdemeanours, or making any other contribution to social utility. Retributivism is, therefore, only one theory of criminal justice. In the psychological literature, a fivefold distinction is sometimes made (following T. Eckhoff, *Justice: Its Determinants in Social Interaction*, 1974) between equity, or fair exchange, where equity is defined as the equivalence of the output to input ratios of all parties involved in an exchange; distributive justice, or fair allocation, involving the one-way distribution of resources, *rights, obligations, or whatever across a category of recipients; procedural justice, or fair procedures and mechanisms, recognizing that an agreed and fair procedure might nevertheless result in a distribution of outcomes that some would define as unjust; retributive justice, or just compensation, dealing with fairness in the allocation of punishments or level of compensation for victimization; and, finally, justice as equality—which may be equality of opportunity, equality of objective outcome, subjective equality (equality of outcomes taking into account need or desert), rank-order equality (in which the allocation of rewards follows normative expectations in order to avoid felt injustice), or equity (equality relative to individual contributions). As will be evident by now this is a subject replete with typologies and codification.

A wide variety of principles are available to regulate social and economic inequalities and so the concept of social justice is the subject of great dispute. Different political ideologies yield different principles of justice. Among the variety of concepts and theories advanced in this way, those of desert, merit, entitlement, equality of outcome, equality of opportunity, need, and functional inequality would seem to be most relevant to sociologists.

Most academic debate about the concept of justice starts with John Rawls's famous 'difference principle', which asserts that inequalities in the distribution of scarce goods (power, money, access to healthcare, or whatever) are justified only if they serve to increase the advantage of the least favoured groups in society (see his *A Theory of Justice*, 1972). What makes this a principle of justice is the idea that justice consists in considering society from an impartial standpoint, in Rawls's case from an imagined 'original position' in which agreement is reached by hypothetical rational self-interested people deprived of information about their talents and attributes, choosing behind a 'veil of ignorance'. According to Rawls, people constrained in this way to choose impartially would be concerned to maximize the well-being of the least advantaged members of society lest they themselves fall into that group, so they will agree to permit inequalities only if these contribute to the welfare of the poor. This proposition then forms part of Rawls's theory of 'justice as fairness', which rests on three principles, which because they may sometimes conflict are ordered in lexical priority as follows: the principle of greatest equal liberty (each person is to have an equal right to the most extensive system of equal basic liberties compatible with a similar system of liberty for all); which takes absolute priority over the principle of equality of fair opportunity (positions are to be open to all under conditions in which persons of similar abilities have equal access to office); which, in turn, takes absolute priority over the difference principle itself, which (as we have seen) requires social and economic institutions to be arranged so as to benefit maximally the worst-off. Note that there is no suggestion anywhere in this theory that people in any sense deserve their advantages.

Theories of justice which demand that people be rewarded according to their differential desert or merit are probably more familiar to sociologists. If justice consists in giving people their due, and those dues are different, then justice seems clearly to require unequal outcomes. However, this approach to justice does then raise the question of what it is that constitutes the bases of desert or merit, and which qualities of individuals it is just to reward. For example, one can make a distinction between those attributes for which an individual can claim responsibility, and those which are his or hers merely by chance. It is by no means clear that justice is served by rewarding the latter. Against the theory of justice as desert, Rawls has argued that even a quality such as ability to work hard is itself a chance attribute, and thus an improper basis for reward.

If notions of desert are allied to the principle of equality of opportunity, then matters become yet more complex, since the latter is open to a variety of interpretations. Does it demand that, however unequal their abilities, people should be equally empowered to achieve their goals? This would imply that the unmusical individual who wants to be a concert pianist should receive more training than the child prodigy. Should people have equal resources to devote to their life-plans, irrespective of ability; or, less drastically, does this principle merely require that people with the same abilities should have equal opportunities to achieve their desired goals (an interpretation which is consistent with the idea that the talented should have more opportunities than the untalented)?

The idea that unequal rewards might be just because people are entitled to unequal resources can be distinguished from arguments based on principles of desert or merit because it is possible to argue that people are entitled to certain goods without in any sense deserving them. Robert Nozick (*Anarchy, State and Utopia*, 1974) maintains that, even if one accepts that each individual's natural assets are arbitrary such that they cannot be said to deserve them, people are still entitled to the fruits of these assets and to whatever else other people choose freely to give them. Desert-based conceptions of justice are, in Nozick's terms, 'patterned' and necessarily conflict with those free exchanges and just transfers which justify an individual's entitlement to resources. Nozick's *libertarian emphasis on property rights and freedom of choice leads to a conception of justice as entitlement which is quite different from the idea that people should get what they deserve.

Friedrich *Hayek (*The Mirage of Social Justice*, 1976) has argued that one cannot justify market outcomes as reflecting merit or desert since luck plays too large a part in determining who gets what. However, in his view, the fact that market outcomes are unintended and unforeseen aggregate consequences means that they are not the kind of thing which it is appropriate to regard as just or unjust. Indeed, the whole idea of social justice is for Hayek a mirage, since it requires us to make the mistake of seeing society as an agent. Interestingly, Hayek concedes that the defence of market outcomes at the level of the general public rests upon the erroneous belief that such outcomes reward merit, and he suggests that such a belief is necessary if people are to tolerate the inequalities that the *market produces. However, his own justification of the market mechanism is quite different, and points instead to its alleged efficiency because it directs scarce resources to where they bring the greatest return, so that even in an unequal distribution the poor are better off than under any other distributive system, since increased *productivity works also to the advantage of those who have least. This argument has obvious parallels with *functionalist theories of stratification.

It will be clear from this brief résumé of only a few of the philosophical arguments about justice that the concept is itself contested; that discussions of justice tend to spill over into disputes about cognate concepts (such as 'efficiency' and 'equality'); and that this is an area in which it is wise to eschew labels in attaching particular views of justice to particular political ideologies. For example, while it is well known that socialists tend to place emphasis on justice as need and equality of outcome, it is perhaps less well known that Karl *Marx considered the desert-oriented distributive principle 'to each according to his labour' as appropriate to the first or lower stage of *socialism, to be superseded by the maxim 'to each according to his need' only in a second or higher stage. Similarly, *liberals tend to endorse the value of equality of opportunity, with inequalities of outcome deemed legitimate if they reflect differences in merit, but then cannot agree either about the conditions that are necessary to ensure equality of opportunity or about what constitutes merit. Some liberals hold a more extreme libertarian position (often confused in popular terminology with *conservatism), and argue both that people are entitled to do as they choose with whatever resources they have acquired legitimately, and that this is more important than equality of opportunity. Contemporary thinkers on the *New Right tend to conflate the principles of entitlement and desert. For example, it is often argued that the market is to be praised because people get out what they put in (with *entrepreneurship and hard work being rewarded), and because markets are the most efficient mechanism for creating wealth which can then *trickle down to the poor. Here, unequal outcomes are justified simultaneously on the grounds that they are needed to give people incentives, and so contribute to social justice by helping the poor, and because they give individuals what they deserve. Old-style conservatives, by contrast, tend simply to regard hierarchy as a good thing, either because inequality is a necessary prerequisite of culture and civilized values, or because they respect tradition and inequality is traditional. From this point of view all talk of the principles of social justice, and perhaps even the notion of social justice itself, is inappropriately rationalist in tenor.

Much of the philosophical literature and political theory of justice has been predominantly normative in character. Like Rawls, most writers have been concerned mainly to identify particular rules which can be used to assess the rightness of an act or institution, in order thereby to encourage specific social arrangements that will promote procedural fairness, just allocation, or equality. However, among sociologists and social psychologists, the discussion has been empirical and descriptive rather than moral and prescriptive.

Psychologists have explored the exchange theories of distributive justice suggested by George *Homans and Stacy Adams, the status-value or status-attribution alternative proposed by Joseph Berger and his colleagues, and the various cost-benefit explanations proffered by certain theorists of social conflict.

Sociological studies of social justice have looked at welfarism, the family, education, and earnings. They have been concerned to uncover popular views about fairness in such distributions. Recent years have seen the emergence of a developing consensus that research into social justice issues could most profitably be pursued within an interdisciplinary framework (see, for example, K. S. Scherer (ed.), *Justice: Interdisciplinary Perspectives*, 1992). This has been attempted empirically by (among others) Gordon Marshall, Adam Swift, and Stephen Roberts, *Against the Odds?* (1997). *See also* MEASUREMENT BY FIAT.

just-in-time system (JIT) This is a system of related production practices which aim to deliver the exact quantity of raw materials, parts, and subassemblies 'just-in-time' for the next stage of *production. Originally associated with Japanese firms, but now more widely diffused, it implies: *flexible production methods; short production runs and rapid changes in product lines; inventory management determined by downstream suppliers rather than forward management planning; and networks of small firms linked by subcontracting.

juvenile delinquency *See* DELINQUENCY.

Kant, Immanuel (1724–1804) One of the greatest, if not the greatest, of all modern philosophers, the German Immanuel Kant has had a profound and lasting influence both in *philosophy itself, and across the full range of intellectual disciplines, including of course sociology. The core of Kant's critical philosophy is generally taken to be his synthesis of the two rival traditions of *empiricism and *rationalism that dominated *epistemology (or philosophical theory of knowledge) in Kant's time. Kant argued, against the empiricists, that there were judgements that were not mere *tautologies, yet were not derived from experience. Kant's great work the *Critique of Pure Reason* (1781) is devoted to the demonstration of this claim and to the systematic derivation of those a priori concepts and categories that are conditions of the possibility of our apprehension of space and time (the 'forms of intuition'), and our making of objective judgements of experience (the 'categories'—causality, necessity, possibility, and others). For Kant, however, the categories, whilst not derivable from experience, could be legitimately applied only within the field of possible experience. To use the categories to offer accounts of 'things-in-themselves', beyond possible experience, was to fall into irresolvable contradiction. So, whilst rejecting a central doctrine of empiricism, Kant nevertheless shared with the leading empiricists a concern to defend the *cognitive status of empirical science against *metaphysical claims to knowledge of 'things-in-themselves' beyond experience.

However, for Kant, thought about 'things-in-themselves' was unavoidable, even if knowledge of them was impossible. This was not least because of the necessity of a rational grounding for objective moral judgement. For an individual to be bound by a moral maxim requires both freedom of will and a unitary personal identity, neither of which is to be found among the contents of experience. Kant's treatment of aesthetics (in the *Critique of Judgement,* 1790) also makes use of ideas (such as 'the form of purposiveness') which can have no application in objective judgements of experience. Despite the anti-metaphysical leanings of the central arguments of Kant's Critique of Pure Reason, therefore, there remains a tension between a realm of objectively knowable objects of experience, on one hand, and unavoidable allusions to an unknowable realm of 'things-in-themselves', on the other. This latter realm is especially required in the grounding of moral and aesthetic judgement and the identity of the perceiving, knowing, and acting *subject.

The principal non-positivist epistemologies that have been influential in sociology derive from various European traditions of interpretation and resolution of these tensions in Kant's philosophy (most especially neo-Kantianism, phenomenology, and hermeneutics—for all of which see separate entries in this dictionary). *Hegel's historical *dialectic of self-realization of the 'Absolute Idea' arose from the critique of Kant's philosophy and went on to inform both the view of history and the epistemology of Marx and Engels.

Kautsky, Karl (1854–1938) A German *socialist politician and social theorist. His *The Agrarian Question* (1899) argued that small-scale peasant production was doomed to disappear in the face of capitalist development, and that social democrats should not seek to defend *peasant interests, their future lying in *proletarianization. For Kautsky, the peasantry embodied the 'backward' social characteristics of isolation, tradition, and individualism. He was opposed to revisionism; that is, the electoral politics of Edward *Bernstein in the 1900s, and adopted a pacifist position in the First World War. He criticized the Bolshevik revolution and its policy of the 'dictatorship of the proletariat', attracting the hostility of *Lenin, who attacked Kautsky as the epitome of the social democratic betrayal of the working class (see *The Road to Power*, 1909, and *The Dictatorship of the Proletariat*, 1918). His major work of 1927 has been translated into English as *The Materialist Conception of History* (1988). *See also* MARXISM.

Kelly, George Alexander (1905–67) An American psychologist who pioneered *personal construct theory and the 'role construct repertory test'. Kelly argued, in *The Psychology of Personal Constructs* (1955), that 'a person's processes are psychologically channelized by the ways in which he anticipates events'. Such constructs are the central subject of psychology. *See also* COGNITIVE THEORY.

Kerr–Siegel hypothesis In an article on 'The Interindustry Propensity to Strike—an International Comparison' (in A. Kornhauser et al., *Industrial Conflict*, 1954), Clark Kerr and Abraham Siegel offered an analysis of inter-industry differences in strike-proneness, and argued that high strike-rates among geographically or socially isolated, cohesive, homogeneous groups of workers (such as longshoremen, miners, and sailors) were a consequence of their *alienation from the wider society and the unpleasant nature of their jobs. First, since the location of the worker in society determines his or her propensity to strike, and location is heavily dependent on industrial environment, then industries will be strike-prone where workers form a homogeneous group isolated from the general community. Moreover, by selection and conditioning, the nature of jobs determines the kind of workers employed: unpleasant, casual, unskilled work attracts (and fosters) tough, combative workers, who will be likely to *strike. A combination of these two theories explains the differential strike-rates observed across industries.

The thesis generated an extensive secondary literature and considerable controversy. Critics argued, among other things, that the strike statistics that formed the basis of the argument were unreliable; that the analysis omitted certain key industries (such as steel) which contradicted the argument; and that the explanation of strike-proneness relied too much on a limited range of structural factors and ignored the attitudes of the different parties involved. *See also* INDUSTRIAL CONFLICT.

Keynesian economics An approach to economic theory and policy derived from the influential writings of the English economist John Maynard Keynes (1883–1946). Prior to Keynes, governments tended to be guided by the argument of *laissez-faire economics that an unregulated economy would tend to move towards full employment, and thence *equilibrium. Keynes argued (in *The General Theory of Employment, Interest and Money*, 1936) that equilibrium could be established before that point was reached, and therefore that governments wishing to achieve full employment had actively to intervene in the economy by stimulating aggregate demand; and, conversely, that if full employment resulted in *inflation they should act to reduce aggregate demand, in both cases by using the devices of tax (fiscal) policy, government expenditure, and monetary policy (changes in interest rates and the supply of credit). Keynesianism, though forming the basis of economic policy in most Western societies for three decades after the Second World War, was itself challenged by the appearance of *stagflation (simultaneous recession and inflation) in the 1970s, and consequently by the economic theories of *monetarism. The dispute between these two approaches currently forms the major axis of disagreement within modern economics.

kibbutzim Agricultural settlements inspired by *socialist and *anarchist ideals, established by Jewish settlers in Palestine, in which working and domestic arrangements, including child-care, are shared by members. They later came to employ wage labour and to form a small part of the Israeli economic system. They are interesting to sociologists primarily as experiments in *egalitarian communal living (see B. Bettelheim, *The Children of the Dream*, 1969). *See also* COMMUNE.

kinesics *See* BODY LANGUAGE.

Kinsey, Alfred (1894–1956) A zoologist who completed the first major large-scale social research into the sexual behaviour of men and women in North America. The findings, based on a sample of 18000 interviews (nearly half of which Kinsey conducted himself), were published as *Sexual Behaviour in the Human Male* in 1948 and *Sexual Behaviour in the Human Female* in 1953. Through the founding of the Kinsey Institute of Sex Research in Bloomington, Indiana, he did much to establish the credibility of such research. His findings were controversial, showing for example that 4 per cent of men in his sample were exclusively homosexual, and a third of men had engaged in homosexual acts. His findings have had an important cultural impact, discussed by P. Robinson in *The Modernization of Sex* (1976).

kinship Kinship is one of the main organizing principles of human society, and kinship systems have been extensively studied by *social anthropologists, for whom they are of particular importance because of their primacy in non-state societies. Kinship systems establish relationships between individuals and groups on the model of biological relationships between parents and children, between siblings, and between marital partners. Relationships established by *marriage, which form alliances between groups of persons related by blood (or consanguineous ties), are usually referred to as affinal relationships. Some social scientists make a distinction between the study of kinship and the study of affinity. All such studies depend on the assumption that these relationships are systematic, entailing the observation of *norms relating to behaviour between those related by kin or affinity. The relationships between parents and children (and by extension between grandparents and grandchildren) determine modes of inheritance as well as the overall political relationships between generations. Like links between siblings, the parent and child dyad can be crucial in establishing *incest rules, which determine not only sexual relationships but also the rules underlying affinity, by denoting prohibited or prescribed marital partners. As the social relationships between husband and wife set up relationships between their respective consanguineous groups, the entire complex of kinship and affinal relationships can be seen to be fundamental to the analysis of political, economic, and social relations in non-state societies.

It should be noted that actual biological relationships are not necessary for status within a kinship system to be established. For instance, it may be more important to establish that a child has a social father, who will take responsibility for its welfare and have a right to the product of its labour, than to find out who the biological father might be. Nevertheless, most kinship systems do operate to establish rights in the sexual, reproductive, economic, and domestic services of women. In *patrilineal societies, where sons inherit from their fathers, all these rights in women rest with the father until a girl marries, at which point they pass in totality to her husband. *Matrilineal societies, on the other hand, focus on the importance of the sibling group. Inheritance passes from mother's brother to sister's son—in other words from uncle to nephew. The variety of ways in which this is organized have been referred to as solutions to the 'matrilineal puzzle'. In the basic forms it means that brothers have rights over their sisters until they marry. At this point they retain reproductive rights, thus controlling their sisters' sons for inheritance purposes; however, sexual rights pass to the husband, as may rights to domestic services. Economic rights to the products of the sister's labour are likely to remain with the brother or sibling group.

Inheritance apart, kinship and affinity rules may also affect residence, relationships between individuals, modes of address, and various other economic and political behaviours. The rules themselves have been investigated through the study of genealogy, kinship terminology, marriage preferences and cycles of social reproduction. Within social anthropology, kinship theories tend to be grouped according to the relative emphasis they place on rules of descent or rules of affinity. In other words, they concentrate on either parent and child relationship rules or on the bonds between groups established through marriage.

Between the 1930s and 1960s, descent theory was predominant, associated largely with the work of Africanist anthropologists, such as Meyer *Fortes, and the theoretical work of A. R. *Radcliffe-Brown. Descent theorists suggest that kinship systems function to make sure that lineage groups persist over time as political entities. This means that relationships within lineage groups must be established and maintained through actual or fictional links traced through either or both parents. Parent-child and sibling bonds are therefore the focus of attention. Descent and succession are stressed in these studies, which are also highly empirical and related to *functionalist theory, entailing that, for descent theorists, kinship systems exist in order to allocate rights and duties in societies.

*Alliance theory is more theoretical, being interested in how the rules setting up links between groups through marriage are generated. Marriage and incest rules are therefore central. This means that, for alliance theorists, kinship systems exist in order to generate marriage possibilities or impossibilities. Much of this perspective is derived from the work of Claude Lévi-Strauss, who designated kinship systems as being either 'elementary' or 'complex'. In the former case, a spouse is selected according to social rules, whereas in the latter the marriage partner is not determined by structural rules but rather by individual choice. However, these are abstract principles rather than descriptions of empirical reality: in practice, all societies have incest rules that define marriage partners according to elementary structures, and all have complex aspects that allow for a measure of situational choice.

In the 1960s and 1970s, controversy between alliance and descent theorists was heated, being part of the debate between functionalist and *structuralist schools in social anthropology. Since then the discussion has cooled, and it is now generally acknowledged that the difference lies more in the level of theory applied, than in either any fundamental difference in concrete kinship systems or necessary adherence to a particular theoretical perspective.

Good introductions include Rodney Needham, *Rethinking Kinship and Marriage*, and Chris Harris, *Kinship* (1990). *See also* FAMILY, SOCIOLOGY OF.

Klein, Melanie (1882–1960) An Austrian-born, second-generation psychoanalyst, trained under Sandor Ferenczi in Budapest and Karl Abraham in Berlin. She moved to London in 1926 and became a major figure in British and world *psychoanalysis, the founder, within the British Psychoanalytic Society, of the Kleinian school.

Her innovations in technique were to analyse young children, substituting play for verbal free-association; to explore the importance of counter-transference—the analyst's feelings about the client; and to undertake the analysis of psychotics. She developed a more elaborate theory of the emotional life of the young baby than did Sigmund Freud. Her argument was that all infants progress through two positions: a paranoid-schizoid position, where bad feelings are projected into the external world, which is then felt to be threatening; and a depressive position, when these feelings are reintegrated into the personality. Thus everybody has the experience of, and at least the distant possibility of regressing to, madness. She gave a clinical meaning to *Freud's concept of the death instinct, dealing with it as destructive envy (hatred), and emphasized the role of unconscious fantasy.

Over recent years her work has been drawn on for purposes of social criticism. For example, her analysis of the early stages of development can be used to understand characteristics of the modern personality (see C. Lasch, *The Minimal*

Self, 1984), and her concern with the play of love and hate has been used to supplement critical theory (see C. F. Alford, *Melanie Klein and Critical Social Theory*, 1989). Her most important papers can be found in Juliet Mitchell (ed.), *The Selected Melanie Klein* (1986). *See also* OBJECT RELATIONS THEORY.

Klein, Viola (1908–73) An Austrian social theorist, she fled to England as a refugee in 1939, becoming a domestic servant. Her second doctorate (obtained in 1944 from the London School of Economics) was published as *The Feminine Character: History of an Ideology* (1946), however her most famous study was conducted with Alva *Myrdal on *Women's Two Roles: Home and Work* (1956, 1968 2nd edn.), an influential volume that was published before the advent of the second wave of *feminism but anticipated many of its arguments.

Kluckhohn, Clyde (1905–60) An American anthropologist who taught at Harvard University and whose writings combined elements of anthropology and psychology. His main publication was *Navajo Witchcraft* (1944), in which he argued that witchcraft within the local society served to channel tensions caused by pressures exerted from the wider society. For a number of years he worked alongside Talcott *Parsons, in the interdisciplinary Department of Social Relations at Harvard, and is generally recognized as having encouraged Parsons to take seriously the Freudian-influenced American cultural anthropology of the 1940s. *See also* CULTURE AND PERSONALITY SCHOOL; MAGIC, WITCHCRAFT, AND SORCERY.

knowledge, sociology of The sociology of knowledge is concerned with the relationship of knowledge to a social base—although what is meant by knowledge and social base is likely to vary from author to author. All the major sociological theorists regarded this as an integral part of their theory. Émile *Durkheim for example, in his sociology of religion, suggested that the basic mental categories by means of which we order the world are rooted in the way we organize society. Max *Weber, in his sociology of religion, gave considerable weight to material conditions influencing the formation of religious beliefs.

*Marxism related knowledge specifically to a theory of *ideology. The social origins of knowledge are seen as related to the possibility of grasping truth. It is sometimes argued that the content of knowledge depends upon social or economic position: the *bourgeoisie will come to look at the world in one way (say in terms of individual competition and survival of the fittest), the *proletariat in another (the point of view of cooperative enterprise and mutual support). These different viewpoints come directly from the experience of each class in the productive process. A more sophisticated tradition, building upon the work of *Hegel and associated with György *Lukács and the Frankfurt School (*see* CRITICAL THEORY), argues that it is the form of knowledge rather than its content that is important. Thus, for Lukács in *History and Class Consciousness* (1923), the thought appropriate to the bourgeois period is marked by formal logic. It is analytic in form, breaking down its subject-matter into component parts, and centres around a number of so-called antinomies—categories such as subject and object which cannot be brought together into a coherent whole. Marxist thought, on the other hand, is claimed to be synthetic, totalizing, and *dialectical. Each form represents the experience of a different social class. For both approaches the proletarian forms of thought are closest to the truth.

The most explicit formulation of the sociology of knowledge as a separate area of study is that of Karl *Mannheim. In *Ideology and Utopia* (1936), he developed the standard non-Marxist view, arguing that a range of social positions (not merely social class) determine forms of knowledge and that it is not possible to grant one point of view greater truth-value than another. However, by virtue of their 'relatively detached' location, intellectuals can mediate between different positions and produce a more complete view.

As a distinct sub-area, the sociology of knowledge seems to begin and end with Mannheim, although various combinations of his ideas (and those of Marxism) can be found in the sociologies of modernity, religion, and science—the last of these often focusing on the knowledge-effect of particular institutions. These discussions are always haunted by the problem of *relativism: how can one make a universal claim that all knowledge is dependent on social position since, presumably, such a claim is itself context-bound? This problem is discussed at length in Werner Stark's *The Sociology of Knowledge* (1958)—still one of the most exhaustive introductions to the classic literature.

Since the 1980s there has been a determined effort to revitalize the field, by sociologists interested in culture, science, religion, and ideology. The development of *cultural studies as a separate discipline has also contributed to this initiative. This work concentrates not on the differing social locations and interests of individuals or groups, but rather on how particular kinds of social organization make whole orderings of knowledge possible. It also expands the field of study from an examination of the contents of knowledge to the investigation of 'forms and practices of knowing'—and so, inevitably, to the structuring of political, cultural, and organizational *discourse. Researchers have looked at the ways in which knowledge is preserved, organized, and transmitted by various media; at how social groups retain and alter their collective memories (for example by 'inventing tradition'); at how organizational structures and practices influence ideas (evident, it is claimed, in the relationship between the structuring of scientific communities and the coherence of particular intellectual *paradigms); and at how authority and *power shape knowledge. For a useful summary of this increasingly diffuse literature see Ann Swidler and Jorge Arditi 'The New Sociology of Knowledge', *Annual Review of Sociology* (1994). *See also* EVANS-PRITCHARD; RELIGION, SOCIOLOGY OF; SCHELER; SCIENCE, SOCIOLOGY OF; SOREL.

Kollontai, Alexandra (1872–1952) A leading *feminist in revolutionary Russia. Her main concerns linked class and revolutionary activity to woman's role and motherhood. Always controversial, she is most noted in sociology for her free-thinking radical analyses of sex and love, which are usefully appraised in Beatrice Farnsworth's *Alexandra Kollontai* (1980).

Kondratieff cycles *See* BUSINESS CYCLE.

Kroeber, Alfred Lewis (1876–1960) An American cultural anthropologist, ethnographer of Native Americans (see his *Handbook of the Indians of California*, 1925), and author of a philosophical and anthropological study of cultural development (*Configurations of Culture Growth*, 1944). The most concise account of his commitment to historical particularism, as against the prevailing *evolutionism, is his article on 'The Eighteen Professions' (*American Anthropologist*, 1915), a forceful statement of the *ideographic approach to the study of social structures, and of his belief that history is determined by cultural patterns and not accidents of personality (see also his 'The Superorganic', *American Anthropologist*, 1917).

Kuhn, Manford (1911–63) A leading *symbolic interactionist, who developed a more quantitative strand of interactionism, and argued that the methodology of the *Chicago School was too vague to permit scientific precision. Kuhn and his colleagues attempted to give operational definitions to such concepts as 'social act' and 'the *self'. The most familiar of his research instruments was the so-called *Twenty Statements Test, which asked people to list twenty responses to the question 'Who Am I?', as a basis for a more objective study of the self.

Kuhn's distinctive approach (sometimes termed the 'Iowa School' of symbolic interactionism) is apparent in the work of Norman K. Denzin, who has undertaken research in the areas of childhood, emotions, alcoholism, life-histories, and film, using a variety of quantitative and qualitative techniques and advocating the research methodology of *triangulation (see *The Research Act: A Theoretical Introduction to Sociological Methods*, 1978, and *Sociological Methods: A Sourcebook*, 1978). Most recently Denzin has described his work as *Interpretive Interactionism* (1990).

Kuhn, Thomas Samuel (1922–1996) American philosopher and historian of science who had a major influence on the development of thinking about intellectual change in sociology and other social sciences. Began his career studying physics at Harvard in the 1940s but converted to the history of science, producing a study of theoretical change in astronomy in his *The Copernican Revolution: Planetary Astronomy in the Development of Western Thought* (1957). Reflecting on the wider implications of this work, he wrote *The Structure of Scientific Revolutions* (1962). His central thesis was that everyday science works within particular paradigms of thought that comprise a framework of 'normal science' in which key assumptions are unquestioningly taken for granted. Only when anomalous observations that cannot be incorporated into these paradigms accumulate do scientists begin to look for alternative ways of seeing the world. It is at such times that 'scientific revolutions' may occur through the invention of new world views that eventually settle down as the basis of a new period of normal science.

Kuhn's work resonated with arguments in the sociology of knowledge that underpinned debates in sociology in the 1960s and 1970s and led the adoption of a rather simplistic form of his argument and so to a growth in relativism and an emphasis on diversity and plurality in theoretical frameworks. His arguments are actually much closer to the forms of realism that have become important in recent social science.

kula ring An exchange cycle that took place in the Trobriand Islands documented by Bronislaw Malinowski in *Argonauts of the Western Pacific* (1922). Twice each year, Trobriand islanders launched their canoes and visited other islands, carrying gifts and local specialities for barter. When they arrived, the travellers gave gifts, bartered, and were feasted by their hosts. These were not simple trading expeditions since the islanders aimed to acquire, from special kula-exchange partners, armlets of white shells (*mwali*) and necklaces of red shells (*souvlava*). These gifts were carried from one island to another in a ring, the armlets in one direction and the necklaces in another, in a constant cycle of exchange called 'kula'.

Kula items had no monetary value and could not be converted into consumer goods. They were merely for display and prestige, similar to a sports trophy that is held only until the next encounter. The shells were highly esteemed by men who sought them from their lifetime partners in exchange: hence the local saying 'Once in kula, always in kula'. Every man in the kula cycle received all of the kula articles at some point, keeping them for a while and then passing them on. The shells were formally transferred and no haggling was allowed. The time-lapse between the gift and counter-gift was an expression of confidence, on the part of the giver, that the partner would return his due. Men performed magic to ensure goodwill and affection so that shells would be returned, since a man's prestige depended on it.

Malinowski chastised writers who referred to kula shells as money. They are better seen as an exchange of gifts in a moral framework. Thus Malinowski used the kula to make the more general point that the economy is embedded in social relations. The kula ring welded together a large number of islands and their economies. He also stressed the political nature of kula. It provided internal status for men, and strengthened political stability among kula trading islands by reinforcing peace. According to Malinowski, the many interactions which came under the ambit of kula (prestige, political influence, trade, and gift-giving) all formed 'one organic whole'. Malinowski's study of kula exchange is thus a major demonstration of the *functionalist method in anthropology. *See also* GIFT RELATIONSHIP; RATIONAL CHOICE THEORY.

SEE WEB LINKS
• Links concerning the kula and the Trobriand Islands (now part of Kiriwina).

labelling (labelling theory) Labelling theory was a major thrust of the sceptical revolution in the sociology of *deviance during the 1950s and 1960s. The orthodox *criminology of the immediate post-war period, both in Britain and America, treated a crime or act of deviance as an unambiguous occurrence that could readily be explained as a product of individual psychology or (even) genetic inheritance. Crimes were committed by criminal types—people with particular psychogenetic attributes or socio-cultural backgrounds.

This *positivist tradition was challenged by members of the *Society for the Study of Social Problems (in the United States) and the *National Deviance Conference (in the United Kingdom), who argued that the established criminology was biased because it favoured authoritative definitions of deviance, was overly deterministic in its view of what caused deviant behaviour, and was uncritical of the thesis that the deviant was a particular type of person. The orthodoxy posed only behavioural and motivational questions about crime: 'Why did they do it?'; 'What sort of people are they?'; and 'How can we stop them doing it again?'. Labelling theorists addressed a number of definitional issues hitherto largely ignored: 'Why does a particular rule, the infraction of which constitutes deviance, exist at all?'; 'What are the processes involved in identifying someone as a deviant and applying the rule to him or her?'; and 'What are the consequences of this application, both for the society and the individual?'

The labelling perspective can be seen as a development of Edwin Lemert's distinction (in *Social Pathology*, 1951) between *primary and secondary deviance; that is, between the initial behaviour (which may arise from a variety of causes), and the symbolic reorganization of *self and social *roles that may occur because of the societal response to any deviation from *norms. The leading American proponent of labelling theory was Howard S. Becker, who argued in *Outsiders* (1963) that deviance is created by society, in the sense that 'social groups create deviance by making the rules whose infraction constitutes deviance and by applying those rules to particular persons and labelling them as outsiders'. From this point of view, deviance is not a quality of the act a person commits, but rather a consequence of the application of rules: 'deviant behaviour is behaviour that people so label'. This position has considerable similarity with some forms of *conflict theory. Stanley Cohen (*Folk Devils and Moral Panics*, 1972) and others developed the proposition that labelling can induce amplification of deviance. That is, attempts at social control may *stigmatize individuals by defining them in dehumanized ways (as thugs, acid-heads, or whatever), and have the unintended consequence of encouraging the deviance they seek to eliminate, by constraining individuals to employ a deviant identity as a means of defence, attack, or adjustment to the problems created by the societal reaction. In this way amplification may occur. An act of non-conformity or alleged deviance is defined as being worthy of attention and is responded to punitively; the deviant is therefore isolated from conventional society; begins to define himself or herself in deviant terms, and to associate with others in a similar position, leading to more deviance; which in turn exposes the group to further punitive sanctions by conformists.

Although labelling theory quickly generated an impressive body of empirical studies it was subjected to considerable criticism during the 1970s. The most common complaints were that it ignored the sources of deviant behaviour; could be applied to only a limited range of criminal activities; was too deterministic in its conception of the labelling process; and neglected issues of *power and social *structure. To those on the political right, the theory seemed tantamount to a claim that many criminals were in fact victims, more sinned against than sinning. It made societal reaction (especially the activities of the police, courts, and other agencies of *social control) the crucial variable. The accusation was often made that this new sociology of deviance seemed more intent on excusing than explaining criminal activity. Labelling theory was particularly vulnerable to this charge since it could be caricatured as offering a crude 'no deviance, leads to slam on label, leads to deviance' model of crime. This perception was heightened by the fact that the theory could most obviously be applied to expressive deviance, and for the large part victimless crimes, such as homosexuality, drug addiction, alcoholism, gang membership, and mental illness. The labelling perspective thus became known in some quarters as 'the sociology of nuts, sluts, and perverts'.

Critics on the political left argued that the theory did not go far enough in its attack on the status quo. By directing attention towards lower-level agencies of social control—the media and social welfare departments for example—it ignored the governing elites in whose interests these institutions actually operated. Labelling theorists studied rule-enforcers rather than rule-makers. Their sympathy for the underdog was not translated into a systematic critique of private property and other allegedly repressive and exploitative structures of capitalist societies. Ironically, some of this criticism later emerged from within the National Deviancy Conference itself, among so-called radical criminologists such as Ian Taylor, Paul Walton, and Jock Young (*The New Criminology*, 1973).

Much of this criticism was undoubtedly unfair and stemmed from a fundamental misunderstanding about the aspirations of the labelling theorists. The definitive defence of the theory is Ken Plummer's 'Misunderstanding Labelling Perspectives' (in D. Downes and P. Rock (eds.), *Deviant Interpretations*, 1979). Plummer points out that the labelling perspective was concerned only with the social processes governing the nature, emergence, application, and consequences of labels. For this reason it could easily be accommodated to studies of deviancy conducted from a variety of otherwise incompatible theoretical standpoints. Many labelling theorists worked within the interactionist tradition, which posits that society is constructed via an exchange of gestures, involving symbolic communication and the negotiation of meaning between reflexive actors. This general perspective is obviously consistent with the particular propositions of labelling theory. But some labelling studies were predominantly *functionalist, *phenomenological, *dramaturgist, or *ethnomethodological in character. It often transpired, therefore, that critiques of labelling theory were actually critiques of its supposedly interactionist or phenomenological premises and propositions. In fact labelling arguments can be accommodated to a range of social theories.

Seen in this light many of the standard criticisms of the theory simply miss the point. Labelling theory does not identify the causes of primary deviance because it does not set out to do so: it offers an explanation of labels rather than of behaviour. Most exponents drew on other sorts of explanations to account for the primary deviance towards which societal reaction was directed. Not even Becker makes the claim that labels themselves are the root cause of deviant behaviour. Nor is there anything inevitable about labelling or amplification. The transition from primary to secondary deviance is a complicated process full of contingencies. Labels may be provisional, negotiable, or rejected. Similarly, it is unfair to complain that labelling theorists ignored large areas of deviant behaviour, since they clearly did not purport to offer a universal explanation for every known form of crime. Rather, proponents made the considerably more modest claim that labelling may alter the direction, intensity, and incidence of the deviant experience. At worst, therefore, labelling theorists can only be accused of setting themselves rather modest aetiological objectives.

Despite many new developments in the study of deviance since the 1970s, labelling theory has remained a prominent influence, especially in North America. Indeed, and ironically (given its radical roots), it may have become something of a new orthodoxy. *See also* CRIMINOLOGY, CRITICAL; DEVIANCE AMPLIFICATION; FOLK DEVIL; MORAL PANIC; SYMBOLIC INTERACTIONISM.

(⊕) SEE WEB LINKS
• A classic paper by Thomas Scheff: 'The Labelling Theory of Mental Illness'. (Subscription)

labour In most sociological contexts this term is synonymous with *wage-labour. However, in *Marxism attention is often drawn to the conflicting interests of 'Labour' and 'Capital'. The former is here a reference to the *proletariat, and alludes to the theory of the *exploitation of labour-power by the capitalist class, or *bourgeoisie. Occasionally, as for example in anthropological discussion of 'labouring' or sociological analyses of *domestic labour, the term may be equated with *work rather than the more restricted category of paid *employment.

labour aristocracy A concept developed by Friedrich *Engels to designate an upper section of the *working class which was in receipt of higher wages and hence liable to be bribed into a surrender of its class interests. The money for this payment was, in Lenin's interpretation of the argument, held to come from *imperialist profits.

The major discussion of the concept has been in relation to the development of class relations in Victorian and Edwardian Britain (the so-called 'labour aristocracy debate' of the 1970s). Among other things, the principal protagonists (who included sociologists of class and culture) disputed the definition of the concept itself; the role of this stratum in promoting working-class militancy and quiescence; standards of living in the immediate aftermath of the Industrial Revolution; conditions of employment, authority in the workplace, and the social construction of *skill; the cultural and political elements in *class consciousness; the emergence of the 'domestic ideal' and the changing role of women in industrial society; and the links between the development of the British working class and 19th-century British *imperialism. The debate petered out—largely unresolved—but yielded a prodigious amount of excellent historical research at both the national and local levels of analysis. A convenient summary of the issues will be found in Robert Gray's *The Aristocracy of Labour in Nineteenth-Century Britain, c.1850–1914* (1981).

labour, division of *See* DIVISION OF LABOUR.

labour-force participation rate This refers to the number of people in *work and *unemployment and those seeking work, as a proportion of a specified baseline population. Rates may vary according to how the base group is defined, for example male, female, the total adult population over 16 years, or the working-age population (16–65 years). Difficulties arise over female participation rates, especially in *Third World countries, because of ambiguity in the definition of women's work. The same applies to child labour.

labour market In a labour market, human effort (or labour power) is made into a commodity, which is bought and sold under terms which in law are deemed to constitute a contract. The purchase and sale of formally free labour developed extensively with *capitalism, but alternative paths to *industrialization (such as *real socialism) have entailed wage employment, though not strictly a free *market for labour. Economists argue that, as with other factors of *production, the market for labour can be understood as a special case of the general theory of prices, with the price (wages or salaries) being determined by supply and demand. However, research on actual labour markets has shown that, in practice, many of the basic conditions assumed by price theory are usually absent. Mobility of workers between jobs is often sluggish or non-existent; the anarchic structure of earnings differentials bears only the loosest relation to labour supply and demand; *discrimination, *labelling, *racism, and *sexism are rife. Economic explanations of labour-market processes have to be supplemented, and sometimes replaced, by sociological analysis, creating a promising field for interdisciplinary research.

*Neo-classical economic theory views exchanges in the labour market as voluntary, and engaged in because, for each party, the results of the *exchange are better than their other options. The labour market is a competitive market because there are many potential buyers for each seller and vice versa. The supply of labour from existing and potential workers and the demand for labour from employers interact so as to reach an *equilibrium price for labour. If the price of labour rises above equilibrium level for any reason, for example due to a national minimum wage or strong *trade-union bargaining, employers will reduce the number of jobs offered. If the price of labour falls, employers will increase the number of jobs offered, all other things being equal. Economic theory of the labour market also posits that both *monopolies and discrimination will disappear in the long run, and are thus unlikely to be enduring constraints on individuals. On the other hand, economic models of the labour market see workers forming a queue for the available jobs, with employers choosing the best first: people with higher qualifications, more experience, and wider skills will be offered jobs before those with less to offer. It follows that the unemployed will always consist of those with few or no qualifications, fewest skills, and least employment experience; and that people with social, psychological, or other problems will be less readily hired. So the model allows for certain forms of rational discrimination.

Many economic models assume that people have perfect information with which to make rational decisions within given constraints, and adjust their offer and demand prices accordingly. Empirical research has persuaded some economists to recognize that information gathering and analysis are costly in time and money, so that market imperfections arise from incomplete or inadequate information, and *satisficing models are accepted as more realistic than maximizing models of behaviour.

Basic to sociological studies of labour markets is the recognition that, although labour effort is nominally bought and sold, it lacks many of the attributes of other commodities in the capitalist economy. These differences in turn go some way to explaining why the market for labour presents such a confusing picture to the price theorist. At least four factors should be considered here.

First, like any service which is bought, there is scope for ambiguity about what precisely constitutes a satisfactory amount of *work (or effort) done in fulfilment of the contract. Ambiguity about what constitutes a fair day's work for a fair day's pay is endemic, especially if there are frequent changes in work tasks. Because this *effort bargaining occurs in even the most routine work situations, then values, custom and practice, administrative rules, and the relative power of employer and employees, are all equally important as the price mechanism in shaping labour-market outcomes.

Second, inequality of wages and conditions reflects the level of organization of the workforce, as well as market competition. Though in legal theory a contract of sale assumes equality of both parties to it, this is inconsistent with the power inequality usual between any worker negotiating individually, and a potential employer. Consequently, in a wide variety of situations and nations since the onset of industrialism, workers have sought to offset this by forming trade unions. *Collective bargaining, when it occurs, undermines standard notions of a market by replacing wage-fixing through the price mechanism by wage-fixing through rules. It also brings law and politics into the regulation of labour matters. The acceptability of collective labour contracts and wage-fixing agreements tends to be a potentially destabilizing political issue everywhere in the industrialized world, as is the legality of the unions and associations which represent the collective worker, to say nothing of the sanctions and stratagems used by both sides during the course of industrial conflict. Most societies have therefore sought to surround the labour market with a body of law and politico-administrative control.

Third, both unions and employers frequently seek to create so-called internal labour markets: that is, networks and hierarchies of jobs to which access is restricted by entry rules and internal promotion. For example, by enforcing job-entry controls, unions can restrict access to craft training and relatively favourable wages and conditions. Employers likewise can segment their demand for labour by varying benefits and promotion, seeking to reward and retain valued workers, while offering others only non-standard or *flexible employment. (Some scholars also claim that internal markets based partly on discrimination and wider prejudice help employers to divide and rule the workplace.) Family and neighbourhood networks frequently reinforce exclusiveness of job access outside the actual workplace, producing extended internal labour markets.

Fourth, there remain many industries and situations where workers are relatively powerless and unorganized, so that pay and conditions can be expected to be less favourable than if workers use their collective strength. Union organization has typically been found to be difficult among workers in small-firm industries, in the retailing and personal services sector, in part-time and subcontracted labour, and among women, ethnic minorities, and young people. Isolation and powerlessness do much to explain the common research finding of widespread low pay and insecurity of work among such groups.

Sociologists have stressed the importance of *labour-market segmentation and have identified the cultural, institutional, and structural factors that help determine people's allocation to one or another market, the imperfections of market processes, the reward systems operating in different markets, and the nature of power relationships in the market. Jill Rubery's essay on 'Employers and the Labour Market' (in D. Gallie (ed.), *Employment in Britain*, 1988) reviews the various theories of labour markets, examines the evidence for flexible employment, and contains a good bibliography of British and American case studies. For examples of empirical analyses see Jill Rubery and Frank Wilkinson (eds.), *Employer Strategy and the Labour Market* (1994). *See also* DIVISION OF LABOUR; HUMAN-CAPITAL THEORY; LABOUR-MARKET SEGMENTATION; OCCUPATIONAL SEGREGATION.

labour-market flexibility A term used to refer to all or some of a variety of features of particular jobs, or of the *labour market as a whole, including: reduced demarcations between categories of worker and flexible job descriptions; the fluidity of workers' movement between jobs, employers, or regions; flexible or non-standard work hours; flexibility of wages; and any other innovation in the organization of employment and patterns of work, such as home-based work, or *telecommuting. In this context, wage flexibility more often means wages that rise or fluctuate in line with company profits and financial performance. *See also* FLEXIBLE EMPLOYMENT.

labour-market segmentation In essence, *neo-classical economic theory sees a market for labour, with buyers and sellers in open competition with each

High span of discretion
and
long-term stable earnings

Primary internal market (PI)	(PE)	Primary external market
Secondary internal (SI) market	(SE)	Secondary external market

Flexible but specific skills

Specialized but general skills

Low span of discretion
and
unstable earnings

Labour-market segmentation. Organizational and firm-specific labour markets

other, which functions in broadly the same way as other markets. There are differences of course. It is recognized that labour is not a completely homogeneous commodity: workers differ in their tastes and preferences for leisure rather than work and for monetary rather than non-monetary rewards; they differ also in *human capital, their investment in education and training, work skills, and experience. But it still makes sense to analyse labour supply and demand in the aggregate.

This model of the *labour market has been refined over the years to accommodate the fact that doctors and dress designers, for example, work in entirely different markets. The British economist Alfred *Marshall first introduced the idea of non-competing groups in the labour market in the 1880s. The most significant dividing-lines have been identified as occupational, geographical, and industrial. Occupational labour markets arise from the *division of labour, increasing differentiation and specialization, with workers unable to switch between occupations requiring significantly different skills and extensive investment in training and qualifications. Nurses and doctors, for example, constitute separate occupational labour markets, even if they work side by side in the same organizations. By restricting entry to an occupation, for example by specifying the minimum qualifications and experience required, those already in it can control the supply of labour and help to push up their wages. Labour markets are also defined spatially, given that neither employers nor workers can move to another location without incurring substantial costs. As a result wages can remain high in big cities, for example, even when there are substantial numbers of unemployed in other parts of the country. The term 'local labour market' is often used in reference to the market for jobs within a particular locale—such as a travel-to-work area, town, or city. Industrial labour markets arise where employers in certain industries require particular skills, or combinations of skill, and seek to retain workers long-term after they have been trained. For example, police officers, civil servants, and coalminers may be mobile across regions of the country and even employers, while exercising the same range of skills in their work, and obtaining similar or industry-standard terms of employment.

The idea of non-competing groups has been developed much further in theories that are identified under the general label of labour-market segmentation theory. The two key formulations are the theories of dual (or split) labour markets and of internal labour markets, both developed in the United States by Peter Doeringer and Michael Piore (*Internal Labor Markets and Manpower Analysis*, 1971) and others (Richard Edwards, Michael Reich, and David Gordon, *Labor Market Segmentation*, 1975), and extended through empirical research. A framework obtained by integrating these two into a single model has since been developed in Europe and is shown in the figure above.

The theory of dual labour markets revolves around the identification of a split between two analytically distinct sectors in the economy and national labour market: a primary sector and secondary sector with quite different wage and employment characteristics and processes. The theory states that job mobility between the two labour markets is very restricted in normal circumstances; in effect workers in the secondary sector are trapped there unless, say, they go to college and obtain higher qualifications. The secondary sector is marked by pervasive *under-employment and *unemployment; jobs are mostly low-skilled, require relatively little training, and can be learnt relatively quickly on the job. There are few barriers to job mobility within the secondary sector. Because the jobs are unattractive there is little incentive to stay, and there are high levels of labour turnover, with workers moving on to other jobs or employers. Wages are generally low, and terms and conditions the poorest offered. Theorists differ in their emphasis on 'bad' jobs in terms of pay and conditions, or on relatively unskilled work, and on whether the primary and secondary sectors also have distinctively different work cultures. The primary sector generally contains the higher-grade, higher-status, and better-paid jobs, with employers who offer the best terms and conditions. In some formulations the emphasis is on occupational labour markets with controlled entry to them; in others the emphasis is on industrial labour markets and the characteristics of employers. The primary sector is sometimes sub-divided into an upper and lower tier. These economic concepts of primary and secondary sectors draw on and have close similarities with sociological theory on social *stratification and *social mobility between classes. Similarly, the theory of internal labour markets has close parallels in sociological debates on the 'Balkanization' of labour markets, industrial feudalism, and the question of property rights in a job. Labour-market segmentation theory has been more accessible to sociologists than most *classical economic theory (*see* LAISSEZ-FAIRE ECONOMICS), and has facilitated multi-disciplinary research on labour-market functioning.

The internal labour market is an administrative unit, such as an office or factory, where the levels of employment and wages are determined by a set of internal administrative rules and procedures. It is quite separate from the external labour market of conventional economic theory, where pricing, allocating, and training decisions are controlled by economic variables. The two markets are connected, with movement between them at specified ports of entry and exit.

Otherwise jobs in the internal market are filled by the promotion or transfer of workers who have already gained entry. Jobs in the internal market are shielded from the direct influences of competitive forces in the external market. Another formulation of this perspective is insider-outsider analysis, which identifies the wage advantage attached to certain labour-market positions, types of employer, or industry.

In a study for the European Commission, R. Loveridge and A. Mok (*Theories of Labour Market Segmentation*, 1979) integrated these theoretical strands into the four-fold classification of firm-specific labour markets shown in the figure above. Jobs in the primary internal segment are those typical of the hard core of stable employees in a firm, need long on-the-job training in firm-specific skills, have security and good promotion prospects, a high span of discretion, and high material rewards. Professional and skilled craft work requiring occupation-specific rather than firm-specific skills, and often supplied on a contract or self-employed basis, would be typical of the primary external segment. The secondary external segment provides jobs that are low skilled, offer little autonomy and responsibility, low and unstable earnings, and poor working conditions, including casual and seasonal work. The secondary internal sector offers jobs that are generally low grade but with some on-the-job training, security, and promotion prospects. The model makes it clear that movement between the primary internal and secondary external segments would be virtually ruled out, with varying amounts and directions of movement between adjacent segments, determined by changes in human capital and employers' responses to the changing economic environment.

Empirical research on industrial societies generally shows women, ethnic minorities, and migrant workers to be concentrated in the secondary labour market. However, social scientists differ as to whether empirical analysis should focus on workers, jobs, occupations, companies, workplaces, industries, or some combination of these.

The concepts of primary and secondary labour markets (or sectors) have now passed into conventional thought, with the primary labour market commonly understood to mean people with secure jobs and good conditions of work in public-sector employment, the large corporations, and highly unionized industries; while the secondary labour market is understood to cover small employers, non-unionized sectors of the economy, and highly fragmented and competitive industries such as retailing, where jobs are less secure and conditions of work and pay generally poorest. *See also* INDUSTRIAL RESERVE ARMY.

labour movement A term applied descriptively to include all organizations representing workers who sell their effort in the labour market. A labour movement may be divided heuristically into its industrial and political wings: the former consists of *trade unions as well as other voluntary associations seeking narrowly defined economic objectives, such as higher wages, greater *industrial democracy, or industrial education; the latter comprises one or more *political parties attempting to influence or control *state power on behalf of labour. Historically, labour movements have been very fragmented. While trade unions and political parties have a formal structure and a clear leadership, the 'movements' that they form are looser networks of individuals, organizations, and groups. There is a long-running theoretical debate about this because of the profound influence of *Marxism and *socialism within labour organizations. These have tended to view labour movements holistically, as embodying the organized working class or *proletariat, thus implying an underlying momentum towards unity between the various elements. Even so, disagreement exists about revolutionary strategy, between *syndicalist expectations of the working class seizing political control through organized industrial action alone, and the *Leninist view that trade-union action must give way to political struggle. Students of the labour movement of a more conservative cast of mind have tended to reflect the outlook of Selig Perlman, a pioneer of labour-relations studies in the United States. Strongly influenced by the example of the American working class, Perlman claimed that labour movements embody what he called a communism of opportunity, expressing limited occupational and communal loyalties, rather than a communism of the intellectuals which sought to unify the whole working class. Certainly, in recent years, much greater attention has been given to the historical, cultural, and institutional diversity of the labour movements of different industrial societies (see M. Regini (ed.), *The Future of Labour Movements*, 1992). *See also* SOCIAL MOVEMENTS.

 SEE WEB LINKS
• The Labour History Archive and Study Centre.

labour power *See* LABOUR THEORY OF VALUE.

labour process Analysis of the labour process may be traced back to Karl Marx's interest in the means by which human labour is harnessed in the creation of products for human need. This process is seen to be socially organized and to vary historically between different *modes of production. Under *capitalism, what appears as a relationship between things or objects in production, is in fact a social relationship between owners of the *means of production and their workforce. The key to understanding this relationship lies at the point of production in the *management of the labour process.

In *Labour and Monopoly Capital* (1974), Harry Braverman attempts to update this thesis, by an analysis of the labour process in the era of monopoly capital. His focus is on the so-called *degradation of work associated with ever-tightening management control. It is postulated that a subordination and *de-skilling of labour will emerge from the combined effects of modern management and new styles of mechanization and *automation. The ideal management objective is the removal of all worker control or autonomy, to be achieved through the specialized division and subdivision of tasks. Skilled craft work is thus reduced to the status of unskilled labour. Taylorism, or *scientific management, which developed at the beginning of the 20th century, is seen as the conscious and systematic expression of this process of degradation. It is argued that one overall effect of the degradation of work will be to produce an affinity between intermediate-level workers (such as routine clerical staff) and the mass of the working class.

Factors which Braverman sees as bound up with the changes he postulates are state regulation of the economy, increasing emphasis on planning, the expansion of clerical work and office computerization, and the emergence of *dual labour markets. Precisely how these developments are linked to his central argument is not made clear—though this is also true of some related criticisms.

Braverman's conceptualization of the process of change has been queried in that it represents a unilinear trend, rather than a complex of factors, which may not necessarily cohere. There could, for example, be different patterns in different industries. Similarly, he is attacked for accepting one model of management as universal, when in fact there are many and varied strategies. For example, bureaucratized management could offer the possibility of incorporating the workforce into the management process, in order to ensure their cooperation. Some contributors to the debate have attempted to extend Braverman's original thesis along these lines. (A good example of the post-Braverman treatment of these issues is R. Edwards's *Contested Terrain*, 1979.) Other questions revolve around the nature and definition of *skill, which is felt to allow more scrutiny than Braverman allows. The connection between the demise of craft skills and the process of *rationalization is argued to be insufficiently explored, whilst the de-skilling hypothesis itself is apparently challenged by a dependence on newly emergent skills. On the specific issue of class relations, Braverman's account seems to under-emphasize the possibility of worker opposition to tightening management control, especially where there are strong *trade unions; whilst, conversely, his equating of worker skill with weaker managerial control has been challenged. His analysis is particularly limited since it addresses only the objective nature of class relations, not the subjective experience of the working class. Again, sympathetic commentators have tried to rectify these shortcomings, in a sustained programme of empirical research. (See, for example, M. Burawoy, *The Politics of Production*, 1975). These criticisms are, however, testament to how influential Braverman's work has been in setting an agenda for debate, much of which has continued to be framed in the original terms of his argument. *See also* PROLETARIANIZATION.

labour relations Labour relations, or industrial relations as it is known in Britain, is the interdisciplinary and somewhat diffuse study of the institutions and rule-fixing processes of the *labour market. Its core subject-matter has always been *collective bargaining between *trade unions or analogous organizations of employees, on one hand, and employers and their associations on the other. A widening of scope has been evident for some years however, as a result of the need to put dealings between organized labour and employers into their legal, historical, economic, political, and sociological contexts. The term 'employee relations', found increasingly in *management writing, was once a synonym for industrial relations; it now usually denotes parts of the field in which management-trade union relationships either play a smaller role or are argued to be inappropriate.

Differences in definition derive partly from the fact that, despite a long history of academic investigation, no single disciplinary core has yet emerged in descriptions and explanations of industrial relations behaviour. Today, therefore, work in the subject includes the following: historical and contemporary aspects of the law of labour contract; the difference in theory and practice between wage-fixing by negotiated rules as opposed to competitive or free-*market processes; reasons for state involvement in labour relations together with historical and contemporary aspects of the politics of employer-employee bargaining; the normative basis of wage differentials and wage negotiation; historical and contemporary causes of *industrial conflict and its relation to class conflict; the relationships between the organized and unorganized sectors of the labour-force; *labour-market segmentation and dualism; the relationship of *employment and wage policy to *social policy; *training, *skill, and *unemployment.

Sociologists, historians, economists, psychologists, lawyers, and others continue to make contributions, often with scant regard for each other. In recent years the notion of industrial relations systems (J. T. Dunlop, *Industrial Relations Systems*, 1958, and T. A. Kochan et al., *The Transformation of American Industrial Relations*, 1986) has been regarded as bringing a degree of unity into studies of the field. Critics of the notion argue that it is incomplete, unhelpfully static in conception, and too broad in scope to be more than a classification device with little or no explanatory power. *See also* LABOUR PROCESS; PERSONNEL MANAGEMENT; TRUST AND DISTRUST.

labour theory of value The idea that labour is the ultimate source of all wealth—a commonplace among the early *political economists. Adam Smith, for example, argued that, in a *market society in which workers owned their own means of production, the prices of goods would be proportional to the amount of labour required to produce them. However, where a class of non-labouring capitalists hired a propertyless class of workers to do the labouring, then competition in the market would establish an average rate of profit, such that capitalists would price goods at a level at which they could pay their workers a fair wage, and retain a profit equal to the average yield on capital. In this way, Smith (and later David Ricardo) used the idea as part of a justification for the existence of, and for the privileges associated with, the ownership of private property.

Later *neo-classical economists somewhat embarrassedly distanced themselves from the theory, on the grounds of its metaphysical and immeasurable quality, preferring instead to argue that, far from prices being determined by the role of labour in the production process, they simply reflected people's subjective preferences (or feelings of so-called utility). By contrast, Karl Marx reformulated the theory such that it became the basis for a whole new way of looking at society, and for criticizing the system of private-property ownership itself.

Almost thirty years elapsed between Marx's first use of the term and the publication of his reformulation in volume i of *Capital* (1867). It appears in chapter 6 and represents the critical moment in the entire text. The earlier chapters lead up to, and the later ones follow from, this proposition. As Marx said (chauvinistically) of the wife of one Dr Kugelman, if she could understand this chapter, even she would be able to understand the remainder of *Capital*.

Some sense of the pleasure that Marx derived from the achievement of this reformulation may be gathered from the way in which, following the method of critique, it is suddenly produced, like a conjurer's rabbit, as a solution to a problem whose appearance of impenetrability he takes great pains to create. This problem is as follows: why do those with money invest in production, when all commodity exchange, as symbolized by the existence of money itself, is the exchange of equivalents? Marx's answer is that, within what had hitherto been 'the hidden abode of production', the investor may find and purchase a unique commodity which, when used, creates more value than it costs. This commodity is labour power. The reason that it possesses this unique attribute is that, with the advent of the capitalist *mode of production, labourers finally lost all rights in their means of production, and therefore both had to and were able to sell their labour power to those with property in the means of production, in order to live.

Thus, when the market rule that all commodities exchange for their equivalents is applied in the realm of production, the result is that labourers are not paid on the basis of what they produce but on the basis of what it takes in the way of food and other necessities of life to enable them to continue presenting themselves and their offspring for work. This, then, is what creates the possibility of 'surplus value'—since the value of the labourer's subsistence ('necessary labour') should be produced, under normal conditions, in less than the total number of hours worked. The result is that capital has at its disposal a quantum of 'surplus labour' whose product it is free to realize for its own sole benefit.

Like most other aspects of Marxist doctrine this particular theory has proved to be highly controversial. Arguably, it has been largely discredited, since not only mainstream economists but also many Marxists themselves have demonstrated its technical deficiencies. One obvious problem, for example, is that the costs of subsistence vary historically and culturally, so that there is no absolute definition of 'necessary labour time'. The quantitative connection between labour and prices in Marxist economics has proved extremely difficult to specify. Conversely, some Marxists have argued that the central position accorded the theory within the Marxian system is unwarranted and indeed unnecessary, since a useful Marxist analysis of the exploitative nature of property relations is possible without recourse to the theory itself. Nevertheless, the labour theory of value (though not necessarily its Marxian variant) remains the principal alternative to orthodox *utility theories of value, and the debate continues (although largely, these days, within highly specialized subfields of economics).

labour union *See* TRADE UNION.

Lacan, Jacques (1901–83) Lacan was a French psychoanalyst and doctor of medicine who reinterpreted the work of Sigmund Freud in the light of the structural linguistics of Ferdinand de Saussure. He trained at the Paris Medical Faculty, in 1963 became Chargé de Conférences at the École Pratique des Hautes Études, and founded the École Freudienne de Paris. He is largely associated with the *structuralist and *post-structuralist movements, and during the 1960s his seminars were a major focus of intellectual life in Paris. His work, which is often obscure and replete with puns and word-plays, has had a considerable influence on feminist theory, because of his argument that Freud's hypotheses must be interpreted symbolically rather than literally; and, in particular, that Freud's controversial idea of 'penis envy' should be treated metaphorically.

The unconscious, Lacan argues, is like language because it operates by using metaphor and metonymy—that is, it works symbolically. His refinement of Freudian theory has been seen by many as crucial because it avoided Freud's controversial and arguably contradictory idea that there are biological 'drives' that reduce all individuals to identical development patterns. Language, according to Lacan, constructs meaning throughout culture, but language is also mutable, so that change is therefore not only possible but also inevitable, both at a social and a personal level. Lacan's theory thus enables the development of *identity and *subjectivity to be seen much more as socially constructed than biologically determined.

Crucial to Lacan's overall theoretical system is his idea of the 'mirror phase' of infant development. He argues that, at around the age of six months, a baby, who has previously thought of itself not as a separate being from its mother, grows aware of being separate. Lacan uses the metaphor of a mirror to illustrate this process, for the baby, looking at the mother as if looking into a mirror, finds an image reflected back which it regards as a coherent and unified whole. In fact, however, the image it sees is the mother/other and not itself. It is this misinterpretation that splits the human psyche into two, because we all identify with something or someone who seems like what or who we want to be, and yet which is in fact separate and alien. This leads to a false belief in the wholeness and stability of the ego, which Lacan sees as a continually restructured process.

As a baby develops, it falls in love with its mother and begins to see the father as threatening to its desire to have the mother to itself. Lacan argues that it is this longing for the mother, and the denial of it by the father who symbolizes culture and the outside world to the baby, which acts to create the unconscious. This process splits the child, the subject, into consciousness and the unconscious, and the whole process is an essential part of a young child's acquisition of language. Awareness of gender difference and the acquisition of gendered subjectivity are also integral to this process. Indeed, the idea of 'difference' is itself fundamental to Lacan's theory.

Lacan is most often referred to by sociologists for his complex decentred conception of the *subject and of gender differences. His most accessible works are probably *Écrits* (1966) and *Four Fundamental Concepts of Psychoanalysis* (1979). Elizabeth Grosz, *Jacques Lacan: A Feminist Introduction*, offers a clear and useful account of his major ideas.

Laing, Ronald D. (1927–89) The best-known British *anti-psychiatrist. Laing's overriding emphasis was on the intelligibility of madness. Drawing on *existentialism, his books explored individual subjectivity (*The Divided Self*, 1960), interpersonal and family dynamics (*The Self and Others*, 1961; *Sanity, Madness and the Family*, 1963), and the wider social context, including the values involved in judgements of sanity and madness (*The Politics of Experience*, 1966). Though he subsequently renounced his more radical views, his ideas still attract attention, and remain controversial. His autobiography, *Wisdom, Madness and Folly* (1985) recounts his first thirty years.

(⊕) SEE WEB LINKS

• An article on sociological aspects of Laing's work, by Susie Scott and Charles Thorpe: 'The sociological imagination of R.D. Laing.' (Subscription)

laissez-faire economics An approach to *economics that asserts the importance of the free, competitive *market of individual suppliers and individual purchasers to the efficient production, distribution, and allocation of goods and services as well as to the maximization of individual choice, and emphasizes the need to keep state regulation to a minimum. Current laissez-faire economic theorizing has its origins in the work of the classical economists, such as David Ricardo, Thomas Malthus, and Adam Smith at the end of the 18th and beginning of the 19th century. In *The Wealth of Nations* (1776) Smith, for example, argued that though individuals in the market would pursue their own self-interest, the market's 'invisible hand' would lead to the realization of the common good.

In the 20th century, the slump of the 1930s was followed by a period in which *Keynesian economics, with its emphasis on state intervention and the value of public spending as a means to reduce unemployment, were dominant. An increasingly *mixed economy, combining public and private enterprise, was developed. However, since the end of the 1970s, following the state's *fiscal crisis and the increasing influence of *New Right philosophies, laissez-faire economics is now once more in the political foreground, with writers such as Friedrich A. *Hayek (*The Road to Serfdom*, 1944) and Milton Friedman (*Capitalism and Freedom*, 1961) providing inspiration. The result has been an increasing *privatization of state activities and a return to an all-pervasive market economy. However, despite its impact on government policies, the criticisms of laissez-faire theorizing are powerful, not least because actual markets bear so little relation to the theorists' idealized models of rational, atomized individuals making choices in the market. In the real world, markets are beset by so-called imperfections: there are often monopolies of supply, imperfect information, few purchasers, external constraints, and so forth. Moreover, individuals' preferences are shaped and limited by *culture and social norms, so reducing choice. The idea of efficient, let alone equitable, allocation via the market is something of a chimera: it functions far more effectively as myth than reality. *See also* LIBERALISM; MONT PELERIN SOCIETY.

language Any verbal or non-verbal *communication engaged in by humans, animals, or even machines. The general field of study which deals with the socio-cultural functions and construction of language is known as sociolinguistics. Sociologists, anthropologists, philosophers, and psychologists all contribute to this area.

The ability of the human race to structure sentences out of essentially arbitrary words which are themselves constructed from individually meaningless sounds (phonemes) is sometimes thought to be the feature that most distinguishes it from other species. All societies have languages that allow humans to express ideas of equal complexity: there is no such thing as a 'primitive' language, although societies may need to borrow or invent new words, in order to express new *concepts.

All human beings possess the ability to learn languages, although brain damage or severe retardation may affect certain areas of language competence. According to Noam Chomsky, children are born with an innate, biological programme that prepares them for how languages are structured. His first book, *Syntactic Structures* (1957), analysed three models of language, arguing that only the third and most complex, involving what he called transformational grammar, is capable of accounting for the infinite range of sentences contained in natural languages. In the same year, the psychologist B. F. Skinner published a study of the acquisition of language (*Verbal Behaviour*), which Chomsky reviewed. Skinner offered a *behaviourist account of language acquisition that was incompatible with Chomsky's ideas about language. Against the behaviourist view that language was acquired through learning in early childhood, Chomsky convincingly argued, in a series of subsequent publications, that a child must be born with an innate linguistic competence—an innate knowledge of the structures of language. It was not possible, he contended, for young children to infer from the language to which they are exposed in the first years of life—its surface structure—the underlying rules or deep structure of language that is necessary to be able to use the language correctly (see especially *Rules and Representations*, 1980).

Others maintain that it is just the child's natural *intelligence that enables it to learn the often very complicated rules and exceptions that structure all language systems. Small children, such as those of international parentage, often have the ability to learn more than one language system. There is fierce debate among linguists as to whether this bilingualism affects the child intellectually—although the basis for some arguments would appear to be more political than scholarly.

The political considerations of bilingualism is just one aspect of the relationship between language and *culture. Languages in many ways reflect the culture of a society, hence the importance that anthropologists place on learning the local language, when studying other societies. For example, languages show how societies classify and evaluate their environment, including kinship relations, the animal kingdom, colours, food, and the natural world. Each society has its own distinctive system of classification which serves in part to maintain boundaries between insiders and outsiders. Mutual comprehension of the cultural as well as the linguistic significance of language used is therefore essential in order to avoid misunderstanding; the translation of culturally constructed concepts and ideas into terms comprehensible to members of another society is a major element of the work not only of anthropologists, but also cross-cultural specialists.

The power of language can be seen in political rhetoric or slogan-making, where single words (such as 'democracy') or phrases (such as 'Black is Beautiful') can mobilize large and diverse groups to political action. Language also demonstrates important divisions within societies that reflect broader political and economic factors. For example, Basil Bernstein has shown that, although middle-class and working-class speech codes are linguistically of equal validity, the working-class (or restricted) code is liable to be discriminated against in the educational arena. A similar phenomenon may be perceived in the relationship between language and regional, ethnic, or religious background. On the other hand, *ethnic groups may utilize their languages as a symbolic means of fostering or developing their own self-identity, or as a means of defence against encroachment by outsiders (as, for example, in the case of Cockney rhyming slang or the rapping style of West Indian youth in Britain). *See also* CONVERSATION ANALYSIS; ELABORATED AND RESTRICTED SPEECH CODES; ETHNOMETHODOLOGY; SAPIR-WHORF HYPOTHESIS; SEMIOLOGY; STRUCTURALISM; WITTGENSTEIN.

langue **and** *parole*   *See* POST-STRUCTURALISM; SAUSSURE.

Lasch, Christopher (1932–94) An American social historian, whose early work was concerned with the history of the American Left, where his political sympathies lay. He subsequently turned to *psychoanalysis and formulated a trenchant critique of modern American society based on the theory of *narcissism (see *Haven in a Heartless World*, 1977, *The Culture of Narcissism*, 1980, and *The Minimal Self*, 1984).

In his later years Lasch launched a defence of American *populism and *communitarianism. For example, in the posthumously published *The Revolt of the Elites and the Betrayal of Democracy* (1995) he attacks America's governing and wealthy elites, who have insulated themselves from the wider society, and feel no responsibility for the welfare of either the poor or the middle classes. As a result, according to Lasch, cities decay, minorities are marginalized, politics are trivialized, crime increases, and society moves towards anarchy. Lasch traces this breakdown to both the ideology of economic *liberalism and the left-wing culture of educational institutions that have given up teaching facts in favour of fashionable theories expressed in (as he sees it) politically correct and incomprehensible jargon.

Critics have argued that Lasch himself sometimes pays scant regard to facts and tends to use evidence loosely; for example, liberals have long recognized that the market needs regulation, and that the poor need some protection by the state. Lasch was also vague about concrete suggestions for improvement, although as a populist he identified himself with the lower middle class of 'small proprietors, artisans, tradesmen and farmers', whose culture he saw as valuing the community (rather than personal ambition) as the highest good, and whom he admired for its 'moral realism, its understanding that everything has its price, its respect for limits, its scepticism about progress' (see, for example, *The True and Only Heaven*, 1991).

late modernity   A term used by writers who do not accept that there has been a transition to a new societal stage of postmodernity, but who do wish to acknowledge that there has been a radical intensification of some of the tendencies of *modernity. Emphases differ but the general position is associated most prominently with the works of Anthony Giddens, Frederic Jameson, David Harvey, and Jürgen Habermas. Whereas postmodernists tend to emphasize fragmentation and centrifugal forces at the cultural level, these theorists focus on the heightening and extension of a range of institutional features that are said to underlie these cultural changes. They also emphasize the continued significance both of centripetal, ordering, forces, and of the possibility for emancipatory politics. For Harvey and Jameson, the fluidities, disjunctions, simulations and forms of nihilism that postmodernism detects and promotes in the cultural sphere are the product of deeper structural changes brought about in the post-industrial, globally networked, period of late capitalism, the era of post-*fordism. Giddens, likewise, emphasizes the intensification and reconfiguration of global capitalism, but in conjunction also with parallel transformations in the capacity for surveillance and administrative control, the nation-state system, and the world military order. Both Giddens and Harvey place issues of time and space at the centre of their analyses. Information, media, and transportation technologies mean that the world has radically shrunk in terms of communication, identity, and the coordination of activities. Giddens draws on Ulrich Beck's notion of 'reflexive modernization' to emphasize the double-bind in which, in an age of heightened complexity, diverse perspectives and an unprecedented access to knowledge about the conditions of activity, such information is inevitably and chronically employed to reorder and redefine that activity, despite the knowledge that the effects will often be perverse.

latent function *See* FUNCTION.

latifundia Large land-holdings in Latin America which originated as imperial grants to settlers from the Spanish crown. With the incorporation of that continent into the world economy they slowly evolved from a form of *feudalism into *capitalist estates producing meat, hides, and crops for export. The distribution of *latifundia* lands through land reform is often seen as a means of promoting economic and social development.

law, sociology of Law—rules of action or statutes established by authorities such as *states—was a central object of theoretical and substantive concern to each of the founding figures of sociology.

Although Karl *Marx did not write a systematic treatise on law, he nevertheless had much to say about it (see M. Cain and A. Hunt, *Marx and Engels on Law*, 1979), including two points which were particularly influential in subsequent studies. The first was that, because the legal system is part of the *bourgeois state, it was an instrument of class oppression. The second was that, because 'the ruling ideas of a period are the ideas of the ruling class', even the most basic of legal concepts (most famously 'rights') are part of the system of bourgeois domination.

Émile *Durkheim likewise did not write a treatise that was specifically devoted to law, although he came closer than Marx in that much of the argument of his *The Division of Labour in Society* (1893) was devoted to explaining why the legal systems of so-called mechanically solidaristic societies are 'retributive', whilst those of organically solidaristic societies should be 'restitutive'. In addition, his *Professional Ethics and Civic Morals* (1950) contains a sustained and significant account of the development of contract and property law during the 19th century.

Finally, and alone amongst the founding figures, Max *Weber did actually write a full-blown treatise on the law. It takes up most of the second volume of his *Economy and Society* (1920) and is a remarkable *tour de force*, covering as it does the theory, history, and social role of the law across a wide variety of different societies. Like Durkheim, but on an entirely different basis, Weber took a much more positive view of the law than Marx, in that he regarded it as an integrative force in society. However, his position was not without a certain ambivalence, since he regarded the law as both an important contributor to the general, historical *rationalization of Western societies (on which point see also his *General Economic History*, 1919–20), and a critical component in the system of legal-rational *domination specific to the most advanced capitalist societies.

Unfortunately, despite the fact that Talcott Parsons periodically returned to the law in the course of his general theorizing, law lost its position as a major focus of macro-sociological work after the death of the discipline's modern founders. Nevertheless, George Gurvitch produced an important study in the 1940s. Because of this neglect, and certainly because of the rise of *empiricism and the existence of a high level of official interest in the results of research related to the operation of the legal system, theoretical issues virtually disappeared from the interests of sociologists of law until the 1970s. In their absence there appeared numberless studies of the police, lawyers, judges, and the court and other regulatory systems, plus many purporting to report on the social impact of various laws. Niklas Luhmann has, however, produced some important accounts of law from the standpoint of his *system theory (in *A Sociological Theory of Law*, 1965, and *Law as a Social System*, 2004).

Recently, the situation has changed. Researchers with theoretical as well as substantive interests in sociological questions about the law have returned to the founders and sought to develop their work so that it can be applied to contemporary societies. Leading examples of such work include Bernard Edelman, *The Ownership of the Image: Elements for a Marxist Theory of Law* (1979); Frank Pearce, *The Radical Durkheim* (1989); and, for the continuation of the Weberian legacy, Roberto Unger, *Law in Modern Society* (1976). There have also been several recent moves to reintegrate theory and empirical work (for an ambitious attempt to do this retrospectively in a textbook format see R. Cotterrell, *The Sociology of Law*, 1984). Why this should be happening is a question for the sociology of knowledge, but it was certainly influenced by the growing importance of *labelling theory in studies of crime. A further reason is the renewed interest in theoretical issues that has marked jurisprudence proper over the same period. Especially in the United States, the established approaches, represented by legal positivism and legal realism, have been challenged by the neo-liberal Law and Economics School (see R. Bowles, *Law and Economy*, 1982), as well as by the much more diffuse Critical Legal Studies Movement.

(⊕) SEE WEB LINKS

- International Journal of Law, Crime, and Justice: the leading socio-legal studies publication (subscription).
- The Socio-Legal Studies Association.

Lazarsfeld, Paul F. (1901–76) An Austrian-born sociologist who founded the Bureau of Applied Social Research at Columbia University. He was a leading authority on American *popular culture, *voting behaviour, and the influence of the *mass media upon society. Among his best-known works are *The People's Choice* (1944) and *Personal Influence* (1955). Lazarsfeld was the principal proponent of *survey analysis in post-war American sociology. His technique of hypothesis-testing via cross-tabulation set standards for quantitative data analysis that were transcended only with the advent of more advanced multivariate modelling techniques. Among his contemporary critics, C. Wright Mills argued that Lazarsfeld's work exemplified *abstracted empiricism, though this charge is hardly justified given Lazarsfeld's explicit interest in *theories of the middle range. More recently, his work has come to be cited as illustrative of sociological *positivism.

Leach, Edmund R. (1910–89) An iconoclastic British *social anthropologist, knighted in 1975, influential in introducing continental *structuralist thought to the Anglo-Saxon world, as an antidote to the prevailing *structural-functionalist orthodoxy. His major research was in the areas of political rhetoric, linguistic categories, kinship, myth and ritual, in works such as *Political Systems of Highland Burma* (1954), *Rethinking Anthropology* (1962), *Genesis as Myth and Other Essays* (1969), *Lévi-Strauss* (1970), *Culture and Communication* (1976), and *Social Anthropology* (1982). His biography is recounted in Stanley Tambiah's *Edmund Leach: An Anthropological Life* (2002).

learning theory The formulation of laws or principles of learning, learning theory is usually identified with *behaviourist 'stimulus-response' models of learning, centred on the process of *conditioning. However, psychologists now view learning as a process involving *cognition and information handling, and as a rule do not attempt to develop highly generalized theories of learning. *See also* AGGRESSION.

Lefebvre, Henri (1901–91) A Marxist, active in the French Communist Party, he joined the Centre d'études Sociologiques, headed by Georges *Gurvitch, in 1948 and carried out studies on peasant communities and rural life. He later moved to the University of Strasbourg. His first major work was *Dialectical Materialism* (1939) in which he adopted a theoretical orientation very close to that of the early *Lukács. This centred on the analysis of *alienation or reification in everyday consciousness, particularly as expressed in privatized consumption and personal relations. He developed this idea in the three volumes of his *Critique of Everyday Life* (1947, 1961, 1981) and in the associated work on *Everyday Life in the Modern World* (1968). He focused on the development and transformation of urban life as a lived space within which work, leisure, and private life all have their focus. Amongst many other works he produced a major theoretical statement of a social theory of space in *The Production of Space* (1974).

legitimacy (legitimation) Legitimation refers to the process by which *power is not only institutionalized but more importantly is given moral grounding.

Legitimacy (or authority) is what is accorded to such a stable distribution of power when it is considered valid.

Max Weber, whose work is central to understanding the complexity of the relationship between power and legitimacy, distinguished 'factual power' and the 'authoritarian power of command' as two *ideal types. The former refers to the subordination exacted on the basis of *interests, where control over goods and services in the market involves the actor submitting freely to that power. As for the latter, in due course naked factual power needs to justify itself, and through the process of legitimation evokes the sense of duty to obey, regardless of personal motives and interests.

Legitimacy may be claimed by those with power on the basis of either traditional, charismatic, or rational-legal grounds. Likewise, legitimacy—and therefore authority—may be accorded to a distribution of power on the basis of tradition, on affectual or emotional grounds usually associated with revelation (charisma), on the basis of value-rational faith or belief in an absolute, or finally on grounds of belief in the legality of the order. The content of the justification for continued domination—its legitimation—constitutes the basis for the differences in such empirical structures of domination as bureaucracies.

Weber distinguishes the legitimacy of an order from its 'validity'. An order becomes more valid as the probability increases that action will be guided by the belief in the existence of a legitimate order. An order is more or less valid, rather than more or less legitimate.

In Weber's writings, it is possible to identify factual power as being concomitant with property and the *market and therefore with *class, legitimate power with a *status order and therefore with status groups. All orders are a mixture of the two, although it is clear that commercial classes, property classes, and social classes are associated with a diachronic movement towards the eventual legitimation of class power buttressed by the status order. The emergence of action guided by custom, habit, convention, legal enactment, and finally religious encoding indicates the stages in the legitimating process of the power of the rulers, and leads eventually to the stable distribution of power. However, when 'the myth of positive privilege' is no longer accepted unquestionably by the masses and the 'class situation' becomes visible as the determinant of an individual's fate, then legitimacy rooted in the status order and its accompanying ideological legitimation can be said to have broken down, and with it that status order itself. Weber does not provide specific accounts of what the factors are which precipitate the legitimation crisis, although the section on the conditions for the formation of communal class action in his famous essay on 'Class, Status and Party' provides some insight into such a scenario.

It is possible to see the ideology of *citizenship as a modern example of a legitimating principle, where the incorporation through the extension of formal civil, political, and social rights provides a status order for the market-generated inequalities of late *capitalism. However, the pressure to provide substantial content to formal rights (actual equality before the law, actual right to property, equal access to the freedom of speech, and the means to participate through social *welfare provision within such a society) may all undermine the legitimating role of citizenship.

legitimation crisis *See* CRITICAL THEORY.

leisure class A term coined by Thorstein *Veblen. In his book *The Theory of the Leisure Class* (1899), Veblen postulates the growth in the United States of an idle and parasitic leisure class. This class is argued to be the product of the competitive struggles of modern business in industrializing America: 'absentee ownership' has isolated it from the 'instinct of workmanship' which Veblen believed was essential to continued technological development of societies. Instead, members of the class are engaged in continuous public demonstrations of their status, a process which Veblen terms 'conspicuous consumption'. This is a form of hedonism involving the ostentatious display and waste of possessions and goods. Documenting the patriarchal character of the class, he showed that women were among the 'objects' put on show as symbols of wealth. This has a specific form which Veblen termed 'conspicuous leisure'. He remarked that leisure itself, though costly, is invisible and offers no particular status advantage. In order to attract public admiration, leisure must be taken in ways that are both wasteful and highly visible—as for example casino gambling, or the use of expensive leisure products like resort clothes, sporting equipment, and the like, which signal wealth and status. He also showed that, while the employment of servants was a display of leisure, an even more conspicuous display of wealth and leisure involved the employment of leisured servants: the conspicuously rich were those who could afford to employ other people to be leisured! Veblen's account is satirical and polemical, and has been criticized for conflating distinct elements of the class, notably the landed gentry, bourgeoisie, and nouveaux riches.

leisure, conspicuous *See* LEISURE CLASS.

leisure, sociology of Leisure generally involves withdrawal from routine activities such as *work, and involvement instead in a pleasurable activity, highly valued by the individual. It may or may not be *productive but it does not involve the social responsibilities attached to one's other social *roles. Playing of games is an obvious example—although so is the hard physical labour associated with rebuilding old cars or steam engines for pleasure.

The sociology of leisure has two main traditions. The first—which has been called the formal approach—consists of empirical studies into relatively discrete problems of which three are prominent: how leisure patterns shift across the *life cycle, as in R. and R. N. Rapoport, *Leisure and the Family Life Cycle* (1975); how work and leisure inter-relate, as in Stanley Parker's *Leisure and Work*, 1983, in which he outlines the interconnections of 'extension' (work and leisure are similar), 'opposition' (they are polarized and demarcated), and 'neutrality' (they are distinct but not polarized); and, finally, research into specific types of leisure, such as cinema attendance, football, or dancing.

By contrast, there is a more historical and theoretical approach, which asks questions about the changing nature of leisure and its varying role in *social change. Two of the most prominent of such arguments are functionalist and neo-

Marxist in tenor. The much criticized *functionalist position, inherent in the 'logic of industrialism' arguments of Clark Kerr et al. (*Industrialism and Industrial Man*, 1960), suggested throughout the 1960s an inevitable movement towards a 'leisure society'. By contrast, neo-Marxists saw an inevitable commercialization of leisure, turning leisure into a *market product. The work of the Frankfurt School of *critical theory also pessimistically analysed the emergence of the 'culture industry' of commercial mass entertainment (popular cinema, sport, television, comics, and so forth) which would exploit individuals and homogenize culture. However, not all neo-Marxists were as pessimistic: those located within the *cultural studies tradition, for instance, argued that much of this culture was used by class fractions as a symbolic means of resisting incorporation into the *dominant ideology (see for example S. Hall et al., *Resistance through Ritual*, 1976).

Despite these debates leisure has rarely been a central concern of sociologists. However, as a consequence of the 'cultural turn' in English-speaking sociology in the early 1990s there were signs of increasing sociological interest in the media, sport, cultural studies, and consumerism, and so the subject of leisure generally may come to feature more prominently in future research (see, for example, C. Rojek's *Capitalism and Leisure Theory*, 1985).

Lenin (Vladimir Ilyich Ulyanov) (1870–1924) A Marxist theoretician and revolutionary, born in Russia, whose early life was characterized by a more or less orthodox *Marxism. However, from the late 1890s he developed a distinctive interpretation of Marx's ideas which has since carried his name. His major works are *The Development of Capitalism in Russia* (1899), commonly held to be his most reputable scholarly piece, *What is to be Done?* (1902), *Imperialism, the Highest Stage of Capitalism* (1916), and *State and Revolution* (1917).

Much of his writing is of historical and partisan interest only. However, a number of his ideas have been debated by sociologists, most notably his thesis that *labour movements (such as *trade unions) are inevitably reformist, seeking only an accommodation with capitalism that improves the workers' lot, so that revolutionary activity on behalf of the *proletariat requires the 'vanguard' of a revolutionary party. The Party will then impose a 'dictatorship of the proletariat', assist the workers to transcend their 'trade-union consciousness' by developing a true (revolutionary) class consciousness, and so eliminate the intra-class divisions ('working-class sectionalism') that undermines the development of *communism. A historical application of this thesis to the class struggles in 19th-century Britain (J. Foster, *Class Struggle and the Industrial Revolution*, 1974) has provoked a heated debate about the nature of the so-called *labour aristocracy in early capitalism.

Lenin also offered an influential analysis of *imperialism; a model of 'democratic centralism', in which lower party and state organizations were accountable to higher ones, with authority resting at the centre in the name of the dictatorship of the proletariat; and a theory of 'uneven development' which challenged the notion that the transition from *traditional society to *modernization is via a smooth and unilinear trajectory. Lenin's argument drew heavily on the earlier work of Nikolai Bukharin (*Imperialism and World Economy*, 1915) and both writers' ideas have been debated well beyond the confines of Marxist intellectual circles.

Lenin was the leader of the Bolshevik Revolution of 1917 and, until his early death from a stroke, the leading politician in the new USSR. Whether everything that flowed out of that revolution finds its origins in Leninism—his particular marriage of revolutionary commitment, Marxist theory, and Russian reality—is still an open (and much debated) question. A useful short introduction to his life and work is Robert Conquest's *Lenin* (1972).

lesbian and gay studies This interdisciplinary field investigates the homosexual—lesbian and gay—experience. Although a first wave of such research can be traced back to the late 19th century (notably the research of Magnus Hirschfield), the major contributions started to appear in the 1970s, in the wake of the rise of a lesbian and gay *social movement. By the 1990s there were courses, institutes, conferences, and publishing houses which specialized in the area. Much of this work has been dominated by sociological research, particularly the ideas of Michel *Foucault, and by the *women's movement. *See also* HETEROSEXISM; HOMOPHOBIA; HOMOSEXUALITY.

less developed countries (LDCs) *See* DEPENDENCY THEORY; THIRD WORLD.

Lévi-Strauss, Claude (1908–2009) A French anthropologist influenced by *Durkheim and *Mauss, he carried out fieldwork in Brazil from 1935 to 1939. He lived in exile in New York during the Second World War and came into contact with the linguist Roman Jakobson, with whom he developed the key ideas of *structuralism. Returning to France, he elaborated these ideas in *The Elementary Structures of Kinship* (1949). His main target was the structural functionalism of *Radcliffe-Brown. His structuralist approach to culture was fully elaborated in *The Savage Mind* (1962) and was then pursued through a massive analysis of myth narratives produced by Native American tribes, published in four volumes between 1964 and 1971 (see, for example, the first volume *The Raw and the Cooked*).

Lévy-Bruhl, Lucien (1857–1939) A French anthropologist working in the tradition of Durkheim who held that 'primitive' peoples possess *collective representations that are 'pre-logical' and mystical (see *How Natives Think*, 1910, and *Primitive Mentality*, 1922). Originally criticized as *ethnocentric, he has been reinterpreted as an early *relativist exploring non-scientized ways of thinking.

Lewin, Kurt (1890–1947) A German-born social psychologist who moved to America in the early 1930s and worked mainly at the University of Iowa and the Massachusetts Institute of Technology. His holistic *field theory, derived from *Gestalt theory but with added social and motivational elements, sees individual behaviour as a function of the psychological field or life-space—that is, the situation of action perceived by the individual in terms of his or her *needs and *goals.

Lewis, Oscar (1914–71) An American anthropologist, who vividly and sympathetically documented the experiences of Mexican and Puerto Rican families, and of what he termed the 'culture of poverty'. His earliest work (*Life in a Mexican Village*, 1951) was a restudy of Tepotzlan, the Mexican village studied by Robert Redfield. His best-known (and best-selling) books, such as *The Children of Sanchez* (1961) and *La Vida* (1966), draw on lengthy interviews and recount in the words of his informants—with whom he became close friends—the life stories of individual families. *See also* POVERTY.

liberalism Although liberalism is usually seen as the *dominant ideology of the Western democracies, with its roots in Enlightenment thought, there are many variations and hybrids of its doctrines. Nevertheless it is clear what liberalism is opposed to: namely, political *absolutism in all its forms, be they monarchist, feudal, military, clerical, or communitarian. In this opposition it attempts to ensure that individuals and groups can resist any authoritarian demands. In practice, this has most commonly meant a split between (on one hand) a public world and a private world where rights are defined, the most common of which are to private property, and (on the other) the free exercise of religion, speech, and association.

Classical liberalism is usually identified with the philosophies of John Locke, David Hume, Jeremy Bentham, and John Stuart Mill (all of whom have separate entries in this dictionary). These writers emphasize the guidance of human beings by enlightened self-interest, rationality, and free choice, and argue for the minimum intervention of the *state in the lives of individuals. It is strongly associated both with economic doctrines of *laissez-faire (as in the writings of Adam *Smith), although the 'New Liberalism' of the late 19th and early 20th centuries (see L. T. *Hobhouse, *Liberalism*, 1911) supported the extension of collective welfare systems. It advocates constitutional guarantees and representative democracy, inalienable rights of citizenship—such as the right to life, to property, to free speech, association, and religion—along with the right to have some say in the running of the country (usually the right to vote)—and, for New Liberals, the right to welfare.

The philosophy of liberalism has been attacked for creating a world of 'possessive individualism' (C. B. Macpherson, *The Political Theory of Possessive Individualism*, 1962). Among sociologists, the key objection has centred upon its (presumed) beliefs in the individual autonomous self, and in the possibility of neutral rules. Both arguments are asocial—assuming the existence of individuals and abstract rules without a society that shapes them. However these sorts of criticisms are often directed at a mere caricature of a particular liberalism. In fact, many liberals recognize the profoundly social nature of its claims, as can be seen, for example, in Susan Moller Okin's *Justice, Gender and the Family* (1989).

There are many divergent strands within liberalism. Some liberals place much more emphasis on economic freedoms but wish for wider government intervention in moral life (the so-called *New Right philosophies of Prime Minister Thatcher and President Reagan). Others stress minimum state intervention in all spheres—a position often identified as *libertarianism. Probably the most celebrated contemporary liberal is the philosopher John Rawls, whose book *A Theory of Justice* (1972) provides an original, formal theory of social contract, in which he aims to provide a moral basis for the just society by conceiving of a contract in which the rights and obligations of citizens would be laid down before they knew of their own social position and lacked knowledge of others'. It is a theory used to good effect in some sociological writings (such as W. G. Runciman's *Relative Deprivation and Social Justice*, 1966). Others who are critical of classical liberalism actually help refine it. Benjamin Barber criticizes 'thin liberalism'—which aims only at representation—in favour of 'strong democracy' in which participation is much more central (see *Strong Democracy*, 1984). Michael Walzer advocates a democracy that can be balanced out over different spheres of social life (see *Spheres of Justice*, 1983). Still others have advocated a feminist liberalism which places the injustices of the family at the centre of the analysis (for example, Susan Moller Okin). *See also* JUSTICE, SOCIAL; MONT PELERIN SOCIETY.

libertarianism An anti-state *ideology which takes the principles of *liberalism to their logical extreme. Libertarianism is rooted in the writings of the 17th-century English political philosopher John *Locke, who insisted upon the priority of individual rights to life, liberty, and property, and 'the elimination of coercive intervention by the state, the foremost violator of liberty'. However, the valuing of individual liberty above all else is also an identifiable strand of *conservative thought, and libertarians form part of the conservative radical right in both the United States and Britain. Modern libertarians include the American philosopher Robert Nozick (*Anarchy, State and Utopia*, 1974), who would reduce the role of the state to that of a mere 'protection agency', and the economist Friedrich Hayek. The latter maintains that the ideal economy and polity is a 'catallaxy'—a spontaneous organization resembling the free market—within which interpersonal relationships are modelled on market exchanges; government is reduced to the minimal tasks of maintaining order and providing those public services which cannot spontaneously emerge because of huge initial capital outlays. This allegedly results in a plurality of personal and social values (see, for example, his 'Principles of a Liberal Social Order', in A. Crespigny and J. Cronin (eds.), *Ideologies of Politics*, 1975).

Libertarians advocate the maximization of individual *rights, the minimization of government, and a free-*market economy. These ideas have found strongest support in the United States, where they mix uneasily with conservatism and neo-liberalism. *See also* JUSTICE, SOCIAL.

life chances A term used in Max Weber's analysis of *class and *status, in particular with reference to the concept of 'class situation'. The ownership of property and the disposal over goods and services in the marketplace, which are outcomes of the distribution of *power in society, determine the 'chance' to realize an individual's goals in social action.

The term subsequently passed into general usage, notably in studies of *social mobility, where the closed nature of a society diminishes the opportunities (chances) for advancement of social classes, women, and ethnic or racialized minorities. It includes chances for educational attainment, health, material reward, and status mobility. See the discussion in Ralf Dahrendorf, *Life Chances* (1979).

life course An expression denoting an individual's passage through life, analysed as a sequence of significant *life-events, including birth, marriage, parenthood, divorce, and retirement. In much modern socio-demographic literature, the term life course has replaced that of *life cycle in analysing these sequences of events, because the former carries fewer normative implications than the latter. *See also* EVENT-HISTORY ANALYSIS.

life cycle A widely used metaphor denoting the passage of an individual through the successive stages of life, from birth to death through childhood, *adolescence, adult life, and old age, and implying a return to infancy in old age. The term is broadly synonymous with those of *life course and life stages.

In some societies, these stages are collectively defined by membership of an age-grade or *age set. In Western societies, certain transition points, such as the age of consent to sexual intercourse, the age of legal majority, or the age when education ceases to be compulsory, are defined and regulated by law, but the stages of the life cycle are otherwise loosely structured and allow a degree of personal choice, for example in the age of marriage. For this reason, research analyses rarely use age alone to define stages in the life cycle, the more common approach being to use marital status and the presence of children in full-time education, or under school-leaving age, who live with the respondent. Among men, the category of prime-age males is often separately identified, especially in *labour-market analyses: these are men in the prime of life, usually defined as aged 25 to 55 years (sometimes 25 to 50 years), when *employment levels are at their highest. Demographic analysts identify fewer life-cycle groups than would sociologists: for them the two dependent groups are children under 15 years and old people aged 65 (or 60) and over, who are supported financially and otherwise by the population of working age or active population.

Life-cycle stage is a variable often used in analyses of employment patterns, housing preferences and needs, patterns of social relationships in the community and the extended family, studies of poverty, and migration patterns. However, although still widely employed, it has dropped out of favour in modern socio-demographic literature because of its normative resonances. *See also* LIFE EVENT.

life event Defined for the purposes of event-history or *life-course analysis, a life event may consist of any demarcated change in demographic, educational, employment, health, or other individual circumstances locatable to a particular point in time. The temporal sequencing of such events may then be analysed to provide information on the interrelationships between different life events.

Major events in the life of an individual would include the age of puberty and *marriage; the birth of any children; death of a spouse, parent, sibling, or other significant person in that person's life; *migration to another region or country; major illnesses; and the onset of physical incapacity in old age. Some would add major events connected with *employment, such as getting a job, redundancy or unemployment, any return to further education in adult life, or changes of employer or occupation; others would treat these as secondary events. Life events constitute significant turning-points in a person's life, in the *roles and activities they are encouraged to adopt, and the groups they interact with, and may be associated with changes in attitudes and values.

life expectancy The number of further years of life a person can expect at a given age. The measure is calculated from a life table, and since it is expressed as an average for persons of that age and sex in a country, depends upon prevailing (current) levels of mortality at different ages within the population or sub-population to which the individual belongs. Since, in all societies, *mortality rates between birth and the first birthday tend to be particularly high, life expectancies at birth are usually considerably lower than life expectancies at year one. As one would expect from variations in mortality rates between countries, life expectancies also vary considerably, being around 30 to 40 years at birth in certain developing countries, and reaching 75 and over for women in the major Western industrialized societies. Life expectancy at birth is a widely used indicator of health standards and social and economic living standards. It is also possible to derive life expectancies for different sub-groups of populations, for example different social classes, providing mortality rates are known.

life history An ideographic approach which provides an intensive account of a life, usually gathered through unstructured *interviewing, but often also involving the analysis of *personal documents such as letters, photographs, and diaries. The approach is clearly akin to the gathering and examination of autobiographies and biographies. There are many early examples of the method, but two classics are those of Wladek, whose life is displayed in some three hundred pages of William Isaac Thomas and Florian Znaniecki's *The Polish Peasant in Europe and America* (1918), and Stanley, in *The Jack Roller* (edited by Clifford Shaw, 1930). Both are associated with the *Chicago School of sociology.

The life-history approach achieved some prominence during the 1920s and 1930s in North America, and prompted a debate over the value of *ideographic versus nomothetic methods. By the late 1930s, the dominant trends had moved towards abstract theory in the work of Talcott *Parsons and quantitative methodology in the work of Paul *Lazarsfeld, so the life-history approach became less prominent in sociological research. From the 1960s onwards, however, there has been a revival of interest in life histories across a range of academic disciplines, as part of the *post-structuralist concern with narratives and the construction of text.

Two main approaches to life history may be distinguished. The more traditional approach aims to provide an objective account of the life in order to throw light on social processes: it may help explore the subjective dimensions of a life, trace the historical connections between a life and a social *structure, or provide access to ambiguity, flux, and social *change. For this reason, the method is frequently used to explore new fields of enquiry, and to complement more statistical and generalizing studies. A more recent approach, however, deals with the interpretive procedures through which biographical work gets done, and with the analysis of life-story production. The distinction between the two approaches is prominent in Norman Denzin's *Interpretive Biography* (1989). *See also* CASE HISTORY.

life stages *See* LIFE CYCLE.

lifestyle A concept that refers to alternative ways of living, usually conspicuous through values and modes of consumption. Such differentials correspond to the concept of *status groups identified by Max *Weber. In British sociology it has often been employed in the *embourgeoisement debate about the nature of the British class structure. In this particular context, it is argued that workers are increasingly adopting middle-class mores and attitudes, such that social class differences are becoming less significant as members of all classes come to share similar patterns of consumption and social behaviour.

More generally, and rather loosely, it refers to contrasting ways of life found among different groups in society, such as the young, unemployed, or deviant. *See also* SUBCULTURE.

lifeworld A *phenomenological concept referring to the everyday world of the shared, ongoing flow of experience, from which we constitute objects and abstract *concepts (see Alfred Schütz and Thomas Luckmann, *Structures of the Life-World*, 2 vols., 1973 and 1983). It has been taken up in the work of *Habermas as a way of understanding the socio-cultural framework of everyday activities that stands in tension with the economic and political systems. *See also* INTERSUBJECTIVITY.

Likert scale A widely used technique for *scaling *attitudes. Respondents are presented with a number of items, some positively phrased and some negatively phrased, which have been found to discriminate most clearly between extreme views on the subject of study. For example, in a study of popular perceptions of social justice, respondents might be presented with items such as 'The distribution of income in the United States is unfair', and 'In our society everyone has an equal opportunity to obtain a good education'. They are asked to rate each item in terms of agreement. Typically, responses are scored using five-point categories (strongly agree, agree, neither agree nor disagree, disagree, strongly disagree), coded as 2, 1, 0, minus 1, and minus 2. These scores are aggregated to form 'summated ratings' or a 'test score'; or may be intercorrelated and *factor analysed, to form a numerical unidimensional scale.

liminality A term introduced by Arnold *van Gennep (*Rites de passage*, 1909), liminality refers to an intermediate ritual phase during *initiation, in which initiates can be considered either *sacred or potentially polluting to the mainstream society because of their anomalous social position. New social rules are commonly taught during the liminal phase, and strong, endearing, and creative bonds often develop between fellow initiates.

lineage *See* DESCENT GROUPS.

line and staff A classification of organizational functions and employees made by *scientific management theorists. The line function refers to the main organizational pattern of hierarchical control and a unified chain of command; the staff function refers to the role of specialists, advising line managers, but not in their chain of command.

linear growth A quantity increasing in line with another variable, in a relationship which approximates to a straight line on a graph.

line of best fit *See* REGRESSION.

linguistic relativity thesis *See* SAPIR-WHORF HYPOTHESIS.

linguistics *See* CONVERSATION ANALYSIS; DISCOURSE; ETHNOMETHODOLOGY; LANGUAGE; SAPIR-WHORF HYPOTHESIS; SAUSSURE; SEMIOLOGY; STRUCTURALISM.

Linton, Ralph (1893–1953) An American cultural anthropologist who undertook fieldwork on the Polynesians. Later, he attempted to develop a systematic cultural science, focusing especially on the relationships between *personality and *society (see *The Cultural Background of Personality*, 1954). His most important book, *The Study of Man* (1936), reconciled the theoretical premises of *functionalism with a historical approach to *culture. He pioneered the concepts of *role and *status, which for him provided the key to understanding the internal consistency of a *social system, because of the importance they play in the relationship between the individual and society.

locality studies *See* COMMUNITY STUDIES.

local labour market *See* LABOUR-MARKET SEGMENTATION.

Locke, John (1632–1702) An English philosopher and political theorist. The 17th-century revolution in physical science found in Locke one of its principal philosophical advocates. Locke combined the leading doctrines of the *empiricist theory of knowledge (that there are no 'innate ideas' and that all of our substantive knowledge is derived from experience) with a commitment to the prevailing mechanical view of the nature of reality and our perception of it. Some properties (colours and tastes for example) were held to be 'secondary', and functions of the effects of external bodies upon our senses, whereas others, the 'primary qualities' (solidity, shape, state of motion, and so on) were held to be 'really in' things themselves. However, at the same time Locke also held that all we are directly acquainted with in perception are our own ideas, so it is difficult to see how this distinction could be sustained. Nevertheless, Locke remains important as one of the founding figures of the enduring alliance between modern science and the empiricist tradition in *epistemology.

Locke's political philosophy is also of continuing importance as an early rational justification for modern constitutional monarchy. As was characteristic for his time, Locke's argument takes the form of a hypothetical state of nature in which humans were supposed to live together without benefit of law or sovereign power. The disadvantages of such a state, though not approaching the catastrophic vision offered by Thomas *Hobbes, would be sufficient to provide good reasons for individuals to enter into a voluntary contract to put themselves under the rule of law and government. However, the state of nature is not so dire that unlimited or absolute power on the part of the sovereign should be tolerated. The citizenry pool their powers in the person of the sovereign on trust that it will be used for their good, and so retain their right to rebellion. Of particular interest in Locke's political philosophy is his analysis of the sources and limits of private property rights, in a world initially held in common by humankind. Since all individuals are held to be owners of their own persons, the mixing of their labour with some part of the material world gives them property rights in what they produce.

However, this is so only on condition that what they take does not go to waste, and that enough remains for others. The institution of money (whose establishment, like governmental power, Locke takes to have been a matter of voluntary agreement) allows for the transfer of property rights, and for the potentially limitless accumulation of wealth. *See also* *LIBERALISM.

lockout *See* INDUSTRIAL ACTION.

Lockwood, David (1929–2014) British theorist concerned with issues of social order and social conflict, Lockwood has also been a major influence on empirical studies of class, especially through *The Blackcoated Worker* (1958) and *The Affluent Worker* series (1968–9). However, his *Solidarity and Schism* (1992) best summarizes his abiding concerns with the problem of order. Throughout his career, Lockwood has been an astute critic of both Parsons's and Marx's sociology and has sought to combine the former's abstractions of value with the latter's abstractions of material circumstances. Thus both consensus and conflict theories of social order are rejected as being one-sided accounts. For Lockwood society cannot be conceived without recognizing both a degree of integration through common norms and an element of conflict arising from the allocation of scarce resources. The distinction he makes between social integration and *system integration is crucial to his approach to the problem of order. Similarly, the distinctions he made in *The Blackcoated Worker*, concerning elements of the class situation of occupations and distinguishing between work situation, market situation and status situation, provided the model for British research on class for the next 30 years and remain influential today. Lockwood's unique contribution has been not simply to understand and use the ideas of the classical sociologists but to tease out what they left unsaid and to make explicit what their own writings left vague. He has combined this with a Weberian attention to historical detail.

logical empiricism *See* VERIFICATION; VIENNA CIRCLE.

logical positivism *See* POSITIVISM; VIENNA CIRCLE.

logical reduction *See* REDUCTIONISM.

logical universals A term sometimes applied in the secondary literature to the major analytical concepts in the writings of Talcott Parsons: that is, the pattern variables, systems problems, and evolutionary universals (all of which are discussed separately in this dictionary).

Lombroso, Cesare (1836–1909) An Italian army physician who developed the theory of the criminal type. Although he modified his views over his life, he is primarily known for studying the physiognomies of criminals, and suggesting that much crime was biological and hereditary, theorizing from *Darwinian evolutionary theory that many criminals were atavistic throwbacks to an earlier and more primitive species. He is often considered to be the founder of modern *positivist criminology.

longitudinal study *See* LIFE HISTORY; PANEL STUDY.

long-wave theory (long-wave cycles) *See* BUSINESS CYCLE.

looking-glass self Charles Cooley's theory of the *self highlighted the ways in which an individual's sense of self is derived from the perceptions of others. Just like the reflections in a mirror, the self depends on the perceived responses of others; or, as he himself puts it, 'each to each a looking glass | Reflects the other that doth pass.'

The looking-glass self has three components: the imagination of our appearance to the other person; the imagination of their judgement of that appearance; and self feelings, such as pride. In Cooley's work, the self is solipsistic, where society essentially comprises 'imagining imaginations'.

Lowie, Robert H. (1883–1957) A student of Franz *Boas, Lowie's book *Primitive Society* (1920) was the first modern survey of social organization in non-Western societies since the decline of *evolutionism. Lowie attacked the theories of Lewis Henry *Morgan on the basis of his own ethnography among Native Americans. His major works (*The Origin of the State*, 1927, and *Social Organization*, 1948) expanded on Morgan's speculative theories of the development of the *state. According to Lowie, the state is based on territoriality, legitimacy, and the monopoly over the means of violence, a far more modern analysis than that of Morgan. However, Lowie insisted on imposing a rigid scientism on his research, which is not really suited to the study of human subjects.

Luhmann, Niklas (1927–98) Trained as a lawyer and worked as a parliamentary adviser until he discovered the work of Talcott *Parsons in 1960. He transferred to an academic career in sociology, first at Dortmund and then at Bielefeld. He published work on organization theory and on law (*A Sociological Theory of Law*, 1965) but then went on to construct a more generalized theory of social systems. This work first appeared in a joint work with Habermas, on whom he had a major influence, and then in his book *Social Systems* (1984). He focused on *social systems as systems of communication operating in environments in relation to which they undergo processes of social differentiation. Each differentiated subsystem operates in terms of a particular 'medium', and the media of money and power play a central role in the overall *integration of the system. This framework has been applied in his *Trust and Power* (1979, originally 1968 and 1975), *Love as Passion* (1986), *Risk* (1991), and *The Reality of the Mass Media* (1996). His final statement of his general theory was *Theory of Society* (1997).

Lukács, György (1885–1971) A Hungarian Marxist philosopher who was a government minister during the short-lived Hungarian revolution of 1919, after which he spent many years in exile in Stalin's Russia, spending a short period there in prison.

Lukács came to *Marxism through both *Kant and *Hegel. His early critical position in *Soul and Form* (1911) and to a lesser extent of *The Theory of the Novel* (1914–5) drew on the ideas of Georg *Simmel. He came to argue that Marxism offers a solution to the *dualisms of classical European philosophy, in particular the reconciliation of subject and object. In *History and Class Consciousness* (1923), he maintains that the experience of the *working class itself is that of the subject and the object of history, and that Marxism is able to construct this experience into a theory of the social totality. The notion of totality is, for Lukács, the most important concept in Marxism, because it enables one to penetrate the appearances of social reality (dominated by *commodity fetishism and *reification), to understand the real human relationships that underlie these surface manifestations. He developed a theory of political organization which reconciles the importance that Lenin gives to the Communist Party with Rosa *Luxemburg's emphasis on spontaneity.

In the 1920s, Lukács's political position came under attack in the Comintern and he concentrated instead on literary theory, developing a notion of socialist realism that goes beyond the crass simplicity of Stalinist orthodoxy, but which never succeeded in coming to terms with literary modernism. The good realist novel is seen as one that portrays underlying social relations rather than surface appearances. See in particular *The Historical Novel* (1937) and *Studies in European Realism* (1946). He criticized trends in German sociology and philosophy in *The Destruction of Reason* (1953). His own view of his life was published in English in 1983 as *Record of a Life. See also* CRITICAL THEORY; IDEOLOGY.

lumpenproletariat Defined emotionally and colourfully by Karl Marx as 'the scum, the leavings, the refuse of all classes', he included amongst their number swindlers, confidence tricksters, brothel-keepers, rag-and-bone merchants, organ grinders, beggars, and other 'flotsam of society' (see *The 18th Brumaire of Louis Bonaparte*, 1852). They were a 'class fraction' in that they constituted the political power-base for Louis Bonaparte in 1848. Here, the financial aristocracy of Louis-Philippe displayed an enormous appetite for wealth created through financial gambles, where both the manner of acquiring that wealth and the enjoying of it went against 'bourgeois law'. In this sense, both the *proletariat and the *bourgeoisie were progressive, advancing the historical process by developing the *labour power of human species-being and their all round capacities, whereas the lumpenproletariat was marginal, unproductive, and also regressive.

Paradoxically, contemporary sociologists are as much concerned with many of the supposedly marginal social categories which Marx dismissed under this label (who are now seen as the victims of modern society), as they are with the major *class protagonists which he situated at the heart of the historical process.

Lundberg, George A. (1895–1966) An influential American sociologist, vigorous proponent of a *neo-positivist approach to the study of social behaviour, most notably in his books *Foundations of Sociology* (1939) and *Can Science Save Us?* (1947). Lundberg argued that, for sociology to be a science, it must model its theories and methods on those of the natural sciences. His work is therefore characterized by *behaviourism and an emphasis on quantification. He was opposed to *introspection, although he accepted the study of values and ideals as a task for sociology, providing these could be defined operationally in an explicit and quantifiable way. Arguing for science over tradition and religious beliefs, he claimed that in science lay the hope for the future, since humanity must become more rational or else fail to survive.

Luxemburg, Rosa (1871–1919) Though born in Poland, Luxemburg is best known as a leading theorist and political leader in the German working-class movement. She vigorously opposed the revisionist current in the German Social Democratic Party, and was imprisoned for her opposition to the First World War. After the war she supported the Russian Revolution, but was sharply critical of the Bolshevik suppression of popular democracy. Her major theoretical work, *The Accumulation of Capital* (1913), argued that *imperialist expansion was necessitated by *capitalism's dependence on a non-capitalist 'third market'. The global triumph of capitalist expansion would also mark its final breakdown. Luxemburg played a leading part in the revolutionary upheaval in Germany which followed the end of the war. She was arrested by army officers in Berlin and clubbed to death by soldiers on her way to prison.

Lynd, Helen Merrell (1896–1982) Helen Lynd was an American ethnographer and social theorist whose most famous books, co-authored with her husband Robert S. Lynd, concerned life in a small Midwestern town. The Lynds lived in the community they studied ('Middletown'—in reality Muncie, Indiana) 1924–6, and published the first volume of the work, *Middletown: A Study in Contemporary American Culture*, in 1929. Their analysis is organized around major activities for community survival, including making a home, earning a living, training the young, and participating in religious and community activities. The second volume, a longitudinal study entitled *Middletown in Transition: A Study in Cultural Conflicts* (1935), was published in the middle of the Depression. In this they described class strains and privileges as being more apparent, although there was little evident workers' solidarity: the radical socio-economic changes of the time did not generate radical class movements. Despite the shared research and authorship, it is more often Robert Lynd who is given most credit for these classic studies.

Helen Lynd was also a teacher and political activist and was subject to harassment during the McCarthy witch-hunts. In 1958 she published *On Shame and the Search for Identity*, a critique of Sigmund Freud and Talcott Parsons, in which she argued that these writers failed to provide either a historical context for or a historical content to their sociological theories. She also published studies of student-teacher interaction in colleges, *Field Work in College Education* (1945), and a historical study entitled *England in the Eighteen Eighties: Toward a Social Basis for Freedom* (1944). Central to all her work was the investigation of human meaning and action.

McDonaldization The author of this term, the American sociologist George Ritzer, defines McDonaldization as 'the process by which the principles of the fast-food restaurant are coming to dominate more and more sectors of American society as well as the rest of the world' (see *The McDonaldization of Society*, 1993). The way in which the hamburger chain prepares food for consumption is taken as an exemplar of Max Weber's theory of the *rationalization of the modern world: the company uses the methods of *scientific management and *fordism to guarantee predictability, efficiency, and calculability to customers. The hamburgers are the same the world over, the restaurants are almost identical, so that customers are guaranteed no surprises. Such rational techniques of production and consumption are, according to Ritzer, being increasingly applied to the *service sector as a whole. We now have junk-journalism (inoffensive and trivial news served up in palatable portions), and 'McUniversities', featuring modularized curricula, delivering degrees in a fast-track pick-and-mix fashion to satisfy all tastes. The diminished quality of these products can only be disguised by extensive advertising which constantly repackages them to look new.

McDonaldization suggests that modern societies are in many respects increasingly standardized, predictable, and uniform. The references to scientific management and fordism are however not entirely appropriate, since the proponents of these earlier strategies for the routinization of production sought to exchange standardized and intensified work for high wages and incentive payments, whereas employment in fast-food restaurants and similar 'McJobs' is characteristically low-paid and insecure. This essentially Weberian view of the trajectory of industrialism is also somewhat at odds with, for example, the theory of *reflexive modernization and the risk society proposed by Ulrich Beck and others—who paint pictures of an increasingly uncertain and unpredictable world.

(⊕) SEE WEB LINKS
• The official website of George Ritzer.

McDougall, William (1871–1938) British social psychologist teaching at Cambridge and Oxford. He was recruited by Alfred Haddon to serve on the anthropological expedition to the Torres Straits. He moved to the United States in 1920, teaching at Harvard (at the invitation of William *James) until 1928 and then at Duke University. He published *An Introduction to Social Psychology* (1908) and *Theories of Action* (1919) before producing his most famous work on *The Group Mind* (1920). This was no metaphysical idea but was a recognition of what *Durkheim referred to as collective representations and was much influenced by the folk psychology of Wilhelm Wundt. It stressed the importance of the cultural construction of personality and the need to study national character. McDougall was interested in Freudian ideas, which he sought to integrate with instinctual responses in his own theory of *emotions (see also *Psychoanalysis and Social Psychology*, 1936).

Machiavelli, Niccolò (1469–1527) An influential Florentine political theorist and humanist. Believing *human nature to be essentially selfish, Machiavelli advocated the need for strong government, notably in *The Prince* and *Discourse* (written between 1513 and 1521). His work has been most influential in *political science, but a number of sociologists have also been intrigued by his theory of statecraft, for example Stanford M. Lyman and Marvin B. Scott (see *A Sociology of the Absurd*, 1970).

machine production *See* FACTORY SYSTEM; INDUSTRIALISM.

MacIver, Robert M. (1882–1970) A pioneering Scottish sociologist who worked at Aberdeen and Edinburgh before becoming chair of sociology at Toronto and then Columbia University in New York. He stayed at Columbia from 1929 until 1950. His classic textbook *Society* (first published in 1931, revised 1937, 3rd edn., 1949, with Charles Page) reveals his concern with developing a systematic, theoretical, humanistic, yet evolutionary sociology, drawing especially on *Durkheim and *Simmel. His prime interests were the *state (*The Web of Government*, 1947) and *community (*Community*, 1928). Full biographical details can be found in *As A Tale That is Told: The Autobiography of Robert M. MacIver* (1968).

macrosociology Macrosociology is usually contrasted with microsociology. The former examines the wider *structures, interdependent social institutions, global and historical processes of social life, while the latter is more concerned with *action, interaction, and the construction of *meaning. In general, theories such as symbolic interactionism, exchange theory, and ethnomethodology are regarded as microsociological theories, whilst Marxism, functionalism, and systems theory are regarded as macrosociological. (All of these theories are treated under separate headings elsewhere in this dictionary.)

Needless to say, however, it is important not to push this distinction too far, since much sociological research is neither clearly in one camp nor in the other, and can be seen as part of a continuing debate over the relationship between social system and social actor. Are micro and macro theories irretrievably autonomous levels of analysis which cannot be synthesized? Is one mode of analysis superior to the other? Is a linkage or even a synthesis possible? Most of the classical theories are concerned with this tension. For example, whilst Max *Weber is often characterized as a sociologist of social action, his work rapidly moves to the analysis of broad historical processes and comparative structures. Similarly, the work of Talcott *Parsons may be seen as an ambitious attempt to create grand theory of a type that would allow units of action to be built up into integrative institutions, with the *pattern variables, for example, being capable of characterizing both two-person interactions and whole societies.

The tension and controversies between these two sociologies take many forms. There are some so-called holists who argue (with Émile *Durkheim) that the logic of sociology dictates a concern with the social *sui generis*, that microsociology cannot capture either the logic of *collective action or the constraints of institutional structures, and is for that reason unsatisfactory. Methodological individualists, by contrast, maintain (among other things) that society is a reification and is always reducible to its component individuals. This is part of a much wider debate over *ontology, in which *realists and nominalists make competing claims about the nature of social reality. Similarly, Anthony Giddens's theory of *structuration and Johnathan A. Turner's *A Theory of Social Interaction* (1988), both of which attempt to transcend the dichotomy of macrosociological and macrosociological concerns, can be contrasted with the position of Alan Dawe, who in a classic paper maintained that 'there are . . . two sociologies: a sociology of social system and a sociology of social action. They are grounded in the diametrically opposed concerns with two central problems, those of order and control. And, at every level they are in conflict. They posit antithetical views of human nature, of society and of the relationship between the social and the individual. The first asserts the paramount necessity, for societal and individual well-being, of external constraint; hence the notion of a social system ontologically and methodologically prior to its participants. The key notion of the second is that of autonomous man, able to realise his full potential and to create a truly human social order only when freed from external constraint. Society is thus the creation of its members; the product of their construction of meaning, and of the action and relationships through which they attempt to impose that meaning on their historical situations' ('The Two Sociologies', *British Journal of Sociology*, 1970). *See also* GALTON'S PROBLEM.

madness *See* MENTAL ILLNESS.

magic, witchcraft, and sorcery The art of performing charms, spells, and rituals, to seek to control events or govern certain natural or supernatural forces. Magic can be good, as in love magic or the canoe magic of the Trobriand Islanders before a hazardous voyage. It can also be malevolent in the sense of witchcraft or sorcery. Sorcery implies magic where powers are intentionally used for a harmful purpose, often involving artificial means. Witchcraft implies the possession of a supernatural power through a pact with evil spirits; this power may be exerted involuntarily. Magic, witchcraft, and sorcery generally function at the level of the individual, and often in opposition to organized *religions. Magical beliefs deal with the individual crises and acts of fate which religious morality cannot explain.

Initial attempts to explain magical beliefs foundered on 19th-century scientism and simplistic psychological theories. For Lucien *Lévy-Bruhl (*Primitive Mentality*, 1922), magic was a form of 'pre-logical thought', which was incommensurable with and antithetical to Western scientific thought. Sir James *Frazer's *The Golden Bough* (1900) postulated an evolutionary progression from magic to religion to science. Bronislaw *Malinowski (*Magic, Science and Religion and Other Essays*, 1948) shared many of the prejudices of earlier approaches towards magic and explained it as an essentially meaningless emotional response to the unknown and otherwise uncontrollable. Magic thus served a psychological function only when technical knowledge was inadequate.

Later anthropological approaches have seen magic as containing a symbolic logic and meaning, and have sought to place it into a context of the cosmology and social relations of the people concerned. This approach derives fundamentally from E. E. *Evans-Pritchard's classic study of *Witchcraft, Oracles and Magic among the Azande* (1937). This was one of the first attempts to study in detail the beliefs and practices relating to magic, witchcraft, and sorcery. The Azande of Southern Sudan invoke witchcraft to explain nearly any misfortune that could befall a person. All deaths are seen to be caused by witchcraft. This explanatory framework does not posit witchcraft as a cause of misfortune. The Azande know that misfortunes are part of life: that houses are eaten by termites and fall down, that people become ill if they drink bad water, and so on. However, witchcraft ideas explain why a misfortune happens to a particular person at a particular time; that is, they answer the vital question 'Why me? Why now?' ('Why did the termites destroy my house, rather than another, and why did it collapse when I was inside, rather than at another time?')

Among the Azande, witchcraft is the domain only of commoners, who use internal psychic powers to do harm. Witchcraft is a physical property, located in the intestines, which allows a witch to go out at night and harm other people. Good magic is seen to be moral, and uses spells, medicines, and herbs as means for fighting witchcraft. Bad magic, or sorcery, is performed only by the Azande nobility, and is seen to be more deadly than witchcraft. Unlike witchcraft, the apparatus of sorcery is external to people, involving spells, rites, and medicines. If a misfortune is significant, a diviner is called in to determine who is the witch causing the malaise, and to convince that person to repent and remove the spell. Accusations tend to occur in disputes where a person is not likely to get retribution through the chief's court. Evans-Pritchard showed how such accusations are related to the points of social tension within Azande social organization. In general, other anthropologists have followed this approach, arguing that witchcraft beliefs are functional to maintaining the order of society by resolving tensions, aggression, and envy. For example, they may function as a levelling mechanism, with individuals who amass too much power or wealth often being accused of acquiring these by means of witchcraft. However, other researchers have argued that witchcraft beliefs generate tensions, as well as helping to resolve them.

Some analysts have located their study of witchcraft within the context of *colonialism. Clyde *Kluckhohn (*Navajo Witchcraft*, 1944) argued that Navajo witchcraft ideas served to channel tensions and aggressions created by the larger White society. In *Moon, Sun and Witches* (1987), Irene Silverblatt argued that female witches formed an integral part of an anti-colonial movement in the Andes.

Ideas about magic and witchcraft have sparked off a lengthy, acrimonious, and unresolved debate about the rationality or otherwise of non-Western peoples, a debate that has grown to engage philosophers and sociologists as well as anthropologists (see, for example, B. R. Wilson (ed.), *Rationality*, 1970). Evans-Pritchard insisted that the Azande have two distinct models of apprehending the world, one mystical and the other mundane, or empirical. These are invoked at different levels of explanation: witchcraft is invoked to explain why tragedy befalls people; how the events themselves occur is explained in a prosaic way which Europeans think to be empirically true. The Azande, according to Evans-Pritchard, are logical but wrong. In opposition to this view, relativists such as Peter Winch (*The Idea of a Social Science*, 1958) have argued that each society constructs its own notions of reality and rationality, and all are equally valid. Anthropologists, therefore, should not judge alien beliefs like witchcraft on the basis of a Western discourse of science. Many of these issues are discussed, and their sociological implications made clear, in Max G. Marwick's 'How Real is the Charmed Circle in African and Western Thought?', *Africa* (1973). *See also* CULTURAL RELATIVISM.

Maine, Sir Henry James Sumner (1822–88) Sir Henry Maine was a pioneer of comparative jurisprudence. Like Lewis Henry *Morgan, he was convinced that the legal basis of 'primitive societies' lay in ties of blood and *kinship. In his two best-known works, *Ancient Law* (1861) and *Popular Government* (1885), he argued for the *evolutionist proposition that the history of human societies showed a progressive move from societies based on *status ascribed through kin ties to advanced politics based on legally binding agreements (or 'contract'). *See also* TRIBE.

male chauvinism A term particularly associated with the 1970s women's liberation movement and used to attack men's attitudes towards women. It suggests blind, arrogant, excessive, and narrow-minded assumptions of innate male superiority, of male ascendancy over women, and of men's pursuit of their own collective interests.

Malinowski, Bronislaw Kaspar (1884–1942) A Polish anthropologist, born in Cracow, where he completed a doctorate in physics and mathematics. A chance reading of Frazer's *The Golden Bough* attracted him to social anthropology. Subsequently, in London, he completed a thesis on the Australian Aborigines. Between 1915 and 1918 he conducted *fieldwork for periods amounting to nearly two years in the Trobriand Islands, New Guinea. Here he developed the now classical methods of intensive fieldwork, pitching his tent in the villages. He stressed the importance of learning the people's language and acquiring the 'native' point of view. In 1927 he was appointed to the first chair in *social anthropology at the London School of Economics, where his seminars attracted and he supervised many now celebrated anthropologists.

Malinowski came to be identified with the theory of *functionalism. All human culture could eventually be reduced to the satisfaction of basic *needs. *Rituals, *kinship patterns, economic exchanges (including the famous *kula ring), were not to be explained in terms of their origins, but their current use. Previous theories which attempted to explain all customs and practices in terms of 'survivals' from some distant era were discredited. Malinowski's emphasis on the current significance alone of institutions meant the neglect of any historical context. He idealized the harmonious *equilibrium of a given society. This ahistorical approach gave the impression that the Trobrianders were still locked in the Stone Age and without underlying conflicts which might generate change. The emphasis on intensive fieldwork with the indigenous people, ideally by-passing the secondary sources of colonial administrators, missionaries, and traders, carried the risk of ignoring the powerful interventions of external and colonial forces. Even the self-contained description of the Trobriand political structure neglected recent changes. Malinowski's posthumously published diary reveals the very visible presence of powerful White outsiders, whom he tried to eliminate both from his participant fieldwork, and from his final texts. His functionalist methodology brought lasting implications, despite the theory's flaws. Anthropologists were encouraged to examine a society holistically. Beliefs, rituals, kinship, political organization, and economic practices could no longer be studied each in isolation, but in terms of their interrelation.

Malinowski published several monographs exploring different aspects of the Trobriands. Of these, *Argonauts of the Western Pacific* (1922), *Crime and Custom in Savage Society* (1926), *Sex and Repression in Savage Society* (1927), *The Sexual Life of Savages* (1929), and *Coral Gardens and their Magic* (1935, 1948) are now classics of the discipline. His international fame brought visits and appointments in Africa and the United States. He was encouraged to pronounce on colonial policies, often in areas where he had no ethnographic knowledge. His function-alism did not foresee self-determination by the colonized. His *A Diary in the Strict Sense of the Term* (1967), often to the consternation of some of his early disciples, has been recognized as an important text for understanding the cross-cultural encounter between the anthropologist and others.

((⊕)) SEE WEB LINKS
• A BBC Radio interview on the life and work of Malinowski.

Malthus, Thomas Robert (1766–1834) An early political economist whose *Essay on Population*, first published in 1798 and frequently revised, had an enormous impact on theories of population. Malthus's father, a liberal English landowner and a friend of *Rousseau, educated his own son until he went to Cambridge. There, Malthus was appointed a Fellow in 1793, and in 1797 he took Holy Orders. In 1805 he became Professor of History and Political Economy at the East India Company College at Haileybury.

In his *Essay* Malthus engaged with the contemporary debate about the per-fectibility of humankind. Against writers such as Godwin and *Condorcet, who believed that the human race was capable of ever greater improvement and happiness, Malthus, drawing on the work of Adam *Smith and David *Hume, pointed to the pressures and difficulties for the human race arising from what he called the 'principle of population'. This was the natural tendency of populations to expand faster than resources. Populations could expand geometrically; resources no more than arithmetically. Inevitably, therefore, actual population growth was checked by insufficiency of resources, either by 'positive' checks (deaths from disease and starvation) or by 'preventive' checks (postponing marriage or sexual abstinence).

Malthus's views have been widely challenged, not least for the implication that attempts to remedy *poverty by increasing resources must be unsuccessful since this only leads to further population expansion and further pressure on the 'necessaries of life', a view that was used to justify the harshness of the 1834 Poor Law Reforms in Britain. Karl Marx, for instance, contended that a population's capacity to feed itself depended primarily on economic and social organization: *capitalism—not population growth—was to blame for poverty.

management Either the process of supervision, control, and coordination of productive activity in industrial and other formal organizations, or the persons performing these functions. As a process, management is conventionally divided into the line or general management of the main goals of the organization, and staff or specialist management dealing with support roles, such as personnel, legal matters, or research and development. A managerial stratum of persons in *industrial society developed as a result of the joint-stock corporation, the growth in size of enterprises, and the expansion of public *bureaucracy. Usage of the term is loose enough to include, at one extreme, directors and other senior staff who have a personal stake of some kind in their companies and are, in effect, also employers; and, at the other extreme, propertyless waged or salaried employees entrusted with, or promoted to, varying levels of supervisory responsibility. Managers in this second sense make up a growing proportion of white-collar workers. An excellent account of the role of ideologies of management in the course of *industrialization is Reinhard Bendix's *Work and Authority in Industry* (new edn., 1974). Mike Reed's *The Sociology of Management* (1989) is a more general textbook. *See also* CONTINGENCY THEORY; LINE-AND-STAFF; MANAGERIAL REVOLUTION.

management of knowledge A term used in the 'new' sociology of education in the 1970s to link the subject with *sociologies of knowledge and *power. It refers to the process by which schools and the educational *curricula control what passes for valid knowledge, together with the methods by which knowledge is recognized as such, and the emergence of deviant paradigms and interpretations is prevented. For a review of the arguments which relate these to the origins and growth of the sociology of education itself see Gerald Bernbaum, *Knowledge and Ideology in the Sociology of Education* (1977). *See also* EDUCATION, SOCIOLOGY OF.

management science *See* ADMINISTRATIVE THEORY; ORGANIZATIONAL CULTURE.

managerial revolution A concept that points to the supposed shift within the modern *corporation from the owner to the professional manager as the controlling figure. This is associated with the declining importance of family ownership and private property in contemporary *capitalism.

The concept originates in a book of that title by James Burnham (1941) who asserted that not only industrial establishments but state agencies and all other significant organizations would become dominated by a new ruling class of managerial professionals pursuing their own interests. It is also associated with Adolf A. Berle and Gardiner C. Means (*The Modern Corporation and Private Property*, 1932), who believed that managers would pursue broader *corporate goals, even at the expense of short-term profitability. *See also* BOURGEOISIE; OWNERSHIP AND CONTROL.

manifest function *See* FUNCTION.

Mann, Michael John (1942–) A British sociologist currently based at the University of California, Los Angeles. He taught at the University of Essex and the London School of Economics before moving to his post in California in 1987. His PhD thesis, undertaken at the University of Oxford, was an investigation of workers in a food production company that relocated from Birmingham to Banbury. Mann reported on their orientations to work and their forms of class awareness in his book *Workers on the Move* (1973). A general view of class consciousness had already been published in a widely read article on 'The Social Cohesion of Liberal Democracy' (1970) and he developed this into the short account presented in *Consciousness and Action Among the Western Working Class* (1973). From the late 1970s his interests extended to wider issues of class and power from the standpoint of comparative and historical sociology. This led him to develop a project for what became a four-volume history of *The Sources of Social Power*, published between 1986 and 2013. Mann set out the argument that power can be seen as having economic, political, military, and ideological sources and that these are differentiated bases for exercising control through despotic and 'infrastructural' mechanisms. He traced changing patterns of power from early tribal forms to modern structures in a way that avoided evolutionary assumptions and developed a powerful historical sociology in the spirit of Barrington Moore and Theda Skocpol. Important adjuncts of this multi-volume work were separate substantial monographs on authoritarian power and ethnic conflict in *Fascists* (2004) and *The Dark Side of Democracy* (2005).

Mannheim, Karl (1893–1947) A Hungarian sociologist who emigrated to Germany and finally to England shortly after Hitler came to power. His most enduring contribution was to the *sociology of knowledge, which he defined as a theory of the social or *existential conditioning of thought. Mannheim viewed all knowledge and ideas as bound to a particular location within the social structure and the historical process. Thus, thought inevitably reflects a particular perspective, and is situationally relative. Mannheim was influenced by both *Marx and *Weber, and in most of his writing he conceives the different social locations of ideas mainly in terms of *class factors or *status groups. For example, he contrasts *utopian thought rooted in the future hopes of the underprivileged, with ideological thought propounded by those benefiting from the status quo. However, Mannheim also gave special attention to generational differences in relation to ideas. A person's *generation, like their social class, gives an individual a particular location in social and historical time and thereby predisposes them to a certain mode of thought.

Although Mannheim saw all thought as relative to social position, he rejected total *relativism. All thought is an authentic expression of a group outlook, but this does not make it false or distorted knowledge. He sought for a method through which each partial truth could be synthesized into a larger, and more objective, picture.

Some of his central and most important ideas can be found in *Ideology and Utopia* (1929), *Essays on the Sociology of Knowledge* (1928), and *Man and Society in an Age of Reconstruction* (1935). David Kettler and Volka Meja have produced a number of important works on Mannheim, including *Karl Mannheim and the Crisis of Liberalism* (1995). *See also* KNOWLEDGE, SOCIOLOGY OF.

manual versus non-manual distinction A broad dichotomy in the study of occupational *stratification, which correlates with many social indicators such as income, health, and educational attainment, as well as conditions of employment broadly defined. It is, nevertheless, based on a value-judgement about the *status and nature of different *occupations in the *working class and the *middle class, according to the amount of mental (non-manual) as opposed to physical (manual) labour they are supposed to require. A closely related distinction is that between blue-collar and white-collar work. Although widely institutionalized in everyday life and in law, attempts to reach agreed operational definitions of manual and non-manual work reveal that the distinction tends to be arbitrary. This is well illustrated by considering *gender differences in occupational position: women doing mental work in white-collar jobs tend not to be accorded either the same pay or prestige as white-collar men. Ambiguity has not prevented sociologists themselves from identifying and describing broad inequalities of *life chances, *lifestyle, and prestige as being associated with so-called manual/working-class and non-manual/middle-class occupations. More sophisticated classifications now used in the sociology of stratification attempt simply to reflect the subjective value element which samples of lay judges themselves employ to distinguish the prestige of jobs; however, the idea that there is a consensus in society about the relative worth of manual or mental labour is itself not borne out by empirical research. *See also* GOLDTHORPE CLASS SCHEME; NEW WORKING CLASS; OCCUPATIONAL CLASSIFICATION; OCCUPATIONAL PRESTIGE.

manufacturing The making of articles and goods for sale as commodities. Manufacturing makes up the greater part of what is sometimes referred to as the secondary sector of the economy. *See also* FACTORY SYSTEM; INDUSTRIAL SECTOR.

Maoism The theory and policies identified with the Chinese revolutionary communist leader Mao Zedong (1893–1976). Mao's relationship to *Marxism is disputed, since many commentators deny either that he made any novel contributions to social theory, or that his writings were distinctively Marxist. He is principally associated with an heretical theory of socialist revolution (*see* REBELLION, REVOLUTION) which accords primacy to the role of the revolutionary *peasantry—hardly surprisingly, given the economically backward circumstances of China in the 1920s, when Mao set out on his political career. Although Marxists continue to dispute vigorously both his relationship to Soviet Marxism, and the practical consequences of his policies on Chinese economic development (especially the effects of the notorious 'Cultural Revolution' of 1966–7), his significance for sociology is limited by the impenetrability of much of his philosophical (as opposed to his political and strategic) writing—a weakness exemplified, for example, in his essays 'On Practice' and 'On Contradiction' (1937).

At various times during the Cold War period, neo-Marxist sociologists turned to Maoist China in the hope of finding a *socialist state that was less wedded to doctrinaire *Marxism than was the Soviet Union, and as a result there are several excellent (though somewhat idealized) ethnographies of life in Maoist China that have achieved almost classic status (including J. Myrdal's *Report From a Chinese Village*, 1965, *China: The Revolution Continued*, 1970, and W. Hinton's *Fanshen*, 1966). However, students would be well advised to balance these with a reading of a more sceptical account, such as Zhang Xinxin and Sang Ye's oral history of contemporary China (*Chinese Lives*, 1986).

Marcuse, Herbert (1898–1979) A German philosopher and social theorist, a member of the Frankfurt School (*see* CRITICAL THEORY). Unlike other members, he remained in the United States after the end of the war, and maintained a commitment to radical politics until the end of his life. He had a strong influence on the ideas of the student left in the 1960s.

His version of critical theory grew out of the mainstream of European philosophy: the work of *Hegel, *phenomenology and *existentialism, and the meeting of these with some aspects of *Marxism. His writings covered politics and aesthetics, as well as philosophical and cultural criticism, and were especially concerned with what he regarded as the *totalitarian tendencies of modern societies. Capitalism had, as he saw it, transcended the economic condition that Marx analysed and the working class had failed to develop as a revolutionary force. He hoped that those groups excluded from the system (for example, Blacks, and for a limited period of their lives, students), might provide a sense of opposition. His most important books were *Reason and Revolution* (1941), a presentation of a Hegelian, critical or 'negative' Marxism, and a vigorous critique of *positivist philosophy; *One Dimensional Man* (1964), concerned with the ways in which modern *capitalism restricts the possibility of opposition; and *Eros and Civilization* (1955), which appropriates some of the more metaphysical ideas of *Freud, particularly his notions of the life and death instincts, into a critique of the way in which modern culture transforms and alienates desire. The best—though highly sceptical—examination of his thought is still Alasdair MacIntyre's *Marcuse* (1970).

marginal employment *See* INFORMAL ECONOMY.

marginalist revolution *See* NEO-CLASSICAL ECONOMICS.

marginalization A process by which a group or individual is denied access to important positions and symbols of economic, religious, or political power within any society. A marginal group may actually constitute a numerical majority—as in the case of Blacks in South Africa—and should perhaps be distinguished from a *minority group, which may be small in numbers, but has access to political or economic power.

Marginalization became a major topic of sociological research in the 1960s, largely in response to the realization that while certain developing countries demonstrated rapid economic growth, members of these societies were receiving increasingly unequal shares of the rewards of success. The process by which this occurred became a major source of study, particularly for those influenced by *dependency, Marxist, and *world-systems theories, who argued that the phenomenon was related to the world capitalist order and not just confined to particular societies.

Anthropologists, in particular, have tended to study marginal groups. This stems in part from the idea that, by looking at what happens on the margins of a society, one can see how that society defines itself and is defined in terms of other societies, and what constitute its key cultural values. *See also* EXCLUSION.

marginal totals (marginals) *See* CONTINGENCY TABLE.

market In both *economics and *sociology a market is understood to be an area over which any well-defined commodity is exchanged between buyers and sellers. Such commodities are considered to be of two kinds—goods and services. The total amount of a commodity produced and available for purchase is referred to as the supply of the commodity, while the total amount being sought for purchase is termed the demand. Because human wants are, in themselves, potentially infinite, it should be noted that in the study of markets demand must be effective, that is to say backed by money or purchasing power.

Note that a market need not be a physical location—as in the case of a Stock Exchange. It is any arrangement for bringing buyers and sellers together. Improvements in telecommunications networks have speeded up communication to such an extent that financial markets and commodity markets are now international in scope. The central purpose of certain regional political initiatives is to create larger integrated markets for goods and services, such as the European Economic Community, or the proposed Latin American Economic Community.

Mainstream economic theory mostly assumes that competition in markets is perfect. That is to say, there is a large number of buyers and sellers, none of whom can exert undue individual influence on the process by which the market price is fixed. Perfect competition, it is argued, ensures that there is an inherent tendency for supply and demand to adjust to each other through the prevailing price which, if all participants act rationally, will rise or fall according to the relative scarcity of the commodity and the competitive efficiency with which it is supplied by producers and purchased by consumers. Competition also explains the relationship between markets: all products are in competition with each other for a share of consumers' limited purchasing power, and all producers are in competition for access to a limited total stock of raw materials, machinery, labour, and investment capital. The competitive process will then penalize any departures from rationality among producers or consumers by driving them out of the market altogether.

Market economies are seen as placing the individual consumer in command of production. Each individual, using income derived in the main from his or her own productive activities, expresses his or her desires and preferences by the way he or she distributes this income for the various goods and services available in markets. This economic theory is associated with a political theory which places the citizen, as a voter, in ultimate authority over the production of public goods, such as education services, weapons, or art. The market system is thus argued to be democratic in essence.

A market is not the only method of allocating goods and services since a central planner could achieve the same result. One of the longest-standing debates in economics has been over which is the more efficient method. Hence the *command economies of *socialist countries are contrasted with the market economies of *capitalist countries. In the market economy, also called free economy or free enterprise economy, the greater part of the activities of production, distribution and exchange are conducted by private individuals or companies rather than by the government, and government intervention is kept to a minimum. Exceptions are sometimes made in the provision and distribution of health services and education services, which are funded by and organized by central or local governments, in which case the term *mixed economy would be more appropriate.

Markets are recognized to have some obvious disadvantages. They tend to have *trade-cycles which mean that resources are periodically not fully employed. In the case of labour, under-utilization means *unemployment, which threatens workers' living standards and this may in turn have a wide range of social as well as economic effects. An uncontrolled market system produces undesirable outputs as well as the goods and services sold on the market. The classic example now is environmental pollution, with waste products being dispersed into the atmosphere, rivers, and oceans. Markets have no morals. The production and sale of weapons, access to basic health care, scientific research, artistic products, and religious services are determined entirely by the level of demand for them. Most societies have value systems which are not wholly consistent with and subservient to the amoral functioning of the market, so that market outcomes may at times be judged to be socially unacceptable. Disadvantages such as these are quite separate from a range of practical imperfections in the functioning of any market. For example markets work best when there is perfect information available to all buyers and sellers, so that demand for commodities and the supply of them interact until prices reach an *equilibrium. In practice, full information may not be available, or only at disproportionate cost, or information may be unequally distributed among market participants.

Since few social scientists have been entirely happy with the notion of perfect competition, one fruitful area for collaboration between economics and sociology is the attempt to develop a systematic account of how the empirical world supports or departs from the competitive ideal. From the outset, economics has sought to understand the distortions to economic processes introduced by any government which attempted to displace the effects of unregulated economic transactions with the political allocation of resources and commodities, even within a single society. Departures occur, however, because of *monopoly and other concentrations of economic power and interest; or because of cultural or administrative barriers. All of these issues are central to the concerns of the sociologist of *economic life but it is only in the study of *labour markets that any real attempt at integrating economic and social theory has occurred.

One of the few exceptions to this generalization is Robert E. Lane's *The Market Experience* (1991), which comprehensively reviews the literature on the market economy, drawing on material from economic philosophy, economic anthropology, economic psychology, and the sociology of work. Controversially, Lane argues that the research evidence from these fields offers a powerful critique of market economics, notably by demonstrating that two of its major premisses are mistaken: namely, that (contrary to mainstream economic theory) work is not a disutility, but is in fact one of the two major sources of lifetime satisfaction; and that monetary income, although a source of utility which does compensate for sacrifices at work, contributes little to a person's sense of well-being. *See also* CAPITALISM; LABOUR MARKET.

market research Qualitative and quantitative research on the tastes, values, and perceptions, on the personal, household, and neighbourhood characteristics, and on the purchasing behaviour, of individual consumers of (or industrial customers for) equipment and services. Usually carried out by agencies who specialize in this activity, although some large companies have their own market-research divisions, and some market research companies are also involved in academic research (for example large-scale surveys) on a contract basis.

market situation *See* CLASS POSITION.

market socialism *See* COMMAND ECONOMY.

marriage Marriage is traditionally conceived to be a legally recognized relationship, between an adult male and female, that carries certain rights and obligations. However, in contemporary societies, marriage is sometimes interpreted more liberally and the phrase 'living as married' indicates that for many purposes it makes no sense to exclude cohabitation. It should be noted, however, that even this more liberal definition usually excludes *homosexual couples. Although cohabitation is increasingly accepted, and is now the normal prelude to marriage, people continue to make a distinction between living together and a 'proper' wedding and marriage.

Much recent sociological research, both in Britain and America, has been concerned with the growing fears that marriage as an institution is in decline. These fears stem from two roots, the first being concern for increasing marital breakdown and subsequent divorce, and the second the fact that marriage is going out of fashion, with more people cohabiting and even rearing children outside matrimony. Certainly, divorce is on the increase, and if current divorce-rates in Britain continue then one in three marriages is likely to end in divorce. In recent years, the median age at first marriage has increased and teenage marriages have declined significantly, with a growing proportion, albeit still a small minority, never getting married. At the same time, rates of cohabitation are increasing, with it now being virtually the norm to cohabit before marrying. Moreover, an increasing number of children are conceived and born outside marriage. Looking at these statistics, one might reasonably conclude that the future of marriage looks bleak, but marriage still remains the preferred way of life for the vast majority of the adult population. Even among those whose first marriage fails, a majority are sufficiently optimistic to marry a second time.

Why do people marry? In Western societies, the emotional aspects of marriage are stressed, and what Lawrence Stone calls *affective individualism prevails (see *The Family, Sex and Marriage in England, 1500–1800*, 1977). Choice of a mate is influenced primarily by the desire for a relationship offering affection and love— although, as Peter Berger observes, the 'lightning shaft of Cupid seems to be guided rather strongly within very definite channels of class, income, education, racial and religious background' (see *Invitation to Sociology*, 1963). The tendency for people of similar backgrounds to marry (marital homogamy) is strong, but there is no clear understanding of why it occurs, or whether the degree of rigidity in mate selection differs among different social groups. Surprisingly, some recent American research suggests that the higher the class position, the less the homogamy (M. Whyte, *Dating, Mating, and Marriage*, 1990). The same study also indicates that homogamy is a poor predictor of marital success.

Concern with marital success and marital adjustment has played an increasingly prominent part in recent research. As David Morgan (*The Family*, 1985) suggests, marriage has become 'medicalized', with therapists and marriage-guidance counsellors at the ready to tackle marital problems and enhance marital quality. This raises the question of how marital success should be measured. Clearly, stability is not a sufficient indicator, as some couples stay together even though they are totally miserable, whereas others divorce, despite having a relationship that some would envy. A variety of marital quality inventories have been developed and recently it has been recognized that marital quality and martial problems are in fact independent. For example, conflict and arguments may be signs of caring and engagement in some marriages.

Marriages clearly face different problems at different times of the *life-cycle, and raising a *family, especially for parents of younger children, is associated with high marital strain. Remarriages appear to be at greater risk of breaking up than first marriages, especially when step-children are involved. This may be in part because remarriage is an incomplete institution, in the sense that societal expectations and *norms still reflect the traditional expectation that marriages will last a lifetime. As Anthony Giddens has pointed out, terms like 'broken marriages' and 'broken homes' embody the traditional ideal and have unfortunate negative connotations, especially regarding children whose parents are separated or divorced.

Increasingly, research is focusing on the interrelationship of employment and family life, including marriage. The primary focus has been on how women's employment has affected the marital relationship. Using longitudinal surveys, American researchers have found that women who contribute a higher share of the household income are more likely to divorce than women who contribute a lower share, or housewives. It may be that wives who become less dependent upon their husbands financially are no longer willing to tolerate a subservient position—and have the resources that enable them to leave. Another important question is whether the employment of women has led to greater *egalitarianism within marriage. Some family researchers have painted a rosy picture of how families are becoming more symmetrical, whereas others continue to exercise scepticism, asserting that the traditional division of labour within the home persists, even when women also hold full-time employment.

Jessie Bernard (*The Future of Marriage*, 1972) has claimed that there is not one marriage but two—the wife's marriage and that of the husband. Studies have consistently shown that marriage tends to be more beneficial for men than for women, with married men being in better psychological health, and showing fewer symptoms of *stress than married women. Some feminists who see marriage as an oppressive institution have urged women not to marry. The inequalities of marriage, however, are reflections of the inequalities of the sexes in society. As Chris Harris states, 'it is to be expected that however great the formal equality between the spouses, wives' sense of inequality in marriage will persist as long as they cannot, for whatever reason, participate on equal terms with men in the labour market' (*Family and Industrial Society*, 1983). Bernard goes further, suggesting that the metamorphosis of housewife to bread-winner sends tremors through every relationship. Dual-earning marriages are sowing the seeds of change. However, despite the dire statistics, marriage seems to be a rather resilient institution; perhaps, very gradually, the benefits for both husband and wife will become more balanced. *See also* ROLE, CONJUGAL; DOMESTIC DIVISION OF LABOUR; DUAL-CAREER MARRIAGE; FAMILY, SYMMETRICAL; GROUP MARRIAGE; HOUSEHOLD ALLOCATIVE SYSTEM.

Marshall, Alfred (1842-1924) An English economist, author of the highly influential *Principles of Economics* (1890), and (among other things) contributor to the *marginalist revolution (*see* NEO-CLASSICAL ECONOMICS) of the 1870s in economics. Marshall is principally of interest to sociologists because, in *The Structure of Social Action* (1937), Talcott *Parsons reviews his work and claims to find therein a significant critique of the notion of marginal utility in an implicit theory of values. Parsons argued that values fall logically outside the analytical scheme of economics, and provides a justification for the theoretical framework of sociology in general and Parsons's 'action frame of reference' in particular.

Marshall, Thomas H. (1893-1982) An English sociologist and professor of sociology at the London School of Economics. He is best-known for his theory of *citizenship, developed from the ideas of his colleague *Hobhouse. He argued (in *Class, Citizenship and Social Development*, 1963) that citizenship has expanded from legal rights (such as a fair trial) in the 18th century, to political rights (such as voting) in the 19th century, to welfare rights (such as social security payments) in the 20th century. These *rights were institutionalized in law courts, parliament, and the *welfare state. He developed the notion that modern societies are 'hyphenated societies' in *The Right to Welfare and Other Essays* (1981), because they are organized around the conflicting principles of *welfare, *class, and *democracy. He also wrote an influential study of social policy (*Social Policy in* *the 20th Century*, 1965). His concept of citizenship continues to be influential although it has been criticized. For example, he neglected the idea of *industrial democracy as a further stage in the development of citizenship rights. His account is also said to be Anglocentric and evolutionist (see M. Mann, 'Ruling Class Strategies and Citizenship', *Sociology*, 1987). His ideas exerted a significant influence on the work of numerous distinguished sociologists, including (in the United States) Robert Merton, S. M. Lipset, and Reinhard Bendix; and (in Britain) Ralf Dahrendorf, A. H. Halsey, David Lockwood, and Lydia Morris.

Martineau, Harriet (1802–76) Harriet Martineau was effectively the first woman sociologist. Martineau, who was English and of Huguenot origin, wrote the first systematic treatise in sociology, carried out numerous cross-national comparative studies of social institutions, wrote a handbook on observational methods, and translated Auguste Comte's *Cours de philosophie positive* into English. A professional and prolific writer, she popularized much social-scientific information by presenting it in the form of novels. Feminist, critic, social scientist, and atheist, she matched her activism about the issues of slavery and the 'Woman Question' to her arguments for equal political, economic, and social rights for women. She undertook many pioneering methodological, theoretical, and substantive studies in the field that would now be called sociology: the analysis of women's rights, biography, disability, education, slavery, history, manufacturing, occupational health, and religion all came within her gamut.

One of her best-known works, *Society in America* (1837), compared American moral principles with observable social patterns, and outlined a yawning gap between rhetoric and reality. Martineau's *How to Observe Morals and Manners* (1838) is arguably the first systematic methodological treatise in sociology, in which she outlined a positivist solution to the dilemma of reconciling intersubjectively verifiable and observable data with unobservable theoretical entities. She tackled the classic methodological problems of bias, sampling, generalization, corroboration, and interviews, as well as outlining studies of major social institutions such as family, education, religion, markets, and culture. Long before Marx, Weber, or Durkheim, Martineau also studied and wrote about social class, suicide, forms of religions, domestic relations, delinquency, and the status of women. Her neglect by sociologists in subsequent years is therefore often cited as an illustration of the ways in which academic sociology has until more recently excluded women sociologists from its agenda.

(⊕) SEE WEB LINKS
• Includes extracts from essays by Martineau.

Marxism The body of theory and diverse political practices and policies associated with (or justified by reference to) the writings of Karl *Marx and Friedrich *Engels. For a substantial part of the 20th century, and until the closing years of the millennium, Marxism was the alleged organizing principle of societies which contained more than one-third of the earth's population. Its influence on culture, history, sociology, politics, economics, and philosophy is explained and documented in David McLellan (ed.), *Marx: The First Hundred Years* (1983).

However, one of the best treatments is still to be found in C. Wright Mills, *The Marxists* (1962), which offers an especially useful introduction for students of sociology.

In one way the political success of the Social Democratic Party (SPD) in establishing itself as the principal voice of the German working-class movement in the 1880s was unfortunate for the further development of Marxism as an intellectual system. This success encouraged the premature systematization of the somewhat inchoate ideas of Marx and Engels around their economic core, so that they could better serve as the doctrinal basis for what was a rapidly developing international movement (the German-led Second International). Engels's own contribution to this process, as represented by his formulation of the doctrine of *dialectical materialism, was probably critical.

There was a direct political consequence of the *economically determinist nature of this systematization was a political one; namely, the fusing within social-democratic thought of Marxism's revolutionary ideas with an acceptance of so-called bourgeois *democracy. (Nothing could prevent the replacement of *capitalism by *socialism so there was no need to challenge the fundamental rules of the democratic system.) The person most often credited with this accomplishment was the SPD's leader Karl *Kautsky. Almost as soon as Kautsky's 'orthodox Marxism' became the dominant current within his party, it was challenged from both the right (by Eduard *Bernstein's revisionism), and the left (by Rosa *Luxemburg's spontaneism). Bernstein criticized the retention of Marxism's revolutionism, whilst Luxemburg was opposed to the acceptance of parliamentarianism. Luxemburg's ideas briefly challenged the dominance of those of the orthodoxy, during the course of the ill-fated Spartacist Uprising of 1918, which took place in Berlin. But Bernstein's ideas eventually triumphed over the orthodoxy, long after his death, when the SPD finally abandoned Marxism in 1959.

In terms of global politics, however, what was vastly more important than these German oppositional currents in determining the fate of both socialism and Marxism for most of the 20th century was an oppositional current that arose in Russia in the early years of the century. This was the Bolshevism fashioned by *Lenin, during the course of his struggle with the Russian equivalent of German orthodox Marxism, namely Menshevism. For the reasons set out by Herbert *Marcuse in his *Soviet Marxism* (1958), the establishment of Marxism-Leninism or *Stalinism as the ruling *ideology of the Soviet state led to the self-strangulation of the most influential body of Marxist thought as a creative and critical enterprise.

During the 1920s a number of new approaches to Marxism, based on *Hegel and the early work of Marx, were produced. György Lukács and Karl Korsch were the most influential, though their works were denounced by the Soviet-led orthodoxy. Antonio Gramsci produced a related set of ideas, but he was imprisoned and had little influence at the time. A further strand of thought was the *critical theory that developed at Frankfurt in the years before the Nazi rise to power. All of these approaches to Marxism had their greatest impact when rediscovered in the renewal of interest in Marxist theory during the 1960s and 1970s. A negative feature of this renewal was that Marxism has continued to be driven by internal disputes between different groups claiming to represent the authentic tradition established by Marx and Engels. The most acrimonious of these debates involved competing 'structuralist' and 'humanist' interpretations, and probably reached its nadir in the debate about the work of *Althusser, as for example in E. P. Thompson's vitriolic attack on structural Marxism in his *The Poverty of Theory* (1978).

The significance of this human and intellectual tragedy was then hugely magnified by the Comintern's (and latterly the Third or Communist International's) successful export of these ideas to much of the rest of the world, most notably to China. By contrast, although it was of course powerfully influenced by the rise of Marxism-Leninism, Marxism retained much of its critical political and intellectual edge in the non-communist world. In the underdeveloped world it helped to stimulate and guide numerous national liberation movements— although there has been considerable dispute about precisely what might be the specifically Marxist elements in some of these movements (on which point see Aiden Foster-Carter's celebrated article on 'Neo-Marxist Approaches to Development and Underdevelopment', in E. de Kadt and G. Williams (eds.), *Sociology and Development*, 1974). In the developed world it has played an equally vital role in the emergence of the welfare state and latterly the new *social movements.

Despite Marxism's complicity in the crimes associated with Marxism-Leninism, it remains a highly significant element in the pursuit of knowledge and social justice in the post-communist world. *See also* ANARCHISM; HUMANISM; POST-MODERNISM; STRUCTURALISM.

Marxist sociology *See* ABSOLUTISM; ANALYTICAL MARXISM; ASIATIC MODE OF PRODUCTION; CAPITAL; CAPITALISM; CENTRE-PERIPHERY MODEL; COLLECTIVE CONSUMPTION; CONTRADICTORY CLASS LOCATION; CRIMINOLOGY, CRITICAL; CRITICAL THEORY; EDUCATION, SOCIOLOGY OF; LEISURE, SOCIOLOGICAL STUDIES OF; RACE, SOCIOLOGY OF; SCHOOL CLASS; STATE; STRUCTURALISM.

Marx, Karl (1818–83) A German social theorist, founder of revolutionary *communism, and in sociology of *historical materialism. Marx began studying law at the University of Bonn and completed his studies at the University of Berlin. Soon after arriving in Berlin, he joined an iconoclastic and bohemian intellectual group (who were to become known as the Young Hegelians), and took up philosophy. After completing his studies in 1841 he became a journalist on, and later the editor of, a radical bourgeois newspaper called the *Rheinische Zeitung*. Rather unluckily, Tsar Nicholas I of Russia happened to read an attack on himself that Marx had penned, and prevailed upon the Prussian government to close the paper down.

In 1843 a jobless Marx married his childhood sweetheart, Jenny von Westphalen, and moved to Paris. During the two years he spent in Paris, Marx met and quarrelled with many of the leading radicals of the time, including the anarchists Bakunin and Proudon, and the poet Heinrich Heine. More important for his own development were some of the unknown people he met, especially the socialist artisans and Friedrich *Engels, the son of a German manufacturer who was already managing his father's factory at Manchester in England. Engels was to become Marx's lifelong friend, collaborator, and much-put-upon patron.

Marx's more or less simultaneous discovery of *socialism and the works of the British *political economists, principally Adam *Smith, David Ricardo, and James Mill, enabled him to distinguish himself clearly from his Young Hegelian mentors and so lay the foundations for his own theoretical system. Of the three manuscripts he wrote during this period, only the two historically less significant ones were published, *The Holy Family* and *The Poverty of Philosophy*. Very likely, as would still be the case today, this was because these two were studies of better-known contemporaries rather than statements of an original position by an unknown author; this was not true of the third text, that which has become known as *The Economic and Philosophical Manuscripts of 1844*. These early publications did little to create a reputation for Marx. By contrast, the ideas outlined in the *Manuscripts* provided him with the intellectual sustenance necessary to sustain himself over a long career as an émigré activist and private scholar, a career marked by poverty and academic as well as political neglect (the interest of Tsar Nicholas proving to be short-lived). Moreover, although the *Manuscripts* were not published until the 1930s, their appearance even then was a major intellectual event and had a profound effect on Marxist scholarship, especially in the 1960s and 1970s. For some, they represented the key to a hitherto suppressed humanistic Marxist and socialist tradition that provided a basis for the criticism, not only of *capitalism, but also of all 'actually existing socialisms', whether Stalinist or social-democratic. For others, they made explicit and so allowed the identification and removal of anachronistic, non-scientific traces in Marx's mature theory, and restored its explanatory potential.

The *Manuscripts* are most often celebrated for the passion with which the concept of *alienation (the wage-worker's lack of control over the production and disposal of his or her product) is presented, but equally noteworthy is the general nature of the argument of which this concept is a part. This is because the argument represents an accessible as well as an extremely powerful instance of the mode of argumentation that has become known as critique: that is, exposing the often unjustified assumptions upon which intellectual positions commonly rest. In what still seems like a striking instance of lateral thinking, Marx chose to go about his 'settling of accounts' with his philosophical past by applying the method of critique to the aforementioned British political economists, and drawing conclusions about the validity of *Hegel's theory of history. What he discovered was that both bodies of thought unproblematically assumed that inequality and all of its attendant sufferings follow from the accident of birth. Thus what Marx shows is that wherever one looks in the conceptual schema of the political economists what one finds is that it rests upon the unjustified assumption of the prior existence of private property.

Marx's own explanation for the existence of private property remains very under-developed in the *Manuscripts*, resting as they do on the concept of alienation. Instead, he is far more concerned to spell out what he sees as the consequences of the psychological and social estrangements that follow from this lack of control, and the resulting universal human need for revolution (*see*

REBELLION, REVOLUTION). It was to take him a further twenty years to specify exactly why alienation occurred.

Marx made his first move towards this goal just one year after he wrote the *Manuscripts*, in the short text that has become known as *The Theses on Feuerbach*. Feuerbach was the 'Young Hegelian' to whom Marx owed most. The critique of his ideas was eventually to have a significance which extended far beyond Marx's own theoretical system. The thought that launched not just *Marxism but *structuralism more generally is most concisely crystallized in the sixth thesis, which states that 'the essence of man is not an abstraction inherent in each particular individual. The real nature of man is the totality of social relations.'

Once Marx had in this way defined his starting-point, he moved rapidly on to the specification of the concrete nature of these relations. In *The German Ideology* of 1846, also unpublished at the time, he used the terms 'productive forces', *division of labour, and 'internal intercourse' or *ideology to conceptualize them, and on this basis was able to distinguish four different forms of society covering the whole span of human history: primitive communism, ancient or slave society, *feudalism, and capitalism. He also began to explore the issue of how one form was succeeded by another. His suggestion was that, over time, contradictions gradually developed within each form of society because of the constraints imposed upon the development of the productive forces by the ruling ideologies of property. These contradictions resulted in struggles over the distribution of any surplus between the *classes created in all societies (except communist ones) by the organization of the division of labour. Marx identified the principal classes of capitalist societies as the *bourgeoisie and the *proletariat.

The theory lying behind the concept of class was still incomplete since the theoretically critical varying modes of surplus appropriation had yet to be specified. Nevertheless, Marx was clearly extremely excited by the analytical possibilities opened up by his possession of this concept, and he spent the next ten years writing empirically orientated texts in which he sought to demonstrate them. Among the most important of these were *The Communist Manifesto* (1848), *The Class Struggles in France* (1850), and *The Eighteenth Brumaire of Napoleon Bonaparte* (1852).

It was not until 1857, and nine years after he had settled in London, that Marx returned seriously to his theoretical studies and the problem of what it was about the ways in which particular *forces of production, divisions of labour, and ideologies of property were combined, which divided people into classes. The result of these labours were the eight hundred or so pages that have become known as *The Grundrisse* (1858). Because Marx was by now a reasonably well-known journalist, he at last found a publisher for his theoretical work. With great difficulty Marx managed to extract a slim volume entitled *A Contribution to a Critique of Political Economy* (1859) from *The Grundrisse*. Its publication was a resounding failure, and with the exception of the famous *base versus superstructure metaphor contained in its Preface, the text itself appears to have been incomprehensible even to many of his closest friends. Marx and his publisher lost interest in publishing any more volumes of such material. This was unfortunate because it meant that it was to be several more years before Marx was forced to present the missing link in his economic theory, the *labour theory of value, and to elaborate upon its consequences in a publishable form. This he finally did in 1867 when the first volume of *Capital* appeared. Two more volumes were published posthumously in 1885 and 1893. Chief amongst the theoretical deductions drawn from the labour theory of value in these later volumes was the theory of crisis he constructed around what he termed 'the tendency of the rate of profit to fall' and its 'counteracting influences'.

In sum, then, Marx died having solved (for himself at least) the principal problem remaining in his economic theory; namely, why should the mode of appropriation of surplus that is specific to capitalism organize those engaged in production into two antagonistic classes? What he did not do was to specify what consequences, if any, his new-found theoretical precision might have for his understanding of the mode of surplus appropriation specific to the other social forms that he had identified. Nor did he enlarge on the more or less incidental remarks he had made throughout his career on such topics as the *state, *ideology, class, *law, *socialism, and (of all things) *communism. One ironic consequence of this unevenness in the development of Marx's thought was that the humane concerns underlying his economic theory were forgotten by many later Marxists, as they often ruthlessly acted upon the extremely powerful, but very partial political and social insights produced by the same theory.

Of the countless biographies and expositions of his thought, David McLellan's *Karl Marx: His Life and Thought* (1973) still commends itself, for its clarity and attention to detail. Marxist sociology has, of course, been both controversial (sometimes self-consciously so) and heavily criticized. Much of this is discussed elsewhere in this dictionary (see especially those topics listed under the heading 'Marxist sociology'). *See also* CAPITAL; CLASS CONSCIOUSNESS; MARXISM; MEANS OF PRODUCTION; MODE OF PRODUCTION; RELATIONS OF PRODUCTION.

(SEE WEB LINKS
• Marx and Engels Internet Archive.

Masaryk, Tomáš (1850–1937) A Bohemian social theorist who became the first President of the Czech Republic, holding office from 1918 to 1935. He undertook a pioneering study of suicide (*Suicide and the Meaning of Civilization*, 1881) that used statistical methods to show that suicide rates reflect the inner spiritual character of a culture and that it was the disintegration of Catholicism in Europe that had generated high levels of suicide. In his later study of *The Spirit of Russia* (1912) he saw societies as dynamic systems of organizations and associations held in a state of interdependence through their cultural values.

masculinity The characteristics of, and appropriate to, the male sex. Although feminists would argue that most sociology has been by men, about men, and for men, the problem of analysing men and masculinity as issues in their own right remained relatively neglected until (ironically) the advent of second-wave *feminism itself. Thus, for example, studies of delinquency or of social class were in effect the study of boys and men, but did not see *gender itself as a concern. The issue of masculinity was largely ignored and gender served as a taken-for-granted variable.

There were some notable exceptions. Margaret *Mead's comparative work suggested the cultural basis for, and relativity of, masculinity and femininity (a finding subsequently challenged by Mead's critics). Likewise, from the perspective of *functionalism and *role theory, Talcott *Parsons described the *sex roles of men and women as instrumental and expressive respectively. Parsons and his colleagues argued that such roles were internalized by young children and led to a neat division of labour in adult life, with men and women becoming well integrated into the social system, hence enabling it to function smoothly. In psychology, too, the idea of the male role was present, often coupled with the view that much of masculinity was a defence against an *identity crisis, serving to mask men's essential vulnerability (see, for example, J. Pleck's *The Myth of Masculinity*, 1981).

Nevertheless, it was not until the 1970s that the topic of masculinity as such started to be more extensively researched, largely as an offshoot of the *women's movement, proponents of which suggested that the problem of *patriarchy was in fact 'the problem of men'. Pioneering studies of gender roles and masculinity were conducted by Mirra Komarovsky, examining the functional significance and cultural contradictions of sex roles (see her *Blue Collar Marriage*, 1964, and *Dilemmas of Masculinity*, 1976). Subsequently, with the development of the so-called Men's Movement, studies of masculinity began to appear in greater numbers. Andrew Tolson (*The Limits of Masculinity*, 1976) attempted to demonstrate that masculinity had to be located within a wider social framework of class, education, work, and age. Masculinity, like femininity, was far from a uniform cultural product, but itself assumed many dimensions. The centrality of seeing masculinity not as an essence but as a product of cultural and historical forces became paramount. By the 1980s, Men's Studies had become established as a specialist area of inquiry replete with its own internal schisms, theoretical debates, differing emphases, and divergent politics (see, for example, T. Carrigan et al., 'Toward a New Sociology of Masculinity', *Theory and Society*, 1985, or A. Brittan, *Masculinity and Power*, 1989).

Whilst some sociologists have continued to use and develop traditional role theory, others have drawn from the work of feminist scholars and gay and lesbian studies, and have highlighted the prominence of patriarchy, heterosexism, and power for the analysis of masculinity. In Robert Connell's work, for example, there has been an increasing emphasis not on masculinity per se but on gender relations organized largely through power (see his *Gender and Power*, 1987).

In 1990 Kenneth Clatterbaugh (*Contemporary Perspectives on Masculinity*) reviewed the whole field, and suggested there were several distinct theoretical stances with respect to the sociological issue of masculinity. The first continued a conservative line of thought, seeing masculinity as universal, unchangeable, and rooted largely in biology. Pro-feminist positions, by contrast, generally followed the analyses laid down by feminist theory, both in its liberal and radical versions. Third, there were the advocates of Men's Rights, who argued that men also were the victims of patriarchy and *sexism. Fourth, a newly emerging position suggested the need for men to regain their spiritual roots, an argument exemplified in Robert Bly's *Iron John* (1991). Finally there were a range of arguments which linked the study of men with class, race, and gay issues. *See also* CULTURE AND PERSONALITY SCHOOL.

Maslow, Abraham H. (1908–70) An American psychologist who developed a theory of *self-actualization from his observations of well-functioning individuals. He is often seen as the leading proponent of the so-called Third Force in psychology—emphasizing *humanism and *existentialism over *behaviourism and *Freudianism. *See also* NEEDS, HIERARCHY OF.

mass communication *See* COMMUNICATION; MASS MEDIA, SOCIOLOGY OF.

mass culture *See* POPULAR CULTURE.

mass hysteria A psycho-social phenomenon whereby people in large groups behave in a similar and often emotional manner. Often used (somewhat *ethnocentrically) in trans-cultural psychiatry, together with the term collective epidemics, in reference to the pressure to conform to group *norms in the societies of the *Third World.

mass media, sociology of A medium is a means of *communication such as print, radio, or television. The mass media are defined as large-scale organizations which use one or more of these technologies to communicate with large numbers of people ('mass communications'). Dependent upon innovations in the electronics and chemicals industries, the period between 1860 and 1930 was a formative moment for the mass media. These years saw the development and introduction of still photography, moving photography (cinema), cable telegraphy, wireless telegraphy, the phonograph, the telephone, radio, and television. These new technologies formed part of the wider transformation in *popular culture during this period and typified the new more intensive capitalization of the leisure industries and their associated concern to address mass audiences.

As defined by C. Wright *Mills in *The Power Elite* (1956), the mass media have two important sociological characteristics: first, very few people can communicate to a great number; and, second, the audience has no effective way of answering back. Mass communication is by definition a one-way process. Media organizations are *bureaucratic and (except in societies where all media are state-controlled) corporate in nature. Media output is regulated by governments everywhere, but the restrictions vary from very light advisory regulation (for example no cigarette advertising or nudity on TV), to the most comprehensive forms of censorship in *totalitarian societies.

Mass media dominate the mental life of modern societies, and therefore are of intense interest to sociologists. From the earliest studies in the 1930s, the main concern was with the power implicit in new media technologies, especially radio and television. Adolf Hitler's successful use of radio for propaganda was an object lesson in the possible dangers. The concept of *mass society added force to the idea that the electronic media might create an Orwellian situation of mind control, with passive masses dominated by a tiny elite of communicators.

Early studies by Harold Lasswell, Paul Lazarsfeld, and others seemed to show that media effects were indeed direct and powerful—the so-called 'hypodermic' model of influence. But more intensive research revealed that mass communications are mediated in complex ways, and that their effects on the audience depend on factors such as class, social context, values, beliefs, emotional state, and even the time of day.

Media research has expanded enormously since the 1960s, with most attention going to television as the most pervasive medium (D. McQuail's *Mass Communication Theory*, 1983, is an excellent introduction and overview). Four distinct areas of research can be distinguished. First, media content studies, concerned with the cultural quality of media output, or with specific biases and effects such as *stereotyping or the promotion of anti-social behaviour and violence, especially on children's television. Second, patterns of ownership and control, the integration of more and more media into a few large *corporations, cross-media ownership, and the increasing commercialization of programming. Third, *ideological influences of the media in promoting a total pattern of life and thought. Fourth, the impact of electronic media on democratic politics via agenda-setting, the distortion and reduction of news, deflecting public attention from social problems, and the use of television advertising in political campaigns.

Some critics have suggested an even more fundamental influence of television. Since the first modern newspapers were published in the early 17th century, mass media have been linked to the spread of literacy and education. Neil Postman (in *Amusing Ourselves to Death*, 1985) is among those who have argued that the electronic and visual media have reversed the trend towards greater literacy and understanding, and are in the process of destroying the foundations of traditional education.

The national organization of the press and broadcasting (radio and television) was a distinctive feature of these mass media throughout the 20th century. However, a number of writers have argued that this organization of the mass media has increasingly been challenged, especially since the 1960s. Most clearly in relation to television broadcasting—the pre-eminent medium of the post-war years in Europe, America, and a good deal of Asia—it is argued that we live in a transitional period. In Britain, this is characterized as a movement from an era dominated by a conception of public-service broadcasting based upon channel scarcity, a national service, and a particular set of communication technologies (including terrestrial broadcasting), to a new age of global media corporations, new technologies, and more segmented (as opposed to mass) audiences. Government policy in Britain has been central to this process. A neo-liberal concern to open up media markets to greater competition has challenged public-service notions of broadcasting as dealing in social goods. This has been accompanied by a shift away from seeing the audience of radio and TV as citizens to seeing them as consumers being offered choice. Opening up media markets has primarily offered new opportunities to emerging global media organizations such as Time Warner, Sony, and News Corporation. These corporations have been concerned to detach audio-visual markets from the space of national cultures. New generic channels (dedicated to sport or news or movies) have spearheaded the new service, carried along new delivery systems (satellite, cable and telephone lines), funded by new forms of payment (subscription or pay-per-view).

Many of these developments have been made possible by the new technologies of computer processing and satellite broadcasting. New forms of broadcasting have become possible and channels of communication have proliferated. The mass media have become associated with the growth of a *cybersociety. Underpinning these developments has been not only the tighter integration of the media sector, but also the convergence of entertainment and information businesses with the telecommunications industry. Driving forward this process of convergence has been a concern to reap the rewards of media synergy. It has been argued that there are four dimensions to this process (see Paul du Gay (ed.), *Cultures of Production/Production of Culture*, 1997). The first concerns 'synergies of software'. This refers to the simultaneous presentation and promotion of a performer or author across a range of media, entertainment products, and leisure goods. In practice this means linking together in a highly systematic way discrete forms such as audio recordings, still images in books or magazines, T-shirts, advertising, film, TV broadcasts, home video, and computer games. The second form of synergy refers to the integration of software and hardware. The electrical goods manufacturer Sony's decision to buy CBS Records and its listing and back catalogue of artists ('software') represents one example of this phenomenon. The third form of synergy concerns the convergence of previously distinct hardware components and is the result of new micro-processing systems and digital technology. Popularly known as 'multi-media', this enables still and moving photos, sound, and text to share the same (digital) format. Finally, new media synergy is possible through new technologies of distribution. The key development here is the fibre-optic cable, which can deliver media products and services such as movies or banking along its length. In doing so it lays the basis for the so-called information super-highway.

Discussions concerning the social and cultural implications of this reconfiguring media landscape have focused around the issues of democracy, access, and the creation of new public spheres. Positively, developments such as pay-per-view and subscription are seen to introduce an element of consumer responsiveness into programming, whilst the more developed forms of interactivity associated with video, digitalization, and the *Internet allow consumers to organize their own way through particular media experiences. The Internet is also seen to offer positive possibilities for groups previously marginal to the mass media to organize themselves and establish a space of communication and identity.

In a more negative vein, however, critics have pointed to the increasing gap between the so-called 'information rich' and the so-called 'information poor' in the new media universe. Access to the new technologies looms large in this argument, and with it questions of social marginalization, where groups are denied opportunities to express themselves via these new means of representation. What is striking here is the enormous concentration of ownership across media production, reproduction, and distribution. In this sense, although the new media may represent greater social and cultural diversity in their range of products, this is not reflected in the social make-up of the media corporations themselves. See the useful discussion in Nicholas Garnham, *Emancipation, The Media and Modernity* (2000).

Mass-Observation An independent social research organization created in 1937 in Britain by anthropologist Tom Harrisson, sociologist Charles Madge, and film-maker Humphrey Jennings. Their aim was to undertake ethnographic studies of everyday life using a large panel of volunteers who kept diaries and recorded their social observations in response to regular directives. They produced studies of street activities on Coronation Day in 1937, workers on holiday in Blackpool, work at a war factory, and drinking behaviour in Bolton pubs. Jennings produced a number of documentary films related to the studies. Their work continued until 1949, when Mass-Observation became a conventional *market-research company. A selection from the studies can be found in A. Calder and D. Sheridan, *Speak for Yourself: A Mass-Observation Anthology*, (1984). The Mass-Observation archives have been mined for a number of compilations and television dramas. An overview of their work can be found in Nick Hubble's *Mass-Observation and Everyday Life* (2006).

mass society The modern image of mass society, although not the label, begins with the French aristocrat Alexis de *Tocqueville, who toured the United States in the 1830s in search of the secret of *democracy. He was struck by the similarity of ideas and values among the people, and speculated that such a society might fall victim to a mass or herd mentality which he called 'the tyranny of the majority'. Tocqueville's classic description of mass society has echoed through the whole subsequent history of social theory: 'an innumerable multitude of men, all equal and alike, incessantly endeavoring to procure the petty and paltry pleasures with which they glut their lives. Each of them, living apart, is a stranger to the fate of all the rest. His children and his private friends constitute to him the whole of mankind. As for the rest of his fellow-citizens, he is close to them but he sees them not; he touches them but he feels them not.'

Nineteenth-century sociologists shared many of de Tocqueville's concerns about the emerging culture of industrial societies. Émile *Durkheim diagnosed *anomie in the new order, and Max *Weber focused on the dead hand of *bureaucracy. Ferdinand *Tönnies, in *Gemeinschaft und Gesellschaft* (1887), reflected unfavourably on the crowded, urban, mass societies then emerging in Europe.

These ideas were largely ignored or dismissed as elitist nostalgia until the 1950s, when sociologists and political scientists began to write about the immediate past history of *totalitarianism in Europe and the Soviet Union. In *The Politics of Mass Society* (1959), William Kornhauser argued that populations cut adrift from stable *communities, and having uniform and fluid values, would be highly vulnerable to the appeals of totalitarian mass movements.

Max Horkheimer, Theodore Adorno, and others of the Frankfurt School (*see* CRITICAL THEORY) focused their attention on the narrowly ideological nature of 'mass culture', and a whole critical literature developed around this perspective. Herbert *Marcuse in *One Dimensional Man* (1964) developed this line of argument to its fullest extent, asserting the absolute *hegemony of mass culture and the impossibility of social change. Salvador Giner provided a comprehensive summary of both conservative and radical theories in his 1976 book *Mass Society*.

The term mass society has fallen out of fashion in sociology, but the principal themes of the theory remain important. The recent work of Robert Putnam (*Bowling Alone: The Collapse and Revival of American Community*, 2001) on *social capital has once again raised this issue, returning to the ideas of Tocqueville. *See also* COMMUNITARIANISM.

master status Each individual occupies a number of *status positions, some ascribed (such as sex or race), and some achieved (such as educational level or occupation). The master status of an individual is one which, in most or all social situations, will overpower or dominate all other statuses. The term was coined by American sociologist Everett Hughes in the 1940s, with special reference to race. Occupation, race, and sex may all function as master statuses in Western societies, and can produce powerful contradictions and social dilemmas when important status positions contradict perceived *roles and *stereotypes—for example the female astronaut, or the African-American surgeon. In these situations, social actors must make status decisions, which may take the form of denial (the astronaut labelled 'unnatural' or the physician as 'exceptional'); or responses may take the form of exclusion, or the acceptance of a new master status. Master status influences every other aspect of life, including personal *identity. Since status is a social label and not a personal choice, the individual has little control over his or her master status in any given social interaction.

material culture *See* CULTURE, ADAPTIVE AND MATERIAL.

materialism In sociology and related disciplines, the word materialism has three quite distinct meanings which are, however, to some extent interconnected, and very commonly confused with each other. The first meaning is drawn from popular moral or political controversy, according to which materialism refers to a prevailing pattern of desire for mere sensory enjoyments, material possessions or physical comfort, at the expense of any higher moral or spiritual values or concerns. This usage is generally pejorative.

The second meaning is to designate a range of metaphysical positions (philosophical views about the fundamental nature of reality). Though recognizably materialist metaphysical positions were advocated as early as the 5th century BCE in Greece, promulgation of materialism as a modern world-view dates from the 17th and 18th centuries CE in Europe. Whereas in classical times matter had been opposed to form, the dominant early modern contrast was between matter and spirit or mind. *Descartes's metaphysics reduced all existence to two fundamental substances: matter, characterized by extension, the substance of bodily existence; and mind, not spatially located, and characterized by thought. The contemporary advances in the science of mechanics provided the basis for early modern philosophical accounts of matter, and also seemed to hold out the promise of ultimately accounting for all phenomena in mechanical terms. The early chapters of Thomas *Hobbes's *Leviathan* are a remarkable early example of such a materialist attempt (*contra* Descartes) to account for human mental operations such as perception, memory, volition, the emotions, foresight, reasoning, and so on, in terms of the concepts of mechanics.

In a period during which clerical authority and political power were closely intertwined, such doctrines were bound to be seen as radical and subversive in their implications. In the 19th century *socialist and *communist doctrines were associated with materialism, by advocates and opponents alike. However, with changes in science and especially with the development of the life-sciences, the content of materialist doctrines also shifted. Organic (as distinct from mechanical) metaphors became more prominent, and processes of development and historicity entered into philosophical representations of the material world. These features were particularly evident in the mid-19th century materialist revolt against the German idealist tradition, led by Feuerbach, *Marx, and *Engels.

These thinkers rejected both *idealism and the narrower reductive forms of materialism that had been based on mechanics, and that had been incapable of taking full account of sensuous existence, of the emergence of conscious and active human subjects. These phenomena were, however, to be understood not by any concession to idealism; but, rather, by taking advantage of the increasingly complex and sophisticated account of matter itself, as made available by ever-advancing scientific knowledge. Engels later came to systematize the principles of this philosophical approach under the title dialectical materialism.

The third meaning of materialism in familiar sociological usage is also associated with Marx and Engels. In this meaning, materialism asserts the primacy of need-meeting interaction with the natural environment both to the understanding of human social structures and patterns of conflict, and also to long-run sequences of historical change. Though there is an obvious affinity between this doctrine and metaphysical materialism, they are quite logically independent of one another. The later writings of Marx and Engels contain attempts to define and classify the basic variant forms of human society in terms of the social organization of the activities of material production, distribution and consumption. The *modes of production thus distinguished were held to have their own distinctive patterns of social dominance, subordination, and conflict, as well as definite tendencies for historical change, and possible transition to new forms. Cultural forms, ways of thinking, and political institutions were held to be characteristic of each mode.

This approach to social explanation, so-called 'historical materialism', is often criticized for its over-emphasis on economic life at the expense of political or cultural processes. Arguably, however, both Marx and Engels distanced themselves from such economic determinist or reductionist interpretations of their work. Partly this is a matter of the non-correspondence between their concept of 'mode of production', on one hand, and the set of activities conventionally labelled 'economic', on the other. Also, however, even in societies where there are institutional separations between economic and political, artistic, and other practices, historical materialism asserts that such non-economic activities have their own *relative autonomy within a range of sustainable possibilities whose limits are set by the economic structure. One of the most challenging problems addressed by 20th-century Marxists has been to provide more rigorous and empirically defensible accounts of these relationships. It is arguable that historical materialism, with its emphasis on need-meeting interactions with nature, is only beginning to reveal its full potential towards the close of the 20th century, as social scientists increasingly turn their attention to environmental problems.

material justice *See* JUSTICE, SOCIAL.

maternal deprivation John *Bowlby's term for the absence of the maternal care considered necessary for later mental health. Subsequent research sought to specify child-care requirements—such as love, attachment, and stimulation—and the respective effects of their lack or distortion. *Feminists denounce the idea for its ideological role in subordinating women to *motherhood. Supporters of the theory hold that it is the *activity* of 'mothering' that is important, not the gender of the person who undertakes it.

mathematical sociology Mathematical sociology uses mathematics (including logic and information science) to formalize theoretical propositions and model empirical social processes. Examples include the algebraic formalization of *measurement theory; use of *graph theory and finite mathematics in *sociometry, social *network analysis, and studies of kinship; and the extensive use of probabilistic Markov chains for modelling *social mobility and *stratification. The specialist *Journal of Mathematical Sociology* covers the field.

The work of the American sociologist Leo A. Goodman is typical of this approach. Goodman, who has substantive interests in demography, social mobility, and stratification generally, has pioneered the use of *loglinear and latent structure techniques in the analysis of *contingency tables. *Analysing Quantitative/Categorical Data* (1978), a collection of ten articles published between 1970 and 1975, is a representative collection of his writings. For a more recent example see *The Analysis of Cross-Classification Having Ordered Categories* (1984). *See also* NEO-POSITIVISM.

matriarchy There are two uses of the term matriarchy. The first is identical to common usage, denoting a type of social organization in which mothers head families, and *descent may be reckoned through them. The occurrence may be idiosyncratic rather than the basis of social structure.

The second usage, which is speculative and based in *evolutionary theories, refers to a society in which mothers hold the main *power positions. This theory was popular in the 19th century; it was, for example, a vital ingredient in Friedrich *Engels's *Origin of the Family, Private Property and the State* (1884). Engels argued that early hunter-gatherer societies, in which property rights did not exist, would have been ruled by women because of their reproductive powers. However, once land and goods became private property, in the development of sedentary agriculture or pastoralism, it became important for men to ensure the legitimacy of their offspring in order to transfer wealth by descent. Thus arose the system of *patriarchy, in which men began to control the reproductive power of women, who lost the political power they had enjoyed under matriarchy.

Like all evolutionary theories the claim that human prehistory was characterized by a shift from mother-right to father-right fell out of favour in the early 20th century. Despite the attractiveness of this speculation for feminist theory, there is no accredited evidence from either archaeology or anthropology for the existence of matriarchy in this second sense, at any time in history or in any human society.

matrilineal Matrilineages are unilineal *descent groups that claim real or fictive kinship through maternal ties to a common ancestress through known genealogical links. In matrilineal systems, inheritance is traced from the maternal uncle (mother's brother) to the nephew (mother's son). The tendency is to preserve the economic and political identity of the sibling group. The means by which this is ensured entail control of women's labour, sexuality, and reproductive powers, by distributing them between husbands and brothers. Matriliny should thus never be considered as a system which somehow empowers women—and should not be confused with *matriarchy.

Mauss, Marcel (1872–1950) Originally trained as a philosopher at the Universities of Paris and Bordeaux, Mauss spent his professional life as a researcher, despite never acquiring a doctorate. With his uncle, Émile *Durkheim, and in the company of an impressive group of sociologists, anthropologists and historians that included Henri Hubert and Robert Hertz, he founded the influential journal *Année sociologique*, in which most of the fundamental ideas of social anthropology were first explored. Mauss's influence on *social anthropology cannot be overstated. Through exploring the nature of *gift relationships (*The Gift*, 1925) he exposed the principles of reciprocity that are unchallenged in either functionalist or structuralist anthropology. Indeed, it can be argued that the structural anthropology of Claude Lévi-Strauss would be unthinkable without its basis in the work of Mauss, not only with respect to reciprocity but also classification (see Durkheim and Mauss, *Primitive Classification*, 1903). The sociologies of exchange relations and belief systems have both been influenced by Mauss's ideas. However, despite the pathbreaking nature of his work, Mauss tended to write essays and critiques rather than books, often in collaboration with others of the *Année sociologique* group, and among sociologists his work has probably not received either the attention or credit that it rightly deserves. *See also* RATIONAL CHOICE THEORY.

Mayo, Elton (1880–1949) Founder of *human relations theory. He led the interpretation of the *Hawthorne Studies and worked closely with Lloyd *Warner at Chicago University. His work stressed the importance of the 'informal' organization of interpersonal relations that surround the *formal structure of work organization stressed by *administrative theory. He criticized the so-called rabble hypothesis that *social order requires hierarchical control. Instead, cooperation is seen as an inherent and necessary condition for society, but is obstructed by slow adaptation to technical change—which *management can resolve by fostering appropriate social skills in the workforce.

Mead, George Herbert (1863–1931) A leading American pragmatist, philosopher of the *Chicago School, and one of the founders of the sociological tradition that came to be known after his death as *symbolic interactionism. He referred to his work as *social behaviourism.

Mead's contribution is most frequently seen as centring upon the development of a theory of *Mind, Self and Society*, the title of his posthumously published book (in 1934). In this work, he laid the foundations for a sociological social psychology, emphasizing the following: an analysis of experience located firmly within society; the importance of *language, *symbols, and *communication in human group life; the ways in which our words and gestures bring forth responses in others through a process of role-taking; the reflective and reflexive nature of the *self; and the centrality of the 'act'.

But Mead's work went well beyond this. Indeed, as John Baldwin has argued in his book *George Herbert Mead* (1986), Mead provided a much wider 'unifying theory' for sociology, which anticipated, at one level, developments in sociobiology, and at another, broad historical transformations. Uniting all this was his unswerving commitment to the role of science in human affairs. 'The scientific method', he wrote, 'is the method of social progress.'

Mead fostered a position sometimes designated 'objective relativism': he often refers to the 'objective reality of perspectives'. There are many accounts of reality possible, depending upon whose standpoint is taken. History, for example, is always an account of the past from some person's present. A theory of the social construction of *time was another major aspect of Mead's work.

When Mead died he had not published a unified statement of his ideas. His four posthumous books are edited versions of his lecture notes and of notes recorded by his students. This gives much of his written work an unsatisfyingly incomplete and piecemeal character. (An unknown, previously unpublished, book by Mead has recently been discovered: *Essays in Social Psychology*, written in 1910 and published in 2001.) Despite this, his influence on modern sociology has been enormous. For a selection of his writings see Anselm Strauss (ed.), *George Herbert Mead on Social Psychology* (1964); and for a valuable bibliography, see Richard Lowry, 'George Herbert Mead: A Bibliography of the Secondary Literature', in *Studies in Symbolic Interaction*, 1986. *See also* REFERENCE GROUP.

SEE WEB LINKS
• The full text of Mead's paper on 'The Social Self'.

Mead, Margaret (1901–78) An American cultural anthropologist and student of Ruth *Benedict. She argued that personality patterns were culturally rather than biologically determined. Her celebrated *Coming of Age in Samoa* (1928) has been attacked by *sociobiologists. It was based on rather insubstantial fieldwork and could be reassessed for reasons which do not discredit her discipline (see Derek Freeman, *Margaret Mead and Samoa*, 1984). She pioneered a critical study of *gender in *Sex and Temperament in Three Primitive Societies* (1935). Her many field trips included the South Pacific Islands, New Guinea, and Bali, and are vividly described in the autobiographical *Blackberry Winter* (1972). She popularized *social anthropology, partly by challenging *ethnocentrism in the *dominant ideology of the United States. She was marginalized by what she saw as the male world of academia, and remained attached to New York City's American Museum of Natural History, moving from assistant to curator. *See also* CULTURE AND PERSONALITY SCHOOL.

mean *See* CENTRAL TENDENCY (MEASURES OF).

meaning (meaningful action) It would be difficult to imagine any sociological study which did not, implicitly or explicitly, look at how people think about the social world and social relationships—in other words at the meanings that the social has for individuals and groups. Indeed, some schools of thought argue that meaning is the only object for *sociology, as against those which look for causal explanations by reference to, for example, social *structures.

The concept of meaningful action is most closely associated with Max *Weber, who distinguishes it from behaviour; that is, from merely physical movement to which the actor does not attach a meaning (for example blinking). Meaningful social action, by contrast, is action directed towards others and to which we can attach a subjective meaning. In this sense, praying alone in a church is meaningful action, as is participating in a church service. Most later theorists accept that these distinctions cannot easily be maintained and take the view that attaching a meaning to something ('mere behaviour') is itself an action; and, moreover, a social action because it draws on a socially constructed and accepted language. *See also* ACTION THEORY; INTERPRETATION.

means of production The means that are used to produce goods and services, including the social relations between workers, technology, and other resources used. The term is prominent in Marxist theory, since *Marx's characterization of *capitalism hinges on the distinction between those who own the means of production (capitalists), and those who have nothing to sell but their own labour power (proletarians).

means-testing *See* SELECTIVE VERSUS UNIVERSAL BENEFITS.

measurement Measurement raises four main issues for the sociologist: representation (how many properties of the empirical world can best be modelled?); uniqueness (how unique are the resulting measurement numbers?); appropriate statistics (what indices may legitimately be used to summarize the measures?); and meaningfulness (what do the measurement numbers signify?).

For any given domain of interest, a measurement representation or model states how empirical data are to be interpreted formally. Measurement involves a relationship between empirical phenomena and the formal or numerical system chosen to represent it. Most social and psychological attributes do not strictly have numerical properties, and so are often termed 'qualitative' or 'non-metric' *variables, whereas properties such as wealth are termed quantitative or metric.

Quantitative measures occur at a hierarchy of levels of measurement of increasing complexity. At the nominal level, things are categorized and labelled (or numbered), so that each belongs to one and only one category (for example, male $= 0$, female $= 1$). At the level of ordinal measurement, the categories also have a (strict) order or ranking. Interval-level measurement requires that equal differences between the objects correspond to equal intervals on the scale (as in temperature). At the ratio level, the ratio of one distance to another is preserved, as in moving from (say) miles to kilometres. Most textbooks on survey research explain the different levels of measurement, with examples, and describe the statistics and techniques that are appropriate to the different levels (see, for example, D. A. de Vaus, *Surveys in Social Research*, 1985, 1991).

measurement error *See* CODING; ERROR (SAMPLING AND NON-SAMPLING).

mechanical management systems *See* CONTINGENCY THEORY.

mechanical solidarity *See* DIVISION OF LABOUR; SOCIAL ORDER.

media *See* MASS MEDIA, SOCIOLOGY OF.

median *See* CENTRAL TENDENCY (MEASURES OF).

medicalization A concept made fashionable by Ivan Illich and Michel *Foucault, the term commonly denotes the spread of the medical profession's activities, such as their increasing involvement in the processes of birth and dying. Greater power is usually assumed to follow increased pervasiveness. For that reason, the term may also be used to imply expansionist, imperialist strategies.

medical model An imprecise but widely used term. The characteristics of the medical model are rarely specified. The term sometimes refers to the framework of assumptions underpinning the relationship between doctor and patient. Erving *Goffman, in *Asylums* (1961), viewed the medical model as a particular version of a more general 'tinkering services' model that assumes a technically expert server and an individual client with an object in need of repair. In medicine the object is the body, and Goffman explored the special characteristics of this 'medical servicing' relationship.

More commonly, the term medical model refers to medicine's ideas and assumptions about the nature of illness, notably its natural scientific framework and its focus on physical causes and physical treatments. As such the term is frequently invoked in the context of ideological and political debates and inter-professional rivalries in which the relevance of this particular set of ideas is called into question. One problem with the term is that it suggests a uniformity of medical ideas about causation and treatment that does not fit the empirical diversity very well, since doctors do not focus exclusively on physical factors, even in relation to physical illness. For this reason some prefer the term 'bio-medical model', since it clearly indicates the focus on the biological, and allows that there are other medical models. An alternative model of health and illness, employed by some doctors but especially favoured in nursing circles for its greater breadth, is a 'bio-psycho-social models' encompassing the biological, psychological, and social aspects. However, attempts to integrate these three terrains present considerable problems, and the term is arguably more rhetoric than reality.

medical sociology *See* MEDICINE, SOCIOLOGY OF.

medicine, sociology of A field of sociology that focuses on medicine as a set of ideas and practices. However, exact delineation of the field is problematic. In the first place, there is disquiet about identifying a field of sociology in terms of its relation to another profession. This issue has often been raised by drawing a contrast between sociology in medicine and the sociology of medicine. Sociology in medicine, it is argued, works within the constraints and parameters of medicine, accepting its objectives and priorities. Sociology of medicine adopts a more detached, critical approach, in which the sociological enterprise has priority over the medical. According to this argument, the sociology of medicine is consequently a legitimate field of sociology, whereas sociology in medicine is not. However in both cases the field is still defined in relation to medicine. Other writers prefer a broader designation of the territory, such as the sociology of healing or of healers, or the sociology of health-care systems, in order to make it clear that doctors are not the only group involved in healing or the only components of the health-care system. There are a range of health carers such as nurses and physiotherapists, as well as informal carers, whose work needs to be examined and should not be subsumed under the umbrella of medicine. A further problem with the delineation of the field concerns the relation of the sociology of medicine to the *sociology of health and illness. Many would argue that the sociology of medicine necessarily embraces the sociological study of health and illness, since these are the core of medicine's concern; others would argue that the focus should be rather narrower and concentrate on medicine as a *profession, and that the sociology of health and illness should be treated as a separate field of study.

Notwithstanding these territorial difficulties, the sociology of medicine, broadly defined, has flourished since the 1950s. Although its roots lie in part in the social medicine of the inter-war years and earlier, its sociological impetus came primarily from Talcott *Parsons's influential work on the medical profession and the *sick role, which put medicine and illness into the mainstream of sociology.

Leaving aside the questions concerning health and illness, the sociology of medicine in its narrower definition focuses on two major issues. A first and dominant concern is to analyse the nature, extent, and origins of the power of the medical profession, and the relation of the medical profession to other allied professions. The work of Eliot Freidson in *The Profession of Medicine* (1971), with his emphasis on autonomy as the defining feature of a profession, exemplifies this tradition. It has been further developed by a number of feminist writers, such as Ann Oakley, who have examined the exclusionary tactics deployed by the medical profession in the *medicalization (a term particularly associated with Ivan Illich's study *Medical Nemesis*, 1976) of events such as childbirth—a medicalization that not only excludes the female midwife but also increases the powerlessness of women who are giving birth.

Doctor-patient relationships constitute the second major focus of the sociology of medicine, with work ranging from in-depth studies of doctor-patient interactions, including analyses of tape-recorded doctor-patient exchanges, to large-scale surveys of doctor-patient satisfaction, the time spent with patients, and so forth. The care of the dying has received especial attention, as has the socialization of medical students. Ruth Laub Coser's *Life in the Ward* (1962) illustrates this tradition.

However, whilst these two areas will no doubt remain at the core of the sociology of medicine, it seems likely that the activities of the medical profession will be increasingly located within the context of the study of other health workers and the wider health-care system (see U. Gerhardt, *Ideas about Illness: An Intellectual and Political History of Medical Sociology*, 1989). Emily Mumford's *Medical Sociology* (1983) is one of the many textbooks dealing with this specialism.

megalopolis In ancient Greek, a large planned town. Used by Lewis Mumford (*The Culture of Cities*, 1940) to refer to a great *metropolis growing uncontrollably, and now to denote a very large, functionally interconnected system of cities and suburbs. *See also* CONURBATION; METROPOLITAN STATISTICAL AREA.

melting-pot The idea that societies formed by immigrants from many different cultures, religions, and *ethnic groups, will produce new hybrid social and cultural forms. The notion comes from the pot in which metals are melted at great heat, sometimes melding together into new compounds, with greater strength and other combined advantages. *See also* ASSIMILATION.

membership group *See* REFERENCE GROUP.

members' methods A term used by *ethnomethodologists to refer to the methods by which people make sense of activities to themselves.

meme A term introduced by Richard Dawkins in 1976 (*The Selfish Gene*) to refer to cultural symbols, intended as a specific analogue to the gene in biology. Memes are seen as the objects of variation and selection and are argued to be the means of cultural transmission and evolution through processes of communication and imitation. Although presented as a novel idea, and widely taken by *evolutionary psychologists as a striking innovation, the part played by cultural symbols in evolution was already well understood by sociologists and anthropologists. The parallel between the gene and the cultural symbol was first made by the biologist Alfred Emerson in the 1950s and was taken up by Talcott *Parsons as the central idea in the analysis of cultural systems. Similarly, ideas on cultural diffusion through imitation were central to the work of Gabriel *Tarde almost a century earlier than Dawkins's book. In the hands of some adherents to Dawkins's work, the idea of the meme has been used far too broadly and simplistically.

mental illness A disputed concept (see, for example, the entries elsewhere in this dictionary on Laing and anti-psychiatry) founded on the everyday contrast between mind and body which, when applied to illness, generates an opposition between two contrasting types of illness—mental and physical. Mental illnesses are illnesses characterized by the presence of mental pathology: that is, disturbances of mental functioning, analogous to disturbances of bodily functioning. Like physical illness the concept is, therefore, fundamentally evaluative and linked to issues of *social control and regulation. The disturbances of thought and feeling that characterize mental illness, such as delusions, hallucinations, excessive elation, or *depression, are often associated with behaviour that is considered bizarre, awkward, disruptive, or disturbing. It is this disturbed and disruptive behaviour that, more than anything else, leads to mental illness being treated as a very distinctive form of illness, requiring special services and attention. What seems to be particularly problematic within society is the apparent irrationality and loss of reason that mental pathology involves. Mind and reason are the distinctive hallmarks of human beings, and their loss (full or partial), if not taken to be a sign of supernatural powers, is generally viewed as profoundly disturbing and threatening. Mental illness is therefore usually more *stigmatizing than other forms of illness (obvious exceptions are diseases such as AIDS, other sexually transmitted diseases, and to a lesser extent cancer).

Historically, the medical concept of mental illness has its basis in lay judgements of mental states, which were embodied in notions such as insanity and lunacy—real madness—as well as in concepts such as 'troubled in mind', 'mopish', and 'distracted', which encompassed the less severe forms of psychological disturbance. Then as now these terms were applied to persons whose behaviour seemed in some way inexplicable or irrational. Deviant or delinquent it might be, but it could not be understood as readily as the usual forms of *delinquency, often because it involved a rejection of what was highly valued in society.

Present-day medical conceptions of mental illness are still intimately linked to lay judgements of what is rational, reasonable, and appropriate. However, *psychiatry has embraced and transformed the everyday lexicons, classifying and listing a diverse set of mental illnesses. These range from conditions such as Alzheimer's disease, which are known to involve brain pathology, through the archetypical mental illnesses such as schizophrenia and manic depression (which belong to the group of psychoses), to conditions such as anxiety states, phobias, and obsessions (frequently termed neuroses), as well as to the so-called behaviour disorders such as alcoholism, anorexia nervosa, drug addiction, and sexual deviations.

Psychiatrists' lists of mental illnesses provide a formal specification of the boundaries of mental illness, however the boundaries are changing and contested. The distinction between mental illness and physical illness is itself highly problematic. It is most obviously made in terms of manifest pathology, but is often not clear-cut, with many illnesses having mental and physical symptoms; once we turn to causes the distinction is even more problematic and the idea of two mutually exclusive categories of illness soon founders. An identifiable mental pathology may well have physical causes, as in the case of Alzheimer's disease; equally, some physical pathologies such as ulcers have mental causes (as the concept of *psychosomatic illnesses allows). Indeed, the interrelation of mental and physical has frequently been used to justify attempts to integrate mental health services with other health services. In practice, where the boundary is set between mental and physical illness is a matter of convention, and depends on ideas about causation as well as on the extent of the manifest mental and behavioural problems.

The boundary between mental illness and *deviance ('madness and badness') is equally problematic, especially in relation to behaviour or personality disorders, where symptoms are very obviously behavioural. Analytically the distinction is one of referent: mental illness is a judgement of mind, deviance one of behaviour. However, since observations of behaviour are the basis for judgements of mind, in practice confusions and difficulties arise. Here, as on its other margins, changing conventions are involved in determining the boundaries between the two, as in the increasing tendency to see child abuse less as a form of deviance than as indicative of underlying mental pathology. Finally, there is the boundary between what is normal and abnormal mental functioning. Again this boundary is largely set by changing conventions, and as with other boundaries its location also varies from individual to individual, according to social background and circumstances.

Ideas about the causes of mental illness vary. Psychiatry, by virtue of medicine's emphasis on physical processes, has focused on physical causes and treatment and given them primacy, frequently and mistakenly seeing physical explanations as precluding the necessity for any examination of the place of psychological and social factors. In contrast, a number of sociologists and social theorists have made significant contributions to the understanding of the social causes of mental illnesses, as for example in the case of George Brown and Tirril Harris's work on depression, or feminist analyses of anorexia nervosa.

However, the sociological contribution to the understanding of mental illness also derives from the analysis of mental illness as a social construct. This construct, as is noted above, sets the boundaries of normal, acceptable mental functioning in different cultures and societies, and as such is part of the social regulation of human conduct. *See also* COMMUNITY CARE; SICK ROLE.

(((∰))) SEE WEB LINKS
• The National Institute of Mental Health (US).

mental labour *See* MANUAL VERSUS NON-MANUAL DISTINCTION.

mercantile capitalism *See* CAPITALISM.

mercantilism A much disputed term for the expansion of national economic power that has become confused with nationalism, protectionism, and autarky. It refers specifically to the economic theories and strategic thinking which guided relationships between states in early-modern Europe. The term gained popular currency through Adam *Smith's critique of the 17th- and 18th-century 'mercantile system' in *The Wealth of Nations* (1776).

According to Smith, mercantilism is particularly concerned with the conditions under which the *state might intervene in the economic sphere in order to secure a favourable balance of trade. The central characteristics of the mercantilist system were an obsession with policies designed to encourage exports of manufactured goods and provision of imported raw materials, and to discourage imports of manufactures and loss of domestically produced raw materials.

merit *See* JUSTICE, SOCIAL.

meritocracy A social system in which *status is achieved through ability and effort (merit), rather than ascribed on the basis of age, class, gender, or other such particularistic or inherited advantages. The term implies that the meritorious deserve any privileges which they accrue. In practice it is difficult to find reliable measures of merit about which social scientists—or anyone else, for that matter—can agree.

The term was coined by Michael Young in *The Rise of the Meritocracy 1870–2033* (1958) to refer to government by those identified as the most able high achievers, with merit defined as intelligence plus effort. His fantasy attempted to foresee the extreme consequences of a society that fully implemented the goal of equality of opportunity through the educational system, with the most able rising to the upper echelons, leaving intellectual dullards to carry out humble manual work. The book warned that the new focus on intelligence and ability in the educational system merely institutionalized inequality of intellectual ability in place of inequality based on social class. Since judgements about what constitutes effort are inescapably moral (does a lazy genius merit rewarding? And, if so, why not a hardworking dullard?) the term remains highly contested (see, for example, John Goldthorpe, 'Problems of "Meritocracy"', in Robert Erikson and Jan O. Jonsson (eds.), *Can Education be Equalized?*, 1996). *See also* ACHIEVEMENT; JUSTICE, SOCIAL.

Merleau-Ponty, Maurice (1905–61) A French phenomenological philosopher who was especially concerned with the relationships between the body,
consciousness, and the outside world; one-time friend and colleague of Jean-
Paul *Sartre. His work on language is often seen as linking *phenomenology and
*structuralism. Merleau-Ponty's most important book is *The Phenomenology of
Perception* (1945). His work has become more influential with growing interest in
the sociology of the *body.

Merton, Robert King (1910–2003) Robert Merton was born Meyer R.
Schkolnick on 5 July 1910 in Philadelphia, Pennsylvania, the son of immigrants
from Eastern Europe. He spent most of his working life at Colombia University,
New York. His doctoral dissertation, published in 1938 as *Science, Technology
and Society in 17th Century England*, became a seminal text in establishing the
sociology of science as a significant field of study in its own right. In twelve single-
authored books and collections of essays, Merton also made path-breaking
contributions to the sociology of the *professions in general and the medical
profession in particular, to the sociology of *mass communications (with Paul
*Lazarsfeld), to the sociology of *racism, and to microsociology.
    At the height of his powers when there were fewer than 1000 sociologists in the
United States, it is difficult to overestimate Merton's influence on the institutional
development of American sociology. He combined the influence of classical
European theorists, particularly *Durkheim and *Simmel, with a commitment
to theoretically informed empirical research reinforced by his association with
the Colombia Bureau of Applied Social Research. He placed the emphasis on
'disciplined inquiry' on the basis of theories of the middle range that were
explicitly opposed to the excesses of both empirically empty grand theory and
theoretically empty data gathering. The magisterial *Social Theory and Social
Structure* remains one of the classic works of 20th-century sociological theory.
It includes brilliantly crafted pieces on the theory of *reference groups, manifest
and latent *functions, *middle range theory, and social structure and *anomie,
which are central statements of his distinctive version of structural-functionalism, a more dynamic, open, liberal and research oriented version than that
proposed by *Parsons.

messianic movement The term is derived from the religious concept of the
'Messiah', from the Hebrew word for 'anointed one', who is sent to humanity to
bring about a new age or the Kingdom of God. Jesus Christ was regarded by the
early Christian church as the Messiah. In the sociology of religion, the term is
used more generally to refer to any *social movement which is based on the
expectation and anticipation of a coming Messiah, who will release people from
their current misery. Messianic movements, especially in *Third World societies,
are typically associated therefore with *deprivation; messianic beliefs offer hope
for a better world. Messianic movements are often based on a synthesis of
Christian and aboriginal belief systems, in which Christian themes of salvation
are blended with indigenous world-views.

There is much debate in sociology about whether messianic beliefs are irrational. Some anthropologists claim that messianic movements are rational responses to a world which appears, from the point of view of native peoples, to be out of control and irrational. From a Marxist perspective, messianic movements are an effect of the alienation of aboriginal peoples, whose social reality has been destroyed by white colonialism and oppression. *See also* MILLENARIANISM; NEW RELIGIONS.

meta-narrative *See* POSTMODERNISM.

metaphysics The most ambitious of all philosophical projects is to devise a theory of the nature or structure of reality, or of the world as a whole. This project is commonly termed metaphysics, and its intellectual viability has been widely challenged in 20th-century Western philosophy. Metaphysics flourished in classical Greece, and also in the context of scientific revolution in 17th-century Europe. Philosophers such as *Descartes, Leibniz, and Spinoza thought that a systematic use of reason could lead them to a view of the nature of the world, which turned out to be very different in character from our ordinary, everyday understanding of it. But science, too, had this consequence. The philosophers Immanuel *Kant and David *Hume are the sources of modern scepticism about the pretentions of metaphysics. For both thinkers, significant use of language is possible only within the bounds of possible experience. Metaphysicians appear to make sense by using words drawn from everyday language, but in using these words to speak about a world beyond the limits of possible experience they fall into contradictions and incoherence. Some modern analytical philosophers have defended a more modest vision of metaphysics—'descriptive' as distinct from 'speculative', or 'revisionary'—as the attempt to analyse and describe the framework of basic concepts and their relationships underlying everyday and scientific discourse.

metatheory (metatheoretical beliefs) *See* AXIOM.

Methodenstreit *See* GEISTESWISSENSCHAFTEN and NATURWISSENSCHAFTEN; IDEOGRAPHIC VERSUS NOMOTHETIC APPROACHES.

methodological artefact *See* ARTEFACTS, STATISTICAL AND METHODOLOGICAL.

methodological pluralism During the 1970s sociologists were prone to argue that a long-standing positivistic hegemony in sociology had crumbled, and that the idea that there was one style of social research (underpinned by a unified *philosophy of social science and *methodology) had given way to the realization that there were many such styles. The *positivist orthodoxy was usually associated with the names of Talcott *Parsons (leading theorist of *functionalism) and Paul *Lazarsfeld (principal proponent of so-called *abstracted empiricism). The new methodological pluralism was a consequence of the emergence of *phenomenological and *structuralist sociologies, the fragmentation of *Marxism into sectarian neo-Marxisms, and the emergence of philosophical *relativism. Some observers employed the alternative terms epistemological pluralism or epistemological anomie to describe the now seemingly normless situation in which many different theories of knowledge or paradigms competed for sociological primacy. One commentator, Paul Feyerabend (*Against Method*, 1975), argued that, even in the natural sciences, researchers often changed what they were doing and how they did things. They had no single method as such; indeed, successful science demanded that there be no slavish adherence to a single method, but required instead a state of epistemological anarchy. Feyerabend, therefore, declared himself to be against method and in favour of such anarchy.

In large part these various labels are interchangeable. Each implies a rejection of methodological exclusiveness, and each rests on a somewhat misleading contrast with a positivist orthodoxy which never actually existed, since neither functionalism nor abstracted empiricism ever held hegemonic sway over the theory and practice of sociology during the previous period. Marxism, *idealism, and *symbolic interactionism (to take only the most obvious examples) offered ever-present philosophical and methodological alternatives.

methodology The word is sometimes used to refer to the methods and general approach to empirical research of a particular discipline, or even a particular large study, although the term 'research techniques' is perhaps more apt in this context. The principal concern of methodology is wider *philosophy of science issues in social science, and the study of how, in practice, sociologists and others go about their work, how they conduct investigations and assess evidence, how they decide what is true and false. The topics addressed include whether the *social sciences are in fact sciences; whether the social scientist needs to understand a sequence of social actions to explain it fully; whether there are laws in the social sciences which can predict as well as explain; whether research can be, or should be, value-free; causation and causal powers; inductive and deductive theory; verification and falsification; and other problems in the philosophy of knowledge and science (most of which are treated under separate headings in this dictionary). *See also* NEO-KANTIANISM; NEO-POSITIVISM.

methodology, feminist There have been a number of proposals that feminist social science—or social science in general, or even science in general—requires a new *methodology. Some of these have been concerned with *research design, some with *epistemology, and some with *ontology. Proposals for feminist research methods have either been directed to the elimination of unconscious sexist bias in research, when a male perspective and double standards are taken for granted, or to the replacement of supposedly *objective structured interviews and quantitative analysis by more reflexive and interactive unstructured interviews and a method of writing sociology that is said to allow the subjects to speak for themselves.

In terms of epistemology, one view is that striving after objectivity, truth, and control over nature is a masculine urge; women are thought to make less of a distinction between knower and known, self and other, mind and body, subject and object, and to be more tolerant of ambiguity and multiple truths. Another influential idea has been that of the 'feminist standpoint', the idea that women, as a subordinated group, are in a better position to arrive at an adequate representation of social reality than men, who are too caught up in their project of control. This epistemological advantage is not necessarily reflected in women's actual beliefs and attitudes but requires a feminist political effort and analysis. It leads towards an understanding of society which incorporates reproduction, bodily work, and intimate relations—the concrete realities of women's everyday existence—rather than working with abstract notions of isolated individuals making rational choices. The 'standpoint' position sees feminism as being capable of getting a truer picture of reality than masculinist science (Sandra Harding, *The Science Question in Feminism*, 1986; Dorothy Smith, *Writing the Social*, 1998). In terms of ontology, then, it is a *realist position. In this respect it differs from feminist *postmodernism, which is sceptical about all claims to scientific objectivity, sees all knowledge as being produced in specific historical and local situations, and recognizes important differences among women (of race, class, ethnicity, and sexual orientation), as well as between women and men.

metonym (metonymy) *See* DESIRE.

metropolis From the ancient Greek for mother and city, it denotes large urban centres and surrounding suburbs, often capital cities. Various statistical and descriptive definitions have been proposed. *See also* CONURBATION; MEGALOPOLIS; METROPOLITAN STATISTICAL AREA.

metropolis-satellite relationship *See* DEPENDENCY THEORY.

metropolitan area *See* CONURBATION.

Metropolitan Statistical Area A functional geographical classification of urban areas (formerly S[tandard]MSA), it comprises a large population nucleus and adjacent communities having a high degree of economic and social integration with the nucleus. Urban areas may contain more than one MSA (these are P[rimary]MSAs), and more than one PMSA (these are C[onsolidated]MSAs). *See also* CONURBATION; MEGALOPOLIS; METROPOLIS.

Michels, Roberto (1876–1936) A German sociologist and economist who wrote on a wide range of issues including nationalism, fascism, secularism, power, élites, intellectuals, and social mobility. Excluded from academic positions in Germany, he settled in Italy and took the name Roberto. He is most famous for the study of the leadership of left-wing democratic parties to be found in *Political Parties* (1911).

With particular reference to the Social Democratic Party in Germany, Michels explored the role of political leaders in shaping demands and aspirations, and in mobilizing popular support for Party initiatives. He was particularly interested in the ways in which organizational dynamics inhibit the realization of radical objectives. He concluded that all organizations have oligarchical tendencies, a proposition which he formulated as an 'iron law of oligarchy', which states that 'it is organization which gives birth to the domination of the elected over the electors, of the mandatories over the mandators, of the delegates over the delegators. Who says organizations says oligarchy.' According to Michels, as a political party grows and becomes more bureaucratic, it is increasingly dominated by officials who are committed to internal organizational goals rather than social change, and by middle-class intellectuals who pursue their own personal objectives which are usually different from those of the party rank-and-file. He also noted the process of *embourgeoisement within parties, as working-class leaders become more middle-class as a result of social mobility, and so less committed to radical objectives. As a consequence, even in democratically governed organizations, a schism develops between the rulers and the ruled. Organizational procedures are often employed to stifle popular initiatives. Michels championed more heroic, principled forms of leadership, which would withstand incorporation. He was highly critical of political compromise.

Empirical researchers of Michels's iron law have found it difficult to demonstrate that the institutionalization of radical parties is in fact the product of the embourgeoisement of their leaders. It has also been argued that Michels's theory may have been valid for the early period of the development of socialist parties in Europe, and as a description of the élitist tendencies of the Bolshevik Party which sponsored a form of bureaucratic domination in Russia, but that the theory has since been undermined by widespread awareness of the dangers of oligarchy itself. A host of other processes have also intervened to create revisionist rather than revolutionary left-wing parties. Michels's theory has also been applied to *trade unions, and used to explore the way in which, as organizations, they have become ends in themselves rather than a means to an end. Much of this secondary literature is summarized in Seymour Martin Lipset, 'Introduction' to the English-language translation of *Political Parties* (1962).

microdata Data-sets containing information on individual respondents to an enquiry, be they persons, households, or organizations such as schools or companies. Microdata are virtually always anonymized, with not only names and addresses omitted to preserve confidentiality, but also detailed geographical or industry codes sometimes deleted or broadbanded to obscure identities. *See also* AGGREGATE (COLLECTIVITY).

microsociology *See* MACROSOCIOLOGY.

middle class (middle classes) In many ways this is the least satisfactory term that attempts in one phrase to define a class sharing common work and market situations. The middle stratum of industrial societies has expanded so much in the last hundred years that any category that embraces both company directors and their secretaries must be considered somewhat inadequate.

In popular perception, all white-collar work is middle class, but sociologically it is necessary to sub-divide this class into distinct groups sharing similar market, work, and status situations. Although used widely in everyday discourse, it has less application as an analytical concept in the analysis of *social class. For example, John H. Goldthorpe (*Social Mobility and Class Structure in Modern*

Britain, 1980) distinguishes the *service class of senior managers and professionals; the junior or subaltern service class of lower professionals such as teachers, junior managers, and administrators; routine non-manual workers such as clerks and secretaries; and owners of small businesses (the traditional petit-bourgeoisie). Conventionally, the service class is referred to as the upper-middle class; the junior service class as the middle class proper; and the others as the lower-middle class. Thus defined, in Britain the upper-middle class comprises some 10 per cent of the population; the middle class accounts for around 20 per cent; and the lower-middle class takes in a further 20 per cent. Taken together, therefore, the middle class is the largest single class in the overall structure.

However, some sociologists (especially those of a Marxist persuasion) would not accept that most routine white-collar workers were middle class, on the grounds that their employment situation is generally equivalent (or even inferior) to that of many working-class people. They prefer to call this group the *new working class. This is not a view which most white-collar workers themselves share, nor one which is substantiated by sociological evidence. Equally, the term 'middle class' is now often used by journalists and politicians to refer to what might better be called the 'middle mass' of those earning somewhere close to average incomes. Evidence from Gordon Marshall et al.' national study of *Social Class in Modern Britain* (1984) shows that ordinary people are somewhat more discriminating. For example, 35 per cent of the sample defined the middle class as *professionals; 11 per cent mentioned managers; only 7 per cent talked of the middle class as being all white-collar workers.

As with the term *upper class, distinctions can be made between the 'old' and 'new' middle class. The former generally refers to the *petite bourgeoisie and independent professionals (whose existence as distinct groups pre-dates the 20th-century expansion of the class as a whole), while the latter refers to all other elements of the middle class: that is, salaried professionals, administrators and officials, senior managers, and higher-grade technicians who together form the service class, and routine non-manual employees, supervisors, and lower-grade technicians who form a more marginal middle class (or, in Marxist terms, a new working class). It could be argued that the term 'middle class' should be abandoned when analysing the economic differentiation of classes. It may be better used as a term in popular *class imagery to define positions in a hierarchy of levels and applied to social classes only when this definition becomes a central part of the *identity of members of the class. *See also* CLASS POSITION; CONTRADICTORY CLASS LOCATION; PROLETARIANIZATION.

middle class, new *See* CONTRADICTORY CLASS LOCATION; PROLETARIANIZATION.

middle-range theory Advocated by the distinguished American sociologist Robert Merton in *Social Theory and Social Structure* (1957) to bridge the gap between the limited hypotheses of *empiricist studies and grand abstract theory of the sort produced by Talcott *Parsons. He describes middle-range theories as 'theories that lie between the minor but necessary working hypotheses that evolve in abundance in day to day research and the all-inclusive systematic efforts to develop unified theory that will explain all the observed uniformities of social behaviour, organization and social change'. Merton consistently argued for, and demonstrated the necessity of, this sort of work in a long series of convincing sociological essays in such areas as structural-functional theory and the sociologies of science, deviance, organizations and occupations. Many of the concepts developed in these theories have become part of the basic sociological lexicon (and are therefore given separate entries in this dictionary): retreatism, ritualism, manifest and latent functions, opportunity structure, paradigm, reference group, role-sets, self-fulfilling prophecy, and unintended consequences. The idea of middle-range theory has directly and indirectly been an important influence on the way many sociologists see their work. The full range of the discussion stimulated by Merton's work is most evident in the excellent collection of commentaries edited by Jon Clark et al., *Robert K. Merton: Consensus and Controversy* (1990).

migration, internal *See* INTERNAL MIGRATION.

migration, sociology of Migration involves the (more or less) permanent movement of individuals or groups across symbolic or political boundaries into new residential areas and communities. Sociological studies of migration are diverse and usually form part of larger problems in (for example) research into *kinship, social *networks, or *economic development. It is conventional to distinguish push from pull factors in the analysis of migration. The former (for example high rates of unemployment in the area of origin) are usually viewed as inducing migration of a conservative, security-maximizing nature, while the latter (economic expansion in the host country or region) are said to encourage risk-taking and income-maximizing migration. A distinction is also made between external migration (between countries) and internal migration (between regions).

There is a considerable literature on rural-urban migration in developing countries, and this has confirmed the importance of family and friends in the destination area, as an explanatory variable for the rate of migration out of particular areas of origin (see for example B. Banerjee, 'Rural-Urban Migration and Family Ties', *Oxford Bulletin of Economics and Statistics*, 1981). Employers have often made use of kin networks in recruiting 'green labour' from one area or country to another. (This topic is discussed fully in M. Grieco's *Keeping it in the Family*, 1987.)

The issue of kin-connected entry and recruitment strategies is also addressed in the other major sociological literatures on migration in the fields of employment studies and ethnic relations. Studies of job-search behaviour have identified the practices of chain employment and chain migration, where the successful migration of one family member creates a chain of opportunities for the whole kin network, as for example in Gary Mormino's study of early 20th-century Italian emigration to Tampa, which shows that the core of the local Italian community originated from only three villages in south-west Sicily and one community in Palermo ('We Worked Hard and Took Care of Our Own', *Labour History*, 1982). This literature often has an ethnic dimension, evident also in Tamara K. Haraven' study of Irish, Italian, and French-Canadian emigration into the New England mill-towns during the same period ('The Labourers of Manchester, New Hampshire, 1912–1922', *Labour History*, 1975). An excellent study in this vein is Ewa Morawska's *Insecure Prosperity: Small Town Jews in Industrial America, 1890–1940* (1996). A powerful argument on the nature and consequences of ethnic migration is presented in Stephen Castle's and Godula Kosack's controversial and much-discussed thesis that the extensive foreign migrant workforce that moved to the advanced industrialized countries of Europe during the years of post-war affluence in the 1950s and 1960s served the twin functions of dividing the indigenous working class and creating a new *reserve army of labour (*Immigrant Workers and Class Structure in Western Europe* 1973). Others have argued that such immigrants form part of an *under-class, since they are discriminated against in markets for employment, labour, and housing, and therefore cannot be assimilated into the indigenous class structure. An important comparative study is Lydia Morris's *Managing Migration: Civic Stratification and Migrants' Rights* (2002). One specifically Marxist interpretation is that migrant labour (in Britain and elsewhere) constitutes a 'racialised fraction of the working class', the explanation for which cannot be reduced simply to the existence of labour shortages which migrant labour power often serves to address. (These differing interpretations are reviewed in R. Miles, *Racism and Migrant Labour*, 1982.)

It used to be believed that migration implied separation from kin, a thesis consistent with the functionalist view that the *extended family is in decline in urban industrialized countries, although it is now accepted that the relationship between family, employment, and migration is more complex and historically contingent than hitherto suggested. As early as 1940, Conrad M. Arensberg and Solon T. Kimball (*Family and Community in Ireland*) pointed out that geographical dispersal did not destroy familial bonds of obligation and affection, so that (for example) Irish peasants having emigrated to urban America still sent back money to relatives at home. *See also* CULTURAL THEORY; DIASPORA; LABOUR-MARKET SEGMENTATION.

militancy Willingness to engage in oppositional rhetoric and action. Often used with reference to *trade-union activities, it may be industrial (concerned with advancing wages and conditions), or political (concerned with the position of the working class as a whole). Which is uppermost has as much to do with national cultures and traditions as with economic conditions.

military and militarism It is conventional wisdom that sociologists have tended to neglect military concerns. In fact this is a somewhat misleading claim, since not only have numerous studies taken the military as a substantive area of interest, but (more importantly) it is hard to see what, if anything, is specifically sociological about militarism and war. The threat of global annihilation, implicit in the Cold War antics of the superpowers, would seem to be a subject of rather more than merely sociological interest.

In any case, Kurt Lang's *Military Institutions and the Sociology of War* (1972) offers an early review of relevant literature, and an annotated bibliography of more than 1300 items on organized violence. These suggest that sociological studies of the military may conveniently be considered under three headings. First, there has been extensive research into the involvement of the military in politics, both in the developed and developing world. C. Wright *Mills's account of the American *military-industrial complex during the Cold War period is a good example of the former. During the 1980s, in a significant extension of this tradition of study, some prominent social theorists (notably Anthony Giddens) and historical and comparative researchers (including Michael Mann) began investigating the relationship between military changes, on one hand, and (the more usually explored) economic, political, social, and ideological changes on the other. In a more limited way, the endemic militarism (that is, the tendency to look for military solutions to political problems and conflicts) in some parts of the developing world is examined fully in volumes such as J. J. Johnson's *The Role of the Military in Underdeveloped Countries* (1962), which both identifies some of the many forms which militarism can take in politics (direct rule, indirect influence, strategic alliances), and also offers a long list of factors which predispose towards military intervention in government in particular societies (relative strength of armed forces, political stalemate, administrative corruption, and so forth). (It should be noted, however, that there is little or no agreement about precisely which of these factors are most important.)

Second, one might point to the attention given to the topics of war and violence in the sociological theories of Social *Darwinists and *evolutionists such as the Polish social theorist Ludwig Gumplowicz (1838–1909) and the Austrian Gustav Ratzenhofer (1842–1904), both of whom extended their theories about the origins of conflict between social groups to include the military struggles between states. Gumplowicz traced such violence to an insurmountable hatred that allegedly exists between different races, on account of their lack of a common blood-bond, and hypothesized that wars between states express an urge for conquest that arises from a desire for improved economic conditions at the expense of other groups. Ratzenhofer (a field-marshal and president of the supreme military court of Austria) produced a typology of *interests which were said to be rooted in *human nature and governed social life, these being procreative, physiological, individual (self-assertion), social (group welfare), and transcendental (religion). These generate conflict between groups (because of an innate human predisposition to obey primary impulses and to hate), but at the same time form the basis of social order, since this struggle for existence soon becomes organized on a group basis and leads eventually to the appearance of (competing) nation-states.

Finally, there are a large number of studies of different aspects of the military as a formal organization, including such classics as Samuel A. Stouffer et al., *The American Soldier* (1949), Samuel E. Finer's *The Man on Horseback* (1962), and Morris *Janowitz's *The Professional Soldier* (1960). Many of these studies have identified social phenomena of more general theoretical and substantive importance (such as the experience of relative *deprivation investigated by Stouffer and his colleagues). By far the best overview of this literature, and still probably the best introduction to the field as a whole, is Janowitz's *Sociology and the Military Establishment* (3rd edn., 1974). A good overview of the field and update is Martin Shaw and Colin Creighton (eds.), *The Sociology of War and Peace* (1988). *See also* IMPERIALISM.

military capitalism *See* MILITARY-INDUSTRIAL COMPLEX.

military-industrial complex A term used to describe the alleged dependence of advanced capitalist economies on the marriage of economic and military-political objectives during the period of the Cold War. A number of sociological studies of this phenomenon were undertaken, the best-known of which is probably C. Wright Mills's *The Power Elite* (1956), in which he argued that the homogeneous governing clique in post-war America represented an alliance of economic, military, and political power, and (contrary to the arguments of *pluralists) had established the USA as simultaneously a 'private corporation economy' and a 'permanent war economy' within which 'virtually all political and economic actions are now judged in terms of military definitions of reality'. Mills's account of the American power elite, and the 'military capitalism' it encouraged by perpetuating the arms race, was echoed in later studies. Fred J. Cook described America as a 'warfare state' in which political life was dominated by military definitions of foreign policy and economic rationality (*The Warfare State*, 1962). Similarly, John Kenneth Galbraith's study of *The New Industrial State* (1967) argues that Cold War imagery served to stabilize aggregate demand in the American economy, since 'if the image is one of a nation beset by enemies, there will be a responding investment in weapons ... [and so] ... in public affairs as well as in private affairs, and for the same reasons, we are subject to contrivance that serves the industrial system'.

The main problems with this interpretation of the American social structure were that it was difficult to verify empirically (much of Mills's own evidence is perhaps best described as circumstantial) and that it was implicitly *functionalist (witness Galbraith's claim that the weapons competition between the United States and USSR 'is not a luxury: it serves an organic need of the industrial system as now constituted'). *See also* ELITE.

Millar, John (1735–1801) A leading figure in the *Scottish Enlightenment of the late 18th century, who is sometimes acknowledged as an early sociologist, on the grounds that his essay on *The Origin of the Distinction of Ranks* (1771) offers a theory of the evolution of societies (which connects forms of property-holding to types of authority and government), and an early account of the *division of labour in society (see W. C. Lehmann, *John Millar of Glasgow, 1735–1801: His Life and Thoughts and his Contributions to Sociological Analysis*, 1960).

millenarianism A term used to refer to a religious movement which prophesies the coming of the millennium and a cataclysmic end of the world as we know it; or, more formally, which anticipates imminent, total, ultimate, this-worldly, collective salvation. Examples include Christadelphianism, Mormonism, Seventh Day Adventism, Fifth Monarchy Men, North American Indian Ghost

Dance Movement, and Jehovah's Witnesses. As will be evident from this list of examples, these movements display great variation in the degree of activism expected among followers; the extent to which they are Messianic or charismatic; and the organizational structure of the movement as a whole.

Millennial movements occur inside all religions, including early *Christianity and *Islam, but also develop outside organized religions. Millenarianism therefore can take many different forms. However, it usually involves explosions of discontent, a rejection of the status quo, and the proposal that the coming millennium will see the installation of a new social order. This new society is usually constructed as *egalitarian and just. Millenarianism often develops in a colonial situation and can have grave consequences for the dominant political order. There is little chance of political compromise since the followers of millenarian movements are not afraid of death; for example, they have been known to run against the guns of an army, believing that the millennium is about to end anyway. Millennial doctrines are often anti-reproduction, and ban sexual intercourse and the planting of crops, since there will be no next year. There is always the tension within millenarianism between an other-worldly message with no earthly content and one where the divine returns into the political process to rule justly. Inevitably, the millennium does not come, and the movement collapses. It either fades away or part of the message is recovered and institutionalized—as in the case of Christianity.

The best-known modern examples of millenarianism are the so-called cargo cults in Melanesia. These usually believe that the ancestors or a culture hero are on their way back to this world in a magic ship to create a timeless order that has been interfered with by Europeans. There will be the return of a cargo of precious material goods to their rightful Melanesian owners, bringing about an era of universal happiness and plenty, where the colonized people will be liberated from White domination. Explanations of the emergence of these cults abound. Peter Worsley (*The Trumpet Shall Sound*, 1957) argues that Melanesian cargo cults are not irrational 'madness', but are the result of frustrations caused by *colonialism. The movements are fundamentally opposed to *imperialism and use a religious idiom to attempt to explain the power of colonizers. This mystical power comes from the ability of Whites to intercept riches (cargo) bound for local peoples. Millenarianism is invoked as a last resort in dealing with this power when political opposition has failed. Alternative interpretations include those of Kenelm O. L. Burridge (*Mambu*, 1960), who argues that cargo cults express certain moral and emotional imperatives in Melanesian society, and Peter Lawrence (*Road Belong Cargo*, 1964), who offers a historical and structural account which emphasizes the 'mismatch' between Western and Melanesian norms of reciprocity and *exchange.

At a more general level, the numerous theories of millennial movements as a whole include interpretations in terms of relative *deprivation; those which see such movements as being rooted in the strains associated with rapid social *change; and some which emphasize the social isolation, disruption, and normlessness characteristic of situations of *anomie. A fairly representative selection of such accounts will be found in the collection edited by Sylvia L. Thrupp (*Millennial Dreams in Action*, 1962).

Mill, John Stuart (1806–73) An English philosopher, proponent of *liberalism and *utilitarianism, and social reformer. Mill publicized the works of Auguste Comte in Britain, critically developed the *utilitarian works of his own father James Mill (1773–1836) and his godfather Jeremy Bentham, and attempted to provide 'a general science of man in society' in his *A System of Logic, Ratiocinative and Deductive* (1843).

Mill's relevance to many contemporary sociologists lies in his logical classification of the methods properly to be applied in the human sciences, that is, the five 'methods of experimental inquiry': of difference (comparing two particular instances which are alike in every respect except the one which is the object of inquiry); indirect difference (comparing two classes of instances which agree in nothing, excepting the presence of a specific circumstance in one case, and its absence in the other); agreement (where two or more instances of the phenomenon under investigation have only one circumstance in common, which is then hypothesized to be the cause of the phenomenon); concomitant variation (the method of establishing statistical correlations between aggregates); and the method of residues (in which the investigator studies only one instance of a phenomenon, eliminates all those effects of the causes of which he or she already possesses a clear knowledge, and then concentrates on clarifying the relationships between the residual causes and effects). Mill raised objections against all of these kinds of experimental method, which he regarded as inappropriate to the study of society. However, he also rejected pure deductive methods, and suggested instead that the most suitable methods for a general science of society were the 'concrete deductive method' (which today would be termed the 'hypothetico-deductive method') and the 'inverse deductive method'. The former involves the statement of a clear hypothesis, making of inferences from this, and testing of predictions by reference to artificial manipulation of empirical data (as in a laboratory experiment). Often, however, the social sciences proceed in the opposite manner: from empirical generalization, from which one has to try to generate hypotheses which will satisfactorily explain generalizations about events that have already happened, and in this way arrive at causal explanations of social processes.

The earlier utilitarians had been staunch liberals, but Mill's *liberalism recognized a role for political intervention and the pursuit of social justice. He was a Liberal MP for a period, sitting as a radical member of the party, and he took a great interest in the development of *socialist ideas. His treatise on *The Subjection of Women* (1869) was an early argument against inequality between the sexes.

Mills, C(harles) Wright (1916–62) An American sociologist whose most important work was published during the 1950s. As a radical on the political left, he was an unusual figure in American sociology at this time, taking up a position that might be better described as liberal-populist rather than socialist. His most important substantive studies were probably *White Collar* (1951), an analysis of the American middle class, and *The Power Elite* (1956) in which he argued that the United States was governed by a set of interlocking and self-perpetuating elites.

He is remembered primarily for *The Sociological Imagination* (1959)—an excellent introduction to and outline of the *humanist impetus behind sociology as a discipline. The sociological imagination is the sociological vision, a way of looking at the world that can see connections between the apparently private problems of the individual and important social issues. He argues for a humanist sociology connecting the social, personal, and historical dimensions of our lives, and which is critical of *abstracted empiricism and *grand theory alike. Useful sources include *C. Wright Mills: Letters and Autobiographical Writings* (edited Kathryn Mills with Pamela Mills, 2000), and *C. Wright Mills and the Sociological Imagination: Contemporary Perspectives* (edited Ann Nilsen and John Scott, 2013). *See also* MILITARY-INDUSTRIAL COMPLEX; POWER ELITE; UNEMPLOYMENT.

Minitab *See* COMPUTER PACKAGES.

minority group Since the 1930s this term has been applied to social groups that are oppressed or *stigmatized on the basis of racial, ethnic, biological, or other characteristics. Louis *Wirth, for example, defines a minority group as 'a group of people who, because of their physical or cultural characteristics, are singled out from the others in the society in which they live for differential and unequal treatment and who therefore regard themselves as objects of collective discrimination'. However, seen in these terms, a minority group could in fact constitute a numerical majority in any society—for example Blacks in South Africa. It might be more useful, therefore, to distinguish between groups which are actually a minority in numbers and those which are marginal in terms of their access to power. The study of minorities has recently been linked to the study of deviance, exclusion, labelling, stigma, racism, the authoritarian personality, homophobia, and sexism (all of which are given separate entries in this dictionary). *See also* MARGINALIZATION.

mirror phase (of infant development) *See* LACAN, JACQUES.

miscegenation Literally 'mixing of races', a *racist term denoting sexual relations between different races, especially White and Black. Miscegenation was promoted in some systems—for example Portuguese colonialism and the Baha'i religion—as a means of overcoming artificial *ethnic barriers. The concept is treated pejoratively in racist ideology as a source of social and economic degeneration.

misogyny Literally, hatred of women. Kate Millet brought the idea of misogyny to the fore in *Sexual Politics* (1970), where she provided a broad theoretical base for radical *feminism. She argued that patriarchal power creates a sexist society and that sexual politics grounded in misogyny result in women's oppression both within the private realm and within social institutions such as the class system and the education system. Andrea Dworkin and Susan Brownmiller pointed to important links between misogyny and men's sexual violence towards women, while Susan Griffin suggested connections between militarism and misogyny. Adrienne Rich defined misogyny as institutionalized, organized, normalized hostility and violence against women. Feminist psychoanalysts, following in particular the work of Melanie *Klein and the *Object Relations School, have argued that misogyny is rooted in the infant's primitive rage towards its mother in the context of a society in which child-rearing is almost invariably carried out by women. Nancy Chodorow (*The Reproduction of Mothering*, 1978) contends that only the full participation of men in infant care would eradicate the roots of misogyny.

mixed economy An economy that combines elements of the *market economy with elements of a *command economy; that is, combines characteristics of *capitalism and *socialism. In a mixed economy, some but not all of the activities of production, distribution, and exchange are organized by the state, and the state generally plays a larger role in setting policy, rules, and objectives, and in controlling labour, than would occur in a purely market economy.

The term is sometimes used more loosely to refer to an economy that includes any elements other than a pure market economy, for example pockets of subsistence farming in particular areas of the country.

mob A solidaristic, focused, acting *crowd. A mob intending to effect a lynching is the classic case.

mobility, occupational *See* OCCUPATIONAL MOBILITY.

mobility, social The movement—usually of individuals but sometimes of whole groups—between different positions within the system of social stratification in any society. It is conventional to distinguish upward and downward mobility (that is, movement up or down a hierarchy of privilege), and intergenerational from intra-generational or career mobility (the former referring to mobility between a family of origin and one's own class or status position, the latter to the mobility experienced during an individual career, such as respondent's first job compared to his or her present job). Other distinctions—most notably that between structural and non-structural mobility—are more contentious.

Most sociological attention has focused on intergenerational mobility, in particular the role of educational achievement as compared to that of social background or of *ascriptive characteristics such as *race, in explaining patterns of occupational attainment. Although there have been many case studies of *elite recruitment (for example P. Stanworth and A. Giddens' *Elites and Power in British Society*, 1974), the most popular research instrument has been the large-scale sample *survey, and the most common points of comparison have been *occupations. Some sociologists have studied social mobility in pre-industrial contexts (see, for example, H. Kaelble, *Historical Research on Social Mobility*, 1977), and others in contemporary developing countries such as India (see A. Beteille, *Caste, Class and Power*, 1965), but the great majority of studies have dealt with the modern industrialized West and, to a lesser extent, the former communist states of Eastern Europe.

The study of social mobility has a long sociological pedigree, extending back to the mid-19th-century writings of Karl *Marx and John Stuart *Mill, with major contributions in the early 20th century from Vilfredo *Pareto (who proposed a theory of the 'circulation of elites') and Pitirim *Sorokin. The now vast literature on the subject is inextricably entangled with wider discussions of (among other things) education, gender, culture, power, statistical techniques, and the role of theory in social research.

A key early view was that of Sorokin (*Social Mobility*, 1927), who wrote that 'channels of vertical circulation exist in any stratified society, and are as necessary as channels for blood circulation in the body'. In an argument that prefigures the later *functionalist theory of stratification, he suggested that these 'staircases' or 'elevators' are necessary to the efficient allocation of talents to occupations, and that failure to achieve this promotes inefficiency and disorder. However, unlike Kingsley Davis and Wilbert E. Moore writing two decades later, Sorokin did not then conclude that high rewards were necessary to motivate individuals to undertake training for functionally important positions in society. More plausibly, he maintained that the incumbents of these positions were able to exploit their strategic occupational roles, in order to attract material and other privileges. Sorokin was particularly interested in the role of educational institutions in allocating people to the various occupational positions. Anticipating the radical critiques of the new sociology of education of the 1970s, he argued that schools function primarily as 'a testing, selecting, and distributing agency'; in other words, they merely certify children for particular positions in the *labour-market, rather than promote each individual's abilities or encourage the development of talent.

Confronted by this potentially vast field of interest, it is useful for heuristic purposes to view the modern literature on social mobility as a dispute between two divergent research programmes which have set the terms of discussion for this subject since 1945, and continue to dominate the field even today. On one hand, there are those investigators who view mobility in the context of a social hierarchy, within which individuals can be ranked according to income, educational attainment, or socio-economic prestige. On the other, there are those who set it within the context of a class structure, embracing social locations defined by relationships prevailing within labour markets and production units. During the 1950s and 1960s, the former hierarchical perspective was dominant, culminating in the so-called *status-attainment tradition of mobility studies emanating principally from the United States. This was increasingly challenged, during the 1970s and 1980s, by researchers schooled within or influenced by the European tradition of class analysis.

The status-attainment programme sees the principal interest of mobility studies as being an attempt to specify those attributes which are characteristic of individuals who end up in the more desirable rather than the less desirable jobs. Characteristically, these studies investigate the extent to which the present occupational status of individuals is associated with the status of their family of origin, rather than individual achievements such as educational attainment. One virtue of this approach, as compared to earlier cross-tabulations of father's occupation by son's occupation, was that it disentangled at least some of the processes that linked the generations. For example, researchers explored the effects of father's education on son's occupational attainment, and showed that these were distinct from the effects of father's occupation. Most studies maintained that son's education was the crucial link between family background and occupational success, arguing that as much as half of the association between the two was mediated via education, with children from more privileged family backgrounds being higher educational achievers than their poorer peers. Later researchers extended the field of interest to include data on income, with most concluding that the impact of family background on earnings is substantial, but operates entirely indirectly through educational and occupational attainment.

Most of these studies employed the statistical techniques of *regression analysis (and in particular *path analysis). Most were also underpinned by a tacit adherence to a liberal model of *industrial societies as increasingly homogeneous, middle class, *meritocratic, and open. Typically, therefore, they tended to conclude that structural shifts in advanced industrial economies (especially the expansion of managerial, professional, and administrative occupations) created more 'room at the top' and so increased the opportunities for upward social mobility of individuals from working-class origins. This increasing social fluidity was reinforced by a progressive shift from ascriptive to achievement criteria as the dominant factors determining status attainment, a movement towards meritocratic selection that, together with the prevailing high rates of social mobility, undermined the potential for class formation and class conflict in industrial societies. Peter M. Blau and Otis D. Duncan's *The American Occupational Structure* (1967) is generally held to be the paradigmatic example of a study of social mobility within the status-attainment tradition.

The Blau-Duncan model prompted an enormous number of related and derivative studies. Whatever their differences and similarities, however, they all rested upon the assumption that occupations can be ranked within a status hierarchy about which there is a wide degree of consensus within and between societies. In some studies this social hierarchy was conceptualized narrowly as being one of *occupational prestige. In others it was generalized to include additional wider aspects of *socio-economic status. Rather than dispute the details of the occupational hierarchy, however, European class analysis came increasingly to challenge the basic premiss of the status attainment research programme; namely, that social mobility was most appropriately viewed as a matter of hierarchical occupational attainment among competing individuals.

The class analysis tradition starts from the rather different assumption that individuals are born into distinct social *classes, membership of which has clear consequences for life-chances, values, norms, life styles, and patterns of association. Representatives of this tradition argue that the socio-economic status scales at the heart of the status-attainment perspective display many unresolved methodological weaknesses. Most importantly, because these scales are a composite measure of popular judgements about the relative prestige or social standing of the various occupations, they rank alongside each other, as having similar levels of socio-economic status, occupations which have quite different structural locations. For example, skilled manual workers may have the same prestige score as routine clerical workers and self-employed shopkeepers, or office supervisors may be ranked alongside farmers and schoolteachers. In other words, the synthetic categories of the scale typically contain occupational groupings that are subject to different structural forces: because of sectoral and other changes in the occupational structure, some occupations will be in expansion, others in contraction, and some will be static. Such heterogeneity merely muddies the water of mobility: it is impossible to distinguish adequately the various structural influences on mobility from those which originate in other factors, and impossible also therefore to isolate hierarchical effects (family background, educational attainment, or whatever) from other effects of a non-hierarchical kind (such as changes in the occupational division of labour, industrial or sectoral growth and decline, government policies of protection, and so forth).

The class analysis programme of social mobility research, initiated in the 1970s, abandoned the Blau-Duncan form of occupational prestige-scaling in favour of discrete class categories whose members shared similar positions within labour markets and production units. In Europe probably the most widely used class categories are those devised by John Goldthorpe (*see* GOLDTHORPE CLASS SCHEME) for the Oxford Mobility Study during the 1970s, a class scheme which attempts to aggregate occupational groupings whose members share similar 'market situations' and 'work situations' (a theory of class which Goldthorpe derived from his earlier collaboration with David *Lockwood during the Affluent Worker Study of the 1960s). In the United States, the '*new structuralism' of the 1970s alerted some analysts of social mobility to the importance of labour-market influences on mobility trajectories, and led to the emergence of 'multiple regression Marxists' (such as Erik Olin Wright) who adapted the methods of Blau and Duncan to a theoretical stance which pointed to the importance of ownership, authority, and autonomy in the workplace.

Along with this new theory went new methods and conclusions. Class analysts argued that mathematical techniques of *loglinear modelling were better suited to the analysis of mobility data, both because they did not require ordinal-level data (and therefore unsubstantiated assumptions) about a status hierarchy, and because they allowed researchers analysing a standard mobility matrix (a *contingency table cross-tabulating class origins against class destinations) to distinguish absolute or total mobility rates (including those changes in mobility occasioned by shifts in the occupational structure) from changes in social fluidity or openness within the structure as such (relative rates). Applied to the same sorts of large-scale data-sets as were used within the status-attainment programme, the class analysis perspective and the new techniques of loglinear modelling suggested that the liberal assumptions of the earlier studies were unwarrantably optimistic. In most industrialized societies absolute levels of mobility have indeed increased significantly over the past three-quarters of a century, in accordance with the growth in skilled non-manual occupations, but relative mobility chances have remained largely unaltered throughout this period. More room at the top has not ensured greater equality of opportunity to get there, since proportionately more of the new middle-class jobs have been captured by the children of those already in privileged class locations. As a result, the association between an individual's class of origin and eventual destination has remained remarkably stable across successive birth-cohorts, despite economic expansion, educational reform, and redistributive social policies.

In the mid-1980s, Goldthorpe (together with collaborators in Sweden and Germany) designed the CASMIN (Comparative Analysis of Social Mobility in Industrial Nations) Project, an intensive comparative study of this problem. The project produced data which show that the mobility profiles of advanced societies are more complex than is allowed within either the liberal theory of industrial society or Marxist accounts of capitalist society. The most important findings suggest that, measured in absolute rates, the amount and pattern of mobility displays considerable variation across societies; that relative rates (or fluidity patterns) display a 'large commonality' across societies; and that changes in social fluidity over time follow a pattern of 'trendless fluctuation' rather than showing evidence of a general increase. In short, therefore, there is no long-term 'loosening' of the class structure, no increase in 'fluidity', and (by implication) no move towards meritocracy.

Each of these research programmes disputes the principal substantive conclusions arrived at by the other. The relevant journals are littered with acrimonious exchanges about matters of theory and method. Sometimes these leave outsiders puzzled or bemused: one sceptical observer has described the field as a 'set of statistical techniques in search of a problem'. Others argue that, for a variety of different reasons, debates about social mobility continue to raise the fundamental issues of the discipline as a whole. For example, feminists have pointed to the fact that most mobility studies are based on samples of males only, and this has prompted wide-ranging discussion of the relevant 'unit of mobility analysis' (individual or family), the nature of so-called cross-class families (where two adult wage-earners are in different class positions and have different mobility trajectories), and the implications of the occupational *division of labour by sex for mobility studies. The best overview of these and other related debates is Anthony Heath's *Social Mobility* (1981).

However, much dispute in the area is of a highly specialized and technical, rather than theoretical, nature. The longest-running controversies hinge on the possibility of distinguishing structural and non-structural sources of mobility. In earlier studies, some sociologists attempted to distinguish between structural (or net) and circulation (or exchange) mobility, the former being that amount of mobility required by the structure of the table itself (the fact that, if the marginal totals showing the distribution of fathers and that of sons are regarded as being fixed, then their differences mean that some respondents must fall into the off-diagonal cells in the table). The percentage of respondents who were mobile because of the very structure of the table was said to represent the amount of structural mobility in a society. Circulation mobility was then simply the difference between the total number of respondents who were mobile and those defined as being structurally mobile. However, both of these concepts are statistical artefacts with no clear substantive interpretation, so the somewhat artificial distinction between structural and circulation mobility has given way to a dispute about the concepts of absolute and relative mobility rates. In any origin-to-destination mobility table, the row and column marginal totals (say, the distribution of fathers as compared to sons) will be different, an asymmetry that is due in part to changes in the occupational structure itself (such as, for example, sectoral shifts of the kind noted above). The use of loglinear techniques (based on the technique of *odds ratios) permits the calculation of relative mobility chances which allow for (exclude) that portion of total mobility that is due to changes in the marginal distributions of the table. Many class analysts insist that this technique therefore distinguishes meaningfully between mobility which is the result of changes in the shape of the class structure and that which reflects changes in its degree of openness. Critics maintain that the concept of relative mobility is no less artificial than that of structural and circulation mobility since, whether or not social mobility is caused by sectoral shifts alone, absolute or overall mobility is 'real'—whereas respondents do not experience the ahistorical and acontextual phenomenon of 'relative mobility chances'. In part this is also a dispute about the relationship between occupational mobility and class mobility; and, therefore, is inescapably a debate about the very definition of social class itself. *See also* CONTEST AND SPONSORED MOBILITY.

mobilization (mobilization model) The process by which a group goes from being a passive collection of individuals to an active participant in public life. (Demobilization is thus the reverse process.) Used in this way, the term has had a wide currency in sociology, and has been applied in particular to studies of *collective action in the literatures on *modernization, *social movements, and *revolution (*see* REBELLION, REVOLUTION). Mobilization is usually seen as *resource mobilization; that is, significant gain over the control of assets, where assets may be viewed as coercive (weapons, armed forces, technologies), utilitarian (goods, money, information), or normative (loyalties or obligations) in nature—a typology suggested by Amitai Etzioni in *The Active Society* (1968). The most complete formal statement of the theory, illustrated by a range of subject-matters to which the mobilization model of collective action can be applied, is Charles Tilly's *From Mobilization to Revolution* (1978). *See also* COLLECTIVE BEHAVIOUR.

mobilization of bias *See* COMMUNITY POWER.

mode *See* CENTRAL TENDENCY (MEASURES OF).

model This is a term which has been given a wide variety of different meanings by sociologists. In some cases it has been used as a synonym for *theory, but in others as a reference to a system of abstract concepts at a more general level than a theory. Equally, it is used to refer to a statistical model, as in *causal modelling. Whichever definition is used the essence of a model is that it requires the researcher to engage with theory and thus avoid *empiricism.

At root, models seek to simplify phenomena, as an aid to conceptualization and explanation. In sociology *structural-functionalism is a model in the first two senses suggested above, since it provides a broad frame of reference (a meta-theory which states that society is like an organism) and a set of conceptual propositions (a theory showing how the parts of society are integrated and make a contribution to the functioning of the whole). Where a hypothesis about the relationship between concepts is specified, and the concepts can be measured, we may speak of an operational model. These models are sometimes expressed diagrammatically, and may be set out more formally in mathematical terms, as for example in a *regression model or *loglinear model. Model building, a key aspect of *mathematical sociology, involves the refinement of models from the stage of a flow diagram to a formal mathematical expression. Causal models may be of either type. Whatever form it takes, a model is an aid to complex theoretical activity, and directs our attention to concepts or variables and their interrelationships. *See also* MULTI-LEVEL MODELS; MULTIVARIATE ANALYSIS.

modelling *See* CAUSAL MODELLING; MODEL.

mode of production Within Marxist theory, this is the constitutive characteristic of a society or social formation, based on the socio-economic system predominant within it—for example *capitalism, *feudalism, or *socialism.

Mode of production was conventionally defined in terms of the interaction of the *relations and *forces of production; that is, the system of ownership of the means of production, and the level of development of the latter. For Karl *Marx, this formed the foundation or base of all social systems, and from it other social, economic, ideological, and political relations were derived. Considerable debate took place within Marxism as to how far the other areas of social activity—the *superstructure—could be derived from the socio-economic *base, or mode of production, and how far they enjoyed an autonomy. Friedrich *Engels remarked that the economic sphere was determinant 'in the last instance', summing up this ambiguity, and initiating an unresolved debate about the *relative autonomy of politics and ideology from economic conditions.

*Marxism also analysed societies in which more than one mode of production was present, either because the society was in transition from one to the other, or because subordinate modes survived or were even maintained by the dominant one through a process of 'articulation' of modes of production—as for example in the case of slavery within the early capitalism of the Americas, or capitalist sectors within predominantly socialist societies.

Modernism Modernism is the generally accepted term to describe the sweeping changes that took place, particularly in the arts and literature, between the late 19th century and the beginning of the Second World War. There is, however, no clear demarcation by date, and although the term *postmodern is increasingly used to describe changes since the Second World War, there are some who argue Modernism persists, and others who see its demise as having occurred much earlier. Roland Barthes, a French *semiologist, saw Modernism as a pluralization of world-views that resulted from the evolution of new classes, technology, and communications that were gathering momentum in the mid-19th century, while the English novelist and essayist Virginia Woolf regarded it as a historic opportunity for change in human relationships and the human character.

Although there is little unanimity as to when it began or exactly what its characteristics were, stylistically Modernism is usually depicted as a movement that explored the limits of the classical aesthetic forms of realist representation and narrative. Artists became more self-conscious of the techniques that made their art possible. Friedrich *Nietzsche, often regarded as one of the first modernists because of his proclamation that 'no artist tolerates reality', argued that the aim of art should be its own self-realization, and that art itself makes life. His emphases on the individual and the drama of the artist's own consciousness were influential in a number of ways for the development of Modernism, as were Sigmund *Freud's theories of the unconscious, and the importance he placed on sexuality.

Impressionism, Post-Impressionism, Expressionism, Cubism, Futurism, Symbolism, Imagism, Vorticism, Dadaism, and Surrealism: all of these movements sprang from what is generally called Modernism, and all were, to varying degrees, subversive of the realist or romantic impulse and disposed towards abstraction. In music, Modernism was characterized in music by atonalism, in poetry by *vers libre*, in fiction by stream of consciousness writing, while in architecture it is associated with functionalism. But Modernism was not just a movement associated with the arts. Rather, it was a broad intellectual movement affecting, and affected by, technological, political, and ideological changes and developments of the time. Einstein's theory of relativity, the discovery of X-rays, the beginning of the mass production of cars, and, crucially, shattering new developments in warfare during the First World War, all encouraged generalized views of crisis, fragmentation, and introversion. *See also* POSTMODERNISM.

modernity A term used to characterize the stage in the history of social relations, dating roughly from the end of the 18th century, that is characterized by the democratic and industrial revolutions. While *modernism is a relatively recent intellectual movement in the arts, modernity refers to much earlier and more enduring social conditions. Strong arguments can be made to the effect that sociology as a discipline developed as a response to the advent and challenges of modernity. Modernity is typically contrasted with traditional forms of society along lines parallel to *Tönnies's distinction between *Gemeinschaft and *Gesellschaft, or *Durkheim's contrast between mechanical and organic solidarity. More recently the comparison has been with postmodernity, which is argued to have superseded modernity, or with *late modernity, which is said to entail a radical intensification of tendencies already embedded within modernity.

In the traditional forms of society relations had been built primarily upon small scale, homogeneous and closely regulated communities. Strongly held beliefs, values, and norms existed alongside repressive laws and severe punishments for nonconformist transgressions. Close, face-to-face ties with familiar others predominated, as did an unquestioning acceptance of ascribed social status. The transition from tradition to modernity involved a mass migration from the countryside to newly expanding cities, a rapid growth in production for exchange and the rise of the money economy, and the development of a specialized division of labour. The differentiation and specialization of functional tasks meant that connections between people in this type of society were increasingly based on mutual interdependence at a distance rather than on emotional involvement based on face-to-face interaction. Correspondingly, the basis of solidarity became weaker and more abstract, allowing for the growth of individuality and freedom. Peter Wagner's *A Sociology of Modernity* writes of the enduring tension within modernity between the structures and values that encouraged this extension of liberty and the partly contradictory structures and values of discipline and order. A concurrent development generating ambivalence within the modern individual was a feeling of rootlessness and nostalgia for more communal forms of solidarity.

Other dimensions of modernity included the consolidation of the nation-state as the locus of political organization and symbolic allegiance, and the rapid expansion of *bureaucracy as a technically efficient, calculable, and predictable means of organizing the many administrative tasks required to impose order on modernity's complexity. *Weber wrote of the way in which the dominance of rational calculation—what he called *rationalization—over more emotional, affective or spiritual forms of apprehension led to a progressive disenchantment of the social world. *Simmel emphasized the role played by monetary exchange in consolidating the impersonal and calculative nature of the relations between people in conditions of modernity, and also the similar role played by the encroachment of the pressures of clock time into everyday consciousness. He also highlighted the relentless assailing of the senses and the disjointed, fragmentary nature of experience in modernity's cities, and the cold and blasé attitudes that developed as a corresponding means of subjective self-protection. In similar vein *Parsons formalized the effects of modernity on forms of social interaction in his celebrated 'pattern variables'. Interaction within modernity was said to be characterized by: generalized criteria (universlism rather than particularism); by the criteria of performance and related credentials (achievement rather than ascription); by attention to only limited aspects of a person (specificity rather than diffuseness or holism); and by an instrumental, means-end, rationality that distances itself from emotional involvement (neutrality rather than affectivity).

Some Marxists have argued that the resurgence of concerns with modernity in light of the debates about post- or late modernity serves an ideological function in deflecting attention away from the centrality of capitalism to social relations. Theorists of modernity from Ulrich *Beck through Anthony *Giddens to Zygmunt *Bauman reject this argument, arguing for a more pluralistic understanding in which capitalism is one amongst several of the defining systemic features of modern society. Capitalism is thus seen alongside, and as interweaving with, other features of modernity such as industrialism, surveillance and administrative control, and the centralization of the means of violence. In Giddens's work each of these features is connected to a parallel institutional dimension of globalization: the world capitalist economy, the international division of labour, the nation-state system, and the world military order. Beck argues that the unintended 'risk' consequences of industrialism, from the dangers of nuclear power to the poisoning of food, are at least as important as the dynamics of capitalism. In *Modernity and the Holocaust*, Bauman focused attention on the huge destructive potential within the apparent 'civilizing process' of modernity. The Nazis' destruction of the Jews and others in the gas chambers of central Europe during the Second World War was not the result of a regression to premodern ways but was a direct product of modernity, one that is ever present. It was a consequence of the modernist impulse to engineer and control the social environment brought together with a combination of the modern state's unprecedented centralization of power and the modern bureaucratic mode of administration. The functional division of labour and instrumental rationality embedded within the latter routinely produce a distance from the victims of political and administrative decisions that is both spatial and moral, and its correlates are moral invisibility and indifference. *See also* ADORNO; FOLK-URBAN CONTINUUM; *GEMEINSCHAFT* and *GESELLSCHAFT*; GENOCIDE; INDUSTRIALISM; TRUST AND DISTRUST; URBAN SOCIOLOGY.

modernization (modernization theory) The process of becoming modern; the development of *modernity. The term can be applied to the ideas of all the theorists concerned with this process. It is often used in a narrower sense to refer to theories that became popular in the early 1960s, as a consequence of the efforts by a group of development specialists in the United States to develop an alternative to the Marxist account of social development. The classic statement is Clark Kerr et al., *Industrialism and Industrial Man* (1960).

In its most sophisticated variants, this modernization theory explains modernization by reference to the onset of the process that Talcott *Parsons refers to as *structural differentiation. This is a process which may be triggered in many different ways, but which is most likely to be initiated by changes in either technology or values (as in Parsons's 'pattern variable' schema). As a result of this process, institutions multiply, the simple structures of traditional societies are transformed into the complex ones of modern societies, and values come to bear a striking resemblance to those current in the United States of the 1960s.

A good example of the genre is the work of the American comparative sociologist Alex Inkeles, best known for his many studies of the attitudinal aspects of modernization, mostly using survey data and psychological tests to explore 'the process whereby people move from being traditional to become modern personalities' (see, for example, his article on 'Industrial Man' in the *American Journal of Sociology*, 1960, and the jointly authored *Becoming Modern*, 1974). These sorts of studies of national character and personality type are also now thought to be contentious. As a result of the growing debate over modernity and postmodernity the term modernization has come to be used more widely, without implying the specific arguments of Parsons, Kerr, and Inkeles. *See also* DEVELOPMENT, SOCIOLOGY OF.

moiety The two or more primary subdivisions in a political or kinship grouping. Some writers restrict the meaning of this term to exogamous groups, whereas others prefer a wider usage, referring to any dual organization (as, for example, in Claude Lévi-Strauss, *The Elementary Structures of Kinship*, 1969).

monetarism An economic theory that posits that the whole economy of a country can be managed through control of the money supply, that is, money in circulation or the cost of credit. The main policy levers are central bank operations to put more or less money in circulation; interest rates, which are raised and lowered to discourage or encourage credit purchases and bank loans; and direct government control over the volume of lending by banks and other financial institutions. Economists disagree as to the relative effectiveness of monetarist policies—as compared, for example, with fiscal policy—in regulating the level of economic activity. They also differ as to the priority to be given to the cost of credit, credit controls, and the quantity of money in circulation, as the focus of monetarist policies.

monism Any philosophical theory that states that all being may ultimately be referred to a single category. *Historical materialism is often described as monist because of its emphasis on determination by the economic *base. The term is also applied more loosely to any causal account that attaches sole importance to a single explanatory factor.

monoculture See CASH CROP.

monogamy A system in which one man marries one woman. Where partners divorce and marry other partners, occasionally repeating the pattern more than once, the term 'serial monogamy' may be used.

monopoly In general terms, monopoly refers to exclusive possession or control of some resource by a single actor or group of actors. In an economic context, it refers to market concentration and imperfect competition; that is, the dominance by one firm of a particular commodity market which gives it the power to set prices, rather than be subjected to price competition with other firms. In real life, few markets are dominated by one firm alone; more common is domination by a small number of firms, a situation which is commonly referred to as *oligopoly. Where two or more businesses reach a formal or informal agreement to limit competition among themselves, for example by fixing similar prices or agreeing separate marketing areas, they are said to form a cartel.

monopoly capitalism See CAPITALISM.

monotheism This is the belief in a single, transcendental God, who is revealed to human beings through events occurring in history. It is contrasted with polytheism or the belief in many gods. *Islam, *Judaism, and *Christianity are the classical illustrations of religions based on the idea of a single, omnipotent, and omniscient Creator. Examples of polytheism include the supernatural beliefs of classical Greece and Rome, *Hinduism, *Buddhism, Shinto, and numerous indigenous religions of Africa and the Americas. Polytheism is particularly condemned in Islam, where *shirk* (or associating another deity with Allah) is regarded as a form of atheism. See also *THEISM.

Montesquieu, Charles Louis de Secondat, Baron de (1689–1755) Best known for his satirical commentary on early 18th century Parisian life (the

Persian Letters, 1721) and for his later masterpiece *The Spirit of the Laws* (1748), Montesquieu was a leading figure of the French Enlightenment, and arguably one of the founding figures of modern *social science. His work in political philosophy explicitly recognized cultural diversity and related the different types of government and law to locally prevailing environmental conditions, institutions, and mores. These ideas were profoundly influential on the thinkers of the *Scottish Enlightenment (especially *Hume, *Ferguson, and *Smith). Montesquieu was also a formative influence on Émile *Durkheim. Many commentators have tended to scorn Montesquieu's inclusion of climate and terrain among those conditions which shape law and government, though the more recent concerns with environmental questions have qualified that judgement. An excellent introduction to his work and its sociological significance is given in Raymond Aron's *Main Currents in Sociological Thought* (1965).

Mont Pelerin Society, The An informal and international association of scholars and public figures dedicated to the generation and dissemination of liberal ideas through its world-wide network of members. Described by one of its founders, the economist Friedrich *Hayek, as a 'kind of international academy of political philosophy' having the aim of 'regenerating the ideas of classical liberalism and in order to refute socialism'.

The Society first met in 1947, when socialist interventionist views were in the ascendant, in the Hôtel du Parc on Mont Pelerin sur Vevey in Switzerland. Its members were concerned about the decline of *liberalism and the threat to their vision of the free society posed by the post-1945 political settlement in favour of *collectivism in democratic-capitalist regimes and the authoritarian *socialism of the Soviet empire. Distinguished scholars who have belonged to the Society include Carlo Antoni, Frank H. Knight, Michael Polanyi, Karl *Popper, Lionel Robbins, George J. Stigler, Carl Iverson, Ludwig von Mises, Milton Friedman, James M. Buchanan, and Gary S. Becker.

The Society did not attempt to shape the formation of government policy directly, being more a 'meeting of minds' than a physical organization or pressure group, but there are those who claim that, by waging a constant 'battle of ideas' against interventionism, individual members exerted considerable indirect influence on the world of politics generally, and contributed significantly to the revival of liberalism in the West in the 1980s. The Society continues to act as a network for the effective dissemination of liberal ideas. There is an interesting official history by R. M. Hartwell (*A History of the Mont Pelerin Society*, 1995).

moral career *See* CAREER.

moral community A term used by Émile *Durkheim to describe traditional rural communities, in contrast to cities. The moral community is characterized by social integration (extensive and intimate attachments) and by moral integration (a set of shared beliefs about morality and behaviour). In modern usage, any small group with these qualities, such as a religious sect or military unit, may be termed a moral community.

moral crusade A campaign centred around a *social movement or organization and concerned with a symbolic or moral issue such as alcohol or pornography. Classic sociological accounts of moral crusades include Joseph R. Gusfield's study of the Temperance Movement, *Symbolic Crusade* (1963), and Louis A. Zurcher et al., *Citizens for Decency* (1976). The term is part of the wider theory of *moral enterprise introduced in Howard Becker's *Outsiders* (1963). *See also* MORAL PANIC.

moral enterprise Within *labelling theory, there is an interest in how rules are produced and enforced, an issue which Howard Becker (in *Outsiders*) calls moral enterprise. Moral enterprise thus refers to the processes involved in creating an awareness of issues and following them through into the statute-book. Moral entrepreneurs are those who are the active promoters of morality: the rule-makers, campaigners, and enforcers. *See also* MORAL CRUSADE; MORAL PANIC.

moral entrepreneur *See* MORAL ENTERPRISE.

moral hazard A problem created by the tendency for the group in receipt of a benefit (such as a welfare benefit) to grow in size as a consequence of the virtually costless (to the individual) availability of certain social benefits. Thus, for example, Charles Murray (*Losing Ground: American Social Policy, 1950-80*, 1986) has argued that the breakdown of traditional family structures and the rise of illegitimacy in the post-war United States is partly a consequence of the availability of new welfare benefits for unmarried mothers.

moral panic The process of arousing social concern over an issue—usually the work of moral entrepreneurs (*see* MORAL ENTERPRISE) and the mass media. The concept was used most forcefully by Stanley Cohen in *Folk Devils and Moral Panics* (1971), with reference to the concern over the teenage styles of Mods and Rockers in England in the mid-1960s, but it has since been applied in the analysis of the societal reaction to many other social problems, including football hooliganism, child abuse, AIDS, and numerous adolescent *subcultural activities. Useful overviews are Erich Goode and Nachman Ben-Yehuda, *Moral Panics: The Social Construction of Deviance* (1994) and Ken Thompson, *Moral Panics* (1998). *See also* LABELLING.

moral statistics Numerical data which are generally held to be indicative of *social pathology. These would include, for example, statistics on suicide, divorce, mental health, illegitimacy, and abortion. In certain 19th-century European societies (most notably France and Britain), such data were widely cited in debates about social reform—although they were usually deployed in very unsociological (indeed unsophisticated) ways.

morbidity statistics Morbidity (illness) statistics are widely used by epidemiologists in the analysis of ill-health within human populations. There are two major types of morbidity rate: the prevalence rate and the incidence rate. The prevalence rate gives an indication of the number of individuals in a population suffering from a particular condition at any time, while the incidence rate shows how many individuals develop a condition within a particular period of time, usually one year. Morbidity rates are generally presented for specific conditions rather than as a general rate, and may be reported as absolute numbers within a year (for example, 200 cases of rabies), or as incidence rates per thousand population, to facilitate comparisons between different sub-populations (such as sexes, age groups, or occupations). Unlike *mortality rates, which are uniquely reported in *official statistics, morbidity statistics are available from a variety of sources, including official statistics on contagious diseases and other notifiable illnesses, hospital in-patient records, records of claims for sickness benefit, and local or national interview surveys which obtain self-report data on ill-health.

mores Mores refer to moral rules or ways of behaving that most members of a society believe are essential for maintaining standards of decency. Mores are vigorously enforced and transgressions punished by either group disapproval and sanction or, where mores become laws, by legal action. *See also* FOLKWAYS.

Morgan, Lewis Henry (1818–81) A New York State lawyer whose interest in the ethnography of native Americans led him to develop a kinship classification system (*Systems of Consanguinity and Affinity of the Human Family*, 1871) that eventually yielded a conjectural history of the family (*Ancient Society*, 1877) which was the basis of Friedrich *Engels's work on the origins of the family and the state.

Morgan was an evolutionary theorist (*see* EVOLUTIONISM), whose project was to examine the *progress of human society from a state of original promiscuity to modern monogamy, which he saw as the basis of the modern state. He contrasted tribal forms of *communitas* with modern forms of *societas*, a distinction that was closely related to that made by Ferdinand Tönnies between *Gemeinschaft* and *Gesellschaft*. Although his conjectural history is no longer taken seriously, the moral link between family and state persists in the 20th century, not only in political thought but also in *functionalist theories of the *family.

mortality (mortality rate) The death rate, usually standardized by age and sex, to facilitate comparisons between areas and social groups. It provides a measure of health risks, improvements in the quality of health care, and the comparative overall health of different groups in the population. It is thus used as a reliable indicator of social and economic change, and of comparative standards of living, as well as by epidemiologists who are interested in monitoring the risk of death from infectious diseases and other causes. A variety of mortality rates are used, each with its own purpose, with the overall national death rate used as the starting-point for comparisons between areas and social groups in a society.

The crude death rate is the number of deaths in a year per 1 000 population in a defined geographical area. In effect a refined version of the absolute number of deaths, this is not very informative, as so much depends on the sex-ratio and age-structure of a population. Crude death rates can be calculated on an age-standardized basis, typically calculated separately for men and women, to produce overall Standard Mortality Ratios (SMR) for each sex, or for both sexes combined, for a given area or social group. The SMR compares age-specific death rates for a given area or social group with national average age-specific death rates. It is calculated by taking the actual or observed number of deaths in the group of interest and dividing by the expected number of deaths—the number that would have occurred if age-specific death rates in the group of interest were equal to the national averages for the year. Age-specific crude death rates and SMRs can also be calculated to identify the age-groups accounting for mortality rates above or below the national average. *See also* MORBIDITY STATISTICS.

mortification *See* *DESOCIALIZATION.

Mosca, Gaetano (1858–1941) An Italian political theorist and proponent of the theory of elite domination. In his most famous book *The Ruling Class* (1896), he argued that there are inevitably two classes of people, the rulers and the ruled. The former is a highly stable, privileged stratum that enjoys wealth, power, and honour. Unlike *Marxists, he did not see this as an exclusively economic class. He also rejected the *liberals' view that the transition to industrial society would end the rule of elites over the masses.

While the ruling class may become heterogeneous as a result of increased social mobility and elite circulation, it nevertheless remains oligarchical. Even in communist societies, there is an organizational need for leadership, and in consequence elite dominance. Like Roberto *Michels, Mosca believed that liberal democracy was a sham, and its ideals could not be realized. It merely hides the inevitability of domination by the ruling elite. Mosca was particularly critical of the symbolic role of political leaders who convinced the masses to support them by means of a mystifying ideology or 'political formulae'. Such self-justification perpetuates elite dominance. That said, he later acknowledged that industrial society consists of multiple social forces, at least some of which the ruling class must try to assimilate. These societies are not entirely closed where a range of interests must be accommodated: this hinders the development of an overly centralized bureaucracy. *See also* ELITE THEORY.

motherhood A term encompassing the practical realities and social signifi-cance of being a mother. The nature of sociological interest in mothering (the process) and motherhood (the condition) has varied over time. Prior to the 1970s, the focus was either on having children as a demographic event (where women rather than men were typically the unit of analysis), or on child-rearing. In both cases the child was the centre of attention, whether as a numerical addition to the population, or as a potential adult member of society. On one hand, patterns of fertility were examined: the age of childbearing, the spacing of births, family size, contraceptive use, illegitimacy, and so forth. On the other hand, the concern was with the impact of the mother's (and to a lesser extent the father's) behaviour on the child, and hence on the subsequent adult. Sociological analyses drew on anthropologists' influential cross-cultural studies of child-training and psychologists' analyses of child development (in both cases the Freudian legacy was strong). Sociological work located child-rearing within the broader framework of the process of *socialization—a process occurring at all stages of life and involving a range of agents, not just parents, in which individuals are trained to accept the prevailing social *norms. Given the marked empirical differences in maternal and paternal roles, research on childhood socialization inevitably showed some awareness of *gender differences, but tended simply to take them for granted. Indeed, macro-theoretical analyses, like that of Talcott *Parsons, asserted the functional necessity in advanced industrial societies of women's role in child-care within the home.

The *feminist movements of the 1970s had a marked impact on the sociological study of motherhood, critically questioning the parental division of labour, although empirical studies showed and continue to show that the bulk of parenting is carried out by women. One consequence of this attention to gender differentiation was an interest in *fatherhood. Feminism also equally importantly shifted the attention from the mother as a producer and creator of children to the mother herself. In the first place, the experience of being a mother has been placed centre-stage. Second, the impact and significance of motherhood on women's position in society and on the gender division of labour has been addressed by a range of feminist theorists. Women's experience of both having and rearing children, the significance of motherhood to women's identity, and the cultural pressures to have children have all been explored in a range of empirical studies, most notably those of Ann Oakley. Many of these studies have challenged the common assumption that women have some instinctive desire to have children and to care for them, and have also examined the dissatisfactions and frustrations of being a mother, especially if one is confined to the home. Not surprisingly, some feminist theorists have suggested that it is the biological fact of childbearing that is the key source of women's oppression, a view developed most fully in Nancy Chodorow's *The Reproduction of Mothering* (1978). However, such claims have been hotly contested, and feminists' views on the significance and value of motherhood in women' lives are a matter of vigorous debate. *See also* MATERNAL DEPRIVATION.

motivation crisis *See* CRITICAL THEORY.

motive (motivation) *See* INTERPRETATION; PSYCHOANALYSIS; SANCTION; VOCABULARIES OF MOTIVE.

Moynihan Report The name conventionally given to the volume on *The Negro Family: The Case for National Action*, published by the US Department of Labor in 1965, and authored by the American social scientist and politician Daniel P. Moynihan.

Moynihan assembled a highly selective account of existing research into *poverty in the United States and seemed to place responsibility for being poor on the victims themselves. The reason given was that the 'lower-class subculture'—in particular that of Blacks—was said to be dominated by 'matriarchy', emasculated males, educational failure, crime, delinquency, and drug addiction, all of which ultimately were attributable to the breakdown of the family structure. In the words of the report, 'At the heart of the deterioration of the fabric of Negro society is the deterioration of the Negro family. It is the fundamental source of weakness of the Negro community at the present time ... The white family has achieved a high degree of stability and is maintaining that stability. By contrast, the family structure of lower class Negroes is highly unstable, and in many urban centres is approaching complete breakdown.' Moynihan argued that 'so long as this situation persists, the cycle of poverty and disadvantage will continue to repeat itself'.

The Report provided the basis for a presidential speech that established new federal policy goals, provoked a public political controversy, attracted a host of academic and other critical reactions, and became a prominent issue in the civil rights debate and movement. Much of the discussion and many of the issues were later restated in relation to the concepts of the *culture of poverty, *cycles of deprivation, welfare dependency, and the *underclass. For a commentary on the Report and an assessment of its significance in shaping American public policy and race relations see Charles A. Valentine, *Culture and Poverty* (1968).

multi-cultural society A society characterized by cultural pluralism—as in the cases of the United States and post-war Britain. As an ideal, multi-culturalism celebrates cultural variety (for example linguistic and religious diversity), and may be contrasted with the *assimilationist ideal assumed in many early studies of race, ethnicity, and immigration.

multidimensional scaling Data such as *attitude items often cannot be represented in one dimension. A representation can be sought in a space of two or more dimensions. The purpose of multidimensional scaling (MDS) is to seek as good a representation of the data as possible in as few dimensions as possible. It has significant similarities with *factor analysis.

In the simplest case (non-metric Euclidean distance MDS), data are thought of as giving information on the similarity or dissimilarity between pairs of objects, as positive correlations can be interpreted as similarities and the purpose of MDS is to represent each variable as a point in a low-dimensional space so that the distance between the points accurately reflects the relative size of the data similarities and dissimilarities. It has been used successfully on a wide range of sociological and psychological data (see J. B. Kruskal and M. Wish, *Multidimensional Scaling*, 1978).

multi-level models A set of closely related approaches to examining the links between macro- and micro-levels of social phenomena. Multi-level (also known as 'contextual' or 'hierarchical') models in sociology attempt to identify the effects of social context on individual-level outcomes.

The idea that individuals are affected by and respond to their social surroundings is fundamental to sociology as a discipline. Among the classic sociologists, Durkheim studied the impact of community structure on suicide rates, and Weber the impact of religious communities (such as the Protestant sects) on economic conduct. However, since the mid-1980s, new theories have been developed and new statistical techniques applied to a variety of sociological problems, and these represent a significant advance over earlier approaches.

Multi-level models explain micro-level outcomes either by showing that the parameters of models specified at the micro-level (where micro-level outcomes are explained by micro-level covariates) are a function of context, or by showing that micro-macro relationships can be expressed in terms of characteristics of the context, in the form of macro-level variables. Although multi-level models promise greater understanding of precisely what context means, and how it may affect individual outcomes in which sociologists are interested, the approach is not without its problems. Robust statistical estimates for model parameters can be hard to provide if models are too complicated.

multinational corporation A form of *capitalist enterprise in which the financial structure, managerial control, and integration of productive activity span national boundaries and are oriented to international (or global) *markets. *See also* INDUSTRIAL INTEGRATION.

multivariate analysis Univariate analysis consists in describing and explaining the *variation in a single variable. Bivariate analysis does the same for two variables taken together (covariation). Multivariate analysis (MVA) considers the simultaneous effects of many variables taken together. MVA models are often expressed in algebraic form (as a set of linear equations specifying the way in which the variables combine with each other to affect the dependent variable) and can also be thought of geometrically. Thus, the familiar scatter-plot of individuals in the two dimensions representing two variables can be extended to higher-dimensional (variable) spaces, and MVA can be thought of as discovering how the points cluster together.

Mumford, Lewis (1895–1990) An architectural writer who was much influenced by Patrick *Geddes. In *Technics and Civilization* (1934) and *The Culture of Cities* (1938) he set out an evolutionary model of city growth, stressing the determining role of technology. He traced the way that technology could increase human capacities. He was interested in the close relationship between human power and mechanical power and introduced the idea of the 'megamachine' to refer to the hierarchical systems of human actors through which massive works of construction could be achieved. His later work (*The City in History*, 1961; *The Myth of the Machine*, 1964) saw technology as a source of oppression and alienation, and he became far more pessimistic about the future.

mutualism *See* ANARCHISM.

Myrdal, Alva (Alva Reimer, 1902–86) Swedish educator, feminist, social scientist, politician, reformer, diplomat. Active life-long member of the Swedish Social Democratic Party to which she contributed intellectually, solely and with her economist husband Gunnar *Myrdal, with works on the social and economic importance of child-friendly education and a family- and women-friendly welfare state, and in practice as government investigator, minister, ambassador and UN delegate. She first gained international fame with her book on the Swedish welfare state, *Nation and Family* (1941), and as Director of UN Department of Social Affairs and later UNESCO's Department of Social Science (1949–55), the first woman to hold high international posts. Here she worked for international social science collaboration over social development and political democratization. With British sociologist Viola *Klein she wrote the first comparative empirical work on women and changing labour market participation, *Women's Two Roles* (1956). After a period as Ambassador to India, she turned to the politics of peace and disarmament, for which she gained the Nobel Peace Prize in 1982.

Myrdal, Gunnar (1898–1987) Swedish economist internationally known for his critical work on hidden values in economic and social theory and the interrelationship between economic, social and institutional conditions (Nobel Prize in Economics, with von Hayek, 1974). An active member of the Swedish Social Democratic Party, with his wife Alva he wrote an influential intellectual manifesto offering a social and economic rationale for a family-friendly welfare state. On the invitation of the Carnegie Corporation he led the largest ever research project on race relations, resulting in *An American Dilemma* (1944). In this he emphasized the need for value explicitness in social research, the American 'creed' of equality and democracy as a value yardstick against which to interpret the mass of evidence on the 'vicious circles' of prejudice and discrimination. He later turned to issues of international economics, poverty and development studies, the major outcome of which was his large study *Asian Drama* (1968).

myth A sacred or religious tale whose content is concerned with the origins or creation of natural, supernatural, or cultural phenomena. The anthropological meaning differs from that which implies an untruth. Myths have been studied as fractured sources of *oral history, as clues to the society's dominant values, as a 'social charter', and (by Claude Lévi-Strauss) for their universal structures.

Nadel, Siegfried Frederick (1903–56) Nadel came to British social anthropology from a background in psychology and philosophy at the University of Vienna, where he had already gained a doctorate. He studied at the London School of Economics under Seligman and Malinowski and carried out fieldwork in West Africa, largely among the Nupe of Nigeria (see *A Black Byzantium*, 1942, and *Nupe Religion*, 1954). His theoretical work attempted to link sociology, social anthropology, and psychology in a single frame of analysis (see *The Foundations of Social Anthropology*, 1942). His relatively early death, when he was at the height of his powers, undoubtedly contributed to the decline in interest in his work among the next generation of social scientists.

narcissism Used in everyday life to indicate self-love and egoism, the concept has a more technical meaning to orthodox *psychoanalytic theory. Primary narcissism refers to the love of self which, *Freud argues, must precede the ability to love others. This stage of development is also typified by the opposite of self-love—self-hatred. Secondary narcissism is identifying with, and then introjecting, an object (person) making it part of oneself. A 'narcissistic object choice' involves identifying with a person on the basis of that person's similarity to oneself.

The concept has been extended by the American social historian Christopher *Lasch (*The Culture of Narcissism*, 1980, and *The Minimal Self*, 1984) into an instrument of social analysis and criticism. Lasch, who is unusual on the political Left for promoting the virtue of family life, argues that modern society has crippled human abilities for love and commitment. The social changes associated with modernity (the development of large bureaucracies and technological change), and consequent changes in family relationships (especially the comparative absence of the father), have allegedly made it difficult to develop beyond narcissism. The dominant personality type of modern society is said to be internally impoverished, fluctuating between exaggerated self-love and self-hatred, consequently needing parasitic relationships to reinforce the former; it is unable to tolerate frustration, inadequacy, and strong feelings, due to a lack of ego-development. Lasch sees a number of cultural phenomena—from the emphasis on health and sporting achievement through to the New Left of the 1960s, sexual liberation movements, and much modern feminism—as manifestations of narcissism. The narcissistic personality is often successful in the outside world, but feels an inner emptiness, and concentrates on survival rather than investing in the future.

narrative A basic way human beings have of apprehending the world and giving it a coherence, and most social science has recently been touched by what has been called the 'narrative' or 'interpretive turn'. A new discipline—narratology—has slowly emerged which takes as its central task the analysis of stories and narratives. There are a wide range of theories of narrative: Raman Selden and Peter Widdowson in *A Reader's Guide to Literary Theory* (3rd edn., 1993) for instance suggest thirteen: dialogical, hermeneutic, critical, neo-Aristotelian, psychoanalytic, feminist, deconstructive, reader-response, Marxist, formalist, semiotic, structuralist, and post-structuralist theories. Combining several strands of thought, narratives are usually seen to be composed of several key elements.

'Story' is the most basic element—and usually implies as Gary Kenyon and William Randall aptly put it in their book *Restorying our Lives* (1997), 'someone telling someone about somebody doing something'. Stories are about someone trying to do something, and what happens as a result. Who all these people are and what they are all doing becomes the feature of the story. Usually it will imply some kind of 'mere' sequence of events with some kind of moral point ('and the moral of the story is . . . '). 'Plots' are more complex: they are the dynamos of stories, they turn them on. In formal (Russian) narrative theory, a 'story' (fabula) is raw material awaiting organization by the author, whilst a 'plot' *(sjuzet)* is the literary device. Following Aristotle, it is the 'arrangements of the incidents'. More clearly, we could say that a story must usually have a dynamic tension which adds momentum, gives a coherence and makes the story interesting: we can speak of a plot 'thickening' to indicate events that grab the reader's interest. As Kenyon and Randall again pithily say: 'no trouble, no tale; no ill, no thrill; no agony, no adventure'. 'Plot carries us from initial calm through ensuing conflict to eventual climax, conclusion and (once more) calm'. Usually plots take on a sequence—a beginning, middle, and end (though in some experimental modernist and all postmodern plots, linear time is dissolved or seriously weakened); they often have 'epiphanies' (or major crises) which shape the dynamic. Closely linked to plots are the key 'themes' that start to organize a life. These are the repeated content clusters in stories. And finally these thematic lines eventually become recognizable as falling into definite patterns, types, and structures often performing definite functions. Langdon Elsbree in his *The Rituals of Life: Patterns in Narratives* (1982) has argued that there are a relatively few 'archetypal actions', 'elementary ritual modes affecting the way we apprehend a story' and suggests these are: (1) establishing, consecrating a home; (2) engaging in a contest, fighting a battle; (3) taking a journey; (4) enduring suffering; (5) pursuing consummation.

The idea of narrative has entered sociology in several major ways. First, sociological theories have themselves been classified as kinds of narratives, lending coherence to social life. Donald Levine's *Visions of the Sociological Tradition* (1995) has thus located such narratives as positivist, pluralist, synthetic, humanist, contextual, and dialogic. Others, such as Ken Plummer's *Documents of Life—2* (2001) have stressed the importance of focusing upon human lives themselves to see how the story of their life can be analysed as a narrative structure. David Maines has argued that sociology has now reached its narrative moment, as a central tool for looking at communication (in the *Sociological Quarterly*, 1993). And for still others the very act of writing sociology is a mode of narrative creation. Laurel Richardson's *Writing Strategies* (1991) has more specifically suggested five kinds of broad narrative that may be found in sociology: everyday life narratives, autobiographical narratives, biographical narratives, cultural narratives, and collective stories. In looking seriously at the narrative forms of social science writing, a much greater sensitivity to matters of aesthetics, argumentation, genre, and metaphor is generated.

In short, narrative has now entered sociology as an important method for analysing and understanding social life.

national bourgeoisie *See* COMPRADOR.

national character *See* CULTURE AND PERSONALITY SCHOOL; MODERNIZATION; NATIONALISM.

National Deviance Conference (NDC) The name given to a group of radical and critical criminologists (*see* CRIMINOLOGY, CRITICAL) and deviance theorists in the United Kingdom, who met regularly at York University, between 1967 and 1975. They were strongly identified with *labelling theory. Typical of the publications associated with the group are Stanley Cohen (ed.), *Images of Deviance* (1971), and Laurie Taylor and Ian Taylor (eds.), *Politics and Deviance* (1973).

nationalism Sentiment, aspiration, and consciousness are all terms applied to what constitutes nationalism, or the valuation of the nation-state above all else. However, it also entails certain assumptions about the will to self-determination, the existence and indeed desirability of diversity, the superiority of the sovereign *state over other forms of rule, and the centrality of national loyalty to political power as a basic form of *legitimation. Authors as diverse as Émile Durkheim and Lenin have argued that the prerequisite of genuine, solidaristic internationalism is mature nationalism, which alone recognizes the commonalities of diversity. However, others maintain the concept involves spurious notions of natural boundaries, and merely provides a convenient political epithet for both Left and Right alike (see A. D. Smith, *Theories of Nationalism*, 2nd edn., 1983, and *National Identity*, 1991).

Variants of nationalism have tended to move away from the German version associated with the writings of J. G. Herder, which stressed the organic unity and ties of a nation, emphasizing subordination to the whole (in this case the state), a sense of mission, national purity, and the soul of a nation. This form of organic nationalism was more affectual than other West European rational associational nationalisms. There were also differences between German and Slav nationalisms, the latter tied to liberationist mobilization rather than irredentism, and to a nationalist *intelligentsia rather than the whole people or *Volk*.

In his classic book on *The Idea of Nationalism* (1945), Hans Kohn distinguishes 'Western' type nationalism of the kind that emerged in England and France during the period 1600–1800 from the 'Eastern' type of nationalism that appeared in later centuries. In the former case, the nation is identified with the masses and with popular forms of politics, and thus serves to provide a cultural justification for an already existing political structure. In the latter, nationalism is used to justify the creation of nation-states in economically and politically less-developed parts of the world, by redrawing political boundaries in conformity with ethnographic demands—in other words it provides a justification for the invention of states and political processes. This distinction, like most other subsequent typologies of nationalism, serves descriptive and normative purposes; that is, it both classifies the types of nationalism found in the modern world, and simultaneously declares these to be politically valuable or dangerous forms. The Western variant is authentic, liberal, democratic, and good, while the Eastern is alien, ethnic, racist, and generally bad.

A similar, subsequent, and currently controversial typology distinguishes between 'civic nationalism' and 'ethnic nationalism' (see for example Liah Greenfeld, *Nationalism: Five Roads to Modernity*, 1992). The former equates nationality with *citizenship; is defined primarily in political or legal terms; implies a commitment (embraced voluntarily) to certain duties and rights; and can therefore be acquired and lost. The concept of civic nationalism means that some individuals can be without a nationality at all. Ethnic nationality, on the other hand, is rooted in biological necessity rather than individual choice. It runs in families and is believed to be an inherited characteristic. People are born into a particular nationality, which then determines their interests, sentiments, and sense of attachment to a particular nation. This distinction is appealing to many Western and liberal observers, because it allows them to differentiate between the idea of a freely chosen, politically decent nationalism (such as one might find in the civic pride of Americans), and the nationalism that celebrates inherited cultural identity (of the type that is found in, and causes conflict within, many East European countries).

Many of the typologies of nationalism have been accused of being Eurocentric, and of failing to address Latin American and emerging African post-colonial nationalisms, and the artificiality of imperially imposed boundaries upon tribal lands which were more fluid than the nation-states which followed.

Some writers have suggested that nationalism is itself a modern religion—or is at least akin to what elsewhere in sociology has been called a *civil (or civic) religion. Indeed, there are specifically 'religious nationalisms', associated mainly with Islam and Judaism but evident also in, for example, the recent histories of Poland and Ireland (where Roman Catholicism has formed a central element in the national—secular—identity). Others maintain that nationalism is an essentially secular form of consciousness, so that the most which can be claimed is a functional equivalence between religion and nationalism.

Some accounts of nationalism appear deterministic. For example, Ernest Gellner's writings (see *Nations and Nationalism*, 1983) suggest that history can be seen as a succession of changing technologies, each of which generates the need for a specific socio-political order, and that nationalism is the style of politics that is best suited to the current (industrial) technology (because industrial societies, unlike agrarian ones, need homogeneous languages and culture in order to work efficiently). According to Gellner, 'a man without a nation... provokes revulsion', so where nationalism does not exist it is (as it were) necessary to invent it. In Gellner's account, emphasis is placed less on spontaneous collective aspirations (of the 'civic' kind) or culture ('ethnic' considerations), than upon the deliberate (and necessary) nation-building policies of government elites (or aspirant governments), pursued by means of public education and the culture industries. Perhaps not surprisingly Gellner's account has been criticized as materialist and functionalist. In social psychology, the social identity theory (SIT) of Henri Tajfel (see *Human Groups and Social Categories*, 1981) and his associates traces nationalism to (possibly innate) human tendencies to affiliate in social groups, and then act in furtherance of these groups. Within this particular research paradigm, social identities are viewed as integral aspects of an overall sense of self; those rooted in racial or national groups are found to be particularly important for self-esteem; and so it is difficult for people not to think nationalistically, to feel loyalties to their given (even if 'imagined') national community, and to pursue its particular interests against those of other nation-states. (For a summary of SIT research in European social psychology see Michael A. Hogg and Dominic Abrams, *Group Identifications*, 1988.)

The post-communist transformations in Russia and Central Europe raise the possibility of examining hypotheses about the relationships between nation-building, in terms of the search for new sources of social identification, and the advent of *capitalism. In particular, the 'value vacuum' created by the collapse of official Marxism-Leninism has provided for a burgeoning of nationalist and populist *ideologies, although these often refer to the nationalism of 'small nations' which do not possess the attributes necessary for full-blown nationalism.

National Socialism *See* FASCISM.

National Statistics Socio-Economic Classification (NS-SEC) There are many ways of measuring socio-economic position: income, education, and occupation have all been used for this purpose, both separately and together. However, in the UK the traditional approach has been to measure socio-economic position via a socio-economic classification and specifically by *social class as a measure of the social structure. This tradition dates back to 1913 with the creation of the *Registrar General's Social Classes (RGSC). RGSC brought together into each of its classes occupations of similar 'social standing'. It was used by researchers in both government and universities to analyse fertility, mortality, and morbidity. The point of these analyses was to show that health inequalities are the outcome of causal processes that are inextricably linked with the basic structure of society. For example, RGSC revealed a health gradient such that people in Classes I and II (professionals and managers) had consistently better health and longer lives than people in Classes IV and V (partly skilled and unskilled occupations).

The RGSC was modified many times between 1913 and 1991 but, useful as it was empirically, it was unclear what it was actually measuring and, indeed, whether it was still necessary for government to produce this type of classification. Hence, in 1994 the government commissioned the Economic and Social Research Council (ESRC) to review RGSC. The result was the creation of the

National Statistics Socio-Economic Classification (NS-SEC) which became the official UK measure of social class from 2001 and is used in the analysis of all government social surveys as well as census data.

Like the RGSC, the NS-SEC is an occupationally based classification. The basic information required to create the NS-SEC is occupation (coded to the occupational unit groups (OUGs) of the Standard Occupational Classification) and details of employment status (whether an employer, self-employed or employee; whether a supervisor; and number of employees at the workplace). The main analytic version of the classification has eight classes, the first of which can be subdivided. The NS-SEC was developed from a social class measure created by the Oxford sociologist John *Goldthorpe. Thus, as with the *Goldthorpe class scheme, the NS-SEC has been constructed to measure the employment relations and conditions of occupations. Conceptually these are central to delineating the structure of socio-economic positions in modern societies and helping to explain variations in social behaviour and outcomes.

The NS-SEC distinguishes four basic employment positions: employers, the self-employed, employees, and those involuntarily excluded from paid employment. Within the category of employers, a further distinction is made between large and small employers according to the number of employees in the organization. Employees are sub-divided into classes according to the type of contract they have with their employer. Two basic contract types are distinguished—the labour contract and the service relationship. Labour contracts involve a relatively short-term and specific exchange between employers and employees of money (a wage) for effort. This is the situation which pertains for the whole working class, although its most basic form is found in the case of routine occupations in class 7. The service relationship, however, is typical for managerial, professional, and senior administrative positions, and its basic form is found in class 1. This form of contract involves a longer-term and more diffuse exchange in which employees render service in return for both immediate and future compensation (a salary, regular pay reviews, perks of various types, a career, generous pension schemes, etc.). Other types of employee, for example, clerical and technical workers in class 3, are defined as intermediate in terms of employment regulation, having contracts with elements of both the service relationship and the

---

The National Statistics Socio-Economic Classification

1	Higher managerial and professional occupations
	1.1　Large employers and higher managerial occupations
	1.2　Higher professional occupations
2	Lower managerial and professional occupations
3	Intermediate occupations
4	Small employers and own account workers
5	Lower supervisory and technical occupations
6	Semi-routine occupations
7	Routine occupations
8	Never worked and long-term unemployed

labour contract. The excluded comprise those who have never worked but would wish to, and the long-term unemployed. However, other non-employed persons, such as those who look after a home, the retired, the short-term unemployed, the sick and disabled, etc., are classified according to their last main occupation. Full-time students can also be treated similarly if required. In this way, it is possible to classify most of the adult population within the NS-SEC.

The NS-SEC has been shown to be a good discriminator in terms of earnings, unemployment experience and duration, smoking behaviour, morbidity, mortality, and subjective health.

(SEE WEB LINKS)
• The National Statistics Socio-Economic Classification website.

nativism In sociological contexts, this term is used most commonly to refer to the negative, *ethnocentric responses of native-born populations towards immigrants. The classic study of such responses is John Higham, *Strangers in the Land: Patterns of American Nativism 1860–1925* (1955).

nativistic movement *See* MESSIANIC MOVEMENT; NEW RELIGIONS.

natural area A term used in *urban ecology to denote an area inhabited by a population that shares common 'social heritage, occupation, interests, or other distinguishing cultural possessions' (A. Hawley, *Human Ecology*, 1950). In short, a distinctive *community. In theories of environmental determinism (*see* ENVIRONMENT), physical zones are seen as defining natural areas such as *pays* and regions. *See also* CONCENTRIC ZONE THEORY.

natural experiment An experiment in which the *independent variable is not artificially manipulated, but rather changes naturally in terms of its level or presence, so that these alterations can be used to monitor its effect and attempt to determine its impact upon a *dependent variable or variables. Such studies are understandably rare in sociology, although one example is provided by John Gaventa's study of quiescence and rebellion among Appalachian coal miners (*Power and Powerlessness*, 1980), which investigates the impact of historically variable *power relationships (most notably the mobilization of bias, *see* POWER) involving large business corporations in local communities.

naturalism In sociology and moral philosophy the term naturalism has several distinct but related uses that are frequently confused with one another. In moral philosophy, naturalism is the thesis (*contra* *Hume's famous denial that 'ought' can be derived from 'is') that moral judgements can be deduced from (or are a type of) factual statements. In sociology, however, the most common use of the term derives from the long-running dispute about whether sociology can be a science in the same sense as the natural sciences; and, relatedly, whether its methods should be based on those of the natural sciences. Naturalism in this usage of the term ('methodological naturalism') is the view that sociology is, or can become, a science, and that the methods of the natural sciences—experiment, inductive generalization, prediction, statistical analysis, and so on—are directly, or by analogy, usable by sociologists. Anti-naturalists argue that a radically different methodological approach—closer to literary criticism, textual interpretation, or conversational analysis—is required.

Generally implicit in this methodological dispute are disagreements of an *ontological kind about the nature of the subject-matter of *sociology (and the other human sciences). In general terms, the opposition may be characterized as a dispute about whether human beings and their social life should be understood as a part of nature, continuous with the subject-matter of other sciences, or whether humans represent a radical discontinuity, a qualitative exception in the order of nature. In this area the dispute between naturalists and anti-naturalists clearly overlaps with that between *materialists and *idealists. However, further distinctions need to be made if we are to make sense of the different positions commonly taken up by sociologists. Ontological naturalists can themselves be divided into two broad groups. Those (such as, for example, *sociobiologists) who take the view that sociology may become a science through direct annexation as a sub-division of the existing natural sciences (evolutionary biology, in the case of the sociobiologists), may be termed 'reductionist naturalists'. Other ontological naturalists insist that humans and their social life are a part of nature, but nevertheless recognize that *language, *culture, complex forms of normatively ordered social life, and so on, establish a distinct order of reality ('emergent properties') that poses special challenges for scientific investigation. Émile *Durkheim, for example, recognized the *sui generis* reality of social life, its irreducibility to the facts of biology or psychology, yet advocated a methodology modelled upon that of the natural sciences.

natural law The ambiguity of the term natural law rests upon a metaphorical link between regularities in nature and the authoritative regulation of human activity. In its latter use, 'natural law' refers to principles of law and morality, supposedly universal in scope and binding on human conduct. In medieval Christian theology natural law was held to be a God-given system, but from the Reformation onwards, attempts were made to give natural law secular foundations in human nature and reason. In the *Leviathan* of Thomas *Hobbes, for example, 'laws of nature' provide rational grounds for the social contract, and so for the establishment of political authority. Since the 18th century, legal theory has tended to be hostile to the notion of natural law—the conventional, socially and historically formed character of law being more commonly emphasized. However, the increase in moral authority attaching to human *rights since the Second World War owes much to the natural law tradition.

The idea of the natural world as created by God, and so being subject (like human society) to God's authority, led to the metaphorical extension of the notion of natural law to refer to regularities in nature. Here, again, the idea had its religious and its secular adherents, though from the scientific revolution of the 17th century, the principal division was between rationalists and empiricists. The former tended to attribute necessity to the laws of nature, some of them (such as Leibniz) supposing these to be rationally demonstrable from a priori principles. The empiricists held that knowledge of the laws of nature could be established only on the basis of observation and experiment. On this view the regularities summarized in laws of nature could not justifiably be held to have any necessity about them. Our expectation that such regularities would continue into the future, however unavoidable in practical life, was (David *Hume argued) nevertheless rationally ungrounded, and a mere habit of mind.

natural selection *See* DARWINISM.

nature versus nurture debate The common description of the controversy over the relative importance of *heredity (nature) and *environment (nurture) in the causation of human behaviour. The debate has been particularly important in certain fields of sociology, including education (with a focus on the heritability of *intelligence), *crime (with, for instance, dispute over the idea of an inherited criminal personality), and *gender divisions (with heated debate over the importance of biology to observed differences in male-female behaviour). Recent discussions have centred on the implications of research into the *human genome.

Naturwissenschaften *See* GEISTESWISSENSCHAFTEN and NATURWISSENSCHAFTEN.

need A need is something that is deemed necessary, especially something that is considered necessary for the survival of the person, organization, or whatever. The concept is widely used in the social sciences, with especial attention being placed on so-called human needs. Needs are commonly contrasted with wants (or desires), needs referring to things that are necessary, wants to those that are desired. Since the concept itself suggests that needs ought to be satisfied, it has frequently been invoked in the rhetoric of political and policy debates, notably in support of claims for action and intervention. It is central to discussions of *poverty and *deprivation and to *welfare—a term referring to the meeting of human needs. Not surprisingly, however, the specification of needs is strongly contested. It is not too difficult to get agreement over a list of basic requirements for survival—such as the physiological and material needs for food, sleep, and shelter. However, determining necessary levels of these requirements is more difficult. Moreover, although academics and policy-makers may agree on a core of basic human needs, many would dispute whether this exhausts the set of basic human needs. Some would wish to include psychological and social needs, such as the need for love and care, for companionship, for the opportunity to learn, and so forth, as universal requirements. It has also been suggested that such needs can be viewed hierarchically. There is disagreement, too, over whether needs should be defined in absolute or relative terms, should be assessed objectively or subjectively, and indeed over the value of the concept itself.

Sociologists, especially those of a functional persuasion, have also used the concept of need in studying the functioning of societies. Talcott *Parsons, for example, explicated the functional prerequisites of the *social system—the things necessary for the survival of the society—such as adequate motivational support for the system itself. In a similar vein, Marxists talk of the needs of capitalism, mentioning most frequently the needs for production, reproduction, and legitimation. However, critics have pointed both to the difficulty of identifying the needs of society with any precision, and to the frequently *tautological nature of the endeavour. *See also* NEEDS, HIERARCHY OF.

needs, hierarchy of The central concept in Abraham *Maslow's theory of *self-actualization. He proposed that human desires are innately given and exist in an ascending hierarchy. Basic physiological needs—food, sleep, protection from extreme hazards of the environment—must first be met. Then the needs for safety and security become paramount: we need some kind of order, certainty, and structure in our lives. Once these are met the third need, to belong and to love, comes into play. Fourth in the hierarchy is the need for self-esteem—for both self-respect and esteem from other people. When all these needs have been met, the fifth and highest need emerges: namely, the need for self-actualization, or the desire to become everything that one can become. As Maslow states in *Motivation and Personality* (1970), 'a musician must make music, an artist must paint, a poet must write if he is to be at peace with himself. What a man can be, he must be. He must be true to his own nature.' Part of Maslow's research involved the study of self-actualized people, and he provided substantial listings of the characteristics of such individuals. His work has led to the study of 'peak' experiences, and the growth of a transpersonal, often more spiritual psychology.

negative correlation *See* CORRELATION.

negotiated order A theory developed largely within *symbolic interactionism by Anselm Strauss to depict social organization occurring in and through people negotiating with each other. Designed in part as a response to the view that interactionists had no tools for analysing social *structure and were too subjective, the theory attempts to depict social organization as an active achievement of social actors, and not as a static or reified concept. It can be traced back to a number of classic sources: George Herbert *Mead's dialectical concept of society; Herbert *Blumer's idea of the interpretive process and the joint act; Robert *Park's characterization of society as a succession of conflicts, accommodations, and assimilations; and Everett Hughes's concern with institutional flexibility. The term is stated and developed most explicitly, however, in the writings of Anselm Strauss and his colleagues, especially *Psychiatric Ideologies and Institutions* (1963), and his later book *Negotiations* (1978). Strauss depicts social order as 'something at which members of any society, any organization, must work. For the shared agreements... are not binding for all time... review is called for... the bases of concerted action (social order) must be constituted continually, or "worked out"'. The theory highlights emergence, change, and temporality; the embedded and contextual nature of order; the omnipresence of specific power relations; and the constant segmentation and fragmentation of social orders.

neighbourhood *See* COMMUNITY.

neo-classical economics Economics, as an academic discipline, is predominantly the study of the allocation of scarce resources to alternative uses via market prices. The dominant paradigm in modern *economics is neo-classical theory which developed from the so-called marginalist revolution pioneered by Carl Menger, Leon Walras, and William Jevons in the late 19th century. This holds that prices are determined by marginal *utility (of consumers) and marginal *productivity (of factors of production). Neo-classical theories are based on simple behavioural models at the micro-level (households, firms) which assume perfect information, freedom of movement, individual choice, optimizing and rational decision-making. The basic conditions for these models are private enterprise, consumer sovereignty, and market-clearing prices. Institutional influences on individual behaviour are defined exogenously as given characteristics and do not form part of the basic behavioural model. However, *game-theoretic approaches have been developed recently to explain individual behaviour within institutional rules.

neo-colonialism A term often applied to the economic situation of many former colonies after political independence has been secured. Neo-colonialist interpretations of economic development in the *Third World suggest that, as a budget-saving and humanitarian act, political decolonization nevertheless left intact the West's monopolistic control over the production and marketing of goods in the former colonies. By using international law, corporate property rights, and the power of major commercial banks the former colonial powers could retain economic influence and control over their former dependent territories. In Marxist discourse this phenomenon is usually termed neo-imperialism.

Under neo-colonialism, as under direct colonial rule, the relationship between centre and periphery (or metropolis and satellite) is said to involve the export of capital from the former to the latter; a reliance on Western manufactured goods and services which thwarts indigenous development efforts; further deterioration in the terms of trade for the newly independent countries; and a continuation of the processes of cultural Westernization which guarantee the West's market outlets elsewhere in the world. The operations of transnational corporations in the Third World are seen as the principal agents of contemporary neo-colonialism, since (at least within *dependency theory) these are seen as exploiting local resources and influencing international trade and national governments to their own advantage. *See also* CENTRE–PERIPHERY MODEL; COLONIALISM.

neo-Darwinism *See* DARWINISM; GENE.

neo-imperialism *See* NEO-COLONIALISM.

neo-Kantianism The growing popularity of scientific *materialist world-outlooks in mid-19th-century Germany provoked intellectual and cultural resistance in the shape of neo-Kantianism. This movement was very diverse, and had a pervasive influence in the humanities and social sciences in Germany from 1860 onwards. The historian of philosophy Kuno Fischer called for a 'return to Kant' in 1860, and the call was answered by many of Germany's leading intellectuals, including Friedrich Albert Lange, Heinrich Rickert, Wilhelm *Windleband, and Wilhelm *Dilthey. In its broader cultural and political significance the movement included liberal-humanist resistance to the increasingly virulent racism of the German Social *Darwinist movement led by the materialist Ernst Hasckel, as well as moderate conservative hostility to materialism as associated with revolutionary *socialism.

More narrowly, the neo-Kantians were concerned to establish a bulwark against the spread of natural scientific methods into the sphere of the humanities and social sciences. *Kant's critical philosophy (in their various interpretations of it) provided resources for this project in two ways. First, the duality in Kant between a perceptible and therefore knowable world of 'appearances', and a world of 'things-in-themselves' presupposed in morality, freedom, aesthetics, and the unity of the self, could be employed as the justification for a radical separation between the natural sciences and the 'human', 'cultural', or 'historical' sciences. Sometimes this distinction was made in terms of the radical differences of subject-matter between the two complexes of disciplines, and sometimes (as in the work of Rickert) in terms of the distinctive character of our interest in the two domains. According to the latter view, our concern in the natural sciences is with objects of experience in so far as they are instances of universal laws, whereas in the cultural sphere our interest is in particular meaningful expressions in virtue of their relevance to values. Moreover, the distinctive character of the objects of the cultural sciences as complexes of meaning requires a distinctive form of understanding (*Verstehen*) not reducible to the sensory perception typical of natural scientific method.

The second way in which Kant was important for the neo-Kantians was his philosophical method. The neo-Kantians (and others, such as Dilthey, who, though sharing many of the preoccupations of the neo-Kantians, was not strictly one of their number) sought not only to establish the autonomy of the human, historical sciences from the natural sciences, but also to parallel Kant's philosophical defence of natural science with an analysis of the conceptual and methodological conditions for objective knowledge of human historical and cultural expressions. Neo-Kantianism was profoundly influential in providing the philosophical and methodological basis for German interpretative sociology, of which the most important representatives were Georg *Simmel and Max *Weber. Later, leading figures in the distinctive 20th-century tradition of Western Marxism (such as György *Lukács) derived their main philosophical orientation from neo-Kantianism, as did the French sociologist Émile *Durkheim, and the founding figure of cultural anthropology Franz *Boas. *See also* GEISTESWIS-SENSCHAFTEN and NATURWISSENSCHAFTEN.

neo-liberalism A loosely knit body of ideas that became very influential during the 1980s and that were premissed upon a (slight) rethinking and a (substantial) reassertion of classical *liberalism. The most prominent neo-liberals are *libertarians, enthusiastic advocates of the *rights of the individual against those of the 'coercive state', chief amongst whose protagonists are Milton Friedman, Friedrich *Hayek, and Robert Nozick. As these names suggest, neo-liberalism has had far more influence in economics and political science than in sociology.

neo-Marxism A term loosely applied to any social theory or sociological analysis that draws on the ideas of Karl *Marx and Friedrich *Engels, but amends or extends these, usually by incorporating elements from other intellectual traditions—such as, for example, psychoanalysis (as in the case of *critical theory), Weberian sociology (as in Erik Olin Wright's theory of *contradictory class locations), or anarchism (as in the example of critical *criminology).

neonatal mortality *See* MORTALITY RATE.

neo-positivism A movement in early 20th-century American sociology which blended together the three themes of quantification, *behaviourism, and *positivist epistemology. Its principal proponents were Franklin H.*Giddings and George A. *Lundberg, although the *mathematical sociology of writers such as George K. Zipf (1902–50) can be seen as a development of neo-positivist theory.

In his *Studies in the Theory of Human Society* (1922), Giddings offered a qualified defence of behaviourism, arguing that 'psychology has become experimental and objective. It has discriminated between reflex and conditioning'. He also insisted that 'sociology [is] a science statistical in method' and that 'a true and complete description of anything must include measurement of it'. Similarly, Lundberg maintained that sociology could be modelled on the natural sciences, and should observe the behaviour of human beings in social situations but without reference to concepts such as feelings, ends, motives, values, and will (which he described as 'the phlogiston of the social sciences'). Like Giddings, Lundberg argued that science dealt in exact descriptions and generalization, both of which required 'the quantitative statement'. He emphasized the importance of attitude scales in this context, and insisted (in common with earlier positivists) that science cannot formulate value statements, and that sociology must be a science in this mould.

In so far as neo-positivism had a lasting influence on the development of American sociology, this is perhaps best seen in later mathematical sociology, as for example in Richard M. Emerson's attempt to integrate mathematical theory and exchange theory (reported in J. Berger et al. (eds.), *Sociological Theories in Progress*, 1972). There are those (see, for example, J. Gibbs, *Sociological Theory Construction*, 1972) who continue to insist that the most important criterion of a scientific theory is testability, and that only a mathematically formalized theory is empirically testable.

network analysis The term network refers to individuals (or more rarely collectivities and *roles) who are linked together by one or more social relationships, thus forming a social network. Examples of relationship links include *kinship, *communication, *friendship, authority, and sexual contact. When individuals are represented as a point and links as a line, the pairwise choices or relations can be arrayed in a table (called a sociomatrix) and the network drawn from this information is often referred to as a sociogram, which features centrally in *sociometry, an elaborate but simple form of analysis pioneered by J. L. Moreno in the 1940s. The mathematical basis of much network analysis is *graph theory.

Initially, much work concentrated on small-group and institutional structures, describing individual points (stars and isolates) and forms of cohesion (clique-detection), but after the 1950s network analysis concentrated more on structural characteristics, such as 'bridges' (persons who formed the only link between strongly connected groups), 'balance' (the tendency of highly cohesive groups to polarize), and more refined definitions of cliques. In the 1960s and beyond, the analysis of social networks was strongly influenced by developments in *mathematical sociology under Harrison White, became much more highly theoretical, and now supports its own journal (*Social Networks*). White was the focus of a highly productive and innovative group of students and staff at Harvard University in the 1960s and 1970s, and is best known for insisting upon social rather than individualistic concepts (for example, movement of clergy vacancies versus movement of individual clergymen), and for developing block-modelling techniques for studying the 'structural equivalence' of network members sharing the same pattern of contacts. Recent developments have been concerned with the issue of *multidimensional scaling and similar methods to represent networks in social space and to use sophisticated computer techniques to depict these spaces visually.

Three main foci typify work in the area of network analyses. Egocentric networks are rooted in a single individual and depend usually on that individual's report of his or her network (such as, for example, E. Bott's study of the effect of overlap between spouses' networks, *Family and Social Network*, 1957). Systemic networks are constructed from all the participants in the network, and concentrate on the structure of the network itself, as in Mark Granovetter's identification of the importance of the 'weak tie' in obtaining new job information—whereby new information comes not from those who are in one's close circle of interaction, but from those in one's network who have access to different sources (see *Getting a Job*, 1974). Finally, diffusion studies explore the shape and form of flows within the networks, as in the processes of innovation, rumour, or *epidemiological diffusion. For an introduction to key ideas see John Scott, *Social Network Analysis* (3rd edn., 2012) and the more advanced discussion in Stanley Wasserman and Katherine Faust, *Social Network Analysis* (1993). An overview of the field as a whole can be found in John Scott and Peter Carrington (eds.), *The Sage Handbook of Social Network Analysis* (2011). *See also* BALANCE THEORY.

(()) SEE WEB LINKS
• A key site for resources on social network analysis.

neurosis Initially a disorder of the nerves, although Sigmund *Freud distinguished 'actual' and 'psycho-neuroses' (the latter having psychological origins), and the term is now used in this latter sense. Frequently contrasted with *psychoses, neuroses are considered less severe, involving an exaggerated response to reality, such as excessive fear (phobia) or anxiety. Some psychiatric classifications eschew the concept for its aetiological implications. Neuroticism is sometimes identified as an important personality dimension. *See also* DEPRESSION; MENTAL ILLNESS.

neurotic anxiety Anxiety of sufficient severity to be deemed clinical; that is, indicative of a pathological, not a normal state. Psychiatric classifications specify that the anxiety can be diffuse, may involve attacks of panic, and is not attributable to real danger.

neurotic depression An alternative label for reactive depression, it is commonly contrasted with the more severe psychotic or endogenous depressions, although the distinction is now challenged. Worry, tearfulness, feeling worse in the evening, and difficulty in making decisions are considered typical. The hallucinations, delusions, agitation, retardation, and early wakening considered symptomatic of psychotic depression are not usually present. *See also* DEPRESSION.

neutralization of deviance (neutralization of guilt) *See* VOCABULARIES OF MOTIVE.

new deviance theory *See* CRIMINOLOGY, CRITICAL; DEVIANCE; LABELLING; NATIONAL DEVIANCE CONFERENCE.

new international division of labour *See* INTERNATIONAL DIVISION OF LABOUR.

New Left The label commonly applied to *humanist dissidents from *communist parties and to followers of Western Marxism during the period of the Cold War. The contrast is with the Old Left—that is, pro-Soviet communism. It later came to include revivals of Trotskyism and *anarchism, and such Marxisms as *Maoism. The New Left developed in the late 1950s as a self-conscious Marxist and radical intelligentsia, particularly in the United States and Britain, which was critical of *capitalism and *state socialism of the Soviet model in equal measure. It sponsored a number of journals of which *New Left Review* was the most prominent. The movement was given additional impetus by the Soviet invasions of Hungary in 1956 and Czechoslovakia in 1968.

newly industrializing countries (NICs) The dozen or so countries that, in the 1970s and 1980s, achieved high levels of industrial output and penetration of external markets. These include the so-called Four Little Dragons (Hong Kong, South Korea, Singapore, and Taiwan), a group of Latin American countries including Brazil and Mexico, and a handful of late industrializing states in Europe such as Spain and (for a time) Yugoslavia. The emergence of the NICs was seen by *neo-classical economists as significantly undermining the claims of *dependency theorists that less developed nations were doomed to stagnation because of their inability to compete with the West for markets. However, the success of the NICs has been contingent on a considerable degree of state intervention, in order to secure the conditions favourable to *industrialization. The NICs therefore offer no simple formula by which the *Third World can emulate its more industrialized counterparts.

new middle class *See* CONTRADICTORY CLASS LOCATION; PROLETARIANIZATION.

new penology In a series of influential publications Malcolm Feeley and Jonathan Simon (see especially J. Simon, *Poor Discipline*, 1993) have argued that a fundamental shift occurred in crime control strategies in the last decades of the 20th century, which has seen the emergence of a 'New Penology' at the expense of an 'Old Penology'. Their analysis of the new discourses, objectives, and techniques in penal policy has opened up important debates over the cast of recent trends in criminal justice and the nature of a *risk society. In particular, they identify how *crime is increasingly addressed through strategies of risk management based on actuarial techniques (such as statistical distributions, probability calculations, and systemic goals) to minimize offending.

Their overall argument is that, while the 'Old Penology' was preoccupied with establishing guilt and diagnosing the appropriate treatment of the individual offender, the 'New Penology' is no longer concerned with such matters. Instead, it takes crime for granted and accepts that *deviance is widespread. Crucially, it rejects the traditional interventionist philosophies of reform, transformation, and reintegration and is instead concerned with identifying, classifying, and managing groups assorted by levels of dangerousness. They chart how penal discourse has shifted from concentrating on an individual's criminal motivation and moral character to the management of aggregate crime rates using risk assessment technologies. The new goal is not to eliminate crime but to manage dangerous populations, especially through controlling the activities of the *underclass by criminalizing poverty.

There is much evidence to suggest that actuarial techniques and discourses of risk are multiple and mobilized in different ways in various parts of the criminal justice systems of Europe and North America. Preventive detention, offender classifications, parole decisions, life sentences are all using such devices to manage and assess the risk posed by offenders. Yet the scale of these transformations cannot be overestimated as they range from the policing of streets, through to judges passing sentence and encompass not only life on prison landings but have also spread out to shopping centres, 'gated communities', and urban governance more generally.

Although critics tend not to dispute the description of the 'New Penology', there is considerable debate over how 'new' many of the trends are, the precise extent to which they have replaced 'old' concerns, and the way the account ignores the increasingly punitive language of vengeance also articulated by governments over this same time period. *See also* CRIME; DEVIANCE; RISK SOCIETY; UNDERCLASS.

new religions (new religious movements) This concept refers to two separate religious phenomena. First, there are the new religions of aboriginal and tribal people in the *Third World, which are the result of an interaction between local, indigenous religions and *Christianity, and to a lesser extent *Hinduism and *Buddhism. Various terms have been given to such religions: *messianic, nativistic, and revitalization religions. They are seen by anthropologists to be responses or adjustments by relatively powerless people to their social dislocation in the face of direct or indirect colonialism. They often borrow the radical theology of early Christianity to express a profound symbolic protest.

Second, there are new religions in the developed, industrial societies of the West, which are often associated with youth movements and the counter-culture. These are often syncretist, borrowing elements from many different religious and philosophical traditions. Sociologists have claimed that such religions satisfy the psychological and social needs of young people seeking a meaning for life which they cannot find in the mainstream religious traditions. Examples include the Divine Light Mission, Hare Krishna, the Unification Church, and Scientology. They are often termed 'movements' because they are looser and more diffuse than established religions and have some of the characteristics of a *social movement.

Numerous typologies of the latter will be found in the literature. For example, in *The Elementary Forms of the New Religious Life* (1984), Roy Wallis offered a three-fold distinction which identified world-rejecting, world-affirming, and world-accommodating types. The first of these represent attempts to escape from the impersonality, materialism, bureaucratization, and individualism of modern life. The International Society for Krishna Consciousness, Children of God, and Unification Church ('Moonies') are cited as examples. By comparison, movements such as Scientology, Transcendental Meditation, and the Japanese Soka Gakkai claim to offer practitioners greater success in achieving goals already set by the status quo, including individual material advancement, psychological well-being, and social popularity: they are therefore world-affirming. Finally, innovatory religions with a world-accommodating orientation carry few implications either for individual conduct in, or for rejection of, the larger secular world, since their primary purpose is to provide stimulation for personal and spiritual experiences. Religions such as the Charismatic Renewal and Neo-Pentecostalism simply instruct adherents to live life (however it is lived) in a more enthusiastically religious manner.

Wallis's typology is, however, only one of many possible classifications. Some idea of the alternatives, and of the enormous literature now available on this general topic, can be gained from Thomas Robbins's lengthy bibliographical essay on 'Cults, Converts and Charisma', *Current Sociology* (1988). *See also* SECULARIZATION.

(⊕) SEE WEB LINKS
- The official site of INFORM, providing sociologically informed material on new religions.

New Right A political philosophy and its proponents, particularly associated with the Thatcher and Reagan administrations in Britain and the United States during the 1980s, that represented a radical break with social democratic values—most visibly in rhetoric but also in practice. Frequently listed beliefs include commitment to the free *market, to individual freedom, and to the reduction of state intervention and *welfare; a *populist morality; and authoritarianism (*see* AUTHORITARIAN PERSONALITY).

During the 1980s, some sociologists built on New Right ideas to argue that their discipline had come to be dominated by the *domain assumptions of a Leftist or Social Democratic political agenda, being implicitly opposed to the market and obsessed by issues of *inequality. In one of the most elegant of such critiques, Peter Berger offered fifty propositions about prosperity, equality, and liberty, which link the attainment of all three closely to the aggressive pursuit of a free-market *capitalism (see *The Capitalist Revolution*, 1986). *See also* MONT PELERIN SOCIETY.

new social movements *See* SOCIAL MOVEMENTS.

new technology Any set of productive techniques which offers a significant improvement (whether measured in terms of increased output or savings in costs) over the established *technology for a given process in a specific historical context. Defined thus, what is seen as *new is obviously subject to continual redefinition, as successive changes in technology are undertaken.

At the time of writing, the current new technologies that are of most interest to sociologists are the information and communications technologies based on microelectronics, the application of which is said by some to be revolutionizing the organization of work. Among the trends which have been identified as alleged consequences of these technologies are those towards de-skilling, proletarianization, automation, telecommuting, flexible employment, just-in-time systems, and the creation of dual or split labour markets and a new international division of labour—all of which are dealt with separately in this dictionary. The assumed effects of new technology sometimes form the basis for apocalyptic accounts of wholesale social change—as, for example, in the theories of post-industrial and self-service societies.

Systematic sociological research invariably reveals that all of these tendencies and theories are overstated by their authors, and that the social and political impact of new technologies is complex and contingent, being subject to variations in managerial strategies, worker resistance, and a host of other cultural and political circumstances (see, for example, the series of case studies reported in B. Wilkinson's *The Shopfloor Politics of the New Technology*, 1983).

new working class A term associated with the thesis that process workers in *automated industries, and white-collar workers in large industrial *corporations, possess the potential to assume the historic revolutionary role of the *proletariat anticipated by *Marxism. Both groups have become productive workers in the functional sense that their expertise is indispensable to the most advanced sectors of the capitalist *labour process. Yet, at the same time, it provides them with the intellectual tools to recognize and challenge the power structure of *capitalism and the (from their point of interest) allegedly irrational *market system by which it is accompanied. Though most recently associated with Serge Mallet, and other members of the *Sociologie du Travail movement in France, the argument that 'engineers' are in some sense a new revolutionary vanguard may be found in the writings of Thorstein *Veblen and the Technicist Movement.

In *La Nouvelle Classe ouvrière* (1965), Mallet argued that the old working class of the archaic industries (coal-mining and such like) could no longer envisage an alternative society. Rather, 'only the strata of the active population who are involved in the most advanced processes of technological civilization are up to formulating alienations and envisaging superior forms of development'. Modern industries (such as oil-refining and chemicals) are characterized by automation, which is said to increase the responsibility and involvement of workers in enterprises; to make obvious the links between the well-being of the firm, the workers' pay, and his or her expertise; and so encourage employees to campaign for greater control over management of the processes of production. Plant-based unionism (*syndicalisme d'entreprise*) further encourages workforce solidarity, and 'the more the modern worker reconquers *at the collective level* the occupational autonomy he lost during the mechanization phases of work, the more trends develop towards a demand for control.' By restoring issues of autonomy and control to the centre-stage of the struggle between labour and capital, the new working class transcends the narrow economism (wage-orientation) of its predecessors, and comes to form the vanguard of a grassroots revolutionary movement for socialism.

For a thesis that was (at best) weakly substantiated by some rather questionable data, Mallet's argument proved remarkably influential in the Western industrial sociology (not to say the industrial and political turmoil) of the late 1960s, although systematic research soon made its empirical weaknesses obvious (see, for example, D. Gallie's *In Search of the New Working Class*, 1978). Factual inaccuracies aside, the thesis also suffered from *technological determinism, analogous to that which underpinned the alternative arguments proffered by the *embourgeoisement theorists; a failure to take the power of the *state seriously; ambiguity about precisely which strata of employees were involved (Mallet identifies two types of 'new worker'—process workers and technicians—but both groups include a list of rather vague occupational categories); and serious imprecision, both in defining central concepts (such as automation), and in specifying the precise causal mechanisms linking technical milieu, high earnings, and unionization of employees.

Recent empirical work stimulated by the new working-class thesis shows that it greatly oversimplifies and even exaggerates the extent to which the latest technologies of large-scale industrial production transform traditional distinctions between mental and manual labour (*see* MANUAL VERSUS NON-MANUAL DISTINCTION). On the other hand this research yielded much evidence that the objective class situation (though not necessarily the class consciousness) of much white-collar work is being affected by information technology. However, in the opinion of some writers, the more precarious global markets of the late 20th century have ushered in an era of post-fordism and *flexible employment, involving smaller-scale firms and more traditional craft-based forms of production, as a result of which automated technology and large-scale production, and along with it the thesis of the new working class, appears *passé*.

Nietzsche, Friedrich (1844–1900) A German philosopher, one of the great (if not the greatest of) modern iconoclasts, Nietzsche has been read as the precursor of such varied phenomena as Nazism and *postmodernism. Essentially, he appears to have been outraged by the lack of reflexivity among philosophers and scientists who failed to apply to their own thoughts the rigorous questioning they applied to those of others, a reaction which led him to dispute the supposed *rationalism, scientism, and *humanism of modern Western societies. Against this, he upheld the ideals of individualism, self-reliance, competition, and élitism. The three terms that summarize both the reasons for the continuing controversy over his thought, and the results of his own self-questioning, are 'nihilism', 'will to power', and 'superman'. Among those said to have been influenced by his works are Max *Weber and Michel *Foucault. Most of his books are available in good modern translations. Amongst the best-known are *The Gay Science* (1882), *Thus Spoke Zarathustra* (1883–92), *Beyond Good and Evil* (1886), *On the Genealogy of Morals* (1887), and *Ecce Homo* (1908).

nomads (nomadism) Terms used to refer to groups who move from place to place, without a year-round permanent residence; bedouins are an example. Anthropologists have distinguished two broad types based on hunting-gathering and pastoralism respectively. The extent to which *hunter-gatherers or *pastoralists are independent of other sedentary groups is empirically variable. In the *ideal type they are economically self-sufficient. A third nomadic group, excluded from the classical typology, are Gypsies, who are always interdependent with another economy, within which they provide occasional goods and services. Groups may be semi-nomadic—as in the case of some contemporary Lapps. See Judith Okely, *The Traveller-Gypsies* (1983).

nominalism, philosophical *See* REALISM; TARDE.

nomothetic *See* IDEOGRAPHIC VERSUS NOMOTHETIC APPROACHES.

non-decision-making A concept that emerged in critiques of decision-making approaches current in studies of *power carried out from within *pluralism. Non-decision-making is the ability to operate behind the scenes to prevent issues from entering the sphere of decision-making. As a hidden and largely unobservable process it is difficult to study empirically. However, failing to study non-decision-making, it is argued, leads to a superficial view of power that does not come to grips with its reality. The key source is Peter Bachrach and Morton Baratz, *Power and Poverty* (1970). *See also* COMMUNITY POWER.

non-participant observation A research technique whereby the researcher watches the subjects of his or her study, with their knowledge, but without taking an active part in the situation under scrutiny. This approach is sometimes criticized on the grounds that the very fact of their being observed may lead people to behave differently, thus invalidating the data obtained, as for example in the famous case of the so-called *Hawthorne effect. To overcome this, researchers normally observe a number of similar situations, over a period of time. Although video-cameras can now be used in non-participant observation, this too may alter (indeed almost certainly will alter) the behaviour of the research subjects. *See also* PARTICIPANT OBSERVATION.

non-response The proportion of people among those invited to participate in an interview, *survey, or other study, who choose not to take part or are unobtainable for other reasons. Non-response covers all causes of non-participation: refusals, people who are away temporarily on holiday for example, and non-contacts for other reasons. Those who are found to be outside the scope of the survey are classified as ineligible and excluded altogether. Ineligibles would include people who had died or moved to an area outside the survey area, businesses that had closed down, and demolished addresses. Non-response is a good indicator of response bias: as a general rule the higher the proportion of non-respondents to a survey, the greater the degree of bias among those who chose to participate. Rules of thumb for acceptable levels of survey response vary, but 60 per cent would generally be regarded as the bare minimum, with 75 per cent regarded as very good, and anything above that as excellent. Non-response above 40 per cent would normally be regarded as high enough to vitiate the results obtained from a survey or study, as non-participants roughly equal participants.

In industrial societies, there are periodic declines in survey response rates, as reflected in all the regular major national surveys which monitor response-rates very closely. Declining response rates are met with renewed efforts to encourage participation, and reassure people on doubts about confidentiality and uses of the data. But they indicate that the survey method could become over-utilized, and that people are becoming increasingly well informed about social research and its uses. *See also* SAMPLING; SAMPLING ERROR.

non-standard worker (non-standard employment) These terms refer to forms of *employment that lack the job-stability and entitlement to fringe benefits, union membership, and the social security of full-time, stable ('standard') employees. Non-standard employment includes part-time work, temporary work, fixed-term contracting and subcontracting, self-employment, and homework. Non-standard forms of employment are thought to have grown in recent years with the increase in *flexible production methods. *See also* LABOUR-MARKET SEGMENTATION.

non-verbal communication Forms of communication which do not rely on the spoken or written word. Facial gestures and hand signals can often give messages to another person without a word being said. In some cultures, for example, the reverse 'V' sign or a single-finger gesture often speaks louder than words. Most such forms of communication, including rude gestures, are culturally specific in their meanings. *See also* BODY LANGUAGE.

norm (social norm, normative) In sociology a norm is a shared expectation of behaviour that is considered culturally desirable and/or appropriate. Norms are similar to rules or regulations in being prescriptive, although they lack the formal status of rules. Actual behaviour may differ from what is considered normative and, if judged by existing norms, may be deemed *deviant. Consequently the concept is intimately linked to issues of social regulation and *social control and to the dominant sociological problem of *social order. In this sense the idea of what is normative is crucial to lay and sociological understandings of social interaction. The terms norms and normative are, however, also frequently used in a statistical sense to refer to what is common or typical, whether of behaviour or some other phenomenon.

The sociological concept of norm is closely allied to that of *role, which is commonly defined as a set of norms attached to a social position. Parsons suggested that norms are beliefs about what individuals ought to do, and become part of a person's motivation through *socialization, so that people come to act in conformity with the norms of their society precisely because they want to conform. There has been a recognition that the norms defining roles should not be seen as fixed or rigid. Interactionist sociology (with its focus on the negotiation of meanings), *ethnomethodology, and *postmodernist theory, all tend to emphasize the complexity and diversity of meanings, and the shifting and fragmented nature of individual identities and the norms that underpin them. From this point of view, norms are perceptions of what actions will lead others to validate an *identity (rather than personal beliefs), so that people are thought to conform to norms in order to demonstrate to themselves and others that they are a particular kind of person. Other theorists, notably Marxists, have emphasized the importance of *power and coercion in sustaining or replacing normative consensus in the maintenance of social order.

normal curve *See* NORMAL DISTRIBUTION.

normal distribution In common usage, normality is treated as synonymous with natural, conventional, acceptable, or ordinary. In statistics, normality is defined as the most commonly occurring, the numerically most frequent type, which is then used as the base-line for identifying the unusual and the statistically rare.

The normal distribution is a hypothetical mathematical distribution that provides an idealized model for comparison with observed variable distributions, and is the most commonly used mathematical model in *statistical inference. In form it is a symmetrical, bell-shaped curve. The normal distribution for any particular *variable is defined by its mean and standard deviation.

The mathematical properties of the normal distribution can be used to estimate the proportion in a sample falling above or below any particular reading or measurement for any variable to which the model is being applied. In many circumstances it will serve as a reasonable model, even in cases where observed variable distributions appear to be rather inadequate approximations to normality. *See also* VARIATION (STATISTICAL); CENTRAL TENDENCY (MEASURES OF).

normalization The *normal distribution is one of the key distributions providing the basis for probability statistics, so that when a particular distribution is not normal, some transformation of the data may be attempted so as to achieve a normal distribution—for example charting the logarithms of values instead of the values themselves. This is known as normalizing the distribution.

normal science *See* PARADIGM.

normative functionalism *See* PARSONS.

normative order Any system of rules and shared expectations governing a particular social situation. The concept occurs most frequently in *functionalist theory, especially the normative functionalism of writers such as Talcott *Parsons, where the various elements of the normative order (notably shared value-commitments but also obligations of membership and sentiments of loyalty) operate to secure *social order. The centrality of the societal normative order to Parsonian accounts of social stability is evident in his claim that 'societal order requires clear and definite integration in the sense, on one hand, of normative coherence and, on the other, of societal "harmony" and "coordination". Moreover, normatively-defined obligations must on the whole be accepted while conversely, collectivities must have normative sanction in performing their functions and promoting their legitimate interests. Thus, normative order at the societal level contains a "solution" to the problem posed by Hobbes—of preventing human relations from degenerating into a "war of all against all"' (*The System of Modern Societies*, 1971). This is probably as concise a statement of the organizing principle of Parsons's sociological theory as occurs anywhere in his voluminous writings. *See also* CONSENSUS; HOBBES.

normative power *See* COMPLIANCE.

normative theory Hypotheses or other statements about what is right and wrong, desirable or undesirable, just or unjust in society. The majority of sociologists consider it illegitimate to move from explanation to evaluation. In their view, sociology should strive to be value-free, objective, or at least to avoid making explicit *value-judgements. This is because, according to the most popular philosophies of the social sciences, conflicts over values cannot be settled factually. Moral pronouncements cannot be objectively shown to be true or false, since value-judgements are subjective preferences, outside the realm of rational inquiry. Marxist sociologists generally subscribe to a different view of the relationship between facts and values, arguing with *Marx that 'the philosophers have only interpreted the world, in various ways; the point... is to change it'.

The majority of sociological enquiries are therefore analytical and explanatory. They do not pose normative questions such as 'Which values ought to provide for social order?' and 'How ought society to organize itself?'

However, some contemporary sociologists have attempted to find non-relativist foundations for solutions to ethical issues, for example by identifying those moral principles that ought to regulate social relationships and institutions. Derek L. Phillips (*Toward a Just Social Order*, 1986) has advanced the controversial argument that since claims about truth and knowledge (no less than statements about what ought to be) rest on consensus among a community of enquirers, both explanatory and normative theories share the same *epistemological status, and are therefore equally open to rational justification.

This sort of normative theorizing is still a minority pursuit within the discipline, although sociologists generally are often subject to accusations that their analyses are tacitly normative, as being biased by non-scientific values and political objectives.

norm of reciprocity *See* RATIONAL CHOICE THEORY.

nuclear family *See* FAMILY, NUCLEAR.

nurture *See* NATURE VERSUS NURTURE DEBATE.

Oakley, Ann (1944–) A British sociologist, writing from a feminist stand-point on issues of gender, work, family relations, and social policy. She has also written a number of novels, an autobiography, and intellectual studies of Richard Titmuss (her father) and Barbara Wootton (*A Critical Woman: Barbara Wootton, Social Science and Public Policy in the Twentieth Century*, 2011). She established her reputation with the publication of the influential book *Sex, Gender, and Society* (1972), which established the distinction between sex and gender and the importance of both as topics of sociological discussion. A series of books on housework, pregnancy, and motherhood followed (*The Sociology of Housework*, 1974, and *Subject Women*, 1981, being among these). Subsequent studies explore these issues in relation to health and the body, focusing especially on the intervention of medical practices. She has written on gender and method, exploring the relationship between qualitative research and randomized control methods, and has written a reflection on her own research practices. She has investigated wider issues of health and the body and produced a major study of environmental issues (*Gender on Planet Earth*, 2002). In 2011 she received a Lifetime Achievement Award from the British Sociological Association.

(((⊕))) SEE WEB LINKS
- Her own website is http://www.annoakley.co.uk/

objective (objectivity) In the dispute between those who view sociology as actually or potentially a science, and those who advocate some other model of intellectual activity (such as textual interpretation, the sympathetic understand-ing characteristic of interpersonal dialogue, or the struggle for self-clarification on the psychoanalyst's couch), the concept of objectivity is an important weapon. The term objective may refer to an attitude of mind deemed proper to a scientific investigator: detached, unprejudiced, open to whatever the evidence may reveal. Alternatively, it may be applied to the method of investigation employed, or to its outcome—some theory or substantive knowledge-claim. Much of what is taught in courses on sociological method are procedures designed to protect investiga-tions from *bias in the collection or interpretation of evidence: random sampling, the use of controls, piloting of questionnaires with alternative wordings, and so on are designed to eliminate biases and ensure objectivity. A study conducted in the appropriate spirit of scientific objectivity, having rigorously employed such methods, may justifiably claim to be objective in the further usage of adequately representing the object of study, rather than the subjective wishes and prejudices of the investigator.

Opponents of the scientific model for sociological enquiry often argue that objectivity (in attitude, method, or outcome) is either unobtainable or inappropriate in sociology. This may be because of what are deemed to be special features of sociology (and other social sciences) or it may be that (as in the case of some radical feminist critiques of 'logo-centrism') objectivity is rejected as an appropriate or attainable standard for any form of enquiry, including the natural sciences. This often involves a stance of epistemological *relativism.

Objectivity as an attitude on the part of the investigator may also be rejected as inappropriate in signalling a morally or politically reprehensible detachment in relation to other human beings, or as unattainable, given the sociologist's own unavoidable social or political engagement. Such views often set subjectivity against objectivity. This may lead to the claim that only an expression of shared *values, or mutual activity on the part of investigator and subject of research, could elicit the required inter-subjective understandings.

Recent discussions have rejected this opposition of subjectivity and objectivity and have seen the possibility of avoiding relativism and achieving an objective account that is properly grounded in the diversity of standpoints from which knowledge can be pursued. While sociology, and other branches of social science, must be responsive to its own social and historical location and to the embodied character of the sociologists who engage in it, knowledge can be achieved that is both impartial and empirically valid. These issues are explored in Gayle Letherby et al., *Objectivity and Subjectivity in Social Research* (2013).

Object Relations Theory Since its formulation by Sigmund *Freud, psychoanalytic theory has developed into many distinct schools of thought. One of these is the so-called Object Relations School, which was originally associated with the names of (among others) W. R. D. Fairbairn and D. W. *Winnicott, but also much influenced by the work of Melanie *Klein. In essence, Object Relations Theory offers a much more social view of psychological development than does the earlier Freudian account, seeing individuals as formed in relation to, and seeking connection with, other individuals. Instead of Freud's notion of libidinal stages of child development, it emphasizes the gradual differentiation of the self through the formation of reflections of experiences of real people from earliest infancy, or in other words of internal 'objects'. The term 'object' denotes the person or persons (or his or her inner representatives) with whom a subject is intensely involved emotionally. It is these initial experiences with other people, according to the theory, that structure and form later relationships.

A central aspect of Object Relations Theory is the primary attachment of infants to their mothers. Feminist theorists have been attracted to this emphasis on the centrality of the maternal, and have drawn on the theory to develop a causal account of gender difference. Gender differences, it is argued, originate in the infantile development process in which female and male infants experience different patterns of struggle to separate from the mother. For example, Nancy Chodorow (in *The Reproduction of Mothering*, 1978) describes how personality develops in terms of both innate drives and relations with other people, or 'objects'.

observation *See* COVERT OBSERVATION; NON-PARTICIPANT OBSERVATION; OVERT PARTICIPANT OBSERVATION; PARTICIPANT OBSERVATION.

observer bias This refers to the cultural assumptions which all researchers bring to their work and which help determine their method of research and their observations. It has been argued by some that all enquiry (including 'pure' science) is simply a reflection of such biases. In any event, researchers are usually encouraged to make any known biases explicit in reporting their findings, in order to assist others wishing to reach a judgement as to the *validity of the results.

occupation An economic role separated from household activity as a result of the growth of markets for labour. Such roles form part of a wider economic *division of labour in an industrial enterprise, formal organization, or socio-economic structure. *See* LABOUR MARKET; OCCUPATIONAL CLASSIFICATION; OCCU-PATIONAL SEGREGATION.

occupational career *See* CAREER.

occupational classification The smallest unit of an occupational classifi-cation is the concept of a job, defined as a set of tasks to be performed by an individual, and commonly identified by a job title. Occupation is often synony-mous with job but may refer to a group of similar jobs identified with a common occupational title. Jobs and occupations can be described not only in terms of tasks, but also in terms of associated characteristics such as *skill, responsibility, earnings, entry qualifications, and prestige (*see* STATUS). More diffuse character-istics may derive from the incumbents of occupations, such as lifestyle, cultural mannerisms, and so forth.

Occupational classifications are essentially ways of grouping and ranking jobs and occupations. Systems of classification vary according to which criteria are given priority during the exercise, and these may differ depending upon the purpose of the intended analysis, and the theoretical framework deployed. Most classifications are developed by national census offices for the production of national employment data, the most common classification being the Inter-national Standard Classification of Occupations (ISCO) developed by the International Labour Organization, of which there are now several versions distinguished by their year of first publication (hence the 'ISCO-68' and 'ISCO-88' classifications). The latest (1988) classification is based on the concepts of job ('the set of tasks and duties executed') and skill (both in terms of skill level, or 'the complexity and range of the tasks and duties involved', and skill specialization, defined by 'the field of knowledge required, the tools and machinery used, the materials worked on or with, as well as the kinds of goods and services pro-duced'). This yields a pyramid whose hierarchical structure consists of ten major groups, at the top level of aggregation, subdivided into 28 sub-major groups, 116 minor groups, and 390 unit groups. Thus, for example, within major group 4 (clerks), sub-major group 41 is office clerks, which includes minor group 412 (numerical clerks), comprising the two unit groups 4121 (accounting and book-keeping clerks) and 4122 (statistical and finance clerks). The US Census Bureau and UK Office of National Statistics produce their own—rather different—classifications.

In sociology, occupational data are commonly used for the analysis of *status attainment and *occupational mobility, so consistent criteria of classification and a hierarchical arrangement of grouped data are sometimes considered important. Class theorists who focus on work situation and market situation favour classifications of occupations based on sources and levels of income, employment status, or conditions of employment, the best example being the Goldthorpe Classes (referred to in some countries as the Erikson-Goldthorpe-Portocarero Classes), which are derived in the British case from the UK census office classification of occupations and employment statuses (see R. Erikson and J. H. Goldthorpe, *The Constant Flux*, 1992). Those who equate social class with social status have often used subjective assessments of *occupational prestige as the basis of class standing, as for example in the Hope—Goldthorpe Scale of Occupational Prestige (see J. H. Goldthorpe and K. Hope, *The Social Grading of Occupations*, 1974).

Most occupational classifications are said to embody a male bias, reflected in the way occupations are distinguished, grouped, and ranked. Occupations filled largely by women are frequently grouped together at a very low level of aggregation (as, for example, in the case of clerical occupations) so that they cannot subsequently be disaggregated and relocated as circumstances change. Similarly, the skill and status level of occupations dominated by women may be underestimated, possibly distorting the location of such occupations in some subsequent derived status classifications.

Social and economic change continually modifies the occupational structure and limits the capacity of any particular classification to reflect this structure over time. Continual updating is therefore necessary, although this then further complicates the process of identifying changes in the occupational structure over time, since some of these may simply be artefacts of the changing classification itself.

occupational community *See* IMAGES OF SOCIETY.

occupational mobility Often wrongly called *social mobility. It refers to the movement of an occupational group itself, or of an individual member of an occupation, or of an occupational vacancy, through the stratification system of social space. Studies of the Hindu *caste system illustrate the first; father-son occupational achievement the second; and Harrison White's study of clergy vacancy-chains the third.

Most studies assume a unidimensional gradation of *occupations in terms of their prestige or *status against which movement is then assessed. Thus, 'downward' mobility refers to loss, and 'upward' mobility to increase in occupational prestige. An important distinction is to be drawn between *within* or intragenerational mobility (for example career patterns) and *between* or intergenerational mobility (for example caste mobility or father-son achievement). Following classic studies in the United States and Europe, many national studies now exist of status achievement of children (especially sons) from their parental origins, symbolized by the Father-Son Turnover Table, which indicates the occupational destination of the offspring of parents in a given occupational category, and conversely, the parental occupational origins of children now in a given category. The analysis of this table forms the core of many conventional studies of occupational mobility, but structural models, which interrelate the complex network of dependence of variables affecting achievement, are now the preferred form of analysis. *See also* STATUS ATTAINMENT.

occupational prestige Occupational prestige refers primarily to the differential social evaluation that is ascribed to jobs or *occupations. What people know about jobs, or how people view occupations, is to a greater extent a given; much more variation exists in the value that they ascribe to them.

To ask how people rate the 'general standing' of an occupation (the most common question) is taken to be a measure of occupational prestige and hence of the social *status of occupations, though many other criteria have been proposed, including 'social usefulness' as well as 'prestige' and 'status' themselves. In order to obtain the scale of occupations (which is invariably taken to be national in application), respondents' ratings are aggregated, typically by taking either the average or, as in the classic American study by C. C. North and P. K. Hatt in 1947 ('Jobs and Occupations: A Popular Evaluation', *Opinion News*), by taking the percentage who adjudged the occupation as having 'excellent social standing'. The resulting aggregate rank-order gives the scale. Variations in ratings are given little attention, though they are often considerable and consistent, and it is a matter of some dispute whether there exist consistent social differences in perception and evaluation. Much has been made by structural-functionalists of the extent to which different national averaged rankings correlate, but this is probably due as much to the necessary restriction to a few very familiar stereotypical occupations, as to any widespread cross-national consensus.

Occupational prestige scores feature centrally in a wide range of empirical sociological studies of social class formation, educational attainment, and occupational inheritance through *social mobility, though their substantive and methodological meaning is sometimes obscure. The most widely used scale of occupational prestige in comparative studies of occupational mobility is probably the so-called Treiman Scale (see D. J. Treiman, *Occupational Prestige in Comparative Perspective*, 1977). *See also* STATUS ATTAINMENT.

occupational segregation The division of labour, in the context of paid *employment, as a result of which men and women (or members of different ethnic or religious groupings) are channelled into different types of occupational roles and tasks, such that there are two (or more) separate labour forces. It is conventional to distinguish vertical job segregation, by which (say) male or white employees are concentrated in the higher-status and better-paid positions, from horizontal job segregation (where the different sexes or ethnic groups work in different types of occupation—men are engineers, women are typists, and so on). This distinction is discussed further in the entry on the *division of labour.

It is important not to confuse occupational segregation (which refers to those processes by which individuals or groups holding particular jobs are kept apart, so that there is little effective competition between them) with *labour-market segmentation (the term usually applied to the differentiation of *labour markets into discrete firm-specific segments, each offering different career rewards, conditions of employment, and so forth). There is no necessary relationship between the two, since there are societies where the sexes are separated into different sorts of occupations, but women enjoy relatively good working conditions and career opportunities (at least when compared with other societies in which there is a similar degree of occupational segregation by sex).

Occupational segregation by sex is widespread in all industrialized societies (although it occurs to varying degrees); segregation by ethnic group is more common in the United States than Europe; occupational segregation by religion occurs less frequently (although, for example, to some extent there are still separate labour markets for Protestants and Catholics in Northern Ireland).

Measurement problems loom large in empirical studies of occupational segregation. What proportion of workers in one occupation as against another need to belong to a particular ethnic group in order for us to speak meaningfully of occupational segregation? To what extent must one sex rather than the other dominate the higher-grade and higher-paid occupations before vertical job segregation can be said to exist? One popular measure of horizontal segregation is the *dissimilarity index, but various alternative coefficients of both vertical and horizontal segregation are in common use, including for example the coefficient of female representation (which is calculated for each of the major occupational groupings by dividing its female share of employment by the female share of total employment). Many of these indices are sensitive to the degree of detail in the *occupational classification that is being used—the more detailed the classification, the greater the degree of occupational segregation that tends to be identified—an important point when comparisons are being made across time and nations (since crossnational standardized occupational classifications are still encountered relatively infrequently in both social *surveys and *official statistics). Researchers are increasingly aware that any single number index of occupational segregation is unlikely to reveal patterns of change within the occupational structure. One alternative is to measure the differences between integrated and segregated occupations in terms of their relative importance across groups and time. These sorts of measurement problems are analogous to those discussed in the literature on *social mobility.

Various theories of *patriarchy and *human capital link the segregation of men and women in employment to the *domestic division of labour. Ethnic segregation in employment is also addressed by human-capital theory, but more commonly explained as a consequence of *discrimination, or (historically) as a legacy of *colonialism. Catherine Hakim's *Key Issues in Women's Work: Female Heterogeneity and the Polarisation of Women's Employment* (1996) contains a comprehensive review of the measurement problems and competing explanations for occupational segregation by sex; offers an empirical study of employment data for a number of industrial societies; and suggests a (controversial) interpretation of workforce polarization and women's subordination in terms of beliefs about the sexual division of labour in the home and the ideology of sexual differences in general—rather than the more commonly suggested consequences following from inequalities of opportunity between the sexes.

occupational socialization The learning of attitudes and behaviours necessary to recognized and sustainable competence within a context of employment. These include skills acquired through training, informal work norms, and peer-group values and relationships.

occupational structure This refers to the aggregate distribution of *occupations in society, classified according to skill level, economic function, or social status. The occupational structure is shaped by various factors: the structure of the economy (the relative weight of different industries); *technology and *bureaucracy (the distribution of technological skills and administrative responsibility); the *labour market (which determines the pay and conditions attached to occupations); and by *status and prestige (influenced by occupational *closure, lifestyle, and social values). It is difficult to attach causal primacy to any one of these factors; moreover, their role in shaping the occupational structure changes over time, as society changes. For example, during the early phase of European *industrialization, the dominance of *manufacturing made for a preponderance of manual occupations, while in recent times the shrinking of this sector, together with the growth in services, has made for an expansion of white-collar occupations. The distinction between *manual and non-manual occupations has also become blurred.

The occupational structure is described and analysed by means of various classificatory schemes, which group similar occupations together according to specific criteria such as skill, employment status, or function. Such classifications are also used as a basis for the empirical analysis of economic and social class. *See also* INDUSTRIAL SECTOR; OCCUPATIONAL CLASSIFICATION.

Oedipal stage (Oedipus complex) *See* PSYCHOANALYSIS.

official statistics Statistical information produced, collated, and disseminated by national governments, their agencies, and the international bodies which link them. These data are almost invariably nationally representative, because they are obtained from complete *censuses or very large-scale national sample *surveys, and they usually seek to present definitive information conforming to international definitions and classifications or other well-established conventions. The impersonal character of official statistics, and their resistance to innovation, stand in sharp contrast to statistics and data-sets from other sources: academic research, market research, independent research institutes, commercial organizations, local, regional, and state bodies.

Official statistics used invariably to be published in large tomes and preserved in book libraries as the definitive record. This method of dissemination underlined their inflexibility, forced the results of enquiries to be presented in a relatively small number of selective statistical indicators and indexes, and is disappearing rapidly with extensive use of information technology. In the 1990s and beyond, government statistical information is far more likely to be disseminated as computer tapes of anonymized *microdata, as data subsets on diskette, or as specially compiled harmonized time-series on diskette with monthly updates sent through national and international computer networks or the telecommunications system. Instead of finding the statistics one needs in a printed volume, interested parties may now have to create and extract them from a diskette with built-in software, or dial into a national-user-service computer centre from a desk-top terminal and extract the figures required from regularly updated databases. Many printed tables are now also published in online form, allowing a more flexible use of the data.

As yet, national governments have refused to pass legislation permitting large-scale data linkage between government agencies, and such a proposal would require a system of unique identity-card numbers (or other referencing system) for each person in the population, to be used from birth to death. Data protection policies currently impede such a development within the commercial sector also, although area-based social profiles are widely used in Western industrial societies. Until such time as massive government data-banks are permitted, the only information held by central government agencies is that supplied directly to them by citizens in response either to public enquiries, or to regulations that specify events to be formally recorded in public records and the like.

Almost all official statistics originally came from registers in which were recorded the details of specified events as and when they occurred: births, deaths, marriages, divorces, crimes, certain contagious diseases, and later notifiable diseases such as cancer, AIDS, and so on. Similar procedures are involved in administrative records of non-compulsory activities, such as claiming unemployment benefits. A decreasing proportion of data comes from these sorts of records. Their chief advantage is that they constitute complete censuses of the events in question, and are thus reliable, up-to-date, and cheap to use as sources of statistics. The obvious disadvantage is that only a fairly narrow range of information lends itself to being collected through such procedures. While the fact of a death may be easy to record, its cause may be more arguable; and other related factors are simply too complex to deal with in that way, however relevant. Certain statistics are still obtained from compulsory registrations and administrative records—for example hospital records of patient illnesses, police records of crime, and records of people claiming various types of social insurance benefits. But they are supplemented with, and increasingly replaced by, specially designed data collections: compulsory censuses of population, housing, and employment, and voluntary interview surveys with national samples of the whole adult population or particular sections of it.

Censuses are usually carried out only once a decade, and are supplemented by a range of regular surveys that provide statistical information on a quarterly basis, an annual basis, or at less frequent intervals. Most countries now have an annual multipurpose household survey to collect social and economic data in the intercensal decade. In Germany it is called the microcensus and in the United States the Current Population Survey; in most other countries it is called the Labour Force Survey; and it collects a much wider range of information than the census it replaces. In addition there is a great variety of other data collections using survey methods with personal, postal, or telephone questionnaires to collect information of a kind that can be coded and quantified to produce statistics on a great range of matters: earnings and incomes; trade; illness, health, and usage of the medical services; housing, job change, and migration; household expenditure patterns; the Retail Price Index; national economic accounts; government expenditures; patterns of food consumption and nutrition; any experience as the victim of crime; leisure activities; travel patterns to work, for business, and for leisure; international travel, immigration, and emigration. In addition there is a huge range of *ad hoc* sample surveys carried out by national governments on a wide variety of topics of public concern, sometimes on a once-off basis, sometimes with repeat surveys every five, ten, or twenty years.

The exact number and variety of regular and *ad hoc* national government-funded surveys varies in line with local needs and circumstances. In many cases they are funded and carried out jointly with other bodies, such as independent research institutes, international bodies, charitable foundations, or commercial organizations. The dividing-line between 'official' and 'non-official' statistics and data-sets is being eroded by the change of emphasis from public-sector records and registers, which are necessarily a government preserve, to interview surveys, which are available to all sectors of society, and may even be more successful if carried out by a non-governmental agency.

The use of official statistics, especially of *criminal statistics, has been subject to much criticism. Those who study the social organization and production of statistics see them not as resources (towards an explanation of a particular social phenomenon), but as topics of investigation in their own right. In an early paper ('A Note on Official Statistics', *Social Problems*, 1962), John Kitsuse and Aaron Cicourel argued that criminal statistics should not be taken as objective indicators of the *crime-rate, but instead should be examined as displays of social organization—of the work of statistics-keeping agencies. Similarly, Jack Douglas in *The Social Meanings of Suicide* (1967) suggested the same treatment should be accorded Émile Durkheim's suicide statistics, by treating them as the problem to be explained rather than as an objective or true measure of the suicide rate. There is a clear connection between this work and the *ethnomethodological critique of sociology as a 'folk discipline' which takes commonsense meanings for granted. This critique has been formulated as 'ethnostatistics' by Robert Gephart (*Ethnostatistics*, 1988), who defines the enterprise as 'the study of the construction, interpretation, and the display of statistics in quantitative social research'. See the general reviews in Ruth Levitas and Will Guy, *Interpreting Official Statistics* (1996).

(⊕) SEE WEB LINKS

- UK website for National Statistics.
- US Census Bureau.

Ogburn, William Fielding (1886–1959) An early *Chicago sociologist, President of the American Sociological Association in 1929, his prime interest was in processes of social *change, and in this context he developed the concept of *cultural lag. A good selection of his work will be found in *On Cultural and Social Change* (1964).

oligarchy Any form of government in which there is 'rule by a few'; for example, by members of a self-regulating *elite having *domination over a larger society. *See also* MICHELS; POLITICAL SOCIOLOGY.

oligopoly Competition amongst the few, where perceptions of competitors' policies and reactions to perceived intentions count for more than price-output considerations. Duopoly (control exercised by two competing agencies) is a special case of oligopoly, and a concrete example of the problems this creates for competition and the entry of new actors into the market is demonstrated by the privatized UK electricity supply industry, which is a very effective duopoly. *See also* MONOPOLY.

ontology Any way of understanding the world, or some part of it, must make assumptions (which may be implicit or explicit) about what kinds of things do or can exist in that domain, and what might be their conditions of existence, relations of dependency, and so on. Such an inventory of kinds of being and their relations is an ontology. In this sense, each special science, including sociology, may be said to have its own ontology (for example, persons, institutions, relations, norms, practices, structures, roles, or whatever, depending on the particular sociological theory under consideration). The core of the philosophical project of *metaphysics is to provide an ontology of the world as a whole. In some versions of metaphysics this takes the form of an attempt systematically to order the relations between the ontologies of the special sciences.

open-ended question An interview question that has no predetermined reply categories. The respondent's reply must be written down by the interviewer verbatim, and coded after all interviews are completed, or grouped into broad categories of reply for verbatim quotes in a report. *See also* CLOSED RESPONSE; CODING.

open groups *See* CLOSED GROUPS AND OPEN GROUPS.

open societies and closed societies These terms were introduced by Karl *Popper in his book *The Open Society and its Enemies* (1945), and further explored in *The Poverty of Historicism* (1957). Popper argued that both science and human history are essentially indeterminate and fluid. Applied to social theory, this produced Popper's lively and devastating attack on *historicism. Theories such as those of Plato, *Hegel, and *Marx, which proposed the existence of laws of history and a knowable human destiny, were dismissed by Popper as scientifically insupportable and politically dangerous. He proposed that all such theories would lead to *authoritarian and inhumane regimes, which he called closed societies because they were closed to the normal processes of change. Open societies by contrast were based on the activity, creativity, and innovation of many individuals, and would develop unpredictably through *piecemeal social engineering. They are those societies in which social policies are monitored for unintended consequences, openly criticized, and altered in the light of such criticism. Such societies must be both *liberal and *democratic, in the sense that it must be possible to remove from office rulers who fail to respond to justified criticism. The implied contrast, of course, was between the *totalitarian regime of what was then the Soviet Union (as a closed society) and the Western democracies (as open societies).

Popper's arguments were rightly seen as decisive logical refutation of the very foundations of *Marxism—both its claim to scientific status, and its claim to reveal the course of future history.

operant conditioning or learning *See* CONDITIONING.

operational definition (operationalization) The transformation of an abstract, theoretical *concept into something concrete, observable, and measurable in an empirical research project. Operational definitions are pragmatic and realistic indicators of more diffuse notions. For example, one way of operationalizing the concept of social class might be to ask people what type of job they do, and code their replies as either 'working class' or 'middle class'. An alternative operationalization of the same concept would be to ask respondents to which class (if any) they felt they belonged. As will be seen from this example, operational definitions are crucial to the process of *measurement, and are often the most controversial aspect of any research design.

operational model *See* MODEL.

opinion polls The measurement of opinions on specific issues through *interviews with a representative *sample of the group whose views are to be described. Polls are often referred to by the name of the interviewing company, as in Gallup poll. The most common topics in polls are voting intentions and political party support, views on the government of the day and its policies, and views on major current public issues; hence opinion polls are regularly used to forecast election results, often successfully. Opinion polls were an important source of data for social scientists for decades before social *surveys became widespread; for example, Gallup polls provide data as far back as 1937 in Britain. Some polling companies now seek to create cross-national comparative data-sets.

opportunity structure Developed by Richard A. Cloward and Lloyd B. Ohlin in their book *Delinquency and Opportunity* (1960), this concept attempts to link the Mertonian theory of *anomie to the *Chicago School tradition of cultural transmission and *differential association, in order to produce a general theory of delinquent *subcultures linked to differential opportunities for crime. When pathways to success are blocked (for example through failed schooling), other opportunity structures may be found and these can lead to diverse patterns of *deviance. They identified three major delinquent opportunity structures: criminal, retreatist, and conflict. Their argument was influential in establishing new careers programmes in North America during the 1960s. *See also* SUBCULTURE.

oral history An approach to writing history that relies in large part on *interviews with older people who provide retrospective data on the events, attitudes, and activities of their childhood, adolescence, and adult life—in effect a transfer of the interview *survey method from sociology to *social history, or the large-scale collection of *life-histories. There is an internationally organized Oral History Society with its own journal (*Oral History*) and a number of national Oral History *data archives. The standard text is Paul Thompson's *The Voice of the Past* (1978). The articles in Thompson's *Our Common History* (1982) are typical of the field.

The time-periods and topics that can be covered by this approach are clearly restricted, and typically include a focus on family life, social structure and social relationships, employment in the market sector, work in the informal economy, leisure activities, perceptions of major public events, and attitudes and values as reconstructed in old age. In a fascinating study of childhood delinquency (*Hooligans or Rebels? An Oral History of Working-Class Childhood and Youth, 1889–1939*), Stephen Humphries demonstrated that hooliganism, vandalism, teenage gangs, and classroom rebellions have a long history among underprivileged children and youths, and are not simply a product of recent social changes in contemporary societies. Oral history interviewing can be used in a rough equivalent to the national survey (with samples truncated by the deaths of age-cohort non-survivors), studies of local communities, and case studies of particular social phenomena, such as the changing pattern of home-based employment.

Oral history now tends to emphasize the shared memories of a social group and their role in sustaining social solidarity: rather than seeing oral history as providing information about what *actually* happened, it is seen as providing information on what people typically *believe* to have happened. Oral history discloses the *myths that groups maintain about their past (see Raphael Samuel and Paul Thompson (eds.), *The Myths We Live By*, 1990).

(⊕) SEE WEB LINKS   **o**
• The Oral History Society, with links to resources.

order, social *See* SOCIAL ORDER.

organic analogy Used by many 19th-century sociologists to bring out the holistic, or systemic, aspects of social life. Inspired by advances in biology, Herbert *Spencer, Albert Schäffle, René Worms, and many others explored the differentiation of structures and their functions. It was strongly opposed to *individualism. The differences between society and living organisms are well rehearsed, but it is the ability to handle the problems of social *conflict and the limits beyond which the plasticity of society cannot go that are its principal limitations. *See also* FUNCTION; SOCIAL ORDER.

organic composition of capital The ratio between constant and variable capital in total *capital, measured in value terms. In lay terms this can be understood as the capital/labour ratio, or the proportion of output contributed by raw materials, machinery and other inputs, relative to labour. Karl *Marx thought the organic composition of capital would rise with the development of capitalism because of labour-displacing technical change. *See also* CAPITAL-INTENSIVE PRODUCTION.

organic solidarity *See* DIVISION OF LABOUR; ORGANIC ANALOGY; SOCIAL ORDER.

organization *See* FORMAL STRUCTURE; ORGANIZATION THEORY.

organizational culture The values, norms, and patterns of action that characterize social relationships within a formal organization. This concept came to the fore in a series of British and American management texts of the 1980s, which attempted to explain either (or sometimes both) the difficulties of Western businesses in coping with economic recession, and the challenge of the Japanese. Many of these texts—including best-selling accounts by William G. Ouchi (*Theory Z*, 1981), Thomas J. Peters and Robert H. Waterman (*In Search of Excellence*, 1982), Walter Goldsmith and David Clutterbuck (*The Winning Streak*, 1984), Richard Tanner Pascale and Anthony G. Athos, *The Art of Japanese Management*, 1981), and Terence Deal and Alan Kennedy (*Corporate Cultures*, 1988)—simply reiterate the insights of the *Human Relations perspective on industrial relations. (Ouchi, for example, explicitly calls for 'a redirection of attention to human relations in the corporate world'.) Deal and Kennedy, on the other hand, largely reiterate the analysis and conclusions reached earlier by Tom Burns and G. M. Stalker (in *The Management of Innovation*, 1961), notably those regarding the workings of *plural social systems within organizations, and the necessity of matching management systems to their economic and political environments. In short, this is an extensive and curiously influential concept and literature, given that it seems to be just so much rediscovering of some commonplace sociological wheels. *See also* CONTINGENCY THEORY.

Organizational Design Movement Also known as the 'neo-human relations school' or 'organizational psychology', this was a group of writers who were influential in American and European business schools in the 1960s. The most notable theorists were were Douglas McGregor (*The Human Side of the Enterprise*, 1960), Rensis Likert ('New Patterns of Management', in V. Vroom and E. L. Deci (eds.), *Management and Motivation*, 1970), and Chris Argyris ('Understanding Human Behaviour in Organizations', in M. Haire (ed.), *Modern Organization Theory*, 1959). What these writers shared was a conviction that conventional formal organizations (*See* FORMAL STRUCTURE) embodied the (regressive) psychological assumptions of their designers, that such organizations often resulted in psychological distress for individuals working within them, and that better organizational structures were possible. Each built loosely on the theories of Abraham H. *Maslow. These ideas became one of the principal elements feeding into the later Quality of Work Life Movement (*see* QWL MOVEMENT).

organizational reach In his extensive historical study of *The Social Sources of Power* (vol. i, 1986), the British sociologist Michael Mann offers a fourfold typology of types of organizational reach, a term he uses to describe the characteristics of social power networks. One dimension of the typology distinguishes between the extensive and intensive *power of organizations; that is, 'the ability to organise large numbers of people over far-flung territories in order to engage in minimally stable cooperation' (extensive power), as against 'the ability to organise tightly and command a high level of mobilization or commitment from the participants' (intensive power). The other dimension of the typology distinguishes authoritative and diffused power; that is, 'power actually willed by groups and institutions' (including definite commands and conscious obedience), as against power which 'spreads in a more spontaneous, unconscious, decentred way throughout a population' (for example an understanding that certain shared social practices are natural or moral). Examples of the four forms of organizational reach thus generated include an army command structure (intensive and authoritative), militarist empire (extensive and authoritative), a general strike (intensive and diffused), and market exchange (extensive and diffused).

organization man Originally the title of an influential book (published in 1956), a classic of American *pop sociology by William H. Whyte, which claimed that white-collar employees in large organizations are dominated by corporate life and loyalties. In cutting themselves off from friends, families, and communities, organization men came to assume a new 'bureaucratic, personality structure'. This favoured conformity, a privatized *life-style in mass-produced suburbia, and subverted the American values of competitive *individualism.

organization theory (sociology of organizations) In practice these terms are used interchangeably, although the former has a slightly wider remit than the latter as it also covers work by non-sociologists, including those who are concerned to provide advice to management on how organizations should be designed and operated.

As various forms of organization pervade social life some difficulty also attaches to the definition of those which are the subject-matter of the sociology of organizations. In a useful discussion of this problem David Silverman (*The Theory of Organizations*, 1970) has suggested that the 'formal organizations' with which this branch of sociology is concerned have two distinguishing features: they arise at an ascertainable moment in time, and they exhibit patterns of social relations that are less taken for granted than those in non-formal organizations (such as the family) and which organizational participants often seek to co-ordinate and control. In consequence, considerable attention is paid to both the nature of these social relations, and to planned changes in them.

Early organization theory developed along two parallel tracks, reflecting its dual sociological and managerial origins. The growth of industrial societies in the 19th century involved the expansion of large-scale organizations—especially those of the *factory and the *state. The former of these gave rise to the doctrines of *scientific management, associated with Frederick William Taylor, and the latter provided the exemplar which Weber had in mind when developing his ideal-typical account of the structure of *bureaucracy. Both these theories concentrated on analysing the structures of organizations; that is, the nature of the various positions occupied by organizational personnel, the powers and duties attaching to these positions, and their relationship to the work required to carry out the explicitly stated goals of the organization. Both also viewed organizations as hierarchical structures, essential for the managerial control of work.

However, in the 1930s and 1940s, a variety of studies (such as those of the *human relations movement, by Chester Barnard, and the now classic study of the Tennessee Valley Authority by the sociologist Philip Selznick) opened up a second area for analysis: the study of the social processes occurring in organizations, often with a particular emphasis on how informal, 'unofficial' social relations could constrain or even subvert the official goals of the organization, and with organizations as cooperative rather than hierarchically controlled social institutions.

There now exists an immense variety of sociological studies of organizations and theories about them. Indeed, most of the major schools of sociological theory have contributed to this literature. Stewart Clegg and David Dunkerley (*Organization, Class and Control*, 1980) identify four major groupings among the diverse approaches. These are as follows.

Typologies of organizations: involving attempts to classify organizations according to a variety of key characteristics, such as who benefits from their operations, or how they obtain compliance from their members. Works by Peter Blau, Amitai Etzioni, Robert Blauner, and Tom Burns and G. M. Stalker are among the best known of such studies.

Organizations as social systems: an approach particularly identified with Talcott *Parsons's structural-functionalist theory of action and with Philip Selznick and Robert Merton's more focused work on organizations. Organizations consist of *social systems in interaction with other social systems (therefore 'open systems') whose values and goals are oriented to those of the wider society. According to Parsons, key requirements for organizational maintenance (which is seen to be the overriding goal of any organization) are those which apply to all social systems; namely, adaptation, goal attainment, integration, and pattern (or value) maintenance. Organizations as empirically contingent structures: an approach particularly associated, in the United Kingdom, with research at the University of Aston. The typological and social systems approaches have difficulty in clearly defining the organization as a theoretical object. (Is it defined solely by a set of typological characteristics? Or, if it is an open system, where are the system boundaries to be drawn?) The Aston Programme applies insights derived from psychology, together with statistical techniques such as *scaling and *factor analysis, to relate measures of organizational performance to different dimensions of organizational structure (such as the degree of specialization of tasks and centralization of authority). The latter are then related to independent contextual variables such as size, technology, and location of the enterprise. This essentially *empiricist approach is subject to all the usual criticisms which apply to such a methodology.

An early contribution to the basis of organizational analysis in theories of action was that of Herbert A. Simon in his work on *satisficing. Later work, for example by David Silverman, is influenced by *phenomenological sociology (especially ethnomethodology) and interactionism (*see* SYMBOLIC INTERACTIONISM). Instead of reifying the organization (referring to organizational goals and needs as if the organization, like a human being, could have such things) organizations are here analysed as the outcome of motivated people attempting to resolve their own problems. They are socially constructed by the individual actions of members having habituated expectations of each other. This approach throws doubt on whether it makes sense to refer to organizations as institutions which pursue organizational goals. In any event, there have been many studies which show (for example) that official goals may bear no relationship to actual or operative goals; that organizations frequently have multiple and conflicting goals; and that goal displacement may occur. The informal culture of work within organizations has been and continues to be extensively studied by sociologists influenced by the *Chicago School of sociology. This tradition is illustrated in the work of, for example, William F. Whyte (*Human Relations in the Restaurant Industry*, 1948), Donald Roy ('Quota Restriction and Goldbricking in a Machine Shop', *American Journal of Sociology*, 1952), and Howard Becker (*Boys in White*, 1961).

A great deal of organization theory has been criticized for its normative (in this case pro-managerial) bias; for its individualistic analysis of the members of organizations (that is, for being more informed by psychological, than by socio-logical perspectives); and for embodying an inadequate analysis of how wider relations of power and control in society affect and are affected by organizations (in other words for concentrating mainly on the internal exercise of managerial authority and attempts to subvert it).

Useful textbooks on organization theory include Peter M. Jackson, *The Political Economy of Bureaucracy* (1982) and Lex Donaldson's more polemical *In Defence of Organization Theory* (1985). *See also* ADMINISTRATIVE THEORY; BOUNDED RATIONALITY; CONTINGENCY THEORY; FLEXIBLE EMPLOYMENT; FORDISM; FORMAL STRUCTURE; GOAL-DISPLACEMENT; HAWTHORNE STUDIES; LINE-AND-STAFF; MICHELS; ORGANIZATIONAL CULTURE; SCIENTIFIC MANAGEMENT; SYSTEMS THEORY.

organized crime All profitable *crime is socially organized, but this term is usually reserved for situations where a large number of people in a hierarchical structure are engaged in an ongoing pattern of criminal activities. The most common activities are extortion and the provision of illegal goods and services, such as drink, drugs, gambling, money-lending, and prostitution. All of these involve continuous relations with the victims or clients, who have contact with the lower echelons of the organization. To be successful, therefore, organized or syndicated crime involves some degree of corruption or intimidation of the police or other agents of law-enforcement. It is often thought to be synonymous with a secret society, such as the Tongs of the Chinese diaspora, the Camorra of 19th-century Naples, the Mafia of Sicily, and Cosa Nostra in the United States. It seems more likely that if such societies exist at all, they do not actually run criminal activities, but rather act as fraternal organizations for some of the racketeers. The myth of the secret society helps the criminals by intimidating victims and helps the authorities because it justifies police ineffectiveness. It is often fuelled by racism, though criminal activities themselves are usually ethni-cally mixed. Organized crime is associated with violence and threats in the course of extortion, but also in the maintenance of control over subordinates, struggles for power within groups, and struggles for monopoly control between groups.

oriental despotism A concept popularized by the German sociologist Karl Wittfogel, an early member of the Institute of Social Research at Frankfurt (*See* CRITICAL THEORY) who fled the Third Reich in 1933, and spent much of the rest of his academic career in the United States (see his *Oriental Despotism*, 1957). Wittfogel, an expert on Chinese civilization, was a controversial figure who seems, during the course of a colourful career, to have traversed the political spectrum from Stalinism to McCarthyism. His fame rests largely on the dispute engendered by his concept of oriental despotism and his analysis of the so-called 'hydraulic society'.

In his early work, Wittfogel described China as having experienced *feudalism, on the grounds that the Chou state was based on the collection by ruling clans of tithes, in the form of communal labour by *peasants working on public fields. Subsequently, a transition from labour-rent to rent-in-kind and money-rent implies that the feudal relation between the peasant communities and local lords gave way to 'oriental despotism', in which the primary mode of extracting surplus value from direct producers became money-rent paid to the centralized *state. Although Wittfogel is by no means clear about the sequence of events (in his later work Chou China is reclassified as an instance of oriental despotism), he argues that the transition between the two *modes of production was prompted mainly by the expansion and intensification of agriculture by means of large-scale irrigation, control of which necessitated coordination by a centralized state. This is the so-called 'hydraulic hypothesis', which states that irrigation is a major cause of the emergence of centralized political authority, and is thus a significant force in the development of early civilizations. *Oriental Despotism* considers this thesis in relation, not only to China, but also wider Marxist arguments about the *Asiatic mode of production.

Wittfogel's work has been criticized as empirically unsound, inconsistent, ecologically *determinist, and implicitly *functionalist. However, his characterization of the agrarian state bureaucracy of early hydraulic societies prompted an enormous literature on state formation and class relationships in South-east Asia, and he has also been described as a sophisticated multilinear evolutionist.

orientations to work *See* WORK, SUBJECTIVE EXPERIENCE OF.

original income *See* INCOME DISTRIBUTION.

Ossowski, Stanislaw (1897–1963) A noted Polish sociologist and philosopher. Together with his wife Maria Ossowska, a philosopher in her own right, he published extensively in the philosophy and psychology of science. However, it was the publication of *Class Structure in the Social Consciousness* in 1957, after the barren Stalinist years when sociology had ceased formally to exist in Polish universities, which projected him into the sociological limelight.

This work was a typology of the various views of class, social structure, and social processes, and the intellectual milieu from which they emerged. He argued vigorously against the crude bipolar *Marxist class analysis of the time. More importantly, he articulated a view in which the existence of *status privilege and economic *inequality persists, even after the formal abolition of the *class system. In particular he sought to introduce the importance of the study of subjective perceptions of inequality, of attitudes, and to research what was new, inherited, or even absent within the supposedly classless societies of *real socialism. He also drew attention to similarities between *capitalist and *socialist societies, in the way in which they presented their societies as classless, and attempted to remove the bases for 'group solidarity amongst the underprivileged'. The nationalization of the means of production may have been a necessary condition for moving towards the kind of society envisaged by the Marxist-Leninists, but it was certainly not a sufficient condition, and he asserted that many old forms of inequality had re-emerged in a new guise.

Ossowski had the intellectual breadth as well as the moral courage to write this treatise at a time when even the discussion of *social stratification with reference to socialist peoples' democracies was taboo. He displayed his socialist concerns alongside intellectual rigour and scholarly autonomy and thus set the foundations for a sociology which survived and flourished in conditions of repression where in other countries of real socialism it all but disappeared.

other-directedness A term coined by David Riesman (*The Lonely Crowd*, 1950), referring to a *personality type which seeks approval and acceptance from others—as opposed to inner-directedness, acting independently, and according to a personal moral code. Other-directedness is said to result from a bureaucratic society geared to consumption. Subsequent volumes entitled *Faces in the Crowd* (1952) and *Individualism Reconsidered* (1954) further explored Riesman's thesis that the American character was moving from inner-directedness to other-directedness with the advance of *industrialization and growth of population density.

out-group In his classic study of *Folkways* (1906), William Graham *Sumner observed that people tend to like their own group (the in-group) over other competing or opposing groups (the out-group). The terms are closely linked to the concept of *ethnocentricism.

outlier An extreme value in a statistical distribution. The outlier lies beyond the normal or typical range of values and may distort the calculation of certain averages or other summary statistics.

outwork (outworking) These terms refer to the *employment of individual workers by firms outside the firm workplace—usually in workers' own homes. The employer supplies materials (and possibly machinery) and workers are paid on a piece-rate basis. It commonly involves light assembly work. *See also* HOMEWORK.

overdetermine (overdetermination) Terms devised by Sigmund *Freud to denote multiple determinations—and hence interpretations—of dreams. The concept was subsequently used by Louis *Althusser in *For Marx* (1966) to indicate multiple historical causation. Althusser contrasted this view of causation with the *Hegelian notion of simple contradiction. He argued that revolutions occurred when a combination of factors—a 'ruptural unity'—was present.

over-socialized conception of man A phrase devised by the American sociologist Dennis Wrong, as part of his critique of *functionalism in general, and the sociology of Talcott *Parsons in particular. Wrong rejected Parsons's views on *socialization and social integration. In 'The Oversocialised Conception of Man' (*American Sociological Review*, 1961) he argued that Parsons's account of socialization had completely lost sight of the tension that Sigmund *Freud identified in the contrast between *human nature and the requirements of civilized *social order. Wrong rejected the view that social actors are simply acceptance-seekers; rather, he argued, human beings should be seen as social without being entirely socialized. The term has also come to be used in relation to the criticisms that Harold Garfinkel has levelled against Parsons for his emphasis on conformity to cultural norms.

overt participant observation *Participant observation carried out with the agreement of the subjects being studied. This agreement may be tacit or formally expressed. In the latter case, the sociologist makes it clear that social science research is being undertaken, and the subjects themselves are then invited to give explicit permission for the research to proceed. In the former, the researcher also reveals his or her identity as an outsider, but states the purposes of the study less clearly, usually in the form of a general statement of interest in the subjects 'in order to write a book' about them. If this is sufficient to gain entry to the field, then no further details are offered to those being studied, unless specifically requested by the subjects themselves. Most researchers enjoy telling the story of how they gained entry to the field; indeed, often this is crucial to understanding the research, since the relationship that is established between researcher and subjects may well affect the quality of the data obtained. Most published accounts of overt participant observation therefore report in some detail on the observer's assumed role in the group or society being studied.

over-urbanization *See* URBANIZATION.

ownership and control There has been much debate about whether, in advanced Western capitalist societies, ownership and control of the means of production has come historically to be dispersed throughout a greater proportion of the population. In the classic statement of this thesis (R. Dahrendorf's *Class and Class Conflict in Industrial Society*, 1959), there is an increasing separation of ownership and control. Subsequent sociological studies investigated, and debated, the empirical relationship between the two.

Adolf A. Berle and Gardiner C. Means (*The Modern Corporation and Private Property*, 1932) argued that a separation of ownership from control in larger American corporations during the 1930s, was transferring economic power from owner entrepreneurs (capitalists) to managers. The growth in scale of industrial enterprise has meant that the number of individuals holding shares has increased to such an extent that no individual, or even group of individuals, can have a significant controlling interest. This long-term process of dispersal creates a power vacuum which can be filled only by a professional salaried *management without significant property.

Marxists have taken a different view. Rudolf Hilferding, for example, maintained that the characteristic form of advanced *capitalism is a fusion of monopoly capital in banking and manufacturing into 'finance capital', or capital not restricted to one sphere of industry. Banks, insurance companies, pension funds, investment trusts, manufacturing, and other commercial corporations all own shares in each other. Large industrial enterprises are controlled not by managers but by bankers. Cross-shareholdings are reinforced by a complex web of interlocking directorships—and sometimes by kinship and friendship ties—which restricts 'effective ownership' to a financial *oligarchy, comprising only a few hundred or few thousand individuals, organized into financial groups or knots of financial power. The capitalist class consists of finance capitalists.

Considerable research effort has been expended in the attempt to decide between these views. How much, and which parts, of a corporation need to be organized into a coordinated financial grouping before strategic control of a particular corporation can be secured? The most convincing answer to these questions will be found in the works of John Scott (*Corporate Business and Capitalist Classes*, 1997). Control in large enterprises, he argues, corresponds neither to management control nor to minority bank control but to 'control through a constellation of interests'. This is found in enterprises where financial intermediaries are the dominant shareholders, but none is able, individually, to exercise minority control. Where the largest twenty voting shareholders collectively hold sufficient shares for minority control, these comprise a diverse constellation of controlling interests, and no stable coalition can exercise full powers of minority control. In this situation, the members of the Board of Directors can achieve some degree of autonomy from any particular interest, and the nature of the capitalist class is much more complex than either of the earlier interpretations would suggest. An important and influential argument is that of Maurice Zeitlin, *The Large Corporation and The Capitalist Class* (1989). *See also* BOURGEOISIE; INTERLOCKING DIRECTORSHIP.

(⊕) SEE WEB LINKS

- A review of comparative studies of contemporary forms of ownership, by John Scott: 'Networks of Corporate Power: A Comparative Assessment.' (Subscription)

Paine, Thomas (1737–1809) The pre-eminent pamphleteer and radical democrat of the American Revolution. Paine was born in England and came to America in 1744. His 1776 revolutionary pamphlet *Common Sense* was enormously popular. In the spirit of Locke, Paine proclaimed that 'Government even in its best state is a necessary evil; in its worst state an intolerable one.' Paine wrote many pamphlets during the war, becoming an articulate spokesman for *democratic and *egalitarian institutions in the new nation. In 1791–2 he published *The Rights of Man*, defending the doctrine of natural rights against Burke. Briefly imprisoned in Paris during the period of Revolutionary Terror, Paine returned to the United States in 1802.

panel study A study that provides longitudinal data on a group of people, households, employers, or other social unit, termed 'the panel', about whom information is collected over a period of months, years, or decades. Two of the most common types of panel are age cohorts, people within a common age band, and groups with some other date-specific common experience, such as people graduating from university, having a first child, or migrating to another country in a given year or band of years. Another type is the nationally representative *cross-sectional sample of households or employers that is interviewed at regular intervals over a period of years. Because data relate to the same social units, change is measured more reliably than in regular cross-sectional studies, and sample sizes can be correspondingly smaller, while remaining nationally representative, as long as non-response and sample attrition are kept within bounds. These are the key problems for panel studies, as initial samples are eroded by deaths, migration, fatigue with the study, and other causes. Another problem is that people become experienced interviewees, leading to response *bias. For example, they may report 'no change' since the previous interview, so as to avoid detailed questioning on changes that have in fact occurred.

Data are usually collected through interview *surveys with respondents in the panel, with other informants (such as parents, doctors), with their spouses and other members of their household. With the respondent's permission, data from administrative records may be added, such as information from educational or medical records, which are usually more precise than the respondent's recollection. A panel element is sometimes added to regular cross-sectional surveys, and *rotating sample designs are a hybrid between panel study and regular survey.

Because they yield longitudinal data, panel studies offer possibilities for examining the relationships between individual *life-histories, *cohort effects, and period effects due to social *change. A number of specialized techniques have therefore been developed for analysing these data (see, for example, J. S.

Coleman, *Longitudinal Data Analysis*, 1982). Nick Buck et al. (eds.), *Changing Households* (1994), is a good example of the range of substantive issues that can most usefully be addressed using panel data—in this case those from the British Household Panel Study. Topics include, for example, changes in household composition, patterns of residential mobility, and stability in voting intentions over time. This volume also contains a useful overview of the methodological problems involved in conducting panel surveys.

SEE WEB LINKS

• The Institute for Social and Economic Research, responsible for the principal longitudinal and panel studies in Britain.

panopticon A term first used by Jeremy Bentham in 1791 to describe his idea of an 'inspection house' to be used for surveillance purposes in public institutions such as prisons, asylums, and workhouses. The panopticon was a circular construction of open single 'cells', built around a central inspection tower, by means of which both the inspector and the inmate were under constant surveillance. Michel Foucault discussed the idea at length in *Discipline and Punish* (1975) and describes the panopticon as an apparatus of power by virtue of the field of visibility it creates. Because it made inmates always conscious of being visible, he argued, an automatic functioning of power was ensured. As a consequence of constant surveillance, individuals became ensnared in an impersonal power relation which both disindividualized the power relationship itself, and individualized those subjected to it. Foucault saw this as an essential development in, and metaphor for, the increasing surveillance, hierarchy, discipline, and classifications of modern society, by means of which individuals became ever more regulated and controlled by impersonal institutions. The idea of the panopticon as discussed by Foucault has also been important and influential in recent theories of the *gaze.

pantheism *See* TRANSCENDENTALISM.

paradigm In ordinary speech the word paradigm designates a typical example or model to be replicated or followed. This connotation is carried over into the technical use of the term introduced by the philosopher and historian of science Thomas Kuhn, and thence into a wide range of sociological contexts. The term paradigm plays a key part in Kuhn's account of the practice which he calls 'normal' science. In 'normal' (that is non-revolutionary) periods in a science, there is a consensus across the relevant scientific community about the theoretical and methodological rules to be followed, the instruments to be used, the problems to be investigated, and the standards by which research is to be judged. This consensus derives from the adoption by the scientific community of some past scientific achievement as its model or paradigm. Scientific training in the discipline involves familiarization with this paradigm, or its textbook representations. To acquire the status of a paradigm, a scientific achievement must offer sufficiently convincing resolutions of previously recognized problems to attract the adherence of enough specialists to form the core of a new consensus. It must also have enough unresolved problems to provide the puzzles for subsequent research practice within the research tradition it comes to define.

The concept revolutionized thinking about the philosophy of science. Until the mid-20th century, at least in the English-speaking world, philosophy of science was conducted largely in abstraction from the history or social realities of scientific practice. Generally, an ideal-typical model of science (sometimes, as in the work of Sir Karl Popper, this was explicitly prescriptive) was subjected to philosophical analysis, and its key features commended as demarcation criteria separating science from pseudo-science, religious faith, speculative *metaphysics, or other (usually less worthy) activities. Kuhn's major work, *The Structure of Scientific Revolutions* (2nd edn., 1970), was one of the first successful attempts to pose philosophical questions about the nature of scientific knowledge by way of a serious conceptualization of the history of the sciences.

Kuhn's account challenges widespread assumptions about scientific progress as the piecemeal accumulation of knowledge, and about scientific rationality as a formal process of matching theory to evidence. His alternative vision is of a discontinuous history, in which periods of consensual normal science were interspersed with crises and intellectual revolutions, some of which called into question the most fundamental *epistemological assumptions of science itself. Far from advancing in a cumulative, gradual way, revolutionary changes in science therefore involve abandonment of much previously accepted knowledge, and proceed by abrupt qualitative transitions of perspective. By contrast, normal science displays few of the features—bold conjecture, preparedness to abandon assumptions in the face of the evidence, and so on—widely attributed to scientists in Popperian and *empiricist philosophies of science. Routine puzzle-solving in terms provided by a shared conventional paradigm is how Kuhn characterizes the great majority of scientific activity in non-revolutionary times.

The attention Kuhn gives to the role of the scientific community, its shared norms, its role in the resolution of periods of revolutionary crisis, the organization of scientific communication and education, as well as the recognition of extra-scientific pressures in the instigation of scientific revolutions, all ensured that his work would be influential amongst social scientists, well beyond the circles of philosophers and historians of science. In sociology, his work was of great importance in enabling sociology of *knowledge to extend its scope to include the natural sciences. It was also important in discussions about the history and nature of sociology itself, and of the significance of a persisting lack of consensus around a single paradigm in *sociology, and indeed the other *social sciences. Was the persistence of rivalry between alternative perspectives evidence that sociology was still in its 'pre-paradigmatic' (that is, pre-scientific) stage; or, rather, did it suggest that the model of 'scientific consensus' was permanently unattainable, or inappropriate to sociology? Though Kuhn was himself a determined anti-relativist, many of his arguments pointed in a relativist direction, and his work was widely used by those whose main aim was to debunk the view of science as an especially authoritative form of knowledge and to see sociology as a 'multiple paradigm' science.

(⊕) SEE WEB LINKS

- A critical discussion of the use of the idea in sociology, by Douglas Lee Eckberg and Lester Hill: 'The Paradigm Concept and Sociology: A Critical Review'. (Subscription)

paradigmatic and syntagmatic *See* SAUSSURE.

paralanguage The various non-semantic aspects of speech (such as volume, pitch, and emphasis) by which individuals communicate meaning.

parallel cousin This is a term used in kinship theory to denote first cousins who have related parents of the same sex; in other words, their mothers are sisters or their fathers are brothers. In some societies there are rules that forbid marriage between parallel cousins. *See also* CROSS COUSIN.

parallel descent A term applied by social anthropologists to a form of arranging descent that does not result in groupings containing both sexes: instead, there are matrilineal groups of females, and patrilineal groups of males. In such systems, the purposes for which the female groups exist are strictly limited, for example to the holding of certain forms of property. It has been argued that the term may be a misnomer, since the system to which it applies exists alongside the familiar marriage arrangements, as for example among the Apinaye of Brazil, who practise what is essentially a patrilineal system according to which men exchange sisters for wives.

paranoia (paranoid reactions) In *psychoanalysis, paranoia involves the projection of internal threatening feelings onto the external world, which is then experienced as persecutory. Psychoanalysts concerned with society are interested in the way paranoid reactions can be mobilized for political purposes (see for example T. Adorno et al., *The Authoritarian Personality*, 1950).

para-religion Since the 1960s, the proliferation of *cults, *sects, *private religions, *invisible religions, and esoteric belief-systems in general has left sociologists of *religion struggling to define their core subject-matter. It has seemed increasingly unsatisfactory simply to assume that religion happens in churches (or, indeed, that Churches are necessarily concerned primarily with the promotion of religion). As a result there have been numerous attempts to impose order on the field. In one such effort, A. L. Greil and T. Robbins (eds.) (*Between Scared and Secular*, 1994) distinguish between religions (as conventionally understood), on one hand, and 'para-religions' and 'quasi-religions' on the other. Para-religious phenomena 'involve expressions of ultimate concern' but make no claim to be religions because no supernatural beliefs are involved. Examples include psychotherapy as practised in a communal setting and ritualistic aspects in corporate and consumer life. Quasi-religions do make supernatural claims but these are 'anomalous given the American folk category of "religion"'. Occultism, New Age spiritualism, astrology, and Scientology are cited as exemplars. The fact that the last of these has been involved in a long history of political and legal wrangling in order to have itself recognized as a Church illustrates the difficulties of defining clear boundaries in this particular sphere of sociological interest.

parasuicide *See* SUICIDE.

parenthood (parenting) *See* CHILDHOOD; FAMILY, SOCIOLOGY OF; FATHERHOOD; MOTHERHOOD.

Pareto principle A principle of welfare economics, derived from the writings of Vilfredo Pareto, stating that a legitimate welfare improvement occurs when a particular change makes at least one person better and, without making any other person worse off. A market exchange which affects nobody adversely is considered to be a 'Pareto-improvement' since it leaves one or more persons better off. 'Pareto optimality' is said to exist when the distribution of economic welfare cannot be improved for one individual without reducing that of another.

The principle rests on three assumptions: that each individual is the best judge of his or her own welfare; that social welfare is exclusively a function of individual welfare; and that if one individual's welfare is augmented, and nobody's is reduced, then social welfare has increased. Since these assumptions are empirically questionable, and probably embody value-judgements about well-being and satisfaction, they are somewhat controversial. It has also been argued that they constitute a rather weak basis for welfare judgements, since they explicitly forbid interpersonal comparisons, are concerned entirely with the subjective choices of individuals, and privilege the position occupied by the status quo (since any move from the status quo which was vetoed by one person would not be considered a Pareto-improvement). Most sociologists object to Paretian welfare economics because of its silence on the initial distribution of resources.

Pareto, Vilfredo (1848–1923) An Italian economist and sociologist, subject of an extensive treatment in Talcott Parsons's *The Structure of Social Action* (1937) as a co-founder of the 'voluntaristic theory of action', but since largely ignored by sociologists.

Already famous for his contributions to equilibrium theory as a mathematical economist, in his later years Pareto turned his hand to sociology, and in 1916 published his *magnum opus* the *Trattato di sociologia generale* (translated in four volumes as *The Mind and Society* in 1935). Pareto is probably best known today for being the first person to use the term 'elite' to refer to the few who rule the many, though the substantive idea owes more to *Mosca. He also exerted an early influence on the development of social *systems theory. Samuel E. Finer's *Vilfredo Pareto, Sociological Writings* (1966) contains a useful selection of his most important sociological texts, together with a substantial introductory essay by Finer himself. *See also* ELITE THEORY; PARETO PRINCIPLE.

pariah group In the narrow sense, a pariah is an untouchable or an outcast found in the *caste system of stratification; however, the term is often used more generally to refer to any outsider. *See also* EXCLUSION.

Parkinson's law A principle formulated by the British political scientist C. Northcote Parkinson (*Parkinson's Law*, 1958) to the effect that 'work expands so as to fill the time available for its completion'.

Park, Robert Ezra (1864–1944) A leading member of the *Chicago School, who introduced the work of Georg Simmel to a generation of American sociologists, mainly indirectly and via the widely used textbook *Introduction to the Science of Sociology* (1921) co-authored with Ernest W. Burgess. Park and Burgess were leading practitioners of *human ecology. Much of the theory of what came to be called 'classical human ecology' was stimulated by Park's writings and teaching at Chicago (see, for example, his definitive article on 'Human Ecology' in the *American Journal of Sociology*, 1936). Park argued that the basic process underlying social relationships was *competition; however, because of human interdependence due to the *division of labour, this competition always involves elements of unplanned cooperation (thus yielding 'competitive cooperation'). In this way, people come to form symbiotic relationships, both at the spatial and cultural levels. These ideas are developed in the collection of essays (many by Park himself) on *The City* (1925) and his monograph on *Human Communities* (1952).

parliamentary government A system of government which allocates public decision-making powers to a house of elected representatives, or parliament, typically including decisions on national laws and regulations, the government budget and fiscal policy, and declarations of war with other nation-states. Specific arrangements vary widely between countries, for example regarding the frequency of elections, the number of chambers in parliament, who is entitled to vote, whether voting is obligatory or optional, how votes are converted into a number of appointed representatives, rules which affect the number of political parties or independent representitives, and the relationship between elected representatives and the head of state or the government. The common feature of such systems is that they seek to achieve a proper balance between governmental power and governmental responsiveness.

parole* and *langue *See* POST-STRUCTURALISM; SAUSSURE.

parsimony (parsimonious) The principle that the best statistical model among all satisfactory models is that with the fewest parameters. Hence, more generally, the principle asserting that if it is possible to explain a phenomenon equally adequately in a number of different ways, then the simplest of explanations (in terms of the number of variables or propositions) should be selected.

Parsons, Talcott (1902–79) For some twenty to thirty years after the Second World War, Talcott Parsons was the major theoretical figure in English-speaking sociology, if not in world sociology. An American who worked all his life in the United States, apart from a brief period of postgraduate study in Europe, his sociological theory (most often labelled structural-functionalism or normative functionalism) was commonly seen as a product of modern, affluent American society, where structural social conflicts had been largely eliminated or were of a transient nature, and where there appeared to be a general social cohesion and shared adherence to democratic values. Parsonian theory came under increasing criticism as the post-war consensus itself showed signs of dissolving, particularly under the impact of the Vietnam War.

From the beginning, Parsons set out to provide an integrated, totalizing theory for sociology, bringing together into a unified whole the diverse insights of the major founders of sociology. In particular this involved an attempt to integrate Weber's individualism and Durkheim's holism. His focus was on ideas, *values, *norms, and the integration of individual actions oriented to norms and values into overarching *social systems.

For Parsons, the prime task was to develop a set of abstract, generalizing concepts describing the social system. The main criterion by which we can judge such a set of concepts is their rational coherence, and they can then be used to derive propositions about the world. In his first book, *The Structure of Social Action* (1937), he argued that the classical sociological theorists could be seen as moving towards a voluntaristic theory of action, conceiving of human beings as making choices between means and ends, in a physical and social environment that limited choices. A central aspect of the social environment is the norms and values by which we make our choices. Within this context, actors aim at maximum gratification, and behaviour and relationships that achieve this goal become institutionalized into a system of status *roles. This is the social system and it presupposes three other systems: a personality system (the actor himself or herself); a cultural system (or wider values giving coherence to the norms attached to status roles); and a physical environment to which the society must adjust.

Parsons then built up an elaborate model of systems and subsystems. In order to survive, each system must meet four 'functional prerequisites': four basic requirements that must be fulfilled. These are *adaptation (to the physical environment); *goal attainment (a means of organizing its resources to achieve its goals and obtain gratification); *integration (forms of internal co-ordination and ways of dealing with differences); and latency or pattern-maintenance (means of achieving comparative stability). Each system, therefore, develops four specialist subsystems in the process of meeting these requirements. This is one of Parsons's most famous taxonomic devices—the so-called AGIL schema.

This was then developed into an *evolutionary view of history as moving from the simple to the complex, societies developing rather as amoeba, through a process of splitting and then reintegration. Systems and subsystems are organized into a cybernetic hierarchy, those systems which have a high level of information (such as the cultural system, including norms and values), controlling systems which have a high level of energy (such as the human biological system).

The four systems mentioned above—cultural, social, personality, and biological—form what Parsons calls the general system of action. Each system corresponds to a functional prerequisite. Similarly, the social system itself has four subsystems, these being (in hierarchical order) the socialization system (pattern maintenance); the societal community or institutions of social control (integration); the political system (goal attainment); and the economic system (adaptation). Each of these can, itself, be seen in terms of further, more specialized, subsystems.

We can also analyse actions, social relationships, and whole systems according to what Parsons calls pattern variables—or choices between pairs of alternatives. For example, in any relationship we may treat its object as unique, or as an example of a general class (this is the dilemma between particularism and universalism); may draw on or ignore emotional commitments (affectivity versus affective neutrality); may value something or someone for their own sake or for what can be done with it or them (quality versus performance); and may relate to all aspects of an object or to one only (diffuseness versus specificity). Institutions tend to cluster round opposing poles: in the family, for example, relationships are particularistic, affective, quality-oriented, and diffuse; in a factory they are typically universalistic, affectively neutral, performance-oriented, and specific.

These ideas were developed over some 40 years, Parsons's other main works being *The Social System* (1951), Towards a General Theory of Action (with Edward Shils, 1951), *Societies: Evolutionary and Comparative Perspectives* (1966), and *The System of Modern Societies* (1971). His structural-functionalism is perhaps best understood as a vast classificatory scheme, enabling us to categorize any level of social life, at any level of analysis. Its level of abstraction meant that it is not surprising that C. Wright Mills's labelling of the approach as *grand theory has stuck, though the language and style is no more complex than that used in many more recent theoretical approaches. The explanations that it offers are of a *functionalist nature and many of the criticisms directed at Parsons's work have been criticisms of functionalist explanations as such. It has also been criticized for its abstraction and lack of connection with empirical research; for its social determinism (although it is a theory of social action it seems that, ultimately, systems prescribe the activities of each actor); for its implicit conservatism; and its inability to take account of action oriented to material rather than normative interests.

Parsonian theory seemed to disappear in the 1970s, with rising interest in a wide range of other theories, but in recent years there has been a renewal of interest (see, for example, J. Alexander, *Action and its Environments: Towards a New Synthesis* (1988), and R. Munch, *Theory of Action: Towards a New Synthesis Going Beyond Parsons* (trans. 1987). These approaches generally go under the name neo-functionalism or, sometimes, system theory. However, American and German neo-functionalism are markedly more open than the original. *See also* ACTION THEORY; CONSENSUS; EQUILIBRIUM; EVOLUTIONARY UNIVERSALS; NORMATIVE ORDER; SCHOOL CLASS; SICK ROLE; SYSTEM INTEGRATION AND SOCIAL INTEGRATION; STRUCTURAL DIFFERENTIATION.

(⊕) SEE WEB LINKS
- A review of recent reassessments of Parsons's work, by David Sciulli and Dean Gerstein: 'Social Theory and Talcott Parsons in the 1980s'. (Subscription)

participant observation A research method that aims to gain a close and intimate familiarity with a given area of study (such as a religious, occupational, or deviant group) through an intensive involvement with people in their natural environment. The method originated in the *fieldwork of *social anthropologists and in the urban research of the *Chicago School. John Lofland's study of the Moonies in *Doomsday Cult* (1966), Laud Humphreys's study of homosexuals in *Tearoom Trade* (1970), and William Foote Whyte's study of the gang (*Street Corner Society*, 1955) are classic exemplars. Such research usually involves a range of methods (all of which are separately discussed elsewhere in this dictionary): informal interviews, direct observation, participation in the life of the group, collective discussions, analyses of the personal documents produced within the group, self-analysis, and life-histories. Thus, although the method is usually characterized as qualitative research, it can (and often does) include quantitative dimensions.

The central methodological problem of such research is balancing adequate *subjectivity with adequate *objectivity. Since a major aim of participant observation is to enter the subjective worlds of those studied, and to see these worlds from their point of view (a method akin to the notion of understanding or *Verstehen*), the problem of adequate subjectivity is posed directly: how can researchers know that they are accurately representing the point of view of the other, rather than imposing their own views upon the research subject? On the other hand, simply to stay with the subject's own view may risk the problem of conversion and 'going native', thus being able to see the world only from the point of view of the research subject or subjects. Here the problem of maintaining adequate objectivity is posed: namely, that of maintaining enough distance to be able to locate the subject's view in a wider theoretical and social context. Participant observers are forever trapped in this dilemma: too much detachment weakens the insights that participant observation brings, but too much involvement will render the data of questionable value for social science. The most comprehensive discussion of these issues is T. S. Bruyn's *The Human Perspective in Sociology* (1966).

Participant observation may take several forms. In a classic article on 'Roles in Sociological Field Observation' (in the journal *Social Forces*, 1958), Raymond L. Gold distinguishes four roles that may be adopted within such research. They are ranged along a continuum of involvement, from complete participant through participant-as-observer and observer-as-participant, to complete observer. This taxonomy again captures the subjectivity versus objectivity dilemma: the first position approaches 'going native' whereas the last may well be too distant and uninvolved to generate insights into the subjective aspects of behaviour. *See also* COVERT OBSERVATION; OVERT PARTICIPANT OBSERVATION.

participation rate *See* LABOUR-FORCE PARTICIPATION RATE.

participatory democracy The 20th-century reincarnation of the ancient Greek ideal of government by the people (*demos*). Participatory *democracy is direct democracy, in the sense that all citizens are actively involved in all important decisions. The youth and student movements of the 1960s, in Europe and America, adopted direct democracy with enthusiasm. In practice, this meant that all debates and decisions took place in face-to-face meetings of the whole group. Direct democracy was especially important in the American New Left, the French and British student movements, the early women's movements, and the anti-nuclear and peace movements of the 1960s and 1970s. It was also a feature of the ecological and community movements that survived into the 1980s and 1990s. The difficulty with participatory democracy is a practical one—that it complicates and slows down the decision-making process. Its strength is that it binds individuals to the group through their active involvement in all decisions.

By general agreement, participatory democracy can be effective only in groups with 500 or fewer active members.

partisan dealignment *See* VOTING BEHAVIOUR.

party, political *See* POLITICAL PARTIES.

passive resistance A tactic of non-violent resistance to authority pioneered by Mahatma Gandhi in his campaign against the British government in India in the 1930s and 1940s. Passive resistance has since become an accepted way for minorities to place moral pressure on majorities. It failed in Czechoslovakia in 1968, but had great success in the American Civil Rights Movement between 1955 and 1964, when many thousands of activists were arrested for violating racial segregation rules in the South, culminating in the Civil Rights Act of 1964. The tactic has also been widely used by peace movements, anti-nuclear-power movements, and anti-abortion movements. In general, passive resistance involves groups of protesters occupying some public or forbidden space, and allowing themselves to be arrested or otherwise harassed by authorities, without offering any violence in return. The power of passive resistance is essentially moral. The images it creates can sway public opinion via the *mass media, and may create guilt and uncertainty among politicians and power-holders. *See also* CIVIL DISOBEDIENCE.

passive worker thesis *See* FATALISM.

pastoralists (pastoralism) A nomadic or semi-nomadic form of subsistence which is mainly dependent on herds of domesticated animals. Those groups who move according to regular seasonal routes for pasture are called transhumant. Pastoral nomads are found in most areas of the world, including Southern Europe. Many have faced pressures of enforced settlement.

paternalism A loosely defined term that is often attached to social relationships within which the dominant partner adopts an attitude and set of practices that suggest provident fostering care for his or her subordinates. The concept carries implications of unwelcome meddling in the lives of the latter by the former. It also alludes to gross inequalities in access to, and exercise of, *power.

A wide variety of social relationships have been described and analysed as characteristically paternalist, including those between husbands and wives, master and slave, employer and employee. The relationship between certain factory owners and their employees, for example during the early phase of industrialization in the West, has often been viewed in this way. The former group exerted almost unrestrained power over the latter. However, as a tactic for securing *social control, the early mill-owners attempted to convert power relations into moral ones; or, in the terminology of Max Weber, to translate *domination into traditional authority. This was to be achieved by the institutionalization of such practices as periodic gift-giving, charitable religious and educational activity, provision of company housing and insurance schemes, and support for company-affiliated voluntary associations and clubs. One of the most systematic studies of this form of paternalism, which examines employer domination and operative responses in the Northern textile mills of Victorian England, is Patrick Joyce's *Work, Society and Politics* (1980).

The suggestion is often put that paternalism, practised in this way, is a device for managing and legitimating overtly and potentially disruptive hierarchical and exploitative relationships: it serves the interests of men rather than those of women, the ruling class rather than the proletariat, or of White masters as opposed to Black slaves. However, it has proved difficult to demonstrate empirically that the ritualistic (usually *deferential) responses of subordinates to the paternalistic strategies of their superiors indicate identification with or approval of the status quo, rather than merely an external and calculated management of impressions (or what has been called 'the necessary pose of the powerless').

path analysis A form of multiple *regression, in which coefficients are computed by stipulating the structure of hypothesized causal relationships (or paths) between *variables, in an explicitly formulated *causal model. The causal connections are conceived as unidirectional paths in a path diagram. In essence, therefore, the technique is merely a diagrammatic representation in which the variables are assumed to have a temporal ordering (see H. B. Asher, *Causal Modelling*, 1983).

pathology Strictly speaking, the scientific study of organic diseases, their causes and symptoms (hence, 'pathologist'). However, pathological suggests morbidity and abnormality, so the term has also been extended to certain branches of *psychiatry and *criminology, most obviously in the widespread use of the term 'psychopath'. In sociology, pathology was once held to be analogous to deviance and social problems or 'social disease' (notably in the work of Émile *Durkheim), and the concept also blurs into the associated notion of *social pathology (see, for example, E. Lemert, *Social Pathology*, 1951, and B. Wootton, *Social Science and Social Pathology*, 1959).

pathology, social *See* SOCIAL PATHOLOGY.

patriarchy Literally 'rule of the father', the term was originally used to describe social systems based on the authority of male heads of household. It has now acquired a more general usage, especially in some feminist theories, where it has come to mean male domination in general, as reflected in the systematic disadvantaging and oppressing of women in employment, politics, and domestic life. Sociological and feminist research has documented a huge variety of instances of patriarchal domination—many of which are described elsewhere in this dictionary. A central theoretical overview and account of patriarchy is that of Sylvia Walby in *Theorizing Patriarchy* (1990). *See also* DOMESTIC DIVISION OF LABOUR; FEMINISM; LABOUR MARKET.

patrilineal A term used in *kinship theory to denote the tracing of kinship through the male line. The term *agnatic is also used. A patrilineal group is a *descent group that traces its ancestry to a single male ancestor and acts as a corporate group for political purposes. Patrilineal systems depend on the principle of passing on property and status from father to legitimate son. However, like legitimacy, membership of a lineage may not only be through actual blood ties but can be socially ascribed.

patrimonialism A form of political *domination described by Max *Weber (*Economy and Society*, 1920), in which authority rests on the personal and bureaucratic power exercised by a royal household, where that power is formally arbitrary and under the direct control of the ruler. This last criterion implies that domination is secured by means of a political apparatus staffed by slaves, mercenaries, conscripts, or some other group (not a traditional land-owning aristocracy) which has no independent power-base. By controlling the instruments of power in this way, the patrimonial ruler can extend personal grace and favours, at the expense of traditional limitations on the exercise of authority. Where an extreme development of the ruler's discretion has occurred then patrimonial authority shades into what Weber calls 'sultanism'. He cites certain traditional African and Oriental societies as examples of patrimonial bureaucracies (the Chinese Empire is an obvious case), and suggests that these systems are relatively unstable, because they encourage palace revolts as the only means of voicing dissent. The absence of a 'rational-legal' *state and *bureaucracy also, in his view, acts as a significant hindrance to the development of modern (Western-type) capitalism.

patron-client relationship The roots of the patron-client relationship have been traced by some to the dependence of plebians on patricians in the Roman Empire. However the relationship is perhaps more obvious in the system of servitude known as *serfdom that was widespread in Europe in the Middle Ages. The various systems of tenancy that followed the fall of the ancient societies of Greece and Rome had a common factor in that a large number of those who worked the land were unfree. They were tied to both land and landlord by bonds of service. The system of servitude in Europe was as much a system of authority as it was an economic adaptation. Prestige for the lord lay in the protection of as many serfs and dependent tenants as possible: hand in hand with this prestige went military capacity and political power.

While the system of serfdom was established by law, the dependency of tenants was ensured through a mixture of economic and religious ties, which are covered by the general terms 'patronage' and 'clientage'. These set up a relationship between a politically and economically powerful patron, usually a landlord, and a weaker client. While the relationship may be regarded as socially necessary and honourable by both parties, its inequality makes it a potent source of *exploitation. The ties established may link two families over many generations and may be reinforced by accumulated debts that make the client fundamentally unfree.

The economic means of establishing patron-client relationships nearly always have their basis in systems of landholding, such as share-cropping. Client families may be lent money, seed or goods by the patron, in order to see them through bad seasons, often in return for the unpaid labour of client family members. This can be regarded as benevolent, but also creates debts that may never be paid off. This is one of the underlying factors in systems of debt bondage (sometimes called bonded labour) that are widespread in India, although forbidden by both national and international law.

The ties of patron-clientage were basic to the system of land tenure and agricultural production in *feudal Europe, where they still persist in Northern Mediterranean countries. *Clienteliumo* is the basis of the varied contractual relationships throughout Southern Italy, for example. Its essence is not the fixed and contractual but rather the informal and flexible. It is a face-to-face relationship, and many writers stress its importance in giving clients a degree of political power, through their support of the patron in his external political activities.

The conquerors and colonists of Latin America imported many of the values and legal institutions of feudal Europe, including patron-client relationships. The pre-dominance of Roman Catholicism in Latin societies links this system of asymmetrical political and economic relationships to the system known as *compadrazgo*, or godparenting. The godparent-godchild relationship established in baptism is actually a link between two sets of parents, the biological and the spiritual. In systematic *compadrazgo*, the child links a powerful godparent, who is supposed to ensure its spiritual welfare, to economically and politically weaker natural parents. Coparenting ties, once established, give the natural parents the right to call on the godfather for material assistance and legal support. In return, their obligation is to support the political activities of the godfather, and to work for him when he requires it. Being a godfather confers prestige as well as economic and political advantages. Although the term patron-client relationship is not always used within or about *compadrazgo*, it clearly applies.

Compadrazgo is a form of fictive kinship that enables actual kin networks to be extended. In the Arab world, the transition from kin-based networks to the more complex relationships of modern states is also marked by extensive political patronage, although this is not nearly so strongly characterized by economic exploitation as the form found in Latin societies. Despite stressing the asymmetry of the patron-client relationship, writers on this area emphasize the political content: the role of the patron as a cultural broker, and a system of obligations that is moral rather than monetary. Clients may become wealthy, but they do not lose their jural status as clients.

For anthropological accounts of this form of (what has been called) 'lop-sided friendship' see Julian Pitt-Rivers, *The People of the Sierra* (1954) and Michael Kenny, *A Spanish Tapestry* (1961).

pattern variables See Parsons.

peasants (peasantry) In common usage refers to rich smallholders, *sharecroppers, or landless labourers, in a vast range of historical and cultural contexts. Social scientists, on the other hand, have devoted a good deal of time and passion to arguing over the exact definition.

Attempts to define peasant economies, particularly in Marxist theory, in such a way as to link social groups as diverse as feudal tenants, independent farmers, and rural day-labourers. These have variously stressed the importance of the peasant family as a unit of both production and consumption, the relationship of capitalist to non-capitalist agriculture, the use of family labour in a rural setting, and the exploitation of poor, or relatively poor, agricultural producers. There have been attempts to define a peasant *mode of production, through the notion of the family-labour farm, as well as assertions that the peasantry is a class. The latter is related to debates about the revolutionary potential of the peasantry—again particularly among Marxist theorists.

Among social anthropologists, peasants have been defined by their cultural habits and norms, by narrowness of vision, and clinging to *tradition. These attempts to characterize peasants as a generic human type have been littered with typologies that try to agglomerate all the different social and economic forms that are variously called peasant. However, as with Marxist economics, no precise or useful definition has been produced, and the term is best regarded as an imprecise socio-economic category of descriptive rather than heuristic usefulness.

There are extensive literatures on the social structure of peasant societies and on peasant movements and *rebellions. The writings of Eric R. Wolf still offer one of the best introductions to these topics (see *Peasants*, 1966, and *Peasant Wars of the 20th Century*, 1971).

pedagogy The science or art of teaching. Some sociologists of education use the term 'pedagogical practices' with reference to the methods and principles that inform educational techniques, and make a distinction between the expressed pedagogy (which the teacher purports to use), and his or her observed pedagogy in practice. The former may be liberal (or 'progressive'), emphasizing the needs and autonomy of the individual child, whereas the latter may be conservative (aimed at preserving the authority and expertise of the teacher as a professional). This distinction is therefore analogous to that between the formal and *hidden curriculum.

peer group A set of individuals who, sharing certain common characteristics such as age, ethnicity, or occupation, perceive themselves and are recognized by others as a distinct social collectivity. The group is seen to have its own *culture, *symbols, *sanctions, and *rituals, into which the new member must be *socialized, and according to which those who fail to comply with group norms may be ostracized.

Peirce, Charles Sanders (1839–1914) One of the founders of *pragmatism and *semiology whose work has generally been neglected in both traditions. One of his key ideas is embodied in the maxim to 'consider what effects, which might conceivably have practical bearings, we conceive the object of our conception to have. Then, our conception of these effects is the whole of our conception of the object'. Pragmatism for Peirce is not a theory of truth but a theory of meaning. His semiological writings introduce the idea of 'indexical signs', a reference to the fact that a token may have different meanings in different contexts, an insight that is basic to the *ethnomethodological principle of the 'indexicality' of all language.

penology The study of the management and punishment of criminals. The term is associated with the 19th-century movement in penal reform, which redefined prisons as correctional rather than retributive establishments, and at that time described a large number of interested parties (including reformers and lawyers) and a discrete debate. However, in its contemporary usage it normally refers to specific sociological or criminological studies of punishment and deterrence, rather than a separate intellectual or academic discourse.

perception The faculty of acquiring sensory experience. Study of the processes by which we gather and interpret visual information is largely the province of social psychologists, who have identified several general principles ('laws') of perception, and also some effects upon it of (among other things) motivation and attention. The former includes the phenomenon of the 'figure-ground contrast'; that is, how we perceive objects distinctly from their surroundings. This can be studied via so-called *projective tests. 'Constancy' is also a principle of perception; that is, objects maintain perceptual stability through transformations of various types, such as alterations in size and proportion. The most systematic attempt to study the organization of perceptual phenomena is probably that of the *Gestalt ('form', 'figure', or 'holistic') psychologists, who emphasize the role of innate patterning in visual perception, although *behaviourist approaches have also been influential, notably in America. *See also* ATTITUDES; ATTRIBUTION THEORY; COGNITIVE THEORY.

personal construct theory A social psychological theory developed by George Alexander Kelly in *The Psychology of Personal Constructs* (1955), which argues that 'a person's processes are psychologically channelled by the ways in which he anticipates events'. Like *phenomenology, *social constructionism and *symbolic interactionism, the theory therefore examines the ways in which people construct *meanings. In this case, the orientation is to the future, the argument being that a person's personal constructs (the distinctive categories by which he or she orders close interpersonal relationships or role-constructs) are an anticipation of future events in terms of similar events experienced in the past. Kelly devised the 'repertory grid technique' (the generalized form of an earlier 'role-construct repertory test') as a way of revealing these personal constructs to the researcher. Subjects are asked to distinguish *triads of people known to them into a series of similar pairs and different individuals, and to explain their selections, in this way building up a series of binary distinctions unique to the respondent, and by means of which he or she is said to anticipate events. The structure of categories that is then mathematically derived from these distinctions is said to correspond to the structure of the psychological space utilized by the individual at a particular point in time. The technique was originally applied to the detection of mental disorder but has since been used more widely.

personal documents These are documents, used in social science, that record part of a person's life—most frequently in their own words. The most obvious examples are letters, diaries, biographies and *life-histories, but the term can be stretched to include many other items from photographs to inscriptions on tombstones. (The surprisingly wide sources of data are fully described in K. Plummer's *Documents of Life—2*, 1983.) Personal documents aim to capture the subjective side of a person's life and are valuable as part of an *ideographic research strategy. They are often used in the early and exploratory stages of research but can also be used as *case studies for *theory generation and *falsification. Personal documents were particularly popular in the work of some of the early *Chicago sociologists: for example, Clifford Shaw gathered many life-histories of delinquents, and the classic study by William Isaac Thomas and Florian Znaniecki *The Polish Peasant in Europe and America* (1918) analysed a series of letters, as well as presenting a major life-history. *See also* DOCUMENTARY RESEARCH.

personal income *See* INCOME DISTRIBUTION.

personality One of several concepts used by social scientists to refer to the individual (others include *self and *identity). The concept has its origins in the Latin word *persona* (meaning 'mask'), and refers to the set of more or less stable characteristics, as assessed and judged by others, that distinguish one individual from another. These characteristics are assumed to hold across time and place and to underlie behaviour. The term personality consequently refers to the individual as object (the object of external evaluation) whereas the concept of self refers to the individual as subject (as the source of action and self-reflection).

Like *attitude, the notion of personality is primarily invoked in the attempt to predict or explain individual behaviour, and refers to what an individual brings to a situation that belongs to them. However, whereas attitudes are object-specific—that is, they are directed towards specific persons or things—the term personality refers to broader, more general orientations and tendencies. The underlying assumption is that behaviour is a function of two factors—personality (or attitudes) and situation—the relative importance of the two varying from situation to situation. Some situations almost entirely override personality differences (a fire in a cinema creating widespread panic); others allow personality differences to flourish.

The precise way in which personality is conceptualized and measured varies enormously. These is an underlying tension between the concept's connotations that each individual is unique, with a distinctive personality which should be described as a whole, and the demands of *positivist science for generalizations based on the exploration of standard personality characteristics across a range of persons. The former suggests an *ideographic approach to personality, in which the description and analysis of the unique individual is the focus, whereas the latter suggests a nomothetic approach in which the emphasis is on studying a range of people and examining shared characteristics. This is usually associated with more atomistic and fragmented models of personality. To some extent, however, this opposition is deceptive since most approaches to personality attempt both to develop general models of personality and to describe individual cases.

The Freudian theory of personality has been most widely used in the detailed examination of an individual's personality, as in *Freud's own classic case-histories, like those of Dora and the Wolf Man. These detailed analyses are, however, grounded in a general theory of personality which, in its best-known version, delineates a tripartite personality structure of id, ego, and superego. Behaviour is the result of the dynamic interplay of the forces of id, ego, and superego, and the individual's personality is determined by his or her success in progressing through the different stages of psycho-sexual development during the first five years of life.

Freudian theorizing has been most influential in clinical contexts where the particular individual is the focus and it is necessary to describe and examine the individual's personality in detail. This is mainly accomplished through observations made in the course of diagnostic interviews and therapy. However, *projective tests have also been widely used in clinical contexts, as an aid to the exploration of personality dynamics. Within academic psychology, nomothetic approaches have been more usual, and there has been a greater focus on the development of standardized measures of personality. One common approach has been the so-called trait approach. The term trait refers to a personality characteristic or disposition—a tendency to act or react in certain ways—and the trait approach seeks to identify the key personality traits, to describe individuals in terms of these traits, and to examine the association of these traits with behaviour.

The American psychologist Gordon *Allport, in his study *Personality* (1937), developed the idea of personality traits, sorting through the enormous number of words in everyday language used to describe individuals and grouping and selecting them on a common sense, intuitive basis. He emphasized the uniqueness of the individual and the interconnectedness of personality traits, and his concerns were more ideographic than nomothetic. In contrast, Raymond B. Cattell used *factor analysis to select out a far more restricted list of independent personality traits, and developed a personality test to measure them. He conceptualized sixteen traits as bipolar dimensions of personality: such as dominance versus submission, radicalism versus conservatism, emotional sensitivity versus toughness. In a similar vein, Hans Eysenck further reduced the number of personality factors, postulating that the two key personality dimensions are extraversion-intraversion and neuroticism. Although the factor analytic techniques used by Cattell and Eysenck have been strongly criticized, the type of pencil-and-paper tests of personality they generated have been widely used.

Sociology's relation to the study of personality has often been ambivalent if not overtly hostile. *Durkheim's assertion of the need for a distinctively sociological explanation of suicide led him to reject the relevance of psychological factors such as 'psychopathic states'. There has been a general tendency to see personality as belonging to the domain of psychology rather than sociology. What this means in practice is that some measure of personality may be included in a social survey simply to establish that observed differences are not due to personality. However some sociologists, notably Talcott *Parsons, have attempted to explore the possible relationships between personality and social structure. Drawing on the work of cultural anthropologists who linked culture and personality, work which was itself strongly influenced by Freudian theorizing, these sociologists have examined not only the way in which personality is shaped by social forces, but also the fit between personality characteristics and the social organization (whether the broader society or some more restricted institution or organization such as a business company or religious group). Max Weber's *Protestant Ethic and the Spirit of Capitalism* (1905) can be viewed as one such study. *See also* AUTHORITARIAN PERSONALITY; CULTURE AND PERSONALITY SCHOOL; MASS SOCIETY; NARCISSISM.

personnel management Within organizations that employ people, this is the function with policy responsibility for the selection and recruitment of staff, training, performance assessment, career development, disciplinary proceedings, pre-retirement advisory work, equal opportunities policies, pay bargaining, and industrial relations. In small organizations these functions may be combined with other management responsibilities; in large organizations a substantial separate department may be involved in setting policy, its implementation, and in keeping up to date with developments in labour law. In recent years the newer alternative term 'human resource management' has come into use, reflecting the increased importance of this function in labour-intensive service-sector industries.

Peter principle A principle which states that employees tend to be promoted to a level above the level at which they are competent and efficient, a process which creates incompetent senior management in any organization.

petite (or petty) bourgeoisie Defined by Karl Marx as a 'transitional class', in which the interests of the major classes of *capitalist society (the *bourgeoisie and the *proletariat) meet and become blurred, the petite bourgeoisie is located between these two classes in terms of its interests as well as its social situation. It represents a distinctive form of social organization in which petty productive property is mixed with, and owned by, family labour. Small shopkeepers and self-employed artisans are the archetypes.

Marx derides what he sees as the petit-bourgeois self-delusion that, because it combines both employment and ownership of the *means of production, it somehow represents the solution to the class struggle. This class was progressive in a limited sense, as witnessed by its claims at various times for cooperatives, credit institutions, and progressive taxation, as a consequence of felt oppression at the hands of the bourgeoisie. However, these were (in terms of the Marxist view of history) strictly limited demands, just as the ideological representatives of this class have been constrained by their own problems and solutions (see Marx's essay on 'The Class Struggles in France 1848–1850').

This traditional 'petty' bourgeoisie (the widespread adoption of the pejorative epithet speaks volumes about the limitations of *Marxism), discussed by Marx in his own writings, was replaced by the 'new petty bourgeoisie' identified by Marxist writers such as Nicos Poulantzas, and consisting of engineers, supervisors, and other modern additions to the class structure who, on the basis of ideological, political, and economic criteria, are unproductive wage-earners but who are none the less carriers of ideological domination. Erik Olin Wright, for his part, found small employers to occupy a *contradictory class location between the petty bourgeoisie proper and the bourgeoisie itself. The application of a whole range of criteria extracted from Marx's writings does little to eradicate the essentially derogatory meaning of the term.

According to Marx, concentration and centralization of capital was eventually to throw the petty bourgeoisie into the ranks of the increasingly immiserated *working class, just as the peasantry were to become *proletarianized despite their attachment to the land. However, the urge to self-employment, to own the means of livelihood, coupled with the growth of the services sector and the persistence of 'shopkeepers', mean that this class continues to defy not only elimination but also neat categorization into the proletariat, the *middle class, or salariat, and as such it is usually accorded the status of a survival from a previous era. The values that its members are commonly deemed to represent—of entrepreneurship at the grassroots level, self-help, individualism, family, and careful husbanding of resources—mean that, however buffeted by recessions and mounting bankruptcies, the petite bourgeoisie continues to provide a stereotyped model of past virtues. However, research suggests that it is here to stay, since the tendencies of modern capitalist society seem to have no uniform effects on its situation: in some countries its position is weakening, while in others it is numerically and politically in the ascendant (see F. Bechhofer and B. Elliott (eds.), *The Petite Bourgeoisie: Comparative Studies of the Uneasy Stratum*, 1981).

For the emerging capitalism of post-Soviet societies in Eastern and Central Europe, it represents a potent image of small-scale (and therefore the only successful form of) privatization, at least to date. Paradoxically, it was the survival of the petty-bourgeois mentality within the second economy of these largely statist societies which contributed in large measure to the collapse of Soviet-style communism (see I. Szelenyi, *Socialist Entrepreneurs*, 1988). It also led to the identification of property ownership with political freedom, and therefore propelled these societies towards an almost uncritical commitment to universal *privatization as the panacea for previous ills.

petty accumulation *See* CAPITALISM.

petty bourgeoisie *See* PETITE BOURGEOISIE.

petty commodity production A Marxist concept which refers to a form of *production in which: the producer has ownership or *de facto* possession of the *means of production; the goods or services produced are commodities (that is, sold through the market); the producer does not systematically hire wage workers, but may use unpaid family labour; the scale of production is small and there is little *capital accumulation. This concept is widely used in the study of peasants, family farmers, and artisans. *See also* SIMPLE COMMODITY PRODUCTION.

phenomenology (phenomenological sociology) Phenomenology is a philosophical method of inquiry developed by the German philosopher Edmund Husserl. It involves the systematic investigation of consciousness. Consciousness, it is argued, is the only phenomenon of which we can be sure. It is assumed that our experience of the world, including everything from our perception of objects through to our knowledge of mathematical formulae, is constituted in and by consciousness. To trace this process of constitution, we have to disregard what we know about the world, and address the question of how, or by what processes, that knowledge comes into being. This strategy is known as bracketing or phenomenological reduction.

On the face of it phenomenology does not seem to offer much inspiration to sociology. Husserl started with individual consciousness and found himself in trouble over establishing that other people actually exist. It is less surprising that phenomenology was developed principally by the major *existentialist thinkers of the 20th century. An important link to sociology was established by a pupil of Husserl, Alfred Schutz, who fled the rise of fascism in Europe and combined his work as a philosopher, in the United States, with work as a banker. His *Phenomenology of the Social World* (1932) sets out the basic principles of phenomenological sociology. It describes how, from a basic stream of undifferentiated experience, we construct the objects and our knowledge of these objects that we take for granted in our everyday lives. The basic act of consciousness is (first-order) typification: bringing together typical and enduring elements in the stream of experience, building up typical models of things and people, and building a shared social world. The job of the sociologist is to construct second-order typifications: a rational model of the social world based on the (first-order) theories which actors offer to explain their own activities. Schutz talks about sociology as creating a world of rational puppets which we then manipulate to discover how people might act in the real world.

Phenomenology became a resource for sociologists in the late 1960s as many of the orthodoxies of the post-war period were rejected. Its most lasting influence has been on *ethnomethodology. Peter Berger and Thomas Luckmann, in *The Social Construction of Reality* (1966), offered a general social theory based on phenomenology, claiming to combine the features of theories both of social action and social structure: the social world is constructed through processes of typifications, which then take on an objective quality, above and beyond the social groups who produce them. Around the same time, this notion of objectification was connected by some authors to Karl Marx's theory of alienation, in an attempt to produce *humanist forms of *Marxism. One source of inspiration for this work was Husserl's later studies of science, which argued that the sciences had become divorced from the fabric of human experience, and were in fact obstructing (alienating) our understanding of ourselves.

A few of these ideas have fed into the sociological mainstream but there is no distinctive phenomenological school of sociology now in existence. *See also* COMMONSENSE KNOWLEDGE; INTERPRETATION.

Phillips curve In a famous article on 'The Relation Between Unemployment and the Rate of Change of Money Wage Rates in the United Kingdom, 1861–1957', published in the journal *Economica* (1958), the economist A. W. Phillips argued that an inverse relationship existed between *unemployment and wage *inflation in the UK throughout the period in question. The rate of change in money wages tended to be high in conditions of low unemployment and low (or even negative) when unemployment was high. Thus, the so-called Phillips curve suggested that maintenance of full employment would necessarily involve some inflation, whereas inflation was only likely to be reduced by an increase in unemployment.

philosophy As an intellectual activity, philosophy is the most broad-ranging of the academic disciplines, since it addresses a wide range of interlinked questions about the nature of understanding, logic, language, and causality, many of which occur in the various other sciences. The sociologist is most likely to encounter philosophical debate in the fields of epistemology and ethics—both of which branches of philosophy are dealt with elsewhere in this dictionary.

The philosophy of the social sciences is a recognized specialism among sociologists, and asks questions about (among other things) the processes of concept-formation, the relationships between theory and evidence, the place of values, nature of motivation, role of language, and the nature of proof in the social sciences generally and sociology in particular. Again, many of the most significant arguments and most influential schools of thought concerning these issues have been treated separately, as discrete items in this dictionary.

It has sometimes been argued that much of what passes as sociological *theory (for example in the works of Anthony Giddens) is actually social philosophy, since it consists mainly of *metaphysical speculation about the human condition, rather than concrete or testable propositions about social life. However, this is probably a minority view, although there is quite widespread agreement that sociology has in the past (most obviously during the 1960s) suffered from an excessive reflexivity and obsession with exploring the epistemological foundations of the discipline. *See also* HISTORIOGRAPHY; METHODOLOGICAL PLURALISM.

philosophy of social science *See* PHILOSOPHY; SCIENCE, SOCIOLOGY OF.

phratry In many pre-industrial societies, social organization is based on kinship groups through descent in either the male or female line, but these kinship groups are then aggregated according to non-kinship principles into larger groups which (in some cases) the anthropologist Lewis H. Morgan termed 'phratries'. Examples include several American Indian and Australian Aboriginal tribes. In other societies, extended kinship groups include the clan (usually a matrilineal descent group), and gens (patrilineal descent group). It is now common to designate as phratries any grouping or association of clans which recognize some relationship to each other. Often, therefore, phratries are organized around either a division of labour or distinct ritual functions. Moieties (the division of societies into two groups, based on any principle, such that there is a dual organization of the whole) are a particular form of phratry. However, all of these terms are subject to the vicissitudes of context, and have sensibly been used in very different ways. Students of kinship groups therefore have to live with a great deal of variation in the use of (sometimes poorly chosen) terminology—and are strongly advised to verify specific definitions and usage in particular circumstances.

Physiocrats (Physiocratic Thought) A school of social theory associated with the writings of the French political economist François Quesnay (1694–1774) and others. Physiocratic thought is mainly of interest to sociologists for its influence on (in curiously equal measure) Adam Smith and Karl Marx. The Physiocrats criticized the *mercantilist belief that wealth originated in exchange, and accorded priority instead to the land, arguing that improved farming techniques, fiscal reform, and free trade in agricultural produce would stimulate *capital accumulation, *surplus value, and wealth generally. Smith endorsed the principle of *laissez-faire and applauded the Physiocratic emphasis on private property as the key to improved living conditions. Marx, in his turn, described Quesnay as the founder of modern *political economy, since his works introduced to modern economics the notions of *capital and the interdependence of production, circulation, and distribution in a surplus-producing economy. Although Marx's attribution of this insight is now quite widely shared, the Physiocrats are generally criticized for glorifying the concept of the agricultural surplus, and failing to realize that there was also a surplus attributable to labour.

Piaget, Jean (1896–1980) A Swiss psychologist who made a major and distinct contribution to theories of human intellectual development, arguing that individuals actively make sense of the world, rather than merely being *conditioned by it.

Piaget conducted a long series of experiments with children which led him to the conclusion that they pass through successive stages of cognitive development. He distinguishes four such phases, each characterized by its own distinctive logic, and each associated with the development of particular intellectual skills. In the sensorimotor stage (from birth to approximately 18 months), the child does not know that it exists as a separate object, and therefore cannot distinguish between its *self, its actions, and the external objects upon which it acts. Its intelligence is expressed only in terms of sensory and physical contact with the environment. The pre-operational stage (from about age 2 to 7 years) is characterized by an increasing command of *language, and an ability to think about concrete objects which are not actually present, but also by extreme egocentrism. At this stage of development children cannot take the role of others. They also lack understanding of abstract concepts such as causality, quantity, and weight. In the stage of so-called concrete-operations (which lasts from about the ages of 7 to 11 or 12), children start to classify objects, can take the role of others and understand the nature of cause and effect, but still have difficulty thinking about abstract concepts without referring these to real events or particular images with which they are familiar (hence 'concrete' operational stage). Finally, in the formal operations stage (12 years onwards), the young person is able to create his or her own classificatory systems and thus to achieve formal and abstract thought. Adolescents can apply general rules to particular problems, reason logically from premises to conclusions, and think in terms of *theories and *concepts. Not all adults progress to this final stage however, since many people have great difficulty comprehending abstract concepts, and so do not move beyond the phase of concrete operations. Abstract thinking is dependent upon a social environment which exposes the individual to formal cognitive reasoning: the internal processes of the mind only develop through social inter-action. Piaget argued that the various stages of cognitive development were the same cross-culturally; however, since the content of cultures varied, the partic-ular beliefs that people learned in each of the stages would vary in time and place. If the surrounding culture teaches that cause and effect are related to magic then, clearly, this is how the individual will come to interpret the world.

Piaget's approach to intellectual development and the notion of developmen-tal stages has been a major influence in *cognitive psychology. Unlike most other psychologists, who have been concerned with behavioural aspects of cognition (such as short-term memory), Piaget has highlighted the *epistemological ques-tions surrounding the definition and categorization of knowledge. His theories of child intellectual development have also been incorporated by some teachers and educationalists into methods of teaching young children. Most of his exten-sive writings are now translated into English (see H. E. Gruber and J. J. Voneche (eds.), *The Essential Piaget—An Interpretive Reference and Guide*, 1977).

piecemeal social engineering In *The Poverty of Historicism* (1957), the philosopher Sir Karl Popper criticized *historicist (notably *communist and *fascist) attempts to foretell the future, and argued that the holistic social exper-iments based on these theories were doomed to failure, because the course of human history is strongly influenced by the growth of knowledge, and we cannot (rationally or scientifically) predict the future growth of scientific knowledge. Rather, by analogy with the central role of piecemeal experiments in the sciences, he argues that the only form of social engineering that can be rationally justified is one which is small-scale, incremental, and continuously amended in the light of experience. The crucial point about this approach is that it is based on trial and error rather than a prior historicist vision; or, as Popper puts it, 'we make progress if, and only if, we are prepared to *learn from our mistakes*: to recognize our errors and to utilize them critically instead of persevering in them dogmat-ically'. Piecemeal social engineering is, therefore, nothing less than the introduc-tion of (Popper's conception of) scientific methods into planning and politics.

pie chart (pie graph) A form of descriptive statistics in which data are pre-sented graphically or pictorially as in the hypothetical illustration shown here. It gives the relative proportions of people who are admitted to universities, based on social-class background. The distribution has been divided into four social classes (salariat, self-employed, routine clerical, working class), and the 'pie' has been divided into 'slices' proportional in size to the frequency of university admission in the various categories. The principal advantage of this way of presenting data is that it makes it easy to see the proportion of the total pie obtained by each category. Where the primary intention of the presentation is to compare the relative sizes of categories then a conventional *bar chart is to be preferred.

pillarization This term is a translation of the Dutch word *Verzuiling*, first used by the political scientist J. P. Kruyt to describe the peculiar nature of the social

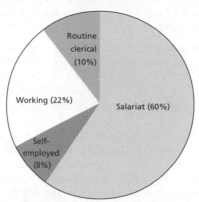

Pie chart. Social class origins of university entrants

structure and political institutions in the Netherlands, although it has since been applied elsewhere (for example with reference to Belgium). For much of the 20th century, Dutch society was divided by cross-cutting class-based and religious cleavages into four dominant interest groups or blocs—Catholics, Protestants, Socialists, and Liberals—around which formed 'virtually all politically and socially relevant organizations and group affiliations' (A. Lipjhart, *The Politics of Accommodation*, 1968).

Both religious blocs incorporated sections of the working and middle classes, whereas the secular forces divided along class lines (working-class Socialists; middle/upper-class Liberals). Separate political parties represented each bloc (two for the Protestants) and politics was characterized by bargaining and accommodation between them. Many other social institutions were similarly constituted: for example, trade unions, media, voluntary associations, social welfare, and education. Patterns of élite formation, friendship, marriage, job recruitment, and other social relations were also affected.

pilot study Any small-scale test of a research instrument (such as a question-naire, experiment, or interview-schedule), run in advance of the main fieldwork, and used to test the utility of the research design. Pilot studies therefore vary in size and nature. Interview-schedules for a large-scale *survey may be piloted on a substantial sub-sample of the relevant population—perhaps as many as 500 respondents. In-depth interviewing techniques, on the other hand, may be ade-quately piloted on only a few acquaintances and friends. Quantitative sociologists and social survey research agencies will insist on full briefing and debriefing of interviewers who conducted the pilot, in order to identify and rectify logistical and analytical difficulties in the research design, including (for example) ambiguous questions, incorrect routeing or filtering through the *questionnaire, replies which cannot be *coded, and items about which there appears to be no variance (*see* VARIATION, STATISTICAL) in the responses. If the difficulties are substantial a second pilot may also be required in order to confirm that the amendments to the original design have proved effective.

Pitt-Rivers, A. Lane-Fox (1827–1900) A controversial and eccentric aristocrat who was a general in the British army, landowner, archaeologist, anthropologist, and government inspector. He has been called the 'father of scientific archaeology', having excavated over forty classic sites in the United Kingdom. He was also an anthropologist and follower of Charles Darwin, advocating a gradualist *evolutionary doctrine.

placebo A treatment that has no physical or direct effect, and is administered to a *control group in experimental research, in place of a treatment whose effects are being studied. This usually happens only in medical research; in social research, control groups are rarely offered a placebo experience or treatment.

In the medical context, a substance lacking known pharmacologically active ingredients is given to the sick in order to please them: that is, for possible beneficial effects arising from faith in the powers of treatment (the placebo effect). Placebos are also widely used as controls in evaluating the therapeutic efficacy of the active components of new drugs. Conventionally, the experimental treatment is given to cases selected at random, with the ineffective placebo given to all other cases, even though they are suffering from the same illness. In the 'double blind' situation, even the person administering the treatments does not know which is which, as the medicines are made to look the same, to prevent him or her inadvertently communicating their knowledge to recipients.

planned economy *See* COMMAND ECONOMY.

plantations Plantation economies developed in the course of European economic and social expansion, particularly in Latin America and South-east Asia. They are associated with a large-scale, limited range of export-oriented, staple-crop production in tropical or sub-tropical environments.

The traditional form of plantation was associated with *slave labour. The socio-economic system that resulted was, in many cases, regarded as synonymous with the organization of colonies because of the investment of foreign capital and transfer of wealth from periphery to core. Historical changes have led to a variety of modern forms of plantation, ranging from those based in labour-intensive cultivation (often making widespread use of migrant or other unskilled unfree labourers), to more capital-intensive agro-industrial enterprises. In general, plantation agriculture is regarded as being exploitative of labour, land, and developing nations.

pluralism The term refers primarily to two major and very different bodies of work in political science. Most commonly, it refers to a body of American, empirically oriented that was highly influential during the 1960s, though it originated in the work on group conflict undertaken by Arthur Bentley at Chicago (see *The Process of Government*, 1905). Largely on the basis of studies of political decision-making in local *communities, most famously exemplified by Robert Dahl's *Who Governs?* (1961), the pluralists argued that the United States was a *democratic society because political power was widely distributed amongst the competing *interest groups that operated therein: none of these groups was all-powerful and each was powerful enough to secure its own legitimate interests. The empirical claims made by the pluralists have been subjected to serious criticisms by scholars working within the Marxist and élitist traditions (see, for example, G. W. Domhoff, *Who Rules America?*, 1967), who argue that visible exercises of power may disguise the fact that some groups wield power in less obvious ways, and that expressed political preferences are not necessarily equivalent to objective (or 'real') *interests. Nevertheless, this variety of pluralism continues to exercise considerable influence as a body of normative political theory (see, for example, Dahl's *A Preface to Economic Democracy*, 1985).

Less commonly, the term also refers to a body of British political theory, associated with such names as George Douglas Howard Cole, John Neville Figgis, and Harold J. Laski, which attracted equal attention in the 1920s. It argued that the sovereign power, whose concentration in the *state is accepted by all other political theories save that of the *anarchist tradition, should not simply be competed for, but should in addition be distributed amongst the self-governing associations of *civil society. This latter body of work appeared to have died a death until it was exhumed by Paul Hirst in his *The Pluralist Theory of the State* (1989). According to Hirst, the 'associationalism' of the British pluralists may be combined with the American stress on group competition to produce a concept of 'associational democracy', which provides a model for a socialist polity which contrasts sharply with that provided by the social democratic and Marxist-Leninist traditions. *See also* COMMUNITY POWER; ELITE THEORY; GUILDS; MILITARY-INDUSTRIAL COMPLEX; POWER ELITE.

pluralism, epistemological *See* METHODOLOGICAL PLURALISM.

plural social systems In the 1960s the industrial sociologist Tom Burns argued that *organization theorists were mistaken to assume that individuals within organizations act solely in accordance with the formal purposes of the enterprise, since they may well be motivated by concerns that conflict with those of the organization itself. Rather, organizations can be conceived as the simultaneous working of at least three *social systems, only one of which is the formal authority system in terms of which all decision-making overtly takes place. There is also a career system, within which people compete for advancement, and a political system in which individuals and departments compete for power. Thus, within firms, one should expect to find 'conflict [about] the degree of control one may exercise over the firm's resources, the direction of the activities of other people, and patronage (promotion and the distribution of privileges and rewards)'. In short, a 'plurality of action systems' are available to the employee, who 'may invoke any of them as the dominant reference system for this or that action, decision or plan' (see 'On the Plurality of Social Systems', in J. R. Lawrence (ed.), *Operational Research and the Social Sciences*, 1966). Burns's research was important in demonstrating that it was naïve for organizational theorists to conceptualize the firm as a unitary system which could be equated with the formal structure set down in the organization chart or blueprint.

plural societies Societies which are divided into different linguistic, ethnic, religious, or racial groups and communities. Arguably, this description could apply to almost any *society, with the result that the term is sometimes (unhelpfully) treated as synonymous with 'multi-cultural society' and applied to states as different as the contemporary United States and Brazil. Originally, however, the concept had a more limited application. It referred to those states in the developing world created by *colonial rule—notably Burma and Indonesia—in which different *ethnic groups occupied distinct places in the *division of labour, existed as largely self-contained *communities, and therefore felt little or no sense of obligation to the national society (see J. S. Furnivall, *Colonial Policy and Practice*, 1948). In other words, not only is there cultural heterogeneity, but also formal diversity in the institutional systems of kinship, religion, education, recreation, and economy (and sometimes, though not always, government).

In plural societies, people of different ethnic origins meet only in the marketplace, where the various groups must trade and exchange goods and services with each other. No common 'social will' therefore develops to restrict the exploitation of the members of one group by members of another. In order to prevent market anarchy, some social framework has to be devised to govern inter-group transactions; in the case of Indonesia, the major attempted resolutions of the plural dilemma have included the imposition of a *caste system, of the rule of a common law, a *nationalist *democracy, and *federalism. A good account of the rise and (partial) demise of pluralism in that society is W. F. Wertheim's *Indonesian Society in Transition* (1956).

Later writers (including, for example, M. G. Smith, *The Plural Society in the British West Indies*, 1965) extended Furnivall's usage to include the post-colonial and multiracial societies of the Caribbean and South Africa—which were seen as being socially and culturally pluralist (if not strictly so in terms of the division of labour). The principal critics of the plural societies thesis have been *Marxists, who have attempted to translate observed ethnic or cultural ('ideological') inequalities into underlying class conflicts, and to highlight relationships of *dependency between developed and developing societies.

Polanyi, Karl (1886–1964) An influential and internationally renowned Austrian-born economic historian, and brother of the philosopher Michael Polanyi. He taught widely throughout Europe and the United States, and has a substantial and continuing influence in sociology because of the way in which his empirical studies undermine many of the assumptions of *neo-classical economic theory.

His best-known publication is *The Great Transformation* (1944)—which has a foreword by Robert M. MacIver—in which he seeks to document the causes of the two world wars, the depression of the 1930s, and the basis of the 'new order' of the mid-20th century. His was a stringent study of the consequences of the emergence of the 'world market' and the manner in which society can protect itself against its consequences. He warned against promoting the economy to the point at which power becomes highly concentrated, economic decision-making escapes human control, and human dignity and freedom are threatened. This economism could destroy society by undermining social cohesion; it requires that the economy be embedded within relations of *social control similar to those found in *traditional societies.

His other major publications, notably the co-authored *Trade and Markets in the Early Empires* (1957) and the posthumously published *The Livelihood of Man* (1977), develop Polanyi's so-called substantivist critique of *liberalism, challenging the idea that freedom and justice are inextricably tied to the free market, and documenting the various ways in which economic processes in any society are necessarily shaped by its cultural, political, and social institutions.

Polanyi was a genuinely interdisciplinary scholar: an entry on him is also likely to be found in dictionaries of economics, history, anthropology, and political science. Most recently, his work has become part of the debate around the possibility for a 'Third Way' in the transition from *communism to the *market. Untrammelled market economics, as exported by most Western advisers, are seen by some East European social scientists and policy-makers as likely to create the kinds of problems associated with the self-regulating market that Polanyi documents across a range of historical examples. The opposition between the 'logic of the economy' and the 'logic of society' are particularly acutely felt by these post-communist societies as they leave their protective states and face the uncertainties of a rapid transition to the market.

polarization The tendency towards concentration at two opposing extremes. Many sociological typologies are descriptions of polar types or extremes: one obvious example is Ferdinand Tönnies's distinction between *Gemeinschaft* (community) and *Gesellschaft* (association), observed by sociologists in a large number of diverse contexts. The term polarization, however, strictly refers to the segregation and opposition of two unequal groups at opposite ends of a distribution of resources. It was in this sense that *Marx referred to the polarization of *bourgeoisie and *proletariat.

The term has also been used in empirical contexts. For example, on the basis of research on the Isle of Sheppey, R. E. Pahl (*Divisions of Labour*, 1984) identified a process of social polarization which was said to be producing in Britain a division into 'work rich' and 'work poor' *households. Pahl argued that opportunities in both the formal and informal sectors of the economy tended to cluster in the same households; or, put somewhat differently, that households whose members were *unemployed did not (indeed according to Pahl could not) compensate for this by informal economic activities in the hidden, underground, or so-called *black economy.

policy research Social scientific research which has non-university groups as its main intended audience (although the results may in practice also interest academic audiences). For the most part such research attempts to apply social scientific findings to the solution of problems identified by a client. The term 'applied sociology' is also given to such exercises. For example, the development of *game theory was funded by the US Department of Defence with reference to its relevance to military strategy, but it has also made a fundamental contribution to social science theory.

Policy research may be descriptive, analytical, or deal with causal processes and explanations; it may evaluate a new or existing policy programme, describe examples of best practice, measure social change, develop projections on the basis of large-scale modelling exercises, or consist of large-scale experimental research in real-life settings running for years and even decades. Most policy research espouses a multi-disciplinary approach and avoids narrowly disciplinary jargon. Thus policy research is rarely explicitly sociological, even if sociology contributes more than any other discipline to the theoretical foundations, design, and methodology of a study.

In principle, policy research will focus on actionable or malleable social factors to a greater extent than theoretical research. For example, the family may be the most important source of sex-role or racial stereotypes, but policy research would focus on the role of the public educational system in changing children's perceptions in directions considered desirable. Policy research has created some multi-disciplinary hybrid fields of study, such as industrial relations (*see* LABOUR RELATIONS) and *social policy. When carried out in the commercial sector the term 'consultancy work' is often preferred. For a review of the issues and an account of some interesting case studies see Martin Bulmer (ed.), *Social Policy Research* (1978). *See also* BLACK REPORT; BROKEN WINDOWS THESIS; COLEMAN REPORT.

political behaviour The term refers to any form of (individual or collective) involvement in the political process, or any activity which has political consequences in relation to government and policy. This broad definition embraces both legitimate forms of political participation (such as *voting in elections, activism in *interest groups, or *social movements) and illegitimate political activities (including *coups d'état, terrorism, and revolutions (*see* REBELLIONS). While formal participation aims at containing social conflict within the extant political system, so that the political order remains stable, dissent which cannot be channelled via existing political structures is likely, not only to pursue changes in policy, but also to challenge the political order itself. The study of political behaviour also embraces the study of inactivity and apathy, as well as the analysis of political *ideologies, *values, and *attitudes as the basis of participation and non-participation in the political sphere.

political crime Historically, the term refers to conspiracy, and the actual deed of challenges to political rulers or sacred authority. Political criminals were likely to suffer much more gruesome punishment than ordinary or common criminals. Over time, however, the meanings of the term—and indeed attitudes toward political criminals themselves—have undergone significant shifts.

For example, politically motivated crimes came to be redefined as offences against the *state in Western Europe during the 19th century, and there were also debates about whether offenders such as the Suffragettes and the Fenians should be dealt with in the conventional criminal justice system because of their self-proclaimed political status. By the late 20th century the political criminal had been transformed into the 'arch-criminal'—the terrorist—who uses illegitimate violence against innocent *citizens. However, human *rights campaigners and some criminologists have also raised questions about the way in which the state itself can use its monopoly of force in a criminal way, in the pursuit of socio-political and military objectives (for example through torture, disappearance, and *genocide). Some writers even argue that only states can be truly terrorist because they have the wholesale capacity to deploy terror as a systematic mode of *domination and governance (see, for instance, N. Chomsky, *The Culture of Terrorism*, 1988).

political culture The *norms, *values, and *symbols that define and help to legitimate the political power system of a society (for example, in the United States, the constitution, democracy, equality, the flag). When a political culture collapses or is thrown into doubt, a crisis of *legitimacy is created, as happened in Central Europe and the former USSR in 1989–91. Political culture, like *culture in general, is made up of fragments of received knowledge which people in a given society take to be truth. Scandals, revelations, failures, and political disasters can quickly undermine citizens' faith in the whole system. For this reason the preservation of political culture is a major preoccupation of politicians and state bureaucrats at every level.

The modern use of this term dates from the period after the Second World War. Gabriel Almond and Sidney Verba's *The Civic Culture* (1963) is a classic comparative study of political attitudes and democracy in five countries, aiming to show how cultural development and political development move hand in hand. The value of the concept does not depend on this particular political agenda. More recent research has tried to distinguish between 'real' political cultures (which citizens actively believe in and support) and 'imposed' political cultures (which are no more than artificially created ideologies imposed on citizens by threat or force). A question for the future is how once-powerful political cultures like those of the United States and the old Soviet Union will adapt to the centrifugal pressures of *ethnicity and *nationalism.

political economy In the strict sense, an influential body of writings on economic questions associated principally with the French and English Enlightenment of the 18th century, and which culminated in the economic theories associated with Adam Smith. However, because the 19th-century classical economists who built on Smith's ideas continued to refer to their work as political economy, some vagueness and broadening of the use of the term occurs in social science literature. It is, in fact, in the broad sense rather than the narrow sense that classical *sociology is widely viewed as a critique of political economy.

Early political economy resulted from the combined influence of the following: the progressive substitution of *rationalism and science for the religious modes of thought in philosophy, and the attempted application of empirical methods to moral and social questions; the rise of *capitalist *industrialism and the need to give an intellectual and ideological account of the emergent economic order; hostility to the so-called *mercantilist policies still being pursued by governments and which attributed the prosperity of states to a favourable balance of foreign trade. Though political economy was never a unified doctrine, its characteristic outlook stemmed from attempts to show that surpluses of value originate from *production, in particular from productive labour, rather than trade as such. For the *Physiocrats (and to some extent perhaps Smith himself), agriculture is the only source of surplus, but political economy from Smith onward also recognized the importance of *manufacture and the overall organization of productive activities through the *division of labour. This, they argued, should not be hampered by mercantilist efforts to control prices, wages, and money. Indeed, money is a mere symbol of value, not its source.

Though Smith's famous treatise in support of free-market exchange, *The Wealth of Nations* (1776), is taken as the beginning of the modern discipline of economics, he and his distinguished contemporaries of the *Scottish Enlightenment (such as Adam Ferguson) also wrote about a wide range of social, moral, and historical issues, much of which can be viewed as early sociology. However, the sociological element implied a more holistic view of society than did the economic doctrines. The latter are sharply individualistic, and in stressing the role of self-interest as the basis of cooperative order, contain in embryo form some key elements of what has since come to be known as *rational choice theory. But the later separation of economics from other disciplines would have been wholly alien to early political economy. This separation owes much to the fact that the so-called classical economists of the next generation, notably David Ricardo and his disciples among the 19th-century English *utilitarians, began to abstract the economic ideas from the rest and to formalize them—a process which has continued ever since. Despite their many divergences in outlook and purpose, Karl Marx, Max Weber, Émile Durkheim, and the other founders of sociology shared a conviction that the abstraction of the economic from other aspects of social life ignored crucial questions about the nature of modernity and capitalist production itself.

A recent development in modern economic theory, developed in the USA, goes under the name of 'political economy' and has nothing to do with radical or Marxist versions to which the label is more commonly applied. This literature applies neo-classical principles to areas outside the economy, such as public policy, focusing on artificially induced scarcities ('rents') which are produced by political pressure exerted by economic interest groups.

So-called radical political economy is a term associated with the renaissance of *Marxist thought in the 1960s. Hostile to functionalist-dominated academic sociology and economics in the United States and Britain, it sought to transcend the (from its point of view) ideological disciplinary divisions in social science, by developing a common basis in a resurgent *historical materialism. *See also* NEO-CLASSICAL ECONOMICS.

political parties Formal organizations for representing the aims and interests of different socio-economic forces in the political sphere—although not all societies have a party-political system of government. Political parties are the organizational means by which candidates for office are recruited and ideologies are propagated. Parties seek to organize and dominate the organs of government and to provide national leadership.

Party systems also take a variety of different forms, from the multi-party system at one extreme, to the one-party monopolistic state at the other. Multi-party systems (often with two principal parties) are strong in liberal democratic societies like Britain, the United States, France, and Germany, while the dominance of one political party is especially evident in African countries such as Kenya and Zimbabwe. It has been suggested that the type of party system is linked to the stage of development of a society, but local historical and political factors are probably more important in influencing the type of system that emerges.

Political sociologists have focused on political parties as organizations and studied their organizational dynamics. Issues of interest include the socio-economic background of leaders, activists, and supporters; the socio-political ideologies espoused by parties; the distribution of *power between the different collectivities embraced by the party organization; and the techniques for mobilizing support. A major pioneering study of political parties was conducted by the German sociologist Robert *Michels. In his study of organizational power, he noted the *oligarchical tendencies of party leaders and officials who come to dominate the party, as it becomes increasingly *bureaucratic. Their beliefs and attitudes, directed towards their own personal goals, are invariably less radical than those of rank-and-file members. Furthermore, where organizational procedures are used to stifle popular aspirations, radical objectives are inhibited. However, evidence from research elsewhere suggests that the oligarchical tendencies of party leaders should not be overstated, especially in accounts of the institutionalization of political parties.

Political scientists have also explored the role of parties in the political process and the extent to which different political regimes may be described as open or closed. The *liberal view is that political parties, along with *pressure groups and other *interest groups, engage in competition for power as the representatives of different socio-economic groups in society. As a result of open competition, power in *pluralist political systems is non-cumulative and shared. This benign view of the role of political parties in liberal democracies has been the subject of much criticism. It has been argued that certain groups dominate the political decision-making process—most obviously those who dominate in the economic realm. Furthermore, while observable party politics is worthy of study, the more subtle forms of power (such as agenda-setting) should not be ignored. Thus, while liberals emphasize the important role of political parties in representative democracies, *neo-Marxists play down their significance. In capitalist societies, it is argued, since the dominant economic power is also the ruling class, parliamentary politics is illusory, and simply an ideological strategy which diverts attention away from the real sources of political power.

Many have argued that this Marxist view of political parties and power is at least as unsophisticated as the liberal alternative. True, power may be concentrated, but it is possible for the views of ordinary people to influence political outcomes. In this respect, political parties are not inconsequential, and play an important role in the political sphere of advanced capitalist societies.

political science An academic discipline that studies *power and the distribution of power in different types of political systems. Political scientists inquire as to the sources of power, how it is exercised and by whom, how processes of constraint and control operate, who gains and who loses in power struggles. All of these topics raise further issues of political alignment, organization, conflict, and stability within political systems. The study of power takes various forms, from the investigation of individual political attitudes and behaviour, to the examination of *state activities at a national and international level. Increasingly, from an initial narrow interest in the machinery of government, political science has broadened its terrain and now overlaps with *political sociology in many of its substantive topics and theories. Dennis Kavanagh's *Political Science and Political Behaviour* (1983) is a good guide to the American and British literature.

In the narrow sense, the study of politics and power involves an examination of the various political institutions, such as the state, government, *political parties, *interest groups, and other non-government intermediary organizations active in the business of policy-making. The state, in particular, has been the subject of much attention since it dominates the political process in liberal democracies. However, taking a wider view, the operation of power is not confined exclusively to formal institutions and institutional activities. Rather, power lies also in non-decision-making processes which may lie outside the political system: for example, the power of business groups within capitalist economies is considerable. Political scientists, particularly those engaged in historical and comparative research, are also increasingly interested in the exercise of power across the world economy and in terms of international relations, rather than merely within particular nation-states. *See also* POLITICAL BEHAVIOUR.

political socialization The process of induction into a political system—by acquiring information on political symbols, institutions, and procedures, learning the role of a passive or active member of the polity, and internalizing the value-system and *ideology supporting the whole enterprise. The process can be understood and analysed both as individual learning and as cultural transmission by the community as a whole. Nations perpetuate their political traditions by inducting new generations into established patterns of thought and action—through the educational system, the mass media, the workplace, the neighbourhood committee, as well as through political institutions themselves. In Third World countries, where new political institutions may be created or existing structures reformed within short periods of time, the educational system, mass media, and community structures may all be used explicitly as means of political education and re-education. In older and more stable polities, the political socialization functions of social agencies are latent rather than manifest, often subtle enough to be invisible and publicly denied.

Studies of political socialization look at the degree of ideological stability over the life-cycle; the relationship between political attitudes and active participation; the selection and socialization of political elites (for example through the educational system); social class patterns of behaviour and anomalies (such as working-class conservatism and so-called false consciousness); the relationship between personality traits and political orientations; induction into political roles; and the relative influence of family, school, and workplace on political ideas and behaviour. *See also* POLITICAL CULTURE; SOCIALIZATION.

political sociology The branch of *sociology that is concerned with the social causes and consequences of given power distributions within or between societies, and with the social and political conflicts that lead to changes in the allocation of *power. A major focus of political sociology is the description, analysis, and explanation of the *state, the institution which claims a monopoly of the legitimate use of force within a given territory, and constitutes possibly the largest single concentration of power and *authority in any society. Whereas *political science deals mainly with the machinery of government, the mechanisms of public administration, and the formal political realm of elections, public opinion, pressure groups, and political behaviour, sociological analysis of political phenomena is concerned rather more with the interrelationships between politics, social *structures, *ideologies, and *culture. Even if the state is the most common object of study, political sociology deals more broadly with the study of the sources and utilization of power, authority, and influence in all social contexts including, for example, the family, friendship groups, clubs, and local communities. Power relationships in the labour market and the workplace could also be included, but are now usually studied under the label of industrial relations instead. A political system is any persistent pattern of human relationship that involves (to a significant extent) power, rule, or authority. Hence it is possible to study the politics of stateless societies, which have not yet developed any formal central institutions to monopolize power, but still have decision-making and rule-making processes which may be dominated by some members more than others.

Political sociology has been concerned with *political parties as social institutions and relations between members and party leaders—for example in the widespread apathy of the majority of members that can leave greater power to the leadership, and in the iron law of oligarchy (*see* MICHELS), which argues that leaders of an organization tend to substitute their own self-interests for those of the organization and seek to retain their positions of power to serve these interests. It addresses the phenomena of despotic and *totalitarian regimes as well as parliamentary *democracies, seeking to explain the origins and stability of specific political regimes and institutional structures. Studies of political participation, especially through the electoral system, address the interest theory of political behaviour which argues that people choose options that maximize their narrow self-interests and wider class interests rather than the public good. Political sociology has concentrated attention on *elites, their membership, and the wide gap separating them from the ruled classes. In one view 'the study of politics is the study of influence and the influential . . . The influential are those who get most of what there is to get . . . Those who get the most are the elite; the rest are mass' (H. Laswell, *Politics: Who Gets What, When, How*, 1958). Political sociology studies the manifestation and regulation of conflict, including social protest behaviour and the causes of revolutions; the formation and activities of *interest groups (which are often not self-aware) and formal *pressure groups; political ideologies, *political cultures, and the formulation of political opinion and *public opinion; *political socialization in childhood, adolescence, and adult life, through educational institutions and experiences in the workplace. Analyses of the tensions and cleavages which arise from the social and economic order are often carried out on a comparative basis in order to show how political choices are made from among the full range of possible or available alternatives.

Political sociology employs all the methods of sociological analysis and attitude research, including *case studies of individual organizations, or particular local, state, or national governments; *opinion polls; interview *surveys of electors, political participants, and political representatives; documentary evidence and content analysis to study political ideologies and government policy-making; and mathematical modelling of decision-making processes and outcomes. Comparative cross-national studies are more common than in other fields of sociology. Robert E. Dowse and John A. Hughes, *Political Sociology* (2nd edn., 1986) is a good introductory text. *See also* COMMUNITY POWER; POWER ELITE; PSEPHOLOGY.

poll *See* OPINION POLLS.

polyandry A term denoting the marriage of one woman to two or more men. It is a rarely encountered form of marriage and usually occurs when one woman marries two or more brothers, in which case it is known as either adelphic or fraternal polyandry. One motive in this case would be the maintenance of land and property within one family, because inheritance passes to the children, who are all regarded as being offspring of the same father(s).

polygamy Although strictly speaking this term denotes the concurrent marriage of one sex to two or more members of the opposite sex, some writers appear to use it to mean marriage of one man with two or more women, which should properly be termed *polygyny.

polygyny A term denoting the concurrent marriage of one man with two or more women. This is not uncommon and is widespread in human societies. Where the women involved are sisters it is termed sororal polygyny. Some writers appear to use *polygamy rather than polygyny to denote this kind of marriage, although strictly speaking, polygyny and *polyandry are both versions of polygamy.

polytheism *See* MONOTHEISM.

Popper, Sir Karl Raimund (1902–94) An Austrian philosopher who, after an early period of teaching in New Zealand (1937–45), worked for most of his adult life at the London School of Economics and Political Science (where he became Professor of Logic and Scientific Method).

Popper made a number of major contributions to the *philosophy of social science and *epistemology, which provoked much discussion and some controversy at the time, but rightly remain highly influential throughout the mainstream of the social sciences. These include his formulation of the principle of *falsification, his critique of *historicism, his concept of the *open society, and arguments in favour of *piecemeal social engineering. All of these are discussed at length elsewhere in this dictionary. His earlier works—*The Open Society and its Enemies* (1945), *The Poverty of Historicism* (1957), *The Logic of Scientific Discovery* (1959), and *Conjectures and Refutations* (1963)—spell out all of his most important arguments. Later volumes, many of which were written after his retirement in 1969—including *Of Clouds and Clocks* (1966), *Objective Knowledge* (1972), *Quantum Theory and the Schism in Physics* (1982), and others—elaborate upon these by applying his ideas to studies of the natural sciences.

Popper was knighted in 1965, but remained curiously isolated from the philosophical mainstream throughout his professional life, mainly (it is often said) because he was never a professor at the Universities of Oxford or Cambridge.

pop sociology Given that many of the concerns of *sociology have an immediate connection to everyday life in general, and social problems in particular, sociology perhaps more than other academic disciplines is open to a stream of popularizations. Almost anybody, it seems, can call themselves a sociologist—even without formal professional training.

Four kinds of pop sociology can be distinguished. First, anyone who elects to comment on or write about social matters may be seen as a pop sociologist. Second, there are many sociologists who see it as an important part of their professional work to make their ideas and findings accessible to a wider social audience than those found in universities and colleges. They may even work alongside *social movements in an attempt to achieve this, or aim to popularize their work through publishing their writing outside academic journals. They may also be regular media commentators on the issue of their concern. Thirdly, there are academics who find in the course of their work that their studies have received a certain prominence (for example, sensational findings on crime and drugs), and who are momentarily forced into the public eye, often against their will and sometimes against their talents. Some of these may enjoy short-run celebrity status. Finally, there is a special group who conduct sociological studies intended for popular consumption. For example, Vance O. Packard, an American journalist and freelance writer, became a well-known popularizer of sociology through books such as *The Hidden Persuaders* (1957) and *The Ultra Rich* (1989).

Being able to draw a clear line between academic sociology and pop sociology is therefore not always easy.

popular culture Culture denotes all the knowledge, technologies, values, beliefs, customs, and behaviours common to people. While simple societies may have only a single integrated culture that is shared by everyone, complex societies can accommodate many layers and levels of *cultures and *subcultures.

One important distinction is between popular culture and what is usually called high culture. The latter includes things like classical music, serious novels, poetry, dance, high art, and other cultural products which are usually appreciated by only a relatively small number of educated people. Popular culture, sometimes also called mass culture, is far more widespread and accessible to everyone. The main business of popular culture is entertainment and, in Europe and the United States (for example), it is dominated by sports, television, films, and recorded popular music. The distinction between minority and majority cultures may often involve a value judgement in favour of high culture.

Traditionalists from Wordsworth on have lamented the poor quality of popular culture. Liberal and radical critics have been more inclined to support the popular as an authentic expression of public taste, and to dismiss the remote products of high culture as elitist. Sociologists have become involved in the analysis of popular culture because it provides a window into public consciousness, and is an important element of solidarity within social classes and of division between them. *Conflict theorists focus on the production of popular culture by large, capitalist *corporations, and suggest that the product may be not only inauthentic but also an instrument of ideological *domination.

Studies of popular culture overlap with those of subcultures, *youth cultures, *ideology, *leisure, and the *mass media. Ian Chambers, *Popular Culture* (1986) and Tony Bennett et al., *Popular Culture and Social Relations* (1986), indicate the range of topics which can be subsumed under this general heading. *See also* CULTURAL STUDIES.

population In its most general sense, a population comprises the totality of the people living in a particular territory (*see* DEMOGRAPHY), but it has a more specific meaning in statistics. In statistical terms, a population refers to the aggregate of individuals or units from which a *sample is drawn, and to which the results of any analysis are to apply—in other words the aggregate of persons or objects under investigation. It is conventional to distinguish the target population (for which the results are required) from the survey population (those actually included in the sampling frame from which the sample is drawn). For practical reasons the two are rarely identical. Even the most complete sampling frames—electoral registers, lists of addresses, or (in the United States) lists of telephone numbers—exclude sizeable categories of the population (who fail to register to vote, are homeless, or do not possess a telephone). Researchers may sometimes deliberately exclude members of the target population from the survey population. For example, it is standard practice to exclude the area north of the Caledonian Canal from the sampling frame for national sample surveys in Great Britain, on the grounds that the Northern Highlands are so thinly populated that interviews in this area would be unacceptably expensive to obtain. However, for most sociological purposes, this particular gap between the target and survey populations is not deemed to be significant—although, in a survey of 'attitudes to public transportation in thinly populated areas', it would clearly be problematic. *See also* STATISTICAL INFERENCE.

population studies *See* DEMOGRAPHY.

populism A term that entered the vocabulary of American politics with the formation in 1892 of the Populist Party. Most of the party's supporters were small farmers in the South and especially the West of the country. The principal plank in the party's platform was the idea that their supporters' grievances against the banks (who always seemed far too keen to foreclose on their mortgages) and the railroad companies (who were able to charge exorbitant haulage rates because of their monopoly positions) would be best resolved if the state nationalized the land and the railways.

Today, the term is most often used within Marxist and neo-Marxist circles in a broadened and transformed sense to refer to any political movement which seeks to mobilize the people as individuals, rather than as members of a particular group, against a state which is considered to be either controlled by vested interests or too powerful in itself (see, for example, E. Laclau, *Politics and Ideology in Marxist Theory*, 1978).

Populism has been a potent political force in developing countries—Peronism in Argentina is an obvious example—and has emerged as a major phenomenon in post-Soviet Central and Eastern Europe. In both cases the connections with *nationalism are important.

positional good A commodity (including goods, services, occupations, or other social relationships) that is either scarce in an absolute or socially imposed sense, or subject to *crowding or congestion through more extensive use. Examples would include everything from top jobs, pleasant tourist locations or desirable residential areas, to front seats at the opera.

What these diverse goods and situations have in common is that the satisfactions obtained from them derive in part from scarcity and social exclusiveness. Moreover, shortfalls in the supply of such items cannot be overcome by *economic growth alone, since (to put the matter at its most simple) expansions in *productivity do not change the fact that not everyone can be President of the Company and not everyone can have tickets to the Super Bowl. In *Social Limits to Growth* (1976), Fred Hirsch identified a wide range of jobs and goods that are subject to positional competition, and argues that affluent societies are increasingly prone to distributional conflict over facilities and services that cannot be acquired or used by all without spoiling them for all.

positive discrimination Policies and practices that favour groups (mainly ethnic groups and women) who have historically experienced disadvantages (usually in the fields of employment and education). In the United States the alternative terms 'affirmative action' and 'reverse discrimination' are also widely used. It is argued by advocates of positive discrimination that, given the existing structure of *inequalities and *stereotypes, the policy is necessary in order to create equality of opportunities with historically privileged groups. However, it is highly controversial, and has generated much legal and political debate. Most sociological interest focuses on the implications of positive discrimination for the concept and practice of equality of opportunity. *See also* JUSTICE, SOCIAL.

positive reinforcement *See* CONDITIONING.

positivism A term that, through overuse and misuse, has become an almost meaningless term of abuse that can be applied to almost any kind of *empirical research that appears not to pay sufficient attention to the complexity of social meanings. In fact, the term has a quite specific and much narrower meaning and should be used only in this sense.

The acknowledged founder of this positivism or 'the positive philosophy' was the French philosopher and social scientist Auguste *Comte (1798–1857). Comte also invented the term 'sociology' to describe his proposed positive science of society.

Positivism is, above all, a *philosophy of science. As such, it stands squarely within the *empiricist tradition. *Metaphysical speculation is rejected in favour of 'positive' knowledge based on systematic observation and experiment. The methods of science can give us knowledge of the laws of coexistence and succession of phenomena, but can never penetrate to the inner 'essences' or 'natures' of things. As applied to the human social world, the positive method yields a law of successive states through which each branch of knowledge must pass: first theological, then metaphysical, and finally positive (or scientific). Since the character of society flows from the intellectual forms which predominate in it, this gives Comte a law of the development of human society itself. The phase of anarchy and revolution through which France had recently passed resulted from intellectual anarchy. Irresolvable disputes on metaphysical questions such as the Divine Right and the sovereignty of the people must now give way to a positive science of society. Well-grounded knowledge would form the basis of consensus, and could also be applied to remove the causes of disorder, just as natural-scientific knowledge had been applied in the taming of nature.

Comte's work was much admired by John Stuart *Mill, amongst others, and positivism became very popular in the latter part of the 19th century. Comte's views shifted later in his life, under the influence of Clotilde de Vaux. He came to see that science alone could not have the binding-force for social cohesion, as he had earlier supposed. He argued that the intellect must become the servant of the heart, and advocated a new 'Religion of Humanity'.

However, Comte's wider and continuing influence in social science derives almost exclusively from his earlier writings. Today, positivism signifies adherence to an empiricist view of the nature of science, and the project of a scientific approach to the study of social life on the empiricist model. In the case of the social sciences, this is most commonly taken to mean a modelling of the methods of social science on those of natural science; the attempt to discover social laws analogous to the law-like regularities discovered by natural sciences; and an absolute insistence on the separation of facts and values. The close link between the empirical knowledge generated by these methods, and questions of political or industrial policy, is also very much in line with Comtean social engineering.

The religious and political aspects of Comte's arguments have not found wide acceptance, but the core idea of positivism as formal, empirical research has won wide acceptance. This has often been seen in relation to the radical empiricism and scientism advanced in the early decades of the 20th century by the Vienna Circle and whose advocates defined themselves as 'logical positivists'. This is usually considered to be the major influence on modern, 20th-century sociological positivism, via the philosophy of the social sciences advanced by such theorists as Ernest Nagel (*The Structure of Science*, 1961) and Carl G. Hempel (*The Philosophy of Natural Science*, 1966), and as exemplified in the work of Paul Lazarsfeld.

Criticisms of positivism commonly focus on the inappropriateness of natural-scientific methods in the human or social sciences. Consciousness, cultural norms, symbolic *meaning, and intentionality are variously held to be distinctive human attributes which dictate a methodological gulf between natural science and the study of human social life. However, following the work of Thomas S. Kuhn, Paul Feyerabend, and others, it has also become common to reject the empiricist account of the natural sciences. Since the positivist proposal for a unified science of nature and society is premised upon empiricism, these questions have to be considered afresh, on the basis of alternative views of the nature of science. This has been the basis of the extended and misguided criticism of empirical and, particularly, forms of quantitative research as positivist.

A qualified defence of positivism, which specifically takes issue with much (misguided) sociological criticism, is mounted in Percy S. Cohen's 'Is Positivism Dead?', *Sociological Review* (1980). In an innovative article on 'Seven Types of Ambiguity' (*Theory and Society*, 1997), Andrew Abbott argues that 'proclamations against positivism often mask an arbitrary unwillingness to think formally about the social world. One asserts that the world is constructed of ambiguous networks of meaning, argues for the complexity of interpretations and representations, and then simply assumes that formal discussion of the ensuing complexity is impossible.' Abbott argues this is untrue, and shows that formal and empirical research can be a source of untapped information about those multiple meanings.

positivist criminology *See* CRIMINOLOGY, POSITIVIST.

post-colonialism Originated in the work of the Subaltern Studies Group in their studies of Indian history. Influenced by the British Marxist tradition of writing history 'from below', they sought to speak on behalf of the colonized subjects rather than to write history from the standpoint of the colonial authorities. Partha Chatterjee (*Nationalist Thought and the Colonial World*, 1986) and Ranajit Guha (*Elementary Aspects of Peasant Insurgency in Colonial India*, 1983) were the key figures. The aim was to let subaltern, or subordinate, voices be heard and to break with the dominant colonial discourse. Related ideas that have influenced contemporary post-colonialism include those of the Franz Fanon and Edward Said (*Orientalism*, 1978), while related ideas have also been developed within Black nationalist thought in the United States.

Epistemologically, the post-colonial viewpoint proposes a standpoint theory of knowledge, according to which knowledge and ideas are shaped by the perspective of a social group, and this perspective, in turn, is shaped by the social location of the group in historical distributions of material and cultural resources. For some this has implied a *relativism and a denial of *objectivity, according to which knowledge derived from a post-colonial standpoint must remain separate and distinct from that produced from the standpoint of the colonizer, rather than being integrated into any larger sociological or historical account. In this respect, post-colonial theory has many similarities with *feminist standpoint theories and the arguments of Marxists such as *Lukács.

Contemporary engagements with *post-colonialism that also draw on *post-structuralist ideas are those of Giyatri Spivak (In *Other Worlds*, 1988) and Homi Bhaba (*The Location of Culture*, 1994). *See also* HYBRIDITY.

post-fordism *See* FLEXIBLE EMPLOYMENT; FORDISM.

post-industrial society (post-industrialism) Terms popularized by the publication of Daniel Bell's *The Coming of Post-Industrial Society* in 1973. According to Bell, a post-industrial society is one where knowledge has displaced property as the central preoccupation, and the prime source of power and social dynamism. It is therefore also one in which technicians and *professionals are the 'pre-eminent' social groups, as well as one in which the *service industries are more important than *manufacturing. *See also* KNOWLEDGE SOCIETY.

postmodernism This term, in its current use, originated in aesthetic discussion to describe movements in art during the 1960s (such as the work of Andy Warhol) that broke with *modernism, played with a variety of fragmentary aesthetic forms, and made no claim to representational realism. The emphasis on plurality, diversity, and relativity encouraged some intellectuals to promote a wider reconstruction of thought. These claims were made in texts by such writers as Jean-François Lyotard and Jean Baudrillard, augmented by a particular reading of a further selection of texts by *post-structuralists such as Jacques Lacan, Roland Barthes, Michel Foucault, and Jacques Derrida. (It should be noted, however, that most if not quite all of these thinkers would deny the applicability of the label to their work—a fittingly ironic state of affairs, some would say.) However, what it is that this body of theory (and its architectural, cinematic, and literary equivalents) has in common, is certainly much less settled.

Despite the fact that he neither invented the term nor claimed a very broad meaning for it (the word itself is commonly credited to Arnold J. Toynbee), it was Lyotard's announcement in 1979 (*The Postmodern Condition*) that the inhabitants of the advanced *capitalist societies had been living in a postmodern world since at least the early 1960s, which made postmodernism a topic of sociological interest. What he did that was new was to declare that postmodernism was a generic social condition, and not just a new creative style or body of theory: it is a condition in which there is a widespread if belated recognition that the two major myths or 'meta-narratives' that have legitimated scientific (including social scientific) activity for the past two hundred years, are no longer widely believed.

On one hand, 'The Myth of Liberation' has been rendered incredible by the complicity of all the sciences in the great crimes of the 20th century, including the Holocaust, the Soviet gulags, and the creation of weapons of indiscriminate mass destruction. On the other, 'The Myth of Truth' has been rendered incredible by the sceptical thoughts of historians and philosophers of science (as, for example, in the *relativism of Paul Feyerabend and Thomas Kuhn)—in other words, the disbelief of those who are supposed to know. The net result of such a generalized 'incredulity towards meta-narratives', according to Lyotard, is that the inhabitants of advanced capitalist societies now live in a world in which the following is the case: there are no guarantees as to either the worth of their activities or the truthfulness of their statements; there are only 'language games'; and there are no economic constraints on the cultural realm.

Perhaps surprisingly, it is the American Marxist literary critic, Fredric Jameson, who has provided the most concrete and influential description of what the culture of this supposed new world looks like. In so doing, he may also be read as specifying what it was that the postmodernists and their precursors are either sensitive to, or have been instrumental in producing (see his *Postmodernism, or the Cultural Logic of Late Capitalism*, 1984). According to Jameson, a survey of recent aesthetic, philosophical, and social criticism reveals multiform 'senses of the end of this or that', and as a result projects an image of a culture that is assertively concerned with surfaces, and hence exhibits a certain 'depthlessness'; is voraciously hungry for variations in surface decoration and hence very adept at pastiche and careless of historical time; is aware of its own depthlessness, and hence characterized by both a penchant for irony, and a certain 'waning of affect' or chariness as regards the expressing of strong emotions; is fascinated with, and hence productive of, schizophrenic psychological conditions; and, finally, is strikingly utopian on the grounds that what you dream is what you might get.

Postmodernity, in whatever guise it appears, thus implies the disintegration of modernist symbolic orders. It denies the existence of all 'universals', including the philosophy of the transcendental self, on the grounds that the discourse and referential categories of modernity (the subject, community, the state, use-value, social class, and so forth) are no longer appropriate to the description of disorganized capitalism. There is instead a new culture of 'paralogy'—of imagination, inventiveness, dissensus, the search for paradox, and toleration of the incommensurable. Postmodernism is therefore characterized by 'a pluralisation of lifeworlds'. Its most conspicuous features are, to quote Z. *Bauman (*Intimations of Postmodernity*, 1992), 'variety, contingency, and ambivalence', the 'permanent and irreducible *pluralism* of cultures, communal traditions, ideologies, "forms of life" or "language games"'.

The term itself is now applied as an adjective to a large number of theoretical positions. For example, there is now a recognized 'postmodern feminism', represented in the work of (among others) Luce Irigaray, Hélène Cixous, and Julia Kristeva. In Kristeva's case, the label is usually justified by reference to her suspicion of and deconstructive attitude towards all *essentialisms, including those propounded by feminists. A very useful English-language introductory selection of her work may be found in Toril Moi, *The Kristeva Reader* (1986).

In all these discussions it is important to distinguish between theories of postmodernity as a social condition and the aesthetic movement of postmodernism itself, though this distinction is often overlooked. Sociologists have been largely concerned to argue about whether or not a postmodern social condition exists; and, if it does, why it exists. Perhaps strangely, few even of those who accept that the condition exists have asked themselves what, if anything, would or should happen to sociology itself, if it took postmodernist ideas seriously. By far the best sociological treatment is David Harvey's *The Condition of Postmodernity* (1989)—a text which makes this whole difficult literature readily accessible to the uninitiated.

The implications of postmodernist theory for the actual conduct of sociological analysis and research are perhaps best understood in relation to an (all too rarely encountered) concrete illustration. For example, the field of class analysis has been subjected to a sustained postmodernist critique, most notably in a series of critical essays by Jan Pakulski and colleagues (see J. Pakulski and M. Waters, *The Death of Class*, 1996; S. Crook et al., *Postmodernization*, 1992), who maintain that postmodernity entails 'the final erosion of boundaries between the knowledges and practices of science and those of other domains', then it follows (as they conclude) that the truth claims of social science 'enjoy no guaranteed salience or guaranteed cognitive privilege', that 'sociology is quite free to tell what stories it likes about change or any other matter', and that 'these stories are part of a more general economy of discourse in which they must fight to find an audience and establish a salience in competition with other stories, and in the absence of guarantees'. In other words sociology has the same epistemological status (*see* EPISTEMOLOGY) as beliefs in fairies or flying saucers, or assertions of racial prejudice. However, this commits us irrevocably to the cultural madhouse in which 'anything goes'. It should also be noted that if the resolution of language games is linked solely to the exercise of power, then the result is invariably a totalitarianism in which the definitions that stick belong to those who wield the biggest stick. The important task for contemporary thought is to work through the many important critical points made by postmodernist writers without abandoning the commitment to *objective social research. *See also* CULTURAL STUDIES.

post-structuralism A broad-based and interdisciplinary movement that originated in France during the 1960s and spread rapidly to other countries. Post-structuralism's prime achievement has been to rediscover and extend the radical analytical possibilities inherent in *Saussure's theory of *language as a significatory rather than a representational phenomenon. According to its proponents, these possibilities were obscured for a long time by the scientistic readings of Saussure which dominated the work of linguists, as well as such other usages as those associated with the likes of Louis *Althusser, Nicos *Poulantzas, Claude Lévi-Strauss, and other *structuralists.

More specifically, its achievement had been to rediscover the possibilities implicit in Saussure's insistence that language aligns the two aspects of all signs (their 'signifiers' or physical images, and their 'signifieds' or mental images) without any referent to the extra-linguistic world. Putting the point another way, what excited the post-structuralists were the analytical possibilities created by the realization that words (and signs more generally) may mean something, without referring to anything in the extra-linguistic world; and, therefore, that all language and language-borne phenomena (philosophies, ideologies, sciences and even whole societies, for example) might be far more autonomous, in relation to other social phenomena, than had hitherto been suspected.

The scientistic appropriations of Saussure's theory which for so long obscured the theory's more radical implications did so because their authors made the claim that *their* words, if no others, were verifiable accurate depictions of what they referred to, whether the latter objects were aspects of language, literature, kinship systems, or modes of production. However, with the exception of the pioneering Jacques Lacan, rather than return to Saussure directly and try to reformulate what had become known as 'the structuralist tradition' on a non-scientistic basis, the leading post-structuralists sought to counter scientism by resorting to bodies of thought which were located outside of the tradition itself—for example, the philosophies of *Nietzsche, in the case of Michel Foucault, and *Heidegger in that of Jacques Derrida. Whichever strategy was adopted, the result was similar in that in each case the conclusion arrived at was that there was both more and less to words than met the eye: more, in that even individual words always carry 'traces' of other words and texts (Derrida), provide evidence of and for the 'unconscious' (Lacan), and project power as elements in 'discourse' (Foucault); less, in that, for Lacan and Derrida (if not necessarily Foucault), words were no longer understood to carry aspects of the extra-linguistic world into thought.

The full *relativistic implications of the post-structuralist critique are perhaps most easily seen in the work of the French social theorist Jacques Derrida. The starting-point of Derrida's self-differentiation within the structuralist tradition, and therefore of his post-structuralism, is his claim to have detected a residual *humanism within the former. This humanism inheres in the unconscious privileging of speech over writing which, ironically, underpins Saussure's decision to make *langue* (language as an established system of rules and units) rather than *parole* (language in use as actually produced speech) the object of study of linguistics. In Derrida's view it is the spoken rather than the written language that Saussure is concerned to elucidate. This privileging of speech, or 'phonocentrism', betrays a 'metaphysics of human presence' buried deep in the heart of the text that has commonly been supposed to be the founding document of the non-humanist approach to the study of social phenomena. Such a metaphysics, because it unconsciously privileges the speaker, vouchsafes not just the possibility of stable meanings, but also the possibility of a knowable truth, and for no convincing reason.

On the basis of this insight, which may be found in the opening essay of his *Of Grammatology* (1967), Derrida proceeds to elaborate on the method, if that is not too strong a word, that made it possible. The essential elements of this are: that writing should not be disprivileged, compared to speech, but that both should simply be taken as instances of 'texts'; special attention should be paid to the decorative and rhetorical aspects of the text (especially if it is one that makes claims to any special rigour); and, finally, the reader should be given an authority as a 'meaning-giver' that is at least equal to that commonly ascribed to the author. Under these conditions, the pursuit of meaning becomes the pursuit of an endlessly receding horizon, whose centripetal movement (*différance*) is the product of the proliferation of connotations (*traces* or *grams* for Derrida) that occurs whenever we use (as we must) other signifiers to define what is signified by any particular signifier. In other words, the true meaning of a text can never be known, and nothing can ever be said about it that is anything other than a provisional account of its 'intertextual' nature.

In sum, Derrida provides a means, not so much of subverting truth claims, but of showing how the texts wherein such claims are made subvert (or 'deconstruct') themselves. The deconstructive method would appear to possess great power when applied to texts that either claim or are claimed to validate themselves (for example religious scriptures). It does not, however, appear to possess the same degree of meaning-deferring power when applied to texts that either do not claim or cannot be claimed to validate themselves. Such texts (those of the social and natural sciences for example) have recourse to modes of validation which refer to phenomena that are beyond their boundaries. Notwithstanding the fact that neither these modes of validation nor the interpretation of their results are innocent of complicity with the texts or counter-texts involved, the possibility of external validation remains ever present, and cannot be denied by deconstructionists without involving them in a self-contradictory claim to know the truth.

The significance of post-structuralist ideas for sociology has been twofold: on one hand, to stimulate new methods of approach to old problems, especially in relation to the study of the ideological realm; and, on the other, to stimulate apocalyptic thoughts about the impossibility of sociology. That said, some authorities have claimed that sociology might profit from a sustained programme of deconstructive readings which would enhance the reflexivity of its practitioners, by drawing their attention to the self-subverting sub-texts that are imported into their discourse, with the myriad metaphors upon which they too often depend in order to make their meanings clear. For a measured assessment (which nevertheless opens with the statement that 'structuralism, and poststructuralism also, are dead traditions of thought') see Anthony Giddens, 'Structuralism, Post-structuralism and the Production of Culture', in Anthony Giddens and Jonathan Turner (eds.), *Social Theory Today* (1987). *See also* EPISTEMOLOGY.

potlatch *See* GIFT RELATIONSHIP; RATIONAL CHOICE THEORY.

Poulantzas, Nicos (1936–79) Greek by origin, Poulantzas made his name in France, as (together with Louis Althusser) the leading representative of so-called structuralist Marxism. The first book of his to gain significant attention was his *Political Power and Social Classes*, which was published in the midst of the 1968 troubles in France. In it he outlined the concept with which his name is normally associated—the *relative autonomy of the capitalist *state. This concept, and the 'regional theory' of the political of which it was a part, were then applied to an analysis of the rise of *fascism in the inter-war period (*Fascism and Dictatorship*, 1970).

In the years that followed, Poulantzas devoted himself to purely theoretical matters, and in 1974 published his *Classes in Contemporary Capitalism*, which was an extensive elaboration of the anti-humanist concept of class that he had first mooted in 1968. His last two books were a study of the collapses of the Iberian dictatorships (*The Crisis of the Dictatorships*, 1975), and an intervention into several then contemporary disputes in sociological theory (*State, Power, Socialism*, 1978). The latter is noteworthy for its trenchant critique of Michel *Foucault's conception of power in capitalist societies.

Poulantzas made a significant contribution to the reconstruction of *Marxism and (some have argued) to sociology generally, although it has also been suggested that the latter has yet to be fully appreciated, thanks to the combination of his own early death and changes in academic fashion (see R. Jessop's *Nicos Poulantzas: Marxist Theory and Political Strategy*, 1985).

poverty A condition in which resources, usually material but sometimes cultural, are lacking. It is common to distinguish between absolute and relative definitions of poverty. Poverty defined in absolute terms refers to a state in which the individual lacks the resources necessary for subsistence. Relative definitions, frequently favoured by sociologists (especially when studying poverty in advanced industrial societies), refer to the individual's or group's lack of resources when compared with that of other members of the society—in other words their relative standard of living. It is, in this sense, *deprivation relative to the standards enjoyed by others and regarded as normal or typical in a particular society. Since relative poverty is a matter of differences in levels of material resources—that is, of inequalities in their distribution across a society—measures of relative poverty are potentially no less objective than those of absolute poverty. They are not simply a matter of subjective feelings of poverty, though such feelings may be of importance when analysing the consequences of poverty.

Subsistence definitions of poverty are of considerable value in examining Third World poverty, and international studies show that the overall level of poverty measured in subsistence terms is very high, with some studies suggesting that almost half of those in low-income countries live in absolute poverty. The very high level of poverty is unquestionable even though very precise measures of poverty are hard to obtain in societies where income gives only an imprecise indication of access to the means of subsistence. Significantly, the classic studies of poverty in Britain by Charles Booth and Seebohm Rowntree also used subsistence definitions and identified rather high levels of poverty, though not as high as those of present-day Third World societies. Booth, in his seventeen-volume study of *The Life and Labour of the People in London* (1889–1903), used income as a measure of poverty. Introducing the concept of a *poverty line, a level below which families were unable to meet the necessities for subsistence, he provided evidence that somewhere near one-third of the whole population in London were in poverty. Rowntree's study of poverty in York at the turn of the century also used a subsistence definition. However, he introduced rather more precision by trying to determine the basic diets necessary for subsistence and then calculating the income needed to provide these subsistence diets, with an allowance for clothing and housing. His evidence showed some 15 per cent of York's population were in primary poverty, with earnings insufficient to meet basic needs. Adding in secondary poverty, where earnings were sufficient but were spent on other things, some 28 per cent were living in obvious want or squalor. His 1936 survey, using modified measures, yielded figures of just under 7 per cent and 18 per cent respectively. By 1950 poverty in Britain appeared almost to have disappeared following the introduction of the *welfare state, and Rowntree concluded that fewer than 2 per cent were in poverty.

In the 1960s, however, poverty was 'rediscovered'. In Britain, writers such as Brian Abel-Smith and Peter Townsend argued that the measures of poverty used by researchers such as Rowntree had not been properly adjusted to take account of changes in the purchasing power of incomes over time, and so were underestimating subsistence poverty. (A parallel story can be told about the United States—for which see the references at the end of this entry.) They also contended that poverty was better defined in relative than in absolute terms. Families might have sufficient resources for survival, but this did not mean they had enough to keep themselves warm or to afford the new consumer durables (such as televisions or fridges) which were coming to seem increasingly necessary, or to participate in the social and leisure activities enjoyed by other families. They were consequently excluded from the 'ordinary social life of the community'. Abel-Smith and Townsend used as a measure of relative poverty a family's position *vis-à-vis* social security (welfare payment) levels, finding nearly 15 per cent of the population in poverty. Subsequent studies, such as Townsend's monumental study *Poverty* (1978), refined the measures of relative poverty and continued to show significant proportions in poverty—proportions that seemed to increase during the 1980s with growing inequality and reductions in welfare provision. Recent figures suggest that perhaps one in five of the British population are in poverty, although these are the subject of much controversy, as indeed are the poverty figures for almost all advanced industrial societies.

The immediate causes of poverty vary over time and over the life cycle. Booth and Rowntree found low and irregular earnings were a major cause. (Rowntree showed that at least half of primary poverty in 1897–98 was due to low wages and over a fifth to large families.) However, Rowntree's 1936 study suggested that *unemployment and old age were more significant causes than formerly. By the time of Townsend's study, the main immediate causes were low pay, loss of the breadwinner, ill-health, unemployment, and old age, with the key groups in poverty being the elderly, single parents, the long-term sick and disabled, the low-paid, and the unemployed. Women are over-represented amongst the poor—a finding that has led some writers to talk of a feminization of poverty.

This mapping of change in the immediate causes of poverty indicates that it is economic and structural factors and social misfortune, not individual weakness in the form of idleness or imprudence, that are the major causes of poverty. Indeed, in order fully to understand poverty, it is necessary to examine the general distribution of wealth and of social *inequality in society. A range of theories attempt to do this. Liberal neo-classical accounts stress the role of the *market in distributing resources in relation to talents, skills, and motivations, arguing that poverty is necessary to provide a system of incentives to individual effort, and that those who end up in poverty lack the appropriate talents and skills. Subsidizing the poor can interfere with the smooth functioning of the market. However, such accounts, though they refer to structural features, are none the less often associated with assumptions that individuals are themselves to blame for their poverty: it is their attitudes, beliefs, and behaviour that are at fault. This argument has been applied to the family and the social group, not just the individual, via concepts such as the 'culture of poverty': that is, a cultural milieu characterized by fatalism, resignation, and idleness, which is antithetical to achievement, hard work, and self-reliance, and tends to be passed on between generations. Such views have, however, been challenged by a range of empirical studies of the lives of the poor.

In contrast, Marxist accounts emphasize the role of *capitalism and capitalist interests in generating poverty, both nationally and internationally. The argument here is that capitalism is based on the exploitation of labour and this applies both nationally and globally. Depending on the state of capitalist development and the particular requirements of capitalists, there may be a need for cheap labour and pressures to keep wages down, for a high level of unemployment, and for a minimization of welfare benefits, so that profits are maximized. Stripped of its Marxist gloss, the argument is that the level of poverty is a function of the nature of economic organization, and of processes concerning both the distribution of wealth and of welfare benefits. It is less that poverty is necessary to the smooth-running of the market, but that it may be politically and economically advantageous for those with power to pursue policies that increase rather than diminish inequality and poverty.

The extensive sociological literature on poverty overlaps with that on *race, *ethnicity, *subcultures, the *underclass, and *stratification generally—more so in the United States than in Britain (see R. H. Haveman, *Poverty Policy and Poverty Research*, 1987). On the 'rediscovery' of poverty in the United States during the 1960s see the Appendix by Julius Wilson and Robert Aponte, 'Urban Poverty: A State-of-the-Art Review of the Literature', in Wilson (ed.), *The Truly Disadvantaged* (1987). A comprehensive overview is John Scott's *Poverty and Wealth* (1994).

(⊕) SEE WEB LINKS
• The Child Poverty Action Group: a campaigning and publicity organization.

poverty line The 'line' that sets the boundary, and consequently the numbers, of the poor. There is much controversy over where and how it should be drawn. In Britain, the most common definition of poverty involves drawing the line in terms of the receipt of income support ('social security'), formerly supplementary benefit payments. Families and individuals who receive such support are deemed to be in poverty.

poverty trap The situation low-income individuals or families may face when taking up paid employment or securing higher earnings, if the loss of means-tested state welfare benefits and/or new income tax payments are equal to, or even exceed additional earnings. The poverty trap is, consequently, a deterrent to work. *See also* SELECTIVE VERSUS UNIVERSAL BENEFITS.

power Power is the concept that is at the heart of the subject of social *stratification. It is therefore not surprising that we have seen so many disputes concerning its meaning (including disputes about what particular sociologists meant when they used the term in the past).

Perhaps the best known of all the definitions is that of Max Weber in his essay 'The Distribution of Power within the Political Community: Class, Status, Party' (in *Economy and Society*, 1920). Max Weber defined power as 'the chance of . . . men to realise their own will in a communal action even against the resistance of others who are participating in the action'. He regarded power as the fundamental concept in stratification, and *class and *status as its two principal dimensions. Elsewhere in his work he saw command or *domination as a third dimension. Broadly speaking, classes were the outcome of a distribution of economic power (in Weber's terms, market and property relationships) and status was a normatively defined social power. Domination involving differences of authoritative power was the basis of *elite formation. Hence, for Weber, the differential distribution of power leads to a situation where *life-chances are also differentially distributed; that is, the ability to obtain economic, social, and political resources is unequally distributed. Weber took this view in a fairly explicit attempt to counter the crude *Marxism of his day, which made too easy an elision between economic control and political rule. He wished to make clear his view that power need not depend solely on the possession of economic resources.

If we examine Weber's definition, it obviously has built into it a notion of conflict and intention. The notion of intention can be seen in the view of someone or some group 'carrying out their will'. This implies a quality of conscious, rational, and calculated action in pursuit of a specific goal. Now, this may well characterize some power relationships, but does it characterize them all? Can power be exercised unwittingly? Should we perhaps see power as involving the achievement of one's preferences—whether by intention or not— rather than as the pursuit of one's will? The other problem we can see in Weber's definition is the assumption of conflict or antagonism which it incorporates. As various critics have noted, the definition suggests that A has power over B to the extent that he or she overcomes the resistance of B if it is offered, implying that— at least some of the time—the interests of B are being sacrificed to those of A. Weber was certainly interested mainly in power in situations of conflicting interests. Many sociologists since Weber have assumed that power involves— even provokes—subordinate resistance which must be overcome by superordinates. Weber held that power can also arise in a consensual context where subordinates accept it as being used legitimately. Where power is used over subordinates who attribute genuine *legitimacy to superordinates he spoke of authority. The idea of power used in an apparently consensual context also leads to further problems. For example, where legitimacy is attributed in a power relationship, does this legitimacy flow from subordinate to superordinate, implying authority (which is what Parsons and many political scientists would say); or is legitimacy imposed from above, by 'swinging' of social norms, implying manipulation (a view which has firm roots in Marxism, especially the Gramscian notion of ideological *hegemony)? As Alvin Gouldner (*The Coming Crisis of Western Sociology*, 1970) noted, 'power is, among other things [the] ability to enforce one's moral claims. The powerful can thus *conventionalize* their moral defaults.' These are clearly very different from power which rests on force or manipulation. Yet we have to remember that all of these terms refer to types of power relationships.

Many studies of political power have focused on formal decision making within state apparatuses. In a much-cited discussion (*Power: A Radical View*, 1974), Steven Lukes follows Peter Bachrach and Morton S. Baratz (*Power and Poverty: Theory and Practice*, 1970) in criticizing these studies for investigating simply one face of power. The second face—so-called 'non-decision making'—involves the 'mobilization of bias', or manipulation of the political agenda by powerful groups, taking decisions which prevent issues from emerging and becoming subject to formal decision-making. This was also recognized by David *Lockwood, who observed that 'power must not only refer to the capacity to realise one's ends in a conflict situation against the will of others; it must also include the capacity to prevent opposition arising in the first place. We often hear that the study of power should concentrate on the making and taking of important decisions. But in one sense power is most powerful if the actor can, by manipulation, prevent issues from coming to the point of decision at all' ('The Distribution of Power in Industrial Society—a Comment', in J. Urry and J. Wakeford (eds.), *Power in Britain*, 1973).

Lukes goes on to advocate the investigation of a third face of power, seeing it as also involving the prevention of people from having grievances in the first place, or as Lukes puts it 'by shaping their perceptions, cognitions and preferences in such a way that they accept their role in the existing order of things'. Thus, certain issues never arise, so neither do decisions to include or exclude them from the political agenda. Lukes also argues that competing concepts of power reflect differing moral and political values concerning the conception of *interests. Lukes concludes that power has to be seen as an 'essentially contested concept'—subject to irresolvable dispute between theorists with differing values. His radical view denies that interests are simply consciously expressed wants, for these may be shaped by a social system which serves the powerful by suppressing people's recognition of their real interests. (Note the parallel here with the Marxist notion of *false consciousness.)

Finally, we should consider power resources. Power is a dispositional concept: it refers to the possibility of a certain action occurring rather than to its actual occurrence. So, power is a potential quality of a social relationship, and as such rests on actors' access to power resources. Quite obviously, in an advanced capitalist society, economic resources such as wealth and control over jobs are vital, but many other power resources exist: for example, organizational capacity, numerical support, competence, expert knowledge, control of information, occupation of certain social positions, control of the instruments of force, and reputation for power itself. The last of these is a unique power resource: it depends not on the actual possession of power but the mere belief by others that it is possessed. Equally, one does not have to own a power resource, but only to control it: senior civil servants and managers provide examples. Between all these potentials for power, and their manifestation, lies one's willingness (and efficiency) to use it. Potential power depends upon certain attributes. Manifest power, however, is revealed not by attributes but through social relationships; and part of the definition of a social relationship is its reciprocal nature. Consequently, the exercise of power involves feedback: A acts, B reacts, A reacts to B's reaction, and so on. Subordinates must have some effect on superordinates for there to be any relationship at all—a point noted long ago by Georg Simmel.

We can begin to see, then, how complex and difficult a concept power is to handle. The issues raised in this entry are discussed in Dennis Wrong's *Power* (1979) and, more fully, in John Scott's *Power* (2001). Though explicitly critical of Weber's views on power, much of the work of Michel Foucault has interestingly extended this view. Of particular importance is Foucault's *Society Must be Defended* (1975–6, trans. 2003), which locates his own arguments firmly within *conflict theory. *See also* BUREAUCRACY; COMMUNITY POWER; COMPLIANCE; GATEKEEPING; MICHELS; ORGANIZATION THEORY; ORGANIZATIONAL REACH; POLITICAL PARTIES; REFERENT POWER; STATE.

power dependence Power is often characterized as 'zero sum'. That is, *power is something that A has over B, such that if A gains in power B correspondingly loses. However, the notion of power dependence suggests that power is also a relational concept, such that the power of A is dependent on B. The exercise of power is an exchange of resources and so A needs B—is dependent on B—in order to exercise power. An example is evident in Britain, where the power of the Prime Minister is dependent on the Cabinet recognizing his or her authority, and implementing his or her decisions.

power elite A concept developed by C. Wright Mills in his book of that name (published in 1956) and used by him to refer to the American ruling elite. According to his analysis this was an *elite which was composed of business, government, and military leaders, bound together by the shared social backgrounds of these leaders and the interchange of personnel between its three segments. Mills's text provoked considerable controversy. A representative selection of liberal and radical responses, together with a retrospective essay by Mills himself, will be found in G. William Domhoff and Hoyt B. Ballard (eds.), *C. Wright Mills and the Power Elite* (1968). *See also* MILITARY-INDUSTRIAL COMPLEX.

power, referent *See* REFERENT POWER.

pragmatism (philosophy of) An influential and important, perhaps the central, North American philosophy. It rejects the quest for fundamental, foundational truths, and shuns the building of abstract philosophical systems. Instead, it suggests a plurality of shifting truths grounded in concrete experiences and language, in which a truth is appraised in terms of its consequences or use-value. It is a down-to-earth philosophy, born in a period of rapid social change, which seeks to unify intelligent thought and logical method with practical actions and appeals to experience. William James, in his *Pragmatism* (1907), neatly summarizes the perspective when he states that 'the Pragmatic method ... is to try to interpret each notion by tracing its respective practical consequences. What difference would it practically make to anyone if this notion rather than that notion were true?'

Pragmatism has sometimes been maligned as the philosophy of capitalism—since it has an apparent emphasis upon the 'cash value' of ideas. While differing significantly in emphasis, its key proponents are generally agreed to be Charles Sanders Peirce, John Dewey, William James, and George Mead. It is identified with the *Chicago School of sociology and was important in shaping the theory of *symbolic interactionism.

praxis A philosophical term referring to human action on the natural and social world. It emphasizes the transformative nature of action and the priority of action over thought. It is often, but not always, associated with *Marxism and especially the work of Antonio Gramsci.

preference theory Preference theory seeks to provide an empirically based, predictive explanation for the differentiated choices women make between productive work and reproductive work in rich modern societies, after the contraceptive revolution gave women control over their own fertility. It posits that women are heterogeneous in tastes and preferences, being divided into three distinct groups: a minority of work-centred women who often remain childless by choice (about 20 per cent of the adult population); a minority of home-centred women who usually have many children and do little paid work (about 20 per cent of the adult population); and a majority of adaptive women who seek to combine paid work in the labour market with childbearing and child-rearing. Preference theory states that the three groups differ qualitatively, for example in responsiveness to particular social and economic policies, to the point where they have conflicting interests on certain policy issues. The theory constitutes a break with sociological and economic theories that treat all labour as essentially homogeneous. See Catherine Hakim, *Preference Theory* (1998).

prejudice Prejudice, in normal usage, means preconceived opinion or bias, against or in favour of, a person or thing. While it is important to remember that biases can be positive as well as negative, nevertheless the term most commonly refers to a negative or unfavourable *attitude towards a group, or its individual members. Prejudice is characterized by *stereotyped beliefs that are not tested against reality, but rather have to do with a person's own feelings and attitudes. Gordon Allport, in his classic book *The Nature of Prejudice* (1954), defines prejudice as 'an antipathy based upon a faulty and inflexible generalization. It may be felt or expressed. It may be directed toward a group as a whole, or toward an individual member of that group.' Some people are more prone to prejudiced outlooks than others: psychoanalytical theories point to an *authoritarian personality type that is more likely to hold the sort of inflexible attitudes associated with prejudice.

Prejudice became a very popular term in social psychology during the 1920s and 1930s, partly out of a concern with the development of attitude theory (and new techniques for scaling attitudes such as the *Bogardus social distance scale); partly because of a concern with the widespread existence of hostility to ethnic minorities in the United States and the rise of anti-semitism in Europe; and partly due to a generalized concern with *minority groups. The original tradition of prejudice research reached its peak with the publication of two major books: Theodor Adorno et al., *The Authoritarian Personality* (1950) and Gordon Allport's *The Nature of Prejudice* (1954). The former provided the most detailed analysis of the personality foundations of prejudice; the latter attempted a synthesis of research findings, trying to integrate the psychological, structural, and historical foundations of prejudice. Although much research has continued in this tradition, the term has also been heavily criticized within sociology, notably for its individualistic implications.

Sociological definitions of the term tend also to stipulate that prejudice violates some social norm such as rationality, justice, or tolerance. Over-generalization, prejudgement, the refusal to take account of individual differences, and thinking in stereotypes all violate rational thought. Similarly, in so far as the net effect of prejudice is to place the individual or group at some disadvantage that is not merited, prejudice is inherently unjust. Prejudice also involves intolerance and even the violation of human dignity. Zygmunt *Bauman, in *Thinking Sociologically* (1990), suggests that prejudice results in double moral standards. What the members of the in-group deserve as of right will be an act of grace and benevolence if done for the people of the *out-group. He goes on to insist that 'most importantly, one's own atrocity against out-group members does not seem to clash with moral conscience'. Identical actions are called different names, alternatively loaded with praise or condemnation, depending on which side has undertaken them. One person's act of liberation is another's act of terrorism.

Prejudice is both a consequence of and a reinforcement for the existence of in-groups and out-groups, which embody the distinction between 'them' and 'us'. In-group and out-group attitudes are intrinsically related, because in-group feeling results in out-group sentiment, and vice versa. It could almost be claimed that one side derives its identity from the fact of its opposition to the other. In this sense the out-group is necessary for the cohesion and emotional security of the in-group, and an out-group might need to be invented, if one does not already exist. A classic but ethically disturbing example of how an in-group and out-group were experimentally created is described in Muzafer Sherif and Carolyn Sherif, *An Outline of Social Psychology* (1956). The authors structured activities at a boys' camp such that two specially created clubs had to compete with each other for rewards. The respective members soon developed hostility towards, and stereotypes of, each other—despite initially having equal numbers of friends in each club. The authors conclude that these stereotypes must have been created rather than learned.

Groups also tend to close ranks when an enemy is at hand. Prejudice, by magnifying the vices of the enemy, ensures that norms of justice and tolerance no longer apply. Prejudice does not always result in any hostile action, but when prejudice is made manifest it can range from (at minimum) avoidance or discrimination, through to mass extermination, as in the Holocaust.

pre-operational stage *See* PIAGET.

pressure groups Groups of persons, employers, or other organizations joining together to represent the interests of a particular sectional group *vis-à-vis* governments, the public at large, or other *interest groups. Pressure groups, lobby groups, and interest groups are distinct from other clubs or social groups, in that their explicit purpose is to mobilize *public opinion in support of their aims and to put pressure on decision-making bodies to agree to and support their demands, be they for the continuation of the existing state of affairs or for some change or innovation. Pressure groups coexist with other forms of interest aggregation, such as political parties, seeking to influence rather than to govern. Interest groups may develop into political parties by adopting a more open, less restricted platform; and some pressure groups have a special relationship with a political party, as illustrated by trade unions and the Labour Party in Britain.

A distinction is sometimes drawn between protective and promotional groups, the former defending a section of society, the latter promoting a cause. The first category includes trade unions, professional associations, employer and trade associations, and motoring associations defending the interests of car owners.

The second category would include societies seeking to prevent cruelty to animals or to children, groups arguing for or against censorship, and the Campaign for Nuclear Disarmament. The distinction between the two types of interest group is obviously not watertight. For example, *trade unions frequently campaign for national minimum wage laws as a means of defending the interests of their members, although the case is always offered as being in the public interest.

prestige *See* STATUS.

primacy effect This refers to the process by which early information colours our perception of subsequent information. The common sense notion that first impressions are the most compelling is not always correct. First impressions may count most because subsequent information is more difficult to absorb—although recent information may be remembered most clearly. *See also* RECENCY EFFECT.

primary and secondary deviation Introduced by Edwin Lemert in his *Social Pathology* (1951), the distinction is central to *labelling theory. Primary deviation refers to differentiation which is relatively insignificant, marginal, and fleeting: individuals may drift in and out of it. Secondary deviation is deviance proper. It is a pivotal, central, and engulfing activity to which a person has become committed. The mechanism by which marginal *deviance and casual rule-breaking become more central depends upon labelling or the societal reaction.

primary group *See* COOLEY.

primary sector *See* INDUSTRIAL SECTOR.

primitive communism A term usually associated with Karl Marx, but most fully elaborated by Friedrich Engels (in *The Origin of the Family*, 1884), and referring to the collective right to basic resources, egalitarianism in social relationships, and absence of authoritarian rule and hierarchy that is supposed to have preceded *stratification and *exploitation in human history. Both Marx and Engels were heavily influenced by Lewis Henry Morgan's speculative evolutionary history, which described the 'liberty, equality and fraternity of the ancient gentes', and the 'communism in living' said to be evident in the village architecture of native Americans. Engels worked this notion into the evolutionary theory of *historical materialism, arguing that the transition to subsequent *modes of production involved the change from production for use to production for exchange, and transformation of communal family relations and equality between the sexes to individual families as economic units and female subordination. The thesis has been much debated in anthropology (see, for example, E. Leacock, 'Marxism and Anthropology', in B. Ollman and E. Vernoff (eds.), *The Left Academy*, 1981), where dispute centres on the nature of property rights, status, and authority among so-called primitive peoples.

primitive society A term used to refer both to the earliest societies and to recent examples with simple technology. It fell into disfavour as a description of any society of recent centuries, since none are relics of an earlier evolutionary stage, and each has its own history and development. Moreover, improvisation of existing materials is subtle, not simple. No equivalent term has yet proved more suitable as a term to describe such societies, though Robert Redfield has proposed the term 'folk society'.

primogeniture The tradition, principle, or law by which the right of succession to property and title falls to the first born. In theory this can be through the male or female line although the former is more common.

principle of population *See* Malthus.

Prisoner's Dilemma A paradigmatic instance in *game theory, taking its name from a story of two prisoners, who are interrogated separately and cannot communicate with each other. There is insufficient evidence for the police to convict either prisoner of armed robbery, so that unless they confess, each will receive a relatively light sentence of one year's imprisonment for illegal possession of firearms. The prosecuting authorities offer each prisoner a deal, whereby they may confess and turn state's witness against the other prisoner (putting him away for ten years), while they themselves will be set free. The catch is that, if both prisoners confess, each will be convicted of armed robbery and sent to jail for six years. The dilemma facing the individual prisoner is whether or not to confess. The self-interested prisoner is better off confessing, no matter what his partner does, since if both prisoners see the issue in this way they will each spend a maximum of six years in jail. If, on the other hand, each could be sure that the other would act in the group interest (rather than pursuing self-interest), both would hold out, and each spend only a year in jail. The worst possible outcome would be to act in pursuit of the group interest while one's partner acted self-interestedly—since ten years in jail would be the result. The case of the Prisoner's Dilemma is commonly used to illustrate the dangers of committing the *fallacy of composition and to explore the conditions of *collective action. *See also* ALTRUISM.

private religion In conventional sociological terms, religion is a public activity involving communal practices (such as worship and sacraments), and commonly shared beliefs. In modern society, where there has been some *secularization of religion, some sociologists argue that religion can only survive as a more private set of beliefs or feelings. Max Weber, in his essay on 'Science as a vocation', argued that religion would continue only 'in personal human situations, in pianissimo'. The concept is occasionally used as equivalent to *invisible religion.

private sphere and public sphere *See* PUBLIC SPHERE VERSUS PRIVATE SPHERE DISTINCTION.

privatism The tendency for people in advanced *industrial societies to spend their lives less in the public domain and more within the confines of the nuclear *family. In other words, increasing 'home-centredness' and 'nuclear familycentredness', and withdrawal from the public realm of community organizations and activities, such as those associated with the church, union, pub, or political party. A forceful statement of the argument is Richard Sennett's *The Fall of Public Man* (1977). Sennett's main theme is that of the dissolution of the 'public culture' (the street life and social intercourse of the café and local marketplace) and the rise of privatism. The extent of this phenomenon, and the allegedly secular trend towards it, are both contested by the majority of sociologists. First significantly developed in work on affluent workers (*see* EMBOURGEOISEMENT), the most useful contemporary assessment is Fiona Devine's *Affluent Workers Revisited* (1992). The process of privatism should not be confused with that of *privatization.

privatization The transfer of responsibilities from the state to the private sector of the economy (see E. S. Savas, *Privatizing the Public Sector*, 1982). Privatization takes many forms, depending on the nature of the responsibilities concerned, and to whom they are transferred. It may involve the highly publicized transfer of the ownership of the property and assets of public corporations or of local authority housing. Equally, it may involve the more gradual and less publicized running down of state provisions, subsidies, and regulation. A commitment to privatization has been a hallmark of conservative governments in Britain and many other West European countries during the 1980s. For an interesting case study see Timothy Barnekov et al., *Privatism and Urban Policy in Britain and the United States* (1989). By far the largest programmes of privatization were initiated after the fall of the *communist regimes in the former state socialist societies of Eastern Europe. The term should not be confused with the more obviously sociological concept of *privatism, though each word is sometimes used with the meaning given to the other.

probability (probability distribution) *See* DISTRIBUTION (STATISTICAL OR FREQUENCY); SAMPLING; SIGNIFICANCE TESTS; STATISTICAL INFERENCE.

problematic A structuralist Marxist term, popularized by Louis Althusser, which refers to 'the particular unity of a theoretical formation', the interdependence of its component concepts, and the way in which this facilitates the posing of certain problems and issues while excluding others from consideration (see *For Marx*, 1965). Althusser contrasts the openness of scientific problematics (specifically the mature works of Marx) with the closed problematics of various *ideologies (idealism, classical political economics, and so forth). What allegedly distinguishes the two is that the latter operate within a 'closed space' or 'vicious circle of the mirror relation of ideological representation' within which all problems are posed in ways that prejudge the solutions (see *Reading Capital*, 1968).

problem family A colloquial and pejorative label used by workers in social agencies and by the public to refer to families whose behaviour or social conditions they deem in some respect problematic. Its generalizing and *stigmatizing properties have led to strong criticisms of its use.

Problem (or Tragedy) of the Commons An example in *game theory that is used to explore problems of resource distribution (see G. Hardin, 'The Tragedy of the Commons', *Science*, 1968). The use of commons (publicly available land on which farmers graze their cattle) becomes a problem when one such farmer reasons that he or she can expand his or her herd since this small addition to the total stock will contribute little harm to the available pasture. However, if other farmers reason likewise, these incremental additions to the stock using the land lead to overgrazing and thus the destruction of the resource itself. In other words, if each individual in this situation rationally pursues his or her own short-term interest while disregarding others similarly pursuing theirs, then the long-run consequence is that everyone loses their share in the collective resource.

problem of theodicy *See* RELIGION, SOCIOLOGY OF.

procedural justice *See* JUSTICE, SOCIAL.

production The transformation of resources, which include time and effort, into goods and services. Resources are understood always to be too scarce to provide for all wants and needs, so there is an emphasis on the efficiency of production, or *productivity. Similarly, the costs of choosing certain goods and services are not measured by the money spent on them, but by the opportunity cost of the alternative uses of the available resources. *See also* GROSS NATIONAL PRODUCT.

productivity The ratio of output to input. Neither element is easy to measure completely or consistently over time; they are often converted into money values. Labour input can be expressed in numbers of workers, total number of hours worked, or wage costs in a given period. Similar choices exist for other factors of production. Outputs may be measured in differing ways, some physical (such as the number of items made), some related to value (such as the sale price or value added). Different measures can produce wide variations in the resulting values for productivity. Typical examples are volume of output per human hour worked or per machine hour; or sales value per dollar labour costs or per dollar invested.

productivity bargaining A form of *collective bargaining in Britain in which higher rates of pay are traded against employees' acceptance of greater flexibility in work tasks and functions, or other changes in working practice, or where *productivity payments are related directly to volume of output.

profane versus sacred distinction *See* SACRED VERSUS PROFANE DISTINCTION.

professions (professionalism, professionalization) Respectively a form of work organization, a type of work orientation (*see* WORK, SUBJECTIVE EXPERIENCES OF), and a highly effective process of *interest group control. As an organizational form, a profession includes some central regulatory body to ensure the standard of performance of individual members; a code of conduct; careful management of knowledge in relation to the expertise which constitutes the basis of the profession's activities; and, lastly, control of numbers, selection, and training of new entrants. Max Weber contrasted professions with *bureaucracy, and regarded them as the paradigm form of collegiate authority, in which rational-legal power is based on representative democracy and leaders in principle are first among equals.

The work orientation of the professional supposedly entails exclusive concern with the intrinsic rewards and performance of a task, and is typically associated with personal services involving confidentiality and high *trust, as found for example in medicine, education, religion and the law. In the mainstream of the sociology of work and organizations, professionalism is contrasted with bureaucracy, and the so-called bureaucratic mentality.

Recent sociological work has tended to view professionalization as the establishment of effective interest-group control over clients with socially constructed problems as a method of exercising *power in society. This approach treats professional ethics as an ideology, rather than an orientation necessarily adhered to, or meaningful in practice. Entry and knowledge controls function as a form of status exclusion from privileged and remunerative employment In this respect, professional organizations make an interesting comparison with trade unions, for although formal professional ethics preclude *collective bargaining and *industrial conflict, in practice many associations have found themselves becoming more unionate, whilst many unions practise quasi-professional job-entry control. From the huge literature of potential relevance to this entry (much relevant material occurs, for example, in discussion of *labour markets, *gender, and the sociology of *medicine) see Andrew Abbott, *The System of Professions* (1988) and Eliot Friedson, *Professional Powers* (1986). *See also* CLOSURE.

profit *See* CAPITAL; ENTREPRENEUR; LABOUR THEORY OF VALUE.

progress The idea of progress, conceived as the increasing sophistication of knowledge and the improving quality of life, has been the driving force of Western civilization for at least three hundred years. During the 20th century, the same idea was adopted, with variations, by virtually every culture on earth. In the *Third World, development and *modernization are taken to be synonymous with progress.

The history of the idea of progress is complex, and even the meaning of the word is fundamentally disputed. Contemporary scholars disagree over whether the philosophers of classical antiquity had any expectation of progress in its modern sense. Robert Nisbet in *The History of Progress* (1980) finds some evidence that they did. But cyclical theories of civilization's rise and decline were far more common in the ancient world, and continued to be supported into the modern age by such distinguished scholars as Montesquieu, Helvetius, Gibbon, and Spengler. Another tradition of thought about human history is entirely pessimistic, seeing nothing but decline from an earlier golden age.

The idea of a universal history of human progress was developed during the 18th century, in the works of Voltaire, Turgot, Herder, and Kant, among others. With *Kant we arrive at the fully developed idea of a unified human race moving towards the ideal of a 'universal *civil society' founded on *justice and based on the maximum individual freedom for all.

It is no exaggeration to say that philosophers in the 18th and 19th centuries became obsessed with the idea of progress. As hopes of a spiritual heaven faded, people's thoughts turned to the dream of heaven on earth, achieved through progress. The 18th-century idea had five elements: the continuing Deistic belief in Benevolent Providence, an essential optimism about the meaning of human life and destiny; the belief that history was not a chaos, but moved through predictable stages according to knowable laws; the belief in posterity, fulfilling the promise of progress and honouring the forerunners who had made it possible; the centrality of knowledge as the driving force of progress; the belief in the ultimate perfectibility of humankind. There was a powerful element of religious nostalgia in all this, and many historians have argued that the whole progressive ideology down to the present day is a mirror-image of Christianity, with the secular *utopia substituting for the promise of paradise (see, for example, C. L. Becker, *The Heavenly City of the Eighteenth-Century Philosophers*, 1932).

While the French Revolution dealt a severe setback to this optimistic 18th-century philosophy, two of the most secular elements were carried forward into the 19th century, with earth-shaking results: the centrality of knowledge and the search for laws of history. Saint-Simon, and more especially Comte, combined these two elements with Kant's vision of a universal human history to produce an enormously influential theory of progress. Comte proposed that humanity evolved as the human mind evolved, and that human history could be divided into three distinct stages based on the level of human understanding. The Theological Stage was characterized by primitive, animist religious beliefs. The Metaphysical Stage (just ending, Comte believed, in his own time) produced more sophisticated and abstract religions. The emerging Positive Stage would be an era completely defined by science and rationality, which would produce an earthly utopia. Although criticized then and later, Comte's grand theory entered into Western consciousness. Its rational, scientific utopia was the very model of modernity.

Karl Marx came to his theory of progress by way of a different philosophical tradition, but there seems little doubt that Comte and Saint-Simon were influences. Hegel's highly abstract theory of history envisaged the progress of the human spirit towards perfect apprehension of itself and the world. Marx grounded this vision in reality by relating progress to economic struggles. His theory of *historical materialism predicts that the final utopian state (communism) will be brought about through the inexorable workings of economic laws.

Spencer's theory of Social *Darwinism is another example of the 19th-century fascination with progress. Social Darwinism was more fashionable in the United States than in Europe. It linked progress to the growth and increasing complexity of societies, and especially to the natural mechanism of the survival of the fittest, which Spencer believed would create the best possible society, if allowed to do so.

For most of the 20th century, theories of progress followed the pattern of the 19th—optimistic, rationalistic, and increasingly materialistic. Sociology contributed its share in the form of early functional and *post-industrial theories which predicated a future society of harmony and prosperity based on science. At the century's end, however, the idea of progress seemed to be in eclipse. The great utopian ideologies have self-destructed at enormous cost. Science has not produced a moral utopia for most of humanity, and the future is clouded by environmental doubts. *See also* ENVIRONMENT; POSTMODERNISM.

prohibition Prohibitions are powerful, (theoretically) enforceable, and sanctionable social and/or legal restrictions on certain behaviours, events, or other activities—including, for example, sexual 'deviations', drug-taking or trafficking, and trade in endangered species.

The term is often applied to the period (1919–33) during which alcohol production was outlawed in the United States. Sponsored by various religious and political *moral entrepreneurs and economic interest groups, and described at the time as a 'noble experiment', the social consequences of prohibition were highly damaging and the experiment ultimately proved to be insupportable.

Prohibitions frequently produce innovative, illegal counter-responses, and in this case criminal entrepreneurs maintained the illegal supply of alcohol. High profits and competition led to violence. Otherwise non-criminal individuals were caught up in the criminalization of a previously normal social activity. The rapid expansion of *organized crime was also a legacy of the American experiment.

projection This term is used in two senses by social scientists. Most commonly it refers to prediction or inference from existing data as to what will happen in the future. However, in a *psychoanalytic context, it describes the unconscious process in which the individual attributes to others his or her own emotions and impulses. Sigmund Freud regarded it as a common *defence mechanism, used by the ego to control unacceptable feelings, thereby helping to reduce anxiety.

projective tests A type of test, primarily used by psychologists in clinical contexts, designed to measure overall personality dynamics rather than discrete personality traits or dimensions. The tests involve presenting subjects with a relatively unstructured task, such as completing a sentence, or describing a vague shape or picture. The assumption is that, in responding to the unstructured task, individuals project their own ideas and feelings onto the stimulus. Variations in response are held to reflect differences in *personality.

The underlying principles of projective tests—the generic term was not introduced until the late 1930s—derive from psychoanalytic theorizing, particularly the idea of *projection, and the principle of free association. Probably the earliest projective test was the Word Association Test, described by Francis Galton in 1879, in which the individual has to respond to each word on a list with the first that comes into mind. The paradigmatic projective test is undoubtedly the *Rorschach Test, first outlined in 1921, consisting of a set of ink-blots. Other projective tests include the *Thematic Apperception Test, the *Object Relations Test, and various sentence completion tests.

Analysis of an individual's test responses involves psychodynamic interpretation and comparison with population norms. Although attempts have been made to produce standardized scoring systems, detractors point to poor scoring standardization, inadequately established norms, and low validity, condemning the tests as unscientific. Proponents of the tests argue that the very richness of the responses and the scope they offer for clinical interpretation and evaluation is the source of their value in assessing personality dynamics.

proletarianization This label is applied to the process by which sections of the *middle class become absorbed into the *working class. In *The Manifesto of the Communist Party* (1848), Karl Marx and Friedrich Engels argued that capitalism would encourage a polarization in the class structure, between the 'two great hostile camps' of the *bourgeoisie (business owners) and *proletariat (working class). Intermediate groupings, such as small producers and self-employed artisans, would gradually disappear. The middle class of white-collar workers would also join one or other of the hostile camps.

Class analysts have long criticized Marx and Engels for ignoring the growing importance of the so-called new middle class of advanced capitalist societies: the expanding numbers of managers, administrators, and professionals. In reply, Marxist sociologists have maintained that the *Manifesto* deliberately paints an abstract picture of a pure type of capitalist system, whereas Marx's writings elsewhere acknowledge the complexities of actually existing societies. It is certainly true that in *Capital*, volume i (1867), for example, Marx observes that the development of joint-stock companies tends to generate a separation of the labour of *management from the ownership of *capital. The former is conducted by a growing army of 'officers [managers] and NCO's [supervisors], who command during the labour process in the name of capital'.

The debate was given new impetus by Harry Braverman's claim, in *Labour and Monopoly Capital* (1974), that many groups of hitherto middle-class workers (notably routine clerical employees and skilled artisans) were being effectively proletarianized by having their labour dehumanized or *de-skilled. According to Braverman, such a process was endemic to capitalist societies, since the imperatives of capitalist production compelled those who owned or managed industry to fragment tasks according to the principles of *scientific management, in order to sustain profits and maintain control over labour. Braverman's work attracted much comment and provided the theoretical foundations for numerous neo-Marxist studies of the *labour process.

Although Braverman's own data have largely been discredited, the popular perception is that debate about proletarianization remains unresolved, because participants have yet to agree about the criteria by which the process is to be measured. At least four different conceptions of proletarianization can be identified in the literature. For some commentators the argument is one about the relative size of classes. Proletarianization in this sense implies a growth in the proportion of working-class places in the overall class structure. Others have looked at social mobility data, attempting to calculate the likelihood of individuals being proletarianized by downward mobility into the working class, either from middle-class backgrounds or during the course of an occupational career. For these authors it is people, rather than places in the structure, that constitute the subjects of the process. A third criterion refers to the labour process itself. Some researchers have argued that many seemingly non-proletarian places in the class structure (such as those occupied by routine clerical workers) have often been so de-skilled, in terms of job content and the routinization of tasks, that they are indistinguishable from those occupied by the manual working class. A final criterion refers to proletarianization in its socio-political sense; that is, the extent to which certain middle-class groups within the labour-force come to identify themselves as working class or as allies of the working class, and so to share its political aspirations and culture.

One clear finding from the empirical research is that proletarianization may be present according to one criterion but absent according to another. For example, many routine clerical workers share proletarian conditions of employment (in terms of income, fringe benefits, autonomy at work, and chances of promotion), but display a typically middle-class socio-political profile (in terms of voting behaviour, propensity to join trade unions, and class self-identification). *See also* DEGRADATION-OF-WORK THESIS; EMBOURGEOISEMENT.

proletariat Karl Marx's *working class under *capitalism. Accorded the role of prime vehicle of revolutionary and emancipating change through its forma-tion, ascendancy, and eventual triumph, the proletariat is today diminishing in size, political potency, and (it is sometimes claimed) internal cohesion and identity. It has even lost its headline position in Russia.

Formulated out of Marx's early writings on *alienation, the proletariat repre-sented the creation, loss, and eventual re-appropriation of the central defining feature of human essence or species being, namely labour-power (*see* LABOUR THEORY OF VALUE). Containing as it did both the needs whose fulfilment drove history along, as well as the powers or potential required to fulfil and generate new needs, labour-power was the means through which humanity was created. Labour so conceived abolished the distinction between humanity and nature, and subordinated the latter to its service. The enslavement of this labour-power (in the form of the productive worker under capitalism generating surplus value), and its eventual liberation after the necessary passage through the various historical epochs, was the core of the historical process. It is the continuous dynamic of the development of labour-power which generates the impetus to the growth in productive forces and their transmission through history which gives that history its coherence. If history is the history of the class struggle then it is a struggle to free this labour-power, and thus also the proletariat, which epito-mizes the enslavement of this labour power and whose liberation will therefore be a universal liberation. This is the basis of the Marxist theory of *historical materialism.

This *humanistic conception of the proletariat is in accord with the ethical thrust of all of Marx's writings, and underpins the subsequent more structurally rigid definitions gleaned from readings of *Capital*. It suggests that, for Marx, class was a process of becoming, both of the proletariat to maturity, and of humanity to control of its developed capacities forged through the historical process. It was not (as it subsequently became in the so-called boundary debate, *see* CONTRA-DICTORY CLASS LOCATION) the application of rigid formulae or criteria based upon relationships to the means of production, the productive (of surplus value) versus unproductive labour distinction, or supervisory and managerial hierarchies of control or autonomy. These exercises only succeeded in identifying an ever-diminishing category of those who were meant (in Marxist theory) to be growing in size, scope, and intensity.

There are, according to Marx, historical factors which propel the proletariat to take up its historical task. The combination of capital creates for the mass of workers a common situation and common interests. The *commodity fetishism, which stands in the way of the individual's attempts to gain true control over his or her 'social interconnectedness', is overcome through the multi-dimensional concomitant processes associated with the intensification of the class struggle, the emergence of *class consciousness, and its transfer into class action. As the proletariat emerges victorious, on the wings of the proletarian dictatorship, it not only regains political control over the state but also economic and eventually moral control over its productive life-processes.

property Property and property rights are central to *capitalist societies. Perhaps because they are largely taken for granted in this context they have received relatively little attention from sociologists. By comparison, political philosophers and economists have debated the nature of property at length, and fiercely contested its origins (see F. Snare, 'The Concept of Property', *American Philosophical Quarterly*, 1972, and E. G. Furubotn and S. Pejovitch, 'Property Rights and Economic Theory', *Journal of Economic Literature*, 1972).

Possibly the most influential modern explanation of the origins of private property is John Locke's theory of natural rights, which states that property ownership rests on the individual's *rights to use whatever is in the natural environment and is deemed necessary for the satisfaction of needs, and the right to own whatever one has expended labour upon (provided it is not then wasted). Locke's theory thus provides three criteria for a naturally just distribution of property: namely, need (or possibly desire), expenditure of labour (which includes creative entrepreneurship), and use (which some have interpreted as exploitation and accumulation).

Since Locke's theory held that property was that which a man had 'mixed his labour with', it offered a potential challenge to the early-modern status quo (although Locke himself had set out to defend this), on the grounds that it implied it was neither natural nor just for the privileged few in society to enjoy the surplus created by the labour of the many. *Utilitarianism met this challenge, with the argument that private property and its laws had no origins or justification other than *utility: that is, the rules of property arise out of conventions which experience has shown to be the most useful for the promotion of human happiness. For example, David Hume considered the principal rules establishing title to property to be those of present possession, first possession, long possession, accession, and succession, and argued that the justice of these rules was rooted in the history of social experience. The present system was the 'right' system because it had clearly evolved in response to people's needs. Since this approach offered not only an explanation but also a justification for the existing distribution of property it became central to the philosophy of classical *liberalism during the 19th century.

The *conservative reaction to this philosophy of property opposed the principles of utility with those of tradition, experience, and stewardship. Conservatives conceived of property as a partnership between the generations, epitomized by the continuity of the landed estate, of which the landowner was a steward who served (rather than owned) the property, under the obligation of maintaining allegiance to the status quo and thus preserving a stable social order.

The Scottish political economists—John Millar, Adam Ferguson, and Adam Smith—extended the analysis of property relations to take account of *class formation. This, in turn, encouraged Karl Marx to offer the first systematic sociological account of the importance of property, stressing the links between property ownership, political domination, and ideological representations. In Marx's formulation, property is power, and the different forms of property define the 'social conditions of existence' upon which rises the *superstructure of the *state, *civil society, and *ideology. Somewhat later, Max Weber also argued that 'property and lack of property are . . . the basic characteristics of all class situations', although he accepted that the propertied classes were highly differentiated in the types of property they held and the meaning which they gave to its utilization.

This last observation opens up the issue which dominates contemporary sociological discussions of property. These have moved away from considering ideologies of property and the social organization of propertied strata, and concentrated attention instead on the *consumption of property, notably the diverse ways in which ownership of certain types of property (for example houses, cars, and clothes) shapes social relations and social meanings, and plays an important role in the construction of social *identities.

Most sociologists have been concerned with private property. However, noncapitalist forms of property ownership (including possession of symbolic property) have been extensively studied by anthropologists, and sociologists have recently extended their analyses to include state or collective ownership, and inheritance. The best short introduction to the topic is Andrew Reeve's *Property* (1986). For a sociological case study of the material and symbolic significance of property see Peter Saunders, *A Nation of Home Owners* (1989). *See also* BOURGEOISIE; COLLECTIVE CONSUMPTION; CONSUMPTION, SOCIOLOGY OF; CONSUMPTION SECTORS; GIFT RELATIONSHIP; OWNERSHIP AND CONTROL; PRIVATIZATION; PUBLIC GOOD.

prostitution, sociological studies of The provision of sexual favours for financial reward has probably been institutionalized in the form of prostitution in every society that has had a coinage. It has nearly always involved the prostitution of women to men, though male prostitution, especially to male clients, is not uncommon.

Kingsley Davis proposed a functional theory which saw prostitution as a safety-valve, helping maintain the respectability of marriage. Prostitution certainly flourished during the Victorian period of rigid sexual morality. But feminists have pointed out that prostitution provides no safety-valve for women, and indeed controls them by labelling those who are not chaste as whores. Victorian prostitution was connected with a double standard of morality, which was much more permissive for men than for women. Sociological studies of prostitutes show that their motivation is mainly economic and it seems likely that the number of prostitutes increases when there are fewer other job opportunities for women. International movements of prostitutes are nearly always from poor countries to richer ones. There are few studies of clients, though a Norwegian study found that while most of them are 'Mr Average', there are a number of single men who have difficulties relating to women who go to prostitutes quite frequently.

In Britain prostitution itself is legal, but soliciting in public, 'kerb-crawling', brothel-keeping, procuring, and living on the 'immoral earnings' of a prostitute are all illegal. Here, the commonest ways of working are as a street-walker, as an individual call-girl who advertises her telephone number, or in association with apparently legal work as a club hostess, escort, or masseuse. In some countries prostitution is regulated by the state, with prostitutes being required to register (and often to have regular medical tests), or with prostitution confined to designated red light districts or registered brothels.

See Allegra Taylor, *Prostitution* (1991) and Julia O'Connell Davidson, *Prostitution, Power and Freedom* (1998).

protestant ethic (protestant ethic thesis) The set of values embodied in early Protestantism, which has controversially been linked to the development of modern *capitalism, most famously in Max Weber's classic essays on *The Protestant Ethic and the Spirit of Capitalism* (1905).

Initially this relationship appears paradoxical, since Protestant beliefs did not embrace the idea of economic gain for its own sake, yet clearly this is an essential (and novel) component of capitalism. Weber's argument is that, whilst capitalism had existed elsewhere in elementary form, it had not developed on anything like the scale seen in modern Europe. Its emergence here was a result of the relatively wide endorsement of the idea of accumulating capital as a duty or end in itself. This, in itself, is an irrational attitude: there is no rational reason why we should choose work against either leisure or consumption. For Weber, religion provides the key to understanding this peculiarly modern orientation to everyday life, since religion entails a choice of ultimate values which cannot be justified on rational grounds. Once we have chosen such a value, however, we can pursue it by rational means: it makes sense to talk of rational and irrational ways of realizing an ultimate value. (For example, if I were to choose communism as an ultimate value, it would be irrational of me to join a conservative political party.) Weber's argument is that the rational pursuit of the ultimate values of the ascetic Protestantism characteristic of 16th- and 17th-century Europe led people to engage in disciplined work; and that disciplined and rational organization of work as a duty is the characteristic feature of modern capitalism—its unique ethos or spirit.

The crucial link to Protestantism comes through the latter's notion of the calling of the faithful to fulfil their duty to God in the methodical conduct of their everyday lives. This theme is common to the beliefs of the Calvinist and neo-Calvinist churches of the Reformation. Predestination is also an important belief, but since humans cannot know who is saved (elect) and who is damned, this creates a deep inner loneliness in the believer. In order therefore to create assurance of salvation, which is itself a sure sign (or proof) of election, diligence in one's calling (hard work, systematic use of time, and a strict asceticism with respect to worldly pleasures and goods) is highly recommended—so-called 'this-worldly asceticism'. In general terms, however, the most important contribution of Protestantism to capitalism was the spirit of *rationalization that it encouraged. The relationship between the two is deemed by Weber to be one of *elective affinity.

This interpretation of the origins of Western capitalism provoked a huge response and even today continues to generate controversy. It was not intended, as is sometimes claimed, to be an alternative to Marxist accounts which offer explanations based on the economy. Weber argued against any simple, one-sided, or reductionist explanation of the rise of capitalist society. Protestantism did not cause modern capitalism, but it was one necessary pre-condition of its appearance. Much of the enormous secondary literature is reviewed in Gordon Marshall's *In Search of the Spirit of Capitalism* (1982). Despite a range of objections on empirical and theoretical grounds, particularly concerning lack of clarity in the argument, the thesis remains influential. A number of translations exist. Parsons translated Weber's slightly revised version of 1920 (in 1930), which was subsequently retranslated in 2002 by Stephen Kalberg. The original essays of 1904–5 have been translated by Peter Baehr and Gordon Wells (published in 2002). Unfortunately, all these translations have been published with the same book title. Weber's various responses to his principal critics have been brought together in David Chalcraft and Austin Harrington (eds.), *The Protestant Ethic Debate* (2001).

Proudhon, Pierre-Joseph (1809–65) An autodidactic French brewer, early *socialist thinker, and militant, who popularized the sayings 'God is evil' and 'property is theft'. He is widely regarded as the founder of political *anarchism, although his own followers applied the term 'mutualism' to their beliefs, emphasizing the need for justice as the means of ending conflict in society. Proudhon advocated production *cooperatives and mutual interest-free banking as the basis for reorganizing society. His doctrine was located between extreme individualistic anarchism and those who envisage an anarchist communism. He emphasized the violent passions of individuals and the need for the family to control these. His *Economic Contradictions, or the Philosophy of Poverty* (1846) provoked a major rejoinder from Karl Marx.

psephology The study of elections, voting patterns, and electoral behaviour, and the forecasting of election results. This became a specialist field of *political sociology with the spread of regular opinion polls on voting intentions, major post-election interview surveys, access to population census statistics for small areas, and sophisticated data analysis and modelling packages.

psyche *See* PSYCHOANALYSIS.

psychiatry A medical speciality, whose boundaries have always been contested, which focuses on the care and treatment of mental disorders. It developed as a professional grouping in the first half of the 19th century: the term was coined in Germany in 1808 and was more widely used in Europe and America from the 1840s. Medical interest and specialization in insanity was not new. However, the establishment of lunatic hospitals and asylums (first voluntary then public) from the mid-18th century onwards, provided a solid foundation for the emergence of psychiatry as a profession. The asylum offered new opportunities for observation, treatment, and training, and new powers like certification that facilitated *professionalization. Associations of asylum doctors were founded in Britain in 1841, the United States in 1844, and France in 1847; the first journals were published in Britain in 1854, the United States in 1844, France in 1843, and somewhat earlier in Germany.

In the 1820s to 1840s, medical interest in lunacy and therapeutic optimism were both high. Practitioners were often eclectic, many supporting moral treatment, which emphasized the therapeutic value of an ordered environment in building up inmates' capacities for self-control and self-esteem. However, higher-status practitioners were soon deterred from asylum work by the residency requirements in larger institutions, which restricted the opportunities for private practice, and by the predominance of pauper patients. Moreover, as the asylums grew and were increasingly filled with inmates having chronic and intractable problems, the medical role became primarily custodial rather than therapeutic. Increasing medical emphasis on the natural sciences was largely reflected in routine autopsies in the effort to identify brain *pathology.

Two major changes occurred in the first half of the 20th century. First, psychiatric work outside the asylums expanded, much of it on a private basis for more affluent patients, many with problems that Sigmund Freud identified as psychoneurotic. His influence on office psychiatry was considerable, especially in the United States, where private practice flourished. Second, there were major efforts to transform asylums into proper hospitals, and in the 1930s physical treatments such as electroconvulsive therapy (ECT) and psychosurgery (to be followed in the 1950s by new drug therapies) were developed, encouraging a new therapeutic optimism.

Both developments underpinned the acceptance of a policy of *community care in the 1950s, initially as a supplement to asylum care, then as an alternative—the one representing a diversification of the locus of care and an increased role for psychiatry across a wider spectrum of conditions, the other a break with old pro-institutional and custodial models of care, a change facilitated by the introduction of voluntary admission in Britain in 1930 and the resulting decline in compulsory detention.

The implications for psychiatry of the subsequent run-down of mental hospitals and the shift to work in the community cannot yet be fully assessed. The loss of the old empire of the mental hospital has undoubtedly reduced psychiatrists' power, as has (to some extent) the development of multi-disciplinary teams. The power of psychiatrists now resides largely in their rights over prescribing and their expertise in the natural sciences. However, developments in biological psychiatry and the neurosciences could cut back the domain of illnesses deemed mental, to the advantage of neurologists and at the expense of psychiatry. *See also* ANTI-PSYCHIATRY.

psychoanalysis A psychological theory and a method of treatment of psychological disorders, developed initially by Sigmund Freud, and extended in a variety of ways by later psychoanalysts. James A. C. Brown's *Freud and the Post-Freudians* (1964) is still a good introduction to the various schools.

The core of psychoanalysis is the theory of the unconscious and the structural model of the psyche as consisting of three interrelated systems of id, ego, and superego. The unconscious comprises ideas and feelings that are unacceptable, either because they are experienced as internally threatening to the existence of the individual, or because they are experienced as threatening to society. These ideas might be sexual in origin (Freud), aggressive and destructive (Melanie Klein), or connected with early experiences of fear and helplessness (D. W. Winnicott). The id is seen as the source of drives demanding immediate satisfaction, and the superego as internalized parental and social authority, the work of the ego being to mediate the resultant conflicting demands.

Freud's account of dreams provides the most elaborate analysis of the workings of the unconscious. He begins by stating that all dreams are wish fulfilments: they provide a fantasy satisfaction of desires that have been repressed into the unconscious. The unconscious itself is timeless and does not mature: we remain, at this level, infantile throughout our lives, demanding immediate satisfaction. Neither is it subject to the laws of logic, desiring contradictory things at the same time, a feature of human life often recognized when people point out that love and hatred of the same person are closely connected. When we sleep the repression of our unconscious desires is relaxed. However, they do not appear directly in our dreams, but are censored through processes that Freud refers to as dream work, of which there are four types: condensation, or the merging of several thoughts into one dream symbol (for example, a policeman in a dream might stand for a range of authority figures in life); displacement, in which a desire is displaced onto an object in some way connected with the original, perhaps by chance or similarity (thus, in the hackneyed example, we might dream of sexual intercourse as a train going through a tunnel); symbolization, or the turning of ideas into pictures (for example, dreaming of setting a table, but laying knives and forks without handles might indicate a feeling of being unable to handle a situation); and, finally, secondary revision, the rational gloss we put on a dream, turning it into a manageable story as we remember it. Freud thought that dream analysis should concentrate on symbols, rather than the story, which is merely a disguise.

The analysis of dreams leads to the central feature of psychoanalytic treatment—free association. The patient is asked to talk about whatever comes into his or her head in connection with the symbol, and from this a pattern of meaning emerges which allegedly takes us back to the original unconscious thoughts (see Freud's *The Interpretation of Dreams*, 1900).

Over recent years these ideas have been taken up in particular by *structuralist and *post-structuralist thinkers in various disciplines: as a theory of literary criticism, for example, when a text is read as a dream; as a theory of the production of meaning; and as providing a so-called decentred theory of the subject. The Marxist philosopher Louis Althusser incorporated the idea of a 'symptomatic reading' into his epistemology as a way of identifying the underlying structure (or *problematic) of a theory.

Freud's theory of sexual development is probably the most widely known aspect of psychoanalysis. The child is seen as developing initially through oral, anal, and phallic stages, where the libido is expressed and satisfied at different points of contact between the body and the outside world—the mouth, anus, and genitals. Individuals can become arrested at or regress to any of these levels. However progress through them is the same for both sexes. An essential element of Freud's argument is that we begin life as bisexual, if not polymorphously perverse, and that heterosexuality is an often tenuous achievement, involving the subordination (repression or sublimation) of *homosexual and other desires. This is achieved largely but not entirely unconsciously through the Oedipal stage of development. Both sexes take the mother as the first love-object. In the case of the little boy, sexual feelings towards his mother cannot be physically realized, and are experienced by him as a challenge to the father. This puts him in danger because of the father's superior strength and power. The danger is experienced as a threat of castration, and in the face of this threat combined with the promise of a woman of his own when he reaches puberty, the boy relinquishes his desire for his mother. The little girl has to make a more dramatic change from mother to father as the primary love-object. According to Freud, she experiences herself as already castrated, leading to early identification with her mother (see *Three Essays on the Theory of Sexuality*, 1905).

This theory has played a prominent role in the development of modern *feminism. For many it established Freud as irredeemably in favour of *patriarchy; for others it provides a basis for an analysis of patriarchy. Juliet Mitchell, a British feminist, Marxist, and psychoanalyst, was the first modern feminist to defend Sigmund Freud, arguing that psychoanalysis offers a description and analysis of patriarchy, rather than a prescription for male domination (see *Psychoanalysis and Feminism*, 1976).

Freud's analysis of the development of the sexual object choice involves an understanding of the process by which the infant first of all seeks satisfaction through its own body (primary *narcissism) and then through identifying with and introjecting the mother as part of its own psyche. Whereas classical psychoanalysis and Freud concentrated on the Oedipal stage, the development of psychoanalytic theory in Melanie Klein's work and British psychoanalysis in general focused on very early relationships with the mother, so that some feminists have tried to explain the development of gender differences in terms of the distinctive relationships between mothers and their young male and female children.

Psychoanalytic theory is not a monolithic block, but has developed through different national schools, and these schools tend to relate to social theory in different ways. The principal link between British psychoanalysis and social theory has been via feminist accounts of mothering. French psychoanalysis, through Lacan, has been associated with post-structuralism in general and post-structuralist feminism in particular. American ego psychology was incorporated by Talcott Parsons as a general theory of *socialization. A general review can be found in Ian Craib's *Psychoanalysis: A Critical Introduction* (2001). *See also* BOWLBY; CRITICAL THEORY; JUNG.

psychohistory The *psychoanalytic study of historical figures, or of the *Weltanschauung* of a particular historical period, based on the attempt to relate Sigmund Freud's theory of psychological development to prevailing social conditions and institutions; or, in the case of specific individuals, to significant *life-events. A noted practitioner is the American psychoanalyst Erik Erikson, whose *Childhood and Society* (1950) and *Life History and the Historical Moment* (1975) are typical of the genre. See his *Young Man Luther* (1958) and the early example in Victor Branford's *St Columba* (1912). Max Weber's life and work were analysed in this way by Arthur Mitzman in *The Iron Cage* (1969).

psychology Variously defined as the science of behaviour or the science of mind, psychology emerged as a distinct discipline in the second half of the 19th century, with the work of researchers such as Wilhelm Wundt (1832–1920) who founded the first experimental laboratory of psychology in Leipzig. Much of the focus of the discipline has been on identifying the general mechanisms involved in processes such as *perception, *learning, motivation, and memory, although there has been some attention to individual differences, especially in relation to *intelligence and *personality.

Academic psychology has tended to be strongly *positivist in orientation and the experimental method has been widely used—characteristics reflected in the strong support for *behaviourism which became the dominant approach in Anglo-American psychology from early in the 20th century through to the 1960s. The major focus of behaviourism was on learning and the approach was associated with a strong emphasis on *environment and a rejection of the importance of innate factors in the development of human behaviour. Since the 1960s there has been a shift towards more *cognitive approaches and acceptance of some innate capacities, with considerable attention paid to the way in which information is handled and processed. There has also been a renewed interest in neuropsychology. The experimental, positivist orientation remains, as does the long-standing hostility to *psychoanalysis and other psycho-dynamic psychologies, although some psychologists and some departments are more eclectic than others. Certainly, both humanist and feminist psychology now usually find a place within the terrain of academic psychology.

As with other disciplines the delineation of fields changes over time. The older terrains of abnormal psychology or psychopathology have now been transformed and broadened into the field of health psychology. An important and long-standing area that has developed since the first decade of this century is that of social psychology. William McDougall published his *Introduction to Social Psychology* in 1908, though its terrain is ill-defined. Within the framework of psychology, social psychology focuses especially on the study of face-to-face social interaction, making considerable use of experimental studies of small *groups. There is, however, a more sociological social psychology, particularly influenced by *symbolic interactionism, and employing methods such as *participant observation.

There is a large selection of introductory social psychology texts from which to choose. Leonard Berkowitz, *A Survey of Social Psychology* (3rd edn., 1986) and Louis A. Penner, *Social Psychology* (1986) are both fairly comprehensive in their coverage. A useful overview of theoretical approaches is James Schellenberg, *Masters of Social Psychology* (1979). From a *symbolic interactionist standpoint, the classic text is A. R. Lindesmith, A. L. Strauss, and N. Denzin, *An Introduction to Social Psychology* (8th edn., 1999). See also EVOLUTIONARY PSYCHOLOGY; SOCIOBIOLOGY.

psychometrics The measurement, representation, and analysis of psychological variables, primarily using mathematics, statistics, and computing. Of special relevance to sociology are the topics of the measurement of *intelligence, psychophysics (quantification and interrelation of physical variables and their subjective counterparts), scaling methods, and artificial intelligence models. Psychometric methods are now widely used in job-selection processes and interviews, though their validity in identifying the best candidates or the best characteristics can be seriously questioned.

psychopath The *psychiatric label for individuals, commonly young males, who behave in disruptive, antisocial ways, showing little guilt or strong emotional ties. By way of explaining the behaviour, *psychoanalysts point to a failure of superego development, *learning theorists to an inability to learn from experience. Whether psychopathy is a mental disorder is contested. Barbara Wootton asserted the impossibility of differentiating such a behaviourally delineated condition from *delinquency.

psychosis A severe mental illness often contrasted with *neurosis. Psychosis is characterized by disordered thought, feeling or perception, as in delusions or hallucinations, and is said to involve loss of contact with reality. Organic psychoses have known bodily causes, functional psychoses do not, although they are often assumed. The two major psychoses are *schizophrenia and manic *depression.

psychosomatic illness Influenced by psycho-dynamic thinking, the term psychosomatic became widespread from the 1930s onwards, initially indicating a general approach to illness emphasizing a mind/body interaction. The concept usually denotes certain bodily illness, such as ulcers, with presumed psychological causes. However, attention to psychosocial stressors across the illness spectrum suggests the difficulty of maintaining any strict differentiation between the psychosomatic and the physical. *See also* *autonomy; STRESS.

psychotherapy An imprecise term that may embrace a wide variety of psychological methods of treatment, group or individual, provided by specialist therapists for the treatment of mental and behavioural problems (usually non-psychotic). Psychotherapy may include directive therapies involving suggestion, such as hypnosis, as well as non-directive, behavioural, and psycho-dynamic therapies. Narrowly defined, it denotes psychoanalytic therapies, excluding full *psychoanalysis.

psy-complex The set of professions dealing with the psyche: psychology, psychiatry, psychoanalysis, psychotherapy, psychiatric nursing, and psychiatric social work. The term derives from the work of Michel *Foucault and French *post-structuralists such as Jacques Donzelot and Robert Castel, who analysed the role of the social and 'psy' professions in regulating family life, sexuality, mind, and rationality. A useful discussion is in Nikolas Rose, *Inventing our Selves* (1998).

public administration The bureaucratic systems and their procedures which serve the government and implement its policies. Hence also the field of study which describes and analyses policy development and policy imple-mentation processes.

public good (collective good) Public goods were defined initially by Paul Samuelson ('The Pure Theory of Public Expenditure', *Review of Economics and Statistics*, 1954) as those where person A's consumption of the good did not interfere with person B's consumption. Ezra J. Mishan (*Introduction to Norma-tive Economics*, 1981) prefers to designate these as 'collective goods'.

Both terms refer to collectively funded services that either cannot be provided by the *market or which particular governments choose to supply from public funds. Some goods and services cannot be priced accurately and hence cannot be efficiently supplied by private industry. 'Non-excludability' refers to services which cannot be withheld from any individual, even if they refuse to pay for it—such as street-lighting. 'Impossibility of rejection' means people cannot abstain from consumption, even if they wish to do so—such as the 'protection' offered by wars and national defence, even to pacifists. 'Non-rivalness in consumption' means a service supplied to one person is automatically supplied to others at no extra cost—as illustrated by a radio station, whose transmission costs are not determined by the number of listeners. The arguments for collective provision are often extended to other services, such as education, which are consumed by individuals as well as benefiting the economy and society as a whole.

In societies with exceptional natural resources that are exploited by the state, such as oil-rich countries, public goods are funded by the revenues from state enterprises and equivalent income. In most societies, public goods are funded from direct and indirect taxation, with more or less debate over how the funding burden should be distributed in relation to levels of use or benefit, and over which services should be funded as a public good and which purchased privately on the market. Services often treated as public goods, not always exclusively, include: national defence; public security, education, health services, fire and other emergency services, telecommunications networks, road, rail, and air networks and transport services, the preservation of national monuments, water supply, national radio and television services. Arguments offered in favour of public ownership of such services include economies of scale, national interest, the case for worker participation in enterprises, and the indirect social benefits (externalities) which would be ignored by private producers. Arguments against include the inefficiencies resulting from lack of *competition, and unlimited demand generated by the absence of any pricing of services consumed. Many public goods cannot be valued easily—for example by carrying out *cost-benefit analyses on their provision.

The concept of public goods has been considerably extended since Samuelson's formulation and a number of competing typologies are now available. For example, some writers prefer to distinguish public goods and welfare goods, the latter being those goods provided by a public agency to consumers (the public) free or at a cost below production cost. The objective of providing these is to redistribute goods in order to increase the total *welfare of society.

Similarly, Richard Cornes and Todd Sandler (*The Theory of Externalities, Public Goods and Club Goods*, 1986) distinguish between public and private goods according to whether consumers are excludable (particular persons can be excluded from the benefits) or non-excludable (particular persons cannot be excluded from the benefits), and whether there is rivalry or non-rivalry in the consumption of the benefits (benefits are divisible or indivisible). By cross-classifying these two dimensions of *property rights, one can then distinguish between private goods (excludable, having rivalry in consumption, as with most consumer goods available in the *market); public goods (non-excludable, non-rivalry in consumption, such as the protection given to all Americans, whether they pay for it or not, by American nuclear weapons); club goods, or impure public goods, which are excludable but only partly (initially) non-rival in consumption (as in an exclusive golf club, where an exclusion criterion acts like a boundary, but once you are in the club its resources are a pure public good, unless membership exceeds carrying capacity, such that *crowding leads to either deterioration of the good or competition for access to it); and, finally, positional goods, or impure private goods, with rivalry in benefits and where consumers are at least partly non-excludable (as where goods are initially pure private goods, but during their consumption something happens to change their character, for example 'bandwagon effects' among consumers lead even those who do not intend to consume the good to share in some of the benefits or losses, through conspicuous consumption or conspicuous waste).

These sorts of distinctions have had a significant impact on economic theory, and are central to *game theory and theories of rational action; however, sociologists have been, on the whole, rather slow to explore their significance (for example for theories of *collective action). *See also* EXTERNALITY; FREE RIDER; POSITIONAL GOODS.

public interest The indivisible collective interests of a *community or *society as judged by the commentator. The provision of public goods is argued to be in the public interest—although practice varies on how wide the net is cast. *See also* PUBLIC GOOD.

public opinion An ill-defined concept, used in many ways, but perhaps most generally it refers to the approval or disapproval of publicly observable positions and behaviour, as expressed by a defined section of a society, and (usually) measured through *opinion polls. Consequently, it is often taken to be synonymous with 'what the polls report'—about morality, favoured consumer brands, politics, or whatever. The two groups most commonly surveyed under this label are adults of working age (variously defined as people aged 16, 18, or 20 to 60 or 65 years), and all adults over the age of compulsory education, including the elderly and retired (typically defined as people aged 16 or 18 and over).

public sociology This term describes the idea that sociology should engage with the public on issues that are relevant to it. It is designed to establish a style of sociology that contrasts with mere 'professional sociology' and is normally used to suggest that the discipline of sociology should not limit itself to what are portrayed as the narrower intellectual concerns and interests of its professional practitioners. The term is therefore used normatively to challenge both the subject matter of the discipline and its focus, and is intended to encourage the discipline to address public issues of topical concern and to do so in a manner that involves active engagement with public constituencies and groups affected by them. Most adherents use the term also to call for greater political involvement by sociologists in issues of injustice, unfairness, and inequality, which tends to restrict engagements to civil society groups and communities amongst the dispossessed, poor, and the powerless. The term was popularised by Michael Burawoy in his 2004 Presidential Address to the American Sociological Association. In his subsequent role as President of the International Sociological Association he has continued to internationalize the term and advance its use within the global discipline. The idea that sociology should have a public focus, however, is very long-standing and the term itself pre-dates Burawoy and can be found in writings by Herbert Gans and Ben Aggar in the USA and Baruch Kimmerling in Israel, although Burawoy captured the global discipline's uncertainty about its normative purpose at the time of the new millennium in the context of neo-liberal complaints about the economic benefits of universities and whole subject areas, and has done most to popularize it.

In one sense all sociology is public in that professional sociologists have always used the discipline to engage with the political, social, economic, and cultural ideas of the time. Sociology's historical origins are in dispute of course, but few doubt that its progenitors wrestled with issues of profound social change in politics, economics, and cultural life in an attempt to diagnose and improve the human condition, irrespective of which century or in which place we locate sociology's roots. Throughout the 20th century, the period when the discipline of sociology became more professional and specialized, there were calls from some sociologists for greater public engagement, most notably Raymond Aron in

France, Charles Wright Mills in the USA, and Peter Townsend in Britain. These three exemplars represent the diversity of public sociology prior to its popularization in the 21st century. Mills's sociological writings were calls for political radicalism by sociologists motivated by US domestic and foreign policy, in which he famously argued that the sociological imagination should transform people's private troubles into public issues. Aron was a public intellectual, writing newspaper columns and using sociology to engage with issues in French culture and politics. Townsend, on the other hand, became actively involved in practical ways in dealing with issues of poverty that his research disclosed, co-founding the Child Poverty Action Group and the Disability Alliance.

In Burawoy, public sociology was seen as a research agenda that focused on the concerns of what he called local organic communities within and underneath civil society that are provoked by their social structural and class location. This engagement was with organic communities both as co-participants of sociological research, which they might help to formulate and design, and as special audiences of sociological research, with targeted programmes of dissemination designed to allow the research to speak to their situation. Critics of public sociology are largely supportive of its intent to reshape the normative value of the discipline but they argue that public sociology needs to become a teaching strategy as well as a strategy for civic engagement in which the discipline also develops closer links with governments, policymakers, and power elites who share responsibility for dealing with the problems affecting organic communities. Engagements upwards tend to be with the bodies precisely with the resources capable of making a difference to the lives of organic communities. Debates about public sociology thus get to the very core of sociology's normative purposes in impacting on the lives of ordinary people and to the nature of the engagements best to achieve this. Burawoy's statement can be found in the *American Sociological Review* (2005) and a good recent discussion is John Brewer's *The Public Value of the Social Sciences* (2013).

⊕ SEE WEB LINKS
• Michael Burawoy's website.

public sphere versus private sphere distinction The public versus private distinction in Greek philosophy was based on a public world of politics and a private world of family and economic relations. In modern sociology, the distinction is normally used in reference to a separation of home and employment, a juxtaposition which has been seen as the basis for a traditional gendered *division of labour.

Public Use Sample (PUS) An anonymous sample of records from the decennial population census. In the United States, these have been made available to researchers from the 1960 Census onwards, at the 1 per cent and 0.1 per cent levels. Following practice in the United States, similar data-tapes have been released in Canada, and—since 1991—in Britain (where they are termed *SAR, or Samples of Anonymised Records).

purdah An Urdu word meaning 'curtain' or 'screen' and referring to a system of *sex-role differentiation marked by strong physical and social *segregation. Purdah is maintained by the segregation of physical space within the household and by the use of articles of clothing such as the veil. It is largely associated with *Islamic religion and culture but immensely variable in the form and degree of observance amongst Islamic peoples.

p

qualitative versus quantitative debate A *methodological issue in sociology with arguments for and against a distinction between qualitative and quantitative studies. The debate arises from a more deeply rooted distinction drawn between different *epistemological positions. Quantitative methodology has generally been associated with *positivist epistemology and is usually regarded as referring to the collection and analysis of numerical data. Qualitative methodology, on the other hand, is generally associated with interpretative epistemologies and tends to be used to refer to forms of data collection and analysis that rely on understanding the *meanings of social phenomena. The debate became prominent in the 1970s as a result of a backlash against the status accorded to the 'scientific' stance of positivist methodology in sociological writing. In these works, sections on qualitative data—if they were included at all— usually referred to them as involving 'soft' techniques of interest only in respect of providing intuitions or hunches for the formulation of *hypotheses, that could then be tested more rigorously using quantitative or 'hard' data. Growing interest in *phenomenological approaches in the 1970s led to scepticism about the relevance of the natural scientific model of research for the *social sciences.

It has increasingly been recognized that qualitative and quantitative approaches are complementary and that no viable understanding can be achieved without the use of both. An early example is Norman Denzin's strategy of *triangulation, while more recent work has stressed the idea of 'mixed methods'. Practising researchers have recently suggested that the distinction between the two types of data is considerably more blurred than is suggested in the theoretical debate. It has also been pointed out that different methodologies are not necessarily tied to particular epistemological positions, and that there are an increasing number of techniques of analysis that defy classification into a simplistic dualist typology. Nevertheless, some still hold that the epistemologies underpinning the different types of a data are so divergent that any attempt at combination or reconciliation is impossible. The continuing debate is paralleled in part—but only in part—by the distinction between *macrosociology and microsociology. Some researchers adopt the position of there being a substantive difference between observing and analysing regularities and associations at the macro-level of social structures, institutions, and aggregate data, and observing or analysing interactions and causal processes at the micro-level of human actors. The former tends towards quantitative analysis while the latter encourages interpretive understanding.

In an important recent intervention, Gary King et al. (*Designing Social Inquiry: Scientific Inference in Qualitative Research*, 1994) have pointed out that although there are various *styles* of social-scientific research there is only one *logic* of scientific inference. The logic of good quantitative and good qualitative research designs does not therefore differ.

quality of life The idea of (improving) quality of life is central to many community programmes, to public policy, to development initiatives, and to much social legislation. However the concept itself is controversial.

The most commonly used indicators are straightforwardly economic—such as per capita GNP—but increasingly even economists recognize that these are crude measures of a citizen's quality of life. An alternative 'capability approach' suggests that the quality of life each person leads corresponds to the freedom that he or she has to live one kind of life rather than another. This is reflected in the combination of doings and beings ('functionings') that are possible, ranging from elementary matters such as being properly nourished and healthy, through to much more complex functionings such as having self-respect, preserving human dignity, and taking part in the life of the wider community. This approach suggests that an adequate measure of quality of life must be plural and should recognize that distinct components of well-being are irreducible to each other.

The Level of Living Surveys set up by the Swedish government to measure the welfare of individuals, and conducted periodically since 1968, use a wide variety of indicators. These measure (among other things) health and access to health care (ability to walk 100 metres, various symptoms of illness); employment and working conditions (unemployment experiences, physical demands of work); education and skills (years of education, qualifications obtained); housing (amenities, and number of persons per room); security of life and property (exposure to violence and thefts); and recreation and culture (vacations, access to leisure facilities)—as well as the more obvious economic resources (income, wealth, property, and so on).

Debates about the quality of life are not unlike discussions of *poverty and *deprivation; for example, the same issues of cultural relativism are raised, and similar measurement problems arise. Should measurement be related to the needs or resources of individuals? Which indicators should be used and how can these be summarized to give an overall picture of quality of life? (How do we compare a rich man who suffers from an untreatable illness which interferes with his enjoyment of life and a poor woman who keeps perfect health and enjoys life?) For a useful and wide-ranging discussion of the concept and the many methodological issues it raises see Martha Nussbaum and Amartya Sen (eds.), *The Quality of Life* (1993).

quasi-religion *See* PARA-RELIGION.

queer theory An approach to social theory that suggests that established theory has been dominated by both deep assumptions of heterosexuality and the male/female gender binary divide and proceeds to challenge such assumptions. It emerged around the mid to late 1980s in North America, both as a response to a hetero-normative sociology and as a humanities/multi-cultural based response to a more limited 'lesbian and gay studies'. Studying homosexuality as a form of deviance is abandoned; instead the interest lies in a logic of insiders/outsiders and transgression. Both the heterosexual/homosexual binary and the sex/gender split are challenged.

With Foucault as an influence, the roots of queer theory are usually seen to lie in the work of Eve Kasofsky Sedgwick who, in *The Epistemology of the Closet* (1990) argued that 'many of the major nodes of thought and knowledge in 20th century Western culture as a whole are structured—indeed fractured—by a chronic, now endemic crisis of homo/heterosexual definition, indicatively male, dating from the end of the 19th century... an understanding of any aspect of modern Western culture must be, not merely incomplete, but damaged in its central substance to the degree that it does not incorporate a critical analysis of modern homo/heterosexual definition'.

Judith Butler's work (in *Gender Trouble*, 1990, for instance) is also seen as queer. For her, there can be no claim to any essential gender: it is all 'performative', slippery, unfixed. As Nicki Sullivan suggests in her *Critical Introduction to Queer Theory* (2003), if there is a heart to queer theory, then it must be seen as a radical stance around sexuality and gender that denies any fixed categories and seeks to subvert any tendencies towards normality within its study. All sexual categories are open, fluid, and non-fixed (which means modern lesbian, gay, bisexual, and transgender identities are fractured along with all heterosexual ones).

The most common objects of study of queer theory are textual—films, videos, novels, poetry, visual images. And its most frequent interests include a variety of sexual fetishes, drag kings and drag queens, gender and sexual playfulness, cybersexualities, polyarmoury, sado-masochism, and all the social worlds of the so-called radical sexual fringe.

Many gays, lesbians and feminists themselves see no advance at all in a queer theory which, after all, would simply 'deconstruct' them, along with all their political gains, out of existence. The term is also provocative: a pejorative and stigmatizing word from the past is reclaimed by that very stigmatized grouping who have renegotiated its meaning. As such it has a distinct generational over-tone. Younger academics love it; older ones hate it. And with this it serves to write off the past worlds of research and create new divisions.

It also brings a category problem: what Josh Gamson (1995) has described as a 'Queer Dilemma' (in Nardi and Schneider's *Social Perspectives in Lesbian and Gay Studies*, 1998). He claims that there is simultaneously a need for a public collective identity (around which activism can galvanize) and a need to take apart and blur boundaries. As he says: 'fixed identity categories are both the basis for oppression and political power'. Whilst it is important to stress the 'inessential, fluid and multiple sited' forms of identity emerging within the queer movement, he can also see that there are very many from within the lesbian, gay, bisexual, and transgender movement (LGBT as it is currently clumsily called) who also reject its tendency to deconstruct the very idea of gay and lesbian identity—hence abolishing a field of study and politics when it has only just got going. Radical lesbian feminist Sheila Jeffreys (*Unpacking Queer Politics*, 2003) is also particularly scathing, seeing the whole queer movement as a serious threat to the gains of radical lesbians in the late 20th century. By losing the category of woman-identified woman and radical lesbian in a fog of (largely masculinist) queer deconstruction, it becomes impossible to see the roots of women's subordination to men. She also accuses it of a major elitism. The languages of most of its proponents ape the language of male academic elites, and hence lose all the gains that were made by the earlier more accessible writings of feminists who wrote for and spoke to women in the communities and not just other academics.

Outside the world of queer theorists—in the world of 'straight sociology'—it has been more or less ignored, has had minimal impact, and the approach has been ghettoized. But for a new generation of gender and sexuality theorists it is seen as a radical critique.

SEE WEB LINKS
• A good site with information and resources.

questionnaire A document containing all the questions, closed and open-ended, for a *survey. Normally, a separate questionnaire is used for each respondent to a survey, providing enough space for answers to be recorded, and subsequently *coded for computer-based analysis of all replies to each question. Questionnaires range from the postcard, with a few questions to be filled in by respondents, to long documents to be filled in by trained interviewers. Good questionnaires require a great deal of care and effort, to ensure that the questions are clear and easy to answer, to exclude leading questions unless by conscious design, to prompt and probe respondents' recollections of events that may not always be very recent, and to shape the interview overall so that it is a pleasant and interesting experience for respondents. Special techniques have been developed for questions on sensitive topics, interviewing on life-cycle events and work histories, questions on attitudes, values, and preferences. Questionnaires must also be structured to ensure that people are correctly filtered into or past particular sections—for example, someone who has not been in employment for many years should not be asked questions about their work, and so on. Questionnaires help to standardize *interviews, increasing the consistency of enquiry and response, but they cannot completely eliminate *interviewer bias.

The many design factors that should be borne in mind when constructing a questionnaire are discussed widely, but see particularly Howard Schuman and Stanley Presser, *Questions and Answers in Attitude Surveys: Experiments on Question Form, Wording, and Content* (1996). *See also* CLOSED RESPONSE; OPEN RESPONSE.

Quételet, Lambert Adolphe Jacques (1796–1874) A Belgian statistician, author of *On Man and the Development of Human Facilities, An Essay on Social Physics* (1835), who applied the mathematics of probability to social phenomena and demonstrated the importance of statistics to social science. Quételet argued that, in the case of social phenomena, the distribution usually follows a *normal curve—a conclusion reached by (among other things) observing the height of soldiers in a regiment. However, his work was for a long time ignored by social scientists, and it was not until the early 20th century that his writings were rediscovered.

race The placing of the term 'race' in inverted commas is now seen by some sociologists as a useful way of indicating that this manner of categorizing individuals and population groups is not based on any biologically valid distinctions between the genetic make-up of differently identified 'races'. Racial categorization is frequently (though not always) based on phenotypical differences; that is, differences of facial characteristics, skin colour, and so forth. But these do not correlate with genotypical differences (differences in genetic makeup). Nor, reputable scientific opinion now agrees, are there innate differences of *personality, *intelligence, and so forth, between populations categorized on either of these bases. The sociology of race is largely concerned with examining the causes and consequences of the socially constructed division of social groups according to their so-called race, regardless of whether this is legitimated by reference to any of the above factors, or none of them (as, for example, in the case of anti-semitism).

However, a feature of this definition of race as a social construct is that it downplays the extent to which sectors of the population may actually form a discrete ethnic group; that is, share certain characteristics on the basis of common historical origin, close-knit patterns of social interaction, and a sense of common identity. Developments such as the Black Power movement in America in the 1960s, and the growth of ethnic minority cultural and political movements (especially among the young) have stimulated sociological research on the nature and forms of *ethnicity. Again, this is a highly controversial field of study. Some sociologists argue that such studies, particularly when they involve research into what may somewhat ethnocentrically be defined as deviant *sub-cultures, can confirm or reinforce racist attitudes and racial *discrimination by the majority population. A related danger is that of the indiscriminate *labelling or *stereotyping of a racially defined minority as an ethnic minority (that is one which has a common culture and lifestyle) when this is not the case. There has also been a tendency, when ethnic minorities are studied in isolation from the wider society, to view their distinctive *lifestyles as a simple legacy of their past history, failing to recognize the ways in which these are shaped and changed by their current location in racially divided societies. In general, such research exaggerates the extent to which minorities are located in relatively enclosed ethnically defined social structures, separate from those of the majority society.

The location of racially defined groups in the stratification system of the wider society is a much-debated issue. Its salience partly reflects the historical circumstances in which this branch of sociology has developed: the legacy of *slavery and continuing immigration of non-White minorities in the United States, the history of *colonialism, and the more recent immigration of minorities from the Third World in Europe. There are several competing approaches (for an overview see R. Miles, *Racism*, 1989).

The *functionalist theories, largely developed in the United States from around the time of the First World War by Robert Park and others, assume an eventual *assimilation of racially defined minorities into the *stratification system of the majority host society and the restoration of *social equilibrium which has been disturbed by their arrival. Racial prejudice and discrimination is a temporary phenomenon occurring in this difficult period of readjustment. Emphasis is here placed on the need for minorities to abandon their imported values and lifestyles and accept those which it is assumed characterize the host society. This theory has been heavily criticized for its *ethnocentric assumption that assimilation is (or ought to be) the outcome of host-immigrant encounters; for ignoring the possibility that continued conflict or some form of racial pluralism might occur; and for its underestimation of the empirically observable extent and persistence of racial prejudice and discrimination.

A more sophisticated approach, illustrated most clearly in the work of John Rex, builds upon Weberian premises. What Rex calls 'race relations situations' involve a particular type of intergroup *conflict and result in racially categorized groups being distinctively located in the overall system of social stratification. In empirical work in the United Kingdom, Rex employs a Weberian concept of class to analyse differences in Black and White *life-chances, and concludes that 'race' and racial discrimination result in Blacks being located at the bottom of and outside the main White class structure. In so far as this is creating distinctive forms of consciousness and political action then a Black *underclass is in the process of formation.

Early Marxist theories (notably, O. C. Cox, *Class, Caste and Race*, 1948) proposed a far simpler connection between race and class, seeing racism as a rulingclass *ideology which developed under capitalism in order to divide—and hence help control—Black and White workers who shared a common and fundamental class *identity. This argument has been heavily criticized as historically inaccurate and irredeemably functionalist—explaining the origins of racism by means of the functions which it has sometimes served under capitalism. A considerable range of neo-Marxist and post-Marxist approaches (between which controversy often rages) have subsequently been developed. These seek to provide a less deterministic account of the relations between race, class, and capitalism. For example, Robert Miles (*Racism and Migrant Labour*, 1982) analyses the construction of so-called 'racialized class fractions' in advanced capitalist societies. An up-to-date overview of theoretical arguments can be found in John Solomos *Race, Ethnicity and Social Theory* (2013).

Sometimes rather separated from these theoretical debates (though also generated by and contributing to them) there are a wide range of empirically grounded sociological inquiries by American sociologists. These include studies of racial belief systems; the extent and nature of racial discrimination and disadvantage; the politics of 'race' and the impact of state policies on racialized minorities; and the distribution, concentration, and *segregation of minority populations—especially in housing-and *labour markets. Examples here might include Lee Rainwater's excellent (though controversial) study of Black families in a federal housing project (*Behind Ghetto Walls*, 1970); Howard Schuman et al.'s survey of *Racial Attitudes in America* (1985); and *Black Men, White Cities* (1973), Ira Katznelson's comparative study of the political responses to Black migration to the Northern cities of the United States and in the United Kingdom. The best summary of the evidence for Britain is David Mason's *Race and Ethnicity in Modern Britain* (2nd edn., 2000).

(⊕) SEE WEB LINKS

• Ethnic and Racial Studies: the leading journal in the field. (Subscription)

racialism (racism) Racialism is the unequal treatment of a population group purely because of its possession of physical or other characteristics socially defined as denoting a particular race (*see* RACE). Racism is the deterministic belief-system that sustains racialism, linking these characteristics with negatively valued social, psychological, or physical traits. For an informative comparative study of racism in the United States and the Netherlands see Philomena Essed, *Understanding Everyday Racism* (1991). *See also* INSTITUTIONAL RACISM.

racialization The social processes by which a population group is categorized as a race.

racism, institutional *See* INSTITUTIONALIZED DISCRIMINATION.

Radcliffe-Brown, Alfred Reginald (1881–1955) Radcliffe-Brown was one of the most influential of the founding figures of *social anthropology, through his teaching in universities in England, North America, South Africa, and Australia. He was less noted for his field studies (see *The Andaman Islanders*, 1922) than for his teaching, yet he was the first to have an anthropological training as an undergraduate at Cambridge, and the first to hold a Chair in Social Anthropology at Cape Town, Sydney, Oxford, and Chicago.

In his theoretical approach Radcliffe-Brown owed much to Émile Durkheim, stressing the importance of structure in society, and of the *functions of different institutions. This has led to criticisms of his approach as too rigid and mechanistic. However, he was clearly an excellent teacher, his influence being represented more by the range of students he influenced than by his (relatively small) published output. He preferred to publish definitive studies of what he called 'comparative sociology' that set out the rules governing human social relationships. Probably the most widely read of these works is still *Structure and Function in Primitive Society* (1952), an accepted classic of social anthropology, setting out clearly many of the concepts that are now taken for granted in the discipline.

radical criminology *See* CRIMINOLOGY, CRITICAL.

range *See* VARIATION (STATISTICAL).

rational choice theory A theory of action that sees individual self-interest as the fundamental human motive and traces all social activities back to acts of rational calculation and decision-making that are supposed to have produced them. Such theories can be traced at least as far back as the classical *political economy of the 18th century, the most familiar example being Adam Smith's theory of the *division of labour, expounded at the start of *The Wealth of Nations* (1776). According to Smith, the hidden hand of the free *market leads prudent self-interested individuals to promote the public welfare, even though that was never their intention. The modern discipline of economics, which grew out of political economy, has developed a highly abstract and increasingly mathematical version of this theory, according to which prices and the allocation of scarce resources can be explained by the rational maximization of *utility by economic actors in relation to their monetary outlays. The apparent success of this sophisticated and relatively unified body of theory inevitably led to the suggestion that the same method might be applied more widely across the social sciences.

One of the best-known examples of this is the 'exchange theory' of George Homans and Peter Blau. Homans saw all human activity as motivated by the desire to gain 'rewards' and avoid 'costs', understanding these as referring to all things—and not just money—that are relevant to human goals and purposes. People enter into social relations only if they are likely to gain a 'profit', and Homans saw all stable interactions as social relations in which each participant is able to secure a profit. If a relationship becomes loss-making for either participant, then he or she will withdraw and will 'spend' their efforts in more profitable ways. Homans derived a whole series of predictions from such assumptions about rational calculation, but the most sophisticated extension of the argument was in Blau's *Exchange and Power in Social Life* (1964). Blau offers a 'structural' version of exchange theory that goes beyond Homans's psychological reductionism and argues that 'reciprocal exchange of extrinsic benefits' between actors may be absent or incomplete—as, for example, where *power relations are involved. Blau shows how exchange assumptions can be used to build accounts of the formation of work groups and hierarchies in organizations.

Economists such as Gary Becker (1930–2014) (see *The Economic Approach to Human Behavior*, 1976) have tried to apply many of the models developed within economics to such activities as love and intimacy within families and engagement in criminal acts. Rational-choice concepts have also been pursued enthusiastically in *political science, where writers such as Anthony Downs and Mancur Olson have explored the calculative considerations behind political commitment, voting behaviour, protest movements, and both voluntary and coerced collective organization. This mathematical and propositional approach to action has been developed within sociology by Karen Cook, who has linked them to *network analysis and *organization theory (*Social Exchange Theory*, 1987), and James Coleman (*Foundations of Social Theory*, 1990). General elaborations of the approach using formal models of rule-following have been set out by Robert Axelrod in *The Complexity of Cooperation: Agent-Based Models of Competition and Collaboration* (1997).

The most striking recent approaches to rational choice theory have, surprisingly, come from within *Marxism in the so-called 'analytical Marxism' of Jon

Elster, John Roemer, and others. Elster defines rational action theory as 'first and foremost normative. It tells us what we ought to do in order to achieve our aims as well as possible. It does not, in the standard version, tell us what our aims ought to be . . . From the normative account, we can derive an explanatory theory by assuming that people are rational in the normatively appropriate sense.' Its central explananda are actions. These actions should be the best way of optimizing an individual's desires, given his or her beliefs, and these desires and beliefs must themselves be rational (or at least internally consistent). In forming their beliefs, people must collect the right amount of evidence, a decision that itself must be subject to the canons of rationality. In other words, 'rational action involves three optimizing operations: finding the best action, for given beliefs and desires; forming the best-grounded belief, for given evidence; and collecting the right amount of evidence, for given desires and prior beliefs' (see *Solomonic Judgements: Studies in the Limitations of Rationality*, 1989; *Making Sense of Marx*, 1985).

A similar general claim is made by John Goldthorpe, who argues that sociology is best served by a version of the theory that refers to action that can be treated as subjectively rational and so has rationality requirements of an intermediate kind; recognizes that there is a need to delimit what can count as such action and so focuses attention primarily on situational understanding; and is therefore a special rather than a general theory. However, although he accepts that certain modes of action fall outside the scope of such theory, he is convinced that the rational action approach offers greater promise than do any other available alternatives (for example those which emphasize the importance of cultural traditions, values, and norms).

These arguments that there are limits to rational choice explanations echo *Durkheim's claim that not everything in the contract is contractual, that is, rational exchange cannot itself be the source of settled, morally regulated social order, but instead presupposes it. Social sentiments must be embodied in *symbols (or *collective representations) of society's obligatory rules and commands that define the scope remaining for the pursuit of individual interest. Thus, it might be suggested that approaches such as *symbolic interactionism provide a more general approach to social action and one within which theories of rational choice might find their place as specialized applications.

Stated in these rather limited terms it is hard to see how anyone might object to Elster's theory of action. Elster is careful to specify the limits and failures of rationality in the explanation of action (for example, where action is non-instrumental and grounded in social *norms). However, many have remained sceptical of attempts to apply rational choice theory in sociology (notably its exchange-based form), for at least three reasons. First, the success of economic theory depends on there being a definite currency in the market exchange, available to both the individual and the theorist, which can be used as an independent measure of the relation between action and advantage. Happiness, social acceptance, prestige, and influence have been offered as equivalent to monetary currency, but these individual goals are also frequently in competition with each other and the explanation of social order calls for an understanding of how such fundamental *values are prioritized. Further, this understanding must avoid circularity. Different orderings of values cannot be explained by the advantage (or value) they might have for the actor. Secondly, the theory is invulnerable to refutation, since particular actions of individuals are treated by rational-choice theorists as both the object of explanation and as proof of the theory: whatever action occurs, even if it has unpleasant consequences for the individual, by definition yields a greater advantage than if the action did not occur. (In other words the theory veers towards *tautology.) Finally, a venerable tradition in sociology regards the occurrence of exchange between individuals as an effect rather than a cause of social order, because stable relationships of exchange depend on a pre-existing minimum of *trust and law enforcement. (For an excellent overview of the relevant issues here see H. C. Bredemeier, 'Exchange Theory', in T. Bottomore and R. Nisbet (eds.), *A History of Sociological Analysis*, 1979.)

It is worth noting the existence of an alternative tradition of rational choice and exchange theory associated with anthropological studies of the more rudimentary social relations of pre-modern societies. Examples of this approach include the study of reciprocal *gift exchange by Émile Durkheim's nephew, Marcel Mauss (*The Gift*, 1925). This was one of the first to examine gift-giving ceremonies, among tribal and archaic societies, which embody what has since come to be known as the norm of reciprocity. A further example is Bronislaw Malinowski's study of the *kula of the Trobriand Islanders and Franz Boas's study of the potlatch among native North Americans. In these and many other cases, purely utilitarian exchange was secondary to the prestations (or obligatory gift-giving) incumbent on whole clans, tribes, or families, and which could include courtesies, entertainments, ritual, military assistance, women, children, dances, and feasts. The gifts and payments were never separated from those making and receiving them: the communion and alliance they establish are indissoluble and thereby the exchanges contain an important instrumental element. They symbolize the compulsion to make an equivalent or value-added return for gifts and assistance received and to give them when demanded. Out of and alongside this grows a social economy of bartering and economic exchange (see Peter Ekeh, *Social Exchange Theory*, 1974). *See also* HAYEK; MONT PELERIN SOCIETY.

(⊕) SEE WEB LINKS
• The home page of Gary Becker.

rationalism Used loosely to indicate a rejection of faith or religion, and more strictly a view that all knowledge can be expressed in the form of a system, and that, in principle, everything can be known. In sociology it is sometimes used to refer to the alternative offered by Max Weber to the *empiricist natural science model. The strong version of rationalism, that knowledge (at least in the social sciences) comes from reason alone (as opposed to sense-experience), is sometimes supported by writers as different as Weber, Talcott *Parsons, and Louis Althusser. More recently, rationalism has been regarded by those labelled as postmodernist as a failed product of the Enlightenment; but, as Jürgen Habermas points out, such an argument is itself a rational one, and therefore self-defeating.

It is difficult to see how any attempt to know the social world can avoid at least some rationalist assumptions. *See also* EPISTEMOLOGY; IDEAL TYPE.

rationality (rational action) *See* ACTION THEORY; BOUNDED RATIONALITY; CRITICAL THEORY; ETHNOMETHODOLOGY; FORMAL RATIONALITY; INTERPRETATION; MAGIC, WITCHCRAFT, AND SORCERY; MEANING; PHENOMENOLOGY; RATIONAL CHOICE THEORY; RATIONALIZATION; WEBER, MAX.

rationality, formal *See* FORMAL RATIONALITY; FUNCTIONAL RATIONALITY.

rationalization Just as it is impossible to understand Karl Marx's concerns without seeing the centrality of labour power and its alienation into capital, so also it would be equally difficult to grasp the intellectual coherence of Max Weber's writings without understanding what Alvin Gouldner has termed the 'metaphysical pathos' associated with his vision of the rationalization of everyday life. This progressive disenchantment of the world, the eradication of mystery, emotion, tradition, and affectivity, and its replacement by rational calculation, informs much of his research and writing. It has created a whole industry among students of his work, who continue to debate the issue of whether or not Weber offers a fully developed theory of rationalization, and (if so) where precisely in his writings it is to be found (see, for example, S. Lash and S. Whimster (eds.), *Max Weber, Rationality and Modernity*, 1987).

Weber saw modernization as a process of rationalization that affects economic life, law, administration, and religion, eliminating traditional ideas and customary practices in favour of formally rational criteria. It underpins the emergence of *capitalism, *bureaucracy, and the legal *state. The essence of the rationalization process is the increasing tendency by social actors to the use of knowledge, in the context of impersonal relationships, with the aim of achieving greater control over the world around them. However, rather than increasing freedom and autonomy, rationalization makes ends of means (slavish adherence to the rules within modern bureaucracies are an obvious example), and imprisons the individual within the 'iron cage' of rationalized institutions, organizations, and activities.

Commentators have remarked that, in his concern over the rationalizing tendencies of modern societies, Weber was more pessimistic in the prognosis for human freedom than any of his contemporaries. *Marx at least foresaw an emancipating revolution, whereas for Weber the only antidote to rationalization was the emergence of the *charismatic figure. *Socialism, Weber claimed, would create an even more confining cage, since it would combine *formal rationality with substantive rationality. Whereas the *market had counteracted bureaucratic state power under capitalism, socialism would see the two combined. That it was toppled in its Soviet variant by the charismatic individuals and movements of Walesa, Solidarity, Havel, and Civic Forum would seem to provide some optimistic respite, in the face of all-encompassing disenchantment. *See also* REFLEXIVE MODERNIZATION.

rational state *See* ABSOLUTISM.

Ratzenhofer, Gustav (1842–1904) *See* MILITARY AND MILITARISM.

reaction formation A *psychoanalytic concept denoting one type of *defence mechanism. When a feeling or idea is felt to be especially threatening it may be dealt with by enthusiastically embracing its opposite. Thus a man who is threatened by his own homosexual feelings might engage in aggressive heterosexual behaviour.

realism In everyday use realism is commonly attributed to caution, or moderation in one's aspirations—the converse of *utopianism. The word is also used to describe a variety of approaches in literature and the visual arts in which accurate depiction of reality is the aim. Each of these uses involves a contrast between human thought or imagination, on one hand, and an external reality independent of mind, on the other. The notion that reality has a cognitive or normative authority over the mind is also generally present. In philosophy, realism signifies the assertion of the existence of a reality independently of our thoughts or beliefs about it. Controversy has centred especially on the question of whether universals (for example properties such as 'redness' or 'softness') really exist, or whether they are functions of our use of language ('nominalism').

Realism as a metaphysical doctrine is challenged by a range of sceptical arguments. Both in classical Greek philosophy and in the early modern period, sceptical arguments commonly began by appealing to our experience of such phenomena as dreams, illusions, and hallucinations, in which our senses mislead us. Since this does, unquestionably, sometimes happen, how do we know that it does not always do so? How can we be sure that, on any particular occasion, what we seem to observe may not turn out to have been illusory? More recently these arguments have been supplemented by analogous challenges to our ability to secure reliable reference to external reality in the use of language. Since we have no access to the world that is not mediated by thought or language, what independent check have we upon the reliability of what we think or say?

Such sceptical arguments do not necessarily lead to a denial of a reality independent of thought. It is possible to hold that there is such a reality, but that we cannot know its nature (or, perhaps, that we cannot know that we know). More commonly, such *epistemological scepticism lapses into phenomenalism, solipsism, or some other form of denial of the existence of a reality independent of mind, thought, or language.

In the philosophy of science, *empiricists tend to be sceptical about the existence of the entities (many of them unobservable) postulated by scientific theories. On this view, the *concepts of such entities are just convenient summaries of actual or possible observations, or grounds for prediction. Scientific realists, on the other hand, argue that the theories in question should be understood as claiming existence for the entities (sub-atomic particles, retro-viruses, or whatever) they postulate. These claims may, of course, be either true or false. Many sociological opponents suppose that scientific realists are committed to an uncritical acceptance of the knowledge claims of science. This is not so. They are, rather, committed to an interpretation of those claims as claims about the nature of a reality which exists and acts independently of our knowledge or beliefs about it. Realists may be as sceptical as anyone else about whether those claims are true. The problem for the anti-realists is to make any sense at all of what science is about; and, in particular, of what it might be for scientific knowledge-claims to turn out to be false.

The leading British figure in the late-20th-century revival of realist metatheory in philosophy and the social sciences is Roy Bhaskar (1944–2014). He and his associates have recently developed a form of scientific realism (variously termed 'transcendental' or 'critical' realism) which is offered as a comprehensive alter- native to both empiricism and *conventionalism in the philosophy of science. (The reference to critical is intended to indicate that the pursuit of knowledge is or should be emancipatory.) Activities such as scientific experimentation and the application of scientific knowledge are held to be unintelligible except on the assumption of a world independent of our beliefs about it. It is also necessary to distinguish the real causal powers and mechanisms of which science seeks knowledge, from the actual flow of events triggered by the activity of these mechanisms. The actual must, in turn, be distinguished from the empirical—that small sub-set of events which are observed by someone. Bhaskar claims that this view of science is applicable to both the human and the natural sciences in a way which is able to take fully into account the radical differences in the natures of their objects. Chief among his many publications are *A Realist Theory of Science* (2nd edn., 1978), *The Possibility of Naturalism* (1979), *Scientific Realism and Human Emancipation* (1986), and *Reclaiming Reality* (1989).

((⊕)) SEE WEB LINKS
• The Centre for Critical Realism.

realist criminology *See* CRIMINOLOGY, REALIST.

real socialism With the non-applicability of the terms *socialism and *com- munism, given the divergence of the reality of Soviet socialism from the ideal as interpreted within the corpus of the Marxist-Leninist classics, an alternative term was required. 'Actually existing socialism', 'developed socialism', and 'state socialism' were just some of the contenders suggested by supporters and detrac- tors alike. 'Real socialism', which emerged as the favoured caption, implied that the economic political, and social make-up of the Soviet bloc societies was in fact a distinct *mode of production, with its own immanent tendencies, which could not be grasped either by reference to the concepts of Western social science or by the instruments of official communist ideology.

Its defining feature was the primacy of politics over economics and the inter- twining of the two. Although the features of capitalism (such as distinctive property rights, and markets of commodities, capital, and labour) were absent, this did not imply the existence of socialism. The latter would have required the organization of the economy along collective lines, with cooperation through a plan which articulated the interests of the direct producers, and tied consump- tion, production, and investment together, through the human logic of expressed (rather than imposed) needs. State ownership of productive means in fact led to a property vacuum. Absent ownership rights fostered corruption, eroded motivation, distorted managerial priorities, and diverted state energies into control rather than planning and directive functions. The power of lobbies replaced societal interest formation and articulation. The primacy of the *nomenklatura* system undermined professional and expertise criteria of performance, dissipated the mechanisms of accountability, and vested power in the hands of groups who ruled this monocentric society and whose aim was the maximization of power over a non-controllable economy. Party, state bureaucracy, security apparatus, and military formed a *power elite, presiding over a bureaucratically centralized, segmented society. Extensive economic growth exhausted the natural and human resources of countries tied into patterns of dependence devoid of an economic logic but rooted within the overriding needs of the military-industrial complex. Soft budgets, poor labour discipline, the politicization of the workplace, the use of the factory-based welfare system to impose labour discipline in the absence of unemployment, all became attributes of the system of redistribution. Economic interests, rather than being based upon economic rationality, were distorted by this redistributional mechanism. Finely graded occupational and hierarchical privilege incorporated most of the population into an artificial set of dependencies.

For its part, society was effectively classless, although forms of social *closure existed—particularly within the *partocracy* and the intelligentsia. Social atomization and amorphous structures were juxtaposed to the burgeoning second society where social self-organization existed around the satisfaction of interstitial but authentic needs. These social relations substituted for the absence of *civil society, the missing meso-level, connecting the individual and family to the state-sponsored organizations and institutions, and sought to break out of the segmentalism and opaqueness which allowed the rulers to manipulate sections of society, often against each other.

An interesting insider's view of real socialism is offered in Rudolf Bahro's Marxist critique of the East German State (*The Alternative in Eastern Europe*, 1977). Bahro identifies a fundamental contradiction in actually existing socialism, and not in class terms, but as the production of a 'surplus consciousness' that can transform society.

It is impossible at this stage to provide anything like a satisfactory characterization of real socialism, for it is only in the leaving of it that one can see clearly its economic and political axial principles, its major institutional contours, and social residues. Health crises, environmental despoliation, a debilitated work ethic, poverty, criminality, political malaise, and the almost endless litany of other failings of this system of imposed modernization tend to detract from some of its undoubted achievements.

rebellion (revolution) Relatively rare but historically important events in which an entire social and political order is overturned, usually by violent means, and reconstructed on new principles with new leaders. The word revolution has come to be applied loosely to any dramatic social *change—as in 'industrial revolution', 'computer revolution', 'style revolution', and so forth. But its central meaning is still political. It is difficult to make a sharp distinction between a political revolution and a rebellion, although some have argued that the term 'revolution' should be reserved for those instances in which the new governing elite attempts to make fundamental changes in the social structure of the post-revolutionary society, whereas rebellions are more limited political upheavals involving only the replacement of one ruling group by another. On this criterion, rebellions clearly shade into revolutions, depending upon one's judgement as to the scope and intensity of the social changes that follow the seizure of power.

The prototypes of all modern revolutions were the American and French Revolutions of 1776 and 1789. Both had a clear political agenda, and both resulted in a complete transformation of power relationships. In this century, the Russian Revolution of 1917 and the Chinese Revolution of 1948 had similar dramatic results. Not all revolutions in recent history have been socialistic or egalitarian, or even modernizing; many have been anti-democratic or right-wing. Fundamentalist Islam has swept through the Middle East, most notably in the revolutionary downfall of the Shah of Iran in 1979. The 1990s witnessed a 'reverse revolution' in many former communist states.

Probably the most influential theory of revolution in sociology has been the *historical materialism of Karl Marx and Friedrich Engels. However, it should be recognized that *Marxism has come to embody several (by no means compatible) theories of revolution, including for example the theory of the dictatorship of the proletariat advanced by *Lenin and of peasant revolution proffered within *Maoism. Many subsequent sociological studies of revolutionary change are explicit critiques of the Marxist view of history in general and of revolutions in particular.

Most studies of rebellions and revolutions have necessarily been historical, and have focused on causes and processes. Theories that stress social disequilibrium, rising expectations, and relative *deprivation are plausible, but have not proved highly explanatory or predictive. In more recent work, Theda Skocpol has formulated a theory of revolution which stresses the inability of institutions to cope with normal crises (*States and Social Revolutions*, 1979), and Charles and Louis Tilly have proposed a historical model in which rebellions arise opportunistically out of a shifting balance of power and resources (*The Rebellious Century 1830—1930*, 1975). Skocpol's theory was particularly controversial. She proposes a macro-level, structural analysis, which makes a sharp distinction between political revolutions (leadership changes) and social revolutions (which transform the whole of society). Arguing against monocausal explanations of social revolutions (for example rising expectations, class conflicts) she proposes a complex, fluid model which emphasizes the differences between *states, the role of external factors such as international economic competition, and the availability of grievance channels for different social classes. (This focus on the complexity of revolutionary social change is continued in her later work, including her edited and co-edited volumes on *Vision and Method in Historical Sociology*, 1984, and *Bringing the State Back In*, 1985).

revolutionary change in a society is never complete, and the outcomes are highly variable. Elements of the old order live on, as they did in France after 1789 and Russia after 1917, confounding the idealistic intentions which launched the revolution.

recency effect A recency effect is the tendency for individuals to be most influenced by what they have last seen or heard, because people tend to retain the most complete knowledge about the most recent events. However, under certain circumstances, *primacy effects prevail and sometimes the first rather than the last event will be the most influential.

recidivist (recidivism) Any person who is convicted of a crime on more than one occasion; a person who re-offends. Recidivism is usually measured in relation to the type of last sentence or last offence, as percentages re-offending, or re-convicted, within one, two, five, or ten years.

reciprocity *See* COMPADRAZGO; RATIONAL CHOICE THEORY; GIFT RELATIONSHIP; KULA RING.

redemptive movement *See* SOCIAL MOVEMENTS.

Redfield, Robert (1897–1958) An American anthropologist who, in 1930, published a study (*Tepoztlan: Life in a Mexican Village*) that outlines an ideal-typical construct of *folk society. Subsequently he suggested that the spread of urban-based civilization transforms folk societies. Depending on their social and cultural characteristics, individual settlements can be placed along an evolutionary *folk-urban continuum.

According to Redfield, folk societies are small, isolated, non-literate, and socially homogeneous. There is strong group solidarity and kinship, a common culture rooted in tradition and religion, behaviour is personal and spontaneous rather than impersonal and law-bound, and there is little intellectual life. Urban societies are characterized by the converse traits: loss of isolation, heterogeneity, social disorganization, secularization, and individuality.

Redfield's *ideal types encapsulate a distinction between industrial-urban and pre-industrial societies which others (such as Ferdinand Tönnies and Émile Durkheim) had earlier espoused. His work greatly influenced *rural sociology and community studies. However, in 1951 Oscar Lewis published a re-study of Tepoztlan (*Life in a Mexican Village: Tepoztlan Restudied*), examining aspects of village life—especially its economy, demography, and politics—which Redfield had ignored. His findings undermined Redfield's account of folk societies, which tended to gloss over conflict, poverty, and disorganization, and to present an idealized account of primitive societies. Lewis also rejected the over-simplified and ahistorical classification of individual settlements implicit in Redfield's approach. Later work on urban communities found this ideal type, and the concept of the folk-urban continuum, equally deficient.

reductionism In its most general usage, the term reductionism denotes any intellectual strategy for reducing apparently diverse phenomena to some primary or basic explanatory principle. For example, reductionist forms of *materialism as applied to the natural sciences have attempted to explain the distinctive properties and powers of living beings in terms of the concepts and laws of chemistry. Attempts to explain patterns of difference in measured human intelligence, or social differences between men and women, in terms of genetic or physiological differences are commonly criticized by sociologists as examples of misguided *biological reductionism. Some forms of *Marxism, in which economic relations are supposed wholly to determine social and political life, are also commonly criticized as economic reductionism. Distinctions may usefully be made between logical reduction, in which the aim is to reduce the laws of the more superficial science to the more basic one; semantic reduction, in which the language of one science is defined in terms of the other; and explanatory reduction, in which the aim is to show that the phenomena of one science can be explained as effects of mechanisms identified in another.

reference group The term reference group was coined by Herbert Hyman in *Archives of Psychology* (1942), to apply to the group against which an individual evaluates his or her own situation or conduct. Hyman distinguished between a membership group to which people actually belong, and a reference group, which is used as a basis for comparison. A reference group may or may not be a membership group. Theodore Newcomb (*Personality and Social Change*, 1943) used reference groups to help explain the changing values and attitudes of students at Bennington, a liberal women's college. Many of the women who came from politically conservative backgrounds developed increasingly liberal attitudes over the course of their college careers, as they came to identify more with the college faculty, and less with their family of origin and home communities. The girls who changed most, according to Newcomb, were those 'characterized by independence from their parents, a sense of personal adequacy in social relations, and modifiability of habits in achieving their goals'. Here, the college is regarded as a positive reference group, but one might view the parents as a negative reference group for their somewhat rebellious offspring.

In these early uses reference group was not well defined, nor was it linked in any clear way to social psychological and sociological theory. One distinction that is commonly made is that between functionalist studies, which highlight the functions of reference groups either in providing a normative standard or a comparative reference-point, and the *symbolic interactionist approach which views reference groups as shared world-perspectives providing meaning to the self.

Robert Merton and Alice Kitt provide a systematic functionalist formulation of the concept in their classic 'Contribution to the Theory of Reference Group Behaviour' (in R. K. Merton and P. F. Lazarsfeld (eds.), *Continuities in Social Research: Studies in the Scope and Method of 'The American Soldier'*, 1950). Their essay was stimulated by Samuel Stouffer's *The American Soldier* (1949), which reported that soldiers' feelings of *deprivation were less related to the actual degree of hardship they experienced, than to the living standards of the group to which they compared themselves. Merton and Kitt point out that relative *deprivation is a special case of comparative reference group behaviour. Merton later distinguishes reference groups and interaction groups (in *Social Theory and Social Structure*, 1957). The latter are a more general part of the individual's social environment—but neither set normative standards for the individual nor serve as a standard of comparison. He also specifies the circumstances under which an individual will select a membership or a non-membership group for normative reference, and claims that non-membership groups are likely to be chosen in highly mobile societies. Thus, an aspiring individual may emulate the lifestyle and attitudes of the local elite, in the hope of raising his or her own status. In a much-cited study of *Relative Deprivation and Social Justice* (1966), W. G. Runciman argues that attitudes to inequality (including people's feelings of relative deprivation) are a function of their restricted reference groups, although this argument has been criticized since it is clear from Runciman's evidence that the causal relationship in question could equally well run in the other direction.

The interactionist conception of reference group flows from George Herbert *Mead's idea of the generalized other. According to Mead, in the acquisition of a *self people move through very specific role-playing in the play and game stages of self-development (for example assuming roles of parents and peers); but in the later stages—known as the generalized-other stage—are able to assume the attitude of their whole community towards themselves. The generalized other thus serves both as a major anchorage in the wider social world and as a mechanism of social control. People come to see the world from the perspective of those who share their world in the wider community. From this starting-point Tamotsu Shibutani developed the idea that reference groups were in fact perspectives: 'a reference group becomes any collectivity, real or imagined, envied or despised, whose perspective is assumed by the actor'. It is, in other words, 'a group whose outlook is used by the actor as the frame of reference in the organization of his perceptual field' ('Reference Groups as Perspectives', *American Journal of Sociology*, 1954). More recently, this idea has been extended in the 'social world perspective' of Anselm Strauss and his colleagues (*Studies in Symbolic Interactionism*, 1978), in an attempt to capture 'universes of discourse' which transcend particular groups—such as 'medical worlds' or 'gay worlds'.

The question of the usefulness of the concept of reference group is still unanswered. Some critics claim it raises more issues than it solves. One of the basic problems is that we do not know what determines which group an individual will select or when. Indeed, it seems likely that a person will employ a variety of different reference groups at different times, and with respect to different goods. Another problem therefore concerns the degree of specificity or generality of reference groups. A study may indicate that a person's political orientation is influenced by his or her college peers, but it is not clear whether the same reference group is also likely to influence that person's views on (say) sexual morality or religion. However, although the concept of reference group may lack rigour and precision, it does seem to provide useful insights into social behaviour and continues to be widely used in the explanation of (for example) patterns of wage-bargaining and religious affiliation.

referent power In one of the many available typologies of *power, J. R. P. French and B. Raven ('The Bases of Social Power', in D. Cartwright (ed.), *Studies in Social Power*, 1959) distinguished five types of power, according to their sources. These are the (self-explanatory) 'reward' and 'coercive' types: 'legitimate power' that stems from holding an office acknowledged to convey rights of decision-making over others (in other words authority); 'expert power' stemming from possession of a limited skill, ability, or access to scarce knowledge; and 'referent power' or the ability of one person to influence others because of the latter's degree of identification with the former. Like other typologies of power, it is hard to see how this one is exhaustive, since it omits (for example) power stemming from control of a strategic channel of communication.

reflexive modernization A term devised by the German social theorist Ulrich Beck, and that refers to the way in which advanced modernity 'becomes its own theme', in the sense that 'questions of the development and employment of technologies (in the realms of nature, society and the personality) are being eclipsed by questions of the political and economic "management" of the risks of actually or potentially utilized technologies—discovering, administering, acknowledging, avoiding or concealing such hazards with respect to specially defined horizons of relevance' (see his *Risk Society: Towards a New Modernity*, 1986, trans. 1992).

In Beck's periodization of social change, simple modernity is synonymous with the development of *industrial society, and the new reflexive modernity with the emergence of the so-called risk society. Risk society is a condition in which the growth of knowledge has everywhere created 'manufactured uncertainty' (for example the risk of ecological disaster) that leads to an increasing reliance on scientific expertise to alleviate the effects of earlier applications of science. Whereas industrial society was concerned primarily with the production and distribution of goods, risk society is organized around the management and distribution of 'bads' or dangers, not only with those associated with physical risk deriving from the application of technological processes but also with the consequences of risky organizational activity and social relations. Reflexive modernity—an intermingling of continuity and discontinuity that is said to be evident, for example, in the critique of science developed by the Green movement—dissolves those 'forms of the *conscience collective*' (such as class culture and family roles) 'on which depend and to which refer the social and political organizations and institutions in industrial society'.

More specifically, according to Beck, during the 1950s 'the unstable unity of shared life experiences mediated by the market and shaped by status, which Max Weber brought together in the concept of social class, began to break apart. Its different elements (such as material conditions dependent upon specific market opportunities, the effectiveness of tradition and of precapitalist lifestyles, the consciousness of communal bonds and of barriers to mobility, as well as networks of contact) have slowly disintegrated'. This 'individualization of social inequality' means that, 'under the conditions of a welfare state, class biographies, which are somehow ascribed, become transformed into reflexive biographies which depend on the decisions of the actor'. Increasingly, therefore, everyone must take the risk of choosing between a huge array of disparate social identities, lifestyles, opinions, and groups or subcultures. Attachments to social classes become weaker, people are separated from the traditional support networks provided by family or neighbourhood, and work loses its importance as a focus of conflict and identity formation. Ascribed differences—of ethnicity, gender, age, and nationality—provide the basis for new lifestyles and self-conceptions that replace class solidarities. In Marxist terms, this is capitalism without classes, but with new and still emerging forms of differentiation and inequality.

Beck has worked collaboratively with Anthony Giddens to develop his ideas (see, for example, Ulrich Beck, Anthony Giddens, and Scott Lash, *Reflexive Modernization*, 1994).

reflexive sociology *See* GOULDNER.

reflexivity *See* ETHNOMETHODOLOGY.

reformative movement *See* SOCIAL MOVEMENTS.

Registrar General's Classification An official scheme of class analysis used in British surveys and censuses for much of the 20th century. In sociological work it was largely superseded by the *Goldthorpe class scheme. The new *NS-SEC classification has now replaced it for official studies and is beginning to be used in sociological work.

regression (regression analysis) A term used originally to describe the fact that if, for example, parents' and children's weights are measured, the children's weights tend to be closer to the average than are those of their parents: unusually heavy parents tend to have lighter children and unusually light parents tend to have heavier children. This phenomenon was referred to as 'regression to the mean'.

In statistics, regression refers, in the simplest case, to fitting a line on a plot of data from two *variables, in order to represent the trend between them. Regression assumes that one variable (the *dependent variable) is determined by the other (*independent) variable and that the relationship is linear. The value of the slope of the line is often interpreted as the overall effect of the independent variable. In multiple regression, simple regression is extended to more than one independent variable. The area is covered in M. S. Lewis-Beck, *Applied Regression—An Introduction*, 1990). *See also* OUTLIER EFFECTS.

regulation theory A loose-knit body of empirically oriented, political-economic theory that originated in France in the 1970s, as part of the general effort then being made to overcome the limitations of Marxism's economic *reductionism. According to what is sometimes referred to as the Parisian School, the concepts necessary to overcome this reductionism are the following: 'regime of accumulation', which refers to the organization of consumption as well as that of production; 'mode of growth', which relates the regime of accumulation to the *international division of labour; and 'mode of regulation', which refers to the national and international, institutional, and ideological framework which facilitates the reproduction of particular regimes of accumulation and modes of growth. The best-known claim made by the regulationists is that the use of these concepts enables one to distinguish two successive modes of regulation in the history of 20th-century capitalism—*fordism and post-fordism.

Representative works in English include Michel Aglietta, *A Theory of Capitalist Regulation: The U.S. Experience* (1976, trans. 1979); Mike Davis, *Prisoners of the American Dream* (1986); David M. Gordon, Richard Edwards, and Michael Reich, *Segmented Work, Divided Workers: The Historical Transformation of Labour in the United States* (1982); and Alain Lipietz, *Mirages and Miracles* (1987). An important critical elaboration is Bob Jessop and Ngai-Ling Sum's *Beyond the Regulation Approach: Putting Capitalist Economies in their Place* (2006).

Reich, Wilhelm (1897–1957) A controversial Marxist neo-Freudian whose work stressed the importance of the physical body, especially the functions of the orgasm. He saw the mechanisms of repression found in the *authoritarian family leading to the creation of a character armour and a rigid conforming *personality type, and he saw the role of society as structuring this conformity into a compulsive morality (see, for example, *The Mass Psychology of Fascism*, 1942, and *The Sexual Revolution*, 1936). He anticipated many of the ideas of the Frankfurt School (*see* CRITICAL THEORY) on *mass society, became a guru of the Free Love counter-culture movement, but died in the United States dismissed as a crank.

reification The error of regarding an abstraction as a material thing, and attributing causal powers to it—in other words the fallacy of misplaced concreteness. An example would be treating a *model or *ideal type as if it were a description of a real individual or society. In Marxist theory, reification is linked to people's *alienation from work and their treatment as objects of manipulation rather than as human beings, and was popularized by György Lukács, but the term is given a variety of meanings by different schools of Marxist thought.

reinforcement *See* CONDITIONING.

relations of production Once Karl Marx had concluded that what labourers sold under *capitalism was not their labour but their labour-power (*see* LABOUR THEORY OF VALUE), and so opened up a new dimension of analysis, he was able to shed his dependence on the inherited term *division of labour as a means of conceptualizing what happens in production. Instead, he coined the term 'relations of production' to refer to the social relations specific to a particular *mode of production, and reserved division of labour (these days the 'technical division of labour') for the concrete, structural composition and organization of production relations.

In chapter 7 of volume i of *Capital*, Marx specifies the relations of production specific to capitalism as being two-fold. The first or control relation is described as follows: 'the labourer works under the control of the capitalist to whom his labour belongs; the capitalist taking good care that the work is done in the proper manner, and that the means of production are used with intelligence, so that there is no unnecessary waste of raw material and no wear and tear of the implements beyond what is necessarily caused by the work'. The second or ownership relation is specified far more generally: 'the labour process is a process between things that the capitalist has purchased, things that have become his property. The product of this process belongs, therefore, to him, just as much as does the wine which is the product of a process of fermentation completed in his cellar.'

The sum total of the relations of production comprise what Marx referred to (somewhat problematically) as the 'economic structure' of capitalist society, or its 'real foundation'. As such, they also account for the division of that society into *classes (the 'social division of labour'), again somewhat problematically since the nature of control and ownership has changed vastly since Marx's time. Although he did not specify them himself with any great precision, Marx also clearly thought that distinctive sets of production relations could be identified for other modes of production, and later writers have addressed this problem at some length (see, for example, B. Hindess and P. Hirst, *Pre-capitalist Modes of Production*, 1975). *See also* BASE.

relative autonomy The renewal of Marxist theory inaugurated by Louis Althusser and his associates in the 1960s had as one of its aims the rescue of Marxism from the charge of *economism (or *economic determinism). According to Althusser, the social totality consisted of four distinct sets of practices—economic, political, ideological, and theoretical—in complex combination with one another. None of these practices should be thought of as reducible to any of the others. On the contrary, each has its own 'relative autonomy' within limits set by its place in the totality. Critics have argued that in the absence of any specification of what these limits might be, the concept lacks explanatory content. The most sustained attempt to apply the concept in substantive analyses will be found in the works of Nicos Poulantzas.

relative deprivation *See* DEPRIVATION; REFERENCE GROUP.

relative mobility *See* MOBILITY, SOCIAL.

relative poverty *See* POVERTY.

relativism The word relativism is used loosely to describe intellectual positions which reject absolute or universal standards or criteria. Thus, epistemological relativism is the view that there are no universal criteria of knowledge or truth. What counts as true is a function of criteria which are internal and so relative to local cultures, historical periods, or socio-political interests (the scientific community, the ruling class, revolutionary proletariat, and so forth). The critiques of *positivism which were influential in the 1960s and 1970s often (mistakenly) advocated some form of relativism as the only alternative. The subsequent work of Michel Foucault, linking 'regimes of truth' with power relations, added to the currency of relativist perspectives in sociology and related disciplines. Moral relativism, likewise, is the view that there are no objective moral standards. This view, like epistemological relativism, has become especially influential through the popularization of the work of the German philosopher Nietzsche by Foucault and others. Though often welcomed by sociologists in a spirit of tolerance and respect for cross-cultural difference, it is often forgotten that these views have strong historical links with political irrationalism, and (in particular) with European Nazism. It should be remembered that, from the standpoint of a thoroughgoing moral relativism, the values of respect and tolerance themselves have no general validity, but are mere peculiarities of particular, localized moral traditions (for example liberalism).

One of the most forceful statements of a thoroughgoing relativism can be found in the works of Paul Feyerabend. In a series of controversial polemics against scientific objectivity, method, and rationality, Feyerabend refers to himself as a 'flippant Dadaist'. In *Against Method* (1975) he uses historical studies of scientific change (as had Thomas Kuhn) to show that for each proclaimed methodological principle of science, an at least equally good case could be made for adopting its opposite. The purpose of the argument was to weaken faith in method as such. The only principle Feyerabend was prepared to support was, famously, 'anything goes'. In subsequent writings (such as *Science in a Free Society*, 1978, and *Farewell to Reason*, 1987), Feyerabend has made clearer the moral and emotional basis of his relativism. He sees a world increasingly dominated by a Western industrial-scientific way of life, which eliminates cultural diversity, destroys the environment, and impoverishes life. The key culprits in this scenario are science and its associated claims to *objectivity and reason. This trio are so corrupted by their incorporation into global monotonization that they should be abandoned in favour of a free-for-all in which magic, witchcraft, traditional medicine, and other alternatives have equal access to power and resources.

Against Feyerabend it has been argued that misuse of science by powerful interests is not a sufficient reason for abandoning all the actual or possible benefits which might flow from its detachment from those interests. It might also be argued that the abandonment of reason has been historically no less destructive than its misuse. *See also* CULTURAL RELATIVISM; METHODOLOGICAL PLURALISM; PARADIGM; POSTMODERNISM.

relativism, cultural *See* CULTURAL RELATIVISM.

reliability When sociologists enquire as to the reliability of data, or of a measurement procedure, they are questioning whether the same results would be produced if the research procedure were to be repeated. Reliability embraces two principal forms of repetition: temporal reliability (the same result is obtained when the measurement is repeated at a later time); and comparative reliability (the same result is obtained when two different forms of a test are used, the same test is applied by different researchers, or the same test is applied to two different samples taken from the same population). Reliability raises many technical problems for the sociologist. For example, having once interviewed someone, a repeat interview may be contaminated by the earlier experience.

Reliability is usually contrasted with *validity—whether or not a measurement procedure actually measures what the researcher supposes it does. However the two are not perfectly independent. One may have a highly reliable measure which is not valid: for example, we might measure IQ by standing subjects on a weighing machine and reading off the numbers, an extremely reliable procedure in both senses; but body-weight is hardly a valid indicator of IQ. A highly unreliable measure, on the other hand, cannot be valid. *See also* VARIABLE.

religion Religion is a set of beliefs, *symbols, and practices (for example *rituals), which is based on the idea of the *sacred, and which unites believers into a socio-religious community. The sacred is contrasted with the profane because it involves feelings of awe. Sociologists have defined religion by reference to the sacred rather than to a belief in a god or gods, because it makes social comparison possible; for example, some versions of *Buddhism do not involve a belief in God. Some have argued that political ideologies such as communism can be the basis of a *civil religion. Religion is also contrasted with *magic, because the latter is thought to be individualistic and instrumental. *See also* INVISIBLE RELIGION; NEW RELIGIONS; SECULARIZATION; SOCIOLOGY OF RELIGION.

religion, sociology of The scientific study of religious institutions, beliefs, and practices had its origins in *Marxism and the neo-Hegelian critique of religion, but it is primarily associated with the late 19th-century research into religious phenomena by Émile Durkheim, Georg Simmel, William Robertson Smith, Ernst Troeltsch, and Max Weber. A psychoanalytic theory of religious behaviour was also developed by Sigmund Freud (in, for example, *Civilization and its Discontents*, 1930). The sociology of religion should be distinguished from religious sociology, which has been employed by the Roman Catholic Church to improve the effectiveness of its missionary work in industrial societies, but it is related to both the phenomenology and anthropology of religion.

The sociology of religion should be seen as a critique of 19th-century *positivist theories, which were concerned to explain the origins of religion on rationalist and individualistic assumptions. This positivist tradition regarded religion as the erroneous beliefs of individuals which would eventually disappear when scientific thought became widely established in society. It was assumed, for example, that *Darwinism would undermine the religious belief in a divine creator. Religion was thought to be irrational.

The sociology of religion, by contrast, was concerned with religion as nonrational, collective, and symbolic. It was not interested in the historical origins of religion in 'primitive society'. Religion was not based on erroneous belief, but responded to the human need for meaning. It was not individualistic but social and collective. It was about *symbol and *ritual rather than belief and knowledge. The growth of scientific knowledge was therefore irrelevant to the social functions of religion.

Émile Durkheim's *The Elementary Forms of the Religious Life* (1912) is the classical statement of this sociological perspective. He defined religion as 'a unified system of beliefs and practices relative to sacred things, that is to say, things set apart and forbidden—beliefs and practices which unite into one single moral community called a Church, all those who adhere to them'. By 'elementary forms' Durkheim meant the basic structures of religious activity; he rejected as unscientific any inquiry into the primitive origins of religion, concentrating instead on the social functions of religious practices. He rejected also the rationalist critique of belief by focusing on practices relevant to the *sacred. His approach has remained fundamental to a sociological understanding of religion.

The sociology of religion has thus been bound up with the problem of defining religion and distinguishing religion from *magic. It has largely abandoned the idea that religion is a collection of beliefs in God. There has been an emphasis instead on practice in relation to the sacred. Alternative perspectives have defined religion as the ultimate concern which all human beings have to address. Many sociologists have subsequently identified the religious with the social.

There are two generally contrasted traditions in the sociology of religion: those of Durkheim and Weber. Whereas Durkheim was interested in the social functions of religion in general, in relation to social integration, Max Weber was primarily concerned with the problem of theodicy (any explanation of the fundamental moral problems of death, suffering, and evil) and the comparative study of the salvation drive. Weber identified two major religious orientations towards the world—mysticism and asceticism—in his *The Sociology of Religion* (1922). He was especially interested in religious attitudes towards economics and eroticism. He argued that inner-worldly asceticism (or the ethic of world mastery) represented the most radical attempt to impose a rational regulation on the world. He explored this theme in *The Protestant Ethic and the Spirit of Capitalism* (1905).

Some sociologists have claimed that, in modern societies, there has been a profound process of *secularization (or religious decline) as a consequence of urbanization, cultural pluralism, and the spread of a scientific understanding of the world. This thesis has also been challenged by sociologists who argue that religion has been transformed rather than undermined.

The sociology of religion was originally at the theoretical core of sociology as a whole, because it was concerned to understand the character of rational action, the importance of symbols, and finally the nature of the social. It has been argued, however, that contemporary sociology of religion has lost this analytical importance, because it has concentrated on narrow empirical issues such as the pattern of recruitment to the Christian ministry. The comparative study of world religions, which was fundamental to Weber's approach, has been neglected.

Alan Aldridge's *Religion in The Contemporary World* (2002) and Steve Bruce's *Religion in the Modern World from Cathedrals to Cults* (1996) both offer an excellent introduction to most of the topics raised in this entry and to the field as a whole. *See also* CIVIL RELIGION; INVISIBLE RELIGION; PRIVATE RELIGION; PROTESTANT ETHIC THESIS; RELIGION; RELIGIOUS REVIVAL; SECT.

(⊕) SEE WEB LINKS

• The Society for the Scientific Study of Religion.

religiosity In *The Religious Factor* (1961), Gerhard Lenski (1924–2015) analyses variations in orientations to economic and political issues, highlighting the differences between Jews, Protestants, and Catholics, partly in terms of an influential typology of the dimensions of 'religiosity'—which he identifies as orthodoxy or belief, association (or religious attendance), devotion (dealing with such aspects as prayer), and communality (the degree of segregation of the religious group).

religious innovation Any change in religious practice, organization, or belief is religious innovation. The major world religions such as *Islam and *Christianity have developed orthodox bodies of belief, custom, and practice, which are regarded as part of a sacred tradition. Religious innovation is thus seen as a departure from orthodoxy, because it is a threat to tradition. Since religious innovation is inevitable, there is a permanent tension between belief in the unchanging nature of orthodox tradition, and the actual social change of religious organizations. *See also* SCHISM.

religious nationalisms *See* NATIONALISM.

religious revival A term applied to mass movements which are based upon intense religious excitement. Periodic religious revivals, which seek to restore commitment and attachment to the group, are a regular sociological feature of religious traditions. The evangelical revival of the 18th century included the Moravians and the Methodists. Revivalism has been a common phenomenon in the United States. *See also* EVANGELICAL; SECT.

remunerative power *See* COMPLIANCE.

Renner, Karl (1870–1950) Along with Hilferding he was a leading figure in Austro-Marxism. He represented the Socialists in the Austrian parliament and became Chancellor and Minister of Finance in 1918–20 and was President of the Assembly in 1930–3. In 1945 he again became Chancellor (President) of the new Austrian Republic. He published works on the political conflicts of nation-states, but became best known for *The Institutions of Private Law and their Social Function* (1904). This argued that legal institutions operate in contexts of material relations that give them a distinct social function that may not correspond in a one-to-one way with their formal codification. Thus, large corporations may be based around private property but in fact sustain concentrated control by finance capitalists. His later work, published posthumously, set out the idea of a growth in size and significance of a managerial and professional 'service class', an idea that has been taken up by such writers as John Goldthorpe.

repertory grid *See* PERSONAL CONSTRUCT THEORY.

replication Repeating a study, in exactly the same format, to check whether the same results are obtained a second or subsequent time (usually by a different researcher). One variation is simultaneous replication of the same study, either in the same context, or in contexts carefully selected for their known variation on one key variable. There can also be replication via *secondary analysis of a major data-set, to re-test hypotheses, and to assess the impact of the particular program or software employed in the original analysis.

Arguably, and for a variety of reasons, not nearly enough resources in the discipline are devoted to replicating results: the effort, cost, and time involved in conducting social *surveys usually preclude systematic replication; funding agencies are less likely to pay for investigations which seek only to confirm earlier findings; and there is little kudos for researchers (and, one suspects, not much career advancement) to be had in reproducing existing studies. (In psychology, by comparison, the dominant *experimental methods lend themselves to the widespread use of replication studies.) However, although whole surveys are all too infrequently replicated, individual questions and batteries of questions often are—especially where these have been assembled into *scales (for example to measure *attitudes or *personality traits).

Strict replication shades gradually into the idea of a 're-study'. Re-studies are also in a sense replications, but are usually conducted at time intervals such that observable differences from earlier findings can reasonably be attributed to real change in the subjects or processes under investigation, rather than to either chance or measurement error in the original study. Prominent and informative re-studies include the two community studies of the English town of Banbury, conducted by Margaret Stacey and her colleagues in 1948–51 and 1966–8 (compare *Tradition and Change*, 1960, and *Power, Persistence and Change*, 1975), and the studies by Robert Redfield and Oscar Lewis of Tepoztlan in Mexico (in 1926 and 1943 respectively). Redfield depicts the community in question as an ideal-typical type of *folk society (smooth functioning, well-integrated, contented, well-adjusted) whereas Lewis paints a picture dominated by individualism, fear, lack of cooperation, envy, schism, and mistrust. Each party accused the other of methodological failings (for example asking the wrong questions of the wrong informants). The celebrated disjuncture between the two accounts was eventually resolved, when a further investigation revealed that the society had in all probability changed dramatically in the intervening years, due to increases in population pressure and a programme of radical land redistribution (see P. Coy, 'A Watershed in Mexican Rural History', *Journal of Latin American Studies*, 1971). *See also* RELIABILITY.

representation Representation refers to the way in which images and texts reconstruct, rather than reflect, the original sources they represent. Thus a painting, photograph, or written text about a tree is never an actual tree, but the reconstruction of what it seemed to be or meant to the person who represented it. If it *were* a tree, it could not then be a photograph, painting, or text.

Representation is an important concept in *semiology, *linguistics, *Marxism, and *feminism, and points to an aspect of the way in which *meaning is constructed. It can therefore be understood as contributing importantly to social processes. Feminists argue that representation is continually creating, re-creating, and endorsing *stereotypical ideas of gender *identity. All media images—for example in advertising or cinema—are constructed by somebody, for a specific purpose with a specific audience in mind, although they are usually presented as if they were a 'slice of reality'. To try and understand what they mean, and how they construct meaning, it is important to examine what lies behind the image or : who constructed it, where and when, for what purpose, and for which ticular audience's *gaze. Because watchers rarely have access to this process, ages in particular tend to classify complex ideas into apparently simple mean- s; they thus deny contradiction and ambiguity, and representations become e myths which are nevertheless accepted as 'real'. Feminist critics of pornog- phy have used the idea of representation to develop theories of how pornography functions in society, and how it is represented in relation to class, race, and gender (see S. Kappeler, *The Pornography of Representation*, 1986; and E. Chaplin, *Sociology and Visual Representation*, 1994).

representationalism   *See* SAUSSURE.

representativeness   The ability to give a reasonably accurate portrayal of the research subject's characteristics and known diversity. As applied to *survey samples, or *case study samples, this is judged by the extent to which key characteristics of the *sample are the same as the characteristics of the *population from which the sample was selected. In relation to single cases, the criterion would be the typicality of the case selected. The term is also applied to research reports, for example to assess whether verbatim quotations, incidents described in detail, or other selectively reported results reflect the full variety and weight of the results obtained. *See also* SAMPLING ERROR.

repression   *See* PSYCHOANALYSIS.

repressive state apparatus   *See* IDEOLOGICAL STATE APPARATUS.

reproductive labour   *See* DOMESTIC LABOUR.

reproductive technologies   A term applied by feminists to technologies used for regulating biological reproduction. They include technologies of contraception and abortion (such as the pill and IUD), childbirth (foetal monitoring), and infertility (for example the much-publicized *in vitro* fertilization). The term, implicitly contrasting the technological with the natural, usually suggests an overly interventionist application of science, and a wresting of power away from individuals themselves, usually women.

research design   The strategic plan for a research project or research programme, setting out the broad outline and key features of the work to be undertaken, including the methods of data collection and analysis to be employed, and showing how the research strategy addresses the specific aims and objectives of the study, and whether the research issues are theoretical or policy-oriented. Hence also, the process of developing such a document, choosing between alternative types of study, their relative size, whether *triangulation will be employed, and adjusting plans to the available resources and timetable. *See also* QUALITATIVE VERSUS QUANTITATIVE DEBATE.

research ethics   The application of moral rules and professional codes of conduct to the collection, analysis, reporting, and publication of information about research subjects, in particular active acceptance of subjects' right to privacy, confidentiality, and informed consent. Until recently *sociologists (and social scientists generally) often displayed arrogance in their treatment of research subjects, justifying their actions by the search for truth. This trend is now being redressed, especially in industrial societies, with the adoption of formal codes of conduct, and greater emphasis on ethical research procedures. Ethical issues are most salient in relation to *case studies and other research designs which focus on very few cases (with the risk that they remain identifiable in reports). Public opinion now resists invasions of privacy for genuine research purposes just as much as for publicity seeking mass media stories, as evidenced by periodic increases in survey non-response, despite the fact that anonymity is effectively guaranteed in large-scale data collections.

There are three key issues. Research subjects' right to refuse to cooperate with a study is clear-cut in relation to interview *surveys, but is not always observed in relation to case studies, especially when *covert observation is employed. Research subjects' right for information supplied to researchers to remain not only anonymous but also confidential in the broader sense is rarely disputed, but again may be difficult to observe in practice, especially when analyses of study results reveal more than may be intended. The right to give or withhold informed consent, if necessary after the research has been completed, ensures that research results are not made public without the subjects' knowing agreement. These and other issues are raised in Martin Bulmer (ed.), *Social Research Ethics* (1982) and Ray Lee, *Doing Research on Sensitive Topics* (1993). See also ETHICS.

research methods See ATTITUDES; CASE HISTORY; CASE STUDY; CONTENT ANALYSIS; DOCUMENTARY RESEARCH; INTERVIEW; LIFE HISTORY; MULTI-LEVEL MODELS; OFFICIAL STATISTICS; PANEL STUDY; PARTICIPANT OBSERVATION; PERSONAL DOCUMENTS; QUALITATIVE VERSUS QUANTITATIVE DEBATE; RESEARCH DESIGN; RESEARCH ETHICS; SECONDARY ANALYSIS; SURVEY; TRIANGULATION.

reserve army of labour See INDUSTRIAL RESERVE ARMY.

residues See ELITE THEORY.

residues, methods of See MILL.

resocialization The relearning of cultural norms and sanctions, on their return to a social system, by those who voluntarily or involuntarily left that system (such as prisoners re-entering society or expatriates returning from abroad) so that they can again be fully accepted within that system. For a fascinating case study—which arrives at some surprising and controversial conclusions—see Roger Goodman, *Japan's 'International Youth'* (1990).

resource mobilization Resource mobilization refers to a distinct perspective for understanding *social movements, emphasizing the critical role played by material resources. Earlier studies of social movements tended to view them as spontaneous or hysterical reactions to high levels of frustration. Resource mobilization stresses rationality, and the importance of adequate funding, leadership, and organization.

respondent Someone who offers information to a researcher, for example in response to a *questionnaire, or during the course of an *interview. The term 'informant' is often used when informal research techniques (such as unstructured interviews) have been employed. See also CASE.

response rate The percentage of an eligible random *sample that agrees to participate in an interview survey. There is no response rate in a *quota sample. *See also* NON-RESPONSE.

restrictive practice An industrial and commercial agreement or arrangement which operates in restraint of free competition even though it may be within the law. The term originates from political and managerial usage but has come to be quite commonly used in the study of *labour relations. For example, restrictive practices might be agreements fixing the prices to be charged for goods, services, or labour, or the quantity supplied, or the conditions of supply. In relation to restrictive labour practices, a large degree of judgement and convention determines whether rules or procedures are regarded as proper safeguards for the customer and the wider public, or are regarded as unjustifiable and reprehensible restrictions. A typical example is the extent to which certain types of employment are restricted to people with specified qualifications and experience, or to those who are members of a *closed shop. *See also* INDUSTRIAL CONFLICT.

re-study (re-studies) *See* REPLICATION.

retirement centre A town, coastal zone, island, or other geographical area to which many people move when they retire from employment, because of the temperate climate, tax regime, or good leisure facilities. As the elderly form an increasingly large share of the population in Western industrial societies, complete towns and housing developments are built for them in retirement centres—notably, for example, in the United States.

retreatism *See* ANOMIE.

retributive justice *See* JUSTICE, SOCIAL.

retrograde amnesia Loss of memory of events and experiences occurring prior to an illness, accident, injury, or traumatic experience such as rape or assault. The amnesia may cover events over a longer or only a brief period. Typically, it declines with time, with earlier memories returning first.

reverse discrimination *See* POSITIVE DISCRIMINATION.

revitalization movement *See* MESSIANIC MOVEMENT; NEW RELIGIONS.

revolution *See* REBELLION.

revolutionary science *See* PARADIGM.

Rex, John Arderne (1925–2011) Born in South Africa but spent his career in Britain, working at the Universities of Leeds, Birmingham, Durham, Aston, and Warwick. He developed a sociology that drew on Max *Weber to develop an alternative to the dominant structural functionalist approach. His *Key Problems of Sociological Theory* (1961) contrasted theories of consensus with those of conflict, as had his contemporaries Ralf Dahrendorf, Lewis Coser, and David

*Lockwood. Rex's version of *conflict theory was firmly based in a Weberian sociology of class that he used to reconstruct Marxist ideas about class dominance. Rex's main interests lay in ethnic relations and he saw this conflict theory as providing a more general framework for understanding social conflict in all its forms. With Robert Moore, he undertook an influential study of a district in Birmingham, exploring the 'housing classes' formed on the basis of an ethnically divided labour market (*Race, Community, and Conflict*, 1967) and he later extended this in a project undertaken with Sally Tomlinson (*Colonial Immigrants in a British City*, 1979). His theoretical reflections on race and colonialism were published in *Colonialism and the City* (1973) and his more general sociological arguments in *Sociology and the Demystification of the Modern World* (1974). He continued to develop his comparative sociology of race relations and multiculturalism, publishing this in *Ethnic Minorities and the Modern State* (1996).

rhizome A botanical term indicating subterranean stems such as bulbs, tubers and couchgrass, with a multiple, lateral, and circular system of ramification, different from roots and radicles which tend to grow by means of binary divisions. The term was given a philosophical twist by French philosophers Gilles Deleuze and Félix Guattari, who used it to open the second volume of their influential 'Capitalism and Schizophrenia' series, *A Thousand Plateaus* (1980). For Deleuze and Guattari, the rhizome described what they called 'substantive multiplicities'—that is, multiplicities that are not simply attributes of an assumed unity (such as 'multiple identities' for example).

Deleuze and Guattari start by opposing the rhizome to the root-tree, arguing that Western metaphysics has always manifested a basic preference for roots and trees over stems, flows, and rhizomes. The tree presupposes the notion of a single pivotal tap-root or foundation out of which all structures are produced by way of binary division (or what they call the process by which the One becomes Two and Two becomes Four and so on). Two examples of this mode of thinking are Chomsky's generative grammar which, in their opinion, reduces the radical rhizomaticity of patois, slangs, and specialized languages to a normative universal structure censoring all singular variations; and psychoanalysis, which literally roots a rhizomorphous unconscious capable of creative deterritorializations and connections, to the parents' bed or to the tap-root of the Oedipal triangle. The rhizome, they claim, can help us to formulate some of the principles which describes all multiplicities as such beyond the botanical realm. As such, the rhizome is not a metaphor for something else (such as modes of social organization), but it is a concept which aims to offer a more radical understanding of ontological processes as dynamic and mutating assemblages.

The most popular sociological use of the rhizome concept has been as a means to describe the socio-technical structure of the Internet—which, according to some authors, presents several key rhizomatic principles. However, the notion of the rhizome can in principle offer a useful alternative to hermeneutic understandings of social processes (thus sidestepping the need to search for 'deep meanings'); to approaches that identify and separate distinct levels of natural/

social organization (physical, biological, economic, social, technical, cultural, economic, etc.), which a rhizomatic approach would consider as always operating simultaneously as assemblages; or to *post-structuralist perspectives that put signifying linguistic models at the heart of all sociological understanding (to which the notion of the rhizome would oppose a-signifying semiotic chains).

Rickert, Heinrich (1863–1936) *See* GEISTESWISSENSCHAFTEN and NATURWISSENSCHAFTEN.

rights The idea of 'rights' has been championed in many different ways throughout history. However, the modern Western conception of rights may be traced through the English Magna Carta to the US Declaration of Independence and Constitution, and the French Declaration of the Rights of Man and the Citizen.

In the wake of international concern over the Holocaust, on 10 December 1948 the General Assembly of the United Nations proclaimed a Universal Declaration of Human Rights, which included the right to 'life, liberty and security of person', 'recognition everywhere as a person before the law', 'freedom of movement', 'a nationality', 'freedom of thought, conscience and religion', 'freedom of peaceful assembly and association', and 'freedom to take part in government'.

In sociology, rights are usually seen to develop out of specific communities: they are social inventions that play an important—and contested—role in political life. For instance, in abortion politics in the United States, one side claims the 'right to life' whilst the other claims the 'right to choose'. The concept of *citizenship evokes notions of rights—as well as those of obligations (see B. S. Turner, *Citizenship and Capitalism*, 1986). There is also an extensive literature on *property rights (see, for example, S. R. Munzer, *A Theory of Property Rights*, 1990). For a general introduction see Lydia Morris, *Rights: Sociological Perspectives* (2006). *See also* CIVIL RIGHTS; COLLECTIVISM; LIBERALISM.

riot A sudden upsurge of collective violence, often directed at property, sometimes at persons in authority. There is considerable taxonomic dispute about the precise definition of the term, and the point at which collective unrest becomes riot, rather than (say) merely civil disorder. The issues here are not merely academic, since acts of collective violence often raise questions of legitimacy (especially when they are directed against the State itself), and can be discredited by those against whom they are directed by means of being labelled as a form of criminal lawlessness. For example, G. Rudé's study of *The Crowd in History* (1964) shows how the revolutionary crowd in European history was identified by the ruling classes as a frenzied criminal mob, while E. P. Thompson's reading of late 18th-and early 19th-century English history (*The Making of the English Working Class*, 1964) suggests that a similar process occurred in respect of Luddism. Stanley Cohen's study of the British Mods and Rockers in the mid-1960s is an exemplary account of the contested labelling that often surrounds the *moral panics which are associated with hooliganism and can promote a public discourse of riot.

Much media and other public discussion of riotous behaviour—be it in the contexts of labour militancy, ethnic unrest, or youth *subcultures—therefore promotes a 'lunatic fringe' or 'criminal riff-raff' theory of such activities. Sociologists who have explored the underlying causes of riots have tended, rather, to view them as symptomatic of structural social tensions. Thus, for example, research into the urban riots in the United States in the 1960s showed that these had wide local support and participation, were not orchestrated by a lawless and unrepresentative criminal minority, and could therefore much more plausibly be seen as broad group responses to shared grievances (see, for example, A. Oberschall, 'The Los Angeles Riot of August 1965', *Social Problems*, 1968). *See also* COLLECTIVE BEHAVIOUR.

risk society A term brought into the centre of social theory with the publication in 1986 of German sociologist Ulrich Beck's *Risk Society: Towards a New Modernity*. Beck distinguishes between pre-industrial notions of fate, associated with the plagues, famines, and natural disasters that were felt to be beyond human control, and the ideas of risk assessment that developed along with modernity. Risk assessment based on calculable decisions involved legal definitions and both private and socialized forms of insurance against the manufactured dangers and hazards of industrial society. The welfare state, with its insurance against the risks of unemployment, ill health, and old age, was a clear example of a collective hedging of risks.

The *Risk Society*, however, is concerned with a further stage, dating roughly from the Second World War, in which industrial society is confronted with uninsurable risks. The dangers of the nuclear and chemical age, the corruption of food chains, the effects of global warming, the pollution of the seas, and the possibility of global financial collapse are but the most salient of these risks. Such risks are typically global rather than national in character, and fail to respect traditional boundaries between rich and poor, the powerful and the powerless. The foundations of Enlightenment-inspired *modernity are called into question as *trust in the major institutions of society is undermined by their seeming inability to mitigate the experience of the large-scale hazards which they themselves have produced. Both Beck and Anthony Giddens emphasize the connection of risk to the process of reflexive modernization in which social agents are forced to confront the systematically produced unintended social and environmental consequences and side-effects of industrialism. Attempts at management often lead, once again, to perverse consequences. Beck notes the development of a new 'subpolitics' that extends the reach of reflexive questioning so that the dominance of technical reason itself is called into question, leading to a challenge from a more broadly envisioned morality and politics to the hegemony of the narrow rationality and judgement of scientific experts. *See also* REFLEXIVE MODERNIZATION.

risky-shift effect A social psychological term, referring to the observed tendency for people to make more daring decisions when they are in groups, than when they are alone.

rites of passage The *rituals associated with a change of status, for example from youth to adulthood, and from unmarried to married state. In his classic study by the same name, Arnold van Gennep distinguished rites of separation, rites of segregation, and rites of integration. Rituals associated with a change in status were identified as having these three stages. Between each there are clear symbolic demarcations.

ritual Generally, an often-repeated pattern of behaviour which is performed at appropriate times, and which may involve the use of *symbols. *Religion is one of the main social fields in which rituals operate, but the scope of ritual extends into secular and everyday life as well. For example, the dramaturgical sociology of Erving *Goffman makes extensive reference to 'interaction rituals', the various ritualized codes of everyday behaviour by which actors cooperate in acknowledging a shared reality and preserve each other's sense of self (see his *Interaction Ritual: Essays on Face-to-Face Behaviour*, 1967).

The Durkheimian approach (*The Elementary Forms of the Religious Life*, 1912) makes a strong distinction between the *sacred and the profane and locates rituals firmly in the former category. For Durkheimians, rituals create social solidarity, which is necessary to hold society together. Durkheim reduced ritual to social structure since he asserted that, through rituals, people correctly represent to themselves the pattern of relations in society. For Durkheim, the unit of significance in ritual is action, since action causes beliefs, not vice versa. Durkheim thus accorded to ritual a primary *epistemological role—insisting that the necessary building-blocks of thought are transmitted through the shared 'effervescence' of ritual. Christel Lane's *The Rites of Rulers: Ritual in Industrial Society* (1981) is a fascinating contemporary example of a Durkheimian interpretation of the socialist rituals of the former Soviet Union.

The Marxist approach to ritual, by contrast, proposes that rituals transmit only *false consciousness. They mystify their participants by misrepresenting the pattern of social relations in the society (see, for example, M. Bloch, *From Blessing to Violence*, 1986).

A framework for categorizing the general structure of rituals was proposed by the Belgian anthropologist Arnold van Gennep (*The Rites of Passage*, 1909). Van Gennep wrote that a person is not just born into society, but has to be re-created through *rites of passage as a social individual, and accepted into society. He outlined three stages in such rites, which transform the social identity of the initiand: separation, or the detaching of an individual from his or her former status; liminality, where the initiand is in 'limbo', having been detached from the old status but not yet attached to the new; and reincorporation, in which the passage from one status to another is consummated symbolically.

A common criticism of sociological interpretations of ritual is that analysts have merely imposed their own meaning on the events. G. Lewis (*Day of Shining Red*, 1980) argues that the search for meaning in rites outweighs the concern for what people may feel about them; that is, the emotional aspects. Thus rituals become like crossword puzzles—to be decoded in the hands of anthropologists and sociologists. Lewis argues that rituals must be understood in the terms of the participants' own meanings as well as those of the analyst.

Rivers, William Halse Rivers (1864–1922) Trained in medicine and developing an early interest in psychiatry, he became lecturer in psychology at Cambridge. He was recruited to the Torres Straits expedition in 1898, along with William McDougall and began a career in anthropology. His first important work was *The Todas* (1906), followed by *Kinship and Social Organization* (1914) and *The History of Melanesian Society* (1914). His early work had drawn on *evolutionism, but in 1911 Rivers converted to *diffusionism. One of his early students at Cambridge was Alfred Radcliffe-Brown, to whom Rivers introduced Durkheim's ideas on social structure. During the First World War he took a post as psychiatrist in a military hospital treating 'shell shock' patients, one of his most famous patients being the novelist Siegfried Sassoon. This period in his life has been fictionalized in Pat Barker's *Regeneration* (1995). It was at this time that he began to seriously study *Freud, and he summarized his own ideas on this in *Instinct and the Unconscious* (1920). He died suddenly in 1922. Rivers's life is recounted in Richard Slobdin's *W. H. R. Rivers* (1997).

role (social role, role theory) Role is a key concept in sociological theory. It highlights the social expectations attached to particular social positions and analyses the workings of such expectations. Role theory was particularly popular during the mid-20th century, but after sustained criticism came to be seen as flawed and became less widely used. However the concept of role, properly understood, remains a basic tool for sociological understanding.

There are two rather different approaches within role theory. One develops the social anthropology of Ralph Linton and gives a structural account of roles situated within the social system. Here, roles become institutionalized clusters of normative rights and obligations: Talcott Parsons's celebrated account of the *sick role is a good example. An alternative approach is more social-psychological in tenor and focuses upon the active processes involved in making, taking, and playing at roles: it is part of the traditions of *symbolic interactionism and *dramaturgy, the latter of which analyses social life through the metaphor of drama and the theatre.

The structural account of roles locates a position in society, such as that of a teacher, and then tries to describe the standard bundle of rights and duties associated with an ideal type of this position. These expectations, which are socially based, constitute the role. Any given person will possess a number of statuses (for example mother, teacher, golf-captain), and these constitute a status set, with each status harbouring its own role. Every role brings a number of different partners, each with their own set of expectations, so that a teacher (for example) may have students, colleagues, heads, governors, and parents as role partners, each of whom makes somewhat different expectations upon his or her behaviour. The sum total of the expectations of these partners is the role-set. When these expectations are in disagreement, as is frequently the case, sociologists talk of role conflict and role strain. In the Parsonian system of social theory, these role patterns are defined through the so-called pattern variables, or choices between pairs of alternative *norms. This theory is a useful *heuristic device for mapping the organization of societies through normative patterns, but some uses of it have tended to oversimplify normative expectations by assuming too much consensus in society, and by reifying the *social system. A sophisticated version that properly recognizes conflict is Ralf Dahrendorf's *Homo Sociologicus* (1968), at one time controversial, now unwarrantably neglected.

The contrasting social psychological view is focused much more upon the dynamic aspects of working at roles: it examines the interactions in which people come to play their roles rather than describing the place of these roles in the social structure. Here, the emphasis is on the ways in which people come to take the role of the other (role-taking), construct their own roles (role-making), anticipate the responses of others to their roles (*see* ALTERCASTING), and finally play at their particular role (role-playing). In some versions of this theory (for example that propounded by Erving Goffman), attention is given to the ways in which roles are performed: sometimes people may embrace their parts fully (role embracement) and play out the details of their role in cherished detail. At other times they may perform their parts with tongue-in-cheek (role distance)— showing that they are much more than the simple role they play. Or they may play roles cynically in order to manage the outcomes of the situation (impression management). In all of these accounts the concern is with the dynamics of working at roles, where roles are not fixed expectations, but emergent outcomes. Perhaps the most useful accounts of this approach to role theory are to be found in Goffman's *The Presentation of Self in Everyday Life* (1959) and *Encounters* (1961).

role, conjugal The distinctive roles of the husband and wife that result from the *division of labour in the family. In her classic study of *Family and Social Network* (1957), Elizabeth Bott observes that one spouse was usually responsible for supporting the family financially, and another for the domestic tasks involved in house-keeping and child-care. But there was considerable variation in the degree to which the conjugal roles were separated. While Bott did not regard conjugal roles as class-determined, nevertheless joint conjugal roles tended to be associated with middle-class marriages. In their study of *Family and Kinship in East London* (1957), and again in their later book *The Symmetrical Family* (1973), Michael Young and Peter Willmott argued that, even among the working class, there is a shift towards joint conjugal roles, with the 'companionable' marriage now accepted as the ideal. However, while more recent empirical studies suggest that the traditional division of labour is becoming less rigid, it is clear that inequalities remain. Time-budget studies reveal that there has been remarkably little change in who does the household chores, although husbands may help out a little more around the home. Nevertheless, even when wives are working full-time, the full sharing of chores around the house is still unusual, and cases of working women married to 'house-husbands' are rare enough to be newsworthy. There is also little evidence that conjugal differences in power and control have disappeared. Studies of money-management in the household suggest that payments of house-keeping allowances to wives are common, with many wives still not knowing how much their husbands earn. All of these issues—the domestic division of labour, household time allocation, and patterns of money allocation within households—are given a rigorous empirical treatment, from the point of view of their implications for changing conjugal roles, in Michael Anderson et al. (eds.), *The Social and Political Economy of the Household* (1994). *See also* DOMESTIC DIVISION OF LABOUR; FAMILY, SOCIOLOGY OF; HOUSE-HOLD ALLOCATIVE SYSTEM; JOINT CONJUGAL ROLES; SEGREGATED CONJUGAL ROLES.

role model A *significant other, upon which an individual patterns his or her behaviour in a particular social *role, including adopting appropriate similar attitudes. Role-models need not be known personally to the individual: some people model their behaviour in particular roles on the real and legendary example provided by historical figures. Role models tend to provide ideals for a particular role only, rather than a pattern to be emulated across all the constit-uent roles of an individual's life and *self.

Rorschach Test A widely used *projective test, developed by Hermann Ror-schach (1884–1922) and influenced by *psychoanalytic thinking, especially the idea of free association. The test explores *personality by examining the subject's responses to relatively unstructured stimuli: ten symmetrical ink-blots. Various scoring systems analyse location, content, use of form and colour, comparing these with established norms.

Rose, Arnold M. (1918–68) An American sociologist, a somewhat eclectic *symbolic interactionist who adopted an intermediate position between the *humanistic approach of the *Chicago School, and the more *positivist stance of Manford *Kuhn and his followers at Iowa. Rose argued that the interactionist perspective was compatible with a range of research techniques—including both *participant observation and the social *survey. This methodological and theo-retical pluralism is evident in the widely used collection of essays on *Human Behavior and Social Processes* (1962), edited by Rose and with contributions from (among others) Howard Becker, Ralph Turner, Herbert Blumer, Robert Dubin, Herbert Gans, and Manford Kuhn, all of whom are seen as offering an interac-tionist approach to the study of society.

Rousseau, Jean-Jacques (1712–78) A controversial social philosopher and educationalist of the French Enlightenment, whose writings centred around the development of *social contract theory, a theory of *human nature as essentially open but subsequently enchained, and a *democratic theory of government. Rousseau's status as an early social theorist depends upon the reader's attitude to the many contradictions in his work. In different places he argued both that scientific inquiry should be shunned, since it corrupted public virtue, yet himself offered systematic studies of social inequality; and insisted that nature and society were in irreconcilable contradiction, yet offered a theory of the state which presupposes the ability of individuals to reconcile their own interests with those of others, and to identify with the general will as expressed in the sovereign body. His major text is probably *The Social Contract* (1762)—although the conception of a legitimate polity that he set out has been much more influential in political philosophy than sociology.

routinization of charisma *See* CHARISMA.

Rowntree, Benjamin Seebohm (1871–1954) A company director and chairman (1923–41) of Rowntree (a chocolate manufacturer) in York, Seebohm Rowntree was also a social reformer, philanthropist, and social researcher, with strong interests in industrial and labour management and in *poverty. He is best-known to sociologists for his detailed empirical studies of poverty in York.

His reforming spirit owed much to his Quaker origins and the strong influence of his father's ideas. He joined the family business when aged 18 and became the company's first Labour Director, implementing a range of reforms: an eight-hour day in 1896, a pension scheme in 1906, a five-day (44-hour) working week and works councils in 1919, a psychology department in 1922, and profit-sharing the following year. These changes were founded on Rowntree's concerns for the needs of workers, whose improved welfare was, he believed, also likely to promote industrial efficiency—a philosophy of scientific management elaborated in books such as *Human Needs of Labour* (1918).

Inspired by Charles Booth's studies of poverty in London, Rowntree decided to assess the extent of poverty in York, carrying out his first survey in 1897–8. *Poverty: A Study of Town Life* appeared in 1901. Rowntree adopted a subsistence definition of poverty, attempting to measure the resources necessary for maintaining physical efficiency. He distinguished primary poverty (where resources were insufficient to maintain efficiency) and secondary poverty (where earnings were sufficient but were spent on other things)—a distinction he subsequently accepted was problematic. The first study showed some 15 per cent of respondents were living in primary poverty. His subsequent studies in 1936 and 1950 employed somewhat modified measures and showed some reduction in poverty.

rules of correspondence A major problem for empirical researchers is the nature of the connection between the language of theory and the language of observation. Rules of correspondence is a term sometimes applied to the means, criteria, and assumptions underlying attempts to connect these two levels, by means of common expressions (see B. Hindess, *The Use of Official Statistics in Sociology*, 1973). In sociology, the passage from observation to conceptualization and back again requires a close examination of the manner in which our observations are organized and categorized (for example according to statistical criteria, tacit knowledge, or background expectancies), as well as to the operationalization of the concepts deployed to organize data.

ruling class *See* ELITE THEORY; MOSCA.

rural sociology Rural sociology has been powerfully influenced by *anti-urbanism, producing a stereotypical view of rural society as stable and harmonious. The claim that certain social characteristics were typical of villages rather than towns was made by Ferdinand Tönnies in his discussion of the *Gemeinschaft* versus *Gesellschaft* distinction between different forms of social association. Later, Robert Redfield and others adopted a more simplistic view, claiming that rural (folk) societies were inherently characterized by (for example) traditional and close-knit family social networks, consensus rather than conflict, and ascribed not achieved statuses.

Such ideas provided the basis for an empiricist rural sociology, notably in the United States, where it supported state policies legitimated by a Jeffersonian conception of rural life. Much rural sociology consisted of *community studies, effectively fact-gathering exercises to assess just how close the *community came to exhibiting the ideal-typical rural way of life, and what was eroding this idyllic vision in practice. After 1945, and especially through its influence on international bodies such as the United Nations Food and Agriculture Organization, this approach spread beyond America. However, its main concern remained that of rural development in advanced industrial countries. Major advances in the analysis of Third World rural change came more from the sociology of development and peasant studies. In state socialist countries, rural sociology was also relentlessly empiricist, although here it served policies of rural transformation rather than preservation.

By the 1960s these ideas about a rural way of life could no longer be sustained. Oscar Lewis, Ray Pahl, and others had shown that the countryside is as much characterized by allegedly urban as by supposedly rural forms of social association, conflict, and cohesion. However, much mainstream rural sociology remains obstinately wedded to the old paradigm, or is little more than *abstracted empiricism.

In the 1970s, there was promising new work on the nature of capitalist agricultural production, and its social consequences for rural populations and the wider society. The emergence of a new sociology of agriculture occurred alongside a similar transformation of urban sociology. This paradigmatic shift opened up many new areas of research, for example regarding the peculiar nature of land as a factor of production, the role of differing patterns of land-ownership, and the study of rural power structures and *social stratification. However, much of this work was deterministic, merely a reading off of the social consequences of rural change from the presumed logic of capitalist agricultural development.

Later studies move beyond these simplicities, exploring the historically and geographically variable nature of agricultural production, and its social consequences. Conceiving agriculture as a complex process of commodity-production, research topics include globally organized 'food regimes', the role of *agribusiness (including its relation to state policies and use of new technologies), and agricultural credit systems. Theories derived from peasant studies and the sociology of development have also been influential. Topics such as environmental issues and the non-agricultural rural economy appeared in the 1980s, widening the research agenda still further. A good bibliographical essay is Howard Newby's 'Rural Sociology' (*Current Sociology*, 1980).

rural-urban continuum *See* FOLK-URBAN CONTINUUM.

r

sacred (sacred versus profane distinction) For Émile Durkheim and subsequent sociologists of *religion, the recognition of the absolute nature of the distinction between these two terms was and has been fundamental to their sub-discipline, both as a *social fact and as something to be explained. Durkheim's classic statement of the distinction is that 'Sacred things are those which the [religious] interdictions protect and isolate; profane things, those to which these interdictions are applied and which must remain at a distance from the first' (*The Elementary Forms of the Religious Life*, 1912). Sacred phenomena are therefore considered extraordinary and set apart from everything else.

Saint-Simon, Claude-Henri de Rouvroy, Comte de (1760–1825) A most unusual French aristocrat who lived through remarkable times. His powerful liberal and republican sympathies saved him from the guillotine during the French Revolution, and after the Bourbon restoration he developed a system of ideas about social *progress. What he created has been called the 'characteristic ideology of industrialism': that everyone must work and be rewarded according to merit, that all progress is based on science, and that the society of the future will be peaceful, prosperous, and run on strictly scientific principles. Saint-Simon gathered a band of enthusiastic disciples who were regarded as radicals and even socialists—although there was not much about his system that would be called socialist today. From 1817 to 1824, when they quarrelled, Auguste Comte worked with Saint-Simon, whose influence on the younger man's theories is clear—it was Saint-Simon who first advocated *positivism as a means of social transformation. See Robert B. Carlisle, *The Proffered Crown* (1987).

salience Salience refers to the centrality of a particular *attitude, *identity, or *role. Salient events are those that are relatively important or are the focus of attention. Thus, at election time, politicians are anxious that the salient issues are the ones most favourable to their party.

sample survey *See* SURVEY.

sampling A method for collecting information and drawing inferences about a larger *population or universe, from the analysis of only part thereof, the sample. *Censuses of the population are an expensive way of monitoring social and economic change, and are carried out infrequently, usually at ten-year intervals. Sampling allows *surveys of the complete population of a country, or sub-sections of it, to be carried out far more cheaply and frequently, and with resources devoted to improving the depth and quality of the information collected, in contrast with the shallow information obtainable from censuses. Sampling is also used in other contexts—for example as quality control in manufacturing industry. Within social science its use as the basis of sampling methodology and *inferential statistics has contributed enormous improvements in the cost-effectiveness of empirical research.

There are two forms of sampling. In probability sampling, each unit in a population has a known probability of selection: for example, in a population with half women and half men, there is a 50% probability of selecting a woman. In non-probability sampling, the proportions of individuals in the population are not known. With probability sampling, probability statistics can be used to measure quantitatively the risk of drawing the wrong conclusion from samples of various sizes. It seems intuitively obvious that if one in two cases is randomly selected from a population, the risk of the half so selected being unrepresentative of the whole group is far lower than if one in fifty were selected. The higher sampling fraction of one in two must give more reliable information than the sampling fraction of one case in fifty. But the actual sample size is even more important in determining how representative the sample is. A sample of about 2500 persons has broadly the same reliability and representativeness, whether it comes from a population of 100 000 persons or one million persons. Samples of 2000–2500 are in fact the most common size for national samples, especially when a fairly narrow range of characteristics is being studied.

There are a variety of sample designs for probability sampling. A random sample, or simple random sample, is one in which each case has an equal chance (or equal probability) of selection, so that the techniques of probability statistics can then be applied to the resulting information. A common variation on this is the stratified random sample: the population being studied is first divided into sub-groups or strata, and random sampling is applied within the strata. For example, random sampling might be applied to both the male and female groups of a population of political representatives, but using a sampling fraction of one person in twenty from the numerous male group and a sampling fraction of one person in two from the relatively small female group. Another common variation is two-stage or multi-stage (also known as complex) sampling. For example, random sampling is first used to select a limited number of local areas for a survey, and then a second stage of random sampling is applied to selecting persons or households or companies within the random sample of areas. The two stages can be extended to three or more stages, if necessary, so long as the eventual sample remains large enough to support analysis. All these sampling designs use random sampling in the final selection process, producing a list of persons from the electoral register, household addresses, company names, or other cases which constitute the final issued sample. All of them must be included in the study, with no substitutions allowed. For this reason, interviewers working on a random sample survey will exert great effort to persuade potential respondents to participate in the study. Failure to achieve interviews with the complete sample can produce *non-response bias in the resulting data. The calculation of *sampling errors for complex sample designs is statistically far more complicated than in the case of simple random samples.

Once the sampling fraction and sample size are known, probability theory provides the basis for a whole range of statistical inferences to be made about the characteristics of the universe, from the observed characteristics of the sample drawn from it. Most of the relevant calculations and *significance tests are supplied in the SPSS software package. Statistics textbooks supply details of the underlying calculations.

Methods of non-probability sampling include the *snowballing technique and the use of a quota sample. In a quota sample, interviewers are instructed to achieve interviews with fixed numbers (quotas) of people with specified characteristics (age, sex, class, etc.). Selection of individuals continues until each quota is filled.

Good researchers bring a great deal of substantive knowledge to bear on assessing the *validity and *reliability of survey results, and they supplement statistical measures with other methods for increasing confidence in the reliability of sample survey results, and the interpretations placed on them. These methods include *triangulation; repeat surveys (as illustrated by *opinion polls); literature surveys which yield information on earlier *replications; as well as theoretical assessments. Statistical measures of reliability, association, or significance are not the same as assessments of the substantive importance of a result. Social surveys can sometimes be over-engineered, in seeking (for example) to establish whether the exact incidence of something is 31 per cent or 36 per cent, whereas in practice all that matters is whether it is about one-third.

sampling error The principal aim of any *sampling procedure is to obtain a sample which, subject to limitations of size, will reproduce the characteristics of the population being studied, especially those of immediate interest, as closely as possible. In practice two types of error will arise from any sampling procedure: first, sampling bias may arise in the way the selection is carried out; and second, random sampling error may arise in the sample obtained, due to chance differences between the members of the population included, or excluded, from the sample. Total sampling error in the sample issued for interviewing consists of these two taken together. The key difference between the two is that random sampling error decreases as the sample size is increased, whereas sampling bias is not eliminated or reduced in that way: it is a constant characteristic unless steps are taken to improve the quality of sample selection. An important source of sampling bias is a sampling frame (a list of the members of the total population of interest from which a sample for study is to be drawn) which does not in fact cover all of the intended population. For example, there may be systematic differences between people who do or do not enter themselves on the electoral register or own a telephone, so that lists of such persons are not completely representative of the adult population. Another source of bias is random sampling that is not in practice completely random, because the lists and records used as the sampling frame are not put together randomly, but presented in some systematic manner not known to the researcher using them. *See also* NON-RESPONSE.

sanction (social sanction) Any means by which conformity to socially approved standards is enforced. Sanctions can be positive (rewarding behaviour that conforms to wider expectations) or negative (punishing the various forms of deviance); and formal (as in legal restraints) or informal (for example verbal abuse). The term 'informal social controls' is sometimes applied to the last of these. As will be obvious, the list of possible sanctions in social interaction is huge, as is the range of their severity. Sanctions do not have to be activated to be effective; often the anticipation of reward or punishment is sufficient to ensure conformity. For example, in his famous article on *vocabularies of motive, C. Wright *Mills argued that the availability of a socially acceptable motivational account of behaviour was crucial to facilitating social action—and that, where such a rhetoric was lacking, the mere anticipation of probable sanctions (ranging from embarrassment to imprisonment) was often sufficient to restrain the behaviour in question. There is considerable latitude in the sociological interpretation of sanctions and their functioning. For example, *Marxists and *conflict theorists are likely to situate the terminology of sanctions in a conceptual context dominated by notions of *power and *social control, whereas *systems theorists and *normative functionalists will emphasize *socialization and maintenance of value *consensus.

sanskritization *See* CASTE.

Sapir-Whorf hypothesis This hypothesis of linguistic relativity argues that (to quote one of its authors) language 'is not merely a reproducing instrument for voicing ideas, but is itself a shaper of ideas, the programme and guide for the individual's meaningful activity'. In short, language determines (or shapes) our perceptions of reality. The classic literary example of this is the 'newspeak' of the *totalitarian rulers of George Orwell's 1984. The most famous commonly cited examples in social science are probably those of the Hanunoo, who have 92 names for rice, each conveying a different reality, and the Eskimo, who have over a hundred words for snow, though these overstatements have been questioned by later studies. What remains valid is the claim that fine differentiation permits cultures to see important facets of their society and environment more clearly and in different ways from others.

This is an important theory and there is broad truth in the argument that *language plays a role in shaping reality. But it should not be overstated and collapse into extreme *relativism: there seem also to be linguistic universals, or features common to every language; and words are often invented to reflect, rather than construct new phenomena in reality.

SAR Sample of Anonymized Records from the population and housing *census. This term was adopted in Britain instead of the term Public Use Samples (PUS) used in the USA and Public Use Microdata Files (PUMF) used in Canada for these types of anonymized *microdata tapes. Such data-sets are available for varying sizes of sample and for individual persons and, often separately, for families and/or households. Data are available for the most recent censuses and for 19th-century censuses for which the full manuscript records are already publicly available under the 100 years confidentiality rule.

Sartre, Jean-Paul (1905–80) A French *existentialist writer and philosopher who attempted to develop a *humanist critique of and philosophical foundation for *Marxism. His most accessible work of interest to the social sciences is *The Problem of Method* (1957) but see also *Being and Nothingness* (1943) and *The Critique of Dialectical Reason* (1960).

satisficing A term used in economic theory to describe how people make *rational choices between options open to them and within prevailing constraints. Herbert A. Simon (*Administrative Behaviour*, 1957) argued that decision-makers can rarely obtain and evaluate all the information which could be relevant to the making of a decision. Instead, they work with limited and simplified knowledge, to reach acceptable, compromise choices ('satisficing'), rather than pursue 'maximizing' or 'optimizing' strategies in which one particular objective is fully achieved. Satisficing is sometimes also referred to as a strategy of disjointed incrementalism.

The adoption of satisficing models instead of maximizing models of behaviour has been found useful in the theory of the firm and corporate behaviour. For example, to maximize its profits a firm needs complete information about its costs and revenues, which in practice is available only after the event. Satisficing models replace the search for the optimum outcome, which may be unattainable, with rules of thumb and compromises which work well enough. *See also* BOUNDED RATIONALITY; ORGANIZATION THEORY.

Saussure, Ferdinand de (1857–1913) A Swiss linguist who is generally considered to have been the founder of modern structural linguistics and, therefore, the grandfather of *structuralism. The revolutionary nature of Saussure's work only became clear somewhat fortuitously when, three years after his death, some of his former students published a book based upon notes they had taken in the course of his lectures. This is the text that has come down to us as *The Course in General Linguistics*.

According to the traditional representational theory, *language consists of humanly created and ceaselessly modified *symbols which name, and so may be understood more or less complicatedly and problematically to stand for, the things and happenings that humans wish to talk about.

Saussure deploys two sets of oppositions (*langue* versus *parole* and synchronic versus diachronic) in order to demarcate a rather different object of study: that is, not the diachronics (historical changes or dynamics) of *parole* (language in use), but the synchronics (system of relationships) of *langue*—or, the socially embedded, structural and tangible aspects of language, that explain its persistence and hence its capacity to serve as a medium of communication. The most common translation of *parole* is 'speech', but Saussure intended the term to apply to written language as well. *Langue* is often translated simply as 'language', but 'tongue' is more strictly accurate.

What persists, and how, is specified and explained by two further sets of oppositions: signified versus signifier, and syntagmatic versus associative (the latter of which is today usually termed paradigmatic). A 'signifier' is a differentiated graphic or sound image. A 'signified' is a differentiated item of thought or a mental image (note, not the thing or happening that the image might be about, which is commonly termed 'the referent'). Together, signifier and signified produce a 'sign', which according to Saussure is an 'unmotivated' or arbitrary combination which is the product of the syntagmatic and paradigmatic relations specific to a particular language. In this context, a syntagmatic relationship unites elements present in a speech chain, whereas paradigmatic relationships unite terms in a mnemonic series. Thus, in the syntagm (or sentence) 'I'm cold', the word 'cold' has a syntagmatic relationship with 'I'm', but a paradigmatic relationship with the words 'cool', 'chilly', and 'freezing'. To elaborate this thesis further, we may note that a sign gains value or meaning syntagmatically according to its linear position in *discourse, for example as determined by grammar; it also gains value paradigmatically according to what signs could have been substituted for it but were not (as determined, for example, by the nature of a particular lexicon).

In sum, for Saussure languages do not consist of individually created and recreated representations, but rather of signs that are the product of extra-individual structures or systems of differences (such as alphabets, grammars, and lexicons). This displacement of the individual from the centre of concern in the analysis of so manifestly social a phenomenon as language is the move that initiated the so-called structuralist revolution. As a result, there remains no better or more essential introduction to this revolution than Saussure's *Course*. Sadly, however, a large number of sociological advocates as well as critics of structuralism appear never to have read it, with the result that their writings are replete with confusions, especially over what is meant by the term 'signified'. *See also* SEMIOLOGY.

scales (scaling) A form of measurement technique based on the observation of supposed common cultural meanings or shared social interpretations. One common sociological use of this technique is to devise measures of social prestige or social standing through occupational scaling—as, for example, in the Hope-Goldthorpe scale of *occupational prestige (see J. H. Goldthorpe and K. Hope. *The Social Grading of Occupations*, 1974). However, the most frequent application of scaling techniques in sociology is probably in the measurement of *attitudes and *personality traits, in which field a number of specialist scaling techniques have been devised. *See also* AUTHORITARIAN PERSONALITY; MULTI-DIMENSIONAL SCALING; SEMANTIC DIFFERENTIAL.

scapegoat One blamed, punished, or *stigmatized for the misdeeds of others, after the classic atonement tale in Leviticus 16, in which one of two goats was sent into the wilderness after having the sins of the people symbolically placed upon it. Scapegoating theory has been developed in social science to examine the basis of *prejudice (as in the work of Gordon Allport), and is implicit in much deviance theory, especially *labelling theory and the work of Émile Durkheim on the functions of deviance. Thomas S. Szasz uses it in *The Manufacture of Madness* (1970) to explain the hostility towards the mentally ill.

Scheff, Thomas (1929–   ) An American sociologist who converted to sociology after a first degree in physics. Studying at the University of California,

Berkeley, where both Herbert Blumer and Erving Goffman were then located, he took a symbolic interactionist approach to social issues and has made major contributions to social psychology. His first book was the path-breaking and highly influential *Being Mentally Ill* (1966), which was widely read in relation to the work of Goffman and Becker on mental illness and deviance. Echoing some of the arguments of Laing and of Szasz, Scheff provided a more rigorous sociological account of the family and professional dynamics behind the generation of mental illness. He developed his work into a sociology of emotions, looking especially at shame, revenge, and similar emotions of collective significance in war, violence, and nationalism (*Microsociology: Emotion, discourse and Social Structure* 1990; *Bloody Revenge* 1994). Most recently he has been working on the expression of emotions in popular music, focusing on the uses of the language of 'love' and concluding that most songs relate more to jealousy, disappointment, and estrangement than they do to love. This has been published as *What's Love Got to Do With It? The Emotional World of Pop Songs* (2011).

Scheler, Max (1874–1928) Director of the Institute for Social Scientific Research and Professor of Philosophy at the University of Cologne from 1919, Scheler was important in the development of *phenomenology, the *sociology of knowledge, and the sociology of culture. Under the influence of Friedrich Nietzsche and Edmund Husserl, Scheler attempted to avoid the *relativism of the sociology of knowledge by adopting an *essentialist view of *human nature in his philosophical anthropology, which was also shaped by his own Roman Catholic beliefs. He recognized the plurality and relativism of belief systems but argued that human nature was universal. For Karl Marx's 'base/superstructure' metaphor Scheler substituted a 'life/spirit' dichotomy. He held a pessimistic view of modern industrial society, which he saw as a corruption of genuine values. His principal works were *Ressentiment* (1912), *The Nature of Sympathy* (1913), *Problems of a Sociology of Knowledge* (1926), and *Man's Place in Nature* (1928). Scheler's contribution to the sociology of knowledge has been unwarrantably neglected.

schism A break or division in a social group, especially in a *church or a *sect. Schisms are common in *evangelical Christian movements, where there is a special emphasis on conformity to orthodox belief and practice. Schism is also a common organizational problem in radical political movements.

schizophrenia A *psychosis, more broadly defined in the United States than Britain, typically characterized by delusions or hallucinations, usually developing in late adolescence, and regarded as paradigmatic of madness. The term was introduced in the early 20th century and applied to a condition identified in the mid-19th century as dementia praecox. Evidence indicates genetic predisposition but also the aetiological importance of *environment. Ronald *Laing, however, highlighted the family processes generating behaviour diagnosed as schizophrenic.

school (schooling) Both an institution and a method of education. A process of learning and management of socially approved knowledge, involving an approved *curriculum and pedagogy, paid professional educators, compulsory attendance of pupils, and school grouping.

school class A type of learning situation: a method by which *schools function as organization by grouping their pupils according to various pedagogic principles. Learning in school classes entails a clear status distinction between the pupil group, and one or more professionals (teachers, instructors, or lecturers), charged with providing education (that is, a legitimate *curriculum). Some of the most important insights into class interaction have come from the Durkheimian tradition, notably through the work of Basil Bernstein, emphasizing the cognitive impact of the hidden (as opposed to the visible) curriculum and pedagogy of the classroom. Ethnographic studies, influenced by *symbolic interactionism, have emphasized the roles and moral *careers of both teachers and pupils. Both groups create meanings about what is going on: for example, when pupil conformity is negotiated in exchange for relaxation of the demands of the official curriculum; or when *self-fulfilling *labels are attached to pupils and become the source of fixed behaviours and attainment. Sociologists from the mainstream traditions of sociology have tried to analyse the relation between such micro-processes and the reproduction of function and power on a macro level. A classic paper by Talcott Parsons stressed the progressive shift in classroom dynamics from the particularism of the elementary years (which supposedly mirrors the child's family) to the universalism of later stages (which anticipates the *labour market and *employment). More recently, Marxist writing in the United States and Britain, drawing on a range of historical, statistical, and ethnographic data, has claimed that classroom learning is mainly significant in socializing a docile labour force for capitalist industry. *See also* ELABORATED AND RESTRICTED SPEECH CODES.

school grouping An organizational constraint in mass education systems. So-called inter-school groupings define types of *schools and the relation between them. Intra-school grouping defines the internal allocation of pupils to *school classes. Conflicting school pedagogies in use typically cause grouping to vary by age, gender, *educability, or cultural factors such as religion and language.

Schreiner, Olive (1855–1920) Olive Schreiner was the best-known feminist theorist and writer of the 1880s through to the 1920s. Her writings sold in large numbers, were rapidly translated into numerous languages and reached wide audiences in Europe, North America, Russia, Japan, and China as well as Britain and southern Africa. Best known now for her novel *The Story of An African Farm*, Schreiner's writings spanned a number of conventionally separate genres (including the novel, short story, allegory, political essay, polemic and theoretical treatise, as well as some thousands of letters), which she crafted to produce a highly distinctive analytical 'voice'.

Schreiner developed a materially-based socialist and feminist analysis of 'labour' which led her to theorize social and economic change, divisions of labour in society and between women and men, and capitalism and imperialism, around innovative ideas about how—and by whom—economic and social value was produced. And she combined this with a keen analytic interest in interpersonal relations, between women as literally or politically sisters, between 'respectable' and sexually outcast women, between 'New Women' and so-called 'new men', and within the family. Her writings on economic and political life in South Africa critiqued British imperialism; provided a radical analysis of the relationship between 'race' and capital; opposed the South African War of 1899–1902 and emphasized its origins in imperialist provocation; supported federation rather than union as the form that the South African state should take; insisted on equal political rights for all and increasingly promoted those of black people; opposed the development of segregationist policies after the Union of South Africa in 1910; and recognized the importance of social movements in achieving greater social justice.

Schreiner's analysis of 'race' and racism changed from liberal patronage to a much more radical position. In *The Political Situation* she developed the idea of 'race parasitism', seeing whites in southern Africa as dependent on the labour of black people, and later she supported the embryonic African National Congress and black women resisters of early pass laws. In *Woman and Labour* and linked essays, Schreiner developed the parallels between 'race' and sex oppression, recognizing that capitalism and its divisions of labour for the first time make it possible for women to become economically completely unproductive and made dependent on men and analysing this as 'sex parasitism'.

She also theorized social care as fundamental to the production of value in social life, and perceived the people who did it (mainly women) as thereby learning a more ethical way of behaving. However, she is by no means a maternalist feminist, and in 'The dawn of civilisation' analysed human aggression and capacity for violence and warfare as equally shared between the sexes, albeit taking usually gendered forms. In addition, 'gender' was something Schreiner analysed (without using this actual term) in social constructionist terms. She strongly disagreed with the essentialism of the major precepts of Darwinism, and rejected the idea that biological sex determined *any* social behaviour, instead perceiving this as almost entirely responsive to social context.

Schreiner did not produce a programmatic or systematic body of feminist social theory. Instead, her work was produced *ad hoc* in response to particular circumstances, and might be written about in a range of genres. While this makes it difficult to evaluate her theorizing by the usual sociological criteria, it does mean that her work is still both fascinating and highly accessible. Her work is discussed in Liz Stanley, *Imperialism, Labour and the New Woman: Olive Schreiner's Social Theory* (2002).

Schumpeter, Joseph (1883–1950) A Moravian historical economist, whose interdisciplinary work addresses issues of interest to sociologists, and who taught throughout the Habsburg Empire, Germany, and the United States. Schumpeter himself saw sociology and economics as complementary disciplines, and often wrote about subjects which are today considered to lie within the province of the former, for example social class and imperialism.

Like both Karl Marx and Max *Weber, Schumpeter was interested in the origins and development of the *capitalist system, and attached similar importance to the profit-generating and risk-taking *entrepreneurs who pioneered new products and techniques. This, together with his interest in the links between *business cycle theory and capital formation, are characteristic features of the Austrian School of Economics—of which Schumpeter can therefore be seen as a direct descendant. His books included *Theory of Economic Development* (1912), *Business Cycles* (1939), and the best-selling *Capitalism, Socialism and Democracy* (1942). In the last of these, Schumpeter warned against both the tendency for entrepreneurs to be replaced by a more conservative class of industrial administrators, and the necessity of economic planning to encourage socialism. *See also* IMPERIALISM.

Schutz, Alfred (1899–1959) *See* INTERPRETATION; PHENOMENOLOGY.

science, sociology of A specialism, originating in the United States, which studies the normative and institutional arrangements that enable science to be carried out; or, as Robert Merton puts it, 'a subdivision of the sociology of knowledge, dealing . . . with the social environment of that particular kind of knowledge which springs from and returns to controlled experiment or controlled observation' (see 'Studies in the Sociology of Science', part 4 of his *Social Theory and Social Structure*, 1968). The best-known classic studies are those by Merton himself, who investigated the consequences of modernity for the development of science, including (for example) the effects of the rise of ascetic Protestantism and the spread of democratic ideals. Many of these investigations are gathered together in his *The Sociology of Science* (1973). During the 1970s it became conventional to distinguish this literature from the European (largely British) dominated 'sociology of scientific knowledge' (often referred to simply as 'SSK'), which is concerned more directly with what is counted as 'science'—and why. The content of scientific knowledge is largely ignored within the former approach, which tends to assume both universal standards of logic and rationality, and fixed points in the physical world and in Nature. Proponents of the latter view, on the other hand, initiated a *relativist revolution which drew attention to the *social construction of scientific knowledge—and claimed no access to a Truth or Reality beyond this human activity.

Not surprisingly these two traditions are often represented as being in competition or even opposition. The earlier American writers tended to be interested in how societies could be arranged so that truth would emerge. This focus (which is evident, for example, in B. Barber's *Science and the Social Order*, 1952) is perhaps best understood against the background of European *totalitarianism. The more recent British contributions ask how it is that certain conclusions about the physical and mathematical worlds are deemed to be correct in particular societies at certain times, and can therefore be seen as a manifestation of the wider *phenomenological revolution in the social sciences during the 1970s, a sociological parallel to the 'linguistic turn' in philosophy. (The writings of Ludwig Wittgenstein are a common source of inspiration.) This so-called 'strong programme' in the sociology of scientific knowledge is most closely associated with

David Bloor, Barry Barnes, Steve Shapin, and Andrew Pickering. Told in these terms, it is possible to see the European literature as a critical reaction against the traditional normative approach to the subject, however this undoubtedly exaggerates the *epistemological differences between the two research programmes. According to Harry Collins, for example, the relationship between the two is one of 'cognitive tangentiality with . . . an admixture of academic antagonism' (see 'The Sociology of Scientific Knowledge', *Annual Review of Sociology*, 1983). Certainly, practitioners working in the cognate fields of the philosophy of science and the history of science have addressed both literatures in more or less equal measure, in the former case to defend rational progress in science against the relativist critique, and in the latter to contribute historical case studies to the discussion and development of sociological theory. The contrast should therefore be seen very much as a heuristic device. Thomas S. Kuhn's (American) work on the relativistic implications of the concept of *paradigms shows that the boundary between the two approaches was by no means hard and fast.

Both traditions have sponsored substantial programmes of empirical research and vigorous theoretical discussion. For example, European researchers have investigated the mechanisms involved in producing scientific knowledge, and shown that merely following the rules for the conduct of 'proper science' does not fully explain the outcome of research, or how scientific controversies are resolved in practice. These sorts of studies usually involve both close familiarity with the technical details of the areas of science under investigation, and detailed *interviews with the members of particular scientific communities and networks, although a minority of researchers have adopted the anthropological technique of *participant observation (perhaps by working as a technician in a research laboratory). Researchers utilizing the former technique tend to focus on scientific accounts, notably the meaning that the actors give to their professional activities, whereas the anthropological approach encourages observations of scientific life and behaviour. In both cases, the final sociological report is itself often highly specialized, requiring considerable familiarity, on the part of the reader, with the scientific field under investigation. On the other hand, some sociological studies of scientific knowledge manage to be both engaging and revealing, as for example in the case of the many investigations of so-called 'fringe sciences' (such as parapsychology).

The best overview of this relatively small, but dynamic and well-organized sociological field, is Andrew Pickering's introduction to his *Science as Practice and Culture* (1992)—a volume which also contains a representative sampling of recent contributions by many of the leading contemporary practitioners. A highly readable collection of case studies is summarized and discussed in Harry Collins and Trevor Pinch, *The Golem: What Everybody Should Know about Science* (1993). Perhaps the most stimulating recent work in this area is that of Bruno Latour in *We have Never been Modern* (1991) and *Pandora's Hope* (1999).

scientific knowledge, sociology of *See* SCIENCE, SOCIOLOGY OF.

scientific management A leading example of *technicism and a theory of work behaviour based on the highly influential and controversial writings of

Frederick William Taylor (1856–1915). Taylorism sought to eradicate the industrial inefficiency and loss of leadership supposedly due to the growth in scale of enterprises and the *managerial revolution. It sought a new legitimacy and discipline for management by basing it on the authority of science—time-and-motion studies. The result would be a supposed mental revolution in which worker-management conflict would be replaced by: scientific redesign of supervision and work organization, including the celebrated notions of functional foremanship, and a thinking department to research into task performance; detailed study and fragmentation of individual tasks so as to identify the 'one best way' to be adopted by all workers; selection and motivation of workers to give systematic matching of tasks and abilities; and incentive payments to determine by scientific (implicitly incontestable) means 'a fair day's work for a fair day's pay'. In this way, individual economic reward was to be linked directly to task completion, as the only means of compelling workers to labour—the assumption being that, unlike management, workers are of limited intelligence, innately idle, and driven by a need for immediate gratification.

Scientific management was the beginning of systematic work study in industry, and impressed not only industrialists (notably Henry Ford) but also leading figures elsewhere, including Lenin. However, it was resisted strongly at grass-roots level by workers, trade unionists, and even managers, because of its very tight control of personal work-life. Taylor viewed workers as if they were, or ought to be, human extensions of industrial machinery. Scientific management (or 'Taylorism') ignores the nature of work as a social process, has a dehumanized view of workers, and treats work motivation in crude instrumental terms—defects later criticized by the '*Human Relations' school of industrial organization and organizational sociology. In recent sociological studies of the *labour process, a lively controversy has surrounded the question of whether Taylorism was unique, or expressed a general tendency for capitalism to divide mental from manual labour (*see* MANUAL VERSUS NON-MANUAL DISTINCTION).

scientific method *See* GEISTESWISSENSCHAFTEN and NATURWISSENSCHAFTEN; *METHODOLOGY; RESEARCH METHODS; SOCIAL SCIENCE.

scientific revolutions *See* PARADIGM.

Scottish Enlightenment An intense period of intellectual endeavour and activity that took place among the social and cultural elite of late 18th- and early 19th-century Scotland. It included such expressions as painting (Allan Ramsay, Henry Raeburn, and others), architecture (Robert Adam and his brothers John and William), literature (Robert Burns, Walter Scott, and others), and engineering (James Watt, Thomas Telford, John Rennie, and other builders of steam-engines, canals, and bridges). One prominent strand of thought concerned the study of people as social and sociable beings. This was the central interest of the philosophers of the Scottish Enlightenment, such as David Hume, Adam Smith, William Robertson, Adam Ferguson, and John Millar. These were the five leading literati of what may fairly be said to be a distinct 18th-century Scottish School of social philosophy that constitutes an important source of sociological thinking (see Charles Camic, *Experience and Enlightenment: Socialization for Cultural Change in Eighteenth-Century Scotland*, 1983).

The Scots were characterized by a common disagreement with the *Hobbesian premise that society arose out of a *social contract made by individuals as a means of self-preservation against each other's otherwise selfish passions. By contrast, they took it as axiomatic that people were naturally social, that their capacities were meaningless outside a social context, and that societies were the natural state of humanity. This view was underpinned by an *evolutionism, which saw humankind as having progressed from a 'rude' to a 'refined' condition, although they also offered the (rather sophisticated) view that this temporal movement did not necessarily imply betterment. A third characteristic of the Scottish School was its insistence that the study of society should be totalizing, dealing with 'all that people did in societies', from the holding of private property to the practice of music. Where the various luminaries disagreed with each other was in the attempt they then made to identify the few general principles by which one could order and systematize history.

It is generally recognized that the Scottish philosophers made an important independent contribution to the economic thought of the 19th century, to Marxist political economy, and to the development of the concept of the *bourgeoisie and its place in the *capitalist order. Ferguson was undoubtedly a forerunner of modern *conflict theory.

screening instruments Measuring instruments used in epidemiological studies and social surveys to screen for illness in community (non-patient) samples. The aim is to identify untreated illness; that is, illness independent of contact with a clinician. Many of the instruments use quite brief symptom checklists, often offering a general measure of health and ill-health, rather than of specific illnesses. Despite their deficiencies, measures such as the General Health Questionnaire (GHQ) are widely used in social research.

seasonal unemployment *See* UNEMPLOYMENT.

Second Industrial Revolution *See* INDUSTRIAL REVOLUTION.

Second World *See* THIRD WORLD.

secondary analysis Any further analysis of an existing data-set which presents interpretations, conclusions, or knowledge additional to, or different from, those presented in the first report on the data collection and its results. Some disciplines, such as economics and demography, rely almost entirely on data collected by others, especially *official statistics. With improved access to *microdata from major government *surveys, sociologists are also using secondary analysis of such data to complement, or replace, analysis of new data-sets (see C. Hakim, *Secondary Analysis in Social Research*, 1982).

(⊕) SEE WEB LINKS

- The UK Data Archive, incorporating Qualidata: the major archive of data-sets available for secondary analysis.

secondary groups *See* COOLEY.

second-order constructs *See* PHENOMENOLOGY.

sect (sectarianism) The sociology of religion developed a model of religious organization which is referred to as the 'church-sect typology'. As originally formulated by Max Weber (*The Sociology of Religion*, 1922) and Ernst Troeltsch (*The Social Teaching of the Christian Churches*, 1912), it was argued that the *church type attempted to embrace all members of a society on a universalistic basis. The church, as a result, is a large, bureaucratic organization with a ministry or priesthood. It develops a formal orthodoxy, ritualistic patterns of worship, and recruits its members through socialization rather than evangelical conversion. The church is in political terms accommodated to the state and in social terms predominantly conservative in its beliefs and social standing. By contrast, the sect is a small, evangelical group which recruits its members by conversion, and which adopts a radical stance towards the state and society. The medieval Roman Catholic Church was the principal example of a universalistic church; sects include Baptists, Quakers, and Methodists.

Contemporary sociologists have modified this typology by identifying the *denomination as an organization which is midway between the sect and the church, and by defining various sub-types of the sect. Bryan Wilson ('An Analysis of Sect Development', *American Sociological Review*, 1959) defined four different sub-types in terms of the various ways in which they rejected social values or were indifferent to secular society. These sub-types are the conversionist (such as the Salvation Army), the adventist or revolutionary sects (for example Jehovah's Witnesses), the introversionist or pietist sects (for instance Quakers), and the gnostic sects (such as Christian Science and New Thought sects). These sub-types have different beliefs, methods of recruitment, and attitudes towards the world. The processes of social change within these sects are thus very different. Wilson is also the author of the best recent account of sects (*The Social Dimensions of Sectarianism*, 1992). Many sociologists have added *cult to this typology of religious organizations.

sectoral cleavages *See* CONSUMPTION SECTORS.

secularization (secularization thesis) Secularization is the process whereby, especially in modern industrial societies, religious beliefs, practices, and institutions lose social significance. The decline of religion is measured by religious attendance, commitment to orthodox belief, support for organized religion in terms of payments, membership, and respect, and by the importance which religious activities such as festivals assume in social life. It is argued that, on these criteria, modern societies have gone through a process of secularization in the 20th century.

The secularization thesis maintains that secularization is an inevitable feature of the rise of *industrial society and the modernization of *culture. It is argued that modern science has made traditional belief less plausible; the pluralization of *life-worlds has broken the monopoly of religious *symbols; the *urbanization of society has created a world which is individualistic and *anomic; the erosion of family life has made religious institutions less relevant; and *technology has given people greater control over their environment, making the idea of an omnipotent God less relevant or plausible. In this sense, secularization is used as a measure of what Max Weber meant by the *rationalization of society.

Critics of the secularization thesis argue that it exaggerates the level of commitment to organized religion in pre-modern societies; implicitly equates secularization with the decline of *Christianity, and these two issues should be kept separate; underestimates the importance of *new religious movements in so-called secular societies; cannot easily explain important variations between industrial societies (such as the United States and Great Britain) in terms of the nature and rate of secularization; fails to consider the role of religion in *nationalist culture such as in Poland and Ireland; and overlooks secular alternatives to religion (such as *humanism) which may function like a religion without involving a belief in the sacred (see, for example, the works of D. Martin, such as his *The Religious and the Secular*, 1969, or *A General Theory of Secularization*, 1978).

Peter L. Berger (*The Social Reality of Religion*, 1969) has argued that human beings require a 'sacred canopy' in order to make sense of the world, because meaninglessness is a threat to our need for an orderly universe. Thomas Luckmann (*The Invisible Religion*, 1963) suggests that modern societies have an *invisible religion. Supporters of the secularization thesis, such as Bryan Wilson (see his *Religion in Sociological Perspective*, 1982) maintain that the diversity, plurality, and fragmentary nature of new religious movements, youth cultures, and counter cultures are in fact evidence of the church's loss of social authority. Where religion appears to flourish, for example in the United States, it is primarily as a channel for nationalist sentiments. Therefore, when sociologists examine the complex relationship between ideology, nationalism, and religious change, it is clear that there are many different patterns of secularization. *See also* CIVIL RELIGION.

segmentary societies *See* ACEPHALOUS.

segmented labour markets *See* LABOUR-MARKET SEGMENTATION.

segregated conjugal roles Segregated conjugal *roles are those in which the husband and wife have a clear differentiation of tasks and a considerable number of separate interests and activities. *Marriages where couples also have separate social ties and obligations tend to be less durable.

segregation Social processes that result in certain individuals or social groups being kept apart with little or no interaction between them. An almost universal type of segregation is achieved by separate public toilet facilities for men and women. The tendency for people with a common culture, nationality, race, language, occupation, religion, income level, or other common interests to group together in social or geographical space produces varying degrees of natural, voluntary, *de facto* segregation in patterns of private residence, business districts, educational institutions, clubs, leisure, and other activities.

Even when patterns of segregation appear to emerge naturally, state policy may seek to destroy them, in the interests of achieving greater social integration and related benefits. One example from the United States are the experiments with busing children to schools outside their home area in order to achieve more racially mixed school populations. Equal opportunities and anti-discrimination policies seek to reduce existing levels of job segregation by race or sex.

In other cases state policy actively imposes *de jure* segregation: that is, a form of segregation imposed by the state, enforcing the rigorous separation of persons or social groups, and backed by law. Certain Islamic states enforce the segregation of men and women in public places and even in private homes. From 1948 to 1991 the policy of apartheid in South Africa enforced the segregation of Whites and non-Whites in marriage, area of residence and employment, and in public and private services. See also COLEMAN REPORT.

selection effects *See* SAMPLE SELECTION BIAS.

selective versus universal benefits A major dispute concerning the organization of welfare regimes, addressing the issue of whether *welfare should be delivered selectively to those in need, or universally as claims that individuals make of each other as members of a community. Advocates of the former strategy argue that selective benefits are targeted towards those in greatest *need and therefore do most to relieve suffering. The advantage of the latter approach is claimed to be that it obviates the need for means testing: that is, provision of the benefit only after a bureaucratic (by implication demeaning) investigation and assessment of income and wealth which demonstrates need (usually in the form of inability to pay). Communitarians also argue that the universal approach has the effect of promoting social solidarity as against the individualistic sentiments of selective entitlement. However, making certain welfare goods and services universally available can have some unintended consequences, as for example when placing a ceiling on property rents simply discourages landlords from letting, or where security of tenure and rent subsidies in public-sector housing encourage people to stay in these properties irrespective of need. See also COLLECTIVISM.

self (the self) In sociology, the concept of self is most frequently held to derive from the philosophies of William James, Charles Cooley, and George Mead, and is the foundation of *symbolic interactionism. It highlights the reflective and reflexive ability of human beings to take themselves as objects of their own thought. For Mead, 'it is the self that makes the distinctively human society possible' (see *Mind, Self and Society*, 1934). In this work, a distinction is usually drawn between two aspects of the self: the 'I', which is spontaneous, inner, creative, and subjective; and the 'Me', which is the organized attitudes of others, connects to the wider society, is more social and determined. The 'Me' is often called the self-concept—how people see themselves through the eyes of others— and is much more amenable to study. The self evolves through *communication and *symbols, the child becoming increasingly capable of taking the role of others. Mead's discussion highlights this growth through the 'play', 'game', 'and generalized other' stages. The generalized other refers to the organized attitudes of the whole community, enabling people thereby to incorporate a sense of the overarching community values into their conception of self.

Among more recent writings on the self, those of Morris Rosenberg are particularly interesting, especially in relation to the study of *youth cultures (see, for example, the co-authored *Black and White Self-Esteem*, 1972). In *Conceiving the Self* (1979), Rosenberg differentiates the content, structure, dimensions, and boundaries of the 'self-concept', which is defined as 'the totality of the individual's thoughts and feelings having reference to himself as an object'. The content embraces 'social identities' (groups or statuses to which the individual is socially recognized as belonging, such as Black, female, or whatever) and 'dispositions' (tendencies to respond as a Black, female, and so forth, which the individual sees himself or herself as possessing). The relationship among the various social identities and dispositions gives the structure of the self. The attitudes and feeling one has about one's self are given on a series of dimensions (including salience, consistency, and stability). Rosenberg also distinguishes the extant self (our picture of what we are like); the desired self (what we would like to be like); and the presenting self (the way we present ourselves in a given situation). Finally, the boundaries of the self-concept refer to the so-called 'ego-extensions' to which it is applied, such as shame in one's humble origins, or pride in one's fashionable clothes.

The concept is also used in therapy, counselling, and psychology in somewhat different ways, highlighting the self as an inner need or potential. Social psychologists routinely deploy an armoury of associated and derived concepts, including self-awareness (focusing attention inward on one's self), self-conception (the view one has of one's 'real' self), self-disclosure (revealing one's 'true' self to another), self-images (transient concepts of self that change across situations), and self-perception (the processes by which individuals come to think about and know themselves). *See also* GOFFMAN; IDENTITY; MASLOW; SELF-ACTUALIZATION.

self-actualization The theory most associated with Abraham Maslow, who argues from his studies of well-functioning people that there is a hierarchy of human *needs, each having to be met before a person can achieve his or her full potential. In ascending order, the needs are physiological, security, love and belonging, esteem and status, and finally 'actualization': that is, the desire to become everything that one can become. Or, as Maslow puts it, 'What a person can be, he or she must be'. *See also* NEEDS, HIERARCHY OF.

self-fulfilling prophecy A concept introduced into sociology by Robert Merton (see his *Social Theory and Social Structure*, 1957), and allied to William Isaac *Thomas's earlier and famous theorem that 'when people define situations as real, they are real in their consequences'. Merton suggests the self-fulfilling prophecy is an important and basic process in society, arguing that 'in the beginning, a *false* definition of the situation evokes a new behaviour which makes the originally false conception come *true*. [It] perpetuates a reign of error'.

The logical converse of a self-fulfilling prophecy is the self-destroying prophecy: that is, a situation in which a prediction (including a sociological generalization) is undermined precisely because of widespread familiarity with the prediction or generalization itself. For example, predictions of crowd trouble at a sporting event may forestall the anticipated violence, if probable troublemakers foresee a huge police presence and therefore stay away from the venue. Note, however, that such predictions can equally well become self-fulfilling prophecies—as those likely to become involved in spectator violence are attracted by the publicity given to the event. No little sociological (and police) effort has been spared in the attempt to determine which is the more likely outcome in particular instances. *See also* UNINTENDED OR UNANTICIPATED CONSEQUENCES.

self-image *See* SELF.

self-management Any system of industrial production which attempts through worker councils, factory committee, or peer group supervision to place all or part of the management function in the hands of employees themselves. *See also* INDUSTRIAL DEMOCRACY.

self-perception *See* SELF.

self-psychology A development in American *psychoanalysis pioneered by H. Kohut (*The Analysis of the Self*, 1971) which shifts the focus of analysis from the ego to the self—basically one's sense of wholeness and togetherness. This means in practice an encouragement of narcissistic grandiosity which, it is argued, is able to modify itself as it comes into contact with the outside world. The therapist adopts an empathic rather than an analytic attitude to the patient. Daniel Stern, a developmental psychologist, has developed a theory of child development around these ideas which emphasizes the carer's ability to understand and communicate with the infant (*The Interpersonal World of the Infant*, 1985).

self-service economy An economy in which a large and increasing proportion of household expenditure is invested in durable goods (such as tools and machinery) which allow consumers to produce services for themselves (rather than buying the services as in a service economy). Two processes are said to be encouraging this trend in some advanced capitalist societies: technical innovation leading to cheaper and simpler capital machinery; and rising labour costs (see J. Gershuny, *After Industrial Society?*, 1978). *See also* INDUSTRIAL SECTOR; SERVICE INDUSTRIES.

semantic differential A method devised by C. E. Osgood and his colleagues to study the *connotative meaning of cultural objects, using a set of bipolar rating scales (for example sweet/sour, good/bad), in order to elicit data (see C. Osgood, G. Suci, and P. Tannenbaum, *The Measurement of Meaning*, 1957). When scales are intercorrelated and *factor analysed, three general components repeatedly appear, both for different objects and cross-culturally: evaluation, potency, and activity. The technique can be used to compare the responses of one individual to different objects, experiences, concepts, or whatever; and of groups of individuals to same stimuli. It has been used in a variety of settings including market research and therapy.

semantic reduction *See* REDUCTIONISM.

semantics That branch of the study of *symbols that deals primarily with the development of the meaning of words. Sometimes viewed as a branch of *linguistics, sometimes as a sister discipline, semantics attempts to study the attribution of meaning to words, and how these are combined to produce complex meaningful utterances; the nature of *meaning itself; and the difficulties people experience when meaning is confused or distorted. Semantics is a background influence in areas such as, for example, *ethnomethodology and *post-structuralism. *See also* MEAD; PIAGET.

semi-colonialism A term used, classically by Lenin and Mao Zedong (*see* MAOISM), to describe states that in the late 19th and early 20th centuries were penetrated by imperial capital, trade, and political influence, but that preserved their juridical independence. Examples include Persia, China, Thailand, Afghanistan, Yemen, and Ethiopia. Factors seen as enabling such countries to maintain their independence include the strength of indigenous states, geographical remoteness, lack of desirable resources, cultural and military resistance, and (most importantly) competition between Great Powers. Semi-colonial status often meant states avoided significant capitalist development. The term has sometimes been misapplied to Japan. *See also* COLONIALISM; NEO-COLONIALISM.

semiology (semiotics) The study of signs and sign systems. Charles Peirce proposed the term 'semiotics', while Ferdinand de Saussure proposed 'semiology'. However, Saussure's ideas have been the more influential and have come to be described by Peirce's term. This semiology owes much to the structural linguistics of *Saussure and developed as part of the upsurge of *structuralism during the 1970s. It proved especially attractive to sociologists interested in the analysis of *ideology—particularly those with a Marxist or feminist background.

The concept of the sign is taken from Saussure (*Course in General Linguistics*, 1916). It is seen as a combination of signifier (the material element, sound, or marks on paper) and signified (the concept with which the signifier is associated). The two are bound together like the two sides of a piece of paper. Saussure emphasized the conventional nature of signs. There is no necessary relationship between the sign and its referent; rather, the relationship is socially agreed. We could call our hands 'daffodils', and flowers 'hands', and nothing would change in the world: it is just that we commonly agree that the daffodil is a flower and the things at the end of our arms are hands. The meaning of any particular sign is defined by its relationship to other signs in the system. For example, we understand the meaning of 'up' in relation to the meaning of 'down', and cannot conceive of one without the other. Saussure's distinction between speech and tongue is also important: speech refers to individual speech-acts; language to the structure of signs out of which the speech-acts are formed.

The French structuralist literary critic Roland Barthes is one of the foremost proponents of semiology. Sociologically, his most important book has been *Mythologies* (1957), in which he subjected various apparently innocent aspects of French popular culture—for example wrestling and steak-and-chips—to a semiotic analysis which reveals their ideological content. Food, for example, may be seen as a language or code. Each item of food is a sign and there are socially agreed rules governing the combination of signs. In some cultures, for example, one does not combine sweet and savoury items. Barthes develops the concept of the sign to analyse what he regards as modern myths. A mythology occurs where one complete sign then becomes a signifier for something else. A picture of an eagle, for example, is at one level a picture of an eagle—a simple sign. On another level, however, it can represent the determination and toughness of the American nation. Similarly, different forms of food carry a meaning beyond the realm of mere nourishment: caviar and hamburgers are more than simply alternative things to eat. By and large this type of analysis is formal: it shows us how sign systems work but it needs to draw on other sociological ideas to connect those workings to wider social processes. *See also* LANGUAGE.

semi-periphery *World-systems theorists originally conceptualized global power relations in terms of core (metropolitan) capitalist states and their weaker underdeveloped dependants in the periphery. The concept of the semi-periphery was subsequently devised in recognition of the inadequacy of the bipolarity of the original formulation. It referred to those nation-states which were neither core nor peripheral but somewhere in between. These societies remained dependent, and to some extent underdeveloped, despite having achieved significant levels of industrialization.

semi-proletariat A wage labour-force that is not wholly dependent on the wage for economic subsistence. Typically this occurs where wage-workers retain access to land, working it themselves or via members of their family. The term also includes seasonal workers, who spend part of the year on peasant plots, and part working in the harvests for wages.

sensorimotor stage *See* PIAGET, JEAN.

serfdom This is a form of unfreedom, akin to *slavery but associated with *feudalism, principally in medieval Europe. This system of servitude, which tied particular tenants and their heirs, for life, to landlord masters through ties of fealty, was simultaneously a system of authority and economic adaptation.

serial monogamy *See* MONOGAMY.

service class A term first used by the Austro-Marxist Karl Renner (*Wandlungen der modernen Gesellschaft*, 1953) to describe employees in government (civil servants), private economic service (business administrators, managers, technical experts), and social services ('distributive agents of welfare'). Subsequently adopted by the British sociologist John H. Goldthorpe, to describe those whose employment relationship is based on a code of service rather than a labour contract, and so involves trust as a key element with autonomy as its corollary. In the so-called *Goldthorpe class schema, the service class (his Class I) therefore refers in the main to professional, senior administrative, and senior managerial employees, for whom autonomy and discretion are a necessary part of the work situation. Since the reference to 'service' can sometimes be misleading (members of the service class are not all employed in the service sector or *service industries) some writers prefer to translate Renner's concept as 'salariat'.

service industries A loosely defined group of labour-intensive economic activities centred around finance, sales, distribution (transport, retailing, whole-saling), and a plethora of businesses and professions giving personal care in various forms. Optimistic theories of *industrialization speak of the rise of a future service (or service-dominated) economy. More sanguine interpretations regard a large service sector as symptomatic of *deindustrialization or of the salience of finance over industrial *capital. *See also* INDUSTRIAL SECTOR.

service sector *See* INDUSTRIAL SECTOR; SERVICE INDUSTRIES.

sex discrimination *See* SEXISM.

sexism Sexism is discrimination on the basis of sex. It ranges from the blatant to the covert: as, for example, when a token woman is appointed so that an employer appears to be committed to a policy of equal opportunities. Sexism occurs at different levels, from the individual to the institutionalized, but all forms combine to preserve *inequality. Normally, sex discrimination operates against women and in favour of men (as, for example, in the case of access to privileged occupational positions), however the obverse is not entirely unknown.

sexism, institutionalized *See* INSTITUTIONALIZED DISCRIMINATION.

sex ratio Conventionally defined as the number of males per 1 000 females in the population of a society. More boys than girls are born each year, but the excess number of males at birth is gradually reduced by the higher male *mor-tality rate, to an age-point where the number of women begins to exceed the number of men. In most countries, the overall sex-ratio is below 1 000, with women outnumbering men. However, since the Second World War the sex ratio has been rising in many Western industrial societies, so that the excess of females is now confined to older age-groups. In Britain, for example, the cross-over point rose from age 25 in 1901–10 to age 47 in 1930–2 and to age 57 years in 1980–2. Due to improvements in health care, and the (relative) absence of wars, men now outnumber women for most of their lives in many countries. Other factors affecting the sex ratio are sex-selective migration patterns, and the female infan-ticide practised in countries where females are treated as socially inferior.

The sex ratio is regarded as an important social indicator. It affects marriage rates, women's labour-market participation rates, and (it has been argued) sex roles.

sex roles Until the 1970s this was the main way that sociology conceptualized the differences and relations between women and men, seeing them as a product of *socialization rather than biology. It has been subjected to the same criticisms as *role theory in general, but also because it masks power and inequality between the sexes.

Sex roles prescribe the different ways men and women are supposed to act and the different tasks they are expected to undertake. In advanced industrial societies, most women are found in the home or in service occupations, in other words in 'women's work'. Men spend their lives in a variety of careers outside the home and their work is often better paid and of higher status than that of women. Why do these sex-role differences occur? There are several competing theories. The biological and psychological perspectives emphasize inherent differences, which can range from genetic selection to biological tendencies that favour the nurturing qualities of women and the more aggressive and instrumental temperament of men. According to *functionalists, sex roles are complementary, and the male and female division of labour increases the stability of the family. This viewpoint has been criticized by feminist writers who emphasize the power aspect of traditional sex roles. Feminists assert that sex roles are essentially a way of keeping women subservient to men and are the result of a *patriarchal society in which men preserve their own self-interest by maintaining the status quo. Traditional women sometimes regard feminism with suspicion; however, in the main, both men and women's attitudes are shifting in favour of more *egalitarian sex roles. The evidence suggests, however, that sex-role behaviour is far more resistant to change. *See also* DOMESTIC DIVISION OF LABOUR; FEMININITY; LABOUR MARKET; MASCULINITY; ROLE, CONJUGAL; SEXUAL DIVISION OF LABOUR.

sex, sociology of The study of sexuality was not a major concern in sociology until late in the 20th century. None of the major figures in the discipline seems to have attached any importance to the topic as an area for research or analysis, though Georg Simmel produced some important essays. Instead, a number of disciplines other than sociology made it a particular focus, and from these sociologists simply borrowed relevant materials.

Three traditions seem particularly important in this context. The first is the biomedical, culminating in the laboratory tradition of Masters' and Johnson's sex laboratories. A second tradition is the psychoanalytic. Some of this writing has involved a sociological dimension, notably when considering the links between sexual drives, repression, and social order. Thus, in the works of Wilhelm Reich, Herbert Marcuse, and Norman O. Brown—loosely described as the 'Freudian Left'—sexuality has been seen as a major foundation for *social order. A third tradition is that of the social *survey, associated with the work of Kinsey. Here, wide-ranging surveys are conducted of people's sexual behaviour, or of 'who does what with whom, when and where'. This particular tradition has been very important for sociology: using survey techniques the frequencies of various sexual behaviours have been estimated; class, region, age, and gender correlations examined; and shifting patterns of sexuality throughout the latter part of the 20th century suggested. These three 'sexological' traditions have been intelligently discussed and analysed in Paul Robinson's *The Modernization of Sex* (1976) and Janice M. Irvine's *Disorders of Desire* (1990).

Whilst sociology has often drawn upon these external traditions it was not until the 1960s that the discipline as such began to develop a stance of its own. A major contribution will be found in the writings of John Gagnon (1931–2016) and William Simon (*Sexual Conduct*, 1973), and in similar studies contributing to the emergence of a new perspective on sexualities, a perspective that may be referred to as the constructionist view of sexuality. Gagnon and Simon both worked at the Kinsey Institute from the mid-1950s to the mid-1960s, but whilst conducting work in the survey tradition (primarily on sex offenders and homosexuality), they became increasingly disillusioned with the behavioural, biological, and atheoretical accounts of sexuality that dominated sexology. Starting to build the elements of a theory of sexuality that was sociological, they suggested that biology was no more important in the sexual sphere than any other, that the idea of powerful sex drives may well be a myth, and that human sexuality was open to a wide range of socio-cultural variation. They argued for a move away from a language dominated by biological metaphor to one which could see sexuality as symbolic and scripted.

In recent writings on sexuality, the influence of Michel Foucault, *feminism, and *social constructionism is obvious. Each of these is critical of the notion of 'sex as natural' and they have highlighted the ways in which sexuality and *gender are socially organized. See Jeffrey Weeks, *Sexuality and its Discontents: Meanings, Myths and Modern Sexualities* (1985) and Jeffrey Weeks, Janet Holland, and Matthew Waites (eds.), *Sexualities and Society: A Reader* (2003). *See also* HETEROSEXISM; HOMOSEXUALITY.

(⊕) SEE WEB LINKS

• Links provided by the Sociology of Sexualities section of the ASA.

sex-typed If certain attributes or pursuits are considered appropriate only for one sex then they are sex-typed. For example, computing science is becoming increasingly sex-typed, with few women entering the profession. In general, sex-typed behaviour is becoming less rigid, so that (for example) it is no longer considered unmanly to cry.

sexual division of labour A term referring to the specialized gender roles of male breadwinner and female housewife; or, in the terminology of Talcott Parsons (*Family, Socialisation and Interaction Process*, 1956), the 'instrumental' and 'expressive' roles. This particular division of labour by sex is usually associated with the separation of workplace from home which followed *industrialization in the West. Anthropological research shows that most pre-industrial societies also distinguish 'men's tasks' from 'women's tasks', although the sexual division of labour so identified may not correspond to the Western stereotype described above. For example, in some societies growing crops and weaving are tasks for women, whereas hunting and making pots are the responsibility of men. *See also* DIVISION OF LABOUR; DOMESTIC DIVISION OF LABOUR; SEX ROLES.

shamanism A term, originating from Siberia, used to describe diverse religious activities in a large number of technologically simple societies. The shaman is a part-time, non-institutionalized, *charismatic religious specialist whose power emanates from his or her perceived ability (often enhanced by mind-altering drugs) to contact external spiritual forces; and, through them, to prescribe solutions to technological, political, and social problems of their own society.

shanty towns Improvised housing settlements, usually but not exclusively associated with *Third World cities. Common characteristics include illegal occupancy of land (squatting); concentration on land of low economic value (such as riverbanks or rubbish-tips); self-built housing; overcrowding; a lack of public utilities and social services; and low-income households. Over time, individuals and neighbourhoods may improve their circumstances, introducing considerable variation within and between shanty towns.

share cropping The general term given to a variety of arrangements whereby landowners receive a portion of the harvest ('share of the crop') from those whom they allow to work their land. A classic example developed after the end of the Civil War in the United States. Freed Black slaves demanded their 'forty acres and a mule', and by 1868 share cropping was the dominant economic arrangement in southern agriculture.

Various explanations have been offered for the emergence of share cropping. One emphasizes favourable economic preconditions, such as a large class of landholders, combined with shortage of labour, and lack of incentives to mechanize. Neo-classical economists argue that share cropping is a rational market response advantageous to both sides. However, an alternative explanation suggests that this arrangement typically meets the preferences of neither party, and arises through a 'constriction of possibilities' and only when all other alternatives have been defeated. (In the American South, for example, Blacks wanted full economic independence while White plantation owners sought an equivalent to slave labour.)

For an excellent case study see Edward Royce, *The Origins of Southern Share-cropping* (1993). *See also* PEASANTS.

Shaw, Clifford (1896-1957) A *Chicago sociologist and pioneer of the *life-history method, who collected over 200 life-histories of delinquents during his time at the Institute of Juvenile Research, the most famous being *The Jack-Roller: A Delinquent Boy's Own Story* (1930)—subsequently re-studied by Jon Snodgrass in *The Jack-Roller at Seventy* (1982).

sib A term used in some American cultural anthropology texts to refer to any unilineal descent group—known elsewhere in anthropology as a *clan.

sick role A concept popularized by Talcott Parsons. He argued (in *The Social System*, 1951) that whilst disease involves bodily dysfunction, being sick—that is, being identified and accepted as ill—is a *role governed by social expectations, of which he listed four. First, exemption from normal social role responsibilities: this exemption must be legitimated by some authority, often a medical practitioner. Second, exemption from responsibility for being ill, which means that the sick must be looked after. Third, since sickness is deemed undesirable, the sick are obliged to want to get better; and also, fourthly, to seek technically competent help and cooperate in trying to get better.

The concept draws attention to the social regulation of illness: to the mechanisms that guarantee the compliance of sick persons, help to restore them to health, and ensure that only the genuinely sick are exempt from normal responsibilities. It also provides a means of analysing the motivational factors involved in illness. Indeed, Parsons suggested that because of these motivational components (he was influenced here by Freudian theorizing), illness could be considered a special form of *deviance, functional to the social system in directing deviant tendencies away from group formation, solidarity, and successful claims to legitimacy.

Critics have questioned the universality of Parsons's specification of the expectations governing the sick role, the extent to which illness is motivated, the model's relevance to long-term sickness, and his focus on what is functional for society. None the less, the concept of the sick role has been central to sociological thinking about health and illness, and its importance would be hard to overestimate.

sign (signs) *See* POST-STRUCTURALISM; SAUSSURE; SEMIOLOGY.

significance tests A variety of statistical techniques are used in empirical social research in order to establish whether a relationship between sample *variables may be extended to the *population from which the *sample was drawn. These techniques assess the rarity, unusualness, or unexpectedness of the results obtained. Significance tests are the technique of analysis by which statistical inferences concerning the relationship between two or more variables in a sample can be generalized to a population.

In using a significance test, the researcher aims to investigate whether interesting differences in the research results are due to *sampling error rather than to genuine differences in the population. If a significance test statistic lies within a range that has a very small probability of occurring by chance, then it can be assumed that the empirical findings are real or significant.

Significance tests offer various levels of significance or confidence, stating that a particular result would only occur by chance less than one in a thousand times, less than one in a hundred times, or less than one in twenty times. Depending on the degree of certainty required by the researcher, results at any of these levels might be accepted as significant, but the 'less than one chance in a thousand' level is regarded as the safest assurance that research results would so rarely arise by chance that they must be true reflections of the real world.

There are a large number of tests of significance and associated measures, including the z-score test, the t-test, the Mann-Whitney U-test, the chi-square test, and Spearman's rank correlation coefficient. These all have various purposes and those used by sociologists are provided by such packages as SPSS and SAS, but a textbook should be consulted to ensure a test appropriate to the data-set is chosen.

Statistical significance is not the same thing as the substantive importance of a research finding, which is determined by theory, policy perspectives, and other considerations. In effect, a research finding may be trivially small and relate to an unimportant subject, but still attain statistical significance. Consequently, some critics have argued that tests of statistical significance are often used unthinkingly and wrongly, and given undue weight in reports on research findings.

significant others This concept, which is derived from the Meadian theory of the *self, highlights the ability of social actors to take the role of others. There are many others whose roles may be taken—ranging from those of strangers to that of the whole community. Significant others are those who have an important influence or play a formative role in shaping the behaviour of another. Since Mead, the concept has entered general and even popular use, as in Armistead Maupin's novel *Significant Others*. In popular discussion it is often misused as a term to describe (partly ironically) a person's husband, wife, or partner.

signifier *See* POST-STRUCTURALISM; SAUSSURE; SEMIOLOGY.

Simmel, Georg (1858–1918) Simmel is generally considered to be the most neglected of the creators of modern sociology (although more so in Britain than in the United States). He published some twenty-five volumes and over three hundred essays during his lifetime. Born a Jew, but later baptized into Christianity, he spent most of his life in Berlin, gaining a full professorship at Strasburg only four years before his death. This late recognition of such a prolific scholar signposts his maverick nature—as well as a certain anti-semitism on the part of some of his peers. He was one of a number of talented artists, scholars, and intellectuals who would meet regularly at Max Weber's house in Heidelberg.

Simmel's work is almost impossible to summarize or systematize and he was himself opposed to such attempts. In many ways he is a sociologist who seems dismayed by the very possibility of sociology. His style and approach differs from that of the other classical sociologists by virtue of its fragmentary and piecemeal character. Simmel wrote short essays, vignettes of social life, rich and textured in their detail of the microscopic order, but wholly unsystematic and often unfinished. His range of inquiry was vast and varied: from books on Kant and Goethe, through studies of art and culture, and on to major analyses of religion, money, capitalism, gender, groups, urbanism, and morality. Even love is among his many topics. Details, rather than abstract generalization, are given prime position in Simmel's work: he argued that, whilst it was not possible to understand the whole or the totality in itself, any fragment of study may lead one to grasp the whole. Thus, in *The Philosophy of Money* (1900), he proclaims 'the possibility . . . of finding in each of life's details the totality of its meaning'. He saw this particular work as providing a more secure foundation for *historical materialism and he was a major influence on the work of the Marxist philosopher György *Lukács.

For Simmel there are three kinds of sociology. General sociology is a programme of method—'the whole of historical life in so far as it is formed societally'. Formal sociology studies 'the societal forms themselves'—the 'forms of sociation'. Finally, there is philosophical sociology, which he defines as 'the epistemology of the social sciences'. He wrote most often about the second of these, formal sociology, which is best seen as the centre of his enterprise. The 'forms of sociation' are the forms in which our interaction develops. (See the partial translation of his key work in K. Wolff (ed.), *The Sociology of Georg Simmel*

(1950).) His most famous short essays—'The Stranger', 'The Metropolis and Mental Life', and his essay on social conflict (all in D. N. Levine (ed.), *Georg Simmel on Individuality and Social Forms*, 1971)—are part of his formal sociology, and this is the sociology that has been most influential in the United States.

Simmel's work was enormously influential in the development of early North American sociology. He was an important mentor for Robert Park and other members of the *Chicago School. Some of Simmel's ideas may also be found in the functionalism of Robert Merton (particularly his *reference group theory and *role theory) and of Lewis Coser (notably his theory of social conflict).

Simmel came to see social forms as dominating the life process, as a form of alienation, and his development of his own very individual method—and indeed of the essay form itself—was an attempt to resist this. In this respect he has been likened to the impressionists in the world of art—constantly trying to create new forms which are closer to our experience of the flux of life. It is no surprise that he has been seen as a precursor of *postmodernism.

Almost any of David Frisby's numerous publications about Simmel give a good account of his sociological significance and relative neglect (see, for example, his *Georg Simmel*, 1984). *See also* FORMALISM; URBAN SOCIOLOGY.

simple commodity production This is a deductive Marxist concept which describes the production of commodities without surplus value: that is, without wage labour and capitalist profit. The definition is similar if not synonymous with *petty commodity production, although some Marxists argue that unlike the latter it is a logical, rather than a historical or empirical category. The term itself was more often used by Friedrich Engels than by Karl Marx himself.

situs A differentiation of *role or *status that is not associated with an evaluation of superiority or inferiority. *Clan memberships may be situs distinctions, as may *cohort distinctions, and even occupational sector—where, that is, the occupations are deemed to be of equal prestige and worth.

skewness A measure of asymmetry in frequency *distributions. The skew in a distribution is the degree to which frequencies trail towards extreme scores in one direction away from the majority of cases. Negative skew means cases trail to the left and positive skew involves trailing to the right. It is important to know the shape of a distribution in order to know what measures (for example of central tendency) can best describe it.

skill In everyday speech, skill means a relatively precise set of manual or mental techniques that, though they may depend on aptitude, have to be learned through training or schooling. Sociological work, though not denying this aspect of skill, is primarily concerned with the management of skill; that is, how skill is defined, constructed, and recognized. Since the publication of Harry Braverman's work in the 1970s, much scholarship has been devoted to examining Karl Marx's claim that 'valorization' in the capitalist *labour process requires a continual attempt to de-skill expensive forms of labour. *De-skilling means either the disintegration and mechanization of craft techniques; or a refusal adequately to recognize established or new capabilities still required of the worker. The latter is very common in women's employment. Many writers, Marxist and non-Marxist alike, argue that de-skilling is not inevitable. Workers, individually or through *trade unions, may resist mechanization, or insist that de-skilled processes are reserved for workers with established training, who continue to be paid a premium for their displaced skills. Also, employers may upgrade (or 'upskill') workers: because they wish to recognize and retain dependable or experienced workers; or to control and inhibit labour unrest; or because, notwithstanding Marx, the development of technology has created new skills in place of older ones. In any case, jobs may be de-skilled without necessarily implying the de-skilling of individual workers, or indeed the labour-force as a whole. A selection of empirical case studies are reported in Roger Penn et al. (eds.), *Skill and Occupational Change* (1994). *See also* ABILITY.

slavery Slavery may refer to a variety of forms of unfreedom, such as *serfdom and bonded labour. However, it is normally associated with chattel slavery, in which the human being is a thing to be bought or sold, and does not have the status of personhood. Chattel slavery is thus distinguished from other forms of slavery by its property dimension. Slaves are not paid for their labour or services (even in cases where they can handle money or economic transactions). Thus they can be regarded as instruments of production.

There are both historical and recent cases of enslavement of peoples conquered in warfare. In modern, early capitalist situations, chattel slavery was used as an efficient (or, more accurately, cheap) labour system by the planters and slave-owners of the Americas between the 15th and 19th centuries, with the labour supply ensured through the slave trade.

*Plantation slavery could only exist through a codified legal system and mechanisms for its enforcement. These modern slave systems also existed in mining enterprises and industrial production. In plantation slavery the slave is the property of the master. By contrast, in the enslavement of whole peoples by conquest, the slave becomes the property of the whole society. The difference rests in the fact that plantation slavery is found in state societies and conquest slavery in pre-state societies.

There is a huge literature documenting the history of slavery: see, for example, E. Fox-Genovese, *Fruits of Merchant Capital* (1983) and Robin Blackburn's major trilogy *The Making of New World Slavery* (1997), *The Overthrow of Colonial Slavery* (1988), and *American Crucible: Slavery, Emancipation and Human Rights* (2011). An important comparative study is Orlando Patterson, *Slavery and Social Death* (1983). *See also* COMPADRAZGO; PATRON-CLIENT RELATIONSHIP.

SEE WEB LINKS
- The International Slavery Museum, Liverpool.
- Slave narratives held in the US Library of Congress.

Small, Albion W. (1854–1926) An American sociologist, less known for his substantive contributions to sociology than for his role in establishing (in 1892) the prototypical and for many years the leading sociology department, at the University of Chicago. Founder of, and prolific contributor to, the *American*

Journal of Sociology (1895), he was responsible for publishing translations of Simmel's essays and the works of other European sociologists. He established close links between the Chicago sociologists and those in Germany. His publications include *General Sociology* (1907), *Adam Smith and Modern Sociology* (1907), and *The Meaning of the Social Sciences* (1910).

Smith, Adam (1723–90) An eminent Scottish philosopher and social theorist, Professor of Logic then Moral Philosophy at the University of Glasgow, whose influential publications include *The Theory of Moral Sentiments* (1759), *An Inquiry into the Nature and Causes of the Wealth of Nations* (1776), and *Essays on Philosophical Subjects* (1795).

Smith is best known as an economist—although even *The Wealth of Nations* is much more than simply a treatise on economic affairs. A total philosophy of society, rather than a narrowly economic perspective on social action, is suggested by passages such as the following: 'Commerce and manufactures gradually introduced order and good government, and with them, the liberty and security of individuals, among the inhabitants of the country, who had lived before almost in a continual state of war with their neighbours, and of servile dependency upon their superiors.'

Smith's exposition of the *division of labour (which precedes his analysis of prices, resources, and distribution) is concerned to show that it is by dividing the labour process into increasingly specialized roles that industry advances and nations become rich. The first three chapters of *The Wealth of Nations* locate the origins of the division of labour in the propensity peculiar to human nature 'to barter, to truck and to exchange'; explain how this is limited by the extent of markets; and observe its effects in massively increased production, as in the celebrated example of the manufacture of pins, such that ten people prepared to break this process down into its constituent eighteen parts will produce 48 000 pins in a day, whereas each working on their own could hope only to make a fraction of this total. In Smith's view, the division of labour increased production by increasing the dexterity of the worker, who was able to concentrate on fewer processes; by saving time, in making the concentration of the worker task-specific; and by encouraging the invention of labour-saving devices.

However, Smith was not blind to the deleterious effects of the division of labour, and accepted that, where individuals were confined to performing only one or two limited and repetitive operations, this could render them 'as stupid and ignorant as it is possible for a human character to become'. He advocated the expansion of education as a means by which governments could combat the atomization and alienation implicit in the advanced division of labour. Unlike later classical economists, he also envisages the state taking an active and wide-ranging part in the organization of social affairs, going beyond the mere provision of justice, defence, and public works. There is, therefore, an ambivalence in his writings that has tended to be overlooked by free-market economists (but see E. G. West, 'Adam Smith's Two Views of the Division of Labour', *Economics*, 1964).

Smith, Dorothy Edith (1926–   ) Born in England, she studied sociology at the London School of Economics and then carried out work for a PhD at the University of California, Berkeley, where she taught from 1946-66 and became involved in the early women's movement. She subsequently worked at the University of British Columbia and the University of Toronto and is currently based at the University of Victoria. Her earliest works were on issues of mental illness, where she applied a feminist perspective. Exploring the relations of feminism, Marxism, and symbolic interactionism, she produced the influential book *The Everyday World as Problematic* in 1987. Here she developed the basis of an approach to the sociology of knowledge that focused on the 'relations of ruling', which she saw as a more general term than the idea of class relations commonly employed. She argued that knowledge is socially constructed under relations that give authority to speak to certain people and deny this to others. She showed that mainstream knowledge has been constructed by male authority figures. The differential experiences of men and women are the bases for their differing views of the world and knowledge can be challenged only by challenging the power relations that underpin these differing experiences and perspectives on knowledge. The argument was fully developed in *The Conceptual Practices of Power* (1990). Her most recent work is *Institutional Ethnography* (2005), in which she expands on the methodological implications of her argument.

(⊕) SEE WEB LINKS
• Smith's own biographical reflections can be found at her website.

snowballing technique (snowball sample) Snowball samples begin from a core of known elements and are then increased by adding new elements given by members of the original sample. They are so called on the analogy of the increasing size of a snowball when rolled down a snow-covered slope. Such samples are often used where there is no available *sampling frame listing all the elements for the *population of interest, for example illicit drug-users. Hence snowball samples are not random and not statistically representative of the population under consideration. They are, therefore, not amenable to inferential statistical techniques.

social action *See* ACTION THEORY; AGENCY; INTERPRETATION; MEANING; SEQUENCE ANALYSIS; SOCIAL BEHAVIOURISM.

social administration The study of social arrangements and policies aimed at meeting social needs—especially state *welfare systems. Academic social administration has typically adopted a practical, problem-solving, reforming approach, frequently criticized as being empiricist, prescriptive, and narrow; theoretically informed approaches to welfare are now more common. However, as the processes of transferring responsibilities for public welfare from the state to the private sector proceed, public-sector directors and managers increasingly replace administrators, and in this context the term social administration sounds somewhat dated. The social administration approach to social policy is well represented by the work of Brian Abel-Smith, whose influential books include *A History of the Nursing Profession* (1960), *The Hospitals, 1800–1948* (1964), *The Poor and the Poorest* (1965), and *Value for Money in the Health Services* (1976).

social anthropology The study of the entire range of cultures and societies in the world, although originally the discipline tended to concentrate on non-Western and so-called primitive societies. There are significant overlaps with *sociology, but also important contrasts. Historically, sociology has tended to study Western societies, and this has generated methodological and theoretical (as well as substantive) differences between the two disciplines. Most importantly, Western sociologists, studying their own society, could take the context for granted before isolating specific aspects for hypotheses in empirical research. Social anthropologists, by contrast, could take nothing for granted, and developed a holistic (*see* INDIVIDUALISM) method without inappropriate hypotheses for an unpredictable context.

Anthropology grew out of a curiosity about other cultures as described in accounts by explorers, traders, and missionaries, from the late 15th century onwards. The discipline emerged as an organized intellectual pursuit from the mid-19th century, when learned societies were founded in France, the United States, England, and Germany. The earliest theories were *evolutionist. The British anthropologist Edward Tylor posited a theory of social evolution which suggested stages from animism (*see* TOTEMISM) to *religion and *monotheism. Other evolutionist theories of the 19th century claimed that *primitive societies were remnants of the distant past in a hierarchy of *progress. Seemingly incomprehensible customs were described as 'survivals'. By the end of the 19th century, social evolutionism and its controversial hierarchy of human groups was replaced by theories of *diffusion and migration. Similarities or differences between cultures were explained by the spread of influences from some cultures or by the movement of peoples. Diffusionists encouraged the cumulative collection of customs for universal comparisons, although it is now widely acknowledged that such comparisons are fraught with difficulties, since there can be few shared definitions for cross-cultural phenomena. In the early 20th century, Bronislaw Malinowski argued that customs should be explained in terms of their current *function, although post-war anthropologists have rejected the crudities of functionalism, preferring instead to interpret cultural practices in terms of their current meaning. Structuralists such as Claude Lévi-Strauss have suggested that similarities between some cultures are to be explained by the limited number of possibilities open to humanity rather than by direct contact between societies.

This transformation in anthropological theory has been accompanied by a revolution in research methods. The early tradition of armchair anthropology is well represented by the work of James Frazer, who attempted to synthesize others' disparate findings around the globe into a speculative theory of origins. Generally, however, professional anthropologists at the turn of the century moved from reliance on evidence from outsiders' accounts to that from their own expeditions. Franz *Boas visited the Canadian Eskimos; Charles Seligman (1873–1940) visited New Guinea. With few exceptions, the material was acquired through interpreters in standardized interviews, which risked problems of translation and the loss of unique insights from the people themselves. Malinowski has been credited with the fundamental shift in methods. By the mid-1920s, and following his example, anthropologists were encouraged to live for periods of one or more years among the peoples whose language they had to learn. Emphasis was on the interrelationship of different aspects of a culture or the social *structure, thus challenging speculative history, especially since there were often no written records. There was a move away from the sweeping comparison of isolated cultural traits to the intensive and holistic analysis of one culture by the specialist fieldworker.

In Britain contemporary social anthropology is separate from the specialized study of biological aspects of humanity. Physical anthropology has become concerned with palaeontology, genetics, and even primates. The physical and social dimensions of social anthropology were more closely linked in the 19th century, when it was mistakenly believed that existing primitive societies were lower down in a scale of social as well as physical evolution. British social anthropology is generally identified with figures such as Malinowski and A. R. Radcliffe-Brown, though the latter was equally happy to call himself a comparative sociologist. Both were influenced by Émile Durkheim, and although their functionalism has been largely discredited, they left a lasting legacy of studying societies holistically and systematically. Anthropologists from the British school tend to have produced monographs on the politics, kinship, religion, and economy of a specific society. Casual priority is not given to one sphere. Some Marxist anthropologists have given priority to the *mode of production. Others have elaborated the power of *ritual and *symbolism, although not necessarily rejecting the primacy of economic and power relations.

In the United States, by contrast, anthropology is still taught in universities as a unitary discipline. There, cultural anthropology is the closest equivalent to British social anthropology, and is identified with such names as *Boas, Ruth *Benedict, and Margaret *Mead. Elsewhere in Europe, ethnology embraces the geographical and historical, and has included folklore.

Modern social anthropology has developed an approach which is relevant for any area, Western or non-Western, and in ways which are distinctive. It challenges *ethnocentrism, being ready with cross-cultural comparisons, yet is alert to possible universals. The practice of long-term *participant observation is now standard. Social anthropology aims to make other cultures familiar, but it simultaneously makes the anthropologist's own culture strange, exposing the taken-for-granted as in need of explanation. The discipline moved long ago from an emphasis on pre-literate societies to literate ones and to areas with world religions. It has been extended more systematically to the study of *peasant and urban groups, to both the powerful and the powerless, and the full range of capitalist societies. After the independence struggles of former colonies, the Vietnam War, and the liberation politics of the late 1960s, anthropologists became more alert to the politics of research. A less economistic *Marxism influenced the study of pre-capitalist societies. A new *feminism fed into the critical study of *gender across cultures. Studies were made by Western anthropologists of *socialist and *communist societies. The number of non-Western and indigenous anthropologists increased. Greater use was made of historical records to enhance the study of oral traditions. The role of the anthropologist as detached observer has been seriously questioned and, in some cases, resolved by a greater self-awareness. *Racism has been clarified in contrast to ethnocentricism. Not only the content but also the style of writing have been open to experimentation. Literary traditions and the humanities are drawn on to enhance the recreation of cross-cultural experience. Meanwhile, others still emphasize the discipline's scientific status. There can be no unitary anthropology, given this multiplicity of approaches, but the discipline continues to flourish in universities throughout Europe and North America. Although sociology and social anthropology have been established as separate disciplines, the intellectual differences between them should not be overstated and the two may be regarded as comparable enterprises.

social area analysis A variant of *urban ecology associated with the work of Eshref Shevky and Wendell Bell and their associates (see especially E. Shevky and M. Williams, *The Social Areas of Los Angeles*, 1949, and E. Shevky and W. Bell, *Social Area Analysis*, 1955). The original formulation offered an almost wholly descriptive account of residential differentiation in urban Los Angeles, distinguishing its social areas in terms of three (by no means clearly constructed) indexes of social rank, degree of urbanization, and segregation. The subsequent theoretical rationale, which emerged during the later study of San Francisco, hinges on the key concept of societal 'scale'; that is, 'the number of people in relation and the intensity of these relations'. The results of increasing scale are then identified with Louis Wirth's propositions about *urbanism as a way of life. In the Shevky-Bell model, increasing societal scale is synonymous with the emergence of urban industrialized society, the prime mover for which is changes in the economy (caused, in turn, by technological innovation). In a later revision of the model, Dennis C. McElrath ('Societal Scale and Social Differentiation', in S. Greer (ed.), *The New Urbanization*, 1968) departs from this *economic determinism, attributing changes in scale to changes in industrial organization and the distribution of skills, on one hand, and the aggregation of population and redistribution of resources in favour of cities, on the other. A large number of studies employing the social area model—most of which take the validity of the basic scheme for granted—were conducted (mainly in the United States) during the 1950s and 1960s. Readers will have noticed—as did critics at the time—that, despite the aura of sophisticated quantitative analysis pervading this literature, many of the central concepts and causal relationships are ill-defined. The discussion of social trends accompanying *urbanization fails to explain why, or how, social differentiation actually occurs. Ultimately, the model fails to relate the effects of modernization to the axes of residential differentiation, and the latter have to be hitched to some other theory if they are to advance beyond the level of mere description. The best general account of the theory, which is now largely of historical interest only, is Duncan Timms's *The Urban Mosaic* (1971).

social behaviourism A term sometimes applied to the social theories of George Herbert *Mead. Mead wanted to distinguish his interest in social action—the observable activities of human beings—from the *behaviourism of contemporary psychologists such as John B. Watson. The latter attempted to exclude all reference to mental events and subjective experience (goals, cognitions, and such like) from explanations of human behaviour. For Watson and other behaviourists, these subjective experiences were epiphenomenal, and unnecessary for the scientific prediction of behaviour. Mead, by contrast, was interested in the role of communication in explaining social acts. In his social behaviourism, human beings are distinguished from other animals by their ability to imagine themselves in the place of the other, and so anticipate his or her response. Language, gesture, communication, and role-taking are thus central to the symbolic interaction by which the *self is constructed, and which forms the basis of social life.

social capital A concept originally devised by James Coleman to describe the types of relations that exist between individuals as located within both families and communities, and that are said to exert a strong influence on levels of educational achievement (see James S. Coleman and Thomas Hoffer, *Public and Private High Schools: The Impact of Communities*, 1987). The concept parallels those of physical and human capital in economics. Coleman and Hoffer argued that deficiencies in social capital—such as would follow from single-parenthood, decreased parental involvement with the child or with family activities, and low levels of interaction between adults and especially parents in local communities—were detrimental to development in *adolescence.

Coleman maintained that 'the social capital for a young person's development resides in the functional community, the actual social relationships that exist among parents, in the closure exhibited by this structure of relations, and in the parent's relations with the institutions of the community. Part of that social capital is the set of norms that develop in communities with a high degree of closure'. Closed networks, giving rise to functional communities, foster among children living therein such things as conformity to school norms, an interest in academic matters, and avoidance of deviance. Lack of interaction between parents and children, and between parents and other adults, fosters open networks, lack of communication, lack of adherence to and enforcement of norms and of family control, all of which reduces the probability of building up *human capital and increases opportunities for deviant behaviour.

It has been suggested that this argument represents a significant shift in Coleman's thinking about academic socialization from his earlier work. In his classic *The Adolescent Society* (1961), Coleman stresses the importance for *adolescence and educational achievement of the *youth cultures within schools, whereas the concept of social capital emphasized the out-of-school influence of the family as it interacts with the larger community. However, it has also been observed that it is possible to marry the two accounts, by considering the possibility that social capital (lack of parental monitoring, the decision to reside in particular neighbourhoods, and to establish ties with some but not other types of parents and institutions in the local community) exerts an indirect influence on peer-group selection among children; that is, that social capital is an indirect determinant of the *subcultures in which young people become involved, both in the community and at school.

S

More recently, the concept has been taken up by Robert Putnam (*Bowling Alone*, 2000) and used to describe the networks of relations that people are involved in by virtue of their membership in voluntary associations and their participation in informal activities. Putnam distinguishes the 'bonding' capital that reinforces exclusive interaction and homogeneity (kinship, community, locality) from the 'bridging' capital that brings different types of people together (voluntary associations, political activities, religious participation). Bonding is the basis of mechanical solidarity, while bridging promotes organic solidarity. Taking up the theme of Alexis de Tocqueville, Putnam argues that the total volume of social capital has been declining in America. Individuals are far less involved in voluntary associations and other forms of bridging relations than formerly and so there is a breakdown in *social solidarity. People engage in solitary activities in an individualized way and they no longer have the social relations that formerly sustained a sense of trust in and loyalty to the institutions of their society.

The idea has come to be used widely in empirical research, complementing *Bourdieu's idea of *cultural capital. A useful conceptual overview can be found in John Field's *Social Capital* (2003). *See also* CULTURAL CAPITAL; HUMAN CAPITAL.

social change *See* CHANGE.

social class *See* CLASS.

social constructionism Social constructionism is a general term sometimes applied to theories that emphasize the socially created nature of social life. Of course, in one sense all sociologists would argue this, so the term can easily become devoid of meaning. More specifically, however, the emphasis on social constructionism is usually traced back at least to the work of William Isaac Thomas and the *Chicago sociologists, as well as the *phenomenological sociologists and philosophers such as Alfred Schutz. Such approaches emphasize the idea that society is actively and creatively produced by human beings. They portray the world as made or invented—rather than merely given or taken for granted. Social worlds are interpretive nets woven by individuals and groups.

The term formally entered the sociological vocabulary through Peter Berger and Thomas Luckmann's *The Social Construction of Reality* (1966), which attempts an innovative synthesis of the ideas of Émile Durkheim and George Herbert *Mead. For Berger (1929-2017) and Luckmann (1927-2016), the basic features of social order are captured in the principle that 'Society is a human product. Society is an objective reality. Man is a social product'. Their major case study of social constructionism was religion (see Berger's *The Social Reality of Religion*, 1969), but at the same time the *labelling theory of deviance was being developed and popularized, suggesting in parallel fashion that deviance is socially constructed. Similarly, within the sociology of education, researchers were deploying arguments derived from the work of Mary Douglas and Basil Bernstein to the effect that educational knowledge was also socially constructed. From a number of somewhat different sources, therefore, the more general phraseology of constructionism emerged—

and the term lost much of its original distinctive meaning (as, for example, in G. Suttles, *The Social Construction of Community*, 1972).

In psychology, a linked term—constructivism—is often associated with the work of Jean Piaget, and refers to the process by which the cognitive structures that shape our knowledge of the world evolve through the interaction of environment and subject.

Social constructionism is often contrasted with so-called *essentialism because it moves away from the ideas of the naturally given or taken for granted and questions the social and historical roots of phenomena. *See also* EMOTION, SOCIOLOGY OF.

social contract A theory of social order that was popular in the 17th and 18th centuries, although the idea goes back to Plato. The social contract is an unwritten agreement between the state and its citizens, in which the relative rights and duties of each are expressed. Thomas Hobbes, John Locke, and Jean-Jacques Rousseau propounded three of the most famous contracts, each describing an ideal rather than a real distribution of power. Hobbes argued that security and order could only be achieved by a contract in which all citizens would give up all their individual powers to a central power (the Sovereign), in return for the protection of life and property. Locke suggested an almost opposite strategy of minimal and revocable government, his contract being grounded in the 'natural laws' of acquisitiveness and self-interest (a view which found its way almost unchanged into the American system of government); Rousseau imagined a contract requiring complete equality and democratic participation based on the expression of a 'General Will'. Social contract theory, because of its fanciful and imaginative nature, has not been congenial to modern social scientists. But it still raises many interesting questions about the nature and purpose of government, and the characteristics of the ideal society.

social control A term widely used in sociology to refer to the social processes by which the behaviour of individuals or groups is regulated. Since all societies have *norms and rules governing conduct (a society without some such norms is inconceivable) all equally have some mechanisms for ensuring conformity to those norms and for dealing with *deviance. Social control is consequently a pervasive feature of society, of interest to a broad range of sociologists having differing theoretical persuasions and substantive interests, and not just to sociologists of deviance. The sociological issue is not the existence of social control, but determining its precise nature, and identifying the mechanisms at work in particular social contexts. By whom is control exercised? What techniques of control are employed? How far can and do individuals or groups resist processes of social control? In whose *interests does control operate? The answers to such questions vary greatly. *Normative functionalists tend to suggest that social control is of value to society as a whole, since it is essential to the maintenance of *social order; others point to the sectional interests that are served in the process of social control, emphasizing the lack of normative consensus, the differences in *power that are involved, and the close linkage between power and control.

Analyses of the main forms of social control differ. A common distinction is between repressive or coercive forms of control—so-called hard techniques, including direct physical constraint—and the softer ideological forms of control that operate through the shaping of ideas, values, and attitudes. The former techniques are particularly characteristic of institutions such as the police and the military, the latter of institutions such as the *mass media. The best recent discussions of the topic are Stanley Cohen's *Visions of Social Control* (1988) and Jack P. Gibbs's *Control: Sociology's Central Notion* (1989). *See also* CRIMINOLOGY; CRIMINOLOGY, FEMINIST; FOUCAULT; SANCTION; TRUST AND DISTRUST.

Social Darwinism *See* DARWINISM.

social demography A field of study concerned with the analysis of how social and cultural factors are related to population characteristics. Its major focus is the impact of social and cultural factors on demographic features of society, such as patterns of marriage and childbearing, the age-structure of the population, life-expectancy, and so forth. In addition, however, social demography also encompasses examination of the social consequences of demographic change. Since the demographic characteristics of a society or social group are themselves social phenomena, and the immediate product of the social (but also biological) events of birth and death, in one sense the demographic study of any human population is a form of social demography. However, whereas *demography itself is primarily concerned with determining and measuring population characteristics and the interrelationship between demographic variables, social demographers seek to understand and explain these demographic patterns. In so doing they draw on the expertise of sociology as well as of demography.

The three main variables underlying population change are fertility, mortality, and migration, variables themselves associated with factors such as age at marriage, the proportions marrying, contraceptive use, levels and types of morbidity, rural-urban migration, and so forth. All receive attention from social demographers, who seek to understand these processes in terms of a range of standard social factors such as the levels and distribution of income, levels of education, the position of women, religion, and economic development. The possible linkages between variables are usually studied by means of social *survey and *correlational techniques. Regrettably, theorization in the field tends to be underdeveloped and restricted to simple models, and there is relatively little attention to *meaning. The way in which *culture may shape individuals' ideas and beliefs receives, with some significant exceptions, rather little attention. *Ethnographic techniques are little utilized. The result of this narrowness of approach is that social demography, like demography itself, remains relatively isolated from the mainstream of sociology.

social differentiation *See* STRUCTURAL DIFFERENTIATION.

social distance Refers to similarity or closeness based upon social *variables measured on *scales—as in some studies of *occupational mobility, or in the Bogardus social distance scale. The latter measures social distance by the willingness to allow various ethnic groups to degrees of intimacy (for example,

'Would you accept a [Saudi Arabian] as a member of your golf club?...as a husband to your daughter?'). Methods of *multi-dimensional scaling are often used to represent such social *space and distance. The term is also used in *network analysis to refer to the total number of links in the network that separate two individuals or groups.

social dynamics and social statics *See* COMTE.

social ecology *See* HUMAN ECOLOGY.

social engineering Planned social change and social development; the idea that governments can shape and manage key features of society, in much the same way as the economy is managed, assuming that adequate information on spontaneous trends is available through *social indicators and *social trends reports. For example, the extent of women's employment is clearly determined in part by government policy to promote or impede women's paid work. *See also* PIECEMEAL SOCIAL ENGINEERING.

social evolution *See* EVOLUTIONISM.

social exchange *See* RATIONAL CHOICE THEORY.

social fact Ways of thinking, feeling, and acting that are experienced by individuals as external and constraining, and that are general throughout a social group. The term originated with Émile Durkheim, who used it to refer to the objects of sociological analysis, as distinct from the facts studied by psychology or biology. Social facts include *roles, *institutions, monetary systems, *language, and the measurable rates of such activities as crime, suicide, and poverty. Durkheim gave particular emphasis to what he called *collective conscience and *collective representations. Social facts result from collectively elaborated and therefore authoritative rules, maxims, and practices, both religious and secular. They constitute practices of the group taken collectively and thus impose themselves and are internalized by the individual. Because they are collectively elaborated they are moral and therefore constrain individual behaviour. The interesting problem for sociologists concerns the gap between the ideal representations and the material social organizations and their constituent actions— as, for example, between the socially approved norms and the actual practice. The characteristics of social facts have been interestingly explored in Margaret Gilbert's *On Social Facts* (1989).

social fluidity *See* FEATHERMAN-JONES-HAUSER HYPOTHESIS; MOBILITY, SOCIAL; ODDS RATIO.

social forecasting An approach to social theory that attempts to outline the probabilities of a range of historical tendencies. The classic example is Daniel Bell's *The Coming of Post-Industrial Society* (1973), which carries the subtitle 'A Venture in Social Forecasting'. Bell distinguishes his enterprise from earlier (discredited) attempts to formalize rules of prediction pertaining to particular social circumstances. Social forecasting, by contrast, attempts only to outline probabilities, and is possible only where 'there are regularities and recurrences of phenomena'; or where there are trends whose direction 'can be plotted within statistical time-series or be formulated as historical tendencies'; and where 'one can assume a high degree of rationality on the part of the men who influence events'. Since (as Bell admits) these conditions rarely obtain, social forecasters are often restricted to specifying the constraints within which certain policy decisions can be made effective, rather than predicting the results of particular decisions.

social formation A Marxist concept, largely synonymous with 'society', that refers to the institutional context which provides the conditions of existence of the *mode of production. The term was devised by the structuralist Marxist Louis *Althusser as a substitute for society, because he thought that the latter was too strongly marked by what he regarded as pre-Marxist humanist conceptions of social life as being (ultimately) the product of individual human beings. For this reason, its presence in a text normally indicates that the author works with a *structuralist conception of social life, according to which social relations as such—rather than their bearers—are what determine what happens within societies. (It is worth noting that Marx himself rarely used the term.) For Althusser, a social formation is a complex of concrete economic, political, and ideological relations, bound together and given their particular character as capitalist, feudal, or whatever by the fact that the economic relations are, in his words, 'determinant in the last instance'. Many of those who continue to use the term now reject this residual *reductionism.

social geography See HUMAN GEOGRAPHY.

social group See DYAD; GROUP; TRIAD.

social history Any study of the past which emphasizes predominantly 'social' concerns. Since much modern social history deals with the very recent past there is considerable overlap with the substantive concerns of *sociologists.

As a recognizable specialism, social history blossomed during the 1960s and 1970s, a self-conscious reaction against what was taken to be the elitism of established practice in political and economic history. For many practitioners, the new social history was synonymous with 'expressing the voice of the common people', and this is reflected in the rapid expansion of interest in the values, lifestyles, and everyday experiences of ordinary men and women. This new substantive terrain was explored by an expanded range of methods and techniques (including, for example, those of *oral history) and an explicit attention to theory. A proliferation of new journals (for example, *Social History, History Workshop Journal, Journal of Social History, Journal of Interdisciplinary History*) sprang up to act as outlets for the new materials uncovered in this way. Important general statements can be found in the work of Peter Burke, most notably *History and Social Theory* (1992).

A significant minority of social historians themselves have voiced concerns about the extent to which their speciality has rapidly become diluted by indiscriminate importing of concepts, theories, and methods from cognate disciplines (notably sociology). For example, among other complaints it has been alleged that too much contemporary social history is itself empiricist, and consists merely of mindless accumulation of data on a particular subject of popular concern merely because these data exist, rather than the pursuit of interesting historical problems or questions; that the obsession with model-building has led to indiscriminate application of (what are recognized elsewhere to be) problematic concepts and arguments derived from *functionalism, *modernization theory, *structuralism, and so forth; that the significance of political and economics factors has been lost and that there is a widespread tendency to make unsubstantiated (usually trite) generalizations about the 'mentality' or 'collective mind' of the masses during some (usually ill-defined) period of interest. In short, for some critics at least, contemporary social history has become a sort of retrospective cultural anthropology, with a premium placed on the use of exotic sources and grandiose (often untestable) generalizations. (For a bad-tempered and polemical—but none the less telling—critique along these lines see T. Judt, 'A Clown in Regal Purple: Social History and the Historians', *History Workshop Journal*, 1979.)

However, this is surely to paint too negative a picture of what is undoubtedly a growing and dynamic interdisciplinary area, having some overlap with, and being of considerable relevance to, sociology itself. A much more positive picture of the methods of social history is painted in Arthur Stinchcombe's *Theoretical Methods in Social History* (1978). Of direct relevance to sociology are the large number of excellent social histories of working-class culture (see, for example, W. H. Sewell, *Work and Revolution in France*, 1980; J. Cumbler, *Working Class Community in Industrial America*, 1979; A. Dawley, *Class and Community: The Industrial Revolution in Lynn*, 1976); of politics and class formation (R. Aminzade, *Class, Politics and Early Industrial Capitalism*, 1981; D. Montgomery, *Worker's Control in America*, 1979; J. W. Scott, *The Glassworkers of Carmaux*, 1974); of the formation of nation-states (V. G. Kiernan, 'State and Nation in Western Europe', *Past and Present*, 1965; A. Ludke, 'The Role of State Violence in the Period of Transition to Capitalism', *Social History*, 1979; H. Rosenberg, *Bureaucracy, Aristocracy and Autocracy*, 1958); and of social change and the family (T. K. Haraven, 'Modernization and Family History', *Signs*, 1976; D. Levine, *Family Formation in an Age of Nascent Capitalism*, 1976; J. Scott and L. Tilly, *Women, Work and Family*, 1978). Feminist social historians have been particularly influential and have moved women's history well up the research agenda (see, for example, the excellent studies by S. O. Rose, *Limited Livelihoods*, 1992, and L. Davidoff and C. Hall, *Family Fortunes*, 1987). In all of this it is, of course, a moot point where social history ends and sociology—especially *historical sociology—begins.

social indicators Easily identified features of a society which can be measured, which vary over time, and are taken as revealing some underlying aspect of social reality. For example, the Retail Prices Index is used as a measure of *inflation, which in turn is taken as a key indicator of economic performance. In general, the most commonly used indicators are derived from *official statistics, and include *unemployment figures, health and *mortality data, and *crime-rates. Quite frequently social indicators are used to assess the extent to which a society is 'progressing'. Similarly they can be used to predict what might happen. For these reasons, social indicators are an important aspect of policy-related studies, and are widely used by governments. There is a well-defined area of research and a specialist scientific journal dedicated to the derivation and discussion of satisfactory social indicators. *See also* INDEX.

social inequality *See* INEQUALITY.

social institution *See* INSTITUTION.

social insurance A state-administered system of contributions-based income-maintenance cover for unemployment, sickness, and retirements, and occasionally other events too. Systems vary between local and national states: some are funded through general taxation as well as contributions; income maintenance payments are often for fixed durations rather than indefinite periods; most systems have eligibility requirements, in addition to a contributions record, which serve to exclude many women and young people.

social integration *See* SYSTEM INTEGRATION AND SOCIAL INTEGRATION.

social interaction *See* ACTION THEORY; DRAMATURGY; FORMALISM; NEGOTI-ATED ORDER; SEQUENCE ANALYSIS; SOCIAL INTEGRATION AND SYSTEM INTEGRA-TION; SYMBOLIC INTERACTIONISM.

social media Networked database platforms that combine public with personal communication. The earliest use of the term was in 2004 when it was coined as a marketing tool for a business conference in California. As a result, its uses in academic literature are still contested and often imprecise, as researchers attempt retrospectively to repurpose a slogan as a theoretical concept that can explain emerging and fast-developing communication practices. Like the related term *Web 2.0*, the term *social media* was an attempt to describe certain common features of emerging web-based media and technology platforms and their business models, and it is now generally taken to refer to profile-based platforms such as *Facebook, LinkedIn*, and *Twitter*. However, the term also draws attention to broader shifts in everyday communicative practices and expectations in the media environment. Social media blur the distinction between the broadcast model of public messages sent to nobody in particular, and personal mediated communication between specific individuals, such as phone calls, email, letters, or text messages. Social media allow people to say or make things, to share those things with others, and for that sharing to be visible to still others. The relationships and experiences of the individual user thus take on a public quality, while more familiar forms of media content become the focus of personal communication which is visible to others.

The term originally emphasized connectivity between users, and also between those users and the Web-based platforms. Social media tools allow users to participate in communication networks and to establish their own networks of relationships, connections, friends, or colleagues with whom they can interact through these services. Communication can flow in multiple directions between multiple combinations of people, although it may be misleading to use the phrase many-to-many communication, as the numbers involved in a given communicative event may be quite small. A key tension surrounding social media derives from the kind of network topology used by some of the largest such platforms. The Internet itself is a distributed, end-to-end network, like the road system or the electricity grid. This has been an important driver of innovation and adoption, as anyone with the necessary skills and resources is able to add to the Net without negotiating with some central authority or remaking the overall infrastructure of the network. But the biggest and most significant social media platforms are centralized networks that run on the larger end-to-end network of the net. All communication between two users of *Facebook*, for example, has to go through 'Facebook', a closed and centralized proprietary network of a type that some critics—including web inventor Tim Berners-Lee— contend is establishing itself as a replacement for the more open end-to-end Net.

Acts of sharing are central to social media, not the output, in the same way that creativity is the input in the creative industries. Social media platforms are built around a particular conception of the database. The business model is to sell uses of their users' personal information and data to other businesses, and to have the users build the database by using the service: every time a user posts a video, likes a photo, searches for a product or sends a message to a friend, this interaction becomes a new part of the database and adds to its value for the company. Social media firms are business-to-business enterprises, whose users are not the customers but the product. The bigger the database, the more value it has, so users are prompted to share more—images and ideas; emotions and opinions—which make the platform more valuable. This has resulted in a series of controversies about privacy and visibility, which stem from users being positioned by social media services to share ever-more access to their data and information, at times in ways which have confused or surprised significant numbers of those users.

Social media firms are media companies that do not themselves produce media content. Rather, they provide a platform for others to do so. In some cases, this is the basic service offered, in the way that a photo-based social media tool allows its users to upload photos. In other cases, it is a much larger and more complex set of products and services, built around the provision of an Application Programming Interface (API) that allows third-party software developers to produce add-on services, such as games, to run on the platform provided by the social media firm.

social mobility *See* MOBILITY, SOCIAL.

social movements An organized effort by a significant number of people to change (or resist change in) some major aspect or aspects of society. The term was first used by *Saint-Simon in France at the turn of the 18th century, to characterize the movements of social protest that emerged there and later elsewhere, and was applied to new political forces opposed to the status quo.

Nowadays, it is used most commonly with reference to groups and organizations outside the mainstream of the political system. These movements, often now abbreviated to NSMs (New Social Movements), in the latter decades of the 20th century became an increasingly important source of political change. Sociologists have usually been concerned to study the origins of such movements, their sources of recruitment, organizational dynamics, and their impact upon society.

Social movements are purposeful and organized forms of *collective behaviour. Examples of social movements would include those supporting civil rights, gay rights, trade unionism, environmentalism, and feminism. Examples of collective behaviour would include riots, fads and crazes, panics, cultic religions, rumours, and mass delusions. Social movements are one of the basic elements of a living *democracy, and may be catalysts of democracy and change in authoritarian societies.

Social movements are not themselves formal organizations or *political parties, but are looser networks of individuals and groups that may embrace a number of such organizations (see Mario Diani, 'The Concept of Social Movement', *Sociological Review*, 1992). Thus, a labour movement may embrace various trades unions, cooperatives, socialist parties, and working men's clubs, without being reducible to any of these. Individuals, groups, and organizations that comprise a social movement are united by their common goals and concerns and their involvement in common action. They operate outside the regular political channels of society, but may penetrate quite deeply into political power circles as *interest groups. Their goals may be as narrow as legalizing marijuana, or as broad as destroying the *hegemony of the capitalist world system; they may be revolutionary or reformist; but they have in common the active organization of a group of citizens to change the status quo in some way. Under the broad banner of a social movement (such as for example 'the peace movement') many individual social movement organizations (SMOs) may operate in a relatively independent way, sometimes causing confusion and conflict within the movement itself.

An early typology of social movements, developed by David F. Aberle (*The Peyote Religion among the Navaho*, 1966), classifies social movements along two dimensions: the locus of change sought (society or individuals), and the amount of change sought (partial or total). The four categories derived from this classification are transformative, reformative, redemptive, and alternative. These are (respectively) movements which aim at the complete restructuring of society (for example *millenarian movements); those which attempt to reform some limited aspects of the existing order (such as nuclear disarmament groups); movements which seek to lead members away from a corrupt way of life (as in the case of many religious sectarian groups); and, finally, those which aim to change only particular traits of the individual member (for example Alcoholics Anonymous). The first two of these are therefore aimed at changing (all or part of) society; the latter pair at changing the behaviour only of individual members.

The dramatic visibility of social movements, and their challenge to the mainstream of society, has made them an object of great sociological interest. Many studies have focused on their expressive and irrational qualities, emphasizing the pathological elements of social movements, as for example in Eric Hoffer's *The True Believer* (1951) and Theodor Adorno et al.'s *The Authoritarian Personality* (1950). The wave of non-violent, largely middle-class social movements in the 1960s and 1970s produced more positive lines of research and analysis. Great attention was paid to the objective and subjective conditions of social movement activity: many theorists like Seymour Martin Lipset blamed the alienating conditions of mass society. Marxists and neo-Marxists proposed new forms of class division and class conflict as underlying causes. Others explored the effects of *relative deprivation and rising expectations on the mobilization of citizens. Still other studies followed the stages of social movement development, from the initial recognition of a grievance to the fully developed movement organization: Neil Smelser's 'value added theory' remains a classic of this type (see *Theory of Collective Behaviour*, 1963). In his account, six sequential determinants of development are identified, each one progressively narrowing the range of possible outcomes. These determinants are structural conduciveness (the broadest social conditions necessary for the movement to occur); structural strain (a sense of injustice or malaise); the growth and spread of a generalized belief (such as an ideology which offers answers to people's problems); precipitating factors (events that trigger action); mobilization of participants for action (for example via conversion); and, finally, the operation of social control. In the 1970s still more detailed evidence of social movement dynamics came through multivariate analysis (T. Gurr, *Why Men Rebel*, 1970).

'Resource mobilization' theories of social movements are particularly influential in North America, while 'identity-oriented' theories are more common in Western Europe. The former is exemplified in the work of Mayer N. Zald and John D. McCarthy (*The Dynamics of Social Movements*, 1979), who discuss movements as organizations, and focus especially on the needs of such organizations to mobilize resources. These theories investigate the range of resources that have to be mobilized by groups, examine the ways in which such resources are deployed, and consider the actions by which authorities may attempt to limit such resources. Within this perspective, the term 'resources' takes on a wide array of meanings, including economic resources, ideologies, rhetoric, and symbols. Factors like leadership, communications networks, available time, money, and business or political connections are seen as crucial in explaining the growth and success or failure of social movements. Identity-oriented theories, by contrast, see social movements as a special type of social conflict which is at the heart of modern society and social change. Thus, according to the French sociologist Alan Touraine, 'the concept of social movement [should be] at the centre of sociology' (*The Return of the Actor*, 1988). This perspective sees social movements as the central groups in the new social politics and realignments (for example the Women's Movement, and the Ecological Movement) and as sources of new political identities. Indeed, Touraine's method of intervention not only treats social movements as one of the most fundamental forms of citizen action, but also requires that sociologists join the action not just to study but to encourage it. Few British or American sociologists have followed Touraine into this delicate territory, and most sociology of social movements involves the *objective analysis of organizations and political processes.

social network *See* NETWORK; ANALYSIS.

social order Explanations of social order, of how and why societies cohere, are the central concern of *sociology. The 'Hobbesian problem of order', for example, preoccupied those classical sociologists faced directly with the apparent consequences of *industrialization and *urbanization: the demise of *community, disruption of primary social relationships, loss of authority on the part of traditional agencies of *social control, and general instability associated with rapid social *change in the 19th century.

There are essentially two types of explanation of social order, which can be linked with the names of Émile Durkheim on one hand, and Karl Marx on the other. The former, associated also with Talcott Parsons and the *functionalist school of thought, focuses on the role of shared *norms and *values in maintaining cohesion in society. For Durkheim, this emphasis arose out of his critique of *utilitarian social thought, popular especially among social and political theorists such as Herbert Spencer in Britain, who focused on mutual self-interest and contractual agreements as the basis of social order in increasingly complex industrial societies. For Durkheim, by comparison, questions of morality were central to the explanation of social integration. In his view, the 'mechanical solidarity' of pre-industrial societies rested on shared beliefs and values, located primarily in the *conscience collective*. However, the advent of industrial society sees the emergence of a new form of 'organic solidarity', based on interdependence arising out of *socialization and differentiation (*see* STRUCTURAL DIFFERENTIATION). Moral restraints on egoism arise out of association and form the basis of social cohesion. While Durkheim did not deny the existence of *conflict and the use of force, especially in periods of rapid social change, Parsons underlined the importance of a prior moral consensus as a necessary pre-condition for social order. He saw organic solidarity as a modified form of the *conscience collective* and argued that the acceptance of values by the internalization of norms is the basis of integration and social order in modern societies. Because of the importance which he attached to a shared body of norms and values, Parsons was persistently criticized for over-emphasizing consensus, and for neglecting conflict and change in his sociological analyses.

The second explanation of social order derives from the Marxist tradition within the discipline and offers a materialist rather than a cultural account of cohesion. Marx emphasized inequalities in material wealth and political power in *capitalist societies. The distribution of material and political resources is the source of conflict between different collectivities—social classes—who want a greater share of those resources than they may already enjoy. Conflict implies there is no moral consensus and social order is always precariously maintained. It is the product of the balance of *power between competing groups, whereby the powerful constrain weaker groups, and cohesion is sustained through economic compulsion, political and legal coercion, and bureaucratic routine. While many Marxists have increasingly embraced cultural accounts of social order, for example by explaining working-class *incorporation through a *dominant ideology, others have noted that economic and political coercion has proved a remarkably effective source of stability, especially where power is legitimated as authority. Nevertheless, persistent conflict implies tension and change, rather than enduring stability.

In the most original recent contribution to the theoretical debate about social order, David *Lockwood (*Solidarity and Schism*, 1992) has demonstrated that neither Marxian nor Durkheimian theory satisfactorily resolves the issues, since each approach is forced to employ residual categories which turn out to be the central analytic elements of the other. In Durkheim's work, the concept of moral classification is the key to social structure, whereas for Marx it is production relations. That is, one theory emphasizes the socially integrative structure of *status, the other the socially divisive structure of *class. However, Durkheim cannot explain how anomic declassification (disorder) occurs or is structured (schismatic) without introducing concepts of power and material *interests into his schema, whereas Marx cannot explain the persistence of capitalist societies without recourse to a generalized category of *ideology which introduces the (unanalysed) conceptual problem of the nature and variability of consensus.

Explanations of social order tend to be macro-theories which focus on society as the unit of analysis, although studies of family obligations, crime, and leisure (to cite but a few examples) raise issues of social order at the micro level. Quite different accounts of how social order is reproduced during face-to-face interaction will be found in the writings of symbolic interactionists, in dramaturgy, ethnomethodology, and exchange theory (all of which are discussed separately elsewhere in this dictionary). The best general account of the various theories and the issues they raise is Dennis Wrong's *The Problem of Order: What Unites and Divides Society* (1994). *See also* FATALISM; HOBBES; SOCIAL CONTRACT; SOCIAL INTEGRATION AND SYSTEM INTEGRATION.

social organization *See* FORMAL STRUCTURE; ORGANIZATION THEORY; PARSONS; SYSTEMS THEORY.

social pathology An early form of *deviance theory, no longer in wide use, which drew upon the organic metaphor to suggest that parts of societies, like parts of bodies, could suffer breakdown and disease. *See also* PATHOLOGY.

social policy Precisely what counts as a social policy is a matter of debate. Both words are problematic. The term policy commonly refers to a more or less clearly articulated set of ideas about what should be done in a particular sphere, which is often set down in writing, and usually formally adopted by the relevant decision-making body. It differs from a plan in that plans specify in detail the way in which objectives are to be achieved, whereas a policy is typically formulated at a more general level, indicating only objectives and the intended direction of change. In academic contexts, however, the term policy is usually not restricted to formally adopted policies, since lack of action and continuation of the status quo (even if not formally agreed) itself constitutes a policy.

The term social is even more problematic. The most common interpretation is that social policies are government policies (both central and local) that are directed towards meeting the social *needs of the population (social needs usually being interpreted as welfare needs), with the list including policies concerning social security, health, housing, education and (sometimes) law and order. However, such a view of social policy is arguably too narrow, since it directs attention to policies generated specifically within the usual list of welfare fields. It ignores key policy areas that also have a profound impact on *welfare, especially areas usually assigned to the domain of economic policy, such as fiscal policies and policies on inflation and economic growth. Whilst these are properly labelled 'economic policies', they are also 'social policies'—or policies with major implications for welfare, which cannot be excluded from the field of social policy. Equally, it is argued that exclusive concentration on government policies is mistaken, and that one should also include the policies of religious and charitable bodies as well as of private corporations (as, for example, in consideration of pensions policies)—a position that has become increasingly necessary with the *privatization of arrangements for welfare.

There have been a range of approaches to the analysis of social policy, although much of the work has been developed in departments of *social administration, outside the framework of sociology. The so-called social administration approach to social policy dominant in the 1950s and 1960s has, however, been widely criticized as atheoretical, and Marxist approaches were especially influential amongst sociologists in the 1970s (see, for example, I. Gough's *The Political Economy of the Welfare State*, 1979). More recently, T. H. Marshall's analysis of *citizenship (see his *Sociology at the Crossroads*, 1963) has once again shaped discussions of welfare and social policy. There is also a greater focus on comparative social policy (with the insularity of British writers on social policy showing signs of waning). The impact of feminist scholarship has also been considerable, with much greater analysis of the role women play in welfare provision, for example through informal care of the sick and disabled, and also greater attention given to women as the recipients of social welfare. *See also* EVALUATION RESEARCH; POLICY RESEARCH.

social problems A generic term applied to the range of conditions and aberrant behaviours which are held to be manifestations of social disorganization and to warrant changing via some means of *social engineering. Typically, these problems include many forms of deviant behaviour (such as crime, juvenile delinquency, prostitution, mental illness, drug addiction, suicide), and of social conflict (ethnic tensions, domestic violence, industrial strife, and so forth). Most of these topics are discussed under discrete headings in this dictionary. In the complex social *structures of modern *industrial societies, individuals and groups are differentially exposed to these hazards, and people occupying different *statuses and *roles tend to differ in their appraisal of social situations and in their views as to what constitutes a social problem requiring a solution. For this reason, the range of possible social problems is almost infinite, and can include phenomena as diverse as declining standards of literacy and the demise of the work ethic. Similarly, the proposed solutions are also variable, and this too is (at least partly) due to the different interests and values of the various parties involved.

social protest *See* CIVIL DISOBEDIENCE; PASSIVE RESISTANCE; REBELLION; SOCIAL MOVEMENTS; STRIKE.

social psychology *See* PSYCHOLOGY.

social science A general label applied to the study of *society and human relationships. The development of social sciences, during the course of the 19th century, followed on the development of natural science. The designation of an area of study as a social science usually carries the implication that it is comparable in important ways to a natural science. Of the various disciplines that study human beings, *psychology is often seen as a natural rather than a social science, and *economics most frequently regarded as a comparatively unproblematic social science. *Sociology, social *psychology, politics, and geography have a more problematic status, while history is perhaps least often designated as a science.

Discipline boundaries are by no means always clear and the generic term social science usually covers most or all of the disciplines mentioned. All, to various degrees, are engaged in debates about the nature of science and scientific status. Are the social sciences directly comparable to the natural sciences, or does the fact that their object of study is human make them different? And, if they are different, in what sense (if any) are they scientific? Sociologists, in particular, have addressed these questions more or less continuously from the time of the classical theorists onwards. *See also* METHODOLOGY.

social security State-administered means-tested systems of income maintenance that are intended to prevent people falling into or remaining in *poverty. Some are citizenship-based, others are residence-based. *See also* WELFARE STATE.

social solidarity One principal theme in the work of Émile Durkheim concerns the sources of moral and therefore *social order in society. In particular, Durkheim was concerned to elaborate the connection between the individual and society, in a time of growing individualism, social dislocation, and moral diversification. In his famous treatise on *The Division of Labour in Society* (1893) he juxtaposed the solidarity of resemblance, characteristic of segmented, opaque societies where 'mechanical solidarity' prevailed, to the solidarity of occupational interdependence in morally dense societies characterized by 'organic solidarity'. The transition from one to the other was neither obvious nor inevitable—as he was the first to admit in his afterwords on abnormal forms of the *division of labour. In subsequent writings, Durkheim sought to make suggestions as to the institutional solutions to the problems of moral regulation and social integration in contemporary societies, in particular suggesting the importance of the 'occupational association' (a sort of modern equivalent of the medieval guild) as a mediator between the individual and society. In the *Elementary Forms of*

Religious Life (1912), social solidarity—society—was found to be the very object of collective worship.

social stability *See* CHANGE; PROGRESS; SOCIAL CONTROL; SOCIAL ORDER; SOCIAL SOLIDARITY.

social statics and social dynamics *See* COMTE.

social statistics Quantitative information about social groups, including *census and *demographic data, used for descriptive policy and inferential analysis. As an application of statistical theory, increasing attention has been given to models of influence and measurement, and to *multivariate models of analysis.

social status *See* STATUS.

social stratification *See* STRATIFICATION.

social structure *See* STRUCTURE.

social survey *See* SURVEY.

social system The concept of system appears throughout the social and natural sciences and has generated a body of literature of its own ('general *systems theory'). A system is any structured or patterned relationship between any number of elements, where this system forms a whole or unity. It is assumed that a system has an *environment and thus there is the requirement of *boundary maintenance. There is an interchange between a system and its environment. It is further assumed that systems will tend towards an *equilibrium state or homeostasis. The idea of the social system was heavily shaped by the social philosophy of Lawrence J. Henderson, who was inspired by Pareto (see Henderson's *Pareto's General Sociology*, 1935), and by the biologist Walter B. Cannon (see *The Wisdom of the Body*, 1932). Talcott Parsons, who was influenced at Harvard by Henderson's interpretation of Pareto, is the sociologist who, through the development of the theory of *structural functionalism, is most generally associated with the elaboration of systems theory.

The *functionalism of Talcott *Parsons offers the most influential employment of systems theory in sociology (see especially *The Social System*, 1951). In Parsonian terms, social system can refer to a stable relationship between two actors, to societies as a whole, to systems of societies, or indeed any level between these. All are analysed principally in terms of their so-called cybernetic aspects; that is, as systems of information exchange and control, where equilibrium is maintained through symbolic exchanges with other systems across boundaries. In economic systems, for example, the exchange is not usually direct but mediated by money. Power is the medium of exchange in political systems. Parsons's ideas have been extended in the neo-functionalism of Jeffrey Alexander and the systems theory of Niklas Luhmann (*Social Systems*, 1984).

Anthony Giddens (*Central Problems in Social Theory*, 1979) and others have stressed that the properties of systems are produced and reproduced by structured and routine social practices. The systematic properties of social systems thus have to be grounded in the nature of social action. A useful overview of the whole area is Walter Buckley's *Sociology and Modern Systems Theory* (1967).

social systems, plural *See* PLURAL SOCIAL SYSTEMS.

social trend A notable pattern of change displayed by a *social indicator or *index. The term is also used more loosely to refer to national social reports which present unvarying distributions, as well as *time-series data showing change.

social work The generic term applied to the various organized methods for promoting human welfare through the prevention and relief of suffering. In the late 19th century, social work was largely voluntary (notably as a charitable activity on the part of middle-class women), and aimed primarily at the alleviation of material *poverty. In the period since the Second World War, social work practice has become increasingly *professionalized, and now has a much wider remit embracing emotional and mental as well as economic well-being.

Contemporary social work tends to suffer from a lack of differentiation from the various other social services which comprise the modern *welfare state. In Britain, for example, social workers have no legal obligation (and no practical resources) to deal with issues of *unemployment, housing, and poverty—all of which are the responsibility of other social services. What they are expected to deal with is the wide range of problems which diminish the 'quality of inner life': for example, problems and crises associated with adoption, fostering of the young and old, marital reconciliation, sexual and physical abuse, and people's relationships with one another generally.

There are several models of social work practice. The 'problem-solving' approach involves the social worker in reinforcing the client's emotional and organizational resources to deal with his or her difficulties. The various 'psycho-social therapies' stress the need for prior psycho-social diagnosis as a prerequisite to psycho-social treatment. Partly as a reaction against the deterministic and mechanical view of action implied in these approaches, 'functionalists' have emphasized the role of the social worker in helping (rather than treating) the client, by sustaining an appropriate supporting relationship with him or her. Other models are oriented towards behaviour-modification, crisis-intervention, and short-term task-centredness. In reality, practice tends to be characterized by eclectic pragmatism, rather than adherence to a specific method. Strong recent influences include feminist theory and anti-oppressive practice. Good recent overviews are Malcolm Payne, *Modern Social Work Theory* (1991), for Britain, and J. Heffernan et al., *Social Work and Social Welfare* (2nd edn., 1992), for the United States.

Not surprisingly, many outside observers have expressed concern at the periodic psychotherapeutic takeover of social work; similarly, given its inherently moral character, social work practice has been subject to repeated controversy involving those who view it as primarily a political tool—either for promoting or hindering *social justice.

social world perspective *See* REFERENCE GROUP.

social worlds A term which is frequently applied to 'universes of discourse' through which common symbols, organizations, and activities emerge. They involve cultural areas which need not be physically bounded. Typical examples might be the 'social worlds' of surfing, nursing, politics, or science. The Gay Community is a self-conscious social world. The concept has a long but vague history in *symbolic interactionism and is discussed most clearly by Anselm Strauss (in Norman Denzin's edited *Studies in Symbolic Interaction*, 1978).

socialism An economic and political system based on collective or state ownership of the *means of production and distribution—although, like *capitalism, the system takes many and diverse forms.

After almost two hundred years of socialist thought the collapse of Soviet *communism has broken the grip of the Marxist-Leninist imprimatur on the provenance of this concept. However, the concerns that have been addressed by those who espoused or eschewed the cause still remain. The dichotomies of freedom and equality, individual and collective rights, and even the nature of the historical process (with its voluntaristic and deterministic connotations) all remain very much to the fore. To some extent these problems are now raised afresh since the system of 'actually existing socialism' or *real socialism as it was called tended to put into suspended animation many of the processes which addressed these questions. Capitalism resurgent in Eastern Europe once again raises the questions of the limit to individual *rights, the nature of the common good, and *liberalism versus communitarianism (*see* COLLECTIVISM). Ethnic and national minorities, with their historically defined differences and animosities for so long cryogenically preserved, have starkly raised the question of collective rights and seeming historical inevitability.

Socialism as a doctrine, or some would say a *utopia, is generally agreed to have been spawned as a reaction to capitalism. The Durkheimian version was rooted in the desire simply to bring the *state closer to the economy, society closer to the realm of individual activity, and sentient parts to each other: in this way the pathologies of capitalism (including anomie) would be mitigated and eventually relieved. Socialism was a cry of pain which did not demand equality of condition but simply a genuine equality of opportunity. The imposition of the former, Durkheim argued, would destroy the very conditions for a healthy society, and society could not demand that which was against its interests for survival.

Max Weber, on the other hand, saw in socialism an accentuation of the process of rationalization commenced under capitalism. He derided the intellectuals who wanted to marry formal to substantive rationality in the socialist state, or as he put it '*bureaucracy in the state and in the economy', which would simply create the 'cage of future bondage'.

The English tradition of so-called ethical socialism argues for forceful government intervention in market processes, state control of the conditions of labour, a *collectivist social policy and strong *welfare state, as represented in the non-revolutionary and pragmatic gradualism of the *Fabians. This vision of socialism emphasizes the values of liberty, fraternity (particularly the importance of *citizenship as a counter to the inequalities of social *class), and equality, and is most explicitly spelled out in A. H. Halsey and Norman Dennis's *English Ethical Socialism* (1988). It is opposed to *historicism and places moral motivation at the centre of human conduct and social organization. It is also opposed to Marxism-Leninism. The writings of T. H. Marshall and R. H. Tawney are typical of the tradition.

This particular philosophy of socialism has had a strong influence on British empirical sociology, obvious for example in the 'political arithmetic' approach to the sociology of education, which has been concerned with comparing the chances of children from different social backgrounds reaching successive stages in the education process. The work of Halsey himself is typical. Halsey's early studies of inequalities in access to education and educational attainment set much of the research agenda of the sociology of education in Britain during the 1960s and 1970s, and were influential in formulating the social policies of comprehensive and compensatory education, while his later work has continued to draw attention to the importance of schools (rather than academic ability) as a determinant of educational achievements (see *Social Class and Educational Opportunity*, 1961, and *Origins and Destinations*, 1980).

However, Karl Marx's views on the socialist future and the advent of communism have been the most pervasive in their influence on the definition of the letter, if not the spirit, of socialism. For Marx, socialism implied the abolition of markets, capital, and labour as a commodity. In fact, second economies, black markets, and other forms of private activity were never eradicated in state socialist societies, even under Stalinism. Very soon, 'market socialism' came to the rescue of the distributive as well as production shortcomings of the planned, *command economy. Free labour was in fact dragooned and disciplined by subservient trade unions, and self-management only surfaced at times of crisis or in managerial forms, as in Poland and Yugoslavia. Shortage, rather than the surplus promised by the abolition of the anarchy of capitalist production, was testified to by food queues and price riots. Accumulation within the heavy industrial sector continued, as the bureaucratic state maintained its power by any means, including importing foreign technology rather than provide autonomy to any segment of society. If socialism meant anything it was the creation of *social justice and the transition from the labour standard to the needs standard. In fact, socialism did not even create a working *meritocracy, but only a political class of the *nomenklatura*, and despite its commitment to a leading role for the working class, it rewarded workers simply by promoting them into political and white-collar positions in an obvious process of inclusion.

The absence of key civil rights (freedom of speech, person, conscience, movement, property ownership) and political rights (assembly and franchise)—obviated, it was claimed, by the victory of the vanguard Party—was in no way compensated for by the socialist 'welfare state' or the satisfaction of need away from the realm of exchange value. Environmental despoliation characteristic of socialist industrialization, mortality and morbidity rates so bad as not to be publishable, gender divisions disguised by the common impoverishment, subsidies to housing and food consumption which provided an extra dimension to the cumulative inequality generated by the socialist system of redistribution— all of these factors and more provided a sorry summary of the achievements of actually existing socialism. Until the very end, ideologists within the Party clung to their socialist rhetoric and slogans, despite the fact that any generation which might have believed in them was by now in a minority.

The overnight collapse of the mass parties in Eastern Europe, and their almost total rejection even in the face of massive impoverishment, is perhaps the major indictment of socialism as it was practised in the Soviet bloc. How it affects the credibility of the doctrine, and what emerges to fill the value vacuum left by its demise, remains to be seen. Nationalism, populism, and varieties of neo-corporatist solutions have already sought to take over the constituency of the political left as socialism still dares not to speak its name. *See also* ANARCHISM; BERNSTEIN; PLURALISM; SAINT-SIMON; SOREL.

socialism, democratic *See* STATE CAPITALISM.

socialism, real *See* REAL SOCIALISM.

socialization Socialization is the process by which we learn to become members of society, both by internalizing the *norms and *values of society, and also by learning to perform our social *roles (as worker, friend, citizen, and so forth).

There is an ongoing dispute about the relative importance of *nature versus nurture (or hereditary and environment) in human development. Current thinking prefers to recognize the interdependence of the two, rather than the exclusive importance of either one. A related debate concerns the extent to which humans are over-socialized. Are humans ruled by their social manners and role-playing skills to the extent that basic human instincts are eradicated? This debate pits the psychological perspective of *Freud, which views socialization as working against our natural inclinations and drives, against the *functionalist perspective that sees socialization as essential for the integration of society. Recent studies have focused on social class differences in socialization, some of which have to do with language (see B. Bernstein, *Class, Codes and Control*, 1971), others of which are more concerned with differences in value orientation (see M. Kohn, *Class and Conformity*, 1969).

Socialization is no longer regarded as the exclusive preserve of *childhood, with the primary agents being the family and school. It is now recognized that socialization continues throughout the life-course. This is often studied through a distinction between primary and secondary socialization. It is also recognized that socialization is not simply a one-way process, in which individuals learn how to fit into society, since people may also redefine their social roles and obligations. Any understanding of socialization must therefore take account of how the process relates to social change. In this sense, some schools of sociological theory imply an allegedly 'over-socialized conception of man in society', in that they overstate the extent to which values are internalized and action is normative in orientation—a charge often levelled, for example, against normative functionalism (see D. Wrong, 'The Oversocialized Conception of Man', *American Sociological Review*, 1961).

societal reaction In the *labelling theory of deviance, the societal reaction refers to the range of formal and informal agencies of *social control—including the law, media, police, and family—which, through their responses towards the deviant, greatly affect deviance outcomes. For Edwin Lemert (*Social Pathology*, 1951), far from control necessarily reducing deviance, it may actually generate, structure, or amplify deviance. *See also* DEVIANCE AMPLIFICATION; PRIMARY AND SECONDARY DEVIATION.

society Generally, a *group of people who share a common *culture, occupy a particular territorial area, and feel themselves to constitute a unified and distinct entity—but there are many different sociological conceptions (see D. Frisby and D. Sayer, *Society*, 1986). More loosely, it refers to human association or interaction generally, as in the phrase 'the society of his friends'.

In everyday life the term society is used as if it referred in an unproblematic way to something that exists 'out there' and beyond the individual subject: we speak of 'French society', 'capitalist society', and of 'society' being responsible for some observed social phenomenon. On reflection, however, such a usage clearly has its problems: for example, is British society a clear unity, or can we also talk of Welsh, Scottish, and Northern Irish societies? And, even within England, are there not wide cultural differences between (say) north and south? Is there one capitalist society—or many? Nor is a society the same thing as a nation-state. The former Yugoslavia clearly contained several societies: Croat, Slovenian, Serbian, and so on.

While many sociologists use the term in a commonsense way others question this use. Some *symbolic interactionists, for example, argue that there is no such thing as society: it is simply a useful covering term for things we do not know about or understand properly (see P. Rock, *The Making of Symbolic Interactionism*, 1979). Others, such as Émile Durkheim, treat society as a reality in its own right (see *The Rules of Sociological Method*, 1895).

Some sociologists have tried to develop more specific concepts to replace that of society. The Marxist theoretician Louis Althusser, for example, suggested the term *social formation: a combination of three levels of relationships (economic, ideological, and political) which can have varying connections with each other (see *For Marx*, 1969). Anthony Giddens, arguing against the identification of society with the nationstate, prefers to talk about *social systems and *institutions which may or may not be limited by national boundaries (see his *A Contemporary Critique of Historical Materialism*, 1981). Recent debates about the nation *state and the national economy have raised the question of whether *globalization is also undermining the autonomy of territorially defined societies. We may be experiencing the dissolution of national society and so need a *Sociology Beyond Society* (John Urry, 2000). *See also* FORMALISM; FUNCTION; GOFFMAN.

Society for the Study of Social Problems (SSSP) A North American organization of sociologists, formed in 1951, as a body aiming to present a more radical and critical approach to deviance and social problems than the American Sociological Association. In its earliest days, it was dominated by *labelling theory, as exemplified in Howard S. Becker (ed.), *The Other Side* (1963). The British *National Deviance Conference was in part inspired by this organization, which is now a major part of American sociology. A good overview of its activities can be found in the review of its work published on the occasion of its 25th anniversary in the journal *Social Problems* (1976).

sociobiology A recently developed academic discipline, particularly popular in the United States, based upon the tenet that all animal and human behaviour is ultimately dependent upon genetic encoding moulded through evolutionary history by the processes of selection. This all-encompassing theme, according as it does with many common-sense assertions about *human nature, is sufficient to have attracted an enormous quantity of media attention. The spotlight has focused particularly on its most well-known popularizing authors: Edward O. Wilson, who coined the term itself in his *Sociobiology: The New Synthesis* (1975); and Richard Dawkins, author of *The Selfish Gene* (1976). Wilson, an American biologist and authority on ant behaviour, also provided the first definition of the new sub-discipline as 'the systematic study of the biological basis of all social behaviour'.

In the mid-1970s sociobiology brought together into a supposedly coherent theoretical synthesis the work of previous authors on the relationship between animal and human behaviour, including Konrad Lorenz, Robert Ardrey, and Desmond Morris. It was anticipated, at least by Wilson, that all social and biological sciences would eventually be regarded merely as branches of sociobiology. Unsurprisingly, many sociologists and anthropologists have been deeply suspicious of the ultimately all-encompassing claims of this synthesis, and have drawn attention to the enormous cultural diversity of human societies—a diversity which challenges the frequently androcentric and *ethnocentric assumptions of much sociobiological writing. For example, serious questions have been raised by Marshall Sahlins concerning the theoretical adequacy of sociobiology, and its claims to be a respectable academic discipline in its own right (*The Use and Abuse of Biology*, 1976). Many social scientists have challenged its use of scientific evidence (see, for example, P. Kitcher, *Vaulting Ambition*, 1985). Others have linked the emergence of sociobiology in the United States to a conservative backlash against the radicalism of the 1960s (see S. Rose, *Not in our Genes*, 1984).

The general response of sociobiologists to these criticisms has been gradually to admit more that is *environmental into their analytical framework, whilst still retaining an adherence to the ultimate determining effect of biology, at least in any aspect of behaviour attributed with evolutionary significance. Wilson, for example, has more recently argued that 'genes hold culture on a long leash'. Whilst some academic analysis has become relatively sophisticated and complex, the level at which much sociobiological argument is expressed (particularly in its more popular versions) remains alarmingly *reductionist.

The sociobiological enterprise is now well established, being supported by a raft of academic journals (including *Ethology and Sociobiology, Human Nature,* and *Evolutionary Anthropology*), and two interdisciplinary associations (the Human Behavior and Evolution Society and the European Sociobiological Society). In a sympathetic review of the field, François Nielsen argues that sociobiological and evolutionary thinking will increasingly affect sociology in a number of areas, including (for example) the study of sex and gender roles, collective action, and altruism (see 'Sociobiology and Sociology', *Annual Review of Sociology*, 1994). It has to be noted, however, that sociobiologists and evolutionary psychologists seriously caricature sociology and, in their criticisms of it, they rely on reiterations of one poorly researched paper (John Tooby and Leda Cosmides, in Barkow, Cosmides, and Tooby (eds.), *The Adapted Mind*, 1992) and quote few actual sociological arguments that espouse the view that they are criticizing. A critical review of some key concepts can be found in Peter Dickens, *Social Darwinism* (2000).

socio-economic status Any measure which attempts to classify individuals, families, or households in terms of indicators such as occupation, income, and education. One of the first major uses of socio-economic status can be found in the social class measures introduced by the British Registrar-General in 1911. *See also* STATUS ATTAINMENT.

sociogram *See* NETWORK ANALYSIS; SOCIOMETRY.

sociolinguistics *See* CONVERSATION ANALYSIS; ETHNOMETHODOLOGY; LANGUAGE.

sociological imagination *See* MILLS.

sociological intervention A technique practised by the French sociologist Alain Touraine, which advocates the active intervention of the sociologist in the *social movement that forms his or her subject, in order to expose the 'actual social relations' that lie behind the 'mesh of approved and organized practices'.

His analysis of post-industrial society focuses on the extraordinary powers of control inherent in the uses of information technology. These powers give human beings the ability literally to make history (historicity), but citizens in general have little access to them. For this reason, Touraine gives primary political importance to social movements in which groups of citizens organize to challenge the dominant forms of knowledge, and to propose alternatives. The sociologist attempts to create a research situation within which the social movement can represent fully the nature of the struggles in which it is engaged. Touraine therefore advocates four research practices: entering into a relationship with the social movement by organizing its militants as groups; encouraging these groups in their militant roles; explaining the historical context of the movement to its activists; and participating in the self-analysis of the militant group's situation by interpreting what took place during the sociological intervention itself.

With his co-researchers at the École des Hautes Études en Sciences Sociales in Paris, Touraine embarked in the 1960s on a series of dramatic 'sociological interventions'. The researchers joined the French student movement, the anti-nuclear movement, the regional Occitan movement, and the Polish

Solidarity movement. Going beyond *participant observation, they became actively engaged in the political ideas and actions of those groups as a way of understanding them more fully. Theoretically, this approach has been labelled *actionalism. This combination of sociological fieldwork with active Marxism (praxis) and more subjective theories of social action was highly controversial. Probably its most successful product was the study of the French student and worker movement of 1968.

The most complete account of the technique, and its theoretical justification, will be found in Touraine's *The Voice and the Eye* (1978). Just how far removed this is from the conventional view of the sociologist as neutral or *objective observer or recorder of the facts is evident in Touraine's claim that 'the supreme moment of the intervention devoted to the students' movement was dominated by a lengthy discussion between the militants and the research leader, who introduced with great vigour into the group the theme of knowledge and its social utilization, which to his mind, represented the only stakes capable of elevating the student struggle to the level of a social movement.'

sociological jurisprudence A term coined by the American jurist Roscoe Pound (1870–1964) to describe his approach to the understanding of the law. Central to Pound's conception was the very suggestive idea that in modern societies the law represents the principal means through which divergent *interests are brought into some sort of alignment with one another. Unfortunately, perhaps because he was a jurist rather than a sociologist, he did not combine this insightful conception with a developed understanding of how these interests were formed and why some of them came to be privileged over others within the legal system. A sociologically informed account of Pound's work, which places it in the context of the historical development of the sociology of law, will be found in Alan Hunt, *The Sociological Movement in Law*, 1978.

Sociologie du Travail A sociology of work, associated with the writings of certain French sociologists of the 1950s and 1960s, which provided at the time a refreshing critique of the factory-bound perspective of mainstream (mostly Anglo-Saxon) industrial sociology. This literature re-established the links which Karl Marx had sought to forge between, on one hand, changes in work organization, technology, and production; and, on the other, personal alienation, class, and sociopolitical relationships. Leading figures were Georges *Friedmann, Michel Crozier, Pierre Naville, Alain Touraine, and Serge Mallet, many of whose works have now been translated into English. Mallet's work stimulated an important debate about the existence of a *new working class, but like much Sociologie du Travail, its iconoclasm was limited by *technicism and *technological determinism. Its influence on left-oriented research and thought in English has now been considerably eclipsed by more recent debates about *skill and *de-skilling, the *labour process, post-*fordism, and flexible employment. Michael Rose's *Servants of Post-Industrial Power?* (1979) is an excellent English-language history and analysis of the movement's theories and work.

sociology It has been argued that the very origins of the word 'sociology', from the Latin *socius* (companion) and the Greek *ology* (study of), indicate its nature as a hybrid discipline that can never aspire to the status of a *social science or a coherent body of knowledge. The discipline itself has an ambivalent genealogy and a controversial recent history as the newest of the social sciences to establish itself in universities in the English-speaking world. In Britain, for example, this did not happen on a large scale until the 1960s, when sociology departments were often accused of instigating student unrest. The difficulty of defining the subject is indicated by the easiest possible form of this entry: namely, a cross-reference to every other entry in the dictionary, which includes theories and concepts from philosophy through to economics. Of all the social sciences it is sociology that most closely scrutinizes *change and *conflict in the wider society. The range of the discipline, and the importance of the arguments that are disputed within it, still make it the most exciting of the social sciences.

Historically, the word itself was first used by Auguste *Comte, although a concern with the nature of *society can be found throughout the history of Western thought. However, it was not until the 19th century, in the aftermath of industrial revolution and consequent political upheavals, that we see a concern with society as such as a direct object of study. In Comte's work, sociology was to be the highest achievement of science, producing knowledge of the laws of the social world equivalent to our knowledge of the laws of nature. We could then determine, once and for all, what sort of social changes were possible and so alleviate the political chaos that followed the French Revolution. It is often argued that this is a profoundly conservative reaction to the liberal optimism of the Enlightenment: against notions of individual freedom and unlimited social *progress, sociology asserts the importance of the *community, and the comparatively limited possibilities that exist for social change. Similarly, in his book *The Sociological Tradition* (1967), Robert Nisbet has argued that much classical sociology reflects a generalized hostility to the industrial and political revolutions of that period. *Marxists also maintain that, as the discipline developed during the 19th century, it was clearly as a bourgeois social science—a reply and alternative to the increasing political and intellectual influence of *historical materialism. At the same time, however, sociology has often been taken up by social reformers: even the positivism of Comte was important in the growth of reform movements during the late 19th century. An alternative to this account of the history of sociology is the argument, found most clearly perhaps in the work of Talcott Parsons (see especially *The Structure of Social Action*, 1937), that in the late 19th and early 20th centuries sociology broke free of its earlier ideological shackles and established itself as a science proper, especially in the work of Max Weber and Émile Durkheim. Neither of these histories is adequate, as the recent work of Anthony Giddens has shown, although most sociology courses still point to the achievements of Marx, Weber, and Durkheim (and, in the United States, George Herbert *Mead) in laying the theoretical foundations of the modern discipline.

In its present form, sociology embraces a range of different views concerning both what a social science should comprise, and what might be the proper subject matter of sociology in particular. The latter provides perhaps the best way of making sense of the discipline. There are three general conceptions of the object of sociological interest—although these are not mutually exclusive. All three can be said to define the study of society but what is meant by society is in each case rather different.

The first states that the proper object for sociology is social *structure, in the sense of patterns of relationships which have an independent existence, over and above the individuals or groups that occupy positions in these structures at any particular time: for example, the positions of the nuclear family (mother, father, children) might remain the same from generation to generation and place to place, independently of the specific individuals who fill or do not fill those positions. There are two main versions of this approach: Marxism, which conceptualizes the structures of *modes of production, and Parsonian structural-functionalism which identifies systems, sub-systems, and *role structures.

A second perspective deems the proper object of sociology to lie in something that we might call, with Durkheim, *collective representations: meanings and ways of cognitively organizing the world which have a continued existence over and above the individuals who are socialized into them. *Language itself is the paradigm case: it pre-exists our birth, continues after our death, and as individuals we can alter it little or not at all. Much modern *structuralist and *postmodernist work (in particular *discourse analysis) can be seen as part of this tradition.

Finally, there are those for whom the proper object of sociological attention is meaningful social action, in the sense intended by Max Weber. The implicit or explicit assumption behind this approach is that there is no such thing as society: merely individuals and groups entering into social relationships with each other. There are widely differing ways in which such interaction can be studied, including Weber's own concerns with rational action and the relationships between beliefs and actions; the *symbolic interactionist concern with the production, maintenance, and transformation of *meanings in face-to-face interaction; and the *ethnomethodological study of the construction of social reality through linguistic practices.

A moment's reflection will confirm that, between them, these three possible candidates for sociological study almost exhaust the range of what one is likely to meet during the course of social relationships. It is no surprise, then, that sociology is sometimes seen (at least by sociologists) as a queen of the social sciences, bringing together and extending the knowledge and insights of all the other (conceptually more restricted) adjacent disciplines. This claim is perhaps less true now than during the period when sociology was expanding rapidly, but despite inevitable specialization among its practitioners there is still a strong totalizing tendency in the discipline, as a perusal of the work of Anthony Giddens or Jeffrey Alexander will establish. Indeed, Giddens himself argues that sociology emerged as an attempt to make sense of the profound social transformation between traditional and modern societies, and as that change continues and gathers pace so the attempt to understand it becomes more important.

Hence sociology is, and is likely to remain, both an attractive and internally divided discipline, and a discipline which attracts a great deal of criticism, especially from those who—for whatever reason—are most resistant to social change. *See also* CULTURAL STUDIES; RATIONAL CHOICE THEORY; SOCIAL ACTION; SOCIAL ORDER; SYSTEM INTEGRATION AND SOCIAL INTEGRATION.

See also individual entries on the sociologies of AGEING, (THE) BODY, CONSUMPTION, DEVELOPMENT, EDUCATION, EMOTION, *(the) family, FOOD, HEALTH AND ILLNESS, KNOWLEDGE, LAW, LEISURE, MEDICINE, RACE, RELIGION, SCIENCE; and entries on DEVIANCE, ECONOMIC SOCIOLOGY, ENVIRONMENT, GENDER, MILITARY AND MILITARISM, ORGANIZATION THEORY, POLITICAL SOCIOLOGY, POP SOCIOLOGY, RURAL SOCIOLOGY, URBAN SOCIOLOGY, WELFARE.

( ) SEE WEB LINKS
- The British Sociological Association.
- The European Sociological Association.
- The American Sociological Association.
- The International Sociological Association.

sociometry A term coined by J. L. Moreno in 1934 in *Who Shall Survive?* and originally developed as part of a sociodrama approach to interpreting social *structure. Sociometry systematizes information from individuals in a *group, concerning who prefers to associate with whom (or often the behavioural parallel of who associates with whom), in terms of a specified basis or for a given purpose. An early use by Moreno was to reallocate dormitory sleeping arrangements to minimize conflict among reform-school inhabitants. Initial use thus tied the sociometric test (for example naming friends) to it having direct consequences, though this is now less common. The number of sociometric choices allowed may be either fixed ('name three best friends') or not ('give as many names as you wish'); may be ordered; or may express the strength of the link. Originally, analysis of sociometric data centred on the number of choices received and given and the resulting point properties, such as stars and isolates receiving very many and no choices respectively. The information is drawn as points and lines on a single diagram called the sociogram, where individuals receiving most choices are located at the centre, and isolates at the periphery. Sociometry is widely used in education and other small-group contexts for understanding clique-structure, and has its own journal, *Sociometry*. It has largely been subsumed by social *network analysis.

socio-technical system A term devised to avoid the rather simplistic *technological determinism in much mainstream *organization theory. It was coined by the Tavistock Institute of Human Relations in Britain, and used in the theory of organizational choice which guided their programme of applied research.

Though accepting the conventional wisdom of industrial sociology and the *Human Relations Movement that in-plant technical factors affect the quality of social relationships at work, the Tavistock researchers argued that technology merely constrains human action, rather than rigidly determining behavioural outcomes. Conscious choice can build good human relations into the technical workflow. Indeed, for any productive problem there is typically a range of technologically equivalent solutions, with differing implications for human relations.

By emphasizing the element of choice, and the mutual influence of technology and the social systems of the workplace, the Tavistock researchers sought to move away from technological determinism towards greater appreciation within management of the need for consultation, innovation, flexibility, and an open mind in the design of work processes and procedures. The consultancy and action research work which led to the formulation of socio-technical systems was carried out in the coal-mining and textiles industries in Britain and India in the 1940s and 1950s, and seemed to show that work teams which operated a flexible allocation of tasks and jobs achieved higher *productivity, lower absenteeism, and fewer accidents than work teams with a rigid division of labour and inflexible 'segregated' task groups.

The Tavistock studies were criticized for underestimating the difficulties of reconciling economic, technical, and social efficiency. However, the idea of the socio-technical system (though not the term itself) has passed into conventional thinking about work organization, flexibility issues, and the impact of technical change.

solidarism This term refers to a belief in the sharing of aims and interests. Solidarity is valued as a source of strength and resistance, and by implication, for its single-minded unity of purpose. A belief in solidarity as an end in itself, rather than a means to an end, was said to characterize the traditional working-class occupational *community. In such settings, shared experiences of work and community life were said to generate and sustain strong feelings of fraternity, together with the values of mutual aid and participation. This sense of belonging was also said to be the source of working-class *collectivism, although there has been little evidence to substantiate the case empirically, and it is doubtful whether such solidarism was ever as coherent and unified as has been claimed. Recent work is reviewed by Graham Crow in *Social Solidarities* (2002). *See also* IMAGES OF SOCIETY; WORK, SUBJECTIVE EXPERIENCE OF.

solidaristic orientation to work *See* WORK, SUBJECTIVE EXPERIENCE OF.

sorcery *See* MAGIC, WITCHCRAFT, AND SORCERY.

Sorel, Georges (1847–1922) After a long career as an engineer in France, Sorel resigned to become an independent scholar, and in the 35 years before his death published a stream of books and articles on social theory, Marxism, and the philosophy of the social sciences (most notably *Reflections on Violence*, 1908, and *The Illusions of Progress*, 1908). As editor of *Le Devenir social*, he introduced theoretical *Marxism into France, and sided with Eduard Bernstein in rejecting Marxism's pretensions to be scientific. However, rather than abandon revolutionary activity for reformism, he argued for an extreme form of anarcho-*syndicalism. His significance for sociology lies in his writings on myth and violence. His analysis of the functions of *myth in society complements Karl Mannheim's later writings on utopia. There is, in fact, a developed (though largely unacknowledged) theory of *ideology in his writings. According to Sorel, many of the central tenets of Marxism were themselves myths, aimed at, and capable of, mobilizing working-class mass action against *capitalism (most notably in the case of the 'myth of the general strike'). His arguments that violent confrontation can be noble and civilizing, that the future is unknowable, and that there is nothing to suggest civilized men and women will ever wholly renounce violence to advance estimable causes, punctured the Edwardian belief that progress would necessarily lead to peaceful settlement of all disputes, and more generally are still a powerful counter to the tendency among some social theorists towards an optimistic *historicism.

Sorokin, Pitirim Alexandrovich (1889–1968) Born in Russia of humble origins, imprisoned and under threat of death, Sorokin was exiled in 1922, and found his way to the United States, where he eventually became Professor of Sociology at Harvard. During his career he published over thirty books on a wide range of topics including *The Sociology of Revolution* (1925), *Social Mobility* (1927), *Rural Sociology* (1930), and *Social and Cultural Dynamics* (4 vols., 1937–41). The last of these offers a cyclical theory of social *change, which sees societies oscillating between three different types of 'mentalities', the sensate (emphasizing the role of the senses in understanding reality), ideational (religious ways of thinking), and idealistic (transitional types between the two). A prolific and profoundly iconoclastic sociologist (see, for example, his *Fads and Foibles in Modern Sociology and Related Sciences*, 1956), Sorokin's work is generally recognized as provocative and (in many respects) pioneering, yet later generations have been remarkably uninfluenced by it (with the notable exception of his analysis of *social mobility).

space Sometimes understood as the empty expanse within which objects are located, space is better understood as itself produced by the arrangement and rearrangement of objects. Material objects have a size and shape that constitutes their spatial extension. The arrangement of all such objects in a configuration or manifold is what is referred to as space. Thus, space itself has both shape and size.

The physical view of space is that particles and larger physical objects are in a state of constant motion and their movements generate the gravitational and other forces through which matter is attracted and repulsed to form the complex arrangement of space. Views of space derived from Albert Einstein combine it with *time as space-time and understand space as 'curved' in shape and finite (though immense) in extent as a result of the causal interdependencies established among the myriad physical entities that comprise the material world.

A sociological view of space recognizes that human interaction occurs within physical space-time but constitutes a distinct social space. Human beings are material entities whose movement involves them in relations with a material environment and specific material objects. The social relations that they form as a result of their movements is a social *structure with a definite shape and extent and so any social structure comprises a social space. Sociologists who recognize the centrality of social change and the need to study processes over time have therefore pointed to social structures as phenomena of social space-time.

For *Durkheim, space and time were fundamental categories in the formation of collective representations: central features of the ways in which humans organize and understand their experience of the world. Durkheim's approach to space emphasized the importance of social morphology, an idea developed in particular by Maurice *Halbwachs, who argued that social relations are projected out into space at the same time as they embed themselves in nature and so produce a particular pattern of settlements, routes, and boundaries. Important sociological studies of social morphology include Engels's description of Manchester in *The Condition of the Working Class in England* (1845), Charles Booth's studies of poverty in London, and the works of Chicago sociologists on *The City* (Park and Burgess, 1925). This work has influenced the development of urban sociology in writers such as Manuel Castells in *The Urban Question* (1972) and the approach has been powerfully extended by Henri Lefebvre in *The Production of Space* (1974).

Social space is not coterminous with physical space and particular fields or spaces of action may extend beyond specific physical locales or may connect a number of distinct physical locations. Thus, cultural scenes, art worlds, and musical subcultures are cultural spaces constituted by the activities of musicians, artists, audiences, producers, media specialists, and others with a specific interest in common but who come together in a single place only rarely, if ever. All social structures, to a greater or lesser extent, are separated from physical locations in this way, though they can never be completely disconnected from their material environment and context. *See also* CHICAGO SOCIOLOGY; TIME.

Spencer, Herbert (1820–1903) Encyclopaedic Victorian thinker who was internationally famous in his own time, and was especially admired in the United States. Many of his ideas have entered Western culture as conventional wisdom—or at least as conventional prejudices—yet few people read his books or remember his name today.

Born in the English Midlands of Nonconformist parents, Spencer became a railway engineer and a draughtsman. After a time he moved into journalism and began to produce a steady stream of books which are the basis of his reputation in social science. The complete bibliography is formidable, but includes *Social Statics* (1851), *First Principles* (1862), *The Study of Sociology* (1873), and *First Principles of Sociology* and *Descriptive Sociology* in parts through the 1870s and 1890s. (For a full account, which discusses Spencer against the social background of his time, see J. D. Y. Peel, *Herbert Spencer*, 1971.)

Spencer was the sociological prophet of the high Victorian era. Unlike Marx, he saw nothing but *progress in the Industrial Revolution. Spencer interpreted *society as a living, growing organism which, as it becomes more complex, must self-consciously understand and control the mechanisms of its own success. The most important of those mechanisms was the intense competition for resources which Spencer labelled 'the survival of the fittest' (anticipating Darwin's 'natural selection' by several years). Spencer believed that the unrestricted application of this principle would eventually lead to the best possible society.

His ideas were adopted with enthusiasm in America, notably by William Graham Sumner, and remain to this day the foundation of *libertarian and *laissez-faire social and economic theories.

Spengler, Oswald (1880–1936) Started his adult life as a schoolteacher but a small inheritance allowed him to live independently. His most famous work *Decline of the West* (1919) owed a great deal to the earlier arguments of the Russian cultural theorist Nikolai Danilevsky. Spengler argued that all civilizations followed a similar lifecycle of birth, maturity, and death. Human history, then, shows a sequence of cultures following each other as each reaches the end of its natural life and is overtaken by another. He saw himself living in the period of decline for Western civilization, which would finally end by the year 2000. He published some other works, but none had the success of his first. Though marked by numerous factual errors, his approach has inspired a number of other theorists to explore the clash and succession of civilizations.

spiralism (spiralist) A type of middle-class occupational *career pattern involving rapid geographical mobility in pursuit of occupational advancement. Many modern *organizations expect such geographical mobility from staff in the course of career promotion.

sponsored mobility *See* CONTEST AND SPONSORED MOBILITY.

SPSS The Statistical Package for the Social Sciences, commonly known as SPSS, is one of the most widely used software packages among academic sociologists. Developed in the United States by social scientists, it provides a range of facilities, including tabulation, *multivariate analysis, and virtually all the tests of statistical significance appropriate for sample survey data. SPSS was originally developed for mainframe computers, but has been increasingly used on personal computers. Market researchers who require report-quality output, and researchers working with large government-produced statistical *surveys and *censuses, sometimes use other, more efficient and more powerful software and programming languages. Sociologists have been reluctant to abandon SPSS in favour of more powerful packages that are easier to use. *See also* COMPUTER PACKAGES.

spurious correlation A correlation between two *variables when there is no causal link between them. A famous spurious correlation often quoted in the literature is that between the number of fire engines at a fire and the amount of damage done. Once the size of the conflagration is controlled for—that is, that large fires cause more damage and therefore require more fire engines to extinguish them—the original implied relationship disappears. Note also that it is not really the correlation which is spurious, but rather the implicit causal model: there are indeed more fire engines at fires where the greatest damage is done, but it is not the fire engines which cause the damage.

stagflation A combination of *inflation and stagnation in the economy. A situation that arose in Britain and other economies since the late 1960s, as accelerating inflation fed through into price expectations and wage demands.

Stalinism A term that is generally identified with the economic, political, and social features imposed on Russia after 1929, until the first de-Stalinization attempt under Khrushchev in 1956. The period of High Stalinism commenced in 1934 with the purge trials subsequent to the Kirov murder. Physical terror and concentration or labour camps, exile, and forced population movements, extermination, famine, and the total breakdown of social bonds of trust were just some of its features. One major characteristic was the forced collectivization of 100 million peasants, the legacy of which is still apparent in the food shortages and poverty-stricken countryside of much of the former Soviet Union. Forced *industrialization and the first two Five-Year Plans saw the imposition of a harsh labour discipline as the country was put on a war footing and smoke-stack industries became the hallmark of socialist progress. All this was overseen by a *command economy which produced pathologies among worker and manager alike.

Ideologically, the system was underpinned by dialectical materialism of the most mechanical kind, as rooted in *MELS*—the writings of Marx, Engels, Lenin, and Stalin—with the first three used to elaborate Stalin's own 'cult of personality'. Socialist *realism stunted the arts and culture. It is even questionable as to whether Stalinism helped the Soviet Union to survive the Nazi invasion in 1941, since not only was Stalin shown to be in gross error over the intentions of his partner in the Molotov-Ribbentrop Pact, but the depredations of the purges (particularly within the Officer Corps) had left the army leaderless.

Stalinism was not just the personal construct of one man. It was rooted in the Bolshevik seizure of power and the closure of the Constituent Assembly in 1918, after unfavourable elections. It was presaged by the practices adopted during War Communism and its aftermath the Kronstadt Revolt, The Tenth Party Congress in March 1921 and banning of factions within the Party, as well as the defeat of the opposition from the Left (Leon Trotsky) and Right (Nikolai Bukharin)—all of which created the blueprint and the practical means for Stalin's subsequent policies. Stalinism as terror was always associated with Yezhov, Yadov, Beria, and the security apparatus, allowing Stalin to distance himself from the atrocities. This enabled him to foster the image of Popular Hero of the Motherland War, Father of the Nations, and Great Strategist, and evade responsibility for the 20 million war dead and the equal number lost through the terror. By the time of Stalin's death in 1953, Soviet society was permeated with suspicion, corruption, inefficiency, and waste, ruled over by the KGB and a demoralized Party. However, the USSR was a major world nuclear power with surrounding nations in thrall, and this sense of superpower status was to keep the neo-Stalinist system which he bequeathed functioning at least until 1991. *See also* COLLECTIVISM; MARXISM.

standard deviation *See* VARIATION.

standardization In order to facilitate comparisons between different groups, data are standardized to some common basis. The simplest method is converting frequency counts into percentages, so that all values are shown to the common base of 100, or into decimal fractions of the total sum treated as unity (1.00). If the arithmetic mean (*see* CENTRAL TENDENCY (MEASURES OF)) and standard deviation (*see* VARIATION) are known, values can be divided by the standard deviation, thus treating the mean as the centre of the data and each case as a plus or minus deviation from it; the procedure is repeated for all sub-groups to be compared. Other procedures are used, depending on the methods of analysis to be applied to the data. *See also* INDEX.

standardized mortality ratios *See* MORTALITY RATE.

state A distinct set of *institutions that has the authority to make the rules which govern a *society. It claims, as Max Weber argued, a 'monopoly on the use of legitimate violence' within a specific territory. Hence, the state includes such institutions as the armed forces, civil service or state *bureaucracy, judiciary, and local and national councils of elected representatives (such as a parliament). Consequently the state is not a unified entity. It is, rather, a set of institutions which describe the terrain and parameters for political conflicts between various interests over the use of resources and the direction of public policy. Frequently there are conflicts over policy and resources, between elected politicians and non-elected civil servants, or between politicians in different parts of the state. It is therefore difficult to identify a state's *interests, since different parts of the state apparatus can have different interests and express conflicting preferences.

It is also difficult to identify the boundaries of the state. Older administrative perspectives see the state as a clearly defined set of institutions with official powers. Others, including Marxist theorists such as Antonio *Gramsci and Louis Althusser, question the distinction between the state and *civil society and argue that the former is integrated into many parts of the latter. For example, Althusser maintains that civil organizations such as the Church, schools, and even trade unions are part of the *ideological state apparatus. It is, indeed, increasingly difficult to identify the boundaries of the state. Many parts of civil society are given institutional access to the state and play a role in the development of public policy. The state also funds a number of groups within society which, although autonomous in principle, are dependent on state support. In addition, the boundaries of the state are continually changing, for example through *privatization (transferring responsibilities from the civil service to private contractors) and the creation of new regulatory bodies. Often the nature of these quasi-autonomous organizations is ambiguous: it is simply not clear whether they are part of the state or part of civil society.

A further important issue in relation to the state is the nature of state *power. The state as a set of institutions cannot act. It is the various actors within the state who make decisions and implement policy. This raises the important issue, much debated in recent years, of state autonomy. *Pluralists generally see the state as acting in the interests of groups in society. State actions are therefore reactions to group pressures. For some pluralists, the state provides an arena for *pressure group conflicts to take place, state policy being determined by the outcome of these conflicts. For others, the state is actually captured by pressure groups, while a third view is that the state determines what is in the national interest by arbitrating between the demands of the various interest groups.

For Marxist theorists, however, the role of modern states is determined by their location in capitalist societies. According to Nicos Poulantzas, for example (*Political Power and Social Classes*, 1968), capitalist states rule in the long-term political interest of capital. This raises the question of how the putative interests of capital are translated into state actions. So-called instrumentalists (such as R. Miliband, *The State in Capitalist Society*, 1969) argue that members of the state *elite come from the same social background as the capitalist class and so they share the same interests as the owners of capital and are linked to them via a whole panoply of social and political interconnections. As a result the state acts more or less at the behest of the capitalist class. Poulantzas, by contrast, argues that the question of who controls the state is irrelevant. Capitalist states act on behalf of the capitalist class, not because state officers consciously contrive to do so, but because the various parts of the state apparatus are structured in such a way that the long-term interests of *capital are always to the fore and dominant.

Both the Marxist and pluralist approaches to the state may be said to be society-centred: that is, they view the state as reacting to the activities of groups within society, be they classes or pressure groups. However, other writings on the state (for example, the works of Eric Nordlinger and Theda Skocpol) suggest that state actors are to an important degree autonomous. In other words, state personnel have interests of their own, which they can and do pursue independently of (sometimes in conflict with) the various groups in society. Since the modern state controls the means of violence, and the various groups within civil society are dependent on the state for achieving any policy goals they may espouse, the relationship between state and civil society is asymmetrical and state personnel can (to some extent) impose their own preferences on the citizenry.

In his writings on the social sources of power, Michael Mann outlines two types of state autonomy. The first is despotic power, where the power of the state derives from force, and so is limited to the territory over which the ruler can exercise terror. However, in modern societies, state power is more likely to be infrastructural. Here, the state increases its power by negotiating administrative relationships with different groups in society, in order to develop its capabilities for intervening in particular areas of policy. The concept of infrastructural power suggests that the state-centred versus society-centred dichotomy is too simplistic. State actors do have interests but these interests develop in relation to groups in society. Moreover, in order to develop the means of intervention, state actors are dependent on allies in society. Force cannot be the only means of state power and, therefore, state actors do have to make concessions.

Any definition of the state has to recognize its complexity. Its boundaries are not clearly defined and constantly changing. It is the site of internal conflicts not only between different organizations but also within organizations. There is no single state interest but, rather, various interests within different parts of the state. These interests are neither solely state-centred nor wholly society-centred but develop instead through bargaining between different groups in civil society and different state actors. Christopher Pierson's *The Modern State* (1996) is a good place to start when considering these various issues.

There is also an extensive literature on state formation. The issue here is one of identifying the processes by which states emerge. Can the formation of states be explained primarily in terms of the interests and struggles of social classes, or are other non-class actors involved? Is state formation best viewed in terms of the internal dynamics and conflicts in a given country, or are there international dynamics involving, for example, conflicts of war or economic domination? Is there a discernible historical pattern in the emergence of capitalist states? Was the formation of national states in the West associated with the emergence of capitalism? These and related issues are pursued in Gianfranco Poggi's *The Development of the Modern State* (1978), and Charles Tilly's *The Formation of National States in Western Europe* (1975). *See also* MILITARISM; MILITARY-INDUS-TRIAL COMPLEX; POWER ELITE.

state capitalism A label that has been applied to at least three different forms of economic organization: the taking over by a *state, within a capitalist society, of major sections of the economy (also known as *etatisme* or sometimes as 'democratic socialism'); the necessary maintenance of a capitalist sector within a society in transition to *socialism (as developed by Lenin in the early 1920s); and the thesis that the Soviet Union was not a socialist society, but simply another variant of *capitalism, as a result of the bureaucratic control of the productive system through state ownership (a proposition advanced by Marxist critics of the USSR from the 1930s onwards). *See also* COMMUNISM.

stateless societies A general term that is often applied to *acephalous or segmented societies, which lack a centralized *state authority, but is occasionally (though incorrectly) extended to include those societies which have a political system based on an acknowledged chief or traditional ruler, and therefore lack a clearly defined state apparatus.

state monopoly capitalism *See* COMMUNISM.

state socialism *See* COMMUNISM; REAL SOCIALISM.

statistical control Statistical techniques for excluding the influence of spec-ified *variables in an analysis. For example, if the data from a sample *survey showed a strong association between unemployment and clinical depression, one might want to control for the effect of social class. Partitioning the data by class (middle versus working) would establish whether or not the relationship between unemployment and depression is constant across all classes. Similarly, an observed association between class and clinical depression might well disap-pear, once a control is introduced for unemployment. (Working-class people are no more likely to suffer from depression than middle-class people, but they are more likely to be unemployed, and the unemployed are more likely to be depressed than are those in work.)

statistical inference The process by which results from a sample may be applied more generally to a *population. More precisely, how inferences may be drawn about a population, based on results from a sample of that population.

Inferential statistics are generally distinguished as a branch of statistical analysis from descriptive statistics, which describe variables and the strength and nature of relationships between them, but do not allow generalization. The ability to draw inferences about a population from a sample of observations from that population depends upon the *sampling technique employed. The importance of a scientific sample is that it permits statistical generalization or inference. For example, if we *survey a simple random sample of university students in Britain and establish their average (mean) height, we will be able to infer the likely range within which the mean height of all university students in Britain is likely to fall. Other types of sample, such as *quota samples, do not allow such inferences to be drawn. The accuracy with which we are able to estimate the population mean from the sample will depend on two things (assuming that the sample has been drawn correctly): the size of the sample and the variability of heights within the population. Both these factors are reflected in the calculation of the standard error. The bigger the standard error, the less accurate the sample mean will be as an estimate of the population mean.

Strictly speaking, therefore, inferential statistics is a form of inductive inference in which the characteristics of a population are estimated from data obtained by sampling that population. In practice, however, the methods are called upon for the more ambitious purpose of prediction, explanation, and hypothesis testing.

statistical interaction A statistically established relationship between two (or more) *variables such that the *values of one vary in some systematic way with the values of another. Statistical interactions between two or more independent variables can significantly complicate certain types of *multivariate analyses where *independent variables are assumed to be independent of (orthogonal to) each other.

status (social status) Two meanings have been given to the word 'status' in sociology. In its weakest form, it simply refers to the position that a person occupies in the social *structure, such as teacher or priest. It is often combined with the notion of social *role to produce the idea of a status-role. It is preferable to use the word 'position' for this, as less confusion with the more specific meaning given to the word will result.

In its stronger and more specific meaning it refers to a form of social stratification in which social positions are ranked and organized by legal, political, and cultural criteria into status groups. There are many versions of this approach to status. For example, the legal theorist Sir Henry Maine argued that we can conceptualize the history of Western society in terms of a transition from status to contract: that is, from a *feudal organization of hierarchically organized strata, to *market relations between individuals who are bound together by contracts. Max Weber adopted a similar historical view of the relationships between classes and status groups in his famous remarks on *power. Weber defined status position in *Economy and Society* (1920) as the 'effective claim to social esteem'. These status positions confer both negative and positive privileges, and status is typically based on a special *life-style, and a formal training. Status is expressed through and maintained by exclusionary practices such as marriage, conventions and customs, and common living arrangements. An aggregate of persons with a common status position form a status group which enjoys a common esteem and certain status monopolies over the resources of the group. Status groups are competitive because they seek to preserve their monopolistic privileges by excluding their rivals from enjoyment of these resources. Finally, depending on the dominant pattern of social *stratification, Weber distinguished between status society and class society.

Critics have noted that, especially in American sociology, the concept of status as a central notion of sociology was eroded, because it came to mean little more than a person's subjective evaluation of his or her position in the status hierarchy (that is 'prestige'). The conflicting and competitive features of status-group relations were translated into the idea of status seeking by individuals (as in 'prestigious roles', 'prestige ranking', and so forth). Among many American sociologists, *class and status came to be used interchangeably, as both concepts were used to measure subjective evaluations of positions in a system of social stratification.

Various attempts have been made to rescue the concept of status by arguing that it involves an objective organization of entitlements and privileges, which in many cases are guaranteed by law and the state, and not simply a subjective awareness of personal esteem. The best short introduction to the concept is Bryan S. Turner's *Status* (1988) and the wider issues are discussed in John Scott's *Stratification and Power* (1996). *See also* CITIZENSHIP; CLOSURE; ESTATE.

status, achieved Any social position held by an individual as a result of his or her personal accomplishments in open formal or market competition with others. The position of (for example) university professor, doctor, or auto-mechanic is usually gained via competitive examination, followed by successful entry into the job market. It is conventional to contrast achieved status with ascribed status. The latter refers to those social positions to which a person is allocated either by birth or by family background and which cannot (if at all) be altered according to individual accomplishments. Examples would include positions ascribed on the basis of race, ethnicity, or gender.

The distinction between *achievement and *ascription is heuristic and by no means absolute. Arguably, for example, an individual's social class standing might be an achieved or an ascribed status—depending on whether the researcher chooses to define class in terms of occupational attainment or family background. Similarly, some apparently achievement-based outcomes (including examination performance and occupational attainment themselves), can at least in part reflect ascriptive mechanisms—such as gender discrimination or race prejudice. *See also* MERITOCRACY; STATUS.

status, ascribed *See* ASCRIPTION; STATUS, ACHIEVED.

status attainment (**status-attainment theory**) An extensive literature investigating how educational achievements and other indicators of *skill and *ability translate into jobs ranked according to *socio-economic status or *prestige. The classic studies are those by Peter M. Blau and Otis Dudley Duncan (*The*

American Occupational Structure, 1967) and David Featherman and Robert Hauser (*Opportunity and Change*, 1978).

The status-attainment programme attempts to explain *social mobility patterns by identifying those attributes which seem to facilitate the movement of individuals into desirable occupations. To what extent are occupational outcomes shaped by family of origin rather than personal attributes such as educational attainment? This approach depends upon the assumption that individuals are allocated to positions ordered in a continuous unidimensional hierarchy. In some studies, this social hierarchy was conceptualized narrowly as being one of *occupational prestige—most commonly, how people rate the relative 'general standing' of different occupations. In others, it was extended to include additional aspects of socio-economic status, such as income and years of schooling. For a useful overview of the major contributions see D. J. Treiman and H. B. G. Ganzeboom, 'Cross-National Comparative Status-Attainment Research', *Research in Social Stratification and Mobility* (1990).

In the original Blau-Duncan model for the United States in 1962, the total correlation between son's current occupation and father's occupation was found to be 0.405. This could be decomposed into an indirect effect via education of 0.227 (57 per cent) and an effect net of education (direct or through the son's first job) of 0.178 (43 per cent). In this same study, the ratio of the effect of education on current occupation to the direct effect of father's occupation on current occupation was calculated to be 2.9 to 1, a finding which led Blau and Duncan to conclude that *achievement was more important than ascription in determining occupational status in mid-20th-century America.

The later so-called Wisconsin Model, developed by William H. Sewell and his associates, continued in the Blau-Duncan mould by relating the family background and ascribed characteristics of students to their occupational status via the mediation of ability as well as educational achievement. Various Wisconsin studies showed that family background affected educational and occupational outcomes through its effects on parental and peer influences and on the shaping of educational aspirations. Academic ability was also found to have a strong effect on educational attainment (independently of social origins) and an effect on occupational attainment through its impact on educational and occupational aspirations. In other words, both schooling and family background affected status attainment, mainly through effects transmitted by social psychological processes.

The implications of these findings for arguments about *equality of opportunity and *meritocracy soon became a matter of controversy. Some observers (such as Robert Hauser) took them to mean that status attainment in the United States was mainly a meritocratic process since the effects of family background could (apparently) be overcome by those attributable to schooling. Others (including Christopher Jencks) argued that such results undermined meritocratic interpretations of the status attainment process because both ascription and achievement continued to exert a substantial influence on mobility outcomes. Moreover, Jencks and his colleagues maintained that the importance of family background was underestimated in the Wisconsin model, and that of aptitude and aspirations overestimated, because of measurement errors in the original studies (see, for example, the exchange between Hauser, Jencks, and others in the journal *Sociology of Education*, 1983).

This approach to the study of social inequality remains controversial. The sociological concept of 'socio-economic status' which was regularly used as the dependent variable (that which people attain) in status attainment research has a bizarre history and referent. In the most widely used index of socio-economic status (that devised by Duncan), an occupation's socio-economic status is determined by a weighted combination of the average income and years of schooling characteristic of those in the occupation (although the reasoning behind this is never explained), while the weights are those that best fit perceptions of the occupational prestige attaching to people in certain specific occupations. (For the details see Duncan's classic article on 'A Socioeconomic Index for All Occupations', in A. Reiss (ed.), *Occupations and Social Status*, 1961.) Is this then a measure of the occupation's prestige or its socio-economic resources?

Other versions of the theory take occupational prestige as a dependent variable. These sorts of scales depend upon the assumption that individuals are allocated to positions along a dimension of 'social standing' that is embedded in a societal consensus about social honour in general and honorific vocations in particular. There is considerable dispute about whether or not such an assumption is tenable. Since this seems to imply that *social order rests upon consensual values, and that the prestige hierarchy is a function of widespread convergence in moral evaluations, the approach has been criticized as an extension of the *functional theory of stratification—although its practitioners strenuously deny this charge.

During the 1980s, and in response to criticism by proponents of the new structuralism, researchers examining occupational outcomes within the explanatory framework of status attainment attempted to incorporate structural limitations as well as socialization processes within their explanations. That is, they moved away from the question of how family of origin and educational attainment affect occupational placement, towards analysis of the impact on occupational outcomes of variation in labour-market structures and processes. This change of emphasis was an attempt to overcome the perceived failure of status-attainment research to consider how structural effects impact upon educational and occupational attainment. The result was something of a hybrid between the status-attainment and class analysis traditions (see, for example, Larry Griffin and Arne Kalleberg, 'Stratification and Meritocracy in the United States: Class and Occupational Recruitment Patterns', *British Journal of Sociology*, 1981). For a review of this later literature see Kalleberg, 'Comparative Perspectives on Work Structures and Inequality', *Annual Review of Sociology* (1988).

status consistency *See* STATUS CRYSTALLIZATION.

status crystallization A term devised by the American sociologist Gerhard Lenski (1924–2015) (see 'Status Crystallization: A Non-Vertical Dimension of Status', *American Sociological Review*, 1954). Lenski argues that inconsistencies in *status attributes lead to status ambiguity which in turn creates social tension. However, the concept itself does not refer to attitudes and expectations, but to the felt status incongruence. It was left to later writers (such as George *Homans) to take such notions as status crystallization and status integration, combine them with the concepts of relative *deprivation and *reference groups, and in this way show their relevance for broader debates about social justice.

Subsequently, in the work of East European sociologists such as Wlodzimierz Wesolowski (see *Classes, Strata and Power*, 1966), status crystallization became the basis for a major school of social *stratification. These authors took the indicators of status—such as *occupational prestige, *ethnicity, education, and income—and sought to measure the degree of crystallization (consistency or congruence); that is, whether or not individuals, *roles, or *groups were being ranked consistently across a range of status criteria, with high salaries attached to high-prestige occupations, and so forth. Crystallization could have consequences for role conflict, mental health, and social tension, particularly if awareness of status inconsistency emerged.

This approach was adopted by sociologists in communist societies during the 1960s and 1970s, in the attempt to introduce research concerning the extent of social inequality under *real socialism, without broaching the taboo question of social *class. Their general argument was that, in post-revolutionary societies, social class in the Marxist sense had lost its determining power over *life-chances, but that social positions comprising status attributes, although decomposed or decrystallized, could re-emerge in a status-consistent form. This would point to the resurgence of systematic or structured social stratification and ultimately lead to social *closure.

status degradation ceremony *See* DEGRADATION CEREMONY.

status frustration A concept developed by Albert Cohen in *Delinquent Boys* (1956), and used to explain working-class male *delinquency as being a *reaction formation towards middle-class values of success, as embodied in the school. Delinquent boys experience status frustration and invert the middle-class values of the school to create a delinquent *subculture. Cohen's argument forms part of the *anomie and strain traditions of delinquency and subcultural analysis.

status group *See* STATUS; STRATIFICATION.

status, master *See* MASTER STATUS.

status set An array of social positions (for example factory-worker, mother, church-goer) found in one person. The term was introduced by Robert Merton in *Social Theory and Social Structure* (2nd edn., 1957). This uses the general, and now outmoded, terminology of *status.

status situation *See* CLASS POSITION.

stem family *See* FAMILY, STEM.

stereotype (stereotyping) Derived from the Greek (*stereos* = solid, *typos* = mark), and applied in the late 18th century as a technical term for the casting of a papier mâché copy of printing type, the concept was developed by the North American journalist Walter Lippman in his book *Public Opinion* (1922) to mean the fixed, narrow 'pictures in our head', generally resistant to easy change. It usually carries a pejorative meaning—in contrast to the sociological process of typification. The concept has been widely used in studies of *crime and *deviance, where assumptions about the character and likely behaviour of members of particular social groups have been shown to make them more or less likely to become the subjects of police action, court conviction, and imprisonment. It is a central idea in *labelling theory. *See also* DEVIANCE AMPLIFICATION; GENDER STEREOTYPES; PREJUDICE.

stigma Although the term has a long history (in classical Greece it referred to a brand placed on outcast groups), it entered sociology mainly through the work of Erving Goffman (*Stigma*, 1960). It is a formal concept which captures a relationship of devaluation rather than a fixed attribute. Goffman classifies stigmas into three types—bodily, moral, and tribal—and analyses the ways in which they and *societal reactions to them affect human interactions.

stimulus discrimination A phenomenon identified in *behaviourist learning theory: the individual learns to distinguish, for response purposes, between similar stimuli.

stimulus generalization In *behaviourist learning theory the concept denotes the way in which responses, initially conditioned to a particular stimulus, are also evoked by other stimuli that bear some similarity to the original.

Stouffer, Samuel A. (1900–60) An American sociologist and quantitative methodologist who, during the Second World War, directed social research in the US War Department. His research there culminated in his most famous work, *The American Soldier* (1949), which made major contributions to social *psychology and *survey methodology, as well as developing the concept of relative *deprivation. *See also* REFERENCE GROUP.

strain theories of delinquency *See* ANOMIE.

stratification The term stratification in sociology is usually applied to studies of structured social *inequality; that is, studies of any systematic inequalities between groups of people, which arise as the unintended consequence of social processes and relationships. When we ask why there is *poverty; why Black people or women in the United States are disadvantaged *vis-à-vis* (respectively) Whites and men; or what chances someone born into the *working class has of achieving a *middle-class position; we are posing questions about social stratification.

Social stratification is thus at the heart of *macrosociology—the study of whole societies, in comparative perspective, in an attempt to understand processes of social stability and *change. Social stratification begins from Weber's limiting cases of the more traditional *status-based society (for example, societies based on *ascriptive categories such as *estates and *castes, or where there is *slavery so that inequalities are legally sanctioned), and the polarized but more fluid *class-based society (typical of the modern West), where there is a greater element of *achievement, where economic differences are paramount, and inequality is more impersonal. Status formation and class formation thus represent the two extreme poles of *social integration—the ways people in a society relate one to another.

Studies of social stratification have three objectives. The first is to establish the extent to which class or status systems predominate at the societal level such that they are constitutive of modes of social action. Hence, to make the claim that Britain is a class society one would need to show that class relationships underlie predominant modes of social action, and represent the fundamentals of social integration. The second is the analysis of class and status structures and the determinants of class and status formation: for example, to pose questions such as why there is no *socialism in the United States, or why the British working class did not produce a *communist revolution, is to pose questions about the degree of class formation in society. Many sociological and historical studies have attempted to explain variability in the degree of such class formation. Finally, social stratification documents inequalities of condition, opportunities and outcome, and the ways in which groups maintain class or status boundaries. In other words, it addresses the question of social *closure, and investigates those exclusionary strategies by which groups maintain their privileges and other groups seek to gain access to them. Often class and status interact in interesting ways. For example, advantaged classes may attempt to develop the characteristics of status groups in order to routinize, justify, and thereby maintain their privileges: the *nouveaux riches* the world over are notorious proponents of this strategy. Similarly, the complex articulation of class, *race, age, and *gender differences have come increasingly to interest researchers investigating the multifarious processes of social stratification in modern societies: the work of Joan Huber is a good illustration of this development (see, for example, *Sex Stratification*, 1983).

At the most general level, therefore, social stratification is concerned in different ways with the issues of class and status-group formation as the key to understanding social integration; that is, the extent to which social relationships are cohesive or divisive, and the consequences of this for *social order. Useful overviews are John Scott, *Stratification and Power* (1996) and Rosemary Crompton, *Class and Stratification: An Introduction to Current Debates* (3rd edn., 2008).

stress An imprecise concept, popular in everyday discourse to refer to any kind of feeling of anxiety or pressure. In its strict academic use, however, it has a precise meaning. It may refer to external situational pressures (stressors) or to the responses to them (stress reactions)—responses usually assumed to have physical and psychological components, such as raised pulse-rate and adrenalin levels, and feelings of anxiety and discomfort. In either usage it is commonly invoked as a key factor in explanations of bodily and mental ill-health, various forms of under-performance, and deviant behaviour. Its attraction to social scientists lies in its potential to link features of the individual's present or recent social situation to some specified outcome.

Much of the sociological debate focuses on identifying and measuring the domain of the stressful. Some researchers assume only negative occurrences like divorce or unemployment are stressful, others any situation involving significant change (for example marriage, job promotion, or moving house); some incorporate only life-events, others include ongoing difficulties; some employ standardized measures (for example the Social Readjustment Rating Scale), others assess subjective meanings, arguing that what is stressful for one may not be stressful for another. However, subjective assessments of stressful experiences are problematic since they may be contaminated by the very feelings generated by that experience, as for example in the case of clinically *depressed individuals who retrospectively identify a particular life-event as stressful in order either to cooperate in treatment or to facilitate self-understanding of their (otherwise mysterious) illness. George Brown and Tirril Harris, in their influential study *Social Origins of Depression* (1978), measure meaning not by direct subjective evaluations but through contextual evidence about values, objectives, and circumstances.

Of increasing interest in the field is the identification of factors such as social support that mediate between stressful situations and responses to them. Brown and Harris term these 'vulnerability' or, conversely, 'coping' factors, examining situationally generated rather than biological vulnerability.

strike A form of *industrial action involving withdrawal of labour such as to constitute a temporary breach of the employment contract. Effective strike action means preventing the use of an alternative labour force, usually through picketing the workplace, so causing the partial or total cessation of production until the matter in dispute is favourably resolved. Strikes are the characteristic sanction of *trade unions and in this form are often characterized as official. Unofficial or wild-cat strikes arise from spontaneous, even unorganized walk-outs or action, by unrecognized rank-and-file leaders. Strikes are also used as a method of social and political protest, the withdrawal of labour or cooperation aimed at influencing government or state policies. Hence the 'political strike' or, where all or much of the population is involved, the 'general strike'. *See also* INDUSTRIAL CONFLICT; KERR-SIEGEL HYPOTHESIS.

strike-proneness *See* INDUSTRIAL CONFLICT.

structural adjustment A package of policies associated with loans to *Third World countries by the International Monetary Fund and the World Bank. There are three elements: stabilization (the control of *inflation by restricting the rate of increase of the money supply via the budget deficit); liberalization (a reduction in government intervention in product and factor *markets in order to bring domestic prices more in line with world prices); and *privatization of public-sector institutions to improve the technical efficiency of production. Structural adjustment policies have had negative distributive effects in the short run, because of high prices and raised *unemployment, and long-run effects have been variable.

structural differentiation A concept associated with *evolutionary theories of history and with structural functionalism. Societies are seen as moving from the simple to the complex via a process of social *change based on structural differentiation. The process may be imagined, in its simplest form, as an amoeba dividing, redividing, then redividing again. So-called simple societies are tribal societies where everything happens within and through the *kinship system. In modern complex societies there are separate institutions of education, work, government, religion, and so forth, while the family now has more specific and limited *roles—such as early *socialization. Differentiation involves the increasing specialization of different subsystems and institutions within the society.

A classic statement may be found in the work of the Israeli comparative and historical sociologist Shlomo N. Eisenstadt (see especially 'Social Change, Differentiation and Evolution', *American Sociological Review*, 1964), now unfashionable, mainly because of its association with the *modernization theory of the 1960s. This neglect is probably unwarranted, since Eisenstadt offers a sophisticated theory of change that goes a long way beyond traditional evolutionary theories, and represents the most systematic attempt yet to deploy the concept of structural differentiation in substantive analyses (as for example in *Modernization, Protest and Change*, 1967, and *Revolution and the Transformation of Societies*, 1978).

Talcott Parsons sees the process as involving three stages: a process of differentiation; a process of adaptation and reintegration; and, finally, the establishment of a more general system of *values which holds the more complex society together. The impetus towards differentiation comes from the need for a society to adapt to its physical and social environment. The basic evolutionary idea can be found in Herbert Spencer, is developed and applied to a particular instance by Neil Smelser (*Social Change in the Industrial Revolution*, 1959), and expounded at the most general level by Parsons himself (*Societies: Evolutionary and Comparative Perspectives*, 1966).

Evolutionary theories such as this have been much criticized by sociologists during the past two decades. Anthony Giddens, for example, in *The Constitution of Society* (1984) argues that simple societies are actually not simple at all, and that the mechanism of adaptation is too vague and general to explain social change.

structural functionalism *See* FUNCTION; FUNCTIONAL THEORY OF STRATIFICATION; MALINOWSKI; PARSONS; RADCLIFFE-BROWN.

structuralism At the most general level the term is used loosely in sociology to refer to any approach which regards social *structure (apparent or otherwise) as having priority over social action.

More specifically, however, it refers to a particular theoretical perspective that became fashionable in the late 1960s and early 1970s and which spread across a range of disciplines including *social anthropology, *linguistics, literary criticism, *psychoanalysis, and *sociology. Its influence on sociology came from several directions: Claude Lévi-Strauss's structural anthropology and semiotic analysis of cultural phenomena in general; Michel Foucault's work on the history of ideas; Jacques Lacan's psychoanalysis; and the structural Marxism of Louis Althusser.

Basic to the approach is the idea that we can discern underlying structures behind the often fluctuating and changing appearances of social reality. The model is *Saussure's structural linguistics and the notion that a language can be described in terms of a basic set of rules which govern the combination of sounds to produce meanings. For Lévi-Strauss and *semiotics generally, these underlying structures are categories of the mind, in terms of which we organize the world around us. For Lévi-Strauss, but not necessarily others, such categories can always be understood as binary oppositions (for example up/down, hot/cold). Structural Marxism replaced these mental categories by positions in *modes of production (such as those of labourer versus non-labourer) and substituted relationships to the means of production for the rules governing the production of meaning.

The basic principle is perhaps most visible in the writings of Lévi-Strauss. He acknowledged three influences: namely, geology, psychoanalysis, and Marxism. All three reveal hidden (unconscious) laws or structures beneath surface manifestations, but that is the extent to which he pursued the implications of the latter two. In contrast to the tradition inspired by Bronislaw *Malinowski, Lévi-Strauss was less interested in detailed, holistic studies of specific societies, but rather in potential universals and common structures of the mind. He examined an array of exotic classification systems and myths, *Mythologies* (four vols., 1964–71), arguing that they could be reduced to binary oppositions, while also demonstrating the complexity and richness of imagination among different peoples. *Totemism* (1962) and *The Savage Mind* (1962) reveal hidden logic and intriguing transformations in what might otherwise have been dismissed as mere superstitions: so-called primitives had a science of the concrete. Similarly, in the bulky and formidable *The Elementary Structures of Kinship* (1949), he aimed to show that the multiplicity of kinship systems could be reduced to just two types—either generalized or restricted exchange.

Whatever the form of structuralism, however, certain implications about the nature of the world necessarily follow. The first is that the underlying elements of the structure remain (comparatively) constant, and it is the varying relationships between them that produce different languages, systems of ideas, and types of society. The emphasis therefore shifts away from looking at distinct entities towards concentrating on the relationships between them—to the extent, indeed, of arguing that those things which appear to us as discrete entities are the artefactual products of relationships. This emphasis on relationships is carried much further by *post-structuralism.

Secondly, there is the implication that what appears to us as solid, normal, or natural, is in fact the end result of a process of production from some form of underlying structure. This is perhaps most startling in literary criticism, where even the realist novel is shown to be as much the result of a process of artistic production as its most avant-garde counterpart: it is not simply a good copy of something that exists 'out there' in reality. This idea has now become commonplace in, for example, sociological studies of gender, where it is often argued that masculinity, femininity, homosexuality, and so forth are social constructions. Similarly, it is frequently argued that scientific knowledge is not knowledge of a real, external world, but rather the result of certain social processes and ways of thinking that we call scientific.

Thirdly, structuralism transforms our commonsense notion of individuals: they too are seen as the product of relationships, rather than as the authors of social reality. Structuralism replaces the ontologically privileged human subject with a decentred conception of the self. Whereas structuralist Marxism would see the individual as a mere bearer of social relations (of ownership and non-ownership of the means of production), others conceptualize individuals as the product of *discourses and the relationships between discourses. This shift in perspective is often placed in a steady progress of our understanding of the world—a process of so-called decentring. Thus, with Copernicus came the realization that the earth was not the centre of the universe; with Darwin the realization that human beings were not the centre of creation but a product of evolution; with Marx the realization that human beings were not the producers but the product of social relations; and with Freud the realization that individuals were not the conscious agents of choice but the product of unconscious desires. Indeed, at the height of the popularity of structuralism, it was common to talk of the death of the subject—the demise of the idea of individuals acting and choosing voluntarily. Some granted the role of agency instead to the underlying structure itself, and talked of 'language speaking people', 'books reading people', and so forth. This more extreme view has moderated with the development of post-structuralism.

Finally, structuralism heralded a change in our conception of history, away from the idea of a comparatively steady evolutionary development, with one form of society leading on to another, towards a view of history as discontinuous and marked by radical changes. The root of this shift in perspective lies in the distinction between diachrony and synchrony. The former refers to changes of which we are most immediately aware. If we take *language as an example, then a language can be seen to change over a shorter or longer period, as new words and phrases enter general usage while others disappear. However, it can be argued that the structure remains constant throughout, since the changes are produced by new combinations already provided for or contained within the underlying rules. This constancy occurs at the synchronic level. Similarly, in the case of societies, it is possible to argue that the underlying structure of (say) capitalism remains the same and determines the history of apparent social change, this being the change that we actually experience. A change in the type of society itself would involve a much more dramatic shift in the underlying structure.

Structuralism (at least in its radical form) is no longer as fashionable as it was, although some of the above ideas have had an influence beyond structuralist circles. Its sociological significance is discussed fully in C. R. Badcock, *Lévi-Strauss, Structuralism and Sociological Theory* (1975).

structural mobility *See* MOBILITY, SOCIAL.

structural unemployment *See* UNEMPLOYMENT.

structuration A concept devised by, and central to, the sociological theory developed by the British social theorist Anthony *Giddens. Structuration theory is a social ontology, defining what sorts of things exist in the world, rather than setting out laws of development or suggesting clear *hypotheses about what actually happens. It tells us what we are looking at when we study society rather than how a particular society actually works. Giddens criticizes and rejects theories such as *functionalism and *evolutionary theory, which he regards as closed systems, insisting that social phenomena and events are always contingent and open-ended. He attempts to transcend the traditional division in sociology between *action and *structure by focusing on 'social practices' which, he argues, produce and are produced by structures. Structures, for Giddens, are not something external to social actors but are rules and resources produced and reproduced by actors in their practices. He also emphasizes the importance of time and space for social theory and social analysis: his historical sociology then explores the different ways in which societies bind these together.

There is no obvious single statement of structuration theory. Giddens began his project with a revision of the classical thinkers in sociology (*Capitalism and Modern Social Theory*, 1971), and this led in turn to the major formulations of structuration (*Central Problems in Social Theory*, 1979, and *The Constitution of Society*, 1984), although these have been developed further in a major enterprise in historical sociology (*A Contemporary Critique of Historical Materialism*, 1981; *The Nation-State and Violence*, 1985; and *The Consequences of Modernity*, 1990). There is now a considerable secondary literature (see, for example, I. J. Cohen, *Structuration Theory*, 1989). Several fairly scathing critiques—which, among other things, accuse Giddens of 'reinventing the wheel' where sociological theories of action, structure, and change are concerned, and structuration theory in particular of obscurantism and empirical emptiness (drawing a parallel with the theoretical work of Talcott Parsons)—will be found in Jon Clark et al. (eds.), *Anthony Giddens: Consensus and Controversy* (1990). A comprehensive review of Giddens's work can be found in Steven Loyal's *Anthony Giddens* (2003). A highly sophisticated approach to structuration—in the form of structural 'morphogenesis'—has been taken by Margaret Archer in *Realist Social Theory* (1995). *See also* GIDDENS.

structure (social structure) A term referring to any recurring pattern of social behaviour; or, more specifically, to the ordered interrelationships between the different elements of a *social system or *society. Structure is generally agreed to be one of the most important but also most elusive concepts in the social sciences (see W. H. Sewell, 'A Theory of Structure', *American Journal of Sociology*, 1992). It is sometimes used rather loosely to refer to any observable 'pattern' in social activities, and empirical researchers, for example, have referred to statistical distributions of occupations and employment as disclosing the social structure of a society. More typically, however, it is seen as designating the actual arrangement of individuals and groups into those larger entities that Durkheim saw as social facts. The term largely originated as an application of ideas from biology, where the structure of an organism is the anatomical arrangement of its various organs. Social systems were seen as organized around an 'institutional' arrangement of individuals that defined their actual relations to each other. Most clearly expounded in structural functionalism, the institutions of a society are clusters of norms and meanings, drawn from the *culture, that define the expectations that people hold about each other's behaviour. It is through these expectations that specific *roles and reciprocal role relationships are defined. A social structure does not, however, consist only of such institutional connections. People act upon the institutionalized role expectations and so come into definite and recurrent relations with each other. Although there is rarely a perfect correspondence between institutionalized expectations and actual social relations, the term social structure designates this crucial combination of institutions and relations as constituting the 'anatomy' of a society. Social structure, then, comprises both 'institutional structure' and 'relational structure'.

Unlike the structure of a building or an organism, a social structure is not directly visible. It is evidenced in the observable movements and actions of individuals, but it cannot be reduced to these. The core institutional norms and meanings are cultural phenomena that exist only as shared ideas and representations in the minds of individuals. For this reason, *socialization into a culture is central to the maintenance of a social structure. Writers on *structuration have emphasized that social structure is carried and has its effects because it is embodied in individuals through their socialization and provides them with dispositions and tendencies to act in particular, structured ways. Thus, a recent discussion has emphasized that the concept of social structure must be seen as resting upon this 'embodied structure' (José Lòpez and John Scott, *Social Structure*, 2000).

Some structural theories have emphasized the determining capacity of social structure as against human *agency. Talcott Parsons, for example, has been criticized for overemphasizing socialization in a common cultural system and, therefore, depicting human actors as lacking in any freedom or autonomy. They are seen as passively acting out the roles into which they have been socialized. This is not, however, inherent in a structural approach. Marxism, for example, recognizes clashes and contradictions between elements of social structures, and active human agency is essential in resolving these contradictions. *See also* FORMALISM; FUNCTION; SOCIAL ORDER; STRUCTURALISM.

structure, formal *See* FORMAL STRUCTURE.

subculture Widely used to refer to a local or specializaed culture embedded in a larger culture. The term is used in subcultural theories to refer to the formation of specific meanings and values as a collective solution to, or resolution of, problems arising from the blocked aspirations of members, or their ambiguous position in the wider society. Thus subcultures are distinct from the larger *culture but borrow (and often distort, exaggerate, or invert) its symbols, values, and beliefs. The concept is widely used in the sociology of *deviance—particularly in studies of *youth culture.

In the American tradition, a major influence has been Robert Merton's refor-mulation of Émile Durkheim's concept of *anomie, whilst the influence of the *Chicago School is also important to note. Albert K. Cohen (*Delinquent Boys*, 1955) argued that delinquent subcultures developed around adolescent status problems. He described the *status frustration of young working-class men, taught at school to aspire to middle-class values, yet remaining tied to their limited, working-class *opportunity structures. Faced with a lack of legitimate opportunities, status could only be achieved within a subculture of oppositional, expressive, hedonistic, and non-utilitarian values. Walter Miller ('Lower-Class Culture as a Generating Milieu of Gang Delinquency', *Journal of Social Issues*, 1958) argued that delinquent subcultures were rooted in aspects of working-class culture; and, rather than being merely a reaction to middle-class society, were more an expressive emphasizing of the 'focal concerns' of the parent culture. Richard A. Cloward and Lloyd B. Ohlin (*Delinquency and Opportunity*, 1960) combined elements of the anomie approach with Edwin Sutherland's theory of *differential association, identifying 'strain' as a result of the perceived blocking of legitimate means to attain internalized, conventional (middle-class) goals. Some youths resolved this strain by turning to the illegitimate opportunity structures of the local working-class community. Apart from legitimate opportu-nities these also offered 'criminal' or 'conflict' means of succeeding. 'Retreatist' behaviour (such as drug-taking or alcohol use) signalled a double failure to succeed in the spheres either of legitimate or illegitimate enterprise.

British subcultural studies have drawn heavily upon the American tradition, but frequently provided new perspectives: for example, in terms of the ways youth experiences British working-class culture (D. Downes, *The Delinquent Solution*, 1966); the bohemian hedonism of middle-class youth subcultures (J. Young, *The Drugtakers*, 1971); the idea of subcultures as arenas of 'cultural resistance through ritual' (S. Hall and T. Jefferson (eds.), *Resistance through Rituals*, 1976); and 'reading' the meaning of style in subcultures (R. Hebdige, *Subculture: The Meaning of Style*, 1979).

Subcultures can arise, according to some authors at least, as forms of symbolic resistance within social institutions which reflect aspects of the social organiza-tion of wider society, including schools (D. Hargreaves, *Social Relations in a Secondary School*, 1967) and prisons (G. Sykes, *The Society of Captives*, 1958), or can provide wider networks for those seeking to assert the sense of difference they feel, for example as homosexuals (see K. Plummer, *Sexual Stigma*, 1975). Feminist writers have explained the absence of girls from street youth culture by reference to a feminine 'bedroom subculture' (see A. McRobbie and J. Garber, 'Girls and Subcultures', in S. Hall and T. Jefferson (eds.), *Resistance through Rituals*, 1976).

Subcultural theories can be criticized on several grounds. They can overdraw differences between (and, relatedly, overemphasize the internal homogeneity of) groups identified by, for example, their social class or their age. A consistent failing in subculture studies has been their neglect of women and non-white groups.

The idea of a subculture implies difference from a dominant, superordinate host culture, yet it can be argued that the plurality and fragmentation of modern or postmodern culture erodes the significance of the former concept. Stanley Cohen has proffered a fairly damning critique of the 'resistance through rituals' tradition of British subcultural theory, arguing that the exercises of decoding and deciphering the subcultural styles in question (punk, skinhead, or whatever) are politically partisan, and ultimately unconvincing, since they nowhere address themselves to the explicit intentions of the research subjects themselves (*Folk Devils and Moral Panics*, 2nd edn., 1980). *See also* COLEMAN.

subemployment *See* UNDEREMPLOYMENT.

subject (the subject) A term used in preference to alternatives such as 'actor' and 'individual' by writers in the *structuralist tradition. Its use indicates a rejection of what such writers regard as the *humanist assumptions carried by the alternative terms. More specifically, what the use of the term minimally indicates is a rejection of the idea that individual human beings are the sole originators of social relations. Whether or not its presence also indicates that subjects are simply the bearers of social relations, and/or the sole substance of sociality, varies from author to author. *See also* ALTHUSSER.

subjectivity The self-conscious perspective of the person or *subject. This is invariably contrasted with *objectivity and is used pejoratively by *positivistic social scientists. By contrast, it is seen as crucial within hermeneutics. Structuralist, Marxist, and psychoanalytic theories have suggested how the subject is constructed. *See also* INTERPRETATION; MEANING.

sublimation A term used by *psychoanalysts, to refer to the unconscious process by which a sexual impulse is deflected, so as to express itself in some non-sexual and socially acceptable activity. For example, a child may wish to play with faeces, but in the light of parental disapproval may play with pies or make clay models instead (see C. Brenner, *An Elementary Textbook of Psychoanalysis*, 1974).

subordinate value system *See* DUAL CONSCIOUSNESS.

subsistence economy An agrarian economy based on production for consumption rather than exchange. Such economies are characterized by low levels of production, yielding a surplus capable of meeting little more than the basic necessities of life, and tend to be seen by development agencies as a major constituent of Third World poverty and a cause of underdevelopment.

substantive rationality *See* FORMAL RATIONALITY.

suburbanism This term refers to social and cultural characteristics that some sociologists have claimed typify suburban residents. Accounts of suburbanism as a way of life differ widely but commonly refer to the dominance of younger, middle-class, and family-oriented patterns of work and social life; a high level of social activity based on friendship rather than kinship networks; and a considerable degree of uniformity, even conformity, in style of life. A series of studies—notably by the American sociologists Herbert Gans and Bennett Berger—largely undermined these claims, showing that suburban areas vary considerably in class and age composition, and in patterns of social life, so that suburban life-styles and social relations are not determined by physical location ('suburbia') as such. Like the 'folk' and 'urban' ideal-types, the suburban ideal-type is largely a myth. The best general overview of this literature is David C. Thorns, *Suburbia* (1972). For an interesting case study of processes of social control in the suburbs see M. P. Baumgartner, *The Moral Order of a Suburb* (1988). *See also* ORGANIZATION MAN; SUBURBANIZATION.

suburbanization Suburbanization denotes the process by which cities expand peripherally, initially by out-migration of population and economic activity from dense urban cores, to less dense contiguous settlements. Developments in transport technology—such as railways, tramways, and improved roads—have aided suburbanization.

There are several partially competing explanations of the process. Economists and geographers stress the importance of competition in urban land markets, driving out activities which can no longer afford to locate centrally, and of market developments which make suburban business location desirable. Sociological studies have shown how individuals are motivated to relocate in suburbs to improve their quality of life. Marxists and others have traced the links between suburbanization and capital accumulation. Each account has some relevance to understanding this complex social and geographical phenomenon. *See also* COLLECTIVE CONSUMPTION; CONCENTRIC ZONE THEORY; SUBURBANISM; URBAN SOCIOLOGY.

suicide Commonly defined as the intentional killing of oneself. Often associated with Émile Durkheim, the study of suicide was a major area of research in 19th-century sociology. Key studies included Emilio Morselli, *Suicide: An Essay on Comparative Moral Statistics* (1879) and Thomas Masaryck, *Suicide and the Meaning of Civilisation* (1881). In his classic study *Suicide: A Study in Sociology* (1897), Durkheim defined it as 'every case of death which results directly or indirectly from a positive or negative act, accomplished by the victim himself which he knows must produce this result'. Controversially he did not require that the death must be intentional, arguing that intentions are hard to identify. Consequently he extended the definition, including for example heroic military deaths, where there is no chance of survival but no specific intention to kill oneself.

Durkheim chose to study suicide because it seemed to illustrate perfectly the necessity for and value of sociological explanation: a patently private, individual act, which was, none the less, subject to social forces and required a distinctively sociological explanation. He maintained that the tendency to suicide depended not on individual psychology or features of the physical environment, but on the nature of the individual's relation to society. Suicide as an individual action represented the failure of social solidarity and was indicative of the ineffectiveness of social bonds. He distinguished four main types of suicide according to

s

causation. Altruistic and egoistic suicide depend on the individual's integration or attachment to social groups. In altruistic suicide the individual is too strongly integrated into society—a society which encourages or even requires the individual to sacrifice his or her own life (as when a wife is expected to commit suicide on her husband's death). Conversely, in egoistic suicide the individual is insufficiently integrated into society, and so is not subject to the collective forces that prevent suicide—and, indeed, experiences an isolation and detachment conducive to it. Anomic and fatalistic suicide reflect the regulation of individuals by shared norms. Anomic suicide occurs as a result of normlessness, when the individual's passions, ambitions, and appetites are increased to a level where they cannot find satisfaction. Fatalistic suicide, on the other hand, is likely to occur when commitment to group norms is excessively strong.

Durkheim's analysis has been criticized on numerous grounds: for his definition of suicide and the mismatch between this definition and that embodied in the suicide statistics he employs to substantiate his argument; for his classification of types of suicide in terms of cause (so-called aetiological classification) which incorporates into the classification the very causal links he is seeking to establish; for his extreme polarization of social and psychological explanations (where complementarity should be assumed); and for using aggregate data to make inferences about individuals (the so-called *ecological fallacy).

A major strand of subsequent sociological discussions concerns the limitations of *official statistics of suicide. Jack D. Douglas, influenced by the work of interactionists and *ethnomethodologists, argued in *Social Meanings of Suicide* (1967) that what was defined or treated as suicide differed from culture to culture, thereby calling into question cross-cultural and historical comparisons of suicide rates, or even data on suicide generated by different coroners. However, it does not follow that suicide statistics have no value in analysing the social causes of suicide; rather, that they need to be treated with exceptional care. One must assess the impact of social and cultural factors on the construction of suicide statistics as well as the tendency to commit suicide. Significantly, the tradition developed by Durkheim has continued, and a range of studies have provided some empirical support for his ideas and evidence of the impact of social factors (such as unemployment) on levels of suicide.

One important development has been the attention to attempted or parasuicide, frequently claimed to be a very different phenomenon from successful suicide, and representing a cry for help. However, some authors argue that the distinction between attempted and successful suicide is a matter of contingency, and it is wrong to exclude unsuccessful cases from the analysis.

The theoretical basis and empirical adequacy of Durkheim's explanation is most fully explored in Whitney Pope's *Durkheim's Suicide* (1976).

Sumner, William Graham (1840–1910) An early American sociologist and noted laissez-faire Social *Darwinist. Influenced by the works of Herbert Spencer, he argued that social life was governed by natural laws (as binding as those governing the physical world), the most basic of which stipulated evolutionary struggle and the survival of the fittest (meaning the most industrious and frugal).

He accepted that societies could ensure the survival of the weakest (for example through welfare programmes) but regarded this as a stimulus to social decline. These beliefs have attracted the usual criticisms levelled against other varieties of *economic determinism. In *Folkways* (1906) he argued the moral *relativist position that each human group has its own appropriate *folkways, *mores, and *institutions—the various group habits that, by trial and error, seem to be best suited to the particular circumstance prevailing at the time. The possible contradiction between this argument, and the belief in the universal superiority of folkways that support a *laissez-faire economy, is not addressed in Sumner's work. He also coined the widely used terms in-group, *out-group, and *ethnocentrism. For the last two years of his life he was president of the American Sociological Association.

superego *See* PSYCHOANALYSIS.

superstructure Like the term *base, that of superstructure was imported into Marxist discourse on the authority of Marx's reference to the sphere of production as being the 'real foundation, on which rises a legal and political superstructure and to which correspond definite forms of social consciousness', which appears in his *Preface to a Contribution to a Critique of Political Economy* (1859). Conventionally, therefore, the superstructure of a society comprises its political and cultural (or ideological) realms. Issues such as how the superstructure relates to the base, precisely what it consists of and the nature of its internal dynamics, were discussed by Marx when he spoke of *ideology and the *fetishism of commodities. Since Marx's time these issues have been approached through such concepts as *hegemony and *discourse. The net result has been that the architectural metaphor upon which the distinction between the base and the superstructure conventionally rests is no longer an adequate summary of the complex relations that are now understood to obtain between the economic and the other realms of society. Arguably, as commentators such as G. A. Cohen have observed, Marx himself did not intend such a crude view of unidimensional and unidirectional causality. *See also* MODE OF PRODUCTION; SOCIAL FORMATION.

surplus value *See* CAPITALISM; EXPLOITATION; LABOUR THEORY OF VALUE.

surveillance A term now most closely associated with Michel Foucault and seen as an aspect of the disciplinary *power through which societies control and regulate their populations. His best-known discussion is in *Discipline and Punish* (1975), where he discussed the idea of the 'panopticon' model of the prison, where each prisoner is under constant observation from a central point. This approach has been taken up by many writers who seek to examine the growth of electronic and other forms of surveillance in contemporary societies. See, for example, David Lyon's *Surveillance Society* (2001).

survey (social survey) At first, a survey was any systematic collection of facts about a defined social group, and the term is still used in this way. The term survey is therefore not necessarily synonymous with 'questionnaire survey', since other methods of data collection (such as observation of behaviour) may be employed in a survey. In practice, however, most sociological surveys are based on written *questionnaires. More precisely, the term usually refers to data collections that employ both *interviewing and *sampling to produce quantitative data-sets, amenable to computer-based analysis. Sampling and interviewing are employed in many other research designs. It is the combination of the two that has led to the social survey, or sample survey, becoming the most important single type of social research, used by all the *social sciences, *market research, and *opinion polls.

Surveys can be used to provide descriptive statistics for national, regional, or local populations; to examine the clustering of social phenomena; to identify the social location and characteristics of subgroups for more intensive follow-up case-study research; and to analyse causal processes and test explanations. In recent years sociological survey analysis has been greatly extended to include the sophisticated *multivariate modelling techniques that are common in econometrics. One of the main attractions of the sample survey for both policy research and theoretical research is its transparency and accountability: methods and procedures can be made visible and accessible to other parties, unlike research designs that depend heavily on the contribution of individual researchers. The key disadvantage is that surveys normally use structured questionnaires, which constrain an enquiry to paths fixed at the start of fieldwork. Other criticisms which are sometimes levelled at surveys are that numerical variables rarely provide adequate operationalizations of sociological constructs; the highly asymmetric power relation between researcher and interviewee is detrimental to the quality of the data collected; they provide a false aura of *objectivity which makes their results vulnerable to political manipulation. Many of these criticisms can be overcome by good survey design and implementation.

Surveys can collect information on individuals, roles, social networks, social groups such as households or families, organizations such as schools, workplaces, or companies. In most cases the information is provided by individuals, but the information collected may be about any social unit of interest, with larger and more complex units requiring multiple interviews to avoid the information limitations or bias of a single informant. Surveys are used to study poverty, social stratification, social mobility, political orientations and participation, work and employment, and virtually all the issues addressed by sociologists and other social scientists.

Survey interviews may be personal, postal, or conducted by telephone. Telephone surveys are particularly common in the United States, where most households have telephones, and the size of the country makes face-to-face interviewing of a nationally representative sample of the population prohibitively expensive (see P. J. Lavrakas, *Telephone Survey Methods*, 1987). Major surveys, especially national surveys, are now carried out by specialist fieldwork agencies or national research institutes that have the necessary resources for questionnaire design, sample design, sample selection from available registers or other sampling frames, fieldwork planning and supervision, training and debriefing of interviewers, *coding of completed questionnaires, consistency checks, and editing of the resulting data-tape. Such agencies often become centres for methodological research on sampling, survey techniques, and design.

CAPI (Computer Assisted Personal Interviewing) and CATI (Computer Assisted Telephone Interviewing) techniques are increasingly used. These involve the interviewer in coding the answers given by each respondent directly onto a data-tape or file, using a personal or laptop computer, at the time of interview. This saves both time and money in the overall survey process, but does mean that particular care must be taken over matters of questionnaire design at the outset, to ensure that there are no filtering or other errors in the final interview schedule.

Most academic research consists of *ad hoc* surveys, carried out on a one-off basis, to address defined theoretical and other issues. *Ad hoc* surveys often employ the smallest sample size necessary to achieve representativeness, typically 2000 respondents for a national survey, relying heavily on *statistical inference to generalize the results to the target *population. National opinion polls are carried out on a regular basis, but again employ the smallest sample size necessary to achieve representativeness, and necessitate the use of tests of statistical significance. With the change of emphasis from administrative records and registers to interview surveys as the basis of *official statistics, a great variety of regular surveys are also carried out by national governments. These involve quite different orders of magnitude to the typical *ad hoc* survey, with national samples of 5000–250000 per year; samples as large as this begin to make tests of statistical significance as redundant as they are with *census data, except when data subsets are analysed. In effect, the variety of surveys is now so wide that it ceases to be a homogeneous category of social research. Regular surveys may involve repeat cross-sectional surveys at defined intervals, such as annually every spring, or be carried out on the basis of continuous year-round interviewing so as to smooth out any seasonal variations in the activities covered. The USA Current Population Survey (CPS) and some equivalent Labour Force Surveys (LFS) employ *rotating sample designs which offer many of the advantages of data from *panel studies for measuring changes over time in the phenomena under study.

Surveys make demands on respondents and require their active cooperation to be successful. They require that respondents adopt the role of interviewee, in effect the role of citizen and commentator on their own lives, and the lives of those around them. This interviewee role has developed over decades in Western industrial societies, and there is increasing recognition that it is not universally understood or accepted in other cultures. For example, in some cultures it would be impolite to express open disagreement with the perceived or expected views of an interviewer, thus invalidating the invitation for respondents to express their own views. Surveys also make information demands that can be difficult to meet in societies where literacy and personal record-keeping are less widespread—so that even dates of birth may be difficult to recall accurately. New techniques of data collection are being developed for surveys in Third World countries and societies with different cultures and social conventions.

There are numerous textbooks on how to design and conduct surveys. Catherine Marsh's *The Survey Method* (1982) stands out as an elegant defence of the technique against critics who object that surveys are invariably superficial and merely descriptive.

sustainable development Defined in *Our Common Future*, the Report of the 1987 World Commission on the Environment and Development (the 'Brundtland Report'), as 'development that meets the needs of the present without compromising the ability of future generations to meet their own needs'. Rather than predicting greater environmental decay and hardship in a world of ever-diminishing resources, the Report foresees 'the possibility of a new era of economic growth, based on policies that sustain and expand the natural environmental resource base'.

*Economic growth and *modernization have historically been pursued aggressively by nation-states, as a means not only of satisfying basic material needs, but also of providing the resources necessary to improve quality of life more generally (for example with respect to access to health-care and education). However, most forms of economic growth make demands on the *environment, both by using (sometimes finite) natural resources and by generating waste or pollution. This jeopardizes growth for future generations. The philosophy of sustainable development attempts to resolve this dilemma by insisting that decisions taken at every level throughout society should have due regard to their possible environmental consequence. In this way, the right kind of economic growth—based on biodiversity, the control of environmentally damaging activity, and replenishment of renewable resources such as forests—is generated, and this can protect or even enhance the natural environment. Present-day economic development is therefore rendered compatible with investment in environmental resources for the future.

Although it is understandably hard to find authorities who are prepared to argue against the idea of sustainable development (it is in fact widely applauded by almost all governments and their agencies), it is often difficult for governments (which tend to be accountable to electorates over short-term periods such as five years or so) to accept the political consequences of promoting sustainable development, for example by imposing tolls or fines for the use of cars in cities (on the principle that the 'polluter should pay'). Moreover, the environment is shared and is largely a *public good, so that to a considerable extent its protection requires *collective action. In practice, therefore, this has proved hard to organize because of the usual *free-rider problems.

symbol Most generally, any act or thing that represents something else. More particularly, the smallest meaning-unit in the semantic fields of *ritual, dream, or *myth. In *psychoanalysis, a symbol is an act or object representing a repressed unconscious desire. Symbols usually signify many things; that is, to use Victor Turner's phrase (*The Forest of Symbols*, 1967), they are *multi-vocal. The link between symbol and referent is not always arbitrary, as with sign, but may be motivated by an association of attributes (for example, the crown as a symbol of monarchy).

Much of the research on symbolism has been done by social anthropologists rather than sociologists. For example, in *Purity and Danger* (1966), the British anthropologist Mary Douglas uses cross-cultural examples, including Hinduism, the Old Testament, and Western beliefs in hygiene, to argue that dirt is the symbol for matter out of place in a society's classification system. Clifford Geertz, the American cultural anthropologist and noted proponent of symbolic anthropology, has argued that human behaviour is fundamentally symbolic and therefore laden with *meaning for social actors. The primary task of the ethnographer is to understand the 'webs of significance' which people themselves have spun. Thus, for Geertz, anthropology (and by implication sociology) is not an experimental science, looking for universal laws, but an interpretative science in search of meaning. 'Deep Play: Notes on the Balinese Cockfight' (in *Daedalus*, 1972) is a classic example of Geertz's symbolic analysis. *See also* SAUSSURE; SEMIOLOGY; SYMBOLIC INTERACTIONISM.

symbolic interactionism A leading American theory that focuses upon the ways in which *meanings emerge through interaction. Its prime concern has been to analyse the meanings of everyday life, via close observational work and intimate familiarity, and from these to develop an understanding of the underlying forms of human interaction. Heavily influenced by *pragmatism, the *Chicago tradition of sociology and the philosophical writings of George Herbert *Mead, the term itself was coined by Herbert Blumer in 1937.

The theory has four key foci. The first highlights the ways in which human beings are distinctly *symbol-manipulating animals. It is through symbols that they, alone of all the animals, are capable of producing *culture and transmitting a complex history. Interactionists are always concerned to study the ways in which people give meaning to their bodies, their feelings, their selves, their biographies, their situations, and indeed to the wider social worlds in which their lives exist. Research strategies such as *participant observation are employed, which enable the researcher to gain access to these symbols and meanings, as in Howard S. Becker's *Art Worlds* (1982) and Arlie Hochschild's *The Managed Heart* (1983). There is a broad affinity here to *semiology, but unlike at least some positions in semiology which seek the structures of language, interactionists are more concerned with the ways in which meaning is always emergent, fluid, ambiguous, and contextually bound. R. S. Perinbanayagam has provided an important account of meaning in interactionism in his book *Signifying Acts* (1985).

This leads to a second theme: that of process and emergence. For the interactionist, the social world is a dynamic and dialectical web, situations are always encounters with unstable outcomes, and lives and their biographies are always in the process of shifting and becoming, never fixed and immutable. Attention is fixed, not upon rigid structures (as in many other versions of sociology), but upon streams of activity with their adjustments and outcomes. Concepts such as *career, *negotiated order, becoming, encounters, and *impression management are central to this approach.

A third focus of interactionism highlights the social world as precisely that—interactive. From this point of view there is no such thing as a solitary individual: humans are always connected to 'others'. The most basic unit of interactionist analysis is that of the *self, which stresses the ways in which people can (indeed must) come to view themselves as objects, and assume the *role of others through a process of role-taking. This idea is clarified in Charles Horton Cooley's notion of the *looking-glass self and Mead's more general idea of 'the self'.

A fourth theme, derived from Georg Simmel, is that interactionism looks beneath these symbols, processes, and interactions in order to determine underlying patterns or forms of social life. Interactionists seek 'generic social processes'. Thus, while they may study the life-experience of doctors, dance-band musicians, drug-users, and the dying, they can detect common processes at work in all such seemingly disparate groupings. A good example is Barney Glaser and Anselm Strauss's *Status Passage* (1967), which provides a formal, interactionist theory of status changes.

Symbolic interactionism developed in the University of Chicago, in the first few decades of the 20th century, and first achieved prominence when the Chicago School came to dominate early American sociology. However, it again became very influential during the 1960s, as a challenge to the dominance of Talcott Parsons and *Grand Theory (sometimes being referred to, during the heyday of functionalism, as 'the loyal opposition'). It was particularly influential in the development of the *labelling theory of deviance, but also in such fields as occupational research (Everett Hughes), medical sociology (Anselm Strauss), and in the study of classroom interaction. Strauss has pioneered a number of developments in interactionist theory. From his early work on identity (in *Mirrors and Masks*, 1969) to his formulation of the concept of *negotiated order, his work exemplifies a major methodological concern with qualitative research (usually, for him, in medical settings), the development of appropriate strategies for doing such research (the so-called *grounded theory approach), and the building of case-study theory which moves beyond itself into a more formal sociology. His work on dying patients (with Barney Glaser) is an exemplary study of all these concerns (see, for example, *Awareness of Dying*, 1967, *Time for Dying*, 1968, and *Anguish*, 1977).

In the 1970s interactionism attracted considerable criticism for its neglect of social structure, power, and history. More recent interactionist writings have shown this critique to be misguided; and, in the process, have revitalized the theory. For example, Sheldon Stryker has attempted to enunciate a version of symbolic interactionism which more clearly relates the conventionally microsociological concerns of that perspective to the organizational and societal levels of analysis, mainly by an imaginative restatement of role theory. In particular, Stryker has been concerned with the idea of 'role-making', the active creation of roles (rather than mere 'taking' of them), where some social structures permit more such creativity than do others (see, for example, *Symbolic Interactionism: A Social Structural Version*, 1980).

In the 1990s interactionism has provided analyses of a range of new phenomena, and has become more theoretically sophisticated (some might say eclectic) in creating links to postmodernism (in the work of Norman Denzin), feminism, semiology, and cultural theory. The best collection of interactionist writings, and one which gives a good indication of the tradition's virtues and limitations, is Ken Plummer's *Symbolic Interactionism* (2 vols., 1990). *See also* FORMALISM; GOFFMAN; KUHN.

symmetrical family *See* FAMILY, SYMMETRICAL.

synchrony *See* SAUSSURE; STRUCTURALISM.

syncretism In a religious context, syncretism refers to the worship of one god using the form or tradition of another god. Thus, for example, the Hebrew prophets constantly condemned the tendency to revert to worshipping Yahweh using forms associated with local 'baalim' or deities.

syndicalism A political movement or ideology that promotes workers' control through the medium of the workplace. It was particularly strong in France, Italy, and Spain in the late 19th and early 20th century, but was extinguished in the 1930s.

syndicated crime *See* ORGANIZED CRIME.

syntagmatic and paradigmatic *See* SAUSSURE.

synthesis The combination of two (or more) contradictory phenomena to produce something qualitatively new. The term is usually associated with the dialectical logic employed by some Marxists: for example, the economic contradictions of capitalism and the class conflict they generate, together produce socialism.

system integration and social integration These terms were first coined by the British sociologist David *Lockwood, in order to indicate what he saw as fundamental problems in both the normative *functionalist theories of the 1950s, and the *conflict theories of writers such as Ralf Dahrendorf and John Rex, which set out to criticize functionalist approaches.

Social integration refers to the principles by which individuals or actors are related to one another in a society; system integration refers to the relationships between parts of a society or social system. Despite the use of the word 'integration' there is no assumption that the relationships so described are harmonious. The terms social integration and system integration can embrace both order and conflict, harmony and contradiction.

The major source of social integration that sociologists have identified in advanced capitalist societies is the *class system. In *feudal society, the system of estates played an equivalent role, as did *caste in Indian society. In general (and following Max Weber's precepts about social stratification), status-based societies are likely to lead to harmonious forms of social integration, and class societies to conflictual forms of social integration. System integration, on the other hand, is a reference to the way in which different parts of a social system (its institutions) interrelate. Any adequate macrosociological theory of *change must attempt to link social integration with system integration. However, in Lockwood's original essay on social integration and system integration, he noted how conflict theorists emphasize the conflict between groups of actors as the basic motor of social change, while normative functionalists downplay the role of actors and seek to emphasize the (functional or dysfunctional) relationships between the institutions of society. For Lockwood, neither approach is adequate, precisely because each deals with only one side of the *agency versus *structure problem or couplet. The task of sociological theory is to overcome this *dualism.

Beyond this, Lockwood's distinction points to those crucial features which need to be examined in any theory of social change. To illustrate this he notes how Karl Marx's theory of capitalist society refers to growing class antagonisms (social integration) which are related to the contradictions between the *forces of production and the *relations of production (system integration). That is, for Marx, system contradictions are linked to the actions of groups who respond to the contradictions by seeking to change or preserve the existing society. It is contradictions at the system level which lead to social (class) conflict: system integration is related to social integration. More recently, Anthony Giddens has also sought to use this distinction. Initially he employed it in a similar manner to Lockwood, but in his more recent work he seeks to use it as a way of replacing the micro versus macro distinction (and, thereby, the problems of agency and structure). Social integration comes to refer to situations where actors are physically 'co-present' and system integration to where they are not. This is unsatisfactory because face-to-face interactions (co-presence) are not confined to micro-processes. (Consider, for example, a meeting in Britain between the Secretary of State for Employment and the General Secretary of the Trades Union Congress, to discuss industrial relations law.)

In summary, used as Lockwood originally intended, the distinction between social integration and system integration is fundamental to any theory which seeks to unite micro and macro levels of analysis. The writings of Jürgen Habermas contain a cognate distinction between 'life-world' and (social) 'system'. *See also* CRITICAL THEORY; MACROSOCIOLOGY.

system problems *See* PARSONS; SYSTEM THEORY.

system theory (systems analysis) A theory of societies as *social systems. The most important formulation of a theory of social systems was that of Talcott *Parsons, who argued (in *The Structure of Social Action*, 1937) that the basic analytical component of a sociological theory of an action system is the unit act, which involves an actor, an end or goal, a situation composed of conditions and means, and norms and values by which ends and means are selected. An action system is a structured collection of unit acts. He then defined a social system as 'a mode of organization of action elements relative to the persistence or ordered processes of change of the interactive patterns of a plurality of individual actors' (*The Social System*, 1951). Parsons argued that a social system is faced by two major problems. One is the (external) problem of the production and allocation of scarce resources; the other is the (internal) problem of achieving social order or integration. This notion gave rise to Parsons's famous development of four subsystems, which respond to the external and internal 'functional prerequisites of a system of action', namely adaptation (economy), goal-attainment (polity), integration (societal community), and latency (socialization). This was defined as the AGIL model of the social system. These subsystems are connected by flows of inputs and outputs, which Parsons called 'media of exchange' (*Economy and Society*, 1956). These are money (A), power (G), influence (I), and commitments (L). The equilibrium of a social system depends on these complex exchanges between the various subsystems.

Social systems theory has been much criticized, principally because it involves an overemphasis on *social order rather than social *conflict and does not provide a satisfactory theory of social *change (since it merely describes the process of differentiation). Although these criticisms have been widely accepted, the 1980s saw a revival of interest in systems theory by writers who sought to overcome them. The American neo-functionalists (see J. C. Alexander, *Neo-functionalism*, 1985) have argued that it is possible to develop Parsonian sociology as a perspective which can explain social change and conflict. There has also been a major development of social systems approaches in Germany. For example, Niklas Luhmann has rejected the idea that human individuals are aspects of social systems, which he defines as a system of communicative acts. Systems, according to Luhmann, function to reduce the complexity of meaning. Consequently, he has been interested in the system problems of successful communication on the basis of the development of codes. For him, the principal media of communication are truth, love, money, and power. (See *The Differentiation of Society*, trans. 1982, and *Social Systems*, 1984.) *See also* ORGANIC ANALOGY; PARSONS; SOCIAL SYSTEM.

S

taboo The term taboo derives from the Tongan 'tabu', meaning 'sacred' or 'inviolable'. However, its contemporary use is broader, most generally meaning a social and often *sacred prohibition put upon certain things, people, or acts, which render them untouchable or unmentionable. The most famous taboo is the near-universal *incest taboo, prohibiting sexual or marriage relations between particular categories of kin. According to both Sigmund Freud (*Totem and Taboo*, 1938) and Claude Lévi-Strauss (*The Elementary Structures of Kinship*, 1969), society itself originated with the incest taboo. Other authors have stressed the function performed by taboos in society. Raymond Firth (in *Symbols Public and Private*, 1973) interpreted taboo as a mechanism of *social control. In *Purity and Danger* (1966), Mary Douglas drew attention to the way in which the taboo serves as a social marker, creating and maintaining social classifications.

tabula rasa Also known as the blank-slate or white-paper thesis, a name for the radically *empiricist view of the mind and knowledge which inspired so-called associationism in psychology. According to John *Locke, the contents of the mind are written on it by experience as if it were white paper, a view comparable with modern *behaviourist theories which try to account for mental processes as a product of external stimulus and behavioural response. Steven Pinker (*The Blank Slate*, 2002) is the latest in a line of evolutionary psychologists and *sociobiologists who have claimed that sociology has adopted a 'Standard Social Science Model' according to which human minds are tabula rasa subject only to *social construction. In fact, sociological arguments are far more sophisticated and complex on this point, and the only work that such critics cite in support of their claimed SSSM is the *behaviourism that most sociologists have rejected.

tabular presentation Quantitative social science results are most commonly presented in the form of an analytic table. Tables should fulfil two main criteria: they should be easy to read; and they should support the inference drawn by the analyst. All tables should have a clear self-explanatory title; give the number of cases on which the statistics are based; and should include only the critical information relevant to the point that the table illustrates.

The most basic type of analytic table is the percentage table. The simplest percentage table is the univariate type which presents the distribution of answers to a single question. A two-way (or two variable) table shows the relationship between a *dependent and *independent variable. For example, in the table, the hypothetical responses to a question 'In general, how do you like sociology?' are broken down by sex. These hypothetical data would illustrate that male students are more positive about sociology than are female students. In order to be sure that the difference is not simply due to *sampling error it would be necessary also to include the associated *significance test. However, no table can show whether or not the difference is of substantive importance, and the scientist must establish in the text why the results matter. *See also* CONTINGENCY TABLE.

	Men (%)	Women (%)
I like it very much	48	38
I like it somewhat	40	42
I dislike it	10	18
Don't Know	2	2
	100	100
N =	(301)	(389)

Tabular presentation. Male and female attitudes to sociology

tacit knowledge (tacit understanding) *See* COMMONSENSE KNOWLEDGE.

Taeuber, Irene B. (1906–74) An American statistician and demographer who nurtured the development of demography within sociology, especially in the 1930s and 1940s, and was the premier editor of *Population Index*. A feminist and humanist, she was nevertheless committed to the ideal of scientific objectivity. Taeuber is well-known for her important international population studies, particularly her demographic work in East and South-east Asia. *The Population of Japan* (1958), a demographic survey of Japan from the start of the literate period until 1955, was her *magnum opus*.

Taft, Jessie (1882–1961) An early *Chicago sociologist who wrote her doctoral thesis on 'The Women's Movement from the Standpoint of Social Consciousness' (1913)—with George Herbert *Mead as her doctoral chair. The most influential of her numerous subsequent publications addressed issues of *social work (see V. Robinson, *Jessie Taft: Therapist and Social Work Educator*, 1962).

take-off An idea derived from the American economic historian Walt W. Rostow 's *Stages of Economic Growth* (1953). Rostow postulated five such stages: traditional society; preconditions for take-off; take-off to maturity; drive to maturity; and maturity. In this way he claimed to identify a recognizable stage in a country's history, lasting perhaps 20–30 years, during which the conditions required for sustained and fairly rapid *economic growth are consolidated, and beyond which growth is more or less assured. The theory assumes that levels of capital investment are crucial to initiating economic growth. Rostow applied this schema to the problems of the then developing countries; and (indirectly) influenced and justified American foreign and overseas-aid policies towards the Third World.

Although the concept of a take-off to self-sustaining economic growth has been influential, Rostow's argument was subsequently the object of a sustained critique by *dependency theorists in sociology, most notably in a famous and much-reproduced article by Andre Gunder Frank ('Sociology of Development and Under-development of Sociology', 1967) which castigates Rostow (among others) for ignoring the history of *imperialism and *neo-colonialism. The theory is now widely discredited but the idea of a take-off point remains part of the language of economic development.

Tarde, Gabriel (1843–1904) A lawyer interested in criminological ideas, his first works were critical of the environmental focus of the Italian criminologists such as *Lombroso. He became Director of Criminal Statistics in the French Ministry of Justice. Tarde adopted a psychologistic approach and in the 1880s began to write more generally about processes of 'imitation'. He saw societies comprising a small minority of creators and innovators and a mass of followers who simply imitate the actions of those they see around them. Imitation, then, is a basic means of cultural transmission (*The Laws of Imitation*, 1890). He saw innovations spreading through societies along chains of imitation, radiating out in networks of diffusion, and his work has been influential among those studying the diffusion of innovations. Following his appointment as a professor in the Collège de France, he wrote on opinion and crowd behaviour. His individualism brought him into conflict with *Durkheim. One of his least-known works is a science-fiction novel on the consequences of global climate change (*Underground Man*, 1896).

task-orientation versus time-orientation distinction A distinction employed in industrial sociology to indicate contrasting orientations to work and forms of labour discipline. In the narrow sense, task-oriented workers relate the measurement of time to naturally occurring phenomena and cycles, such as 'the time between sunrise and sunset', the seasons of the year, or (quite simply) 'the time it takes to complete the task in hand'. The important point is that there is a complete disregard for the artificial units (minutes, hours, and 'working days') of clock-time. Anthropological and historical evidence suggests that this attitude to work—in which labour is oriented to the completion of specific tasks with a minimal demarcation between *work and *leisure—was prevalent among traditional tribal and Western pre-industrial societies alike. The invention of clocks—or rather their utilization by employers as a means of measuring labour-inputs—generated (after well-documented initial resistance among workers) a labour discipline in which time was the principal currency. Effort was now bought and sold by the hour; time was 'spent' rather than 'passed'; and the 'time-effort bargain' could be budgeted like any other commodity. The classic analysis of the change in work-discipline that accompanies the shift between task-orientation and time-orientation is E. P. Thompson's 'Time, Work-Discipline, and Industrial Capitalism' (in *Past and Present*, 1967).

In contemporary usage, the application of these concepts has become some-what broader, with task-orientation and time-orientation often being treated as synonymous with 'solidaristic' and 'instrumental' orientations to work respectively. *See also* WORK, SUBJECTIVE EXPERIENCE OF.

tautology The use of words to repeat (unnecessarily) the same statement or meaning. For example, the statement that 'Britain is an island and surrounded by water' is a tautology, since islands are by definition so described. Tautological explanations are similarly true by definition, or circular, and therefore unfalsifiable. Sociological explanations which locate the origins of social institutions in their effects tend to take this form. Thus, for example, some early functionalist anthropologists (including Bronislaw *Malinowski) were prone to argue that, because certain (exotic) social practices (such as witchcraft) existed, then they must have a social function—and that one could assume they had that function precisely because the practices themselves existed.

Tawney, Richard H. (1880–1962) An English economic and social historian, social reformer, and *egalitarian social philosopher. He was equally well known as a historian and champion of socialism—in both of which roles he exerted a significant influence on early British sociology during the post-1945 period. His classic texts on *Equality* (1920) and *The Acquisitive Society* (1931) exemplify the English tradition of *Fabianism and ethical *socialism. His best-known historical publications are probably *Religion and the Rise of Capitalism* (1926), *Land and Labour in China* (1932), and *Business and Politics under James I* (1962). Numerous collections of his essays are also in circulation (see, for example, *The American Labour Movement and Other Essays*, 1979). Tawney was a committed Christian and this informed his criticism of the exploitative elements of *capitalism. He argued that *citizenship, equality of opportunity, *collectivism, and a *corporate society were necessary to eradicate the injustices associated with social class and inherited wealth. Social equality required also that the principles of liberty, equality, and fraternity operate on the factory floor. His is still an original critique of the excessive *individualism threatened by capitalism and of the inefficiencies (for example the creation of *poverty) in the free *market.

taxonomy A taxonomy (or typology) is a classification. To classify social phenomena is not to explain them. For example, sociologists of religion commonly use a taxonomy of religious organizations which embraces the categories of church, denomination, sect, and cult. This classifies religious groupings according to their organizational structure (for example bureaucratic or informal), adjustment to the prevailing order (world-rejecting, world-accommodating, and so forth), and principal mode of recruitment (ascribed membership by birth or achieved membership by voluntary attachment). This particular classification does not explain why certain individuals practise religion, while others do not, nor does it offer a theory of how religious organizations arise or develop. In practice, however, many sociological taxonomies are implicitly aetiological (causal). A well-known example is *Durkheim's classification of the types of *suicide—egoistic, altruistic, anomic, and fatalistic—a taxonomy which also embodies a theory about why people kill themselves intentionally.

Taylor, Frederick William (1856–1915) The founder of *scientific management, who developed controversial theories of work-study and industrial efficiency, in the conflict-ridden American steel industry at the end of the 19th century. Taylor achieved national renown but his hostility to trade-union controls on effort, and his *technicism directed at financial interests, provoked both political and industrial opposition.

Taylorism *See* SCIENTIFIC MANAGEMENT; TAYLOR.

technicism A belief that *technocracy is desirable or inevitable. Also a broad *social movement, especially influential in the United States during the early 20th century (the Technocracy Movement), calling for the elimination of the price system in favour of the government of industry and society by scientific or engineering principles. *See also* TECHNOCRACY.

techniques of neutralization *See* DELINQUENT DRIFT; VOCABULARIES OF MOTIVE.

technocracy A revolutionary or governing *elite composed of, or drawn from, technical experts. *See also* BOURGEOISIE.

technological determinism A theory of social *change, characteristically one of *evolutionary *progress or development, in which productive technique obeys a logic or trajectory of its own; and, in the process, acts as the principal determinant of institutions and social relationships. Since literal technological determinism is clearly untrue, most such theories also invoke a *cultural lag between the introduction of a technology, and its full social impact. It should not be confused or equated with *historical materialism. *See also* CULTURAL MATERIALISM.

technological society Some writers argue that there is a distinctive type of society, typically emergent from various forms of *industrialism, in which *technology and a *technocracy increasingly determine the nature of institutions and change. Optimistic versions include much *technicism and the so-called convergence thesis (*see* INDUSTRIAL SOCIETY) favoured by many American functionalists of the 1950s and early 1960s. An early, more pessimistic, account is given by Jacques Ellul in *The Technological Society*. In the tradition of the *Sociologie du Travail, technology is treated as a form of alienation, and as domination by artefacts. The growing interest in alternative technology, ecology, and the environment may be regarded as a reaction born of an analogous interpretation of late 20th-century industrialism.

technology A term used rather loosely in sociology, to mean either machines, equipment, and possibly the productive technique associated with them; or a type of social relationship dictated by the technical organization and mechanization of work. For an interesting comparative analysis of the historical and cultural importance of technology in human societies see Jack Goody's *Production and Reproduction* (1975).

technology, new *See* NEW TECHNOLOGY.

technostructure *See* BOURGEOISIE.

telecommuting White-collar employment that allows the worker to work in his or her own home, or in a neighbourhood work centre, communicating with an employer through a terminal which is connected with the employer's computer either directly or via the telecommunications network. Although much discussed as a revival of cottage industry, and as an illustration of *labour-market flexibility, there were almost no true examples of this work arrangement in Europe by the early 1990s. Most people who used desktop computers at home still used conventional forms of communication, such as the postal service, or face-to-face meetings with employers and clients. However, there are cases of telecommuters working for a firm in another country or continent. Exaggerated claims of the incidence and growth of telecommuting are attributable to the rediscovery and revival of home-based employment in industrial societies, the vast majority of which does not involve computers or telecommunications networks. *See also* INTERNET.

teleology A teleological explanation either explains a process by the end-state towards which it is directed; or explains the existence of something by the *function it fulfils. In sociology, the former tends to be confined to theories of purposive human action, whereas the latter is a feature of functionalism. It is widely argued that teleological explanations are admissible only with reference to individuals and groups since they alone have explicitly formulated purposes or goals. Societies, by contrast, set themselves no such objectives. *Evolutionary and *systems theories, as well as theories which imply a historical logic or inevitability (such as *historical materialism), are often criticized as being unacceptably teleological—although there have been controversial attempts to argue that even these explanations can be translated into conventional causal accounts.

terrorism A contested concept generally applied to actual or suggested violence connected to political aims. It is notoriously difficult to define because 'terrorism' may be deployed as a relative, emotive, pejorative, or ideologically driven label. Subjective elements of the 'terrorism' label are often conveyed through the terrorist versus freedom fighter maxim. Whilst this notion articulates the moral relativism at stake, a confusion and conflation of the goals and activity of terrorism undermine its conceptual value. Further controversies exist regarding the scant focus on activities of states and their proxies in many conceptions of terrorism. In recent years these debates have led to the emergence of 'critical terrorism studies'. Drawing from the broader field of critical security studies and the Frankfurt School, and seeking distinction from more 'orthodox' studies (e.g. scholarship characterized as working within 'top-down' dissident-focused definitions of terrorism), critical terrorism studies place explicit increased attention on the role of the state as an arbitrator of insecurity and violence. (See the edited collection *Critical Terrorism Studies: A New Research Agenda* by Jackson, Gunning, and Breen Smyth (2009).

Usage of term has incorporated a heavy emphasis on violent jihadi extremism since the attacks in New York, Washington, and Pennsylvania on 11 September, 2001 ('9/11'). However, brief reflection on the shifting meaning of terrorism reveals much greater breadth, complexity, and mutability. During the French Revolution (1789–1799) terrorism was associated with anti-monarchist violence, and thus serving the protection of democracy, and throughout the second half of the twentieth century the term was variously used to describe the activities of anti-colonial struggles, far left groups, right-wing extremists, ethno-nationalists, criminal gangs, and state sponsorship of dissents. During the 21st century, many countries have dilated their legal definitions of what constitutes terrorism. For example, most of those currently imprisoned for terrorism-related offences in the UK have been prosecuted for non-violent activities such as the 'encouragement' of terrorism, membership of a proscribed organization, or withholding information that might prejudice an investigation. Such is the degree of contestation and the impossibility of reaching definitional consensus in the international setting, that the UN refrained from providing a working definition of terrorism until 2004, previously creating initiatives governing specific activities such as hijacking, or instructing member states to develop their own meanings. The existing UN definition (UN Security Council Resolution 1566) focuses on the use, threat, or suggestion of violence to achieve political change but has attracted controversy through its denial of a 'just cause'. Critics have pointed out that the UN's explicit statement that such activities are 'under no circumstances justifiable' leaves open the possibility that any action against repressive regimes may be easily labelled as terrorism and thus attract additional repressive responses.

Scholarly attention to terrorism increased rapidly after 9/11 yet still remains heavily concentrated in the political sciences, most notably in the field of international relations. However, this period has seen growth in contributions from other social science disciplines, particularly social psychology. Stephen Vertigans's *Sociology of Terrorism: People, Places and Processes* (2011) is one of the few studies in sociology, and the topic remains comparatively under-represented in this field. Among the studies that do exist are analyses of the interaction of individuals and their environments, small group dynamics, *anomie, subcultural theory, and the visceral attractions of transgression. Sociologically informed analyses of counter-terrorism are more numerous and most common among these are approaches that draw on elements of socio-legal studies, political sociology, and human geography to examine associated practices of social control.

tertiary sector *See* INDUSTRIAL SECTOR.

theism A term which refers to the belief in the existence of a divine being, especially in the existence of a single God, who is thought to be personal and who is the Creator of the universe. Theism involves the idea of divine revelation, and consequently is contrasted with deism, the rational belief in divinity independently of faith in a revealed truth. *See also* MONOTHEISM; RELIGION.

theodicy In *metaphysics, representation of the world as God's creation offered a method of demonstrating that the world must have certain characteristics, often ones which contradicted commonsense experience. Thus, from God's goodness and omnipotence it could be deduced that the created world must itself be good, despite the appearance of evil and suffering. The philosophical optimism of Leibniz and his followers ('all is for the best in the best of all possible worlds') was ruthlessly satirized by Voltaire in *Candide*. The role of theodicies as reconciling, conservative *ideologies has been noted by Max Weber among other sociologists of religion, but they may also have critical implications.

theodicy, problem of *See* RELIGION, SOCIOLOGY OF.

theology The systematic study of religious beliefs and systems of thinking about God (or gods), often from within a given tradition, such as *Judaism or Catholicism. Theology is not far removed from *philosophy and the *sociology of religion when considerations of meaning and empirical manifestations of religion are primary.

theories of the middle range *See* MIDDLE-RANGE THEORY.

theory A theory is an account of the world which goes beyond what we can see and measure. It embraces a set of interrelated definitions and relationships that organizes our concepts of and understanding of the empirical world in a systematic way. Thus, we may establish a statistical relationship between poverty and crime, but to explain that relationship we might have to employ a number of theories: about people's motivations, the social meanings attached to poverty and crime, and the structural constraints which keep sections of the population in poverty.

Generally speaking there are three different conceptions of theory in sociology. Some think of theory as generalizations about, and classifications of, the social world. The scope of generalization varies from theorizing about a particular range of phenomena to more abstract and general theories about society and history as a whole. Others believe that theoretical statements should be translated into empirical, measurable, or observable propositions, and systematically tested. Thus, in the example above, we should test assumptions about motivations, social meanings, and so forth. This approach is usually characterized (rather unhelpfully) as *positivism. Finally, yet others argue that theory should explain phenomena, identifying causal mechanisms and processes which, although they cannot be observed directly, can be seen in their effects. For example, Marxists might use the alleged contradiction between the forces and relations of production (unobservable) to explain fluctuations in the levels and development of class struggle (observable). The label *realism is sometimes attached to this view. *See also* AXIOM; RATIONAL CHOICE THEORY; HYPOTHESIS; PHILOSOPHY.

theory-laden statement A statement about the world is said to be theory-laden if it presupposes or rests upon a *theory—in other words if it is not a pure observation. Many philosophers of science (including, for example, T. S. Kuhn, *The Structure of Scientific Revolutions*, 1962) argue that all observations are in some sense theory-laden.

therapeutic community Residential units run on psychodynamic lines, first introduced for wartime rehabilitation, then developed for those with neurotic and behaviour disorders. The aim is to create a therapeutic environment in which patients are actively involved in their therapy and the hierarchy between therapist and patient is fractured. Interpersonal interactions are analysed in regular group meetings.

thick description Intensive, small-scale, dense descriptions of social life from observation, through which broader cultural interpretations and generalizations can be made. The term was introduced in the philosophical writings of Gilbert Ryle, and developed by Clifford Geertz in anthropology, especially in his celebrated study of the Balinese cockfight (see his *The Interpretation of Cultures*, 1973, and *Local Knowledge*, 1983).

Third World By analogy with the 'third estate' in the French Revolution, a group of states independent of the two main camps in the Cold War. The term was originally used in the late 1940s to denote a potentially neutral bloc in Europe, but from the early 1960s referred to countries of the developing world, as distinct from the 'first' (developed) capitalist and 'second' (communist) worlds.

(⊕) SEE WEB LINKS
- The Third World Network: an information and pressure group providing news on trade and politics.

Third World entrepôt A term with three distinct (though similar) meanings: originally, a port used by colonial powers to deposit goods that were eventually destined for sale elsewhere; sometimes used to describe cities which receive migrants from less developed countries; often applied to cities or regions, usually in the poorer states, with a large commercial sector geared mainly to exporting primary products from the hinterland.

Thomas, Dorothy Swaine (1899–1977) An American sociologist of population and demographic studies. Her published work also includes a study of Japanese-American evacuation and resettlement during the Second World War (*The Salvage*, 1952; *The Spoilage*, 1969). She married William Isaac Thomas in 1935 and became the first woman president of the American Sociological Association in 1952.

Thomas Theorem The classic aphorism, stated by W. I. Thomas, that 'When people define situations as real they are real in their consequences'. *See also* SELF-FULFILLING PROPHECY.

Thomas, William Isaac (1863–1947) A student, instructor, and ultimately an influential professor at the University of Chicago, who collaborated with Florian

Znaniecki to produce *The Polish Peasant in Europe and America* (1918), which pioneered the use of *personal documents and *life-histories. His theory of the 'definition of the situation' suggested that 'when people define situations as real they are real in their consequences'. In 1927 he served as president of the American Sociological Association.

time-and-motion studies *See* SCIENTIFIC MANAGEMENT.

time-budget studies Surveys and other studies which require participants to keep time-use diaries, to report the activities occupying each hour of each day for a fixed period of time, such as a week or month. For a review and examples see Jonathan I. Gershuny and Graham S. Thomas, *Changing Times* (1984).

time orientation *See* TASK-ORIENTATION VERSUS TIME-ORIENTATION DISTINC-TION.

time-series data Data about a social phenomenon or phenomena which are ordered in time. In sociology the most common form of time-series data are those derived either from *censuses or *panel studies, although *opinion-poll surveys and some administrative records offer opportunities for time-series study. Occasionally, two or more unrelated *ad hoc* *surveys have asked similar sorts of questions of similar populations, and allow an approximation to time-series analysis. In Britain the Central Statistical Office hosts a time-series data-bank, which contains information on some 2 000 variables.

time, sociological study of Time is a measure of duration and depends upon particular cultural ideas that give it meaning. Western scientific cultures have given rise to precise ideas of clock and calendar time that can measure the duration of physical and social objects in terms of the passage of minutes, days, years, etc. There are, however, other competing conceptions of time by which the duration and occurrence of social events are marked and around which human activities and their consequences are organized and given meaning. This may involve 'epochs' and 'eras' related to particular *generations, periods related to meals and bodily processes, and the rhythms of everyday activities. Social life is organized through a variety of timetables and biographical narratives of life-stages, *status passages, and *careers.

A distinction that is sometimes drawn in sociological theory is that between the idea of *durée*, as the unstoppable personal flow of a person's experience, and la longue *durée*—the broader, almost timeless history of people relating to their environment in broad spans of history. The former leads to a social psychology of time—as described in the work of William *James; the latter encourages a historical concern with temporal structures, as in the work of Fernand *Braudel. *La longue durée* is the long time-period which forms a vast and critical backdrop to a whole frame of social life, and is often dominated by a particular organizing mode, such as religion ('the Christian era') or politics (for example 'the Modern World and Capitalism'). Important studies are E. Zerubavel, *Hidden Rhythms: Schedules and Calendars in Social Life* (1981), and B. Adam, *Time and Social*

Theory (1990). *See also* change; EVOLUTIONISM; LIFE CYCLE; LIFE HISTORY; PRO-GRESS; SEQUENCE ANALYSIS; TASK-ORIENTATION VERSUS TIME-ORIENTATION.

Titmuss, Richard Morris (1907–73) A key figure in the study of *social policy and *social administration in the post-war period. Titmuss was one of a group of British academics (notable others were Brian Abel-Smith and Peter Townsend) who made a major contribution to the study of social *needs and *welfare provision at a time when the welfare state was expanding. Without formal academic training, his interest in social policy developed while he was working in an insurance office in the 1930s, and he began to write books such as *Poverty and Population* (1938) and *Our Food Problem* (1939). These led to his appointment as official historian to the War Cabinet in 1942. There he wrote a volume entitled *The Problems of Social Policy* which was published in 1950. Also in that year he was appointed as Professor of Social Administration and Head of Department at the London School of Economics and Political Science, where he developed a strong organizational base and research team, whose work typified the reforming social administration approach to social policy. He was also active in political and wider public life, serving on various government committees, and as an adviser to the Labour Party. Subsequent publications included *Essays on the Welfare State* (1958), *Income Distribution and Social Change* (1962), and *The Gift Relationship* (1970). The last of these is a justly celebrated comparative study, offering a convincing critique of the use of the market to secure an adequate supply of blood for hospitals, and a powerful analysis of altruism.

An opponent of means-tested benefits (*see* SELECTIVE VERSUS UNIVERSAL BENEFITS), Titmuss did not believe that welfare services could solve problems of social inequality, but they could help to ameliorate them.

Tocqueville, Alexis de (1805–59) An early French sociologist who travelled to the United States between 1831 and 1832 to observe *democracy at work. His classic work *Democracy in America* (1835–40) identifies within democracies a tension between equality and liberty which cannot easily be reconciled. Since democracy tends to undermine hierarchy, it discourages the formation of inter-mediate groupings between the individual and society, and therefore promotes tendencies towards individualism and centralization which, if unchecked, will result in an authoritarian state. This proposition was illustrated in a systematic comparison of France and the United States. The post-revolutionary history of the former country revealed the dangers of attempting to impose equality without first establishing the liberty of self-government: administrative centralism fostered revolutionary despotism. In the case of the United States, the well-entrenched constitutional principle of *federalism provided for a multiplicity of intermediate voluntary associations, and a decentralized mode of government to which people had ready access, and in which they could participate. In both cases, however, Tocqueville warned against the 'tyranny of the majority', by which 'every citizen, being assimilated to all the rest, is lost in the crowd'. His work is thus the starting-point for many debates about the nature of *mass society (including, for example, D. Reisman's *The Lonely Crowd*, 1950, and R. Bellah's *Habits of the Heart*, 1985).

Tönnies, Ferdinand (1855-1936) A German sociologist and founding member of the German Sociological Association. He is most famous for his distinction between *Gemeinschaft* (community) and *Gesellschaft* (association). The distinction refers to the different types of relationships supposedly characteristic of small-scale and large-scale societies respectively. In the former, where the population is largely immobile, *status is *ascribed and the family and church play important roles in sustaining a clearly defined set of beliefs, emotional and co-operative relationships flourish. The village and small community are therefore characterized by *gemeinschaftlich* relationships. However, these dissolve into contractual and impersonal relationships as the *division of labour grows more complex, so that large-scale organizations and cities express *gesellschaftlich* social forms. Tönnies lamented the loss of *community and what he saw as the increasing dominance of *competition and *individualism in modern urban society. In this respect he was a critic of *utilitarianism, a pessimist, and conservative. The distinction between *Gemeinschaft* and *Gesellschaft* parallels Émile *Durkheim's contrast between mechanical and organic solidarity—and shares many of the same weaknesses.

total institution A term introduced by Erving *Goffman in *Asylums* (1961) to analyse a range of institutions in which whole blocks of people are bureaucratically processed, whilst being physically isolated from the normal round of activities, by being required to sleep, work, and play within the confines of the same institution. Prisons and mental hospitals are Goffman's key examples, but he suggests others including concentration camps, boarding schools, barracks, and monasteries. In his book, Goffman analyses the lives of inmates and custodians within such institutions, and emphasizes the inevitable *bureaucratic regimentation and manipulation of residents in the interests of staff. He also identifies tendencies to resistance in the informal inmate culture—or 'under-life'—of the institution. The term became very popular, during the 1960s, as part of a wider critique of the mechanisms and regimes of *social control in advanced industrial societies. *See also* DECARCERATION.

totalitarian (totalitarianism) The term appears to have originated with the Italian fascists under Mussolini and with the philosopher Giovanni Gentile. Meaning 'comprehensive, all-embracing, pervasive, the total state', the label was applied to a variety of empires and orders of rule, and in general to rightist regimes; that is, until the period of the Cold War, when it gained renewed currency.

Typically, it combines a syndrome of attributes that can be objectively assessed with a number of emotive connotations which are less open to investigation, as for example when it is equated with terms such as 'evil empire'. The political scientists Carl Friedrich and Zbigniew Brzezinski were primarily responsible for shifting the meaning away from *fascist regimes and toward reformulating it as a paradigm for Stalin's Soviet Union. Their six defining elements were intended to be taken as a mutually supportive organic entity and comprised the following: an elaborate, total *ideology, making *chiliastic claims, with a promise of a *utopian future; a single mass party, typically led by one person; a system of terror, physical or psychic; a monopoly of the means of communication; a monopoly on arms; and central direction and control of the economy through *bureaucratic co-ordination (see *Totalitarian Dictatorship and Autocracy*, 1963).

This approach evoked reactions from those who claimed that the Soviet system, both politically and as a social entity, was in fact better understood in terms of *interest groups, competing *elites, or even in quasi-class terms (using the notion of the *nomenklatura* as a vehicle for the new *class). The use of the term became intertwined with Cold War stances, and in social science the explanatory power of the concept was questioned, not least because of its ahistorical and generalizing nature. It fell into disuse during the 1970s, although the notion of 'post-totalitarianism' featured in the debates around the reform-ability of the Soviet system. In due course, as the Soviet system crumbled, opponents of the concept claimed that the transformation of the USSR under Gorbachev proved that the Soviet system was not totalitarian. Proponents argued that the *homo sovieticus* could now be identified more clearly and that, in any case, the factors leading to its collapse were exogenous. There is little doubt that the system of *real socialism did generate a form of one-party rule, based around a tendency towards a personality cult, with a specific teleological ideology, censorship and terror, statist economy, and a monopoly on violence for which there are few competitors in other types of society even of the most repressive kind. An examination of its legacy will become possible as the affected societies seek to build democracies and create markets on the basis of citizenship rights.

total war A form of warfare, characteristic of modern *industrial society, involving the maximum mobilization of social and economic resources of a country for armed conflict, usually entailing the exposure of the civilian popula-tion and economy to enemy attack. The idea has particularly been explored in the work of Arthur Marwick (*War and Social Change in the Twentieth Century*, 1977, and his edited collection *Total War and Social Change*, 1988). As a form of warfare it is distinct from regional or local war, and from nuclear conflict (see M. Shaw, *Dialectics of War: An Essay in the Social Theory of Total War and Peace*, 1988).

totemism An association between human groups or individuals and specific animals or plants which entailed ritualized observances and sometimes eating avoidances. The term was first drawn to the attention of Westerners by J. Long in *Voyages and Travels* (1791), being derived from the American Indian Algonquin language. The ensuing debates read like a history of anthropological theory.

J. F. McLennan searched for the origins of totemism, asserting it to be a remnant of animism (the belief that natural phenomena, animate and inanimate alike, are endowed with spirits or souls which effect consequences in society). William Robertson Smith argued that people had totems because they expected something beneficial from them. James *Frazer argued that totemism existed where 'savages' had no knowledge of the role of the human male in conception. Émile *Durkheim took totemism as the most elementary form of religious life and suggested that it was the clan worshipping itself. Bronislaw *Malinowski offered a matter-of-fact explanation: namely, that in order to survive, people had to have detailed knowledge and control over animals and plants, especially the indispensable species. E. E. *Evans-Pritchard questioned functional utility as an explanation. The most useless animals could be the object of ritual attention. The relationship between humans and animals could be seen as metaphorical. Meyer *Fortes linked the perceived relations between humans and animals to those between living men and their ancestors. Claude Lévi-Strauss concluded that the differences between animals or plants were used by humans to affirm differences between themselves. Animals were 'good to think with' and were just one example of humanity's need to classify. His arguments stimulated further studies of animal symbolism in both non-Western and Western societies.

Touraine, Alain (1925-) A French sociologist who initially studied history and philosophy before studying sociology with Talcott Parsons at Harvard in 1952. Returning to France, he began a series of studies of French industry and worker organization, focusing especially on the implications of technological change. His work combines a strong awareness of issues raised within Marxist theory with a firm and clear commitment to ideas drawn from contemporary sociological theory. He set out a classic and influential account of post-industrialism in *The Post-Industrial Society—Tomorrow's Social History: Classes, Conflicts and Culture in the Programmed Society* (1969). His key focus has been on the idea of the social movement, cast in terms of an historically informed action theory that focused on the issue of collective action. Active in the student revolts of 1968, he set up the Centre for the Study of Social Movements in Paris in 1979. His study of the student movement was presented in *May Movement: Revolt and Reform* (1968) and he developed his approach to social movements through studies such as *Anti-nuclear Protest: The Opposition to Nuclear Energy in France* (1980). His larger theoretical framework has been developed in a number of major studies. His foundational work *Sociologie de l'action* (1965) has not been translated into English, but translated works include *The Self-Production of Society* (1973), *The Voice and the Eye* (1978), and *Return of the Actor* (1984). Recent publications are *Critique of Modernity* (1992), *Can We Live Together?* (2000), *Le monde des femmes* (2006), and *Après la crise* (2010).

Toynbee, Arnold John (1889–1975) Son of a social worker and nephew of an economic historian (also called Arnold, and inventor of the phrase *industrial revolution), Toynbee trained as a historian and worked on the Survey of International Affairs at Chatham House. He began a major world history in the form of a comparative sociology of civilizations. His work was inspired by that of *Spengler, but Toynbee's approach emphasized the conflict of groups as the driving force in social and cultural development. The *elites heading societies, he argued, faced challenges posed by their environmental circumstances and, if their societies are to survive, they must devise appropriate and effective responses to these challenges. Toynbee's work was published in twelve volumes between 1933 and 1961.

tracking (streaming) A widespread practice in American elementary and secondary school systems, tracking attempts to homogenize classrooms by placing students according to a range of criteria which may include pupils' performances on standardized aptitude tests, classroom performance, perceived personal qualities and aspirations, and social class and ethnic origin. Different tracks typically offer different curricula, types of student-teacher relationship, and educational resources. The higher college tracks have been found to be more intellectually demanding, with better resources, and more favourable teacher expectations of pupils. Studies have highlighted the implications of tracking in terms of its negative psychological consequences for those placed in the lower tracks, reinforcement of ethnic and social class segregation, and perpetuation of inequality in society. The practice, issues, and debates have their British equivalent in the system of so-called streaming.

trade cycle The well-documented tendency for the level of business activity to fluctuate over a regular short-term period with peaks and troughs occurring around a longer-term upward growth trend. Both short-term and long-term cyclical fluctuations in the economy are a major factor in unemployment and are the subject of bitterly contested explanations in economics. *See also* BUSINESS CYCLES.

trade union Any organization of employees established in order to substitute, or attempt to substitute, *collective bargaining for individual bargaining in the *labour market. Unions seek generally to ensure that earnings and conditions are governed by rules applied consistently across their membership—although many unions also have broader social and political aims. Some are also professional associations.

It is customary to classify unions into types, according to the constituency from which they recruit, in the following way: craft (exclusive to skilled workers); occupational (all workers in an occupation regardless of industry); industrial (all workers in an industry regardless of occupation); general (amalgamations of occupational and industrial organization); and enterprise (all workers in a single company or plant). However, in practice, the typology breaks down in the face of the complexities of actual trade unionism. Numerous controversies surround unions. Can they, in the long run, raise labour's income-share in the face of market forces? How far are they an expression of a limited trade-union consciousness as against a common *class consciousness oriented towards the pursuit of the interests of the labour movement as a whole? How are they affected by the particular goals, traditions, and political culture of their leaders, and of the rank-and-file? Do they embody an inherent contradiction between their democratic or populist origin and the oligarchy necessary to effective leadership? There are extensive sociological literatures addressing all of these questions. *See also* CORPORATE SOCIETY; LENIN; MICHELS; PROFESSIONS; UNIONATENESS.

trade-union consciousness *See* LENIN.

tradition (traditions) A set of social practices that seek to celebrate and inculcate certain *norms and *values, implying continuity with a real or imagined past, and usually associated with widely accepted *rituals or other forms of *symbolic behaviour. Research has established that many traditions which are popularly perceived to be of long standing are in fact relatively recent inventions. Examples include the distinct Highland culture (of kilts, tartan, and bagpipes) of Scotland, a late 18th- and early 19th-century creation; the lifetime employment system in Japan, which was created in the 1920s to bolster a strategy of economic *modernization; and the supposedly indigenous political and economic traditions of many African societies (which were in fact invented by colonial authorities in order to make the necessary connections between local and imperial political, social, and legal systems). Some fascinating case studies along these lines are reported in Eric Hobsbawm and Terence Ranger (eds.), *The Invention of Tradition* (1983).

traditional society The term 'traditional society' is usually contrasted with industrial, urbanized, capitalist 'modern' society. It incorrectly groups together a wide range of non-modern societies, as varied as contemporary hunting and gathering groups on one hand, and medieval European states on the other. It is a judgemental term, often implying negative traits associated with being backward, primitive, non-scientific, and emotional, although it is sometimes linked with a mythical golden age of close-knit family values and community. *See also* GEMEINSCHAFT *and* GESELLSCHAFT.

training, sociology of Training implies preparation for a specific task or *role by ordered instruction. Academic sociologists often contrast training with education. Sociologically, however, training should be conceptually opposed to *schooling, leaving discussion of the educational merits of either to others. Training is carried out preparatory to employment, during the course of it, or for domestic work. Although in large industrial firms it is often formalized in separate training workshops, and is increasingly found in schools themselves, such instruction should, in principle, be considered as training so long as the quantity and quality of the *curriculum is shaped by commercial and labour-market criteria, rather than by broader pedagogies governing the management of knowledge in schools. The relationship between schooling and training is enormously variable across industrial societies, and is the subject of interesting comparative research, suggesting (for example) that it is an important element in *economic growth and the effective use of *human capital. Training is also of considerable significance to mainstream sociological concerns. These include debates about skill, the labour process and labour market, the relationship between the subjective experience of work and class consciousness (or the lack of it), trade unions, and unionateness (all of which are discussed under separate headings elsewhere in this dictionary). The theoretical debates surrounding training, together with an insightful case-study, are discussed in David Lee et al., *Scheming for Youth* (1990). *See also* EDUCATION, SOCIOLOGY OF; VOCATIONALISM.

trait *See* PERSONALITY.

transcarceration *See* DECARCERATION.

transcendentalism The belief that God stands outside and independent of the universe of which He is the Creator. It is normally contrasted with the idea of immanence—the belief that God dwells in the world. The doctrine of immanence is common in pantheism, in which human beings and Nature are thought to be aspects of an all-inclusive divinity. *Monotheism is normally transcendentalist. *See also* RELIGION; THEISM.

transformative movement *See* SOCIAL MOVEMENTS.

transhumance The seasonal movement of herd animals, together with the herding population, between regions, as pasture becomes available (often between highlands and lowlands). Transhumant populations, such as the Saami of Arctic Scandinavia and the Nuer of Southern Sudan, differ from nomadic peoples in that their movement is regular, annual, and seasonal, rather than migrational.

transinstitutionalization A process whereby individuals, supposedly dein-stitutionalized as a result of *community care policies, in practice end up in different institutions, rather than their own homes. For example, the mentally ill who are discharged from, or no longer admitted to, mental hospitals are frequently found in prisons, boarding-houses, nursing-homes, and homes for the elderly.

transmitted deprivation *See* CYCLE OF DEPRIVATION; DEPRIVATION.

transsexual A person born into one sex who crosses over into the other, requiring sex surgery to change the sex organs, and being fully trained into the gender role of that sex. The ideal for many transsexuals is to pass completely and imperceptibly into the other sex and gender. Transsexualism was invented as a clinical phenomenon during the mid-20th century, but it is of great sociological interest in the study of gender and deviance. *See also* TRANSVESTISM.

transvestism The process of cross-dressing or wearing clothes appropriate to the opposite sex. Usually applied in the case of men who dress temporarily as women—and not to be confused with either *transsexuality or *homosexuality. Cross-dressing assumes many forms across different cultures. It was diagnosed as a condition in the West in the late 19th century. Transvestism is an important topic in the study of gender presentation, for it often involves men passing (masquerading) as women, and is more generally a significant factor in the sociology of dress (see, for example, D. Feinbloom, *Transvestites and Transsexuals*, 1975).

trend, social *See* SOCIAL TREND.

triad A triad, or three-person group, is often the least stable of small groups, as there is a tendency for triads to divide into a *dyad and an isolate. Two weaker members may form a coalition against the stronger third, or the weakest member may gain power by dividing the other two.

triangulation The use of at least two theoretical perspectives, research methods, or data-sets for research on one issue or theme, using each to complement and verify the other and in order to achieve robust research results.

Examples are the combined use of micro-level and macro-level studies and of *qualitative and quantitative methods. The approach was elaborated most extensively by Norman K. Denzin.

tribe (tribalism) This term usually denotes a social group bound together by kin and duty and associated with a particular territory. Members of the tribe share the social cohesion associated with the family, together with the sense of political autonomy of a nation. In *Ancient Law* (1861), Sir Henry *Maine identified tribalism with a pre-civilized stage of human society, and the derogatory use of the term to denote emotional, pre-scientific, and irrational behaviour, unfortunately still lingers in the modern usage.

trickle-down effect A term associated with *neo-classical economics, referring to the alleged tendency for economic growth in an unequal society to benefit the population as a whole, via the eventual downward percolation of wealth to the lowest strata. This thesis is usually deployed against the view that state intervention is necessary in order to eliminate poverty. *See also* JUSTICE, SOCIAL.

Troeltsch, Ernst (1865–1923) A German philosopher and theologian, contemporary and close friend of Max Weber, who also made a major contribution to the sociology of religion (see his *The Social Teaching of the Christian Churches*, 1911, and *Protestantism and Progress*, 1912). Like Weber—whom he influenced greatly—Troeltsch was interested in the interrelationship of the material and ideal elements in social life. Again, like Weber and in criticism of Karl Marx, he insisted that religious beliefs could act as an independent variable influencing the development of material factors. His 'church-sect typology' subsequently proved influential in characterizing religious movements. *See also* SECT.

Trotsky, Leon (Leon Lev Davidovich Bronstein Trotsky) (1879–1940) A Bolshevik revolutionary leader, Foreign Minister, and Commissar of War after the 1917 Revolution, who was ousted by Stalin in 1927, exiled in 1929, and murdered in Mexico in 1940. In 1938 he founded the Fourth International in order to oppose Stalin. He is mainly remembered as the theorist of 'permanent revolution', and of the USSR as a 'degenerated workers' state', in which the *bureaucracy functioned as a new ruling class (*see* ELITE).

trust A strong tradition in sociology argues that stable collective life must be based on more than mere calculations of self-interest and that, even in a business situation, an element of trust is essential. Émile *Durkheim's celebrated phrase that 'in a contract not everything is contractual' states this position most succinctly.

One of the most influential recent discussions of trust (A. Giddens, *The Consequences of Modernity*, 1990) defines it as 'confidence in the reliability of a person or system' and provides a useful summary of the chief issues which are raised by this concept. Giddens observes that some properties of trust apply regardless of the type of society under discussion. The human condition is essentially uncertain and threatening, but for day-to-day purposes, the upbringing of most members of society protects them from deep-seated anxiety by the development of 'basic trust' in others and in 'taken-for-granted' ways of living. Several traditions in psychology and psychoanalysis ascribe bizarre, aggressive, and disturbed behaviour to the failure of parents to transmit a sense of basic trust to their offspring, with the result that both the inner self and the external environment are perceived as unreliable and hostile.

That the onset of modernity fundamentally alters both the sources and the objects of basic trust is suggested by the classical and more recent writings alike. The broad consensus of this work is that modernity undermines the salience of kinship ties, breaks the hold of the local community, and questions the authority of religion and appeals to tradition. Giddens attributes these effects to various 'disembedding mechanisms' which detach social relations from local contexts and 'restructure them across indefinite spans of time and space'. There are two classes of such mechanisms, both of which require a more abstract form of trust than in pre-modern circumstances: namely, symbolic tokens (the prime example being money), and expert systems (where trust is placed in a body of reflexive knowledge). The distancing of social relations in time and space, however, requires a learned ability to maintain trust and simultaneously tolerate absence. Modernity is therefore double-edged, since it threatens our 'ontological security', that is, our confidence in the continuity of personal identity and in the social and material environment. It also increases the likelihood of risk and anxiety as well as demanding trust in abstract systems.

Arguably, trust is a neglected and underdeveloped notion in sociological analysis, although there are clear signs of an awakening of interest (see, for example, Barbara Misztal, *Trust in Modern Societies*, 1996). In this newer literature, issues of trust tend to be linked to wider discussions of rational action theory (*see* RATIONAL CHOICE THEORY) and *game theory. To date, however, the main usage of the concept in a substantive research context has been in the comparative sociology of labour relations and management. For example, Alan Fox (*Beyond Contract*, 1974) proposed a distinction between labour-management systems with a low-trust and a high-trust 'dynamic' (ethos and methods of control), arguing that it could be applied to differences in both individual organizations and national bargaining structures. The amount of discretion allowed to the worker is related to remuneration and working conditions, job security, supervisory style, policy towards collective bargaining, and so on. Whereas British and American management styles historically have tended to reflect a low-trust dynamic, Germany and Japan are cited as examples of high-trust industrial cultures. It is important to note, however, that high-trust methods may be adopted by industrial management for calculative reasons, and may in the longer term be perceived by the workforce as manipulation, or the attempt to manufacture consent.

Fox's dichotomy has been rediscovered (and relabelled) by several later authors. For example, Andrew Friedman (*Industry and Labour*, 1977) contrasts managerial strategies of 'direct control' (close supervision, minimal worker responsibility, use of coercive threats), with those of 'responsible autonomy' (encouraging workers to identify with the goals of the enterprise, and to police their own efforts, by granting them authority, status, and responsibility).

However, regardless of the terminology in which the contrast has been presented, it is vulnerable to the criticism that patterns of managerial control in the real world are more complex, and cannot be reduced to any dualist view of strategy. General discussions of trust can be found in Niklas Luhmann's *Trust and Power* (1968) and Barbara Misztal's *Trust in Modern Societies* (1996).

Turner, Victor (1920–83) A British social anthropologist who elaborated the study of *ritual and *symbolism. His main fieldwork was among the Ndembu in Africa, where he made detailed interpretations of colour symbols, *rites of passage, and healing ceremonies, as well as a micro-study of village politics (see *Schism and Continuity in an African Society*, 1957, and *The Forest of Symbols*, 1967). Developing Arnold van Gennep's idea of *limen* or threshold, he explored the concept of *liminality in pilgrimage and Western society, in *The Ritual Process* (1969).

Tylor, Sir Edward Burnett (1832–1917) An English Victorian anthropologist who was the first to teach *social anthropology under its name at Oxford, beginning in 1884. He is best known for formulating the first well-known definition of *culture as 'that complex whole which includes knowledge, belief, art, morals, law, custom and any other capabilities and habits acquired by man as a member of society'.

In *Primitive Culture* (1871), Tylor contributed to the development of the tools of comparative religion, especially with his theory of animism (*see* TOTEMISM), which he saw as a primordial form of primitive religion. Tylor was a proponent of *evolutionary theory, deeming some aspects of culture to be functionless survivals from the past, and seeing other elements as survival strategies. One of his famous statements on this subject was that, in the history of societal evolution, the choice facing many peoples was 'to marry out or die out'. In this way, by creating alliances through intermarriage, potentially threatening groups could be co-opted.

Tylor was ground-breaking in his use of social arithmetic—the use of statistics in the analysis of societies through his method of 'fluctions' or what would today be called *correlation. Using such methods, he demonstrated convincingly that the avoidance of in-laws by daughters or sons was based upon choice of residence at marriage. If residence is uxorilocal, the son would be expected to avoid his in-laws, but if residence is virilocal, the daughter is more likely to practise such behaviour. On the basis of this evidence, Tylor proceeded to explain other customs, including the presence of certain kinship terms. This style of analysis, which interwove distinct cultural practices, contributed to the development of *functionalism, which later became the first major paradigm of modern British social anthropology.

typification *See* IDEAL TYPE; PHENOMENOLOGY.

typology *See* TAXONOMY.

unconscious *See* PSYCHOANALYSIS.

underclass The extensive and acrimonious sociological debate about the underclass stems from a predominantly American literature which addresses two phenomena that are argued to be related: namely, high levels of youth unemployment, and an increasing proportion of single-parent households. Concern with single parenthood stems from the fact that this is the largest category of welfare dependence by virtue of Aid to Families with Dependent Children (AFDC). The Black population is disproportionately affected by both joblessness and single parenthood.

The term itself suggests a group which is in some sense outside the mainstream of society—but there is much disagreement about the nature and source of their exclusion. One interpretation, advanced most strongly by Charles Murray (*Losing Ground*, 1984), is that *welfare dependency has encouraged the break-up of the *nuclear family household, and *socialization into a *counter-culture which devalues work and encourages dependency and criminality. An alternative structural view, advanced by William Julius Wilson and others, emphasizes the failure of the economy to provide secure employment to meet demand, and the consequent destabilization of the male-breadwinner role. The former sees the source of exclusion to lie in the attitudes and behaviour of the underclass population; the latter situates it in the structured inequality which disadvantages particular groups in society.

The precise nature of this structural disadvantage is itself a matter of intense dispute. One central disagreement is about whether the problems of the disadvantaged Black population lie in their colour or their class position. Early in his work, Wilson makes reference to 'a vast underclass of black proletarians—that massive population at the very bottom of the social class ladder, plagued by poor education and low-paying, unstable jobs' (see *The Declining Significance of Race*, 1978). This conceptualizes the underclass as a Black phenomenon, defined in terms of vulnerability in the *labour market, and without reference to behavioural or moral factors. However, in a later study (*The Truly Disadvantaged*, 1987), Wilson writes of 'individuals who lack training and skills and either experience long-term unemployment or are not members of the labour force, individuals who are engaged in street crime and other forms of aberrant behaviour, and families that experience long term spells of poverty and/or welfare dependency'. The emphasis has here shifted slightly: there is no explicit reference to 'race'; unstable unemployment has become absence of employment; and the definition has expanded to include criminality and welfare dependence (thus incorporating a cultural dimension into Wilson's essentially structural approach).

Though discussion about the nature and extent of underclass membership has been most fully developed in the USA, the ideas which underpin it are by no means unfamiliar in Britain, not just in the upsurge of concern about (welfare) 'dependency culture' in the 1980s, but through studies dating back to the 1960s and 1970s, and perhaps most notably the literature on so-called *cycles of deprivation. Other work in the 1970s focused on the disadvantage of inner-city Blacks in Britain, with (for example) John Rex and Sally Tomlinson arguing that systematic disadvantage in both employment and housing leads to a neighbour-hood activity which is an expression of collective class awareness, such that 'there is some tendency for the black community to operate as a separate class or an underclass in British society' (*Colonial Immigrants in a British City*, 1979).

Charles Murray has played a considerable role in placing the concept of the underclass back on the political as well as the sociological agenda, but often in a highly controversial manner. In recent work he has argued that 'the difference between the United States and Britain was that the United States reached the future first'. Using metaphors of 'plague' and 'disease', he suggests that an underclass defined by illegitimacy, violent crime, and drop-out from the labour force is growing, and will continue to do so because there is a generation of children being brought up to live in the same way (*The Emerging British Under-class*, 1990). This conclusion would seem to be undermined by the research emanating from the earlier debate about cycles of deprivation.

Unemployment has always posed a problem for stratification studies based on occupational ranking, and the notion of an underclass has been adopted by some class analysts, in an attempt to resolve this difficulty. W. G. Runciman ('How Many Classes are there in Contemporary British Society?', *Sociology*, 1991) argues that below the *working classes of skilled and unskilled manual workers there is a distinct underclass, a term which 'stands not for a group or category of workers systematically disadvantaged within the labour market but for those members of British society whose roles place them more or less permanently at the economic level where benefits are paid by the state to those unable to participate in the labour market at all ... They are typically the long-term unem-ployed'. However, this definition is of questionable value, for strictly speaking it applies not to the unemployed, who are at least notionally still participant in the labour market (albeit unsuccessfully), but rather to those more conclusively outside: namely, the aged, the long-term sick, and the severely disabled.

Another British sociologist, Anthony Giddens (*The Class Structure of the Advanced Societies*, 1973), defines the underclass as composed of people who are concentrated in the lowest-paid occupations, and are semi-employed or chronically unemployed, 'as a result of a "disqualifying" market capacity of a primarily cultural kind'. Duncan Gallie has explored the potential for cultural cohesion and collective self-awareness as defining characteristics of the underclass, and concluded that the non-standard employment patterns and long-term unemployment of the 1980s may have provided a structural basis for a distinctive underclass, but not for its cultural underpinning (see

'Employment, Unemployment and Social Stratification', in his *Employment in Britain*, 1988). Most of the recent American and British literature is discussed extensively in a debate about the evidence for and against the existence of a separate underclass, published in the *British Journal of Sociology* (1996).

The final word on the concept should perhaps therefore be left to Herbert Gans ('Deconstructing the Underclass', *Journal of the American Planning Association*, 1990), who concludes that 'underclass is a quite distinctive synthesizing term that lumps together a variety of highly diverse people'. It probably has more value as political rhetoric than as a meaningful sociological concept.

underconsumption, theories of The notion of underconsumption posits a persistent shortfall in the demand for consumption goods which creates a tendency towards overproduction and stagnation in *capitalist economies. It results from the conflict between capitalists' desire to restrain the tendency of real wages to rise and their need to realize surplus value through the sale of commodities. The term has been linked to theories of *imperialism and *under-development, in that markets in the *Third World are sometimes targeted to absorb the excess commodities produced in the First.

underdevelopment A term associated with *dependency theory and used to describe the condition of poverty and economic stagnation characteristic of many Third World societies. It implies that these societies are not simply suffer-ing from lack of development, but also that they have not achieved the expected levels of development which would have occurred, had they not been exploited by the advanced capitalist states.

underemployment Suboptimal utilization of labour, also termed sub-employment. Visible underemployment involves working fewer hours than a person normally works, or prefers to work. Invisible underemployment involves underutilization of a person's skills, qualifications, or experience in a job that is lower grade than their usual job, or involves a skills mismatch, and may lead to low productivity and low income. The majority of part-time jobs are taken voluntarily in preference to full-time jobs, and so do not constitute visible underemployment. However, part-time jobs often involve invisible underem-ployment, for example when they are taken by women who revert to less skilled work on their return to the *labour market after an absence for child-rearing.

understanding *See* ACTION THEORY; MEANING; NEO-KANTIANISM.

unemployment The state of being unable to sell one's labour-power in the *labour market despite being willing to do so. In practice, unemployment is difficult to identify and measure, because willingness to be employed is partly affected by the extent and nature of demand for one's services. As a result, official definitions imposed by government employment agencies are affected by polit-ical theories about the causes of being unwilling or unable to be employed, on one hand; and, on the other, by the rules allowing registration as out of work and eligible for such *welfare benefits as may be on offer.

Unemployment was used by C. Wright *Mills as a graphic illustration of the distinction between private troubles and public issues which he considered basic to sociology. Research on the unemployed has repeatedly shown that unemployment is rarely explicable simply as a private or individual problem of insufficient motivation and aptitude. It is, rather, a public issue caused by the failure of *market processes.

Economists distinguish various causes of unemployment, the chief two of which are the structural decline of industry in a region or nation, and cyclical variations in economic activity. The former generates shifts in the occupational structure which render particular skills obsolete, as for example might follow technological innovation, changes in the market for goods and services, or the decision by companies to close or relocate their operations. The latter occurs when firms lay off workers (perhaps temporarily) during periods of economic recession. Other forms of unemployment include frictional unemployment (which is due to workers voluntarily switching jobs) and seasonal unemployment (when a change in the seasons reduces demand for particular types of workers, for example those involved in agriculture, or in the recreation and leisure industries).

Unemployment is a major factor in *poverty, especially where the unemployed experience spells of joblessness alternating with so-called sub-employment, that is, low paid and uncongenial work with a high degree of insecurity of tenure. The unemployed must also endure the stigma of being unable to conform to the prevailing *work ethic of Western societies—despite their own typically strong desire to find work.

There is an enormous sociological literature on the process of becoming unemployed and its social and individual consequences. A good place to start is Marie Jahoda's *Employment and Unemployment* (1982). An excellent series of empirical studies—examining the relationships between unemployment and (among other things) attitudes to work, household work strategies, psychological health, marital dissolution, welfare, deprivation, and involvement in social networks—is reported in Duncan Gallie et al. (eds.), *Social Change and the Experience of Unemployment* (1993). *See also* UNDEREMPLOYMENT.

uneven development A term used within later Marxist theory to denote the process by which *capitalism transforms the world as a whole but does so in different ways, developing the productive and social forces in some areas, but (as part of the same process) restricting or distorting growth in others. It may be contrasted with the earlier Marxist belief in capitalism as producing a uniform world in its own image.

unilineal descent *See* DESCENT GROUPS.

unintended or unanticipated consequences It is an old saying that things do not always turn out as we expect. The theme of the unintended consequences of action therefore has an understandably long pedigree in the social sciences. Many sociological observers have distinguished between the stated purpose or intent of social actions, and their generally unrecognized, but objective functional consequences. William Isaac *Thomas noted how the co-operative institutions of Polish peasants served not just their specific objectives but also functioned to forge cohesion. More recently, Lewis Coser has argued that conflicts are not always destructive for an organization, but may, by their adaptive or safety-valve function, play a part in maintaining organizational stability (see *The Functions of Social Conflict*, 1965).

The classic sociological example of unanticipated consequences is found in Max Weber's thesis about the connection between the *protestant ethic and the spirit of modern capitalism. The Calvinist doctrines of predestination and this-worldly asceticism had the unintended consequence of creating a climate suitable for the growth of capitalism by encouraging the accumulation of capital as a duty or end in itself. More recent illustrations are given by Jon Elster in *Nuts and Bolts for the Social Sciences* (1989). One example deals with the way in which *opinion polls can affect election outcomes. The publication of pre-election polls may actually alter the outcome of the election, either because they cause people to switch and support the leading candidate, or because people cast a sympathy vote for the apparent underdog. Of course, if everyone opted for the underdog, this would have the strange result of awarding victory to the less popular candidate. A somewhat similar example of the unintended is provided by the *Hawthorne Studies, where the presence of the researchers inadvertently changed the behaviour of the workers they were studying, a phenomenon since designated the 'Hawthorne effect'.

According to Robert Merton (*Social Theory and Social Structure*, 1949) the unintended consequences of actions are of three types: those which are functional for a designated system and therefore comprise latent *functions; those which are *dysfunctional for a designated system and are latently dysfunctional; and those which are irrelevant to the system since they have no functional consequences. As soon as these types are applied to a specific situation there are problems. Obvious questions include 'Dysfunctional for whom?' and 'Performing a latent function for what?' Moreover, it makes no sense to use unanticipated consequences to explain the function, because the consequences were not known at the time. An unanticipated consequence could, however, influence future actions. Think of a child throwing a tantrum in order to get an ice-cream. If the tantrum has the unintended consequence of attracting adult attention, then attention-seeking rather than ice-cream may motivate future tantrums.

Unanticipated consequences are important at the micro-level as social actors are often mistaken in their interpretation of the situation and can, by their action, bring unanticipated results. A special case of this is the *self-fulfilling prophecy, in which the pronouncement of an erroneous belief may evoke behaviour that (apparently) vindicates that belief, thus making the prophecy come true. The *labelling theory of deviance postulates precisely such a mechanism. Thus, to quote the early formulation by Frank Tannenbaum in *Crime and the Community* (1938), 'the very process of making the criminal is a process of tagging, defining, identifying, segregating, describing, emphasizing, making conscious and self-conscious; it becomes a way of stimulating, suggesting, emphasizing the very traits that are complained of'. Unanticipated consequences are also important at the macro-level because so many events occur unintentionally. As Adam Ferguson observed, 'History is the result of human action, not of human design.' *See also* ACTION THEORY; FUNCTION.

unionateness The nature and level of *trade-union *militancy and willingness to use *strikes or other forms of *industrial conflict to pursue the interests of labour. Also, the qualitative aspect of trade-union strength or weakness, as against the quantitative completeness (or so-called density) with which a union recruits from its potential constituency.

unit act *See* SYSTEMS THEORY.

unit of analysis *See* UNIT OF ENQUIRY.

unit of enquiry This is the unit—for example individual, household, corporation, or whatever—about which information is required in a research project. Students often confuse the unit of enquiry (sometimes also called the unit of analysis) with the *sampling unit. The two need not be the same for any particular study. Thus, one may sample households, and then collect information (from one or more of its members) about all individual residents. Here, the sampling unit is the household, and the unit of enquiry is the household member.

univariate analysis *See* MULTIVARIATE ANALYSIS.

universal benefits *See* SELECTIVE VERSUS UNIVERSAL BENEFITS.

unobtrusive measures Techniques for collecting data without the knowledge of respondents. Two types—the covert and the indirect—may be identified. The former include, for example, *covert participant observation, undisclosed note-taking, or use of one-way mirrors. The latter involves the use of *personal documents and other records which might offer indirect measures of variables such that the need for interaction between the investigator and his or her subjects is obviated. (For example, student satisfaction with new educational practices might be assessed by inspecting records of attendance at classes and rates of switching between course, rather than direct interview or questionnaire.) The justification of such methods is that, because respondents are unaware of their status as research subjects, their activities are unaffected by certain potential biases in the research situation itself—such as the desire to please the investigator. Although some of these techniques (most notably covert observation) are now frowned upon by professional sociological associations as being ethically suspect, the imaginative use of existing documentary sources for novel research purposes is occasionally very effective, although one is normally working 'against the grain' of the data since they have usually been collected for purposes other than those embodied in the research. *See also* INTERVIEW BIAS; RESEARCH ETHICS.

unstructured interview *See* INTERVIEW.

u

upper class As a concrete, descriptive term in British studies of *social stratification, the upper class is a dominant social class that owes a great deal to its close *status affinities with the 'aristocracy'. The latter is the (often hereditary) noble class, comprising peers (in medieval England the dukes, marquesses, earls, viscounts, and barons) and landed magnates (or 'gentlemen'). However, while the aristocracy is an important symbolic element of the upper class, it does not completely account for its membership today. As a dominant class, it comprises the *bourgeoisie or capitalist class. The upper class is a property-owning class living from earnings made from the ownership, control, and exploitation of property such as land, capital, large businesses, or share holdings, and whose members enjoy superior, traditionally grounded status privileges. Proportionally, therefore, this is much the smallest class, perhaps as little as 1 per cent of the population. The *power which the ownership of property confers is out of all proportion to the size of a dominant class. Many members of this class effectively control large companies, either directly via their positions within these organizations, or more subtly through their occupation of key positions in the financial sector. Some of these individuals also have leading positions in politics and other spheres of public and cultural life. Through their involvement in politics, a dominant class may become a ruling class.

In Britain there have been important status distinctions within the upper class, between those who have 'old money', and the *nouveaux riches*. The highest status tends to be conferred on the landed upper classes, the true aristocracy, as represented by individuals such as the Duke of Westminster (the wealthiest individual in the UK after the Queen). Often they operate exclusionary strategies against the *nouveaux riches*, for example, by restricting the membership of very exclusive aristocratic clubs. 'New money' confers less status—though by no means less power. Hence, it is no accident that the *nouveaux riches* have long sought to acquire a more aristocratic status via inclusionary strategies, such as the purchase of landed estates, intermarriage with the aristocracy for themselves or their children, and the education of their children in elite schools.

Popular conceptions of the upper class correspond more with old money than with new. In their survey of social class in Britain in 1984 (*Social Class in Modern Britain*), Gordon Marshall and his colleagues discovered that two-thirds of their sample referred to the upper class in terms of status factors, for example rank or title; two-fifths of the sample mentioned income; and one-third referred to occupation. Only one-quarter of the sample mentioned property ownership as the defining characteristic of the upper class—although sociologically this is its key feature.

Similar dominant classes exist in all capitalist societies, though they are not always formed into a status-defined upper class. Important sociological work on the British upper class is to be found in the voluminous writings of John Scott (see, for example, *The Upper Class*, 1982, and *Who Rules Britain?*, 1991). Comparative work can be found in Tom Bottomore and Robert Brym (eds.), *The Capitalist Class* (1989). See also CLOSURE; ELITE; OWNERSHIP AND CONTROL.

urban agglomeration See CONURBATION.

urban ecology Urban ecology, pioneered by *Chicago sociologists in the 1920s, was central to the development of *human ecology. Indeed the two terms are often used interchangeably.

Urban ecology applies principles derived from biological science to the explanation of spatial distribution in urban populations. This is said to result from 'biotic' competition for territorial advantage by human groups, each constituted by social basis, for example, common class position or ethnicity. Groups occupy distinctive 'natural areas' or neighbourhoods. The *concentric zone model proposed by Ernest Burgess is an ecological representation of this urban system. The ecological concepts of invasion, domination, and succession describe the stages of change occurring as groups relocate due to competitive pressures. However, unrestrained biotic competition makes social order impossible, so a second level of social organization ('culture') overlays and limits territorial competition. This involves communication, consensus, and co-operation, seen in both the natural areas occupied by socially homogeneous groups, and in city-wide mechanisms of integration, such as mass culture, the media, and urban politics.

Few sociologists now accept the biologically derived assumptions underlying urban ecology. However, the urban ecologists' use of Chicago as a research laboratory contributed greatly to the development of empirically grounded sociology and its research methods, influencing directly the development of urban sociology, community studies, cultural sociology, the study of deviance and illness, social and religious movements, the family and race relations, and rural sociology. The recollections by Helen MacGill Hughes of her training in Chicago shed an interesting light on the (at times naïve) methodology of urban ecology (see 'On Becoming a Sociologist', *Journal of the History of Sociology*, 1980).

urbanism Urbanism refers to patterns of social life thought typical of urban populations. These include a highly specialized *division of labour, growth of instrumentalism (*see* WORK, SUBJECTIVE EXPERIENCE OF) in social relationships, weakening of kin relationships, growth of *voluntary associations, normative pluralism, *secularization, increase in social *conflict, and growing importance of the *mass media. In a key paper published in 1938 ('Urbanism as a Way of Life', *American Journal of Sociology*) Louis *Wirth sought to ground these patterns in three general characteristics of cities—size, density, and social heterogeneity. However, later research showed that attempts to link social and cultural characteristics deterministically with physical locations are misconceived. *See also* URBAN SOCIOLOGY.

urbanization Narrowly defined, urbanization refers to city formation. The earliest cities date from about the fourth millennium BCE. In the Middle Ages the expansion of long-distance trade and mercantile capitalism stimulated the growth of major European cities. There is significant controversy about the relationship between urbanization, *feudal decline, and the growth of *capitalism.

Most sociological attention has focused on the large-scale urbanization accompanying industrialization and the emergence of modern societies. Although there is no invariant relationship between levels of economic development and urbanization, the term 'under-urbanization' is often used to describe the situation in (former) state socialist countries, where the growth of industrial agglomerations is not matched by a sufficient expansion of housing and urban infrastructure for the workforce. Similarly, the term 'over-urbanization' is applied to Third World cities which have large populations that cannot be absorbed into the formal economy. As the social changes accompanying industrialization diffuse throughout national territories the sociological significance of urbanization diminishes. In such urbanized societies the term may carry a wider meaning, signifying possession of an advanced industrial economy, and modernized social structure. *See also* URBANISM.

urban managerialism A Weberian-influenced theory of urban processes proposed by R. E. Pahl and others. Urban managers (local government officials and finance officers, for example), controlling access to scarce resources such as housing and education, largely determine the socio-spatial distribution of the population. The theory placed issues of power, conflict, and the role of market and state institutions at the centre of *urban sociology.

urban social movements Organizations formed by residents to protest about, or make demands for changes in, the urban environment and urban services. The term was originally applied narrowly by Manuel Castells to those urban movements which contributed to wider revolutionary social change. *See also* SOCIAL MOVEMENTS.

urban sociology Sociological concern with *urbanization began with *sociology itself, for it was the rapidly growing 19th-century industrial cities that first supported those social relationships and structures which inspired the new discipline. Most early sociologists shared the anti-urban bias of much Victorian thought and writing—and a correspondingly romanticized view of rural life. A key concern was the apparent breakdown of *community and *social control consequent upon urbanization.

Georg *Simmel (*The Metropolis and Mental Life*, 1903) incorporated these concerns in a brilliant, impressionistic discussion of urban lifestyles and personality, viewing the social organization and culture which typified urban areas as the consequence of large population aggregates, thus linking causally the physical characteristics of cities with the social characteristics of their inhabitants. Simmel's analysis and ideas, derived from Darwinian *ecology, shaped the *Chicago School of urban sociology—the dominant paradigm from the 1920s to the 1950s. The most famous summation of this paradigm occurs in an article ('Urbanism as a Way of Life', *American Journal of Sociology*, 1938) in which Louis *Wirth derives ideal-typical social characteristics of urban life (*urbanism) from three apparently universal features of cities—large size, high density, and social heterogeneity.

Chicago urban sociology stimulated important empirical research. However, by the 1960s the paradigm had disintegrated and the sub-discipline was a sociological backwater. Empirically, the work of researchers such as Herbert Gans (in the United States) and R. E. Pahl (in Britain) disproves any necessary connection between urban location (hence Wirth's universal features of cities), and particular *lifestyles. Theoretically, this approach involves a form of *naturalism, reifying physical characteristics of cities, falsely identifying these as the causes not the consequences of social processes, and erroneously concluding that social patterns occurring in cities are caused by cities.

This suggests that to derive typical or characteristic patterns of social life from supposedly universal physical or demographic features of cities is to commit not just an empirical but also an epistemological error. Nevertheless, there have been several more recent attempts to provide a new unifying theoretical paradigm for urban sociology, including neo-Weberian theories of *housing classes and *urban managerialism; so-called non-spatial urban sociology focusing on *consumption-sector cleavages; and neo-Marxist perspectives centring on *collective consumption.

The last of these defined the new urban sociology of the 1970s. Its most important text was Manuel Castells's *The Urban Question* (1977). Drawing on the structuralist Marxism of Louis *Althusser and Nicos *Poulantzas, Castells developed an elaborate account of the so-called structures and practices of capitalist urbanization, suggesting that modern (monopoly) capitalism was increasingly dependent on state-supplied urban goods and services (or 'collective consumption') to ensure adequate reproduction of its labour force. This led to rising conflict between the *state and urban *social movements. The latter, in alliance with workplace struggles, might bring about revolutionary change in capitalist societies as a whole.

The Urban Question offered a seemingly powerful analysis of capitalist urbanization. It certainly inspired much new work in urban social theory and research. However, this tended to show that key aspects of Castells's formulation were theoretically and empirically wanting, notably his definition of cities as 'spaces for collective consumption', the importance given to urban social movements, and his structural-Marxist conception of the *relatively autonomous state. Subsequently, indeed, in *The City and the Grassroots* (1983), Castells abandoned Marxist theory, and adopted a less dramatic view of the potential effects of urban social movements. In later work (*The Informational City*, 1989, and, in particular, his three-volume study on *The Information Age*, 1996–8) he argues that the revolution in information technology marks a major new phase in capitalist production and consequential patterns of urban and regional development.

None of these more recent approaches has attained the degree of intellectual dominance formerly exercised by the Chicago School (although the influence of neo-Marxism is still substantial). However, they have resulted in extensive research (frequently of an interdisciplinary nature) on topics as diverse as the political economy of urban and regional development, urban politics, and social movements, and the relationship between space and the social structure (see D. T. Herbert and D. M. Smith, *Social Problems and the City*, 1989). Much of this literature has informed more general sociological concerns, such as social *stratification, collective social action, and the distribution of *power. While the search for a theoretically delimited urban sociology has failed, urban social research contributes substantially to sociology, and indeed other social sciences. *See also*

BUSINESS IMPROVEMENT DISTRICTS; COMMUNITY STUDIES; PARK; SUBURBANISM; URBAN ECOLOGY.

Urwick, Edward Johns (1867–1945) A student of the liberal theorist T. H. Green, along with Bernard and Helen *Bosanquet, he worked for the Charity Organisation Society at Toynbee Hall in the East End of London. In 1897 the Society reformed itself as a training body for social workers and took the name 'School of Ethics and Social Philosophy', later 'School of Sociology'. Urwick was appointed as its first director. Financial difficulties led the School to merge with the London School of Economics in 1912, becoming its Department of Social Science and Administration. Urwick was joint Head of Department, along with *Hobhouse. Urwick left the LSE in 1924, having been invited by Robert *MacIver to join him at Toronto to teach social policy in the Department of Political Science. He set up the Department of Social Service in 1928 and headed this until his retirement in 1937. Early works on youth, delinquency, and wealth were followed by his principal book *The Social Good* (1927) which was published shortly after he left Britain and set out an evolutionary theory of moral progress and citizenship. He developed an idealist view of society as a system of moral representations.

use value *See* COMMODIFICATION.

utilitarianism The name given by John Stuart *Mill to a leading tradition of economic *liberalism in political and moral philosophy and social theory. As a political and moral philosophy, utilitarianism is epitomized by a famous slogan coined by Jeremy *Bentham, 'the greatest happiness of the greatest number'. The most sophisticated version is to be found in the work of the philosopher David *Hume, but Hume's arguments equating goodness and utility are rejected by Adam *Smith in his moral writings, even though Smith is often misleadingly cast as a utilitarian in modern sociological literature. Utilitarianism flourished in late 18th-century and early 19th-century Britain, but European and American thinkers propounded similar notions. Bentham and his followers argued that the respective 'happinesses' of each individual are additive (the so-called utilitarian calculus of pleasure and pain) and that the test of the rightness of individual or social action is to maximize the sum of individual *utility.

Utilitarians often erroneously justified both their moral doctrines and their advocacy of *laissez-faire politics by means of an embryonic rational *choice theory of society, which goes back at least as far as the writings of Thomas *Hobbes, and which is sometimes known as egoistic hedonism. It asserts that individual action is always the product of the pursuit of (implicitly selfish or self-referencing) pleasure and avoidance of pain. Later utilitarians include Herbert Spencer and John Stuart Mill himself, whose father James Mill had been a leading representative of the school in its heyday. John Stuart Mill struggled to retrieve some of the ambiguities and banalities to which the moral and social theory led, and because of his writings both on method and on substantive issues, he is sometimes considered as an early sociologist. However, most of the acknowledged founders of sociology were critical of the tradition of liberal *political economy within which utilitarianism emerged, and which it helped to develop. As a result the label utilitarian is often somewhat indiscriminately applied (for example by Talcott Parsons in *The Structure of Social Action*) to the whole tradition of economistic methods and theories in social science.

utility In economic theory, utility is defined as the benefit or satisfaction which is derived from the consumption of a commodity. In 18th-century moral philosophy, it meant 'the greatest happiness principle': actions are right if they tend to promote happiness. Early sociologists, for example Émile Durkheim, criticized the utility principle, because it provided an inadequate explanation of *social order.

utopia (utopianism) A utopia is an imaginative account of a perfect society or ideal commonwealth. The term, which is often used derogatively to mean unrealistic, is derived from Sir Thomas More's *Utopia* (1516). Many literary sources have explored the ideas of utopian and dystopian communities, ranging from William Morris's *News From Nowhere*, through George Orwell's *1984* and Aldous Huxley's *Brave New World*, to Margaret Atwood's *The Handmaid's Tale*. Auguste *Comte saw social reconstruction as involving scientifically guided change in utopian directions. This argument was developed in the works of *Geddes, *Branford, and *Mumford as the idea of 'eutopia': a positively achievable ideal society rather than an arbitrary and unrealistic goal (See Mumford's *The Story of Utopias*, 1922). A number of small utopian communities, often based on simple anarchist and communist ideas, have been established as attempts to introduce new principles of social organization.

In sociology the idea of utopia has often been seen in terms of the sociology of knowledge of Karl *Mannheim. In *Ideology and Utopia* (1929), Mannheim claimed that subordinate groups and classes are attracted to utopian beliefs that emphasize the possibilities of change and transformation, whereas dominant social classes typically adopt an ideological outlook which emphasizes stability and continuity. For Mannheim, the radical views of the Anabaptist sects were examples of utopianism. However, Mannheim's interest in utopianism also had a philosophical and religious dimension: it is the capacity for utopianism which ultimately defines *human nature, that is, the capacity to imagine alternative futures.

Mannheim's perception of the relationship between utopianism and human *ontology was also shared by the Marxist social philosopher Ernst Bloch, whose *The Principle of Hope* (1959) examined the role of dreaming, fairy stories, utopian philosophies, and fantasies in human societies. For Bloch, utopianism was an anticipatory consciousness which is ubiquitous. Utopias have two dimensions, material and subjective, which he expressed in terms of the Not-Yet-Become and the Not-Yet-Conscious. Bloch's ideas were a protest against the failures of organized *communism in Eastern Europe.

The utopian strands in Karl *Marx's theory of communism are retained in even the most revisionist of contemporary *neo-Marxisms. The work of André Gorz is typical in this respect. Born in Austria, Gorz became one of the leading social and political theorists of the French New Left, and for a time edited *Les Temps* *modernes*. He wrote numerous short, popular articles, and a series of influential books including *Ecology as Politics* (1980), *Farewell to the Working Class* (1982), *Paths to Paradise* (1985), and *Critique of Economic Reason* (1989). Though strongly influenced by Marxist ideas, and especially by Sartre, Gorz continually attempted to revise this heritage in the light of his own analyses of contemporary social changes, and his distinctive vision of a possible utopian future. His earlier work proposed a strategy for the labour movement based on an alliance between the declining 'traditional' working class and a growing 'new' working class. The meaninglessness and alienation of work in advanced capitalism were conditions shared by these different groups. Subsequently, however, Gorz ceased to assign to the working class in any form the revolutionary role expected by classical Marxism. Technological change in advanced capitalist societies is bringing about fundamental changes in the social structure: 'worker-producers' are increasingly outnumbered by a heterogeneous population in insecure, part-time, or temporary work, in other words a growing 'post-industrial neo-proletariat'. At the same time, the obsession with economic growth and the commitment to the work ethic are increasingly destructive of both nature and of personal life in society. New *social movements, especially ecological politics, point the way to a future in which class and domination are ended. A basic income will be provided independently of work. Technology will be employed to reduce to a minimum that element of unrewarding labour which remains necessary for the meeting of need. Meanwhile, such necessary labour as is required will be shared equally among the population. The progressive reduction in the working week made possible by these arrangements will free people for a creative, autonomous, and convivial use of their time and energies.

Gorz's work has been subjected to searching criticism in Boris Frankel's *The Post-Industrial Utopians* (1987). For a more general treatment of the topic see Ruth Levitas, *The Concept of Utopia* (1990). *See also* COMMUNE; MESSIANIC MOVEMENT.

(⊕) SEE WEB LINKS

• Utopia Britannica, dealing with British utopian communities.

u

validity The property of being genuine, a true reflection of attitudes, behaviour, or characteristics. A measure (such as a question, series of questions, or test) is considered valid if it is thought to measure the concept or property which it claims to measure. For example, it might be contested whether the answers to a question about job satisfaction are a valid indicator of alienation from modern society; the holding of paid employment on the part of a woman is a valid indicator of a feminist consciousness; or the divorce rate in the United States is a valid indicator of the extent of social stress in that society. The validity of an attitude scale, or of the answers obtained by a question in an interview, is ultimately a matter for judgement, but techniques have been developed to supplement a researcher's own views, which may not be representative.

Rules of thumb have been developed which rule out certain types of question completely. For example, it is generally held to be pointless enquiring long after the event about the attitudes and reasons linked to a decision or choice made many years ago, on the grounds that views tend to be reconstructed with the benefit of hindsight. Arguments of validity rule out proxy interviews for anything except the most basic factual data, such as someone's occupation, if even that. Logical validation, checking for 'face validity' in theoretical or commonsense terms, continues to be the most important tool, which is strengthened by employing as wide a range of people as possible to make the checks. This can be extended into the use of panels of experts, judges or juries who are in fact ordinary people who have close familiarity with the topic in question, and can judge whether questions and classifications of replies cover all the situations that arise, and are appropriately worded. Another approach is to present the research instrument to groups of people who are known to have particular views or experience, and see whether it differentiates adequately between the groups. However, the ultimate test is whether the research tools, and the results obtained, are accepted by other scholars as having validity. It is rare for researchers to submit their work to the scrutiny of the research subjects themselves, though this sometimes happens in policy research. Population *censuses are unique in having post-enumeration *surveys after each census to check data validity and general quality.

There are many different definitions of validity in the available literature. It is clear that different authors use the terminology in different ways. Part of the problem is that most of the relevant discussion takes place among psychologists, who also provide many of the examples and established procedures for testing for validity, but it is not clear that these always translate easily into sociological contexts.

One elementary and useful distinction sometimes made is that between criterion and construct validity. The former refers to the closeness of fit between a measure (let us say a concept) and the reality that it is supposed to reflect. For example, the *Goldthorpe class scheme is intended as and claims to be a measure of 'conditions and relations of employment', in particular the material and other benefits of the 'service relationship' as against that of the 'labour contract'. However, for practical reasons its *operationalization is effected via data about each individual's occupational title (teacher, nurse, or whatever) on one hand, and employment status on the other (manager, employee, self-employed, and so on). One could therefore investigate the criterion validity of the Goldthorpe scheme by drawing a sample of individuals from within each of the social classes represented in the classification, and then collect independent data relating to the actual conditions and relations of employment of these respondents, for example evidence about their location on an established career ladder and incremental salary scale, enjoyment of enhanced pension rights, and of a certain autonomy in how they use their time at work. In other words, one would examine the degree to which the Goldthorpe classes measure those aspects of employment that they are said to measure, using independent criteria of the concept under investigation.

Construct validation, on the other hand, involves an assessment of whether or not a particular measure (a concept or whatever) relates to other variables in ways that would be predicted by the theory behind the concept. For example, in the case of Goldthorpe (or any other) social classes, one would expect—if this measurement of class was valid—that the social classes so identified would be readily differentiated in terms of (say) voting behaviour, levels of educational attainment, and inequalities in health (or literal 'life-chances'). These are the sorts of things that, from our understanding of the theory of social class, we anticipate will be associated with the class location of individuals. For this reason construct validity is sometimes also referred to as 'predictive validity'—rather misleadingly, perhaps, since one is here simply looking for correlations, rather than offering predictions about how weak or strong these correlations will be in actuality. Moreover, the term 'construct validation' is itself sometimes applied to the whole validation process, including those aspects earlier discussed under the label of criterion validity.

Arguably, all definitions and concepts of validity are to some extent circular, in the sense that one is attempting to confirm that a sociological construct (a classification, concept, or variable) actually measures what it claims to measure, by comparing that construct with something else (other indicators) that one hopes and assumes are independent of the original measurement. A useful discussion of the many complexities raised by this troublesome notion will be found in R. A. Zeller and E. G. Carmines, *Measurement in the Social Sciences* (1980). For elaboration of the example provided above, and an illustration of how tests for validity are conducted in practice, see Geoffrey Evans and Colin Mills, 'Identifying Class Structure: A Latent Class Analysis of the Criterion-Related and Construct Validity of the Goldthorpe Class Scheme', *European Sociological Review* (1998). *See also* RELIABILITY; VARIABLE.

value A word with several quite different meanings: in statistical analysis of quantitative data-sets, the value is the score or figure observed on a particular *variable for a particular case, or in specific circumstances, that is, it is a quantified amount. In economics the *labour theory of value states that commodities are exchanged according to the amount of labour embodied in them, except in the Marxian theory of exploitation, which states that employers extract a surplus and hold wages down by creating a reserve army of labour. In attitude research, values are ideas held by people about ethical behaviour or appropriate behaviour, what is right or wrong, desirable or despicable. In the same vein, philosophers treat values as part of *ethics, aesthetics, and political philosophy.

Regarding values as a type of social data, distinctions are often drawn between values, which are strong, semi-permanent, underlying, and sometimes inexplicit dispositions; and *attitudes, which are shallow, weakly held, and highly variable views and opinions. Societies can usually tolerate highly diverse attitudes, whereas they require some degree of homogeneity and consistency in the values held by people, providing a common fund of shared values which shape social and political consensus. It is usually held that the sociological theories of normative functionalists (or *consensus theorists) in general, and of Talcott *Parsons in particular, overemphasize the importance of shared values in maintaining *social order.

More generally, all *sociology is concerned with value issues, and many of the classical writers—most notably Éile *Durkheim and Max *Weber—discussed the role of values in social research at some length. At this more philosophical level, the issues for sociology would seem to be twofold. First, since society itself is partially constituted through values, the study of sociology is in part the study of values. Second, since sociologists are themselves members of a society and presumably hold values (religious, political, and so forth), sociological work may become embroiled in matters of value—or even (as *Marxists might put it) matters of *ideology. Indeed, some have argued that, for this reason, sociologists may be incapable of the value-neutrality expected of scientists more generally.

These sorts of *epistemological debates about the role of values in social science can impinge on sociological work at three stages: first, in the decision to study a particular topic such as religion or homosexuality, where issues of value-relevance are raised; second, in the actual execution of a study, where the issues of bias, value neutrality, and *objectivity are raised; and, finally, in the consequences of particular theories or research for society, where the issue of 'value effects' is raised. In practice, most sociologists accept that such sharp distinctions cannot readily be made, and the various value issues overlap.

One of the defining characteristics of philosophical *positivism is that it takes the sciences (including social sciences) to be value-neutral or value-free—the expectation being that scientists will (or at least should) eliminate all biases and preferences at each stage of their studies. Value-neutrality is therefore indispensable for a scientific sociology. Similarly, sociology is considered to have a purely technical character, reporting findings that carry no logically given implications for policy or the pursuit of particular values. In marked contrast, Marxists argue that every stage of sociological analysis is riddled with political and moral assumptions and consequences, such that sociology is itself irredeemably an *ideological enterprise. However, most sociologists hold positions somewhere between these extremes, arguing (for example) that although the choice of research areas must raise matters of value, the execution of a study should be as impartial as possible, and the findings presented neutrally, at which point the way such findings are put to use by others will again raise value (that is, policy) issues. A frequently encountered pragmatic solution to the apparently intractable epistemological issues raised by the question of values is the suggestion that sociology is always bound up with ethics, politics, and values, and since it cannot purge itself of them, sociologists should make the underlying debates explicit.

Some of the classic value debates involved such notables as C. Wright Mills, Howard S. Becker, Alvin Gouldner, George Lundberg, Robert Lynd, and Gunnar Myrdal (most of whose works are treated elsewhere in this dictionary). However, the major methodological statement is still to be found in the essays contained in Max *Weber's *The Methodology of the Social Sciences* (1904–18), especially those sections where he discusses the philosophical basis of 'value-relevance' as a principle of concept formation. Here, Weber argues (following the epistemology of Heinrich Rickert (*see* GEISTESWISSENSCHAFTEN and NATURWISSENSCHAFTEN) that reality is infinitely complex and conceptually inexhaustible; that the natural and social sciences typically use generalizing and individualizing modes of concept formation; and that the objects of the latter are distinguished by being imbued with meaning and values. Value-relevance, for Weber, governs the selection of facts in the social and historical sciences by clarifying the value inherent in a situation or phenomenon under analysis. Of course, there are always several possible plausible interpretations of the values underlying cultural phenomena, and consequently several different points of view from which one might conceptualize the phenomenon (or 'historical individual') to be explained. However, once a historical individual is constructed for a particular inquiry, 'objectively one-sided' social scientific knowledge becomes possible through the discovery of causal relationships between the value-relevant description of the object of enquiry and antecedent historical factors, because the formation of these relationships is governed by the established rules of scientific procedure. If the particular value-standpoint according to which the object of enquiry has been conceptualized does not facilitate an explanation of the phenomenon which is both meaningfully and causally adequate, then there may be other values inherent in that phenomenon which permit a more satisfactory explanation to be constructed. This complex argument is described in full in Thomas Burger's *Max Weber's Theory of Concept Formation* (1976). *See also Normative Theory.*

value-relevance *See* VALUE.

van Gennep, Charles Arnold (1873–1957) An ethnologist of Dutch and French parentage whose *Rites of Passage* (1909) is a classic in the social anthropological study of ritual. He encouraged an ethnographic approach to the study of European folklore. *See also* RITES OF PASSAGE.

variable In the physical sciences, variables are the characteristics of entities which are physically manipulated, such as the heat or volume of a substance. In the social sciences, the term refers to attributes which are fixed for each person or other social entity, but which are observed to be at different levels, amounts, or strengths across samples and other aggregate groups. Variables measure a social construct (such as social class, age, or housing type) in a way which renders it amenable to numerical analysis. Thus, the key feature of a variable is that it is capable of reflecting variation within a population, and is not a constant.

There are various difficulties involved in the process of creating variables from constructs (*operationalization). The central considerations here are *validity (that the variable is a true *measurement of the construct it is aimed at) and *reliability (that its measurement is reliable).

Variables may be measured at different levels of measurement, but the basic distinction is between continuous variables such as income, and categoric or discrete variables such as class. Relatively few social variables are continuous—forming interval scales such as income or age. Most are discrete, forming ordinal and nominal scales, such as highest educational qualification obtained, or sex, respectively. The different levels of measurement have implications for the types of analysis that can be undertaken.

variance *See* CAUSAL MODELLING; SEQUENCE ANALYSIS; VARIATION (STATISTICAL).

variation (statistical) The greater part of empirical research is concerned with the characteristics of groups, or aggregate social entities, rather than individual cases; that is, with men or women in general, rather than any particular man or woman. A range of statistical measures of association are employed to describe the features of groups, or types of case in the aggregate. The mean, mode, and median provide measures of central tendency, the most common or typical values in the distribution, that coincide when the variable follows a *normal distribution. Measures of dispersion attempt to concentrate information about the general pattern in single summary statistics. These include the range, mean deviation, quartile deviation, decile range, and the standard deviation, which is by far the most important. One of the properties of the normal distribution is that about 68 per cent of all cases are contained within one standard deviation on either side of the mean, about 95 per cent lie within two standard deviations, and some 99.73 per cent lie within three standard deviations on either side of the mean. The standard deviation of a distribution thus summarizes a great deal of information about the overall dispersion, the degree of clustering or concentration around the mean. *See also* MEASUREMENT; SAMPLING.

vassalage *See* FEUDALISM.

Veblen, Thorstein Bunde (1857–1929) A leading social critic of American industrialism, whose writings inspired so-called institutional economics, and influenced figures such as John Kenneth Galbraith and C. Wright Mills. The son of Norwegian immigrants, Veblen held several university posts, but his formal career was ruined by his outspoken and unconventional behaviour. His often eccentric writings are full of bitter satire and heavy irony and, arguably, their quality eventually suffered from his personal disappointments.

Veblen took the principal ideologies of late 19th-century entrepreneurial *capitalism, in particular evolutionism and price theory, and turned them back on the society in which they flourished. In *The Theory of the Leisure Class* (1899) he drew on fashionable evolutionary anthropology, comparing the *conspicuous consumption and conspicuous leisure (*see* LEISURE CLASS) of the financially successful classes with the display rituals of 'barbarians' in tribal societies. He showed himself acutely aware of the 'barbarian' status of women and their continued exploitation by men in 'civilized' societies. In *The Theory of the Business Enterprise* (1904), and in numerous articles criticizing neo-classical price theories, he developed a systematic account of how the mechanism of the market in reality engenders waste, fraud, and the exploitation of the industry and inventiveness of the worker. His notion of 'pecuniary business interests' may, in some ways, be compared with the concept of finance capital developed by his Marxist contemporary Rudolf Hilferding. However, Veblen himself rejected the utopian character of Marxism, and at one time pinned his political hopes on a version of *technicism. That Veblen, though unfashionable, remains important is attested to by the fact that many of his ideas and concepts have become commonplace in the social sciences.

verification In *empiricist philosophy, knowledge-claims are accepted as scientific only if they are verifiable. To verify a statement is to provide evidence, generally of an empirical or observational kind, for believing it to be true. In logical empiricism the meaning of a statement was treated as equivalent to its method of verification, and only verifiable statements were accepted as meaningful. In non-empiricist philosophies of science, and in less extreme forms of empiricism, it is accepted that evidence may give good reasons for believing in the truth of a statement, whilst falling short of verification in the sense of conclusive proof. *See also* VIENNA CIRCLE.

verificationism *See* VIENNA CIRCLE.

verstehen *See* INTERPRETATION.

vertical integration *See* INDUSTRIAL INTEGRATION.

victimless crime An activity classified as a *crime in the laws of a country, which may therefore be prosecuted by the police or other public authorities, but which appears to have no victim in that there is no individual person who could bring a case for civil damages under civil law. Unlike (say) a case of theft, the damage is to society as a whole, and to notions of morality, proper conduct, and so on. Examples might be drinking alcoholic beverages, reading Marxist literature, homosexuality, gambling, or drug-taking, in societies where such activities are prohibited. *Corporate crime is sometimes regarded as a type of victimless crime. Here again, the damage could be seen to be to the business community as a whole, or to notions of trust and probity in financial matters which provides the necessary underpinning to the whole system; or the victims can be seen as the mass of shareholders, customers, and trading partners who have each sustained a tiny fractional share of the damage done. The concept is polemical, arguing in effect that certain crimes should not be prosecuted by the police, or should be decriminalized.

victimology The study of victims of *crime, including such aspects as patterns of offence, place of incident, characteristics of and relationship between victim and offender, and the like. The field has recently been stimulated by the increased availability of victim surveys which provide data on the hidden incidence of crime. Common but sometimes controversial key themes include the idea that some individuals may be more prone to victimization than are others, and that some victims contribute to or 'precipitate' their victimization, for example because of their style of dress or by frequenting risky locations. The implications of the latter argument have been criticized within *feminist criminology. Victim support organizations have developed in order to campaign for appropriate services and policies.

Vienna Circle In the 1920s and early 1930s, the *empiricist tradition of philosophy of science was reinvigorated by a group of philosophers, mathematicians, and scientists (including some social scientists) at the University of Vienna. The group included Moritz Schlick, Rudolph Carnap, Otto Neurath, Kurt Gödel, and others. The Vienna Circle had a significant influence on Sir Karl *Popper and Ludwig *Wittgenstein, though neither were members. The logical empiricist, or *positivist philosophy of the circle was particularly influential in the English-speaking world, partly due to the work of A. J. Ayer, and also to the affinities between this approach and that of Bertrand Russell. In important respects the new philosophy of science was a response to the turn-of-century revolution in physical science. The project was to tie scientific knowledge-claims so tightly to supposedly indubitable observation-reports, that all speculative, *metaphysical, unprovable elements would be removed from the privileged domain of science. In the most extreme version, the empirically unprovable would be denied even the status of meaningful utterance, a doctrine sometimes referred to as *verificationism.

visual sociology Although modern sociology and photography appeared almost simultaneously at the start of the 19th century, their lives have for the most part been quite separate. A few early texts—such as Frederic Thrasher's *The Gang* (1927)—used photographs to illustrate the research, but in the main sociologists tended to ignore visual images. This was not true of all other social scientists; for example, many anthropologists worked with visual images and film to great effect, as in Margaret *Mead and Gregory Bateson's *Balinese Culture* (1942), while the documentary film has proved invaluable to social historians.

More recently, however, a branch of sociology known as visual sociology has flourished. Visual sociology usually has one of two major concerns. Much of it uses photography (and increasingly video and film) as a research tool to facilitate the gathering of data. Alternatively, visual images may be used as data in their own right, usually as part of a sociological study of *culture, in which film and other artefacts may be examined, often with the aid of *semiotics. The recent work of the American interactionist Howard Becker illustrates both developments, pioneering the role of photography in sociology (discussed in his book *Doing Things Together*, 1986), and observing the nature of art work (in his *Art Worlds*, 1980).

(⊕) SEE WEB LINKS

- Good accounts of this area can be found in Gillian Rose's *Visual Methodologies* (2001) and a special issue of online journal *Forum: Qualitative Social Research* 9, 3 (2008).

vital statistics Statistics of births, deaths, and marriages within a country, which provide the essential basis for *demography. They include crude rates matching vital events to total populations, and more sophisticated measures of fertility, nuptiality, and mortality. Their quality depends on the accuracy of vital-event registers. State registration is now usual (in Britain since 1837); church registers formerly provided some vital-event data.

vocabularies of motive A concept outlined by the literary critic Kenneth Burke as one of his five dramatistic terms: who, what, when, where, and why? The term was first developed sociologically by C. Wright *Mills (in *American Sociological Review*, 1944) to capture the language by which people describe their motivations and account for their conduct. The important point is that Mills's idea is not rooted in a psychology of motivation: he was not interested here in *needs, drives, or inner compulsions, as was (for example) Sigmund *Freud. Rather, his concern was with the ways in which people talk about their motives, in particular social contexts. Motivational talk is usually part of a wider *ideology, such that certain stated motives will be much more acceptable in given contexts than in others, and motivational statements are hence relative. For instance, irrespective of the underlying psychological motivation, a thief may make different motivational claims about his thieving behaviour to his peers, his family, the court-room, to a criminologist, or even to him- or herself. The contexts and *significant others shift what will be said in the motivational account.

Sociologists have been concerned with the ways in which such talk helps interaction proceed smoothly. They have explored the sources of motivational statements, classified their different varieties, and examined the consequences of their acceptance or rejection. A cluster of linked terms have been developed. Gresham Sykes and David Matza have developed a theory of *delinquency that depends upon the delinquent employing a vocabulary to neutralize the legitimacy of the dominant order. These 'techniques of neutralization' include denying the victim, condemning the condemners, denying injury, denying responsibility, and appealing to higher loyalties (*American Sociological Review*, 1957). Stanford M. Lyman and Marvin B. Scott have developed this idea into a more general theory of 'accounts', as part of their *existential sociology (discussed in their *A Sociology of the Absurd*, 2nd edn., 1990). They examine the patterning and consequences of different 'excuses' and 'justifications' that are offered when something untoward occurs and people are asked to explain what has happened. John P. Hewitt and Randall Stokes have also introduced the term 'disclaimers' to cover those situations in which people 'want to ward off the negative implications of something they are about to do or say'. Such statements take the form 'I'm not prejudiced, but...' (*American Sociological Review*, 1975).

Analysing motivational talk in this way has become part of dramaturgical sociology, ethnomethodology, labelling theory, symbolic interactionism, and the sociologies of knowledge and language (all of which are treated separately elsewhere in this dictionary).

vocationalism An educational philosophy or pedagogy, claiming that the content of the curriculum should be governed by its occupational or industrial utility, and marketability as *human capital. *See also* TRAINING, SOCIOLOGY OF.

voluntarism A term usually contrasted with *determinism, voluntarism denotes the assumption that individuals are the agents of their actions, and have some control over what they do. Voluntarism's alliance with action contrasts with the deterministic emphasis associated with *structure. By accepting human unpredictability, voluntarism renders sociological analysis more difficult, though arguably more interesting. Voluntaristic theories place issues of decision, purpose, and choice at the forefront of sociological analysis. In *The Structure of Social Action* (1937), Talcott Parsons develops a voluntaristic theory of action, so called because it includes normative elements, subjective categories, choices about means and ends, and effort.

Voluntarism in social science raises the philosophical issue of free will: namely, the belief that choice means freedom, in the sense of individuals being free to will what they will. Most sociologists—even those of a voluntaristic persuasion—recognize that individuals can only do otherwise than they do within limits (perhaps of a cultural or psychological kind). That is, a residual determinism is implied, even though social action is typically not reduced to physical and biological variables.

voluntaristic theory of action *See* PARSONS.

voluntary associations Any public, formally constituted, and non-commercial organization of which membership is optional, within a particular society. Examples include churches, political parties, pressure groups, leisure associations or clubs, neighbourhood groups, and (sometimes) trade unions and professional associations. In some theories of *democracy, emphasis is placed on the important role such groups can play in fostering participation in the *civil society, and thus in maintaining social order.

von Restorff effect An effect named after the *gestalt psychologist who first studied it, whereby individuals learn unusual or different items most rapidly, as for example in the case of a list in which all the items are printed in black ink except for one which is printed in red.

voting behaviour Voting is the main form of political participation in liberal democratic societies and the study of voting behaviour is a highly specialized sub-field within *political science. The analysis of voting patterns invariably focuses on the determinants of why people vote as they do and how they arrive at the decisions they make. Sociologists tend to look to the socio-economic determinants of support for political parties, observing the correlations between class, occupation, ethnicity, sex, age and vote; political scientists have concentrated on the influence of political factors such as issues, political programmes, electoral campaigns, and the popularity of party leaders on voting behaviour. However, both disciplines share much the same terrain, and increasingly have tended to overlap in their analytical approaches (see M. Harrop and W. L. Miller, *Elections and Voters: A Comparative Perspective*, 1987).

A number of different (but not mutually exclusive) approaches to the explanation of voting behaviour can be distinguished in the literature. Structural (or sociological) approaches concentrate on the relationship between individual and social structure, place the vote in a social context, and examine the effects on voting of such variables as social class, language, nationalism, religion, and rural-urban contrasts. Ecological (or aggregate statistical) approaches relate voting patterns to the characteristic features of a geographical area (ward, constituency, state, or whatever). Social psychological approaches relate voting decisions to the voter's psychological predispositions or attitudes, for example his or her party identification, attitudes to candidates, and such like. Finally, rational-choice approaches attempt to explain voting behaviour as the outcome of a series of instrumental cost-benefit calculations by the individual, assessing the relative desirability of specific electoral outcomes in terms of the issues addressed and policies espoused by the different parties or candidates. Each of these broad approaches tends to be associated with different research techniques and each makes different assumptions about what motivates political behaviour.

In Britain there has been a long-running debate about whether the influence of social class on voting behaviour has declined (the so-called 'class dealignment thesis'), and about the extent to which this process is associated with the dilution of loyalty to the two major parties (the Conservative Party and the Labour Party) which have dominated the political system since the Second World War (the 'partisan dealignment thesis'). Proponents of these arguments (see, for example, B. Sarlvik and I. Crewe, *Decade of Dealignment*, 1983) argue that both absolute class voting (the overall proportion of the electorate who vote for their 'natural' class party) and relative class voting (the relative strength of the parties in different classes) have declined continuously since the late 1960s and that this is connected to the decline in the share of the Conservative and Labour Party votes. They attribute this dealignment to a number of underlying social changes: changes in the occupational structure, the decline in the size of the manual working class, social mobility, and growth of cross-class families—all of which are said to undermine the socio-economic cohesiveness of class. As a result of class fragmentation, issues have become a more important influence on how electors vote, and voters evaluate the political parties as self-interested individuals rather than on a collective or class basis.

In a similar vein, proponents of the thesis of *consumption-sector cleavages argue that increasing fragmentation has reduced the political distinctiveness of social classes, and that as a result of the growing importance of consumption, differences between those who are dependent on public rather than private consumption of goods and services (like housing, transport, education, and health) are the source of new political alignments. These sectoral distinctions have replaced class as the most salient structural cleavage, both in terms of debate between the political parties and in terms of voting behaviour. The private consumption of goods and services increases the propensity to vote Conservative while those dependent on public provision vote Labour. As with the theory of class and partisan dealignment, that of consumption sectoral cleavage emphasizes the growing importance of the media in shaping individual interests, and the particularly damaging effects of these changes on working-class support for Labour.

However, opponents of this view (such as A. Heath, et al. *Understanding Political Change*, 1991) argue that class dealignment is a consequence of partisan dealignment rather than a cause. While absolute levels of class voting have declined, 'trend-less fluctuation' in relative class voting suggests that social classes still retain their political distinctiveness. Indeed, class remains the major influence on voting behaviour; and, furthermore, consumption cleavages such as housing tenure (which are not especially novel) are merely correlates of class, and do not have important independent effects on voting behaviour. Calling for what they call an 'interactionist' approach to the analysis of the relationship between social structure, party performance, and vote, Heath and his colleagues argue that Labour's electoral failure in the 1980s was largely the result of across-the-board political failures (rather than underlying social changes), principally the policy failures of the 1964–70 Labour governments, the increasing number of third party (Liberal) candidates standing in working-class constituencies, the failure of the Labour Party to devise a credible economic policy, and its internal disunity. Class origins and class attitudes still influence how people vote—although class organizations like the Labour Party have not always been successful in mobilizing this potential in the political sphere.

In recent years, studies of voting behaviour have become a methodological minefield, as advances in techniques for the analysis of large-scale data-sets have fuelled existing controversies between different theories and models of voting behaviour. Concluding their admirable and exhaustive review of this literature, Jeff Manza, Michael Hunt, and Clem Brooks observe that the relationship between class and voting in the capitalist democracies of Western Europe and North America shows no evidence of being subject to a universal process of class dealignment, and that, at this juncture, 'only one conclusion is firm: in no democratic capitalist country has vote been entirely independent of class in a national election' ('Class Voting in Capitalist Democracies since World War Two: Dealignment, Realignment, or Trendless Fluctuation?', *Annual Review of Sociology*, 1995). On the debates in the United States in particular see Richard G. Niemi and Herbert F. Weisberg, *Controversies in Voting Behaviour* (1993).

(⊕) SEE WEB LINKS

• The British Election Study, University of Essex.

wage-labour *Employment as an employee for a specified weekly wage or monthly salary, normally on terms and conditions determined by the employer, whose offer may be constrained by employment law, collective-bargaining agreements, or pressure from trade unions. The term is often used to emphasize the weak bargaining position of people who have only their own labour to sell, and may be exploited. *See also* WORK.

Wallas, Graham (1858–1932) A leading member of the Fabian Society, he was a close associate of Beatrice and Sydney *Webb and was actively involved in the London County Council and the London School Board. In 1895 he was offered the directorship of the London School of Economics but preferred to take a teaching role. He spent the rest of his academic life at the LSE, holding the Chair of Politics from 1914 to 1923. His main ideas were formed during his studentship at Oxford, where he encountered the English idealism of T. H. Green and Bernard Bosanquet. In *Human Nature in Politics* (1908), he argued that biological conditions and cultural forces were more important than the rational calculation stressed by *utilitarianism. He stressed the crucial role played by cultural traditions and customs in forming the 'social heritage' of a society (*Our Social Heritage*, 1921). He stressed the importance of taking an empirical, rather than an ethical, approach to politics. His best-known book is, perhaps, *The Great Society* (1914).

Wallis, Roy (1945–90) A British sociologist of religion, whose more general writings include notable studies of *social movements (particularly *moral crusades), and of the place of actors' motivational accounts in sociological analysis. An early study of the Church of Scientology (*The Road to Total Freedom*, 1976) generated the typology of ideological collectivities shown below. Cults and sects are both religiously deviant by comparison to the normatively sanctioned or respectable church and denominational orthodoxy. Unlike sects, however, cults are 'pluralistically legitimate' in the sense that membership is perceived to offer but one of a variety of possible paths to salvation. Sects, on the other hand, purport to offer adherents a unique access to such rewards.

In a subsequent study of contemporary *sectarianism (*The Elementary Forms of the Religious Life*, 1984), Wallis offered a tripartite typology of *new religious movements, distinguishing between 'world-rejecting', 'world-affirming', and 'world-accommodating' types.

wants *See* NEED.

war, total *See* TOTAL WAR.

	Respectable	Deviant
Uniquely legitimate	Church	Sect
Pluralistically legitimate	Denomination	Cult

Wallis, Roy. Roy Wallis's typology of ideological collectivities

Ward, Lester Frank (1841–1913) One of the pioneers of American sociology, founder of a psychological evolutionism, which (contrary to Herbert *Spencer) ascribed an important role in evolution to human mentality. Self-educated from boyhood, Ward enlisted in the Union Army in 1863, and finally gained his university degrees through evening study. He was a geologist and palaeontologist until the age of 65—when he accepted a professorship in sociology at Brown University (where he continued to teach until his death). In 1906 he was elected to be the first president of the American Sociological Society. Greatly influenced by Comte and Spencer, Ward's sociology is organized around a theory of *evolution. This process is described in terms of stages, these being the result initially of 'genesis' (spontaneous blind forces), but latterly of 'telesis' (purposive actions of humans based on knowledge and the anticipation of consequences). Ward conceptualized sociology as the systematic study of social forces, these being psychic in nature, and resulting in a continuous process of 'social synergy' by which new structures were created. He is significant mainly because his works, particularly his discussion of telesis, anticipate the emphasis that 20th-century sociology was to place on *culture (see *Dynamic Sociology*, 1902; *Pure Sociology*, 1903; and *Applied Sociology*, 1906). There is a useful introduction to his writings in Ronald Fletcher, *The Making of Sociology*, vol. i (1971).

Warner, William Lloyd (1898–1970) A leading American sociologist of the 1930s and 1940s. Among his many projects was the major and influential *community study of Newburyport in New England life in the early 1930s, published in five volumes (the so-called 'Yankee City' studies) dealing with class, community, factory life, ethnic groupings, and religion and symbolism. The first of these (*The Social Life of a Modern Community*, 1941) spells out in detail the ahistorical *functionalism that underpins Warner's sociology—and which is acknowledged as its most serious weakness. He later studied the more industrial city of Morris, Illinois (*Democracy in Jonesville*, 1949). As one commentary has observed, Warner's work has so often been criticized that it is perhaps time to call a moratorium, although it should also be acknowledged that he broke an academic taboo and opened up discussion of *stratification in the United States—even if his notion of class absorbed the three analytically distinct concepts of class, status, and party into one vertical dimension of so-called class, and is (in fact) a measure of prestige. An abridged version of the Yankee City series as a whole was published in 1963.

wealth The term is often used in studies of social inequality to refer simply to a person's whole stock of financial resources, as contrasted with 'income', which is the flow of financial resources received over a particular time period. In this sense, it is possible to measure total 'national wealth' and to examine the share of different groups in this distribution (*see* INCOME DISTRIBUTION). Many studies of *poverty contrast the share in national wealth received by the poorest with that received by the richest groups in the population. This leads to purely statistical, and arbitrary, measures of what it is to be 'wealthy'.

A second meaning of wealth allows a properly sociological concept of wealth and the wealthy to be formed. Townsend developed an idea of poverty as relative deprivation, according to which the poor are defined as those who are deprived of resources relative to the standard of living accepted as normal in their society. They are deprived relative to other citizens. On this same basis, the wealthy can be defined as those who are privileged or advantaged relative to what is normal for the citizens of their society. (See John Scott, *Poverty and Wealth*, 1994.) Deprivation and privilege should be seen as complementary terms, as two contrasting departures from the normal lifestyle of the citizen. From this point of view, deprivation and privilege are polarized conditions of life. If the 'poverty line' is the point in the distribution of resources below which deprivation and a decline into poverty occurs, then a 'wealth line' can be defined as the point in the distribution of resources above which privileges and advantages escalate dispro-portionately to any increase in resources. To have wealth and to be wealthy is to live above the wealth line.

Webb, Beatrice (Potter) and Webb, Sidney James (1858–1943); (1859–1947) Noted authors of a definitive *History of British Trade Unionism*, and leading thinkers and activists of the so-called *Fabian socialist movement, who made a distinguished contribution to the development and characteristic outlook of the British Labour Party. They founded the London School of Economics as a social science institution and were responsible for introducing the teaching of sociology. In *Methods of Social Study* (1932) they produced a pioneering text on social research methods. The Webbs' own work on *trade unions shows a distaste for the strong craft tradition in Britain and looks forward to a time when state regulation of minimum wages, together with social insurance, will make unions obsolete. Their *socialism was distinguished for its advocacy of building democratic socialist institutions by steady accretion, though they later became enthusiastic advocates of Soviet communism. The welfare consensus between the political parties of post-1945 Britain owed much to their ideas.

Weber, Alfred (1868–1958) German economist, brother of Max, who contrib-uted to theories which explain patterns of industrial location as the outcome of competition for the most advantageous (cost-minimizing/profit-maximizing) locations; and, through this, to the development of geography as a social science. However, he is perhaps best known to sociologists for his cultural sociology (see *Fundamentals of Culture-Sociology*, 1920–1), in which he analyses the relation-ship between the growth of knowledge (especially science and technology) and the 'culture' (or 'soul') of civilizations.

Weber, Max (1864–1920) Weber, together with Émile Durkheim, is often regarded as the founder of modern sociology as a distinct social science. His work is the more complex and ambitious, still providing a rich source for interpretation and inspiration. His life, too, possesses a certain fascination. A mental breakdown in 1897 was followed by four years of intellectual inactivity. His wife Marianne was an early feminist, and the Webers were the heart of the most impressive intellectual circle in early 20th-century Germany, centred on regular Sunday seminars at their Heidelberg home. Max Weber's contribution to sociology was immense. He offered a philosophical basis for the social sciences; a general conceptual framework for sociology; and a range of learned studies covering all of the great world religions, ancient societies, economic history, the sociology of law and of music, and many other areas.

Whereas Durkheim's attempt to found a science of sociology was based on the scientific *positivism of his day, Weber's intellectual training was in the *neo-Kantian school of philosophy associated with the names of Wilhelm *Windelband and Heinrich Rickert (*see GEISTESWISSENSCHAFTEN* and *NATURWISSENSCHAFTEN*), dominant in Germany at that time. This philosophy involved a radical distinction between phenomena (the external world we perceive) and noumena (the perceiving consciousness). In Weber's sociology, this became a distinction between the natural and social sciences, the latter concerned with the forms in which we apprehend the world. Thus, whilst we might wish to establish universal laws in the natural sciences, this was not the task of the social sciences—since their interest is in the *causal explanation and understanding of social actions in their particular historical contexts. At the same time, human society was not a matter of chance but of 'probabilities', and what made social science possible was the fact that human beings act rationally for at least a large part of the time.

The proper object of social science, then, is social action: action directed towards significant others and to which we attach a subjective *meaning. Sociology attempts an interpretative account of such action using an *ideal-type methodology. Weber developed a fourfold classification of social action: traditional action undertaken because it has always been so performed; affectual action based on or driven by emotion; value-rational action directed towards ultimate *values; and end-rational or instrumental action. Only the last two of these fall within the scope of rational action—although Weber also argued strongly that there can be no rational choice either of ends or ultimate values. However, once these have been adopted, they can certainly be pursued by more or less rational means. Weber saw the development of modern societies as a process of increasing *rationalization in which the world loses its mystery. The growth of large-scale modern *bureaucracy is a major part of that process and one of Weber's criticisms of socialism was that it would simply hasten this 'disenchantment' of life.

On a philosophical level, Weber's other main contribution was a theory of value-freedom, a complex formulation often mistakenly interpreted as a naïve belief in objectivity. For Weber, the choice of science and of sociology was a value choice, which could not be justified in terms of instrumental rationality. This was true also of the selection of a particular object of study. However, once these choices were made, a sociological study could be value-free in the sense that its rational coherence was subject to the criticisms of the scientific community. What might be meant by rational, however, was itself open to historical change. In this sense, social scientific work is hemmed in by values, not only the values of the individual sociologist but also those of the community of social scientists and the prevailing culture as a whole.

It is common to juxtapose Weber to Marx, and to see him as developing an alternative sociology, at once both more scientific and more bourgeois. In fact Weber's intellectual mentors are numerous and diverse. For example, in formulating the *protestant ethic thesis (often read as an alternative to Marxist accounts of the rise of *capitalism), Weber was explicitly building upon earlier theories of capitalism and of money propounded by Werner Sombart and Georg Simmel. Weber does, however, provide an important alternative to Marxist conceptions of class and politics. For Weber, class is defined not by relationship to the means of production, but by the sharing of a common market position leading to shared *life chances. This has enabled sociologists to talk about, for example, housing classes (owner-occupiers, tenants of private rentals, and so forth) as well as classes defined by possession of skills and other marketable assets. Beyond this he introduced the concept of *status group as an important element of stratification: that is, groups differentiated according to positive or negative honorific criteria, and sharing a common style of life (such as *ethnic groups or *castes). He also argued that organized conflicts over *power were an important aspect of social life and one not necessarily linked to economic class conflict.

There is considerable disagreement about Weber's political views, which are as ambivalent and complex as many of his sociological analyses. Was he, as some have claimed, a precursor of fascism; or, as seems much more plausible, a sophisticated liberal? The problem is that, as with much of his other work, his political writings do not fit the rather simplistic categories into which social theorists now try to fit them.

His publications are as voluminous as they are diverse, but his most important works (all available in English translation) are probably *Economy and Society* (1920), *The Protestant Ethic and the Spirit of Capitalism* (1904), *General Economic History* (1919-20), *The Religion of China* (1915), *The Religion of India* (1916), *Ancient Judaism* (1917), and the essays on methodology collected and translated as *The Methodology of the Social Sciences* (ed., Edward Shils, 1949). Marianne Weber's fascinating biography of her husband (*Max Weber: A Biography*, 1926) is a sociological classic—though frequently economical with the truth about Weber's private and public life. *See also* ABSOLUTISM; ACTION THEORY; CHARISMA; DOMINATION; FEUDALISM; FORMAL RATIONALITY; HINDUISM; INDUSTRIAL SOCIETY; INTERPRETATION; LAW, SOCIOLOGY OF; LEGITIMACY; PATRIMONIALISM; PROTESTANT ETHIC; RELIGION, SOCIOLOGY OF.

W

(⊕) SEE WEB LINKS
- The official guide to Weber's collected works (in German and English).
- A site dedicated to Weber and his work.

welfare Refers to the well-being of individuals or groups and, by implication, those measures which can help to ensure levels of well-being through provision of education, health services, managed housing, and social security benefits. Thus where the state takes responsibility for such measures we can speak of a *welfare state.

More recently, the term welfare has come to be associated specifically with means-tested benefits provided by some states to alleviate destitution. This use of the term is current in the USA, but is also used elsewhere. Due to the negative connotations often attached to means-tested benefit receipt this can confusingly result in formulations which are apparently the reverse of those strictly implied by the term welfare, such as welfare-dependent. The use of welfare to imply social security benefits rather than a wider range of provision can also be found in the phrase 'welfare rights', which nevertheless stresses entitlement and normally covers non-means-tested as well as means-tested benefits.

In comparative literature the term 'welfare regimes' encompasses not only the ways in which the state guarantees welfare but also the role of the market and the family in ensuring the well-being of citizens, and particular groups of citizens. This move beyond a focus on the state alone is important given the different combinations of approaches to welfare that can be found, and the ways that responsibility for different elements are delegated to different parts of the triad across different countries. (See G. Esping-Andersen, *The Three Worlds of Welfare Capitalism*, 1990.) Feminist analysis has also stressed the importance of considering the gender implications of different forms of welfare regime, and that men and women's welfare may not be equally ensured by the same configuration of provision (e.g. J. Lewis's, 'Gender and the Development of Welfare Regimes', *Journal of European Social Policy*, 1992).

Marxists have been sceptical of the motivation behind moves towards a more active state role in achieving individuals' or groups' welfare. Marx and Engels in *The Communist Manifesto* described activism for social policy development as stemming from bourgeois socialists' reluctance to grasp the necessity of fundamental change. And others have regarded concessions at the level of benefits, health provision, and so on as representing attempts by those in power to pacify and distract the working classes. On the other hand, there are those who would argue that activism is impossible without some guaranteed level of security, and thus even if the motivation for conceding unemployment benefits or free health care is to pacify workers, the effect is to enable them to campaign more effectively for further or more fundamental change.

Influential discussions of the key role of the state in promoting welfare can be found in R. M. Titmuss's work, for example, in his *Essays on 'The Welfare State'* (1958) (despite his distaste for the term, 'welfare state' itself). Titmuss stressed the need for universalism in public welfare provision as well as 'positive discrimination' to compensate those bearing the social costs of a rapidly changing society. He argues his position on the grounds of social justice, supported by detailed critical analysis of the operation of the state and of the views of his opponents. The emphasis on social justice, in this case associated with the nature of citizenship, can also be found in T. H. *Marshall's work on *Citizenship and*

Social Class (1950), in which he posits the development of rights associated with citizenship from civil through political to social. State promotion of welfare has also been argued not simply to have benefits at the level of the individual but to be important in creating social cohesion, developing common values and thus contributing to national identity and unity.

It has been argued that state commitment to welfare is under pressure or even on the decline with fears of a crisis of the welfare state in the face of the rise of libertarian values and economic and demographic pressures (I. Ferguson et al., *Rethinking Welfare*, 2002). However, others have argued that in fact welfare provision once constructed is very hard to dismantle, given the number of interests in maintaining—or even extending—it. And cuts in spending have been applied relatively selectively where they have occurred.

The flavour of the different positions on welfare can be gathered from C. Pierson and F. G. Castles, *The Welfare State Reader* (2000); while an account of the range of philosophical and ideological positions is to be found in V. George and P. Wilding, *Ideology and Social Welfare* (1994). G. Esping-Andersen puts forward the challenges facing the welfare state in *Why we Need a New Welfare State* (2002).

welfare state A term referring to a form of capitalist society in which the state takes responsibility for a range of measures intended to ensure the well-being of its members, through providing education for children, access to health care, financial support for periods out of the labour market, and so on. It gained currency in Britain and internationally in the late 1940s following the post-war establishment of a range of British public welfare systems (*see* BEVERIDGE REPORT). Welfare states differ widely, however, in the ways in which they make such provision: for example, whether there is an emphasis on insurance contributions of paid workers and building up entitlement, whether provision is targeted at the less well-off and means-tested, or whether provision is conditional primarily on citizenship. Increasingly, then, there is an interest in recognizing the diversity of welfare states (and their potential for development in different directions) rather than seeing the welfare state as a universal category with transparent meaning. A good discussion of these points can be found in Allan Cochrane et al., *Comparing Welfare States*, 2nd edn., 2001).

Weltanschauung A German term that refers to the 'world-view' or 'philosophy of life' of different groups within society. For example, it is sometimes argued that the long-term unemployed have a fatalistic outlook, the middle classes an individualistic approach to life, while members of the working class hold a set of beliefs and attitudes which emphasize collectivism. Sociologists have posed a number of interesting questions around this topic. Do particular social groups actually adhere to identifiable world-views? If so, how do individuals come to hold specific images of society, and what is the relationship between membership of a group and an individual's subjective representations of it? The major problem confronting sociologists who address these issues is that of defining and describing a world-view itself. What beliefs and values may be said to constitute a world-view? Should we even expect people to hold to consistent world-views, given that (for example) research on *class imagery suggests that, more often than not, people's attitudes and values are inconsistent or ambiguous, and rarely form a coherent whole? In short, use of this term usually points to a certain imprecision in an argument, and almost invariably indicates that data appropriate to the particular case are wanting.

Westermarck, Edvard Alexander (1862-1939) A Finnish sociologist, anthropologist, and philosopher, who (as a Professor at the London School of Economics) was one of the founders of academic sociology in Britain. His best-known work is *The History of Human Marriage* (1891) in which, using an early form of comparative anthropological study, he attempted to refute the (then fashionable) thesis that our earliest human ancestors lived in sexual promiscuity. Together with Franz *Boas, Westermarck was a pioneer of fieldwork (mainly in Morocco), who communicated directly with his subjects, attempting to learn their languages and at least observe (if not participate in) their culture at first hand. His decontextualized use of the comparative method (aimed at uncovering correlations between institutions, across a range of societies, isolated from the *social system of which they formed a part) was superseded by *functional approaches in the 1920s and 1930s, which analysed local communities as functioning wholes, and his magnum opus is today of only historical interest. His other books included *The Origin and Development of Moral Ideas* (1912) and *The Future of Marriage in Western Civilization* (1936).

white-collar crime A term introduced by Edwin Sutherland in the 1940s in order to draw attention to the illegalities and misdeeds of 'captains of industry' and other middle-class members of the business world (see his 'White-Collar Criminality', *American Sociological Review*, 1940, or *White-Collar Crime*, 1949). The great value of the idea was to redress the imbalance in *criminology's obsession with *crimes of the working class. The concept tends to be used very broadly, to include both activities carried out by employees against their employer (embezzlement, pilfering), and activities undertaken by corporate executives on behalf of the corporation itself (such as violation of anti-trust regulations or stock-market rules). Strictly speaking the latter should more accurately be designated *corporate crime.

white-collar work *See* MANUAL VERSUS NON-MANUAL DISTINCTION.

Windelband, Wilhelm (1848-1915) A prominent figure in the German *neo-Kantian movement, Windelband is chiefly remembered for his monumental *A History of Philosophy* (1893, 1901), in which he outlines the classic distinction between nomothetic and *ideographic approaches to science.

Winnicott, Donald Woods (1896-1971) A British paediatrician and *psychoanalyst whose work on the mother-baby relationship directed attention to the infant's environment and to 'good-enough mothering'. Often discussed by modern feminist writers on parenting, his most accessible book is *The Child, the Family and the Outside World* (1964).

Wirth, Louis (1897–1952) Born in Germany, he studied in the United States, where he became a leading figure in *Chicago sociology during the 1930s. His doctoral thesis was published as *The Ghetto* (1925), and he maintained his interests in city life, minority group behaviour, and mass media throughout his influential career. He is best known as the author of a classic (and much discussed) essay on 'Urbanism as a Way of Life'. For a sampling of his work, together with a comprehensive bibliography, see Louis Wirth, *On Cities and Social Life* (1964). See also URBAN SOCIOLOGY; URBANISM.

Wisconsin Model *See* STATUS ATTAINMENT.

witchcraft *See* MAGIC, WITCHCRAFT, AND SORCERY.

Wittgenstein, Ludwig J. J. (1889–1951) Though he was born in Vienna and lived in Austria until 1912, Wittgenstein is often regarded as the most important English-language philosopher of the 20th century. His extraordinary achievement was to have produced two profoundly influential but mutually incompatible philosophies in the course of his relatively short academic career.

Wittgenstein's early philosophical work was influenced by Bertrand Russell's *Principles of Mathematics*, and its most complete expression was the *Tractatus Logico-Philosophicus*, first published in German in 1921 and then in English in 1922. At the core of this work was a view of *language and *meaning, according to which each sentence is a picture of some possible state of affairs. Sentences are combinations of names, which, in some ultimate analysis, must refer unambiguously to simple objects. For this relationship of picturing between reality, language, and thought to be possible, they must share a common logical form. But this logical form is, of course, not in the world and so cannot itself be pictured in language. Similarly, moral values and the relation of the self to the world are not states of affairs which can be pictured in language. These are *metaphysical matters about which nothing meaningful can be said and about which one must be silent. Wittgenstein's early work was often misunderstood as sympathetic to the anti-metaphysical verificationism of the *Vienna Circle. However, unlike the adherents of that school, Wittgenstein acknowledged the depth and seriousness of metaphysical questions, whilst denying their answerability.

Wittgenstein's later philosophy emerged piecemeal, in notebooks written during the 1930s and 1940s, and in his lecture courses at Cambridge during the same period. It took the form of a devastating critique of the very view of language and meaning to which his earlier philosophy had been committed. The major source for this later philosophy is the *Philosophical Investigations* (published posthumously in 1953).

This work begins with descriptions of a series of imaginary 'language-games' in the course of which Wittgenstein tries to dispel the powerful temptation to think that there must be some single underlying essence of all language, that this essence consists in some relation of representation of the world, and that words function primarily or exclusively through naming. As described by Wittgenstein, language-games are rule-governed human practices, in which the meaning of utterances is given by the part they play in the context of the practice.

Generally, the meaning of a word or sentence is its use in such a practice, and so meanings can be as diverse as the practices and purposes to which humans may put them. Similarly, the rules governing language use are not somehow fixed for all time by a definition or logical formula, but are established by social practice itself. To give the meaning of a word is to describe the practices in which it is used, to consider how it is learned, and under what circumstances misuse of the word can be corrected.

This, in turn, forms the basis of one of Wittgenstein's most influential and controversial arguments. If meaning depends on use, and use is itself established only in the context of a human practice in which misuse can be detected and corrected, then there can be no such thing as a logically private language. The important consequence of this is that a whole range of pervasive ways of thinking about the language in which we talk about our inner, subjective life have to be rejected. Indeed, widely held images of language itself as an external expression of our inner thoughts are exposed as radically misleading. Wittgenstein insists that if the language in which we talk about our thoughts, dreams, imaginings, sensations, and so on is meaningful at all, then it can only be so in virtue of there being some publicly accessible way of learning how to use it correctly, correct misuses, and so on. As he puts it, an inner process stands in need of an outer 'criterion'.

Wittgenstein has been widely misrepresented as a kind of *behaviourist, but far from denying that we do have an inner life or even that we can meaningfully talk about it, he rather offers a powerful account of what makes it possible for us to do so. The possibility for practices of talking about subjective life to become established, and to be learned by children, is grounded in a repertoire of natural expressions of pain, pleasure, distaste, and so forth, which can reliably and consensually be recognized in the course of living a common 'form of life'. Here, interpretations of Wittgenstein diverge. Is a shared form of life a common natural history, such as might define and distinguish species (Wittgenstein's writings contain often amusing references to the psychological capacities of dogs, or lions), or does it designate the *culture of a people, as in anthropology? The latter interpretation takes some of its followers in the direction of culturally relative views on language, meaning, and rationality. The former interpretation would be consistent with a more naturalistic approach which linked the possibilities of human social and cultural life with certain facts of the natural history of the species.

Wittgenstein's later philosophy has been profoundly influential across the whole spectrum of humanities and social sciences. His account of meaning in terms of rule-governed social practice provided an important means for bringing philosophy and the social sciences back into communication with one another, and offered a powerful challenge to *positivistic forms of social science methodology. It is also arguable that in his rejection of *essentialism, his displacement of representation as the core image for thinking about linguistic meaning, and in his way of treating human subjectivity, Wittgenstein anticipated some key themes of *postmodernism.

For a good short introduction to his work see A. C. Grayling, *Wittgenstein* (1988).

Wollstonecraft, Mary (1759–97) Self-educated writer and social theorist. She worked as a governess and a school teacher and spent much time in France. She produced an early manifesto on human rights and the French Revolution and then the strikingly original and influential *Vindication of the Rights of Woman* (1792). In this book she argued against ideas of the natural inequality of the sexes and held that women were just as capable of the exercise of reason as were men. Her book became a leading text in *feminist thought. She lived with the radical William Godwin from 1796, marrying him when she became pregnant. She died shortly after childbirth. Their daughter, Mary Shelley, was the author of the novel *Frankenstein* (1818).

women's movement This term refers to the mobilization of women around the project of changing and improving their position in society. It is often used interchangeably with 'Women's Liberation Movement' to describe the second wave of *feminism from the 1970s onwards (the first wave being 19th- and early 20th-century feminism culminating in the struggle for votes for women).

Woodward, Joan (1916–71) A British professor of industrial sociology who led the South-East Essex research team in a survey of manufacturing organizations in that area during the 1950s. Her many publications included *The Dock Worker* (1955), *The Saleswoman* (1960; an early and neglected study of service workers), and the influential *Industrial Organisation: Theory and Practice* (1965).

Woodward argued that differences in the organization of work and in behaviour at work (the number of levels of management, area of responsibilities of supervisors, division of functions among specialists, clarity with which roles and duties are defined, amount of written communication, and such like) could usually be traced to the immediate work situation itself. In particular, in the Essex survey, differences in *technology accounted for many of the differences in organizational structure. She produced a widely discussed typology of production systems, distinguished according to their degree of technical complexity, ranging from unit and small-batch production, through large-batch and mass production, to the most complex form of process production. Often accused (unjustly) of technological determinism, Woodward's work was instrumental in setting new standards of empirical research in the sociology of organizations, and in demonstrating the possibilities of systematic comparison as against the (hitherto predominant) isolated case study. *See also* CONTINGENCY THEORY.

Wootton, Barbara (1897–1988) Trained as an economist, and taught the subject to 'Citizenship' students in London, and then taught at Cambridge. After a period as a research worker for the Labour Party and as an extramural teacher, she was appointed as Reader and then Professor of Social Studies at Bedford College (London) and a life peer (from 1958), Barbara Wootton's main contribution was to social policy. She served on numerous public committees, including four Royal Commissions, and wrote extensively on planning, incomes policy, social work, inequality, and delinquency. In *The Social Foundations of Wage Policy* (1955) she anticipated many sociological criticisms of exclusively economic explanations of *inflation. *Social Science and Social Pathology* (1959), which is perhaps her best-known book, applies *utilitarian philosophy and empirical sociology to the enlightened management of society, in the tradition of English ethical *socialism. Her life has been written by Ann Oakley in *A Critical Woman* (2011).

work The supply of physical, mental, and emotional effort to produce goods and services for own consumption, or for consumption by others. Productive work falls into three main categories: economic activity or *employment, unpaid domestic and leisure activities, and volunteer community service. Boundary lines between the three categories are fuzzy and determined by national conventions for surveys and official statistics.

Employment is distinguished from unpaid *domestic labour by the 'third-person criterion': whether the activity could be done by someone else without diminishing its utility. On that basis, schoolwork, studying, participating in sport for exercise, cooking or gardening for pleasure cannot be employment, even if they involve strenuous effort. Similarly, the manufacture of goods and services purely for domestic consumption are excluded from the definition of employment. Volunteer community services involve productive work for community development or to provide services to others, but are normally unpaid, and hence treated as a separate category from employment. *See also* BLACK ECONOMY; HOMEWORK; HOUSEHOLD WORK STRATEGY; INFORMAL ECONOMY.

work ethic The idea of productive labour, or *work, being valued in and for itself by those who do it, encouraging them to invest greater effort than could be achieved by social pressures, incentive payments, or other devices developed by employers to extract maximum output from their workforces. The concept is a unique product of Western European culture; other cultures rely on different social, religious, and political ideologies to encourage productive labour and the fulfilment of social obligations. The idea was derived originally from the *protestant ethic, which presents work as a religious and moral obligation, and is now widely used as a simplified popular version of that concept, especially in the context of explanations for low or high *productivity and *economic growth. The relevant American and British research in sociology, psychology, economics, and political science is reviewed systematically in Michael Rose, *Re-working the Work Ethic* (1985). *See also* ACHIEVEMENT MOTIVATION; ENTREPRENEUR; TASK-ORIENTATION VERSUS TIME-ORIENTATION DISTINCTION; WORK, SUBJECTIVE EXPERIENCE OF.

work groups Formal and informal groups in the workplace that collaborate as a team on work tasks, for short or for indefinite periods of time. The quality circles movement makes work groups central to the production system, with responsibility to study and resolve production problems.

working class The working class is classically defined as the class that must sell its labour-power in order to survive. This was essentially what Karl *Marx meant by the *proletariat. However, this is hardly a satisfactory definition for late 20th-century developed societies. If there is a working class distinct from the rest of society, then there must be distinctive features to its work and market situations, and indeed there are.

First, in terms of market situation, the working class is defined by the fact that it sells its labour-power in discrete amounts of time (paid by the hour) or output piecework) in return for a wage. In the case of work situation, the working class comprises those who are in an entirely subordinate role, such that this is a key feature of their labour contract. Hence the working class basically consists of those who work in manual or blue-collar occupations. However, none of this should be taken to mean that there is one amorphous working class, since there are a number of ways in which the class is divided into distinct groups. One of these is in terms of *skill. There is an upper working class or aristocracy of *labour which consists of skilled workers—occupations such as fitters, electricians, and the like—where incumbents have been apprenticed or learned a trade. These constitute about one-third of the working class. The remainder are in so-called semi-skilled or unskilled occupations. A second division is that between those working in primary rather than secondary *labour markets. Some members of the working class have better paid and more secure jobs (in the primary labour market) than have others. Most skilled workers belong to this primary labour market. Many female and ethnic-minority workers are found in the lower-paid, more insecure secondary labour market, lacking standard labour contracts, pension and illness entitlements, paid vacations, and so forth. It is among this group that both *unemployment and underemployment (where people find that they have periods of employment and unemployment interspersed on a frequent and irregular basis) are most frequently found. The other notable feature of the working class in developed capitalist societies is that it is shrinking, largely due to a combination of technological change (notably *automation), and the decline of the primary and manufacturing sectors. Only about one-third of the economically active would be working class by the definition given here.

The fullest development of the working class in Britain was in the period from the 1890s to the 1950s, when these economic divisions matched and were associated with a complex of cultural and political institutions and practices that gave the working class a cohesive identity and social consciousness organized around so-called 'traditional' working-class communities. These institutions included the Cooperative store, the Labour Party, trades unions, and the working men's club, together with solidaristic orientations to industrial and political action, including solid Labour voting (see Michael Savage and Andrew Miles, *The Remaking of the British Working Class*, 1994). Since the 1950s, these cultural and political aspects of working-class experience have weakened and those who share a working-class market and work situation exhibit a variety of subjective orientations and social identities. Nevertheless, Gordon Marshall et al.'s *Social Class in Modern Britain* (1984) reported that 49 per cent of respondents mentioned being a manual or unskilled worker as the chief characteristic of the working class, and 16 per cent defined the class as those with low incomes. By the time of the empirical work summarized in Michael Savage, *Class Analysis and Social Transformation* (2000), a more diverse range of identifications and aspirational lifestyles were apparent. Some argue that this points to the 'death' of the working class, yet it remains the case that sharp economic contours persist. *See also* PROLETARIAT; MIDDLE CLASS; UPPER CLASS.

working class, new *See* NEW WORKING CLASS.

work orientation *See* TASK-ORIENTATION VERSUS TIME-ORIENTATION DISTINCTION; WORK, SUBJECTIVE EXPERIENCE OF.

work satisfaction *See* JOB SATISFACTION.

work situation *See* CLASS POSITION.

work socialization The process of learning to labour in paid *employment and conforming to the associated ideological structures: internalizing the *norms, *values and *culture of the workplace, employing organization, *profession, or occupational group; accommodating to power and authority relations at the workplace; acquiring the *skills of secondary relationships; complying with the particular *role and functions allocated to the individual worker; and adopting the behaviours preferred by employers (such as punctuality, team spirit, and loyalty). More generally, it involves learning to value the attitudes that reinforce the worth of work in general and the skills involved in doing particular jobs, such as strength, dexterity, numeracy, creativity, analytical abilities, or persuasiveness.

work, subjective experience of In contrast to the relatively stable ideologies which constitute a *work ethic, sociology also looks at the way work is actually experienced by individuals and groups. This includes orientations to work, attitudes in the job, job motivations, and *job satisfaction. Though work is highly gendered, and is carried out as domestic as well as industrial labour, the former was largely invisible until recently and the literature on these topics deals almost exclusively with the subjective experience of paid employment.

The study of orientations to work has developed only recently and is especially associated with research carried out in the late 1960s and 1970s by John H. Goldthorpe, David *Lockwood, and their colleagues and students. Logically, however, it deserves priority, being concerned with the values, purposes, expectations, and sentiments the workers bring to the work situation. In *The Affluent Worker* (1968) Goldthorpe and Lockwood distinguish three ideal-typical orientations to work. Employees with an instrumental orientation see work as a means to an end (the need to acquire income); have a primarily calculating attitude to the employing organization; and do not carry their work experiences and relationships over into other aspects of their lives. By contrast, the solidaristic orientation to work is characterized by an involvement in the task as an end in itself; high job satisfaction and strong identification with the work-group (against the employer); and the carrying over of work relationships and loyalties into an 'occupational community' outside the workplace. Finally, the bureaucratic orientation defines work as a service to the organization, in return for incremental and secure wages; embodies a relationship of trust between employer and employee; pursues status advancement as a central life interest; and carries over self-concepts and social aspirations formed at work into non-work activities and relationships. Michael Burawoy's *Manufacturing Consent* (1979) is a fascinating and much-discussed attempt to link the literature on orientations to work to the Marxist discussion of the *labour process.

w

Past experience is important in developing work orientations. Workers who possess few skills or are stigmatized and discriminated against have little, if any, choice of job. Typically, their work orientations will reflect a vicious circle: the range of insecure, low-paid, and unattractive jobs available reinforces a *fatalistic outlook, which is inimical to building up any long-term identification with a particular employer. Where workers have a genuine choice, work orientations will affect the kind of labour force that is attracted to particular kinds of job. Research findings confirm the commonsense expectation that workers balance out the advantages and disadvantages of jobs according to their personal priorities and self-perceptions, as when they choose (for example) the cosiness of a small-firm working environment, despite the lower rates of pay and poorer fringe benefits characteristic of small-firm employment. The dedicated choice of historically relatively low-paid caring occupations (such as nursing), precisely because of the intrinsic moral satisfaction they offer, provides another example of the importance of work orientation. In contrast, workers with so-called instrumental orientations deliberately accept the boredom of high-paid though intrinsically monotonous jobs (such as assembly-line work), in return for the enhanced leisure and consumption which it makes possible. It has been suggested that such values brought to the workplace will be affected by the system of social stratification within the labour market. Formidable methodological problems arise, however, in disentangling work orientations from the whole complex of subjective perceptions connected with a job or occupation.

Job-related attitudes have been the subject of research for a much longer time, largely because of the preoccupation of industrial sociology with in-plant factors. Studies have sought, not altogether successfully, to show that attitudes vary with such factors as type of occupation, size of firm, and management style. A great deal of this work has relied on attitude scaling, and has sought to standardize and measure common dimensions underlying the complexities of workers' perceptions of their jobs, which can then be used to compare different groups or to contrast attitudes characteristic of particular situations. One familiar such study is Robert Blauner's attempt to decompose *alienation (in its original Marxist usage not an attitude at all) into a number of components such as isolation and meaninglessness to show that these vary with the level of *technology. Such work has been extensively criticized, both for its implication that the agreeableness or otherwise of a job lies in the task itself rather than in the mind of the worker, and for the assumption that formal *scaling can measure in a valid way all the complex factors which shape the subjective experience of industrial work. The literature on work orientations, for all its faults, provided a refreshing critique of *attitude research, as did a switch to the greater use of ethnography in the sociology of work.

Work-motivation studies, of which there have been many since the *Human Relations Movement, tend to reflect managerial preoccupations with discovering what goes on in the worker's mind and in this way securing greater commitment to the task. A major stimulus was the failure of incentive systems of wage payment and the fact that workers appeared to be acting irrationally by restricting their output below the level at which they could, in theory, maximize their short-term money earnings. Motivation in most cases turned out to consist of more than short-term instrumentalism and, among other things, to be affected by management's likely response to workers earning more than the average wage because of the incentive pricing of jobs.

Job satisfaction is also a term primarily associated with managerial interest in securing high productivity and a committed workforce. Satisfaction is a notion which raises acute methodological problems. Not to be satisfied with one's work might be seen as an admission of personal failure in many Western societies, and the earliest, rather unsophisticated studies found that a very high proportion of workers claimed to be contented. However, when the components of job satisfaction are disentangled, it becomes clear that the criteria by which satisfaction is judged vary widely. A particularly well-known distinction is between the extrinsic satisfactions of a job (notably wages, hours, and conditions), and the intrinsic or expressive satisfactions that might also be attached to it, such as opportunities for creativity, sociability, promotion, and social mobility.

Taken as a whole, the literature tends to suggest that intrinsic satisfactions are mostly found among professional and middle-class jobs requiring education and training, which also offer good extrinsic rewards. In contrast very many low-paid industrial jobs available to poorly qualified workers also offer little in the way of intrinsic satisfaction. *See also* HOUSEWORK; INDUSTRY, SOCIOLOGY OF; TASK-ORIENTATION VERSUS TIME-ORIENTATION DISTINCTION.

world-system (world-systems theory) A historical description of the growth of the *capitalist economic system, from centre to periphery, and of the effects of this growth on capitalist and pre-capitalist societies alike. It is associated mainly with the work of Immanuel Wallerstein and his colleagues at the Fernand Braudel Centre for the Study of Economies, Historical Systems, and Civilizations, at the State University of New York at Binghampton (see especially *The Modern World-System*, 3 vols., 1974, 1980, 1989).

The obvious inadequacies of *dependency theory encouraged two elaborations upon it during the 1970s: the theories of *internal colonialism and of centre-periphery. The latter is, strictly speaking, not a theory at all; rather, a *heuristic descriptive device which suggests that changes in the socio-economic structure of society are related to changes in its spatial structure. It is, in fact, a mix of ideas taken from geographical central place theory, classical political economy, Marxism, and theories of regional development. In general terms it provides a highly descriptive form of *social area analysis in which the attributes of populations are catalogued and related to residential location. World-systems theory then gives a further sociological gloss to such accounts by documenting the expansion of capitalism across the globe. Its central propositions are that capitalism is organized globally rather than nationally, that the dominant core regions develop advanced industrial systems and exploit the raw materials of the periphery, and that the modern world is rooted in an international economic order and diverse political systems (whereas pre-modern empires display the opposite pattern).

Although Wallerstein's work is suggestive and has been influential, it does little more than direct attention to the relationships between centre and periphery in this expansion, suggesting a holistic analysis but not (of itself) providing that analysis. Different world-systems analysts have attached the centre-periphery metaphor to different theories in an attempt to explain the relationships they observe. (Wallerstein himself has moved from an early reliance on neo-functionalist categories to an accommodation with Marxist political economy.) There is also some internal disagreement among proponents of the approach as to precisely what factors explain the centralizing tendencies described. Critics—of whom there are many—have also suggested that world-systems theory neglects the effects of endogenous factors generally, and culture in particular, in explanations of social change. In addition to the work of Wallerstein, particularly important contributions have been made by Christopher Chase-Dunn in *Global Formation: Structures of the World Economy* (1998) and in Thomas Hall and Christopher Chase-Dunn, *Rise and Demise: Comparing World-Systems* (1997). *See also* CENTRE-PERIPHERY MODEL; GLOBALIZATION.

( ) SEE WEB LINKS

- The Institute for Research on World-Systems, managed at the University of California at Riverside.

World Wide Web *See* INTERNET.

youth Typically regarded in sociology as an ascribed status, or socially constructed label, rather than simply the biological condition of being young. The term is used in three ways: very generally, to cover a set of phases in the *life cycle, from early infancy to young adulthood; in preference to the rather unsatisfactory term *adolescence, to denote theory and research on teenagers, and the transition to adulthood; and, less commonly now, for a set of supposed emotional and social problems associated with growing up in urban industrial society.

youth culture Strictly speaking a *subculture, the subject of an influential debate between (mainly) functionalist writers and their critics. Youth cultures are explained either by factors in the experience of *adolescence, or by the manipulation of young people's spending and leisure, through advertising and other mass media. The functional separation of home, school, and work supposedly makes teenagers increasingly distinct from adults, more self-aware, and subject to peer-group rather than parental and other adult influences. But the relative affluence of teenagers in the decades after the Second World War, especially if they were in work, also encouraged the growth of a large and profitable market for goods and services specifically directed at young consumers. This has promoted the growth of distinctive youth fashions and styles in clothes, music, and leisure, many of them originating in the United States.

For some writers the cultural clash across generations has displaced social *class as the primary form of conflict in modern industrialism. Yet class itself figures importantly in shaping the content of different youth cultures. Research in the United States distinguished the so-called college cultures of (mainly) middle-class youth from the rough or corner cultures of their working-class counterparts. The former were thought to manage the gap between conformist attitudes to achievement and the otherness of adolescent school life—of which the school itself is often the centre. Corner cultures, in contrast, were viewed as a response to working-class academic failure; centred around the neighbourhood gang rather than the school; and as reflecting a search for alternative, even deviant, status, identity, or rewards. In Britain, however, youth culture was almost exclusively identified with male working-class youth and the *moral panic about its style and aggressiveness. Neo-Marxist studies saw this as a symbolic protest against, for example, the dissolution of the traditional working-class neighbourhood community, and mass control over what were once predominantly working-class forms of leisure (such as soccer). Much of this literature is reviewed in Mike Brake, *The Sociology of Youth Cultures and Youth Subcultures* (1980).

Developments both in sociology and society itself, notably during the 1980s, greatly modified the terms of the debate. Feminist writers pointed to the invisibility of girls in the mainstream literature on youth and have researched gender variations in youth culture. The experiences of youth among ethnic minorities have also received more attention. But, above all, the period since the mid-1970s has seen the demise of the notion of the independent teenage consumer and rebel. The focus of research has switched instead to the youth labour market, and the dependence of young people on the household, as a result of growing unemployment and the vulnerability of youth to *flexible employment. *See also* COLEMAN, JAMES S.

zeitgeist The characteristic spirit (*Geist*) of a historical era (*Zeit*). 18th-century philosophers like Voltaire were intrigued by the idea of 'the spirit of the age', but it was most fully developed by *Hegel. Philosophies and works of art, he argued, cannot transcend the spirit of the age in which they are produced. Their expression is always symbolic and imperfect, and the progress of the human spirit is marked by the greater or lesser degree to which it captures the absolute spirit, or truth itself, beyond the limitations of any particular era. The term *Zeitgeist* has come to be used more loosely to describe the general cultural qualities of any period, such as 'the sixties' or 'the romantic era', and does not carry the strong *historicist connotations of Hegelian philosophy.

zero-sum game *See* GAME THEORY.

zero tolerance A policy argument supporting practical initiatives to curtail antisocial behaviour; more generally, implying no scope for opposition, dispute, or deviation. Criminal acts and incivilities are fixed in time and place but as a cumulative process can lead to the erosion of community and an impression that control has been relinquished. James Wilson and George Kelling (*Broken Windows*, 1982) influentially argued that street vandalism, empty buildings, the flight of local businesses and respectable families, are stages of community deterioration that require strong, early intervention. Famously, from the mid-1990s, New York City police adopted a 'zero tolerance' stance toward minor offences and subsequently claimed dramatic reductions in crime and behaviours such as street begging. However, critics have demonstrated similar changes in urban locations that did not adopt zero tolerance. For supporters, zero tolerance is an element of a scientific approach to crime-mapping, prevention, and improving quality of life; for opponents the approach is uncompromising, aggressive, and persecutes the powerless.

Znaniecki, Florian (1882–1959) Born in German-occupied Poland, Znaniecki was one of the first Polish professors of sociology, initiating the Polish Institute of Sociology and the *Polish Sociological Review*. In 1914 he collaborated with William Isaac *Thomas on *The Polish Peasant in Europe and America*, a study which pioneered new methods (diaries, life-histories, letters); the methodology of the humanistic coefficient, in which the meanings to participants in social action are always considered; and the beginnings of a more systematic account of society. This was developed in his later books, *Cultural Reality* (1919) and *Social Relations and Social Roles* (1965).

zoning The means of publicly regulating land use in North America by allocating territorial areas to particular permitted uses. Originating in New York City in 1916, to protect commercial property values, zoning is often used to prevent lower-income residents moving into *suburban areas. *See also* BUSINESS IMPROVEMENT DISTRICTS.

zone of (or in) transition Defined by the Chicago urban sociologist Ernest *Burgess as an urban area, between the central business district (CBD) and outer rings of working-class and middle-class residence, containing slum housing being displaced by CBD expansion. Inhabited by the poor, ethnic minorities, and socially deviant groups. The term is broadly synonymous with what is nowadays more commonly referred to as the 'inner city'. *See also* CONCENTRIC ZONE THEORY.

Oxford Quick Reference

A Dictionary of Psychology
Andrew M. Colman

Over 9,000 authoritative entries make up the most wide-ranging dictionary of psychology available.

'impressive ... certainly to be recommended'
Times Higher Education Supplement

'probably the best single-volume dictionary of its kind.'
Library Journal

A Dictionary of Economics
John Black, Nigar Hashimzade, and Gareth Myles

Fully up-to-date and jargon-free coverage of economics. Over 3,400 terms on all aspects of economic theory and practice.

'strongly recommended as a handy work of reference.'
Times Higher Education Supplement

A Dictionary of Law

An ideal source of legal terminology for systems based on English law. Over 4,200 clear and concise entries.

'The entries are clearly drafted and succinctly written ... Precision for the professional is combined with a layman's enlightenment.'
Times Literary Supplement

A Dictionary of Education
Susan Wallace

In over 1,250 clear and concise entries, this authoritative dictionary covers all aspects of education, including organizations, qualifications, key figures, major legislation, theory, and curriculum and assessment terminology.

Oxford Quick Reference

A Dictionary of Sociology
John Scott

The most wide-ranging and authoritative dictionary of its kind.

'Readers and especially beginning readers of sociology can scarcely
do better ... there is no better single volume compilation for an up-to-
date, readable, and authoritative source of definitions, summaries and
references in contemporary Sociology.'

A. H. Halsey, *Emeritus Professor, Nuffield College,*
University of Oxford

The Concise Oxford Dictionary of Politics
Iain McLean and Alistair McMillan

The bestselling A–Z of politics with over 1,700 detailed entries.

'A first class work of reference ... probably the most complete as well as
the best work of its type available ... Every politics student should have
one'

Political Studies Association

A Dictionary of Environment and Conservation
Chris Park and Michael Allaby

An essential guide to all aspects of the environment and conservation
containing over 8,500 entries.

'from *aa* to *zygote*, choices are sound and definitions are unspun'

New Scientist

More History titles from OUP

The Oxford Companion to Black British History
David Dabydeen, John Gilmore, and Cecily Jones

The first reference book to explore the full history of black people in the British Isles from Roman times to the present day.

'From Haiti to Kingston, to Harlem, to Tottenham, the story of the African Diaspora is seldom told. This Companion will ensure that the history of Black Britain begins to take its rightful place in mainstream British consciousness.'

David Lammy, MP, former Minister for Culture

A Dictionary of World History

Contains a wealth of information on all aspects of history, from prehistory right up to the present day. Over 4,000 clear, concise entries include biographies of key figures in world history, separate entries for every country in the world, and subject entries on religious and political movements, international organizations, and key battles and places.

The Concise Oxford Dictionary of Archaeology
Timothy Darvill

The most wide-ranging, up-to-date, and authoritative dictionary of its kind.

'Comprehensive, proportionate, and limpid'

Antiquity